East Africa
a travel survival kit
Geoff Crowther
Hugh Finlay

East Africa – a travel survival kit

3rd edition

Published by
   Lonely Planet Publications
   Head Office: PO Box 617, Hawthorn, Vic 3122, Australia
   Branches: PO Box 2001A, Berkeley, CA 94702, USA
                  12 Barley Mow Passage, Chiswick, London W4 4PH, UK
                  71 bis rue du Cardinal Lemoine, 75005 Paris, France

Printed by
   Colorcraft Ltd, Hong Kong

Photographs by

Steve Barnes (SB)	Greg Elms (GE)	Chris Klepp (CK)
Geoff Crowther (GC)	Hugh Finlay (HF)	Debbie Tan (DT)
Rob van Driesum (RvD)	Greg Herriman (GH)	Tony Wheeler (TW)

Front cover: Voi bus stand, Kenya (TW)
Back cover: Burchell's zebra (HF)

Safari Guide illustrations by Matt King

First Published
   September 1987

This Edition
   April 1994
   Reprinted with Update supplement June 1996

Although the authors and publisher have tried to make the information as accurate as possible, they accept no responsibility for any loss, injury or inconvenience sustained by any person using this book.

National Library of Australia Cataloguing in Publication Data

Crowther, Geoff
   East Africa – a travel survival kit.

   3rd ed.
   Includes index.
   ISBN 0 86442 209 1.

   1. Africa, East – Guidebooks.
   I. Finlay, Hugh. II. Title. (Series: Lonely Planet travel survival kit.)

916.76

text © Lonely Planet 1994, except Kenya © Hugh Finlay 1994
maps © Lonely Planet 1994
photos © photographers as indicated 1994
climate charts compiled from information supplied by Patrick J Tyson, © Patrick J Tyson 1994

Geoff Crowther

Born in Yorkshire, England, Geoff took to his heels early on in search of the miraculous, taking a break from a degree in biochemistry. The lure of the unknown took him to Kabul, Kathmandu and Lamu in the days before the overland bus companies began digging up the dirt along Africa's trails.

In 1977, he wrote his first guide for Lonely Planet – *Africa on the cheap* (now *Africa on a shoestring*). He has also written *South America on a shoestring*, travel survival kits to *Korea & Taiwan*, *Korea* and has co-authored guides to *Kenya*, *India*, *Malaysia, Singapore & Brunei* and *Morocco, Algeria & Tunisia*.

Geoff lives in northern New South Wales, Australia, with his wife, Hyung Poon, and son, Ashley Choson, but still spends at least six months overseas each year.

When not travelling or sweating over a hot computer, Geoff devotes his time to landscaping, playing guitar, dreaming up impossible schemes, arguing with everyone in sight, pursuing noxious weeds and brewing Davidson's plum and elderberry wine. To his credit, he remains generally *compos mentis*.

Hugh Finlay

After deciding there must be more to life than a career in civil engineering, Hugh took off around Australia in the mid '70s, working at everything from spray painting to diamond prospecting, before hitting the overland trail.

Since joining Lonely Planet in 1985, Hugh has written the Lonely Planet guide to *Jordan & Syria*, co-authored *Morocco, Algeria & Tunisia*, and has contributed to other Lonely Planet guides including *Africa on a shoestring*, and travel survival kits to *Kenya* and *India*.

Hugh lives in Central Victoria with Linda and daughters Ella and Vera.

This Book

For this edition, Geoff and Hugh both spent time in Kenya writing *Kenya – a travel survival kit*, which appears in full in this edition of East Africa. Geoff also travelled exten-

sively in Uganda, Tanzania, and Zaïre updating those countries. He also briefly visited Rwanda in the company of commanders of the rebel RPF, in between dodging shells and bullets, but decided it wasn't for the average tourist. Pray the gorillas will still be there when the fighting ceases

Geoff has a whole list of people to thank for their help with the research of this edition. Their names appear on page 639.

Hugh would like to thank Paul Cameron at the Australian High Commission for his efforts to revive Hugh's laptop, which suffered a major breakdown in Nairobi; and David Else for his assistance with the mountain sections.

From the Publisher

This edition of East Africa was edited at Lonely Planet's Melbourne office by Miriam Cannell and Alison White. Greg Herriman handled the design, illustrations, title pages and the Safari Guide design, Richard Stewart worked on the Kenya maps, and Geoff Crowther drew the maps for the rest of the book.

Thanks to Matt King for the Safari Guide illustrations and to Ian Foletta and Rob Rachowiecki for assistance in editing the safari guide text.

Thanks also to Alan Rake from the *New African* magazine for up-to-the-minute information on Burundi.

Finally, thanks to all those travellers who took the time and effort to write to us with suggestions and comments, their names appear on page 640.

Warning & Request

Things change – prices go up, schedules change, good places go bad and bad places go bankrupt – nothing stays the same. So if you find things better or worse, recently opened or long since closed, please write and tell us and help make the next edition better.

Your letters will be used to help update future editions and, where possible, important changes will also be included in an Update section in reprints.

We greatly appreciate all information that is sent to us by travellers. Back at Lonely Planet we employ a hard-working readers' letters team to sort through the many letters we receive. The best ones will be rewarded with a free copy of the next edition or another Lonely Planet guide if you prefer. We give away lots of books, but, unfortunately, not every letter/postcard receives one.

Contents

EASTERN ZAÏRE

TANZANIA

FACTS ABOUT THE COUNTRY 494

FACTS FOR THE VISITOR 503

GETTING THERE & AWAY 508

GETTING AROUND 515

DAR ES SALAAM 526

THE COAST 541

NORTH-EASTERN TANZANIA 570

Map Legend

BOUNDARIES

— · — · — · —	........International Boundary
— · — · —	................Internal Boundary
+++++++++++	....National Park or Reserve
- - - - - - -	........................The Equator
· · · · · · · · · ·	........................The Tropics

SYMBOLS

◉ NATIONAL	........................National Capital
● PROVINCIAL	........Provincial or State Capital
● Major	............................Major Town
● Minor	............................Minor Town
■	..........................Places to Stay
▼	...........................Places to Eat
⊠	..............................Post Office
✈	..................................Airport
i	....................Tourist Information
◒	............Bus Station or Terminal
66	...........Highway Route Number
☾ ✝ ⛪ ⛪	......Mosque, Church, Cathedral
∴	........................Temple or Ruin
✚	....................................Hospital
※	....................................Lookout
⚐	.....................Camping Area
⌒	...........................Picnic Area
⌂	......................................Hut
▲	........................Mountain or Hill
═╪═	......................................Gate
·+·+·+·	...................Railway Station
═══	...........................Road Bridge
+++++	........................Railway Bridge
⇒ ⇐	...........................Road Tunnel
→) (←―	........................Railway Tunnel
⌣⌣⌣	...................Escarpment or Cliff
⁓	....Pass

ROUTES

—————	........Major Road or Highway
- - - - - - -	.... Unsealed Major Road
—————	..........................Minor Road
- - - - - -	..... Unsealed Road or Track
═══	.... City Street
+++++++++++	................................Railway
—●—	.... Subway
- - - - - -	..................Walking Track
- - - - - -	.... Ferry Route
++++++++++	.... Cable Car or Chair Lift

HYDROGRAPHIC FEATURES

	.... River or Creek
	..............Intermittent Stream
	........Lake, Intermittent Lake
	................................Coast Line
	................................Spring
	............................Waterfall
	................................Swamp
	.... Salt Lake or Reef
	................................Glacier

OTHER FEATURES

	Park, Garden or National Park
	......................Built Up Area
	... Market or Pedestrian Mall
	.........Plaza or Town Square
	...............................Cemetery

Note: not all symbols displayed above appear in this book

Introduction

If your vision of Africa is of elephants crossing the plain below Kilimanjaro, an Arab dhow sailing into Zanzibar, a million pink flamingos, Maasai tribespeople guarding their cattle, then East Africa is where this vision becomes reality.

This book covers a small group of countries of absorbing interest and diversity. Whatever your interests, East Africa has plenty to see, experience and consider.

Kenya and Tanzania are the heart of African safariland. Some of the most famous reserves are found here, and in a trip to these countries you will probably see everything from rhinos to lions, hippos to baboons, wildebeest to flamingos. Safaris are an experience in themselves, but the reserves themselves are also spectacular, such as the Ngorongoro park in Tanzania, which is in the crater of a colossal extinct volcano, or the

Amboseli park in Kenya, which has Mt Kilimanjaro as a spectacular backdrop.

The reserves of Kenya and Tanzania are the region's best known natural attractions, but certainly not the only ones. The superb Ruwenzori Mountains sprawl across the border between Uganda and Zaïre, while further south are some of the most active volcanoes in Africa, particularly in the Parc National des Volcans in Rwanda. And Rwanda is, of course, famous for its scattered groups of mountain gorillas, which you can also visit. Scuba divers will find plenty to interest them along the coast and around the offshore islands, while other visitors may find lazing on the beach and collecting a suntan quite enough exercise.

If lazing isn't a word in your vocabulary, East Africa offers some wonderful mountains to climb. If you're fit, an assault on Mt Kenya or, best of all, snowcapped Mt Kilimanjaro, the highest mountain in Africa, is within your reach.

East Africa isn't just wildlife and scenery – there are also people, cultures and politics. Politically the region offers as wide a span of Africa's problems and aspirations as you could ask for. At one extreme there's Kenya, where Africa really works and where stability and progress have been the norm, a situation very different from so many other African nations. Tanzania illustrates where the best of African intentions can go disastrously awry, while Zaïre is a victim of pure, untrammelled greed. Burundi is a painful example of the horrors of tribal animosity, and while Idi Amin may be gone, Uganda has far from forgotten him.

The cultures and people of the region are equally interesting. Along the coast, and particularly on islands like Zanzibar and Lamu, you can observe the strong influence of the Arabs, who came first as traders and later as slavers and remained in the region for centuries. Everywhere you'll see the many and varied tribes of the region, particularly the strong-minded Maasai of Kenya. Go there – it's a wonderful region.

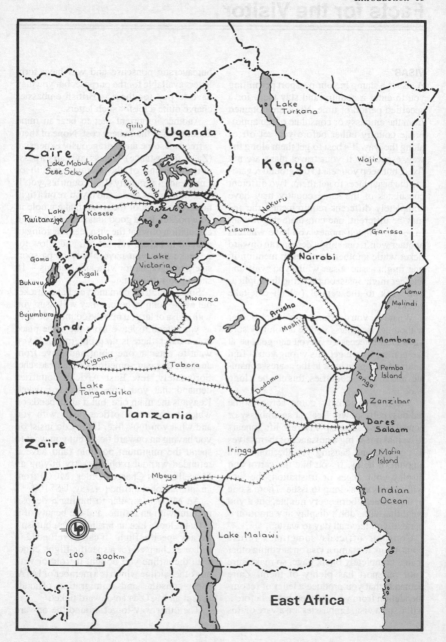

East Africa

Facts for the Visitor

VISAS

A visa is a stamp in your passport permitting you to enter a country and stay there for a specified period of time. Visas are obtained from the embassy or consulate of the appropriate country either before you set off or along the way. It's best to get them along the way, especially if your travel plans are not fixed, but keep your ear to the ground regarding the best places to get them. Two different consulates of the same country may have completely different requirements; the fee may be different, one consulate might want to see how much money you have whereas another won't, one might demand an onward ticket while another won't even mention it, one might issue visas while you wait and another might insist on referring the application back to the capital (which can take weeks).

Whatever you do, don't turn up at a border without a visa unless you're absolutely sure visas aren't necessary or you can get one at the border. If you get this wrong you'll find yourself tramping back to the nearest consulate, and in some countries, this can be a long way.

You'll occasionally come across some tedious, petty-power freak at an embassy or consulate whose sole pleasure in life appears to be making as big a nuisance of themselves as possible and causing you the maximum amount of delay. If you bite the carrot and display your anger or frustration, the visa will take twice as long to issue. There's one of these creeps born every minute, but if you want that visa, don't display any emotion – pretend you have all day to waste.

Consular officials sometimes refuse point-blank to stamp a visa on anything other than a completely blank page, so make sure your passport has plenty of them. Zaïre demands that you produce a letter of recommendation from your own embassy before it will issue a visa. Embassies are aware of this bureaucratic nonsense and will have form letters available for the purpose, but you may have to pay for these – British embassies charge quite a lot for such letters.

Another important fact to bear in mind about visas is their sheer cost. None of them is free and some are outrageously expensive (Zaïre, for instance). Unless you carry a passport from one of the Commonwealth or European Community (EC) countries, you'll need quite a few visas, and if you're on a tight budget, the cost of them can make a hole in your pocket. It's a good idea to make a rough calculation of what the visa fees are going to amount to before you set off, and allow for it. Make sure you have plenty of passport size photographs for visa applications – 16 should be sufficient.

Some countries demand you have a ticket out of the country before they will issue you with a visa or let you into the country. So long as you intend to leave from the same place you arrived, there is no problem, but if you want to enter at one point and leave from another, this can sometimes be a headache. Fortunately, few East African countries demand that you have an onward ticket. Kenya is the main one, but it all depends on which immigration officer deals with you and what you look like. If they do insist on you having an onward ticket but you want to spend the minimum possible (and have it refunded without problems), try buying an Miscellaneous Charges Order (MCO) from an international airline for, say, US$100.

An MCO is similar to having a deposit account with an airline, and the beauty of it is that it looks like an airline ticket, but isn't for any specific flight. It can be refunded in full or exchanged for a specific flight, either with the airline you bought it from or with any other airline which is a member of IATA. Most consular and immigration officials accept an MCO as an onward ticket.

The other way to get around the onward

ticket requirement is to buy the cheapest ticket available out of the country and then get it refunded later on. If you do this, make sure you can get a refund without having to wait months. Don't forget to ask specifically where it can be refunded, since some airlines will only refund tickets at the office where you bought them, some only at their head office.

See individual country chapters for details on visa requirements and the addresses of embassies and consulates.

DOCUMENTS

The essential documents are a passport and an International Vaccination Card. If you already have a passport, make sure it's valid for a reasonably long period of time and has plenty of blank pages on which stamp-happy immigration officials can do their stuff. If it's more than half full and you're going to need a lot of visas, get a new one before you set off. This way you won't have to waste time hanging around in a capital city somewhere while your embassy issues you with a new one. In some countries there is the option of getting a normal-sized passport or a 'jumbo' passport. Get the larger one. US nationals can have extension pages stapled into otherwise full passports at any of their embassies.

Whoever supplies you with your vaccinations will provide you with an International Vaccination Card and the necessary stamps. In most countries you won't be asked to present it, but there's one place you definitely will and that's before boarding a boat to Zanzibar. You will not be allowed to board if you don't have proof of a yellow fever vaccination.

If you're taking your own transport or are thinking of hiring a vehicle to tour certain national parks, get hold of an International Driving Permit before you set off. Any national motoring organisation will fix you up with this, provided you have a valid driving licence for your own country. The cost of these permits is generally about US$5. On the other hand, a national driving licence seems to suffice in most countries for hiring a vehicle.

An International Student Identity Card (ISIC) or the graduate equivalent is also useful in many places and can save you a considerable amount of money, though its usefulness diminishes with each passing year. Possible concessions include airline tickets, train fares, and reduced entry charges to museums and archaeological sites. If you're not strictly entitled to a student card, it's often possible to get one if you book a flight with one of the 'bucket shop' ticket agencies that have proliferated in certain European and North American cities. The deal usually is that you buy an airline ticket and they'll provide you with a student card.

Another useful thing to have is a Youth Hostel Association (YHA) membership card, particularly for Kenya. Some of the hostels will allow you to stay without a card but others will insist that you join up first. Concessions which are possible with an ISIC or a YHA membership card are mentioned in the appropriate chapters.

MONEY

Be careful which currency you take with you, as some is difficult or even impossible to change. US dollars, Canadian dollars, UK pounds, French francs, German marks, Swiss francs and Italian lire are all readily accepted. Australian and New Zealand dollars can be difficult to change except in Nairobi. The problem here is that the exchange rate may not be known. You don't get this with American and European currencies.

See individual country chapters for exchange rates.

Travellers' Cheques & Cash

For maximum flexibility, take the larger slice of your money in travellers' cheques and the rest in cash – say up to US$500. American Express, Thomas Cook and Citibank cheques are the most widely used and their offices generally offer instant replacement in the event of loss or theft. Keep a record of the cheque numbers and the original bill of sale for the cheques in a safe place in case you lose them. Replacement is a whole lot quicker if you can produce this information. Even so, if you don't look clean and tidy, or they don't believe your story for some reason or another, replacement can take time, since quite a few travellers have sold their cheques on the black market, or simply pretended to lose them, and then demanded a replacement set. This is particularly so with American Express cheques. You should avoid buying cheques from small banks which only have a few overseas branches, as you'll find them very difficult, if not impossible, to change in many places.

Make sure you buy a good range of denominations when you get the cheques – US$10, U$20, U$50 and US$100 – so you don't get stuck changing large denomination bills for short stays or for final expenses. Plenty of small cheques are essential for Tanzania if you don't want to end up with a mountain of local currency, since all accommodation over US$10 and all national park fees have to be paid in hard currency. This particularly thorny issue is discussed in greater detail in the Tanzania chapter, and you're well advised to read it *before* you leave home.

Having a credit card and a personal chequebook is an excellent way of having funds to hand. With these, you can generally withdraw up to US$150 in cash per day and up to US$1000 in travellers' cheques per week from any branch of the credit card company or participating banks. This virtually dispenses with the need to buy travellers' cheques in your home country, though you should take some, since you can only avail yourself of this service during banking hours.

With a Visa card, for example, any main branch of Barclays Bank will let you have the local equivalent of US$150 per day without contacting your bank. For any amount over US$150, they'll telex your bank before giving you the money. You don't need a cheque account to do this. Similarly, American Express offices will issue US dollar travellers' cheques up to a certain limit (usually US$5000 every 20 days) against one of their cards and a personal cheque

drawn on your bank. If you don't have a personal chequebook but you do have a credit card, there's usually no problem. Simply present your card and ask for a counter cheque. This is fine even if you don't have an actual cheque account but do have, say, a deposit account. What will happen in that case is that the bank will bounce the cheque which you signed for American Express and American Express will send you a demand for the money or bill your American Express account. If you're on a long trip, you'll obviously have to arrange for someone back home to pay the monthly accounts.

There are American Express offices or agents in Nairobi, Mombasa, Kampala and Dar es Salaam.

National Westminster Eurocheque cards are another possibility. With one of these and a personal cheque, you can withdraw up to UK£100 a day at selected banks in Kenya, Tanzania and Uganda. Nominated banks in Kenya are those of the Kenya Commercial Bank at both Kencom House and Kipande House in Nairobi, at Treasury Square in Mombasa, and in Kisumu and Nakuru; the National Bank of Kenya's main branches in Nairobi and Mombasa; and the Standard Chartered Bank's main branches in Nairobi and Mombasa. In Tanzania, Eurocheque cards can be used at the head office of the National Bank of Commerce in Dar es Salaam, and in Uganda at the head offices of either the Standard Chartered or Uganda Commercial banks in Kampala.

Credit Cards

American Express, Diner's Club, Visa and MasterCard are all widely recognised credit cards which can be used to pay for accommodation, food, airline tickets, books, clothing and other services in most large towns, especially in Kenya (though less so in neighbouring countries). Even Kenyan Railways accepts Visa cards for railway tickets.

Credit cards also have their uses when 'sufficient funds' are demanded by immigration officials before they will allow you to enter a country. It's generally accepted that you have 'sufficient funds' if you have a credit card.

Transferring Money

If you run out of money while you're abroad and need more, ask your bank back home to send a draft to you (assuming you have money back home to send). Make sure you specify the city and the bank branch. Transferred by cable or telex, money should reach you within a few days. If you correspond by mail, the process will take at least two weeks, often longer. Remember that some countries will only give you your money in local currency; others will let you have it in US dollars or another hard currency. Find out what's possible before you request a transfer; you could lose a fair amount of money if there's an appreciable difference between the official and unofficial exchange rates. Kenya is probably the best place to transact this sort of business.

Black Market

You cannot always change travellers' cheques in small places or, of course, when the banks are closed. However, in most places you can use travellers' cheques to pay for accommodation costing over US$10 or national park entry fees (in Tanzania). You should bring some cash with you, though, because it allows you to take advantage of any street rate of exchange (black market). Sometimes you can change travellers' cheques on the black market, but this isn't always the case.

During the 1980s, you could get considerably more for your hard currency on the street in Uganda, Tanzania and Zaïre than you could at the banks. The difference in Kenya was minimal. This has all now changed with the introduction of Forex bureaux in Uganda and Tanzania. Both their currencies are now freely convertible and there's no black market. The situation in Kenya is somewhat complicated – although there's an official exchange rate and Kenyan banks trade at this rate, the international banks (Barclays, Standard Chartered, Grindlays, IBN, etc) trade at close to the black market rate.

In Rwanda and Burundi, virtually everyone changes on the street (assuming they have cash), since there's a significant difference between the bank rate and the street rate.

Zaïre's economic situation is totally crazy, and any comment about the currency would be outdated as soon as it's made. You'd have to be lobotomised to go to a bank in this country. The best thing to do is to establish what the price is for a bottle of Primus beer in local currency. This has always been about US$1. Use that as your exchange rate whether it means you get Z 2,000,000 or Z 3,000,000 to the US dollar.

The black market is a thorny issue. Some people regard it as morally reprehensible, even economic sabotage. It's certainly predatory, but some countries used to overvalue their currency to a degree that was totally Mickey Mouse.

You'll have to make up your own mind about which side of the moral fence you stand on, but one thing is for sure – you won't meet many budget travellers who don't utilise the black market where there's a significant difference between the bank and street rates. And you'll meet plenty of officials – some of them in remarkable positions of authority and in full view of everyone around – who will make it plain that they're interested in swapping local currency for hard cash.

This doesn't mean that you should be blasé and incautious. Quite the opposite. Discretion is the name of the game.

When changing on the black market, have the exact amount you want to change available – avoid pulling out large wads of notes. Be very wary about sleight of hand and envelope tricks. Insist on personally counting out the notes that are handed to you. Don't let anyone do this for you and don't hand over your money until you're satisfied you have the exact amount agreed to. If at any point you hand the notes back to the dealer (because of some discrepancy, for example), count them out again when they're handed back to you – if you don't, you'll probably find that all but the smallest notes have been removed. Some operators are so sharp they'd have the shoes off your feet while you were tying up the laces. Don't allow yourself to be distracted by supposed alarms like 'police' and 'danger'. In many countries you won't have to take part in this sort of minidrama, as money is generally changed in certain shops or with merchants at a market, so it's a much more leisurely process. Whatever else you do, *don't* change actually on the street, as you may be set up by a police undercover agent.

Treat all the official and black market rates given in this book as a guide only. They are correct at the time the book goes to press, but coups, debt crises, devaluations and IMF 'structural adjustment programmes' can alter the picture dramatically. You must check out all prices and exchange rates with your fellow travellers along the way. They are your best source of current information.

Note that currency declaration forms are no longer issued in any of the East African countries.

Costs

It's very difficult to predict what a trip to Africa is going to cost, since so many factors are involved: how fast you want to travel, what degree of comfort you consider to be acceptable, how much sightseeing you want to do, whether you intend to hire a vehicle to explore a game park or rely on other tourists to give you a lift, whether you're travelling alone or in a group, whether you will be changing money on the street or in banks, and a host of other things.

There's only one thing which remains the same in Africa and that's the pace of change – it's fast. Inflation and devaluations can wreak havoc with your travel plans if you're on a very tight budget. You should budget for at least US$10 per day in the cheaper countries and US$20 per day in the more expensive ones. This should cover the cost of very basic accommodation, food in local cafés and the cheapest possible transport. It won't include the cost of getting to Africa, safaris in game parks or major purchases in markets. On the other hand, if you stay in one place for a while and cook your own

---

Money Safety

There is no 'safe' way to keep your money while you're travelling, but the best place is in contact with your skin where, hopefully, you'll be aware of an alien hand before your money disappears. One method is to wear a leather pouch hung around your neck and kept under a shirt or dress. If you do this, incorporate a length of old guitar string into the thong which goes around your neck (the D string should be thick enough). Many thieves carry scissors but few carry wire cutters.

Another method is to sew an invisible pocket inside the front of your trousers. Many travellers prefer a money belt, though I've never been able to understand the rationale for this. First and foremost, it's obvious where your money is. Secondly, it labels you as a tourist and, therefore, someone who doesn't know too much about the place. This is balm to the eyes of a thief or a mugger. So why make it easy? Not only that, but in order to pay for something, you have to open it up and display the bulk of your wealth. You can be sure *someone* will be watching. A sillier invention I've never come across. All I can say is that if you do wear one, keep some small change distributed around various other pockets to pay for things like buses, newspapers, beers, etc. Personally, I wouldn't wear one if you paid me, even if it was empty.

Ideally your passport should be in the same place that you keep your money, but this isn't always possible, as some are either too thick or too stiff. Wherever you decide to put your money, it's a good idea to enclose it in a plastic bag. Under a hot sun, that pouch or pocket will get soaked with sweat – repeatedly – and your cash or cheques will end up looking like they've been through the laundry.

And one last thought: do you know where Nairobi taxi drivers keep their money? All over their body! Shoes, pockets, underpants – you name it. ∎

food, you can reduce daily costs considerably, since you won't be paying for transport and you'll get a better deal on the cost of accommodation.

Bargaining

Many purchases involve some degree of bargaining. This is always the case with things bought from a market, street stall or craft shop. Bargaining may also be necessary for hotels and transport in some places, though these are often fairly standard and you won't be paying any more than the local people. Food and drink bought at restaurants don't usually involve any bargaining – the prices will be written on the menu.

Where bargaining is the name of the game, commodities are looked on as being worth what their owners can get for them. The concept of a fixed price would invoke laughter. If you cop out and pay the first price asked, you'll not only be considered a halfwit but you'll be doing your fellow travellers a disservice, since this will create the impression that all travellers are equally stupid and are willing to pay outrageous prices. You are expected to bargain – it's part of the fun of going to Africa. All the same, no matter how good you are at it, you'll never get things as cheaply as local people do. To traders and hotel and café owners, you represent wealth – whatever your appearance.

In most cases bargaining is conducted in a friendly, sometimes exaggeratedly extroverted manner, though there are occasions when it degenerates into a bleak exchange of numbers and leaden handshakes. Decide what you want to pay or what others have told you they've paid, and start off at a price at least 50% lower than this. The seller will inevitably start off at a higher price, sometimes up to 100% higher, than they are prepared to accept. This way you can both end up appearing to be generous.

There will be times when you simply cannot get a shopkeeper to lower the prices to anywhere near what you know the product should be selling for. This probably means that a lot of tourists are passing through and if you don't pay those outrageous prices,

some mug will. Don't lose your temper bargaining. There's no need to. You can always walk away and come back another day or go to a different shop. It's just theatre.

WHAT TO BRING

Bring the minimum possible. An overweight bag will become a nightmare. A rucksack or backpack is preferable to an overnight bag, since it will stand up to rougher treatment and is easier to carry. Choose a pack which will take some rough handling – overland travel destroys packs rapidly. Make sure the straps and buckles are well sewn on, and strengthened if necessary, before you set off. Whether you take a pack with or without a frame is up to you, but there are some excellent packs on the market with internal frames (eg Berghaus, Karrimor). Take a strong plastic bag with you that will completely enclose the pack. Use it on dusty journeys, whether your pack is in the luggage compartment of a bus or strapped onto the roof. If you don't, you'll be shaking dust out of your pack for the next week.

A sleeping bag is more or less essential. Deserts get very cold at night, and if you'll be visiting mountainous areas, you'll need one there as well. You'll also be glad of it on long bus or train journeys as a supplement to the wooden seats or sacks of potatoes. A sheet sleeping bag – similar to the ones used in youth hostels – is also good when it is too hot to use a normal bag. It's cool and keeps the mosquitoes off your body. It also means you don't have to use hotel sheets if they look dubious.

Take clothes for both hot and cold climates, including at least one good sweater for use at night in the mountains and the desert. Gloves and a woolly hat are very useful if you are planning on climbing mountains. You needn't go overboard, however, and take everything in your wardrobe. Things like T-shirts, cotton shirts and sandals are very cheap in most places and it's usually more economical to buy these things along the way.

In some places, Zanzibar for example, you will seriously offend local people by wearing clothes that reveal large areas of your body. This includes shorts, short skirts and see-through garments. The rules are relaxed at beach resorts, of course, but generally, it's inadvisable for women to wear anything short or overly revealing in Muslim areas (the coastal areas of Kenya and Tanzania) otherwise they may well come in for a lot of hassling by local men or youths. Muslim women in these areas all wear the buibui (the equivalent of the chador or burka in other Muslim countries) though, in East Africa, it doesn't cover the face and is worn with considerably more panache.

Whatever else you do regarding clothing – keep it clean! Go and buy that packet of Omo and get moving in the sink. Grubby Western travellers are a common sight in Nairobi and elsewhere but are not at all appreciated and are often despised by Africans. Take a leaf from their book and make the same effort.

Some people take a small tent and a portable stove. These can be very useful and save you a small fortune, but they do add considerably to the weight of your pack. Camping equipment can be rented in several places in Kenya, as well as in Arusha (Tanzania).

Don't forget the small essentials: a combination pocket knife or Swiss Army knife, needle and cotton, a small pair of scissors, sunglasses, towel and toothbrushes, oral contraceptives, tampons and one or two good novels. Most toiletries – toilet paper, toothpaste, shaving cream, shampoo, suntan lotion, etc – are available in capital cities and large towns, except in Uganda, where there's hardly anything. A water bottle (insulated) is very useful when it's hot or for walking in the mountains. It also enables you to give those dubious water holes a miss and so cut down your chances of getting hepatitis.

POST
Sending Mail
When sending letters, try to use aerograms (air letters) rather than ordinary letters. If you send stamped letters, it's sometimes necessary to ensure the stamps are franked in front of you. There's a chance that unfranked stamps will be steamed off, resold and the letter thrown away. Having said that, I've posted ordinary letters, parcels and postcards back home from every country covered in this book and they have all arrived – and not all of them were franked in front of me.

Travelling Companions

Travelling overland is rarely a solo activity unless you want it that way. Even if you set off travelling alone, you'll quickly meet other travellers who are heading in the same direction or who are returning. Crossroads where travellers congregate are good places to meet other people and team up with someone. The best are Arusha, Dar es Salaam, Lamu, Malindi, Mombasa, Nairobi and Zanzibar.

If you'd prefer to find someone before you set off, check the classified advertisements in national newspapers or the notice boards at colleges and universities before the summer holidays come up. If you're in London, the best publications to look for ads are *Time Out* and *TNT*. In New York, try the New York Student Centre (☎ (212) 695 0291), Hotel Empire, Broadway and 63rd St, or get hold of something like the *Village Voice*.

In some countries, there are specific publications and organisations which cater for intending travellers looking for companions. In the UK, try *The Adventurers*, which is published monthly by Adventurers International (☎ (071) 480 6801), 12 Telford Yard, London E1 9BQ, and costs £1.75 per issue. At the back are two pages of advertisements from travellers seeking companions. There's no charge for inserting an advertisement. Otherwise try Travelmate, 6 Hayes Ave, Bournemouth BH7 7AD, or Odyssey International, 21 Cambridge Rd, Waterbeach, Cambridge CB5 9NJ, both of which gather and distribute intending travellers' details and plans to their members. Membership costs £15 to £25. These agencies are only as reliable as their members are willing to keep the agencies abreast of their plans as they evolve. ■

There's little point in having any letter sent by Express Delivery (called Special Delivery in the UK), as they won't get there any quicker, on average, than an air letter.

Receiving Mail

Have letters sent to you c/o Poste Restante, GPO, in whatever city or town you will be passing through. Alternatively, you can use the mail holding service operated by American Express offices and their agents, if you have their cheques or one of their credit cards.

Most embassies no longer hold mail and will forward it to the nearest poste restante. Plan ahead – it can take up to two weeks for a letter to arrive even in capital cities and sometimes takes much longer in smaller places.

The poste restante services in most of East Africa are pretty reliable, though there are exceptions (Kampala is useless at present).

Mail is generally held for four weeks – sometimes more, sometimes less – after which it is returned to the sender. The service is free in most places, but in others (Tanzania, Rwanda, Burundi), there is a small charge for each letter collected.

As a rule you need your passport as proof of identity. In large places where there's a lot of traffic, the letters are generally sorted into alphabetical order, but in smaller places, they may all be lumped together in the one box. Sometimes you're allowed to sort through them yourself; sometimes a post office employee will do the sorting for you.

If you're not receiving expected letters, ask them to check under every conceivable combination of your given name, surname, any other initials and even under 'M' (for Mr, Ms, Miss, Mrs). This sort of confusion isn't as widespread as many people believe, though most travellers have an improbable story to tell about it. If there is confusion, it's generally because of bad handwriting on the

envelope or language difficulties. If you want to make absolutely sure that the fault won't be yours, have your friends address letters with your surname in block letters and underlined.

Avoid sending currency notes through the post. They'll often be stolen by post office employees no matter how cleverly you disguise the contents. There are all sorts of ways of finding out whether a letter is worth opening up. Still, some people do successfully get cash sent through the mail.

BOOKS

You can walk into any decent bookshop in Europe, America or Australasia and find countless books on Western and Eastern history, culture, politics, economics, religion/philosophy, craft and anything else you care to name. Finding the same thing for Africa is somewhat more difficult except in specialist bookshops. Things are improving, however, but so far only in the large-format, hardback, photo-essay genre.

What you will be hard-pressed to find is a good selection of novels, plays and biographies by contemporary African authors, many of them published by the African branches of major Western publishing houses. Heinemann's African Writers Series offers a major collection of such works but they're generally only available in large African cities. In East Africa, the bookshops of Nairobi carry an excellent selection but the choice is considerably more limited in Tanzania and Uganda. In Western countries, they're to be found only in specialist bookshops.

General Books

There are some excellent but quite expensive photo-essay hardbacks which you may prefer to look for in a library. They include *Journey though Kenya* (Bodley Head, 1982), by Mohammed Amin, Duncan Willets & Brian Tetley. There is a companion volume entitled *Journey through Tanzania* by the same authors and publisher.

Other colourful books on the region include *Africa Adorned* (Collins, 1984) by Angela Fisher; *Ivory Crisis* (Chatto & Windus, 1983) by Ian Parker & Mohammed Amin; *Isak Dinesen's Africa* (Bantam Books, 1985) by various authors; *Africa: A History of a Continent* (Weidenfield & Nicolson, 1966) by Basil Davidson; and *Through Open Doors: A View of Asian Cultures in Kenya* (Kenway Publications, Nairobi, 1983) by Cynthia Salvador. Salvadori also co-authored with Andrew Fedders *Peoples & Cultures of Kenya* (Transafrica, Nairobi, 1989).

In addition to the above, there has recently been a flurry of large-format, hardback books on the various tribal societies of Kenya, especially the Maasai and Samburu, which you'll see in the bookshops of Nairobi and Mombasa.

History, Politics & Economics

There are numerous books on the history of Africa which include *The Penguin Atlas of African History* (Penguin, 1980) by Colin McEvedy, *A Short History of Africa* (Penguin, 1962) by Roland Oliver & J D Fage, and *The Story of Africa* (Mitchell Beazley/Channel Four, 1984) by Basil Davidson. Also excellent reading is *The Africans – A Triple Heritage* (Guild Publishing, 1986) by Ali A Mazrui, which was published in conjunction with a BBC TV series of the same name.

For the origins and development of the coastal Swahili culture and how it has been affected by the arrival of the Portuguese in the Indian Ocean, the standard work is *The Portuguese Period in East Africa* (East African Literature Bureau, 1961) by Justus Strandes. For a radical African viewpoint of the effects of colonialism in general, Walter Rodney's *How Europe Underdeveloped Africa* (Bogle L'Ouverture, 1976) is well worth a read.

Worthwhile contemporary accounts include the extremely readable but rather discouraging *The Africans* (Vintage Books/Random Books, 1984) by David Lamb. Or there's *The Making of Contemporary Africa* (Indiana, 1984) by Bill Freund, and *A Year in the Death of Africa* (Paladin,

1986) by Peter Gill. On contemporary Kenyan politics, it's well worth reading Oginga Odinga's *Not Yet Uhuru* (Heinemann) and *Detained – A Prison Writer's Diary* (Heinemann, 1981) by Ngũgĩ wa Thiong'o, for a radically different view from that put out by the Kenyatta and Moi regimes.

Not exclusively about Africa but very relevant to bilateral and multilateral aid issues, is the *Lords of Poverty* (Mandarin, London, 1991) by Graham Hancock, an exposé of the bungling and waste perpetrated by the UN, IMF, World Bank and others.

The *Africa Review* (NTC Publishing Group, UK) an annual production by World of Information, offers an overview of the politics and economics of every African country as well as detailed facts and figures. It's well balanced and researched and makes no attempt to curry favours with any particular regime.

Travellers' & Other Accounts

Dian Fossey's research with the mountain gorillas of Rwanda is recounted in her book *Gorillas in the Mist* (Penguin, 1983). *The White Nile* (Penguin, 1973) by Alan Moorehead is a superbly evocative account of the exploration of the upper Nile and the rivalry between the European powers.

Journey to the Jade Sea (Paladin, 1974) by John Hillaby, recounts this prolific travel writer's epic trek to Lake Turkana in northern Kenya in the days before the safari trucks began pounding up the dirt in this part of Kenya. Other books to look for include *Initiation* (Penguin, 1985) by J S Fontaine, *A Bend in the River* (Penguin, 1979) by V S Naipaul and *Travels in the Congo* (Penguin, 1927) by André Gide.

Two women's accounts of life in East Africa earlier this century have been recent best sellers. *Out of Africa* by Karen Blixen (Isak Dinesen) is published by Penguin books and has also been made into a hugely popular movie. *West with the Night* (North Point Press) by Beryl Markham has also been a major best seller.

African Fiction

Heinemann's African Writers Series probably has the greatest range of contemporary African authors. There's a list of their writers on the first page of each of their books. Two of Kenya's best authors are Ngũgĩ wa Thiong'o and Meja Mwangi whose books are a good introduction to what's happening in East African literature at present. Ngũgĩ is uncompromisingly (but somewhat dogmatically) radical and his harrowing criticism of the neocolonialist politics of the Kenyan establishment landed him in jail for a year, lost him his job at Nairobi University and forced him into exile. His books, on the other hand, are surprisingly not banned in Kenya even though he was considered a dangerously subversive thorn in the side of the government. Meja Mwangi sticks more to social issues and urban dislocation but has a brilliant sense of humour which threads its way right through his books.

Titles worth reading by Ngũgĩ wa Thiong'o include *Petals of Blood* (1977), *A Grain of Wheat* (1967), *Devil on the Cross* and *Weep Not Child*. Titles by Meja Mwangi include *Going Down River Road, Kill me Quick* (1974) and *Carcass for Hounds* (1974). All these titles are published by Heinemann.

For a hilarious but at times poignant account of the higher education system and its relationship with the political system you probably can't beat *The People's Bachelor* (East Africa Publishing House, Nairobi, 1972) by Austin Bukenya. Though set at Makerere University in Kampala, Uganda, shortly after independence, its theme is relevant to virtually all British ex-colonies. Another author whose books are well known even outside Africa is Chinua Achebe. Although Achebe is a Nigerian and his material is drawn from his experiences in that country, many of the themes and issues are relevant to contemporary East Africa. His most famous title is *Things Fall Apart* (Heinemann, 1958). *Ant Hills of the Savannah*, a much more recent publication, is also well worth reading.

Another Nigerian author who writes about

similar themes is Elechi Amadi. Try his *The Concubine* (Heinemann, 1968).

For writing by women in Africa try *Unwinding Threads* (Heinemann, 1983), a collection of short stories by many different authors from all over the continent.

Travel Guides

Africa on a shoestring (Lonely Planet, 1992), by Geoff Crowther, covers more than 50 African countries, concentrating on practical information for budget travellers. *Kenya – a travel survival kit* (Lonely Planet, 1994) is available as a separate guidebook, but also appears in full in the book you are reading.

Insight Kenya (APA Productions, 1985), edited by Mohammed Amin & John Eames, is another of the popular APA guidebook series with many excellent photographs and a lively text. It concentrates more on the country's history, its peoples, cultures, sights and wildlife rather than on practical information and is a good book to read either before you go or whilst you're there.

Guide to Mt Kenya & Kilimanjaro (Mountain Club of Kenya, Nairobi, 1981), edited by Iain Allan, has been written and added to over the years by dedicated enthusiasts, but is mainly directed at skilled climbers and mountaineers. It contains information on the rock and ice routes, but also has some (very dated) trail descriptions, maps, photographs, descriptions of fauna, flora, climate and geology, even mountain medicine.

More recent practical guides to East Africa are those by David Else. His *Trekking in East Africa* (Lonely Planet, 1993) covers a selection of treks and expeditions in the mountains and wilderness areas of Kenya, Tanzania, Uganda and Malawi, and has plenty of advice and general information about trekking in this part of the world.

The *Camping Guide to Kenya* (Bradt Publications, 1990) covers every camp site in Kenya – the cities, national parks and mountain areas – and contains information and advice for campers and backpackers venturing off the main routes into the more remote areas of Kenya.

Mountain Walking in Kenya (Robertson-McCarta, 1991) covers a selection of walking routes through the mountain and highland regions of Kenya including everything from easy strolls around Lake Naivasha to longer hikes on Mt Kenya. There's an equipment guide as well as accurate maps and colour photographs.

Flora & Fauna Guides

A Field Guide to the Larger Mammals of Africa (Collins, 1986) by Jean Dorst & Pierre Dandelot, together with *A Field Guide to the Birds of East Africa* (Collins, 1963) by J G Williams & N Arlott, should suffice for most people's purposes in the national parks and wildlife reserves.

MAPS

Largely as a result of the prosperous tourism industry, there's a wide range of maps available, although many are just made to look pretty and have very little practical use.

One of the best maps of the region is the Hallwag map *Kenya & Tanzania* which also covers Uganda, Rwanda, Burundi and eastern Zaïre. Covering a similar area, but not as well, is Hildebrand's travel map of *East Africa*. The Michelin maps are usually pretty reliable but the only one which takes in this area (No 155, Southern Africa) covers too wide an area to give enough detail.

The *Tourist Map of Kenya*, printed and published in Kenya, gives good detail and there are a few similar ones.

Macmillan publishes a series of maps to the game parks and these are not bad value at US$3.50 each.

The Public Map Office next to the Kenyatta Conference Centre in Nairobi has a stock of government survey maps covering the whole country. The most popular ones (Mt Kenya, Mt Elgon and those covering the game parks) are often out of stock but it's worth getting hold of these maps if possible.

The only trouble with maps published by the Survey of Kenya other than those available in the bookshops is that they're not available to the general public without official authorisation. This is hard to get and takes time so, if you're a tourist with limited time, you can forget it. Even people with credentials, such as Kenyan residents of the Mountain Club of Kenya (MCK), have great difficulty or find it simply impossible to get hold of detailed maps of the country.

HEALTH

East Africa is a fairly healthy area to visit. Malaria is endemic and you need to take precautions against chloroquine-resistant strains. Chloroquine-based malaria tablets are available over the counter even in tiny stores out in the country. Locally manufactured Maloprim is also available, in Nairobi at least, and at a fraction of the cost you'll pay at home.

In Kenya, tap water is safe to drink but water obtained from other sources, especially wells and bores, should be treated with suspicion.

Travel health depends on your predeparture preparations, your day-to-day health care while travelling and how you handle any medical problem or emergency that does develop. While the list of potential dangers can seem quite frightening, with a little luck, some basic precautions and adequate information, few travellers experience more than mild upset stomachs.

Travel Health Guides

Two useful books are *The Traveller's Health Guide* (Lascelles, London) by Dr A C Turner, and *Preservation of Personal Health in Warm Climates* published by the Ross Institute of Tropical Hygiene, Keppel St, London WC1. Another helpful book on health is David Werner's *Where There is No Doctor: a village health care handbook* (Macmillan Press, London). *Travel with Children* (Lonely Planet Publications, Hawthorn), by Maureen Wheeler, includes basic advice on travel health for younger children.

Predeparture Preparations

Medical Insurance Get some! You may never need it, but if you do you'll be very glad to have it. Medical treatment in East Africa is not free and public hospitals are often very crowded. Don't expect the same quality of medical treatment in an East African public hospital as you get back home either. There are many different travel-insurance policies available and any travel agency will be able to recommend one.

Before you choose one collect several different policies and read through them for an hour or two, as the cost of a policy and the sort of cover offered can vary considerably. Many policies are pitched at the family package-tour market and are not really appropriate for a long spell in Africa under your own steam. Usually, medical insurance comes in a package which includes baggage insurance and life insurance, etc. You need to read through the baggage section carefully as many policies put a ceiling on how much they are prepared to pay for individual items which are lost or stolen. Check the small print:

- Some policies specifically exclude 'dangerous activities' which can include scuba diving, motorcycling, even trekking. If such activities are on your agenda you don't want that sort of policy.

- You may prefer a policy which pays doctors or hospitals direct rather than you having to pay on the spot and claim later. If you have to claim later make sure you keep all documentation. Some policies ask you to call back (reverse charges) to a centre in your home country where an immediate assessment of your problem is made.

- Check if the policy covers ambulances or an emergency flight home. If you have to stretch out you will need two seats and somebody has to pay for them!

Medical Kit A small, straightforward medical kit is a wise thing to carry. A possible kit list includes:

- Aspirin or Panadol – for pain or fever

- Antihistamine (such as Benadryl) – useful as a decongestant for colds, allergies, to ease the itch from insect bites or stings or to help prevent motion sickness

- Antibiotics – useful if you're travelling well off the beaten track, but they must be prescribed and you should carry the prescription with you*

- Kaolin preparation (Pepto-Bismol), Imodium or Lomotil – for stomach upsets
- Dehydration mixture – for treatment of severe diarrhoea, this is particularly important if travelling with children
- Antiseptic, mercurochrome and antibiotic powder or similar 'dry' spray – for cuts and grazes
- Calamine lotion – to ease irritation from bites or stings
- Bandages and Band-aids – for minor injuries
- Scissors, tweezers and a thermometer (note that mercury thermometers are prohibited by airlines)
- Insect repellent, sunscreen, suntan lotion, chap stick and water-purification tablets

* Ideally antibiotics should be administered only under medical supervision and should never be taken indiscriminately. Overuse of antibiotics can weaken your body's ability to deal with infections naturally and can reduce the drug's efficacy on a future occasion. Take only the recommended dose at the prescribed intervals and continue using the antibiotic for the prescribed period, even if the illness seems to be cured earlier. Antibiotics are quite specific to the infections they can treat; stop immediately if there are any serious reactions and don't use it at all if you are unsure if you have the correct one.

Prescriptions & Medications Make sure you are healthy before you start travelling. If you're embarking on a long trip make sure your teeth are OK; dentists are few and far between in Africa and treatment is expensive. If you wear glasses take a spare pair and your prescription. Losing your glasses can be a real problem, although in Nairobi you can get new spectacles made up quickly, cheaply and competently.

In East Africa, medicines which you would normally need a prescription for in your own country are available over the counter (if they have them) at either a chemist (pharmacist) or a dispensary and the price will be much cheaper than what you would pay in the West. You need, however, to check the expiry date as it may have passed. It's also possible that drugs which are no longer recommended in the West (or have even been banned) are still being dispensed in East Africa, so make sure you know what medicine you require.

Immunisations Before you're allowed to enter most African countries you must have a valid International Vaccination Card as proof that you're not the carrier of some new and exotic plague. The essential vaccinations are yellow fever (valid for 10 years) and cholera (valid for six months). While it is generally agreed that cholera vaccinations are a waste of time, many African countries (including Kenya) still require that you have a cholera jab. Good vaccination centres in the West will still stamp your card for you without giving you the shot. In addition, you're strongly advised to be vaccinated against typhoid (valid for three years), tetanus (valid for 10 years), tuberculosis (valid for life) and polio (valid for 10 years).

Gamma globulin shots are also available for protection against infectious hepatitis (type A) but they are ineffective against serum hepatitis (type B). Protection lasts three to six months. There is also a vaccine for type A which provides 100% protection for 12 months (a course of two injections) or for 10 years (with a third, booster, injection), though it is quite expensive. There is a vaccine available for type B but it's only recommended for individuals at high risk. It's also expensive, and the series of three injections takes six months to complete.

You need to plan ahead for these vaccinations, as they cannot all be given at once and typhoid requires a second injection about two or three weeks after the first. Cholera and typhoid jabs usually leave you with a stiff and sore arm for two days afterwards. The other injections generally don't have any effect.

If your vaccination card expires whilst you're away, there are a number of medical centres in Kenya where you can have booster vaccinations. There's usually a small fee for these but sometimes they are free.

Avoid turning up at borders with expired vaccination cards, as officials may insist on your having the relevant injection before they will let you in and the same needle may be used on a whole host of people.

Your local physician can arrange a course of injections for you, or in most large cities there are vaccination centres (including the following) which you can find in the telephone book:

Belgium
> Ministère de la Santé Publique et de la Famille, Cité Administrative de l'État, Quartier de l'Esplanade, 1000 Brussels
> Centre Médical du Ministère des Affaires Etrangères, 9 Rue Brederode, 1000 Brussels

France
> Direction Départementale d'Action Sanitaire et Sociale, 57 Blvd de Sevastopol, 75001 Paris (☎ 4508-9690)
> Institut Pasteur, 25 Rue du Docteur Roux, 75015 Paris (☎ 4566-5800)

Holland
> Any GGD office or the Academical Medical Centre, Amsterdam

Switzerland
> L'Institut d'Hygiène, 2 Quai du Cheval Blanc, 1200 Geneva (☎ (022) 438075)

UK
> Hospital for Tropical Diseases, 4 St Pancras Way, London, NW1. Injections here are free but the hospital is often booked up about a month ahead (☎ (071) 387-4411).
> West London Designated Vaccination Centre, 53 Great Cumberland Place, London W1. No appointment is necessary, and the fees vary depending on the vaccine (☎ (071) 262-6456).
> British Airways Immunisation Centre, Victoria Terminal, Buckingham Palace Rd, London, SW1. Try to book a few days in advance, or you might have to wait around for a few hours before they can fit you in (☎ (071) 834-2323).
> British Airways Medical Centre, Speedbird House, Heathrow Airport, Hounslow, Middlesex (☎ (081) 759-5511).

General Health

The main things which are likely to affect your general health while you're abroad are diet and climate. Stomach upsets are the most likely problem but the majority of these upsets will be relatively minor. Don't become paranoid – trying the local food is part of the experience of travel after all.

Water Avoid drinking unboiled water anywhere it's not chlorinated, unless you're taking it from a mountain spring. Unboiled water is a major source of diarrhoea and hepatitis, as are salads that have been washed in contaminated water and unpeeled fruit that has been handled by someone with one of these infections.

Avoiding contaminated water is easier said than done, especially in the desert, and it may be that you'll have to drink water regardless of where it came from. This is part of travelling and there is no way you can eliminate all risks. Carrying a water bottle and a supply of water-purifying tablets is one way around this. Halazone, Potable Aqua and Sterotabs are all good for purifying water but they have little or no effect against amoebas or hepatitis virus. For this you need a 2% tincture of iodine – five drops per litre in clear water and 10 drops per litre in cloudy water. Wait 30 minutes and it's safe to drink.

In hot climates you sweat a great deal and lose a lot of water and salt. Make sure you drink sufficient liquid and have enough salt in your food to make good the losses (a teaspoon of salt per day is generally sufficient). If you don't make good the losses, you run the risk of suffering from heat exhaustion and cramps.

Food & Nutrition Cheap food from cafés and street stalls tends to be overcooked, very starchy (mainly maize and millet) and lacking in protein, vitamins and calcium. Supplement your diet with milk or yoghurt (where it's available and pasteurised) and fresh fruit or vitamin/mineral tablets. Avoid untreated milk and milk products. Peel all fruit. Read up on dietary requirements before you set off. And watch out for grit in rice and bread – a hard bite on the wrong thing can lead to a cracked tooth.

Rest Adjustment to the outlook, habits and social customs of different people can take a lot out of you. Many travellers suffer from some degree of culture shock. This is particularly true if you fly direct from your own country to an African city. Under these conditions, heat can aggravate petty irritations which would pass unnoticed in a more temperate climate. Exhausting all-night, all-day bus journeys over bad roads don't help if you're feeling this way. Try to take things at a slower pace, and make sure you get enough sleep.

Hygiene Many health problems can be avoided by taking care of yourself. Wash your hands frequently – it's quite easy to contaminate your own food. Clean your teeth with purified water rather than straight from the tap. Avoid climatic extremes: keep out of the sun when it's hot, dress warmly when it's cold.

Hot, dry air will make your hair brittle, so oil it often with, say, refined coconut oil. Take great care of cuts, grazes and skin infections otherwise they tend to persist and get worse. Clean them well with antiseptic or mercurochrome. If they're weeping, bandage them up since open sores attract flies. Change bandages daily and use an antibiotic powder if necessary.

Avoid potential diseases by dressing sensibly. You can get worm infections through walking barefoot, or severe cuts from coral or sea urchin spines by walking over coral without foot protection. You can avoid insect bites by covering bare skin when insects are around, by screening windows or beds or by using insect repellents. Seek local advice: if you're told the water is unsafe due to jellyfish, crocodiles or bilharzia, don't go in it. In situations where there is no information, discretion is the better part of valour.

Medical Problems & Treatment
While the list of medical problems might seem long and off-putting, it isn't meant to be. Most travellers arrive healthy and leave even healthier. If you do pick up something, however, it's useful to know what to do.

Self-diagnosis and treatment can be risky, so wherever possible seek qualified help. Although we do give treatment dosages in this section, they are for emergency use only. Medical advice should be sought before administering any drugs.

An embassy or consulate can usually recommend a good place to go for such advice. So can five-star hotels, although they often recommend doctors with five-star prices.

(This is when that medical insurance really comes in useful!) In some areas of Kenya, standards of medical attention are so low that for some ailments the best advice is to get on a plane to Nairobi.

Prickly Heat
A temporary but troublesome skin condition which affects many people from temperate climates is prickly heat. Many tiny blisters form on one or more parts of your body – usually where the skin is thickest, such as your hands. They are sweat droplets which are trapped under your skin because your pores aren't large enough or haven't opened up sufficiently to cope with the greater volume of sweat. Anything which promotes sweating – exercise, tea, coffee, alcohol – makes it worse. Keep your skin aired and dry, reduce clothing to a loose-fitting minimum and keep out of direct sunlight. Calamine lotion or zinc oxide-based talcum powder helps to soothe the skin. Apart from that, there isn't much else you can do. The problem is one of acclimatisation and shouldn't persist for more than a few days.

Heat Stroke
This serious, sometimes fatal, condition can occur if the body's heat-regulating mecha-

---

Vital Signs
A normal body temperature is 98.6°F or 37°C; more than 2°C higher is a 'high' fever. A normal adult pulse rate is 60 to 80 per minute (children 80 to 100, babies 100 to 140). You should know how to take a temperature and a pulse rate. As a general rule the pulse increases about 20 beats per minute for each °C rise in fever.

Respiration (breathing) rate is also an indicator of illness. Count the number of breaths per minute: between 12 and 20 is normal for adults and older children (up to 30 for younger children, 40 for babies). People with a high fever or serious respiratory illness (like pneumonia) breathe more quickly than normal. More than 40 shallow breaths a minute usually means pneumonia. ∎

nism breaks down and the body temperature rises to dangerous levels. Long, continuous periods of exposure to high temperature can leave you vulnerable to heat stroke. You should avoid excessive alcohol or strenuous activity when you first arrive in a hot climate.

The symptoms of heat stroke are feeling unwell, not sweating very much or at all and a high body temperature (from 39 to 41°C). Where sweating has ceased the skin becomes flushed and red. Severe, throbbing headaches and lack of coordination will also occur, and the sufferer may be confused or aggressive. Eventually the victim will become delirious or convulse. Hospitalisation is essential, but meanwhile get patients out of the sun, remove their clothing, cover them with a wet sheet or towel and then fan continually. Be careful not to cool them down too rapidly; if they start to shiver, their core temperature will rise still further rather than decrease.

Fungal Infections

Hot weather fungal infections are most likely to occur on the scalp, between the toes or fingers (athlete's foot), in the groin (jock itch or crotch rot) and on the body (ringworm). You get ringworm (which is a fungal infection, not a worm) from infected animals or by walking on damp areas, like shower floors.

To prevent fungal infections wear loose, comfortable clothes, avoid artificial fibres, wash frequently and dry yourself carefully. If you do get an infection, wash the infected area daily with a disinfectant or medicated soap and water, and rinse and dry well. Apply an antifungal powder like the widely available Tinaderm. Try to expose the infected area to air or sunlight as much as possible and wash all towels and underwear in hot water as well as changing them often.

Tropical Ulcers

These are sores which often start from some insignificant scratch or blister which doesn't seem to heal up. They often get worse and spread to other areas of the body and they can be quite painful. If you keep clean and look after any sores which you get on your arms and legs (from ill-fitting shoes, accidents to your feet, or from excessive scratching of insect bites) then it's unlikely you will be troubled by them. If you do develop sores which won't clear up then you need to hit the antibiotics quickly. Don't let them spread.

Altitude Sickness

Acute Mountain Sickness or AMS occurs at high altitude and can be fatal. The lack of oxygen at high altitudes affects most people to some extent. Take it easy at first, increase your liquid intake and eat well. Even with acclimatisation you may still have trouble adjusting – headaches, nausea, dizziness, a dry cough, insomnia, breathlessness and loss of appetite are all signs to heed. If you reach a high altitude by trekking, acclimatisation takes place gradually and you are less likely to be affected than if you fly straight there.

Mild altitude problems will generally abate after a day or so but if the symptoms persist or become worse the only treatment is to descend – even 500 metres can help. Breathlessness, a dry, irritative cough (which may progress to the production of pink, frothy sputum), severe headache, loss of appetite, nausea, and sometimes vomiting are all danger signs. Increasing tiredness, confusion, and lack of coordination and balance are real danger signs. Any of these symptoms individually, even just a persistent headache, can be a warning.

There is no hard and fast rule as to how high is too high: AMS has been fatal at altitudes of 3000 metres, although 3500 to 4500 metres is the usual range. It is always wise to sleep at a lower altitude than the greatest height reached during the day.

Motion Sickness

Eating lightly before and during a trip will reduce the chances of motion sickness. If you are prone to motion sickness try to find a place that minimises disturbance – near the wing on aircraft, close to midships on boats, near the centre on buses. Fresh air usually helps, reading or cigarette smoke doesn't.

Commercial antimotion-sickness preparations, which can cause drowsiness, have to be taken before the trip commences; when you're feeling sick it's too late. Ginger is a natural preventative of motion sickness and is available in capsule form.

Diarrhoea

Sooner or later most travellers get diarrhoea, so you may as well accept the inevitable. You can't really expect to travel halfway around the world without succumbing to diarrhoea at least once or twice, but it doesn't always mean that you've caught a bug. Depending on how much travelling you've done and what your gut is used to, it can be merely the result of a change of food. If you've spent all your life living on food out of sterilised, plastic-wrapped packets and tins from the local supermarket, you're going to have a hard time until you adjust.

If and when you get a gut infection, avoid rushing off to the chemist and filling yourself with antibiotics. It's a harsh way to treat your system and you can build up a tolerance to them with overuse. Try to starve the bugs out first. Eat nothing and rest. Avoid travelling. Drink plenty of fluids. Have your tea with a little sugar and no milk. Diarrhoea will dehydrate you and may result in painful muscular cramps in your guts. The cramps are due to a poor salt balance in your blood, so take a small amount of salt with your tea. If you can find it, tincture of opium (known as 'paregoric' and often mixed with kaolin – a stronger version of milk of magnesia) will relieve the pain of cramps. Something else you may come across, called RD Sol, also helps to maintain a correct salt balance and so prevent cramps. It's a mixture of common salt, sodium bicarbonate, potassium chloride and dextrose. Two days of this regime should clear you out.

If you simply can't hack starving, keep to a *light* diet of curd, yoghurt, toast, dry biscuits, rice and tea. Stay away from butter, milk, sugar, cakes and fruit.

If starving doesn't work or you really have to move on and can't rest for a couple of days, try Pesulin (or Pesulin-O which is the same but with the addition of a tincture of opium). The dosage is two teaspoons four times daily for five days. Or try Lomotil – the dosage is two tablets three times daily for two days. Avoid overuse of Lomotil.

If you have no luck with either of these, change to antibiotics or see a doctor. There are many different varieties of antibiotics and you almost need to be a biochemist to know what the differences between them are. They include tetracycline, chlorostep, typhstrep, sulphatriad, streptomagma and thiazole. If possible, have a word with the chemist about their differences. Overuse will do you more harm than good but you must complete the course otherwise the infection may return and then you'll have even more difficulty getting rid of it.

Giardia

Giardia is prevalent in tropical climates and is characterised by swelling of the stomach, pale-coloured faeces, diarrhoea and, after a while, depression and sometimes nausea. Many doctors recommend Flagyl (metronidazole) – seven 250 mg doses over a three-day period should clear up the symptoms, repeated a week later if not. Flagyl, however, has many side effects and some doctors prefer to treat giardia with Tinaba (tinadozole). Two grams taken all at once normally knocks it right out but if not you can repeat the dosage for up to three days.

Dysentery

Dysentery is, unfortunately, quite prevalent in some places. It's characterised by diarrhoea containing blood and lots of mucus, and painful gut cramps. There are two types. Bacillary dysentery is short, sharp and nasty but rarely persistent – it's the most common variety. Amoebic dysentery is, as its name suggests, caused by amoebic parasites. This variety is much more difficult to treat and often persistent.

Bacillic dysentery comes on suddenly and lays you out with fever, nausea, painful cramps and diarrhoea but, because it's caused by bacteria, it responds well to antibiotics. Amoebic dysentery builds up more slowly and is more dangerous. You cannot starve it out and if it's untreated it will get worse and permanently damage your intestines. If you see blood in your faeces persistently over two or three days, seek medical attention as soon as possible.

Flagyl is the most commonly prescribed drug for amoebic dysentery. The dosage is six tablets per day for five to seven days. Flagyl is both an antibiotic and an antiparasitic. It is also used for the treatment of giardia and trichomoniasis. Flagyl should not be taken by pregnant women. If you get bacillic dysentery, the best thing for slowing down intestinal movements is codeine phosphate (30 mg tablets – take two once every four hours). It's much more effective than Lomotil or Imodium and cheaper. Treatment for bacillic dysentery consists of a course of tetracycline or bactrim (antibiotics).

Hepatitis

Hepatitis is a liver disease caused by a virus. There are basically two types – infectious hepatitis (known as type A) and serum hepatitis (known as type B). The one you're most likely to contract is type A. It's very contagious and you pick it up by drinking water, eating food or using cutlery or crockery that's been contaminated by an infected person. Foods to avoid are salads (unless you know they have been washed thoroughly in purified water) and unpeeled fruit that may have been handled by someone with dirty hands. It's also possible to pick it up by sharing a towel or toothbrush with an infected person.

An estimated 10% of the population of the Third World are healthy carriers of type B but the only ways you can contract this form are by having unprotected sex with an infected person or by being injected with a needle which has previously been used on an infected person.

Symptoms of type A appear 15 to 50 days after infection (generally around 25 days) and consist of fever, loss of appetite, nausea, depression, complete lack of energy and pains around the base of your rib cage. Your skin will turn progressively yellow and the whites of your eyes yellow to orange. The easiest way to monitor the situation is to watch the colour of your eyes and urine. If you have hepatitis, the colour of your urine will be deep orange no matter how much liquid you've drunk. If you haven't drunk much liquid and/or you're sweating a lot, don't jump to conclusions. Check it out by drinking a lot of liquid all at once. If the urine is still orange then you'd better start making plans to go somewhere you won't mind convalescing for a few weeks. Sometimes the disease lasts only a few weeks and you only get a few really bad days, but it can last for months. If it does get really bad, cash in that medical insurance you took out and fly back home.

There is no cure as such for hepatitis except rest and good food. Diets high in B vitamins are said to help. Fat-free diets have gone out of medical fashion, but you may find that grease and oil make you feel nauseous. Seeking medical attention is probably a waste of time and money, though you are going to need a medical certificate for your insurance company if you decide to fly home. There's nothing doctors can do for you that you can't do for yourself other than run tests that will tell you how bad it is. Most people don't need telling; they can feel it! Wipe alcohol and cigarettes right off the slate. They'll not only make you feel much worse, but alcohol and nicotine can do permanent damage to a sick liver.

To avoid these problems, think seriously about getting that gamma globulin vaccination. There is also a vaccine available for hepatitis A (brand name Harvix) which provides protection for 12 months, or for 10 years if you choose to have a booster injection as well. There is also a very effective vaccine against hepatitis B, given as a course of three injections over a six-month period, which is an option for those who know their travel plans well in advance of their trip. The course offers protection for about five years.

Typhoid

Typhoid fever is another gut infection that travels the faecal-oral route – ie contaminated water and food are responsible. Typhoid is very infectious and vaccination against it is not totally effective. It is one of the most dangerous infections so medical help must be sought.

In its early stages typhoid resembles many other illnesses: sufferers may feel like they have a bad cold or flu on the way, as early symptoms are a headache, a sore throat, and a fever which rises a little each day until it is around 40°C or more. The victim's pulse is often slow relative to the degree of fever present and gets slower as the fever rises – unlike a normal fever where the pulse increases. There may also be vomiting, diarrhoea or constipation.

In the second week the high fever and slow pulse continue and a few pink spots may appear on the body; trembling, delirium, weakness, weight loss and dehydration are other symptoms. If there are no further complications, the fever and other symptoms will slowly go during the third week. However you must get medical help before this because pneumonia (acute infection of the lungs) or peritonitis (burst appendix) are common complications.

The fever should be treated by keeping the victim cool and dehydration should also be watched for. Chloramphenicol is the recommended antibiotic but there are fewer side affects with ampicillin. The adult dosage is two 250 mg capsules, four times a day. Children aged between eight and 12 years should have half the adult dose; younger children should have one-third the adult dose.

Patients who are allergic to penicillin should not be given ampicillin.

Worms

These parasites are most common in rural, tropical areas and a stool test when you return home is not a bad idea. Worms can be present on unwashed vegetables or in undercooked meat and you can pick them up through your skin by walking bare foot. Infestations may not show up for some time, and although they are generally not serious, if left untreated they can cause severe health problems. A stool test is necessary to pinpoint the problem and medication is often available over the counter.

Tetanus

This potentially fatal disease is found in undeveloped tropical areas. It is difficult to treat but is preventable with immunisation. Tetanus occurs when a wound becomes infected by a germ which lives in the faeces of animals or people, so clean all cuts, punctures or animal bites. Tetanus is known as lockjaw, and the first symptom may be discomfort in swallowing, or stiffening of the jaw and neck; this is followed by painful convulsions of the jaw and body.

Rabies

Rabies is found in many countries and is caused by a bite or scratch by an infected animal. Dogs are a noted carrier. Any bite, scratch or even lick from a mammal should be cleaned immediately and thoroughly. Scrub with soap and running water, and then clean with an alcohol solution. If there is any possibility that the animal is infected medical help should be sought immediately. Even if the animal is not rabid, all bites should be treated seriously as they can become infected or can result in tetanus. A rabies vaccination is now available and should be considered if you are in a high-risk category – eg if you intend to explore caves (bat bites could be dangerous) or work with animals.

Meningococcal Meningitis

Sub-Saharan Africa is considered the 'meningitis belt' and the meningitis season falls at the time most people would be attempting the overland trip across the Sahara – the northern winter before the rains come.

This very serious disease attacks the brain and can be fatal. A scattered, blotchy rash, fever, severe headache, sensitivity to light and neck stiffness which prevents forward bending of the head are the first symptoms. Death can occur within a few hours, so immediate treatment is important.

Treatment is large doses of penicillin given intravenously, or, if that is not possible,

intramuscularly (ie in the buttocks). Vaccination offers good protection for over a year, but you should also check for reports of current epidemics.

Tuberculosis

Although this disease is widespread in many developing countries, it is not a serious risk to travellers. Young children are more susceptible than adults and vaccination is a sensible precaution for children aged under 12 travelling in endemic areas. TB is usually spread by coughing or by unpasteurised dairy products from infected cow's milk. Milk that has been boiled is safe to drink; the souring of milk to make yoghurt or cheese also kills the bacilli.

Bilharzia

This is caused by blood flukes (minute worms) which live in the veins of the bladder or the large intestine. The eggs which the adult worms produce are discharged in urine or faeces. If they reach water, they hatch out and enter the bodies of a certain species of freshwater snail where they multiply for four or more weeks and are then discharged into the surrounding water. If they are to live, they must find and invade the body of a human being where they develop, mate and then make their way to the veins of their choice. Here they start to lay eggs and the cycle repeats itself. The snail favours shallow water near the shores of lakes and streams and they are more abundant in water which is polluted by human excrement. They particularly like reedy areas. Generally speaking, moving water contains less risk than stagnant water but you can never tell.

Bilharzia is quite a common disease in Africa so stay out of rivers and lakes. If you drink water from any of these places, boil it or sterilise it with chlorine tablets. The disease is painful and causes persistent and cumulative damage by repeated deposits of eggs. If you suspect you have it, seek medical advice as soon as possible – look for blood in your urine or faeces that isn't associated with diarrhoea. The only body of water in Africa which is largely free of bilharzia is

Lake Malawi, so keep out of Lake Victoria. As the intermediate hosts (snails) live only in fresh water, there's no risk of catching bilharzia in the sea.

Sexually Transmitted Diseases

Sexual contact with an infected sexual partner spreads these diseases. While abstinence is the only 100% preventative, using condoms is also effective. Gonorrhoea and syphilis are the most common of these diseases; sores, blisters or rashes around the genitals, discharges or pain when urinating are common symptoms. Symptoms may be less marked or not observed at all in women. Syphilis symptoms eventually disappear completely but the disease continues and can cause severe problems in later years. The treatment of gonorrhoea and syphilis is by antibiotics.

There are numerous other sexually transmitted diseases, for most of which effective treatment is available. However, there is no cure for herpes and there is also currently no cure for HIV/AIDS. HIV/AIDS is rampant in Uganda, less so in Kenya and Tanzania but still a serious problem and on the increase. The latest figures put the number of carriers of the HIV virus (the virus that causes HIV/AIDS) at one in 12. Most of those who have it are not aware of the fact, and hospitals (if they ever get to them) are likely to diagnose their symptoms as something more mundane. The obvious way to pick up the HIV virus is to have sex with someone who has the disease. The obvious way to avoid it is to be celibate. Not everyone can do this so if you do have sex make sure you cut the risk as far as you can by using condoms. You are still a long way from 100% safe if you do this but the message has definitely got through and most sexually active Africans living in urban areas carry condoms.

There are two other ways you can pick up the HIV virus. The first is if you need a blood transfusion. Blood donors in Kenya are rarely screened for HIV/AIDS and if you receive blood from an infected donor you will be exposed to the virus. Your options are probably limited if you get into the sort of strife which requires a transfusion. It is also possible to pick up the virus if you are injected with an unsterilised needle. If you do have an injection in Kenya try to ensure that the needle is either new or properly sterilised.

Malaria

Malaria is caused by a blood parasite which is spread by certain species of night-flying mosquito (anopheles). Only the female insects spread the disease but you can contract it through a single bite from an insect carrying the parasite. Start on a course of antimalarial drugs before you set off and keep it up as you travel.

The drugs are fairly cheap in some places but horrendously expensive in others – the USA and Scandinavia in particular. There are basically two types: proguanil (brand name Paludrine in the USA) which you take daily, and chloroquine (brand name Aralen in the USA) which you take once or twice per week (depending on its strength). Both are marketed under various trade names.

In Kenya the parasite is beginning to acquire immunity to some of the drugs, so you will need to take Maloprim in addition to chloroquine, or mefloquine (brand name Larium in the USA). You would be very unlucky to contract malaria if you are taking one or more of these drugs but they are not a 100% guarantee.

Having said that, it's fair to say that many expatriates working in East Africa for long periods of time prefer not to take prophylactics but to treat the disease if and when it occurs. The reasoning behind this is that the prophylactic drugs can have serious side-effects, specifically to the liver and eyes, when taken continuously over a long period of time. I've experienced this myself. These people prefer insect repellants, mosquito nets and screening. So did I for six months – and didn't get malaria.

If you do develop malarial symptoms – high fever, severe headaches, shivering, liver pains and aching joints – and are not within reach of medical advice, the treatment is one single dose of four tablets (600 mg) of chloroquine followed by two tablets (300 mg) six hours later and two tablets on each following day. As an alternative (or in chloroquine-resistant areas) take a single dose of three tablets of Fansidar, or two tablets of Larium followed by two more 12 hours later.

Other than the malaria hazard, mosquito bites can be troublesome and although it's probably useless to say this, *don't scratch the bites*. If you do, and they don't heal quickly, there's a chance of them becoming infected with something else. You'll come across people in Africa pockmarked with angry sores which started out as insignificant mosquito bites – the owners couldn't resist the urge to scratch them. Don't join them. Willpower works wonders, as does antihistamine cream. To keep the mosquitoes off at night, use an insect repellent or sleep under a fan. Mosquitoes don't like swift-moving currents of air and will stay on the walls of the room in these circumstances.

There is not yet a vaccination against malaria, so take those pills.

Trypanosomiasis (Sleeping Sickness)

This is another disease transmitted by biting insects, in this case by the tsetse fly. Like malaria, it's caused by minute parasites which live in the blood. The risk of infection is very small and confined to areas which are only a fraction of the total area inhabited by the tsetse fly. The flies are only found south of the Sahara but the disease is responsible for the absence of horses and cattle from large tracts of central Africa, particularly central and eastern Tanzania.

The fly is about twice the size of a common housefly and recognisable from the scissor-like way it folds its wings while at rest. The disease is characterised by irregular fevers, abscesses, local oedema (puffy swellings caused by excess water retained in body tissues), inflammation of the glands and physical and mental lethargy. It responds well to treatment.

Yellow Fever

Yellow fever is endemic in much of Africa.

Get that vaccination before you set off and you won't have to worry about it.

Cuts & Scratches

Skin punctures can easily become infected in hot climates and may be difficult to heal. Treat any cut with an antiseptic solution and mercurochrome. Where possible avoid bandages and Band-aids, which can keep wounds wet. Coral cuts are notoriously slow to heal, as the coral injects a weak venom into the wound. Avoid coral cuts by wearing shoes when walking on reefs, and clean any cut thoroughly.

Bites & Stings

Bee and wasp stings are usually painful rather than dangerous. Calamine lotion will give relief, or ice packs will reduce the pain and swelling. There are some spiders with dangerous bites but antivenenes are usually available. Scorpion stings are notoriously painful and in Mexico can actually be fatal. Scorpions often shelter in shoes or clothing.

There are various fish and other sea creatures which can sting or bite dangerously (eg jellyfish, stone fish on coral reefs) or which are dangerous to eat. Again, local advice is the best suggestion.

Snakes

To minimise your chances of being bitten always wear boots, socks and long trousers when walking through undergrowth where snakes may be present. Don't put your hands into holes and crevices, and be careful when collecting firewood.

Snake bites do not cause instantaneous death and antivenenes are usually available. Keep the victim calm and still, wrap the bitten limb tightly, as you would for a sprained ankle, attach a splint to immobilise the limb and then seek medical help, if possible with the dead snake for identification. Do not attempt to catch the snake if there is even the remotest possibility of being bitten again. Tourniquets and sucking out the poison are now completely discredited.

Fleas, Lice & Bedbugs

Unwanted passengers you're likely to come across are fleas, lice and bedbugs. There isn't a lot you can do about fleas. They vary considerably in numbers from one season to another; some places have a lot, others none at all. The less money you pay for a bed or a meal, the more likely you are to encounter fleas.

You can generally avoid lice by washing yourself and your clothes frequently. You're most likely to pick them up in crowded places like buses and trains, but you might also get them by staying in very cheap hotels. You'll occasionally meet tribespeople whose hair is so matted and so unwashed that it's literally crawling with lice. However, it takes a while for lice to get stuck into you so you should get a companion to have a look through your hair about once a week to see if you've acquired any eggs. They are always laid near the base of the hairs. If you find any, you can either pick them out one by one (very laborious) or blitz them with insecticide shampoo like Lorexane or Suleo. We've had letters from people who have doused their hair in petrol or DDT. You're certainly guaranteed total wipeout this way, but it does seem mildly hysterical!

With luck you won't come across bedbugs too often. These evil little bastards live in the crevices of walls and the framework of beds where they hide during the day. They look like lice but they move like greased lightning once you become aware of their presence and switch on the light to see what's happening. Look for telltale bloodstains on the walls near beds in budget hotels. If you see them, find another hotel.

Jiggers are nasty small fleas (Tunga penetrans) which burrow under the skin of the feet (usually under the toe nails) to lay their eggs! After incubation the eggs hatch out and you'll have enough fleas to start a circus! The best preventative is to avoid walking around barefoot.

Women's Health

Gynaecological Problems Poor diet, lowered resistance due to the use of antibiotics for stomach upsets and even contraceptive pills can lead to vaginal infections when travelling in hot climates. Keeping the genital area clean, and wearing skirts or loose-fitting trousers and cotton underwear will help to prevent infections.

Yeast infections, characterised by a rash, itch and discharge, can be treated with a vinegar or even lemon-juice douche or with yoghurt. Nystatin suppositories are the usual medical prescription to thrush. Trichomoniasis is a more serious infection; symptoms are a discharge and a burning sensation when urinating. Male sexual partners must also be treated, and if a vinegar-water douche is not effective, medical attention should be sought. Flagyl is the prescribed drug.

Pregnancy Most miscarriages occur during the first three months of pregnancy, so this is the most risky time to travel. The last three months should also be spent within reasonable distance of good medical care, as quite serious problems can develop at this time. Pregnant women should avoid all unnecessary medication, but vaccinations and malarial prophylactics should still be taken where possible. Additional care should be taken to prevent illness and particular attention should be paid to diet and nutrition.

ACCOMMODATION

Except in Burundi and Rwanda, where options for cheap accommodation are very limited, you can usually find somewhere cheap to stay, even in the smallest towns. Options include a wide choice of budget hotels, youth hostels (Kenya only), religious missions, Sikh temples and camp sites. Some of these places (religious missions and Sikh temples) may be free, but if they are, please leave a donation (otherwise it won't be long before they no longer welcome travellers – as has happened in other parts of Africa).

In budget hotels, what you get depends largely on what you pay for, though in general, they're good value. You can certainly expect clean sheets and shared showers in all of them, but you don't always get a fan or mosquito net and, if you're paying rockbottom prices, the showers will be cold.

Very cheap hotels often double as brothels (or 'sperm palaces', as an American companion was fond of calling them), but so do many other more expensive hotels. Theft from hotel rooms generally isn't a problem, though only a fool would tempt fate by leaving money and other valuables lying around unattended for hours at a time. If a place looks safe, it generally is. Check the door locks and the design of keys. Many cheap hotels in Kenya also have a full-time doorman or even a locked grille and they won't let anyone in who is not staying there.

Obviously, you need to take care in dormitory-type accommodation, since you can't lock anything up (unless there are lockers). All in all, the chances of being mugged in a dark alley at night in a dubious part of a city or along a deserted stretch of beach are far greater than having your gear stolen from a hotel room.

There are camp sites of a sort all over East Africa but the facilities offered vary tremendously. Some are nothing more than a patch of dirt without even a tap. Others are purpose-built. Where there's nothing, religious missions will often allow you to camp in their compounds – usually for a small fee. Don't simply camp out in the bush or on a patch of wasteland in a town or city, however. You are asking for problems, and if you leave your tent unattended, there'll be nothing left in it when you get back. In small villages off the beaten track, ask permission first from the village elder or chief before setting up your tent.

Getting There & Away

Many travellers get to East Africa overland as part of a much lengthier journey through the continent. Due to the civil war in Sudan, however, it is no longer possible to go overland down the Nile valley between Sudan and either Uganda or Kenya. The furthest you will get coming down from the north is Khartoum. From there to Kenya or Uganda, you will have to fly. Zaïre, too, has become problematical, due to the conflict between President Mobutu and the Prime Minister Tshisekedi and rioting army troops, but by mid-1993, travellers were again making it through without incident. You should, however, keep your eye on the situation, as it could radically change overnight. At the time of writing (mid-1993), there's a civil war going on in Rwanda and the border with Uganda is closed. This could, of course, change at any time if one of the many 'ceasefires' finally holds and the warring sides reach a reconciliation agreement.

There are no such problems coming up from the south between Zambia or Malawi and Tanzania.

Trying to find a passage on a ship to Africa these days is virtually a waste of time. There are no regular passenger services and you won't get onto a freight ship without a merchant sailor's ticket. Don't believe any rumours that there are such ships.

There are about four or five dhows which do the journey from Zanzibar and Mombasa to Karachi and Bombay each year via Somalia, South Yemen and Oman, but they are extremely difficult to locate and to get onto. The days of the dhows were numbered decades ago, and those you find in Mombasa harbour will only be plying between Lamu, Mombasa, Pemba, Zanzibar and Dar es Salaam.

AIR

Unless you are coming overland, flying is just about the only – and the most convenient – way of getting to Kenya. Nairobi is the main hub for flights and the route on which you are most likely to get a relatively cheap ticket, but it's also worth checking out cheap charter flights to Mombasa from Europe.

Buying an ordinary economy-class ticket is not the most economical way to go, but it does give you maximum flexibility and the ticket is valid for 12 months.

Students and those under 26 can often get discounted tickets, so it's worth checking first with a student travel bureau to see if there is anything on offer. Another option is an advance-purchase ticket which is usually between 30% and 40% cheaper than the full economy fare but has restrictions. You must purchase your ticket at least 21 days in advance (sometimes more) and you must stay away for a minimum period (usually 14 days) and return within 180 days (sometimes less). The main disadvantage is that stopovers are not allowed and if you have to change your dates of travel or destination, there will be extra charges to pay. Stand-by fares are another possibility. Some airlines will let you travel at the last minute if there are seats available just before departure. These tickets cost less than the economy fare but are usually not as cheap as the advance-purchase fares.

Of all the options, however, the cheapest way to go is via the so-called 'bucket shops'. These are travel agencies who sell discounted tickets and advertise in newspapers and magazines. Airlines only sell a certain percentage of their tickets through bucket shops, so the availability of seats can vary widely, particularly in the high season. You have to be flexible with these tickets, though if the agency is sold out for one flight, it can generally offer you something similar in the near future.

Most of the bucket shops are reputable organisations, but be careful, as there is always the occasional fly-by-night operator who sets up shop, takes your money for a bargain-basement ticket and then either disappears or issues you with an invalid or unusable ticket. Check what you are buying carefully before you hand over money, though I've used bucket shops for years and been handed the most weird and wonderful tickets (for example, tickets issued in East Berlin but bought in London for a flight from London to Malaysia with stopovers in New Delhi, Bangkok and Kuala Lumpur).

To/From North America
In the USA, the best way to find cheap flights is by checking the Sunday travel sections in the major newspapers, such as the *Los Angeles Times* or *San Francisco Examiner-Chronicle* on the west coast and the *New York Times* on the east coast. The student travel bureaux are also worth trying – STA Travel or Council Travel.

North America is a relative newcomer to the bucket shop traditions of Europe and Asia, so ticket availability and the restrictions attached to them need to be weighed against what is on offer on the more normal advance-purchase or economy fares.

Return tickets to Nairobi from New York (Air France) cost US$1340 in the low season (1 November to 14 December, 16 January to 24 March, 11-14 April) and US$1525 in the high season (15 December to 5 January, 25 March to 10 April, 15 June to 30 December). From Los Angeles, a return ticket costs US$1525 in the low season and US$1832 in the high season. If you shop around, it's possible to get one-way tickets from New York to Nairobi for as little as US$599 in the low season, and return tickets for US$1099 also in the low season.

From Canada, Air France offers flights from Toronto to Nairobi for US$1340 in the low season and US$1697 in the high season.

It may well be cheaper in the long run to fly first to London from the east coast of the USA using Virgin Atlantic (from around US$140 one way in the low season), or stand-by on the other airlines for a little more, and then buy a bucket shop ticket from there to Kenya with or without stopovers, but you must do your homework to be sure of this. All the main magazines which special-ise in bucket shop advertisements in London will mail you copies so you can study current prices before you decide on a course of action.

To/From Europe
You can find bucket shops by the dozen in London, Paris, Amsterdam, Brussels, Frankfurt and a few other places. In London, there are several newspapers with lots of bucket shop ads which will give you a good idea of current fares, as well as specialist magazines catering entirely to the travel industry.

Trailfinder is a magazine put out three times a year by Trailfinders (☎ (071) 938-3366), 46 Earls Court Rd, London W8 6EJ. It's free if you pick it up in London, but if you want it mailed, it costs UK£8 for three issues in the UK or Eire and UK£12 (US$20) for three issues in Europe or elsewhere in the world (airmail). Trailfinders can fix you up with all your ticketing requirements for any-where in the world as well as insurance, immunisation and books. They've been in business for years and can be highly recom-mended. All the staff are experienced travellers, so they speak your language. Trailfinders is open Monday to Saturday from 9 am to 6 pm (7 pm on Thursday).

Africa Travel Now is a newspaper put out quarterly by Africa Travel Centre (☎ (071) 387-1211), 4 Medway Court, Leigh St, London WC1H 9QX. It's free and, as its name indicates, specialises entirely in travel to and around Africa. It contains an excellent rundown of discounted flight prices to most major cities in Africa, as well as what safaris are available once you get there, along with costs. You can book all your safaris in advance at this place, in addition to getting your airline ticket, if you care to do that. Office hours are Monday to Friday from 9.30 am to 5.30 pm and Saturday from 10 am to 2 pm. As with Trailfinders, they're highly recommended.

London's weekly entertainment guide, *Time Out* (☎ (071) 836-4411), Tower House, Southampton St, London WC2E 7HD, is available from all bookshops and news-agents. Subscription enquiries should be addressed to Time Out Subs, Unit 8 Grove Ash, Bletchley, Milton Keynes MK1 1BZ, UK.

The price of airline tickets from London to Nairobi advertised in the above magazines is around UK£220 one way and UK£385 return. The corresponding fares to Dar es Salaam are UK£ 264/451 respectively.

The airlines used are generally Aeroflot and other Eastern European and Middle Eastern airlines, but this isn't always the case. Both Trailfinders and Africa Travel Centre can also fix you up with multi-stopover tickets which include Kenya and other African destinations.

There are also 'open jaws' tickets available (fly into one city/country and out of another), such as London to Kigali (Rwanda) plus Nairobi to London or vice versa for about UK£400. A specialist in this sort of fare is the Africa Travel System (☎ (071) 602-5091), 6 North End Parade, London W14 0SJ. It offers tickets such as London to Nairobi and Entebbe to London with Sabena for UK£585, London to Nairobi and Dar es Salaam to London with EgyptAir for UK£565, and London to Nairobi and Lilongwe to London with EgyptAir/Ethiopian for UK£685. On these tickets, you make your own travel arrangements between Nairobi and your place of departure.

Africa Travel System can also arrange tickets which take you east to Australasia after Africa, at prices comparable to anything you'll be offered at the bucket shops in Nairobi.

There is no advantage in buying a one-way ticket to Nairobi and then another one-way ticket back to Europe from there. You'll end up paying more than buying a return ticket in the first place. You may also run foul of immigration on arrival in Kenya without an onward ticket and be forced to buy one on the spot – an expensive exercise in lack of forethought.

A round-the-world (RTW) ticket is another economical option if that's what you want to do and have the time, but very few of these include African stopovers; Johannesburg is the most common. Starting and finishing in London with stopovers in Johannesburg, Perth, Sydney, San Francisco, Orlando and Washington, you're looking at around UK£811.

Don't take advertised fares as the gospel truth. To comply with truth-in-advertising laws, UK companies must be able to offer *some* tickets at their cheapest quoted price but they might only have one or two of them each week. If you are not one of the lucky ones, you could find yourself looking at tickets which cost up to UK£50 more (one-way or return). The best thing to do, therefore, is to start looking into tickets well before your intended departure date so you have a very good idea what is available.

Remember that discounted tickets cannot generally be paid for with a credit card. You must pay with cash or with a bank cheque.

To/From Asia

You may safely assume that flying is the only feasible way of getting between the Indian subcontinent and Kenya. There are plenty of flights between East Africa and Bombay, due to the large Indian population in Kenya. There are bucket shops of a sort in New Delhi, Bombay and Calcutta, and most of the discounted tickets will be with Air India. In New Delhi, I'd recommend Tripsout Travel, 72/7 Tolstoy Lane, behind the Government of India tourist office, Janpath.

Typical fares from Bombay to Nairobi are around US$312 return with either Ethiopian Airlines, Kenya Airways or Pakistan International Airlines (PIA; via Karachi).

In Nairobi there are a lot of bucket shops offering tickets to Karachi, Islamabad, New Delhi, Bombay and Calcutta. Most of these will be with Air India or PIA.

To/From Australia

There are no longer tight constraints on ticket discounting in Australia, but for Australians and New Zealanders, there are simply very few route options to Africa. The only direct connections are the weekly Qantas flight from Sydney to Perth and Harare (Zimbabwe), which costs about A$1760 return from Perth (A$1999 from

Melbourne or Sydney) in the low season (16 January to 15 February) and A$2200 from Perth (A$2500 from Melbourne or Sydney) in the high season (1 December to 15 January), and South African Airways' flight from Perth to Johannesburg. A return ticket from Sydney or Melbourne to Johannesburg costs the same as that to Harare; ie around A$1999 in the low season and A$2500 in the high season.

Another option between Australia and Africa is the weekly flight from Perth to Mauritius with Air Mauritius, from where there are twice-weekly flights to Nairobi. The fare is A$2000 from Sydney or Melbourne, and you can have a stopover in Mauritius if you wish. For about A$300 more, you can use another carrier from Melbourne, Sydney or Brisbane to Singapore and hook up with Air Mauritius there. Other cheap options include going via Bombay with Air India, or via Karachi with PIA. The price on either of these routes from Sydney or Melbourne is around A$2600.

It obviously makes sense for Australasians to think in terms of an RTW ticket or an Australia/New Zealand to Europe round-trip ticket with stopovers in Asia and Africa. It shouldn't be too much trouble for a travel agency to put together a ticket which includes various Asian stopovers plus a Nairobi stopover. Having Nairobi added to such a ticket bumps up the price a little, and you may have to go through several travel agencies before you get satisfaction, as many of them know very little about deals via Africa.

It's probably best to start your search for a ticket by looking in the travel section of the Saturday issue of either the *Sydney Morning Herald* or the *Age* and by visiting a student travel bureau. It's also worth writing or telephoning for a copy of *Airfares Guide* from The Travel Specialists (☎ (02) 262-3555), 62 Clarence St, Sydney, NSW 2000. It's been publishing this guide for a number of years now and it will give you a very good idea of what's available.

LEAVING EAST AFRICA

Nairobi is the best city in East Africa (and perhaps in the whole of Africa) to pick up cheap airline tickets for international flights. See the Leaving Kenya section of the Kenya Getting There & Away chapter for routes and costs.

Departure Tax

The airport departure tax for international flights from Kenya or Tanzania is US$20. You must pay this in foreign currency (cash); travellers' cheques and local currency are not accepted. Local currency can be reconverted into US dollars at the airport on presentation of a bank receipt proving you changed sufficient hard currency into local shillings. In Uganda, the departure tax for international flights is US$23, payable in either foreign currency or local currency.

Getting Around

AIR

There's a good network of internal flights within Kenya but much less so in Tanzania, Uganda, Rwanda, Burundi and Zaïre. Most of the internal sectors are serviced by the respective national carrier, but in Kenya and Tanzania, there are also quite a few private companies which operate light aircraft (six to eight-seater twin-propeller planes).

BUS, MATATU & TAXI

Buses are usually quicker than trains or trucks. In Kenya, where there's a good network of sealed roads, you may have the choice of going by so-called 'luxury' bus or by ordinary bus over certain routes. The luxury buses cost more but are not always quicker than the ordinary buses. In Tanzania there's also a choice of 'luxury' and ordinary buses, but only on the main routes: Arusha to Moshi and Dar es Salaam, and Dar es Salaam to Mombasa. Uganda has ordinary buses only. There are very few full-size buses in Burundi and Rwanda – minibuses are the rule. In Zaïre, buses and minibuses are few and far between, so you will be reliant on trucks for transport in most areas.

Most East African countries rely heavily on matatus for transport. They're generally more expensive than ordinary buses but are quicker. In Kenya and Tanzania, you can expect them to be packed to bursting point. Due to overloading, excessive speed, poor maintenance and driver recklessness, matatus in Kenya are not the safest way of getting around. In fact, they can be downright dangerous, and newspaper reports of matatu crashes are a regular feature. In Uganda, Rwanda and Burundi, however, travelling in minibuses is much safer.

Most countries also have share-taxis (which take up to five or six passengers and leave when full) and private taxis. You can forget about private taxis if you're on a budget, but share-taxis should definitely be considered. They can cost up to twice as much as the corresponding bus fare but in some places are only slightly more expensive than a matatu, and they're certainly quicker and more comfortable. They're also considerably safer than matatus.

TRUCK

For many travellers, trucks are the favoured means of transport. They may be the *only* form of transport in some areas. They're not only the cheapest way of getting from A to B as a rule, but you also get an excellent view from the top of the load.

For most regular runs there will be a 'fare', which is more or less fixed and is what the locals pay – but check this out before you agree to a price. Sometimes it's possible to get the truckie to lower the price if there's a group of you (form an impromptu group where possible). Trucks are generally

---

Road Conditions

The main roads of Kenya, Uganda, Rwanda and Burundi are sealed and generally in a good state of repair, though you'll occasionally encounter the odd rough patch. The main roads of Tanzania, however, are often in an appalling state (except for the Namanga to Moshi, Moshi to Dar es Salaam, and Dar es Salaam to Morogoro roads). The situation is similar in Zaïre.

Roads in far-flung rural areas of all East African countries may well be in a bad state of repair, so breakdowns and getting stuck, especially in the wet season, are a regular feature of any journey. Desert roads in north and north-east Kenya may just be a set of tyre tracks left in the sand or dust by previous trucks. Don't pay too much attention to red lines drawn on maps in places like this. Many roads are impassable in the wet season, and on some of them a convoy system may be in operation, so it's only possible to travel at certain times of the day. ∎

cheaper than buses over the same distance, but not always. Most of the time you'll be on top of the load, though you can sometimes travel in the cab for about twice what it costs on top.

There are trucks on main routes to most places every day, but in the more remote areas they may only run once or twice a week. Many lifts are arranged the night before departure at the 'truck park' – a compound/dust patch that you'll find in almost every African town. Just go there and ask around for a truck which is going your way. If the journey is going to take more than one night or one day, ask about food and drink.

TRAIN

Kenyan trains are excellent and are the preferred method of transport where they are available. Tanzanian trains are considerably slower but are still the preferred means of transport, since many roads are in such bad shape that going by bus is a generally uncomfortable experience. Ugandan trains are even slower, and long delays are common. The system has been allowed to run down badly over the last few years and passenger services have been curtailed. You probably wouldn't use them in the eastern part of the country, but they are a possibility if you're travelling west between Kampala and Kasese. Burundi, Rwanda and Eastern Zaïre have no railways.

Although the railway systems of Kenya, Uganda and Tanzania are interconnected, there are no international services.

Third class is usually very crowded and uncomfortable and you may have thieves to contend with, so it's not generally recommended. Second class is preferable and will cost you about the same as a bus over the same distance. Travelling 1st class will cost you about double what a bus would cost but does give you a considerable measure of privacy and comfort.

HITCHING

In Kenya, but less so in the other countries of East Africa, resident expatriates and aid workers with their own vehicles seem to be reasonably generous about offering free lifts. Remember that sticking out your thumb in many African countries is the equivalent of an obscene gesture, though allowances are generally made for foreigners. Wave your hand vertically up and down instead.

A word of warning about lifts in private cars. Smuggling across borders does go on, and if whatever is being smuggled is found, you may be arrested even though you knew nothing about it. Most travellers manage to convince police that they were merely hitching a ride and had nothing to do with the smuggler (passport stamps are a good indication of this), but the convincing can take days.

Free lifts on trucks are the exception rather than the rule, though it depends on the driver. You may have to wait a long time until a free lift comes along, and it's often not worth bothering.

Although many travellers hitchhike, it is not a totally safe way of getting around. Just because we explain how hitching works does not mean we recommend it.

BOAT

There are quite a few possibilities for travelling by boat, either on the lakes inland or along the coast. In particular, there are some amazingly venerable old steamships operating on the lakes. A trip on the MV *Liemba* on Lake Tanganyika is quite an experience.

There are international connections on Lake Victoria (Uganda-Tanzania) and Lake Tanganyika (Burundi-Tanzania-Zambia and Tanzania-Zaïre), but there are no international connections on Lake Victoria between Kenya and/or Uganda and Tanzania, or on Lake Kivu between Zaïre and Rwanda.

Along the coast, there are dhows and a catamaran between Kenya and Tanzania (Mombasa to Pemba, Zanzibar and Dar es Salaam). Between Dar es Salaam and Zanzibar, there's a choice of dhow, regular motorised boat, catamaran and hydrofoil. Further down the coast, there's a fairly regular ship between Dar es Salaam and Mtwara, calling at most small ports en route.

Kenya

Introduction

In past centuries the main visitors to Kenya were the Arab traders who plied their dhows along the eastern coast of Africa. These days it's tourists and adventurers who come to Kenya in large numbers – currently around one million annually – and little wonder as it has an amazing variety of attractions.

For many people Kenya means wildlife and in this field alone it is one of the best places in Africa. Millions of wildebeest on their annual migration, and equally large numbers of pink flamingos massing on the shores of the rift valley soda lakes are breathtaking sights. For sheer majesty it's hard to beat the sight of a herd of elephants crossing the plains with Africa's most famous mountain, the evocative snowcapped Kilimanjaro, rising in the background. Kenya is also the heart of safari country and a trip through a few of Kenya's spectacular reserves is a memorable experience.

If relaxation is on your mind then head for the coast. Mombasa is a town with a history, and from here any of the superb picture-post-card beaches are easily accessible. But without doubt the highlight of the coast is the island of Lamu, where the Arab influence is evident and the pace of life definitely a few steps behind the rest of the country – the perfect place to unwind for a week, or two...

Those people seeking more energetic pursuits will find no shortage of challenges – Kenya has some excellent mountains to climb, especially the popular Mt Kenya with its unusual alpine flora, and the much less visited Mt Elgon in the west on the Ugandan border. Organised camel treks through the semidesert north of the country also attract a steady stream of hardy souls.

The heart of this relatively prosperous country is the bustling capital, Nairobi, a friendly, modern and efficient city where things work and business can be taken care of in a snap – a far cry from so many other African countries where even simple things like a telephone call can be a major exercise. Added to this is the fact that Kenya has excellent air connections with Europe, Asia and elsewhere in Africa, making it the ideal place for a short visit, or the starting or finishing point for a longer sojourn in Africa. Either way it's a great place – don't miss it.

Facts about the Country

HISTORY
The Birthplace of Humanity
The rift valley which runs through the centre of Kenya has been established as the 'cradle of humanity' as a result of the now famous digs of the Leakey family in Olduvai Gorge (Tanzania) and around Lake Turkana (Kenya). Their discoveries of several hominoid skulls, one of which is estimated to be 2½ million years old, have radically altered the accepted theories on the origin of humans.

Before the East African digs, the generally accepted theory was that the ancestors of modern humans were of two different species: ape-like *Australopithecus africanus* and the *Australopithecus robustus*. It was believed one of these died out while the other gave rise to *Homo sapiens*. The Leakey discoveries suggested that there was a third contemporary species, *Homo habilis*, and that it was this one which gave rise to modern humans while both the Australopithecus species died out, leaving no descendants.

Early Settlement
This area of Africa has a large diversity of peoples – Kenya is home to almost every major language stock in Africa. Even Khoisan, the 'click' language spoken by the Bushmen and Hottentots in southern Africa, has its representatives, although these days they are only a tiny community close to the Tana River near the coast. This diversity is clear evidence that Kenya has been a major migratory pathway over the centuries.

The first wave of immigrants were the tall, nomadic, Cushitic-speaking people from Ethiopia who began to move south around 2000 BCE. They were pastoralists and depended on good grazing land for their cattle and goats, so when the climate began to change and the area around Lake Turkana became more arid, they were forced to resume their migration south. They were to reach as far as central Tanzania.

A second group of pastoralists, the Eastern Cushitics, followed them around 1000 BCE and occupied much of central Kenya. The rest of the ancestors of the country's medley of tribes arrived from all over Africa between 500 BCE and 500 CE, though there was still much movement and rivalry for land right up to the beginning of the 20th century. Even today it hasn't ended completely. The Bantu-speaking people (such as the Gusii, Kikuyu, Akamba and Meru) arrived from West Africa, while the Nilotic speakers (such as the Maasai, Luo, Samburu and Turkana) came from the Nile Valley in southern Sudan.

Arab Traders
While migrations were going on in the interior, Muslims from the Arabian peninsula and Shirazis from Persia (now Iran) began to visit the East African coast from the 8th century CE onwards. They came to trade, convert and settle, rather than conquer as they had done in North Africa and Spain. Their dhows would head down on the northeast monsoon bringing glassware, ironware, textiles, wheat and wine and return with ivory, slaves, tortoiseshell and rhino horn.

This trade soon extended right across the Indian Ocean to India and beyond. (Even China entered the fray at one point early in the 15th century, with a fleet of 62 ships and an escort of some 37,000 men, after the king of Malindi had sent the Chinese emperor a gift of a giraffe!) Many of the traders stayed to settle and intermarry with the Africans. As a result, a string of relatively affluent and Islamic-influenced coastal towns sprang up along the East African coast from Somalia to Mozambique, acting as entrepôts for the cross-Indian Ocean trade. Though there was naturally rivalry between these towns from time to time, up until the 16th century life was relatively peaceful. All this was to be rudely shattered with the arrival of the Portuguese.

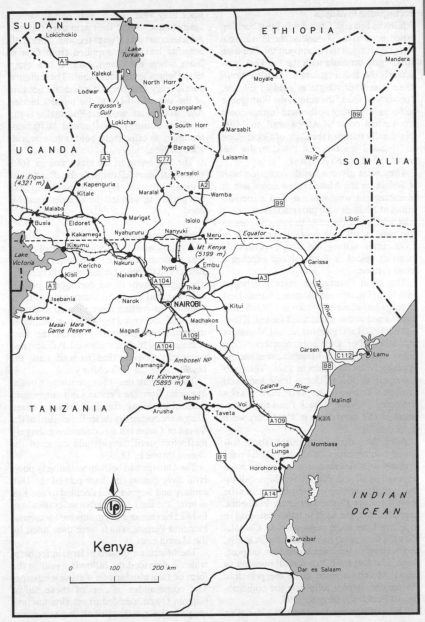

SUDAN

Lokichokio

A1

Kalekol

Lodwar

Ferguson's
Gulf

Lokichar

UGANDA

Mt Elgon
(4321 m) ▲

Kapenguria

Kitale

Malaba

Busia

Eldoret

Kakamega

Kisumu

Lake
Victoria

Kericho

Kisii

Isebania

A1

Musona

Masai Mara
Game Reserve

Magadi

Namanga

TANZANIA

Mt Kilimanjaro
(5895 m) ▲

Moshi

Arusha

Taveta

B1

Horohoro

A14

Lake
Turkana

North Horr

Loyangalani

South Horr

Baragoi

C77

Parsaloi

Maralal

A2

Marigat

Nyahururu

Isiolo

Nanyuki

Nakuru

Naivasha

A104

Narok

NAIROBI

Thika

A104

Machakos

A109

Amboseli NP

Mt Kenya
(5199 m) ▲

Nyeri

Embu

Meru

Equator

A3

Kitui

Galana   River

Voi

A109

Lunga
Lunga

ETHIOPIA

Moyale

Mandera

Marsabit

B9

Laisamis

Wajir

SOMALIA

Liboi

Garissa

Tana   River

Garsen

C112

Lamu

B8

Malindi

Kilifi

Mombasa

INDIAN
OCEAN

Zanzibar

Dar es Salaam

Kenya

0   100   200 km

Portuguese Invaders

While the Spanish Crown was busy backing expeditions to the Americas, the Portuguese were determined to circumvent the Ottoman Turks' grip on trade with the Far East, particularly the trade in spices which were worth more than their weight in gold in Europe. Throughout the 15th century, the Portuguese had been exploring further and further down the western coast of Africa until, in 1498, they finally rounded the Cape of Good Hope and headed up the east coast under the command of Vasco da Gama.

They were given a hostile reception both at Sofala on the Mozambique coast and at Mombasa but were lucky to find a friendly sultan at Malindi who provided them with a pilot who knew the route to India. Da Gama was back again with another expedition in 1502, after selling the first expedition's cargo of spices in Portugal and earning a small fortune.

The main Portuguese onslaught began with Dom Francisco de Almeida's armada of 23 ships and some 1500 men in 1505. Sofala was burned to the ground and looted, Kilwa was occupied and garrisoned, and Mombasa was taken after a naval bombardment and fierce street fighting. Mombasa was sacked again by Nuña da Cunha in 1528. The Arab monopoly of Indian Ocean trade had been broken. Though the Ottoman Turks attempted to wrest it back from the Portuguese in 1585 and again in 1589, they were unsuccessful.

After the original onslaught, there followed two centuries of harsh colonial rule. Tribute was demanded and levies were imposed on all non-Portuguese ships visiting the coastal towns. Severe retribution was the reward for the slightest offence. Economic exploitation came hand in hand with a drive to convert the local population to Catholicism but they never had much success at this, and whenever they abandoned an outpost, those who had been 'converted' reverted to Islam. Mombasa came to be the principle Portuguese outpost following the construction of Fort Jesus there in 1593.

The Portuguese task was made easier since they were able to play one sultan off against another, but their grip over the East African coast was always tenuous since their outposts had to be supplied from Goa in India, where the viceroy had his headquarters. Delays were inevitable. The colonial bureaucracy also became moribund because of the sale of offices to the highest bidder. And, in the final analysis, Portugal was too small a country and lacked sufficient resources to effectively hold onto a worldwide empire.

The beginning of the end came in 1698 when Fort Jesus fell to the Arabs after a siege lasting 33 months. By 1720, the Portuguese had packed up and left the Kenyan coast for good.

Omani Dynasties

The Arabs were to remain in control of the East African coast until the arrival of the British and Germans in the late 19th century. The depredations of the Portuguese period, however, had exacted a heavy price and the constant quarrelling among the Arab governors who succeeded them led to a decline in the trade and prosperity which the East African coast had once enjoyed. Political and economic recovery had to wait until the beginning of the 19th century.

Throughout the 18th century, Omani dynasties from the Persian Gulf entrenched themselves along the East African coast. They were nominally under the control of the Sultan of Oman but this control was largely ineffective until Seyyid Said came to the Omani throne in 1805.

The Omanis had built up a relatively powerful navy during the latter part of the 18th century and Seyyid Said decided to use this to bring the East African dynasties into line. In 1822 he sent an army to subdue Mombasa, Paté and Pemba, which were then ruled by the Mazrui clan.

The Mazruis appealed to Britain for help, which it provided the following year in the form of two warships on a survey mission. The commander of one of these ships, Captain Owen, decided to act first and ask questions later, so the British flag was raised over Fort Jesus and a protectorate was declared. A small garrison was left in charge, but three years later the British government repudiated the protectorate and the flag was hauled down. Seyyid Said reasserted his control the following year, garrisoned Fort Jesus and began to lay out clove plantations on Zanzibar. In 1832 he moved his court to Zanzibar.

19th-Century Colonialism

By the mid-19th century, several European nations were showing an interest in the East African coast, including the British and the Germans. The British were interested in the suppression of the slave trade and when Seyyid Said moved to Zanzibar they set up a consulate at his court. Later an agreement was reached between the British and the Germans as to their spheres of interest in East Africa. Part of the deal was that the Sultan of Zanzibar would be allowed to retain a 16 km-wide strip of the Kenyan coastline under a British protectorate. It remained as such right up until independence when the last Sultan of Zanzibar, Seyyid Khalifa, ceded the territory to the new government.

Since it was occupied by the Maasai pastoralists, the Kenyan interior, particularly the Rift Valley and the Aberdare highlands, remained impregnable to outsiders until the 1880s. Their reputation as a proud warrior tribe had been sufficient to deter Arab slavers and traders and European missionaries and explorers up to that date. But with the rest of Africa being combed by European explorers, Kenya's turn was soon to follow.

Notable early explorers who lived to tell the tale were Gustav Fischer (a German whose party was virtually annihilated by Maasai at Hell's Gate on Lake Naivasha in 1882), Joseph Thomson (a Scot who reached Lake Victoria via the Rift Valley lakes and the Aberdares in 1883), and Count Teleki von Szek (an Austrian who explored the Lake Turkana region and Mt Kenya in 1887). James Hannington, an Anglican bishop who set out in 1885 to set up a diocese in Uganda, wasn't quite so fortunate. He discovered Lake Bogoria (known as Lake Hannington during colonial days) but was killed when he reached the Nile.

By the late 19th century, the Maasai were considerably weakened and their numbers reduced by years of civil war between two opposing factions, the Ilmaasai and the Iloikop. The dispute was about which of the two were the true descendants of Olmasinta, the legendary founder of the tribe. Rinderpest (a cattle disease), cholera, smallpox and famine had also taken their toll between 1880 and 1892. Because of this, the British were able to negotiate a treaty with Olonana (known as Lenana today), the *laibon* (chief, or spiritual leader) of the Maasai. Armed with this treaty, the British were able to construct the Mombasa-Uganda railway through the heart of the Maasai grazing lands. The approximate halfway point of this railway is where Nairobi stands today.

White Settlement

With the railway completed and the headquarters of the colonial administration moved from Mombasa to Nairobi, White settlers began to move into the fertile highlands north of Nairobi in search of farming lands. Their interests naturally clashed with those of the Maasai, prompting the colonial authorities to pressure Olonana into restricting the Maasai to two reserves, one on either side of the new railway. Though this was a blow to Maasai independence, worse was to follow since the White settlers soon wanted the northern reserve as well. In 1910-11 those Maasai who lived there were forced to trek south, despite Olonana's objections.

Though it's probably true that it was the Maasai who had the greatest amount of land taken from them by the White settlers, the Kikuyu, a Bantu agricultural tribe which occupied the highlands around the western side of Mt Kenya, also suffered. The Kikuyu came to nurse a particular grievance about the alienation of land by White settlers later on in the 20th century. (See African Nationalism later in this chapter.) Many of the numerically larger tribes such as the Luo and Luyha and the tribes of the north-east were hardly affected, if at all.

White settlement in the early years of the 20th century was led by Lord Delamere, a pugnacious gentleman farmer from Cheshire, England. Since he was not familiar with the land, its pests and its wildlife, his first ventures – into sheep farming and, later, wheat growing – were disastrous. By 1912, however, following the move to the highlands, Delamere and his followers had put the colony onto a more realistic economic footing by establishing mixed agricultural farms. Other European settlers established coffee plantations about the same time, including Karen von Blixen and her hunter husband, Bror. Her memoirs are to be found in the book *Out of Africa*, which has also been made into a very successful film.

WW I interrupted White settlement of Kenya for four years during which some two-thirds of the 3000 White settlers formed impromptu cavalry units and went off in search of Germans in neighbouring Tanganyika, leaving their wives behind to manage the farms. They were not entirely successful but they did eventually manage to drive the German forces into Central Africa with assistance from Jan Smut's South African units. However, Vorbeck's intrepid unit of 155 Germans and 3000 Africans remained undefeated when the armistice was signed in November 1918. Under the Treaty of Versailles, Germany lost Tanganyika and the British were given a mandate by the League of Nations to control the territory.

Settlement of Kenya resumed after the war under a scheme where veterans of the European campaign were offered land in the highlands, either at rock-bottom prices or on long-term loans. The effect of this was to raise the White settler population to around 9000 by 1920. By the 1950s it had reached 80,000.

African Nationalism

While all this was going on, more and more Kikuyu were migrating to Nairobi or being drawn into the colonial economy in one way or another. They weren't at all happy about the alienation of their land and this led to the formation of a number of associations whose principle concern was the return of land to the Kikuyu.

One of the early leaders of the Kikuyu political associations was Harry Thuku. Shortly after he was arrested for his activities by the colonial authorities in March 1922, a crowd of Africans gathered outside the Nairobi Central Police Station where he was being held. Reports differ as to what happened next but by the time the police had stopped shooting, between 21 and 100 people had been killed.

Thuku was eventually exiled to Kisimayo and was only finally released from jail in 1930 after he had agreed to cooperate with the colonial authorities. His cooperation cost him his leadership of the Kikuyu movement since he was thenceforth regarded as a collaborator. This early Sharpeville led to the politicisation of the Kikuyu and was the start of a sustained campaign for political, social

Jomo Kenyatta

and economic rights. (Sharpeville refers to the notorious massacre by police of unarmed Black demonstrators in 1960 in the town of the same name in South Africa. It signalled the beginning of the ANC's armed struggle against the apartheid regime.)

While Harry Thuku's star was on the wane, that of another member of the tribe was on the rise. His name was Johnstone Kamau, later changed to Jomo Kenyatta, who was to become independent Kenya's first president. Kenyatta was born in 1892 in the highlands north of Nairobi, the son of a peasant farmer. He spent the early years of his life as a shepherd tending his fathers' flocks. When he was in his teens he ran away to a nearby Church of Scotland mission school where he picked up an education.

At the age of 29 he moved to Nairobi. He worked there as a court interpreter and water-meter reader but his real skills lay elsewhere – as an orator. He soon became the secretary for propaganda of the East Africa Association which had been set up to campaign for land reform, better wages, education and medical facilities for Africans. At this time, Africans were barred from hotels and restaurants and were only considered for the most menial jobs within the colonial administration.

Although it was official British government policy to favour African interests over those of the settlers in the event of conflicts, this was often ignored in practice because of the dominance of Lord Delamere's lobby in the Whites-only legislative council which had been formed after the protectorate became a colony. Recognising this, Kenyatta soon moved to join the more outspoken Kikuyu Central Association as its secretary-general.

Shortly afterwards, in 1929, with money supplied by Indians with communist connections, he sailed for London to plead the Kikuyu case with the British colonial secretary. Though the colonial secretary declined to meet him, Kenyatta teamed up with a group called the League Against Imperialism which took him to Moscow and Berlin and then back again to Nairobi. He returned to London the following year and remained there for the next 15 years. He spent his time perfecting his oratory with Trafalgar Square crowds, studying revolutionary tactics in Moscow, visiting cooperative farms in Scandinavia and building up the Pan-African Federation with Hastings Banda (who later became the president of Malawi) and Kwame Nkrumah (who later became the president of Ghana). By the time he returned to Kenya in 1946, he was the recognised leader of the Kenyan liberation movement.

During WW II, the Belgian, British, French and Italian governments all recruited African troops to fight. The overall effect on Africans (as well as soldiers from other colonised peoples) was a realisation that the Europeans were not omnipotent. They could be defeated or, at the least, forced to come to terms with African aspirations for the same benefits and opportunities as their European overlords. Africans had also been trained in the use of arms. When the war ended, therefore, the returning soldiers were in no mood to accept the status quo and began to actively campaign for change.

The main African political organisation involved in the confrontation with the colonial authorities was the Kenya African Union (KAU), first headed by Harry Thuku and then by James Gichuru who himself stood down in favour of Kenyatta on the latter's return from Britain. The Kikuyu Central Association had been banned in 1940 along with many other similar organisations.

Mau Mau Rebellion

As the demands of the KAU became more and more strident and the colonial authorities less and less willing to make concessions, oath-taking ceremonies began to spread among various tribes like the Kikuyu, Maasai and Luo. Some of these secret oaths bound the participants to kill Europeans and their African collaborators. The Mau Mau was one such secret political society which bonded its members, willingly or otherwise, to the organisation via oathing ceremonies. Formed in 1952, it consisted mainly of

Kikuyu tribespeople, and its aim was to drive White settlers out of Kenya.

The first blow was struck early in 1953 with the killing of a White farmer's entire herd of cattle. This was followed, a few weeks later, by the massacre of 21 Kikuyu loyal to the colonial government. The Mau Mau rebellion had started. The government declared an emergency and began to herd the tribespeople into 'protected villages' surrounded by barbed wire and booby-trapped trenches which they were forbidden to leave during the hours of darkness. Some 20,000 Kikuyu 'home guards' were recruited to assist British army units brought in to put down the rebellion and to help police the 'protected villages'. By the time it came to an end in 1956 with the defeat of the Mau Mau, the death toll stood at over 13,500 Africans – Mau Mau guerrillas, civilians and troops – and just over 100 Europeans, only 37 of whom were settlers. In the process, an additional 20,000 Kikuyu had been thrown into detention camps.

Only a month after the rebellion started, Kenyatta and several other KAU leaders were arrested and put on trial as the alleged leaders of the Mau Mau. It's very doubtful that Kenyatta had any influence over the Mau Mau commanders, let alone that he was one of their leaders, but he was, nevertheless, sentenced to seven years' jail in the remote Turkana region after a trial lasting five months. He was released in 1959 but was immediately sent to Lodwar under house arrest.

The rebellion shook the settlers to the roots and gave rise to a number of White political parties with opposing demands, ranging from partition of the country between Blacks and Whites to the transfer of power to a democratically elected African government. It should have been obvious to anyone with eyes to see that the latter view would have to prevail in the end, but it wasn't adopted as official policy until the Lancaster House Conference in London in 1960. The rebellion did lead, however, to an exodus of White settlers who packed their bags and headed off to Rhodesia, South Africa and Australia. At the conference, independence was scheduled for December 1963 and the British government agreed to provide the new Kenyan government with US\$100 million in grants and loans so that it would be able to buy out European farmers in the highlands and restore the land to the tribes from whom it had been taken.

In the meantime a division occurred in the ranks of the KAU between those who wanted a unitary form of government with firm centralised control in Nairobi and the others who favoured a federal set-up in order to avoid Kikuyu domination. The former renamed their party the Kenya African National Union (KANU) and the latter split off under the leadership of Ronald Ngala to become the Kenya African Democratic Union (KADU). Many of the White settlers, who had come to accept the inevitable, supported the KADU.

Kenyatta was released from house arrest in mid-1961 and assumed the presidency of the KANU. Despite his long period of incarceration by the colonial authorities, he appeared to harbour no resentment against the Whites and indeed set out to reassure the settlers that they would have a future in the country when independence came. At a packed meeting of settlers in Nakuru Town Hall in August 1963, he asked them to stay, saying that the country needed experience and that he didn't care where it came from. He assured them of the encouragement and protection of the new government and appealed for harmony, saying that he wanted to show the rest of the world that different racial groups were capable of living and working together. It did the trick. Kenyatta's speech transformed him, in the eyes of the settlers, from the feared and reviled spiritual leader of the Mau Mau into the venerable *mzee* (respected elder) of the post-independence years.

Most of the White settler farms have been bought out by the government over the years and the land divided up into small subsistence plots which support 15 to 20 people. This may well have appeased the pressure for land redistribution in a country with the world's highest birth rate but it has led to a serious decline in agricultural production (and therefore a diminishing tax base for the government) and has threatened to damage the region's delicate ecology. By 1980, Kenya was forced to import half its grain needs whereas in 1975 it was self-sufficient in these. The government is keen to halt the break-up of the 100-odd settler farms which remain but the prospects of being able to do this in a land-hungry nation are not good.

Independence

The two parties, KANU and KADU, formed a coalition government in 1962, but after the May 1963 elections, KANU and Kenyatta came to power. Independence came on 12 December 1963 with Kenyatta as the first president. He was to rule Kenya until his death in 1978. Under Kenyatta's presidency, Kenya developed into one of Africa's most stable and prosperous nations. Unlike many other newly independent countries, there was no long string of coups and counter-coups, military holocausts, power-crazy dictators and secessionist movements. It wasn't all plain sailing but he left the country in a much better state than he found it and, although there were excesses, they were minor by African standards. By the time he died, there were enough Kenyans with a stake in their country's continued progress to ensure a relatively smooth succession to the presidency. Violence and instability would have benefited few people. Kenyatta's main failings were that he was excessively biased in favour of his own tribe and that he often regarded honest criticism as tantamount to treason.

Control of the government and large sectors of the economy still remain in the hands of the Kikuyu, to the social and financial detriment of other ethnic groups. Corruption in high places remains a problem and once prompted J M Kariuki, a former Mau Mau fighter and later an assistant minister in the government, to remark that Kenya had become a nation of '10 millionaires and 10 million beggars'. There are indeed great disparities in wealth. Many destitute squat-

ters and unemployed people, especially in Nairobi, have little hope of ever finding employment – but this is hardly a problem peculiar to Kenya.

In 1964, Kenya effectively became a one-party state following the voluntary dissolution of the opposition KADU party. With it died the party's policy of regionalism, and the two-chamber legislature became the single-chamber legislative assembly. However, when Oginga Odinga, a Luo, was purged from the KANU hierarchy in 1966 over allegations that he was plotting against the government, he resigned from the vice-presidency and formed his own opposition party, the Kenya People's Union. The party was later banned and Odinga was jailed. He was released when he agreed to rejoin KANU, but was imprisoned again in 1969 on spurious charges. After his release in 1971 he was banned from running for public office until 1977.

Similarly, Tom Mboya, an intelligent young Luo who was widely regarded as future presidential material, was murdered by a Kikuyu gunman in 1969. The ambitious Mboya was feared by influential Kikuyu who felt that he might have designs on succeeding Kenyatta as president. J M Kariuki, a very popular Kikuyu who spoke out stridently and often about the new Black elite and their corrupt practices, met a similar fate. He was assassinated in 1975. Other politicians who opposed Kenyatta – however mildly – found themselves arrested and held for long periods, often without trial.

The 1980s

Kenyatta was succeeded by Daniel arap Moi, a member of the Tugen tribe and regarded by Kikuyu power brokers as a suitable front man for their interests. Lacking the charisma of Kenyatta and the cult following which he enjoyed, Moi was even less willing to brook criticism of his regime and his early years were marked by the arrest of dissidents, the disbanding of tribal societies and the closure of universities. There were allegations of conspiracies to overthrow the government whose details were often so labyrinthine they could have come straight out of a modern spy novel. Whether these conspiracies were real or just a convenient façade to justify Moi's consolidation of power is hard to tell since names and details were rarely released.

What certainly was real was the attempted coup by the Kenyan air force in August 1982. It was put down by forces loyal to the government but, by the time it was over, about 120 people had been killed and there was widespread looting of the major shopping areas. Twelve ringleaders were subsequently sentenced to death and 900 others received jail sentences. The entire Kenyan air force was disbanded and replaced by a new unit.

Since then, other alleged conspiracies have come to light but, again, the details are rarely made known. The most publicised of these clandestine opposition groups was Mwakenya which supposedly centred around a number of lecturers at Nairobi University along with the exiled novelist and playwright, Ngũgĩ wa Thiong'o. Certainly Ngũgĩ has made his opposition to the Kenyan government quite plain but there is little evidence to support the claim that he was a leading light behind the movement.

President Moi was re-elected in March 1987 in an election which was most notable for the controversial voting system it employed. Candidates could only run in the secret ballot election after gaining a set percentage of the vote in a preliminary election whereby voters queued behind the candidate of their choice. If the candidate gained more than 70% of the queue vote, they were automatically elected and did not have to take part in the secret ballot election. The outcome was that at least 45 constituencies had no secret ballot as the candidate who had received over 70% of the turnout in the queue vote was automatically elected (it didn't matter that in one case the turnout was less than 9% of registered voters). In other constituencies, the number of candidates was significantly reduced because the nominees failed to win sufficient support at the preliminary election.

After the election, Moi expanded his cabinet to 33 ministers – many on the basis of political patronage – and, as a result, the government's (and therefore Moi's) position seemed totally secure. With the fall of a couple of outspoken politicians in the 1987 elections (amid allegations of vote rigging) it seemed unlikely that parliamentary opposition to Moi on major issues in the immediate future would be anything more than a whisper. Perhaps more significantly, changes to the constitution were rushed through parliament unopposed in late 1987 which gave Moi increased presidential powers, including the right to dismiss senior judges and public servants without redress. The independence of the judiciary had been a much-admired cornerstone of the Kenyan political system ever since independence and the changes were viewed with alarm by many sections of society.

From this point on there ceased to be any effective political opposition within the parliamentary system and the party further strengthened its hold by augmenting the ranks of the KANU Youth Wing who essentially served as pro-government vigilantes. They were frequently unleashed to disrupt demonstrations, harass opposition figures and maintain a climate of intimidation amongst those who might have similar thoughts. Many opposition political leaders were detained without trial during this period.

Yet the government was unable to silence various leaders of the Christian churches (especially the bishops of the Anglican church) who increasingly turned their sermons into political speeches. They were supported by an outspoken critic of government nepotism, Professor Wangui Mathai, the leader of the Green movement. All of them were vilified by both the president and various ministers and there were calls for their removal and even arrest on charges of sedition. Mathai probably suffered most when she was thrown out of her modest offices on University Way and forced to endure a public character assassination blitz whose script could have been put together from the trash scrawled on toilet walls.

But times were changing. Multiparty politics was sweeping Africa and Kenya was not to escape.

The 1990s

With the collapse of Communism in Eastern Europe and the break-up of the Soviet Union, the West's attention was abruptly refocused. No longer was it necessary to prop up corrupt African regimes which grabbed Western aid for all it was worth and pocketed the lion's share of the proceeds in the name of containing Communism. All that was finished.

The Kenyan government quickly found itself under intense pressure from the donor countries to introduce a multiparty system and to name a date for elections if aid were to be maintained. Though it prevaricated for a while, the government, faced with a foreign debt of some US$9 billion, a downturn in the economy, and determined grass-roots opposition in the form of FORD (Forum for the Restoration of Democracy), was forced to capitulate. To drive the point home, aid was suspended by virtually all Western countries in early 1992.

Suddenly, everyone was talking politics everywhere and anywhere and there emerged a clear consensus that FORD would sweep to victory in any election assuming it could keep its act together and that the elections were reasonably 'free and fair'. Unfortunately, the opposition shot itself in the foot in the lead-up to the elections. The principle players were Oginga Odinga, Kenneth Matiba, and Mwai Kibaki. Originally all members of FORD, but unable to stomach the idea of anyone but themselves being the new president, they split the party into three – FORD-Kenya (Oginga Odinga), FORD-Asili (Kenneth Matiba), and the Democratic Party or DP (Mwai Kibaki). From that point on, they had no chance.

In the meantime, Moi, no doubt, watched with glee. But he did more than that. According to the IMF/World Bank, he authorised the printing of KSh 9 billion (over US$250 million), unsupported by foreign currency/gold reserves, which was used to line the pockets of his supporters and blatantly

buy votes for the ruling party (KANU). In the lead-up to the elections, the newspapers were full of pictures and stories of *wananchi* (peasants and workers) lining up to collect their KSh 500, a KANU-emblazoned T-shirt and a cap. Moi knew that full stomachs bought votes even if the economy collapsed shortly after the elections. Which it virtually did.

He also played the tribal card for all it was worth in his home area, allowing the Kalenjin to wreak havoc amongst Kikuyu settlers in the area whilst at the same time denying any complicity with police lack of action. Hundreds were killed and injured in these tribal clashes and thousands left homeless and destitute. Hardly anything has been done since to rehabilitate these people. The violence succeeded in driving Kikuyu (who were clearly not going to vote for KANU) from Kalenjin areas (Moi's home ground).

Another blatant ploy was to postpone the election until the final week of December and to ensure that it fell on a normal working day. Had it not finally been declared a public holiday about a week in advance, thousands of registered voters, particularly in the Nairobi area, would have been unable to travel back to the place where they were registered in order to vote. Moi was aware that he had little support in the Nairobi area and amongst the Kikuyu as the elections results were to show.

To curry the favour of the donor nations, international observers were brought in to monitor a cross section of the polling stations and to decide whether the elections had been 'free and fair'. As far as the voting itself went, the elections were fair to a greater rather than a lesser degree, though the various opposition parties predictably denied this. The trouble was, the observers were flown in only days before the election and, by then, the dirty deeds had been done. Moi and KANU swept to victory yet with only one-third of the total vote. Clearly, the opposition would have won if they had presented a united front but vanity and ambition got in the way.

Vanity and ambition also resurfaced shortly after the elections as several MPs, unable to stomach the prospect of life on the opposition benches, cynically defected to the KANU and were welcomed with glee. Loyalty to the voters who had elected them on an opposition ticket was apparently of no concern to these MPs.

The Future

Once the new Kenyan parliament gets down to serious business instead of staging walk-outs and trading insults (and even fisticuffs), the government will have a much harder job ahead of it. No longer will it be able to do just what it pleases. Outstanding issues which need urgent attention are corruption, the economy and resolution of the chaos in the currency market.

It's perhaps unfair to hammer a fledgling democracy in this way – how long did it take the Europeans and North Americans to get their systems stabilised and how much bloodshed did it involve? – but it's the '90s and the world is a smaller place. What cannot be excused is Moi's cynical sabotage of the economy in the pursuit of continued political power. This has affected everyone and those at the bottom of the economic scale most. Inflation is now rampant and prices are escalating daily, yet wages have remained the same. No doubt things will stabilise before too long since, after all, Kenya does have a diverse economy, but that may not be before major social upheaval.

And it's not just the economy which the government has to deal with but the continuing population expansion of around 4% per annum (one of the highest in the world) which is going to see Kenya's population grow from its present 22 or 23 million to around 37 or 38 million by the end of the century. This is already putting intense strain on health and educational facilities and is likely to result in increasing social, economic and political turmoil. Of the estimated 400,000 school leavers who come onto the job market each year, only around 30,000 manage to find formal jobs. Or, put another way, of the labour pool of some seven million, there are only about one million formal wage-paying jobs. By the end of the century, it's estimated that the labour pool will double.

This is an enormous problem, the solution to which is not at all obvious. The International Monetary Fund (IMF), from which Kenya was seeking loan support, prescribed the usual 'structural adjustment programme' (SAP) which included the sacking of some 45,000 civil servants. To most Kenyans, this was a dangerous and counterproductive measure since, on average, each wage earner in Kenya supports five people. The measure, if carried out, would therefore have directly affected a quarter of a million people. Indirectly, it would have affected the livelihoods of millions more since those affected by the cuts would have been forced to curtail their spending to the very bare essentials.

It seemed obvious to all those on the Kenyan side of the negotiating table that the IMF's SAP was designed not to create jobs but to push unemployment to an unacceptably high level, wipe out small business and put most products out of the reach of the average family. It would also clearly not wipe out corruption but increase it since, as those still in a job would find it harder and harder to make ends meet, the only solution would be to demand higher bribes for any service rendered. A corollary of this for those thrown out of work, their dependants and others who found themselves destitute, would have been a marked increase in crime, particularly robbery and theft. The effects of hard economic times are already plainly visible especially in Nairobi where there has been a vast increase in child beggars, on the one hand, and muggings by teenagers and young men, on the other.

Fortunately, to Kenya's credit, the IMF was thrown out in March 1993. It was a brave move in many ways, but the consequences may be just as traumatic. Most bilateral and multilateral aid is linked to IMF/World Bank approval of a country's economic policies. Without that approval, aid from the USA and Europe may not be resumed. The move incited a hot debate in the country's press about the pros and cons of aid. Some suggested it was a foolhardy decision which would bring further hardship and see Kenya marginalised; others suggested it was about time Kenya stopped relying so heavily on foreign aid and got its own act together. There are merits to both arguments but, when the dust has settled, the problems which led to Kenya's current turmoil will still be there and will have to be constructively addressed. ■

Since then, Moi has continued to rule in much the same fashion as before and the opposition has so far disgraced itself in farcical public conflicts over who should be the opposition leader. This was finally resolved with the choice of Kenneth Matiba – leader of FORD-Asili, the party which gathered the majority of the opposition votes.

GEOGRAPHY

Kenya straddles the equator and covers an area of some 583,000 sq km which includes around 13,600 sq km of inland water in the form of part of Lake Victoria. It is bounded in the north by the arid bushlands and deserts of Ethiopia and Sudan, to the east by Somalia and the Indian Ocean, to the west by Uganda and Lake Victoria, and to the south by Tanzania.

The country can be roughly divided into four main zones: the coastal belt, the Rift Valley and central highlands, western Kenya and northern and eastern Kenya.

Coastal Belt

This area covers some 480 km of Indian Ocean littoral including coral reefs and beaches, the Lamu archipelago, the Tana River estuary (Kenya's principal river) and a narrow, low-lying and relatively fertile strip suitable for agriculture. Beyond this, the land rises fairly steeply towards the central plateau and gives way to bushland and scrub desert.

Rift Valley & Central Highlands

These regions form the backbone of the country and it's here that Kenya is at its most spectacular scenically. The lake-studded Rift Valley runs the whole length of the country from Lake Turkana to Lake Magadi and is peppered with the cones of extinct volcanoes. It's bounded on the eastern side by the thickly forested slopes of the Aberdare Mountains and, further to the east, by the massif of Mt Kenya – Africa's second-highest mountain at 5199 metres. This is the most fertile area of the country and the lower slopes of the mountains are intensively cultivated. Nairobi, the capital, sits at the southern end of the central highlands.

Western Kenya

The west of the country consists of an undulating plateau stretching from the Sudanese border to Tanzania in the south. The northern part, particularly around the shores of Lake Victoria, is fertile, well watered and intensively cultivated and it's here that Mt Elgon (Kenya's second-highest mountain at 4321 metres) is situated. Further south the land gradually merges into scrub and savannah and is suitable only for cattle grazing but it's here that Kenya's largest and most popular wildlife sanctuaries are situated – Masai Mara, Amboseli and Tsavo. To the south of Amboseli rises the spectacular massif of Mt Kilimanjaro – Africa's highest mountain.

Northern & Eastern Kenya

These two regions cover a vast mountainous area of bushland, scrub and desert where rainfall is sparse and where the land is suitable only for cattle grazing. It's this area, however, where Kenya is at its wildest and most untouched by the modern world.

CLIMATE

Because of Kenya's diverse geography, temperature, rainfall and humidity vary widely but there are effectively four zones about which generalisations can be made.

The undulating plateau of western Kenya is generally hot and fairly humid with rainfall spread throughout the year though most of it falls in the evenings. The highest falls are usually during April when a maximum of 200 mm may be recorded, whilst the lowest falls are in January with an average of 40 mm. Temperatures range from a minimum of 14 or 18°C to a maximum of 30 to 34°C.

The central highlands and Rift Valley enjoy perhaps the most agreeable climate in the country though there's quite a variation between the hot and relatively dry floor of the central rift valley and the snow-covered peaks of Mt Kenya. Rainfall varies from a minimum of 20 mm in July to 200 mm in April and falls essentially in two seasons –

March to May (the 'long rains') and October to December (the 'short rains'). The Aberdare mountains and Mt Kenya are the country's main water-catchment areas and falls of up to 3000 mm per year are often recorded. Average temperatures vary from a minimum of 10 or 14°C to a maximum of 22 to 26°C.

The vast semiarid bushlands, deserts and lava flows of northern and eastern Kenya are where the most extreme variations of temperature are to be found, ranging from up to 40°C during the day in the deserts down to 20°C or less at night. Rainfall in this area is sparse and when it does fall it often comes in the form of violent storms. July is generally the driest month and November the wettest. The average annual fall varies between 250 and 500 mm.

The fourth climatic zone is the coastal belt which is hot and humid all year round though tempered by coastal sea breezes. Rainfall ranges from a minimum of 20 mm in February to a maximum of 300 mm in May. The average annual fall is between 1000 mm and 1250 mm. Average temperatures vary little throughout the year ranging from a minimum of 22°C to a maximum of 30°C.

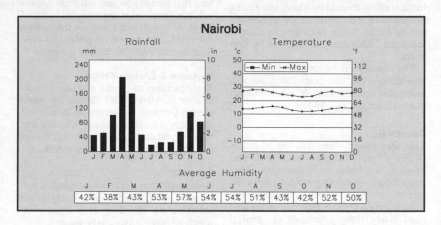

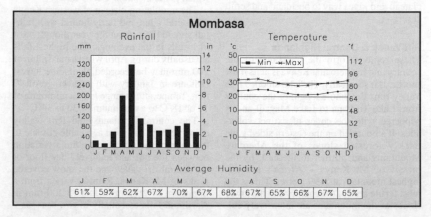

FLORA & FAUNA

Flora

With its range of physiographic regions, Kenya has a corresponding diversity in its flora. The vast plains of the south are characterised by distinctive flat-topped acacia trees, and interspersed with these are equally distinctive bottle-shaped baobab trees and thorn bushes.

On the slopes of Mt Elgon and Mt Kenya the flora changes with altitude. Above about 1000 metres it is thick evergreen temperate forest which continues to around 2000 metres and then gives way to a belt of bamboo forest up to about 3000 metres. Above this height is mountain moorland which is characterised by the amazing groundsel tree *(Dendrosencio)* with its huge cabbage-like flowers, and giant lobelias with long spikes. In the semidesert plains of the north and north-east the vegetation cover is unremarkable, yet very characteristic – thorn bushes seem to go on forever. In the northern coastal areas mangroves are prolific and the trees are cut for export, mainly to the Middle East for use as scaffolding; mangrove wood is termite resistant and is in high demand.

Fauna

Kenya has such a dazzling array of wildlife that game-viewing in the national parks is one of the main attractions of a visit to this country. All of the 'big five' (lion, buffalo, elephant, leopard and rhino) can be seen in at least two of the major parks, and there's a huge variety of other less famous but no less impressive animals.

To aid identification of animals while you're game-spotting on safari, refer to the Safari Guide at the back of this book. For a full treatment of Kenya's animals, *A Field Guide to the Mammals of Africa* (Collins, 1988) has excellent colour plates to aid identification as does the smaller *A Field Guide to the Larger Mammals of Africa* (Collins, 1986). The main trouble with both these books is the relatively poor index (which lists many animals only by their Latin names) and the placement of the colour plates often far from the actual description of

the animals in question. *Animals of East Africa* (Hodder & Stoughton, 1960) has good descriptive notes of the animals' habits and appearance, but the sketches are not the greatest and the notes on distribution are out of date.

The birdlife is equally varied and includes ostriches, vultures, eagles, a wide variety of water birds such as flamingos, storks, pelicans, herons, ibis and cormorants, and others such as the yellow weaver birds which you'll see everywhere. The best reference source for twitchers is *A Field Guide to the Birds of East Africa* by John G Williams. It is widely available in Kenya.

NATIONAL PARKS & GAME RESERVES

Kenya's national parks and game reserves rate among the best in Africa. Obviously the tremendous variety of birds and mammals is the main attraction, and the more popular parks such as Masai Mara Game Reserve and Amboseli National Park see huge numbers of visitors – from the budget campers to the hundreds-of-dollars-a-day Hilton hoppers. In the peak season (from January to February) on a game drive, you can observe at close quarters the daily habits of the prolific Nissan Urvan. Other smaller parks, such as Saiwa Swamp National Park, near Kitale in the country's western highlands, would be lucky to see a handful of visitors a day at any time of year.

In addition to the protection of wildlife, some parks have been created to preserve the landscape itself, and these too can be exciting and rewarding places to visit – places such as Mt Kenya, Mt Elgon, Hell's Gate, Mt Longonot and the Kakamega Forest are all worth investigating.

Marine life is also in abundance and the marine national parks of Malindi and Watamu off the central coast both offer excellent diving possibilities. Shimoni and Wasini islands in the extreme south offer even better opportunities but are much less accessible and developed.

What probably helps to make Kenyan parks such a draw card for the budget traveller is that the competition among safari

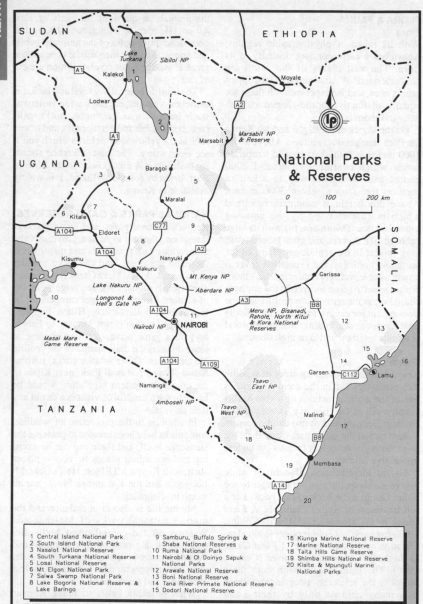

National Parks & Reserves

0   100   200 km

1 Central Island National Park
2 South Island National Park
3 Nasalot National Reserve
4 South Turkana National Reserve
5 Losai National Reserve
6 Mt Elgon National Park
7 Saiwa Swamp National Park
8 Lake Bogoria National Reserve &
   Lake Baringo

9 Samburu, Buffalo Springs &
   Shaba National Reserves
10 Ruma National Park
11 Nairobi & Ol Doinyo Sapuk
   National Parks
12 Arawale National Reserve
13 Boni National Reserve
14 Tana River Primate National Reserve
15 Dodori National Reserve

16 Kiunga Marine National Reserve
17 Marine National Reserve
18 Taita Hills Game Reserve
19 Shimba Hills National Reserve
20 Kisite & Mpunguti Marine
   National Parks

Wildlife Conservation

As Kenya relies so heavily on tourism for income, and because it's the animals which people have chiefly come to see, the government has placed a high priority on wildlife conservation and the eradication of poaching. To this end it has appointed Richard Leakey, grandson of Louis Leakey, head of the Kenya Wildlife Service, and he has not been afraid to stick his neck out and get things done. Poaching patrols are now much more efficient, extremely stiff penalties for poaching are now in effect, and the estimated 500 of the service's Land Rovers which had been left to rot due to lack of maintenance are gradually being refurbished and pressed into service. It was Leakey who recommended that President Moi should take a high-profile stance on Kenya's anti-ivory policy and burn the stockpile of confiscated ivory in 1989. This action got good press coverage abroad but was widely criticised at home by people who thought that the ivory should have been sold and the money (estimated at around US$3 million) put to good use.

It's a moot point since although the tourist industry brings in some US$400 million a year, the budget for the national parks was, until very recently, only a tiny fraction of this amount and depended heavily for its anti-poaching measures on gifts from Western governments and environmental groups.

Yet, despite the risks, poaching still goes on and has virtually become a war between the Kenyan government and the poachers who turn to robbing tourists when denied elephants and rhino. And it's easy to see the reasons for poaching. There is big money in ivory and rhino horn and as long as the Taiwanese government and various Arab governments – notably the two Yemens, Oman and Kuwait – refuse to ban their importation, the slaughter of Kenya's wildlife is likely to continue. A kg of ivory is worth about US$300 wholesale and rhino horn is US$2000 a kg (or up to US$30,000 for a single horn). In the Middle East, rhino horn is prized for dagger handles whilst in China and Korea, in powdered form, it's a supposed aphrodisiac.

Although poaching has been going on for many years, it took on a new dimension in 1972 as a result of the drought in north-eastern Africa which rendered some 250,000 Somali pastoralists destitute as their sheep, goats and camels died by the million. Many drifted south armed with weapons ranging from bows and arrows to WW II guns and found poaching to be a suitable antidote to poverty. Meanwhile, corruption in the Kenya Wildlife Service deepened, with officials taking bribes in return for turning a blind eye to the poachers' activities. By 1976, it was plain that the number of elephants being slaughtered by poachers far exceeded those dying as a result of drought and deforestation and it was estimated that there were over 1300 poachers operating within Tsavo National Park alone.

Worse was yet to come. In 1978, waves of Somalis hungry for ivory and rhino horn and encouraged by official corruption swept across the border and into the national parks, only this time they came with modern automatic weapons issued to them by the Somali government during the 1977 war with Ethiopia. They killed everything in their path including any Kenyan tribal poachers they came across. By the end of the decade, some 104,000 elephants (about 62% of the total) and virtually the entire rhino population had been slaughtered.

There was little improvement during the early '80s despite the setting up of anti-poaching patrols armed with modern weapons, high-speed vehicles and orders to shoot on sight. Part of the reason was the patrols' reluctance to engage the Somalis who have a reputation for toughness and uncompromising violence. By 1989, however, following George Adamson's murder by poachers in the Kora National Reserve and attacks on tourists in other national parks, the Kenyan government signalled its determination to seriously address the problem. Following Leakey's appointment, corrupt wildlife officials were sacked and the anti-poaching units beefed up, even to the extent that 200 US-trained paramilitary personnel were deployed in 1990 on shoot-to-kill patrols.

The measures have had a large degree of success though it appears that some poachers, denied ivory, are turning to robbing tourists. A few tourists have actually been shot dead and others seriously injured but the numbers are very small – less than 10 so far. Put in the context of the huge numbers of tourists who visit Kenya (around 800,000 to a million each year), that's still a pretty good safety record and it's only fair to add that some areas are worse than others. Masai Mara, Amboseli and Samburu are considered safe, for example, whereas parts of Tsavo East and Meru are more dubious. ■

companies for the traveller's dollar is so fierce that a safari of at least a few days is within the reach of the vast majority of travellers. For those at the other end of the scale the competition is equally brisk and there are lodges and tented camps within the major parks which have superb facilities and are a real experience – if you can afford them.

Information

Entry Fees The entry fees to all national parks and to Masai Mara Game Reserve is US$12 per person per day for nonresidents (US$1.50 for residents) plus US$1.50 for a car. Camping costs US$3.20 per person per night for nonresidents, and US$0.80 for residents. Children's entry fees are US$1.35 for nonresidents (US$0.55 for residents) and camping fees US$1.20/0.80. Entry fees to game reserves other than Masai Mara vary because they are administered by local county councils but to be on the safe side it's best to assume they are the same as for national parks. If you find them less, consider it a bonus.

The latest word from the Kenya Wildlife Service is that the above fees are due to rise soon but the exact figures have not yet been agreed on.

Maps If you are driving your own vehicle it's a good idea to equip yourself with maps of the parks before you set out. The best are all published by the Survey of Kenya and obtainable either from the Public Map Office or bookshops in Nairobi. The ones you will need are SK 87 *Amboseli National Park*, SK 86 *Masai Mara Game Reserve*, SK 82 *Tsavo East National Park* and SK 78 *Tsavo West National Park*.

Accommodation

Camping out in the bush is, of course, the authentic way of experiencing an African safari. There's nothing quite like having just a sheet of canvas between you and what you would normally see only on the residents' side of a zoo. Full-on contact with the bush along with its potential dangers and rewards is surely what you are looking for. Anything

---

Minimising Your Impact

In their quest for the perfect photo opportunity some drivers do some crazy things. Again, a healthy dose of common sense goes a long way, but too many drivers are under too much pressure to please their clients with little regard for the effects on the wildlife.

• Never get too close to the animals and back off if they are getting edgy or nervous. On a safari I was on, a female cheetah (with cub) became extremely agitated when she was totally surrounded and hemmed in by a dozen minibuses, all full of excited visitors trying to get their 'shot'. She reacted by dropping the cub and bolting.
• Never get out of your vehicle, except at designated points where this is permitted. The animals may look tame and harmless enough but this is not a zoo – the animals are wild and you should treat them as such.
• Animals always have the right of way. Don't follow predators as they move off – you try stalking something when you've got half a dozen minibuses in tow.
• Keep to the tracks. One of the biggest dangers in the parks today is land degradation from too many vehicles crisscrossing the countryside. Amboseli's choking dust is largely a result of this. Likewise, Masai Mara in November 1992 looked, from the air, as though the East African Rally had been run entirely in the park. There were tyre tracks literally everywhere and they were clearly acting as drainage channels for the rain. If that continues, there won't be much grassland left.
• Don't light fires except at camp sites, and dispose of cigarettes with care.
• Don't litter the parks and camp sites. Unfortunately the worst offenders are often the safari drivers and cooks who toss everything and anything out the window, and leave camp sites littered with all manner of crap. It won't do any harm to point out to them the consequences of what they're doing, or clean it up yourself. ■

more luxurious than this is going to dilute the experience and remove the immediacy of it all.

It's true there are some beautifully conceived and constructed game lodges and, if you have the money, it's probably worth spending a night or two at one or another of them though it's probably true to say they are mainly for those who prefer to keep the bush at arm's length and a glass of ice-cold beer within arm's reach. Or for those who are simply on a package tour or short holiday and prefer creature comforts and predictability to the rigours of camping.

Certainly the way in which some game lodges attract wildlife to their door is somewhat contrived. Hanging up shanks of meat in a tree which a 'resident' leopard comes to feed off 10 minutes later – despite the spotlights – is hardly the essence of Africa. You might as well feed your domestic cat at home and suck on a cold beer. It's only fair to add,

on the other hand, that not all game lodges go in for this sort of circus.

Getting There & Away

Since you are not allowed to walk in the national parks (with the exception of Hell's Gate, Saiwa Swamp and certain designated areas within Nakuru) you will have to hitch a ride with other tourists, hire a vehicle or join an organised tour.

Hitching is really only feasible if the people you get a ride with are going to be camping. Since this requires some considerable preparation in terms of food, drink and equipment, people with their own cars are naturally reluctant to pick up hitchhikers. If they are going to be staying at the lodges then you have the problem of how to get from the lodge to the camp site at the end of the day. Lodges and camp sites are often a long way apart and driving in the parks is not allowed between 7 pm and dawn. You'll then have to

---

Animal Spotting

In the parks and reserves you'll be spending a lot of time craning necks and keeping watchful eyes out for the animals and birds you've come so far to see. There are a few telltale signs, as well as a few things you can do to maximise your chances. Most of them are just common sense but it's amazing the number of people who go belting around noisily expecting everything to come to them:

• Drive slowly and, where possible, quietly, keeping eyes trained not only on the ground ahead but also to the side and in the branches above.
• Go in search in the early morning or the late afternoon, although in the more popular parks such as Amboseli and Masai Mara the animals are actually changing their normal hunting habits to fit in with the tourists, so at midday, when most people are safely back in their lodges stuffing their faces, the carnivores are out hunting in the hope that they may be able to do the same thing – in peace.
• Vultures circling are not necessarily an indication of a kill below, but if they are gathering in trees and seem to be waiting you can reasonably assume they are waiting their turn on the carcass.
• In wooded country, agitated and noisy monkeys or baboons are often a sign that there's a big cat (probably a leopard) around. ■

face the problem of transport the following day for game drives and again when you want to leave. All in all, it can be very problematical and it's probably not worth the effort.

Most travellers opt to go on organised safaris. There are scores of different companies offering safaris and they cater for all pockets and tastes. The cheaper ones involve camping and a degree of self-sufficiency (including erecting your own tent, helping with the catering) and are for people who don't expect much in the way of comfort but do want an authentic experience in the African bush.

For a full description of safari possibilities, costs and company addresses, etc see the Organised Safaris section in Kenya's Getting Around chapter.

The alternative to an organised safari is to get a group together and rent a vehicle. If you're looking for other people to join you on a safari using a rented vehicle then check out the notice boards at the youth hostel and Mrs Roche's in Nairobi. As with safaris, a full description of costs and conditions for vehicle hire can be found in the Getting Around chapter.

GOVERNMENT

Kenya is a multiparty state with the Kenya African National Union (KANU) being the ruling party. The major opposition parties (in order of numbers of seats held) are FORD-Asili, FORD-Kenya, and the Democratic Party (DP). The government consists of the president, who holds executive power, and a single legislative assembly of 188 members, 176 of whom are elected, the rest being nominated by the president. There's a high degree of political patronage.

The judiciary were, until 1987, independent of government pressure and free to interpret both the constitution and the laws passed by the legislative assembly. In that year, however, parliament rushed through a bill giving the president the right to dismiss judges without recourse to a tribunal, thus effectively silencing them as a source of opposition. The measure was viewed with

dismay by many sectors of Kenyan society and has yet to be repealed.

As far as the independence and freedom of action of government ministers is concerned, it would be fair to say that it's very limited. Indeed, it would not be inappropriate to slightly misquote Louis XIV's classic statement: 'L'état? C'est Moi!'

ECONOMY

The cornerstone of Kenya's capitalist economy is agriculture which employs around 80% of the population, contributes some 31% to the GDP, and accounts for over 50% of the country's export earnings. The principal food crops are maize, sorghum, cassava, beans and fruit while the main cash crops are coffee, tea, cotton, sisal, pyrethrum and tobacco. The bulk of the food crops are grown by subsistence farmers on small plots of land whereas most of the cash crops originate from large, privately owned plantations employing contract labour though there's a significant input from smaller growers. Coffee and tea are the largest of the agricultural export earners with annual production being around 120,000 tonnes and 160,000 tonnes respectively.

While such figures might be a healthy sign for the country's balance of payments, there's a great deal of discontent among the small farmers and labourers who are paid a pittance for the tea and coffee which they produce or pick. In 1989-90, the country witnessed riots over this paltry sum. The dispute was handled badly by the Kenya Tea Development Authority (KTDA) and, although several heads rolled and price increases were promised, it was all too little too late. Small growers regularly wait up to a year and more to be paid. The situation is similar in the coffee sector and exacerbated by internationally imposed quotas which limit Kenya's ability to dispose of its stockpile. Coffee exports amounted to about 40% of export earnings in 1987.

On the other hand, tourism has replaced coffee as the country's largest export earner, although arrivals dropped off markedly in 1992 due to the tribal clashes in western

Top: Market, Nairobi, Kenya (TW)
Bottom: Kenyatta Ave, Nairobi, Kenya (TW)

Top: Heading towards South Horr, Kenya (GC)
Middle: Eliye Springs, Kenya (HF)
Bottom: Marich Pass, Kenya (HF)

Kenya and the uncertainty which accompanied the elections held in late December. Estimates of the downturn in tourism ranged from 50 to 70% and, although some sources disputed these figures, there were clearly far less tourists in Kenya in 1992 than there were in previous years. Hopefully things will improve now that the uncertainty which surrounded the first multiparty election has passed. There are also concerns that the continued depletion of the wildlife in Kenya's game parks through poaching may lead to a fall-off, with Tanzania becoming the preferred destination

In addition to agriculture and tourism, Kenya has a relatively well developed industrial base which accounts for some 15% of GDP, though the bulk of this industry is concentrated around Nairobi and Mombasa. The principal manufactures include processed food, beer, vehicles and accessories, construction materials, engineering, textiles, glass and chemicals. Initially, this sector of the economy was developed with import substitution in mind but the bias has now changed in favour of joint-venture, export-oriented industries as a result of the increasing deficit in the balance of payments and IMF loan conditions. (The IMF have since returned after being thrown out in March 1993.) Kenya's external debt of around US$9 billion is still considered to be low but the most worrying thing is the proportion of the country's foreign exchange earnings which go into servicing foreign debt – currently around 35%.

Mining is a relatively small contributor to GNP and centred around the extraction of soda and fluorspar for export. There are other minerals, which include silver, gold, lead and limestone, but these have yet to be developed commercially.

Kenya's major export trading partners are the UK (17%), Germany (11.5%), Uganda (about 9%), the USA (about 7%) and the Netherlands (6.5%).

Some 75% of domestic energy requirements are imported, mainly in the form of oil from Saudi Arabia, but geothermal projects are being developed and there are four hydroelectric plants in operation along the Tana River and the recently completed hydroelectric plant in the Turkwel Gorge.

Kenya's major sources of imports are Saudi Arabia (18.5%), the UK (about 14%), Japan (10%), Germany (8%) and the USA (5.5%).

POPULATION & PEOPLE

Kenya's population stands at around 25 million and is made up almost entirely of Africans with small (although influential) minorities of Asians (about 80,000), Arabs (about 40,000) and Europeans (about 40,000). The population growth rate of 3.8% is one of the highest in the world and is putting great strain on the country's ability to expand economically and to provide reasonable educational facilities and other urban services. It has also resulted in tremendous pressure to increase the area of land under cultivation or for grazing with its associated environmental problems.

Africans

There are more than 70 tribal groups among the Africans, although the distinctions between many of them are already blurred and are becoming more so as Western cultural values become more ingrained. Traditional values are also disintegrating as more and more people move to the larger towns, family and tribal groups become scattered and the tribal elders gradually die off.

Yet even though the average African may have outwardly drifted away from tribal traditions, tribe is still the single most important part of a person's identity. When two Africans meet and introduce themselves they will almost always say right at the outset what tribe they are from. Although nominally Christian for the most part, a surprising number of people still practice traditional customs. Some of the more inhumane customs, such as cliterodectomy (female circumcision), were outlawed by the British, usually with the aid of the local missionaries, but circumcision still remains the principal rite of passage from childhood to adulthood for boys.

Maasai woman

The most important distinguishing feature between the tribes is language. The majority of Kenya's Africans fall into one of two major groups: the Bantu speakers and the Nilotic speakers. The Bantu people arrived in East Africa in waves from West Africa over a period of time from around 500 BCE. Among the Bantu the largest tribal groups are the Kikuyu, Meru, Gusii, Embu, Akamba, Luyha and Mijikenda.

The Nilotic speakers migrated to the area from the Nile Valley some time earlier but then had to make room for the migrations of Bantu-speaking people. Nilotic speaking groups include the Maasai, Turkana, Samburu, Pokot, Luo and Kalenjin. Together these tribal groups account for more than 90% of the total African population in Kenya. The Kikuyu and the Luo are by far the most numerous groups, and between them hold practically all the positions of power and influence in the country.

A third language grouping, and in fact the first migrants into the country, are the Cushitic speakers who occupy the north-east of the country and include such tribes as the El-Molo, Somali, Rendille and the Galla.

On the coast, Swahili is the name given to the local people who, while having various tribal ancestries, have in common the fact that they have been mixing, trading and intermarrying both among themselves and with overseas immigrants for hundreds of years.

Asians

The economically important Asian minority is made up largely of people of Indian descent whose ancestors originated from the western state of Gujarat and from the Punjab. Unlike the situation in Uganda, sensibility prevailed and the Asians here were not thrown into exile, largely because their influence was too great. (Uganda is still trying to get its economy back on track.)

India's connections with East Africa go back centuries to the days when hundreds of dhows used to make the trip between the west coast of India or the Persian Gulf and the coastal towns of East Africa every year. In those days, however, the Indians came as traders and only a very few stayed to settle. This all changed with the building of the Mombasa-Uganda railway at the turn of the century. In order to construct it, the British colonial authorities brought in some 32,000 indentured labourers from Gujarat and Punjab. When their contracts expired many of them decided to stay and set up businesses. Their numbers were augmented after WW II with the encouragement of the British.

Since they were an industrious and economically aggressive community they quickly ended up controlling large parts of the economies of Kenya, Tanzania and Uganda as merchants, artisans and financiers. Not only that, but they kept very much to themselves, regarding the Africans as culturally inferior and lazy. Few gave their active support to the Black nationalist movements in the run-up to independence despite being urged to do so by Nehru, India's prime minister. And when independence came, like many of the White settlers, they were very hesitant to accept local citizenship, preferring to wait and see what would happen. To the Africans, therefore, it seemed they were

Sisal Baskets

Sisal baskets, or *kiondos*, are probably the most distinctive Kenyan souvenir and are now popular and widely available in the West. They are still an excellent buy here and the range is staggering – take a look in the market in Nairobi (although buying here is expensive). They come in a variety of sizes, colours and configurations with many different straps and closures. Expect to pay around KSh 100 for a basic one up to around KSh 300 for a large one with a leather 'neck'. Some of the finer ones have the bark of the baobab tree woven into them and this bumps up the price considerably. ■

Fabrics & Batik

Kangas and *kikois* are the local sarongs and they serve many useful purposes.

Kangas are colourful prints on thin cotton, and each bears a Swahili proverb and are always sold in pairs – one to wrap around your waist and one to carry your baby with on your back – though you can buy just one if you prefer. Biashara St in Mombasa is the kanga centre in Kenya, and here you'll pay upwards of KSh 200 for a pair, depending on quality.

Kikois are made of a thicker cotton and just have stripes. They are originally from Lamu and this is still the best place to buy them, although the kanga shops in Mombasa also stock them. These days they are also made into travellers' clothes in Lamu.

Batik cloth is another good buy and there's a tremendous range, although the good prints are not cheap. The cheapest are printed on cotton and you can expect to pay around KSh 400 for one measuring about one metre by one metre, although the price also varies depending on the artist.

Batiks printed on silk are superior quality and the prices are generally in the thousands rather than the hundreds of shillings. ■

Soapstone

Soapstone carvings from Kisii in the west of Kenya are the main offering. The soft, lightly coloured soapstone is carved into dozens of different shapes – from ashtrays to elephants. The best place for buying Kisii soapstone carvings is not in Kisii, as you might expect, but in Kisumu on Lake Victoria. The only problem is that it's extremely heavy and a kg or two of dead weight in your rucksack is not something to be taken lightly. ■

Makonde

Makonde carvings, which are made from ebony, a very black and very heavy wood, are the best pieces of woodcarving and also the most expensive. This genre of carving had its origins in the highlands on either side of the Ruvuma River in southern Tanzania but, because of its popularity, has been copied by other carvers all over East Africa. Done with inspiration, attention to detail, and an appreciation of the life force which motivates its imagery, it's a suberbly unique art form matched nowhere else in the world. Unfortunately, too many imitators create inferior products. It's not the fact that much of what is passed off as ebony is lighter (and cheaper) wood blackened with Kiwi boot polish that degrades it, but the quality of the carving which is often slap-dash. A quality piece of makonde carving is always superbly finished.

Maybe you don't care too much about this. Perhaps you like what you imagine to be the slightly rough quality of 'ethnic art'. But, if you do, you're not buying makonde. You're buying repro rubbish.

Before you buy any of this type of carving, do the rounds of the expensive craft shops in Nairobi and see what it ought to look like. Better still, buy it in Tanzania where it's much cheaper anyway. And, when you've seen the real thing, don't become too obsessed with ebony. There are some excellent Kenyan carvers even if they do do it on local hardwoods and employ Kiwi boot polish as the finish.

Basically, there are two forms of this art – the traditional and the modern – and they're instantly distinguishable. The modern stuff is pure Modigliani, though the carvers have doubtless never heard of the man or seen any of his works.

The best pieces are to be found in the expensive craft shops and were probably made in Tanzania, but you shouldn't pass up the opportunity of having a good look at what is hawked around the bars of Nairobi. Some of it is good; most of it is rubbish. If you're interested, heavy bargaining is the name of the game. ■

not willing to throw their lot in with the newly independent nations and were there simply as exploiters.

As is well known, Uganda's Idi Amin used this suspicion and resentment as a convenient ruse to enrich himself and his cronies. Uganda's economy collapsed shortly afterwards since Amin's henchmen were incapable of running the industries and busi-nesses which the Asians had been forced to leave.

Asians have fared somewhat better in Tanzania though nationalisation of many of their concerns has considerably reduced their control over the economy. It is in Kenya that they have fared best of all. Here they have a virtual stranglehold over the service sector (smaller hotels, restaurants, bars, road transport and the tourist trade), the textile trade, book publishing and selling, and they are very important in the construction business.

For a time in the 1970s it seemed that there was little future for them in Africa. Governments were under heavy pressure to 'Africanise' their economies and job markets. Even in Kenya thousands of shops owned by Asians who had not taken out Kenyan nationality were confiscated in the early 1970s and Asians were forbidden to trade in the rural areas. Those days appear to have passed and African attitudes towards them have mellowed. What seemed like a widespread demand that they should go 'home' has been quietly dropped and the Asians are there to stay. The lesson of what happened to the economy of Uganda when the Asians were thrown out is one reason for this.

Refugees & the Dispossessed

Kenya, being a relatively stable country with opportunities to make a living or at least working the tourists for hand-outs, is a natural magnet for refugees from strife-torn neighbouring countries. Nairobi and Mombasa and, to a lesser degree, the coastal resort towns, are the favoured destinations. You'll come across plenty of these people on your travels and it's relatively easy for them to remain anonymous if they can make enough money to stay off the streets.

There's nothing remarkable about this – it happens all over the world. What is remarkable in Kenya is the number of unattached teenage and early-20s mothers – many of them Kenyan but also quite a lot from Uganda, Sudan, Ethiopia and even Rwanda. With the break-up of many traditional communities as a result of colonial policies that were designed to bring people into the money economy, and the continuation of this system under post-colonial regimes, there has been large-scale movement of people to urban areas. Most arrive with nothing and are forced to live in overcrowded shantytowns (some 60% of Nairobi's population lives in these places) with little hope of anything resembling a steady job with reasonable pay.

As a result, all the facets of urban alienation can be found in these places with drunkenness, theft and rape (particularly of schoolgirls) being fairly commonplace. But this isn't confined to the major urban areas. It appears to be fairly widespread everywhere outside of traditional tribal areas.

As far as the girls are concerned, once they become pregnant they're expelled from school (in other words, it's the end of their educational prospects) and, as likely as not, rejected by their families, too. In 1986, the number of young girls who found themselves in this position (according to official figures) was 11,000 and it's been rising steadily ever since. The options for those to whom this happens are extremely limited. A few shelters do exist (usually run by Christian organisations) but it's only the lucky few who get in. For the rest, it's very poorly paid domestic work or the flesh market.

Laws regarding the responsibilities of paternity in Kenya either don't exist or are hardly ever enforced – it's definitely a man's world – and establishment Kenyan society remains tight-lipped about the problem. What it remains even more tight-lipped about is the practice of well-to-do Kenyan families recruiting little girls from the bush as domestic servants. Those recruited are even more circumspect.

Though clothed and fed and, if lucky, paid a pittance which varies between US$1 and US$16 a month, these children work on average 15 to 17 hours a day with no days off. Some get no pay at all with just food and clothing provided in lieu of salary. The reason their parents push them into this, apart from the wages which they expect to recoup, is the hope that their children will acquire a training and education of sorts. The reality is often quite different. These girls are often raped by either the man of the house or his sons and thrown out when they become pregnant. Like their more fortunate counterparts who did actually go to school before being expelled, these girls, as likely as not, join the flesh market.

Whatever you may think of prostitution, it's a hard life in Kenya. Minimal rentals, even in rough areas of Nairobi, are around US$50 a month. In better areas it's much more. Add on decent clothes and footwear and medical attention when necessary, that's a lot of money to be made even to make ends meet – let alone save anything. It's not surprising, therefore, that those who do manage to get their heads above water go for the bars and discos frequented by expatriate workers and tourists since it's more lucrative and there is the vague possibility of marriage or, at least, a long-term friendship. Even so, it's not that easy. Ever since the advent of AIDS, there's been a profound reluctance to tempt fate, and prostitutes now carry condoms out of economic necessity as well as to protect themselves from infection.

It isn't just pregnant young girls who find themselves dispossessed of course. The conditions under which young boys have to work in the coffee, sisal and rice plantations are equally onerous and many find their way onto the streets of Nairobi (so-called 'parking boys') and Mombasa along with other jobless adult males.

Blaming the government for this state of affairs is all too easy for those from rich Western countries but is, to a large degree, unfair. Because of Kenya's high birth rate and the limited amount of funds available, the government is already flat out keeping pace with the demand for schools, hospitals and other social services, the transport infrastructure, and paying interest on its foreign loans. Given this, it's unlikely that much can be done in the foreseeable future for those who fall under the category of the dispossessed.

RELIGION

It's probably true to say that most Kenyans outside the coastal and eastern provinces are Christians of one sort or another whilst most of those on the coast and in the eastern part of the country are Muslim. Muslims make up some 30% of the population. In the more remote tribal areas you'll find a mixture of Muslims, Christians and those who follow their ancestral tribal beliefs.

As a result of intense missionary activity from colonial times to the present, just about every Christian sect is represented in Kenya, from Lutherans to Catholics to Seventh Day Adventists and Wesleyans. The success which all these sects have enjoyed would be quite mind-boggling if it were not for the fact that they have always judiciously combined Jesus with education and medicine – two commodities in short supply until recently in Kenya. Indeed, there are still many remote areas of Kenya where the only place you can get an education or medical help is at a mission station and there's no doubt that those who volunteer to staff them are dedicated people.

On the other hand, the situation is often not as simple as it might at first appear. As with Catholicism in Central and South America which found it necessary to incorporate native deities and saints into the Roman Catholic pantheon in order to placate local sensibilities, African Christianity is frequently syncretic. This is especially so where a tribe has strong ancestral beliefs. There are also many pure home-grown African Christian sects which owe no allegiance to any of the major Western cults. The only thing they have in common is the Bible though their interpretation of it is often radically different. It's worth checking out a few churches whilst you're in Kenya if only to get an understanding of where the religion is headed and even if you can't understand the language which is being used, you'll certainly be captivated by what only Africans can do with such beauty and precision – unaccompanied choral singing.

The upsurge of home-grown Christian sects has much to do with cultural resurgence, the continuing struggle against neocolonialism, and the alienation brought about by migration to urban centres far from tribal homelands in search of work. Some of these sects are distinctly radical and viewed with alarm by the government. The Tent of the Living God, for instance, was denounced by the president as being anti-Christ and three of its leaders were arrested at a gathering in Eastleigh, Nairobi, in late January 1990. The charges against them were thrown out of court the following week and the men released, but the government's action was perhaps an indicator of how it intends to deal with such perceived threats to the status quo in the future.

It isn't just the radical sects which worry the government, however. During the agitation for the introduction of a multiparty political system, even mainstream church leaders took to criticising the government from the relative safety of their pulpits. Many were denounced and some came so close to the bone that they were accused of treason and there were calls for their arrest, although none were actually arrested.

As far as Islam is concerned, most Muslims belong to the Sunni branch of the faith and, as a result, the Sunni communities have been able to attract substantial Saudi Arabian funding for schools and hospitals along the coast and elsewhere.

Only a small minority belong to the Shia branch of Islam and most are to be found among the Asian community. On the other hand, Shiites have been coming to East Africa from all over the eastern Islamic world for centuries, partially to escape persecution but mainly for trading purposes. They didn't come here to convert souls, and there was a high degree of cooperation between the schismatic sects and the Sunnis which is why there's a total absence of Shiite customs in Swahili culture today.

Among the Asian community, there are representatives of virtually all Shiite sects but the most influential are the Ismailis – followers of the Aga Khan. As with all Ismailis, they represent a very liberal version of Islam and are perhaps the only branch of the faith which is strongly committed to the education of women at all levels and their participation in commerce and business. It's obvious that the sect has prospered well in Kenya, going by all the schools and hospitals dedicated to the Aga Khan which you will come across in most urban centres.

Hinduism, as is the case in India, remains a self-contained religion which concerns only those born into it. You'll come across a considerable number of temples in the larger urban areas where most of those of Indian origin live. There are literally scores of different sects of Hinduism to be found in Kenya which are too numerous to mention here but many are economically quite influential.

For a superb and very detailed account of each and every Asian-derived sect of both Islam and Hinduism see *Through Open Doors – A View of Asian Cultures in Kenya* (Kenway Publications, Nairobi, 1989), by Cynthia Salvadori. This is a large-format, hardback book with many illustrations, and is on sale in most of Nairobi's bookshops. It's one of the best researched and readable books I've ever come across.

LANGUAGE

English and Swahili (correctly known as Kiswahili) are the official languages and are taught in schools throughout Kenya, but there are many other major tribal languages which include Kikuyu, Luo, Kikamba, Maasai and Samburu as well as a plethora of minor tribal languages. Most urban Kenyans and even tribal people involved in the tourist industry speak English so you shouldn't experience too many problems making yourself understood. Italian and German are also spoken by many Kenyans but usually only among those associated with the tourist trade on the coast.

It's extremely useful, however, to have a working knowledge of Swahili, especially outside of urban areas and in remote parts of the country since this will open doors and enable you to communicate with people who don't speak English. It's also the most common language which speakers of different tribal languages use to communicate with each other. Even tribespeople who haven't been to school will usually be able to speak *some* Swahili. If you're planning on visiting Tanzania then you'll find it extremely useful as it's now the official language there (though English is still used extensively).

Another language you'll come across in Kenya, which is spoken almost exclusively by the younger members of society, is Sheng. Essentially a patois, it's a fairly recent development and, like Swahili, is still evolving. It's composed of a mixture of Swahili and English along with a fair sprinkling of Hindi, Gujarati, Kikuyu and several other Kenyan tribal languages. It originated in the colonial days as a result of the employment of African nannies by Whites to look after their children.

Unless you can speak reasonable Swahili, you probably won't realise it's being spoken since it does sound quite similar to Swahili. One of the keys to know that it's being spoken is in the initial greeting between friends. The greeting will be, 'Sassa!' The response to this can be, 'Besht', 'Mambo' or 'Fit' (pronounced almost like 'feet'). There is then an option to continue in Sheng or any other mutually intelligible language.

The *Swahili Phrasebook* by Robert Leonard is available in the Lonely Planet language survival kit series.

Pronunciation

Swahili vowels are pronounced as follows:

a	as the 'a' in 'father'
e	as the 'e' in 'better'
i	as the 'ee' sound in 'bee'
o	as the 'a' in 'law'
u	as the 'oo' in 'too'

Double vowels, or any two vowels together, are pronounced as two separate syllables. Thus *saa* (time/hour) is pronounced 'sa-a', and *yai* (egg) is pronounced 'ya-i'. There are no diphthongs as in English.

One thing you should know about pronunciation in Kenya is that the majority of Kikuyu are incapable of pronouncing the letter 'r' (much like the Japanese and Koreans). It comes out as 'l'. This can lead to some hilarious pronunciations of certain words in English. Even the Kikuyu laugh at this and one joke which a Kikuyu speaker related to me was to ask me how I thought a Kikuyu would pronounce the following: 'Red lolly on the road.' I'll leave you to work it out. I have a similar joke with my Japanese friend when I ask him to pronounce, 'Are the rafters on the roof?' In Kenya, you'll hear the most common example in bars when a Kikuyu orders a 'Pilsner'. However acute your hearing, there's no-doubt it comes out as 'Prisoner'!

General Rules

Swahili relies heavily on prefixes; adjectives change prefix according to the number and class of the noun. Thus *mzuri, wazuri, vizuri* and *kizuri* are different forms of the word 'good'.

Verbs use a pronoun prefix:

I	*ni*
you	*u*
he/she	*a*
we	*tu*
you	*m*
they	*wa*

and a tense prefix:

present	*na*
past	*li*
future	*ta*
infinitive	*ku*

giving you:

We are going to Moshi.
Tunakwenda Moshi.
Shall I take a picture?
Nitapiga picha?
Juma spoke much.
Juma alisema sana.

Some Useful Words & Phrases

hello*
jambo or *salama*
welcome
karibu
How are you?
Habari?
I'm fine, thanks.
Mzuri.
Goodbye.
Kwaheri.
yes
ndiyo
no
hapana
Thank you.
Asante.

Thanks very much.
Asante sana.

What's your name?
Unaitwa nani?

It is...
Ninaitwa...

How was the journey?
Habari ya safari?

How much/how many?
Ngapi?

Where?
Wapi?

money
pesa

today
leo

tomorrow
kesho

guesthouse
nyumba ya wageni

toilet
choo

eat
kula

sleep
lala

want
taka

come from
toka

there is
kuna

there isn't
hakuna

White people
wazungu

White person
mzungu

* There is also a respectful greeting used for elders: *shikamoo*. The reply is *marahaba*.

Food

food
chakula

rice
mchele or *wali*

bananas
ndizi

bread
mkate

vegetables
mboga

salt
chumvi

meat
nyama

beef
ng'ombe

goat
mbuzi

chicken
kuku

fish
samaki

egg(s)
(ma)yai

milk
maziwa

water
maji or *mai*

Numbers

½	*nusu*
1	*moja*
2	*mbili*
3	*tatu*
4	*nne*
5	*tano*
6	*sita*
7	*saba*
8	*nane*
9	*tisa*
10	*kumi*
11	*kumi na moja*
20	*ishirini*
30	*thelathini*
40	*arobaini*
50	*hamsini*
60	*sitini*
70	*sabini*
80	*themanini*
90	*tisini*
100	*mia*

Facts for the Visitor

VISAS & EMBASSIES

Visas are required by all except nationals of Commonwealth countries (excluding nationals of Australia, New Zealand and Sri Lanka and British passport holders of Indian, Pakistani and Bangladeshi origin), Denmark, Ethiopia, Germany, the Republic of Ireland, Italy, Norway, Spain, Sweden, Turkey and Uruguay. Those who don't need visas are issued a Visitor's Pass on entry which is valid for a stay of up to six months. Three months is the average, but it depends what you ask for.

If you enter Kenya through a land border no-one will ever ask you for an onward ticket or 'sufficient funds'. This isn't always the case if you enter by air. A lot depends on what you look like, whether you're male or female, what you write on your immigration card and which immigration officer you deal with. If it's fairly obvious that you aren't intending to stay and work then you'll generally be given the benefit of the doubt. Put yourself in a strong position before you arrive: look smart, and write the name of an expensive hotel on your immigration card in the appropriate section.

Single women have occasionally been told that 'sufficient funds' in the absence of an onward ticket were suspect 'because women lose money easily'! Perhaps the appropriate rejoinder should be that 'men spend money faster'. To balance these experiences, it should be said that we've never heard of anyone being refused entry to Kenya even if, as a last resort, they've had to buy a refundable onward ticket.

So long as your visa remains valid you can visit either Tanzania or Uganda and return without having to apply for another visa. This does not apply to visiting any other countries. There is, however, a charge at the border for doing this – usually about US$4.

Kenyan Embassies

Visas can be obtained from the following Kenyan diplomatic representatives in:

Australia
 QBE Bldg, 33 Ainslie Ave, Canberra, ACT 2601 (☎ (062) 474788)
Belgium
 1-5 Avenue de la Joyeuse, 1040 Brussels (☎ (02) 230-3065)
Canada
 415 Laurier Ave, Ottawa, Ontario, KIN 6R4 (☎ (613) 563-1773)
Egypt
 20 Boulos Hanna St, PO Box 362, Dokki, Cairo (☎ 704455)
Ethiopia
 Fikre Miriam Rd, Hiher 16 Kebelle 01, PO Box 3301, Addis Ababa (☎ 180033)
France
 3 Rue Cimaros, 75116 Paris (☎ 4553-3500)
Germany
 Villichgasse 17, 5300 Bonn-Bad Godesburg 2, Micael Plaza, (☎ (0228) 356042)
India
 E-66 Vasant Marg, 110057 New Delhi (☎ 672280)
Italy
 Icilio No 14, 00153 Rome (☎ 578-1192)
Japan
 24-20 Nishi-Azobu 3-Chome, Minato-Ku, Tokyo (☎ (03) 479-4006)
Netherlands
 Koninginnegracht 102, 2514 A1, The Hague (☎ (070)504215)
Nigeria
 52 Queens Drive, Ikoyi, PO Box 6464, Lagos (☎ 682768)
Pakistan
 Sector G-6/3, House 8, St 88, PO Box 2097, Islamabad (☎ 811243)
Rwanda
 UN Toit A Toi Bldg, Rue Kadyiro, PO Box 1215, Kigali (☎ 72774)
 Open Monday to Friday from 8.30 am to noon and 2 to 4.30 pm; US$10, two photos, same-day issue for applications before 11.30 am, otherwise 24 hours. No onward tickets or minimum funds required.
Somalia
 Km 4 Via Mecca, PO Box 618, Mogadishu (☎ 80857)

Sudan
  Street 3 Amarat, PO Box 8242, Khartoum
  (☎ 43758)
Sweden
  Birger Jarlsgatan 37, 2tr, 10395 Stockholm
  (☎ (08) 218300)
Tanzania
  NIC Investment House, Samora Ave, PO Box
  5231, Dar es Salaam (☎ 46362/6)
  Open Monday to Friday from 8 am to 3 pm, from
  9 am for visa applications; US$10, two photo-
  graphs, 24 hours.
Uganda
  Plot No 60, Kira Rd, PO Box 5220, Kampala
  (☎ 231861)
  Open Monday to Friday from 8.30 am to 12.30
  pm and 2 to 4.30 pm; US$10, two photos, same-
  day issue for applications before noon.
UK
  45 Portland Place, London W1N 4AS (☎ (071)
  636-2371)
USA
  2249 R St NW, Washington DC 20008 (☎ (202)
  387-6101)
  424 Madison Ave, New York, NY 10017
  (☎ (212) 486-1300)
Zaïre
  5002 Ave de l'Onganda, BP 9667, Gombe,
  Kinshasa (☎ 30117)
Zambia
  Harambee House, 5207 United Nations Ave, PO
  Box 50298, Lusaka (☎ 212531)
Zimbabwe
  95 Park Lane, PO Box 4069, Harare (☎ 792901)

Where there is no Kenyan embassy or high commission, visas can be obtained from the British embassy or high commission.

The cost of visas generally increases with the distance from Kenya, though not by a great deal. In Africa, they generally cost US$10 (sometimes payable in local currency if the exchange rate is stable). Two photos (sometimes three) are required but you normally do not have to show an onward ticket or a letter from a travel agent confirming that you have booked one. Visas remain valid for a period of three months from the date of issue. Apply well in advance for your visa especially if doing it my mail – they can take up to two weeks in some countries (eg Australia). Kenyan visa applications are simpler and less time-consuming in Rwanda, Tanzania and Uganda, and payment is accepted in local currency (see the earlier list for details).

Visas are also available on arrival at Jomo Kenyatta International Airport in Nairobi for US$10.

Visa Extensions

Visas can be renewed in Nairobi at the immigration office (☎ (02) 332110), Nyayo House (ground floor), on the corner of Kenyatta Ave and Uhuru Highway; at the office in Mombasa (☎ (011) 311745), or at immigration on the 1st floor of Reinsurance Plaza, corner of Jomo Kenyatta Highway and Oginga Odinga Rd during normal office hours. A three-month single-entry visa costs US$10 and a 12-month multiple-entry visa US$50 (except in Kisumu where a visa can be renewed for three months free of charge). You must pay in foreign currency. No onward tickets or 'sufficient funds' are demanded (except in Kisumu where they may ask to see an onward ticket but won't refuse you if you don't have one). Remember that you don't need a re-entry visa if you're only going to visit Tanzania or Uganda *as long as your visa remains valid*. Staff at the immigration offices are generally friendly and helpful.

Foreign Embassies in Kenya

Since Nairobi is a common gateway city to East Africa and the city centre is easy to get around, many travellers spend some time here picking up visas for other countries which they intend to visit. If you are going to do this you need to plan ahead because some embassies only accept visa applications in the mornings, others only on certain days of the week. Some take 24 hours to issue, others 48 hours. Some visas (Sudan, for instance) may have to be referred to the country's capital city, but this is rare.

Burundi The embassy is currently not issuing visas and will tell you to get one on arrival at the border.

Egypt The embassy is open Monday to Friday from 9 am to 12.30 pm. The cost of a one month, single-entry visa varies depending on your nationality. For the USA and

Denmark it's US$10.70, for Canada it's US$44 and for the UK it's US$57. For all others it's US$15.60. One photo is required plus you need to show an onward ticket and vaccination certificates for yellow fever and cholera. Visas take 48 hours to issue and you can collect them in the afternoons only from 2 to 3.30 pm.

Ethiopia The embassy is open Monday to Friday from 9 to 11 am and 2.30 to 4 pm. One-month visas cost US$6.85, require one photo and take 48 hours to issue. You must show an onward ticket when applying for the visa.

Madagascar The embassy is open Monday to Friday from 8.30 am to 1 pm and 2 to 5 pm but visa applications are only accepted between 9 am and noon. Visas cost US$11.40, require four photos and are issued in 24 hours.

Malawi The high commission is open Monday to Friday from 9 am to 12.30 and 2 to 4.30 pm. Visas require two photos, cost US$17.15 and are issued in 48 hours.

Rwanda The embassy is open Monday to Friday from 9 am to noon and 2 to 5 pm. One-month visas cost US$5.70, require two photos and take 48 hours to issue. On the application form you will be asked the date you want to enter Rwanda. Think carefully about this as the visa will run from then.

Sudan The embassy is open Monday to Friday from 8.30 am to noon (closed Wednesday). Visas are difficult to get because of the civil war and all applications have to be referred to Khartoum. An onward ticket is necessary so get one of these before you apply.

Tanzania The high commission is open Monday to Friday from 8.30 am to 12.30 and 2 to 5 pm but visa applications are only accepted between 9 am and noon. The cost of a visa depends on your nationality and

ranges from US$6.85 to US$42.85. Canadians pay the most followed by Belgians, Dutch, Italians, Spanish, Swiss and Japanese. Americans, Germans, French and Israelis pay least. Two photos are required and visas are issued in 48 hours (two weeks for Israelis).

Uganda The high commission is open Monday to Friday from 9.30 am to noon and 2 to 4 pm. Single-entry visas cost US$20 for British and Irish nationals and US$25 for all others (US$40/50 respectively for double-entry visas), two photos are required and visas are issued in 24 hours.

Zaïre The embassy is open Monday to Friday from 8.30 am to 12.45 pm and 2 to 5 pm. Visa fees are the same for all nationalities. Single-entry/double-entry visas cost US$75/120 for a month; US$135/180 for two months, US$200/225 for three months and US$270/360 for six months. One-way transit visas (three days) are also available for US$45. Four photos are required and a letter of introduction from your own embassy. The visas take 24 hours to issue.

Zambia The high commission is open Monday to Friday from 8.30 am to 12.30 pm and 2 to 4.30 pm. Visas cost US$8.60, require three photos and take 48 hours to issue.

Francophone Countries The French Embassy issues visas for French-speaking countries which don't have embassies in Nairobi, such as Chad and the Central African Republic.

MONEY
The unit of currency is the Kenyan shilling (KSh), which is made up of 100 cents. Notes in circulation are KSh 500, 200, 100, 50, 20 and 10; coins are KSh 5 (seven-sided) and KSh 1, and 50, 10 and 5 cents.

Treat the following exchange rates as a guide only. The Kenyan shilling continues to depreciate (see the Demise of the Kenyan

Shilling section), so prices in this book are quoted in US dollars to retain some semblance of reality. As of October 1993 the rates were:

US$1 = KSh 120
UK£1 = KSh 179
1FF = KSh 21
DM1 = KSh 75
A$1 = KSh 79

Import and export of local currency is allowed up to KSh 100 and, when you leave

the country, customs officials may ask you if you are carrying any. If you say you are not that's generally the end of the matter. If you're only leaving the country for a short while and intend to return via the same border and don't want to convert all your Kenyan shillings into another currency, you can leave any excess at a border post against a receipt and pick it up again when you get back, but who could be bothered?

When leaving via Nairobi airport it's possible to reconvert any amount of Kenyan shillings to hard currency as long as you have

---

The Demise of the Kenyan Shilling

Throughout the 1970s, 1980s and early 1990s, the Kenyan shilling was East Africa's most stable currency and there was little difference between the official rate of exchange and the parallel (black) market. This all changed in late 1992 when the government, strapped for dollars (and other 'hard' currencies), authorised banks to pay a premium for the exchange of 'hard' currencies into Kenyan shillings – known as the Forex-C. This meant that anyone with dollars (cash or cheques) could walk into a bank, request the premium, and, so long as they changed a minimum of US$500, get whatever were the free-market rate of exchange (which fluctuated between KSh 47 and KSh 51) as opposed to the official rate of exchange of around KSh 35.

The idea was to encourage those with dollars to keep their money in the country and re-invest it and, to this end, those with businesses which received dollar payments, were allowed to keep 50% of their earnings in dollar accounts (known as 'retention accounts'). The measure didn't quite achieve what it had intended to do since speculators began to buy up hard currency wherever they could find it thus driving the shilling down and forcing up the price of imports. Within weeks, the price of just about everything doubled (if you were paying for it in local currency).

Then, in November 1992, the whole scheme was abruptly cancelled when the central bank was unable to honour Forex-C certificates (ie the premium which the banks had paid) due to a lack of 'hard' currency (vehemently denied by the central bank, naturally, but obvious to all concerned).

What happened next was beyond belief. Pressured into multiparty elections (which took place at the end of December 1992) and determined to win, the government flooded the currency market with what was estimated to be KSh 9 billion unsupported by reserves, most of which went into buying votes.

As a result, the currency took a dive and was devalued to US$1 = KSh 46 in January 1993. Concurrently, the black market roared ahead while the major banks prevaricated about what to do.

Enter the IMF and the World Bank which demanded (among other things) that if Kenya's debts were to be rescheduled and a major loan package put in place, then the government would have to withdraw from circulation the KSh 9 billion. The government threw them out but not necessarily over this issue (see the History section in the Facts about the Country chapter for more details). At the same time, dollar retention accounts were cancelled and the central bank demanded that those holding dollars in such accounts sell them to the central bank at the official exchange rate (US$1 = KSh 46) within 48 hours.

There was panic on the currency market and the Kenyan shilling took another plunge but, although the official exchange rate remained at KSh 46 to the US dollar, the international banks (eg Barclays, Grindlays, IBN, etc) began trading at KSh 67 to the dollar, which was very close to the black-market rate of around KSh 72.

At the time of writing, the Kenyan shilling continues to depreciate and probably will not stabilise until late 1993 when it is predicted it will hit US$1 = KSh 150 or thereabouts. ■

the bank receipts to cover the amount. This is only possible at the airport, and not only is the exchange rate a little low but they charge KSh 100 commission. This facility is obviously meant for those who are leaving the country and have excess shillings (which you can't legally export) but they don't ask to see your air ticket at the time so presumably anyone could do this.

It is sometimes still possible to cash US dollar travellers' cheques at banks in Kenya and get US dollars cash for them, but it's difficult. Who wants Kenyan currency under the present circumstances? Barclays and certain other banks will quote a rate for selling dollars (between 3 and 5% higher than the buying rate) but, although you can watch someone right in front of you cashing dollars, they won't sell them back to you. Overcome this hurdle by doing a deal with people who want to sell dollars before they reach the counter.

Naturally, if they won't sell you cash dollars for Kenyan shillings, they're not going to sell you cash dollars for travellers' cheques. Things may change, but, for the present, this is one of your few options.

It may be possible to get cash dollars if you make a withdrawal against your home account using a Visa card at Barclays Bank. So long as you don't want more than US$150 to US$200 per day it takes about 20 minutes but, if you want more, then it has to be referred to your home country and this takes longer.

Your last options are the black market and the casino on Uhuru Highway just below the National Museum. At the latter you can change your travellers' cheques to gambling chips then, after pretending you've been gambling for a while, go back to the cashier and change the chips back to cash dollars.

Bank Charges
Travellers' cheques attract a 1% commission at some banks but none at others. Barclays is probably the best bank to change cheques at since there's hardly any red tape and the transaction takes just a few minutes, though other international banks are just as good.

Banking hours are Monday to Friday from 8 or 9 am to 2 pm and on the first and last Saturdays of the month from 9 to 11 am.

Black Market
Because of the unrealistic official exchange rate and the virtual impossibility of buying dollars from the banks, there is a black market for hard currency in Nairobi (cash or travellers' cheques) and you can get up to 20% above the rate at which the banks are trading. The places to do this are generally well-known among travellers who have been in Nairobi for a little while, so ask around.

Transferring Money
Kenya is a good place to have funds transferred to. It generally takes only a few days. You can collect your money entirely in US dollars travellers' cheques but the money is transferred first into Kenyan shillings then back into dollars. If you have a Visa or American Express card, you can do the same thing directly by going to Barclays or Express Kenya, respectively.

Costs
Despite the chaos on the currency market and spiralling inflation which has seen the price of almost everything double (in Kenyan shilling terms) since the beginning of 1993, prices in US dollar terms have remained fairly stable.

Prices in this book have been quoted in US dollars on the basis of US$1 = KSh 46 (the official exchange rate) but the international banks are trading at a much higher rate so, if you have hard currency, everything costs considerably less. Bear this in mind when considering costs.

The cost of budget accommodation in Kenya is very reasonable so long as you're happy with communal showers and toilets. Clean sheets are invariably provided and sometimes you'll also get soap and a towel. For this you're looking at US$3 a single and US$5 a double and up. It can be slightly cheaper on the coast, especially at Lamu. If you want your own bathroom, costs rise to from around US$5 a single and US$7 a double. Again, it can be slightly cheaper on the coast but more expensive in Nairobi.

There are plenty of small cafés in every town, usually concentrated in a certain area. They cater to local people and you can get a traditional meal for around US$1 or US$2. Often, the food isn't up to much but sometimes it can be excellent. For just a little bit more, the Indian restaurants are great value. Some offer all-you-can-eat lunches for around US$3. The food is not only tasty but you won't need to eat for the rest of the day either. A splurge at a better class restaurant is going to set you back between US$8 and US$15.

The price of beer and soft drinks depends entirely on where you buy them. They're obviously cheapest bought from a supermarket (around US$0.33 for a beer assuming an exchange rate of US$1 = KSh 46). Using this as a benchmark figure, you would be paying around 60% more for them in a basic bar, slightly more than double in a better class bar or restaurant, and up to eight times as much in a five-star hotel!

Public transport is very reasonable and the trains are excellent value. To travel from one end of Kenya to the other (Mombasa to Malaba) on the train in 2nd class is going to cost you about US$38. In 3rd class it's less than half that. Buses are priced about halfway between the 3rd and 2nd-class train fares.

The thing that is going to cost you most in Kenya is safaris. A safari for three nights and four days, for instance, with companies which cater for budget travellers is priced around US$180; seven days costs around US$385. This includes transport, food, hire of tents, national park entry fees, camping fees and the wages of the guides and cooks. In other words, more or less everything except a few drinks and tips.

Car hire is even more expensive and is probably out of reach of most budget travellers. A 4WD Suzuki costs from US$650 to US$900 per week with unlimited mileage; petrol is extra. If you don't want 4WD then a small car, such as a Nissan Sunny, costs around US$420 per week.

Tipping

With such an active tourist industry, Kenya is a country where tipping is expected. Obviously there's no need to tip in the very basic African eateries or hotels, on *matatus* (local minibuses) or when using other public transport. In better restaurants 5 to 10% of the bill is the usual amount, although in these a service charge of 10% will often have been included on the bill (though it's debatable whether the employees ever get it).

If you take a safari then it's also expected that you tip your driver, guide and cook. The majority of employees in this industry earn low wages so it's suggested you be as generous as you feel able to. Around US$1.50 per day per employee is about the right amount. This is the cost per person, and how much you give obviously depends on whether they have worked well to make your safari enjoyable.

WHEN TO GO

There are a number of factors to take into account when considering what time of year to visit Kenya. The main tourist season is January and February, as the weather at this time of year is generally considered to be the best – hot and dry. It's also when you'll find the largest concentrations of birdlife on the Rift Valley lakes, and the animals in the game parks tend to congregate more around the watercourses as other sources dry up, making them easier to spot.

From June to September could be called the 'shoulder season' as the weather is still dry and it's the time of that visual extravaganza – the annual wildebeest migration into the Masai Mara Game Reserve from the Serengeti.

During the long rains (from March to May) and the short rains (from October to December) things are much quieter – places tend to be less full and accommodation prices come down. The rains generally don't affect your ability to get around and see things (although Amboseli National Park can be flooded out), it's just that you may well get rained on, especially in the late afternoon. This is especially so in the highlands and the west of the country.

WHAT TO BRING

Bring the minimum. One thing that many travellers in Kenya find once they actually get there is that they have far too much gear. This is not only an uncomfortable inconvenience, it also means that instead of taking back some special reminders of Kenya you'll be taking back the same extra pullover and jeans that you set off with. Unless it's absolutely essential, *leave it at home!*

A rucksack (backpack) is far more practical than an overnight bag, and is essential if you plan to climb Mt Kenya or do any amount of walking. It is worth buying a good quality bag right at the start – African travel soon sorts out the good stuff from the junk, and if it's the latter you've opted for you'll be cursing it the whole way.

What type of pack you buy is largely a matter of personal preference. I find that the travel packs with the straps which zip into a compartment in the back are excellent. Although expensive, they are a compromise solution to a number of different problems; however, they are not really suited for specialised activities such as climbing or serious walking. Of the other types of packs, internal frame ones seem to be the best as they have less protuberances and straps to catch on things.

A day pack is a worthwhile item, if only for keeping your camera dry and out of the incredible dust which seems to permeate every crack and crevice when you're on safari. For those reasons and for security, it needs to be one which zips shut. Quite a few travellers use the local *kiondos* (woven baskets) which are fine if they suit your purpose.

A sleeping bag is more or less essential if you are travelling overland beyond Kenya or planning to climb mountains, but in the country itself there are enough hotels for you not to need one. On the other hand, carrying a sleeping bag and closed-cell foam mat does give you a greater degree of flexibility and means that if you take a safari you know you'll have adequate gear. Sleeping bags are the one thing which all camping safari companies require you to provide.

There's always much discussion about the pros and cons of carrying a tent, and basically it boils down to what sort of travelling you want to do, and how much weight you're prepared to carry. As with a sleeping bag, a tent is not necessary if you're just travelling from town to town, but carrying your own portable shelter opens up a whole stack of exciting possibilities. The same applies to carrying a stove and cooking gear, so give some careful thought as to what you want to do, and how. On the other hand, the full range of camping equipment can be hired from various places in Nairobi (principally Atul's on Biashara St) and from certain hotels elsewhere in the country (principally the Naro Moru River Lodge on the western side of Mt Kenya).

Quite a few travellers carry a mosquito net, and with the risk of malaria there is no doubt that this is not a bad idea. Personally I have found that with judicious use of insect repellent and mosquito coils, I was never unduly discomfited. On the topic of insect repellent, bring a good supply and make sure that whatever you bring has as the active ingredient NN-diethyl-m-toluamide, commonly known as DEET. This has been found to be the most effective against mosquitoes. Brands which have this include Mijex and Rid. Mosquito coils are what the locals use (when they use anything at all, that is) to keep the mozzies at bay, and local brands such as Doom are available in even the smallest stores.

Clothes need to be both practical and take into account local sensibilities. Although Kenya straddles the equator, the large variations in altitude lead to equally large variations in climate. The coast is hot and steamy year-round, while Nairobi and the western highlands get decidedly cool in the evenings in July and August, so you need to carry one decent warm pullover as well as warm-weather gear. A windproof and waterproof jacket also comes in handy, particularly during the rainy seasons. Most travellers seem to get around in T-shirts and shorts which is fine in most areas, but you should be more circumspect on the Muslim-dominated coast, particularly in Lamu. Here women should wear tops that keep the shoulders covered and skirts or pants which reach at least to the knees. Shorts on men are likewise not particularly appreciated. Civil servants and embassy staff, likewise, do not appreciate scantily dressed travellers and will treat you with disdain.

Overlooked by many people but absolutely indispensable is a good pair of sunglasses. The amount of glare you experience in the bright tropical light is not only uncomfortable but can damage your eyes. A hat which shades your face and neck is also well worth considering. A water bottle is well worth any slight inconvenience it may cause. It needs to be unbreakable, have a good seal, and hold at least one litre.

Also important are little things which can make life just that little bit more comfortable: a Swiss Army knife, a small sewing kit (including a few metres of fishing line and a large needle for emergency rucksack surgery), a 10-metre length of light nylon cord for a washing line along with a handful of clothes pegs, and half a tennis ball makes a good fits-all washbasin plug.

Most toiletries – soap, shaving cream, shampoo, toothpaste, toilet paper, tampons – are available throughout the country.

The one thing that you're really going to appreciate in Kenya is a pair of binoculars, whether they be pocket ones or larger field binoculars. When out in the game parks you can put them to constant use and they are essential for identifying the dozens of species of mammals and birds that you'll come across. If you don't plan on going to the game parks they are are still handy just for the scenery, or perhaps for trying to spot that potential lift coming over the horizon when you're stuck out in the north somewhere...

TOURIST OFFICES

Considering the extent to which the country relies on tourism, there's not much available in the way of printed information, and it's incredible to think that there's not even a tourist office in Nairobi! There are a couple of free pamphlets which go some way towards filling the gap. They are the monthly *Kenya Tourist Guide* (☎ 226206 in Nairobi) published by Rank Communications Inc, and the quarterly *What's On* (☎ 221222 in Nairobi) put out by Nation Newspapers. Both contain articles on subjects of tourist interest plus listings of hotels, restaurants, airlines, embassies, banks, safari and car-hire companies, train and boat schedules, and a considerable amount of advertising (which is why they're free). You can pick them up at the larger hotels and at travel agencies.

The fortnightly *Tourist's Kenya* (☎ 33-7169 in Nairobi) put out by Savers Cards Ltd, hasn't been produced since March 1992, but the staff are still in the office on the 1st floor of Union Towers, Moi Ave, keeping the information on their computers up to date, so they may go back into production soon.

The only tourist offices in the country are the ones in Mombasa on Moi Ave (☎ 31-1231) and in Malindi on Lamu Rd.

The Ministry of Tourism maintains several overseas offices including:

France
    Kenya Tourist Office, 5 Rue Volney, Paris 75002 (☎ 260-6688)
Germany
    Kenya Tourist Office, Hochstrasse 53, 6 Frankfurt A M (☎ 282552)
Sweden
    Kenya Tourist Office, Birger Jarlsgatan 37, 11145 Stockholm (☎ (08) 218300)
Switzerland
    Kenya Tourist Office, Bleicherweg 30, CH- 8039 Zurich (☎ 202-2244)
UK
    Kenya Tourist Office, 25 Brook's Mews (off Davies St) Mayfair, London (☎ (071) 355-3144)
USA
    Kenya Tourist Office, 9100 Wilshire Blvd, Doheney Plaza Suite 111, Beverly Hills CA 90121 (☎ (213) 274-6634)
    Kenya Tourist Office, 424 Madison Ave, New York, NY 10017 (☎ (212) 486-1300)

BUSINESS HOURS & HOLIDAYS

Government offices are open Monday to Friday from 8 or 8.30 am to 1 pm, and 2 to 5 pm. Some private businesses are also open on Saturday mornings from around 8.30 am to 12.30 pm.

Banking hours are Monday to Friday from 9 am to 2 pm. Banks are also open on the first and last Saturday of the month from 9 to 11 am.

Nairobi and Mombasa both have branches of Barclays Bank which stay open until 4.30 or 5 pm Monday to Saturday. The branch at Nairobi airport is open 24 hours.

Outside normal banking hours you may be able to change at one of the five-star tourist hotels, although many are reluctant to help unless you're a guest, and their exchange rates are poor anyway.

Public Holidays

January
   New Year's Day
March-April
   Good Friday
   Easter Monday
   Id al Fitr (end of Ramadan, 1994-95)
1 May
   Labour Day
1 June
   Madaraka Day
20 October
   Kenyatta Day
12 December
   Independence Day
25 December
   Christmas Day
26 December
   Boxing Day

POST & TELECOMMUNICATIONS

The Kenyan postal system is very reliable. Letters sent from Kenya rarely go astray but do take up to two weeks to reach Australia or the USA. Incoming letters to Kenya take around a week to reach Nairobi.

Parcels or books sent by surface mail take up to 4½ months to arrive – but they do get there. I can vouch for this – I've sent plenty of stuff this way.

Postal Rates

The airmail rates in US$ for items posted from Kenya are:

Item	Africa	Europe	USA & Australia
letter	$0.20	$0.30	$0.40
postcard	$0.10	$0.20	$0.28
aerogram	$0.20	$0.20	$0.23

Sending Mail

Kenya is a good place from which to send home parcels of goodies, or excess gear. In the main post office in Nairobi you'll always see at least a couple of people busily taping and wrapping boxes to send home. You have to take the parcel *unwrapped* to be inspected by customs at the post office not later than 3.30 pm. You then wrap and send it. The whole process is very simple and, apart from wrapping the parcel, takes only a few minutes.

There's usually no-one selling wrapping material outside the post office in Nairobi so you need to bring along your own cardboard, paper, tape and string. The cheapest place to get this stuff is the supermarket on Koinange St between Kenyatta Ave and Standard St. Otherwise go to Biba on Kenyatta Ave at the junction with Muindi Mbingu St. Cardboard boxes are usually available free of charge or for a few shillings at supermarkets.

Receiving Mai

Letters can be sent care of poste restante in any town. Virtually every traveller uses Nairobi as a mail drop and so the amount of mail in poste restante here is amazing. The vast majority of it finds its way into the correct pigeonholes though there's naturally the occasional mistake. Most of the mistakes are entirely the fault of the letter writer. Make sure you write the addressee's name in block capitals and underline the surname. (I can only admire the ingenuity of the postal staff in sorting out poste restante letters into the correct pile after seeing the way that some people address letters!) If you're not getting expected letters, try looking under all possible initials including 'M' (for M, Mr, Mrs,

Ms, if you're an English or French speaker), 'S' (for Señor, Señora, etc, if you're a Spanish or Portuguese speaker), etc.

Some travellers use the American Express Clients Mail Service and this can be a useful alternative to poste restante. Officially you are supposed to have an Amex card or be using their travellers' cheques to avail yourself of this service but no check of this is made at the office in Nairobi. The postal addresses in Nairobi and Mombasa are:

American Express Clients Mail Service
    Express Kenya Ltd, PO Box 40433, Nairobi
Express Kenya
    PO Box 90631, Mombasa

The Nairobi office is in Bruce House on Standard St (☎ (02) 334722), while the Mombasa office is on Nkrumah Rd (☎ (011) 312461).

There's also a set-up called Africa Travel Centre that has offices in London, Sydney and Nairobi which offers mail-holding services (and baggage storage). You can have your mail reliably held or forwarded by the centre for a small fee. It also provides a fax service. The addresses are:

London
    4 Medway Court, Leigh St, London WC1 9QX
    (fax (071) 383-7512)
Sydney
    12th Floor, 456 Kent St, Sydney 2000 (fax (02)
    267-3047)
Nairobi
    PO Box 63006, 1st Floor, Union Towers, Moi
    Ave, Nairobi (fax (2) 213445)

Telephone

The phone system works reasonably well, although it can take a number of attempts to get an international connection depending on the time of day.

International Calls International calls are easy to make from Nairobi, Mombasa and Kisumu where you can either go through the operator or dial yourself on a private line. Phonecards used to be available at the Nairobi Extelcoms office and at the Kenyatta Conference Centre in denominations of KSh

200, 400 and 1000 but the supply of them is erratic and you usually have to go through the operator.

If phonecards are still available, there's one card phone in Nairobi at the main post office, and another in the Extelcoms office on Haile Selassie Ave. There are also two in the lobby of the Kenyatta Conference Centre and these are by far the best to use as there's little background noise there. Mombasa, Malindi, Lamu and Kisumu each have one cardphone at the main post office.

Operator-connected calls are also easy to make. The Extelcoms office in Nairobi is open from 8 am to midnight. Again, the Kenyatta Conference Centre is the best place to ring from as there's an international call office in the lobby and this is much quieter and less frantic than the Extelcoms office. It is only open until 6 pm, however.

In other towns, calls can be made from the post office, although there may be some delay in getting through to the international operator in Nairobi.

It's possible to make reverse-charge (collect) calls to the UK, Europe and the USA, but not to Australia. The cost of international calls to any of these destinations from Kenya when going through the operator is US$20 for three minutes.

Calls put through a hotel operator from your room will be loaded at between 25 and 50% so check what they're going to charge you before you make the call.

Local Calls Local and long-distance (STD) calls are also quite straightforward. There are public phone boxes in every town and these all seem to work. The only problem is that there aren't enough of them, especially in Nairobi where you'll find a queue of four or five people at each box. Local calls cost KSh 2, while STD rates vary depending on the distance. Call boxes accept only KSh 1 and KSh 5 coins. When making an local call, make sure you put a KSh 1 coin into the machine first (regardless of what you insert after that). If you don't, you may have problems making your call.

Calls to Tanzania and Uganda are only STD calls, not international.

The STD area codes for the main towns and cities in Kenya are as follows:

Busia	03362
Diani Beach	01261
Eldoret	0321
Embu	0161
Garissa	0131
Isiolo	0165
Kakamega	0331
Kericho	0361
Kilifi	0125
Kisii	0381
Kisumu	035
Kitale	0325
Lamu	0121
Lodwar	0393
Malindi	0123
Maralal	03681
Marsabit	0183
Meru	0164
Mombasa	011
Nairobi	02
Naivasha	0311
Nakuru	037
Nanyuki	0176
Nyahururu	0365
Nyeri	0171
Thika	0151
Voi	0147
Watamu	0122

TIME

Time in Kenya is GMT/UTC plus three hours all year round.

One thing that must be borne in mind is that Swahili time is six hours out of kilter with the way we tell the time, so that noon and midnight are 6 o'clock (*saa sitta*) Swahili time, and 7 am and 7 pm are 1 o'clock (*saa moja*). Just add or subtract six hours from the time you are told and hopefully from the context you'll be able to work out whether the person is talking about am or pm! You don't come across this all that often unless you speak Swahili but you still need to be prepared for it – I met one person who missed the one daily bus from a particular town on two consecutive days because he was at the station six hours late.

ELECTRICITY

Kenya uses the 240 V system. The power supply is usually reliable and uninterrupted in most places though Nairobi has been having problems lately. Power sockets are of the three-square-pin variety as used in the UK, although some older buildings have round-pin sockets. Bring a universal adapter if a power supply is important to you.

MEDIA
Newspapers & Magazines

Tabloid newspapers are printed in both English and Swahili. Of the three English-language papers, the best is the *Daily Nation*, which has a surprising amount of both local and overseas coverage, and is well worth reading on a daily basis if you want to get a feel for what's happening in the country. It has the best cartoons, doesn't shirk from criticising the government and exposing corruption, but balances this with a similar attitude towards the opposition parties. The others are the *Kenya Times* (the KANU party rag) and the *Standard*.

There is also a surprising range of locally produced magazines in both English and Swahili. Principal among these is the *Weekly Review* which is the Kenyan equivalent of Time/Newsweek. Radicals berate this magazine as being a tool of government propaganda but it does, nevertheless, discuss issues in much greater detail than any of the daily newspapers and it's well worth a read. There are plenty of other weekly and monthly magazines, some of them sufficiently critical of the government to occasionally prompt their seizure by the police, and others which are largely titillative such as *True Love* (the 'Dear Claire.....' agony column is often hilarious) and the less silly *Drum*.

Foreign newspapers (up to a week old) in English, French, Italian and German are readily available in Nairobi and Mombasa but vary greatly in price depending on where you buy them. They're expensive at the pavement newsstand next to the New Stanley Hotel in Nairobi, but you can buy the same papers from a man who lays them out on the pavement at the junction of Kaunda and Kimathi Sts much more cheaply.

Current affairs magazines such as *Time, Newsweek, New African* and *South* are also widely available at a controlled price which is printed on the front cover. *New African* is the best of the bunch if you're looking for detailed coverage of African affairs and events. It's published monthly.

Radio & TV

The Kenyan Broadcasting Corporation (KBC) has radio transmissions in English, Swahili and more specialised languages such as Hindi and African languages.

The BBC World Service transmits to East Africa on short wave around 12 hours a day and has programmes in English and Swahili. The *Daily Nation* prints the programme each day. Although frequencies change from time to time, the main ones to try if you have a short-wave radio include: 21470, 17885 and 15420 kHz.

There are two TV channels – KBC and KTN. The latter is better except that it no longer produces its own independent news programmes but takes them from KBC. Many programmes are imported from Europe, the USA and Australia.

FILM & PHOTOGRAPHY

Film

Film is widely available, especially in Nairobi and on the coast, and the price compares fairly well with what you'd pay at home. You'll need plenty of it – Kenya has heaps to photograph, and anyone with a camera inevitably gets very shutter-happy in the game parks looking for that 'perfect' shot.

It's wise to bring films of varying ASA. If you're using a zoom or long focal length camera (recommended) you're going to need film of at least 200 ASA to give you enough light, especially as the best photo opportunities are early and late in the day when the light is not as bright as the middle daylight hours. Higher speed film also makes it possible to take photos with a higher shutter speed, which is important when you're trying to photograph moving animals at the same time as being bumped around inside a minibus.

Some of the lodges have salt licks which the animals are attracted to at night, so with 800, 1600 or higher ASA film, non-flash photos are a possibility.

You'll find Kodak and Fuji 64, 100, 200 and 400 ASA slide film readily available in Nairobi and Mombasa, but 800 ASA is virtually impossible to find. The same is true for colour-negative film. Agfa film is also very difficult to find. As an indication of price, 36-exposure slide film in Nairobi costs US$9.60 (64 ASA), US$11.30 (100 ASA), US$13.60 (200 ASA), and US$15.70 (400 ASA). Colour-print film (36 exposures) costs US$6.70 (100 ASA), US$7.70 (200 ASA), and US$9.60 (400 ASA). B&W print film costs less than colour-print film.

Cameras & Lenses

For serious wildlife photography a SLR (single lens reflex) camera which can take long focal length lenses is necessary. If all you have is a little generic 'snapomatic' you may as well leave it behind. Although they are becoming more sophisticated these days, the maximum focal length is around 110 mm – still too small for getting decent shots.

Zoom lenses are best for wildlife photography as you can frame your shot easily to get the best composition. This is important as the animals are constantly and often quickly on the move. The 70 to 210 mm zoom lenses are popular and the 200 mm is really the minimum you need to get good close-up shots. The only problem with zoom lenses is that with all the glass (lenses) inside them they absorb about 1½ 'f' stops of light, which is where the 200 and 400 ASA film starts to become useful.

Telephoto (fixed focal length) lenses give better results than zoom lenses but you're limited by having to carry a separate lens for every focal length. A 400 or 500 mm lens brings the action right up close, but again you need the 200 or 400 ASA film to make the most of them. You certainly need a 400 or

500 mm lens if you're keen on photographing birdlife.

Another option is to carry a 2x teleconverter, which is a small adapter which fits between the lens and the camera body, and doubles the focal length of your lens, so a 200 mm lens becomes 400 mm. These are a good cheap way of getting the long focal length without having to buy expensive lenses. They do, however, have a couple of disadvantages. The first is that, like the larger lenses themselves, a teleconverter uses about 1½ 'f' stops of light. Another disadvantage is that, depending on the camera and lens, teleconverters can make it extremely difficult to focus quickly and precisely, which is an important consideration when both you and the animals are on the move.

When using long lenses a tripod can be extremely useful, and with anything greater than about 300 mm it's a necessity. The problem here is that in the confined space of the hatch of a minibus (assuming you'll be taking an organised safari) it is impossible to set up the tripod, especially when you are sharing the confined space with at least three or four other people. Miniature tripods are available and these are useful for setting up on the roof of the van, although you can also rest the lens itself on the roof, provided that the van engine is switched off to kill any vibration.

Whatever combination of camera, lenses and accessories you decide to carry, make sure they are kept in a decent bag which will protect them from the elements, the dust, and the knocks they are bound to receive. It's also vital to make sure that your travel insurance policy includes your camera gear if it gets stolen.

Camera Hire & Repair

If you don't have the inclination or the resources to buy expensive equipment but still want some decent pictures of your safari, it is possible to hire SLR cameras and lenses in Nairobi. The best place to do this from is Expo Camera Centre (☎ 221797), Jubilee Exchange, Mama Ngina St, which is run by Mo Hussein, a very friendly and helpful

man. Its busy here everyday of the working week both with local businesses and tourists so you know it must be reliable and that the prices are competitive.

Expo also has a well-equipped repair shop where you can leave an ailing camera to be repaired with confidence. They do an excellent job but they're not cheap (neither is anyone else).

Selling Cameras

With the high duty placed on imported goods, you may be surprised to find that your old used camera is worth quite a bit in Kenya. Obviously the better the condition of the camera, the more it will be worth. There are a few camera shops in Nairobi which deal in second-hand equipment, so check them out. Bear in mind, however, that you'll most probably be paid in Kenyan shillings, so if it's at the end of your stay you'll need to have enough bank exchange certificates to reconvert the shillings to hard currency at the airport.

Film Processing

There are plenty of one-hour film-processing labs in Nairobi, and at least one in all other major towns. They can handle any film speeds. The cost is reasonable and the results just as good as what you'd get back home. Three good places to have this done are Expo Camera Centre, Camera Experts and the lab next to the Coffee House, all on Mama Ngina St. The lab also has a wide variety of film for sale.

Photographing People

As is the case in any country where you are a tourist, this is a subject which has to be approached with some sensitivity. People such as the Maasai and the Samburu have had so many rubbernecks pointing cameras at them for so many years that they are utterly sick to death of it – with good reason. There are even signs up in Namanga and Amboseli saying that it is prohibited to take photos of the Maasai. This doesn't mean that you can't, but just that you'll have to pay for it. Much as you may find this abhorrent, it is nevertheless an aspect of the tourism industry you'll just have to accept – put yourself in their position and try to think what you'd do.

It is of course possible to take pictures of people with zoom lenses but, most of the time, what's the point? By paying or giving some sort of gift, you'll not only get a better picture by using a smaller lens but you'll have some interaction with your subject. You might even get an invitation to see the family (and possibly photograph them).

WOMEN TRAVELLERS

Sexual harassment of women is far less prevalent in Kenya than in many countries though essentially this relates only to White women. If you're Black and walking the streets alone after 7 pm, there's a very good chance you'll be arrested, accused of being a whore and pressured into bribing your way out. KSh 200 is the usual amount. Refuse to pay and you could well spend the night in a cell at the central police station, be taken to court the following morning and fined KSh 1000. According to the people I've met to whom this has happened, you break no ice protesting your innocence even if you're married and your husband happens to be back at a hotel room or elsewhere. It can even happen if you're a Black woman in the company of a White man. The obvious way around this is to take taxis at night if you're going anywhere.

White women come under the category of 'tourists' and enjoy a somewhat dubious though privileged status. If you're a white woman, you may get the occasional hassle but it's rarely persistent if treated with the cold shoulder. There are certain areas in Nairobi where you wouldn't want to walk alone at night, but that applies equally to men, though usually for different reasons.

DANGERS & ANNOYANCES
Theft

Travelling in Kenya is basically trouble-free but you definitely do need to keep your wits about you. The time when you face the biggest risk is within the first couple of days of arriving in the country. The people who

make a living by relieving people of their possessions can often spot new arrivals by their uncertain movements and general unfamiliarity with the place. This is particularly true in Nairobi, and in fact the number of people who get their passports and money knocked off on the No 34 public bus in from the airport is amazing. The thieves use the 'instant crowd' technique, you'll find yourself jostled and before you know it your bag or money-belt strap has been slashed. Personally, I wouldn't use this bus for quids and, instead, take the Kenya Airways minibus, or even a taxi and get into Nairobi with my valuables intact.

Never leave your gear unattended anywhere as chances are it won't be there when you get back, no matter how short a time you are away. In hotel rooms your gear is generally safe but use your common sense – in some places (particularly the real cheapies/brothels) the door locks are purely cosmetic. In Nairobi the danger of theft of your possessions from your hotel room has to be weighed against the risk of having them ripped off on the street. If your hotel and room is secure, it's probably safer to leave valuables there. If you are going out raging at night, only carry as much money as you're likely to need, and leave everything else in your hotel. If your hotel has safety deposit boxes, leave your valuables there.

The place to carry your passport, money and other precious documents is in a pouch against your skin, either around your waist or your neck. Neither method is foolproof but both give a good measure of security and make it much harder to lose things. Leather pouches are far more comfortable to have against your skin than synthetic ones, and the moisture from perspiration is far less likely to turn your precious documents into a soggy pulp.

Small pouches and other wallets worn on the outside of your clothes are like flashing beacons to a thief as are the ubiquitous money belts, yet they continue to be immensely popular. Personally, I wouldn't step out of the hotel with one strapped to my waist. Advertise your valuables, and someone will be watching you. Day packs, especially in Nairobi, instantly classify you as a tourist (and probably one who hasn't been around too long). Elsewhere, they're not quite such a beacon. Minimise the risk by wearing them on your front rather than your back.

If you are the victim of a snatch theft, think twice before yelling 'Thief!' Nairobi people hate thieves, pursue them with a vengeance and, if they can catch them, mete out instant, brutal and often lethal punishment on the spot. One or more thieves lose their lives everyday in Nairobi for this. The police may intervene, but not always.

Confidence Tricks

In Nairobi the chances are you'll come across people who play on the emotions and gullibility of foreigners. People with tales about being 'refugees', usually from South Africa (but it could be anywhere with a political problem), can sound very convincing as they draw you into their net but they all end up asking for money. If you do give any, expect to be 'arrested' by 'plain-clothes police', complete with fake ID cards, who then extract a 'fine' from you on the basis that 'it's illegal to give money to foreigners'. It's actually only illegal to give them foreign currency. Stories such as this abound and the number of travellers who get taken in – sometimes to the tune of hundreds of dollars – is legend. The best policy is to ignore all such requests for money even though by doing this you'll occasionally be turning down what is a genuine request for help.

Another trick in Nairobi is the envelope full of money which gets dropped on the footpath in front of you. The idea is that, as you are reaching to pick it up, someone else (the accomplice of the person who dropped it) grabs it and then suggests to you that, as you both found it, you should go somewhere and share your 'good luck'. If you go along the only thing that will be shared is your money in a side alley somewhere.

Another tried and tested con trick is what appears to be a school student who approaches you with a photocopied sponsor-

ship form headed by the name of a school. He tells you his school needs funds to buy equipment and can you give a donation? Look at the form and you'll find the names of two or three wonderfully philanthropic people (usually from the USA, Germany or the UK) who have apparently donated vast amounts of Kenyan shillings to this worthy cause. If you fall for this then you need your head examined. If the person proves persistent, just ask him to go along with you to a telephone so you can confirm that the request is genuine and that the person is a registered student at the school in question.

The story changes each week. Whatever works gets pumped for all it's worth.

In Nakuru they don't lack ingenuity either. A trick that has been popular for years involves tourists with cars. Locals splash oil on your wheels, then tell you that your wheel bearings, differential or something else had failed, and then direct you to a nearby garage where their friends will 'fix' the problem – for a substantial fee. We've even had reports of oil being splashed on the back wheels and then the driver being told that the rear differential had failed even though the car was front wheel drive! Another vehicle trick is that people on the side of the road will gesticulate wildly to you as you are driving along, indicating that your front wheels are wobbling. Chances are that if you stop you'll be relieved of your valuables.

Mugging

Foreigners (and even experienced expatriates) do occasionally get mugged, but if you're sensible the chances of it happening to you are extremely small. There are certain places in Nairobi and on the coast where it's not recommended to walk at night, but other than that it's just a matter of common sense: don't go out drinking in the nightclubs or bars carrying your valuables and then go rolling home down the street; don't wear your wealth, or you become a very tempting target. Leave valuable jewellery at home, keep cameras out of sight and don't pull out wads of money to pay for something. Always have enough small change for everyday transactions handy and keep the rest concealed. Take a cue from the taxi drivers of Nairobi who stash their money in at least half a dozen places on their body and in various articles of clothing.

Lastly, be wary on crowded matatus. It's not the ragamuffins you should watch but those who appear to be well dressed and on their way home from work. Plenty of these people work the matatus and you, as a tourist, are just one of their targets. Kenyans get hit, too.

And, if you do get mugged, don't listen to anyone who swears blind that he/she can get back what you've lost because they know 'the scene'. You'll end up several hours later being told a sob story or simply never see the person again.

WORK

With the economic downturn in Kenya, it's difficult for foreigners to find jobs, though by no means impossible. The most likely areas in which employment might be found are in the safari business, teaching, advertising and journalism but, except for teaching, it's unlikely you'll see them advertised and the only way you'll find out about them is to spend a lot of time getting to know resident expatriates. You will also need to be able to prove that you have the relevant qualifications and/or experience in the field. Basically the rule of thumb is that if an African can do the job there's no need to hire a *mzungu* (White person).

The most fruitful area in which to look for work, given that you've had some experience and have the relevant skills, is the 'disaster industry'. Nairobi is awash with UN and other aid agencies servicing the famines in Somalia and southern Sudan and the refugee camps along the Kenyan border with those countries. But remember that the work is tough, often dangerous and the pay low. To find such work you would, again, have to spend a lot of time getting to know the expatriates involved in this.

Freelance work in the fields of journalism, literature and the film industry is also possible but, if you get involved in this, make sure you have a cast-iron contract for the work which you do. Too many people neglect to do this, go ahead on a kiss and a promise, don't get paid and/or see their work ripped-off or shelved and end up tearing their hair out.

Work permits and resident visas are not the easiest of things to arrange either. A prospective employer may be able to arrange them relatively painlessly but, usually, you would find yourself spending a lot of money (US$300 minimum) and time at Nyayo House (immigration).

ACTIVITIES
Diving & Snorkelling

Malindi, Watamu, Shimoni and Wasini Island are the spots for scuba diving, the latter two being preferred. At Watamu, diving is from a boat not far offshore. A typical anchor dive is made at 12 to 15 metres depth. Visibility is often only fair and in fact Kenyan diving visibility has a poor reputation due to the plankton in the water. There are, however, usually plenty of fish in the water even if the coral is not that spectacular. A typical dive costs US$30. For more information contact the Dive Shop at the Driftwood Club in Malindi, or the Ocean Sports Hotel at Watamu. Possibilities at Shimoni and Wasini Island in the extreme south are covered in The Coast chapter.

Windsurfing

Most of the resort hotels south and north of Mombasa have sailboards for hire, and the conditions are ideal – the waters are protected by the offshore reefs and the winds are usually reasonably strong and constant. The going rate at most places seems to be about US$3 per hour, more if you need instruction.

Beaches

One of the great attractions of Kenya is the superb beaches which line the coast. Many travellers find themselves staying much longer than they anticipated. This is real picture postcard stuff – coconut palms, dazzling white sand and clear blue water. The only problem is that for the most part the resort hotels have a virtual monopoly on accommodation, although there are a couple of budget options both south and north of Mombasa.

The beach at Diani is one of the best although it's lined solidly with resort hotels. Tiwi Beach, between Diani and Mombasa, is much more low key and you can camp right on the beach at the Twiga Lodge. There are similar possibilities north of Mombasa, although at certain times of year seaweed accumulates on the beach in huge quantities. Lamu doesn't suffer this problem and has some of the best beaches on the coast.

Caving

For information on this adventurous activity contact the Cave Exploration Group of East Africa, PO Box 47583, Nairobi.

Desert Grandeur

There's the opportunity to experience this on either side of Lake Turkana and for a considerable distance south of there on the eastern side of the lake. For most travellers, this is one of the highlights of their trip to Kenya.

On the western side, access to the lake is easy with a bitumen road all the way from Kitale, and there's at least one bus and often a matatu or two every day in each direction. If you're heading up this way then don't miss the opportunity of exploring the Cherangani Hills east of the Kitale to Lodwar road using the Marich Pass Field Studies Centre as your base. Either side offers many challenging possibilities. The Turkana, Samburu and Rendille tribespeople are also fascinating and, like the Maasai, have hung on to their traditional ways. It's certainly an area which you shouldn't miss at any cost.

Climbing & Walking

Mt Kenya is the obvious one, but other promising and relatively unexplored territory includes Mt Elgon on the Uganda border, the Cherangani Hills north of Kitale, the Matthews Range and Ndoto Mountains north of Isiolo, and even the Ngong Hills close to Nairobi. For more information refer to the relevant chapters in this book or contact the Mountaineering Club of Kenya (MCK) at its clubhouse at Wilson Airport (meetings every Tuesday at 8.30 pm – visitors welcome), or at its Nairobi address (☎ (02) 501747), PO Box 45741, Nairobi.

Gliding

The Gliding Club of Kenya has its headquarters in Mweiga near Nyeri in the Aberdares, and there are flights every day except Monday. For more information contact the Gliding Club of Kenya (☎ (0171) 2748), PO Box 926, Nyeri.

Ballooning

Balloon safaris in the game parks are an absolutely superb way of seeing the savannah plains and of course the animals, but without the intrusion of vehicles and dozens of other tourists doing the same thing. The most popular of these trips is that in the Masai Mara Game Reserve. The hot-air balloons depart daily from both Keekorok Lodge and the Fig Tree Lodge just after dawn and return around mid-morning. The flight includes a champagne breakfast on the plains. The cost is US$300. Bookings can be made through Adventures Aloft (☎ (2) 220592), Eagle House, Kimathi St, PO Box 40683, Nairobi; the Fig Tree Lodge; Block Hotels (☎ (02) 335807), PO Box 47557, Nairobi; or directly at Keekorok Lodge.

There's another outfit which offers balloon trips in Taita Hills Game Reserve. Bookings for this can be made through the Hilton International (☎ (02) 334000), PO Box 30624, Nairobi.

Fishing

The Kenya Fisheries Department operates a number of fishing camps in various parts of the country. They are really only an option if you have your own transport as the sites are off the main roads. Before you head off you need to get a fishing licence from the Fisheries Department. Advance bookings are not taken so it's just a matter of turning up at the site. For full details of the exact locations of the camps, see the Fisheries Department in

Nairobi; the office is near the National Museum.

White-Water Rafting

Rafting is still in its infancy in Kenya, perhaps because of the limited possibilities – there are only two major rivers in Kenya, the Athi/Galana and Tana. The Tana flows through relatively flat country so it's sluggish and unsuitable for rafting. The Athi/Galana, on the other hand, has substantial rapids, chutes and waterfalls. The only outfit which can fix you up with a trip down this river is operated by Mark Savage (☎ 521590), PO Box 44827, Nairobi. He has two units of the Avon Ranger 3 river rafts.

A day trip from Nairobi consists of putting in just above Sagana on the Athi River and finishing about four km above the Masinga Dam. The trip starts with about two km of mild rapids followed by six km of smooth water and then two km of Grade 4-plus rapids without a breather and another two km of the same grade but with a few calm stretches for bailing out. This is followed by portage around a waterfall and a further 13 km of smooth water to the take-out point.

There's also an exciting three-day trip available from Yatta Gap on the Athi down to Tsavo Safari Camp (74 km).

ACCOMMODATION

Kenya has a good range of accommodation from the very basic US$2-a-night budget hotels to luxury tented camps in the national parks for up to US$500 a night!

Camping

There are enough opportunities for camping that it is worth considering bringing a tent. It is also possible to hire camping equipment in Nairobi and elsewhere but it's not the sort of lightweight gear you could carry without a vehicle.

There are camp sites in just about every national park and game reserve and these are usually very basic. There'll be a toilet block with a couple of pit toilets, and usually a water tap, but very little else. Private sites are few and far between but where they do exist

they offer more in the way of facilities. Often it's possible to camp in the grounds of a hotel but this is obviously not an option in the bigger towns where space is limited.

Camping out in the bush is also possible though you would be advised to ask permission first. On the coast this is not advisable and sleeping on the beaches would be just asking for trouble.

Just in case you thought that the tented camps in the game parks might be a cheap option – forget it. They are luxury camps with all the facilities laid on, and high prices. The 'tents' barely justify the name – they usually just have canvas or mosquito netting for walls, but otherwise have a roof and bathroom. High, shoulder and low-season pricing policies apply equally to these places as they do to the top-end hotels.

Youth Hostels

The only youth hostels affiliated with the International Youth Hostels Federation (IYHF) are in Nairobi and Malindi. If you like youth hostels, they are fine. At US$2.40 for a dorm bed they are not so cheap but, as usual, they are good places to meet people. There are other places which call themselves 'youth hostels' but are not members of the federation. Some are good, others less so.

Hotels

Real bottom-end hotels (known everywhere as boardings & lodgings – hotels are often only restaurants) are generally brothels first and hotels second. This in itself is not a problem as long as you don't mind the noise, disruption and general atmosphere. Most places don't mind renting out rooms all night, although in some you get distinctly strange looks when they discover that not only do you want the room for the whole night, but that you want to spend it alone! These places are also not all that clean – you'll have to ask for clean sheets, and the shared bathrooms smell – and the rooms are often claustrophobic cells. On the other hand, you do occasionally come across cheap places which are clean and pleasant places to stay, so don't dismiss them totally;

there's usually at least one cheap boarding & lodging in each town. On the plus side, they are cheap; expect a single/double room to cost around US$2.50/3.50.

Things improve dramatically if you have a dollar or two more to spend, though there are always exceptions. For US$4.50/6 a single/double, you will usually get a clean room with private bath (soap and towel supplied). These places often have a restaurant and bar (usually noisy). The only real advantages you get over the cheap places are your own bathroom and toilet and a degree of security.

Those who prefer a mid-range hotel are well catered for. If you're willing to spend US$8 to US$15 a night then you can expect all the basic comforts and sometimes even touches of luxury such as your own shower and toilet with hot water, towels, soap and toilet paper; clean sheets and beds; a table and chair; and often a telephone and room service.

At the top end of the market, accommodation ranges from better than the average mid-range to the five-star international chain hotels which provide the lot with prices to match. These start at around US$20/30 for a single/double and head up from there. Some of these places are old colonial buildings with bags of atmosphere, but most are modern and vary from characterless to the luxurious. The resort hotels on the coast and the lodges in the game parks also fall into this category, although some of the latter are superb places to stay if you can afford it – having animals come to drink at the salt lick in front of your lodge as you sit on the verandah sipping a cool drink is just great, but pleasures such as this can set you back up to US$100 per person for full board, depending on the season.

If you intend to stay in any of the top-range hotels, it's important to know that the price depends on the season. The high season generally runs from 16 December to 31 March and from 1 July to 31 August. The shoulder season is from 1 September to 15 December and the low season from 1 April to 30 June. There's generally also an additional supplement over the Christmas and New Year periods.

FOOD

For the main part, Kenyan cuisine consists largely of stodge filler with beans or a (tough) meat sauce and is really just survival food for the locals – maximum filling-up potential at minimum cost. It is still possible to eat cheaply and well although the lack of variety becomes tedious after a while. People with carnivorous habits are far better served by the local food than vegetarians.

The most basic local eateries (often known as *hotelis*) hardly warrant being called restaurants. These places usually have a limited menu and are open only for lunch – the main meal of the day. If you're on a tight budget you'll find yourself eating in these places most of the time. However, if you have the resources, even in the smaller towns it's usually possible to find a restaurant that offers more variety and better food at a higher price. Often these places are connected with the mid-range and top-end hotels.

Preparing your own food is a viable option if you are camping and carrying cooking gear. Every town has a market and there's usually an excellent range of fresh produce available.

Fast food has taken off in a big way and virtually every town has a place which serves food that rates high in grease and low in price. Fried chips with lashings of lurid tomato sauce are a basic filler, but sausages, eggs, fish and chicken are also popular. In Nairobi there are literally dozens of these places, and they can be handy places to pick up a snack.

The only place where any sort of distinctive African cuisine (other than *nyama choma* or barbecued goat's meat) has developed is on the coast where the Swahili dishes reflect the history of contact with the Arabs and other Indian Ocean traders – coconut and spices are used heavily and the results are generally excellent.

As might be expected with the large number of Asians in Kenya, there are also large numbers of Indian restaurants. In addition, many hotels are owned by Indians and the choice of food available on their menus reflects this. If you like this cuisine, you'll have no problems even in the smaller towns though most of these restaurants are confined to Nairobi and Mombasa.

Vegetarians are not well catered for. Away from the two main cities there are virtually no vegetarian dishes to accompany the starch. Beans are going to figure prominently in any vegetarian's culinary encounters in Kenya! Buying fresh fruit and vegetables in the market can help relieve the tedium.

Snacks

Sambusas are probably the most common snack and are obvious descendants of the Indian samosa. They are deep-fried pastry triangles stuffed with spiced mince meat. Occasionally you come across sambusas with vegetable fillings, but this is usually only in the Indian restaurants. If you can find them freshly made and still warm, sambusas can be excellent. However, more often by the time you get them they are at least several hours old, are cold and have gone limp and greasy from the oil saturation.

Another item that fits into the pure starch category is that curious beast known as the *mandazi*. It's a semisweet, flat doughnut and, once again, when they're fresh they can be very good. They are usually cooked and eaten at breakfast time – often dunked in tea. Should you decide to eat one later in the day, chances are it will be stale and hard.

Something that you don't come across very often but which makes an excellent snack meal is *mkate mayai* (literally 'bread-eggs'). This was originally an Arab dish and is now found in countries as far ranging as Kenya and Singapore. Basically it's a wheat dough which is spread into a thin pancake, filled with minced meat and raw egg and then folded into a neat parcel and fried on a hot-plate. The Iqbal Hotel in Nairobi is a good place to try this snack.

Seemingly on every second street corner someone is trying to make a few bob selling corn cobs roasted on a wire grille over a bed of hot coals. You pay only a couple of shillings for these. Another street-corner snack is deep-fried yams, eaten hot with a squeeze of lemon juice and a sprinkling of chilli powder.

Main Dishes

Basically it's meat, meat and more meat, accompanied by starch of some sort. The meat is usually in a stew with perhaps some potato or other vegetables thrown in, and is often as tough as an old boot. Beef, goat and mutton are the most commonly eaten meats.

The starch comes in three major forms:

Nyama Choma

If you had to name a national dish in Kenya, nyama choma (barbecued goat's meat) would probably be it. In recent years it has become almost a fetish amongst Africans and expatriates alike and, to cater for the demand, hundreds of places have opened up offering just that. Sometimes it's good; sometimes it's tough as old leather. What you get is what you choose from a refrigerated selection of various cuts which you buy by the kg. Once it's barbecued, it's brought to your table by a waiter and sliced into bite-sized pieces along with a vegetable mash (often *matoke*, which is plantains and maize). It's not a cheap option but not expensive either.

The trouble with nyama choma, if you've ever had any culinary experience, is that in no way does it resemble (except in the most expensive establishments) anything similar to marinated and seasoned barbecued meat. Most of the time, you'll take years off the life of your teeth chewing it and end up spending more time with a tooth pick than you spent eating. Marination and the use of herbs, let alone basting, have yet to reach Kenya.

Nevertheless, the Kenyan middle class regard an invitation to nyama choma (and copious quantities of Tusker lager) as a special night out. So don't let me put you off – try it! Maybe this is how Africans keep their beautiful, healthy teeth. ■

potatoes, rice and *ugali*. The last of these is maize meal which is cooked up into a thick porridge until it sets hard. It's then served up in flat bricks. It's incredibly stodgy, almost totally devoid of any flavour and tends to sit on the stomach like a royal corgi, but most Kenyans swear by it. It's certainly the equivalent of mashed potato for the Poms or sticky rice for the Chinese and Koreans but it certainly isn't a culinary orgasm. Freshly cooked it's palatable; when stale, just about inedible. Naturally, you must try it at least once and some travellers actually get to like it, but don't hold your breath! The only thing it has going for it is that it's cheap.

Roast chicken and steak are popular dishes in the more up-market restaurants of the bigger towns. Food in this sort of place differs little from what you might get at home. Cooked red kidney beans are always an alternative to meat and are widely available in local eateries.

Menus, where they exist in the cheaper places, are usually just a chalked list on a board on the wall. In better restaurants they are usually just in English.

The following food list gives some of the main words you are likely to come across when trying to decipher Swahili menus or buy food in the market.

Useful Words

boiled	*chemka*
bread	*mkate*
butter	*siagi*
cup	*kikombe*
curry	*mchuzi*
egg(s)	*yai (mayai)*
food	*chakula*
fork	*uma*
fried	*kaanga*
glass	*glasi*
hot/cold	*moto/baridi*
hot (spicy)	*hoho*
Indian bread	*chapati*
knife	*kisu*
napkin	*kitambaa*
pepper	*pilipili*
plate	*sahani*
raw	*mbichi*

ripe	*mbivu*
roast	*choma*
table	*mesa*
teaspoon	*kijiko*
salt	*chumvi*
sauce	*mchuzi*
soup	*supu*
sugar	*sukari*
sweet	*tamu*
yoghurt	*maziwalala*

Vegetables & Grains

aubergine	*biringani*
cabbage	*kabichi*
capsicum	*pilipili baridi*
carrots	*karoti*
cassava	*muhogo*
garlic	*vitunguu saumu*
kidney beans	*maharagwe*
lettuce	*salad*
maize-meal porridge	*ugali*
mashed plantains &	
maize	*matoke*
onions	*vitunguu*
plantains	*ndzi*
potatoes	*viazi*
rice	*wali*
spinach	*sukuma wiki*
boiled spinach	*sukuma wiki*
tomatoes	*nyana*
vegetables	*mboga*
vegetable stew	*mboga*

Meat & Fish

beef	*nyama ya ngombe*
kebabs	*mushkaki*
meat	*nyama*
meat stew	*karanga*
mutton, goat	*nyama ya mbuzi*
pork	*nyama ya nguruwe*
steak	*steki*
crab	*kaa*
fish	*samaki*
lobster	*kamba*
squid	*ngisi*

Fruit

This is where Kenya really excels. Because of the country's varied climate, there's an excellent array of fruits. The tropical ones are especially good. Depending on the place and the season you can buy mangoes, papaya, pineapple, watermelon, oranges, guavas, custard apples, bananas (many varieties) and coconuts. Prices are cheap and the quality very high.

bananas	ndizi
coconut (green)	dafu
coconut (ripe)	nazi
custard apples	stafeli
dates	tende
fruit	matunda
grapefruits	madanzi
guava	pera
limes	ndimu
mangoes	maembe
oranges	machungwa
papayas	paipai
passionfruit	pasheni
pineapples	mananasi
sugar cane	miwa
watermelon	tikiti

DRINKS
Nonalcoholic Drinks
Tea & Coffee Despite the fact that Kenya grows some of the finest tea and coffee in the world, getting a decent cup of either can be difficult.

Tea *(chai)* is the national obsession and is drunk in large quantities. It bears little resemblance to what you might be used to but as long as you look on it as just a different hot drink and not actually tea it can be quite good. Be warned that it is generally very milky and horrendously sweet. Chai is made the same way in Kenya as it is in India: all the ingredients (tea, milk and masses of sugar) are put into cold water and the whole lot is brought to the boil and stewed. Finding a good honest cup of tea is virtually impossible outside the fancy restaurants. For tea without milk ask for *chai kavu*.

Coffee is similarly disappointing. Instant coffee is generally used, and in small quantities, so, once again, you're looking at a sweet milky concoction. However, as each cup is individually made it's somewhat

easier to order one tailored to your own liking.

Soft Drinks All the old favourites are here, including Coke, Pepsi and Fanta, and they go under the generic term of soda. As with beer, prices vary depending on where you buy. In most places you pay around US$0.25 per bottle but in the more exclusive places you can pay up to US$1. There are no such predictable prices for freshly squeezed fruit juices which range from US$0.50 to US$2 per glass.

Alcohol
Beer Kenya has a thriving local brewing industry and formidable quantities of beer are consumed. It's probably true to say that beer is the most widely available manufactured product in the country. Go to just a tiny group of *dukas* (local stores) by the side of the road somewhere and chances are one of them will either be a bar, or it will stock beer. Sure, it won't be cold, but then even in the most up-market places beer is available both chilled and warm. 'Why warm?' you might ask as your face wrinkles in horror! The answer is because most Africans appear to prefer it that way. I've certainly never seen them drink cold White Cap though you'll occasionally see an African drinking cold Pilsner or Premium.

The beer names are White Cap, Tusker and Pilsner (all manufactured by Kenya Breweries Ltd) and they're sold in 500 ml bottles. They are basically the same product with different labels (though there is a discernible difference in taste) but most people end up sticking to just one brand. The same company manufactures export-quality 300 ml beers – Export and Premium respectively – and these are slightly stronger and more expensive. Guinness is also available but tastes and looks nothing like the genuine Irish article (or even the bastardised but similar variety sold outside of the Emerald Isle in the West and Hong Kong).

Lastly, Kenya Breweries has also brought out a draught version of Tusker which is very good but only available in a few places.

Check the price before ordering – in some places it's cheaper than the bottled variety; in others it costs more (sometimes considerably more).

Beers are cheapest bought from a supermarket where a 500 ml bottle will cost you around US$0.50. Bought from a normal bar, you are looking at US$0.60 to US$0.90. Bought at a bar in a five-star hotel it can cost you up to US$3. This would be exceptional but, as there are no price controls on beer – bars and hotels can charge what they like.

Wine Kenya has a fledgeling wine industry and the Lake Naivasha colombard wines are said to be quite good. This is something that cannot be said about the most commonly encountered Kenyan wine – papaya wine. It tastes foul and even the smell is unbearable.

On the other hand, you can get cheap imported European and even Australian wine by the glass for around US$2 in Nairobi restaurants. This is expensive when compared to the price of beer but is actually not too bad.

Local Brews Although it is strictly illegal to brew or distil liquor this doesn't stop it going on. *Pombe* is the local beer and is usually a fermented brew made with bananas or millet and sugar. You may get the chance to sample it here and there and it shouldn't do you any harm. The same cannot be said for the distilled drinks, known locally as *chang'a*, as these are often very effective poisons – inefficient/amateur distilling techniques ensure various percentages of methyl alcohol creep into the brew. They'll blind you if you're lucky; kill you if you're not. Leave it alone!

THINGS TO BUY

Kenya is an excellent place for souvenirs, although much of the cheap stuff available is just pure junk mass-produced by hand for the tourist trade. Look carefully at what's available before parting with your money.

Nairobi and Mombasa are the main centres but many of the items come from the various regions, so it's often possible to pick up the same at source, although you then have the problem of transporting it.

The best buys include *makonde* carvings, sometimes made from ebony (but often softer woods stained with boot polish), kiondos (woven sisal baskets), jewellery and tribal souvenirs, including colourful Maasai beaded jewellery, the decorated *calabash* (dried gourds) and spears and shields. There are also batiks, local sarongs *(kangas* and *kikois)*, soapstone carvings from Kisii in the west of Kenya, and paintings.

It's possible to pick up something which will look good in your living room back home without spending a fortune but, these days, something of genuine quality and artistry is going to cost real money because there are many skilful artists around who produce works of genuine art (as opposed to tourist tat) and know that there are quite a few tourists around who are very discerning and will pay big bucks for quality. This particularly applies to makonde carvings, jewellery and paintings. In some cases, you can be talking about thousands of US dollars.

If you're interested in quality artwork, spend time doing the rounds of the shops and galleries which deal in it.

Elephant Hair Bracelets

On the streets of Nairobi you'll undoubtedly be approached by hawkers trying to sell you 'elephant hair' bracelets. Despite all the protestations to the contrary, these bracelets are made from reed grass (which is then covered in boot polish), from slivers of cow horn, or simply from plastic. You can safely assume that none of them are the real McCoy. ■

Getting There & Away

AIR

Unless you are travelling overland, flying is just about the only – and the most convenient – way of getting to Kenya. Nairobi is the main hub for flights and the route on which you are most likely to get a relatively cheap ticket, but it's worth checking out cheap charter flights to Mombasa from Europe too.

Buying an ordinary economy-class ticket is not the most economical way to go, but it does give you maximum flexibility and the ticket is valid for 12 months.

Students and those under 26 (under 29 in the USA) can often get discounted tickets so it's worth checking first with a student travel bureau (such as STA Travel) to see if there is anything on offer. Another option is an advance purchase ticket which is usually between 30 and 40% cheaper than the full economy fare, but has restrictions. You must purchase your ticket at least 21 days in advance (sometimes more) and you must stay away for a minimum period (usually 14 days) and return within 180 days (sometimes less). The main disadvantage is that stopovers are not allowed and if you have to change your dates of travel or destination then there will be extra charges to pay. Standby fares are another possibility. Some airlines will let you travel at the last minute if there are seats available just before departure. These tickets cost less than the economy fare but are usually not as cheap as the advance purchase fares.

Of all the options, however, the cheapest way to go is via the so-called 'bucket shops'. These are travel agencies which sell discounted tickets. Airlines only sell a certain percentage of their tickets through bucket shops so the availability of seats can vary widely, particularly in the high season. You have to be flexible with these tickets, although if the agents are sold out for one flight they can generally offer you something similar in the near future.

Most of the bucket shops are reputable organisations, but be careful as there is always the occasional fly-by-night operator who sets up shop, takes your money for a bargain-basement ticket and then either disappears or issues you with an invalid or unusable ticket. Check carefully what you are buying before you hand over money. Having said this, I must add that I've used bucket shops for years and been handed the most weird and wonderful tickets. For example, tickets issued in East Berlin but bought in London for a flight from London to Malaysia with stopovers in New Delhi, Bangkok and Kuala Lumpur. They've all been sweet.

Bucket shops generally advertise in newspapers and magazines and there's a lot of competition and different routes available so it's best to telephone first and then rush round if they have what you want. In Europe, the market for these sort of tickets to American and Asian destinations has been well developed over many years, but little has been available to African destinations south of the Sahara until fairly recently. Fares are now becoming more flexible, and Nairobi is one of a handful of destinations that has plenty of options.

To/From North America

In the USA, the best way to find cheap flights is by checking the Sunday travel sections in the major newspapers such as the *Los Angeles Times* or *San Francisco Examiner-Chronicle* on the west coast, and the *New York Times* on the east coast. The student travel bureaus are also worth trying – STA Travel or Council Travel.

North America is a relative newcomer to the bucket-shop traditions of Europe and Asia so ticket availability and the restrictions attached to them need to be weighed against what is on offer on the more normal advance purchase or full economy fares.

Return tickets to Nairobi from New York (Air France) cost US$1340 in the low season

(1 November to 14 December, 16 January to 24 March and 11-14 April), and US$1525 in the high season (15 December to 15 January, 25 March to 10 April, 15 June to 30 September). From Los Angeles a return ticket costs US$1525 in the low season and US$1832 in the high season. Note that these fares are for students aged up to 29 years.

If you shop around, it's possible to get one-way tickets from New York to Nairobi for as little as US$599 in the low season, and return tickets for US$1099 also in the low season.

From Canada, Air France offers flights from Toronto to Nairobi for US$1340 in the low season and US$1697 in the high season.

To/From Europe

You can find bucket shops by the dozen in London, Paris, Amsterdam, Brussels, Frankfurt and a few other places too. In London, there are several newspapers with lots of bucket shop ads which will give you a good idea of current fares, as well as specialist magazines catering entirely to the travel industry.

Trailfinder is a magazine put out three times a year by Trailfinders at 46 Earls Court Rd, London W8 6EJ (☎ (071) 938-3366), and 194 Kensington High St, London W8 (☎ (071) 937-5400). It's free if you pick it up in London but if you want it mailed it costs UK£8 for three issues in the UK or Eire, and UK£12 or US$20 for four issues elsewhere in the world including airmail postage. Trailfinders can fix you up with all your ticketing requirements for anywhere in the world as well as providing information on insurance, immunisation and books. Trailfinders has been in business for years and can be highly recommended. All the staff are experienced travellers so they speak your language. It's open Monday to Saturday from 9 am to 6 pm (7 pm on Thursdays). There are branch offices at 194 Kensington High St, London W8 7RG (☎ (071) 938-3939), 58 Deansgate, Manchester M3 2FF (☎ (061) 839-6969), and 2 McLellan Galleries, Sauchiehall St, Glasgow G2 3EH (☎ (041) 353-2224).

Africa Travel Now is a quarterly newspaper put out by the Africa Travel Centre (☎ (071) 387-1211), 4 Medway Court, Leigh St, London WC1H 9QX. It's free and, as its name indicates, it specialises entirely in travel to and around Africa. It contains an excellent run-down of discount flights to most major cities in Africa as well as details on safaris which you can book in advance if you care to. Office hours are Monday to Friday from 9.30 am to 5.30 pm and on Saturdays from 10 am to 2 pm. As with Trailfinders, the Africa Travel Centre is highly recommended.

Time Out (☎ (071) 836-4411), Tower House, Southampton St, London WC2E 7HD, is London's weekly entertainment guide and it's available from all bookshops and newsagents. Subscription enquiries should be addressed to Time Out Subs, Unit 8 Grove Ash, Bletchley, Milton Keynes MK1 1BZ, UK.

The price of airline tickets from London to Nairobi advertised in the above magazines is around UK£220 one way and UK£385 return. The corresponding fares to Dar es Salaam are UK£264 one way and UK£451 return. The airlines used are generally Aeroflot and other Eastern European and Middle Eastern airlines but this isn't always the case. Both Trailfinders and Africa Travel Centre can also fix you up with multistopover tickets which include Nairobi and other African destinations on them. Also check out Africa Travel System (☎ (071) 602-5091) at 6 North End Parade, London W14 0SJ, which specialises in airline tickets to Africa.

If you plan to head further east or to Australasia after Africa, Africa Travel System can arrange a ticket at a price comparable to anything you'll be offered at the bucket shops in Nairobi.

There is no advantage in buying a one-way ticket to Nairobi and then another one-way ticket back to Europe from there. You'll end up paying more than if you bought a return ticket in the first place. You may also run foul of immigration on arrival in Kenya without an onward ticket and be forced to buy one on the spot – an expensive exercise in lack of forethought.

A round-the-world (RTW) ticket is another economical option if you have the time, but only very few of these include African stopovers and hardly any include Nairobi. Johannesburg is the most common African stopover. For example, a London, Johannesburg, Perth, Sydney, San Francisco, Orlando, Washington, London ticket costs around UK£811.

Don't take advertised fares as gospel truth. To comply with truth in advertising laws, UK companies must be able to offer *some* tickets at their cheapest quoted price but they might only have one or two of them each week. If you are not one of the lucky ones, you may find yourself looking at tickets which cost up to UK£50 more (one way or return). The best thing to do, therefore, is to start looking into tickets well before your intended departure date so you have a very good idea what is available.

Remember that discounted tickets cannot generally be paid for with a credit card. You must pay with cash or with a bank cheque.

To/From Asia

You may safely assume that flying is the only feasible way of getting between the Indian subcontinent and Kenya. There are plenty of flights between East Africa and Bombay due to the large Indian population in Kenya. There are bucket shops of a sort in New Delhi, Bombay and Calcutta and most of the discounted tickets will be with Air India. In New Delhi I'd recommend Tripsout Travel, 72/7 Tolstoy Lane behind the Government of India Tourist Office, Janpath.

Typical fares from Bombay to Nairobi are around US$312 return with either Ethiopian Airlines, Kenya Airways or Pakistan International Airlines (PIA) via Karachi.

In Nairobi there are a lot of bucket shops offering tickets to Karachi, Islamabad, New Delhi, Bombay and Calcutta. Most of these will be with Air India or PIA.

To/From Australasia

There are no longer tight constraints on ticket discounting in Australia, and fares are continuing to fall, but for Australians and New Zealanders there are still very few route options to Africa. The only direct connections are the weekly Qantas flight from Sydney to Perth and Harare (Zimbabwe) which costs A$1760 return from Perth (A$1999 from Melbourne or Sydney) in the low season (16 January to 15 February) and A$2200 from Perth (A$2500 from Sydney or Melbourne) in the high season (1 December to 15 January), and South African Airways' flight from Perth to Johannesburg. A return ticket from Sydney or Melbourne to Johannesburg costs the same as that to Harare; ie around A$1999 in the low season and A$2500 in the high season.

It obviously makes sense for Australasians to think in terms of a RTW ticket or an Australia/New Zealand to Europe round-trip ticket with stopovers in Asia and Africa. It shouldn't be too much trouble for a travel agency to put together a ticket which includes various Asian stopovers plus a Nairobi stopover. Having Nairobi added to such a ticket bumps up the price a little and you may have to go through several travel agencies before you get satisfaction as many of them know very little about deals via Africa.

It's probably best to start your search for a ticket by looking in the travel section of the Saturday issue of either the *Sydney Morning Herald* or the *Age* and by visiting a student travel bureau. It's also worth writing or telephoning for a copy of *Airfares Guide* from The Travel Specialists (☎ (02) 262-3555), 62 Clarence St, Sydney, NSW 2000. It has been published for a number of years now and will give you a very good idea of what's available.

To/From Ethiopia

Both Ethiopian Airlines and Kenya Airways operate regular direct flights between Nairobi and Addis Ababa.

To/From Somalia

Somali Airlines is defunct and Kenya Airways no longer flies there. There are, on the other hand, plenty of UN and other aid agency aircraft which fly between Mombasa and Mogadishu. If you're interested in getting there, talk to aid workers in Mombasa or Nairobi. I found it was very easy to get a (free) lift there and back.

To/From Sudan

Kenya Airways and Sudan Airways operate direct flights between Khartoum and Nairobi.

To/From Tanzania

The cheapest regular flights from Tanzania to Kenya are between Dar es Salaam and Nairobi on Kenya Airways. A one-way full economy fare is US$123 (but you can find tickets for as little as US$110) though you must add the US$20 departure tax to these prices. There are also flights between Zanzibar and Mombasa (US$45). However, as these are very popular, you'll need to book at least two weeks ahead if you want to be sure of getting a seat. You can forget about Air Tanzania for the present because, although they schedule a Dar es Salaam to Nairobi flight, they have only one jet in their 'fleet' of just two planes and it's fully occupied servicing the Tanzanian domestic routes.

There are also two private companies based in Zanzibar with six and eight-seater propeller planes which occasionally fly between Zanzibar and Mombasa or Nairobi. They are Air Zanzibar (☎ (054) 32512), 302 Kenyatta Rd, Shangani, Zanzibar; and Zan Air (☎ (054) 33670), Malindi, Zanzibar. The price of flights to Mombasa are the same as on Kenya Airways but to Nairobi a ticket costs US$100. To find out if the companies are operating, contact their offices in Zanzibar or keep an eye on the notice boards at Africa House Hotel or the Fisherman Restaurant. Neither company has offices in Mombasa or Nairobi.

LAND

To/From Ethiopia

Since the change of regime in Ethiopia, land borders are once again open. The only

problem is transport. There are buses from Isiolo to Marsabit and Moyale (the border town) but from there transport is problematical. Hitching may be your only option and traffic is sparse until you get further into Ethiopia.

To/From Somalia

There's no way you can get overland from Kenya to Somalia at present (unless you're part of a refugee aid convoy). Even if you attempted it, the Kenyan police or the army would turn you back. Moreover, the entire border area is infested with well-armed Somali *shifta* (bandits) making any attempt to cross it a dangerous and foolhardy venture.

To/From Sudan

As with Somalia, there's no way you can get overland between Kenya and Sudan at present. The furthest north you're going to get is Lokichokio, and you'll be lucky to get that far unless you're with a refugee aid convoy.

To/From Tanzania

Dar es Salaam to Mombasa There are a number of bus companies (such as Coast, Cat and Tawfiq) which do the run from Dar es Salaam to Mombasa via Tanga and vice versa, though usually only once a week in either direction. The trip takes anything from 16 to 24 hours (eight to 12 hours from Tanga). The border crossing at Lunga Lunga (Kenya) and Horohoro (Tanzania) is quite straightforward but it takes as long as four hours to clear all 50 or so people through both posts. The fare from Dar es Salaam to Mombasa is TSh 3000. The Cat bus office in Dar es Salaam is on Msimbazi St close to the Kariakoo Market and the Caltex station.

If you're going to take one of these buses it's worth considering doing the journey partly by train. It's much more comfortable, and costs only about TSh 300 more to take the overnight train 1st class from Dar es Salaam to Tanga. From Tanga you can pick up one of the buses running between Dar es Salaam and Mombasa at around 8 am;

however, there's a chance you may have difficulty getting on. The trip from Tanga to Mombasa costs TSh 700.

You can also do the journey the hard way. From Tanga to the Tanzanian border post at Horohoro there are a couple of buses per day along the rough single-lane dirt road which cost TSh 400. From Horohoro it's a six-km walk to the Kenyan border post at Lunga Lunga and there's very little traffic so hitching is difficult. Once through the Kenyan border post, however, there are frequent matatus for the one-hour journey to Mombasa.

Arusha/Moshi to Nairobi These days the trip between Nairobi and Arusha or Moshi is a breeze. The trip takes five hours and getting through customs and immigration is no problem. There are at least three companies with direct buses/minibuses operating on a daily basis. The most expensive of them is the DHL Shuttle (run by the international courier company of the same name) which leaves Nairobi daily at 8.30 am from the Norfolk Hotel, and from Arusha at 2 pm from the Novotel Mt Meru. The fare from Nairobi is US$17. Advance booking is advisable, and this can be done at DHL, 8th Floor, Town House, Kaunda St, Nairobi (☎ (02) 212804). In Arusha, the DHL office is in the foyer of the Novotel Mt Meru.

A similar shuttle service is operated by Tayler's Travel (☎ (02) 335365), Tubman Rd, Nairobi and on Swahili St, Arusha (☎ 3488).

Much cheaper is the Arusha Express, which operates full-sized buses and has its office in amongst the cluster of bus companies down Accra Rd in Nairobi. In Arusha, the office is at the bus station. Buses leave Nairobi daily except Wednesday at 8.30 am and the fare is US$5.70.

It's also easy, but less convenient, to do this journey in stages, and since the Kenyan and Tanzanian border posts are next to each other at Namanga, there's no long walk involved. There are frequent matatus and share-taxis from Arusha to Namanga every day which go when full and cost TSh 700 to TSh 1300 (negotiable). The taxis normally take about 1½ hours, though there are a number of kamikaze drivers who are totally crazy and will get you there in just one hour. From the Kenyan side of the border there are frequent matatus and share-taxis which go when full and cost US$2.85 and US$4.30 respectively. The journey by taxi takes about two hours, and by matatu about three hours. Both have their depot outside the petrol station on Ronald Ngala St close to the junction with River Rd.

Moshi to Voi The crossing between Moshi and Voi via Taveta is also reliable as far as transport goes (buses, matatus and share-taxis). A matatu between Taveta and Voi (along a bumpy road) takes 2½ hours and costs US$2.60. There's also a train which takes five hours and costs the same.

Musoma to Kisii It's much more difficult to cross the border between Musoma and Kisii via Isebania in the north as there are no matatus or buses which go all the way to the border so you're looking at hiring a taxi or hitching. Hitching is difficult as there's very little traffic. On the other hand, this is one of the routes through to Zaïre which overland trucks use so you may be lucky and get a lift all the way, but trucks don't come through that often.

Serengeti to Masai Mara If you look at any detailed map of the Serengeti National Park and Masai Mara Game Reserve, you'll see that there's a border crossing between Bologonja and Sand River, and so you would assume it's possible to cross here. It is if you're crossing *from* Kenya *to* Tanzania, assuming you have the appropriate vehicle documentation (insurance and temporary entry permit). But officially, it isn't possible to cross in the opposite direction because you must pay the park entry fee to Masai Mara and you must pay it in Kenyan shillings, which you ought not to have since, under Kenyan currency regulations, you're not allowed to export them. And the nearest place where you *might* be able to change money is at Keekorok Lodge, 10 km away. Just imagine! In practice, the border guards/park officials are very helpful, so if you just happen to have a sufficient stash of Kenyan shillings to pay the park entry fees, then like Nelson with his blind eye at Trafalgar, it's a question of 'I see no ships'.

To/From Uganda
The two main border posts which most overland travellers use are Malaba and Busia with Malaba being by far the most commonly used.

Kampala to Nairobi via Malaba
Akamba operates direct buses between Kampala and Nairobi daily which cost USh 15,000, depart at 3 pm, and arrive the following morning. Its office in Kampala is on Dewinton St.

Doing the journey in stages, there are frequent matatus until the late afternoon between Kampala (USh 2500, three hours) or Jinja (USh 1500, two hours) and Malaba. There are also frequent matatus in either direction between Tororo and Malaba (Uganda) which cost USh 250 and take less than one hour. The road has recently been resurfaced and is excellent, although it does mean that the drivers can get up to terrifying speeds. Luckily, there's not much traffic on this road except close to Kampala.

There's also a train from Kampala to Tororo but it only runs three times a week and is diabolically slow. The fare is USh 1950 (3rd class only).

The Ugandan and Kenyan border posts are about one km from each other at Malaba and you will have to walk.

There are trains from Malaba to Nairobi via Eldoret and Nakuru on Wednesdays, Saturdays and Sundays at 4 pm, arriving in Nairobi the next day at 9.30 am. The fares are US$22 in 1st class, US$12.50 in 2nd class and US$4.75 in 3rd class. The trains do not connect with the Ugandan system.

If you don't want to take the train, there are daily buses by different companies between Malaba and Nairobi which depart at around 7.30 pm arriving at about 5.30 am the next day. The fare is US$5.40. If you prefer

to travel by day there are plenty of matatus between Bungoma and Malaba which take about 45 minutes. If you stay in Bungoma overnight there are plenty of cheap hotels to choose from. From Bungoma there are several daily buses to Nairobi which leave at about 8 am and arrive about 5 pm the same day.

The other main entry point into Kenya from Uganda is via Busia further south. There are frequent matatus between Jinja and Busia and between Busia and Kisumu. This border is more convenient to get across because the Ugandan and Kenyan border posts are right next to each other.

SEA
To/From Asia
There are no longer any passenger ships from India or Pakistan to Kenya. Don't believe any rumours that there are such ships. There are about four or five dhows which do the journey from Zanzibar and Mombasa to Karachi and Bombay each year via Somalia, South Yemen and Oman, but they are extremely difficult to locate and even more difficult to get onto. The days of the dhows were numbered decades ago and those you find in Mombasa harbour will only be plying between Lamu, Mombasa, Pemba and Zanzibar.

To/From Tanzania
It's possible to go by dhow between Zanzibar, Pemba and Mombasa plus there's a catamaran, the MV *Flying Horse*, which does the Dar es Salaam to Mombasa run via Zanzibar once a week in either direction (on Mondays from Mombasa). For full details, refer to to the Mombasa section in the Kenya Coast chapter.

There are no steamer services which connect Kenya with Tanzania on Lake Victoria.

LEAVING KENYA
Nairobi is the best city in East Africa (and perhaps in the whole of Africa) to pick up cheap airline tickets for international flights. There is a lot of competition between travel

agencies so most of them lean over backwards to give you whatever discounts they can. They are the equivalent of bucket shops in Europe. Only a few of the airlines sell discounted tickets through these agencies and none of them sell them directly from their own offices. The most common discounters are Aeroflot, Air India, EgyptAir, Olympic Airways, Pakistan International Airlines (PIA) and Sudan Airways and most of the cheap tickets available are for flights to Europe, although there are others to India, Pakistan and Singapore and sometimes to Madagascar, Mauritius and Réunion.

Except on Kenya Airways, all airline tickets must be paid for in hard currency (cash, travellers' cheques or credit card).

The cheapest flight from Nairobi to London costs US$350 (US$330 to Frankfurt or Rome) one way with Sudan Airways. The flight leaves once weekly on Sunday and goes via Addis Ababa, Khartoum and Frankfurt (making it quite a long haul if your destination is London). Kenya Airways flies Nairobi to London nonstop for US$450 return – this is a good deal if you want a return ticket. British Airways also flies Nairobi to London nonstop but the price of an economy-class ticket is US$867 one way.

The cheapest flight from Nairobi to New York costs US$595 one way with Saudia. The flight leaves once weekly on Monday. Remember there's no alcohol aboard Saudia flights. The next cheapest to New York is US$947 one way with Gulf Air. A regular economy-class ticket costs US$1113 one way.

The cheapest flight from Nairobi to Bombay (India) costs US$265 one way with PIA and goes via Karachi. The fare to Karachi with the same airline costs US$230. If Delhi is your destination then the same airline will take you there for US$305 but Gulf Air will do Nairobi to Delhi for US$288. Regular economy-class tickets to Karachi, Bombay and Delhi are US$291, US$312 and US$383 respectively.

The cheapest tickets from Nairobi to Bangkok and Singapore are US$455 and US$527 one way, respectively, on Gulf Air which flies twice a week on Thursday and Saturday via Bahrain. The regular economy-class tickets on this sector cost US$569 and US$658.

Between Nairobi and Sydney/Melbourne, the cheapest fare is US$907 one way and US$1400 return with Gulf Air. The flights leave twice a week on Thursday and Saturday and go via Bahrain and Singapore. A regular economy-class ticket to Sydney or Melbourne is US$1133 one way.

Between Nairobi and Hong Kong, the cheapest fare is US$496 one way, again with Gulf Air. An economy-class fare on this route is US$699.

The cheapest flight between Nairobi and Johannesburg costs US$300 one way on Olympic Airways although Air Malawi is presently offering a return ticket for the same price. How long this will last remains to be seen. A regular economy-class ticket to Johannesburg costs US$372 one way.

Other discounted fares within Africa include the Kenya Airways twice-weekly flight from Nairobi to Kigali (Rwanda) or Bujumbura (Burundi) for US$163 one way (US$326 return). Kenya Airways also offers a 21-day return excursion ticket for US$229, and flies from Nairobi to the Seychelles for US$300 return.

A list of recommended travel agencies can be found in the Nairobi chapter.

Departure Tax

The airport departure tax for international flights is US$20. You must pay this in foreign currency (cash); travellers' cheques and Kenyan shillings are not accepted. Kenyan shillings can be reconverted into US dollars at the airport on presentation of a bank receipt proving you have already changed sufficient hard currency into Kenyan shillings.

Getting Around

AIR

Kenya Airways

Kenya Airways, the national carrier, connects the main cities of Nairobi, Mombasa, Kisumu and Malindi. It's advisable to book in advance and essential to reconfirm 48 hours before departure if you're coming from either Malindi or Kisumu and have to connect with an international flight from either Nairobi or Mombasa airports. Otherwise you may well find that your seat has been reallocated. The flight schedules and fares can be found in the respective city chapters.

Private Airlines

There are also a number of private airlines operating light aircraft which connect the main cities with smaller towns and certain national parks. The airlines are Air Kenya Aviation (☎ (02) 501421), Prestige Air Services (☎ (02) 501211), and Eagle Aviation, and they all operate out of Nairobi's Wilson Airport and Mombasa's Moi Airport.

These airlines connect Nairobi with Mombasa, Kisumu, Nanyuki, Nyeri, Malindi, Lamu and the national parks/reserves of Amboseli, Masai Mara and Samburu. Their services to Eldoret and Turkana are temporarily suspended. Flight schedules can be found under the relevant sections.

BUS

Kenya has a network of regular buses, matatus (normally minibuses), share-taxis and normal private taxis. The cheapest form of transport is by bus, followed by matatu, share-taxi (Peugeot services) and lastly private taxi (expensive). There's not a great deal of difference in journey times between normal buses and matatus, but there's a huge difference in safety.

Bus fares are generally about halfway between what you would pay on the railways in 2nd class but journey times are quicker.

Unlike the trains, which usually travel at night, many buses travel during the day so you may prefer to take a bus if you want to see the countryside. All the bus companies are privately owned but some of them run better buses than others. Coastline Safari, Goldline, Tana River Bus Company, Malindi Bus and Garissa Express are about the best of the bunch. Akamba Bus Service has the most comprehensive network, but its buses are older.

Some Kenyan towns have what you might call a 'bus station', although this is often nothing more than a dirt patch. In others each bus company will have its own terminus though these are often close to each other. There are exceptions and these are indicated on the street maps. Matatu and share-taxi ranks sometimes use the same stations as buses but this isn't always the case, especially in Nairobi.

Nairobi also has the local KBS public buses which run within and around Nairobi.

MATATU

The way that most local people travel is by vehicles known as matatus. (The name comes from 'three', because when matatus first started running it cost three coins to travel.) These can be anything from small, dilapidated Peugeot 504 pick-ups with a cab on the back, to shiny, brightly painted 20-seat minibuses complete with mega-decibel stereos, as found in Nairobi. Most matatu drivers are under a lot of pressure from their owners to maximise profits so they tend to drive recklessly and overload their vehicles. They also put in long working days. Stories about matatu smashes and overturnings in which many people are killed or injured can be found almost daily in the newspapers. Of course, many travellers use them and, in some cases, there is no alternative, but if there is (such as a bus or train) then take that in preference. The Mombasa to Nairobi road is notorious for smashes.

Matatus

Matatus are not just transport. They are Kenya's contribution to world culture. These gaudily painted minibuses, featuring 200-decibel stereo systems pumping out disco beat at bone-conduction level have a crew of three: the driver, who normally hasn't slept for three days, keeping himself going by chewing *miraa* shoots, a bush which contains a natural amphetamine; the conductor, who extracts fares from reluctant passengers; and the tout, a veritable Daddy Cool whose aerial gymnastics on the outside of the minibus ought to be an Olympic event. The tout performs these antics to attract customers.

All Nairobi matatus are individually named and the most popular ones on the Eastleigh run are 'Public Enemy', 'Florida 2000', 'Defending Champion', 'Get in & Die', 'You Move with the Best', and 'You Die Like the Rest'. Driving standards and the frequency of fatal accidents justify these names, yet despite this, matatus are still the preferred mode of local transport. ∎

Overcrowding, on the other hand, isn't confined to matatus. I once counted 136 people getting off a Malindi to Mombasa bus at Kilifi excluding the driver and his mate.

As in most East African countries, you can always find a matatu which is going to the next town or further afield so long as it's not too late in the day. Simply ask around among the drivers at the park. Matatus leave when full and the fares are fixed. It's unlikely you will be asked for more money than the other passengers.

TRAIN

Kenyan trains are a very popular form of travel, despite the fact that the rolling stock, tracks and other essential works have been allowed to deteriorate. The trains generally run on time and are considerably safer than travelling by bus or matatu. The main railway line runs from Mombasa to Malaba on the Kenya-Uganda border via Voi, Nairobi, Nakuru and Eldoret with branch lines from Nakuru to Kisumu, Nairobi to Nanyuki, Voi to Taveta and Eldoret to Kitale.

There are no passenger services on the Nairobi to Nanyuki or Eldoret to Kitale branches. Although the Kenyan tracks are contiguous with both the Tanzanian and Ugandan systems, there are no international services at present. (See the Nairobi chapter for fare details.)

Classes

First class consists of two-berth compartments with a washbasin, drinking water, a wardrobe and a drinks service. There's a lockable door between one compartment and the adjacent one so, if there are four of you travelling together, you can make one compartment out of two, if you wish. They're usually very clean. What you cannot do is lock the door of your compartment from the outside when you go for dinner.

Second class consists of four-berth compartments with a washbasin and drinking water supply. Third class is seats only. All the compartments have fans. Sexes are separated in 1st and 2nd class unless you book the whole compartment. Third class can get a little wearing on the nerves on long journeys especially if they are overnight (which most are). Second class is more than adequate in this respect and 1st class is definitely a touch of luxury as far as budget travel goes.

Reservations

You must book in advance for both 1st and 2nd class – two to three days is usually sufficient – otherwise you'll probably find that there are no berths available and you'll have to go 3rd class. Visa credit cards are accepted for railway bookings. If you're in Malindi and planning on taking the train from Mombasa to Nairobi, bookings can be made with travel agencies and major hotels in Malindi, or by calling the station yourself. Compartment and berth numbers are posted up about 30 minutes prior to departure.

Meals & Bedding

Most trains have a dining car which has dinner and two sittings of breakfast. Meals on the trains used to be quite an experience with plentiful and cheap four-course meals served on starched white linen by smartly dressed waiters. Sadly, these days the meals are neither cheap nor special, and the level of service is generally poor.

All meals must be booked and paid for at the time of purchasing your ticket. Breakfast is US$3.60, lunch or dinner US$6. Cold beers are available at all times.

Bedding is available in 1st and 2nd class, and this too must be booked and paid for when you buy your ticket. A bed roll, which consists of sheets, blankets and pillow, costs US$2.85, and a mattress is available for an extra US$1.70.

CAR & 4WD

If you are bringing your own vehicle to Kenya you should get a free three-month permit at the border on entry, so long as you have a valid *carnet de passage* for it. If you don't have a carnet you should be able to get a free one-week permit at the border on entry after which you must get an 'authorisation permit for a foreign private vehicle' at Nyayo House, Kenyatta Ave, Nairobi, which costs a few dollars but a lot of time queuing. Before you do this, however, get in touch with the Automobile Association of Kenya which is in the Hurlingham shopping centre (signposted) in Nairobi.

When you are driving your own vehicle there are certain routes in north-east Kenya where you must obtain police permission before setting out. This is just a formality but there will be a roadblock to enforce this. The main stretch where this applies is between Isiolo and Marsabit where all transport must travel in convoy at a particular time of day unless you're turning off to go somewhere else (such as Samburu National Park, Wamba or Maralal).

Foreign registered vehicles are not allowed into Kenyan game parks and reserves, which is a major inconvenience if you are travelling this way.

Road Conditions

Kenyan roads in the south-western part of the country – west of a line drawn through Malindi, Isiolo and Kitale – are excellent. In fact they're some of the best in Africa, though sections of the Nairobi to Mombasa road sometimes get badly potholed before resurfacing. North and north-east of this line and in the national parks the roads are all gravel, usually in a reasonable state of repair though there are long sections of corrugated gravel in some parts. Driving on these, at the necessary speed to avoid wrecking a vehicle, can be agony on your kidneys after several hours, especially if you're on a bus which has had a double set of unyielding springs fitted to it. Naturally, there are washouts on some of these gravel roads during the rainy seasons and, under these circumstances, journey times can be considerably longer. Naturally, if a bridge gets washed out, you'll either have to turn back or wait.

Right up in the north on the eastern side of Lake Turkana, especially in the Kaisut and Chalbi deserts, you can make good headway in the dry season and the roads (which would be better described as tracks) are often surprisingly smooth and in good condition. This is certainly true of the road from Wamba to North Horr via Parsaloi, Baragoi, South Horr and Loyangalani, except for the *luggas* (dry riverbeds) between Wamba and Parsaloi for which you'll need 4WD.

After rain, however, it's another story, particularly on the flat parts of the deserts. They turn into treacherous seas of mud, often as much as a metre deep in places. Only a complete fool would attempt to drive in these circumstances without 4WD, sand ladders, adequate jacking equipment, shovels, a tow rope or wire, drinking water and spare metal jerry cans of fuel. This is particularly true of the stretches of track between North Horr and Maikona and on any of the tracks leading off the Marsabit to Isiolo road to South Horr.

To get out of the mud, if you're really stuck, you're going to be entirely dependent on the small number of vehicles which *may* pass by and *may* stop and help (they won't want to get stuck either), or on a passing herd of camels. It's going to cost you money either way. Not only that, but you can sometimes drive for hours only to find that it's impossible to cross a river, which may not even exist in the dry season, and have to drive all the way back again. Fuel is very difficult to find in this region and is usually only available at mission stations for up to three times what you would pay for it in Nairobi – and they'll only sell you a limited amount. Make adequate preparations if you are driving your own vehicle.

Car & 4WD Rental

Hiring a vehicle to tour Kenya (or at least the national parks) is a relatively expensive way of seeing the country but it does give you freedom of movement and is sometimes the only way of getting to the more remote parts of the country. On the other hand, if you're sharing costs, it's quite a feasible option.

There are a number of factors to take into consideration before deciding what type of vehicle to take and which company to go through, and there's no real substitute for sitting down with pen and paper and working out as near as possible what the total cost will be. To do this you'll need as many hire-charge leaflets as you can get hold of and a distances table.

The other major consideration is what type of vehicle is going to be suitable to enable you to get where you want to go. At times other than the rainy season, a 2WD vehicle may be perfectly adequate in some parts of the country including Masai Mara Game Reserve, Amboseli and Tsavo national parks (at least on the main access routes of the latter), but it won't get you to the east side of Lake Turkana and would restrict your movements in the Aberdare and Meru national parks and the Buffalo Springs and Samburu game reserves. Most companies also have a policy of insisting that you take a 4WD vehicle if you're going upcountry and off the beaten track.

Rental Costs This is something of a minefield since the daily/weekly base rates vary quite a lot as do the km (mileage) charges. What initially looks cheap often works out just as expensive as anything else.

To give you some idea of average costs, the base rates for a 2WD saloon car are between US$20 and US$30 per day plus around US$0.30 per km (often with a minimum charge of 100 km) plus insurance of between US$11 and US$20 per day. All-inclusive daily charges with unlimited km are around US$90 per day for one day, with a sliding scale dropping to around US$60 per day if you take the car for one week or more. Limited-km weekly rates start at around US$260 (Payless) for 500 km, and head up to US$375 for 1200 km.

In the next category, an average small 4WD vehicle such as a Suzuki Sierra costs between US$30 and US$45 per day plus insurance plus around US$0.30 to US$0.45 per km. On a daily unlimited-km basis it costs around US$120 (with a minimum of four days), while a weekly limited-km rental costs around US$350 (500 km) or around US$575 (1200 km). Unlimited weekly rental will cost you around US$650 to US$900.

In the highest category – a 4WD Isuzu Trooper or Mitsubishi Pajero, for instance – daily rates vary between US$51 (Habib's) and US$75 (Avis) plus insurance and mileage of around US$0.55 to US$0.70 per km. All-inclusive limited km rates are around US$650 with 500 km and US$1050 with 1200 km. Unlimited weekly rental rates are around US$1300 to US$1500.

Minimum Mileage Conditions Some of the so-called 'unlimited' km rates are not quite that. Some have a ceiling of 1200 to 1400 km per week free after which you pay the excess at the normal km rate. Some companies also offer the option of 500 km or 1200 to 1400 km per week free of charge with corresponding lower or higher base rates. If you are renting on a daily basis, some companies have a 100-km minimum charge, regardless of whether you travel this far or not. If you're not planning on going too far then it may be more economical to opt for the lower free km rate.

Insurance The only way to cover yourself against damage to the hire vehicle and other property is to take out Collision Damage Waiver (CDW) insurance. The thing to really look out for here is the excess payable by you in the event of a collision. With the larger and generally more reputable companies (Avis, Hertz, Europcar, Central, among others) it's generally US$30, but with others (Glory, Market, Payless, Habib's, among others) it's as high as US$750, and this is over and above the US$10 to US$30 or so you pay per day for insurance in the first place! Some companies are less than forthcoming about what your liability is, so make sure you know exactly what the conditions of the rental are – getting hit for US$750 when you think you are insured can come as a rude shock. The reason companies do this is that their own insurance premiums are lower if the customer is liable for a higher amount. Windscreens and tyres are not covered by insurance with any company. If you are renting on an 'unlimited km' basis, CDW is usually included in the charge, but make absolutely sure of this.

The cost of CDW insurance ranges from around US$10 per day for a small car up to US$30 for a large 4WD. Theft insurance is also available from some companies for around US$5 per day.

Deposits There's a wide variation in the deposits charged on hired vehicles. It's usually the estimated total hire charges (base rate and km) plus whatever the excess on the CDW is (from US$30 to US$750, depending on the company). No deposit is necessary if you are paying by credit card.

Drivers' Licences & Minimum Age An international driver's licence or your own national driving licence is standard. Some companies stipulate a minimum age of 23 years but with others it is 25. There are occasionally stipulations about endorsements on licences (clean licences preferred) and that you must have been driving for at least two years.

Maintenance Although it's not always the case, it's probably true to say that the more you pay for a vehicle, the better condition it will be in. It's worth paying attention to this,

especially if you're planning on going a long way. It doesn't necessarily mean that all the cheaper companies neglect maintenance but, as our feedback mail indicates, some certainly do.

The other factor related to maintenance is what the company will do for you (if anything) in the event of a major breakdown. The major companies *may* deliver you a replacement vehicle and make arrangements for recovery of the other vehicke, but with most companies you'll be entirely responsible for getting the vehicle fixed and back on the road. Only when you return it will you be refunded and you'll need receipts to prove what you spent.

Equipment Some companies provide you with adequate tools to tackle breakdowns, others with just sufficient to change a tyre. If you have mechanical skills, it's worth enquiring about what tools are provided. The only company which includes a full complement of camping equipment in their 4WD hire charges is Habib's. With other companies you'll have to hire this separately.

One-Way Rates If you want to hire a vehicle in one place and drop it off in another there will be additional charges to pay. These vary depending on the vehicle, the company and the pick-up and drop-off locations but range from around US$30 (Mombasa to Malindi) and US$100 (Nairobi to Mombasa).

Driving to Tanzania Only the larger (and more expensive) companies cater for this and there are additional charges. Briefly, these are US$28.50 for insurance and US$71.50 for documentation (both payable to the hire company) plus US$100 for Tanzanian road tax (payable to Tanzanian customs on entry).

Rental Agencies At the top end of the market are two companies:

Avis
    Koinange St, Nairobi (☎ (02) 336794)
    Moi Ave, Mombasa (☎ (011) 223048)
    Sitawi House, Malindi (☎ (0123) 20513)
    Two Fishes Hotel, Diani Beach (☎ (0127) 2101)
    Jomo Kenyatta International Airport, Nairobi
    (☎ (02) 822186)
Hertz
    Muindi Mbingu St, Nairobi (☎ (02) 331960)
    Moi Ave, Mombasa (☎ (011) 316333)
    Blue Dolphin Hotel, Malindi (☎ (0123) 20069)

In much the same league but considerably less expensive on weekly rates is Europcar at Bruce House, Standard St, Nairobi (☎ (02) 334722), and also in the Times building, Nkrumah Rd, Mombasa (☎ (011) 226198). It also has branch offices at Jomo Kenyatta International Airport in Nairobi (☎ (02) 822348), Moi International Airport in Mombasa (☎ (011) 433780), Diani Sea Lodge at Diani Beach (☎ (0127) 2114) and at the Blue Dolphin Hotel in Malindi.

Europcar manages an excellent choice of good, reliable companies with well-maintained vehicles and similar rates. What they don't have is large fleets of vehicles, so it's important to book in advance if you want to be sure of getting what you want – particularly a 4WD vehicle. Companies in this category include:

Central Rent-a-Car
    Fedha Towers, Standard St, Nairobi (☎ (02)
    222888)
Glory Car Hire
    Nairobi (☎ (02) 224428)
    Mombasa (☎ (011) 221159)
    Malindi (☎ (0123) 20065)
    Diani (☎ (0127) 2276)
Habib's
    Agip House, Haile Selassie Ave, Nairobi (☎ (02)
    220463)
Market Car Hire
    Market Service Station, on the corner of
    Koinange & Banda Sts, Nairobi (☎ (02) 225797)
Payless Car Hire
    Olympic House, Koinange St, Nairobi (☎ (02)
    338400)
    Saroya House, Moi Ave, Mombasa (☎ (011)
    222629)
The Car Hire Company
    New Stanley Hotel, Standard St, Nairobi (☎ (02)
    225255)

Central is certainly the best in this category with a well-maintained fleet of fairly new vehicles and a good back-up service. Their excess liability on CDW is also one of the lowest (US$28.50). Glory has some decent cars but also has some real bombs – the car I hired between Mombasa and Malindi to update this book was in a diabolical state – almost unroadworthy. A complaint only elicited a 'take it or leave it' response from the staff in Malindi. Market and Payless are owned by the same people and their excess liability on CDW would leave you penniless if you did have an accident (US$570).

For cheap car hire exclusively in and around Nairobi, go to Rent a Beetle (☎ 33-8041/5), 7th Floor, Finance House, Loita St (PO Box 60517), Nairobi. Here you can hire a VW Beetle for just US$24 per day which includes 250 km free. Insurance is optional provided the hirer signs a waiver accepting liability in the event of an accident. Comprehensive insurance is available for an extra US$5. (When you telephone, ask for Don Cornes or Margaret.) It's the cheapest car rental you'll find anywhere in Nairobi.

BICYCLE
Bicycles are basically only in use in cities and there's not many of them. Virtually everybody travels by matatu. Anyone foolish enough to risk cycling along main roads in Kenya must be taking suicide seriously.

HITCHING
Hitching is usually good on the main roads and may well be preferable to travelling by matatu, but if you are picked up by an African driver and are expecting a free lift then make this clear from the outset. Most will expect a contribution at least. Hitching to the national parks, on the other hand, can be very difficult since most people either go on a tour or hire their own vehicle. Apart from that, once you get to the park lodges or camping areas, you will be entirely dependent on persuading other tourists with their own vehicles to take you out with them to view game since walking in the parks is generally forbidden.

Although many travellers hitchhike, it is not a totally safe way of getting around. Just because we explain how hitching works does not mean we recommend it.

BOAT

Lake Victoria Ferry

Ferries connect Kisumu with Kendu Bay, Homa Bay, Mbita, Mfangano and Asembo Bay but there are no international services connecting these Kenyan ports with those of Tanzania or Uganda.

The schedule for the lake ferries can be found in the Kisumu section.

Dhow

Sailing on a dhow along the East African coast is one of Kenya's most worthwhile and memorable experiences. There's nothing quite like drifting along the ocean in the middle of the night with the moon up high, the only sounds the lapping of the waves against the side of the boat and subdued conversation. It's enjoyable at any time of day, even when the breeze drops and the boat virtually comes to a standstill.

There are no creature comforts aboard these dhows so when night comes you simply bed down wherever there is space. You'll probably get off these boats smelling of fish since fish oil is used to condition the timbers of the boat – nothing that a shower won't remove! Take drinking water and food with you although fish is often caught on the way and cooked up on deck over charcoal. Dhows can be picked up in Mombasa, Malindi and Lamu.

Many of the smaller dhows these days have been fitted with outboard motors so that progress can be made when there's no wind. The larger dhows are all motorised and most of them don't even have sails.

Safaris

ORGANISED VEHICLE SAFARIS

There are essentially two types of organised safaris – those where you camp at night and those where you stay in game lodges or luxury tented camps at night. Whichever you choose, safaris typically start and end in either Nairobi or Mombasa, though there are a number of exceptions to this. Apart from transfer to and from Nairobi or Mombasa and driving from one park to another, once you're in a park you'll be taken on a number of game drives – usually two and sometimes three per day. Each drive typically lasts two to 2½ hours and the best (in terms of sighting animals) are those in the early morning and late afternoon when the animals are at their most active. The vehicles used for these drives are six to eight-seater minibuses with roof hatches, Land Rovers, or open-sided trucks.

As a general rule, you'll be left to your own devices between late morning and around 3 pm (except for lunch) though, if you're on a camping safari, you may well be taken to a lodge in the early afternoon to relax over a cold beer or have a swim in the pool (though at some lodges the pool is for guests only). You may also be taken to a lodge after the late-afternoon game drive for the same thing before returning to camp for dinner.

Camping Safaris

Camping safaris cater for budget travellers, for the young (or young at heart) and for those who are prepared to put up with discomfort. They are no-frills safaris, with none of life's little luxuries such as flush toilets, running water or iced drinks. Such safaris can be quite demanding depending on where you go, and you'll be expected to lend a hand. You'll end up sweaty and dusty and there may well be no showers available – even cold ones. On the other hand, you're in for an authentic adventure in the African bush with nothing between you and the animals at night except a sheet of canvas and the embers of a dying fire. It's not at all unusual for elephants or hippos to trundle through the camp at night, or even the occasional lion, and so far no-one has been eaten or trampled on.

Another plus for these safaris is that you'll

probably find yourself with travellers from the four corners of the earth. Truck safaris may have as many as half a dozen people of different nationalities on board.

The price of your safari will include three meals a day cooked by the camp cook(s) though on some safaris you'll be expected to lend a hand in the preparation and clean up. Food is of the 'plain but plenty' variety.

The price will also include all the necessary camping gear except a sleeping bag which you must provide or hire locally. The tents provided sleep two people as a rule and you'll be expected to erect and dismantle it yourself though there are some safaris where the camp is taken on ahead of you and the tents erected by the staff. Tents are invariably of the type which sleep two people and, if you're a single traveller, you'll be expected to share with someone else. If you don't want to do that then you'll be up for a 'single supplement' of between 20 to 25% on the price of the safari which will allow you to have a tent of your own. Mosquito nets are generally not provided so you'll have to hire one yourself or bring along insect repellent either in the form of coils or a skin cream.

You'll need to bring clothing and footwear sufficient to cover you for hot days and cold nights but the amount of baggage which you'll be allowed to bring is limited. Excess gear can usually be stored at the safari company's offices. Don't forget to bring along a torch (flashlight) and pocket-knife – the company will provide kerosene lanterns for the camp but they won't be left on all night.

There are also a number of somewhat more expensive camping safaris available which utilise permanent camp sites with pre-erected tents fitted with mosquito nets, beds and sheets and which have showers (though there's sometimes not enough water for everyone to have a shower).

Remember that at the end of one of these safaris your driver/guide and the cooks will expect a reasonable tip. This is only fair since wages are low and these people will have made a lot of effort to make your trip a memorable one. Be generous here. Other travellers are going to follow you and the last thing anyone wants to find themselves closeted with is a disgruntled driver/guide who couldn't care less whether you see game or not.

Lodge Safaris

The other type of safari is for those who want luxury at night and in between game drives. On these the accommodation is in game lodges or luxury tented camps. There are plenty of beautifully conceived and superbly sited lodges in the main national parks where you can expect a fully self-contained room or cottage, cuisine of an international standard, a terrace bar with ice-cold drinks, a swimming pool and videos and plenty of staff to cater for all your requirements. Many of these lodges overlook a watering hole or salt lick so you can sit on the viewing terrace and watch the animals from there. The watering hole or salt lick will usually be floodlit at night. Some of the lodges put out bait or salt to encourage certain animals to visit the spot and while this is often very contrived, it usually guarantees you a sighting of animals which you'd be very lucky to see otherwise.

There's obviously a considerable difference in price for these safaris as opposed to camping and most of the people who go on them are package tourists with expectations and attitudes of mind quite dissimilar to those who opt for a camping safari. For them it's essentially a holiday rather than in-depth involvement in Africa, its people and wildlife. It's the African bush at arm's length. On the other hand, if you have the money, it's worth staying at the occasional lodge just for the contrast.

Lodge safaris will cost you at least four times what a camping safari costs – and often considerably more. Luxury tented camps are no less expensive than lodges and the more exclusive ones cost up to four times the price of a lodge. They're for people to whom money is no object and who want to experience what it must have been like in the days of the big-game hunters, except that they'll be stalking with cameras rather than guns.

Routes

Whether you take a camping safari or a lodge safari, there's a whole plethora of options available ranging from two days to 15 days and sometimes 25 days. If possible, it's best to go on a safari which lasts at least five days and preferably longer since otherwise a good deal of your time will be taken up driving to and from the national parks and Nairobi. You'll also see a great deal more on a longer safari and have a much better chance of catching sight of all the major animals. Remember that sightings of any particular animal cannot be guaranteed but the longer you spend looking, the better your chances are. A longer safari will also give you the opportunity of having some involvement with the local tribespeople.

A three-day safari typically takes you either to Amboseli or Masai Mara. A four-day safari would take you to Amboseli and Tsavo, to Masai Mara or to Samburu and Buffalo Springs. A five-day safari would take you to Amboseli and Tsavo, or to Masai Mara and Lake Nakuru; whereas a six-day safari would take you to lakes Nakuru, Bogoria and Baringo plus Masai Mara, or to Lake Nakuru, Masai Mara and Amboseli. On a seven-day safari, you could expect to visit at least two of the Rift Valley lakes plus Masai Mara and Amboseli, whereas on an 11-day safari you would take in one or more of the Rift Valley lakes plus Masai Mara, Amboseli and Tsavo; or Mt Kenya, Samburu and Buffalo Springs, Meru, Lake Nakuru and Masai Mara.

Most of the safari companies cover the above standard routes but some also specialise in different routings designed to take you off the beaten track. There are, for instance, safaris which take in Masai Mara, Lake Victoria, Mt Elgon, Saiwa Swamp and Nakuru, and others which take in Mt Kenya, Samburu and Buffalo Springs, Nyahururu, Lake Nakuru and Masai Mara. Other safaris visit Shaba, rather than Samburu and Buffalo Springs, where you'll hardly see another vehicle.

Most companies also offer safaris to Lake Turkana which range from seven to 12 days.

The shorter trips take one or other of the standard routes – Nairobi, Nakuru, Nyahururu, Maralal, Baragoi, South Horr and Loyangalani or Nairobi, Isiolo, Maralal, Baragoi, South Horr and Loyangalani. The longer trips detour from this route and take you to either or both the Matthews Range and the Ndoto Mountains. A full description of the options available can be found in the East of Turkana section in the Northern Kenya chapter.

Costs

There's a lot of competition for the tourist dollar among the safari companies and prices for the same tour are very similar. The trouble is, there are now so many safaris to choose from which offer similar itineraries and options that it's not that easy to compare prices. It depends what you want, though it's still generally true that the longer you go for, the less it costs per day.

For camping safaris with no frills you are looking at an all-inclusive price of around US$65 to US$70 per day on a reducing scale up to 10 days (plus or minus 15%). The price includes transport, food (three meals per day), park entry and camping fees, tents and cooking equipment. The price per day for safaris over 11 days tends to rise somewhat since there's a lot more organisation involved and you'll be going to remote areas where there are no services available so everything has to be trucked in.

Unfortunately, the situation is not as simple as the above suggests. While it may be OK to use the above figure as a benchmark, prices vary widely. A three-day safari to Amboseli and Masai Mara or Amboseli and Tsavo varies from US$180 to US$570. A five-day safari to Amboseli and Masai Mara or to the Rift Valley and Amboseli varies from US$300 to US$800; and a seven-day safari to Amboseli, Masai Mara and the Rift Valley or to Amboseli, Masai Mara and Samburu varies from US$385 to US$1050. In other words, you must do some legwork. Collect as many company leaflets as you can (about a morning's work), decide where you want to go, compare prices, work out what's included and what isn't, and then make your choice. Remember that, generally, what you pay for is what you get. A high degree of personal involvement in camp chores and a willingness to eschew creature comforts usually guarantees a low price. If you want the opposite, it will cost you more. No-one works for nothing.

The prices for safaris which involve staying in lodges or tented camps are considerably higher. Here you're looking at a minimum of US$120 to US$150 per person per night in the lodges and up to US$350 in the luxury tented camps.

The above prices are based on the assumption that you will share accommodation (a tent or room) with one other person. If you don't want to do this then you'll have to pay what's called a 'single room supplement'. This is generally around 20 to 25% extra.

Departure Frequency

This varies a lot from company to company and depends on the season. In the high season, many companies have daily or every second day departures to the most popular game parks – Amboseli, Masai Mara and Tsavo – since there's high demand. To the less frequented parks such as Samburu and Buffalo Springs, Shaba and Meru, they generally leave only once or twice per week. Safaris to Lake Turkana are usually only once weekly. In addition, most companies will leave for any of the most popular game parks at any time so long as you have a minimum number of people wanting to go – sometimes four, sometimes six. In the low season, there are fewer departures.

It obviously makes a lot of sense to either book ahead or to get a group together rather than just turn up and expect to leave the very next morning. Advance booking is essential for the Lake Turkana safaris since they're heavily subscribed. It's also essential for any of the more exotic options described in the Other Safaris section.

Choosing a Company

There is no doubt that some safari companies are better than others. The main factors which make for the difference are the quality and type of vehicles used, the standard of the food, and the skills and knowledge of the drivers/guides. It's equally true that any company can take a bunch of people on safari one week and bring them back fully satisfied, and yet the following week take a different set of people on the same safari and end up with a virtual mutiny. That's an extreme example, but whether a company gets praised or condemned can hinge on something as simple as a puncture which takes half a day to fix and for which there are no tools on board, or a broken spring which involves having to wait around for most of the day whilst a replacement vehicle is sent out from Nairobi. There's obviously a lot which companies can do to head off breakdowns but a broken spring, for example, isn't reasonably one of them on a short safari though you would expect such spares to be on board for longer journeys and certainly on a safari to Lake Turkana.

The other major factor to take into consideration before you decide to go with any particular company is whether they actually operate their own safaris with their own vehicles or whether they are just agents for other safari companies. If they're just agents then obviously part of what you pay is their commission but the most important thing here is, if anything goes wrong or the itinerary is changed without your agreement, you have very little comeback and you'll be pushing shit uphill to get a refund. We get letters about this all the time from travellers to whom this happened.

Unfortunately, the situation isn't that easy to avoid. It's a minefield working out which are genuine safari companies and which are just agencies. Go into any office in Nairobi and, naturally, they all have their own vehicles and, of course, they'll compensate you at the end of the safari if anything goes seriously wrong. Not so if they're just agents. They will already have paid the lion's share of what you gave them to the company which actually provided the vehicles and staff so that gives them very little room for manoeuvre. Likewise, there's no way that the actual safari company is going to provide the agency with a refund.

It's perfectly obvious that quite a few so-called safari companies are merely agencies. Simply pick up half a dozen leaflets from various companies and compare the wording – you'll find that quite a few are identical!

Another aspect of Kenya's safari business is that there's a good deal of client swapping between companies whose vehicles are full and those which aren't. This isn't philanthropy; it's pure business. In other words, you may find yourself on a certain company's safari which is not the one you booked through. The reputable companies won't do this without informing you but the agents certainly will. Getting swapped onto another company's safari isn't necessarily a bad thing but make sure they are members of the Kenyan Association of Tour Operators (KATO). That way, they will be answerable to the association's ethics committee in the event of a dispute.

Despite the pitfalls mentioned here, there are a number of reliable companies offering camping safaris which have their own vehicles and an excellent track record. Most of the people who run them paid their dues driving overland trucks around Africa for years so you can be sure they know the business back to front. The following companies have been listed alphabetically, and are not in order of preference or reliability:

Best Camping Tours
2nd Floor, Nanak House, corner of Kimathi and Banda Sts, PO Box 40223, Nairobi (☎ 29667, 29675).
This is a popular company which offers budget camping safaris on all the main routes ranging from Amboseli or Masai Mara (three to four days) to Amboseli and Tsavo (four days) right through to Amboseli, Tsavo, the Rift Valley lakes and Masai Mara (eight days) to Turkana (eight days).

Blackwing Safaris
PO Box 42532, Nairobi (☎ 891241; fax 882160).
This small company, run by Dave Mascall, caters for discerning clients who want flexibility and quality and who don't want to be crammed into the usual safari minibus. Dave takes only three clients or less at a time and can arrange safaris of any duration within Kenya or Tanzania. He has

excellent equipment and his own private camp site in Masai Mara. His safaris cost a standard US$150 (three clients), US$200 (two clients) and US$250 (one client) per person per day which includes all transport, transfer to and from Nairobi airport, first and last nights at the Boulevard Hotel in Nairobi, all food and drink (including wine and beer), all park entry and camping fees, and the full range of camping and safari equipment.

Bushbuck Adventures
Barclays Bank Bldg, Kenyatta Ave, PO Box 67449, Nairobi (☎ 212975/6/7; fax 218735).
To quote the company's leaflet, 'We do not offer safaris for those requiring all the comforts of home, nor do we offer rock-bottom prices and comparable facilities. We specialise in safaris for (those) who want reasonable comfort while still feeling close to nature'. As a result, they're relatively expensive. Bushbuck has its own camp sites and offers Amboseli (three days, US$570), Masai Mara (five days, US$756), Western Kenya (Masai Mara to Mt Elgon; 12 days, US$1650) as well as a number of more exotic safari options (see later in this chapter).

Eagle Camping & Lodges Safaris
4th Floor, Uganda House, Kenyatta Ave (PO Box 22432), Nairobi (☎ 226192; fax 331276).
This new outfit, run by Charles Ngigi, has received good reports. Charles offers low-budget camping safaris to all the major parks and areas of natural beauty and is an excellent guide and driver. Eagle is worth checking out.

Exotic Safaris
1st Floor, South Wing, Uniafric House, Koinange St, PO Box 54483, Nairobi (☎ 338811; fax 211701).
We have received good reports of this company, which offers a full range of safaris along the standard routes from Amboseli (three days) through lakes Nakuru, Bogoria and Baringo and Masai Mara (six days) to Mt Kenya, Samburu and Masai Mara (eight days) to a 'Turkana Special' which also takes in Samburu (seven days).

Gametrackers Camping Safaris
1st Floor, Kenya Cinema Plaza, Moi Ave, PO Box 62042, Nairobi (☎ 338927, 222703; fax 330903).
Also long-established and reliable, this company offers a whole range of safaris ranging from Amboseli (three days, US$180), to Masai Mara (four days, US$235), Masai Mara and the Rift Valley lakes (six days, US$310), to Turkana (eight days, US$330, two route options), as well as more exotic options (see the Other Safaris section later in this chapter).

Jomima Tours

4th Floor, Spikes Bldg, Kenyatta Lane, PO Box 2215, Nakuru (☎ 212956; fax 42694).

This company could well be useful if you're in Nakuru but not on an organised safari. It offers daily tours to Lake Nakuru, Lake Baringo and the Aberdares plus it also has cars for hire.

Ketty Tours

Moi Ave (PO Box 82391), Mombasa (☎ 315178; fax 311355).

This company specialises partly in short tours of the coastal region (Wasini, Shimba Hills, Gede, etc) but it also offers camping safaris to all the usual parks (Tsavo, Amboseli, Masai Mara, the Rift Valley lakes, and Samburu) ranging from two to 10 days. The average cost per person per day is US$70.

Safari-Camp Services

On the corner of Koinange and Moktar Daddah Sts, PO Box 44801, Nairobi (☎ 330130, 328936; fax 212160).

This company is one of the first in Kenya and has been operating for almost two decades. It is the originator of the legendary 'Turkana Bus' which recently celebrated its 600th departure. (As described in the company's leaflet: 'If you want a hot bath and iced cocktails every night and are prepared to be part of a Leo-Centric-Kombi-Ring by day we advise you to take a tour of Kenya's excellent luxury lodges...Our clients require a sleeping bag, they travel in the back of a dusty truck...We offer authenticity and value rather than luxury, we promise you an involvement with the real Africa and an affinity with the new generation of fellow travellers'.

Its Turkana Bus is one of the best (seven days, US$265) and its Wildlife Bus is just as good (seven days, US$385) but there are also 'lodge-equivalent' camping safaris for those who prefer somewhat better facilities. These include the 'Hemingway' (seven days, US$979) and the 'Hemingway Plus' (10 days, US$1320) which take in Samburu, Nyahururu, Lake Nakuru and Masai Mara using the company's own private camp sites, and 'Vanishing Africa' (14 days, US$2420) which takes in the Rift Valley lakes, Masai Mara and a whole swathe of northern Kenya including Lake Turkana.

Safari Seekers

5th Floor, Jubilee Insurance Exchange Bldg, Kaunda St, PO Box 9165, Nairobi (☎ 226206; fax 334585).

Ground Floor, Diamond Trust Arcade, Moi Ave, PO Box 40126, Mombasa (☎ 228276; fax 228277).

This company has come a long way in the last few years and is well recommended. It offers two three-day safaris (one to Masai Mara and the other to Amboseli), two four-day safaris (one to Amboseli and Tsavo and the other to Masai Mara and Lake Nakuru), a five-day safari to Masai Mara and the Rift Valley lakes, and a seven-day 'special' to Amboseli, Lake Nakuru and Masai Mara. These camping safaris are all priced on the basis of US$65 per person per day.

Special Camping Safaris Ltd

Gilfillan House, Kenyatta Ave, PO Box 51512, Nairobi (☎ 338325, 220072; fax 211828).

This is a small company operated by two people and their Kenyan staff who pride themselves on personal service. They offer Amboseli and Tsavo (four days, US$225), Masai Mara (four days, US$225), Masai Mara and the Rift Valley lakes or Samburu, Shaba and Mt Kenya (both six days, US$350), plus Turkana (10 days, US$370) and a 'game safari special' which takes in Masai Mara, the Rift Valley lakes, Maralal and Samburu (10 days, US$570).

Savuka Tours & Safaris

3rd Floor, Pan Africa House, Kenyatta Ave, PO Box 20433, Nairobi (☎ 725907, 725108).

This outfit is not a member of KATO but we've had good reports of it from those who have taken a safari with them.

Yare Safaris Ltd

1st Floor, Union Towers, Mama Ngina St, PO Box 63006, Nairobi (☎ 214099; fax 213445).

This company specialises in camel safaris but also runs regular safaris, usually on a weekly basis, to Amboseli (four days, US$300), Masai Mara (four/six days for US$350/345), Amboseli and Masai Mara (seven days, US$685), Samburu Game Reserve (seven days, US$520) and Turkana (10 days, US$360). In addition, it operates an excellent hostel/camp site at Maralal which is used by many other safari companies for overnight accommodation. The hostel is also host to the annual Maralal International Camel Derby in October (see the Maralal section for details).

This is by no means an exhaustive list of companies which offer camping safaris nor is there necessarily any implication that others are unreliable – though some are. On the other hand, we do get hundreds of letters from travellers every year describing their experiences with various safari companies. Some get consistently good reports and others get variable reports but there are some which get consistently bad reports. If you do choose a company not listed here don't blame us if you get into strife but do tell us what the problem was and what was done about it (if anything).

KENYA

If you don't want to camp but prefer to stay in a lodge each night then check out:

African Tours & Hotels
Utalii House, Uhuru Highway, PO Box 30471, Nairobi (☎ 336858, fax 218109) and Nkrumah Rd, PO Box 90604, Mombasa (☎ 223509; fax 311022)

Pollman's Tours & Safaris
Koinange St, PO Box 45895, Nairobi (☎ 337998; fax 337171)
Moi Ave, PO Box 84198, Nairobi (fax 314502)
It also has an office in London.

United Touring Company
Fedha Towers, on the corner of Muindi Mbingu and Kaunda Sts, PO Box 42196, Nairobi (☎ 331960; fax 216871)
Moi Ave, PO Box 84782, Mombasa (☎ 31-6333/4; fax 314549)
It also has offices in Europe (London, Munich and Paris), North America (Philadelphia) and the Far East (Tokyo and Singapore).

Vacational Tours & Travel Ltd
Nairobi Hilton, PO Box 44401, Nairobi (☎ 33-7392; fax 210530).

OTHER SAFARIS
Camel Safaris

This is a superb way of getting right off the beaten track and into areas where vehicle safaris don't or cannot go. Camel safaris offer maximum involvement in areas of Kenya which the 20th century has hardly touched, if at all. Most of them take place in the Samburu and Turkana tribal areas between Isiolo and Lake Turkana and you'll have plenty of opportunity to become accustomed to the pace of nomadic life as well as to mingle with the indigenous people. You'll also encounter wildlife though, naturally, sightings of any particular animal and in what numbers cannot be guaranteed.

You have the choice of riding the camels or walking alongside them (except in a few spots where you will be forced to dismount). The camels are led by experienced Samburu *morani* (warriors) and accompanied by English-speaking guides of the same tribe who are well-versed in bush lore, botany, ornithology and local customs. Most travelling is done as early as possible in the cool of the day and a camp site established around noon. Following lunch, you are free to relax during the heat of the day and, in the evening, while the sleeping arrangements and dinner are being organised by the staff, take a walk (along with a guide if you choose). Hot showers are normally available before drinks and dinner are served around a camp fire.

All the companies provide a full range of camping equipment (two-person tents, as a rule) and ablution facilities but they vary in what they require you to bring along. Some even provide alcoholic drinks, though normally you pay extra for this. The typical distance covered each day is between 15 and 18 km so you don't have to be super fit. Far more important is flexibility and a good positive attitude, since no two safaris are exactly alike. Itineraries and routes also change depending on the weather and other factors.

Yare Safaris also host the annual Maralal International Camel Derby from their lodge and camp site at Maralal. The derby includes a full day of races in Maralal on the Saturday of the third week of October, plus a longer 18-day endurance race. For full details see the Maralal section in the Northern Kenya chapter.

The following list of recommended companies which offer camel safaris has been listed alphabetically, and not in any order of preference or reliability:

Desert Rose Camels
PO Box 44801, Nairobi (☎ 228936, 330130; fax 212160).
This company is run by Yoav & Emma Chen and Helen Douglas-Dufresne, and their safaris cover the Matthews Range, Ndoto Mountains and Ol Doinyo Nyiru between Wamba and South Horr. They have no hard-and-fast itineraries; the route depends on the season, the number of days you

have available and personal interests – so they can tailor a safari to your requirements. If, for instance, you wish to make Lake Turkana your final destination, it can be arranged.

As with Yare's safari, you will will be accompanied by experienced Samburu cameleers and guides but, unlike Yare, they do not use a support vehicle. All baggage, camping equipment and food and drink are transported by camels. There are, of course, camels for riding, too.

A seven-day safari costs US$350 per person (one to two people), US$260 (three to five people) and US$210 (six to eight people) and includes all food and drink (even wine and beer), camping equipment (except sleeping bags) and ablution facilities. Specially tailored or longer safaris cost correspondingly more.

Gametrackers
1st Floor, Kenya Cinema Plaza, Moi Ave (PO Box 62042), Nairobi (☎ 338927, 222703; fax 330903).
This company offers a 10-day combined camel safari and vehicle safari which starts and finishes in Nairobi but the camels are used exclusively for transporting baggage. You have to walk alongside them.

The camel trek starts at Laisamis on the Isiolo to Marsabit road and uses local Rendille guides. For the next four days you trek south of the Ndoto Mountains along the Malgis lugga (dry riverbed) and then up to the top of the Ndotos. On the seventh day, you are met by a vehicle and taken to Loyangalani on Lake Turkana. The next day is spent at the lake after which you are driven to Maralal and the final day is spent driving back to Nairobi via Nyahururu and Naivasha.

There are departures twice a month on Monday and the cost is US$430 per person which includes all transport, food and camping equipment (except sleeping bags).

Yare Safaris Ltd
1st Floor, Union Towers, Mama Ngina St, PO Box 63006, Nairobi (☎ 214099; fax 213445).
Its seven-day safari begins and ends at Yare's Maralal hostel. The trek starts at Barsalinga Bridge on the Ewaso Nyiro River (which flows through Samburu and Buffalo Springs game reserves) and it leaves every Saturday.

On the first day of the trek you are transferred by vehicle to the starting point and for the next five days you trek through the bush with your camels and Samburu morani cameleers and guides. Your excess baggage and the camp is moved on ahead of you each day by support vehicle. The camps are equipped with two-person tents, mattresses and showers.

The cost per person is US$360 and includes all transport, food, camping equipment (except sleeping bags), ablution facilities and transfer to

and from Nairobi and Maralal. Alcoholic drinks are your responsibility.

Yare also hosts the annual Maralal International Camel Derby from its hostel just outside of town in the last week of October. It's well worth attending if you're anywhere in the area at the time. Full details can be found in the Maralal section of the Northern Kenya chapter.

Walking & Cycling Safaris

For the keen walker and those who don't want to spend all their time in a safari minibus, there are a number of options.

Bushbuck Adventures
Barclays Bank Bldg, PO Box 67449, Nairobi (☎ 212975/6/7; fax 218735).
This company also offers what is essentially a 14-day walking safari which takes in the Aberdare and Mt Kenya national parks including an ascent of Mt Kenya. The last few days are spent touring Shaba National Reserve in a Land Rover. The cost is US$2270 per person all-inclusive.

Gametrackers
1st Floor, Kenya Cinema Plaza, Moi Ave (PO Box 62042), Nairobi (☎ 338927; fax 330903).
This company offers a four-day walking safari into the Aberdare National Park. The first day is spent getting to Mweiga where you meet your guide after which you head up the forested eastern slopes of the Aberdare Range and make camp. The next two days are spent walking in the area and going on a short game drive if weather permits. The last day is spent driving back to Nairobi. There are two departures each month and the cost is US$265 per person (minimum five people).

Hiking & Cycling Kenya
4th Floor, Arrow House, Koinange St, PO Box 39439, Nairobi (☎ 218336/8; fax 228107).
This company specialises in hiking and cycling safaris although they all involve some transport by road and/or boat. All are camping safaris.

Its shortest safari (eight days) involves climbing Mt Longonot and walking through Hell's Gate National Park (Naivasha), walking along the Mara River into Kipsigis country, through Saiwa Swamp, and the slopes of Mt Elgon. The walks are interspersed with game drives through Masai Mara, a drive through the tea plantations of Kericho and a game drive through Nakuru National Park.

The nine-day safari takes you to Lake Turkana in the footsteps of Count Teleki. It involves a visit to Lake Baringo followed by a hike down into the Suguta Valley and Lake Loigipi in the Rift Valley. Next comes a climb over Teleki's Volcano to the

Jade Sea. Here you are met by a boat which takes you to South Island (where you spend the night) followed by another boat to Loyangalani the following day. On the way back to Nairobi, by vehicle, you call off at Maralal and Samburu National Reserve.

This company also runs a 10-day cycling and vehicle safari which begins in the Ngong Hills and ends up in Nairobi taking in Suswa Volcano, Masai Mara, Lake Nakuru and Lake Bogoria.

There's also a 13-day walking and boating safari which takes in Mt Longonot, Hell's Gate National Park, the Mara River, Saiwa Swamp, Mt Elgon, the Cherangani Hills and Lake Turkana. It also includes game drives through Masai Mara and a visit to the remote Sibiloi National Park (by boat) at the north-eastern end of Lake Turkana. This is a very interesting package and one of the few opportunities you will have to visit Sibiloi (hardly any other safari company includes this park in their itineraries).

Hiking & Cycling Kenya can also arrange a six-day mountain trek up Mt Kenya (Sirimon route) topped off by a visit to Samburu National Reserve.

You're not expected to be an experienced hiker or super fit but you need to be in reasonable shape. Also, you won't be required to carry your luggage on your back – this is taken care of by camels, donkeys, a boat, a vehicle or local porters. You will, on the other hand, be required to share daily camp chores.

The prices include all transport, food, porters, park and camping fees, camping equipment and guides.

Kitich Camp

PO Box 14869, Nairobi (☎ 444288)

PO Box 51, Wamba.

This is a relatively new outfit operated by Toby Stark. The camp is at Ngalia village north of Wamba (which itself is north of Isiolo). Here you can arrange to go walking in the Matthews Range along with a guide (and cooks and porters if you wish). There are no fixed departures or itineraries and you can go walking for any number of days, but you must bring your own tent. Guide fees are US$2.20 per day and a cook can be provided at extra cost (otherwise do your own cooking). The camp site fee at Kitich is US$3.55 per day or you can stay at their permanent tented site for US$68.85 with full board. To get to the camp, there is at least one matatu daily from Isiolo to Wamba around noon and from there you'll have to hitch (very little traffic) or walk (six hours). If this doesn't appeal, pick-up can be arranged in Isiolo or Wamba.

Sirikwa Safaris

PO Box 332, Kitale.

This outfit is run by Jane & Julia Barnley from

their farmhouse/guesthouse and camping site about 20 km outside Kitale on the Lodwar road. They can arrange bird-watching trips to the Cherangani Hills along with a guide (US$5.35 per day for a guide plus US$2.65 if you spend the night out) as well as trips to Saiwa Swamp National Park, Marich Pass, Mt Elgon and the Kongelai Escarpment.

White-Water Rafting

Savage Wilderness Safaris Ltd

PO Box 44827, Nairobi (☎ 521590; fax 501754).

This outfit is run by Mark Savage and is the only one of its kind in Kenya. Depending on water levels, rafting trips of up to 600 km in length and of two weeks or more duration can be arranged, though most trips last between one and four days during which you cover up to 80 km.

One of the most popular short trips (one day's duration) is on the Tana River, north-east of Nairobi. You are picked up from the Norfolk Hotel at 8 am and taken to the put-in point near Sagana where you'll be briefed on safety and other procedures and issued with life jackets and helmets. Then it's off into the water. The first of the rapids is only class (or grade) 3 followed by three km of class 2 and 3 (ideal for learning some of the basic skills needed to tackle the larger rapids further on). That's followed by six km of calm scenic water where birdlife abounds. The last six km are the most exciting, consisting of class 3, 4 and, at certain water levels, class 5 rapids interspersed with short sections of calmer water where the boat can be bailed out. A hearty picnic lunch is included and you should be back in Nairobi by around 5 pm.

This trip departs every Tuesday and Saturday (advance bookings required) or by request any day if there are four or more of you.

Another of the popular short trips is the three-day adventure on the Athi River, south-east of Nairobi between Tsavo East and West national parks. The first day is spent driving to Cottar's Luxury Camp at Kibwezi on the Nairobi to Mombasa road. Here you spend the night. The following morning you leave at about 7 am for the put-in point where you are briefed and issued with life jackets and helmets. After that, it's six to eight hours rafting on both calm and white water after which you return to Cottar's Camp for the night. On the third day, you make a pre-dawn start with a picnic breakfast and tackle the much larger and faster rapids which include small waterfalls and gushing shutes interspersed with short lengths of calmer water. These are followed by a picnic lunch and the drive back to Nairobi.

These trips leave any day of the week subject to a minimum of four passengers.

The most exciting times to go on these white-water rafts are from late October to mid-January and from early April to late July when water levels are at their highest. The Tana River generally maintains a higher water level longer than the Athi.

Balloon Safaris

Viewing a game park from the vantage point of a hot-air balloon is a magnificent experience which you won't ever forget – but it is expensive! The experience of floating silently above the plains with a 360° view of everything beneath you, without safari buses competing for the best photo opportunity, is incomparable. It's definitely worth saving up for!

The flights typically set off at dawn and go for about 1½ hours after which they put down and you tuck into a champagne breakfast. After that, you'll be taken on a game drive in a support vehicle and returned to your lodge. At present, these flights are only available in the Masai Mara and they cost around US$300. There are two outfits:

Adventures Aloft
  Eagle House, Kimathi St, PO Box 40683, Nairobi (☎ 221439).
  This company operates out of Mara Fig Tree Lodge (Radiocall 3725) and you can either book in Nairobi or at the Fig Tree Lodge. The flights also depart from this lodge.
Balloon Safaris Ltd
  Wilson Airport, PO Box 43747, Nairobi (☎ 502850).
  This company operates out of Keekorok Lodge so you can either book through Block Hotels, Rehema House, Standard St (PO Box 47557), Nairobi (☎ 335807) or at Keekorok Lodge. The flights also depart from this lodge.

Flying Safaris

These safaris essentially cater only for the rich and those interested in big-game fishing. They centre around Rusinga Island in Lake Victoria. A light aircraft collects you from your nearest airstrip in the early morning and returns you in time for lunch or an afternoon game drive. In the meantime a motorboat takes you out on Lake Victoria where you can feed and photograph fish eagles and go fishing for Nile perch – the largest freshwater fish in the world. Angling gear is provided. Bookings can be made through Lonrho Hotels Kenya (☎ 723776), PO Box 58581, Nairobi.

SAFARIS FURTHER AFIELD

A few companies in Nairobi offer safaris to the Tanzanian game parks of Lake Manyara, Ngorongoro Crater, Serengeti and Tarangire but most of them are just agencies for Tanzanian safari companies based in Arusha so you might as well go there yourself and organise things from there. It would certainly cost less than doing it in Kenya since you won't be paying the agency's commission.

If your time and budget is limited, however, and you want to take in all or most of the major sights of Tanzania (Serengeti, Ngorongoro Crater, Lake Manyara), Burundi (Lake Tanganyika), eastern Zaïre (the gorillas of Kahuzi-Biéga National Park or Virunga National Park, the chimpanzees of Tongo, and Lake Kivu), and Uganda (Queen Elizabeth National Park, and the chimpanzees of the Kitale Forest), then it's worth thinking about booking an extended safari with one of the companies which offers these kind of safaris in Nairobi. It would certainly save on the time and expense of having to do all the legwork and organisation yourself ·plus the uncertainties of knowing whether you'll be able to join a gorilla or chimpanzee-viewing walk the day after you turn up (this cannot be guaranteed without prior booking).

There are several reliable companies which offer such safaris ranging from 10 to 25 days though, once again, these have been listed alphabetically and not in any order of preference:

Gametrackers
  1st Floor, Kenya Cinema Plaza, Moi Ave (PO Box 62042), Nairobi (☎ 338927; fax 330903).
  This company offers a longer 19-day version of Yare's and Worldwide's 10-day safaris which not only takes in the gorillas at Djomba (Zaïre) and the Queen Elizabeth National Park (Uganda) but also includes the Semliki Valley (pygmies and hot springs) and Kibale Forest (Uganda), Lake Naivasha, Mt Longonot and Hell's Gate National

Park as well as Masai Mara. The safaris begin and end in Nairobi and depart once a month.

The cost is US$790 (or US$660 if you don't want to go to Masai Mara) plus US$75 for food. The price includes everything except visa fees, gorilla-viewing fees, the boat trip on the Kazinga Channel and entry to Kibale Forest. The latter three items amount to US$136.

Kumuka Africa

PO Box 70559, Nairobi (☎ 213123, fax 228107). This UK-based company, which has a subsidiary headquarters in Nairobi, also offers a four-week 'Gorilla Safari' although the gorillas actually only occupy a small proportion of the total. Most of the trip is spent elsewhere in Tanzania, Uganda and Kenya. Kumuka takes you to virtually every interesting place, has good trucks and good drivers, cooks and guides but it does tend to appeal to punters with an 'overland everywhere' attitude which may, or may not, be what you are looking for. The Gorilla Safari costs US$1232 plus US$124, all-inclusive, except visas.

Worldwide Adventure Ltd

1st Floor, Nginyo House, on the corner of Koinange and Moktar Daddah Sts (PO Box 76637), Nairobi (☎ /fax 332407).

This company also offers a 10-day safari in 110 Land Rovers which is almost identical to Yare's safari of the same duration. The only difference is that Worldwide takes in Lake Naivasha and involves no camping at all (accommodation is entirely in budget hotels, except at Kericho on the way out and the way back where you stay at the mid-range Tea Hotel). It costs US$990 which includes everything except lunches, visas and compulsory travel insurance. There are departures every two weeks.

Yare Safaris

1st floor, Union Towers, Mama Ngina St, PO Box 63006, Nairobi (☎ 214099; fax 213445)

Yare pioneered these types of safari back in 1984 and is still the leader. The shorter trips (10 and 14 days) are done in 110 Land Rovers (converted to allow maximum viewing), and accommodation is mostly in budget hotels with occasional camping (in the national parks). Both begin and end in Nairobi. The longer trips (15, 20, 21 and 25 days) are done in trucks with group sizes ranging from 10 to 20 passengers. Accommodation is a mixture of budget hotels and camping.

The 10-day trip takes in Lake Naivasha, the tea plantations of Kericho and on into Uganda. Next it's on to the Zaïre border at Kisoro and the gorilla sanctuary at Djomba, just over the border. After seeing the gorillas, you return to Uganda and visit the Queen Elizabeth National Park including a launch ride up the Kazinga Channel. After that, it's back to Nairobi. The 14-day trip includes all the above but is followed by visits to Serengeti

National Park, Ngorongoro Conservation Area and Lake Manyara National Park after which it's back to Nairobi.

The cost of the 10-day trip is US$1075 and for the 14-day trip US$1425, which includes all transport, accommodation, breakfast and dinner each day and all park entry fees. It does not include the cost of visas, lunches and compulsory travel insurance.

The 15-day truck safari is essentially for those whose main interest is to see the gorilla sanctuaries of Zaïre and it takes in both the Kahuzi-Biéga National Park (eastern lowland gorillas) and the Virunga National Park (mountain gorillas). The safari begins and ends in Kampala (Uganda) and follows a route which takes you first into Tanzania, then Burundi, on into Zaïre and back to Uganda. It costs US$975 (plus a food kitty contribution of US$85) which includes all transport, camping and cooking equipment, food and national park fees. It does not include the cost of visas, compulsory travel insurance or transport between Nairobi and Kampala.

The 21-day safari, starting in Kampala and ending in Nairobi takes a different route so as to include the Queen Elizabeth National Park (Uganda), the Tongo chimpanzee sanctuary (Zaïre), the Kahuzi-Biéga gorillas (Zaïre), Burundi, Serengeti National Park (Tanzania) and Lake Naivasha (Kenya). It costs US$1275 plus US$125 for food and the price includes the same things as the 15-day safari, excluding transport between Nairobi and Kampala.

The 20-day safari is essentially a shorter version of the above but it starts from Bujumbura (Burundi), takes in both Kahuzi-Biéga and Tongo (Zaïre), Queen Elizabeth National Park (Uganda) and ends up in Nairobi. The cost is US$1135 plus US$120 for food.

The 25-day safari is, again, a Land Rover safari but, since this involves only a small group, it allows you a certain flexibility about where you decide to go and what you do. These safaris start and end in Nairobi. The route basically takes in Lake Naivasha and Kisumu in Kenya; Jinja, Kampala, the Semliki Valley (pygmies and hot springs), Kibale Forest (chimpanzees), the Ruwenzori Mountains and Queen Elizabeth National Park, all in Uganda; Virunga National Park (mountain gorillas), Tongo chimpanzee sanctuary, Mt Nyiragongo (volcano), Kahuzi-Biéga National Park (lowland gorillas), all in Zaïre; the Jane Goodall Chimpanzee Sanctuary (Burundi), Serengeti National Park, Ngorongoro Conservation Area and Lake Manyara National Park, all in Tanzania. The cost is US$1495 plus US$280 for food. All the above safaris have regular departures – contact the company for details.

DO-IT-YOURSELF SAFARIS

This is a viable proposition in Kenya if you can get a group together to share the costs since you will have to rent a vehicle and camping equipment. The costs of renting a suitable vehicle can be found under the earlier Car & 4WD section in this chapter.

Doing it yourself has several advantages over organised safaris. The main one is flexibility – you can go where you want, stop whenever you like and stay as long as you like. You don't have to follow the standard tourist routes. Another is that you can choose your travelling companions.

The main disadvantage is the extra effort you have to put in to organise the safari – hiring equipment, buying food and drink, cooking and agreeing among yourselves where you want to go and which route to take. It can also be a worry if none of you have mechanical skills and/or no tools and

the vehicle breaks down. There's also the security of the vehicle and contents to think about if you want to leave it somewhere and go off walking. If you do this then you'll have to pay someone to guard it. Lastly, there's the question of maps especially if you intend to get right off the beaten track. Reasonably good large-scale maps are available in Kenya but the detailed ones are unavailable without going through a great deal of red tape. This means you could find yourself out in the middle of nowhere with not a clue where you're going and have to backtrack.

As far as costs go, it's probably true to say that organising your own safari is going to cost at least as much and usually more than going on a company organised safari. By how much more depends on a lot of factors but mainly the cost of hiring a vehicle and buying fuel. You'll have to sit down and work this out yourself.

Nairobi

Mark Knopfler could almost have been singing about Nairobi when he wrote *Telegraph Road*. Until the late 1800s there was nothing there. It was just a watering hole for the Maasai. Then came the Mombasa to Uganda railway, with its 32,000 indentured Indian labourers from Gujarat and the Punjab, along with their British colonial overlords intent on beating the German colonial push for the Ugandan heartland. Being approximately halfway between Mombasa and Uganda and a convenient place to pause before the arduous climb into the highlands, it quickly became tent city.

Much of the area was still a foul-smelling swamp at this time and game roamed freely over the surrounding plains, yet by 1900 it had become a town of substantial buildings and five years later succeeded Mombasa as the capital of the British East Africa protectorate. Since then it has gone from strength to strength and is now the largest city between Cairo and Johannesburg. The tower blocks of Nairobi can be seen for miles as you crest the hills which surround the plain on which it sits. Yet, in terms of the world's largest cities, Nairobi is still small with a population of about one million. You can walk from one end of the central business district to the other in 20 minutes. And where else in the world would you be able to see lions, cheetahs, rhinos and giraffes roaming free with the tower blocks of a city as a backdrop?

It's a very cosmopolitan place – lively, interesting, pleasantly landscaped and a good place to get essential business and bureaucratic matters sewn up. This is no Third World capital city though there are some very overcrowded slums on the outskirts and even across the other side of the Nairobi River from Kirinyaga Rd. The latter are periodically bulldozed away and burnt down by the city council in the interests of hygiene but it takes only days for them to regenerate!

Like most cities, Nairobi has its crowded market and trading areas, its middle class/office workers' suburbs and its spacious mansions and flower-decked gardens for the rich and powerful. The first is an area full of energy, aspiration and opportunism where manual workers, exhausted matatu drivers, the unemployed, the devious, the down-and-out and the disoriented mingle with budget travellers, whores, shopkeepers, high school students, food-stall vendors, drowsy security guards and those with life's little illicit goodies for sale. It's called River Rd – though, of course, it spans more than just this road itself. One of the funniest yet most poignant yarns I have ever read about an area such as this is to be found in a novel by Kenyan author Meja Mwangi called *Going Down River Road* (Heinemann, African Writers Series). I'd recommend this book to anyone and especially travellers passing through Nairobi. Even if you are not staying in this area you should make a point of getting down there one day just to see how the other half lives on the wrong side of Tom Mboya St.

Elsewhere in Nairobi are all the things you won't have seen for months if you've been hacking your way across the Central African Republic and Zaïre from West Africa or making do with the shortages in Zambia and Tanzania. Things like the latest films on big screens, bookshops, restaurants, cafés and bars full of travellers from all over the world, offices where you can get things done with the minimum of fuss, banks where you can change travellers' cheques in less than five minutes and a poste restante where you sort out your own letters from the pile so you don't end up with that feeling that letters have been put in the wrong pigeonhole. It's a great place to stay for a week or so but if you stay too long it can get expensive because almost everyone you meet wants to do the same as you did when you first arrived

– splurge at the restaurants and drink their fill in the bars and rage in the discos.

Orientation

The compact city centre is in the area bounded by Uhuru Highway, Haile Selassie Ave, Tom Mboya St and University Way. The main bus and train stations are within a few minutes' walk of this area, while the main budget travellers' accommodation area is centred around Latema Rd, just east of Tom Mboya St on the fringe of the bustling and somewhat sleazy River Rd area.

To the west of the centre is one of the more enlightened bits of Nairobi town planning – Uhuru Park. It's a much needed lung for this increasingly crowded city and is a pleasant place in the daytime. At night it becomes a mugger's paradise and should be avoided.

Directly west of Uhuru Park, and still within walking distance of the centre (but *don't* walk at night!), are some of the city's better middle and top-range hotels, the popular youth hostel, a number of government ministries and the hospitals. Beyond here are the sprawling upper middle class suburbs of Ngong and Hurlingham with their large detached houses and carefully tended gardens surrounded by high fences, and guarded by askaris (police) along with prominent signs warning that the premises are patrolled by 'Ultimate Security', 'Total Security', 'Securicor' and the like. These signs are surely one of the most enduring impressions of suburban Nairobi!

North of the centre is the university, the national museum, the International Casino and one of Nairobi's original colonial hotels, the Norfolk. Beyond here is Westlands, another of Nairobi's upper middle class suburbs. North-east of the centre is Parklands, which is home to many of Nairobi's Asian minority and where the Aga Khan Hospital is to be found. Close to the hospital is the popular Mrs Roche's guesthouse. Going east, there are the bustling and predominantly African suburbs of Eastleigh and Pangani along with the country bus station.

South of the city is Nairobi National Park,

and to the park's north-east is Jomo Kenyatta International Airport which is connected to the city by an excellent dual carriageway.

Information

Tourist Office In a city the size of Nairobi, and in a country which relies so heavily on tourism, it seems inconceivable that there is no tourist office, but there isn't.

There is a 50-page booklet called *Kenya Tourist Guide* which is published once a month and the quarterly *What's On* both of which are free and can be found at the better class hotels. There also used to be an 80-page leaflet called *Tourist's Kenya* which was published fortnightly and though publication was suspended in early February 1992, the staff are still working and the owners intend to resume publication soon. Its main outlet was the Thorn Tree Café in the New Stanley Hotel. Like the other publications, it's free.

Money At Jomo Kenyatta International Airport the branch of Barclays Bank is open 24 hours a day, seven days a week. In Nairobi, the bank's branch on the corner of Kenyatta Ave and Wabera St is open Monday to Saturday from 9 am to 4.30 pm.

Post The GPO is on Haile Selassie Ave, although a new post office on Kenyatta Ave is nearing completion and may in fact be open by now. The office on Haile Selassie is open Monday to Friday from 8 am to 5 pm and Saturdays from 9 am to noon. The poste restante is well organised and you are allowed to look through as many piles as you like, plus there's no charge for letters collected. The only trouble is that the counter which deals with it is also one of the few which sells stamps, so the queues are often long.

With the huge volume of poste restante mail here it's not surprising that some letters get misfiled but, surprisingly, it doesn't happen too often. As a favour to other travellers you should pull out any letters you come across which are misfiled so the clerk can get them into the right pile.

This post office is also the best one from

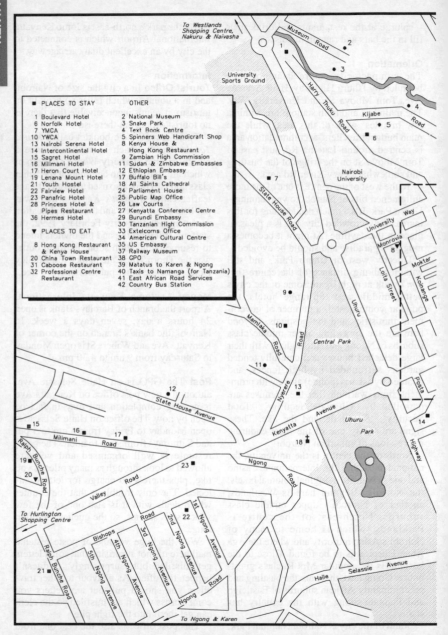

PLACES TO STAY

1 Boulevard Hotel
6 Norfolk Hotel
7 YMCA
10 YWCA
13 Nairobi Serena Hotel
14 Intercontinental Hotel
15 Sagret Hotel
16 Milimani Hotel
17 Heron Court Hotel
19 Lenana Mount Hotel
21 Youth Hostel
22 Fairview Hotel
28 Panafric Hotel
28 Princess Hotel &
   Pipes Restaurant
36 Hermes Hotel

▼ PLACES TO EAT

8 Hong Kong Restaurant
   & Kenya House
20 China Town Restaurant
31 Caboose Restaurant
32 Professional Centre
   Restaurant

OTHER

2 National Museum
3 Snake Park
4 Text Book Centre
5 Spinners Web Handicraft Shop
8 Kenya House &
   Hong Kong Restaurant
9 Zambian High Commission
11 Sudan & Zimbabwe Embassies
12 Ethiopian Embassy
17 Buffalo Bill's
18 All Saints Cathedral
24 Parliament House
25 Public Map Office
26 Law Courts
27 Kenyatta Conference Centre
29 Burundi Embassy
30 Tanzanian High Commission
33 Extelcoms Office
34 American Cultural Centre
35 US Embassy
37 Railway Museum
38 GPO
39 Matatus to Karen & Ngong
40 Taxis to Namanga (for Tanzania)
41 East African Road Services
42 Country Bus Station

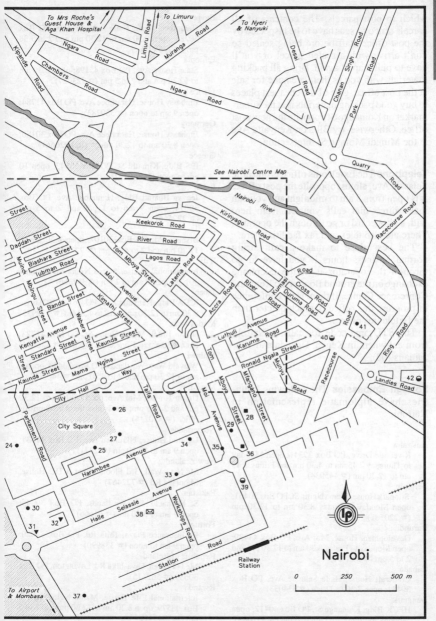

To Mrs Roche's
Guest House &
Aga Khan Hospital

To Limuru

To Nyeri
& Nanyuki

Kiparde
Road

Ngara
Road

Chambers
Road

Limuru Road

Muranga
Road

Desai
Road

Chanan Singh Road

Park
Road

Ngara
Road

Ngara
Road

Quarry
Road

See Nairobi Centre Map

Nairobi River

Racecourse Road

Kirinyago
Road

Street

Daddah Street

Muindi
Mbingu
Street

Biashara Street

Tubman Road

Banda Street

Keekorok Road

River   Road

Lagos Road

Tom Mboya Street

Laterna Road

Accra Road

River   Road

Road

Kumasi
Cross
Road

Duruma Road

Road

Moi   Avenue

Kenyatta Avenue

Kimathi Street

Wabera Street

Standard Street

Kaunda Street

Street

Mama

Ngina

Kaunda Street

Street

Street

Way

Taifa Road

Tom

Luthuli   Avenue

Karume   Road

Ronald Ngala Street

Mfangano Street

Mbuyu   Road

Racecourse   Road

Ring   Road

• 41

40 ⌂

Landies Road

42 ⌂

City   Hall

Parliament   Road

City Square

• 26

• 27

• 25

24 •

Harambee   Avenue

Moi   Avenue

• 34

35 •

29 •

■ 28

■ 36

33 •

39 ⌂

• 30

31 ▼

32 ▼

Haile   Selassie   Avenue

38 ✉

Workshops Road

Road

Station

Railway
Station

Nairobi

0   250   500 m

To Airport
& Mombasa

37 •

IP

which to post parcels. The contents of all parcels sent overseas have to be inspected by the post office staff before being sealed so don't arrive with a sealed parcel or you'll have to pull it apart again. Bring all packing materials with you as there are none for sale at the post office. One of the cheapest places to buy good packing materials is at the supermarket on Koinange St opposite the new post office. Otherwise, try Biba on Kenyatta Ave at the Muindi Mbingu St intersection.

Telephone The Extelcoms office is on Haile Selassie Ave, almost opposite the post office. It is open from 8 am to midnight and you can make direct-dial calls yourself from here with a phonecard or go through the operator. There are also telex and fax facilities here.

The best place to make a call during normal business hours if you have to go through the operator is at the telephone exchange on the ground floor of the Kenyatta Conference Centre. If there is no conference in progress this office is much quieter than the Extelcoms office.

The STD area code for calls to Nairobi from anywhere in Kenya, Uganda and Tanzania is (02).

Foreign Embassies The following countries have diplomatic representation in Nairobi:

Australia
  Riverside Drive, PO Box 39341; open Monday to Thursday 7.45 am to 4.30 pm and Friday 7.45 am to 12.30 pm (☎ 445034)
Belgium
  Silopark House, Mama Ngina St, PO Box 30461; open Monday to Friday 8.30 am to 12.30 pm (☎ 220501)
Burundi
  Development House, Moi Ave, PO Box 44439; open Monday to Friday 8.30 am to 12.30 pm and 2 to 5 pm (☎ 338721)
Canada
  Comcraft House, Haile Selassie Ave, PO Box 30481; open 7.30 to 11 am (☎ 334033)
Denmark
  HFCK Bldg, Koinange St, PO Box 40412; open Monday to Friday 7.45 am to 3 pm (☎ 331088)

Egypt
  Harambee Plaza, Haile Selassie Ave, PO Box 30285; open 9.30 am to 12.30 pm and 2 to 3.30 pm (☎ 225991)
Ethiopia
  State House Ave, PO Box 45198; open 8.30 am to 12.30 pm and 2 to 5 pm (☎ 723027)
France
  Embassy House, Harambee Ave, PO Box 41784; open 9 am to noon (☎ 339783)
Germany
  Embassy House, Harambee Ave, PO Box 30180; open 8.30 am to 12.30 pm (☎ (02) 226661)
Greece
  IPS Bldg, Kimathi St, PO Box 30543; open 10 am to noon (☎ 340722)
India
  Jeevan Bharati Bldg, Harambee Ave, PO Box 30074; open 9 am to 1 pm and 2 to 5 pm (☎ 222566)
Israel
  Bishops Rd, PO Box 30107; open 8.30 am to 12.30 pm and 2 to 4.30 pm (☎ 722182)
Italy
  International House, Mama Ngina St, PO Box 30107; open 8 am to 2 pm (☎ 337356)
Japan
  ICEA Bldg, Kenyatta Ave, PO Box 60202; open 8.30 am to 12.30 pm and 2 to 4.30 pm (☎ 332955)
Madagascar
  Hilton Hotel, Mama Ngina St, PO Box 41723; open 8.30 am to 1 pm and 2 to 5 pm (☎ 226294)
Malawi
  Waiyaki Way, Westlands, PO Box 30453; open 8 am to 12.30 pm and 2 to 4.30 pm (☎ 440569)
Mauritius
  Union Towers, Moi Ave; open 8.30 am to 12.30 pm and 2 to 5 pm; this is also the Air Mauritius office (☎ 330215)
Netherlands
  Uchumi House, Nkrumah Ave, PO Box 41537; open 9 am to 12.30 pm (☎ 227111)
New Zealand
  Mr N G Wall, 3rd Floor, Minet-ICDC House, Mamlaka Rd (☎ 722467)
Pakistan
  St Michael's Rd, Westlands, PO Box 30045; open 9 am to 3.30 pm (☎ 61666)
Portugal
  Re-Insurance Plaza, Taifa Rd, PO Box 34020; open 9 am to noon (☎ 338990)
Republic of Ireland
  Mr J O'Brien, Owashika Rd, Lavington, PO Box 30659 (☎ 562615)
Rwanda
  International Life House, Mama Ngina St, PO Box 48579; open 8.30 am to 12.30 pm and 2 to 5 pm (☎ 334341)

Seychelles
  Agip House, Waiyaki Way, Westlands (☎ 74-8545)
Somalia
  International House, Mama Ngina St, PO Box 30769; open 9 am to 1 pm. This embassy does not presently function and, in fact, anyone can get into Somalia at present without a visa (☎ 224301).
Spain
  Bruce House, Standard St, PO Box 45503; open 10 am to 1 pm (☎ 335711)
Sudan
  Minet-ICDC House, Mamlaka Rd, PO Box 74059; open 8.30 am to noon, closed Wednesdays (☎ 720883)
Sweden
  International House, Mama Ngina St, PO Box 7694; open 8.30 am to 4 pm (☎ 229042)
Tanzania
  Continental House, on the corner of Uhuru Highway and Harambee Ave, PO Box 47790; open 8.30 am to 12.30 pm and 2 to 5 pm (☎ 331056)
Uganda
  Uganda House, Baring Arcade, Kenyatta Ave, PO Box 60853; open 9.30 am to 12.30 pm and 2 to 4.30 pm (☎ 220801)
UK
  Bruce House, Standard St, PO Box 30465; open 8.30 to 11.30 am and 1.30 to 3.30 pm (☎ 335944)
USA
  Moi Ave, PO Box 30137; open 8.30 am to 3 pm (☎ 334141)
Zaïre
  Electricity House, Harambee Ave, PO Box 48106; open 8.30 am to 12.45 pm and 2 to 5 pm (☎ 229771)
Zambia
  Nyerere Rd, PO Box 48741; open 8.30 am to 12.30 pm and 2 to 4.30 pm (☎ 724796)
Zimbabwe
  Minet-ICDC Bldg, Mamlaka Rd, PO Box 30806; open 8.30 am to 12.30 pm and 2 to 4.30 pm (☎ 721045)

Cultural Centres All the foreign cultural organisations have libraries which are open to the public and are free of charge except for the American Cultural Center which is for members only. Both the French and German cultural centres welcome travellers. The addresses are:

Alliance Française
  ICEA Bldg, Ground Floor, Kenyatta Ave. Open Monday to Friday from 10 am to 1 pm and 2 to 5.15 pm; also Saturdays from 9.30 am to noon (☎ 340054).
American Cultural Center
  National Bank Bldg, Harambee Ave. Open Monday, Tuesday and Thursday from 10 am to 6 pm, Wednesday from 10 am to noon and Friday from 10 am to 4 pm (☎ 337877).
British Council
  ICEA Bldg, Mezzanine Floor, Kenyatta Ave. Open Monday to Friday from 10 am to 5 pm and Saturday from 9 am to noon (☎ 334855).
French Cultural Centre
  Maison Française, on the corner Monrovia and Loita Sts. Open Monday to Friday from 10 am to 6 pm and Saturday from 10 am to 1 pm (☎ 336263).
Goethe Institut
  Maendeleo House, on the corner Monrovia and Loita Sts. Open Monday to Friday from 10 am to 6 pm (☎ 224640).
Italian Cultural Institute
  Prudential Bldg, Wabera St. Open Monday to Wednesday from 8 am to 2 pm, and Thursday and Friday from 8 am to 1 pm and 2.30 to 5.30 pm (☎ 220278).
Japan Information Centre
  Postbank House, on the corner of Market and Banda Sts. Open Monday to Friday from 8.30 am to 12.30 pm and 2 to 4.30 pm (☎ 340520).

Travel Agencies To get the best possible deal on an international airline ticket, first make the rounds of the airline offices to ascertain the standard price and then make the rounds of the travel agencies. Always get several quotes as things change constantly. It's sometimes, but not usually, possible to get as good a deal from the actual airline offices as it is from the agencies. European and Asian destinations are the ones to which you'll find the best discounts. This is less so in the case of North American destinations and virtually impossible for Australasian destinations.

Most of the heavily discounted tickets will involve stopovers between connections – on Aeroflot, EgyptAir, Ethiopian Airlines and Sudan Airways, for example. (See the section on Leaving Kenya in the Kenya Getting There & Away chapter for examples of fares.)

One popular agency that gets good reports from many travellers is Bankco Tours & Travel (☎ (02) 336144) on Latema Rd near the New Kenya Lodge. Just as good is Worldwide Adventures (☎ (02) 332407), 1st Floor, Nginyo House, on the corner of Koinange and Moktar Daddar Sts (above Safari Camp Services). This is run by the tall, bearded, bespectacled, Yorkshireman, Philip Jackson. If there's a good deal going, he'll know about it. Worldwide also offers a visa service and can advise you about safari companies, plus it runs some of its own.

Also recommended is Let's Go Travel (☎ (02) 340331) on Standard St close to the Koinange St intersection.

Bookshops There is a good selection of bookshops in the city centre. The Nation Bookshop is on the corner of Kimathi St and Kenyatta Ave, next door to the New Stanley Hotel, and beside it on Kenyatta Ave is the Westland Sundries Bookshop – both are excellent.

On Mama Ngina St there's Prestige Books, next to the 20th Century Cinema. There are others but they don't carry the same range.

Maps There are many maps of Nairobi available in the bookshops but probably the best is the *City of Nairobi: Map & Guide* (Survey of Kenya) in English, French and German which has a red front cover with partially coloured photographs on the back cover. It covers the suburbs as well as having a detailed map of the central area. If you're going to be staying for a long time, however, the *A to Z: Guide to Nairobi* (Kenway Publications), by D T Dobie, is worth buying.

Photography For passport-size photographs, the cheapest place to go is the machine under the yellow and black sign 'Photo Me', a few doors up Kenyatta Ave from the Nation Bookshop on the corner of Kimathi St. It costs US$1.50 for four prints and takes about three minutes. There's another machine on the corner of Tom Mboya St and Accra Rd. You can also get passport photos from the photography shop in Kimathi House opposite the New Stanley

Hotel but here they are marginally more expensive.

For camera repairs or equipment rental the best place is Expo Camera Centre (☎ 22-1797), Jubilee Exchange, Mama Ngina St. Mo Hussein, who runs this place, is a very helpful man and has a well-equipped repair workshop. Expo Camera is also very reliable for developing and printing. Alternatively, try Camera Experts, also on Mama Ngina St, or the Camera Maintenance Centre in the Hilton Arcade.

Medical Services If you need medical treatment try Dr Sheth on the 3rd floor of Bruce House on Standard St. This doctor has his own pathology laboratory if you need blood or stool tests. He charges US$11 per consultation plus laboratory fees. There is also a dentist on the same floor.

Otherwise go to the Nairobi Hospital which has the same scale of charges as Dr Seth. Avoid the Kenyatta Hospital, because although it's free, treatment here is possibly worse than the ailment, according to local residents. The Aga Khan Hospital in Parklands, opposite Mrs Roche's guesthouse, is very good.

For chiropractic treatment the best place to go is the medical centre on Rose Ave, off Argwings Kodhek Rd, just above the Hurlingham shopping centre and before you get to the Hurlingham Hotel. There are several practitioners here and you're looking at around US$7 a session.

For acupuncture there's no better practitioner than Professor Dr Abdul H Mohamed (☎ 744028, 749748), at the Africa (Laser) Acupuncture Centre, 3rd Parklands Ave (diagonally opposite the Aga Khan Hospital), Parklands. He's a little eccentric but has practised acupuncture all over the world and is well regarded by the medical doctors at both the Aga Khan and Nairobi hospitals. He practices Monday to Friday from 11 am to 2 pm and 5 to 6 pm, and on Saturday, Sunday and public holidays from 11.30 am to 1 pm. A session costs US$15.50.

You can get vaccinations at City Hall Clinic, Mama Ngina St. It is open for jabs from 8.30 am to noon and 2.30 to 4 pm Monday to Friday. Yellow fever shots cost US$7.50, cholera US$3, meningitis US$3, typhoid US$7.50 and tetanus US$0.30.

If you want a gamma globulin shot (for hepatitis A) go to Dr Sheth, 3rd Floor, Bruce House, Standard St. The charge is US$12.

Dangers & Annoyances You may hear rumours about Nairobi being a dangerous city at night as far as robberies go. We've certainly had enough letters from people to whom this has happened but never once on any occasion that I've been to Nairobi have I felt uneasy or threatened walking back to my hotel. Perhaps I just look like I know where I'm going or perhaps it's because I always pull out my wallet when someone asks me for a few shillings down a dark alley. And I don't walk across Uhuru Park at night.

The best thing that can be said is to be vigilant. It's no worse than many other cities around the world and there are plenty worse. You should definitely not walk from the centre to the youth hostel or through Uhuru Park or along Uhuru Highway/Waiyaki Way (anywhere between Westlands and the roundabout with Haile Selassie Ave) at night. The area to the north and east of River Rd is also a no-go area late at night. You are asking for trouble. That taxi home may cost you US$2 but could save you a lot of money.

While we're on this subject, don't forget to read the stories in the Dangers & Annoyances section of Kenya's Facts for the Visitor chapter.

National Museum

The Kenya National Museum is on Museum Rd off Museum Hill which itself is off Uhuru Highway. The museum has a good exhibition on prehistoric people, an incredible collection of native birds, mammals and tribal crafts and a new section on the culture, history and crafts of the coastal Swahili people. It's just unfortunate that many of the displays are moth-eaten and tatty these days.

Opening hours are 9.30 am to 6 pm daily and admission is US$2.

The Kima Killer

Early this century when the railway line was being pushed through from Mombasa to Kampala and beyond, a remarkable incident occurred at Kima, a small siding on the line, about 110 km along the track south-west of Nairobi.

A rogue lion had been terrorising the track gangs and had in fact claimed a few victims. In an attempt to eradicate this menace, a superintendent of the Uganda Railways stationed in Mombasa, Charles Ryall, decided to mount a night vigil in a railway carriage specially positioned at the Kima siding. The station staff wanted nothing to do with the escapade and had locked themselves firmly in the station buildings.

Ryall left the carriage door open, in the hope that the lion would be lured in, and sat back with rifle at the ready and waited. Inevitably he fell asleep and just as inevitably the lion showed up. The struggle that ensued caused the sliding door on the compartment to shut and the lion was trapped inside with a firm grip on Ryall's neck. Accompanying Ryall in the carriage were two European merchants who were travelling to Nairobi and had hitched a ride with Ryall, agreeing to the overnight stop in Kima. So petrified were they that one of them ducked into the toilet and bolted the door, while the other watched transfixed as the lion wrested the body out the train window!

A reward was offered by Ryall's mother for the capture of the offending lion but it was only after a trap, baited with a live calf, was devised that the human-eater was snared. It seems there was no reason for the lion to have turned human-eater as it was a healthy beast and there was abundant herds of game animals in the vicinity – it seems it just developed a liking for human flesh.

The railway carriage involved in this incident is today preserved in the Nairobi Railway Museum, while the tombstone of Ryall, which bears the inscription 'He was attacked whilst sleeping and killed by a man-eating lion at Kima', is in the Hill Cemetery, also in Nairobi. ∎

Snake Park

The Snake Park, opposite the museum, has living examples of most of the snake species found in East Africa – some of them are in glass cages, others in open pits. There are also tortoises and crocodiles. Hours and entry charges are the same as for the museum.

National Archives

Right opposite the Hilton Hotel on Moi Ave is the National Archives. It is regarded by many as better value than the National Museum and entry is free. It contains more than the usual documents you'd expect to find in such a building, including photographs of Mzee Kenyatta and Moi visiting different countries, and exhibitions of handicrafts and paintings.

Railway Museum

The Railway Museum is on Station Rd – follow the railway tracks until you are almost at the bridge under Uhuru Highway or walk across the small piece of vacant land next to the Haile Selassie Ave roundabout on Uhuru Highway. In addition to displays of old steam engines and rolling stock, the museum will give you a good idea of Kenya's history since the beginning of the colonial period. There's also a scale model of the venerable MV *Liemba* which plies the waters of Lake Tanganyika between Mpulungu (Zambia) and Bujumbura (Burundi).

It's open daily from 8 am to 4.45 pm; entry is US$1.50.

Parliament House

Like to take a look at how democracy works in Kenya? If so, you can get a permit for a seat in the public gallery at parliament house on Parliament Rd or, if parliament is out of session, you can tour the buildings by arrangement with the Sergeant-at-Arms.

Art Galleries

There's not much in Nairobi in the way of art galleries but this is gradually changing. The Gallery Watatu on Standard St close to Lonrho House is the oldest established gallery and has fairly regular exhibitions as well as a permanent display. Another more recently established gallery is the Kenya Arts Museum (☎ 214801), PO Box 34464, which has displays of Kenyan art and artefacts plus top examples of carvings, jewellery and photography. There's also a shop where you can buy superior examples of this type of work. The Kiwi and Kenyan team which runs this venture is currently negotiating to borrow large private collections for permanent display.

Kenyatta Conference Centre

There is a viewing level on the 28th floor of the centre but the revolving restaurant no longer operates. If you'd like to go up there, you must request a guide at the information desk on the ground floor. He'll expect a tip, but otherwise it's free. You're allowed to take photographs from the viewing level. Access is sometimes restricted when there's a conference in progress.

Activities

Clubs & Societies There are lots of specialist clubs and societies in Nairobi, many of which welcome visitors. Most of the foreign cultural organisations have film and lecture evenings (usually free of charge) at least once or twice a week. Give them a ring and see what they have organised. In addition to these, some local clubs you may be interested in contacting include:

East African Wildlife Society
    Nairobi Hilton, PO Box 20110, Nairobi (☎ 748170).
    This society is in the forefront of conservation efforts in East Africa and it publishes an interesting bimonthly magazine. Membership costs US$35 (US$70 if you want the magazine sent by airmail rather than surface mail) but entitles you to certain reductions in the national parks.
Mountain Club of Kenya (MCK)
    PO Box 45741, Nairobi (☎ 501747).
    The club meets every Tuesday at 8 pm at the clubhouse at Wilson Airport. Members frequently organise climbing weekends at various sites around the country. Information on climbing Mt Kenya and Kilimanjaro is available on the same evening.

Nairobi Chess Club
    PO Box 50443, Nairobi (☎ 225007).
    The club meets every Wednesday to Sunday at 5 pm at St John's Ambulance Headquarters, top floor, Parliament Rd.
Nairobi Photographic Society
    PO Box 49879, Nairobi (☎ 891075).
    Members meet at 8.30 pm on the first and third Thursdays of each month at St John Ambulance Headquarters.

Sports The following clubs all offer facilities for tennis, squash and cricket, and some also cater for football and hockey:

Impala Club
    Ngong Rd, Nairobi (☎ 568684)
Nairobi Club
    Ngong Rd (☎ 725726)
Nairobi Gymkhana
    corner of Rwathia and Forest Rds (☎ 742804)
Parklands Sports Club
    Ojijo Rd (☎ 742938)

Swimming Pools Most of the international tourist hotels have swimming pools which can be used by nonguests for a daily fee of around US$3. The YMCA on State House Rd also has a large pool with springboard which you can use for US$1.50.

Places to Stay – bottom end

There is a very good selection of budget hotels in Nairobi and the majority of them, except for two very popular places outside the city centre, are between Tom Mboya St and River Rd so if you find that one is full it's only a short walk to another. Virtually all the hotels in the city centre suffer from pretty chronic water shortages. Often there is only water for a couple of hours a day, so getting a shower at some of these places can be a bit of an ordeal.

On the other hand, many of the cheaper hotels, such as the Iqbal, the New Kenya Lodge and Mrs Roche's will store baggage for you, usually for a small daily charge. However, you're advised not to leave anything valuable in your left luggage.

Central Nairobi The *New Kenya Lodge* (☎ 222022), on River Rd at the Latema Rd intersection, is a legend among budget travellers and still one of the cheapest places, though many people feel it's a bit past it these days. There's always an interesting bunch of people from all over the world staying there. Accommodation is basic but clean and there's supposedly hot water in the evenings. A bed in a cramped four-bed room costs US$2.35.

The same people who own this also have the *New Kenya Lodge Annex* (☎ 338348) just around the corner on Duruma Rd. Prices here are the same as the old place but it lacks the atmosphere of the former, some of the rooms don't even have windows and security is not what it could be. All the same, it's still quite popular, the staff are friendly, baggage is safe, and the notice board makes interesting reading.

Sharing the legend is the *Iqbal Hotel* (☎ 220914), on Latema Rd, which has also been popular for years and is still a pretty good place. There's supposedly hot water available in the morning but you have to be up early to get it. A night in a three-bed room costs US$3.10, while double/triple rooms cost US$6.15/9.25, all with shared facilities. Baggage is safe here and there's a storeroom where you can leave excess gear if you are going away for a while. The Iqbal's notice board is always a good place to look for just about anything.

If the above two places are full there are three others on Dubois Rd, just off Latema Rd. The *Bujumbura Lodge* (☎ 228078) is very basic and a bit rough around the edges, but it's clean and quiet and very secure. The toilets and showers are clean and there is erratic hot water. It's good value at US$2.10/3.30 for singles/doubles with shared facilities.

The *New Safe Life Lodging* (☎ 221578) is very similar to the Bujumbura and the staff are cheerful. The rooms are somewhat overpriced at US$6 but security is good. The *Nyandarua Lodging* is very clean, quiet and comfortable and you can get a large double room for US$4.25. It also has single rooms but they're just glorified cupboards and not such good value for money at US$2.70. The

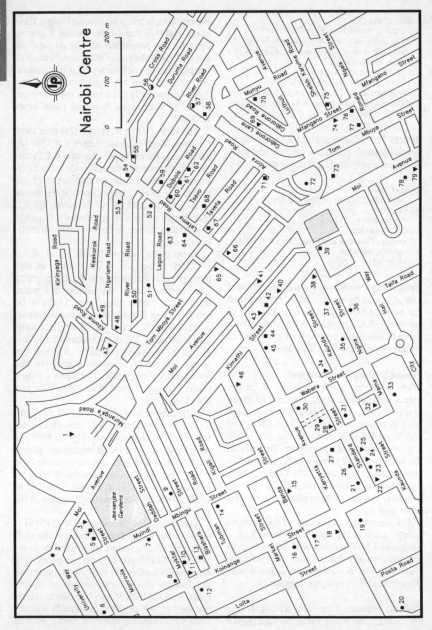

Nairobi Centre

0   100   200 m

■	PLACES TO STAY	25	Calypso Restaurant, Bruce House & British High Commission	14	City Market
				16	New Florida Nightclub
4	Parkside Hotel			17	Air Tanzania & Air Zimbabwe (Chester House)
5	New Garden Hotel	26	The Pub & Akasaka Restaurant		
10	Terminal Hotel				
13	Embassy Hotel	28	Rickshaw Chinese Restaurant	19	Post Office (Under Construction)
27	Sixeighty Hotel				
39	Hilton Hotel	29	Jacaranda Café	20	Immigration (Nyayo House)
42	Oakwood Hotel	32	Café Helena & the Coffee Bar		
44	New Stanley Hotel & Thorn Tree Café			21	Let's Go Travel
		34	Trattoria Restaurant	23	Express Kenya (American Express)
50	Naseem's Lodging	38	Foresta Magnetica		
54	New Kenya Lodge	40	Jax Restaurant	25	Bruce House & British High Commission & Calypso Restaurant
55	New Kenya Lodge Annexe	41	Honey Pot		
		43	Supermac		
58	Sirikwa Lodge	44	Thorn Tree Café & New Stanley Hotel	30	Barclays Bank & Ugandan High Commission
59	New Safe Life Lodging				
60	Nyandarua Lodging	46	Minar Restaurant		
61	Africana Hotel	47	Dhaba Restaurant & Nyama Choma Terrace & Bar	31	Central Car Hire
62	Bujumbura Lodge			33	City Hall
64	Sunrise Lodge & Modern Green Day & Night Bar			35	Prestige Books
		48	Supreme & Mayur Restaurants	36	Rwandan & Somali Embassies
				37	Expo Camera Centre
67	Iqbal Hotel	49	Zam Zam Restaurant	45	Westland Sundries Bookshop & Nation Bookshop
68	Orient Palace Hotel	53	Bull Café		
70	Al Mansura Hotel	65	Growers Café		
71	Solace Hotel	66	Nairobi Burgers	51	Akamba Buses
73	Ambassadeur Hotel	69	Malindi Dishes	52	Bankco Tours & Travel
75	Dolat Hotel	74	New Bedona Café	56	Coast Bus, Goldline, Mawingo, Malaika & Arusha Express Bus Offices
76	Terrace Hotel	79	Zanze Bar & Pagoda Restaurant		
77	Gloria Hotel				
				57	Matatus for Embu, Nanyuki, Isiolo
▼	PLACES TO EAT		OTHER		
				63	Nairobi Bus Union
1	Khyber Restaurant	2	Police Station	64	Modern Green Day & Night Bar & Sunrise Lodge
3	Curry Pot	6	Safari Club		
11	Goldstar Restaurant	7	Afro Unity Bar		
15	African Heritage Café	8	Safari Camp Services & Worldwide Adventures	72	National Archives
18	Harvest Restaurant			78	Florida 2000 Nightclub
22	Beneva Coffee House	9	Atul's Camping Equipment Hire		
24	Dragon Pearl Restaurant	12	Kenya Airways		

only problem here is that the checkout time is a very uncivilised 8.30 am.

Back on Latema Rd, the *Sunrise Lodge* is clean, secure and friendly and there's usually hot water in the mornings and evenings. Dorm beds cost US$2.30, while singles/doubles go for US$3.50/4.60, all with shared bathroom facilities. The front two rooms overlooking the street are the largest and have a balcony but they are right next door to the Modern Green Day & Night Bar which

rages 24 hours a day, 365 days a year, so if you want a quiet room take one of those at the back of the hotel. If you're looking for material for a novel, on the other hand, then take one of these rooms.

Naseem's Lodging on River Rd is a small and friendly place with just a few rooms. Security is good and the place is kept very clean. The US$4.30/6.60 price tag is relatively expensive but it does include breakfast.

Right at the bottom of the scale is the *Al Mansura Hotel* on Munyu Rd. It's basic and the rooms are clean enough but it's really only good for a night if you can't get in elsewhere. Women are likely to feel uncomfortable in this place as it operates as a brothel. A bed in a shared room costs US$1.60, doubles are US$3.10, and there are no single rooms.

Moving up the scale, there are several hotels in the same area. One of the cheapest is the *Gloria Hotel* (☎ 228916), on Ronald Ngala St almost at the Tom Mboya St intersection. Rooms here are good value at US$5.40/5.80 for a single/double. All rooms have bath and hot water, and the price includes breakfast. The only problem here is that some of the rooms cop the noise from the street below.

A couple of doors along from the Gloria is the *Terrace Hotel* (☎ 221636) which has rooms with bath and hot water for US$4.30/4.60 including breakfast. It doesn't win any prizes for friendliness and some of the rooms are noisy, but overall it's not a bad place.

One of the best budget places is the *Dolat Hotel* (☎ 22797), on Mfangano St, which is very quiet and costs US$5.60/7 for singles/doubles with bath and hot water. The sheets are changed daily, the rooms kept spotless and there's 24-hour water. It's a good, secure place with friendly management and quite a few travellers stay here.

Outside the Centre There are two very popular places away from the city centre. *Mrs Roche's*, on 3rd Parklands Ave opposite the Aga Khan Hospital, is, like the New Kenya and the Iqbal, a legend. Mrs Roche has been making travellers welcome for over 20 years and her guesthouse is a favourite with campers and those with their own vehicles as well as those who want a room away from the city centre. There's always an amazing band of people here and the whole place has the general atmosphere of a gypsy camp – there's never a dull moment.

It's situated in a very pleasant area amongst trees and flowering shrubs and is a very mellow place to stay. It's just a pity that some travellers with vehicles seem to disembowel them here and leave the discarded parts lying around for other travellers to camp amongst. Camping costs US$1.20 per night while a bed in a shared room costs US$1.60. Because it's so popular you may have to sleep on the floor for the first night until a bed is available. This is another place with a good notice board, and you can store baggage safely for a small fee.

To get to Mrs Roche's, take a matatu from the junction of Latema Rd and Tom Mboya St right outside the Odeon Cinema. There'll be a sign 'Aga Khan' in the front windscreen. Tell the driver you're heading for Mrs Roche's guesthouse. It's well known. There are several places to eat cheaply in the immediate vicinity and the nearest bar (which also has an excellent barbecue) is the Everest Hotel just up the road. It's a lively place and I've met Mrs Roche there on several occasions!

The other very popular place is the *Nairobi Youth Hostel* (☎ 221789), on Ralph Bunche Rd between Valley and Ngong Rds. Although it was being refurbished and extended when this edition was researched it's reportedly open again. The hostel is often very crowded so is a good place to meet other travellers.

It's very clean, well run, stays open all day and there's always hot water in the showers. The wardens here are very friendly and will lock up gear safely for you for up to two weeks for US$0.30, then it's US$0.50 per day after that. On a day-to-day basis there are lockers to keep your gear in when you go out, but you must supply your own lock. The notice board here (for messages, things for sale, etc) is one of the best in Africa.

A bed in a shared room costs US$2 but you must have a YHA membership card to stay. If not, you'll have to pay a temporary membership fee of US$0.90 per night or join the association for US$4.90 for a year. Any matatu or bus which goes down either Valley or Ngong Rds will drop you at Ralph Bunche Rd. The No 8 matatu which goes down

Ngong Rd is probably the most convenient. You can pick it up either outside the Hilton Hotel or on the corner of Kenyatta Ave and Uhuru Highway. If you're returning to the youth hostel after dark don't be tempted to walk back from the centre of the city. Many people have been robbed. Always take a matatu or taxi.

There is both a *YMCA* (☎ 724066) and *YWCA* (☎ 724699) in Nairobi. The former is on State House Rd and the latter on Mamlaka Rd off Nyerere Rd. The YMCA costs US$5.60 for a dorm bed and US$5.80/10.50 for singles/doubles with shared facilities. Self-contained rooms are US$9.80/14. All the above rates include breakfast. Other meals are available for US$2. You must buy temporary membership to stay here which costs US$1.

The YWCA has dorm beds for US$5.40 (US$29 per month) and double rooms with shared facilities for US$6.70 (US$38 per month). It also has singles/doubles with a washbasin in the new wing for US$9.40/11 (US$51/58 per month) and doubles/family rooms with private bath in the annexe for around US$16/22 (US$89/122 per month). You also have to pay a membership fee of US$1. It takes couples as well as single women.

There's also the very quiet and secure *West End Lodgings* (☎ 750524) on Kijabe Rd, which is clean and has helpful staff. It's only a few cents more than the Iqbal for a double room, yet is far removed from the noise of Latema Rd.

Camping Mrs Roche's is the only place to go if you want to camp. In the high season the limited garden space gets pretty cramped, not only with tents but also with vehicles. It costs US$1.20 per person to put up your tent.

If you want to hire camping equipment (anything from a sleeping bag to a folding toilet seat, tent or mosquito net) the best place to go to is Atul's (☎ 225935), Biashara St. It has the lot and is open Monday to Friday from 8.30 am to noon and 2 to 5 pm and on Saturday from 8.30 am to noon and 2.30 to 4 pm. Hire charges have to be paid in full before commencement of hire as well as

a deposit for each item. The deposits are refunded when hired items are returned in good condition. Identification, such as a passport, is required.

The items for hire are far too numerous to mention here, but there is a list which you can pick up for US$0.60. Advance booking is highly recommended and saves a lot of time. If you'd like a list before going to Kenya, write to PO Box 43202, Nairobi.

Places to Stay – middle
Central Nairobi The *Solace Hotel* (☎ 33-1277), is on the horrendously noisy Tom Mboya St – the matatu drivers here honk and rev their engines to drum up business, and it goes on nonstop from early morning until late at night. Rates are US$12/18 for small, self-contained single/double rooms including breakfast. It's somewhat overpriced and the extra money seems to be mainly for a carpet and phone in the room. If you do stay here make sure you get a room away from the street.

The *Sirikwa Lodge* (☎ 226687) on the corner of Munyu and Accra Rds is a good place in the middle bracket. For US$10/13 you get a clean room with bath, hot water, a phone and breakfast. Accra Rd is somewhat quieter than Tom Mboya St so this place is not a bad bet. Another quiet place is the *Africana Hotel* (☎ 220654) on Dubois Rd between Accra and Latema Rds. The rates are US$8/11 for rooms with bath, hot water and breakfast. It's good value and secure.

Further away from this area, on Tom Mboya St down towards Haile Selassie Ave, is the *Princess Hotel* (☎ 214640), which is popular with VSO volunteers. The rooms are self-contained and cost US$9/12 including a good breakfast. Like all places on Tom Mboya St, the quietest rooms are at the back, though the street is nowhere near as noisy here as further up near Accra Rd. The hotel has its own bar and restaurant. The food is good and the staff friendly.

The *Oakwood Hotel* (☎ 220592), PO Box 40683, is on Kimathi St, right opposite the New Stanley Hotel. It's a very pleasant place to stay and there are 23 self-contained rooms which cost US$34/48 a single/double, and US$55 a triple including breakfast and all taxes. There's constant hot water, a telephone and TV with in-house movies in every room and an overnight laundry service. Other hotel facilities include a bar and restaurant.

The new *Orient Palace Hotel* (☎ 217600) on Taveta Rd is an up-market hotel in a downmarket part of town, but it represents good value at US$44/55 for self-contained air-con rooms. The hotel has a bar and a good Indian restaurant.

The *Ambassadeur Hotel* (☎ 336803), PO Box 30399, is right in the city centre on Moi Ave and is part of the Sarova Hotels chain. It has self-contained singles/doubles for US$34/44 excluding breakfast (US$4.80 extra). The hotel has a bar and, on the ground floor, a good restaurant with lunch/dinner for around US$7.

There's another group of mid-range hotels near Jeevanjee Gardens which we feel are generally better value than those on the River Rd side of Moi Ave, if only for the noise factor and the vehicle fumes, but not everyone agrees.

The *New Garden Hotel* (☎ 33445) and the *Parkside Hotel* (☎ 224033) are both on Monrovia St which runs alongside Jeevanjee Gardens. The New Garden is excellent value at US$5.80 a single with shared bath and US$8.20/9.50 for singles/doubles with private bath. Prices include breakfast. The Parkside has rooms for US$12/15 with bath, hot water and breakfast. The staff are very friendly and the hotel has its own restaurant.

Opposite the Kenya Airways terminal on Moktar Daddah St is the *Terminal Hotel* (☎ 28817), which is also popular with travellers. It offers rooms with clean sheets, hot-water bath, soap and towel for US$8.70 a single, US$10.70 a double and US$11 for a twin (two single beds). There are also triples for around US$15. Breakfast is not included. Some of the rooms are getting a little tatty these days but the staff are friendly and honest, and valuables left in the rooms are safe. There's a same-day laundry service on weekdays (but not at weekends).

Close by is the *Embassy Hotel* (☎ 24087), on Biashara St between Koinange and Muindi Mbingu Sts. Rooms with bath, hot water, soap and towel, cost much the same as at the Terminal but there are also a number of cheaper, smaller singles.

Outside the Centre Most of the other mid-range hotels are along Milimani, Ralph Bunche and Bishops Rds.

Very popular indeed with travellers and expatriates on contract work is the *Heron Court Hotel* (☎ 720740), on Milimani Rd, PO Box 41848. It's a large place and excellent value at US$12/15 for singles/doubles with bathroom, hot water, soap and towels. There are also self-contained apartments with a double bedroom, separate lounge with balcony, bathroom and fully equipped kitchen for US$15/17 a single/double. Breakfast is not included in the room rates. Monthly rates come at a considerable discount. The sheets and towels are changed daily in both types of room, and the hotel facilities include a swimming pool, sauna, massage, guarded car park, shop and 24-hour laundry service. The staff here are friendly and helpful and security is excellent. At the front of the hotel is one of Nairobi's most popular bar/restaurants, Buffalo Bill's, which is open daily from early morning until around 11 pm.

Right at the top of Milimani Rd at the Ralph Bunche Rd intersection is the *Sagret Hotel* (☎ 720933), PO Box 18324, which is of a somewhat higher standard than the Heron Court and offers singles/doubles with bath for US$15/21 including breakfast. The hotel has its own bar and restaurant and accepts Visa and MasterCard.

In between the Sagret and the Heron Court is the *Milimani Hotel* (☎ 720760), PO Box 30715. This is a huge, rambling place popular with expatriates on contract and charges US$25/33 for singles/doubles including breakfast and taxes. There are also more expensive self-contained apartments complete with fully-equipped kitchens. Facilities at the hotel include a swimming pool, bar, beer garden, restaurant and guarded parking.

On Bishops Rd at the back of the Panafric Hotel is the *Fairview Hotel* (☎ 723211), PO Box 40842. Billed as 'the country hotel in the city' (with some justification due to its pleasant garden and quiet location), it offers singles/doubles with shared bath for US$28/48 or US$34/56 with private bath. There are also family units for US$56 and balcony doubles for US$63. All the rooms have a telephone, TV and video service, and prices include breakfast. Other meals average around US$4.70 (set menu) and there's an authentic African buffet every Tuesday and Friday for the same price. The bar has draught Tusker. Guests are entitled to use the swimming pool at the Panafric Hotel.

Further afield, close to Nairobi Hospital, is the *Silver Springs Hotel* (☎ 722451), PO Box 61362, with reasonable singles/doubles at US$26/30.

The *Hurlingham Hotel* (☎ 721920), PO Box 43158, on Argwings Kodhek Rd, west of the Hurlingham shopping centre, is also a popular place to stay. Long-established, it exudes a rustic charm and is set in its own grounds but it's small and often full. Many of the people who stay here return time and time again, so it's best to ring in advance and make sure a room is available. There's a bar and restaurant and it costs much the same as the Silver Springs Hotel.

Places to Stay – top end

In a city the size of Nairobi there are naturally many top-range hotels, some of them in the city centre and others outside this immediate area. If you are planning on staying in one it is worth booking through one of the travel agencies in town instead of paying the so-called 'rack rates' as an agency can often get you a considerable discount. At the Serena, for example, it's possible to get a discount of nearly 40% by booking through United Touring Company.

Central Nairobi In the centre of town, on Muindi Mbingu St between Standard St and Kenyatta Ave, is the *Sixeighty Hotel* (☎ 33-2680), PO Box 43436. This is a large modern hotel and good value at US$44/67 for singles/doubles without breakfast. Better value and with considerably better facilities is the *Boulevard Hotel* (☎ 227567), on Harry Thuku Rd (PO Box 42831). It offers rooms with bathroom, balcony, telephone and radio for US$54/63 a single/double, US$70 a triple including taxes but excluding breakfast. Facilities include a swimming pool, tennis court, restaurant, barbecue, bar, and beer garden.

Also in the centre is the *New Stanley Hotel* (☎ 333233), PO Box 30680, on the corner of Kimathi St and Kenyatta Ave. It was built in 1907 and despite numerous subsequent renovations still has a touch of colonial charm. Singles/doubles (including breakfast and taxes) cost US$79/94 plus there are suites ranging from US$100 to US$180. Facilities include a rooftop swimming pool and, at street level, the popular Thorn Tree Café, though the food is mediocre and service can be agonisingly slow.

The *Hilton Hotel*, PO Box 30624, (☎ 33-4000), on Mama Ngina St near Moi Ave, has all the usual Hilton facilities including a rooftop swimming pool yet, despite the relatively high price, some of the rooms are surprisingly gloomy and tatty. Singles here go for US$98 to US$131 and doubles for US$121 to US$168 plus taxes (30% in total). The nearby *Intercontinental Hotel* (☎ 335550), PO Box 30353, on City Hall Way, is similarly priced and was recently refurbished.

Outside the Centre A little outside of the city centre where Kenyatta Ave turns into Valley Rd is the *Panafric Hotel* (☎ 720822), PO Box 30486. Part of the Sarova Hotels chain, it's a huge, multistorey modern hotel with all the facilities you'd expect. Rooms here cost US$60/80 a single/double, plus there are more expensive suites. Prices include breakfast and all taxes.

Not far from here is the much smaller, more intimate *Lenana Mount Hotel* (☎ 71-7044), on Ralph Bunche Rd between Milimani and Lenana Rds (PO Box 40943). It's a brand new place and has singles/

doubles for US$58/75, as well as superior rooms for US$63/81 including all taxes. Breakfast costs extra.

Also outside the centre in Westlands off Waiyaki Way is the *Jacaranda Hotel* (☎ 448713), PO Box 47557, which is part of the Block Hotels chain. (For reservations, contact Rehema House (☎ 335807; fax 340541), PO Box 47667, Nairobi.) It's a pleasant place to stay and offers singles/doubles for US$50/72 with breakfast, plus there are more expensive triples and suites. Facilities include an imaginative bar, restaurant and a free shuttle bus service into the centre.

At the top of the line are two hotels: the *Norfolk Hotel* (☎ 3355422), PO Box 40064, on Harry Thuku Rd, and the *Nairobi Serena Hotel* (☎ 725111), PO Box 46302, on the edge of Central Park between Kenyatta Ave and Nyerere Rd. The Norfolk is the oldest of Nairobi's hotels – it was built in 1904 – and was *the* place to stay in the old days. It's still extremely popular among those with a taste for nostalgia and the money to spend. All the olde worlde charm has been retained despite facilities having been brought up to international standards. Singles/doubles in the main block cost US$150/160 plus there are suites for US$195 and luxury double cottages for US$290. Breakfast is not included. Meals range from US$9 (breakfast) to US$13 (lunch/dinner). The Norfolk, which is owned by Lonrho Hotels, has a popular terrace bar and restaurant.

The Nairobi Serena is a much more recent hotel and imaginatively designed. It's owned by the Serena Lodges group and has singles/doubles for US$143/175. It has all the facilities you'd expect from a five-star hotel. Even Jimmy Carter stays here.

Places to Eat

For most people with limited means, lunch is the main meal of the day and this is what the cheaper restaurants cater for. That doesn't mean that they're all closed in the evening (though quite a few are). It does mean, however, that what is available in the early evening is often what is left over from lunch time and the choice is limited. If you want a full meal in the evening it generally involves a splurge or eating from a barbecue attached to a bar.

Nairobi is replete with restaurants offering cuisines from all over the world – Italian, Spanish, Japanese, Chinese, Korean, Indian, Lebanese, and Thai. There are also steak houses, seafood specialists, etc and at many places the prices are surprisingly reasonable. For around US$8 per person you can eat well at quite a few of them. For US$10 to US$15 per person you could eat very well at almost all of them and if you spent that much at some of them you'd hardly need to eat anything the next day.

While there is a good selection of restaurants in the city centre, increasing numbers of restaurants are opening up in the suburbs, which makes it difficult if you don't have transport. The two main eating centres away from the downtown area are the Westlands shopping centre, just a km or so north of the centre along Uhuru Highway, and the new Yaya Centre, about three km from the centre on Argwings Kodhek Rd in Hurlingham.

Cheap Restaurants There are a lot of very cheap cafés and restaurants in the Latema Rd/River Rd area and at the top end of Tom Mboya St where you can pick up a very cheap, traditional African breakfast of mandazi (a semisweet doughnut) and tea or coffee. Most of these places would also be able to fix you up with eggs and the like. Since many of them are Indian-run, they also have traditional Indian breakfast foods like samosa and idli (rice dumplings) with a sauce.

For good local food the restaurant in the *Iqbal Hotel* is very popular and is something of a meeting place for travellers. The mkate mayai (minced meat pancake) is excellent, although it does come served with a curious side plate of shredded lettuce with tomato sauce! One gets the feeling that the animals and birds used in the stews here died of plain old age, but the cabbage and potato stew is very good.

The *Malindi Dishes* restaurant in Gaborone Rd is well worth trying at least once. As the name suggests, the food here has the Swahili influence of the coast, and so coconut and spices are used to rev up what is otherwise pretty ordinary cuisine. Main dishes are around US$2, and the usual snacks and burgers are also available.

Also in this area is the *New Bedona Café* opposite the Dolat Hotel on Mfangano St. The food here is mostly fried, but it's cheap and the place is kept very clean. Another ultra-cheap café which is fairly popular is the *Bull Café* around the corner from the New Kenya Lodge on Ngariama Rd.

For a good solid meal (mixing Western and local cuisine) such as steak and matoke (mashed plantains and maize) or maharagwe (kidney beans), try the *Café Helena* on Mama Ngina St opposite the City Hall. It's only open at lunch time and is popular with businesspeople. Meals are priced at around US$2 and are excellent value. The *Coffee Bar* next door is similar although more expensive. Another place at this end of town is the *Beneve Coffee House* on the corner of Standard and Koinange Sts. It has a tasty selection of instant food ranging from stews to curries, fish & chips, sambusa, pasties and a host of other choices. It's self-service and good value.

Very popular with the lunch-time business crowd and said to be one of the cheapest places in Nairobi for the quality of food it offers is the *Jacaranda Café* in the Phoenix House Arcade between Kenyatta Ave and Standard St. A hamburger, chips and salad costs just US$1.50! Similar are the ramshackle wooden eateries between the Railway Museum and Haile Selassie Ave which are jammed with local office workers in three-piece suits at lunch time. It's quite a sight!

If you're staying at Mrs Roche's up in Parklands, the *Stop 'n' Eat* tin shed just up the road offers ugali (maize meal) and ngombe (beef) at very modest prices.

Kenya is the home of all-you-can-eat lunches at a set price and Nairobi has a wide choice of them, most offering Indian food. One of the best is the *Supreme Restaurant* on River Rd, which offers excellent Indian veg-

etarian food for US$2.50 depending on whether you want the ordinary or the 'delux' lunch and whether you want dessert. It also has superb fruit juices.

In the Harambee Plaza building on the corner of Uhuru Highway and Haile Selassie Ave, the *Caboose Restaurant* does an 'African buffet' on Wednesday from 12.30 to 3 pm for US$4, while on other weekdays the usual 'businessman's buffet' costs US$3.

The *African Heritage Café*, which you reach through the African Heritage shop on Kenyatta Ave or through a separate entrance on Banda St, is also highly recommended for lunch. There are actually two parts to the restaurant – the main room adjoining Banda St which tends to be somewhat gloomy and is more expensive and the much lighter barbecue grill in the centre of the building. The food in the barbecue section is excellent and there's a choice of meat, fish or chicken which comes complete with chips and salad. Reckon on spending around US$3 for a meal. Get here early if you don't want to wait for a table as it's a popular place to eat.

The restaurant at *The Pub* underneath the Sixeighty Hotel, on Standard St between Muindi Mbingu and Koinange Sts, offers Western dishes such as steak and chicken, but at US$5 and up, these are not particularly good value. Lunch is served from noon to 2 pm and dinner from 6 to 11 pm. You can get much better value across the road at *Calypso* in the basement of Bruce House. Here you can choose from a limited set menu (which includes meat and seafood) and it won't cost you more than US$2.50. It's a popular place to eat at lunch times. Try their fish pili pili – delicious.

Another good place to go for lunch and well cooked, straightforward food is the *Harvest* on Kenyatta Ave between Koinange and Loita Sts. It's a very pleasant spot to eat.

Jax Restaurant on the 1st floor of the Old Mutual building, Kimathi St, is a very popular place for lunch. It offers a wide selection of beautifully prepared hot meals, a salad buffet and Goan specialities in various dining areas, including an open-air section. There's a licensed bar and you can eat well for US$2.50 and up. It's open from 8 am to 5 pm Monday to Friday, 8 am to 5 pm on Saturday but closed on Sunday and public holidays.

Any of the *Minar* chain of up-market Indian restaurants are a great place to head for on Sunday at lunch time as they do a US$4.50 all-you-can-eat buffet. The food is excellent, the service attentive and there's a good range of both Indian and continental dishes. There are branches on Tom Mboya and Banda Sts in the centre of town, and in the Yaya Centre (1st floor) on Argwings Kodhek Rd, Hurlingham.

Fast Food That well known English staple, fish & chips, has caught on in a big way in Nairobi and there are scores of places offering it. They're all cheap but the quality varies from grease ad nauseam to excellent.

Very popular at lunch time for fish & chips is *Supermac* on Kimathi St, directly opposite the Thorn Tree Café on the mezzanine floor of the shopping centre there. It not only offers some of the best fish & chips in Nairobi, but also serves sausages, salads and fruit juices. Get there early if you don't want to queue.

Also recommended for this type of fast food is the *Prestige Restaurant*, in Tsavo Lane off Latema Rd, which offers large servings of sausage, chips and salad for US$2. It's popular with local people.

The hamburger is all-conquering in Nairobi too, though, surprisingly, none of the US chains have got a foothold in Kenya yet. Too much competition from Indian entrepreneurs perhaps? What has got a solid foothold is the *Wimpy* chain which has branches on Kenyatta Ave, Tom Mboya St and Mondlane St. These places have the usual range of snacks and meals (burgers, sausages, eggs, fish, chicken, milkshakes, etc) costing up to US$4 and are open from 7.30 am to 9.30 pm. Another good café for a meal of burgers, fish or chicken with a mountain of chips and salad for around US$2.50 is *Nairobi Burgers* on Tom Mboya St right opposite the end of Latema Rd. Sweets, soups and ice cream are also served – it's a very popular place.

Also on Tom Mboya St, down near the Princess Hotel, is the fairly new *Pipes Restaurant*. This is a US-style fast-food place with all the usual junk-food snacks.

Breakfast The *Growers Café* on Tom Mboya St is deservedly popular with both local people and travellers and the prices are reasonable. Food on offer includes eggs (boiled or fried), sausages and other hot foods, fruit salads (with or without yoghurt) and good coffee. Another popular breakfast place is the *Honey Pot* on Moi Ave. Here a breakfast of eggs, sausages, juice, toast, jam and tea or coffee is US$1.40.

If you're staying in the Koinange St area, the *Goldstar Restaurant* on the corner of Koinange and Moktar Daddah Sts is a good place for breakfast. For US$1.40 you get juice, cornflakes, eggs, toast, jam and tea or coffee. For a little extra, you can also get bacon and a sausage. Very similar is *Calypso* in the basement of Bruce House on Standard St where you can get an English-style breakfast for the same price.

For a breakfast splurge, try one of the buffets at a major hotel. The *Illiki Café* on the ground floor of the Ambassadeur Hotel on Moi Ave is excellent value. Here you can make a total pig of yourself for US$5. It offers the works – a variety of juices, milk, yoghurt, cereals, porridge, eggs, bacon, beans, sausages, toast, fruits, cakes, you name it.

Most of the other top-end hotels also do buffet breakfasts, although they are more expensive. The best value is offered by the *New Stanley Hotel* where a buffet brekky costs US$7.20. At the *Hilton* you're looking at US$7.50 while the *Intercontinental* charges US$8 and is probably the poorest value among these places.

Mid-Range Restaurants The choice here is legion and spans just about every cuisine in the world. Most of them are mentioned in the *Kenya Tourist Guide* and *Tourists' Kenya* though there's no indication of prices.

Most of the more expensive restaurants are licensed and offer beer, wine and spirits but the major exceptions are the Indian vegetarian restaurants which usually offer only fruit juices and tea or coffee.

Virtually all these restaurants accept one or more international credit cards.

Indian One of the best places in Nairobi for North Indian tucker is the *Dhaba Restaurant* at the top end of Tom Mboya St. A lot of work and thought has gone into the décor here with some fine watercolour murals of Punjabi rural life and ceilings made of mangrove poles and plaster. It's very popular among Indian families, which is a good indication of the quality of the food. The house specialities are the taka-taka meat dishes, which take their name from the noise which comes from the tandoori kitchen as the chef prepares the meat with huge cleavers. Main dishes are in the range of US$3.80 to US$4.50, so expect a full meal to come to around US$7 per person with drinks.

The *Mayur Restaurant* (☎ 331586), above the Supreme Restaurant (see Cheap Restaurants) has been famous for superb Indian vegetarian food for years. It's not bad value at US$4.30 but the hushed atmosphere is a bit daunting. Also excellent is the *Minar Restaurant* (☎ 229999), in Banda St, which specialises in Mughlai dishes and offers buffet lunches and à la carte dinners. Expect to pay around US$8 for a three-course dinner including coffee. The restaurant is licensed, the service friendly and the restaurant is open from noon to 2 pm and 7 to 10.30 pm daily. It also has branches in Tom Mboya St and the Yaya Centre (1st floor) in Hurlingham.

The *Zam Zam Restaurant* (☎ 212128), just off Kilome Rd near the top end of River Rd, is a new place with pleasing décor and good service. The food is good, and remarkably cheap, yet this place remains relatively poorly patronised, perhaps because of its location close to River Rd. Main dishes are all under US$3 and the servings are generous.

Another good and cheap place is the *Safeer Restaurant* in the Ambassadeur Hotel. Despite appearances, this place is not expensive and two people can eat well here for US$6 including a couple of beers. The food is mainly north Indian, and there are complimentary salads, chutney and pickle.

At the Meridien Court Hotel on Muranga'a Rd near the top end of Moi Ave, the *Khyber Restaurant* (☎ 225585) also specialises in Mughlai dishes and offers a buffet lunch. Dinner choices include tandoori chicken, lamb or fish, other special lamb or chicken dishes, seafood, vegetarian dishes and the usual range of Indian breads and sweets. It's licensed and open from 12.30 to 2.30 pm and 7 to 10.30 pm daily including holidays.

West African The *West African Paradise Restaurant* (☎ 741396) is in Rank Xerox House in Westlands. It offers a wide range of food from a number of West African countries and dishes include poulet yassa (chicken with onions and garlic sauce), jollof (rice with onions), and fufu (maize). It's quite different food and is well worth a try if you haven't been to West Africa. The restaurant is open daily from 9.30 am to 9.30 pm.

Chinese Nairobi has a reasonable selection of Chinese restaurants although none of them are cheap. One of the best is the *Hong Kong Restaurant* (☎ 228612) in Kenya House on Koinange St. The soups here at US$2.50 make a meal in themselves, but if you have room for more, main dishes cost around US$2.50 to US$3. This is a surprisingly popular place, especially at lunch time and on Sunday nights.

In Shankardas House, on Moi Ave near the Kenya Cinema, is the recently renovated *Pagoda Restaurant* (☎ 227936). Again, the food here is mainly Szechuan, and you can expect a complete meal to come to around US$8 with drinks.

The *Dragon Pearl* (☎ 340451), in Bruce House on Standard St, also has good Chinese food at prices comparable to the other more expensive restaurants.

Rated as the best Chinese restaurant in town by residents is the *Rickshaw Chinese Restaurant* (☎ 223604), in Fedha Towers, Standard St. It has an extensive menu and the food is delicious. Prices are comparable with the other Chinese restaurants.

Mongolian The only place you'll find this cuisine is at the *Manchurian Restaurant* (☎ 444263), Brick Court, on the corner of Mpak Rd and Brookside Drive in Westlands. Here you choose from a range of marinated meats, vegetables, condiments and spices and have your meal cooked in front of you on giant hot-plates. Leaving out drinks, the price is standard and you can go back as many times as you like for more of the same or something else so don't pile everything onto the first plate!

Thai Nairobi's first Thai restaurant is in the Westlands shopping centre, just a few minutes' north of the city centre along Uhuru Highway. The *Bangkok Restaurant* (☎ 75-1311), Rank Xerox House, Parklands Rd, has a good reputation and is open daily from 12.30 to 2.30 pm and 6 to 10.30 pm.

Italian For Italian food there is the long-running and very popular *Trattoria* (☎ 340855) on the corner of Wabera and Kaunda Sts. It is open daily from 8.30 am to 11.30 pm and both the atmosphere and the food are excellent. There's a wide choice on the menu and à la carte is available at lunch time. In the evening, it's all à la carte. A soup, main course, salad, dessert and a carafe or two of house chianti will relieve you of around US$10 per person. As you might expect, the ice cream here is superb.

Also good is the *Capolinea* in The Mall shopping centre at Westlands. This is more of a café-style place, and this is reflected in the prices – around US$1.50 to US$3 for snacks and sandwiches. Another excellent place away from the centre is the *La Cucina* (☎ 562871) in the Yaya Centre in Hurlingham. It has everything from pasta to steak, home delivery is available, and there's an attached wine bar.

Also worth a try is the *Marino Restaurant* (☎ 227150), 1st Floor, National Housing Corporation Bldg, Aga Khan Walk, just off Haile Selassie Ave. It has a spacious interior

dining area as well as an open-air patio and is open from 9 am to 2 pm and 7 to 10 pm Monday to Saturday; closed on Sunday. There's a wide range of Italian and continental dishes available with main courses priced from US$3 to US$5.

The best of the lot by far, and marginally the most expensive, is the *Foresta Magnetica* (☎ 728009) on the 1st floor of Corner House, at the junction of Mama Ngina and Kimathi Sts. The food here is delicious and beautifully presented plus there's a live band each evening which plays a mixture of Western and African music and, when the majority of people have finished eating, you are free to dance. Check it out by having a drink at the Picino Bar (in the centre of the restaurant) first. A meal will set you back US$10 to US$20 per person depending on whether you have wine. It's open daily until 2 am except on Sunday.

Greek The *Spyros Wine Bar & Taverna* (☎ 750202) is out of the centre in Brick Court, Mpaka Rd, Westlands. It's not cheap, but there's often live entertainment, and plenty of authentic touches, including retsina – at US$15 a bottle!

At the Yaya Centre in Hurlingham there's the *Sugar & Spice (Zorba the Treat)* (☎ 562876), which is a much more modest place serving a wide variety of snacks.

Japanese There's one Japanese restaurant in the city centre, the *Akasaka* (☎ 333948), which you'll find next to The Pub on Standard St between Koinange and Muindi Mbingu Sts. As you might expect, it's done out in traditional Japanese style and there's even a tatami room which you can reserve in advance though mostly it's table and chairs. It offers the full range of Japanese cuisine including tempura, teriyaki and sukiyaki as well as soups and appetisers. A full meal will cost US$6 to US$10 per person. It's licensed and open daily from 12.30 to 2 pm for box lunches, and from 6 to 9 pm for dinner.

Korean The only Korean restaurant in Nairobi is the *Restaurant Koreana* in the

Yaya Centre, Hurlingham. A full meal costs around US$12 and the restaurant is licensed. It's open from noon to 2.30 pm and 6 to 10.30 pm Monday to Saturday and closed Sunday.

Ethiopian The *Daas* Ethiopian restaurant is in an old house, some distance from the centre off Ngong Rd (signposted) and not far from the Adams Arcade shopping centre. The décor includes many Ethiopian artefacts and there's often live music in the evenings. Meals are based around excellent unleavened bread and are eaten with the fingers. Expect to pay around US$6 per person for a full meal including drinks.

Seafood The best seafood restaurant in Nairobi is the *Tamarind* (☎ 338959) in the National Bank building on Aga Khan Walk, between Harambee and Haile Selassie Aves. It offers a wide selection of exotic seafood dishes, and culinary influences range from European to Asian to coastal Swahili. The cuisine is superb as are the surroundings which are decorated in a sumptuous Arabic-Moorish style. Eating here is definitely a major night out as most main courses are priced well over US$7.50 with crab and prawn dishes up to US$15. There's also a special vegetarian menu. It's open for lunch Monday to Saturday from 12.30 to 1.45 pm and daily for dinner from 6.30 to 9.45 pm.

Western The best restaurant for plain meat and vegie dishes (eg sausages and mashed potato) is the *Zanze Bar* (☎ 222532) on the top floor of the Kenya Cinema Plaza, Moi Ave, though a range of other dishes are also available. It's open for lunch and dinner daily but is not strictly a restaurant alone – more a combination of bar, wine bar, live music venue and restaurant. You can also play chess, darts and backgammon here. The food is good, reasonably priced (around US$3 per person), but you must pay an extra US$2.20 entry in the evenings (free during the day).

Nyama Choma For steak eaters who haven't seen a decent doorstep since they left Argentina, Australia, Uruguay or the USA and are looking for a gut-busting extravaganza then there's no better place than the *Carnivore* (☎ 501709), out at Langata just past Wilson Airport. To get there take bus Nos 14, 24 or 124 and tell the conductor where you are going; the restaurant is a one-km signposted walk from where you are dropped off. It's easy to hitch back into the centre when you're ready to go. Otherwise, negotiate for a taxi. Whether it's lunch or dinner you take there's always beef, pork, lamb, ham, chicken, sausages and at least one game meat (often wildebeest or zebra). The roasts are barbecued on Maasai spears and the waiters carve off hunks onto your plate until you tell them that you have enough. Prices include salads, bread, desserts and coffee. Meals here can be surprisingly cheap given the amount you receive and you're looking at US$11 for lunch from Monday to Saturday and US$13 on Sunday; dinner is priced at US$13 daily. This is a very popular tourist restaurant and the car park is usually overflowing with tourist buses.

For something a little less extravagant there's the *Nyama Choma Terrace & Bar*, above the Dhaba Restaurant at the top end of Tom Mboya St. This is a great little place which has nyama choma as well as a number of other Kenyan dishes, and it's dirt cheap.

Highly rated by residents, particularly Africans, is the nyama choma at the *Sagret Hotel*, Milimani Rd. Any day of the week you pass here, you'll see clouds of delicious-smelling smoke rising from the restaurant. The food is OK, relatively cheap and there's usually a good crowd.

For authentic, no-frills Nairobi nyama choma the only place to go is the suburb of Kilmichael, some distance from the centre out past Pangani and Eastleigh. It's certainly not for the squeamish as the goats are slaughtered only a few metres away from where you eat and are then barbecued right in front of you, but there's no doubting the freshness of the meat! This is not a place to go to alone, however, as the people here are not used to seeing *wazungu* and while it's not threatening, it's best to be in the company of a reliable Kenyan. You probably wouldn't find it on your own anyway. There are African prices, as you might expect.

Entertainment

Cinema Nairobi is a good place to take in a few films and at a price substantially lower than what you'd pay back home, but if you don't want scratched films then go to one of the better cinemas such as *The Kenya* on Moi Ave, or *The Nairobi* or *20th Century* on Mama Ngina St. The cheaper ones are on Latema Rd and include the *Odeon* and *Embassy*. There are also two good drive-ins if you have the transport, both have snack bars and bars. Nairobi is also a good place to see an Indian film. If you've never seen one of these then treat yourself one evening. If you have seen them before, you won't need persuading! Check with local papers to see what's on.

Discos There's a good selection of discos in the centre of Nairobi. Single men may or may not find the attention of the many unattached women found in most of them to be exactly what they're looking for but there's never any pressure other than the occasional request for a drink.

Perhaps the most popular disco in the centre of town is the *Florida 2000* on Moi Ave near City Hall Way. Entry costs US$2.20 for men (US$2.70 on Saturday) and half that for women and it's open until 6 am. Also very popular is the *New Florida* (known to resident expatriates as the 'Mad House'), on the corner of Koinange and Banda Sts, which is a most unusually shaped building above a petrol station! Entry charges are the same as the Florida 2000 and it stays open until 5 am. There are floor shows at about 1 am at both discos but they're pretty kitsch and the dancers are obviously bored. Both discos have bars separate from the main disco areas where you can sit down, escape the noise and order a quiet drink, a snack or a meal.

Another popular disco in the centre is *Visions* on Kimathi St which is open daily except Monday from 9 pm. Less popular but probably just as good is the *Hollywood* on

Moktar Daddah St between Koinange and Muindi Mbingu Sts where the entry charges are the same as the above. Further out of town is *Bubbles* at the International Casino, Westlands Rd, just off Uhuru Highway.

There's a live band/disco every Wednesday night at the *Carnivore* in Langata but entry costs US$3 per person. There's usually a good crowd and it makes a refreshing change from the more enclosed and crowded space of the New Florida or the Florida 2000 in town.

Beer in all these places is reasonably priced but other drinks, especially imported liquors, are more expensive. Snacks are available at all of them.

There don't appear to be any rigid dress regulations at any of the discos. Joggers and jeans are quite acceptable as are clean T-shirts, though it's probably true to say that most men wear open-necked shirts and trousers and the local women are always well turned out. Don't turn up wearing grubby clothes – you will not be well received.

Live Music The *African Heritage Café* on Banda St is a popular place to hear live bands on Saturday and Sunday afternoons between 2 and 5 pm. There's a small cover charge.

Also in town, in the next block to the Florida 2000 on Moi Ave and on the top floor of the Kenya Cinema Plaza, is the *Zanze Bar*, which has live music most nights. This bar was extremely popular when it first opened, but with a change of management and the introduction of a US$2.20 cover charge its popularity plummeted. To get the most out of this place, go in a group. Drinks are reasonably priced and the toilets (extremely clean) still have a blackboard on which you can scrawl jokes or obscenities.

Much further out of town, just below the roundabout at Dagoretti Corner on Ngong Rd, is the *Bombax Club* which has live bands every Thursday, Friday, Saturday and Sunday night. Unlike many of the other discos and bars mentioned in this section, this one is frequented mainly by local Kenyans with only a sprinkling of Whites, but the atmosphere is very friendly and convivial. Again, there's a small cover charge. To get there, take a minibus or matatu to Dagoretti Corner from Kenyatta Ave outside Nyayo House, or share a taxi (about US$4).

Bars The *Thorn Tree Café* in the New Stanley Hotel on the corner of Kimathi St and Kenyatta Ave is a bit passé these days but is still something of a meeting place for travellers. The service is generally supercilious and snail-like in pace. Perhaps this is just a ploy by the management to discourage 'shabby' travellers who might lower the tone of the place. Whatever the case, if you sit down between 11 am and 2 pm and 5 and 7 pm for a drink you'll have to order something to eat as well. The best thing about the Thorn Tree is the notice board where you can leave personal messages (but not advertisements of any kind, such as things for sale, or a request for people to join a safari).

Another popular bar (where you don't have to buy a meal in order to have a beer) is *The Pub* on Standard St between Koinange and Muindi Mbingu Sts. It's designed to resemble an English pub (in which it fails miserably) and the beer fridge is a museum piece which rarely has the full range of Kenya Breweries products. Nevertheless, it attracts a remarkable cross section of the population, including people from the British High Commission opposite. It's open from 11 am to 11 pm daily. If you're a single man looking for some action, there are usually plenty of unattached women but it does vary from day to day. That doesn't mean it's solely a pick-up joint – you'll see quite a few businessmen downing a quick beer or three at lunch time. The Pub is part of the Sixeighty Hotel which has another open-air bar, the *Terrace Bar*, on the 1st floor above the entrance lobby.

The liveliest bar in Nairobi by far, however, is *Buffalo Bill's* at the Heron Court Hotel, Milimani Rd. It even got a three-paragraph mention in the National Geographic magazine in May 1990 in an article describing the Rift Valley. Decked out with mock, denim-covered wagons surrounding a central bar and recently taken over by a resilient Frenchman (Fabrice), it's extremely popular with a wide variety of resident expatriates (who are engaged in all manner of professions), tourists, and locals. It's *the* place to go if you're single, but just as much fun for a couple. While it's open all day, every day, until around 11 pm, it only livens up from about 5.30 pm onwards. Most of the women you see here migrate to the Florida 2000 once the bar closes. Meals and snacks are available throughout the day up until around 11 pm. (It's also here that the familiar Nairobi refrain, 'Just imagine! No problem!' originated. You'll undoubtedly meet the originators: Margaret Zemei, 'Cutie' and Gladys.) This is also one of the favourite bars of safari operators in Nairobi.

For an unparalleled spit-and-sawdust binge, put aside a whole evening to join the beer-swilling, garrulous hordes at the *Modern Green Day & Night Bar*, on Latema Rd next to the Sunrise Lodge. This place rages 24 hours a day, 365 days a year and the front door has never been closed since 1968 – except for one day in 1989 during a national census. All human life is here and you need stamina to survive it – teenage girls chewing *miraa* (stimulating leafy twigs and shoots), hustlers, whores, dope dealers and what one traveller once described as 'lowlife Whites'. The jukebox is always on full blast with screaming Indian vocalists or African reggae and the bar is completely encased in heavy duty wire mesh with a tiny hole through which money goes first and beer comes out afterwards. It's a great night out but is definitely not for the squeamish. The back bar is quieter and you're more likely to meet someone whose brains are intact, but this cannot be guaranteed. Beers are always warm.

There are plenty of other African bars which are not quite so wearing on the average person's sensibilities but are still African bars where you're unlikely to see another White. People here are generally very friendly but, in terms of getting back home, it's probably best you go along with a Kenyan friend. Try *Disneys* or the *Heathrow* along Juja Rd, Pangani.

Those looking for more genteel surroundings in which to sip their beer could try the *Ngong Hills Hotel* on Ngong Rd, the beer gardens at the *Boulevard* or *Jacaranda* hotels, or the terrace bar at the *Norfolk Hotel*. Be wary of going for a drink at either the *Big Five* (Intercontinental Hotel) or the *Jockey Club* (Hilton Hotel) unless you have money to burn. At the former, a beer costs US$2.80 (3½ times the normal price).

Theatre At the *Phoenix Theatre*, Parliament Rd, the auditorium is small and the acting professionally competent but it's quite expensive. Check with local papers to see what's on.

Things to Buy

Nairobi is a good place to pick up souvenirs although you do need to shop around. The City Market on Muindi Mbingu St has a good range of items, particularly kiondo baskets, and there's a whole gaggle of stalls in Kigali St behind the Jamia Mosque. It's all a bit of a tourist trap and you need to bargain fiercely.

Even though they originated in Tanzania (and they're still much cheaper there), makonde woodcarvings have caught on in a big way in Nairobi and the shops are full of them. At the cheaper end of the market, however, it's worth looking at the examples which hawkers bring around to the bars where tourists congregate. Buffalo Bill's at the Heron Court Hotel is one of the best places. The quality of the carving varies a lot, but if you're not in a hurry then you can find some really fine examples at bargain-basement prices. Expect to pay around half to two-thirds of the price first asked.

If you're not into bargaining, or want top-quality stuff, there are plenty of 'fixed-price' souvenir shops around, although even at these they'll usually give you a 'special price' if you are obviously not a Hilton hopper. One of the better shops is on the corner of Kaunda and Wabera Sts, and another on Tubman Rd near the corner of Muindi Mbingu St.

If you want to get kitted out in the latest designer 'White hunter' safari gear, there are literally dozens of shops selling all the requisite stuff at outrageous prices.

The Spinners Web describes itself as a 'consignment handicraft shop' which sells goods made in workshops and by self-help groups around the country. They have some superb items, including hand-knitted jumpers, all sorts of fabrics and the huge Turkana baskets. The shop is on Kijabe Rd, around the corner from the Norfolk Hotel.

The gift shop of the East African Wildlife Society in the arcade of the Hilton Hotel has a range of souvenirs and interesting knick-knacks, many of them with an animal theme. It's well worth shopping here as the proceeds go towards conserving Kenya's wildlife rather than to conserving the lifestyle of rich Kenyans.

For a much less touristy atmosphere try the Kariokor Market east of the centre on Racecourse Rd in Eastleigh. It's a few minutes' ride by bus.

Getting There & Away

Air Airlines with offices in Nairobi include:

Aeroflot
    Corner House, Mama Ngina St (☎ 220746)
Air Botswana
    Hilton Hotel (☎ 331648)
Air France
    Fedha Towers, Muindi Mbingu (☎ 217512)
Air India
    Bharati House, Harambee Ave (☎ 334788)
Air Madagascar
    Hilton Hotel (☎ 225286)
Air Malawi
    Sixeighty Hotel, Muindi Mbingu St (☎ 333683)
Air Mauritius
    Union Towers, Moi Ave (☎ 229166/7)
Air Rwanda
    Mama Ngina St (☎ 332225)
Air Tanzania
    Chester House, Koinange St (☎ 336224)
Air Zaïre
    Arrow Motors, Monrovia St (☎ 222271)
Air Zimbabwe
    Chester House, Koinange St (☎ 339522)
Alitalia
    Hilton Hotel (☎ 224362)
British Airways
    International House, Mama Ngina St (☎ 334362)

EgyptAir
  Hilton Arcade (☎ 227887)
El-Al Airlines
  KCS House, Mama Ngina St (☎ 228123)
Ethiopian Airlines
  Bruce House, Standard St (☎ 330837)
Gulf Air
  International House, Mama Ngina St (☎ 214444)
Iberia Airlines
  Hilton Hotel (☎ 331648)
Japan Airlines (JAL)
  International House, Mama Ngina St (☎ 220591)
Kenya Airways
  Nationwide House, Koinange St (☎ 229271)
KLM
  Fedha Towers, Muindi Mbingu St (☎ 332673)
Lignes Aerienne (Seychelles)
  Rehema House (☎ 340481)
Lufthansa
  IPS Bldg, Kimathi St (☎ 335819)
Olympic Airways
  Hilton Hotel (☎ 338026)
Pakistan International Airlines (PIA)
  ICEA Bldg, Banda St (☎ 333900)
Qantas Airways
  Rehema House, Kaunda St (☎ 213221)
Sabena
  International House, Mama Ngina St (☎ 222185)
South African Airways
  Lonrho House, Standard St (☎ 229663)
Sudan Airlines
  UTC Bldg, General Kago St (☎ 225129)
Swissair
  Corner House, Kimathi St (☎ 331012)
Uganda Airlines
  Uganda House, Kenyatta Ave (☎ 221354)
Zambia Airways
  Lonrho House, Standard St (☎ 224722)

Kenya Airways is the main domestic carrier and operates from Nairobi's Jomo Kenyatta International Airport. There are 10 flights weekly to Kisumu (USS$44 one way), 14 flights weekly to Malindi (US$65 one way) and 55 flights weekly to Mombasa (US$65 one way). Fares and can be paid either in US dollars or in local currency (it makes them considerably cheaper if you pay in the latter).

Make sure you reconfirm flights 48 hours before departure and remember that delays are frequent on Kenya Airways.

There are several private aviation companies operating light aircraft which also connect Nairobi with Mombasa, Malindi, Lamu, Nanyuki, Nyeri, Kisumu and the

national parks/reserves of Amboseli, Masai Mara, Samburu and Kiwayu (north of Lamu). These airlines also normally connect Nairobi with Eldoret and Turkana but these services are temporarily suspended. The companies include Eagle Aviation, Prestige Air Services and Air Kenya Aviation. They all operate out of Wilson Airport. There's generally at least one flight a day to each of the above destinations (except to Kiwayu which depends on demand) by each one of these companies. The services to the national parks would, of course, depend on you having a pre-booked safari (and accommodation) which included being picked up from the airstrip at an agreed time.

Let's Go Travel (☎ 340331) prints a leaflet with most of the options and prices and though it's not totally comprehensive it's worth getting hold of a copy. One-way fares to the various destinations from Nairobi are: Mombasa or Malindi (US$45), Lamu (US$112), Kiwayu (US$150), Nanyuki or Nyeri (US$63), Amboseli (US$65), Masai Mara (US$83) and Samburu (US$97). Baggage allowance is 15 kg and excess is charged at the rate of approximately US$1 per kg.

Bus In Nairobi most long-distance bus offices are along Accra Rd near the River Rd junction. For Mombasa there are numerous companies (such as Coast Bus, Akamba, Mawingo, Goldline and Malaika) doing the run, both by day and night. They all cost around US$5, give or take US$0.50 or so, and the trip takes around eight hours with a meal break on the way.

Akamba is probably the biggest company in the country and also has the most extensive network. If you must travel by bus, it's probably the safest and most reliable company. The office is conveniently located on Lagos Rd, just off Latema Rd and very close to Tom Mboya St. Apart from the Mombasa service, it also has daily connections to Isiolo, Nyeri, Nanyuki, Chogoria, Embu and Kisumu. If you're heading for Uganda there is a daily Akamba bus direct to Kampala. It leaves Nairobi at 7.30 pm and arrives in Kampala at 10 am; the fare is US$15.

The main country bus station is just off Landies Rd, about 15 minutes' walk from the budget hotel area around Latema Rd. It's a huge but reasonably well-organised place, and all the buses have their destinations displayed in the window so it's just a matter of wandering around and finding the one you want. There is at least one daily departure and often more to virtually every main town in the country, and the buses leave when full. For more details see Getting There & Away for each place.

Train Trains run from Nairobi to Mombasa every day in both directions at 5 and 7 pm and the journey takes about 13 hours. The fares on the 7 pm train are US$40 in 1st class and US$26 in 2nd class. The 5 pm train fares are slightly less.

The 7 pm train prices are for nonresidents and include dinner, breakfast and bedding (whether you want them or not – no discount if you don't want them). The corresponding fares for residents are US$28 (1st class), US$19 (2nd class) but these do not include meals and bedding. (Meals cost an extra US$3 for dinner, US$1.80 for breakfast and bedding is US$0.70.)

This is a popular run so book your tickets as far in advance as possible, although you shouldn't have any trouble a day or two before. There's also a 'deluxe' day train on Saturday at 7 am arriving in Mombasa at 8.15 pm. On Sunday it does the return from Mombasa. The fares are the same as on the 7 pm night train.

From Nairobi to the Ugandan border at Malaba there are trains on Tuesday, Friday and Saturday at 3 pm arriving at 8.30 am the next day. In the opposite direction they depart Malaba on Wednesday, Saturday and Sunday at 4 pm and arrive at 9.30 am the next day. The fares are US$22 in 1st class, US$12.50 in 2nd class and US$4.80 in 3rd class. En route to Malaba these trains go through Naivasha, Nakuru (US$7.50/4.30 in 1st/2nd class, US$1.50 3rd class), Eldoret (US$14.50/8.40) and Bungoma.

The Nairobi to Kisumu trains depart daily at 6 pm arriving at Kisumu at 8 am the next day. In the opposite direction they depart daily at 6.30 pm arriving at Nairobi at 7.35 am the next day. Depending on demand there is usually an additional train ('express') at 5.30 pm from Nairobi daily for the first week of every month (and sometimes for the second week too) which arrives at Kisumu at 6.40 am the next day. The fares are US$15 in 1st class, US$8.70 in 2nd class and US$3.10 in 3rd class. This is also a popular route and the train is often booked out weeks in advance. If that's the case you may have to rely on the extra coach which is added on the day of departure if demand warrants. Many of the carriages used on the Kisumu run are older than those used on the Nairobi to Mombasa run and are not as comfortable.

The booking office at Nairobi railway station (☎ 335160) is open from 8 am to 7 pm daily. Meals and bedding must be ordered and paid for at the time of buying your ticket, not on the train. See Kenya's Getting Around chapter for full details of meal prices.

Nairobi railway station also has a left-luggage office which is open daily from 8 am to noon and 1 to 6.30 pm. It costs US$1 per item per day.

Share-Taxi This is a good alternative to that dangerous and heart-stopping mode of transport – the matatu. Although you're still likely to be whisked along at breakneck speed, at least it will be in a vehicle that is not carrying twice its rated capacity and has at least a sporting chance of stopping in a hurry if the need arises. Share-taxis are usually Peugeot 504 station wagons which take seven passengers and leave when full. They are much quicker than the matatus as they go from point to point without stopping, and of course are more expensive. Again, most of the companies have their offices around the Accra and River Rds area.

DPS on Dubois Rd has daily Peugeots to Kisumu (US$8, four hours), Busia (US$11.50), Kakamega (US$9.50), Nakuru (US$7.50, two hours), Malaba on the

Ugandan border (US$12), Kitale (US$11.50), and Kericho (US$7.50). On any of these services you pay an extra US$0.60 for the front seat. These departures are only in the mornings so you need to be at the office by around 7 am, and it's a good idea to book one day in advance.

Taxis for the Tanzanian border at Namanga leave from the top side of the service station on the corner of Ronald Ngala St and River Rd. They run throughout the day, take about two hours and cost US$6. (A matatu along the same route is cheaper but takes about three hours.) These days, however, most people prefer to take either a bus direct from Nairobi to Arusha, or a shuttle minibus. The Arusha Express bus leaves daily at 8.30 am and 2 pm (US$5.70) from its office on Accra Rd. The DHL shuttle minibus leaves daily at 8.30 am (US$17) and can be booked through a travel agency. Both of these take about five hours and save a lot of messing about at the border.

Car All the major companies, and many smaller ones, have offices in the city centre, and the bigger ones such as Avis and Hertz have desks at the airport. A comprehensive description of car hire, and a list of companies, can be found in Kenya's Getting Around chapter.

If you just want to hire a car for use in Nairobi and the immediate environs, try Rent a Beetle, 7th Floor, Finance House, Loita St, PO Box 60157, Nairobi (☎ 338041/5). Ask for Don Cornes or Margaret. Here you can rent a VW Beetle for just US$24 per day with 250 km free. Insurance is optional provided the hirer signs a waiver accepting liability in the event of an accident. It's the cheapest you'll find.

Hitching For Mombasa, take bus Nos 13 or 109 as far as the airport turn-off and hitch from there. For Nakuru and Kisumu, take bus No 23 from the Hilton to the end of its route and hitch from there. Otherwise start from the junction of Chiromo Rd and Waiyaki Way (the extension of Uhuru Highway) in Westlands. For Nanyuki and Nyeri take bus Nos 45 or 145 from the central bus station up Thika Rd to the entrance to Kenyatta College and hitch from there. Make sure you get off the bus at the college entrance and not the exit. It's very difficult to hitch from the latter. Otherwise, start from the roundabout where Thika Rd meets Forest and Muranga'a Rds.

Getting Around
To/From the Airport The Jomo Kenyatta International Airport is 15 km out of town off the road to Mombasa. The cheapest way of getting into town is on the city bus No 34 *but* (and this is a big but) you must keep your wits about you! The number of people who

---

Creative Parking

Though the wildlife parks may be Kenya's premier tourist attraction, it's worth strolling around Kenya's other park – Nairobi's kerbsides – to observe the imaginative and often unbelievable way in which drivers utilise every inch of space to park their frequently scratched and battered vehicles. It's virtually impossible to find a spot to park in central Nairobi any day during business hours except Sunday so if there's the slightest possibility of parking another vehicle between two others in any way whatsoever then someone is going to do it! This is often at 90˚ to the adjoining cars with no thought about what happens to either the front or back ends. Neither pavements nor parking meters are any impediment to these people or the danger of having either end wiped out by either harrassed pedestrians or kamikaze KBS bus drivers. If there's simply not an inch to spare that's just too bad and double parking becomes the order of the day. How you get a car out of this miasma is your problem – not that of the people who've boxed you in.

Parking wardens there certainly are, as well as fines for 'illegal' parking but the deterrent effect of them is minimal and, in any case, always negotiable to a degree.

The best areas to view this spectacle are between Kenyatta Ave and University Way and anywhere between Tom Mboya St and the Nairobi River. ■

get ripped off on this bus doesn't bear thinking about. The usual story is that an 'instant crowd' forms, you are jostled and before you know it your bag or money pouch has been slashed or ripped off. It's not much of an introduction to Kenya to lose your valuables on the first day so take the airlines bus if you are at all hesitant. There is generally no problem catching the No 34 city bus to the airport. The fare is US\$0.30 and the trip takes about 45 minutes, more in peak periods.

A safer and far more pleasant way of getting into town is the Kenya Airways bus. This leaves the airline's city terminus on Koinange St at 7, 8, 9, 10 and 11.30 am, and 12.45, 2.30, 4.45, 6.30 and 8 pm. The trip takes about 30 minutes and costs US\$1.40. When coming in from the airport this bus will drop you at any of the hotels in the centre, which is great if you're jetlagged.

The third way to or from the airport is by taxi, and this is really the only option if you have a dawn or late-night flight. The standard fare is US\$9. If you want to share a taxi to the airport, check out the notice boards at the Iqbal and the New Kenya Lodge.

To Wilson Airport (for light aircraft to Malindi, Lamu, etc) take bus Nos 14, 24 or 124 from in front of Development House, Moi Ave, and elsewhere. The fare is US\$0.10.

Bus Buses are the cheapest way of getting around Nairobi, but there is no great need to use them. The only ones you are likely to need are the No 34 to the airport and those mentioned in the Around Nairobi section. Forget about them in rush hours if you have a backpack – you'll never get on and if by some Herculean feat you manage to do that, you'll never get off!

Taxi Other than the fleet of brand new London cabs (which belong to the son of the most prominent politician in the country), Nairobi taxis rate as some of the most dilapidated and generally unroadworthy buckets of bolts that ever graced a city street. Taxis cannot usually be hailed on the street (because they don't cruise for passengers)

but there are taxi ranks at the railway station, the National Museum, the City Market and outside most of the main hotels. At night, you'll find them outside bars and the nightclubs. The cabs are not metered but the fares charged are remarkably standard and few cabbies attempt to overcharge, though they're reluctant to give change if it's KSh 10 or less; US\$2 gets you just about anywhere within the city centre. The same would be true from Ralph Bunche or Milimani Rd to the main post office though they sometimes ask for a bit more as it involves backtracking down the other side of Haile Selassie Ave.

Outside this immediate area, the fare generally goes up to US\$3.50.

Around Nairobi

NAIROBI NATIONAL PARK

This park is the most accessible of all Kenya's game parks, being only a few km from the city centre. You should set aside a morning or an afternoon to see it. As in all the game parks, you must visit it in a vehicle; walking is prohibited. This means you will either have to arrange a lift at the entrance gate with other tourists, go on a tour, or hire a car. Entry to the park costs the usual US\$12 per person plus US\$1.50 for a vehicle.

Nairobi National Park is the oldest park in the country, having been created in 1946. For a park so close to the city centre you can see an amazing variety of animals – with a backdrop of jumbo jets coming in to land at Jomo Kenyatta International Airport which is adjacent to the park! Gazelle, oryx, lions, zebras, giraffes, buffaloes, cheetahs and leopards are all seen regularly. Elephants are not found in this park as the habitat is unsuitable. However, it's in this park that you have one of the best chances for spotting a rhino – they are doing quite well here because poachers prefer more remote areas.

The concentrations of game are higher in the dry season when water sources outside the park have dried up. Water is more plen-

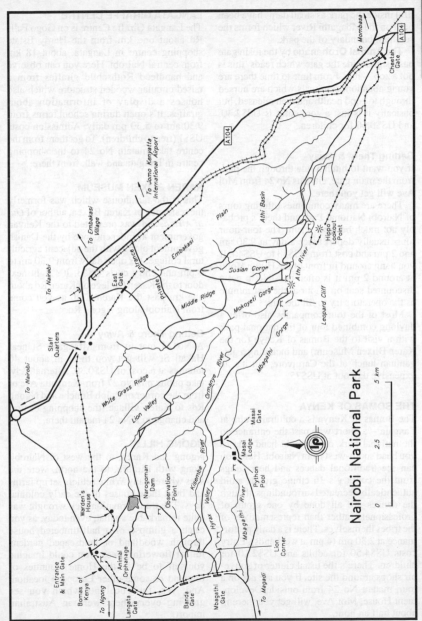

Nairobi National Park

5 km

2.5

To Mombasa

A104

Cheetah Gate

To Jomo Kenyatta International Airport

To Embakasi Village

Athi Basin

Plain

Hippo Lookout Point

Athi River

East Gate

Embakasi

Entrance

Sosian Gorge

Private

Middle Ridge

Mokoyeti Gorge

Leopard Cliff

To Nairobi

Staff Quarters

White Grass Ridge

Lion Valley

Athi River

Ormanye River

Mbagathi Gorge

To Nairobi

Warden's House

Narogoman Dam

Observation Point

Kisembe River

Hyrax Valley

Masai Gate

Masai Lodge

Python Pool

Mbagathi River

Lion Corner

Bomas of Kenya

Entrance & Main Gate

Animal Orphanage

Langata Gate

Banda Gate

Mbagathi Gate

To Ngong

To Magadi

tiful inside the park as small dams have been built on the Mbagathi River which forms the southern boundary of the park.

The **Animal Orphanage** by the main gate has a sign inside the gate which reads 'this is not a zoo' – it is. From time to time there are young abandoned animals which are nursed through to good health and then released, but basically it is just a zoo; entry is US$2.40, and US$0.60 for children.

Getting There & Away
If you want to hitch a ride through the park from the main gate, city bus No 24 from Moi Ave will get you there.

There are many companies offering tours of Nairobi National Park and there's probably not much between them. The four-hour tours usually depart twice a day at 9.30 am and 2 pm and cost from US$33 to US$40. If you hang around in front of the Hilton Hotel at around 2 pm it is often possible to get a discounted seat on a tour at the last minute as the operators try to fill the van.

Most of the tour companies also offer a daylong combined tour of the national park with a visit to the Bomas of Kenya (or the Karen Blixen Museum) and including a gargantuan lunch at the Carnivore, but it's an expensive day out at US$75.

THE BOMAS OF KENYA
The Bomas of Kenya is a cultural centre at Langata – a short way past the entrance to the national park on the right-hand side as you head south-west from Nairobi. Here you can see traditional dances and hear songs from the country's 16 ethnic groups amid authentically recreated surroundings, though the dances are all done by one group of professionals rather than representatives of the tribes themselves. There is a daily performance at 2.30 pm (4 pm at weekends). Entry costs US$4.50 for adults and US$2.10 for children. There's the usual clutter of souvenir shops around the site. If you are not on a tour, matatu No 24 from outside Development House, Moi Ave, will get you there in about half an hour.

LANGATA GIRAFFE CENTRE
The Langata Giraffe Centre is on Gogo Falls Rd about one km from the Hardy Estate shopping centre in Langata, about 18 km from central Nairobi. Here you can observe and handfeed Rothschild giraffes from a raised circular wooden structure which also houses a display of information about giraffes. It's open during school terms from 9.30 am to 5.30 pm daily. Admission costs US$1 (free to children). To get there from the centre take matatu No 24 to the shopping centre in Langata and walk from there.

KAREN BLIXEN MUSEUM
This is the farmhouse which was formerly the residence of Karen Blixen, author of *Out of Africa*, and was presented to the Kenyan government at independence by the Danish government along with the adjacent agricultural college. It's open daily from 9.30 am to 6 pm and entry costs US$3. It's right next door to the Karen College on Karen Rd about one km past the Karen Club as you come from Nairobi along Ngong Rd.

Getting There & Away
A No 24 matatu from Mfangano St near Hakati St will get you there in about 40 minutes at a cost of US$0.30. Alternatively, take public bus No 27 from Kenyatta Ave or from the corner of Ralph Bunche and Ngong Rds to Karen village (the shopping centre) and change to a No 24 matatu there.

NGONG HILLS
Ngong and Karen, to the west of Nairobi, along with Limuru, to the north, were the sites where many White settlers set up farms and built their houses in the early colonial days. The transformation they wrought was quite remarkable so that, even today, as you catch a glimpse of a half-timbered house through woodland or landscaped gardens full of flowering trees, you could imagine yourself to be in the Home Counties of England or some other European location. And, yes, the eucalypts which you see growing everywhere were an Australian import.

There are some excellent views over Nairobi and down into the Rift Valley from various points in the Ngong Hills, but it's unwise to go wandering around alone as people have been mugged here, especially at weekends. What you really need to get a feel for these areas is your own car or, alternatively, that of a resident who is willing to drive you around the place.

Horse riding is also available at Karen at a cost of US$30. Contact Let's Go Travel (☎ 340331) in Nairobi for details.

Ngong Races

Every second Sunday for most of the year there's horse racing at the Ngong Racecourse. It's a very genteel day out, and with an entry fee of US$1.10 for the members' enclosure or just US$0.30 in the public enclosure, it's hardly going to break the bank. There's betting with the bookies or the tote, and while the odds you get are hardly going to set the world on fire, it's great fun to have a punt. You can bet as little as US$0.30 so even the most impecunious should be able to afford a flutter.

Local cynics will tell you that, like everything else in the country, all the races are rigged. It may well be true, but it hardly seems to matter. There's a good restaurant on the ground floor of the grandstand and two bars with beer at regular bar prices. If you don't have transport back to town it's easy enough to find a lift if you talk to people in the members' enclosure. Bus or matatu No 24 from the city centre goes right past the racecourse to the Karen shopping centre.

Places to Stay

There's nowhere to stay in this area of Nairobi but there is an excellent place to eat and drink. This is the *Horseman* (☎ 882033) at Karen village on Langata Rd. Here you have a choice of three restaurants (two open air and one indoors) and a very popular bar (with draught beer) all set in a leafy compound complete with its own pond and croaking frogs. It's straight out of rural Surrey, England. The food in the restaurants (one of which offers barbecued game meats)

is excellent though it is relatively expensive. The bar is often packed in the evenings and usually stays open until early morning, though this cannot be guaranteed – sometimes it closes up shop when business is booming.

LIMURU

Limuru possibly has even more of a 'European' feel than the Ngong Hills, except that there are vast coffee and tea plantations blanketing the rolling hills cut by swathes of conifer and eucalypt forest. It's up here that you'll find the *Kentmere Club* (☎ (0154) 41053), Limuru Rd, Tigoni. This is the quintessential White settlers' club – even more so than the Norfolk Hotel in Nairobi.

The club consists of a series of low, intimate wooden cottages with shingle roofs connected to each other by quaint walkways and bridges. The main block is built in the same style and houses a restaurant and a superb recreation of an English country pub with low ceilings, exposed beams and log-burning fireplaces. If you'd like to rent a cottage the cost is US$30/40 for singles/doubles with shared facilities; breakfast is included in the price. It's a very peaceful place, and the restaurant is excellent.

Not far from the Kentmere Club is the *Waterfalls Inn* (☎ (0154) 40672) with its picnic site, waterfall, viewing point, restaurant and disco. Admission costs US$4.50 per car (with up to six passengers). Pony, horse and camel riding is available.

Another thing you can do in the area is to visit a tea farm. If you've never done this before then it's worth a day out. Visits are organised by Mitchell's *Kiambethu Tea Farm* (☎ (0154) 40756) at Tigoni, about 35 km north-east of Nairobi. Here you'll be shown the whole process of tea production as well as taken on an accompanied walk into the forest to see the colobus monkeys. Visits here come in a package which includes pre-lunch drinks and a three-course lunch, all for around US$15 per person. Groups are preferred and visits are by prior arrangement only.

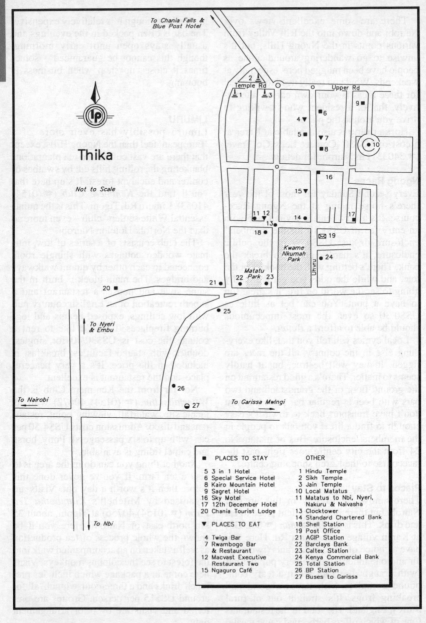

To Chania Falls &
Blue Post Hotel

Temple Rd

Upper Rd

Thika

Not to Scale

Kwame
Nkumah
Park

Uhru

Matatu
Park

To Nyeri
& Embu

To Nairobi

To Nbi

To Garissa Mwingi

■ PLACES TO STAY

5 3 in 1 Hotel
6 Special Service Hotel
8 Kairo Mountain Hotel
9 Sagret Hotel
16 Sky Motel
17 12th December Hotel
20 Chania Tourist Lodge

▼ PLACES TO EAT

4 Twiga Bar
7 Rwambogo Bar
   & Restaurant
12 Macvast Executive
   Restaurant Two
15 Ngaguro Café

OTHER

1 Hindu Temple
2 Sikh Temple
3 Jain Temple
10 Local Matatus
11 Matatus to Nbi, Nyeri,
   Nakuru & Naivasha
13 Clocktower
14 Standard Chartered Bank
18 Shell Station
19 Post Office
21 AGIP Station
22 Barclays Bank
23 Caltex Station
24 Kenya Commercial Bank
25 Total Station
26 BP Station
27 Buses to Garissa

Getting There & Away
KBS public bus No 116 will take you fairly close to the farm. If you have your own transport then take Limuru Rd (C62) past City Park and turn left at Muthaiga roundabout. Seven km further on you reach Ruaka village where you turn right by the signpost for Nazareth Hospital and onto D407 Limuru Rd (otherwise known as Banana Rd). Some 14½ km down this road you'll see a signpost for Limuru Girls' School where you turn right. Go down past the school and take the entrance on the left-hand side signposted 'L G Mitchell'. The Waterfalls Inn (signposted) is 2½ km down the dirt road from the turn-off.

THIKA
Despite its fame due to the popular *Flame Trees of Thika* novel, the town itself comes as something of a disappointment – there's not even many flame trees in evidence! It's appeal lies in the fact that it makes a great escape from the madness of urban Nairobi just 38 km down the road. If you want to get the feel for a small Kenyan agricultural service town, yet still be in commuting range of Nairobi, it could be just the place.

The town's only 'attraction' as such is **Chania Falls**, one km from the centre of town and on the edge of the busy Nairobi to Nyeri road (which thankfully bypasses Thika). The falls are quite small but there's a good view of them from the up-market Blue Post Hotel, which is a pleasant place to stop for a beer.

Places to Stay & Eat
If you decide to stay, there's a good choice of accommodation, particularly in the mid-range area as it seems Thika is also a popular weekend conference venue.

There's a number of similar boarding & lodgings. The *3 in 1* is typical, and costs US$1.80/3.60 for singles/doubles with shared facilities. It's passably clean and not too noisy. Others include the *Rwambogo* and the *Sky Motel*.

The best value rooms in town are at the *12th December Hotel* (☎ (0151) 22140) near the post office. Large doubles cost US$7.50, and singles US$6.30, though these are tiny. Also a good place is the *Sagret Hotel* (☎ (0151) 21786) where the rooms are a little smaller but all have private bath and balcony, and the price includes breakfast. Small vehicles can be parked securely in the hotel courtyard; larger vehicles remain on the street. The cost for rooms here is US$11/17.

Further up the range is the *Chania Tourist Lodge* (☎ (0151) 22547), though it is poor value compared with the Sagret. Rooms here are way overpriced at US$13/15. At the *Blue Post Hotel* (☎ (0151) 22241) you'll pay US$13/19.

All the mid-range hotels have their own restaurants. For a good meal in a regular restaurant try the amazingly named *Macvast Executive Restaurant Two*! Here the waiters are all done up with pink pinstriped shirts and bow ties, but the prices are low and the menu extensive. It's a popular place with the local youths – the TV and the bar at the back are the big drawcards.

Getting There & Away
Matatus leave from a number of places around town. The main matatu stand, used mostly by local matatus, is near the Sagret Hotel. Most long-distance matatus – to Nairobi, Nakuru, Naivasha, Nyeri and Embu – leave from behind Barclays Bank. The trip to Nairobi only takes 45 minutes.

The Coast

This cannot be less than natural beauty, the endless sand, the reefs, the lot, are completely unmatched in the world.

Ernest Hemingway

The coast of Kenya is one of the country's main attractions. It offers a combination of historical sites, trading ports with a strong Arab-Muslim influence, superb beaches and diving opportunities – an area not to be missed.

Mombasa is the coast capital, if you like, and is the first port of call for most people after leaving Nairobi. It is an old trading port with a history going back at least to the 12th century, and the old city here shows heavy influence of the town's previous rulers – the mosques and the Portuguese fort in particular. It has a steamy humid climate but is a pleasant place nonetheless. Unfortunately, many people are in such a rush to get to the beach that they really only transit Mombasa, which is a pity as the city, particularly the old part, is well worth exploring.

To the north it's much the same story, with Malindi being the big coastal resort centre, but there's a couple of interesting attractions here as well – the historical site of Gedi just a short bus ride to the south, and the excellent diving on the coral reef in the offshore Malindi and Watamu marine national parks.

Head further north and you come to the island of Lamu – a beautiful Arab-influenced town which has been something of a travellers' Mecca for years and still draws visitors by the thousands. Despite this it retains the very distinctive personality which attracted people to it in the first place – an easy-going unhurried pace, traditional architecture, and a unique culture which owes a great deal to its Muslim roots.

The people of the coast are the Swahili, and it's here that Kiswahili (Swahili) – the lingua franca of the modern nation – evolved as a means of communication between the local inhabitants and the Arab traders who

first began plying their dhows up and down this coast sometime before the 7th century. Other influences also shaped the language and there is a smattering of not only Arabic but also Portuguese, Hindi and English words.

History

The first traders here appear to have been Arabs from the Persian Gulf who sailed south along the coast during the north-east monsoon, sailing home north with the south-west monsoon. By the 12th century some substantial settlements had developed, mainly on islands such as Lamu, Mandu, Pemba and Zanzibar, as these provided greater security than the coast itself. The main export trade in this early part was in ivory, tortoiseshell and leopard skins, while items such as glass beads from India and porcelain from as far afield as China were finding their way here.

From the 12th to the 15th centuries settlements grew and a dynasty was established at Kilwa (in present-day Tanzania). By the end of this period Mombasa, Malindi and Paté (in the Lamu archipelago) were all substantial towns. The inhabitants were largely Arab but there were also significant numbers of African labourers. Intermarriage was common and, culturally, the settlements were more closely connected with the Islamic Persian Gulf than they were with inland Kenya. Although all these city-states had this common heritage and cultural link, they were all virtually independent and were often vying with one another for power.

So preoccupied were they with their own internal struggles that the coastal centres were quite unprepared for the arrival of the Portuguese in 1498. Before long they were paying tribute to the Portuguese and by 1506 the Portuguese had sacked and gained control of the entire coast. In the century which followed, the Portuguese had raided

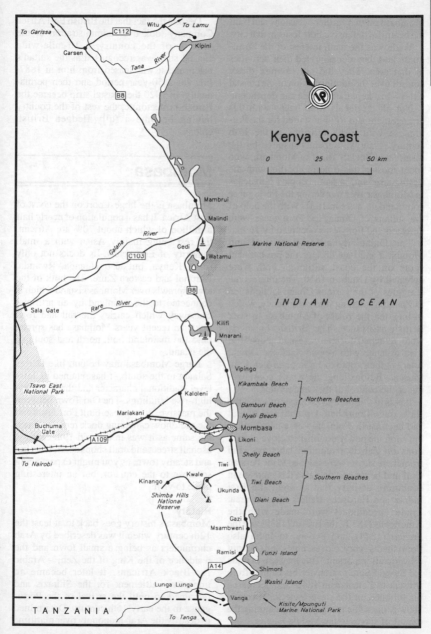

Mombasa on two further occasions and built the beautiful defensive Fort Jesus in that city.

Trade was the main interest of the Portuguese and they concentrated their activities in that area. They did not exercise direct control over the administration of the coastal cities – just kept them in line and dependent.

Not all the locals were happy with this arrangement and trouble started for the Portuguese with local uprisings in the 17th century. They were mainly inspired by the disaffected Sheikh Yusuf of Mombasa, who spent most of his time in conflict with the Portuguese, and in fact occupied Fort Jesus in Mombasa after murdering the Portuguese commandant there in 1631. With the help of the sultans of Oman, the Portuguese were defeated and Fort Jesus occupied by 1698.

The Omani dynasties flourished and Mombasa and Paté became the pre-eminent spots on the coast, although both were defeated by Lamu in 1810. The internecine struggles of the various Omani factions led to Zanzibar coming into ascendancy, which in turn led the rulers of Mombasa to seek British assistance. The British, however, were reluctant to intervene and jeopardise their alliance with Seyyid Said, the Omani ruler, as their route to India passed close to Muscat. Before long the whole coast was under the control of the Omani ruler.

It was in this period of Omani rule that the slave trade flourished. Up until this time it had been carried out only on a small scale, but soon the newly established clove plantations on Zanzibar required labourers, and from there slaves were shipped to the Persian Gulf and beyond. It was also this increase in economic activity that brought the first Indian and European traders into the area. Trade agreements were made with the Americans (1833), the British (1839) and the French (1844), and exports to India also flourished – ivory, cloves, hides and coconut oil were all important. This increase in trade led Seyyid Said to transfer his capital from Muscat to Zanzibar in 1840, and decreased his reliance on the slave trade for revenue. He was thus able to sign a treaty banning the export of slaves to the Middle East.

Despite the fact that the British East Africa Company took over administration of the interior of the country, a 10-mile-wide coastal strip was recognised as the sultan's patch and it was leased from him in 1887, first for a 50-year period and then permanently. In 1920 the coastal strip became the British protectorate, the rest of the country having become a fully fledged British colony.

Mombasa

Mombasa is the largest port on the coast of East Africa. It has a population of nearly half a million of which about 70% are African, the rest being mainly Asian with a small minority of Europeans. Its docks not only serve Kenya, but also Uganda, Rwanda, Burundi and eastern Zaïre. The bulk of the town sprawls over Mombasa Island which is connected to the mainland by an artificial causeway which carries the rail and road links. In recent years Mombasa has spread onto the mainland both north and south of the island.

Large Mombasa may be but, like Dar es Salaam to the south, it has retained its low-level traditional character and there are few high-rise buildings. The Old Town between the massive, Portuguese-built Fort Jesus and the old dhow careening dock remains much the same as it was in the mid-19th century, asphalt streets and craft shops apart. It's a hot and steamy town, as you might expect being so close to the equator, but an interesting place to visit.

History

Mombasa's history goes back to at least the 12th century when it was described by Arab chroniclers as being a small town and the residence of the King of the Zenj – Arabic for Black Africans. It later became an important settlement for the Shirazis and remained so until the arrival of the Portuguese in the early 16th century. Determined to destroy the Arab monopoly over maritime trade in the Indian Ocean, especially with regard to spices, the Portuguese, under Dom Francisco de Almeida, attacked Mombasa with a fleet of 23 ships in 1505. After a day and a half it was all over and the town was burnt to the ground. So great was the quantity of loot that much of it had to be left behind, for fear of overloading the ships, when the fleet sailed for India.

The town was quickly rebuilt and it wasn't long before it regained its commanding position over trade in the area, but peace didn't last long. In 1528, another Portuguese fleet under Nuña da Cunha arrived on the East African coast too late to catch the south-western monsoon which would take them to India, so they were forced to look around for temporary quarters. Naturally, Mombasa was in no mood to welcome them but, unfortunately, Mombasa was at that time engaged in bitter disputes with the kings of Malindi, Pemba and Zanzibar. An alliance was patched together and the Portuguese were again able to take Mombasa, but sickness and constant skirmishing over many months eventually decided the outcome. The city was again burnt to the ground and the Portuguese sailed for India.

The Portuguese finally made a bid for permanency in 1593 with the construction of Fort Jesus, but in 1631 they were massacred to the last person in an uprising by the townspeople. The following year a Portuguese fleet was sent from Goa and Muscat to avenge the killings but was unable to retake the town. By this time, however, the Mombasan ruler had decided that further resistance was useless and, having reduced the town to rubble and cut down all the fruit trees and palms, he withdrew to the mainland. It was reoccupied without a fight by the Portuguese the following year. Portuguese hegemony in the Indian Ocean was on the wane by this time, not only because of corruption and nepotism within Portuguese ranks, but because of Dutch, French and English activity in India and South-East Asia.

The 17th century also saw the rise of Oman as a naval power and it was the Omanis who, in 1698, were the next to drive the Portuguese from Mombasa, after a 33-month siege in which all the defenders were slaughtered. Even this disaster wasn't enough to convince the Portuguese that their days were over and Mombasa was reoccupied. However, the end finally came in 1729 following an invasion by an Arab fleet, a general uprising of the population in which Portuguese settlers were slaughtered, and an abortive counteroffensive which involved the entire military resources of the viceroyalty of Goa.

In 1832 the Sultan of Oman moved his capital from Muscat to Zanzibar and from then until Kenya's independence in 1963 the red flag of Zanzibar fluttered over Fort Jesus. Meanwhile, the British became active along the East African coast. In their attempts to suppress the slave trade, they interfered increasingly in the affairs of Zanzibar until, in 1895, the British East Africa protectorate was set up with Mombasa as the capital (until it was moved to Nairobi) and the Sultan of Oman's possessions were administered as a part of it. When independence came, the Sultan's coastal possessions were attached to the new republic.

During the protectorate years the British confirmed Mombasa's status as East Africa's most important port by constructing a railway from Mombasa to Uganda. It was completed in 1901 using indentured labourers from Gujarat and Punjab in India – hence the origin of Kenya's (and Uganda's and Tanzania's) Asian population.

Information

Tourist Office The regional tourist office (☎ 311231) is just past the famous tusks on Moi Ave and is open Monday to Friday from 8 am to noon and 2 to 4.30 pm, and on Saturdays from 8 am to noon. It has a reasonable map of south-east Kenya and the Kenyan coast for sale but is otherwise geared to big spenders – mainly those who want to stay at a beach resort hotel – so is of little help to budget travellers. You can also buy the local guide books to Fort Jesus and Mombasa Old Town here.

KENYA

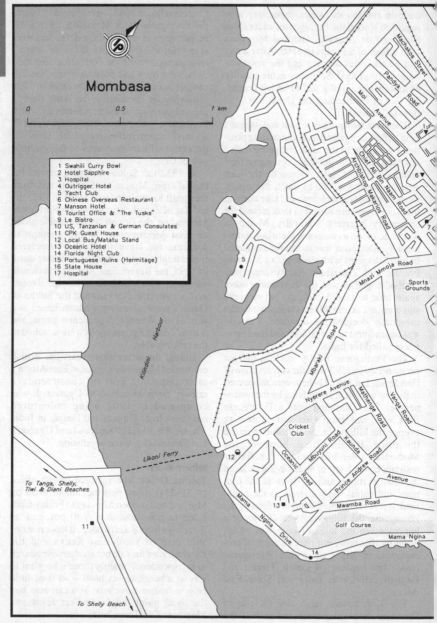

Mombasa

0   0.5   1 km

1 Swahili Curry Bowl
2 Hotel Sapphire
3 Hospital
4 Outrigger Hotel
5 Yacht Club
6 Chinese Overseas Restaurant
7 Manson Hotel
8 Tourist Office & "The Tusks"
9 Le Bistro
10 US, Tanzanian & German Consulates
11 CPK Guest House
12 Local Bus/Matatu Stand
13 Oceanic Hotel
14 Florida Night Club
15 Portuguese Ruins (Hermitage)
16 State House
17 Hospital

Machakos Street
Pandya Road
Moi Avenue
Archbishop Makarios Road
Chief Ali Bin Naam Road

Kilindini Harbour

Mnazi Mmoja Road

Sports Grounds

Mbaraki Road

Nyerere Avenue

Mathenge Road

Venga Road

Cricket Club

Oceanic Road

Mbuyuni Road

Kaunda Road

Prince Andrew Road

Avenue

Mwamba Road

Golf Course

Mama Ngina

Mama Ngina Drive

Likoni Ferry

To Tanga, Shelly,
Tiwi & Diani Beaches

To Shelly Beach

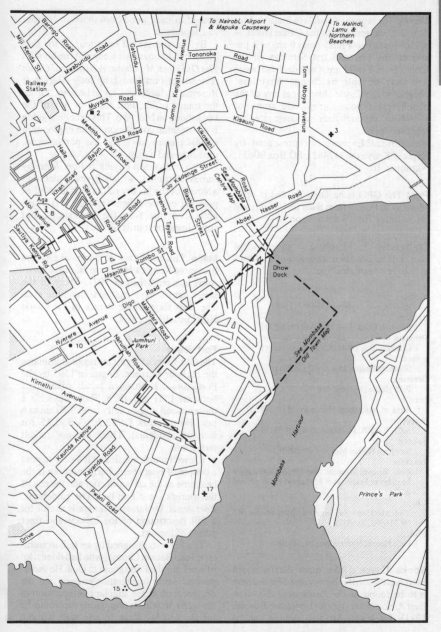

Money The branch of Barclays Bank on Moi Ave, 200 metres west of the Castle Hotel, is open Monday to Friday from 9 am to 3 pm and on the first and last Saturday of the month from 9 to 11 am. Outside these hours you may be able to change travellers' cheques at the Castle Hotel, or at any of the beach resort hotels north and south of Mombasa, although their exchange rates are relatively poor.

American Express is represented by Express Kenya (☎ 312461), PO Box 90631, Nkrumah Rd.

Post The GPO is on Digo Rd and is open Monday to Friday from 8 am to 4.30 pm and on Saturday from 8 am to noon.

Embassies As Mombasa is an important port and tourism town, a number of countries also have consulates here:

Austria
    Raili House, Nyerere Ave (☎ 313386)
Belgium
    Mitchell Cotts Bldg, Moi Ave (☎ 20231)
Denmark
    Liwatoni Bay (☎ 311826)
France
    Southern House, Moi Ave (☎ 20501)
Germany
    Palli House, Nyerere Ave
India
    Bank of India Bldg, Nkrumah Rd (☎ 24433)
Netherlands
    ABN Bank Bldg, Nkrumah Rd (☎ 311043)
Sweden
    Southern House, Moi Ave (☎ 20501)
Tanzania
    Palli House, Nyerere Ave (☎ 228596); open Monday to Friday from 8.30 am to 12.30 pm and 2.30 to 4 pm.
UK
    The Missions to Seamen, Mogadishu Rd (☎ 316502, 316331)
USA
    Palli House, Nyerere Ave (☎ 315101)

Books If you'd like more details about Mombasa's stirring history, the best account is to be found in *The Portuguese Period in East Africa* (East African Literature Bureau, 1971), by Justus Strandes, which can be bought in most good bookshops in Nairobi and Mombasa.

Before you set off on a tour of the Old Town of Mombasa get a copy of the booklet *The Old Town Mombasa: A Historical Guide* (Friends of Fort Jesus), by Judy Aldrick & Rosemary Macdonald. It can be bought from the tourist office, Fort Jesus, or one of the bookshops on Moi Ave. This excellent guide is an essential companion for an exploration of this part of town and has photographs, drawings and a map.

Also well worth buying is *Fort Jesus* by James Kirkman, which gives a detailed account of the history of the Fort, as well as pointing out the salient features. It is available from the fort, the bookshops and sometimes the tourist office.

Maps The best map of Mombasa is the Survey of Kenya's *Mombasa Island & Environs*, last published in 1977. Many of the street names have changed, but little else. The craft shop on the terrace of the Castle Hotel usually stocks it.

Fort Jesus

The Old Town's biggest attraction dominates the harbour entrance. Begun in 1593 by the Portuguese, it changed hands nine times between 1631 and 1875. These days it's a museum and is open daily from 8.30 am to 6 pm. Entry costs US$2.20 (US$0.45 for Kenyan residents). There are no student reductions.

It's well worth a visit and it's easy to pass a couple of hours here. Early morning is the best time as the air is still cool and the rest of the tourists are still in bed. The guidebook, *Fort Jesus*, by James Kirkman is useful for a full description of the history and finer points of the fort.

The fort was designed by an Italian architect, Joao Batista Cairato, who had done a lot of work for the Portuguese in Goa. He incorporated some ingenious elements into the design, such as the angular configuration of the walls, making it impossible for would-be invaders to lay siege to one wall without

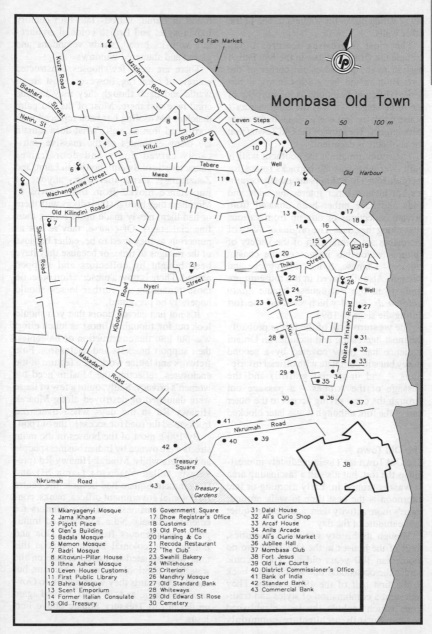

Mombasa Old Town

Old Fish Market

Leven Steps

Well

Old Harbour

Well

0   50   100 m

1 Mkanyagenyi Mosque
2 Jama Khana
3 Pigott Place
4 Glen's Building
5 Badala Mosque
6 Memon Mosque
7 Badri Mosque
8 Kitovuni-Pillar House
9 Ithna Asheri Mosque
10 Leven House Customs
11 First Public Library
12 Bahra Mosque
13 Scent Emporium
14 Former Italian Consulate
15 Old Treasury

16 Government Square
17 Dhow Registrar's Office
18 Customs
19 Old Post Office
20 Hansing & Co
21 Recoda Restaurant
22 'The Club'
23 Swahili Bakery
24 Whitehouse
25 Criterion
26 Mandhry Mosque
27 Old Standard Bank
28 Whiteways
29 Old Edward St Rose
30 Cemetery

31 Dalal House
32 Ali's Curio Shop
33 Arcaf House
34 Anils Arcade
35 Ali's Curio Market
36 Jubilee Hall
37 Mombasa Club
38 Fort Jesus
39 Old Law Courts
40 District Commissioner's Office
41 Bank of India
42 Standard Bank
43 Commercial Bank

being sitting ducks for soldiers in one of the other walls.

The most interesting features today include the **Omani house** in the San Felipe bastion in the north-western corner of the fort. Built in the late 18th century it has served different functions as the purpose of the fort changed – it was the chief warder's house when the fort was a prison in the early 20th century. The view of the Old Town from the roof here is excellent.

The **museum** along the southern wall is built over what was the barracks rooms for the garrison. The exhibits are mostly ceramics but include other interesting odds and ends and have either been donated from private collections or dug up from various sites along the coast. The origins of many of the pieces are a reflection of the variety of cultures which has influenced the coastal culture – Chinese, Indian, Portuguese and Persian. Also displayed in the museum are finds from the Portuguese frigate *Santo António de Tanná* which sank off the fort during the siege in 1697.

The **western wall** of the fort is probably the most interesting and includes an Omani audience hall (now covered by a second storey but still complete with official inscriptions – and unofficial graffiti) and the Passage of the Arches – a passage cut through the coral giving access to the outer part of the fort, although it was later blocked off.

The Old Town

The Old Town isn't as immediately interesting as the fort, but it's still a fascinating area to wander around in. Early morning or late afternoon is the best time to walk around; there's more activity then, and it's very quiet in the middle of the day.

Though its history goes back centuries, most of the houses in the Old Town are no more than 100 years old but you'll come across the occasional one which dates back to the first half of the 19th century. They represent a combination of styles and traditions which include the long-established coastal Swahili architecture commonly found in Lamu, various late-19th century Indian styles and British colonial architecture with its broad, shady verandahs and glazed and shuttered windows.

There are very few houses constructed entirely of coral rag, however. Most are of wattle and daub though they may include coral here and there. Most of the old palm thatch or tile roofing has been replaced with corrugated iron as well. What does remain are many examples of the massive, intricately carved doors and door frames characteristic of Swahili houses in Lamu and Zanzibar. It seems that when anyone of importance moved from these towns to Mombasa they brought their doors with them or had them newly made up to reflect their financial status. Of course, they're not as numerous as they used to be, either because of the ravages of time, or because they have been bought by collectors and shipped abroad. There is now a preservation order on those remaining so further losses should hopefully be prevented.

It's not just carved doors that you should look out for, though. Almost as much effort was put into the construction of balconies, their support brackets and enclosures. Fine fretwork and lattice work are a feature of the enclosures, reflecting the Muslim need for women's privacy. Sadly, quite a few of these were damaged or destroyed along Mbarak Hinawy Rd in the days when oversized trucks used the road for access to the old port.

By 1900, most of the houses in the main streets were owned by Indian businesspeople and traders whilst Mbarak Hinawy Rd (previously called Vasco da Gama St) and Government Square had become the centre for colonial government offices, banks, consulates and business or living quarters for colonial officials. Ndia Kuu housed immigrant entrepreneurs from India, Goa and Europe. The colonial headquarters at this time were situated in Leven House on the waterfront overlooking the old harbour, but shortly afterwards they were moved to Government Square and, in 1910, moved again up the hill to Treasury Square above Fort Jesus.

In later years, as Mombasa expanded along what are today the main roads, many of the businesses which had shops and offices in the Old Town gradually moved out, leaving behind ornate signs, etched glass windows and other relics of former times. Their exact location is described in *The Old Town Mombasa: A Historical Guide*.

You can start your exploration of the Old Town anywhere you like but the main points of interest are marked on the street map. There is a notice in Government Square saying that photography of the old harbour area (but not the buildings) is prohibited. I don't know how serious the authorities are about this since I can't imagine what is so sensitive about the place, but if you want pictures of it there are plenty of narrow streets leading off to the waterfront between the square and the Leven Steps where no-one will bother you.

Harbour Cruises

Those looking for a luxury dhow cruise around the harbour should book a trip with Tamarind Dhow Safaris (☎ 20990, 315569) but be warned that they're not cheap at US$43 for the lunch cruise and US$51 for the evening cruise. The price includes a four-hour cruise around the harbour, a gourmet lunch or dinner (seafood or steak) cooked on board, an on-board live band and transport to/from your hotel. The dhow has its own fully stocked bar. The lunch cruise begins at 10.30 am and the evening cruise starts at 6.30 pm.

There's also another outfit called *Jahazi Marine Ltd* (☎ 472213, 471895) which offers night-time dhow cruises on Monday and Thursday for US$65. The price includes a sundowner cruise with a cocktail past Mombasa Old Town and the fort, a barbecue at Bamburi Nature Park, a torchlit safari through the park, a visit to the casino and the Bora Bora Nightclub and transfers from your hotel.

You can book either of the above cruises direct or at any travel agency or top-end hotel.

Places to Stay

There's a lot of choice for budget travellers and for those who want something slightly better, both in the centre of the city and on the mainland to the north and south. Accommodation up and down the coast from Mombasa Island itself is dealt with separately.

Places to Stay – bottom end

One of the best value places in this category is the *Mvita Hotel*, on the corner of Hospital and Turkana Sts. The entrance is on the first alley on the left-hand side on Turkana St or through the bar on the ground floor on Hospital St. It's Indian-run, clean, quiet and secure, all the rooms have fans and a washbasin and the beds are comfortable. The showers and toilets are scrubbed out daily. Rooms cost US$3.30 a double, but the hotel is often full as it's only a small place. There's a lively bar downstairs (which you can't hear in the rooms upstairs) and at lunch and dinner times barbecued meat and other snacks are available in the back yard.

Equally good value and popular with travellers is the *Cosy Guest House* (☎ 313064), on Haile Selassie Rd, though we have had reports that Salim, the owner, hassles women. It costs US$2.70/4 for singles/doubles, US$6 for triples, all with shared facilities. All the rooms have fans but due to chronic water problems the toilets can stink. The guesthouse will most likely be full if you get there late in the day.

On the opposite side of the road from the Cosy Guest House is the *Midnight Guest House* (☎ 26275) which is a bit scruffy, and the management is not all that friendly, but it would do if you're stuck. There are no singles, and a double with shared facilities costs US$3.60.

Just around the corner on Shibu Rd is the friendly *New Al Jazira Hotel* which has doubles with balcony and shared bath (no fans) for US$3.10. As is the case with many Mombasa hotels, there are no single rooms.

If all these places are full then you could try the *Balgis Lodge* (☎ 313358), on Digo Rd, which is very friendly. It has singles/

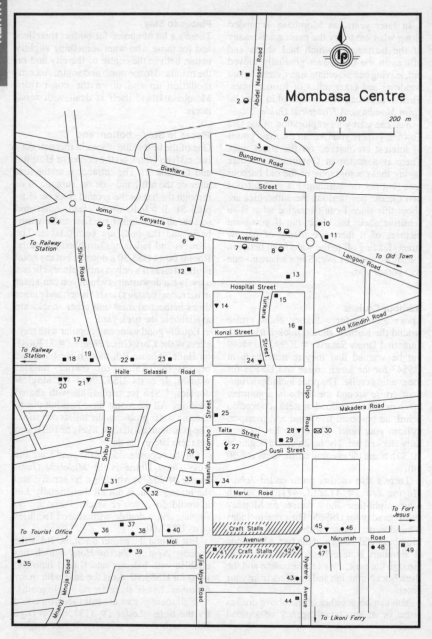

Mombasa Centre

0   100   200 m

■ PLACES TO STAY		26	Splendid View Restaurant
		28	Masumin Restaurant
1	New People's Lodge	32	Pistacchio Ice Cream & Coffee Bar
3	Al Nasser Lodging	34	Blue Fin Restaurant
11	Hydro Hotel	36	Mombasa Coffee House
12	Unity Guest House	42	Fontanella Restaurant
13	Down Town Lodge	45	Hard Rock Café
15	Mvita Hotel	47	Capri Restaurant
16	Balgis Lodge		
17	New Al Jazira Hotel		OTHER
18	Midnight Guest House		
19	Visitor's Inn	2	Buses & Matatus to Malindi & Lamu
20	Cosy Guest House	4	Coast Bus
22	Continental Guest House	5	Bus Station
23	Hotel Fortuna	6	Cat Bus
25	Hotel Hermes	7	Mawingo Buses
29	New Britania Boarding & Lodging	8	Akamba Bus
31	Glory Guest House & ABC Lodge	9	Malindi Taxi Bus
33	Hotel Splendid	10	Market
37	Kilindini Guest House	27	Sheik Jundoni Mosque
41	Castle Hotel	30	GPO
44	Manor Hotel	35	Bahati Book Centre
49	New Palm Tree Hotel	38	Bahari Bookshop
		39	Barclays Bank
▼ PLACES TO EAT		40	Istanbul Bar
		43	Fort Supermarket
14	Geetanjali Restaurant	46	Kenya Airways
20	New Chetna Restaurant	47	Executive Air Services
21	Indo African Restaurant	48	American Express
24	Blue Room Restaurant		

doubles for US$2.70/4 and triples for US$5.40, all with shared facilities. The rooms only have internal windows which makes them pretty hot, but there's also a dorm which has windows overlooking noisy Digo Rd. Another real cheapie which is habitable though very scruffy is the *Down Town Lodge* on Hospital St for US$2.50 per room. Most of the rooms don't have fans.

Heading towards the northern end of town, the *Al Nasser Lodging* (☎ 313032) on Abdel Nasser Rd is good value at US$4.90 for a double with shower.

Another budget hotel in this area, and one which has been popular for years, is the *New People's Lodge* (☎ 312831), on Abdel Nasser Rd right next to where the buses leave for Malindi and Lamu. Some travellers rate this place very highly and it certainly compares very well in price with the others but it is a little tatty and the rooms which face onto

the main road are very noisy. The air also stinks of diesel fumes because bus drivers always rev their engines for up to an hour before they actually leave. The management is friendly, and gear left in the rooms is safe. Rooms cost US$1.70/3.40 a single/double with shared showers and toilets, and US$2.80/5.60/8.40 a single/double/triple with private facilities. There are also four-bed and five-bed rooms with shared facilities for US$4.50/5.60. All the rooms have fans, the sheets are clean and the water in the showers is generally lukewarm. It's a large place and is rarely full. There's a good, cheap restaurant downstairs.

Another place which was once a popular budget hotel is the *Hydro Hotel* (☎ 23784), on Digo Rd at the Kenyatta Ave junction, but it's barely habitable these days and you'd have to be desperate to stay there. In better shape is the *New Britania Boarding &*

Lodging on Gusii St. The hotel entrance is through the downstairs bar and then up the stairs. The rooms are clean and good value at US$2.90.

Not far from the tourist office and similar in price to the other budget hotels is the quiet *Kilindini Guest House* off Shibu Rd.

Somewhat more expensive than the above (but not necessarily better value) is the *Hotel Fortuna*, on Haile Selassie Rd, which costs US$4/5.10 for singles/doubles with private showers and toilets. The *Hotel Fortuna Annex* across the road shares the same reception but is cheaper since the rooms are not self-contained.

Better value is the *Continental Guest House* (☎ 315916) on Haile Selassie Rd near the Hotel Fortuna. Double rooms (no singles) go for US$5.40 with bath and breakfast. It's run by a very friendly guy, but you need to get there early as it fills up quickly. Close by is the similarly priced *Visitor's Inn* on the corner of Shibu Rd. The rooms are self-contained and the price includes breakfast. However, some of the rooms overlook Haile Selassie Rd and so cop the noise. The entrance is on Shibu Rd and is easy to miss.

Places to Stay – middle

One of the cheapest in this range is the new *Unity Guest House* (☎ 221298) just off Msanifu Kombo St. It has self-contained singles/doubles with fan for US$5.60/10 and doubles with air-con for US$17.

Also on Msanifu Kombo St is the *Hotel Splendid* (☎ 220967), a huge place which is rarely full. Singles with shared facilities cost US$6.40, and self-contained doubles/triples are US$12/19. The prices include breakfast. It's an old place but very clean and there's a popular rooftop restaurant which gets sea breezes in the evenings.

Another well-maintained hotel in this category is the *Hotel Hermes* (☎ 313599) on Msanifu Kombo St near the Sheik Jundoni Mosque. The rooms are pleasant, if a little dingy, and self-contained doubles (no singles) with air-con cost US$14 including breakfast.

Not far from here is the *Glory Guest House* (☎ 313204) on Shibu Rd. The rooms are a bit on the small side but are spotlessly clean and well maintained. Self-contained singles/doubles with fan cost US$11/16 plus there are doubles with air-con for US$18. Breakfast is included in the price. There is also an annexe with cheaper rooms and shared facilities. Singles/doubles here cost US$8.90/13.40.

An excellent-value mid-range place is the *New Palm Tree Hotel* (☎ 312169), on Nkrumah Rd. A comfortable self-contained room with fan here costs US$11/15 a single/double including breakfast. The staff are friendly and helpful, and the hotel has its own bar and restaurant.

Places to Stay – top end

One of the cheaper top-end hotels is the brand new *Manson Hotel* (☎ 222356), on Kisumu Rd. It has 84 self-contained rooms which cost US$16/20 a single/double without air-con, US$20/24 with air-con. Prices include breakfast. The hotel has a restaurant (exclusively vegetarian food) but no bar.

Similar in price and also some distance from the centre but close to the railway station, is the brand new *Hotel Sapphire* (☎ 491657) on Mwembe Tayari Rd. All the rooms are self-contained with air-con and cost US$18/27 including breakfast. Children under 12 years of age sharing with parents cost US$4.50 extra. Diners Club cards are accepted.

The most popular hotel and the one with most character is the central *Castle Hotel* (☎ 223403, 221683) on Moi Ave. Originally constructed in 1908, it was Mombasa's premier hotel throughout the colonial period when it was run by a Mr Schwentafsky, otherwise known as 'Champagne Charlie' on account of his notoriously keen interest in female guests. Following WW II, it was allowed to run down but was recently restored to its former glory by Alliance Hotels which has retained the original snow-white façade, the balcony balustrades and the polished wooden floors and grand staircases.

All the rooms have air-con, private bathrooms and colour TV. Singles/doubles cost US$29/40, and children aged between two and 12 years sharing with adults cost an extra US$7.80. The price includes an excellent US-style buffet breakfast. All major credit cards are accepted and there's guarded parking. Amenities include a restaurant and three bars, one of which is the popular open-air Terrace overlooking Moi Ave; virtually every visitor to Mombasa comes to the Terrace at one time or another for a cold beer.

Not quite as old, but another colonial landmark, is the nearby *Manor Hotel* (☎ 314643), on Nyerere Ave, with a wide verandah and surrounding garden. Like the Castle, it's been renovated since it was first built in the 1920s, but is cheaper at US$17 a single with shared facilities. Self-contained singles/doubles with fan are US$19/31, US$25/33 with air-con. Children under 12 years sharing a room with their parents cost US$5.60 extra. Prices include breakfast and there's guarded parking at the rear. Amenities include a restaurant and bars.

Superbly located overlooking the Indian Ocean and with a range of amenities which includes Indian, Chinese and Italian restaurants, a swimming pool and an open-air bar in a garden setting, is the relatively modern *Oceanic Hotel* (☎ 311191/2/3), off Oceanic Rd, not far from the Likoni ferry. Self-contained, air-con rooms in this high-rise hotel cost US$22/31 a single/double and triples US$40 including breakfast. All major credit cards are accepted.

Top of the range is the *New Outrigger Hotel* (☎ 220822) set in landscaped gardens leading down to Kilindini Harbour on the western side of Mombasa Island. All the rooms are self-contained with air-con and have a balcony facing the harbour. Singles/doubles cost US$55/65 including breakfast. The hotel is under Belgian management, the cuisine is French, there's a swimming pool and all credit cards are accepted.

Places to Eat

Mombasa has a good range of restaurants. If you are putting your own food together, or want to stock up with goodies to take down the coast, the Fort Supermarket on Nyerere Ave is well stocked, and there's a wide variety of fruit and vegies in the market on Digo Rd next to the Hydro Hotel.

Places to Eat – cheap

If you are just looking for fish or chicken with chips try the *Blue Fin Restaurant*, on the corner of Meru Rd and Msanifu Kombo St. There's very little variety but it's not a bad place. There's a better choice at the *Blue Room Restaurant* on Haile Selassie Rd. It serves excellent burgers for US$0.60 to US$1, depending on what you have with them, and the fish & chips and Indian snacks are also worth a try.

The *Masumin Restaurant*, opposite the GPO on Digo Rd, does a good full breakfast for US$1.20, and at other times has various curries with rice for US$1, as well as steaks and cheap juices.

The *Mombasa Coffee House* on Moi Ave is a good place for fresh coffee and snacks, and you can also buy coffee beans here.

Indian Food Since many of the restaurants in Mombasa are Indian-owned you can find excellent curries and thalis at lunch time (from 12.30 to around 3 pm) there is often a cheap, substantial set meal available. One which you'll hear nothing but praise for is the *Geetanjali*, on Msanifu Kombo St, which offers a 'deluxe' thali for US$1.50. Both the food and service are excellent.

Similar is the popular *New Chetna Restaurant*, on Haile Selassie Rd directly under the Cosy Guest House. The food here is South Indian vegetarian (with dishes such as masala dosa and idli) and sweets. An all-you-can-eat set vegetarian lunch costs US$1.50.

Excellent tandoori specialities can be found at the very popular *Splendid View Restaurant*, which is opposite, but not part of, the Hotel Splendid. Food on offer includes chicken, lamb, fruit juices and lassis and you can eat well here for around US$1.80. There are tables outside and inside.

Swahili Food For coastal Swahili dishes made with coconut and coconut milk, the

Swahili Curry Bowl, on Tangana Rd off Moi Ave, is recommended. Prices are reasonable. It's also one of *the* places for coffee and ice cream. Don't bother trekking out here on a Sunday as it's closed then.

Another excellent place, and one you should try at least once, is the *Recoda Restaurant* on Nyeri St in the Old Town. It's a hugely popular place amongst the locals and the tables are set up along the footpath. The atmosphere is great and the waiters are keen to explain what is available that day – usually dishes such as beans in coconut, grilled fish, meat, superb chapatis and salad. You may well find yourself coming back here each night (it's not open at lunch time).

Places to Eat – more expensive

Going up in price, the rooftop restaurant in the *Hotel Splendid* catches the breeze in the evenings and has surprisingly moderate prices (from US$1.40 to US$2 for a main meal), though the food is only mediocre. Don't come here with any ideas of having a quick meal, as the service is far from lightning fast.

The new Hotel Sapphire also has the *Mehfil Restaurant* which serves Mughlai and continental dishes.

The *Pistacchio Ice Cream & Coffee Bar* is a small café near the Hotel Splendid. Not only does it have excellent ice cream, but the fruit shakes are great. The buffet lunch or dinner for US$2.20 is not bad value although the selection is limited. À la carte dishes such as spaghetti are also served. It's open daily from 9 am to 10 pm.

For Chinese tucker you could try the *Chinese Overseas Restaurant* on Moi Ave, just north of the tusks. Main dishes are priced around US$3.40.

The *Fontanella Restaurant* is in a shady courtyard on the corner of Digo Rd and Moi Ave. The extensive menu runs the whole gamut from fish & chips (US$1.40) through steaks (US$2.20) to lobster thermidor (US$8.90). It's great for a minor splurge or just a quiet beer or snack.

For a real splurge, head for *Le Bistro*, on Moi Avenue, close to the tusks. This recently opened restaurant and cocktail bar is owned and run by the same Swiss Germans who own the Pistacchio and it's open daily from breakfast to late at night. Both the atmosphere and the food, which includes pizza, pasta, steak and seafood, are excellent. Expect to pay from US$4.50 to US$5.60 for a full meal and a drink, though there are considerably cheaper meals such as toasted sandwiches from US$1.50, hamburgers from US$1.90 and lunch-time specials.

Those keen to dine in an atmosphere as far removed from Kenya as anyone could imagine, and to choose from a range of dishes named after famous musicians, should try the *Hard Rock Café*, Nkrumah Rd, next door to Kenya Airways. It's all somewhat contrived, but popular with Mombasa yuppies (young, 'upwardly mobile' professionals). Before you go for a meal here you need to be absolutely certain that a constant bombardment of heavy rap music will be conducive to the digestive process. A main course plus a drink will set you back around US$6.

Mombasa's best restaurant by far is the *Capri Restaurant* (☎ 311156), in Ambalal House, Nkrumah Rd, opposite Kenya Airways. French-run with a range of continental and seafood dishes, and a well-stocked cellar of European wines, the food here is superb. Nowhere else compares. It's open daily for lunch and dinner but closed on Sunday and public holidays. Expect to pay around US$11 for a full meal. Attached to this restaurant is the *Hunters Snack Bar* which is a good place for an ice-cold beer in air-con surroundings. Down on the ground floor of the same building is a branch of the restaurant called the *Arcade Café* open from 8.30 am to 5.30 pm which serves coffee, fruit juices, milk shakes, pizza, hot dogs, meat pies, sandwiches and ice cream.

Entertainment

For an ice-cold beer in the heat of the day many people go to the terrace of the *Castle Hotel* which overlooks Moi Ave. It's the nearest thing you'll find to the Thorn Tree

Café in Nairobi but the comparison isn't really valid. If you're on a strict budget, don't come here between 11 am and 3 pm as the price of beer is double the usual charge.

If you prefer cheaper beer and a livelier place then go to the *Istanbul Bar* also on Moi Ave, on the opposite side of the road from the Castle Hotel towards the tusks. Though primarily a pick-up joint and delightfully degenerate, it's very popular and attractively set under makuti roofs in the open air. It's undoubtedly one of Mombasa's landmarks with an atmosphere not unlike that of the Modern Green Day & Night Bar in Nairobi. Here you'll find every nutcase in town along with everyone else with a few 'bob' in their pockets to spend on what are remarkably cold beers (given the refrigeration facilities). If you're looking for someone in Mombasa, you'll find them here.

The best night club/disco in town is the *Florida* on Mama Ngina Drive. Built right on the seashore and enclosing its own swimming pool, it's owned by the same people who run the Florida 2000 and New Florida clubs in Nairobi. The atmosphere is much the same but here there are three open-air bars as well as an enclosed dancing area. Entry costs US$1.10 for women and US$2.20 for men (US$1.40/2.70 on Friday and Saturday nights).

Things to Buy

While Mombasa isn't the craft entrepôt you might expect it to be, it's still not too bad. The trouble is that there are a lot of tourists and sailors who pass through this port with lots of dollars to shed in a hurry. Bargains, therefore, can take a long time to negotiate. The main craft stall area is along Moi Ave from the Castle Hotel down to the roundabout with Nyerere Ave. Many specialist craft shops have sprung up in recent years in the Old Town close to Fort Jesus, especially along Mbarak Hinawy Rd and Ndia Kuu.

Along Moi Ave it's mainly makonde woodcarvings, soapstone chess sets and animal or human figurines, basketwork, drums and other musical instruments, and paintings.

Biashara St, which runs west of the Digo Rd intersection, is the centre for fabrics and *kangas* or *kikoi*, those colourful, beautifully patterned, wraparound skirts complete with Swahili proverbs, which most East African women (who aren't Hindus) wear even if they wear it under a buibui (black wrap-around skirt). You may need to bargain a little over the price (but not too much). What you get is generally what you pay for and, as a rule, they cost around US$4.50 a pair (they are not sold singly). Assuming you are willing to bargain, the price you pay for one will reflect the quality of the cloth. Buy them in Mombasa if possible. You can sometimes get them as cheaply in Nairobi but elsewhere prices escalate rapidly.

Getting There & Away

Air Three companies operate flights from Mombasa to Malindi and Lamu. They are Eagle Aviation Ltd (☎ Mombasa 316054/5), Prestige Air Services Ltd (☎ Mombasa 21443), and Skyways Airlines (☎ Mombasa 221964).

Each company has two flights per day in either direction between Mombasa and Malindi and between Mombasa and Lamu. Flights from Mombasa depart at 8.30 am and 2.15 pm and arrive in Malindi 30 minutes later and in Lamu 70 minutes later. The fare to Malindi is US$14.50 one way and US$29 return. Between Mombasa and Lamu the fares are US$68 one way and US$124 return. Children over two years old pay the full fare; those from three to 12 years pay 50%. Check-in time is 30 minutes before departure and the baggage allowance is 10 kg per person. Most of the time you won't be hassled if your baggage weighs over 10 kg but, even if you are, excess charges are minimal (US$0.20 per kg). The airport departure tax is US$1.50 at Malindi and Mombasa but there's no charge at Lamu.

Kenya Airways also flies from Mombasa to Nairobi via Malindi in either direction at least once daily except on Sunday, using F50 propeller planes. If you're relying on these flights to get back to Nairobi to connect with an international flight, then make absolutely sure you have a confirmed booking or, preferably, go back a day before. Don't join the legion of people who are left on the tarmac tearing out their hair because they didn't reconfirm and the flight was full.

Bus & Matatu In Mombasa bus offices are mainly along Jomo Kenyatta Ave. For Nairobi, there are many departures daily in either direction (mostly in the early morning and late evening) by, among others, Coast, Cat, Mawingo, Malaika and Akamba. The fare ranges from US$3.65 to US$4.20 and the trip takes from seven to eight hours including a meal break about halfway.

To Malindi there are also many departures daily in either direction from early morning until late afternoon by several bus companies and matatus. Buses take up to three hours; matatus about two hours. In Mombasa they all depart from outside the New People's Hotel, Abdel Nasser Rd. See the Malindi section for more details, and for the alternative of hiring a share-taxi.

It's possible to go straight through from Mombasa to Lamu but most travellers stop en route at Malindi.

For Tanga and Dar es Salaam in Tanzania, Cat Bus has departures on Monday, Wednesday and Friday at 4 pm. The journey to Tanga takes about eight hours (US$3.20) and all the way to Dar es Salaam about 20 hours (US$8).

For buses and matatus to the south of Mombasa you first need to get off the island via the Likoni ferry (see the later Getting Around section).

Train Trains to or from Nairobi operate in either direction at 5 and 7 pm, arriving at 8 and 8.30 am respectively. The 7 pm train (the so-called 'deluxe service') is the better of the two but costs more. On the 5 pm train you get to see a bit more of the countryside before it gets dark. The fares on the deluxe service are US$40 in 1st class and US$26 in 2nd class, including dinner, breakfast and bedding (whether you want them or not). You should make a reservation as far in advance as possible as demand sometimes exceeds

supply. The booking office at the station in Mombasa is open daily from 8 am to noon and 2 to 6.30 pm.

The left-luggage service at the railway station costs KSh 12 per item per day. It's open from 8 am to noon and 2 to 6.30 pm Monday to Saturday, and from 7.30 to 10 am and 2 to 6.30 pm on Sunday.

Boat Depending on the season, it's possible to get a ride on a dhow to Pemba, Zanzibar or Dar es Salaam in Tanzania. Departure times used to be haphazard, and there were periods when foreigners were prohibited from travelling in this manner. However, this has all changed now and there's a standardised procedure you have to go through. First go down to the dhow registrar's office on Government Square in the Old Town (entry to the compound will cost you KSh 5 which is payable at an office on the right-hand side of the entrance gate) and find out when the next dhow is going.

The next step is to write or type a declaration which reads:

I .... (full name) of .... (country) born on .... (birth date) travelling on passport number .... (number) intend to travel by dhow from Mombasa to .... (destination) on .... (date) at my own risk.

In no way shall I hold the boat captain or the Kenyan government responsible for my safety.

.... (name & address)

Take this to be stamped at the district commissioner's office on Treasury Square (just up from the fort on the left-hand side) and then return to the dhow registrar's office. Here you pay KSh 350 (which is your fare on the dhow), get a receipt and you'll be told which dhow you're going on. Make sure you are well stocked as the trip takes anything up to 36 hours and you get zilch in the way of food or facilities. The toilet is a long-drop perched out over the back of the boat.

If you want something more reliable (but not necessarily frequent), there's now an air-con catamaran, the MV *Flying Horse* which does the run from Mombasa to Zanzibar and Dar es Salaam on a fairly regular basis taking 7½ hours to Zanzibar and 11 hours to Dar es

Salaam. It costs US$50 (1st class), US$40 (business class) and US$30 (deck class) one way. For bookings in Mombasa contact Ketty Tours Ltd (☎ 315178), Eagle Travel Ltd (☎ 316416), Noor Travel Ltd (☎ 31-3276) or Friendly Travels Ltd (☎ 312493). In Nairobi contact A H Khimji (☎ 765993).

If you're interested in yachts or boats to India or the Seychelles it's worth getting out to Kilibi Creek. Most of the people with yachts moor at Kilibi Creek because mooring berths at the Mombasa Yacht Club are very expensive. If you want to make enquiries you can get to Kilibi by going to Tom's Beach, about 1½ km out of Mombasa centre, near the Seahorse Hotel.

Getting Around
To/From the Airport Kenya Airways operates a shuttle bus from its Nkrumah Rd office at 10.20 am, and 2.20 and 5.40 pm. There's a regular public bus which goes to the airport and costs a few cents. Any 'Port Reitz' matatu will take you past the airport turn-off (ask to be dropped off) from where it's about a 10-minute walk. The standard taxi fare is US$4.45.

Taxi Mombasa's superbly beaten up old taxis are not metered so make sure you agree on a fare before stepping in.

Car All the major companies and many of the smaller outfits have offices in Mombasa as well as in Nairobi. Details can be found under Rental Agencies in Kenya's Getting Around chapter.

The Automobile Association of Kenya or AAA (☎ 26778) has its office just north of the tourist office on the road which connects Aga Khan Rd with the railway station. It has a few road maps and may be of use if you have specific questions about road or traffic conditions.

Boat The Likoni ferry connects Mombasa Island with the southern mainland and runs at frequent intervals throughout the night and day. There's a crossing every 20 minutes on average between 5 am and 12.30 pm; less

frequently between 12.30 and 5 am. It's free to pedestrians; KSh 17 for a car. To get to the ferry from the centre of town take a Likoni matatu from outside the GPO on Digo Rd.

South of Mombasa

The real attractions of the coast south of Mombasa are the beaches, and although it is basically all resort hotels, there are a few options for the budget traveller – at Tiwi and Diani beaches.

All the beaches are white coral sand and are protected by a coral reef so there is no danger from sharks when you go swimming. Tiwi is probably the best beach since it's less developed though, like Shelly, it suffers from large amounts of floating seaweed, depending on the season. Diani doesn't have this to anywhere near the same extent but in some places much of the sand has been washed away leaving just a coral bed.

SHELLY BEACH
Shelly Beach is the closest beach to Mombasa and as such, is not a bad place to swim if you just want to day-trip from Mombasa, though, at times, it's like pea soup because of the seaweed problem. There is no budget accommodation available here so forget it for a long stay unless you have plenty of money.

Places to Stay
The cheapest place to stay, but some distance from the beach, is the *CPK Guest House* (☎ 451619) not far from the Likoni ferry. It's a pleasant place, and costs US$5.60 per person with breakfast, full board US$9.40.

One of the few places to stay on the beach itself (other than renting a holiday let) is the *Shelly Beach Hotel* (☎ 451001/2), about three km from the Likoni ferry. As far as resort hotels go it's not a bad place, and seems to be popular with British tour groups. Most people seem to prefer swimming in the pool rather than in the sea just a few metres away. Half-board rates are US$21/33 for singles/doubles, or US$27/47 with air-con. In the off season it may be possible to get a reduction on these rates, but don't expect too much.

Further south are *Savannah Cottages* (☎ 23456) which are self-contained, air-con holiday lets with fully equipped kitchens, bathrooms, lounge and dining areas, and double bedrooms with twin-bunk beds.

Getting There & Away

From the Likoni ferry, take the first turn to the left after the bus stand. From here it's a 30-minute walk and there are occasional matatus and enough traffic to make hitching possible. The Shelly Beach Hotel has its own transport into town, but you pay extra for this.

TIWI BEACH

Next along the coast is Tiwi Beach, also about two or three km off the main coast road, along either one of two gravel tracks (only one of which is signposted 'Tiwi') which wind their way through the coastal scrub. This is the best beach to head for if you're on a budget and/or have your own camping gear. It's also the least developed, though there's not much in the way of beachfront which isn't already spoken for. The good thing here is that the hotels are all low key, consist mainly of individual, largely self-contained, cottages with a central bar and restaurant appealing to independent travellers. It's a totally different world from the package tourist ghetto of Diani Beach. The prices also reflect this difference.

The thing which you must do at this beach is book in advance if you intend to stay during the high season (January, April to early July, August to early September and Christmas/New Year), otherwise you'll probably find them full. It's essential to book ahead for the self-catering lodges at *any* time of year otherwise you probably won't find anyone around who can deal with you. (If the lodges are full, the owners often head off to Mombasa and the 'managers' are not empowered to rent anything out.)

The last thing you need to know is that

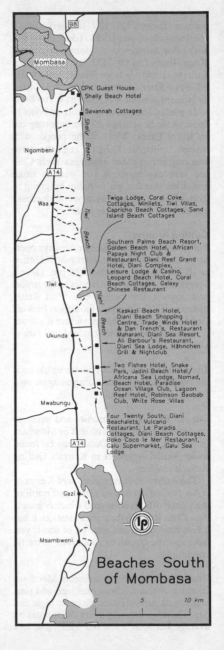

Beaches South of Mombasa

you'll have to bring all your own food and drink if you're staying at a self-catering lodge, though you could, of course, arrange to eat at a lodge which has a restaurant and bar.

Coming from the north, the hotels are: Sand Island Beach Cottages, Capricho Beach Cottages, Maweni Beach Cottages, Tiwi Villas, Coral Cove Cottages, Twiga Lodge, Minilets and Tiwi Beachlets. Most of these are signposted on the main road.

Places to Stay & Eat

Cheapest of the lot (but only by a small margin) is the very popular *Twiga Lodge* (☎ (0127) 2457). It is certainly *the* place to camp along the coast as you can pitch your tent just a few metres from the water plus there's plenty of shade. Camping charges are minimal. Single/double rooms go for US$6.70/13 with breakfast plus there are cottages accommodating four people for US$12 (plus US$3.40 for each extra bed if there are more than four people). There's a restaurant, bar and shop. It's a good place to stay as there's usually an interesting mix of people here.

Right next door to the Twiga Lodge are the *Coral Cove Cottages* (☎ (0127) 4164). The cottages here are similar in price to those at Twiga Lodge and range from those with no facilities to others which are fully self-contained (complete with cooking equipment). It's a very pleasant place to stay and popular with young expatriate workers.

South of Twiga Lodge are the *Minilets* (☎ (0127) 2551), a collection of small, self-contained, cliff-top chalets connected to the beach by a series of paved walkways. Singles/doubles cost US$11/15, and there's a bar and restaurant.

Going further north, *Tiwi Villas* (☎ (0127) 2362) is an attractive complex, again on top of a cliff, with a swimming pool, bar and restaurant. A double cottage here costs US$11, one which sleeps four people US$20, and a more spacious triple US$26.

Further up the coast, the *Capricho Beach Cottages* (☎ (0127) 24630) are a collection of self-contained one, two and three-bedroom cottages with lounge/dining room, verandah and a full range of cooking equipment. You must provide your own bed linen and mosquito nets, though these can be hired with advance notice. In the low season the cottages cost US$15 (up to two people), US$25 (up to five people) and US$30 (up to six people), plus 20% tax. Prices are US$17/35/41 in the high season. The complex has its own swimming pool.

Beyond here, the *Sand Island Beach Cottages* (☎ (0127) 2461) is another group of self-catering and self-contained cottages similar to those at Capricho which range in price between US$15 (up to two people) and US$30 (up to six people) in the low season and US$17 to US$41 in the high season plus 20% tax. There are also campers available with outside toilets and showers which sleep two people for US$4 and US$8 in the low season and US$6 and US$11 in the high season plus 20% tax. Bed linen and mosquito nets must be brought with you unless arranged in advance.

Getting There & Away

The buses and matatus drop you at the start of the gravel access road, from where it's a three-km (45-minute) walk. This road is notorious for muggings so, unless you're part of a group (in which case you can assume you're safe), wait for a lift. There are no buses or matatus but quite a few cars so you shouldn't have to wait long.

DIANI BEACH

Diani is a package-tourist hotel/resort complex. If you're an independent traveller looking for a patch of authentic Kenyan coast and a mellow atmosphere, you'll hate it here. The promotional literature looks very alluring and the architecture can be very imaginative but the clientele is dreadful. Lobotomised European wage slaves on day release wouldn't be too far from the truth.

At least, that's the story as far as the tarmac stretches at the back of this beachfront development. Further south, it does change and you get back into something resembling the Kenyan coast before the 'developers' decided to recreate the Costa Lotta. It's in this area that you'll find Dan Trench's, the only budget accommodation on this part of the coast.

As at Tiwi beach, you need to make advance booking for any of the cheaper places at Diani during the high season otherwise you'll find them full, though some sort of accommodation can usually be found at any time at Dan Trench's.

Information

The village of Ukunda on the main Mombasa to Tanzania highway is the turn-off point for Diani Beach. It's here that you'll find the nearest post office plus a number of basic lodging houses. From here a tarmac road runs about two km down to a T-junction with the beach road which runs several km in either direction north and south. Along this beach road is everything which Diani has to offer.

Do not walk along the road from Ukunda to the beach road. It's notorious for muggings. Avoiding walking is no problem as there are plenty of matatus (and KBS buses) running backwards and forwards all day on their way to or from Likoni.

Places to Stay – bottom end

The only cheap place is *Dan Trench's* (PO Box 8, Ukunda), behind the Trade Winds Hotel. It's not signposted, but if you turn off when you see the sign for the Trade Winds, it's on the right before you get to the Trade Winds entrance gate. Dan unfortunately died some time ago but the place has been taken over by Tony Partridge who is doing a lot of work to improve the facilities. These now include new water tanks, a security wall, laundry service, lighting, and breakfast on request. Camping costs US$1.70 per person per night (no tents for hire) plus there are eight double rooms and one single at US$3.40 per person per night and four self-contained apartments with kitchen, lounge and verandah at US$8.90 per day. It's a mellow place, and there are no security problems. If you're staying here you can use the beach and bar at the Trade Winds Hotel.

Places to Stay – middle

The only places in this category, and even these are not cheap, are the lodges and cottages south of the tarmac on the beach road.

At the southern end, after two km of pot-holed dirt road, is the *Galu Sea Lodge*, a pleasant two-storey building with a swimming pool. Next up, heading north, you come to the *Galu Supermarket* then the *Boko Boko Coco le Mer Restaurant* followed by the *Diani Beach Cottages* (☎ 3348) which cost US$50/69 for singles/doubles with half board. All major credit cards are accepted.

Next up are *Le Paradis Cottages*, the *Vulcano Restaurant* and *Diani Beachalets* (☎ 2180). At the latter, there's a range of self-contained rooms ranging from US$12 to US$14 in the high season (US$7.80/9.10 in the low season) for one bedroom, US$21.35 in the high season (US$14.20 in the low season) for two bedrooms, and US$27 in the high season (US$18 in the low season) for four bedrooms all plus 20% tax.

Further north still, at the beginning of the tarmac, is the popular *Four Twenty South* (☎ 2034). Here there are a number of different cottages which cost between US$17 and US$21 a double in the high season (US$17 and US$13 in the low season) plus US$4 for each extra person. Bookings can be made through Mrs M Martin, PO Box 42, Ukunda, Kenya; Let's Go Travel in Nairobi; or by ringing Nairobi ☎ 744815.

Unless indicated, all the above places to stay are self-catering and kitchen facilities are provided.

Beyond this point you're looking at major expense and the sort of ennui that only major resort complexes can offer.

Places to Stay – top end

The other hotels along this beach cost mega-bucks and are basically for those with money to burn. They range from US$35/45 a single/double to US$44/65 in the low season to *double* and *triple* that in the high season with full board. They all offer much the same – air-con rooms, swimming pool, bars, restaurant, usually a disco, and some have water sports equipment for hire. The better ones (and there are quite a few) have been designed with the environment and local architectural styles in mind; others are not so special.

From north to south along the strip the hotels are:

Southern Palms Beach Resort – US$51/65 a single/double with half board (low season); US$74/93 in the high season (☎ 3721)

Golden Beach Hotel – US$50/100 a single/double with half board (low season); US$105/210 in the high season (☎ 2625)

Diani Reef Grand Hotel – US$72/103 a single/double with half board (low season); US$110/146 in the high season. There are also more expensive deluxe rooms (☎ 2723).

Leisure Lodge & Casino – US$93/121 a single/double with full board (low season); US$136/183 in the high season. There are also more expensive suites (☎ 2011).

Leopard Beach Hotel – US$44/65 with full board (low season); US$104/152 in the high season. There are also more expensive suites and cottages (☎ 2111).

Coral Beach Cottages – US$20/34 for two/three-bedroom cottages (low season) or US$56/66 (high season), but these cottages can only be rented for a minimum period of one year (☎ 2206)

Kaskazi Beach Hotel – US$55/90 for singles/doubles including breakfast (low season); US$125/180 in the high season (☎ 3170)

Trade Winds Hotel – US$42/85 a single/double with full board (low season); US$90/120 (high season)

Diani Sea Resort – under construction.

Diani Sea Lodge – US$74/99 with full board in the high season (☎ 2114)

Two Fishes Hotel – US$47/96 a single/double with full board (low season); US$98/129 in the high season (☎ 2101)

Jadini Beach Hotel/Africana Sea Lodge – US$77/115 a single/double with full board (low season); US$120/185 in the high season (☎ 2726)

Nomad Beach Hotel – US$35/45 a single/double including breakfast (low season); US$100/135 in the high season. This hotel is closed throughout May (☎ 2155).

Safari Beach Hotel – US$85/125 a single/double with full board (low season); US$135/205 in the high season (☎ 2726)

Paradise Ocean Village Club – a private French-owned club not open to the general public

Lagoon Reef Hotel – US$43/72 a single/double with half board (low season); US$76/114 in the high season (☎ 2627)

Robinson Baobab Hotel – US$144/240 a single/double in the high season with full board (☎ 2026)

The Trade Winds Hotel and the Golden Beach Hotel are part of the African Tours & Hotels group. Bookings can be made through them at PO Box 30471, Nairobi (☎ 336858) or at PO Box 90604, Mombasa (☎ 223509).

The Diani Sea Lodge is part of the Welcome Inns Ltd Kenya. Bookings can be made through them at PO Box 86779, Mombasa (☎ 314732).

The Lagoon Reef Hotel is part of the Reef Hotels group. Bookings can be made through PO Box 82234, Mombasa (☎ 47-1771).

The Safari Beach Hotel, Jadini Beach Hotel and the Africana Sea Lodge are all part of the Alliance Hotels group.

Places to Eat
Diani beach is well supplied with shopping centres so you needn't bring everything with you from Ukunda village if you are self-catering, though the fruit and vegetables are naturally more expensive on the beach road than they are in Ukunda.

One of the largest complexes is the *Diani Beach Shopping Centre*, not far from the Trade Winds Hotel/Dan Trench's. It has a supermarket, bank, doctor's surgery, boutiques and a branch of Glory Car Hire. Further north there is *Quinnsworth Supermarket* and, further north again, is *Diani Complex* which has a supermarket, a branch of the Kenya Commercial Bank, a boutique and an Indian restaurant. Way down south beyond the tarmac and not far from the Galu Sea Lodge, is the *Galu Supermarket* which is OK for basics but carries only a limited range of goods.

If you're staying at the southern end of the beach off the tarmac, there's the *Vulcano Restaurant da Lina* (☎ 2004) which is an excellent place to eat, though a bit of a splurge. It's open every night from 7 pm until late and offers a range of classic Italian dishes as well as seafood (lobster, prawns, crabs, calamari and fish). Table reservations are recommended.

Back on the tarmac about half way towards the T-junction are a cluster of restaurants and nightclubs. Here you'll find the *Hähnchen Grill & Nightclub* (which, as the name suggests, is a German restaurant), *Temura's Restaurant* and the *Restaurant Maharani*. The latter is an Indian restaurant and is open daily from 7 to 11 pm as well as for lunch on Saturday and Sunday from 12.30 to 3 pm. In the same area but down a track on the opposite side of the road is *Ali Barbour's* which is an expensive seafood restaurant set in a coral cave between the Trade Winds Hotel and the Diani Sea Lodge.

North of the T-junction are the *Galaxy Chinese Restaurant* (next to the Quinnsworth supermarket) and the *Shan-e-Punjab* Indian restaurant in the Diani Complex. Beyond here, not far from the Diani Reef Grand Hotel, is the *African Papaya Nightclub & Restaurant*.

Apart from the above, many of the beach hotels offer buffet lunches and dinners at the weekends which are open for nonguests. Make enquiries as to which currently offer the best deals and/or the best food. Most are priced in the US$10 to US$15 range.

Entertainment

Apart from the discos in the hotels (which you may have difficulty getting into if you're not a guest), there are now four discos independent of the hotels. Because the clientele is more mixed in these discos they're more lively and worth checking out.

Opposite the Two Fishes Hotel is the *Bush Baby Nightclub*, an open-air restaurant and nightclub which is not a bad place for a bop. Not too far from here is the nightclub at the Hähnchen Grill (see Places to Eat). Almost next door to this is the *Shakatak Disco*. It's probably the best of the lot and entry is free but the price of drinks is outrageous (around three times what you would pay in a reasonable bar!).

Lastly, way up near the northern end of the tarmac, is the *African Papaya Nightclub &*

Restaurant (see the earlier Places to Eat section).

Getting There & Away

Diani is the most accessible beach if you are dependent on public transport. From the Likoni ferry there are KBS buses (No 32) every 20 minutes or so from early morning until around 7 pm. The fare is minimal and the trip takes about 30 minutes.

Plenty of matatus make the trip from Likoni to Diani. They do the journey slightly faster and cost a little more.

When the buses and matatus get to Diani they first head north along the Diani beach road then turn around and go to the southern end of the bitumen where they turn again and head for Likoni. Just tell the driver where you want to get off.

SOUTH OF DIANI

Going south of Diani, you first come to the village of **Msambweni** where you'll see a sign for a now-defunct hotel (the Black Marlin – which is being redeveloped as a semi-private hotel resort). A little further on is another sign for the *Beachcomber Hotel* alongside a surfboard on the left-hand side. This English-run place set on a cliff above a small cove has to be one of the most mellow places on the coast. Unfortunately, because it has a steady flow of regular clients throughout the year, it's not really open to walk-ins but you could try. It's about five km from the main road past the old Black Marlin.

Continuing on south (70 km from the Likoni ferry) you'll come to **Ramisi** and just beyond it is a sign (easy to miss) on the left-hand side of the road indicating 'Lazy Lagoon'. This is the turn-off for Tony Duckworth's camp site at **Bodo** which is 2½ km down the gravel road on the right-hand side.

SHIMONI & WASINI ISLAND

Shimoni is right out at the end of a small peninsula 76 km south of Likoni, and not far from the Tanzanian border. There's not a great deal here apart from the Shimoni Reef

Lodge, but it's the headquarters of the Kisite National Marine Park.

Wasini Island itself is just off the coast of the Shimoni Peninsula. It's well wooded and unspoilt and is the perfect place to relax and experience a Swahili culture virtually untouched by the 20th century and tourism. There are no cars, roads or running water on the island and the only electricity comes from generators.

On a wander around you can come across Muslim ruins, local women weaving mats, men preparing for fishing by mending nets and making fish traps, huge old baobab trees and the extensive 'coral gardens' with its odd-shaped stands of old coral that you can

---

The Swahili People

Although the people of the coast do not have a common heritage, they do have a linguistic link which unites them – Kiswahili (commonly referred to as Swahili), a Bantu-based language which evolved as a means of communication between Africans and foreign traders such as Arabs, Persians and the Portuguese. As might be expected with such diverse input, the Swahili language borrows words from Arabic, Hindi, Portuguese and even English. The word *swahili* is a derivative of the Arabic word for coast – *sahel*.

Arab traders first started plying the coast in their sailing dhows sometime before the 7th century, arriving with the north-east monsoon and sailing home on the south-west monsoon. The main exports were ivory, tortoiseshell and leopard skins, while items such as glass beads from India and porcelain from as far afield as China found their way here.

After the 7th century Islam became a strong influence as traders began settling along the coast. Today the majority of the coastal people are Muslims, although it's a world away from the puritanical forms of Islam which prevail in some places in the Middle East.

Swahili subgroups include Bajun, Siyu, Pate, Mvita, Fundi, Shela, Ozi, Vumba and Amu (residents of Lamu). ■

Siwa Instrument

Typical Swahili Houses

walk through (except at certain times of year when the sea floods it).

Kisite National Marine Park

To visit this park, which is offshore to the south-east of Wasini Island, you'll need to go by boat. See the park headquarters in Shimoni to make arrangements. Entry to the park costs US$4 for nonresidents and US$0.65 for residents. Boats to take you there cost US$4.90 per person (less than 12 people) or US$1.90 per person (12 or more people). If the sea is rough, the boats don't sail so keep an eye on the weather and tides.

Snorkelling & Diving

In addition to the boats which can be hired from the Kisite park headquarters in Shimoni, Masood Abdullah (who runs the Mpunguti Restaurant on Wasini Island) can arrange trips to the marine park. He has his own dhow as well as masks and snorkels.

There's also another outfit which can arrange all this for you known as Kisite Dhow Tours (☎ 2331 in Diani) which operates out of Jadini Beach Hotel on Diani Beach. It offers full-day tours from Shimoni jetty for US$49 (US$65 with transport from Diani Beach) which include a morning's dhow tour and snorkelling in Kisite marine park, a traditional seafood lunch and a guided walk through Wasini Island village. With a little effort, you can arrange all this for much less.

Diving safaris off the Pemba channel (spectacular!) and dhow trips to Kisite National Marine Park can also be arranged from the Shimoni Reef Hotel, but are expensive.

Places to Stay & Eat

The only place to stay at Shimoni is the *Shimoni Reef Hotel* (☎ 471771 in Mombasa; 9 in Shimoni), which is beautifully situated on a bluff overlooking the channel to Wasini Island. The facilities are excellent and it's a very mellow place to stay. The price for singles/doubles with half board is US$43/76 in the low season, US$72/114 in the high

season. The full-board supplement is US$10 per person.

Across the channel on Wasini Island, the only accommodation is at the *Mpunguti Restaurant*, run by Mr Masood Adullah. You can camp here if you have your own gear for US$1.10 per person per night or rent a very clean and pleasant room for US$6.70 per person (half board) or US$10 (full board). Cooking facilities are available for those who prefer self-catering (fish, coconuts, maize flour and rice are for sale in Shimoni and on Wasini, but very little else).

Masood is a very affable character and well organised, and the traditional Swahili food he turns out is delicious. Alcoholic drinks must be brought with you from the mainland – there are none available on the island.

Getting There & Away

There are a couple of direct buses and matatus daily between Shimoni and Likoni. Hitching is also a possibility.

From Likoni there are taxis available to Shimoni, or you can take one of the few KBS buses which do the trip daily. You could also take a matatu towards Lunga Lunga and get off at the Shimoni turn-off, but you'd then have to hitch the 14 km from the main road to Shimoni. It's not that difficult – even the locals do it.

Once at Shimoni (unless you intend to stay at the Shimoni Reef Hotel) you'll have to negotiate a dhow ride across the channel. The price for this depends to a degree on who you meet on arrival, how many there are of you and how affluent you look. If you assume US$18 for the boat (round trip) you won't be too far wrong, though you can get it cheaper.

The same people who run the dhows will also take you to the reefs for snorkelling for much the same price but you'll have to negotiate a price for the hire of snorkelling gear.

SHIMBA HILLS NATIONAL RESERVE

This national reserve is in the hills behind the coast south of Mombasa, directly inland from Diani Beach. The forest setting is beautiful but the game is not prolific. There is a baited water hole at the Shimba Hills Lodge, and so it's possible you'll see leopards and plenty of elephants but not much else. Other animals which frequent the reserve include the rare sable antelope – a tall and compact animal with beautifully curved horns on both the male and female. The adult bull is a dark brown on the upper body and white below, while the female is a lighter brown. The animals are, unfortunately, often killed by poachers for meat, and this is the only reserve where they are found.

Places to Stay

The camp site has a superb location on the edge of the range with views right down to Diani Beach. It's about three km from the main gate, which itself is about three km from the village of Kwale.

The only alternative to camping is Block Hotels' *Shimba Hills Lodge* (☎ 335807 in Nairobi) where singles/doubles with half board cost US$97/124 in the low season (1 April to 30 June) and US$162/206 in the high season. There is an additional supplement of US$19 per person at Christmas and Easter. Note that children under seven years old are not admitted to this lodge. The water hole here is baited to attract a few animals and is floodlit at night.

Getting There & Away

There are KBS buses to Kwale, from where it shouldn't be too difficult to hitch to the park entrance. Once there, however, you may have a long wait for a vehicle back. The road from Kwale to Kinango, the next inland town, actually passes through the northern part of the park and there's a chance of seeing animals from the KBS buses. The No 34 bus runs from Likoni to Kwale.

North of Mombasa

MOMBASA TO KILIFI

Like the coast south of Mombasa, the north coast has been well developed almost two-thirds of the way up to Kilifi with resort complexes which take up much of the beach frontage. Most of them cater to package tourists on two to three-week holidays from Europe but there is scope for individual initiative here and there, though only the Jauss Farm at Vipingo and the 'youth hostel' at Kikambala genuinely fall into the budget accommodation bracket.

As with Shelly and much of Tiwi beaches south of Mombasa, the northern beaches are plagued with seaweed which clogs them and makes swimming an often unpleasant experience. Only at the expensive resort hotels are people employed to minimise this inconvenience by raking it into piles and either burning it or burying it. Elsewhere you literally have to jump into the soup.

Going north from Mombasa the names of the beaches are Nyali, Bamburi, Shanzu, Kikambala and Vipingo.

Mamba Crocodile Village

Mamba Village (☎ (011) 472709) is north of Mombasa on the mainland opposite Nyali Golf Club in the Nyali Estate. It's a crocodile farm set amongst streams, waterfalls and wooden bridges. If you've never seen a crocodile farm with reptiles ranging from the newly born to the full grown, here's your chance. Personally, I've seen a lot of these farms in the past and I don't find them very interesting. They're often just a collection of concrete and wire-mesh cages with thousands of young crocodiles up to five years old, and a few token, fully grown adults to pull in the punters. You pay through the nose to see them, too, even though the owners of the farms are making megabucks selling skins to Gucci and the like.

Bamburi Quarry Nature Trail

Further up the coast, this nature trail (☎ (011) 485729) has been created on reclaimed and reforested areas damaged by cement production activities which ceased in 1971. Once the forest was established, the area was restocked with plants and animals in an attempt to create a mini replica of the wildlife parks of Kenya. At present, animal species represented include eland, oryx, waterbuck, buffaloes, wart hogs, bush pigs, various monkeys and many different varieties of birds. There's also what the owners claim to be an 'orphan' hippo which was introduced as a baby from Naivasha and which has remained bottle-fed ever since. A likely story!

The complex also includes a fish farm, crocodile farm, reptile pit and plant nursery. The centre is open daily from 2 to 5.30 pm. Feeding time is at 4 pm. To get there take a public bus to Bamburi Quarry Nature Trail stop (signposted) on the main Mombasa to Malindi road.

Places to Stay – bottom end

There are very few cheap places to stay on the beaches north of Mombasa. Even places way back from the beach with nothing special going for them can be remarkably expensive.

One of the few genuine cheapies is the *Kanamai Conference Centre* (☎ (0125) 32046) at Kikambala Beach which was previously a youth hostel but is no longer affiliated to the IYHF. Dormitory beds are US$3.90 in either two, six or 10-bed rooms, while self-contained one-bedroom cottages are US$16, two-bedroom US$31, and three-bedroom US$48. Meals are available for US$2.50 for breakfast, US$3.50 for lunch and US$3.90 for dinner – expensive for what is basically ugali and chicken stew. There's also a laundry service.

The trouble with this place is getting there! First you have to take a matatu to Majengo on the Mombasa to Kilifi road (from near the New People's Hotel in Mombasa). Get off when you see a yellow sign saying 'Camping Kanamai'. Go down the dirt track by this sign for about 300 metres and then turn left at the fork. Continue for about three km and you'll find it on the left-hand side by the beach. It's a long, hot walk and lifts are few and far between. With a backpack it's a major effort.

Close by, a little further to the north along the track which runs parallel to the beach, are the *Continental Beach Cottages* (☎ (0125)

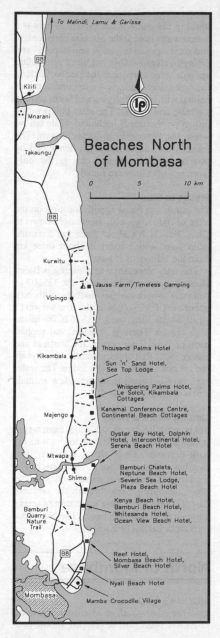

Beaches North of Mombasa

32077) which are good value at US$19.50 per person in the high season (US$21 with breakfast), dropping to US$14 in the low season. Accommodation is in one and two-bedroom self-contained cottages each with lounge, kitchen, bathroom and air-con. It's rarely full and there's a good swimming pool, bar and restaurant and a pleasant beach. Cheap meals (omelette & chips and curries) are available for around US$3. As with the Conference Centre, the only problem about this place is getting there; taxis are expensive.

Right next door to the Continental is *Kikambala Cottages* (☎ (0125) 32032), a very basic place with no pool or restaurant. However, the self-contained cottages are comfortable enough, and cheap at US$35 with two bedrooms, lounge, and kitchen with fridge. You need to be fairly self-sufficient here as there are no shops or cheap restaurants nearby.

If you're staying at either of the above places and want a change of scene or a cold beer, the Whispering Palms Hotel is about 15 minutes' walk north along the beach. Breakfasts here cost US$5.80 and you can use the swimming pool for US$3.90 per day.

A little further north, just behind the Sun 'n' Sand Hotel and about three km off the main coast road, is the *Sea Top Lodge* (☎ (0125) 32184), a small hotel which seems to be a bar first and a hotel second. The cost is US$9.70 for a small but clean double room. There are a few small dukas nearby and the beach is a short walk away. With a little discretion you could probably use the facilities at the Sun 'n' Sand.

Further up the coast at Vipingo, about 40 km north of Mombasa, there is *Timeless Camping* (☎ (0125) 32218) on the Jauss family farm. It consists of a camp site, budget chalets, and two self-contained bungalows on an 85-hectare dairy and tropical-fruit farm with its own quiet and unspoilt silver-sand beach. The camp site is equipped with showers and toilets and costs US$1.95 per person per night. The budget chalets are fairly basic twin rooms with clean beds and mattresses, and toilets and showers have to be shared with those occupying the camp site. The cost for these is US$5.90 per person. The bungalows are fully equipped and cost US$58 for the four-bed one, and US$78 for the large bungalow which sleeps 10 people. Excellent and filling meals are available, no matter which accommodation you are using, and these are very good value at US$2.30 for a half breakfast, US$4.50 with the works, and US$6.10 for lunch or dinner. The bar has the coldest beers on the coast, and there's a well-stocked library. This very laid-back place has a wonderfully informal atmosphere and is the perfect place to drop out for a few days – or weeks. If arriving by public transport, get off at Vipingo village and ring from there; someone will come and collect you. If you have your own transport, take the signposted turn-off to Timeless Camping, on the main road 1.6 km north of Vipingo.

Places to Stay – top end
Virtually all the other hotels along this stretch of the East African coast before you arrive at Kilifi are resort complexes and cater largely for package tourists from Europe. Most of them are so self-contained that many of those staying there hardly ever see anything of Africa other than Mombasa airport, the inside of minibuses, the hotel itself and Black Kenyan waiters. As at the hotels south of Mombasa and at Malindi, many cater almost exclusively for one specific European nationality whether they be British, German or Italian (French people don't feature prominently in East African tourism). There's precious little intermingling.

All the hotels compete furiously with each other to provide the utmost in creature comforts, mellow surroundings, day trips and sports facilities and there's little to choose between them though it's generally true to say that the further you get from Mombasa, the cheaper and less ritzy they become.

Down at Nyali Beach – the closest to Mombasa – even places which don't face the sea and are in no way hotel resorts, and which you might imagine should be fairly cheap given the facilities they offer, can be surprisingly expensive. *Bamburi Chalets* (☎ (011) 485706), for example, which offers self-contained cottages with two bunk beds, two normal beds, shower, cooking facilities, gas stove, refrigerator, and use of a swimming pool cost US$78 per night or US$117 with sea views. The *Cowrie Shell Apartments* (☎ (011) 485971) all have two bedrooms and face the sea, and cost US$58 to US$117 depending on the season. The *Baharini Chalets* (☎ (011) 486302) have only one bedroom and are much cheaper at US$23, but are not great value as there are no cooking facilities.

It's unlikely that if you intend to stay at any of the genuine resort complexes that you'll be reading this book since you'd have reserved your hotel via an agent and your air fares would be included in a package deal. Should you wish to make your own arrangements for staying at any of the resort complexes, however, here's a selection of the hotels.

Nyali Beach The following resorts are at Nyali Beach:

Mombasa Beach Hotel – singles/doubles cost US$114/151 with breakfast (☎ (011) 471861)
Nyali Beach Hotel – US$159/190 with breakfast, US$137/229 with half board, US$195/263 with full board (☎ (011) 471551)
Reef Hotel – singles/doubles for US$99/148 with half board (☎ (011) 471771)

Kenyatta-Bamburi Beach Further north are the following hotels:

Bamburi Beach Hotel – singles/doubles with breakfast cost US$35/46 (low season), US$58/73 (high season); add US$6 for full board (☎ (011) 485611)
Neptune Beach Hotel – US$39/55 with breakfast (low season), US$55/74 (mid-season) and US$105/144 (high season); children aged from three to 12 years pay 50% (☎ (011) 485701)
Ocean View Beach Hotel – US$70/109 with half board (☎ (011) 485601)
Plaza Beach Hotel – US$62/70 with breakfast (low season), US$195/211 with full board in the high season (☎ (011) 485321)

Severin Sea Lodge – US$39/78 for singles/doubles with breakfast (low season), US$94/129 (mid-season) and US$97/136 (high season); children pay 50% (☎ (011) 485001)
Whitesands Hotel – US$55/109 for singles/doubles with half board (low season), US$234/434 for a one-bedroom/two-bedroom apartment (high season). Children pay 75% of the full price and meals cost US$9 for breakfast, US$14 for lunch and US$16 for dinner (☎ (011) 485926).

Shanzu Beach At Shanzu Beach are the following resorts:

Dolphin Hotel – US$58/104 for singles/doubles with full board (☎ (011) 485801)
Intercontinental Hotel – singles/doubles with breakfast cost US$118/150 (low season), US$138/175 (mid-season), and US$152/191 in the high season (☎ (011) 485811)
Oyster Bay Hotel – singles/doubles with breakfast cost US$27/55 (low season), US$35/70 (mid-season), US$39/78 (high season) (☎ (011) 485061)
Serena Beach Hotel – singles/doubles cost US$45/91 with breakfast (low season), US$91/117 (mid-season), US$117/156 (high season). Other meals cost US$12, and children aged three to 12 years pay 50% (☎ (011) 485721).

Kikambala Beach Finally, Kikambala Beach offers the following:

Whispering Palms Hotel – singles/doubles with full board cost US$94/122 (low season), and US$120/165 in the high season (☎ (0125) 32004)
Sun 'n' Sand Beach Hotel – singles/doubles with half board cost US$52/104 in the low season, and US$110/130 in the high season; children are charged 50% of the adult rate (☎ (0125) 32133)

Takaungu Right up at the top end of this long line of beaches close to Kilifi is the village of Takaungu. It's supposedly the oldest slave port on the Kenyan coast – Zanzibar is the oldest. It's worth a visit if you have the time. The local people are very superstitious and no-one goes down to the beach at night except the fishers. If you can speak Swahili you'll hear many weird stories going around which date back to the time of slavery. It's an interesting place right off the beaten track where you won't meet any other travellers.

Rooms can be rented in private houses in

Takaungu for around US$2.60 per night. Ask at the teashops.

For those with slightly less limited resources there's *Takaungu House* (☎ (02) 502491), a luxury house privately owned and run. There are just three bedrooms, but other features include a swimming pool, beach frontage, snorkelling, water-skiing and deep-sea fishing on request. The charge for full board is US$116 per person.

KILIFI

Other than Mtwapa Creek, just north of Mombasa, Kilifi is the first major break in the coastline between Mombasa and Malindi. It has been a backwater for many years, ignored by developers yet coveted by discerning White Kenyans, artists, writers and adventurers from various parts of the world who have gradually bought up most of the land overlooking the wide creek and the ocean and built, in many cases, some quite stunning and imaginative houses. They form a sort of society within a society and keep largely to themselves. Without an introduction, it's unlikely you'll meet them though sailing a yacht into the creek would probably secure you an invitation! Kilifi Creek is a popular anchorage spot for yachties in this part of the world and you can meet them in the evening at the Seahorse Hotel off to the left of the main road on the northern side of the creek.

So why stop off in Kilifi? The answer to this is mainly for the contrast it offers to Mombasa and Malindi, and for the Mnarani ruins on a bluff overlooking the creek on the Mombasa side. Very few travellers ever see these ruins yet they're well preserved and just as interesting as those at Gedi though not as extensive. The beach, too, on either side of the creek is very pleasant and doesn't suffer from the seaweed problem which plagues the beaches further south. The only problem is access, which is mostly through private property, though you can walk along it from the ferry landing at low tide.

The present district centre of Kilifi is on the northern bank of the creek.

Information

Kilifi consists of the small village of Mnarani (or Manarani) on the southern bank of the creek and Kilifi itself on the northern bank. It's a small town which you can walk around within minutes.

There's a good variety of shops (including a small bookshop), a lively open-air market and an enclosed fruit and vegetable market, a post office, a number of basic hotels and two banks. Barclays Bank is open Monday to Friday from 8.30 am to 1 pm and on Saturday from 8.30 to 11 am. The Kenya Commercial Bank keeps the same hours.

Mnarani Ruins

Mnarani, on the southern bank of Kilifi Creek overlooking the ferry landing, was once one of the string of Swahili city-states which dotted the East African coast. Excavations carried out in 1954 showed that the site was occupied from the end of the 14th century to around the first half of the 17th century after which it was destroyed by marauding Galla tribespeople. The principal ruins here include the Great Mosque with its finely carved inscription around the mihrab (the niche in a mosque showing the direction of Mecca), a group of tombs to the north (including one pillar tomb), a small mosque dating from the 16th century, and parts of the town wall and a gate. There's also a large and forbiddingly deep well whose shaft must go down at least as far as the low-tide level of the creek.

Mnarani was associated with **Kioni**, at the mouth of Kilifi Creek on the same side, and with **Kitoka**, about 3½ km south of here on the northern bank of Takaungu Creek. A carved stone with an interlaced ornament, probably from a mihrab, was found at Kioni on the cliff above the creek and is presently in the Fort Jesus museum at Mombasa. The ruins at Kitoka include a mosque similar to the small mosque at Mnarani along with a few houses. All these settlements were subject to Mombasa.

The Mnarani ruins are just above the old southern ferry landing stage and the path to them (about 300 metres long) is prominently

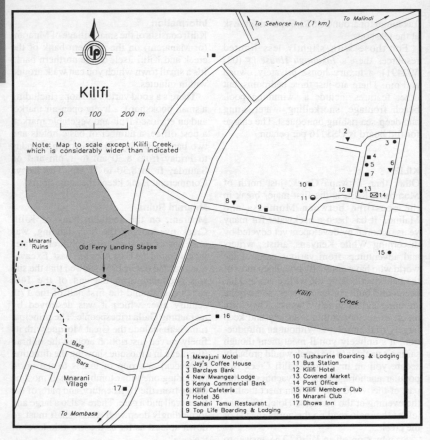

Kilifi

0   100   200 m

Note: Map to scale except Kilifi Creek, which is considerably wider than indicated

To Seahorse Inn (1 km)

To Malindi

Mnarani Ruins

Old Ferry Landing Stages

Kilifi Creek

Bars

Bars

Mnarani Village

To Mombasa

1 Mkwajuni Motel
2 Jay's Coffee House
3 Barclays Bank
4 New Mwangea Lodge
5 Kenya Commercial Bank
6 Kilifi Cafeteria
7 Hotel 36
8 Sahani Tamu Restaurant
9 Top Life Boarding & Lodging
10 Tushaurine Boarding & Lodging
11 Bus Station
12 Kilifi Hotel
13 Covered Market
14 Post Office
15 Kilifi Members Club
16 Mnarani Club
17 Dhows Inn

signposted on the main road. Entry costs US$3.90 but there's often no-one there to collect the fee.

Places to Stay – bottom end

There are a number of cheap places to stay in Kilifi including the *Top Life Boarding & Lodging* (hardboard cubicles), the *Kilifi Hotel*, the *Hotel 36* and the *New Mwangea Lodge* but probably the best place to stay is the *Tushaurine Boarding & Lodging* (☎ (0125) 22486) near the bus station. This is a recently constructed hotel, several storeys high, which offers good, clean, simple rooms with mosquito nets and shared bathroom facilities for US$3.90/5.80 a single/double.

Places to Stay – middle

The best place in this range is the *Dhows Inn* (☎ (0125) 22028) on the main road south of Kilifi Creek. It's a fairly small place with a number of double rooms surrounding a well-kept garden. There's a lively and quite popular bar and restaurant. A room here with mosquito nets and bath costs US$15, though the price is negotiable to a degree. If arriving by bus or matatu, get the driver to drop you right outside, rather than in Kilifi itself in which case you'll have the long walk across the bridge.

On the northern side of the bridge, just off the main road, is the *Mkwajuni Motel* (☎ (0125) 22472). Set in a spacious garden, the rooms are small but very clean and neat, each with a small patio and table and chairs. The motel is only about 10 minutes' walk into town. Single/double rooms cost US$12/16 including breakfast.

Places to Stay – top end

The large resort complex at Kilifi is the somewhat exclusive *Mnarani Club* on the southern side of Kilifi Creek and quite close to the Dhows Inn. It's one of the African Safari Club hotels and so bookings must be made through Mombasa (☎ (011) 485520). The hotel caters largely to package tourists from Germany and Switzerland and it's these people who keep the craft-shop owners of Mnarani village smiling.

Despite its size, the Mnarani Club is hardly visible from the main road or even from a boat on the creek since it's constructed of local materials (including some enormous makuti roofs) and surrounded by beautifully landscaped gardens full of flowering trees.

The other top-range hotel is the *Seahorse Inn* (☎ (0125) 22813), about 1½ km off to the left of the main Mombasa to Malindi road on the northern side of the creek. It's a very pleasant place with individual bandas set in a coconut grove right on the banks of Kilifi Creek, which at this point is a couple of km wide. To stay here will set you back US$51/78 for full board. Like the Mnarani Club, the Seahorse is run by the African Safari Club, so the same applies with bookings.

Places to Eat

A cheap and very popular place to eat both for lunch and dinner is the *Kilifi Hotel* at the bus station. Standard Indo-African fare is on offer, and you can eat well here for around US$2.60. Another popular place, especially

at lunch time, is the *Kilifi Cafeteria* though prices here are somewhat higher.

Across on the southern side of the creek, you can eat at the *Dhows Inn* which has a limited menu of meat and seafood dishes. The only trouble with eating here is that food takes forever to arrive and the quality is variable: sometimes it's good, sometimes it's almost inedible. The average price of a main course is around US$3.

For a splurge, go for a meal at the *Mnarani Club* or the *Seahorse Hotel*. At both places you can partake in the buffet lunch spread for US$6.50, which is excellent value. In the evenings à la carte meals are available for the same price.

Even more up-market is the very agreeable *Sahani Tamu Restaurant* on the northern side of the creek, opposite the Mnarani Club. The food here is mainly Italian and seafood and is very well prepared and presented. Main dishes such as spaghetti are in the US$3 to US$4 range, steaks are around US$6, and seafood dishes from US$9 to US$15. It's well worth the expense and makes a very pleasant evening out. The restaurant is open daily, except Tuesday, from 11 am to 2 pm and 6 to 10 pm.

Entertainment

For a spit-and-sawdust evening on Tusker or White Cap you can't beat the bars in Mnarani village of which there are several, but the amount of action depends largely on how many tourists brave the 200 metres or so of dirt road between the Mnarani Club and the village. Don't expect cold beers at any of these bars.

The bar at the *Dhows Inn* on the other hand is usually pretty lively and you can be assured of cold beer.

The *Mnarani Club* has a nightly floor show – usually of tribal dancing – followed by a live African band which plays until late. Entry to the show and dance costs US$3.90. Nonguests can rent windsurfing equipment from this hotel during the day for US$3.90 per hour.

For a far more informal evening pay a visit

to the *Kilifi Members Club* on the northern side of the creek.

Getting There & Away
All the buses and matatus which ply between Mombasa and Malindi stop at Kilifi but getting on a bus at Kilifi to go to either Mombasa or Malindi can be problematical since they're often full. Matatus are a much better bet.

WATAMU
About 24 km south of Malindi, Watamu is a smaller beach resort development with its own marine national park – part of the Marine National Reserve which stretches south from Malindi. The coral reef here is even more spectacular than at Malindi since it has been much less exploited and poached by shell hunters. In addition, underwater visibility is not affected by silt brought down into the sea by the Galana River.

The coast at Watamu is broken up into three separate coves divided by craggy and eroded headlands and there are a number of similarly eroded islands just offshore. The coral sand is a dazzling white and although there is some shade from coconut palms, you'll probably have to retreat to the cooler confines of a hotel bar or restaurant in the middle of the day. The most southerly cove is fronted entirely by beach resorts and exclusive private houses. The central cove also has many resorts, though they are not as extensive. The northern cove and part of the headland is covered by the rambling Watamu Beach Hotel at the back of which is the actual village of Watamu.

Before tourist development got underway here, Watamu was a mellow little fishing village of makuti-roofed cottages nestled beneath coconut palms and it still retains much of that atmosphere despite the intrusion of souvenir shops, bars and restaurants catering for the tourist hordes. In fact the contrasts are quite bizarre – it's the only place I've seen package tourists in beach wear wandering down the dusty streets of an African village! A lot of development has

taken place on the outskirts of the village and seems destined to continue.

Information
There is a branch of Barclays Bank in the village of Watamu which is open from 9 am to noon on Monday, Wednesday and Friday.

Watamu National Marine Park
The actual coral reef lies between one and two km offshore and to get to it you'll have to hire a glass-bottomed boat. These can be arranged at any of the large hotels or, alternatively, ask at any of the souvenir stalls that line the main road in Watamu. Expect to pay US$15.60 per person. It's worth every cent!

There are also boat trips to a group of **caves** at the entrance to **Mida Creek** which are home to a school of giant rock cod many of which are up to two metres long. Diving equipment is usually necessary to get down to their level since, most of the time, they remain stationary on the bottom.

Places to Stay – bottom end
Budget accommodation has always been something of a problem in Watamu. There are a couple of cheap lodges in the village but they can't seriously be recommended. The *Blue Lodge* charges US$5.90 for a scruffy, stuffy and gloomy double room illuminated by only the feeblest of globes – only for the desperate. The other alternative, *Sam's Lodge*, is no better, though it is marginally cheaper at US$4.60 for a double. Neither place has fans or mosquito nets – which are absolutely essential on the coast.

Another possibility in the village is a private house known as the *Maasai House*. It has one double room for US$9, and another self-contained room for US$9.80. There's a kitchen, big verandah, a garden with a well, and a housekeeper who will cook meals at a reasonable charge. It's a good place to meet the Samburu performers from the Watamu Beach Hotel.

Of the regular lodges, the best value is the family-run *Villa Veronica/Mwikali Lodge* (☎ (0122) 32083), opposite the Hotel Dante Bar & Restaurant. This is a very friendly and

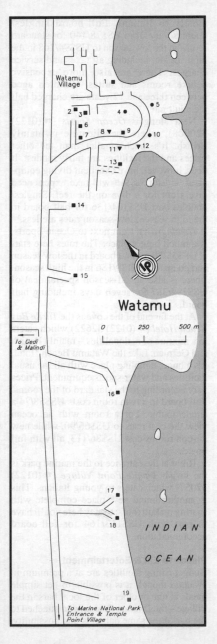

1   Watamu Beach Hotel
2   Sam's Lodge
3   Blue Lodge
4   Bank
5   Bicycle Hire
6   Peponi Cottages
7   Watamu Paradise Restaurant
    & Cottages
8   Come Back Club Tim's Restaurant
9   Villa Veronica
10 Barclays Bank
11 Hotel Dante Bar & Restaurant
12 Happy Night Bar & Restaurant
13 Barracuda Inn
14 Seventh Day Adventist Youth Camp
15 Watamu Cottages
16 Blue Bay Village
17 Ocean Sports Hotel
18 Hemingways Hotel
19 Turtle Bay Beach Hotel

secure place which offers spotlessly clean rooms with fan, mosquito nets, shower and toilet for US$16/19 a single/double including breakfast.

The *Hotel Dante* itself is about the cheapest habitable place, and self-contained doubles (no singles) go for US$14. The price does not include breakfast, but there is a small swimming pool.

The only other place that fits this price bracket is *Watamu Cottages* (☎ (0122) 32211), on the main access road to the village and about 15 minutes' hot walk. These are a good deal at US$15 for a self-contained double including breakfast. The rooms are set in a pleasant garden which also has a swimming pool.

It may occasionally be possible to get a cheap room at the *Seventh Day Adventist Youth Camp* if there's no group there but don't count on it. You can also camp here if you have your own tent. The facilities are minimal though there is a gas cooker which you can use.

Places to Stay – middle

Peponi Cottages (☎ (0122) 32246) consists of a two-storey, makuti-roofed block of rooms which are quite pleasant, if a little small. Each has mosquito netting on the windows, and a balcony runs the length of the building. There's also a small pool. A double costs US$19, which does not include breakfast.

On the main road leaving the village is the *Watamu Paradise Restaurant & Cottages* (☎ (0122) 32062) which has a number of cottages each containing three double bedrooms with fan, mosquito nets and bathroom. A double here costs from US$19 to US$28, depending on the facilities. It's a very pleasant place to stay and there's a swimming pool in the complex.

Places to Stay – top end

Top-end hotels take up much of the beach frontage along each of the three coves. As at Malindi, they're mostly resort-type hotels which cater to package tourists' every need and are quite specific as to the European nationality which they appeal to – German, British or Italian.

At the northern end and next to Watamu village is the rambling *Watamu Beach Hotel* (☎ (0122) 32001), where most of the German tourists stay. It's one of the many hotels operated by the African Safari Club, a German-based organisation, and casual bookings are not encouraged – they don't even know at the reception desk what the tariff is! If you want to stay, bookings can be made at the African Safari Club office in Mombasa (☎ (011) 485520). Room rates start at US$70/90 for full board. The hotel has a swimming pool, and with a little discretion nonguests can use it.

At the northern end of the central cove is the *Barracuda Inn* (☎ (0122) 617074). This is another foreign-owned place and bookings can only be made in Italy! They will let you stay if there's a vacancy, but expect to pay at least US$47 for a double. It has a very pleasant makuti-roofed bar and restaurant area, while the air-con cottages are set back from the beach.

The southern cove sports at least five hotels, all of them of the resort variety. Closest to Watamu village is the *Blue Bay Village* (☎ (0122) 323626), which caters

mostly to Italians. Full-board singles/doubles vary from US$78/140 for standard rooms in the low season to US$94/168 in the high season, including all taxes and service charges. There are also more expensive deluxe rooms and suites. Children aged between three and 12 years are charged half the adult rate.

Next along is *Ocean Sports* (☎ (0122) 320008), where the clientele is mainly British. It's much smaller than the other places and the facilities are fairly modest. It does, however, have excellent diving equipment and for US$19 will take experienced divers out for a dive on the reef. Singles/doubles cost US$104/136 for half board in the high season; low-season rates are less.

Hemingways, right next to Ocean Sports, is a much bigger place. The rates here start at US$53/70 for half board in the low season and go up to US$139/186 in the high season. There is also an off-season special deal of US$294/387 for seven days including half board.

At the far end of the cove is the *Turtle Bay Beach Hotel* (☎ (0122) 32622) which caters to a mixture of nationalities – mainly British and German. Like the Watamu Beach Hotel, it's a huge, rambling place with all the usual facilities and water-sports equipment. Prices vary according to the standard of the rooms. Full board in a twin room costs US$58/74 a single/double. For a room with an ocean view the cost rises to US$66/90, while new air-con rooms cost US$86/113, all with full board.

Right at the entrance to the marine park is the lavish *Temple Point Village* (☎ (0122) 32057) which caters to young Italians. This is another brand new place complete with soaring makuti roofs; to stay here you'll have to part with US$113/164 for full-board accommodation.

Places to Eat & Entertainment

Budget eating facilities are at a premium in Watamu though it is possible to get simple meals at one or other of the local bars in the village – the *Ujamaa Restaurant*, attached to the bar of the same name, is one possibility.

Friend's Corner is a small duka on the road between the Come Back Club and Villa Veronica. It has about the best cheap food in town, although the variety is limited.

The *Hotel Dante* is probably the best of the non-resort restaurants. The service is slow but there's warm beer and a juke box to distract you while you're waiting. Almost opposite is *Come Back Club Tim's Restaurant*, but the food is not up to much and it's hard to think of a good reason to come back, except perhaps to dance in the disco which operates some nights.

The *Happy Night Bar & Restaurant* has ice-cold beers and European-style food, all at Kenyan (rather than lodge) prices, but its opening hours are erratic. It sometimes has live music or disco nights.

For a splurge, the lunch-time buffet meals at the *Watamu Beach Hotel* are a real bargain. For US$6.50 you can dip into the buffet as many times as you like, and the range of dishes is very good. This is one of the few places on the coast where outside guests are openly welcome to use the restaurant – even if they do greet you with 'Guten tag'!

Getting There & Away

Matatus leave from the bus station in Malindi throughout the day. They cost US$0.50 to Watamu and take about 30 minutes. Most of these first go down to the Turtle Bay Beach Hotel after which they turn around and go to Watamu village. On the return journey they generally go direct from Watamu village to Malindi without first going down to the Turtle Bay Beach Hotel.

Getting Around

Bicycles can be hired for US$0.50 per hour or US$2 per day from a place next door to the Nyambene Lodge in Watamu village.

GEDI

Some three to four km from Watamu, just off the main Malindi to Mombasa road, are the famous Gedi ruins, one of the principal historical monuments on the coast. Though the ruins are extensive, this Arab-Swahili town is something of a mystery since it's not mentioned in any of the Portuguese or Arab chronicles of the time.

Excavations, which have uncovered such things as Ming Chinese porcelain and glass and glazed earthenware from Persia, have indicated the 13th century as the time of its foundation, but it was inexplicably abandoned in the 17th or 18th century, possibly because the sea receded and left the town high and dry, or because of marauding Galla tribespeople from the north. The forest took over and the site was not rediscovered until the 1920s. Even if you have only a passing interest in archaeology it's worth a visit.

Entry costs US$3.90 (US$0.75 for students and children) and the site is open daily from 7 am to 6 pm. A good guidebook with map is for sale at the entrance.

The site is surprisingly large and surrounded by two walls, the inner one of which was possibly built to enclose a smaller area after the city was temporarily abandoned in the 15th to 16th centuries. In places it actually incorporates earlier houses into its structure. The site is lush and green with numerous baobab trees. Monkeys chatter in the tree tops, lizards rustle in the undergrowth and large, colourful butterflies flutter among the ruins.

The buildings were constructed of coral rag, coral lime and earth and some have pictures incised into the plaster finish of their walls, though many of these have deteriorated in recent years. The toilet facilities in the houses are particularly impressive, generally in a double-cubicle style with a squat toilet in one and a wash stand in the other where a bowl would have been used. Fancier versions even have double washbasins with a bidet between them.

The other notable feature of the site is the great number of wells, many them remarkably deep.

Most of the interesting excavated buildings are concentrated in a dense cluster near the entrance gate. There are several others scattered around the site within the inner wall and even between the inner and outer walls. Outside the site, by the car park, there's a small museum with some items found on the site. Other items are exhibited in Fort Jesus in Mombasa.

The Tombs

On your right as you enter the site is the Dated Tomb, so-called because the Muslim date corresponding to 1399 has been deciphered. This tomb has provided a reference point for dating other buildings within the complex. Next to it is the Tomb of the Fluted Pillar which is characteristic of such pillar designs found up and down the East African coast. There's another good example of this kind of pillar in Lamu.

The Great Mosque

The Great Mosque originally dates from the mid-15th century but was rebuilt a century later, possibly as a result of damage sustained at the time of Gedi's first abandonment. The mosque is of typical East African design with a mihrab facing towards Mecca. You can see where porcelain bowls were once mounted in the walls flanking the mihrab.

The Palace

Behind the mosque are the ruins of the extensive palace which is entered through an arched door. Once through the doorway, you enter a reception court and then a large audience hall while to the left of this are numerous smaller rooms. Look for the many 'bathrooms' and the room flanking the audience hall with its square niches in the walls intended for lamps. Behind that room is another one with no doorway at all which would probably have been used to store valuables. Entry was by ladder through a small hatch high up in the wall. Beyond this is a kitchen area with a small but still very deep well.

The Palace also has a particularly fine pillar tomb, while to the right is the Annexe with four individual apartments, each with its own courtyard.

The Houses

In all, 14 houses have been excavated at Gedi, 10 of which are in a compact group beside the Great Mosque and the Palace.

They're named after particular features of their design or after objects found in them by archaeologists. They include the House of the Cowrie, House of the Cistern and House of the Porcelain Bowl.

Other Buildings

Follow the signposted path from the Tomb of the Fluted Pillar to the adjoining House of the Dhow and House of the Double Court with a nearby tomb. There are pictures in the wall plaster in these houses.

A path follows close to the inner city wall from the houses to the Mosque of the Three Aisles where you will also find the largest well in Gedi. Beside it is the inner wall of the East Gate from where a path leads to the Mosque Between the Walls; a path cuts back to the car park from here.

Alternatively, from the East Gate you can follow another path right around the inner circuit of the inner wall or divert to the Mosque on the Wall at the southern extremity of the outer wall. The House on the West Wall actually comprises several adjoining houses of typical design while at the northern end of the town there is the more complex North Gate.

Just outside the North Gate is a 'traditional' **Giriama tribal village**, and here the package tourists are entertained with 'traditional' Giriama dances. Unfortunately it's *very* contrived and the dancing girls' costumes look something like a cross between a Hawaiian skirt and a tennis outfit!

Getting There & Away

Take the same matatu as you would to go to Watamu but get off at Gedi village where the matatu turns off from the main Malindi to Mombasa road. From there it's about a one-km signposted walk to the ruins along a gravel road.

It's also possible to get a taxi to take you on a round trip from Malindi for about US$19 with an hour or more to look around the site. This could be worth it if your time is limited and there's a small group to share costs.

Top: Unloading a dhow, Lamu, Kenya (GC)
Bottom: Waterfront, Lamu, Kenya (GC)

Top: Giraffe & calves, Masai Mara Game Reserve, Kenya (GH)
Left: Camel trekking, Ndoto Mountains, Kenya (SB)
Right: Zebra, Amboseli National Park, Kenya (SB)

MALINDI

Malindi was an important Swahili settlement as far back as the 14th century and often rivalled Mombasa and Paté for control of this part of the East African coast. It was also one of the very few places where the early Portuguese mariners found a sympathetic welcome, and today you can still see the cross which Vasco da Gama erected as a navigational aid.

These days, on account of its beaches, it has experienced a tourist boom similar to that north and south of Mombasa, and resort hotels are strung out all the way along the coast. On the other hand, it still retains a recognisable African centre where commerce, business and everyday activities, which aren't necessarily connected with the tourist trade, continue. Cotton growing and processing, sisal production and fishing are still major income earners. It isn't, however, a Lamu or Zanzibar. The streets here are relatively wide and straight and there are few buildings more than a century old.

It's a popular port of call for travellers heading north from Mombasa although the beach here is nothing special and is often choked with seaweed – as are many of the beaches along the coast. The only drawback to Malindi is the brown silt which flows down the Galana River at the northern end of the bay during the rainy season which makes the sea very muddy. For the rest of the year it's perfect and even during the rainy season you can largely avoid the muddy waters by going to the beaches south of town.

Information

Tourist Office There is a tourist office next door to Kenya Airways opposite the shopping centre on the Lamu road. The staff are helpful but have little useful information.

Money Barclays Bank is open Monday to Friday from 8.30 am to 1 pm and 2.30 to 5 pm and on Saturday from 8.30 am to noon. In the low season it's often closed on Saturdays. The Standard Chartered Bank has much the same hours.

Post & Telecommunications The post office is open for international telephone calls from 7 am to 7 pm Monday to Friday and 8 am to 2.30 pm on Saturdays. There is also a cardphone here but, as usual, the supply of cards is erratic.

Immigration There is an office next to the Juma Mosque and pillar tombs on the waterfront (see street map for location).

Warning Don't walk back to your hotel along the beach at night. In past years many people have been mugged at knife-point, although these days the beach appears to be safer. Go back along the main road (which has street lighting) or take a taxi. You also need to exercise caution if returning to the youth hostel late at night.

Town Buildings

Malindi has a pedigree going back to the 12th century and was one of the ports visited by the Chinese junks of Cheng Ho between 1417 and 1419, before the Chinese emperor prohibited further overseas voyages. It was one of the few places on the coast to offer a friendly welcome to the early Portuguese mariners and to this day the pillar erected by Vasco da Gama as a navigational aid still stands on the promontory at the southern end of the bay. The cross which surmounts this pillar is of Lisbon stone (and therefore original) but the supporting pillar is of local coral.

There's also the partial remains of a Portuguese church, which is undoubtedly the one which St Francis Xavier visited on his way to India. A painting of the crucifixion is still faintly visible. Not far to the north are a number of pillar tombs and the remains of a mosque and a palace. Other than this, however, little remains of the old town. The nearest substantial ruins from pre-Portuguese days are at Gedi, south of Malindi.

Malindi National Marine Park

The most popular excursion from Malindi is to the Malindi National Marine Park to the south of town past Silver Sands. Here you can rent a glass-bottomed boat to take you out to the coral reef. Masks and snorkels are provided though they're usually pretty well used and the quality is not what it might be. Fins can be rented for US$1.60 from the kiosk on the beach inside the marine park gate.

The variety and colours of the coral and the fish are simply amazing and you'll be surprised how close you can get to the fish without alarming them. On the other hand, the area is getting a little overused and there's been quite a lot of damage to the coral. Shell collectors have also degraded the area. During the rainy season visibility is severely reduced by the silt in the water which gets washed in from the Galana River.

You can arrange these trips in Malindi – people come around the hotels to ask if you are interested in going. The usual price is US$18 per person which includes a taxi to take you to and from your hotel, hire of the boat and the park entry fee. You may be able to get it for less if you bargain hard but you won't be able to knock too much off this price. The marine park is open daily from 7 am to 7 pm, but the boats only go out at low tide.

Snake Park

Yes, Malindi has the inevitable snake park. It's behind the Sabaki shopping centre on the Lamu road and is open from 9 am to 5 pm daily. Entry is US$4.50 for adults and US$2.35 for children.

Falconry

The falconry has a number of caged birds of prey, as well as a huge tortoise which roams the grounds, and a chimp on a rope – fine if you like that sort of thing. The opening hours and entry fees are the same as for the snake park.

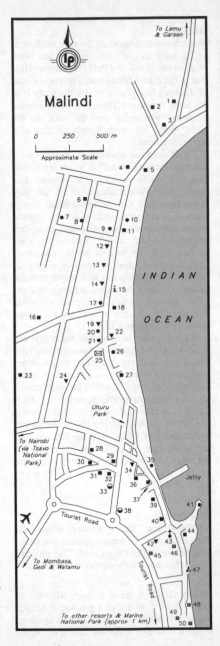

■ PLACES TO STAY

1	Sultan Cottages
2	Eddie's
3	African Pearl Hotel
4	Malindi Cottages
5	Eden Roc Hotel
6	Lutheran Guest House
11	African Dream Cottages
16	Glory Guest House
18	Blue Marlin Hotel, Europcar & Eagle Aviation
23	Fondo Wehu Guest House
27	Lawford's Hotel
28	New Lamu Lodge
29	New Safari Hotel & Garissa Express Bus
30	Wananchi Day & Night Club
31	Salama Lodge
32	Tana Hotel
36	Ozi's Guest House
37	Metro Hotel, I Love Pizza Restaurant & Malindi Fishing Club
39	Travellers' Inn
40	Da Gama's Bed & Breakfast & Baobab Café
44	Scorpio Villas
45	Youth Hostel
46	El Pescatori Restaurant & Sailfish Club
47	Silver Sands Camp Site
48	Driftwood Club
49	Coconut Village
50	Tropical Village

▼ PLACES TO EAT

2	Eddie's Restaurant
12	Malindi Fruit Juice Garden
13	Hermann's Beer Garden, Putipu Restaurant & Stardust Club

14	Trattoria Restaurant
19	Slot Machines Bar & Restaurant
22	Palm Garden Restaurant
24	Urafiki Bar
34	Bahari Restaurant
37	I Love Pizza Restaurant, Metro Hotel & Malindi Fishing Club
40	Baobab Café & Da Gama's Bed & Breakfast
42	Travellers' Café
46	El Pescatori Restaurant & Sailfish Club

OTHER

7	Falconry
8	Snake Park
9	Sabaki Shopping Centre
10	Casino
13	Stardust Club, Hermann's Beer Garden & Putipu Restaurant
15	Tourist Office & Kenya Airways
17	Barclays Bank & Avis
18	Europcar, Eagle Aviation & Blue Marlin Hotel
20	Glory Car Hire
21	Police
25	Post Office
26	Standard Chartered Bank & Prestige Air Services
29	Garissa Express Bus & New Safari Hotel
33	Malindi & Tana River Bus Offices
35	Souvenir Market Stalls
37	Malindi Fishing Club, Metro Hotel & I Love Pizza Restaurant
38	Matatu Stand, Bus Stand & Vegetable Market
41	Vasco da Gama's Pillar
43	Portuguese Church

Scuba Diving

If you'd like to go scuba diving you can do this from the Driftwood Club at the Silver Sands resort. A dive costs US$39 plus the park entry fee (US$7.15). There is also a diving school here for those who wish to learn, but it's not cheap at US$455 for a course.

Deep-Sea Fishing

Kenya is famous for the game-fishing opportunities off the coast. The Malindi Fishing

Club can organise trips at a cost of US$468 per boat for four people including all equipment. Most of the resort hotels can also arrange these trips.

Places to Stay – bottom end

There are a number of cheap, basic lodges in the centre of town, but they're usually fairly noisy at night and you don't get the benefit of sea breezes or instant access to the beach. Most travellers prefer to stay in one of the hotels closer to the beach, although it is not really a swimming beach in the town – you have to go a couple of km south before the beaches improve.

By far the best place is the *Fondo Wehu Guest House* (☎ (0123) 30017) in the western part of town. It's about 10 minutes' walk from the bus station, and you may need to ask directions as it can be a little hard to find the first time. It's run by an English-woman and her Kenyan husband and is a very popular place to stay. Dorm beds in the airy upstairs dorm cost US$3.90, and comfortable single/double rooms cost US$10/14. The price includes an excellent breakfast and free laundry service. Tasty snacks are also available.

Next best is probably *Ozi's Guest House* (☎ (0123) 20318) on the foreshore road. It's kept spotlessly clean, and safe lockers are available for US$0.40 per day. The rooms, all with fans and mosquito nets, cost US$7.80/15 with breakfast in the low season, up to US$12/23 in the high season. Bathrooms and toilets are shared between four rooms. The only problem here is that rooms on one side face the mosque, while those on the other side overlook the Malindi Bus depot – either way you'll be woken early.

Another popular place is the *Silver Sands Camp Site* (☎ (0123) 20412), two km south of town along the coast road. It costs US$1.95 per person to camp here (less in the low season) and there are good toilets, salt-water showers, and freshwater taps but very little shade.

The Silver Sands also has three types of banda for rent. The so-called *Mzuri Huts* are self-contained and cost US$12 for a double. The *White Huts* have two single beds, mosquito nets, screened windows, electric lights and lockable doors but shared showers and toilets for US$7.80 a double. The *Green Huts*, of which there are three, are actually tents under a makuti roof and cost US$6.50 a double. They have mosquito nets, private bathroom facilities and electric lights. There is no single-occupancy tariff, and prices are negotiable if you plan to stay for a while.

Bicycles can be rented for US$3.10 per day or US$0.60 by the hour. The main draw-back here is that there is nowhere to eat or buy provisions, although at the time of writing it seemed a shop/café was under construction which may now be open.

If you are happy with dormitory accommodation, the very friendly *Malindi Youth Hostel* is not a bad choice. It's a fairly relaxed place and there are no silly restrictions – dorms are only segregated if you request it, alcohol is permitted and there is no curfew. The dorms hold four to five people, and the cost of a bed is US$3.10. The kitchen is reasonably well equipped and there's access to a fridge and washing facilities. The hostel is in the southern part of the town, about 10 minutes' walk from the bus and matatu stands.

Also popular in the past has been the *Travellers' Inn*, on the beachfront road just south of the main part of town. It's hard to see the attraction of this place as the rooms are basic and somewhat gloomy, but it is kept immaculately clean and the owner is very friendly. Rooms cost US$9.70 for a double including breakfast, and there's no single tariff.

Da Gamas Bed & Breakfast (☎ (0123) 30295) is a new place just south of the Travellers' Inn. It has received favourable reports from a number of travellers, and the owner, James, is friendly and helpful. The cost of rooms varies from US$7.80/15 to US$12/23 depending on the season.

Also cheap is the *Lutheran Guest House* (☎ (0123) 21098) at the opposite end of town off the Lamu road. This is excellent value and very popular. The rooms are set around a quiet courtyard – very reminiscent of an Indonesian *losmen* – and are clean and well maintained. The cost is a very reasonable US$12 for a double with breakfast (US$16 with private bath). Once again there is no reduction for single occupancy.

Further north again is *Eddie's* (☎ (0123) 20283) which is basically a restaurant with a pool, but there are a few very pleasant rooms. These are all self-contained and have a small patio with table and chairs. It's excellent value at US$13 per person with breakfast, although you are quite a distance from town if you are on foot.

If you want to stay in the noisy town centre there are several places where you can get a double room for around US$5.20 with shared bathroom facilities. They include the *Salama Lodge* and the *New Lamu Lodge*. Also here is the *Tana Hotel* (☎ (0123) 20234) which is very clean and comfortable and costs US$5.90/7.80 for singles/doubles with shared bath or US$12 for a self-contained double. The rooms are all at the back of the building and so are fairly quiet.

Places to Stay – middle
There are few places to stay in this price range and their tariffs vary considerably from one month to another. *Malindi Cottages/Robinson Island* (☎ (0123) 20304) is out on the Lamu road, close to the Eden Roc Hotel, and consists of several fully furnished, self-contained cottages surrounding a swimming pool. Each cottage has two bedrooms, a sitting room, kitchen and verandah. Facilities include a refrigerator, gas cooker, mosquito nets and fans. Each cottage sleeps up to five adults and costs from US$32 to US$47 depending on the season. It's a pretty rough-and-ready place much in need of a major facelift.

Just beyond the Eden Roc Hotel on the Lamu road are *Sea View Cottages* (☎ (0123) 20439) which consists of a number of round, makuti-roofed cottages divided in half to form two double rooms each with its own shower and toilet. The prices here are US$35/43 with breakfast in the low season, rising to US$51/70 in the high season. It's another place which is in need of renovation but it is reasonably close to the centre of the action.

Places to Stay – top end
Malindi's top-range hotels are strung out along the beachfront both north and south of the town centre and more are being built each year. Some are very imaginatively designed and consist of clusters of makuti-roofed cottages in beautifully landscaped gardens full of flowering trees. Others are fairly standard beach hotels. All of them have swimming pools and other sporting facilities and many have a discotheque. They cater mostly, but not exclusively, to package tourists from Europe on two to three-week holidays and they all seem to pitch their business at a specific nationality – British, German or Italian. Very little intermingling seems to take place and you can definitely feel you've come to the wrong spot in some hotels if you don't belong to the dominant nationality. It's a common trait with package tourism anywhere in the world.

Most of the hotels impose a supplement over the Christmas and New Year periods which can be quite considerable (US$19, for example), so bear this in mind if you intend to stay at this time of the year.

If being by the beach is important, it's also worth bearing in mind that the hotels north of town do not have a beach frontage as there is a wide swathe of sand dunes here; those to the south of town don't have this problem.

Right in the town itself are *Lawford's Hotel* and the *Blue Marlin Hotel*, which are managed by the same people (☎ (0123) 20440). Lawford's is the cheaper of the two and in the low season it offers bungalows at the rear for US$47/62, bungalows with a sea view for US$52/70 and air-con rooms with a view for US$55/74, all with half board. In the high season the rates jump to US$55/70, US$66/82 and US$70/86 respectively.

The Blue Marlin offers a somewhat higher class of accommodation with superb facilities and costs US$61/82 for singles/doubles in the low season and US$78/94 in the high season. All prices are for half board and include taxes.

North of town on the Lamu road is the *Eden Roc Hotel* (☎ (0123) 20480), one of the few hotels which seems to have a mixed clientele. It's also one of the few places with tennis courts, though these are not open to nonguests. The hotel is one of the older resorts in Malindi, and certainly not much imagination has gone into its design. The rates are US$45 per person in a bungalow, US$52 per person in a deluxe double, and

US$58 per person for a deluxe suite. All prices include breakfast and taxes.

South of town, the top-range hotels stretch all the way from the path leading to the Vasco da Gama monument down to Casuarina Beach and the Malindi National Marine Park.

First is the *Sailfish Club* (☎ (0123) 20-016), which is a very intimate hotel with only 10 rooms, all of them self-contained and air-con. It's essentially for those interested in big-game fishing and caters largely for private prebooked groups. The cost is US$43 per person including breakfast.

Almost opposite is *Scorpio Villas* (☎ (0123) 20194) which has 17 cottages spread over some 1½ hectares of beautiful tropical gardens, with three swimming pools and just 50 metres from Silver Sands Beach. All the cottages are fully furnished in Lamu style and come complete with your own cook/house steward. There's an excellent restaurant and bar within the complex. It's Italian-owned and Italians form the bulk of the clientele. Full-board charges are US$117/169 to US$156/208 depending on the season.

Further down the beach beyond the Silver Sands Camp Site is the *Driftwood Club* (☎ (0123) 20155). This was one of the first beach resorts to be built at Malindi and it's different from the other hotels as it's used more by individual travellers rather than package groups. Although it gets more of a mixture of nationalities, the clientele is mainly British and White Kenyan. The club offers a variety of rooms from US$23/32 to US$52/68 depending on the season and facilities. The cheaper rooms have shared bathrooms while the more expensive are self-contained and have air-con. All prices include breakfast and taxes. The bar, restaurant and other facilities are open to nonguests on payment of a temporary membership fee of US$1.55 per day, so there's often an interesting mix of budget travellers hanging out by the pool.

Next down the beach is *Coconut Village* (☎ (0123) 20928), where the clientele is mainly Italian. Double rooms with full board

cost between US$74/97 and US$136/156 depending on the time of year (and there are no less than six 'seasons'!). Children under two years old are free of charge and those under 12 years old pay 50% of the above rates. All prices include taxes and service charges. The hotel has a popular open-air, makuti-roofed discotheque which overlooks the beach.

Next door is the *Tropical Village* (☎ (0123) 20256) where, again, the clientele is mainly Italian. Rooms cost US$51/66 including breakfast and US$65/94 for full board. This is one of the most imaginatively conceived places with two huge soaring makuti-roofed areas for the bar/restaurant.

Further south is the *African Dream Village* (☎ (0123) 20119) which is owned by the same people who run the African Dream Cottages on the Lamu road. Unlike the cottages, this is a fully fledged beach resort which has double rooms with shower, toilet, verandah, air-conditioning and telephone, and a range of facilities including a swimming pool, sports centre, bars and restaurant. Full-board rates are US$140/203 while singles/doubles with breakfast cost US$117/156. Meals taken separately are charged at the rate of US$16 for lunch and US$19 for dinner.

Next is the *Silver Sands Villas* (☎ (0123) 20842) which consists of a main building with single and double rooms and a number of two and four-person self-contained villas. Rooms with half board range from US$53/74 to US$84/125, while four-bed villas cost from US163 to US$263 and six-bed villas from US$248 to US$387. All prices include taxes and service charges.

The *White Elephant* (☎ (0123) 20223), further down the beach, has two-storey apartment-type accommodation set in a lush garden complete with swimming pool and games room. The charges range from US$110/169 to US$175/299 for full board depending on the season. There's a temporary membership charge of US$7.80 for nonguests to use the facilities.

Further still are two more resorts – the *Jambo Club* and *Kivolini Hotel*.

Places to Eat – cheap

There's not a lot of choice in this range. The *Travellers' Cafe* in the shopping complex near the Portuguese Church has been popular for years and is a convenient place if you're staying at the youth hostel. It offers Western and African-style meals for between US$2.30 and US$5.20.

Other cheap meals can be found in the restaurants at the hotels in the centre of town. The fare is standard Indo-African. The *Bahari Restaurant* offers much the same sort of thing plus seafood and very good milk shakes. The *New Safari Hotel* is a very popular place with the locals at lunch time. Also worth visiting for its excellent milk shakes and fruit juices is the *Malindi Fruit Juice Garden* on the Lamu road near the casino.

Slightly more expensive but excellent value is the *Palm Garden* on Lamu road opposite the petrol station. Food here is very tasty, and the place is usually packed with escapees from the resorts. The menu is mainly seafoods and curries. The front part of the restaurant serves snacks and light meals, while the makuti-roofed back section (entered from the side street) does full meals. Meals in the snack area include burgers & chips for US$2.70, weiner schnitzel (US$5.50), steaks (US$4.80) and curries (US$2.90).

Ozi's Guest House is also worth checking out for reasonably priced curries (around US$3) though they do have more expensive seafood dishes such as prawns and lobster.

Places to Eat – more expensive

For a splurge, it's worth trying the *Driftwood Club* where you have to pay US$1.55 for temporary membership. This entitles you to the use of the swimming pool, hot showers, bar and restaurant. The prices are very reasonable – lunch for US$7.50, dinner for US$10, good snacks (such as smoked sailfish and prawn sandwiches) from US$1.95, and à la carte seafood main dishes for US$3.30 to US$6.50. It's especially convenient if you are staying at the Silver Sands Camp Site.

I Love Pizza in front of the fishing jetty and close to the Metro Hotel is a popular place for a splurge. As you might expect, it serves Italian food (pizza and pasta for around US$6) and also more expensive meals such as chicken casserole and seafood dishes from US$7.80. It's open from noon to midnight daily. Further south towards the Driftwood Club is the open-air *El Pescatori* restaurant, which is open in the evenings and serves up-market seafood meals.

In the northern part of town near the disco and casino are a couple of places which also cater largely to the resort crowds. At *Hermann's Beer Garden* you can eat German and other continental dishes for US$7.80 and up. It's hardly the place for a quiet meal as the music is always loud. Right next door at the Stardust Club is the open-air *Putipu Restaurant*, where the emphasis is on Italian food. Main dishes are in the US$6 to US$12 range, while pizzas cost US$7.80.

Further north, just off the Lamu road is *Eddie's*, which is probably one of the best seafood restaurants in Malindi as well as having a tastefully intimate atmosphere. It's open from 12 to 2.30 pm and 7.30 to 10.30 pm and there's a swimming pool which you can cool off in before eating your meal. Expect to pay US$4.50 for fish dishes and up to US$16 for lobster.

For superb gelati ice cream, the *Gelateria Bar* in the Sabaki shopping centre has a range of flavours, but it's not cheap. There's a similar place in the courtyard of this complex.

Entertainment

Because Malindi is a holiday resort there are a number bars and discos to visit in the evening, some of which rock away until dawn. The most famous of them is the *Stardust Club* which generally doesn't get started until late (10 or 11 pm) and costs US$3.90 entry (US$7.80 on Saturday night).

There's also a disco at least once a week – usually on Wednesday – at *Coconut Village* past the Driftwood Club and, if you get there early enough, you won't have to pay the entry charge. It's a pleasant place to dance away the evening and you won't drown in perspiration as it's open-air under makuti roofs right on the beach. The bar is incredible and is worth a visit just to see it. It's built around a living tree with one of the branches as the bar top!

Another place which is worth checking out if you want to catch a film is the *Malindi Fishing Club*, right next to the Metro Hotel. It's a very attractive, traditionally constructed building with a makuti roof. There's a bar and snacks are available. The clientele, mainly British, are friendly, although some of the videos they show are decidedly daggy and there's a membership charge of US$0.75.

The liveliest tourist bar is the makuti-roofed *Hermann's Beer Garden*, where the music is loud, the lighting subdued and the girls ever present. One of the liveliest African bars is the *Urafiki Bar & Restaurant* with its deafening jukebox that seems to be playing nonstop. It closes by 11.30 pm and the beers are often lukewarm but, somehow, you don't miss the Arctic fetish for ice-cold beers.

The *Malindi Golf & Country Club*, a couple of km north of town, is open to all comers on payment of a temporary membership fee. Apart from golf, there is tennis, a bar/restaurant, and a library.

Malindi's newest drawcard is the *Casino* on the Lamu road. It has all the usual international games and you can bet as little as US$0.75 on most games. If you happen to be around at midnight, free spaghetti is served! It's open daily from noon until 5 am.

Things to Buy

There's a collection of at least 30 craft shops (tin shacks) on the beachfront near the mosque. Prices are reasonable, though you must, of course, bargain, and the quality is also reasonable. Crafts on offer include makonde carvings, wooden animal carvings, soapstone and wooden chess sets, basketware and the like. If you have unwanted or excess gear (T-shirts, jeans, cameras) you can often do a part-exchange deal with these people.

Getting There & Away

Air Three companies operate flights to Malindi from Mombasa and Lamu. They are Eagle Aviation Ltd (☎ Malindi (0123) 21258, Mombasa (011) 316054, Lamu (0121) 3119), Prestige Air Services Ltd (☎ Malindi (0123) 20860, Mombasa (011) 21443, Lamu (0121) 3055), and Skyways Airlines (☎ Malindi (0123) 20951, Mombasa (011) 221964, Lamu (0121) 3226).

All the above companies have their offices on the Lamu road in Malindi, and all have two flights per day in either direction between Mombasa and Malindi and between Lamu and Malindi. Flights from Mombasa depart at 8.30 am and 2.15 pm and arrive in Malindi 30 minutes later. From Lamu they depart at 10 am and 4 pm and arrive in Malindi 40 minutes later. The fare from Lamu to Malindi is US$49 one way and US$83 return. Children over two years old pay full fare. Check-in time is 30 minutes before departure and the baggage allowance is 10 kg per person. Most of time you won't be hassled if your baggage is over 10 kg but, even if you are, excess charges are minimal. The airport departure tax is US$1.50 at Malindi and Mombasa but there's no charge at Lamu.

Air Kenya Aviation (☎ Mombasa (011) 433982) also operates between Malindi and Mombasa with one flight per day four times a week. The fare is US$56.

Kenya Airways (☎ (0123) 20237) also flies from Nairobi to Mombasa via Malindi in either direction twice daily. If you're relying on these flights to get back to Mombasa or Nairobi to connect with an international flight then make absolutely sure you have a confirmed booking or, preferably, go back a day before.

Bus & Matatu Three bus companies operate between Mombasa, Malindi and Lamu on a daily basis. They are Malindi Bus service, Tana River Bus Service and Garissa Express and they all have offices in Mombasa, Malindi and Lamu. There are several departures daily in either direction between

Mombasa and Malindi which take about 2½ hours and cost US$1.50. There are also matatus which do this run taking about two hours and costing US$3. There's no need to book in advance from Mombasa if you turn up early enough in the morning. In Mombasa the buses leave from outside the New People's Hotel early in the morning. Matatus leave from the same place all day until late afternoon and go when full.

Travellers report that buses travelling between Mombassa/Malindi and Lamu are being held up by Somali bandits. Passengers are forced to hand over their money and possessions. There have been incidents of rape. Because of this, buses are increasingly making the journey in convoy, taking between 12 and 24 hours to reach Lamu from Malindi. An alternative is to fly.

Buses from Lamu to Malindi leave from the mainland between 7 and 7.30 am. The fare from Lamu to Malindi is US$4.50 and the journey takes about five hours. You must book in advance for this journey as there's a heavy demand for tickets.

Tana River Buses also have direct buses to Nairobi at 7 am and 7 pm (around US$7, eight hours), and to Hola at 9.30 am (US$4, six hours).

Garissa Express buses for Garissa leave from outside the New Safari Hotel at 11.30 am daily. The trip costs US$5.75 and as there's no advance booking you need to turn up at 11 am to grab a seat when the bus pulls in.

Share-Taxi It's also possible to find Peugeot 504 station wagons which do the journey between Mombasa and Malindi. They leave when full (seven passengers) and cost US$3 per person. You'll find them at the bus station in Malindi but only in the mornings. Commissioning a normal taxi to take you between Mombasa and Malindi will obviously cost you far more.

Train You can make advance reservations for Kenyan Railways at most of the large hotels in Malindi and at travel agencies, but you'll be charged US$2.60 for the service. All they do for this is make a telephone call to Mombasa railway station. You can do it yourself (☎ (011) 312221) for a fraction of the cost. See the Mombasa Getting There & Away section for information on train fares and timetables.

Getting Around
Glory Car Hire (☎ (0123) 20065), Hertz (☎ (0123) 20069), Avis, and Europcar all have offices on the main street near the Blue Marlin Hotel.

You can rent bicycles from the Silver Sands Camp Site or from Ozi's Guest House. This is probably the best way to get around town unless you prefer to walk.

Lamu

In the early 1970s Lamu acquired a reputation as the Kathmandu of Africa – a place of fantasy and other-worldliness wrapped in a cloak of medieval romance. It drew all self-respecting seekers of the miraculous, the globetrotters, and that much maligned bunch of people called hippies. The attraction was obvious. Both Kathmandu and Lamu were remote, unique and fascinating self-contained societies which had somehow escaped the depredations of the 20th century with their culture, their centuries-old way of life and their architecture intact.

Though Kathmandu is now overrun with well-heeled tourists and the hippies have retired to their rural communes or into business as purveyors of the world's handicrafts, Lamu remains much the same as it has always been – to a degree.

With an almost exclusively Muslim population, it is Kenya's oldest living town and has changed little in appearance or character over the centuries. Access is still by diesel-powered launch from the mainland (though there's an airstrip on Manda Island) and the only motor-powered vehicle on the island is that owned by the district commissioner. The streets are far too narrow and winding to accommodate anything other than pedestrians or donkeys. Men still wear the full length

KENYA

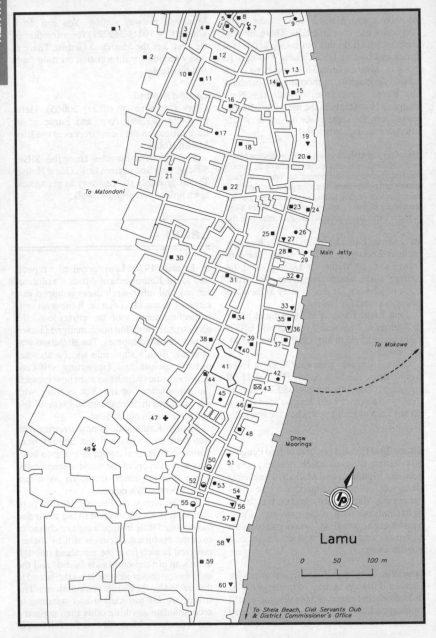

To Matondoni

To Mokowe

Main Jetty

Dhow
Moorings

Lamu

0   50   100 m

To Shela Beach, Civil Servants Club
& District Commissioner's Office

■ PLACES TO STAY

1 Peace Guest House
2 Kishuna Guest House
3 Jannat House
4 Sanctuary Guest House
5 Jambo Guest House
6 Karibuni Guest House
8 Saiga Guest House
10 Starehe Guest House
11 Pool Guest House
12 Pole Pole Guest House
14 Buhari Hotel
15 Salama Lodge
16 Yumbe House
18 Shuweri Guest House
21 Haludy Guest House
22 Sanaa Guest House
23 New Kenya Lodge
24 Casuarina Rest House
25 Lamu Guest House
28 Petley's Inn
30 Sunrise Guest House
31 Paradise Guest House & Amu House
33 Bush Lodge &
    Bush Gardens Restaurant
34 Bahati Lodge
35 Full Moon Guest House & Eagle
    Aviation
36 Hapa Hapa Lodge & Restaurant
37 Lamu Sea Shore Lodging
38 New Century Lodge
39 New Maharus Hotel
44 New Castle Lodge
46 Dhow Lodge
48 Rainbow Guest House
57 Lamu Palace Hotel
59 Bahawaba Lodge

▼ PLACES TO EAT

13 Coral Rock Restaurant
19 Ghai's Restaurant
27 Kenya Cold Drinks
33 Bush Gardens Restaurant &
    Bush Lodge
36 Hapa Hapa Restaurant & Lodge
40 Mid-Town Nyama Chroma
51 New Star Restaurant
54 Swahili Dishis
56 Labanda Restaurant
58 Olympic Restaurant
60 Coconut Juice Garden

OTHER

7 Jamaa Mosque
9 Door Carving Workshops
17 Swahili House Museum
20 Donkey Sanctuary
26 Lamu Museum
29 Prestige Air Services
32 Standard Chartered Bank
35 Eagle Aviation &
    Full Moon Guest House
41 Fort
42 Customs
43 Post Office
45 Market
47 Hospital
49 Riyadha Mosque
50 Malindi Bus Office
52 Tana River Bus Office
53 Gypsies Gallery
55 Garissa Express Office &
    Lamu Book Centre

white robes known as *khanzus* and the *kofia* caps, and women cover themselves with the black wraparound buibui as they do in other Islamic cultures, although here it's a liberalised version which often hugs their bodies, falls short of the ankles and dispenses completely with the dehumanising veil in front of the face.

There are probably more dhows to be seen here than anywhere else along the East African coast and local festivals still take place with complete disregard for camera-toting tourists. The beach at Shela is still magnificent and uncluttered and nothing

happens in a hurry. It's one of the most relaxing places you'll ever have the pleasure to visit.

At least, that was the story until the late 1980s. Since then a number of pressures have been threatening to undermine the fabric of this unique Swahili settlement. The most important is tourism. In the high season several hundred tourists visit Lamu every day, either by air or overland by bus and launch. One of the spin-offs of this influx is that many of the houses at Shela have been bought up by foreigners. As a result, local newspapers (particularly *Mvita*, published in

Mombasa) have begun running scare articles with headlines such as 'Lamu Under Siege', and suggesting that tourism is gradually destroying the culture and even physical fabric of Lamu. It's a moot point but neither entirely right or wrong.

The other major pressure is population increase. It's expected that the town's current population of around 12,000 will increase to 30,000 by the end of the century. To accommodate and provide services for all those extra people is going to take some very sensitive planning.

Tourism certainly distorts centuries-old cultural values and economic patterns and can even destroy them but Lamu urgently needs an injection of cash for preservation, restoration, creation of employment, schools and for a cleanup – particularly of the open drainage system. Tourism could be the source of that cash and, to a large extent, is already. And it's hardly fair to blame tourism for corrugated iron replacing traditional wall and roofing materials. Most tourists would much prefer to see traditional materials used.

History

The 20th century may have brought Lamu a measure of peace and tranquillity but it has not always been that way. The town was only of minor importance in the string of Swahili settlements which stretched from Somalia to Mozambique. Although it was a thriving port by the early 1500s, it surrendered without a fight to the early Portuguese mariners and was generally politically dependent on the more important sultanate of Paté which, at the time, was the most important island port in the archipelago. Until the late 1700s it did manage to avoid the frequent wars between the sultanates of Paté, Mombasa and Malindi following the decline of Portuguese influence in the area.

After that there followed many years of internecine strife between the various island city-states of Lamu, Paté, Faza and Siyu, which only ended in 1813 when Lamu defeated the forces of Paté in a battle at Shela. Shortly afterwards Lamu became subject to the sultanate of Zanzibar which

nominally controlled the whole of the coastal strip from Kilwa to the Somali border (under a British protectorate from 1890) until Kenya became independent in 1963.

In common with all the other Swahili coastal city-states, Lamu had a slave-based economy until the turn of the 20th century when the British forced the Sultan of Zanzibar to sign an anti-slavery agreement and subsequently intercepted dhows carrying slaves north from that island. All that cheap labour fuelled a period of economic growth for Lamu and traders grew rich by exporting ivory, cowries, tortoiseshell, mangrove poles, oil seeds and grains, and importing oriental linen, silks, spices and porcelain.

With the abolition of slavery in 1907, the economy of the island rapidly went into decline and stayed that way until very recently when increased receipts from tourism gave it a new lease of life. That decline, and its strong sense of tradition, is what has preserved the Lamu you see today. No other Swahili town, other than Zanzibar, can offer you such a cultural feast and an undisturbed traditional style of architecture.

Information

Tourist Office There's a seasonal tourist information counter on the waterfront near the dhow jetty, but it's of limited use.

Money The Standard Chartered Bank and the Kenya Commercial Bank, both on the harbour front, are the only banks in Lamu. Standard Chartered is open Monday to Friday from 8.30 am to 1 pm and Saturday from 8.30 to 11 am. In the low season, cashing a cheque can take as little as half an hour but in the high season it can take considerably longer. Get there early.

Books There are some excellent books about Lamu and the Swahili civilisation. The best general account is *The Portuguese Period in East Africa* (East African Literature Bureau, Nairobi, 1971) by Justus Strandes. This is a translation of a book originally published in German in 1899 with up-to-date notes and appendices detailing recent archaeological findings, some of which contradict Strandes' opinions. It's very readable.

Lamu: A Study of the Swahili Town (East African Literature Bureau, Nairobi, 1975), by Usam Ghaidan, is a very detailed study of Lamu by an Iraqi who was formerly a lecturer in architecture at the University of Nairobi and has since devoted his time to research into the Swahili architecture of the north Kenyan coast. You can find both of the above books in most good bookshops in Nairobi or Mombasa and the latter at the museum in Lamu.

If you're going to stay long in Lamu the leaflet-map *Lamu: Map & Guide to the Archipelago, the Island & the Town* is worth buying at the museum bookshop.

Bookshops Apart from the museum, the Lamu Book Centre, next door to the Garissa Express office, has a small but reasonable selection of English-language novels and other books. It's also the only place where you can buy local newspapers, and international news magazines such as *Time* and *Newsweek*. It's open from 6.30 am to 12.30 pm and 2.30 to 9 pm.

Touts Your first introduction to Lamu may not be all that pleasant. As you step off the bus or plane you will be approached by a number of touts (known all along the coast as 'beach boys') who will try to entice you to stay at a particular hotel. They will often make rash promises (bordering on straight-out lies) about the facilities provided by the hotel in order to get you to stay. They usually have nothing to do with the hotels, but receive a hefty commission from the hotel owners. This commission is of course built into the price you pay for the room.

If you don't want any assistance in finding a room, be polite but firm in telling these guys where to get off – they can be amazingly persistent. When you do get to the hotel you want, if a tout is still clinging to you, make it clear to the hotel owner that you have come to the hotel independently and the tout is nothing to do with you.

Many hotels will offer a substantial discount for a longer stay, particularly if things are quiet. If you are planning on staying for a while (and many people do, despite earlier intentions!) it's not a bad idea to pay the full price the first night and then spend a bit of time checking out other places before committing yourself to a place for any length of time – many travellers find somewhere they'd rather stay after paying for a week at the first place.

Town Buildings

Lamu town dates back to at least the late 14th century when the Pwani Mosque was built. Most buildings date from the 18th century, but the lower parts and basements are often considerably older. The streets are narrow, cool and quiet and there are many small courtyards and intimate spaces enclosed by high walls. Traditionally, buildings were constructed entirely out of local materials – faced coral-rag blocks for the walls, wooden floors supported by mangrove poles, makuti roofs and intricately carved shutters for windows. This is changing gradually with the increasing use of imported materials and is one of the factors of great concern to conservationists.

One of the most outstanding features of the houses here, as in old Zanzibar, is the intricately carved doors and lintels which have kept generations of carpenters busy. Sadly, many of them have disappeared in recent years but the skill has not been lost. Walk down to the far end of the harbour front in the opposite direction to Shela and you'll see them being made.

Only a few of the mosques have minarets and even these are small affairs. This, combined with the fact that there's little outward decoration and few doors and windows opening onto the street, makes them hard to distinguish from domestic buildings.

Both in Lamu and in Shela, private developers have recently been allowed to build ugly, modern hotels despite local pressure, but fortunately there is only one in each place. There has been quite an increase in the number of hotels and guesthouses, but as most of them have used existing buildings the fabric and atmosphere of the old town has, by and large, been retained.

Lamu Museum

A couple of hours spent in the Lamu Museum, on the waterfront next to Petley's Inn, is an excellent introduction to the culture and history of Lamu. It's one of the most interesting small museums in Kenya. There's a reconstruction of a traditional Swahili house, charts, maps, ethnological displays, models of the various types of dhow and two examples of the remarkable and ornately carved ivory *siwa* – a wind instrument peculiar to the coastal region which is often used as a fanfare at weddings. There's a good slide show available at the museum – ask to see it. Entry costs US$1.50 (US$0.30 for residents) and the museum is open daily from 8 am to 6 pm.

The museum has a good bookshop specialising in books on Lamu and the Swahili culture.

Swahili House Museum

If the museum stokes your interest in Swahili culture then you should also visit this museum tucked away off to the side of Yumbe House (a hotel). It's a beautifully restored traditional house with furniture and other house wares as well as a pleasant courtyard. Entry charges and opening hours are the same as the main museum.

Lamu Fort

The building of this massive structure was begun by the Sultan of Paté in 1810 and completed in 1823. From 1910 right up to 1984 it was used as a prison. It has recently undergone complete restoration and now houses an impressive walk-through aquarium and natural history museum, as well as the island's library.

Donkey Sanctuary

One of the most unexpected sights on Lamu is the Donkey Sanctuary which is run by the International Donkey Protection Trust of Sidmouth, Devon, UK. Injured, sick or worn-out donkeys are brought here to find rest and protection. As in most societies where they're used as beasts of burden, donkeys are regularly abused or get injured so it's good to see something positive being done for their welfare. The sanctuary is right on the waterfront.

The Beach

The best part of the beach if you want waves is well past Peponi's Hotel at Shela – there's no surf at Peponi's because you're still in the channel between Lamu and Manda islands. There was also a spate of robberies and a couple of rapes way out along this beach several years ago but there's been no repeat of that following a big police crackdown at the time, so it's probably safe to go as far along the beach as you like. It's possible to hire windsurfing equipment at Peponi's.

Matondoni Village

You'll see many dhows anchored in the harbour at the southern end of town but if you want to see them being built or repaired the best place to do this is at the village of Matondoni.

To get there you have a choice of walking (about two hours), hiring a donkey, or hiring a dhow. If you choose the dhow it will cost about US$13 for the boat (so you need a small group together to share the cost) but it usually includes a barbecue fish lunch.

To walk there, leave the main street of Lamu up the alleyway by the side of Kenya Cold Drinks and continue in as straight a line as possible to the back end of town. From here a well-defined track leads out across the island. You pass a football pitch on the right-hand side after 100 metres. Follow the touch line of the pitch and continue in the same direction past the paddock/garden on the left-hand side and then turn left onto another track. This is the one to Matondoni. The football pitch has telephone wires running above it which go to Matondoni and they're almost always visible from the track so if you follow them you can't go wrong. If you don't cut across the football pitch you'll head off into the middle of nowhere and probably get lost – although this can be interesting (old houses, wells, goats, etc).

Set off early if you are walking. It gets very hot later in the day. There's a small café in the village where you can get fish and rice for around US$1.30 as well as fruit juice. There are no guesthouses in the village but a bed or floor space can usually be arranged in a private house if you ask around. An impromptu group of travellers generally collects later in the afternoon so you can all share a dhow ride back to Lamu.

One traveller also recommended a visit to **Kipongani village** where local people make straw mats, baskets and hats. It's a friendly place, and tea and snacks can be arranged plus there's a beautiful empty beach nearby with waves.

Shela Village

Shela village, a 40-minute walk from Lamu, is a pleasant little village well worth a wander around. The ancestors of the people here came from Takwa when that settlement was abandoned in the late 17th century and they still speak a dialect of Swahili which is distinct from that of Lamu. Many have migrated to Malindi in recent years. Don't miss the famous mosque with its characteristic minaret at the back of Peponi's. Many of the houses in this village have been bought up and restored by foreigners in the last few years, so while it has a surprising air of affluence, the languorous atmosphere remains unspoiled. Quite a few travellers prefer to stay in Shela rather than in Lamu town.

To get to Shela, follow the harbour-front road till it ends and then follow the shore line. You will pass the new hospital built by the Saudi Arabian government and a ginning factory before you get to Shela. If the tide is out, you can walk along the beach most of the way. When it's in, you may well have to do a considerable amount of wading up to your thighs and deeper. If that doesn't appeal, there is a track all the way from Lamu to Shela but there are many turn-offs so stay with the ones which run closest to the shore (you may find yourself in a few cul-de-sacs

doing this as a number of turn-offs to the left run to private houses and end there). A popular alternative to walking there is to take one of the frequent motorised dhows which shuttle back and forth between the two villages. This costs US$0.75 per person. In the past few years a number of people have been mugged, and one British tourist was killed, while walking between Lamu and Shela. Although it is safe at the moment, it may be an idea to check locally before setting out.

Dhow Trips

Taking a dhow trip is almost obligatory, and it is a very relaxing way to pass a day. You'll constantly be approached while walking along the waterfront by people wanting to take you out for a trip. The cost is around US$4 per person for four or more people, US$7.80 for less than four people. Five is a comfortable number as the boats are not that big. The price includes fishing and snorkelling, although both are largely fruitless exercises because it's virtually impossible to catch fish at midday, and the best snorkelling is a couple of hours away. A barbecue fish lunch on the beach at Manda is provided, supposedly with the fish you have caught but usually with fish provided by the captain. Make sure you take a hat and some sunblock as there is rarely any shade on the dhows, despite assurances to the contrary.

See the Islands Around Lamu section later in this chapter for details about longer dhow trips.

Places to Stay – bottom end

Lamu has been catering for budget travellers for well over a decade but, in the last few years, budget hotels have mushroomed to cater for the hordes of travellers who come to stay here. As a result, there's a bewildering choice of simple, rustic lodges, rooftops and whole houses to rent. Don't believe a word anyone tells you about there being running water 24 hours a day at any of these places. There often isn't. Water is not an abundant commodity on Lamu and restrictions are in force most of the year. It's usually only available early in the morning and early in the

Dhows

Dhows have been sailing along the coast of East Africa for centuries and, until fairly recently, were the principal trading vessels used between the eastern coast of the continent and the Persian Gulf and India. They once numbered in the thousands but, since the turn of the century, they have declined rapidly in the face of competition from steamships and these days only a few make the journey to the Gulf. Those that remain confine themselves to sailing between the mainland and the offshore islands and between the islands themselves and even then only in certain areas. Their romantic appeal, nevertheless, remains and a dhow trip around the Lamu archipelago is an extremely popular activity amongst travellers.

Essentially, all dhows are wooden vessels – either planked or dug out – along with a rudder, mast and lateen (triangular) sail. Like all sail boats unless motorised, they're completely dependent on the wind but, unlike boats with only square sails, they're capable of tacking into the wind.

There are several categories of dhow and what name is applied to any particular type is often a contentious issue mainly because Swahili has a rich vocabularly of terms for boats. The essential factors, however, are size and shape.

The largest of the dhows are known as *jahazi* which are planked, ocean-going vessels with broad hulls and ruggedly designed to be capable of withstanding constant bumping along rocky shores and submerged coral reefs. They can have either one or two lateen sails. Most have woven coconut fibre matting fixed to their sides to reduce splash and a wooden 'eye' attached to each side of the bow below a decorated or carved tailboard. Dhows of this type built in the Lamu archipelago often have a perpendicular bow whereas those from Zanzibar have sloping bows. A jahazi often has a toilet hanging off the stern of the boat.

Motorised versions of the jahazi are known as *mtaboti* or *mchaboti*. The only difference is that these have an inboard motor instead of a sail.

Smaller craft go under the generic name of *mashua* and there are many different types. Around Lamu they're usually known as *kijahazi*. These dhows differ from the jahazi in being smaller, much narrower in the hull and having only one sail. They can be remarkably fast given a favourable wind and are the ones you're most likely to utilise for trips around Lamu.

Another common type of dhow yet smaller still is the *dau la mwao* – a sort of dugout canoe with a narrow hull, small mast and no keel which sits low in the water and is frequently used for transporting soil, sand and coral rag building blocks. Most do not have a a square stern. A variation of this type from the Kizingitini area is the *mtori* which is somewhat smaller and faster and fitted with a keel. Decoration on mwao and mtori is restrained. It's interesting to note that the mwao is the nearest surviving relative to the *dau la utango* which was the most common type of dhow found along the coast during the 19th century.

There are excellent models of the various types of dhow in the Lamu Museum. ■

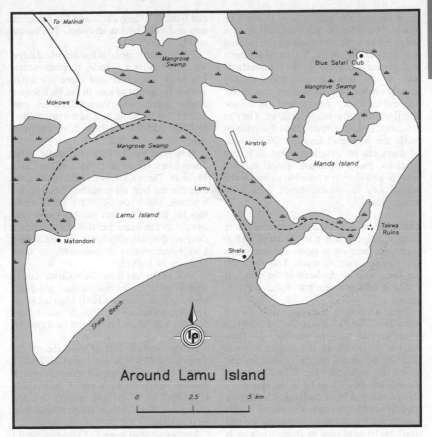

To Malindi

Mangrove
Swamp

Blue Safari Club

Mangrove Swamp

Mokowe

Airstrip

Mangrove Swamp

Manda Island

Lamu

Lamu Island

Takwa
Ruins

Matondoni

Shela

Shela Beach

Around Lamu Island

0   2.5   5 km

evening which, in most cases, means bucket
showers only and somewhat smelly toilets.

Prices are remarkably consistent because
there's a lot of competition though you obviously get what you pay for both in terms of
facilities and position. A dormitory bed or
space on the floor of a rooftop costs around
US$2, a single room between US$2 and
US$5.80, and a double room US$3.10 to
US$7.80. Almost all of these would involve
sharing bathroom facilities but some of the
higher priced doubles might have their own
bathroom. Prices rise in the high season
(August to September) by a factor of up to

50%; at other times there's room for negotiation, particularly if you plan to stay for more
than just a day or two. If a lodge is full when
you arrive but you like it a lot and want to be
first in line for a room, they'll usually let you
sleep on the roof or elsewhere until the following morning.

Where you stay initially will probably
depend largely on what sort of room you are
offered, what's available and who meets you
getting off the ferry from the mainland.

If you plan on staying in Lamu for a while
it's worth making enquiries about renting a
house, so long as there's a group of you to

share the cost. On a daily basis it won't be much cheaper (if at all) than staying at a lodge but on a monthly basis you're looking at a considerable saving. You can share them with as many people as you feel comfortable with or have space for and prices usually include a house steward. Some of the simpler houses can be very cheap indeed and include a refrigerator and cooking facilities. They're available in Lamu town itself but also at Shela and between Lamu and Shela. Some of them can be excellent value and very spacious. You need to ask around and see what is available. It's possible to find some remarkably luxurious places, especially around Shela.

Lamu Town It's virtually impossible to arrange budget hotels in any order of preference since there are so many and conditions and facilities vary so much. This selection has been done on the basis of the cheapest available beds or rooms but implies no preference.

There's a couple of choices right on the waterfront. The *Full Moon Guest House* is a friendly place with an excellent 1st-floor balcony overlooking the water. It costs US$5.80 per room (single or double) and there's one triple room for US$9.80, all with shared facilities. Close by is the spotlessly clean *Lamu Sea Shore Lodging*. It's run by a friendly old Muslim man who has very little time for the 'beach boys', so chances are you won't be brought here by them. Security is good and items left in the rooms are safe. The charge here is US$5.80 for a single or double room.

On the first street back from the waterfront there are a number of other places, most of them pretty basic. Right at the bottom of the pile is the *Badhawaba Lodge* at the southern end of the street. It's clean enough, although about as basic as you can get on Lamu. It's also as cheap as you'll find anywhere, with rooms for US$2.40/3.50. Also on this same street and of a similar standard are the *Dhow Lodge* and the *Rainbow Guest House*.

A definite notch up the scale is the *New Kenya Lodge*, behind the Kenya Commer-

cial Bank. It's fairly clean and has mosquito nets and cold bucket showers. The rooms cost US$4.60/5.50.

Further north again is the *Salama Lodge*, which is run by a friendly Englishwoman. It's basic but clean and there's a small kitchen for guests to use. In the high season double rooms with shared facilities cost US$12, but in the off season the price drops to US$3.90/5.90. All beds have mosquito nets.

Very good value, clean and simple, is the *Lamu Guest House* at the back of the Lamu Museum. There's a choice of different rooms here but the best are probably those on the top floor, which cost US$9.80. There are no fans but the sea breezes and sea views adequately compensate for this. Lower down there are doubles with bathroom and fan for US$18 and smaller doubles with the same facilities for US$13.

Next to the fort is the *New Castle Lodge* which overlooks the main square and picks up sea breezes since it's fairly high up. It has a rooftop dormitory for US$3.50 per bed and doubles with shared bathroom facilities for US$7.80.

At the northern end of town there's the *Saiga Guest House*, which costs US$9.80/12 for self-contained singles/doubles in the high season, dropping to a more reasonable US$4.90/5.90 in the low season. It's not great value. The *Karibuni Guest House* close by is similar.

Further west of town (15 minutes' walk) is the *Peace Guest House* (☎ (0121) 3020) which is clean, provides mosquito nets and morning tea and charges US$2.40 for a bed in a four-bed dormitory, and US$8.50 for a self-contained double. It's a wooden building surrounded by gardens, and there's a modern addition which contains the double rooms. You can also camp here for US$1.95. Facilities include two showers and access to the kitchen. This place has been popular for a number of years and still gets high praise from most travellers who stay here. It's well signposted from the northern part of town near the Buhari Hotel.

Moving further back from the waterfront

there are a number of places in the maze of small streets that make up Lamu town. The *Paradise Guest House* is a large, unrestored three-storey Lamu house. It's very rough and ready but has heaps of atmosphere and is cheap at US$9.80 for a double with attached bath. A cheaper option close by is the *Bahati Lodge*. The rooms are small and somewhat gloomy, but all the beds have mosquito nets. The rooms on the upper floors have the advantage of catching views and the sea breezes. It's certainly a fairly basic place, but is popular and cheap at around US$2/4 for a single/double with shared bath.

Also further away from the waterfront is the *Sunrise Guest House* which is a very friendly place. The rooms however, are extremely basic and have just hardboard partitions. At US$5.80 a double, it's quite a popular place to stay.

Shela Quite a few travellers, especially beach lovers, prefer to stay at Shela village rather than in Lamu itself. There is no real budget accommodation here apart from a few rooms which are let out by the owner of the *Bahari Restaurant*, and these are no great bargain at US$16 for a double.

If you're going to stay here for a while – and it seems most of the people who stay here do – then it's best to ask around for a house to rent and have a small group together to share the cost. Many of the houses here are owned by expatriate foreigners (especially Italians) who have poured vast amounts of money into them but only live here for part of the year. Most of them have been very sensitively upgraded and some are stunning. Quite a lot of them can be rented out so ask around in the restaurants.

Places to Stay – middle
Lamu Town The best value in this range is undoubtedly the *Casuarina Rest House* (☎ (0121) 3123) which was formerly the police headquarters. It offers large, airy rooms with good views and is clean and well maintained. It's good value at US$18/27 a double depending on how long you intend to stay, but like all places it's negotiable to an

extent, and prices are much lower in the off season. There's access to a large, flat, roof area.

A slightly cheaper option is the *Hapa Hapa Lodge* behind the restaurant of the same name on the waterfront. The rooms are clean, huge and simply furnished, and good value at US$27 for a self-contained double, or US$16 with shared bath. Almost next door is the *Bush Lodge*, behind the Bush Gardens Restaurant. There are just three double rooms (US$9.80) and one large triple (US$14), as well as a kitchen for guests' use.

Close to the main square is the *New Maharus Guest House* which has variable prices depending on which floor you stay on. There are no single rooms, and the doubles cost US$12 on the 3rd floor, US$16 on the 2nd floor and US$19 on the 1st floor; all rooms on the 1st and 2nd floors are self-contained, while those on the 3rd floor have shared facilities. It's not great value.

A better bet is the *Haludy Guest House* away from the village. Self-contained rooms in this spacious and airy place cost US$23/31 in the high season, dropping to US$12/16 in the low season. There's a fridge and cooking facilities for those who want to put their own meals together.

One of the most beautiful places in this range is *Yumbe House* (☎ (0121) 3101), close to the Swahili House Museum. It's a four-storey traditional house surrounding a central courtyard which has been superbly and sensitively converted into a hotel with airy terraces and makuti roofs. All rooms are self-contained (towels and soap are provided), spotlessly clean, and there are mosquito nets. It's excellent value at US$19/33, including breakfast.

Another good place in this range is the *Pool Guest House*, so-called because it has a (very small) swimming pool, though this is not always filled. It's a maze of a place and the rooms vary quite a bit, some having sea views and breezes. All are excellent value at US$17/23; half that in the low season.

Also worth trying is *Jannat House*, away from the village. The rates are US$16 for a self-contained room with two traditional single beds, US$14 for a double with shared bath, and there's one enormous family room with four beds at US$31.

The *Buhari Hotel* (☎ (0121) 3172) is a new place with a very pleasant terrace, but variable rooms. The downstairs rooms are small, gloomy and poor value at US$12/23, but the upstairs rooms, particularly those at the front, are very good and cost US$17/29. All rooms are self-contained and have mosquito nets.

Right away from town is the *Kishuna Guest House* (☎ (0121) 3125) but as it is a new building it lacks the character of most of the other places. The rooms are large, self-contained, well furnished and cost US$16/23 a single/double.

Shela The only mid-range places in Shela are whole villas which, as previously described, are available for longer term rental (a couple of weeks or more). Typical is the *Bustani Square*, close to the Stop Over Restaurant on the foreshore. It's a five-bedroom place which can sleep eight people comfortably but more if necessary. The cost is US$58 per night, but this is open to negotiation, depending on how long you want to stay and what time of year it is.

Places to Stay – top end

Lamu Town The best top-range hotel in Lamu itself is *Petley's Inn* (☎ (0121) 3107) right on the harbour front next to the Lamu Museum. It was originally set up in the late 19th century by Percy Petley – a somewhat eccentric English colonist who ran plantations on the mainland at Witu until he retired to Lamu. At the time of writing it is undergoing a major renovation but should be open once again by the time you read this. Facilities include a swimming pool and excellent rooftop terrace (open to nonguests). Expect to pay at least US$39 per person for a self-contained room including breakfast.

Lamu's latest blot on the landscape is the *Lamu Palace Hotel* (☎ (0121) 3272) right on the foreshore. It's the only hotel on the island which has air-con rooms; singles/doubles cost US$39/71 with private bath.

An excellent place in this category is *Amu House* (☎ (0121) 3246) next to the Paradise Guest House in the heart of town. The hotel is a restored 16-century Swahili dwelling and is very comfortably furnished. The price is a very reasonable US$27 including breakfast.

Shela *Peponi's Hotel* (☎ (0121) 3029), at the far end of Shela village and right on the beach, is *the* place to stay if you want a top-range hotel on Lamu. It consists of self-contained, whitewashed cottages with their own verandahs facing the channel between Lamu and Manda islands and is reckoned to be one of the best hotels in the country, both in terms of its position and the quality of its cuisine.

Peponi's is run by young Danish people and up-market informality is the name of the game here. The rates for full board are US$195/286 a single/double, while singles/doubles with breakfast cost US$169/221. Children sharing the same accommodation are charged US$19 to US$84 depending on age and meal requirements. There's a full range of water sports facilities. Advance booking is essential and the hotel is closed during May and June.

Also on the channel is *Kijani House* (☎ (0121) 3235), which has beautifully furnished rooms arranged around a lush and colourful garden. Facilities include a swimming pool, and like Peponi's, it is also closed in May and June. The cost here is US$91/117 for self-contained rooms with breakfast and US$123/175 for full board. Children aged from two to seven years are charged US$39 and US$52 respectively.

In the same area is the *White Rock Pool Guest House* (☎ (0121) 3234). It's fairly sparsely furnished and somewhat tatty, despite being quite new. It too has a swimming pool, and there's also a kitchen for guests to use. Self contained doubles with breakfast cost US$58 in the high season, dropping to US$39 in the low season. It's not particularly good value.

Much more pleasant is the *Island Hotel* (☎ (0121) 3290), another new place but further back from the water. It was built using traditional methods and the upper rooms with makuti roofs and sea views are superb. The lower rooms are a bit cramped. To stay it'll cost you US$52/80 with breakfast, and US$78/117 for full board. Children aged between two and 12 years are charged US$13 for bed and breakfast, and US$25 for full board. The hotel has its own excellent restaurant (open to nonguests), but there is no swimming pool.

A good deal cheaper, and the place to stay if you want to do your own catering, is the *Shela Rest House* (☎ (0121) 3091) not far from the Island Hotel. It too has open makuti-roofed areas and sea views. Two-bedroom apartments with kitchen and fridge cost US$39 for three people and US$52 for four. It's a friendly place and the management can arrange for a cook to prepare your meals if you want a rest from doing it yourself.

Lastly there's the ugly three-storey blot on the foreshore that should never have got past the planning stage – the *Shela Beach Hotel*. This brand new place is unnecessarily large for Shela and could easily have been made smaller to make less of a visual impact. It was still under construction at the time of writing but should be open by now.

Places to Eat – cheap

One of the cheapest places to eat in Lamu is the *New Star Restaurant*. You certainly won't beat the prices and some people recommend it highly, but others visit once and never return. Service is sometimes painfully slow (depending on what you order and the time of day) and the menu is often an unbridled act of creativity, though I thought the food was average. Fish & chips or rice costs US$2.70.

Cheaper still is the very basic *Swahili Dishis* (sic) just off the waterfront. This tiny place caters purely for the locals and serves no-frills African food at rock-bottom prices. Another local eatery is the *Mid-Town Nyama Choma* café on the main square by the fort. There are no prizes here for culinary excel-

lence, but for a cheap meat meal it's the place to go.

For snacks and shakes there's *Kenya Cold Drinks*, a popular place on the road which runs parallel to the foreshore. It also serves more substantial dishes such as steak or fish from US$3.10 and lobster for US$7.10. The service here is very haphazard. The *Bantu Café* in the New Castle Lodge also does basic snacks but on Tuesday and Friday evenings it serves a seven-course meal of local Lamu dishes for US$3.10. This is a good way to sample some local food and, unless you get invited to eat with a family or can hire someone to cook for you, this café is probably the only way to taste coastal cooking in Lamu. You need to book by 3 pm on the day so they know how many to cater for.

On the verandah of the old fort is the *Mazangira Café*, which is another great place for people watching. It serves good juices, as well as snacks and main dishes in the range of US$2.30 to US$3.70.

For consistently good food at a reasonable price there are a handful of very popular restaurants. The menus at all are pretty standard, with fish, seafood, steaks and curries. All do excellent juices and shakes. Despite the excellent seafood available, the seafood meals in Lamu are really very basic.

The first is the *Olympic (Sindbad) Restaurant* on the waterfront overlooking the dhow moorings. Here you can get pancakes with various fillings, grilled fish and salad or a full lunch or dinner of soup, main course and fruit juice. Close by is the *Labanda Restaurant*, which apart from the standard dishes also does poulet yassa, a delicious Senegalese chicken dish for US$5.20. It also serves some vegetarian dishes, which are hard to find on Lamu.

The *Coral Rock* has also been popular for years, although not always under that name. It offers all the usuals including banana pancakes with honey, grilled fish, crab, and lassi. The food is generally OK but the service is careless and I really got the feeling that customers were seen as something of a nuisance. It's open daily, except for Tuesday during the off season.

Somewhat more expensive but very popular is the *Bush Gardens* on the waterfront, next door to the Hapa Hapa Restaurant. It's run by the very personable and energetic 'Bush Baby' who personally supervises the cooking which sometimes makes for slow service but guarantees you an excellent meal. Fish dishes (barracuda, tuna, snapper or shark) cost US$3.50, crab US$7.80, prawns US$6.80 and lobster US$13, all served with chips or coconut rice and salad. Fruit juices are also available. It's arguably the best seafood restaurant in Lamu.

Next door is the *Hapa Hapa Restaurant* which is also very good, and offers a similar range of dishes, including seafood and possibly the best fruit juices and milkshakes in town. Prices are similar to those at Bush Gardens, and it's also a very popular place, especially at breakfast time.

Another place on the waterfront, at the northern end of town, is *Ghai's*. This place gets very mixed reviews, some people think the food is excellent while others come away dissatisfied. The set meal – juice, crab toast with cheese, chips and salad – is good value at US$3.90, while à la carte dishes are much the same price as the other places. It's open daily from 10.30 am to 10 pm.

The rooftop terrace at *Petley's* serves surprisingly cheap food and it's open to nonguests of the hotel. A fixed-price, three-course seafood lunch or dinner is a bargain at US$5.80, and the cheese samosas are excellent.

Many travellers come across a man popularly called 'Ali Hippy' who, for several years, has been offering travellers meals at his house. The meal usually includes lobster, crab, fish, coconut rice and vegetable stew and the whole family entertains you while you eat. Some people come away quite satisfied (it's definitely an unusual evening out) but the majority these days feel it is not worth the US$3 per person.

At Shela, the *Stop Over Restaurant* right on the beach is a popular place to eat or drink and prices are very reasonable though they only offer simple meals. Steaks are US$2.90,

fish dishes US$3.30 and lobster US$9.80. Similar and offering a slightly wider range is the *Bahari Restaurant* on the foreshore near Peponi's.

Places to Eat – more expensive
For an up-market snack or coffee, the café in the *Gypsies Gallery* on the street parallel to the waterfront is worth a try.

For a splurge meal the range is strictly limited. The restaurant at the *Lamu Palace Hotel* is far from cheap and the food is patchy – some nights it's excellent, other times it's practically inedible.

A meal at the *Petley's Inn* outdoor barbecue used to be a pleasant night out, but was being renovated at the time of writing. It should be open by now.

The rooftop restaurant at the *New Mahrus Hotel* touts itself as a classy restaurant but the food is only average and the hygiene suspect.

For a splurge at Shela the *Barbecue Grill* at Peponi's offers delicious food and is open to nonguests. There's a choice of both barbecued fish and meat and a superb range of salads. Also worth trying is the *Barracuda Restaurant* at the Island Hotel. Main dishes cost around US$5.20, while crab and lobster are available for US$14.

Entertainment
Bars There are four places where you can get a beer in Lamu itself but only two of them have cold beers. One of them is the makuti-roofed terrace bar *Petley's Inn* which is a very pleasant place to relax and catch the sea breeze. It's the most popular watering hole on the island and is open to nonguests. On the ground floor of the hotel there's an 'African' bar which serves warm beer at cheap prices. It's a bar with character, though I suspect that once renovation of the rooms is complete, the character will change.

The other place with cold beer is the bar at the *Lamu Palace Hotel* on the waterfront. It's also a good place to catch the breezes, and as you're on ground level it's interesting to watch the passing parade of pedestrians.

The *Police Club* by the police station serves warm beer. It's open in the evenings until fairly late and you don't have to be in the police force to get in. Ask directions from the Garissa Express bus office.

There's another bar at the *Civil Servants' Club* which has a disco on some Friday and Saturday nights. Keep an eye out for advertising posters around the town. Entry costs US$2 and it's a good night out.

Out at Shela, *Peponi's* is a mandatory watering hole and the beer here is always ice-cold. The bar is on the verandah overlooking the channel and beach. It's open all day until late at night.

Getting There & Away

Air Three companies operate flights to Lamu from Mombasa and Malindi. They are Eagle Aviation Ltd (☎ Mombasa (011) 316054, Malindi (0123) 21258, Lamu (0121) 3119), Prestige Air Services Ltd (☎ Mombasa (011) 21443, Malindi (0123) 20860, Lamu (0121) 3055), and Skyways Airlines (☎ Mombasa (011) 221964, Malindi (0123) 20951, Lamu (0121) 3226).

Each has two flights per day in either direction between Mombasa and Lamu, and Malindi and Lamu. Flights from Mombasa depart at 8.30 am and 2.15 pm and arrive in Lamu an hour and 10 minutes later. From Malindi they depart at 9 am and 3 pm and arrive 40 minutes later. In the opposite direction, they depart Lamu at 10 am and 4 pm for both Mombasa and Malindi. The fares are US$68 (Mombasa to Lamu) and US$49 (Malindi to Lamu) one way. Return fares are US$124 and US$83 respectively. Children over two years old pay full fare. Check-in time is 30 minutes before departure and the baggage allowance is 10 kg per person. Most of the time you won't be hassled if your baggage is over 10 kg but, even if you are, excess charges are minimal. The airport departure tax is US$1.50 at Mombasa and Malindi but there's no charge at Lamu.

The airport at Lamu is on Manda Island and the ferry across the channel to Lamu

costs US$0.60. Hotel touts will be waiting for you at the airport and will pursue you all the way. They're very persistent and hard to shake off.

Air Kenya Aviation (☎ (02) 501421 in Nairobi) operates daily flights in either direction between Lamu and Nairobi's Wilson Airport. The fare is US$112 one way and Petley's Hotel is the Lamu agent.

Bus Three bus companies operate between Mombasa, Malindi and Lamu on a daily basis. They are Malindi Bus service, Tana River Bus service and Garissa Express and they all have offices in Mombasa, Malindi and Lamu. The fare from Malindi to Lamu is around US$4.50 and the journey takes about five hours. Buses leave in either direction at 7 or 8 am depending on the company. The fare to Mombasa is US$4.50. The buses from Mombasa to Lamu arrive in Malindi around 8.30 am and leave around 9.30 am so there's a choice of departure times from Malindi if seats are available. It's wise to book in advance as there's a heavy demand for tickets. Garissa Express also operate a daily service between Garissa and Lamu which costs US$9.40 and takes around 10 hours.

The buses terminate at the ferry jetty on the mainland not far from Mokowe. From here you take a motorised ferry to Lamu which costs US$0.60.

Dhow Other than trips around the Lamu archipelago, you can also find dhows sailing to Mombasa. The journey takes two days on average and prices are negotiable. Before you set off you need to get permission from the district commissioner. His office on the harbour front close to the post office and opposite the main quay. It's best if you can persuade the captain of the dhow to take you along here and guide you through the formalities. It shouldn't take more than 1½ hours in that case. Usually they will do this without charging you money but be prepared to pay if the captain is unwilling.

Getting Around

Boat There are frequent ferries between Lamu and the bus terminus on the mainland (near Mokowe). The fare is US$0.60. Ferries between the airstrip on Manda Island and Lamu also cost US$0.60. Between lamu village and Shela there are regular motorised dhows and these too cost US$0.60.

There are also regular ferries between Lamu and Paté Island – see the following section for details.

Islands Around Lamu

A popular activity while you're in Lamu is to take a dhow trip to one of the neighbouring islands. You need a small group (six to eight people) to share costs if you're going to do this but it's very easy to put a group like that together in Lamu. Just ask around in the restaurants or the budget hotels.

Since taking tourists around the archipelago is one of the easiest ways of making money for dhow owners in Lamu, there's a lot of competition and you'll be asked constantly by different people if you want to go on a trip. Negotiation over the price and what is included is essential both to avoid misunderstandings and being overcharged. The price of day trips is usually settled quickly because a lot of travellers will have been on them and the cost will be well known.

Dhow trips are usually superb whoever you go with so it's unfair to recommend any particular dhow or captain but, if you're going on a long trip – say, three days – then it's a very good idea to check out both the dhow and the crew before committing yourself. Don't hand over any money until the day of departure except, perhaps, a small advance (say US$4) for food for a long trip. Also, on long trips, it's probably best to organise your own beer, soft drink and bottled water supplies. And remember that the person who touts for your business is often not the captain of the boat but an intermediary who takes a commission for finding you.

Dhows without an outboard motor are naturally entirely dependent on wind to get them anywhere, though poling – or even pushing – the boat is fairly common along narrow creeks and channels. If you have to pole the boat or you get becalmed out in the channels between the islands, there's no point in remonstrating with the captain. He's not God and there's nothing he can do about it, yet it's surprising how many people imagine otherwise. With that in mind, never go on a long trip if you have a deadline to meet. A three-day trip can occasionally turn into five-day one, although this is unusual.

Likewise, dhows are dependent on the tides. You can't sail up creeks if the tide is out and there's not enough depth of water to float the boat. This will be the main factor determining departure and return times.

To give you some idea of what a longer dhow trip involves, here's a brief description of one which Geoff took with five others:

After discussions with three different intermediaries in Lamu about trips to Kiwayu we made our choice and arranged to meet outside the Kisiwani Lodge at 6 am the next morning. The price was fixed at US$120 for a three-day trip, or around US$6 per person per day including food. Meanwhile we purchased beers and soft drinks from the Kenya Breweries depot and dropped them off at the Kisiwani (the crews will generally do this for you but it will cost more).

Next morning the dhow finally turned up at 7.30 am along with a crew of four and we set off in the direction of the channel between Manda Island and the mainland. Since the wind wasn't in the right direction, the dhow had to tack all the way to the channel by which time it was low tide. There was sufficient water in the channel to just keep the boat afloat – but the wind had dropped completely. There was no alternative but to pole and push the dhow all the way to the end of the channel and naturally we all lent a hand. It took hours.

Once out in the open sea again, the wind picked up and we were able to get close to Paté Island but again the wind dropped and the clouds burst. It looked very much like we and all our gear were about to get a soaking so it was with considerable relief that we discovered the crew had brought along an enormous sheet of plastic.

After the storm, the wind picked up again and we reached Mtangawanda by about 3.30 pm where we got off the boat and had a late lunch cooked by the crew. Despite only having one charcoal burner, they did an excellent job of this and the food was delicious.

Lamu Archipelago

| 0 | 7.5 | 15 km |

INDIAN OCEAN

We set off again about 4.30 pm and headed for Faza with a stiff side wind which enabled us to make good progress for the next two hours. After that it died completely and darkness fell. By 10 pm, it was obvious we were going nowhere that night so the anchor was dropped and a meal prepared (by torch-light!). By now we were all getting to know each other very well and there was a good rapport between crew and passengers. The tranquillity and beauty of a becalmed night at sea added immensely to this. After the meal, we all bedded down as best we could for a night of 14th-century discomfort.

By first light we discovered that seepage through the hull of the boat had brought the water level to well above the toe-boards so it was all hands on deck and bail out with anything to hand. Shortly after this, the wind picked up and we sped our way across the channel between Paté Island and Kiwayu, arriving at about 11 am off the tip of the island. At this point, all the passengers and one of the crew got off the dhow and went snorkelling among the reefs on the eastern side. The dhow, meanwhile, sailed on to Kiwayu village.

We caught up with the dhow again around 3 pm after walking along the beach and climbing over the ridge. Lunch was prepared by the crew (again deli-cious) and we settled down to an afternoon and evening of relaxation – sunbathing, fishing and exploring the village. Those with tents camped on the beach and the others took a banda at the camp site.

Next morning brought heavy rain but by 11 am we were on our way back to Lamu with a strong tailwind and making excellent progress. Just off Faza, however, the wind died again and the captain (rightly) predicted there'd be no more that day so it was Faza for the night at his family's house. But it wasn't that simple getting off the boat! The tide was out and we couldn't sail up the creek to the town. It didn't look like a particularly feasible idea from the relative 'comfort' of the boat but, after some persuasion, we all jumped overboard with our packs on our heads and headed for the shore in thigh-deep water. There were no mishaps but a lot of jokes and laughter. Half an hour later we reached Faza.

The dhow was brought up at high tide and we were given three bedrooms to share at the family house. That evening a superb meal was prepared for us by the captain's family which we ate in the company of what must have been a good proportion of the town's younger children, all fascinated by this strange collection of wazungu that had turned up in town. Though we did offer, the family refused to take any money for the meal and the accommodation.

After the meal, the captain gave us his prediction about the winds next day – pretty pessimistic – and advised us to take the motor launch back to Lamu. The food was at an end, the last beers had been consumed with the meal that night and so, in the end, we all opted for the motor launch rather than another possible two days and a night back to Lamu. He did, on the other hand, firmly offer to take any or all of us back to Lamu on the dhow at no further cost if that's what we preferred.

All things considered, an excellent trip, superb value, great company, quite an adventure and I'd do it again.

MANDA ISLAND

This is the easiest of the islands to get to since it's just across the channel from Lamu and almost everyone takes a half-day trip to the Takwa ruins at the head of the creek which almost bisects the island. The average cost of a dhow to this place is around US$19 shared by however many people you can put together. Sometimes (but not always) this includes a barbecued fresh-fish lunch so settle this issue before you leave.

The extensive Takwa ruins are what remains of an old Swahili city which flourished between the 15th and 17th centuries and which attained a peak population of some 2500. It was abandoned for reasons unknown when the townspeople moved to Shela. The ruins consist of the remains of about 100 limestone and coral houses, all aligned towards Mecca as well as a mosque

and tomb dating from 1683 (1094 by the Islamic calendar). The settlement is surrounded by the remains of a wall and huge baobab trees dot the site. It's maintained by the National Museums of Kenya and entry costs KSh 100.

Just off the north-east coast of Manda is **Manda Toto Island** which offers some of the best snorkelling possibilities in the archipelago. The reefs here are excellent and there are also good beaches. The only way to get here is by dhow.

Places to Stay

Apart from the *camp site* adjacent to the ruins, the only other accommodation option on the island is the very expensive Italianrun and owned *Blue Safari Club* (☎ (01) 338838 in Nairobi) at the northern tip of the island. Accommodation consists of 15 bandas and a separate restaurant and bar. The cost is a mere US$432 per person per day for full board, including drinks and transfers from the airstrip.

Getting There & Away

The trip across to Manda takes about 1½ hours and can only be done at high tide as it's reached by a long mangrove-fringed inlet which is too shallow at low tide. You may well have to wade up the final stretch, so wear shorts. Since you have to catch the outgoing tide, your time at the site will probably not be more than 45 minutes.

It's possible to walk to the Takwa ruins from either the airstrip or the village of Ras Kitau but it's quite a long way and the paths are not too clear.

PATÉ ISLAND

There are a number of historical sites on Paté Island including Paté the town, Siyu, Mtangawanda and Faza. All are still inhabited – mainly by fishers and mangrove-pole cutters – but very little effort has been put into preserving or clearing the remains of the once powerful Swahili city-states and that's not likely to happen until tourist receipts warrant the expense. Indeed, the only foreigners who come to this island are those on dhow trips and the occasional archaeologist so you can expect to be a novelty and treated with friendly curiosity especially by the children.

Accommodation and food on the island is easy to arrange with local families. The cost is negotiable but very reasonable. There are no guesthouses as such except at Faza but there are generally one or two simple restaurants which offer basic meals like bean or meat stews and tea.

Partly because the island is so flat, mosquitoes are a real pest and you're going to need insect repellent. Mosquito coils are for sale in the island's shops.

Paté

The origins of Paté are disputed. There are claims that it was founded in the 8th century by immigrants from Arabia, but recent excavations have produced nothing earlier than the 13th century when another group of Arabs, the Nabahani, arrived and gradually came to exert considerable influence over the other semiautonomous settlements along the coast.

By the time the Portuguese arrived in the early 16th century, Paté's fortunes were on the decline but were given a shot in the arm by the European mariners' interest in the silk cloth for which the town was famous and the introduction by the Portuguese of gunpowder. A number of Portuguese merchants reputedly settled here but their welcome was relatively short-lived, and by the mid-17th century their descendants had withdrawn to Mombasa following a series of uprisings by the Patéans against taxes imposed by the Portuguese authorities.

For the next half century or so, Paté regained some of its former importance and successfully fought off attempts by the Omani Arabs to take it over. Paté's harbour, however, had long been silting up and the city-state was eventually forced into using that of Lamu. The dependency created frequent tensions, particularly as Paté claimed sovereignty over Lamu, and the two were frequently at war. The final crunch came in 1812 when a Patéan army was soundly defeated at Shela. Thereafter, Paté faded into insignificance and lost all importance after the ruling family was driven out by Seyyid Majid in 1865 and was forced to set up the short-lived sultanate of Witu on the mainland.

Today, Paté resembles a down-at-heel Lamu. The narrow, winding streets and high-walled houses are there but the streets are earthen and the coral-rag walls unplastered. Its one redeeming feature is the Nabahani ruins just outside of town. These are quite extensive and include walls, tombs, mosques and houses. They're worth exploring but they've never been seriously excavated or cleared so it can be difficult to get around because of the tangle of vegetation. In addition, local farmers plant their tobacco crops among the ruins and have demolished substantial sections of the walls.

Getting There & Away There is a motor launch which usually leaves Lamu for Mtangawanda (about two hours) and Faza (about four hours) three times a week on Monday, Wednesday and Friday (Tuesday, Thursday and Saturday in the opposite direction). The fare is US$2.60.

From Mtangawanda it's about an hour's walk to Paté town along a narrow footpath through thick bush and across tidal flats but you're unlikely to get lost as the path is easy to follow and you'll probably be walking it together with local people who get off the launch.

The launch doesn't always call at Mtangawanda on the return trip from Faza to Lamu, so it's best to walk across to Faza and take it from there, paying a visit to Siyu on the way.

Siyu

Founded in the 15th century, Siyu was famous not for commerce or military opportunism but as a centre of Islamic scholarship and crafts. In its heyday (between the 17th and 19th centuries) it boasted some 30,000 inhabitants and was the largest settlement on the island though, today, less than 4000 people live here and there are few signs of its former cultural and religious influence.

Though one of the last upholders of coastal independence, Siyu's demise came in 1847 when it was occupied by the Sultan of Zanzibar's troops. The huge fort outside town dates from this period and is one of the largest buildings on the island. It's well worth a visit, as unlike many other Swahili relics, it has undergone considerable renovations.

The modern village displays little of Siyu's former glory and consists essentially of a sprawl of simple mud-walled and makuti-roofed houses.

Getting There & Away The mangrove-lined channel leading up to Siyu is too shallow and silted up to allow the passage of anything but the smallest boats and so cannot be reached directly from the sea by dhow or motor launch. The only feasible access is on foot either from Paté or Faza.

From Paté it's about eight km to Siyu along an earth track through the bush. The first part is tricky since there are turn-offs which are easy to miss so it's a good idea to take a guide with you as far as the tidal inlet. From here on it's easy as the path bears left and then continues straight through to Siyu. This last leg should take you about one hour.

Faza

Faza has had a chequered history. It was destroyed by Paté in the 13th century and rebuilt in the 16th century only to be destroyed again by the Portuguese in 1586 as a result of its collaboration with the Turkish fleet of Amir Ali Bey. It was subsequently re-established and switched its allegiances to the Portuguese during their attempts to subdue Paté in the 17th century but declined into insignificance during the 18th and 19th centuries. These days it has regained some of its former importance after being chosen as the district headquarters for Paté Island which includes part of the Kenya mainland to the north.

Faza has very little to offer in the way of interesting ruins. About the only thing there

is in the town itself are the remains of the **Kunjanja Mosque** right on the creek front next to the district headquarters where the ferries anchor. Even so, most of it is just a roofless pile of rubble though there's a beautifully carved mihrab and some fine Arabic inscriptions above the doorway. Outside town is the tomb of Amir Hamad, commander of the Sultan of Zanzibar's forces, who was killed here in 1844 whilst campaigning against Siyu and Paté.

The modern town is quite extensive and includes a post office, telephone exchange, the district headquarters, a simple restaurant, two general stores and two guesthouses.

It's an interesting place to wander around and easy to strike up conversations with just about anyone – men, women or children. Most of the houses here are mud-walled or coral-rag walled with makuti roofs though concrete and corrugated iron make an occasional appearance.

Places to Stay & Eat The two guesthouses – *Lamu House* and *Shela House* – are essentially family residences but they're more than willing to turn over one or more bedrooms for your use and cook you a delicious evening meal if you need somewhere to stay. The price is negotiable but the family is very friendly.

The simple restaurant mentioned earlier offers bean stews, tea and mandazi for just a few cents and is a popular meeting place for the men of the town.

Getting There & Away The inlet leading up to Faza from the main channel is deep enough at high tide to allow the passage of dhows and motor launches (though at low tide you'll have to walk in over the mud and sand banks from the main channel).

There's a regular motor launch which connects Lamu with Faza via Mtangawanda three times a week on Monday, Wednesday and Friday (Tuesday, Thursday and Saturday in the opposite direction). The fare is US$2.60 and the journey takes four hours. From Faza to Lamu, the launch leaves at about 6 am but you need to be down by the district headquarters about half an hour before that as you have to ferried out to the launch in small boats.

Getting to Siyu from Faza involves a two-hour walk through shambas and thick bush along an earth track. The first hour's walk as far as the disused airstrip is no problem, and there are generally people you can ask for directions if you're unsure. The second half is more confusing and you may need a guide so it might be best in the long run to take a guide with you all the way from Faza.

KIWAYU ISLAND

Kiwayu Island is at the far north-east of the Lamu archipelago and is included in the Kiunga National Marine Reserve. It acquired a reputation some years ago as an exclusive hideaway for rock stars and various other members of the glitterati, both local and foreign. It's unlikely you'll be rubbing shoulders with these people. The main reason for coming here is to explore the coral reefs off the eastern side of the island which the tourist literature rates as some of the best along the Kenyan coast. Personally, I think it's somewhat overrated (Watamu is better) but the dhow trip there is definitely a highlight of a trip to Lamu and I can highly recommend it.

The village on the western side of the island where the dhows drop anchor is quite small but it does have a general store with a few basics. The place to stay here is the *Kiwayu Camping Site* run by a friendly man named Kasim. There are several beautifully conceived bandas to stay in, all constructed out of wooden poles and makuti including one on stilts and another built over a tree. The cost varies between US$13 and US$26 depending on which one you take, but they'll all sleep up to three people. Clean sheets, pillows and mattresses are provided as well as a kerosene lantern and mosquito coil. There are good toilet and shower facilities. Campers can erect their tents here for US$2.60 including use of showers and toilets. You'll pay the same charge even if you camp on the beach below the site since this is also apparently owned by Kasim. There's a covered dining and cooking area for the use of both campers and banda dwellers.

Further up the coast across from Kiwayu on the mainland is the luxury lodge, *Kiwayu Safari Lodge* (☎ (02) 503030 in Nairobi) which gains a listing in Harper's *100 Best Hotels in the World* (the only hotel in Kenya and one of only a handful in Africa to do so) and where the glitterati stay. The cost of a night here is US$248 with full board. There's a speed launch to it from Lamu which takes less than an hour, or flights by Air Kenya Aviation from Nairobi in six-seater planes for US$195 one way. You can forget about going up there for a cold beer if you're staying at the camp site as there's no transport across the channel between the island and the mainland.

Getting There & Away

Virtually the only way to get to Kiwayu is by dhow and, for most people, this would be part of a longer trip from Lamu with stopovers elsewhere. If there's sufficient wind, the return trip to Kiwayu from Lamu takes three days and two nights.

The Rift Valley

In Kenya the Rift Valley comes down through Lake Turkana, the Cherangani Hills, lakes Baringo, Bogoria, Nakuru and Naivasha then exits south through the plains to Tanzania. Together these areas make up some of Kenya's most interesting places to visit. Lake Turkana (dealt with in the Northern Kenya chapter) is a huge lake in the semidesert north, home to nomadic pastoralists and a world away from the tourist minibuses and fancy hotels of the south. The Cherangani Hills provide some excellent walking opportunities and brilliant scenery – and hair-raising roads. More accessible are the central lakes which attract literally hundreds of bird and mammal species – they're a naturalist's dream and a visit to at least one of them is a must.

Volcanic activity is usually an accompaniment to rift valleys, and Kenya has both Mt Longonot and Mt Kenya. Longonot is accessible, easy to climb and certainly the most dominant feature of the landscape as you enter the Rift Valley from Nairobi. Mt Kenya, at 5200 metres, is a challenging climb, although Point Lenana, at 4985 metres, can be reached without specialist equipment. Further south are the vast plains, home of the Maasai, and also home to a profusion of wildlife that you're not likely to come across anywhere else in the world – an area not to be missed.

What is known as the Rift Valley in Kenya is in fact part of the Afro-Arabian rift system which stretches some 6000 km from the Dead Sea in the Middle East, south through the Red Sea, Ethiopia, Kenya, Tanzania and Malawi to Mozambique. There's a western branch of the system which forms the string of lakes in the centre of the African continent: Mobutu Sese Seko (formerly Albert) and Rutanzige (formerly Edward) which make up part of the Uganda-Zaïre border; Kivu on the Zaïre-Rwanda border; and Tanganyika on the Tanzania-Zaïre border. This western arm joins up with the main system at the northern tip of Lake Malawi.

Soda Lakes

Because the shoulders of the rift (see diagram) slope directly away from the valley, the drainage system in the valley is generally poor, and this has resulted in the shallow lakes along the valley floor in

To Lodwar
& Lake
Turkana

To Lake
Turkana

C77

Maralal

Rift Valley

0   25   50 km

Approximate Scale

Loruk

Lake
Baringo

Marigat

Lake
Bogoria

Lake Bogoria
National Reserve

Laikipia Escarpment

Nyahururu

Nanyuki

B5

Mt Kenya
(5199 m)

Nakuru

Nyeri

Lake
Nakuru

Lake Elmenteita

Lake Nakuru
National Park

A104

Lake
Naivasha

Naivasha

A2

Mt Longonot
(2886 m)

A104

Thika

Limuru

Longonot & Hell's Gate
National Park

NAIROBI

Lake
Magadi

A104

A109

Magadi

To Mombasa

Kenya, some of which have no outlet. Due to high evaporation, the waters have become extremely concentrated and the high alkalinity from the area's volcanic deposits makes the perfect environment for microscopic blue-green algae and diatoms, which in turn provide food for tiny crustaceans and insect larvae. These in turn are eaten by certain species of soda-resistant fish.

The water of these soda lakes (Nakuru, Bogoria and Magadi in Kenya, and Lake Natron in Tanzania) may feel a little strange to the touch (it's soapy) and often doesn't smell too pleasant (though this is mostly due to the bird shit). However, the abundant insects and fish are heaven to many species of water bird and they flock here in their millions – it's a twitcher's paradise!

Foremost among the birds is the deep-pink lesser flamingo *(Phoenicopterus minor)*, which feeds on the blue-green algae, and the pale-pink greater flamingo *(Phoenicopterus ruber)*, which feeds on the tiny crustaceans and insect larvae. Also numerous are various species of duck, pelican, cormorant and stork. The highest concentrations of these birds are found where food is most abundant and this can vary from year to year and lake to lake.

Another curious feature of the uplifting of the valley shoulders is the effect this has had on existing drainage patterns, although this of course happened in the last couple of million years. In Uganda, the uplifting caused the White Nile to form a pond (Lake Nyoga) after it left Lake Victoria, flow up what was previously a tributary, and into the northern end of Lake Albert via a circuitous route. Prior to the uplift, the river had flowed direct from Lake Victoria into the southern end of Lake Albert.

Viewpoints

The best place to view the escarpments of the Rift Valley is from the viewpoints which are signposted along the Nairobi to Naivasha road, just past Limuru. Here the road descends into the valley and the views are stunning. Mt Longonot is directly in front while the plains of the Maasai sweep away to the south. Predictably there are souvenir stalls at the viewpoints, but the stuff for sale is some of the worst I've seen in the whole country.

The old road to Naivasha also descends into the rift in this area, and it's the route to take if you are heading for Mt Longonot or Masai Mara, as the new road runs direct to Naivasha. It's also the road used by heavy vehicles and is often in a diabolical state of repair. This road was originally built by Italian POWs in WW II, and there is a chapel at the bottom of the scarp.

Getting There & Around

Lakes Naivasha, Nakuru, Elmenteita and, to

Rift Valley

The rift valley system consists of a series of troughs and areas of uplift known as swells. The troughs, generally 40 to 55 km wide, are along parallel fault lines and are formed by blocks dropping down in relation to the rest of the land. They account for most of the lakes and escarpments in East Africa. The swells are the land on either side of the troughs, and it's on these that you find two of Africa's mightiest peaks – Kilimanjaro (5895 metres) and Mt Kenya (5199 metres) – and lesser peaks such as Mt Elgon (4321 metres) – all extinct volcanoes. The floor of the rift valley is still dropping, although at the rate of a few mm per year you are hardly likely to notice anything!

The rift valley is certainly not one long well formed valley with huge escarpments either side, although this does occur in places (the Rift Valley Province is one such place). Sometimes there is just a single scarp on one side (such as the Nkuruman Escarpment east of Masai Mara) or just a series of small scarps. In some cases uplift has occurred between parallel fault lines and this has led to the formation of often spectacular mountain ranges, such as the Ruwenzoris on the Uganda-Zaïre border. ∎

a lesser extent, Baringo are readily accessible to independent travellers without their own vehicle. There are plenty of buses and matatus and a rail link between Nairobi, Naivasha and Nakuru, and less frequent buses and matatus between Nakuru and Marigat (for Lake Baringo). The other lakes, however, are more remote and there's no public transport. Hitching is very difficult and can be impossible. There's also the problem that lakes Nakuru and Bogoria are both in national parks/reserves, which you are not allowed to walk in – you must tour them in a vehicle.

Renting a vehicle may be expensive for budget travellers but it would certainly work out cheaper for four people to hire a vehicle to visit Naivasha, Nakuru, Bogoria and Baringo than for them all to pay individually for safari company tours. A one-day tour of Lake Nakuru starting from Nairobi goes for around US$40. A two-day tour of lakes Nakuru, Bogoria and Baringo costs about US$150 per person. A car hired for several days and shared between four people would cost considerably less than the total cost of a two-day tour for four people.

MT LONGONOT NATIONAL PARK

Hill climbers and view seekers should not miss the opportunity of climbing to the rim of dormant Longonot (2886 metres), a fairly young volcano which still retains the typical shape of these mountains, although it's far from being a perfect conical shape.

As this is a national park there is an entrance fee of US$12. The scramble up to the rim takes about 45 minutes from the parking area, and to do the circuit of the rim a further 2½ to three hours is needed. If you're feeling game there's a track leading down inside the crater to the bottom, though it's worth hiring a local guide before you set off.

Places to Stay

There's no accommodation in the park or immediate vicinity, but it is possible to camp at the ranger station at the foot of the mountain. If you are just on a day trip you can leave

your gear at the Longonot railway station or the police station.

Getting There & Away

If you don't have your own transport it's a long walk from Longonot railway station on the old road to Naivasha. It's about seven km to the trail head, and even if you have your own car it's wise to pay someone to keep an eye on it, or leave it at the Longonot railway station.

NAIVASHA

There's very little of interest in the town of Naivasha itself. It's just a small service centre for the surrounding agricultural district. Most travellers just pass through here on the way to or from Mt Longonot, Lake Naivasha, Hell's Gate National Park and Nakuru. The main road actually skirts the town so if you're going directly from Nairobi to Nakuru you don't actually pass through Naivasha. It's a good place to stock up with supplies if you're planning a sojourn by the lake as there are very limited stocks in the dukas dotted along the lake-shore road.

The area around Naivasha was actually one of the first settled by wazungu, and the Delamere Estates, originally owned by Lord Delamere, surround the town and stretch away to the west towards Nakuru. Many of the plots around Naivasha are still European-owned, which is hardly surprising given that this was one of the stamping grounds of the Happy Valley set of the 1930s.

The town basically consists of two main roads, a couple of other streets, and everything is within walking distance.

Information

There are branches of both Barclays Bank and the Kenya Commercial Bank on Moi Ave which are open during normal banking hours.

Places to Stay – bottom end

If you need to stay overnight in Naivasha there's a good range of budget hotels. The *Naivasha Super Lodge* has no doubles but

Top: Lion, Masai Mara Game Reserve, Kenya (SB)
Bottom: Oryx, Samburu National Game Reserve, Kenya (SB)

Top: Vulture in flight, Masai Mara Game Reserve, Kenya (SB)
Bottom: Hippo Pool, Masai Mara Game Reserve, Kenya (GH)

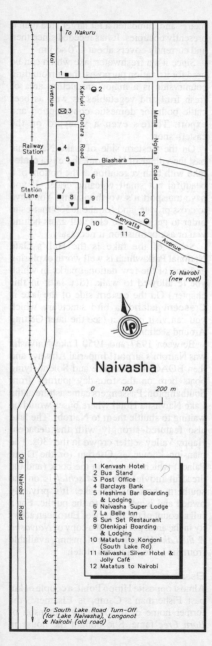

Map labels:
- To Nakuru
- Moi Avenue
- Kariuki Chotara Road
- Mama Ngina Road
- Railway Station
- Station Lane
- Biashara
- Kenyatta Avenue
- To Nairobi (new road)
- Naivasha
- 0   100   200 m
- Old Nairobi Road

1 Kenvash Hotel
2 Bus Stand
3 Post Office
4 Barclays Bank
5 Heshima Bar Boarding & Lodging
6 Naivasha Super Lodge
7 La Belle Inn
8 Sun Set Restaurant
9 Olenkipai Boarding & Lodging
10 Matatus to Kongoni (South Lake Rd)
11 Naivasha Silver Hotel & Jolly Café
12 Matatus to Nairobi

To South Lake Road Turn-Off (for Lake Naivasha), Longonot & Nairobi (old road)

the single beds are large enough for a couple; at US$1.80 these are not bad value.

For something a little less cosy try the *Olenkipai Boarding & Lodging* or the *Heshima Bar Boarding & Lodging*, both of which are adequate and charge around US$2.20 for a double.

There are plenty of other cheap places along Kariuki Chotara Rd.

Places to Stay – middle

For more salubrious lodgings the *Naivasha Silver Hotel* on Kenyatta Ave has self-contained rooms with hot water for US$4.50/6 a single/double. There's an upstairs bar and restaurant.

Very good value if you're alone is the *Othaya Annexe Hotel*, in Station Lane, which is very clean and has self-contained singles (no doubles) for US$6.70. The hotel has its own bar and restaurant.

The best accommodation in town is the rustic *La Belle Inn* (☎ (0311) 20116) on Moi Ave, which is a popular rendezvous for local residents and a watering hole and meal stop for safari companies. The staff is friendly and rates are good value at US$12/15 for singles/doubles with shared bathroom facilities, or US$22/23 with private bath. Prices include breakfast. There's a guarded car park, and all credit cards are accepted.

The new, modern *Kenvash Hotel*, beyond the post office, is not yet complete but may well be by the time you read this.

Places to Eat

If you appreciate good food, there's essentially only one place to eat in Naivasha, *La Belle Inn*. While not 'cheap', it's not too expensive either, and the food is some of the best in Kenya. Soups cost around US$1 and main meals between US$2 and US$3. It's open daily (all day) except Tuesday. The outdoor terrace is also an excellent place to have a beer or a meal despite the occasional clouds of dust raised by trucks on their way further west.

The *Jolly Café* next to the Silver Hotel on Kenyatta Ave is slightly less extravagant and has decent food. For good old no-frills

African stodge try the *Sun Set Restaurant* on the corner of Kenyatta Ave and Kariuki Chotara Rd.

Getting There & Away
Bus & Matatu The main bus and matatu station is on Kariuki Chotara Rd. There are frequent buses and matatus to Nairobi, Nakuru and all points further west. There are also departures for Nyahururu and Narok. Note that matatus to Nairobi leave from the matatu stand on Kenyatta Ave.

Train Travel from Naivasha to Nairobi by train is inconvenient as all the trains pass through in the early hours of the morning. The trains to Kisumu and Malaba pass through in the late afternoon. Unless you are prepared to travel 3rd class, make a booking in Nairobi before arriving in Naivasha.

Hitching It's useless trying to hitch out of Naivasha town to Nairobi without first getting onto the main road. The accepted point for hitching, and where the main road passes closest to the town, is about 500 metres east of the bus station. It's about one km to the main road in either the Nakuru or Nairobi direction.

LAKE NAIVASHA
Naivasha is one of the Rift Valley's freshwater lakes and its ecology is quite different from that of the soda lakes. It's home to an incredible variety of bird species and a focus of conservation efforts in Kenya. Not everyone supports these efforts, however, and the ecology of the lake has been interfered with on a number of occasions, the most notable introductions being sport fish, commercial fish (such as Nile perch), the North American red swamp crayfish, the South American coypu (an aquatic rodent, also called a nutria, which escaped from a fur farm) and various aquatic plants including *salvinia*, which is a menace on Lake Kariba in southern Africa.

The lake has ebbed and flowed over the years as half-submerged fencing posts indicate. Early in the 1890s it dried up almost completely but then it rose a phenomenal 15

metres and inundated a far larger area than it presently occupies. It has receded since then and currently covers about 170 sq km.

Since it's a freshwater lake which can be used for irrigation purposes, the surrounding countryside is a major production area of fresh fruit and vegetables as well as beef cattle both for domestic consumption and export. There's even a vineyard on the eastern shore.

On the western side of Lake Naivasha, past the village of Kongoni, there is a **crater lake** with lush vegetation at the bottom of a beautiful but small volcanic crater. If you have transport it's worth visiting. You have to cross private land for about 500 metres in order to get there, so close all gates behind you or ask permission if necessary.

South of the lake is the Hell's Gate National Park which is well worth exploring and one of the few national parks in which you're allowed to walk. (See later in this chapter.) On the eastern side of the lake is **Crescent Island**, a bird sanctuary which you can visit by boat (see the later Getting Around section).

Between 1937 and 1950 Lake Naivasha was Nairobi's airport! Imperial Airways and then BOAC flew Empire and Solent flying boats here on the four-day journey from Southampton. Passengers came ashore at the Lake Naivasha Hotel where buses would be waiting to shuttle them to Nairobi. The lake also featured strongly with the decadent Happy Valley settler crowd in the '30s. The mansion known as Oserian (or the Djinn Palace) which features in the book (and the dreadful movie) *White Mischief* is on the southern shore of the lake. It's privately owned and is not open to the public. For a full account of the history of European activity in the area, get hold of a copy of *Naivasha & the Lake Hotel* by Jan Hemsing, available from the Lake Naivasha Hotel.

Elsamere
Almost opposite Hippo Point, a couple of km past Fisherman's Camp, is Elsamere, the former home of the late Joy Adamson of *Born Free* fame. She bought the house in

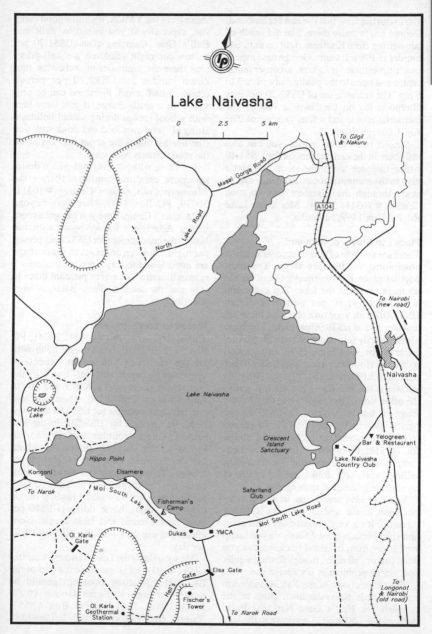

Lake Naivasha

0   2.5   5 km

To Gilgil
& Nakuru

Masai Gorge Road

A104

North Lake Road

Lake Road

To Nairobi
(new road)

Naivasha

Crater
Lake

Lake Naivasha

Crescent
Island
Sanctuary

Yelogreen
Bar & Restaurant

Hippo Point

Kongoni   Elsamere

Lake Naivasha
Country Club

Safariland
Club

Moi South Lake Road

Fisherman's
Camp

Moi South Lake Road

Ol Karia
Gate

Dukas   YMCA

Elsa Gate

To Longonot
& Nairobi
(old road)

To Narok

Hell's
Gate

Ol Karia
Geothermal
Station

Fischer's
Tower

To Narok Road

1967 with the view that she and her husband, George might retire there. She did much of her writing from Elsamere right up until her murder in 1980. It seems George never spent much time there. It is now a conservation centre and open to the public daily from 3 to 6 pm. The entrance fee of US$2.20 includes afternoon tea on the lawn, a visit to the memorial room, and a film-viewing of *The Joy Adamson Story*.

Subject to 24 hours' notice, you can also visit here in the early afternoon for US$4.40 which includes lunch, the same film and a visit to the memorial room. Bookings can be made through the Elsamere Conservation Centre (☎ (0311) 30079), Moi South Lake Rd, PO Box 1497, Naivasha.

Places to Stay – bottom end

There are a couple of budget accommodation possibilities on the lake shore. The most popular place is *Fisherman's Camp* on the southern shore of the lake. You can camp here for US$1.80 per person (children US$1.40) with your own tent plus there are tents for hire at US$0.90 per night. There are also four fully self-contained *bandas* (round, concrete or mud-brick huts with makuti roofs) with four beds in each for US$6.70 per person (children US$4.50) and what is known as the *Top Camp* (up the hill across the other side of the road). Here they have a range of bandas which cost US$3.40 per person (two beds) and US$4.50 per person (four beds) as well as the *Kongoni Cottage* for US$18. Firewood is for sale at both camps plus, at the main camp, there's a store selling beers, soft drinks and ice cream at reasonable prices, but nothing else.

You can also rent boats from the store between 8 am and 5 pm (see Getting Around). It's a very pleasant site with grass and shady acacia trees. Make sure you camp well away from overland trucks unless you want to party all night, though finding a quiet spot isn't a problem as it's a huge site.

The other choice is the *YMCA*, three km back towards Naivasha town close to the turn-off for Hell's Gate National Park. Although it's difficult to get down to the lake shore from the YMCA, it's still a good camp site, especially if you intend to walk into Hell's Gate. Camping costs US$1.70 per person per night (children are half-price) plus there are a number of somewhat run-down bandas for US$2.20 per person (children half-price). Firewood can be provided for a small charge. It gets busy here with school groups during school holidays. Bring all your own food and drink with you (the nearest dukas are about one km down the road towards Naivasha).

For those without tents and with a desire for more creature comforts, there's the *Elsamere Conservation Centre* (☎ (0311) 30079; PO Box 1497, Naivasha), beyond Fisherman's Camp. Here you can get a room in Joy Adamson's former house with full board (the only choice) for US$29 per person per night. Children under seven years of age are not allowed to stay since it's basically a research centre. It's a very pleasant place to stay and the warden, Tony Bates, is very friendly.

Places to Stay – top end

The *Safariland Club* (☎ (0311) 20241; PO Box 72, Naivasha), is a top-end hotel with all the facilities you might expect. A single/double room with full board in the high season (December to March and July to August) costs US$90/130. There are also one-bedroom cottages for US$165 and two-bedroom cottages for US$270. In the low season, singles/doubles cost US$55/80. Prices in the shoulder season are about halfway between those in the high and low seasons. The club accepts all the usual credit cards, and facilities include boat hire (US$27 for four people plus a US$5 landing fee on Crescent Island), horse riding (US$10 per hour), lawn tennis and table tennis. Non-guests can use the swimming pool for US$3 per day.

Very similar is the *Lake Naivasha Country Club* (☎ (0311) 13) and since it's part of the Block Hotels chain, bookings should be made through Rehema House (☎ (2) 335807; fax 340541), PO Box 47557, Nairobi. Singles/doubles with full board in the high season cost US$112/155 plus there are two-bedroom cottages for US$413. In the low season singles/doubles cost US$68/99 and the cottages US$262. Shoulder-season prices are about halfway between those in the high and low seasons.

Places to Eat

If you're not eating at any of the above hotels or camp sites, there's the *Yelogreen Bar & Restaurant* near the eastern end of Moi South Lake Rd. It's a pleasant place for a cold beer plus the food is good and reasonably priced. However, you need your own transport to get here as it's so far from the lake accommodation.

Getting There & Away

The usual access to Lake Naivasha is along Moi South Lake Rd. This also goes past the turn-off to Hell's Gate National Park (both the Elsa and Ol Karia gate entrances). There are fairly frequent matatus between Naivasha town and Kongoni on the western side of the lake. It's 17 km from the turn-off on the old Naivasha to Nairobi road to Fisherman's Camp and costs US$0.20. The road from the turn-off to Kongoni was recently resurfaced and is a beautiful length of tarmac highway.

Getting Around

Motorboats for game-viewing on Crescent Island can be hired from the Safariland Club for US$27 per person for four people, plus a US$5 landing fee on Crescent Island. The Lake Naivasha Hotel also offers trips to Crescent Island for much the same price.

Much cheaper rowing and motorised boats can be hired from Fisherman's Camp, but it's a long way from there to Crescent Island. Rowboats (four people maximum) cost US$1.10 per hour, and motorboats US$11 to US$22 per hour with driver, depending on the boat size. There's also a deposit of US$11.

HELL'S GATE NATIONAL PARK

This park is one of only two parks in the country which you can walk through (the other is Saiwa Swamp near Kitale). The looming cliffs and the Hell's Gate gorge itself are spectacular, and are home to a wide variety of bird and animal life. On a walk through the park it is possible to see zebra, Thomson's gazelle, antelope, baboon and even the occasional cheetah or leopard. Ostriches and the rare lammergeier are also sighted on occasion.

The usual access point is through the main **Elsa Gate**, two km from Moi South Lake Rd. From here the road takes you past **Fischer's Tower**, a 25-metre-high column of volcanic rock named after Gustav Fischer, a German explorer who reached here in 1883. He had been commissioned by the Hamburg Geographical Society to find a route from Mombasa to Lake Victoria but this was about as far as he got, largely because he was unable to get on good terms with hostile Maasai.

The road then continues through the steep-sided gorge and emerges at the **Ol Karia Geothermal Station** – a power project which utilises one of the hottest sources in the world. You can see the plumes of steam rising into the air from many of the viewpoints in the park. Left of here, you'll see Central Tower, another column of volcanic rock similar to Fischer's Tower but much larger. From the geothermal plant the track heads back to the lake shore via the Ol Karia Gate, and emerges in the vicinity of Oserian farm (now a large supplier of cut flowers, fruit and vegetables to the European market) and Elsamere.

The entire walk from the lake road turn-off via Elsa Gate and Ol Karia Gate to the lake shore is 22 km. The distance between the two gates via the lake road is nine km. If you intend walking the whole way through the park (and it's well worth doing so), allow a full day, and take along some drinking water and something to eat. The only drinking water available in the park is at the camp sites. The usual park entry and camping fees apply.

If you don't want to walk through the park it may be possible to arrange a trip by car if you ask around at Fisherman's Camp.

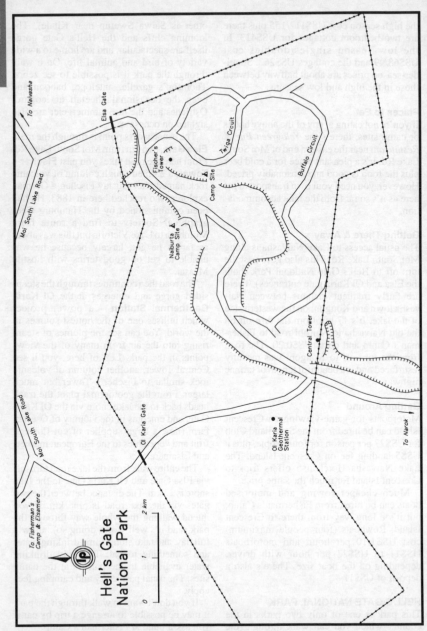

Hell's Gate National Park

To Naivasha

Moi South Lake Road

Elsa Gate

Fischer's Tower

Camp Site

Twiga Circuit

Buffalo Circuit

Naiburta Camp Site

Moi South Lake Road

Ol Karia Gate

To Fisherman's Camp & Elsamere

Central Tower

Ol Karia Geothermal Station

To Narok

0   1   2 km

LAKE ELMENTEITA

Like Lake Nakuru, Elmenteita is a shallow, soda lake with a similar ecology. Flamingos live here too, but in nowhere near the same numbers as at Nakuru. Elmenteita is not a national park, so you can walk around it and there are no entry fees. However, there are few tracks and, as most of the shoreline is privately owned, there's a lot of fencing. We recently had a letter from a woman traveller who attempted to walk around the lake alone and she was not at all impressed by the absence of a warning about how difficult it was. Think twice before attempting it!

The easiest way to get there is to take a matatu along the Naivasha to Nakuru road and get off at one of the signposted viewpoints on the escarpment above the lake. You can either walk down from there or hitch a ride.

KARIANDUSI PREHISTORIC SITE

The Kariandusi site is signposted off to the right of the main road on the way from Naivasha to Nakuru. There's not much to see as the only excavation was carried out by Louis Leakey in the 1920s, although the small museum is worth a look.

NAKURU

Kenya's fourth-largest town is the centre of a rich farming area about halfway between Nairobi and Kisumu on the main road and railway line to Uganda. It's here that the railway forks, one branch going to Kisumu on Lake Victoria and the other to Malaba on the Ugandan border.

It's a pleasant town with a population of 75,000 but is of interest mainly to those who work and farm in the area. The big draw for travellers is the nearby Lake Nakuru National Park with its prolific birdlife. The Menengai Crater and Hyrax Hill Prehistoric Site in the immediate area are both worth a visit (see later in this chapter).

Places to Stay – bottom end

The *Amigos Guest House* on Gusil Rd is a very friendly place to stay and the best value in this range. David, the man who runs it even remembered my face after seven years! The rooms and bathroom facilities are spotlessly clean, towels are provided and there's hot water. Singles/doubles with shared facilities cost US$1.60/3.10, triples are US$4.50. Don't confuse this place with the other Amigos at the junction of Kenyatta Ave and Bondoni Rd. The other one isn't anywhere near as good and can be very noisy because of the upstairs bar.

Around the corner from Amigos are the *City Inn* and the *Gamel Guest House*, though they're more basic than the above. Another good place is the *Tropical Valley Lodge* (☎ 42608) on Moi Rd which has singles/doubles with shared bath for US$2/3.10.

Right in the centre of town is the *Shik Parkview Hotel* (☎ 212345) on the corner of Kenyatta Ave and Bondoni Rd. It's a large place, but whoever designed it surely made a basic mistake since although the single rooms are self-contained (ie have private bathrooms), the doubles are not! The beds are comfortable but what other furniture you get varies. Singles/doubles cost US$4/6.20 with breakfast. The rooms overlooking Kenyatta Ave are noisy. The best thing about this place is its proximity to the bus and railway stations.

You could also check out the *Shiriksho High Life Hotel* on Mosque Rd which is conveniently close to the bus and matatu station but is not a great bargain. It's similar in price to the Shik Parkview, but none of the rooms have private bathrooms.

Places to Stay – middle

Going up in price, an excellent choice is the *Mukoh Hotel*, on the corner of Mosque and Gusil Rds, which is clean and comfortable. Singles/doubles cost US$5.60/7.80 with private bath. Soap and towels are provided and there is erratic hot water. The hotel has its own bar and restaurant, and the management is very friendly.

Not far from the Mukoh and similar in quality is the *Carnation Hotel* (☎ 43522) which has singles/doubles for US$5.80/8.90 with shared bath, or US$7.80/11.10 with

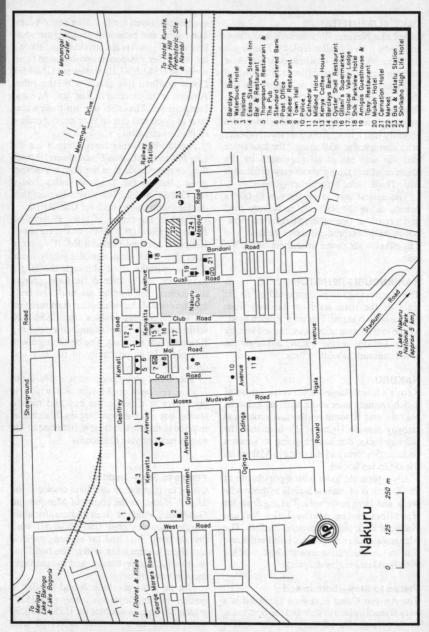

Nakuru

private bath. There's hot water in the bathrooms and the hotel has its own restaurant.

Places to Stay – top end

There's a choice of two top-end places in Nakuru. The *Midland Hotel* (☎ 212123) on Kamati Rd is a rambling old place with self-contained rooms and hot water for US$8.40/14 including breakfast. It has three bars (including the Long Bar) and two restaurants (one outdoor and one indoor).

More expensive but very pleasant is the *Waterbuck Hotel* (☎ 211516/46) on the corner of Government Ave and West Rd, which offers self-contained rooms with balcony for US$21/27 a single/double, and US$33 a triple. The price includes a good breakfast. There are substantial reductions in the low and shoulder seasons. The hotel has its own bar, restaurant and barbecue bar, and the staff are very friendly. Vehicles can be parked safely in the hotel compound which is guarded 24 hours a day.

Further away from the centre on the road to Nairobi and close to the turn-off for Hyrax Hill is the modern *Hotel Kunste* (☎ 212140, 245612) which is a conference centre/hotel. Rates in self-contained rooms are US$10/17 for a single/double, US$26 a triple, including breakfast. Lunch or dinner costs US$3.80.

Further out, several km down the road towards Nairobi, is the *Stem Hotel* which has rooms for US$17 a double with half board. It's only really of interest to those with their own transport.

Places to Eat

For price and quality, the best place to eat is the *Tipsy Restaurant* on Gusil Rd. It's very popular with local people, especially at lunch time. Dishes include Indian curries, Western food and lake fish. The food is very tasty.

The restaurant on the ground floor of the *Mukoh Hotel* is a good place for breakfast and also serves good meals and snacks. For just a coffee and a snack try the *Kenya Coffee House* on the corner of Moi Rd and Kenyatta Ave. You can also buy roasted coffee beans there.

The open-air bar at the *Midland Hotel*,

which offers barbecued chicken and a Sunday curry buffet (chicken or beef), is a popular place to eat especially at lunch time. It's very reasonably priced at around US$1.20 for main courses. The outside bar of the *Waterbuck Hotel* is also very similar. You might also like to check out the *Thompson's Restaurant* between Kenyatta Ave and Kamati Rd.

The *Steele Inn Bar & Restaurant*, next to the Esso station on Kenyatta Ave, is also a pleasant place to eat. It's a little cottage with verandahs in a garden setting and offers chicken or red meat with chips.

Going up somewhat in price, one of the town's best restaurants is the *Oyster Shell Restaurant* (☎ 40946), upstairs on Kenyatta Ave near the Club Rd corner. The menu is extensive and includes Western, Indian, Mughlai and Indonesian dishes. It's open daily for lunch and dinner and is very reasonably priced. Soups are US$0.80 and main courses US$2.70.

Similar in price and quality is the *Kabeer Restaurant* which offers indoor and al fresco dining. It's open daily until 10 pm and offers Indian food (including tandoori), Chinese dishes, seafood and grills. Main courses are priced between US$2.40 and US$2.80 (prawns cost US$5). You can also get a good Indian-style breakfast here, as well as fruit juices and takeaways at lunch time.

Entertainment

Apart from the bars mentioned earlier, there are two discos in Nakuru. The best is *Illusions* on Kenyatta Ave which is open Wednesday, Friday, Saturday and Sunday evenings until early morning. It's quieter than the discos in Nairobi but it has excellent equipment and a good mixture of music. Entry costs US$1.10 and beers sell for normal bar prices.

The other disco is upstairs from the Oyster Shell Restaurant and is open daily until 4 am. Entry costs US$0.55 for women and double that for men.

Getting There & Away

Bus & Matatu The bus and matatu station is

right in the thick of things at the eastern edge of town, near the railway station. It's a pretty chaotic place though generally it doesn't take too long to locate the bus, matatu or Peugeot you want. There are regular departures for Naivasha, Nairobi, Nyahururu and all points west.

Train As is the case with Naivasha, trains often come through in the middle of the night so you're better off going by road, as the buses and matatus arrive in the daytime only. The daily Kisumu and Nairobi trains come through at 12.30 am and 2.25 am respectively, while the Malaba trains are on Tuesday, Friday and Saturday at 8.45 pm. As for travel to Naivasha, you need to make an advance reservation in Nairobi if you're heading west and want 1st or 2nd class.

LAKE NAKURU NATIONAL PARK

Created in 1961, the park has since been considerably increased in size and now covers an area of some 200 sq km. Like most of the other Rift Valley lakes, it is a shallow soda lake. Some years ago the level of the lake rose and this resulted in a mass migration of the flamingos to other Rift Valley lakes, principally Bogoria, Magadi and Natron. What had been dubbed 'the world's greatest ornithological spectacle' suddenly wasn't anywhere near as spectacular. Since then the lake has receded and the flamingos have returned, once again giving you the opportunity of seeing up to two million flamingos along with tens of thousands of other birds. It's an ornithologists' paradise and one of the world's most magnificent sights. Those of you who have seen the film, *Out of Africa*, and remember the footage of the flight over the vast flocks of flamingos, are in for a very similar treat. Simply go up to the lookout on the top of **Baboon Cliffs** on the western side of the lake and feast your eyes on the endless pink masses which fringe the lake.

Don't blame us, though, if the birds are not there in such profusion or even if the lake dries up! The flamingos migrate from time to time if food gets scarce and there's a better

supply elsewhere – usually to Lake Bogoria further north or to lakes Magadi and Natron further south.

The lake is very shallow and the level fluctuates by up to four metres annually. When the water is low the soda crystallises out along the shoreline as a blinding white band of powder which is going to severely test your skills as a photographer. Lake Nakuru last dried up in the late 1950s and, at that time, soda dust storms and dust devils whipped up by high winds made life unbearable for people in the town and surrounding area. In the dry season you'll see these dust devils (like tiny tornadoes) whipping soda up into the air as they course along the shoreline.

Since the park also has areas of grassland, bush, forest and rocky cliffs there are many other animals to be seen apart from birds. One species you'll see plenty of are wart hogs with their amusing way of running with their tails erect. Right by the water you'll come across waterbuck and buffalo, while further into the bush are Thomson's gazelle and reedbuck – there's even the occasional leopard. Around the cliffs you may catch sight of hyrax and birds of prey. There's even a small herd of hippos which generally lives along the northern shore of the lake.

The national park entrance is about six km from the centre of Nakuru. Entry costs US$12 per person plus US$1.50 per vehicle. As in most national parks, you must be in a vehicle. Walking is not permitted so you will either have to hitch a ride with other tourists, rent your own vehicle or go on a tour.

You can only get out of your vehicle on the lake shore and at certain viewpoints. It's a memorable experience being in the proximity of several hundred thousand flamingos feeding, preening, grunting and honking and even more memorable when several thousand of them decide that you're a little too close for comfort and they take off to find a more congenial spot.

Warning Don't drive too close to the water's edge, the mud is very soft! Take your cue from the tracks of other vehicles.

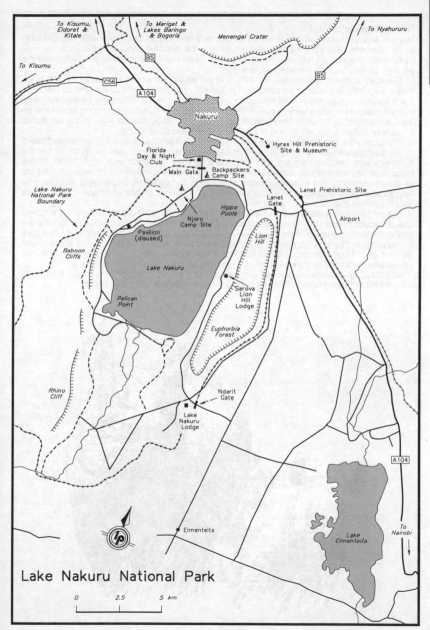

Lake Nakuru National Park

0   2.5   5 km

Rhino Rescue

Many of Africa's animals are threatened by the loss of their habitat due to human overpopulation or by poachers, and it's the poor rhino which is in the greatest danger. The rhino's horn, its trademark, causes the problem – plenty of people covet them and this only serves to push the price up as they become increasingly rare.

The stark statistics are horrific. In 1970, it is estimated that Kenya had about 20,000 black rhinos. By 1985, that number had dwindled to just 425, and rhinos were so few and so scattered that it was becoming increasingly difficult for a lady rhino to meet a compatible gentleman rhino, with the object of creating baby rhinos. With this huge fall in numbers, the price of rhino horns on the black market had soared from US$35 per kg to over US$30,000 per kg – and is still rising. Elsewhere in Africa, the fall in rhino numbers has been equally dramatic.

Rhino horn is a popular ingredient in many Chinese traditional medicines and we have all heard of the supposed effects of rhino horn on the libido. But the major market for rhino horn is the Yemen, where Djambia daggers with rhino horn handles are worth over US$15,000. These fantastic prices are inspiring ruthless tactics from poachers who tote modern weapons and are as likely to shoot as run when confronted by rangers. In 1990, their brazenness reached new heights when they shot not only Kenya's only five white rhinos (in Meru National Park) but first shot the armed guards in order to do so.

The only solution is felt to be the creation of small parks where rhinos can be carefully watched and protected. Funded by Rhino Rescue, an organisation set up in 1986 specifically to save the rhinos, the Nakuru National Park was selected as the first manageable rhino sanctuary. The park is now protected by a 74-km electric fence with guard posts at 15-km intervals. The construction involved over 11,000 fence posts and 880 km of high-tensile wire. An initial group of 19 rhinos was established and there are plans to increase this number, possibly to as many as 60.

Additional sanctuaries are planned but saving the rhino isn't going to come cheap. Donations can be sent to Rhino Rescue, PO Box 1, Saxmundham, Suffolk, IP17 3JT, UK ■

Places to Stay – bottom end

There is a good camping site, known as the *Backpackers' Camp Site* just inside the park gate. Fresh water is available and there are a couple of pit toilets, but you need to bring all your own food. Make sure tents are securely zipped up when you're away from them otherwise the vervet monkeys or baboons will steal everything inside them. If you are backpacking and trying to hitch a ride, the rangers at the gate will let you camp here without paying the park entry until you are successful.

If you have no camping equipment there's the very basic *Florida Day & Night Club* about half a km before the entrance gate.

A km or so further into the park is the *Njoro Camp Site* and this is the one to head for if you have a vehicle. It's a beautiful grassy site under acacia trees and there's firewood, water on tap and the usual pit toilets.

Places to Stay – top end

The first place you come to down the eastern access road of the park is Sarova Hotels' *Sarova Lion Hill Lodge* (☎ (2) 333248; fax (2) 211472). It has all the usual facilities including a swimming pool and open-air bar/restaurant area. High-season prices with full board are US$112/132 for singles/doubles. In the low season, prices drop to US$47/94. There are also more expensive suites. It's a well thought-out site but there are only occasional views of the lake through the thorn trees.

Almost three km beyond the southern end of the lake is the *Lake Nakuru Lodge*, PO Box 561, Nakuru (also 2nd Floor, Arrow House, Koinange St, PO Box 70559, Nairobi ☎ 2249998; fax 230962). Like the Sarova Lion Hill, it has all the usual facilities and consists of a series of shingle-roofed cottages; prices are also similar.

Getting There & Away

If you don't have your own vehicle, the only way into the park from Nakuru is by taxi (unless you can persuade a tourist with a car to take you in). A taxi costs between US$12 and US$15 for three hours, though you'll have to bargain hard for this. Alternatively, contact Jomina Tours & Travel Ltd (☎ 21-2956/7), 4th Floor, Spikes Bldg, Kenyatta Lane, Nakuru. This company runs daily tours to Lake Nakuru.

If you're driving, there's access from three points: the main gate; Lanet, just a few km along the Nairobi road; and Ndari Gate near the southern end of Lake Elmenteita.

MENENGAI CRATER

Rising up on the northern side of Nakuru is the Menengai Crater, an extinct 2490-metre high volcano. The crater itself descends to a maximum depth of 483 metres below the rim. You can drive right up to the edge, where there's one of those totally trivial signs telling you that you're five million km from some city halfway across the world.

To walk up to the crater takes a solid couple of hours, and it really is *up*, but still a very pleasant walk. The views back over Lake Nakuru are excellent, as are the views north to Lake Bogoria once you reach the top. About three-quarters of the way along there is a small group of dukas where you can get basic meals, soft drinks and, of course, the amber fluid.

HYRAX HILL PREHISTORIC SITE

Just outside Nakuru on the Nairobi road, this prehistoric site is open daily from 9 am to 6 pm and admission is US$1.60. The small booklet, *Visitor's Guide to the Hyrax Hill Site*, is available from the museum there.

Archeological excavations were first conducted here in 1937 although the significance of the site had been suspected by Louis Leakey since 1926. Further excavations have been conducted periodically, right up into the 1980s.

The finds at the site indicate three settlements were made here, the earliest possibly 3000 years ago, the most recent only 200 to 300 years ago. From the museum at the northern end you can take a short stroll around the site, starting with the North-East Village where 13 enclosures or pits were excavated. Only Pit D, investigated in 1965, is still open; the others have grown over. The North-East Village is believed to be about 400 years old, dated by comparison with the nearby Lanet site. A great number of pottery fragments were found at the site, some of which have been pieced together into complete jars and are displayed in the museum.

From the village the trail climbs to the scant remains of the stone-walled hill fort near the top of Hyrax Hill, which gave the site its name. You can continue up to the peak from where there is a fine view of the flamingo-lined Lake Nakuru.

Descending from the hill on the other side you come to the Iron Age settlement where the position of Hut B and Hut C is clearly visible. Just north of these huts, a series of burial pits containing 19 skeletons was found. Since they were mostly male, and a number of them had been decapitated, it's possible they were killed in sort sort of fighting. Unfortunately, souvenir seekers have stolen the bones that were displayed.

Virtually underneath the Iron Age site, a Neolithic site was discovered. The Iron Age burial pits actually topped a Neolithic burial mound and a second Neolithic burial mound was found nearby. This mound is fenced off as a display. Between the burial mound and the Nairobi road are more Iron Age pits, excavated in 1974. The large collection of items found in these pits included a real puzzle – six Indian coins, one of them 500 years old, two of them dating from 1918 and 1919!

Finally, following the path back to the museum, there's a *bau* board in a large rock. This popular game is played throughout East Africa.

You are free to walk around the site yourself but a guide is useful. He'll expect a small tip at the end.

LAKE BOGORIA

The two completely dissimilar lakes of Bogoria and Baringo are north of Nakuru off the B4 highway to Marigat and Lodwar.

Lake Bogoria is a shallow soda lake while Lake Baringo is a deeper freshwater lake. They're connected to Nakuru by the B4 road which is a superb, sealed highway the whole way.

Lake Bogoria covers an area of 30 sq km and has a maximum depth of nine metres. As with the other soda lakes in Kenya, Bogoria has no outlet and so the intense evaporation has led to high levels of salts and minerals. The result is that the lake supports no fish at all, but is ideal for blue-green algae, which is a favourite of the flamingos. Bogoria is a national park so there's an entry fee of US$12 per person plus US$1.50 per vehicle.

Most of the birdlife on Bogoria has migrated to the (presently) richer pastures of Lake Nakuru, but the stalwarts (of all species) remain. It's a very peaceful area but it doesn't currently compare with the ornithological spectacle of Nakuru. There are, however, the **hot springs** and **geysers** about three-quarters of the way along the lake going south. They're not comparable with those at Rotorua in New Zealand but if you've never seen geysers before then this is the place. The springs are boiling hot so don't put your bare foot or hand into them unless you want to nurse scalds for the next week.

The land to the west of the lake is a hot and relatively barren wilderness of rocks and scrub, and animals are rare though you may be lucky to catch sight of a greater kudu, impala or klipspringer. The eastern side of the lake is dominated by the sheer face of the northern extremities of the Aberdares.

Places to Stay

There are two camp sites at the southern end of the lake: *Acacia* and *Riverside*, but there are no facilities and the lake water is totally unpalatable. Bring all water and food with you if you are intending to stay at either site. Otherwise, the camp sites are shady and very pleasant.

There's another camp site just outside the northern entrance gate (Loboi). Drinking water is available here and there's a small shop nearby which sells basic supplies (canned food, jam, biscuits, washing powder, soft drinks, etc).

The *Lake Bogoria Lodge* (☎ (037) 42696) is a top-range lodge two km from the northern entrance. It's a very pleasant place set in a well-tended garden, but few people seem to stay here. Rooms cost US$46/71 a single/double, while cottages are US$150. Prices include breakfast but not service charges. With full board, charges rise to US$71/121 plus taxes.

Getting There & Away

There are two entrance gates to Lake Bogoria – one from the south (Mogotio) and another from the north (Loboi). You'll see the signpost for the Mogotio Gate on the B4 about 38 km past Nakuru heading north but, if you take it, you'll probably regret it! Most of this road is good smooth dust or gravel but there is about five km of it which leads down to the southern park entrance which will certainly rip apart any tyres and destroy any vehicle driven at more than a few km per hour. Without 4WD you'd be wasting your time. These razor-sharp lava beds don't end once you reach the park gate but continue for at least as far on the other side. In addition, signposting along the route from the turn-off is almost nonexistent.

A far better entry to the park is from the Loboi Gate just a few km before you reach Marigat on the B4. It's also signposted. From the turn-off, it's 20 km to the actual park entry gate and, although the road was once sealed, these days the bitumen is breaking up badly and you need to drive carefully.

Whichever gate you use, you're going to need your own vehicle since hitching is well-nigh impossible. Very few people visit Bogoria and those who do are usually in tourist minibuses which won't pick you up unless you're booked with them. It *may* be possible to walk into the park since there are no large predators living here (with the possible exception of the occasional leopard) but don't count on it. Officially, you're supposed to tour the park in a vehicle.

LAKE BARINGO

Some 15 km north of the town of Marigat you come to the village of **Kampi-ya-Samaki** which is the centre for exploring Lake Baringo. This lake, like Naivasha, is freshwater. It covers around 170 sq km and has a maximum depth of just 12 metres.

Fauna

The lake supports many different species of aquatic animals and birdlife as well as crocodiles and herds of hippos which invade the grassy shore every evening to browse on the vegetation. You'll hear their characteristic grunt as you walk back to your tent or banda after dark or settle down for the night. They might even decide to crop the grass right next to your tent. If they do, stay where you are. They're not aggressive animals (they don't need to be with their bulk and jaws!) but if you frighten or annoy them they might go for you. And, despite all appearances, they can *move*!

Crocodiles and hippos apart, Lake Baringo's main attraction is the birdlife and the lake is the bird-watching centre of Kenya. People come here to engage in this activity from all over the world. Kenya has over 1200 different species of birds and more than 450 of them have been sighted at Lake Baringo. Some bird-watchers are so keen they're known as 'twitchers' since their primary concern seems to be to rack up sightings of as many different bird species as possible. It's a serious business and the Lake Baringo Club even has a 'resident ornithologist' who leads bird-watching walks and gives advice to guests. A few years ago he set a world record for the number of species seen in one 24-hour period – over 300!

There's a constant twittering, chirping and cooing of birds in the trees around the lake, in the rushes on the lake and even on the steep face of the nearby escarpment. Even if you've had no previous interest in bird-watching, it's hard to resist setting off on the dawn bird walk and the highlight of the morning is likely to be a sighting of hornbills or the magnificent eagles which live almost exclusively on rock hyrax.

Places to Stay – bottom end

There's a superb place to stay just before the village called *Robert's Camp* (☎ Kampi-ya-Samaki 3 – through the operator) where you can camp for around US$2 per person per night; bundles of firewood cost US$0.80. Facilities include clean showers and toilets. There are also three double bandas available with cooking facilities for US$4.50 per person plus 18% tax. I'd strongly recommend the bandas if there is one available but demand is heavy at times and it would be wise to book one in advance (through David Roberts Wildlife, PO Box 1051, Nakuru). The bandas are beautiful, circular, grass-thatched traditional-style houses which are as clean as a new pin and furnished with comfortable beds, table and chairs and mosquito netting at the windows. Showers and toilets are separate and cooking facilities are available for US$4.50. The people here are very friendly and there's a huge land tortoise which ambles around the grounds and appears to be used to the attention it receives.

If you're camping here then you need to exercise some common sense regarding the hippos. Although hippos may graze within just a metre of your tent at night, you should not approach nearer than 20 metres, especially if they have young ones. Don't frighten them in any way with headlights, torches (flashlights) or loud noises and don't use flash photography. No-one's ever been hurt by a hippo in over 10 years but they are wild animals and should be treated with respect.

If Robert's Camp is full or you have no camping equipment then try one of the basic lodges in Kampi-ya-Samaki. The *Hippo Lodge* at the entrance to the village is way overpriced at around US$2 per person for a bed in a basic grubby room. Cheaper but equally basic is the *Lake View Lodge* on the lake side of the town. Rooms here cost around US$1 per person.

There is also a hotel in Marigat if you prefer, though it's quite a way from the lake shore and it's not the world's most interesting place. The *Marigat Inn* is about 1½ km from the signposted main road turn-off.

Singles/doubles with breakfast cost US$4.50/8, and it's very pleasant with its own bar and restaurant.

Places to Stay – top end

Right next door to Robert's Camp is the *Lake Baringo Club*, one of the Block Hotels chain (☎ 335807 in Nairobi for reservations or write c/o PO Box 47557). Singles/doubles with full board are US$39/78 in the low season and rise to US$74/116 in the high season (July and August). Children under 12 years sharing a room with adults stay for free, and pay only for meals (50% of adult meal prices). Facilities at the club include a swimming pool, dart boards, table tennis table, badminton court, a library and a whole range of local excursions including boat trips and bird-watching trips accompanied by an expert.

One-hour boat trips cost US$40 (with a minimum of seven people), bird walks US$4 per person (plus US$2 if you need transport) and camel rides US$2 per half-hour. The club also offers trips to Lake Bogoria for US$38 per person (minimum three people) and to a nearby Njemps village for US$5.50 per person (minimum three people). The Njemps are the local tribespeople who live in villages around the lake shore and practice a mixture of pastoralism and fishing. The club has an arrangement with the headman of the village which you visit so you're allowed to walk around freely and take photographs, though you'll probably be hassled to buy some of the handicrafts produced by the villagers.

The facilities at the club are open to non-guests on payment of a US$2 per person per day temporary membership on weekdays and US$3.30 on weekends, although this fee is waived if you're eating either lunch or dinner there. Use of the swimming pool costs about US$2 per person per day on top of the daily membership fee. If you arrive at the club by vehicle you probably won't be asked for the fee. At 7 pm each evening there's a slide show and commentary featuring some of the more common birds sighted in the area.

Another top-end hotel is the *Island Camp* (☎ (02) 502491, 225941 in Nairobi), which is a luxury tented lodge sited on Ol Kokwa Island in the lake. It is rated highly by those who have stayed there, and is also expensive at US$85/130 for full board. There are 25 double tents each with their own shower and toilet, two bars, a swimming pool and water sports facilities. Activities here include water-skiing (US$45 per hour) and boat trips (US$22 per hour). Boat transfers from the mainland to the island cost US$6.70 return, and the boats leave from a poorly signposted landing on the north side of Kampi-ya-Samaki village. The locals can all point you in the right direction.

Also on the island is the *Saruni Camp* (☎ (02) 333285 in Nairobi), which has eight self-contained double tents, each with views of the lake. Meals are taken in the main mess tent, and the cost of a visit is US$63/102.

Places to Eat

If you're camping at Robert's Camp and want to keep costs down then you'll have to bring your own food with you as well as cooking facilities and equipment (unless you want to cook over a wood fire). Only very basic foodstuffs are available in the village of Kampi-ya-Samaki, and a slightly better choice in Marigat, so bring what you will need from Nakuru.

Those who want to splurge can eat at the *Lake Baringo Club*. As you might expect, the meals here are very good but will cost you around US$6 for breakfast and US$11 for either lunch or dinner. The club is also the only place where you will be able to find a cold beer, and the only place where you can buy petrol and diesel between Marigat and Maralal.

Getting There & Away

There are frequent matatus between Nakuru and Marigat but they don't all continue on to Kampi-ya-Samaki, so you may have to hitch from Marigat or take another of the infrequent matatus which go to the village. In the opposite direction, there's a minibus from Kampi-ya-Samaki at about 7 am which goes to Nakuru and another which comes through later from Loruk at the top end of the lake.

It's an interesting journey between Nakuru and Baringo since the country remains relatively lush and green until you pass the equator where it almost immediately becomes drier and dustier and continues to get more barren and forbidding the further north you go. As you near Marigat there are spectacular mountains, ridges and escarpments.

A gravel track connects Loruk at the top end of the lake with the Nyahururu to Maralal road. It's in good shape if you have your own transport and are contemplating doing the trip. There's no public transport along this road and hitching is extremely difficult.

LAKE MAGADI

Lake Magadi is the most southerly of the Rift Valley lakes in Kenya and is very rarely visited by tourists because of its remoteness. Like most of the Rift Valley lakes, it is a soda lake and supports many flamingos and other water birds. It also has a soda extraction factory, hence the railway line there. A few years ago it was the site of a major rescue operation of young flamingos when drought threatened hundreds of thousands of them because of soda encrustation on their feathers – this doesn't affect the adults.

Magadi is quite different from the lakes to the north as it is in a semidesert area. Temperatures hover around the 38°C mark during the day and much of the lake is a semisolid sludge of water and soda salts. There is a series of hot springs around the periphery of the lake.

Getting There & Away

There is a rail link to the lake shore which branches off from the main Nairobi to Mombasa line but there are no passenger services along it. There's also a minor road from Nairobi (the C58) but there's no public transport along it so you will either have to hitch or have your own vehicle.

The Central Highlands

The Kenyan central highlands comprise the Aberdares, which begin around Limuru just north-west of Nairobi and continue on up to Maralal, plus the massif of Mt Kenya itself. They form the eastern wall of the Rift Valley and are the heartland of the Kikuyu people. Within the main area are two national parks, Aberdare and Mt Kenya.

It's a very fertile region, well watered, intensively cultivated and thickly forested.

The climate, likewise, is excellent. Given these qualities, it's not surprising that the land was coveted by the White settlers who began arriving in ever increasing numbers once the Mombasa-Uganda railway was completed. Here they could grow anything year-round, particularly cash crops which were in demand in Europe. It's also not surprising that the Kikuyu eventually became so disenchanted with the alienation of their

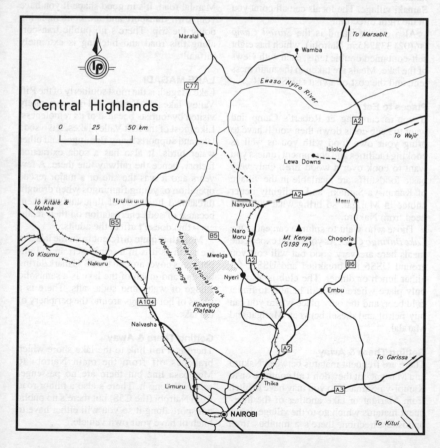

Central Highlands

0   25   50 km

To Marsabit
Maralal
Wamba
Ewaso Nyiro River
C77
To Wajir
A2
Isiolo
Lewa Downs
Nyahururu
Nanyuki
A2
Meru
B5
Iö Kitale &
Malaba
B5
Naro
Moru
Mt Kenya
(5199 m)
Chogoria
To Kisumu
Nakuru
Aberdare National Park
Mweiga
A2
B6
Nyeri
Embu
A104
Kinangop
Plateau
Naivasha
A2
To Garissa
Limuru
Thika
A3
To Kitui
NAIROBI

best land that war erupted between the two groups in the form of the Mau Mau Rebellion. It is probable that this event, more than any other, forced the British colonial authorities to reassess their position and ultimately to grant independence to the country.

While White Kenyan farmers still exist in considerable numbers in the area, their holdings have been reduced and much of the land parcelled out among the Kikuyu. Given the current level of population growth, it's anyone's guess how much longer this subdivision and further encroachment on the forest can continue before the environment is seriously threatened. Soil erosion is a major problem and many plots are too small to support a family. It's true there's still a great deal of forest remaining but with pressure on it for use as construction material and firewood (the most common form of fuel for cooking and heating) there are limits to the expansion of agricultural land. It's important to remember that much of Kenya is scrub and desert.

The Aberdares

Known to the Kikuyu as *Nyandarua*, 'drying hide', the Aberdares were named after the president of the Royal Geographical Society by the explorer Thomson in 1884. The lower eastern slopes were long cultivated by the Kikuyu while the higher regions, with peaks of up to 4000 metres and covered in dense forests and bamboo thickets, were left to the leopard, buffalo, lion and elephant. The arrival of the Europeans saw the establishment of coffee and tea plantations on the eastern side and wheat and pyrethrum farms on the western slopes. Most of this land has now been returned to the Kikuyu. Not all of the higher reaches of the Aberdares, however, are dense forest. There are also extensive areas of mist-covered moors along the ridges and a good swathe of forest out of which the Aberdare National Park was created in 1950.

ABERDARE NATIONAL PARK

This park essentially encloses the moorland and high forest of the 60-km long Kinangop plateau along with an eastern salient reaching down to the lower slopes in the vicinity of Nyeri. Only rarely does this park feature in the itineraries of safari companies and it's even less visited by individual travellers. There are various reasons for this. The main one is perhaps the weather. As on Mt Kenya, rain can be expected at any time and when it arrives, it's heavy. Roads turn into mud slides and 4WD is absolutely essential. The park is often closed during the wet season as a result.

Another drawback (though the wild game would no doubt describe it as a plus) is the difficulty of seeing animals because of the dense forest. This is not savannah like Amboseli and Masai Mara so you have to take your time and stay a few nights, which brings us to the third drawback – finding a place to stay. Though there are three camp sites within the park, facilities are minimal and you're going to need a good tent and warm sleeping gear. Add to this the fact that there's no public transport whatsoever, hitching is virtually impossible and that, as elsewhere, walking isn't permitted without special permission. That essentially puts the Aberdares out of reach of anyone without their own transport. The only other accommodation possibilities are two very expensive lodges, The Ark and Treetops, which you are not allowed to drive to in your own vehicle. You must make advance reservations for both and be driven there in the lodges' transport.

In the dry season it may be possible to walk over the high moorland between the four main peaks if the weather is favourable but you can't do this without the express permission of the game warden at Mweiga north of Nyeri (☎ 24 in Mweiga). If this is what you want to do then it's best to first contact the Kenya Mountain Club in Nairobi before setting out, as they may be planning such a trip.

These sorts of difficulties and/or the

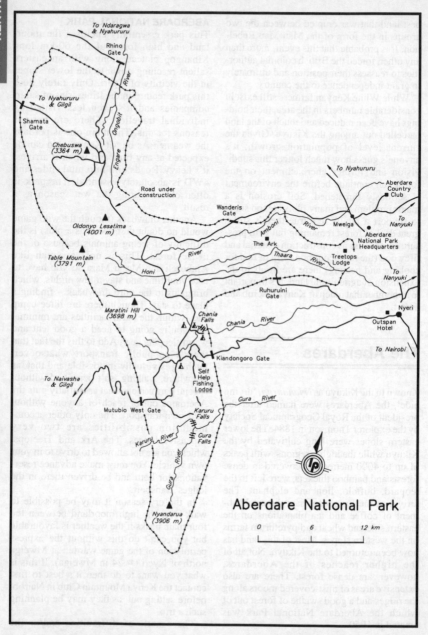

Aberdare National Park

0   6   12 km

expense involved put off most independent travellers but if you're determined to go then the rewards can well justify the effort.

The park does offer a variety of fauna, flora and scenery which you won't find elsewhere except, perhaps, on Mt Kenya. There are also the dramatic **Gura Falls** which drop a full 300 metres, thick forest, alpine moorland and a slim chance of seeing a bongo, black leopard, elephant or rhino. There are also hundreds of species of birds. The major plus about this park is that you'll never feel part of the safari-bus gravy train as you can often do in Masai Mara, Amboseli or Nairobi national parks.

Game Drives

If you can't afford the overnight charges at the lodges there is a somewhat cheaper way of visiting the park and that is to go on a game drive organised by the Outspan Hotel in Nyeri. You can do this into the eastern park area for US$30 per person (minimum two people) for the day excluding park entry fees. You can also rent self-drive vehicles from the Outspan to explore the whole park for US$78 per day.

Game drives organised by the Aberdare Country Club are yet another option, although these aren't particularly cheap either. A game drive in the salient costs US$162 for the whole vehicle for half a day, or US$312 for a full day. A surcharge of 20% is made if you're not staying at either the Country Club or The Ark.

Places to Stay

If you wish to camp in the park, reservations have to be made at the park headquarters at Mweiga (☎ 24 in Mweiga), about 12 km north of Nyeri. The charges are standard.

Both of the lodges are built beside water holes, and animals – especially elephant and buffalo – are lured to them by salt which is spread below the viewing platforms each day. This is obviously a contrived way of getting the animals to turn up but it pulls in the well-heeled punters and they, in turn, keep Lonrho, Block Hotels, Kodak and Nikon in business. What it doesn't do is

anything positive to the immediate environment. Elephants eat a prodigious amount of herbage each day and trample down even more. Buffaloes aren't exactly light on the hoof either. The two combined make sure that the area in front of the viewing platforms resembles a matatu stand which, in turn, makes the smaller and more timid animals reluctant to approach because of lack of cover. I suppose if you pay big bucks, the video has to be good even if it's thin on authenticity.

On the other hand, *Treetops* isn't exactly a 'luxury' lodge with its trestle tables, creaking floorboards, shoe-box sized rooms and shared bathroom facilities, though it does have that yuppie appeal of knowing that you've stayed under the same roof as various crowned heads of Europe and presidents of state – there are even faded mug-shots of the *nomenclatura* on the walls.

Full board (including transfer from Nyeri but excluding park entry fees) at Treetops costs US$134 (ordinary room) and US$266 (suite) per person between 1 September and 31 March, US$165 and US$201 during July and August, and US$84 and US$114 the rest of the year. Children under seven years old are not admitted. You must book in advance through Block Hotels (☎ (02) 335807), Central Reservation Office, Rehema House, Standard St, PO Box 47557, Nairobi. Having booked, you then turn up at the Outspan Hotel in Nyeri by 11.30 am for lunch (included) and transfer to the park at 2.30 pm. It isn't necessary to stay at the Outspan the previous night unless you particularly want to.

The Ark is somewhat better appointed than Treetops and is further into the park but it costs much more, too. Full board here, including transfer from Mweiga but excluding park entry fees, costs US$207/242 from April to June and November to mid-December, and US$377/448 the rest of the year. As at Treetops, children under seven years old are not admitted; children over seven years pay the full adult rate.

You must book in advance through Lonrho Hotels Kenya (☎ (02) 216940),

Bruce House, Standard St, PO Box 58581, Nairobi. Having booked you must turn up at the Aberdare Country Club at Mweiga, 12 km north of Nyeri, on the appointed day and you'll be driven to the lodge.

NYERI

Nyeri is one of the largest towns in the central highlands, the administrative headquarters of Central province, and the usual gateway to Aberdare National Park. It's a lively place with an extensive market, several banks, hardware stores, vehicle-repair shops, bookshops and a plethora of other stores selling everything under the sun. It also has a good choice of hotels and restaurants.

It started life as a garrison town back in the early days of colonialism but was quickly transformed into a trading and social centre for White cattle ranchers, coffee growers and wheat farmers. Their watering holes, in the form of the White Rhino Hotel in town and the Aberdare Country Club at Mweiga are nostalgic reminders of their proclivities, though the White Rhino appears to have accepted inevitable decline.

It's a very green area and intensively cultivated for all manner of vegetables, sugar cane, citrus fruits, bananas, tea, coffee and even that Australian import – macadamia nuts! On a clear day, too (usually early mornings), you can see Mt Kenya in all its snowcapped glory in the distance. Apart from these virtues, however, it's hardly the most magnetic town in Kenya and few travellers stay more than a couple of nights.

The Gliding Club of Kenya has its headquarters at Mweiga, just a short distance north of Nyeri. If you are into soaring, or would like to take a glide over the Aberdares, it's worth getting in touch with the managers Peter & Petra Allmendinger (☎ (0171) 2748), PO Box 926, Nyeri.

Places to Stay – bottom end

If you're down and out, there are some real dives here such as the *New Alaska Hotel* and the *South Tetu Hotel* but they can't seriously be recommended.

One of the best in the budget range is the *Bahati Boarding & Lodging* at the front of the upper bus and matatu stand. It's simple and clean and offers rooms for US$3/4 a single/double without bath, and US$4.60/6 for a self-contained room complete with lurid wallpaper. There's supposedly hot water in the mornings, and the hotel has its own bar and restaurant. It's a convenient place to stay if you're taking an early bus. If the Bahati is full (unlikely), then try the *New 7 Star Boarding & Lodging* across the road. It's cheaper at US$2.70/5.50 but is very basic and somewhat gloomy.

For something a bit better try the clean and relatively new *Nyeri Star Hotel* near the lower bus stand. The large rooms are set around an internal courtyard, and the front rooms (singles only) have excellent views across town to Mt Kenya. All rooms are self-contained and the charge is US$6/9.70. The hotel also has an agreeable bar and quite a reasonable restaurant.

Places to Stay – middle

The most economical place in this range is the *New Thingira Guest House* (☎ (0171) 4769). To get there, turn left and head downhill just after the mosque as you come in on the Nairobi to Karatina road. It's a relatively new place but is poorly managed, and the institute where the building's architect was trained ought to be shut down! The cost for a self-contained room is US$8.50/14, supposedly with breakfast, but you'll be lucky if this ever materialises. An askari (private security guard) is employed to guard the car park overnight.

Slightly more expensive but a much better proposition is the equally modern *Central Hotel* (☎ (0171) 2906) at the top end of town. Self-contained singles/doubles here with hot water cost US$12/16. The hotel has its own bar and restaurant and there's a disco on Friday and Saturday nights.

For a touch of olde-worlde charm at about the same price (though you pay more for nostalgia than the facilities which it offers) there's the old White settlers' watering hole, the *White Rhino Hotel*. It's a popular place

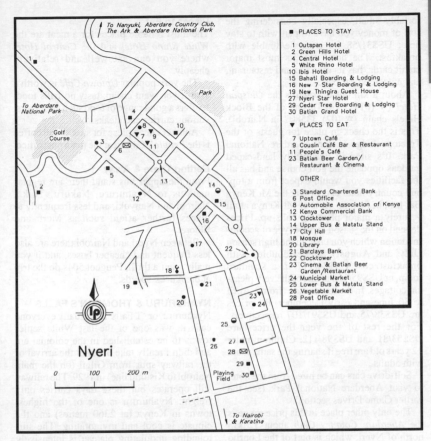

To Nanyuki, Aberdare Country Club,
The Ark & Aberdare National Park

To Aberdare
National Park

Golf
Course

Park

Nyeri

0   100   200 m

To Nairobi
& Karatina

to stay, has a terrace bar, lounge, garden and
quite a cheap restaurant and offers rooms for
US$11/18.50 including breakfast.

At the top of the range is the *Green Hills
Hotel* (☎ (0171) 2017) which sits on the crest
of the hill across the narrow valley opposite
the White Rhino. Unless you have transport
the location is inconvenient and you'll be
much better off in one of the hotels in the
town centre. The hotel is set amongst rolling
lawns and though it has 124 double rooms
it's not high-rise. Rooms cost US$21/33 a
single/double including breakfast and taxes.
There's no charge for children up to 12 years

old occupying the same room as their
parents. There are two restaurants, a bar,
sauna, massage facilities, children's play-
ground, swimming pool and guarded
parking facilities. Checkout time is 10 am.
The staff are friendly and the rooms very
pleasantly decorated and furnished.

Places to Stay – top end

In the town centre, not far from the lower bus
stand, is the modern *Batian Grand Hotel*
(☎ (0171) 4141). Although it's clean, comfortable and well furnished, some of the
rooms (particularly the singles) are uncom-

fortably small, especially considering the sort of money you have to part with to stay here: US$31/58 for a single/double with breakfast. The hotel accepts most major credit cards, has its own bar and restaurant, and a guarded car park.

About a km out of town is the *Outspan Hotel* (☎ (0171) 2424), one of the Block Hotels chain (☎ (02) 335807 in Nairobi). This is the check-in place for guests of the Treetops lodge in the Aberdare National Park. It's sited in beautifully landscaped gardens opposite the golf course and has all the facilities you would expect from a top-end country hotel except that the Mt Kenya Bar has, in fact, no view of Mt Kenya at all – surely a major planning balls-up. Prices depend on the season and the type of accommodation which you take. In the high season (July and August) Singles/doubles with breakfast cost US$84/117 in a standard room, or US$95/123 in one of the very pleasant cottages. In the low season (from 1 April to 30 June and early December) the prices are US$38/75 and US$91/107 respectively. For the rest of the year the prices are US$53/81 and US$98/112. Children under 12 years old are free if sharing the same room with adults.

Self-drive cars can be hired from the hotel to visit Aberdare National Park (see the earlier Game Drives section).

The only other place in this price range is the *Aberdare Country Club* about 12 km north of Nyeri, which is part of the Lonrho Hotels Kenya group (☎ (02) 216940), Bruce House, Standard St, PO Box 58581, Nairobi. Like the Kentmere Club at Limuru and the Norfolk Hotel in Nairobi (also owned by Lonrho), this was once one of the quintessential White planters' watering holes and social foci except that these days it caters for the international leisure set and those with the money to burn on a night or two at The Ark. Full board (including temporary membership) costs US$79/133 for singles/doubles from April to June and November to mid-December, and US$129/168 the rest of the year. Children aged from two to 12 years are charged US$52.

Places to Eat

The most reliable places for a meal are the *White Rhino Hotel* and the *Central Hotel* where you can eat well and relatively cheaply.

The very popular *Uptown Café* is worth a visit if you want cheap, tasty no-frills food. It offers a good range of food such as burgers, various curries and steaks.

Another cheap place for snacks and coffee is the *People's Café* near the main post office.

Getting There & Away

From the upper bus stand there are regular matatus to Nyahururu, Nakuru, Thika, Nairobi and Nanyuki, and less frequently to places further afield such as Meru and Eldoret.

Between Nyeri and Nairobi there are also less frequent and cheaper buses, and if you really want a thrill, Peugeot 504s do the trip at breakneck speeds.

NYAHURURU & THOMSON'S FALLS

Nyahururu, or 'T Falls' as virtually everyone calls it, was one of the last White settler towns to be established in the colonial era and didn't really take off until the arrival of the railway spur from Gilgil (on the main Nairobi to Kisumu line) in 1929. The railway still operates but these days carries only freight. Nyahururu is one of the highest towns in Kenya (at 2360 metres) and the climate is cool and invigorating. The surrounding undulating plateau is intensively cultivated with maize, beans and sweet potatoes and well forested, mainly with conifers. The most interesting approach to the town is probably along the excellent road from Nakuru which snakes up and down through farmlands and forests and offers some spectacular views over the Aberdares.

The falls, on the outskirts of town, are named after Joseph Thomson who was the first European to walk from Mombasa to Lake Victoria in the early 1880s. They're a popular stopover for safari companies en route to Maralal and points further north and are well worth a visit. Formed by the waters of the Ewaso Narok River, the falls plummet

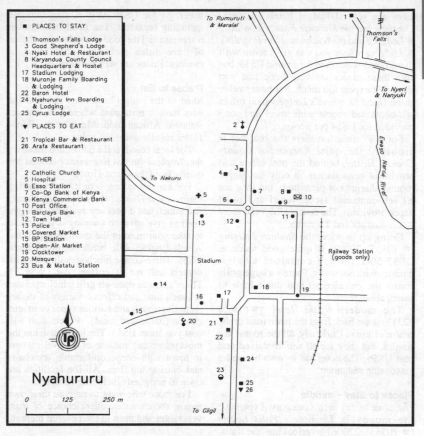

PLACES TO STAY
1 Thomson's Falls Lodge
3 Good Shepherd's Lodge
4 Nyaki Hotel & Restaurant
6 Karyandua County Council
   Headquarters & Hostel
17 Stadium Lodging
18 Muronje Family Boarding
   & Lodging
22 Baron Hotel
24 Nyahururu Inn Boarding
   & Lodging
25 Cyrus Lodge

PLACES TO EAT
21 Tropical Bar & Restaurant
26 Arafa Restaurant

OTHER
2 Catholic Church
5 Hospital
6 Esso Station
7 Co-Op Bank of Kenya
9 Kenya Commercial Bank
10 Post Office
11 Barclays Bank
12 Town Hall
13 Police
14 Covered Market
15 BP Station
16 Open-Air Market
19 Clocktower
20 Mosque
23 Bus & Matatu Station

Nyahururu

0   125   250 m

over 72 metres into a ravine and the resulting spray bathes the dense forest below in a perpetual mist. A series of stone steps leads down to the bottom of the ravine and is the only safe access. Don't attempt to go down any other way as the rocks on the side of the ravine are often very loose. Up above the falls and partially overlooking them (though the view is obscured by a row of ugly souvenir shacks) is the old colonial watering hole, Thomson's Falls Lodge, which has retained much of its quaint atmosphere and is still the most interesting place to stay. The hotel grounds are a popular place for a Sunday

picnic with local families. There's supposedly a US$0.60 charge for using the hotel grounds if you're not staying there, but this is rarely enforced.

Places to Stay – bottom end
The best place to stay if you have camping equipment is the camp site at *Thomson's Falls Lodge* which is very pleasant and costs US$2 per person per night with as much firewood as you need. Campers have access to all the facilities at the lodge including hot showers and toilets.

For those without camping equipment

there are several budget hotels in town. Cheapest are the *Muronje Family Boarding & Lodging* and the *Nyahururu Inn Boarding & Lodging* where you can get a room with shared cold-water bath for around US$3, but both these places are very basic and you shouldn't expect too much. Far better value is the *Good Shepherd's Lodge* which offers self-contained rooms with towel and soap provided for US$4 per person.

For solo male travellers the best bet is probably the quiet *Karyandua County Council Hostel*, behind the post office and provincial headquarters. It only has single rooms (sharing not permitted), but they are all self-contained (soap, towel and toilet paper provided). The cost is US$3 and there is a restaurant and TV room.

Going up in price, the *Stadium Lodging* (☎ (0365) 22002) is quite good value at US$3.50/7 for self-contained singles/doubles with hot water. There's a large grille across the entrance so you don't have to worry about theft.

The modern *Nyaki Hotel* (☎ (0365) 22313) is set back from the main road in the centre of town. Curiously, all the rooms are singles, but they are all self-contained and cost US$6. The hotel has its own bar and a reasonable restaurant.

Places to Stay – middle

The place to stay in this category if you have the money is *Thomson's Falls Lodge* (☎ (0365) 22006) overlooking the falls. Though it's no longer frequented by White planters, it exudes nostalgia and olde-worlde charm with its polished wooden floorboards and log fires. Accommodation is available either in the main building with its bar, lounge and dining room or in separate cottages scattered over the well-maintained lawns. Rooms here are self-contained with hot water and your own log fire, and cost US$30/42 a single/double though there is scope for negotiation.

If you prefer modernity and a place in the centre then the *Baron Hotel* (☎ (0365) 32751) is the choice. It's clean, well-organised and self-contained rooms with hot

water go for US$9.70/14 a single/double including breakfast. The hotel has its own restaurant and the food is good with a choice of three dishes each day – fish, meat or chicken. Prices are very reasonable.

Places to Eat

Most of the budget hotels and many of the bars have a restaurant where you can get standard African food. Meals at the *Baron Hotel* are also excellent value.

For local colour and a barbecued meal, try the *Tropical Bar & Restaurant* around the corner from the Baron Hotel.

For a minor splurge – or if you're staying there – eat at *Thomson's Falls Lodge*. Breakfast, lunch and dinner are available, but you need to give advance warning if you intend to take your meal in the main dining room. A full English-style breakfast costs about US$6. Three-course lunches or dinners with dessert and tea or coffee cost US$9.70. There's also an open-air grill which operates at lunch time and offers a variety of dishes including soups and various types of nyama choma (barbecued meat). A meat dish will cost you about US$3. The lodge also has the most interesting and one of the liveliest bars in town with deep comfortable armchairs and blazing log fires. All the facilities are open to nonguests including campers.

For those who want to prepare their own meals, there's an excellent choice of fruit, vegetables and meat in the covered market.

Entertainment

The *Baron Hotel* has a discotheque every Friday and Saturday night.

Getting There & Away

There are plenty of buses and matatus throughout the day until late afternoon in either direction between Nakuru and Nyeri and Nyahururu. Other destinations served by regular matatus and buses include Nairobi, Nanyuki, Thika, Kericho and Isiolo.

There's also at least one minibus per day in either direction between Maralal and Nyahururu which leaves early in the morning and costs US$4. Get there early if you want a seat. For the rest of the day, hitching is feasible but not easy. The road is surfaced as far as Rumuruti after which it's gravel or *murram* (dirt). Parts of this gravel road are in bad shape but it improves considerably the nearer you get to Maralal.

Mt Kenya Area

Although a distinctly separate massif from the Aberdares, Mt Kenya also forms part of the central highlands. Africa's second-highest mountain at 5199 metres, its gleaming and eroded snow-covered peaks can be seen for miles until the late-morning clouds obscure the view. Its lower slopes, like those of the Aberdares, are intensively cultivated by the Kikuyu and the closely related Embu and Meru peoples, along with the descendants of the White settlers who grow mainly wheat on the grassy and largely treeless plains on the northern side. So vast is this mountain that it's not hard to understand why the Kikuyu deified it, why their houses are built with the doors facing the peak and why it was probably never scaled until the arrival of European explorers.

These days it's every traveller's dream to get to the top and take home with them a memory which money cannot buy.

The mountain is circled by an excellent tarmac road along which are the area's main towns – Naro Moru, Nanyuki, Meru and Embu, along with Isiolo at the extreme north-eastern end. We deal first with the towns along this road and then with Mt Kenya itself since the towns are the jumping-off points for climbing the mountain.

NARO MORU

The village of Naro Moru on the western side of the mountain consists of little more than a string of small shops and houses, a couple of very basic hotels, agricultural warehouses and the famous Naro Moru River Lodge, but it's the most popular starting point for climbing Mt Kenya. There's a post office here but

no banks (the nearest are at Nanyuki and Nyeri).

The other important thing to bear in mind is that the Naro Moru River Lodge has an exclusive franchise on the mountain huts along the Naro Moru route including those at the meteorological ('Met') station so you have to go to this lodge to make bookings. It's all been carefully calculated to sew up the market on this route but that doesn't prevent you from climbing independently so long as you're willing to camp and have the appropriate equipment.

Places to Stay

There are a couple of basic lodges in the village, the *Naro Moru 82 Bar & Restaurant* and the *Mountain View Lodge*, but hardly anyone stays there. Most people head off to the *Naro Moru River Lodge* (☎ (0176) 62622) which is about 1½ km off to the left down a gravel track from the main Nairobi to Nanyuki road. It's essentially a top-range hotel set in landscaped gardens alongside the Naro Moru River but it does have a well-equipped camp site with hot showers and toilets for US$4.50 per person per night. Also at the camp site are dormitory bunkhouses where a bed costs US$6.50. Campers are entitled to use all the hotel facilities.

Those seeking a degree of luxury either before or after climbing the mountain have the option of self-contained 'standard' or 'superior' rooms or cottages. In the low season (24 April to 11 June and 18 September to 17 December) the rooms cost US$36/66 and US$47/81 for half board, while the cottages range from US$36 to US$71. For the rest of the year the prices are US$85/110 and US$98/138 for the rooms, and from US$55 to US$120 for the cottages. The hotel has a swimming pool and a restaurant. There's also a cosy bar complete with log-burning fireplace and decked out with autographed T-shirts of various groups from all over the world who have climbed the mountain at one time or another. American Express and Visa cards are accepted.

The main reason for coming to this lodge if you're an independent traveller is that it's

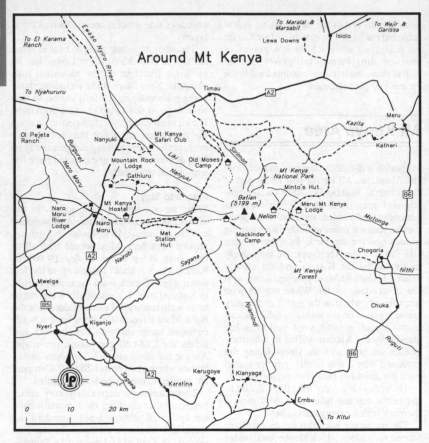

Around Mt Kenya

here you must book and pay for any of the mountain huts which you want to stay at along the Naro Moru route. Those at the Met Station cost US$7.50 and the ones at Mackinder's Camp US$11. You can also pay for the camp sites here which cost US$0.60 (no charge for guides or porters). Members of the Mountain Club of Kenya are entitled to a 25% discount on these prices and the accommodation charges at the lodge.

The other reason for coming to this lodge if you don't have a tent, cooking equipment or appropriate clothing is that it runs a comprehensive hire service which is open daily

from 7 am to 1 pm and 2 to 8 pm. The charges are similar to those at Atul's in Nairobi and are detailed under the description of climbing the mountain.

There's also an excess baggage store which costs US$0.80 per piece. You can use this service whether you're a guest or not.

The only cheap place to stay in the vicinity is the *Mt Kenya Hostel*, about 12 km up the road towards the mountain, off the main road to the right. This is a very popular place with budget travellers and campers and it's run by a very friendly and helpful man named Joseph. Accommodation is available in

The Kikuyu

The Kikuyu number more than three million and their heartland is the area around Mt Kenya. The original Kikuyu are thought to have migrated to the area from the east and north-east over a period of a couple of hundred years from the 16th century, and were actually part of the group known as Meru. Basically they overran the original occupants of the area such as the Athi and the Gumba, although intermarriage and trading did take place.

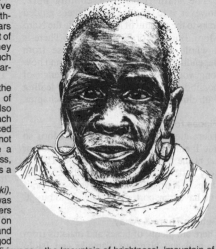

The Kikuyu's new land was bordered by the Maasai and although there were periods of calm between the two groups, there were also times when raids were carried out against each other's property and cattle. Both groups placed a high value on cattle. Intermarriage was not uncommon between them and there are a number of similarities – particularly in dress, weaponry, and dancing – shared by both as a result of their intermingling.

The administration of the clans *(mwaki)*, made up of many family groups *(nyumba)*, was originally taken care of by a council of elders with a good deal of importance being placed on the role of the witch doctor, medicine man and the blacksmith. Traditionally the Kikuyu god (Ngai) is believed to reside on Mt Kenya *(Kirinyaga* – the 'mountain of brightness', 'mountain of whiteness' or 'black and white peak spotted like ostrich feathers') which accounts for the practice of orientating Kikuyu homes with the door facing Mt Kenya.

Initiation rites for both boys and girls are important ceremonies and consist of circumcision in boys and cliterodectomy in girls (the latter now rarely practiced), accompanied by elaborate preparations and rituals. Each group of youths of the same age belong to an 'age-set' *(riika)* and pass through the various stages of life (with associated rituals) together.

Subgroups of the Kikuyu include Embu, Ndia and Mbeere. ∎

either the main building or in a rustic hut, facilities include hot-water showers and cooking facilities. The hostel is signposted on the main road up to the mountain. The advantage of staying here is that it's only about four km to the park entrance gate.

Seven km north of Naro Moru on the Nanyuki road is the *Mountain Rock Lodge* (☎ (0176) 62625), tucked away in wooded surroundings less than a km from the main road. It offers pleasant self-contained cottages with hot showers and fireplaces for US$26/29 a single/double. Rates including breakfast are US$34/44, or with full board, US$53/85. 'Superior' rooms are also available and these cost US$32/39, US$39/52 and US$60/95 respectively. There's also a well-equipped camp site with hot and cold water, toilets, cooking facilities, electricity and ample firewood for US$5 per person per night. Meals in the restaurant cost US$6.50 for breakfast, US$9 for lunch and US$10.40 for dinner. All prices include taxes and service charges. The main block consists of a spacious dining room, bar, lounge and a terrace with a *makuti* (straw or reed) roof. The hotel accepts credit cards.

Horse riding (US$13 per hour), trout fishing (US$6.50 per hour including fishing rod and licence) and bird-watching are some of the activities which the lodge caters for, plus there are traditional dances performed when demand warrants it (US$5 per person with a minimum of six people, or US$104 on demand).

The main reason for coming here, however, is to take one of the hotel's guided treks to the summit of Mt Kenya via the Naro Moru, Burguret or Sirimon routes. There is a whole range of these to choose from depending on where you want to go and how long you wish to take. The full range of possibilities is outlined in the section dealing with climbing Mt Kenya later in this chapter.

Places to Eat

There are no restaurants at Naro Moru so you'll either have to cook your own food or eat at the *Naro Moru River Lodge*. There's very little choice of food available at the shops in Naro Moru so bring your own or, if you have transport, go to Nanyuki to buy it.

Getting There & Away

There are plenty of buses and matatus from Nairobi and Nyeri to Nanyuki and Isiolo which will drop you off in Naro Moru.

The Naro Moru River Lodge also operates a shuttle bus between the lodge and Nairobi on a daily basis. It departs from the lodge at 9 am and from Nairobi at 2.30 pm and costs US$40 one way and US$73 return (not cheap!). In Nairobi you have to book the bus on the 1st floor of College House (☎ 337-501), University Way – ask for Stanley Matiba. In Naro Moru, book at the lodge itself.

The lodge also does transfers to Nanyuki airstrip (US$20 per person) and to the meteorological station for US$78, the park gate for US$39 or the trailhead on the Sirimon route for US$137.

NANYUKI

Nanyuki is a typical small country town about halfway along the northern section of the Mt Kenya ring road and a popular base from which to trek up the mountain via either the Burguret or Sirimon routes. It was founded by White settlers in 1907 in the days when game roamed freely and in large numbers over the surrounding grassy plains.

The game has almost disappeared – shot by the settlers for meat and to protect their crops from damage by foragers – but the descendants of the settlers remain and the town has also become a Kenyan air force base as well as a British army base for the joint manoeuvres conducted by the two armies each year. It's a fairly pleasant town and still has a faint ring of the colonial era to it. There's all the usual facilities here including banks, a post office and a good range of well-stocked stores.

Places to Stay – bottom end

The cheapest place is the *Nanyuki Youth Hostel* (☎ (0176) 2112) at the Emmanuel Parish Centre, Market Rd, but it's pretty basic, even dismal. The showers have only cold water. There are also some simple lodges, including the *Silent Guest House* and the *Juba Boarding & Lodging*.

More expensive but a popular place to stay is the *Josaki Hotel* (☎ (0176) 2181) which has large, clean, self-contained singles/ doubles with hot water for US$4 per person. There's a bar and restaurant on the 1st floor. Secure parking is available. Also popular, but not as good, is the *Sirimon Guest House* fronting the park.

Places to Stay – middle

A short distance from the centre of town along the Isiolo road is the *Simba Lodge*, not far from the Catholic church. Self-contained rooms in this comfortable and quiet hotel cost around US$14/18 including breakfast. Vehicles can be parked in the hotel compound and are guarded by an askari.

Probably the nicest place in this range is the *Sportsman's Arms Hotel* (☎ (0176) 22598), south-east of the town centre and across the river. Run by an Asian lady, Mrs Dia, this was once the White settlers' watering hole as the style of the building and the extensive surrounding lawns indicate. It's certainly a bit rough around the edges these days, but is excellent value at US$12/19. The self-contained rooms are huge and musty, the plumbing antedilu-

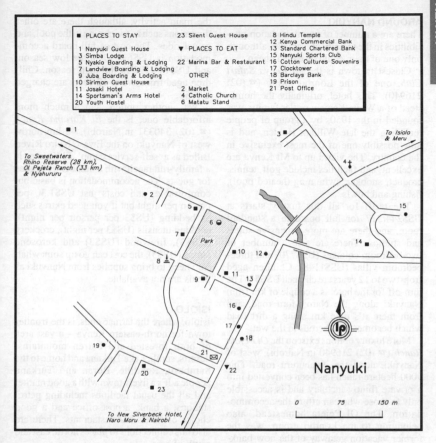

PLACES TO STAY

1 Nanyuki Guest House
3 Simba Lodge
5 Nyakio Boarding & Lodging
7 Landview Boarding & Lodging
9 Juba Boarding & Lodging
10 Sirimon Guest House
11 Josaki Hotel
14 Sportsman's Arms Hotel
20 Youth Hostel

23 Silent Guest House

▼ PLACES TO EAT

22 Marina Bar & Restaurant

OTHER

2 Market
4 Catholic Church
6 Matatu Stand

8 Hindu Temple
12 Kenya Commercial Bank
13 Standard Chartered Bank
15 Nanyuki Sports Club
16 Cotton Cultures Souvenirs
17 Clocktower
18 Barclays Bank
19 Prison
21 Post Office

To Isiolo & Meru

To Sweetwaters
Rhino Reserve (28 km),
Ol Pejeta Ranch (33 km)
& Nyahururu

Park

Nanyuki

To New Silverbeck Hotel,
Naro Moru & Nairobi

0   75   150 m

vian and the whole place has an air of gradual and inevitable decay. The restaurant serves some of the best meals in town at moderate prices, and the bar is lively in the evenings with the British army lads.

Places to Eat

There are very few restaurants in Nanyuki which are not attached to hotels, so take your pick. The *Marina Bar & Restaurant* is a reasonable place to eat in the centre of town and an expats' watering hole. For something a bit more sophisticated, try a meal at the *Sportsman's Arms*.

Things to Buy

There are a number of souvenir stalls and shops set up around town, catering mostly to the British army. The Cotton Culture store on the main street has some interesting items, including beautiful woollen jumpers (US$52) hand-knitted by a local women's cooperative.

Getting There & Away

There are daily buses from Nairobi and Isiolo to Nanyuki as well as minibuses and matatus from Nyeri and Nyahururu which run throughout the day.

AROUND NANYUKI

There are a number of accommodation possibilities in the vicinity of Nanyuki, although only one of them could be called cheap.

Closest to town is the *Mt Kenya Safari Club*, one of the Lonrho group (☎ (02) 216940). This hotel, originally the homestead of a White Kenyan settler family, was founded in the 1950s by a group of people including the late William Holden, and is now possibly one of the most exclusive in the country. The views up to Mt Kenya are excellent, and facilities include golf, tennis, croquet, snooker, swimming (heated pool), fishing and bowls.

The tariff for all this luxury starts at US$244/317 for full board in a standard room, and there are more expensive suites and studios. There are also a number of two-bedroom cottages (US$770) and three-bedroom villas (US$1148). Children aged from two to 12 years are charged US$57. The turn-off for the hotel is a couple of km from Nanyuki along the Naro Moru road, and from there it's nine km along a dirt road which becomes treacherous in the wet.

More luxury options exist on the *Ol Pejeta Ranch* (☎ (02) 216940 in Nairobi), west of Nanyuki along the Nyahururu road. This 9000-hectare ranch has been converted into a private rhino sanctuary and is accessible only to those who can afford the accommodation. The Ol Pejeta homestead, also belonging to the Lonrho group, was the former vacation getaway of the now-bankrupt international financier Adnan Kashoggi. As he was not one to spare any expense, the hotel is lavishly decorated, and still features Kashoggi's four-metre-wide bed! Full-board rates are US$78/130 in the low season (April to June, and November to mid-December) and US$163/208 the rest of the year. More expensive suites are also available. Children under 16 years are *personae non gratae* here.

Also on the Ol Pejeta Ranch is the *Sweetwaters Tented Camp*, where a number of luxury permanent tents (though they are tents in name only) have been constructed beside a water hole (floodlit at night). With the water hole as a focus, game-viewing is the main activity, although there are other diversions such as swimming in the pool, and camel rides. The cost of full-board accommodation is US$63/117 in the low season, and US$144/192 in the high season. Children aged from two to 12 years are charged US$52.

Yet another option, and a much more affordable one, is the *El Karama Ranch* (☎ (02) 340331 in Nairobi), 42 km northwest of Nanyuki on the Ewaso Nyiro River. Billed as a 'self-service camp', El Karama is a family-run ranch with a number of bandas for guests. The accommodation is basic but comfortable, and costs just US$1.30 per person per night but if you need extras such as bedding (US$3 per person per night), cooking utensils (US$3 per night), crockery (US$3), firewood (US$3) and kerosene lamps (US$3), the cost can go up somewhat. You need to bring supplies from Nanyuki as meals are not available.

ISIOLO

Isiolo, where the tarmac ends, is the frontier town for north-eastern Kenya – a vast area of both forested and barren mountains, deserts, scrub, Lake Turkana and home to the Samburu, Rendille, Boran and Turkana peoples. It's a lively town with a good market and all the usual facilities including petrol stations, a bank, a post office and a good choice of hotels and restaurants. There are also bus connections to places north, east and south of here.

The resident population of Isiolo is largely Somali in origin as a result of the resettlement here of Somali ex-soldiers following WW I. It ought, in addition, to be famous for the number of formidable speed bumps which force traffic to a snail's pace on the way into town from the south. There are no less than 21 of these and more still at the northern edge of town!

Information

Isiolo is the last place going north which has a bank (Barclays) until you get to either Maralal or Marsabit. There are no banks on

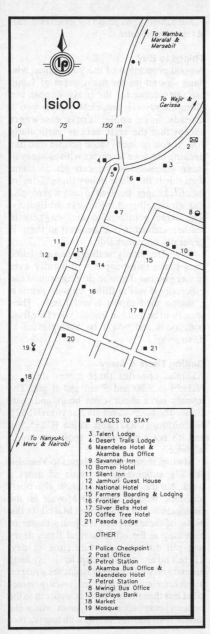

To Wamba, Maralal & Marsabit

Isiolo

0   75   150 m

To Wajir & Garissa

To Nanyuki, Meru & Nairobi

■ PLACES TO STAY
3 Talent Lodge
4 Desert Trails Lodge
6 Maendeleo Hotel &
   Akamba Bus Office
9 Savannah Inn
10 Bomen Hotel
11 Silent Inn
12 Jamhuri Guest House
14 National Hotel
15 Farmers Boarding & Lodging
16 Frontier Lodge
17 Silver Bells Hotel
20 Coffee Tree Hotel
21 Pasoda Lodge

OTHER
1 Police Checkpoint
2 Post Office
5 Petrol Station
6 Akamba Bus Office &
   Maendeleo Hotel
7 Petrol Station
8 Mwingi Bus Office
13 Barclays Bank
18 Market
19 Mosque

the way to or at Lake Turkana (assuming you bypass Maralal).

Likewise, there are no petrol stations north of here until you reach Maralal or Marsabit except at the Samburu Lodge (in Samburu National Park). This doesn't mean that petrol or diesel is totally unobtainable since you can buy it in Baragoi (with ease) and possibly at Christian mission stations elsewhere (with difficulty or not at all if they're low on stock) but you will pay well over the odds for it due to transport costs and irregularity of supply. Stock up in Isiolo.

Travellers about to go to the national parks north of here or to Lake Turkana and who intend to do their own cooking should stock up on food and drink in Isiolo as there's very little available beyond here except at Maralal, Marsabit and (less so) Wamba. There's a very good market in Isiolo adjacent to the mosque for fresh fruit, vegetables and meat. The general stores, too, have a good range of canned food and other items.

Places to Stay – bottom end
There are a number of fairly basic lodging houses available for those tight on funds which include the *Maendeleo Hotel, Farmers Boarding & Lodging, Savannah Inn, Frontier Lodge, Coffee Tree Hotel* and the *National Hotel*, all offering rooms with shared bathroom facilities (cold water only) from US$3.30/4.50 a single/double. The downstairs area of the Frontier Lodge is taken up by a lively bar which sometimes hosts live bands.

The best place to stay, however, is the *Jamhuri Guest House* which is excellent value and has been popular with travellers for a number of years. It's run by Ibrahim and Arden who are both very friendly and will go out of their way to be helpful. The rooms are very clean and pleasant, mosquito nets are provided and the communal showers have hot water in the mornings. Rooms cost US$3/4 a single/double. Belongings left in the rooms are quite safe. Next door to it and similar in price and quality is the *Silent Inn*.

Another possibility is the *Talent Lodge* near the post office. It offers rooms with shared bath for US$1.80/3.50 a single/ double. There is supposedly hot water all day in the showers but this is wishful thinking. The centre of the hotel and the terrace overlooking the street are taken up by a bar so it's not as quiet as the Jamhuri Guest House.

Going up in price, there is the *Pasoda Lodge* which is clean and quiet and offers doubles with bath for US$5.80. There are no singles. The hotel has its own restaurant and bar.

At the top of the budget category is the brand new *Desert Trails Lodge*, clearly visible behind the BP station on the main street. The design of this place is perhaps a little claustrophobic given all the wide open spaces close by, but it does mean the security is good. Rooms are good value at US$4.50/8 with a bathroom shared between two rooms.

Places to Stay – middle
There's only one mid-range hotel in Isiolo and that is the *Bomen Hotel* (☎ (0165) 2225). This three-storey hotel has a total of 40 spacious rooms, tastefully decorated and furnished. Rates are US$16/23 for singles/ doubles with hot-water bath, and prices include breakfast, taxes and service charges. Children under 12 years old are charged 30% of the single rate when sharing a room. The hotel has its own bar and restaurant which serves excellent food at very reasonable prices. Meal times are from 7 to 9.30 am (breakfast), noon to 2.30 pm (lunch) and 7.30 to 10 pm (dinner). Guarded parking is available in the hotel compound.

This is an excellent place to stay if you want to visit the nearby reserves of Samburu or Buffalo Springs but can't afford the charges at the lodges inside the parks or don't want to camp.

Places to Eat
Most of the simple boarding houses also have restaurants where you can eat typical African-style meals for less than US$3. The *Frontier Lodge* has a good café, the restaurant at the *Pasoda Lodge* is one of the better ones, and the *Silver Bells Hotel* does excellent chicken curry for US$1.60.

For a minor splurge, go for lunch or dinner at the *Bomen Hotel*.

Things to Buy
A good proportion of the young men who hang around on the main street of Isiolo are salespeople for the brass, copper and aluminium/steel bracelets which you'll already have come across elsewhere except that the craft here is particularly fine. If you're one of those people who like decking out your forearms with as many of these bracelets as you can get on them, then this is the place to buy them. They're much cheaper here than anywhere else though haggling is, of course, obligatory. The same people also sell daggers in leather scabbards but the craft in these is generally unremarkable.

If you're simply walking around Isiolo then these salespeople will hardly ever bother you but if you're driving around and especially if you're filling up with petrol at a station then expect a real hassle. Their wares will be thrust in front of your face from both sides and you'll be hard-pressed to drive away.

Getting There & Away
Akamba operates three buses daily to Nairobi at 7.30 and 9 am and 8 pm. The journey takes about seven hours and costs US$6. The buses travel via Nanyuki (US$2), Naro Moru (US$2) and Thika (US$5.50), and it's not a bad idea to book one day in advance.

Mwingi Buses operates buses to Marsabit (US$7), supposedly a couple of times a week, but this is very flexible. It also operates less frequent buses to Moyale on the Ethiopian border (US$7 from Marsabit). For either of these services it's just a matter of enquiring at the office several times to try and pin down a departure time or day. There's no alternative except to simply hang around and wait, or either negotiate a ride on a truck (relatively easy and usually somewhat less than the bus fare) or walk out to the police checkpoint north of town where the tarmac ends and hitch a ride with tourists (not so easy). The Mwingi office is an anonymous shopfront at the rear of the Bomen Hotel; just look for the derelict buses out the front.

Mwingi also operates buses to Maralal a few times a week (depending on demand) which cost US$6.50. Again, the departure times are uncertain.

There's no scheduled transport to Wajir and Mandera, north-east of Isiolo, and besides, this area is the domain of the shifta (Somali bandits, usually armed) and only those people with a specific reason (or a suicide wish) should contemplate travelling here. Every morning at 8 am a convoy of vehicles headed for Wajir, Mandera or Garissa leaves the police checkpost. They are mostly trucks and many will take passengers for a fee. If you are heading for Garissa a stop is made overnight in the beautiful little village of **Mado Gashi**. Here the *New Mount Kenya Lodge* is good value at US$2.70 for a large double room.

AROUND ISIOLO
Lewa Downs

Lewa Downs is a privately owned ranch of some 16,000 hectares which has been turned into a rhino and wildlife sanctuary, although ranching activities are still maintained. The entire area has been enclosed by a solar-powered electric fence to keep out stock from neighbouring properties.

Black rhinos from other parts of the country have been relocated here and are now breeding. The ranch also has a small group of the more placid white rhinos, and these are a big attraction, especially since those in Meru National Park were slaughtered a few years ago. Other wildlife abounds, and visitors can expect to see elephants, giraffes, eland, oryx, buffaloes, lions and leopards.

The Craig family run the *Wilderness Trails Lodge* on the ranch, and this is a small, superbly sited stone and makuti thatch set-up with stunning views across to Isiolo and the northern plains. It's a top-end place, so you can expect to part with about US$260 per person per day for full board, but the level of service is excellent and the setting perfect. The lodge is closed during April and May, and from 1 November to 15 December. Bookings must be made in advance through Chris Flatt in Nairobi (☎ (02) 502491).

The Meru

The Meru arrived in the area north-east of Mt Kenya from the coast sometime around the 14th century following invasions of that area by Somalis from the north. The group was led by a chief known as the *mogwe* up until 1974 when the incumbent converted to Christianity and denied his son inheriting the role. A group of tribal elders *(njuuri)* were all powerful and along with the mogwe and witch doctor would administer justice as they saw fit – which often consisted of giving poison laced beer to an accused person. Other curious practices included holding a newly born child to face Mt Kenya and then blessing it by spitting on it, while witch doctors might eliminate one of their rival's sons by putting poison on the circumcision blade.

Subgroups of the Meru include the Chuka, Igembe, Igoji, Tharaka, Muthambi, Tigania and Imenti. ■

KENYA

MERU

Up at the north-eastern end of the ring road around the southern side of Mt Kenya, Meru is an important town which services the intensively cultivated and forested highlands in this part of Central Province. It's quite a climb up to Meru from either Isiolo or Embu and, in the rainy season, you'll find yourself in the clouds up here along with dense forest which frequently reaches right down to the roadside. When the weather is clear there are superb views for miles over the surrounding lowlands. Views of the peaks of Mt Kenya, on the other hand, are hard to come by due mostly to the forest cover.

Although there's a small centre of sorts, Meru is essentially just a built-up area along the main road and, as far as travellers' interests go, there's precious little reason to stay the night there. It's certainly much too far away from any of the route heads leading to the peaks of Mt Kenya to be a suitable base to take off from. The nearest of these begins at Chogoria, about halfway between Meru and Embu.

Meru's main claim to fame is the quality of its miraa. These are the bundles of leafy twigs and shoots which you'll see people all over Kenya (and particularly Somalia and Ethiopia) chewing for its stimulant and appetite-suppressant properties. While it still grows wild here, much of it is now cultivated and it's become a major source of (legal) income for the cultivators and harvesters who supply both the internal market and also export it to neighbouring countries. No doubt the marijuana growers are green with envy!

Meru National Museum

This small museum just off the main road is worth visiting if you're staying here or passing through. It has the usual display detailing the progress of evolution, along with exhibits of stuffed birds, animals and mounted insects, but there's also a small and

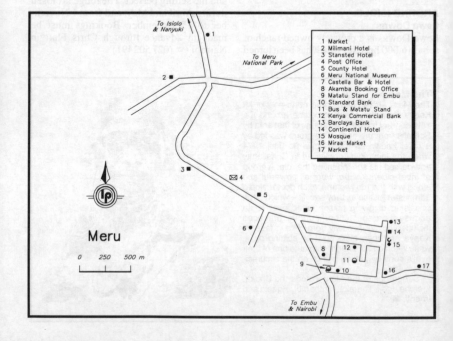

```
To Isiolo
& Nanyuki
                                    1  Market
To Meru                             2  Mlimani Hotel
National Park                       3  Stansted Hotel
                                    4  Post Office
                                    5  County Hotel
                                    6  Meru National Museum
                                    7  Castella Bar & Hotel
                                    8  Akamba Booking Office
                                    9  Matatu Stand for Embu
                                   10  Standard Bank
                                   11  Bus & Matatu Stand
                                   12  Kenya Commercial Bank
                                   13  Barclays Bank
                                   14  Continental Hotel
                                   15  Mosque
                                   16  Miraa Market
                                   17  Market

Meru

0    250   500 m

To Embu
& Nairobi
```

informative section concerning the agricultural and initiation practices of the Meru people and their clothing and weapons. Out at the back of the building are a number of appallingly small and sordid cages containing obviously neurotic and pathetically bored specimens of baboon, vervet monkeys and a caracal cat which someone ought to liberate immediately as an act of sheer pity if not humaneness. There's also a reptile pit with a notice advising visitors that 'Trespassers will be bitten'.

The museum is open daily from 9.30 am to 6 pm except on Sundays and holidays when it's open from 11 am to 6 pm and 1 to 6 pm respectively. Entry costs US$0.40 (US$0.20 for children) and US$0.20 for Kenyan residents.

Places to Stay

Two of the cheapest places to stay in Meru are the *Castella Bar & Hotel* and the *Continental Hotel* in the town 'centre'. They're basic and neither is particularly special. The Castella has a noisy bar downstairs, and a curious sign at reception warns that: 'Combing of the hair in the room is not allowed'. Somewhat better value is the *Stansted Hotel* (☎ (0164) 20360) on the main road past the post office. It is clean, quiet and offers self-contained rooms at US$4 per person including breakfast. The hotel has its own bar and restaurant.

Also good value is the *Milimani Hotel*, further up the hill from the Stansted. It offers good self-contained rooms with hot water for US$7/9.40 a single/double. Vehicles can be parked safely in the hotel compound and at weekends there's a disco. If you don't have transport, this hotel is probably too far from the centre – it's about two km uphill.

The best mid-range hotel is probably the *County Hotel*, again on the main road and close to the turn-off for the museum. It's clean, comfortable, has its own restaurant and lively bar and secure parking. Self-contained rooms cost US$18/31 a single/double with breakfast.

Those with their own transport might like to check out the *Rocky Hill Inn*, about eight km out of town to the north, which is essentially a barbecue and bar but has basic chalets for rent, or the *Forest Lodge*, even further out, which has a swimming pool and pretensions to being a sort of country club with expensive chalets.

Places to Eat

For a good, cheap meal of curried fish (US$1.30) or chicken (US$2.60), try the *Copper Coin* restaurant near the bus stand. Another good bet is the snack bar at the *County Hotel*. Meals cost from around US$1.30 to US$2.60, or there's a three-course set meal which is great value at US$3. The food is unexciting, but it's filling and you can have a beer with your meal. The hotel also has a more up-market restaurant.

Getting There & Away

Meru is served by Akamba buses to and from Nairobi (US$5) with departures from Meru at 7.30 and 9 am, and 8 pm. The buses travel via Chogoria (US$1.30), Embu (US$3) and Thika (US$4.50). The buses can be booked in advance, and the office is in the town centre, just off the main road.

From the matatu park there are regular departures for Isiolo, Embu and Nairobi.

CHOGORIA

The only reason to come to this small town on the lower eastern slopes of Mt Kenya is that it is the access point for the most scenic route up the mountain – the Chogoria route. Guides and porters can be engaged through the Chogoria Guides Club, which is based at the Transit Motel.

Places to Stay & Eat

The choices here are limited. The *Transit Motel* (☎ 96 in Chogoria) is about half an hour's walk up from Chogoria, and has cheap and clean singles/doubles. Camping is also possible for US$2 per person.

The other alternative is the *Forest Station*, at the barrier across the track about five km up the route from Chogoria. The 15 cabins here are fully equipped with kitchens, fireplaces, hot showers and three beds.

The *Lenana Restaurant*, just inside the gates of the hospital, is a good place for cheap, substantial meals.

Getting There & Away

The Akamba buses running between Nairobi and Meru pass through Chogoria, or there are regular matatus to Embu and Meru. The bus trip between Nairobi and Chogoria takes about 3½ hours.

EMBU

On the south-eastern slopes of Mt Kenya, Embu is an important provincial centre but spread out over many km along the main road. It has a famous school and hotel and is set in a very hilly area which is intensively cultivated. It's also the provincial headquarters of the Eastern province though it's on the extreme eastern edge of this and can only have been chosen because of its agreeable climate. Not many travellers stay here overnight, and with good reason since there's nothing much to see or do and it's a long way from the only feasible eastern route up Mt Kenya (the Chogoria route).

Places to Stay

There are quite a few cheap hotels spread out along the main road but most of them are very basic and can't be recommended. Behind a row of shops almost opposite the bus and matatu park is the *Eden Guest House*. While hardly paradise, it offers clean, quiet rooms with shared facilities for US$3/5.

The *Al-Aswad Hotel*, just a little further up the road, has no single rooms, but the doubles are quite good value at US$6. The hotel also has a good restaurant where you can eat for just US$1.30. The *Kubukubu Lodge*, further down the hill from the Eden Guest House, is another reasonable choice.

The *Valley View Hotel* (☎ (0161) 20147), also in this range, has self-contained rooms with hot water for US$7/12 with breakfast. It's clean and tidy and soap and towel are provided, plus the staff are friendly and helpful. The hotel has its own bar and restau-

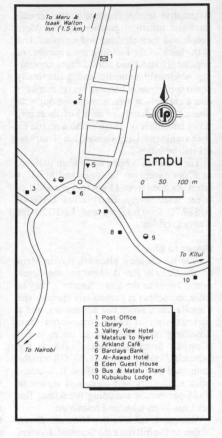

Embu

0   50   100 m

To Meru &
Isaak Walton
Inn (1.5 km)

To Kitui

To Nairobi

1 Post Office
2 Library
3 Valley View Hotel
4 Matatus to Nyeri
5 Arkland Café
6 Barclays Bank
7 Al-Aswad Hotel
8 Eden Guest House
9 Bus & Matatu Stand
10 Kubukubu Lodge

rant, and it's much quieter than the hotels around the bus stand.

If you'd like to splurge then consider a night at the *Isaak Walton Inn* (☎ (0161) 20128), about two km up the main road towards Meru from the town centre. It's right out of the colonial era and set in extensive lawns and gardens with a good restaurant and cosy bar – both with log-burning fireplaces. Originally a farmhouse and set on 3.4 hectares, it has 42 double rooms (described as 'specious' in the promotional leaflet though they no doubt meant 'spacious'!), each with bathroom and hot water plus a balcony. Rates are US$18/23 for singles/ doubles including breakfast. The staff are friendly and helpful and it's definitely *the* place to stay if you have the money. Even if you don't stay here it's definitely worth turning up for a beer or a meal.

Places to Eat
The *Arkland Café*, near the main roundabout in the centre of town, is a good place for a meal or snack at lunch time. If you want the full treatment, head for the restaurant at the *Izaak Walton*.

Getting There & Away
There are daily Akamba buses between Nairobi and Embu and this is the safest way to travel between the two places. The booking office is on the top side of the bus and matatu stand.

Matatus also offer the same service but they are invariably overcrowded – often dangerously so – and the drivers drive like maniacs. 'Accidents' are frequent and often result in everyone on board being killed. This happens on average about once a fortnight so, if you value your life, *don't do this trip by matatu*. It's not that the road is in bad shape – it's an excellent road – but its sweeping curves, high bridges and constant up-hill-down-dale progression seems to encourage total recklessness among drivers. The fare to Nairobi on the matatus is US$4.50 and they terminate on Accra Rd (if you're fortunate to get that far).

The alternative to a bus or matatu is a shared Peugeot taxi, although, if anything, these are more dangerous because they travel faster.

The matatus to Meru are not quite the same hair-raising and dangerous prospect since there's not the same pressure on the drivers, but they're no joy ride either. Take the Akamba bus or a Peugeot taxi in preference.

TREKKING ON MT KENYA
Mt Kenya's highest peaks, Batian and Nelion, can only be reached by mountaineers with technical skills. However, Point Lenana, the third-highest peak, can be reached by trekkers and this is the usual goal for most people. As you might imagine, there are superb views over the surrounding country from Point Lenana and other high points around the main peaks, though the summit is often clothed in mist from late morning until late afternoon.

Safety
It's not surprising that trekking on this mountain is high on many travellers' priority list. However, because Mt Kenya is so easy to reach, and because Point Lenana is not technically difficult, this can create its own set of problems. Many people do the ascent much too quickly and end up suffering from headaches, nausea and other (sometimes more serious) effects of altitude sickness (see the Health section in the introductory Facts for the Visitor chapter for more details). Another problem can be the weather; even though they end up seeing the glaciers on the summits, many visitors go up the mountain without proper gear, completely unprepared for the cold and wet conditions often encountered.

This situation is made worse by some tour companies (and some guidebooks) billing the trek to Point Lenana as an easy hike. It's not unknown for ill-prepared independent trekkers to get hopelessly lost on Mt Kenya, sometimes with fatal results. Most years there are reports of people simply disappearing on the mountain.

So, when planning your trek up Mt Kenya, it is important to realise that this is no small mountain: Point Lenana is just under 5000 metres – not much lower than the Everest Base Camp in Nepal. If you spend at least three nights on the ascent before going to the summit of Lenana, you stand a much better chance of enjoying yourself, and with proper clothes and equipment, you stand a much better chance of surviving too!

If you're not a regular mountain walker, and don't know how to use a map and compass, going up and down anything other than the Naro Moru route, without a competent companion or a local guide, is simply asking for trouble.

The best times to go, as far as fair weather is concerned, is from mid-January to late February or from late August to September.

Here is a letter from a traveller who had a less than ideal trip:

I'm sure thousands of people agree that your books are extremely useful but the travel survival kit is very aptly named.

I went missing for five days on my own on the descent from Point Lenana. I lost my rucksack, sleeping bag and food. I managed to keep an army surplus bag with my camera, purse belt, hypothermia foil and guide book.

By the end of the fourth day the foil was ripped to shreds and gaining inspiration from the street dwellers in London I ripped out pages from the travel survival kit to cover myself with. I also ate some of the pages on Uganda!

Thanks for helping me survive!

Gillian Tree, UK

Books & Maps

Before you leave Nairobi we strongly recommend that you buy a copy of *Mt Kenya 1:50,000 Map & Guide* (1993) by Mark Savage & Andrew Wielochowski. It has a detailed topographical map on one side and a full description of the various routes, mountain medicine, flora & fauna, accommodation, etc on the reverse. This is money well spent and contains everything which most trekkers will need to know. It's stocked by all the main bookshops.

For keen trekkers looking for more information, or for details on wilder routes and some of the more esoteric variations that are possible on Mt Kenya, get hold of Lonely Planet's *Trekking in East Africa* by David Else. This book covers not only Mt Kenya but also a selection of treks and long-distance walks in Kenya, Tanzania, Uganda and Malawi.

Those who intend to do some technical climbing or mountaineering (as opposed to walking) should think seriously about getting a copy of the Mountain Club of Kenya's *Guide to Mt Kenya & Kilimanjaro*, edited by Iain Allan. This is a much more substantial and comprehensive guide, and is also available in all the main bookshops, or contact the Mountain Club of Kenya, PO Box 45741, Nairobi. It may also be available from West Col Productions, Goring-on-Thames, Reading, Berks RG8 9AA, UK, and from Stanford's Map Centre, 12/14 Long Acre, Covent Garden, London WC2E 9LP, UK.

Clothing & Equipment

The summits of Mt Kenya are covered in glaciers and snow, and the temperature at night often drops to below -10°C so you are going to need a good sleeping bag. A closed-cell foam mat is also advisable if you are going to sleep on the ground as it provides the necessary insulation under your body and is far more comfortable than sleeping without one. A good set of warm clothes is equally important and that should include some sort of headgear and gloves. As it can rain at any time of year – and heavily – you will also need waterproof clothing. A decent pair of boots is an advantage but not strictly necessary. A pair of joggers is quite adequate most of the time though it's a good idea to have a pair of thongs, sandals or canvas tennis shoes to wear in the evening if your main shoes get wet.

Remember that it's not a good idea to sleep in clothes which you have worn during the day because the sweat which your day clothes absorb from your skin keep them moist at night and so reduce their heat-retention capabilities.

If you don't intend to stay in the huts along the way you'll need a tent and associated equipment.

Unless you intend to eat only canned and dried food along the way (not recommended) then you'll also need a stove, basic cooking equipment and a water container with a capacity of at least one litre per person as well as water-purifying tablets for use on the lower levels of the mountain. Stove fuel in the form of petrol and kerosene (paraffin) is fairly easily found in towns, and methylated spirits is available in Nairobi, as are gas cartridges although the supply of these is not

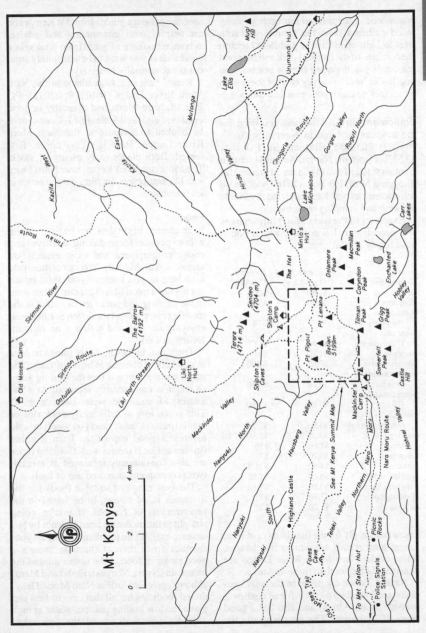

Mt Kenya

0   2   4 km

guaranteed. Except in an emergency, using wood gathered from the vicinity of camp sites to light open fires is prohibited within the confines of the national park and for good reason. If you intend to engage porters then you'll also have to supply each of them with a rucksack to carry your gear and theirs.

Equipment Hire All the gear you need for the trek can be hired in Nairobi at Atul's (☎ (02) 225935), Biashara St, PO Box 43202, or from the Natural Action Mountain Centre (☎ (02) 740214), in the Museum Hill Shopping Mall, PO Box 12516. Atul's also sells some second-hand and locally made trekking and camping equipment.

Examples of the sort of daily hire charges and deposits (in US dollars) which you'll have to pay at Atul's are:

Item	Hire Cost	Deposit
sleeping bag	$1.60-$2.30	$20-$39
air mattress	$1.40	$20
air-mattress pump	$0.40	$9.75
dome tent		
(two-person)	$6	$78
dome tent		
(three-person)	$9.40	$117
gas stove	$1.20	$31
kerosene stove	$0.60	$7.80
water container		
(one litre)	$0.20	$1.60
water container		
(10 litre)	$0.30	$1.60
mess kit		
(one person)	$0.60	$2.30
cooking pot	$0.25-$1.70	$2.30-$7.80
gas lamp	$1.60	$39
kerosene lamp	$0.20	$7
rucksack	$4.60	$71-$130
woollen socks	$0.80	$7.80
woollen gloves	$0.80	$7.80
climbing boots	$2.70	$31
raincoat	$1.20	$23

These rates apply for the first 10 days of hire; longer term rentals are quite a bit cheaper. Rates at the Naro Moru River Lodge are consistently higher than those at Atul's.

Natural Action claims to be the only specialist outdoor shop on the African continent (outside South Africa) and also has a good range of equipment. The guys who run the shop are off-duty guides from Mt Kenya and are helpful with information and advice. Advance booking of gear (from Atul's) is a good idea if you want to be absolutely sure, but is not normally necessary.

Rental gear is also available at the Naro Moru River Lodge (☎ (0176) 22018), PO Box 18, Naro Moru, and is mostly in good condition and well maintained. Gear cannot be booked in advance at the Naro Moru River Lodge. Here it's first come, first served. Both places carry plenty of stock. The Mountain Rock Lodge near Naro Moru also has equipment for hire, but the range is less extensive.

Food
In an attempt to cut down on baggage, quite a few people forgo taking a stove and cooking equipment and exist entirely on canned and dried foods. You can certainly do it so long as you keep up your fluid intake but it's not a good idea. That cup of hot soup in the evening and pot of tea or coffee in the morning can make all the difference between enjoying the trek and hating it or, at least, feeling irritable.

There are, however, a few things to bear in mind about cooking at high altitudes. The major consideration is that the boiling point of water is considerably reduced. At 4500 metres, for example, water boils at 85°C. This is too low to sufficiently cook rice or lentils (pasta is better) and you won't be able to brew a good cup of tea from it either (instant coffee is the answer). Cooking times are also considerably increased as a result (with consequent increased use of fuel).

The best range of suitable foods for the mountain is, of course, to be found in the supermarkets of Nairobi. If you're going straight to the mountain from Nairobi by bus or share-taxi, it's no problem to bring all your supplies from there. Otherwise there's a good range of food in the towns around the mountain (Nyeri, Nanyuki, Embu and Meru) although precious little at Naro Moru. Dehydrated foods are not all that easy to find and given the low boiling point of water at high altitudes you really need the precooked variety. Fresh fruit and vegetables are available in all reasonably sized towns and villages.

Take plenty of citrus fruits and/or citrus drinks with you as well as chocolate, sweets or dried fruit to keep your blood sugar levels high on the trek.

One last thing – and this is important to avoid severe headaches caused by dehydration – is to drink at least three litres of fluid per day. It may also help to avoid the effects of altitude sickness.

Park Fees

Entry fees to the national park are US$12 plus US$1.50 for a vehicle. If you take a

---

Mt Kenya – Geology, Flora & Fauna

Africa's second-highest mountain at 5199 metres, Mt Kenya was formed between 2½ and three million years ago as a result of successive eruptions of the volcano. Its base diameter is about 120 km, and it is probable that when first formed it was over 6000 metres in height and had a summit crater much like that on Kilimanjaro. Intensive erosion, however, principally by glacial ice, has worn away the cone and left a series of jagged peaks, U-shaped valleys and depressions containing glacial lakes or tarns.

In many of these valleys you will come across terminal moraines (curved ridges of boulders and stones carried down by the glaciers) whose position – some as low as 3000 metres – indicates that during the Ice Ages the glaciers must have been far more extensive than they are today. They began retreating rapidly about 150,000 years ago as the climate changed and the process is still going on today. Since records were first kept back in 1893, seven of the glaciers have already disappeared leaving only the current 11, yet even these are getting quite thin. It's estimated that if the present trend continues, there might be no permanent ice left on the mountain in 25 years.

The volcanic soil and the many rivers which radiate out from the central cone have created a very fertile environment, especially on the southern and eastern sides which receive the most rain. Human agricultural activity currently extends up to around 1900 metres in what used to be rainforest, yet which today is still well wooded in many parts. Above this zone, except where logging takes place, stretches the untouched rainforest characterised by an abundance of different species, particularly the giant camphors, along with vines, ferns, orchids and other epiphytes. This forest zone is not quite so dense on the northern and eastern sides since the climate here is drier and the predominant tree species are conifers. Vines, likewise, are absent.

The forest supports a rich variety of wildlife and it's quite common to come across elephants, buffaloes and various species of monkey on the forest tracks. Rhinos, numerous varieties of antelope, giant forest hogs, and lions also live here but are usually only seen in the clearings around lodges.

On the southern and western slopes the forest gradually merges into a belt of dense bamboo which often grows to 12 metres or more. This eventually gives way to more open woodland consisting of hagena and hypericum trees along with an undergrowth of flowering shrubs and herbs.

Further up still is a belt of giant heather which forms dense clumps up to four metres high interspersed with tall grasses. Open moorland forms the next zone and can often be very colourful because of the profusion of small flowering plants which thrive there. The only large plants to be found in this region – and then only in the drier, sandier parts such as the valley sides and the ridges – are those bizarre specimens of the plant kingdom, the giant lobelias and senecios. This moorland zone stretches right up to the snow line at between 4500 metres and 4700 metres though the vegetation gets more and more sparse the higher you go. Beyond the snow line, the only plants you will find are mosses and lichens.

The open woodland and moorland support various species of antelope, such as the duiker and eland, as well as zebras, but the most common mammal is the rock hyrax. Leopards also live in this region and have occasionally been observed as high as 4500 metres! Of the larger birds which you'll undoubtedly see up here are the verreaux eagles (which prey on hyrax), auger buzzards and the lammergeier (or bearded vulture). Smaller birds include the scarlet-tufted malachite sunbird, which feeds on nectar and small flies, and the friendly cliff chat which often appears in search of scraps. ∎

guide and/or porters then you'll have to pay their entry fees too, and these are US$1 per person per night. Camping fees are an additional US$3.20 per person per night.

Guides & Porters

The charges for guides, porters and cooks vary according to the route taken. On the Naro Moru route they are US$4.75, on the Chogoria route they are US$4, and on the Sirimon route a guide or cook is US$10, while a porter is US$6.

Porters will carry up to 18 kg for a three-day trip or 16 kg for a longer trip, excluding the weight of their own food and equipment. If you want them to carry more then you'll have to negotiate a price for the extra weight. A normal day's work is regarded as one stage of the journey – from the Met Station to Mackinder's Camp on the Naro Moru route or from the Chogoria road head to Minto's Hut on the Chogoria route, for example. If you want to go further than this then you'll have to pay them two days' wages even if they don't do anything the following day.

Guides, porters and cooks can be engaged at the Naro Moru River Lodge, the Mountain Rock Lodge or through one of the hotels in Chogoria village and possibly at the park entry gates (though this isn't as reliable). They can also be found by contacting the Naro Moru Porters & Guides Association (☎ (0176) 6205), PO Naro Moru, Naro Moru; or the Chogoria Porters (☎ 88 in Chogoria), PO Box 96, Chogoria, who are based at the Transit Motel in Chogoria. If you're staying at the Mt Kenya Hostel near Naro Moru, Joseph will fix you up if you ask him.

Accommodation

There are quite a lot of huts on the mountain but not all of them are available to the general public. Several are owned by the Mountain Club of Kenya (MCK). A few of these huts are reserved exclusively for use by members, others can be used by the public, although these are all basic and most are in very bad condition.

There are also some larger bunkhouses with more facilities on the mountain. These are owned by lodges outside the park and are mainly for people going on treks organised by these lodges, but they can also be used by independent trekkers. Beds in the large bunkhouses have to be booked and paid for, but there is no reservation system.

On the Naro Moru route, the bunkhouses are at the meteorological station (always called the Met Station), and Teleki Lodge (more usually called Mackinder's Camp), and both can be booked through the Naro Moru River Lodge, or Let's Go Travel in Nairobi.

On the Sirimon route, the bunkhouses are at Old Moses Camp and Shipton's Camp, and both can be booked through the Mountain Rock Lodge.

On the Chogoria route, there are some comfortable bandas at the Meru Mt Kenya Lodge, near the park gate. It costs around US$26 to stay there. Reservations are not always necessary but it's possible to book through Let's Go Travel in Nairobi.

The small MCK huts can be booked and paid for in Nairobi at the MCK clubhouse, or at Let's Go Travel, or at the Naro Moru River Lodge. They cost around US$3, but are generally in such bad condition that very few trekkers use them. If you are going independently and not planning to use the bunkhouses, it's much better to camp than to use these MCK huts.

Officially you can camp anywhere on the mountain but it is usual to camp near one of the huts or bunkhouses as there is often a water supply nearby.

Getting to the Trekking Routes

There are at least seven different routes up the mountain, but only the three main routes are covered here – Naro Moru, Sirimon and Chogoria. The other routes are much harder to follow and there's a real chance you can get lost without decent maps and the ability to read them, and if you have no experience with a compass.

If you intend to do the trek independently then public transport (bus or matatu) along the Mt Kenya ring road is the first step towards getting to the mountain. For the Naro Moru route it's Naro Moru village where there's a prominent signpost on the right-hand side just outside the village on the way to Nanyuki. For the Sirimon route, first go to Nanyuki and then take another matatu about 13 km up the main road towards Isiolo where the route is signposted off to the right. For the Chogoria route all matatus and buses between Embu and Meru stop at Chogoria village, just off the main road.

From where the buses or matatus drop you it's quite a walk to any of the park entry gates but it's possible to find private (though relatively expensive) transport from the main roads to the park entry gates. See the individual routes for details.

If you have your own transport, you can get up to all three of the national park entry gates in 2WD but to get to the road heads beyond that you will need 4WD. Don't attempt these last sections in anything other than that. And don't even expect a small Suzuki 4WD to make it up to the meteorological station on the Naro Moru route in wet weather. The road up there from the park entry gate is diabolical in wet weather. On the Chogoria route, 4WD is essential to get from Chogoria village to the national park entry gate. The top section of the track up through the forest is totally impassable in wet weather, even for 4WDs fitted with snow chains!

Mt Kenya Routes

The normal weather pattern is for clear mornings with the mist closing in from 10 am though this sometimes clears again in the early evening. This means that if you want to make the most of the trek you should set off early every morning and, for the final assault on Point Lenana (the highest point that can be reached by trekkers), you need to make an early start if you want to see the sunrise from the top.

Naro Moru Route

This is the most straightforward and popular of the routes. It's also the least scenic, although it's still a spectacular and very enjoyable trail. You should allow a minimum of four days for the trek up and down this route, or three if you have transport between Naro Moru and the meteorological station, although doing it this quickly if you're not acclimatised is asking for altitude sickness.

Naro Moru to the Met Station Your starting point here is the village of Naro Moru on the Nairobi to Nanyuki road where the turn-off for the mountain is well signposted. To get there, take one of the daily Akamba buses from Nairobi to Naro Moru. The depot is on Lagos Rd in Nairobi and the buses can be booked in advance. You can also get to Naro Moru from Nyeri by matatu though these are often crowded.

The first part of the route takes you along a relatively good gravel road through farmlands for some 12 km (all the junctions are signposted) to the start of the forest where there's a wooden bridge across a small river. A further five km brings you to the park entry gate at 2400 metres. Having paid your fees, you continue on another eight km to the road head and *Met Station Hut* (3000 metres) where you stay for the night.

If your time is limited you can cut out this part of the trek by taking the Naro Moru River Lodge's Land Rover all the way to the meteorological station. This costs US$78 per person, plus the driver's park entry fee and US$3 for the vehicle shared by up to eight people. It's also possible to take this vehicle just as far as the park entry gate for US$39 per person. You don't have to be on one of the lodge's organised treks to use this vehicle. Hitching is also possible but the chances of a lift *up* the mountain are limited – it's easier to get a ride on the way down.

The Met Station to Mackinder's Camp On the second day you set off up the Teleki Valley along a well-marked path past the police signals station and up to the edge of the forest at around 3200 metres. From here you scale the so-called Vertical Bog and up onto a ridge from where you can see Mackinder's Camp. The route divides into two here and you have the choice of taking

KENYA

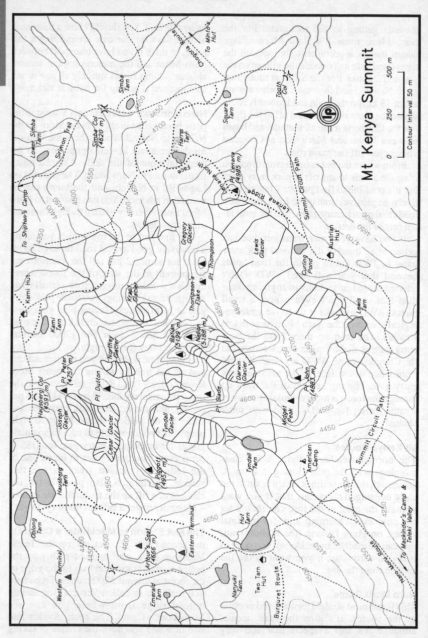

the higher path, which gives the best views but is often wet, or the lower path which crosses the Naro Moru stream and continues gently up to *Mackinder's Camp* (4160 metres). This part of the trek should take you around 4½ hours. Here you can stay the night (bunkhouse or camping). The stone cabins at Mackinder's are quite comfortable with two large dorms. The bunk beds have mattresses, there are toilets, and drinking water is available. The caretaker here checks your bunkhouse booking receipts.

Mackinder's Camp to Point Lenana On the third day you can either rest at Mackinder's Camp (to help acclimatise) or aim for Point Lenana. From Mackinder's to Point Lenana takes about four to five hours, so it's usual to leave around 2 am (you'll need a torch or flashlight) to reach the summit of Lenana in time for sunrise. From the bunkhouse, continue up the valley past the ranger station to a fork in the path. Keep right, and go across a swampy area, followed by a morrain and then up a very long scree slope – this is a long, hard slog. You reach Austrian Hut about three to four hours from Mackinder's. This is about one hour below the summit of Lenana, so it's a good place to rest before the final push for the summit. This section of the trek, from Austrian Hut up to Point Lenana, takes you up a steep ridge and then across the edge of a snow-covered glacier. In good weather, the going is fairly straightforward, but in bad weather you should not attempt to reach the summit unless you are experienced in trekking in mountain conditions or have a guide. Plenty of inexperienced trekkers have come to grief on this section, falling off icy cliffs or even disappearing into crevasses.

To avoid the long slog in the dark, it is also possible to walk from Mackinder's to the *Austrian Hut* on the third day, stay there, then go for the summit of Lenana on the morning of the fourth day. However, conditions at Austrian Hut are very basic, so you need to be well-equipped.

Those who are camping and not staying at either Mackinder's Camp or the Austrian Hut

have a third choice of where to spend the night. This is the so-called *American Camp*, which you get to by branching off left along a minor track just before the swampy area and above the ranger station. It's an excellent camp site on a grassy meadow.

Return Routes From Point Lenana most people return to the Met Station back down the same route. Assuming you get to Point Lenana early in the day, you can reach the Met Station on the same day.

Alternatively, you can return to Austrian Hut then walk north and north-west around the base of the main peaks to reach the top of either the Sirimon or Chogoria routes, and go down one of those routes. This is on the Summit Circuit path (described briefly in the Sirimon Route section), which is reckoned to be one of the most exciting trekking routes in East Africa. Completely circling the mountain, you cross several major cols, and get great views of the peaks and glaciers from all angles. The Summit Circuit path can also be demanding and potentially dangerous. Many people have got lost on this trail and you should not attempt it unless you have plenty of time, proper equipment, and a map and compass that you know how to use.

Sirimon Route
This is the least used of the three main routes but the driest. It is also the longest approach to Point Lenana, and involves some serious sections of trekking. If you are inexperienced in high mountain conditions, this route should not be attempted without a local guide. You should allow a minimum of five days to undertake this trek.

Take the same Akamba bus as to Naro Moru but continue on to Nanyuki. If you want to start walking up the mountain the same day as you leave Nairobi on this route, you need to take the earliest possible bus leaving Nairobi otherwise you'll probably have to stay in Nanyuki for the night and leave the following day.

To get from Nanyuki to the start of the Sirimon route, take one of the frequent matatus going to Timau on the main road towards Isiolo and tell the driver you want to be dropped off at the start of the Sirimon track (signposted). If you go over a fairly large river (the Sirimon River) then you've gone too far. The start of the route is about 13 km from Nanyuki.

Turn-Off to Old Moses Camp On the first day you walk from the main road to the park entrance gate (about 10 km) and on from there to the road head at 3150 metres (a further nine km). The going is straightforward to this point. At the road head there's a good camp site and a bunkhouse called *Old Moses Camp*. If you have your own vehicle then you'll need 4WD for the last five km as the road is in bad shape. Transport to the gate or the road head can also be arranged at the Mountain Rock Lodge.

Old Moses Camp to Shipton's Camp On the second day you leave Old Moses Camp, aiming uphill on a gradually deteriorating track. After about one hour you reach a fork – the left branch goes to the Liki North Hut, although this route is not used much. Take the right branch, which leads to a path over two ridges into the Mackinder Valley. Look out for red and white marker posts. The path leads up the east side of the valley, eventually crossing the Liki Stream and passing Shipton's Caves (in an obvious cliff on the left side of the path) before reaching *Shipton's Camp* bunkhouse and camp site. From the road head at Old Moses Camp to Shipton's Camp takes about seven hours. Shipton's Camp is a good place to spend two nights and have a rest day to help acclimatise. However, if you're feeling OK, one night here is sufficient.

Shipton's Camp to Point Lenana Both of the ways around the Summit Circle path, from Shipton's Camp to Point Lenana, are among the most spectacular trails on the mountain (indeed, in all of East Africa), but either route is strenuous and can be hard to follow – even in good weather. When visibility is poor the trails can be very difficult to follow and many people get lost. It is not uncommon for inexperienced trekkers to head down the wrong valley and then become hopelessly lost in the forest. Use common sense – if you can't use a map or compass, or are inexperienced in mountain conditions, don't go this way without a local guide. Also, if you are camping at American Hut or sleeping at Austrian Hut, make sure you are fully equipped for cold conditions.

Via American Camp From Shipton's Camp you join the Summit Circuit path, so on the third day you can go west or east of the main peaks to reach Point Lenana. If you want to go west, go straight up the valley side from Shipton's, keeping the main peaks to your left, to reach Kami Hut (which is in very bad condition) and then continue up a long scree slope to reach the Hausberg Col. From here you drop down into the next valley to reach Hausberg Tarn and Oblong Tarn. Follow the path between the tarns, then go up again to the col between the summit of Arthur's Seat and the Western Terminal. Aim south from here, passing Nanyuki Tarn to your right, to reach Two Tarn Hut, from where you drop down to American Camp at the head of the Teleki Valley. You can camp here or go down to the nearby Mackinder's Camp bunkhouse. From Shipton's Camp to American Camp by this route takes about four to five hours. On the fourth day you can reach Point Lenana (as described in the Naro Moru Route section).

Via Austrian Hut Your second choice from Shipton's is to go east of the main peaks, up the head of the steep-sided valley to Simba Col, or up the large scree slopes to Harris Tarn. From both of these points you can reach Simba Tarn, then Square Tarn. From Square Tarn you aim south, through Tooth Col (next to a large, jagged pinnacle) and then gradually up to reach Austrian Hut. From Shipton's Camp to Austrian Hut by this route takes about six hours. On the fourth day you can reach Point Lenana (as described in the Naro Moru Route section). If you are going east of the main peaks and don't feel like going for the summit of Lenana, from Simba Col you can join the Chogoria route and drop down to Minto's Hut.

There is another route from Harris Tarn direct to the summit of Lenana up the north face, which means you can go from Shipton's up to Lenana then down to Austrian Hut in one day. However, this option is very serious (and impassable after snow) and should only be tackled by experienced trekkers, or by groups with competent local guides.

Return Routes From Point Lenana you can retrace your route down to Shipton's and go back down the Sirimon route, or return via the Naro Moru or Chogoria routes.

Chogoria Route

This route, from the eastern side of the mountain, is undoubtedly the most beautiful of the access routes to the summit and certainly the easiest as far as gradients go. This is a good route if you've got a tent and some trekking experience. From Minto's Hut there are breathtaking views of the head of the Gorges Valley and the glaciers beyond.

To get started on this route, take an Akamba bus from Nairobi direct to Chogoria village, or one first to Embu and then a matatu to Chogoria. Unless you get to Chogoria village early in the day, you will probably have to spend the night in Chogoria before setting off up the mountain, as the first day's hike is a long slog. It's about 30 km from the village to the park entry gate up the forest track with nowhere to stay en route.

Chogoria to Park Entry Gate The first day is spent walking up to the park entry gate at 2990 metres through superb rainforest and on into the bamboo zone. You have the choice here of staying at the *Meru Mt Kenya Lodge*, near the park entry gate, or continuing on a further three km to the small MCK's *Urumandi Hut*. At the road head itself (3200 metres), six km from the park entry gate, there's also an excellent camp site.

It's possible to hitch all the way to the park entry gate from Chogoria as at least one

official vehicle does the run most days between the village and the Meru Mt Kenya Lodge, though there's no set timetable. There may also be people staying at the lodge who can help out with lifts. Alternatively, if you want guaranteed transport, this can be arranged at one of the hotels in Chogoria village. Natural Action (see the earlier Equipment Hire section for details) also has a base and transport here.

Park Entry Gate to Minto's Hut The second day is spent walking from either the Meru Mt Kenya Lodge, the Urumandi Hut or the road head camp site to Minto's Hut with spectacular views all the way. The route is well defined and first crosses a stream then climbs to a ridge which it follows all the way to Minto's Hut. You need to bring water with you as there are no sources en route. From the road head to Minto's Hut should take you about 4½ to five hours. You can stay at *Minto's Hut* for the night, although recent reports suggest that it is in a pretty dire state – dirty and rat-infested – or head further up the valley where there are a number of sheltered camp sites.

Minto's Hut to Austrian Hut On the third day you continue to the head of the Gorges Valley, a steep climb across scree slopes, aiming south-west to reach Square Tarn. The last section of this leg of the route is very steep.

From the tarn the route becomes the Summit Circuit path, continuing south through Tooth Col (to the east of Point Lenana), after which it descends briefly and then goes up across a scree slope to the right to reach Austrian Hut. The route is marked with cairns in some places but it is still easy to get lost, especially in mist or snow. The section between Tooth Col and Austrian Hut is where most trekkers get lost. It is essential to realise that there is another huge valley (called Hobley Valley) in between the Gorges and Teleki valleys. The route goes *around* the head of the Hobley, not down into it. From Minto's to Austrian Hut should take about three to four hours.

Austrian Hut to Point Lenana From Austrian Hut you can scale Point Lenana (allow another hour) the same day or stay there for the night and make the ascent the following morning, as described in the Naro Moru Route section.

Return Routes From Point Lenana you can retrace the route back down to Minto's Hut which should take about two hours after which it's a further three to five hours back down to the Meru Mt Kenya Lodge. Alternatively, from Austrian Hut you can descend to Mackinder's Camp, and then return via the Naro Moru route.

Organised Treks

If your time is limited or you'd prefer someone else to make all the arrangements for a trek on Mt Kenya, there are several possibilities.

The Naro Moru River Lodge (☎ (0176) 22018), PO Box 18, Naro Moru, does a range of trips, all of which include a guide/cook, porters, all meals, park entry fees, camping fees, and transport to and from the road heads. The standard five-day trip takes you up and down the Naro Moru route using the lodges' own bunkhouses. The cost is US$480 per person in a group of eight, or US$754 for one person. Shorter trips are available at reduced cost.

The Mountain Rock Lodge (☎ (0176) 62625), between Naro Moru and Nanyuki, also offers a range of organised treks, usually up and down the Sirimon route, taking from three to six days and using its own bunkhouses en route. Costs vary according to the number of days you wish to spend on the mountain and the number of people in the party, though it's cheapest with a group of

eight or more people. A three-day direct trip to Point Lenana via the Sirimon route costs US$507 to US$273 per person (one to eight people respectively); a four-day trip along the same route is from US$630 to US$358 per person.

A four-day trip going up the Sirimon and down the Naro Moru routes costs from US$644 to US$370, while a five-day trip going in on the Sirimon trail and out via the Chogoria route costs from US$884 to US$543. All prices include park entry fees, guide and porter fees, food, transport to and from the road heads, accommodation, and a special half-board deal at the lodge itself.

There are several safari companies in Nairobi which offer Mt Kenya treks, but most of these companies just sell the treks operated by Naro Moru and Mountain Rock lodges, charging you an extra commission in the process. However, some companies are running their own treks, and these include:

Kenya Hiking & Cycling
  Arrow House, Koinange St, PO Box 39439, Nairobi.
  This company's Mt Kenya trek goes up the Sirimon route and down the Naro Moru in five days, staying at bunkhouses. The cost is US$520 including transport to and from Nairobi (☎ 218336).
Natural Action Ltd
  Nairobi National Museum, PO Box 12516, Nairobi.
  A standard five-day Mt Kenya trek goes up the Chogoria route and down the Naro Moru, following more unusual paths for some of the way. The cost is around US$754 per person. Even if you don't take one of its treks, Natural Action provides information for trekkers, sells books and maps, and hires out equipment. There's also a trekkers' message board which you can use to find trekking companions, buy and sell gear and so on (☎ 740214).

Western Kenya

Western Kenya is an area with many attractions, but is often overlooked by travellers, and you won't find a single safari minibus out this way either. For this reason alone it's worth spending a bit of time exploring here, just to get the feel of Kenya without the tourists.

The countryside is, for the most part, beautiful rolling hills, often covered with the bright green bushes of vast tea plantations. Further west you have Lake Victoria and the regional capital of Kisumu on its shore. From here there are plenty of possibilities – just a short distance to the north lies the Kakamega Forest with its lush vegetation and abundant wildlife. Further north still, close to the regional town of Kitale, are the national parks of Mt Elgon (well worth exploring)

Western Kenya

0   25   50 km

- Sigor
- Cherangani Hills
- Kapenguria
- Saiwa Swamp National Park
- Tot
- Kapsawar
- Mt Elgon (4321 m)
- Endebess
- Mt Elgon National Park
- Kitale
- C45
- A1
- Kimilili
- B2
- Malaba
- Bungoma
- Webuye
- A104
- A1
- A109
- UGANDA
- Busia
- Eldoret
- A1
- A104
- Kakamega
- A1
- Asembo
- Kisumu
- B1
- B1
- To Nakuru
- Rusinga Island
- Mfangano Island
- Kendu Bay
- A1
- Kericho
- Lake Victoria
- Homa Bay
- Kisii
- A1
- TANZANIA
- Migori
- Isebania

and Saiwa Swamp, where the only way of getting around is on foot and the attraction is the rare sitatunga or marshbuck deer.

If you have your sights set on more distant horizons, head west for Busia or Namanga and Uganda, or south to Isebania and across the border into Tanzania.

This area is the home of Kenya's Luo people. Numbering around two million they make up the third-largest ethnic group in the country. Marginalised politically, you'll nevertheless find them a friendly people. The atmosphere in this part of the country is in sharp contrast to that of the central provinces.

Getting Around

This is the most densely populated part of the country so the road system is good and there are hundreds of matatus of varying shapes and sizes plying the routes. Accidents are unnervingly common, but these seem to happen more amongst the very small matatus which are usually dangerously overloaded. The small-truck sized matatus are a lot safer as they generally travel more slowly and can carry loads with greater ease.

One annoying factor of matatu travel in this region is the way the destination changes suddenly depending on the number of passengers. So if your matatu is supposedly going from, say, Kakamega to Kitale and it gets to Webuye and everyone gets out, it's a fairly safe bet that you will have to as well. When this happens, and you have paid the fare to the final destination, the driver will find you a seat in another vehicle and fix things with its driver. You will get there in the end, but it may take longer than you think. It took me three matatus to get from Kisumu to Kisii, despite being told when I boarded the first two that they were going all the way.

Lake Victoria

With an area approaching 70,000 sq km, Lake Victoria is obviously the major geographical feature in this part of the continent. Unlike the lakes further west, Victoria is not part of the rift valley system, and so is wide and shallow (only 100 metres deep) compared with, say, Lake Tanganyika which is nearly 1½ km deep.

Lake Victoria touches on three countries – Uganda, Tanzania and Kenya – but it's not possible to take a boat between Kenya and Uganda and/or between Kenya and Tanzania. The only possibilities for lake excursions in Kenya are the ferries which run from Kisumu to Kenyan ports further south.

Bilharzia is prevalent in Lake Victoria so don't swim in the water or walk in the grass along its shores – this is the hideout of the snails which are the host for the parasitic flukes which invade your body. (See the Health section in the introductory Facts for the Visitor chapter for more information.) Admittedly, you face only a very small risk of contracting bilharzia if you spend only a short time here.

KISUMU

Although it hardly feels like it, Kisumu is Kenya's third-largest town. It has a very easy-going, almost decaying, atmosphere, possibly partly due to the fact that with the cessation of international ferry services on the lake, and the decline in through traffic to Uganda, it's a bit of a dead end these days. It was a busy port from early this century right up until the East African Community split up in 1977, and it seems that from this point on the town has just been marking time.

Don't be put off by that though, as it's the ideal place to head for from the east of the country as the travel connections are excellent, especially by rail. There's also enough to do in the town itself to make it an interesting place to stop for a few days.

If you've arrived from the higher country further east the first thing that you will notice is the heat and humidity. Kisumu is always a good few degrees hotter than say Nairobi and the steamy conditions only add to the general torporific air.

Orientation

Kisumu is sited on the gently sloping shore of Lake Victoria. Although it's a fairly sprawling town, everything you are likely to need is within walking distance. The main drag is Oginga Odinga Rd and along it are virtually all the shops, the banks and the post office.

The railway station and ferry jetty are close together about five minutes' walk from Oginga Odinga Rd, while the noisy bus and matatu station is on Jomo Kenyatta Highway behind the market, about 10 minutes' walk from the centre.

Most of the cheap hotels are in the area between Oginga Odinga Rd and Otiena Oyoo St. The mid-range and top-end hotels are mostly along Jomo Kenyatta Highway plus there are others further afield. The best access to the lake itself is at Dunga, a small village about three km south of town along Nzola Rd.

Information

The GPO is in the centre of town on Oginga Odinga Rd and is open Monday to Friday from 8 am to 5 pm and Saturday from 9 am to noon. If you need to make international calls there is a cardphone outside and you can dial direct. Phonecards are sold at the post office.

The British Council Library, also on Oginga Odinga Rd, has newspapers and magazines and quite a good library. It's open from 9.30 am to 1 pm and 2 to 5 pm Monday to Friday, and 8.30 am to 12.45 pm on Saturday. Behind it is the UK Voluntary Service Overseas (VSO) office.

Immigration is on the 1st floor, Reinsurance Plaza (behind Deakons Supermarket), on the corner of Oginga Odinga Rd and Jomo Kenyatta Highway. The officials here are friendly and helpful and will renew your visa for up to three months. It all takes just five minutes, there's no fee or photos required, though you will be asked for an onward ticket (tell them you left it in your hotel for safekeeping).

The best bookshop in town is the well-stocked Sarit Bookshop on Oginga Odinga Rd diagonally opposite the post office.

Kisumu Museum

It comes as something of a surprise to find this excellent museum here – it's probably the best in the country and is well worth a visit. It's on Nairobi Rd within easy walking distance of the centre and is open daily from 9.30 am to 6 pm; entry is US$1.10.

The displays are well presented and wide ranging in their variety. There's a very good collection of everyday items from the various peoples of the area, including agricultural implements, bird and insect traps (including a white-ant trap!), food utensils, clothing, furniture, weapons, musical instruments, and a fairly motley collection of stuffed birds and animals including an amazing centrepiece of a lion riding on a wildebeest.

Outside there is a traditional Luo homestead consisting of the husband's mud and thatch house, and separate houses for each wife. There's usually a man near the homestead who will show you around for a few shillings and point out the salient features. Also outside are the inevitable crocodile and tortoise enclosures which are small and a bit depressing.

Market

Kisumu's market is one of the most animated in the country, and certainly one of the largest. Whether you're in the market for a bag of potatoes or are just curious, it's worth a stroll around. You can cut through to the bus station through the hole in the back wall of the market compound.

Hippo Point

Hippo Point is at Dunga, about three km south of town, and the café on the point is a good place to head for. There were no hippos in evidence when I visited but it's a pleasant spot all the same. Known as Dunga Refreshments, it is well signposted once you get out of town along Nzola Rd. This place also has the only camp site in Kisumu.

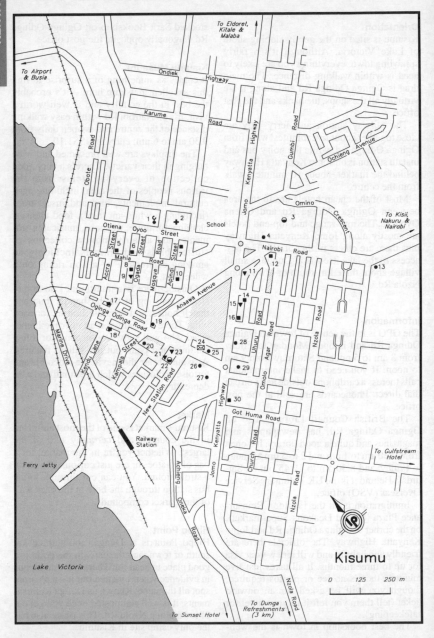

To Eldoret,
Kitale &
Malaba

To Airport
& Busia

Ondiek   Highway

Karume   Road

Gumbi Road

Kenyatta Highway

Ochieng Avenue

Obote Road

Jomo

Omino

Crescent

To Kisii,
Nakuru &
Nairobi

School

1 ♀
2 ✚

3 ⊖

4 ●

Nairobi   Road

●13

Otiena Street
Oyoo   Street

Gor   Street

Mahia   Street

Ogada   Street

Apindi   Street

Accra

Mosque   Road

5
6
7
8
9
10

11 ▼

12

Anaawa Avenue

14
15 ▼
16

Uhuru Road

Nzola Road

Agar Road

17

Oginga Odinga Road

19 ●

18

Kendu Lane

Kampala Street

New Station Road

20 ●
21
22
23 ▼
24 ⊠
25 ●
26 ●
27 ●
28 ●
29 ●
30 ●

Omolo Road

Got Huma Road

Ferry Jetty

Railway
Station

Lake   Victoria

Jomo   Kenyatta   Highway

Church Road

Anding Road

Oneko Road

Nzola Road

To Gulfstream
Hotel

Kisumu

0   125   250 m

To Dunga
Refreshments
(3 km)

To Sunset Hotel

Places to Stay – bottom end

The cheapest option for accommodation is the *YWCA* (☎ 43192) on the corner of Omolo Agar and Nairobi Rds which has dorm beds (three people per room) for US$1.10 with shared facilities. It also has self-contained double rooms which vary from US$1.80 to US$2.20 per person. The Y takes both men and women and there's a canteen where you can get basic meals.

The best area for a cheap hotel is that between Oginga Odinga Rd and Otiena Oyoo St.

Very popular with expatriate volunteer workers is the *Razbi Guest House* (☎ 42-152), upstairs on the corner of Oginga Odinga Rd and Kendu Lane. It's very secure (there's a locked grille at the top of the stairs), the rooms are spotless and a towel and soap are provided. The rates are US$1.90/2.90 for singles/doubles with shared cold-water bath. There's certainly no confusion between the showers and toilets here – one of the toilets is labelled 'Urine'!

Somewhat more basic is the *New Rozy Lodge* (☎ 41990) on Ogada St which has singles/doubles with shared bath for US$1.90/2.70. It's hardly 'new' but the staff is friendly.

Two streets east of Ogada St is Apindi St where you'll find a choice of three basic lodges. The first is *Safina Lodge* which has singles/doubles for US$1.80/2.50 and triples for US$3.10, all with shared facilities. Next up is *Mirukas Lodge* which has similar rooms for the same price. Next door is *Nasim's Lodge*, the best of the bunch, which is excellent value (apart from the saggy beds) at US$2.20/2.80 for self-contained singles/doubles with clean sheets and hot water. At this price, you won't find better.

Back on Oginga Odinga Rd, there's another slightly more expensive hotel which is, nevertheless, good value. This is the *Mona Lisa Guest House* (above the restaurant of the same name) which has singles/doubles with shared bath for US$2.20/3.40 or US$3.40/4.50 with private bath. There's hot water supposedly 24 hours a day. Around the corner, the *Talk of the Town Coffee House* has rooms at a similar price. Singles/doubles with shared bath cost US$2.20/3.40 or US$4/5.40 with private bath. There's hot water in the mornings and evenings.

Campers should head for *Dunga Refreshments* (☎ 44023) at Hippo Point, right on the shores of Lake Victoria three km south of town. It takes nearly an hour to walk it, or you can take a taxi for US$2.20. It's a well-run place with good facilities but there's little shade. Camping here costs US$1.80 per person plus there's also a dormitory block which costs US$4.50 per bed with shared facilities. The complex includes a very pleasant restaurant with reasonably priced meals (omelette and chips for US$1.90 or main meals of chicken, fish or mutton for US$2.50). It also caters for vegetarians, and fruit juices and cold beers are available. It's a mellow place to stay and highly recommended.

Places to Stay – middle

The *Black & White Boarding & Lodging*, in the centre of town, has singles/doubles for US$4/5.90 and triples for US$7.40, all including breakfast. Bathrooms are shared by three rooms and there is hot water. Close by is the *New Victoria Hotel* (☎ 2909) on the corner of Kendu Lane and Gor Mahia Rd. It's good value, especially if you get one of the front rooms with a balcony and views of Lake Victoria. Rates (including breakfast) are US$4.60 a single with shared bath or US$8/12 for a double/triple with private bath. The hotel also has a good restaurant.

The *Lake View Hotel* is aptly named and has spacious rooms as well as a bar and restaurant. Bed and breakfast in self-contained rooms with hot water here costs US$6.70/9.40 a single/double. It's good value for the price and very clean, plus the staff are friendly and helpful.

Opposite the Lake View is the *Western Lodge* (☎ 42586) which only has single, self-contained rooms at US$5.40.

Just off Jomo Kenyatta Highway close to the Imperial Hotel is the *Hotel Inca* (☎ 40158) which is also good value. It's a large place and offers well-furnished, very clean, self-contained rooms with fan and hot water for US$5.60/10. There's a bar and restaurant and the staff are friendly.

Places to Stay – top end

The best hotel in this range is the charming *Hotel Royale* (☎ 44240) on Jomo Kenyatta Highway. It's an old hotel with a gleaming white façade, open-air terrace bar and polished wooden floorboards. It's twin is the Castle Hotel of Mombasa and, like the Castle, has been recently refurbished. If you have the money, and can get one of the rooms on the 1st floor, it's excellent value at US$15/22 for self-contained singles/doubles including breakfast. Some of the rooms on the ground floor are gloomy, so ask to see a room first before booking in. The hotel has its own very good restaurant, and credit cards are accepted.

The *Imperial Hotel* (☎ 41485), also on Jomo Kenyatta Highway, is a much newer place with five-star facilities. The cheapest rooms with all the facilities you would expect cost US$37/42 a single/double plus there are deluxe rooms for US$42/46. There are also more expensive apartments and suites. There's a rooftop bar, two restaurants (breakfast US$3.40, lunch/dinner US$5.60) and a swimming pool, but the pool is tiny and hemmed in by the building.

On the southern edge of town, the *Sunset Hotel* (☎ 41100/4), in Impala Lane (off Jomo Kenyatta Highway), does indeed have views of the sunset, and of the lake, from each room. There's also a swimming pool and a good, if expensive, restaurant (US$8/10 for lunch/dinner). Bed and breakfast costs US$38/50 for singles/doubles and US$70 for triples throughout the year. All credit cards are accepted. The hotel is part of the African Tours & Hotels group so reservations are also possible in Nairobi.

There's also the *Gulfstream Hotel* (☎ 43927) off to the east of town which is very well appointed but inconvenient if you don't have your own transport. Standard singles/doubles here cost US$13/15, plus there are luxury suites for US$24 without breakfast. The hotel has two bars and a restaurant.

Places to Eat

One of the most popular restaurants for those on a budget as well as expatriate VSO workers is the *Talk of the Town Coffee House* just off Oginga Odinga Rd. It has a wide variety of good cheap meals and is a popular place for breakfast, though is open all day.

It's a friendly place and you can meet lots of people here. Similar is the *Mona Lisa Restaurant*, on Oginga Odinga Rd.

The *New Victoria Hotel* also does an excellent breakfast of juice, papaya, eggs, toast, butter and tea or coffee for about US$1. It's open for breakfast from 7 to 9 am and also serves standard dishes such as steak, chicken and chips.

For stand-up-and-eat or takeaway greasy-spoon food there's the *Chicken Palace*, the *Wimpy*, or *Rafiq Refreshments & Fast Burgers* all on Jomo Kenyatta Highway.

For a splurge, go for lunch or dinner (especially the latter) at the *Hotel Royale* and soak in the atmosphere. Both the service and the food are excellent. And talk about service! All you have to do is blink and there'll be a waiter there asking if everything is alright! Food at the *Imperial Hotel* is equally good. A meal at either will cost US$6 to US$10 per person.

If you're out at Hippo Point, don't forget *Dunga Refreshments* which has good food at budget prices plus you can eat outside right on the water's edge.

Entertainment

Everyone in search of action goes to the excellent disco/bar/restaurant complex called *Octopus Night Club* on Ogada St. It's a weird and wonderful place, and has three bars (The Pirate's Den, the Fisherman's Wharf, and the Captain's Wives) where you can also get meals or snacks, as well as the actual disco. Beers are sold at normal prices and the disco is a good rage. You haven't seen Kisumu until you've been here.

Things to Buy

Kisumu is about the best place to buy Kisii soapstone carvings and there are pavement stalls set up on the northern side of Oginga Odinga Rd near the British Council Library.

The Wananchi Craft Shop near the town hall is a cooperative selling crafts made by local women, and there are some interesting items.

Getting There & Away

Air Kenya Airways has 11 flights weekly to Nairobi. The trip takes one hour and costs US$44. You can pay in local currency which makes the flight a good deal cheaper. Kenya Airways (☎ 44055/6) is in the Alpha building on Oginga Odinga Rd.

Bus & Matatu Buses and matatus leave from the large bus station just north of the market for Busia, Kakamega, Homa Bay, Kitale, Nakuru, Kericho and Nairobi.

It's possible to book Nairobi buses in advance at the bus station. Both Coast Bus (US$3.80) and Akamba (US$4.45) have once-daily buses to Nairobi which travel at night. Re-Union Buses (US$3.35) also has a daily departure. These are the best buses to use as they operate on a regular schedule. Nyayo Buses and JA Buses also cover similar routes, but their schedules are unreliable.

Nissan matatus go to Nairobi (US$4.45), Busia (on the Ugandan border, US$1.55), Homa Bay (US$0.90), Isebania (on the Tanzanian border, US$3.35), Kakamega (US$0.90), Kitale (US$2.90), Malaba (on the Ugandan border, US$1.80) and Nakuru (US$2.65).

There are also shared Peugeot taxis to Nairobi (US$8) which leave when full.

Train There are trains to Nairobi daily at 6.30 pm, arriving at 7.35 am the next day. Depending on demand there is often a second daily train. Fares to Nairobi are US$15.10 in 1st class, US$8.70 in 2nd class and US$3.10 in 3rd class. It's advisable to book in advance. The booking office at the station is open daily from 8 am to noon and 2 to 4 pm.

Car For car rental see Kamba Travel (☎ 28-131) on Jomo Kenyatta Highway in the red-roofed building diagonally opposite the Hotel Royale and in front of Reinsurance Plaza.

Boat With the demise of the international services, the Lake Victoria ferries now only go to places close to Kisumu such as Kendu Bay, Homa Bay, Asembo Bay and Mfangano Island. There are three classes on the MV *Reli* and only 2nd and 3rd classes on the MV *Tilapia* and MV *Alestes* but none of them is ever very crowded, so 2nd or 3rd class is quite OK.

The MV *Reli* has the following services from Kisumu on Wednesday and Sunday:

	Arrival	Departure
Kisumu	–	9 am
Kendu Bay	10.50 am	11.05 am
Homa Bay	1.55 pm	2.25 pm
Asembo Bay	5 pm	8 am (next day)
Homa Bay	10.35 am	11.05 am
Kendu Bay	1.55 pm	2.10 pm
Kisumu	4 pm	–

The MV *Alestes* leaves Kisumu on Tuesday (9.30 am) but doesn't return until Saturday (5.30 am). In the meantime it services other lake ports such as Homa Bay and Mfangano Island so it's of limited interest to travellers other than those who want to stay at Homa Bay or Mfangano Island for four nights.

The MV *Tilapia* provides the following service from Kisumu on Tuesday, Friday and Sunday:

	Arrival	Departure
Kisumu	–	9 am
Kendu Bay	10.50 am	11.10 am
Homa Bay	2 pm	2.30 pm
Asembo Bay	5 pm	8 am (next day)
Homa Bay	10.35 am	11.05 am
Kendu Bay	1.55 pm	2.10 pm
Kisumu	4 pm	–

The fares from Kisumu to Kendu Bay are US$0.90/0.65/0.35 in 1st/2nd/3rd class, to Homa Bay US$1.55/1.20/0.55, to Asembo Bay US$2.10/1.65/0.65, and to Mfangano Island US$2.80/2/1.

AROUND THE LAKE
Kendu Bay
This small lakeside village has little to offer apart from a somewhat strange volcanic lake a couple of km from town. There's basic accommodation in the town, and the ferry jetty is about one km away.

Homa Bay
This is a very nondescript yet surprisingly busy town on a small bay in Lake Victoria. Most of the action involves transporting agricultural products from the area to Kisumu. Nearby is the intriguing volcano-shaped **Mt Homa** and the small **Ruma National Park**.

Places to Stay & Eat There are several budget hotels along the main road from the ferry, but none are anything to rave about. They basically service the lust of those who frequent the bars out front. Take your pick.

If, on the other hand, you have money to spare, there's the very pleasant *Homa Bay Hotel* (☎ (0385) 22070) set in its own grounds on the shore of the lake. It's part of the Msafiri Inns group so you can book it in Nairobi. A good room here facing the lake costs US$20/25 a single/double or US$40 a triple including breakfast. Other meals cost US$4.90. It's a mellow place to relax if you want to get away from it all for a few days.

Getting There & Away Most people come here by ferry but there's plenty of transport (bus and matatu) from here to Kisumu, Kisii, Migori and Isebania (Tanzanian border).

Rusinga Island
Mbita is the town on Rusinga Island which is connected by a causeway to the mainland. The only remarkable thing about the island is the mausoleum of Tom Mboya on the northern side of the island – he was born here in 1930 and was shot dead by police in 1969 during political unrest. (See the History section in the Kenya Facts about the Country chapter for more details.)

There are matatus to Homa Bay, as well as the ferry services to Kisumu, Mfangano Island and Homa Bay.

Mfangano Island
There's little to see here and very little in the way of facilities. The small fishing community is about as far off the beaten track as you can get in Kenya.

There is one cheap hotel and the island is

connected to the mainland by the ferry mentioned in the earlier Kisumu Getting There & Away section.

Western Highlands

The western highlands are the agricultural heartland of Kenya and they separate Kisumu and Lake Victoria from the rest of the country. In the south around Kisii and Kericho lie the vast tea plantations, while further north around Kitale and Eldoret it's all fertile farming land.

The towns of the highlands are really just small agricultural service towns, much the same as you'd find in similar areas in Australia or the USA – and they're about as interesting. For visitors, the attractions of the area lie outside these towns – the tea plantations around Kericho, Kakamega Forest near Kakamega, Mt Elgon and Saiwa Swamp

national parks both near Kitale, and the Cherangani Hills which lie north-east of Kitale and Eldoret.

KISII

As you might expect, this is where Kisii soapstone comes from but it's not on sale here at all, the simple reason being that Kisii sees very few tourists and those that do come this way tend to just keep moving. You can, however, visit the quarries if you like. Not much happens in Kisii, and even the locals will tell you that it's 'a remote place'. On the other hand people are friendly, and as so few tourists come here you'll be regarded with curiosity.

Kisii is the main centre of the region known as the **Gusii Highlands**, home of the Gusii people. The Gusii, numbering around one million, are a Bantu-speaking people in the middle of a non-Bantu area; the Maasai to the south, Luo to the west and north and

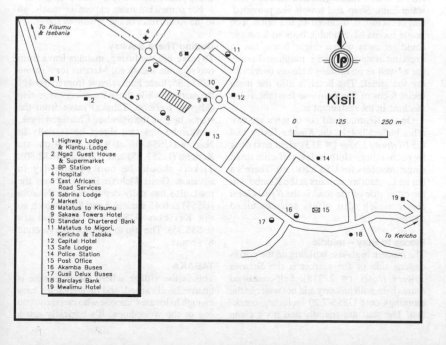

1 Highway Lodge & Kianbu Lodge
2 Ngau Guest House & Supermarket
3 BP Station
4 Hospital
5 East African Road Services
6 Sabrina Lodge
7 Market
8 Matatus to Kisumu
9 Sakawa Towers Hotel
10 Standard Chartered Bank
11 Matatus to Migori, Kericho & Tabaka
12 Capital Hotel
13 Safe Lodge
14 Police Station
15 Post Office
16 Akamba Buses
17 Gusii Delux Buses
18 Barclays Bank
19 Mwalimu Hotel

Kisii

0   125   250 m

To Kisumu & Isebania

To Kericho

Kipsigis to the east all speak unrelated languages.

The town centre is compact and, as usual, the market is the liveliest place in the town during the day.

Whilst you're here, it's worth making the four-hour round trip to the top of nearby Manga Ridge from which the views – especially over Lake Victoria – are magnificent. You can also see Kisumu in the distance and the tea plantations of Kericho behind you.

Places to Stay – bottom end

There are two excellent places to stay in Kisii. The cheaper one is the relatively new *Sabrina Lodge*, just around the corner from the matatu park. It's a very friendly place and has rooms with shared facilities for US$2.60/4 a single/double. The hotel also has a bar and restaurant.

Somewhat more expensive is the *Safe Lodge* (☎ 202950), opposite the BATA shop, which has friendly staff and costs US$3.40/4.50 for singles/doubles with hot-water bath. Soap and towels are provided, and breakfast is included in the price. The single rooms have double beds so a couple could get away with a single. It also has an excellent restaurant and a rough and ready bar as well as an upstairs balcony overlooking the street. The hotel is also the main social focus of the town – at least the video machine in the restaurant is.

On the Kisumu road out of town are two other budget hotels, the *Kianbu Lodge* and the *Highway Lodge* (☎ 213), right next door to each other. Both offer self-contained singles/doubles for US$2.20/3.80. There's a bar and restaurant upstairs at the Kianbu. On the other side of the road is the *Ngaũ Guest House* which also offers self-contained rooms.

Places to Stay – middle

The modern high-rise building on the north-eastern side of the market is the *Sakawa Towers Hotel* (☎ 21218). Self-contained rooms here with balcony and hot water in the mornings cost US$5/7.20 including breakfast. The staff are friendly and it's a clean

place to stay. Towels are provided and there's a bar and restaurant on the 1st floor.

At the eastern end of town is the modern *Mwalimu Hotel* in its own compound. Self-contained singles/doubles cost US$5/7.60 including breakfast. The hotel has a popular bar, terrace, beer garden and restaurant. There's also guarded parking.

The most pleasant place to stay in this range is the *Kisii Hotel* which is set in its own gardens (complete with turkeys) on the western side of town. It's a single-storey building with a popular bar and restaurant and has self-contained doubles (no singles) for US$8.70.

Places to Eat

For breakfast try the restaurant in the *Safe Lodge*. For less than US$1 you get juice, fruit, cereals, eggs, sausage, toast and tea or coffee – good value – and there are also good meals. The fact that there is a video and that beer is served makes this a gregarious and lively place, especially in the evenings.

For somewhat more expensive meals, go to the *Kisii Hotel* or the *Mwalimu Hotel*.

Getting There & Away

To make life confusing, matatus leave from two separate locations. Matatus for Kisumu (US$1.35, three hours) leave from in front of the market, while those for everywhere else (Migori, Kericho, Tabaka) leave from the station up past the Standard Chartered Bank.

Akamba has two direct buses daily to Nairobi (US$4.10) at 9 am and 9 pm via Kericho (US$1.55) and Nakuru (US$2.80). Tickets should be booked one day in advance. Gusii Deluxe Buses, across the road, also has daily departures for Nairobi (US$4) at 6.45 am and 5 and 8 pm which go via Kericho (US$2.20) and Nakuru (US$3.35). The trip to Nairobi takes around 8½ hours.

TABAKA

This is the village where the soapstone is quarried and carved, and on arrival it's easy enough to locate someone who can show you one of the workshops. It's basically just a cottage industry and there are few people who actually work the stone for a living – to most people it's just a handy way to supplement a meagre income made from agriculture.

To get there, take one of the fairly infrequent matatus from Kisii.

KERICHO

Tea – it's everywhere! This is the heart of western Kenya's tea plantation area and the rolling hills are a uniform bright green. Kericho's climate is perfect for growing tea, mainly because of the afternoon showers which fall every day of the year. Yes, Kericho is a wet place, but the showers are generally only brief and, apart from benefiting the tea bushes, they make the area green and pleasant.

The town takes its name from the Maasai chief, Ole Kericho, who was killed by the Gusii in the 18th century in a battle over land – the Maasai had been in the area for years and didn't appreciate the Gusii moving in, though the Gusii themselves were being pushed out by the advancing Luo. The area today is the home of the Kipsigis people, who are part of the greater Kalenjin group.

PLACES TO STAY
1 Cheap Hotels
5 Tea Hotel
6 Tas Lodge
9 Mid-West Hotel
10 Njekimi Bar & Restaurant
11 Mwalimu Hotel
12 Mother Hotel
16 Sugutek Hotel

OTHER
2 Bus & Matatu Stand
3 Market
4 Police
7 Kobil Station
8 Shell Station
13 Law Courts
14 Snow Day & Night Club
15 Post Office
17 Standard Chartered Bank
18 Barclays Bank
19 Town Hall
20 Caltex Station
21 Hindu Temple
22 Hospital

To Nakuru

Harambee Road
John Kericho Road
Moi Road
Isaac Salat Road
Lane
Tengecha Lane
Uhuru Road
Kenyatta Road
Tengecha Road
Temple Road
Moi Highway
Hospital Road

Kericho

0   100   200 m

To Kisii & Kisumu

The name *Kalenjin* (literally 'I tell you') was given in the '50s to the group of Nandi-speaking tribes, including the Pokot, Nandi, Kipsigis and Marakwet.

There's not a great deal to the town itself but it's not a bad place to stop for the night.

Information
The post office and the two main banks are all on Moi Highway. The banks are open Monday to Friday from 8 am to 1 pm and on Saturday from 8.30 to 11 am.

Tea Plantations
The closest plantation to town is behind the Tea Hotel, itself once owned by the Brooke Bond company. If you walk through the hotel grounds behind what was the service station and out through the back gate, the path leads through the tea bushes to the hotel workers' huts. If you're lucky there may be picking in progress.

It may be possible to organise a tour of a plantation and processing plant through the Tea Hotel.

Places to Stay – bottom end
There's not a lot of budget hotel accommodation available in Kericho but check out the *Sugutek Hotel* on Tengecha Rd and the *Njekimi Bar & Restaurant* on John Kericho Rd. At either you'll get a basic single/double room for US$1.60/2.40 with shared facilities.

There are also a few more boarding & lodging places on the road below the matatu station but they're really basic.

Campers should head for the *Tas Lodge* where you can camp in the pleasant grounds for around US$1 per person per night.

Places to Stay – middle
The *Tas Lodge* (☎ 21112) on the Nakuru road (Moi Highway) is about the best in this range. The hotel has a pleasant garden setting including an open-air bar under makuti roofs. Self-contained singles/doubles with hot-water shower cost US$3.40/5.60 including breakfast. In the centre of town there's the more modern *Mwalimu Hotel* which has

a popular bar and restaurant. Singles/doubles with private bath cost US$8/10.20 including breakfast.

Places to Stay – top end
The cheapest of the top-range hotels is the modern *Mid-West Hotel* (☎ 20611) which has standard singles/doubles with private bath for US$14/18 and deluxe singles/doubles for US$16/19, plus there are more expensive suites. Prices include a substantial breakfast and all taxes. The hotel has its own bar and restaurant.

At the top of the line is the grand old *Tea Hotel* (☎ 30004/5) which was originally built by the Brooke Bond company in the 1950s for its managers but which is now managed by African Tours & Hotels (☎ (2) 336858). It's set in its own well-tended grounds and exudes an atmosphere of days gone by. The rooms are spacious in the extreme, especially the two suites at the back overlooking the tea plantations. All the rooms are self-contained with hot-water showers. Rates (inlcuding breakfast) are US$18/21 for singles/doubles, US$38 for triples, plus there are suites with two double beds for US$44. Other meals cost US$3.40 (lunch) and US$4 (dinner). There's a popular bar/lounge area which sprawls over much of the ground floor and out onto the terrace. The staff are friendly and there's guarded parking.

Places to Eat
For basic African stodge and stews the *Mother Hotel* on Uhuru Rd does as good a job as any, as does the restaurant in the *Sugutek Hotel* on Tengecha Rd, which has chips, chicken, ugali, etc.

The restaurant in the *Mwalimu Hotel* is a little more sophisticated, while the US$3.10/4 set lunch/dinner in the *Mid West Hotel* is good value. The buffet lunches and dinners at the *Tea Hotel* are also good but somewhat more expensive. On the other hand, there is a grand piano which you are welcome to use if you feel like playing some Mozart or Elton John.

The Gusii

The Gusii number around one million and inhabit an area in the western highlands east of Lake Victoria. The area is dominated by Nilotic speaking groups with just this pocket of the Bantu-speaking Gusii. Being a relatively small group, the Gusii were always on the move following influxes of other groups into their existing lands.

After migrating to the Mt Elgon area sometime before the 15th century, the Gusii were gradually pushed south by the advancing Luo, and over the next couple of centuries came into conflict with the Maasai and the Kipsigis. They finally settled in the hills here as the high ridges were easier to defend. Having fought hard for their autonomy the Gusii were unwilling to give it up to the British and suffered heavy losses in conflicts early this century. Following these the men were conscripted in large numbers into the British army.

The Gusii family typically consists of a man, his wives and their married sons, all living together in a single compound. Large families served two purposes: with high infant mortality rates the survival of the family was assured, and the large numbers facilitated defence of the family enclosure. Initiation ceremonies are performed for both boys and girls, and rituals accompany all important events. Death is considered not to be natural but the work of 'witchcraft'. The Gusii were primarily cattle keepers but also practiced some crop cultivation and millet beer was often an important ingredient at big occasions.

As is the case with many of Kenya's ethnic groups, medicine men *(abanyamorigo)* had a

Gusii in traditional dress

highly privileged and respected position. Their duty was to maintain the physical and mental wellbeing of the group – doctor and social worker combined. One of the more bizarre practices was (and still is) the removal of sections of the skull or spine to aid maladies such as backache or concussion. ■

For a real spit and sawdust experience, call in for a beer at the *Snow Day & Night Club* on Isaac Salat Rd.

Getting There & Away

The matatu station is fairly well organised, with matatus on the upper level and minibuses and buses on the lower level.

As is the case throughout the west, there is plenty of transport in any direction. Nissan minibuses and matatus leave regularly for Kisumu. The companies running buses to

Nairobi have small offices at the matatu station.

If you are hitching, the turn-off to Kisumu is about two km south of town along the Kisii road, so you need to get there first, either on foot or by matatu.

KAKAMEGA FOREST RESERVE

The Kakamega Forest Reserve is a superb slab of virgin tropical rainforest in the heart of an intensively cultivated agricultural area. It is home to a huge variety of birds and animals and is well worth the minimal effort required to get to it.

The Forest Department maintains a beautiful four-room rest house here, as well as a large nursery for propagating trees and shrubs used for ceremonial occasions around the country and for planting in the area. The workers are very friendly and it's no problem to get shown around.

The forest near the rest house is very dense and there are paths leading all over the place. For that reason, and certainly for a greater appreciation of the forest flora & fauna, it's worth engaging one of the staff to guide you around. Leonard is the most well-known guide. He is friendly and his knowledge of the trees and birds is extensive. Binoculars and wet-weather gear are essential (it usually rains heavily every afternoon for a couple of hours). For that reason it's best to arrive in the morning as you usually have to walk a few km to reach the rest house. The driest period here is from December to April, but even then it rains daily.

Places to Stay & Eat

The *Forest Rest House* is a superb place to put your feet up for a few days. It's an elevated wooden building with a verandah which looks directly on to the seemingly impenetrable Kakamega Forest. There are only four double rooms but they all have a bathroom and toilet. Blankets are supplied but you need to have your own sleeping bag or sheet. The rooms cost US$1.50 per person plus you can also camp for a few cents. If the rest house is full when you arrive, and you have your own sleeping gear, it is usually possible to sleep on the verandah for next to nothing. If you want to be sure of a room, book in advance through the Forest Ranger, PO Box 88, Kakamega.

The only problem here is food. Basically you need to bring your own and preferably something to cook it on, although it is possible to cook on a fire. There's a small kiosk which sells beer, tea and soft drinks (sodas) and also cooks basic meals at lunch time. Evening meals are cooked on request (beans or corn and rice is about the limit), but you need to make sure they know you are coming as the kiosk closes at 6.30 pm. You can get basic meals and supplies from a small group of dukas about two km back towards Shinyalu.

Getting There & Away

The Forest Rest House lies about 12 km east of the A1 Kisumu to Kitale road, about 30 km north of Kisumu. Access is possible either from Kakamega village on the main road when coming from the north, or from Khayaga also on the main road when coming from the south. From both places dirt roads lead east to the small market village of Shinyalu, from where it's a further five km to the rest house, signposted to the left. There are matatus from Kakamega to Shinyalu, and even the occasional one from Khayaga to Shinyalu.

If you want to walk – and it is beautiful walking country – it's about seven km from Khayaga to Shinyalu, or about 10 km from Kakamega to Shinyalu. These roads become extremely treacherous after rain and you may prefer to walk when you see how the vehicles slip all over the road. There's very little traffic along either of the roads but you may get a lift with the occasional tractor or Forest Department vehicle. Whatever means you employ to get there, allow half a day from Kitale or Kisumu. From the turn-off to the rest house the dirt road continues on to Kapsabet so you could also come from that direction but it is a long walk if you can't get a lift.

KAKAMEGA

The town of Kakamega is on the A1 route, 50 km north of Kisumu and 115 km south of Kitale. About the only reason to stay here is if you are heading for the Kakamega Forest and arrive too late in the day to walk or get a vehicle. It's also the last place to stock up with supplies if you're heading for a forest sojourn.

The town has the usual facilities – a couple of banks, a post office, market and the ubiquitous boardings & lodgings.

The Akamba

The traditional homeland of the Akamba people *(Ukumbani)* is the region east of Nairobi towards Tsavo National Park. They migrated here from the south several centuries ago in search of food, mainly the fruit of the baobab tree which was accorded great nutritional value.

The Akamba were great traders and ranged all the way from the coast to Lake Victoria and up to Lake Turkana. Ivory was one of the main barter items but locally made products such as beer, honey, iron weapons and ornaments were also traded. From the neighbouring Maasai and Kikuyu they used to obtain food stocks as their own low-altitude land was relatively poor and couldn't sustain the increasing population which followed their arrival in the area.

In colonial times the Akamba were highly regarded by the British for their intelligence and fighting ability and were drafted in large numbers into the British army. Thousands lost their lives in WW I. When it came to land, however, the British were not quite as respectful and tried to limit the number of cattle the Akamba could own (by confiscating them) and also settle more Europeans in Ukumbani. The Akamba response was the formation of the Ukamba Members Association, whose members marched en masse to Nairobi and squatted peacefully at Kariokor Market in protest. After three weeks the administration gave way and the cattle were eventually returned to the people.

All adolescents go through initiation rites to adulthood at around the age of 12, and have the same age-set groups common to many of Kenya's peoples. The various age-set rituals involve the men, and the women to a lesser extent, gaining seniority as they get older. Young parents are known as 'junior elders' *(mwanake* for men, *mwiitu* for women) and are responsible for the maintenance and upkeep of the village. Once his children are old enough to become junior elders themselves, the mwanake go through a ceremony to become a 'medium elder' *(nthele)*, and later in life a 'full elder' *(atumia ma kivalo)* with the responsibility for death ceremonies and administering the law. The last stage of a person's life is that of 'senior elder' *(atumia ma kisuka)* who is responsible for the holy places.

Akamba subgroups include Kitui, Masaku and Mumoni. ∎

A *kiinga* basket, used for storing grain

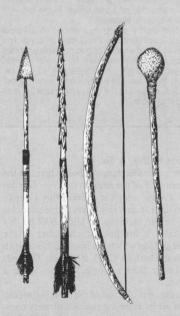

Traditional weapons of the Akamba

The Luo

The Luo people live in the west of the country on the shores of Lake Victoria. Along with the Maasai, they migrated south from the Nile region of Sudan around the 15th century. Although they clashed heavily with the existing Bantu-speaking people of the area, intermarriage and cultural mixing took place readily.

The Luo are unusual amongst Kenya's ethnic groups in that circumcision is not practiced in either sex. This practice was instead replaced by something that one can imagine being almost as painful – the extraction of four or six teeth from the bottom jaw. Although it is not done that much these days, you still see many middle-aged and older people of the region who are minus a few bottom pegs.

Although originally cattle herders, the Luo have adopted fishing and subsistence agriculture. The family group consists of the man, his wife (or wives) and their sons and daughters-in-law. The house compound is enclosed by a fence, and includes separate huts for the man and for each wife and son. (There is a good reconstruction of a Luo village in the grounds of the Kisumu Museum.)

The family group is member of a larger grouping of families (dhoot), several of which in turn make up a group of geographically related people (ogandi) each led by a chief (ruoth). Collectively the ogandi constitute the Luo tribe. As is the case with many tribes, great importance is placed on the role of the medicine man and the spirits. ■

Luo Chief

Places to Stay & Eat

There's a limited range of hotels here. At the bottom end of the scale is the *New Garden View Lodge*, which is conveniently close to the matatu station and offers singles/doubles with shared facilities for US$1.80/2.60. It's basically a brothel. Much better is the *Franca Hotel* which has two-bed rooms with hot-water bath for US$3.40 a room. The beds are larger than a single, but not quite a double.

At the opposite end of the scale is the *Golf Hotel* set in its own grounds with very comfortable, self-contained rooms for US$35/40 a single/double or US$65 a triple including breakfast. There's a bar, restaurant (lunch/dinner for US$6/7) and barbecue area. It's also a great place to relax with a cold beer even if you're not staying here.

Getting There & Away

The matatu station is at the northern edge of town. There are buses, matatus or Peugeots to Kisumu, Webuye, Kitale, Nairobi and Busia. Hitching is not too difficult.

ELDORET

There is little to see or do in Eldoret but it may make a convenient stop for the night in your peregrinations around the western highlands, particularly if you are heading to or from the Cherangani Hills which lie to the north of Eldoret.

The town has benefited hugely from the

university here and that has led to a lot of new development.

Information

The post office is on the main street, Uganda Rd, and is open Monday to Friday from 8 am to 5 pm and Saturday from 9 am to noon. Also on the main street are branches of Barclays and Standard Chartered banks.

For car rental, check out the Eldoret Travel Agency (☎ 33351) on Kenyatta St.

Places to Stay – bottom end

For a rock-bottom hotel, check out either the *New Paradise Bar & Lodging* on the corner of Uganda Rd and Oginga Odinga St, or the *Top Lodge*, also on Oginga Odinga St. Neither has much to offer other than a bed and they're basically short-time brothels.

Much better is the *Mahindi Hotel* (☎ 31520) which is close to the bus and matatu station and is good value at US$2.70 a single with shared bath or US$3.40/5.60 for singles/doubles with private bath. The hotel has a restaurant, and the noise from the Silent Night Bar downstairs can sometimes be distracting. Very similar and also close to the bus station is the *New Miyako Hotel* (☎ 22954) which charges US$2.70 a single with shared bathroom facilities and US$3.40/4.50 for self-contained singles/doubles. There's hot water in the showers and the hotel has an upstairs bar.

Also in this same area is the *Sosani View Hotel* which offers singles/doubles with hot-water bath for US$2.70/4.50. The hotel has its own bar and restaurant.

Places to Stay – middle

A popular place to stay in this range and one of the cheapest is the *New Lincoln Hotel* (☎ 22093) which is quiet and has guarded parking if you're driving. Self-contained rooms are good value at US$5.70/8.10 including breakfast. The staff are friendly, there's hot water in the showers and the hotel has its own bar and restaurant.

Up in price, the somewhat characterless *White Castle Motel* (☎ 33095) on Uganda Rd offers bed and breakfast for US$10/19 a single/double. There's a bar and restaurant on the ground floor.

The pick of the hotels in this range is the recently refurbished *Eldoret Wagon Hotel* (☎ 62270/1/2) on Oloo Rd. This hotel was built years ago in the colonial era and was once a watering hole for White settlers. It still exudes a certain charm but the open verandah where you used to be able to sit and drink a cold beer has now been entirely enclosed. The bar memorabilia, however, is still intact. Self-contained singles/doubles including breakfast cost US$10/17. Credit cards are accepted. The bar keeps 'English' hours: 11 am to 2 pm and 5 to 11 pm.

Places to Stay – top end

The only top-end hotel here is the modern *Sirikwa Hotel* (☎ 31655) which has rooms for US$30/40 a single/double, US$54 a triple including breakfast. All major credit cards are accepted and the hotel has the only swimming pool in Eldoret. Meals in the restaurant here cost US$3.40 (lunch) and US$4 (dinner).

Places to Eat

A popular lunch-time spot is *Otto Café* on Uganda Rd. It offers good cheap Western-style meals such as steak, chicken, sausages, eggs, chips and other snacks. Another good place for snacks is the *Spark Milk Bar* on Oginga Odinga St.

For a slightly more up-market meal or snack try the popular *Sizzlers Café* on Kenyatta St, near the Eldoret Travel Agency. Here you'll find a whole range of burgers, curries, steak and sandwiches. Also good is *Gilma's Restaurant* on Oginga Odinga St.

For a splurge, eat at either the *Eldoret Wagon* or *Sirikwa* hotels.

One of the liveliest bars in town is the *Midnite Cave* near the top of Oginga Odinga St.

Getting There & Away

Air Light aircraft flights between Nairobi and Eldoret are temporarily suspended.

Bus & Matatu The bus and matatu station is

KENYA

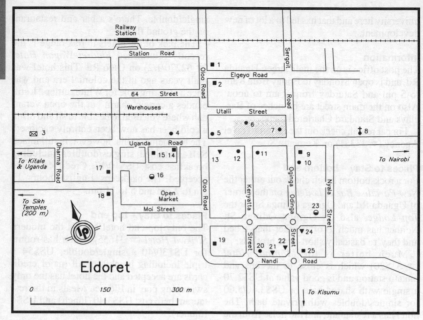

Eldoret

0   150   300 m

■	PLACES TO STAY	▼	PLACES TO EAT		6	Town Hall
1	Eldoret Wagon Hotel	13	Otto Café		7	Library
2	Sirikwa Hotel	21	Sizzlers Café		8	New Church
9	New Paradise Bar &	22	Gilma's Restaurant		10	Midnite Cave
	Lodging	24	Spark Milk Bar		11	Standard Chartered
14	White Castle Motel					Bank
15	Mahindi Hotel		OTHER		12	Barclays Bank
17	New Miyako Hotel				16	Bus & Matatu Station
18	Sosani View Hotel	3	Post Office		20	Eldoret Travel Agency
19	New Lincoln Hotel	4	Police		23	Akamba Bus
25	Top Lodge	5	National Bank of Kenya			

in the centre of town, just off Uganda Rd.
Buses, minibuses, Peugeots and matatus
depart throughout the day for Kisumu,
Nakuru, Naivasha, Nairobi, Kericho and
Kitale.

Train There are services three times a week
to Nairobi on Wednesday, Saturday and
Sunday at 9 pm, arriving the next day at 9.30

am. Trains to the Ugandan border at Malaba
depart on Wednesday, Saturday and Sunday
at around 4 am.

CHERANGANI HILLS
The beautiful Cherangani Hills are part of the
rift valley system and extend for about 60 km
from the north-east of Eldoret. They form the
western wall of the spectacular **Elgeyo**

Escarpment. You could easily spend weeks exploring here, and never come across another mzungu.

The area is best explored on foot as the roads are rough and some of those which scale the Elgeyo Escarpment are incredibly steep. In wet conditions the roads in this area become treacherous. For serious exploration you would need to get copies of the relevant Survey of Kenya maps to the area, which are almost impossible to get (see the Maps section in the introductory Facts for the Visitor chapter). Otherwise contact Jane or Julia Barnley of Sirikwa Safaris, PO Box 332, Kitale, who can organise ornithological tours of the hills along with a guide at a very reasonable price. Jane and Julia also run an excellent guesthouse and camp site 23 km north of Kitale (see the Kitale section later in this chapter for full details).

The hills are dotted with small towns and although none of them have any recognised accommodation, it should be possible to arrange something with the local people (ask the village chief or ask in the bars). If you have a tent it's just a matter of finding a good spot and asking permission.

From Eldoret it should be possible to hitch, or even find a matatu, as far as **Kapsowar**, 70 km to the north-east in the **Kerio Valley** and right in the heart of the hills. Coming from the north there is a road which starts from Sigor at the Marich Pass and finds its way to Kapsowar via Tot and the impossibly steep escarpment road, but don't expect much in the way of transport along it.

The hills are the home of the Marakwet or Markweta people (part of the greater Kalenjin grouping) who migrated here from the north. They found the area provided good safety, and that the streams were ideal for agriculture as the rainfall was low. To this end they have made good use of, and extended, the water-distribution channels which were already in existence when the Marakwet first migrated to the area. The channels distribute the water to all the small shambas in the hills.

For further details on these hills, see the Marich Pass section in the Northern Kenya chapter.

KITALE

Kitale is another in the string of agricultural service towns which dot the western highlands. It does have an interesting museum but its main function for travellers is as a base for explorations further afield – Mt Elgon, Saiwa Swamp National Park – and a take-off point for the trip up to the western side of Lake Turkana. As such it's a pleasant enough town and can make an enjoyable stopover for a couple of days.

Information

The post office is on Post Office Rd (surprise, surprise) and is open the usual hours. It's possible to make international calls but these have to be made through the operator in Nairobi, and this takes time.

Kitale has the usual banks and a busy market.

Kitale Museum

The museum has a variety of indoor exhibits, including good ethnographic displays of the Turkana people. The outdoor exhibits include traditional homesteads of a number of different tribal groups, the inevitable tortoise enclosure and an interesting biogas display.

Probably most interesting is the small **nature trail** which leads through some virgin forest at the back of the museum. There are numbered points along the way; the small guidebook available from the craft shop in the museum explains the points of interest.

The museum is open Monday to Friday from 7.30 am to 6 pm, Saturday from 8 am to 6 pm and Sunday from 9 am to 6 pm; entry is US$1.10.

Places to Stay – bottom end

Best of the usual bunch of cheapies/brothels is the *Star Lodge*. Good-sized rooms upstairs cost US$2.20 a double with shared bath, but cop a bit of noise from the road below.

Very similar is the *Kahuroko Boarding & Lodging* where self-contained singles cost

US$2.70 and doubles with shared bath US$2.20. It's getting run-down these days but is still OK for a night. Another cheapie is the *New Mombasa Hotel* which offers clean singles with shared facilities for US$1.80 though there's a very noisy bar on the 1st floor. The *Hotel Mamboleo* is much quieter, though the rooms are somewhat gloomy. Self-contained singles/doubles here cost US$2.20/3.40 plus there's hot water in the showers.

Other travellers have recommended the *New Kitale House* next door to the Mamboleo which offers beds with clean sheets and shared bath for just US$1.40. The *Executive Lodge*, on Kenyatta St, has self-contained singles for US$3.40, but no doubles.

If you want to camp, the only place in the area is *Sirikwa Safaris,* about 23 km north of Kitale on the Kapenguria road. It's run by Jane and Julia Barnley at their farmhouse and is a beautiful place to stay. Jane and Julia are very friendly and know the western highlands like the back of their hand, plus they're great conversationalists. Stay here and feel right at home! You won't regret the little effort it takes to get here. Camping with your own tent costs US$2.70 including the use of firewood, hot showers, flush toilets and electricity. If you don't have your own tent, that's no problem as there are also 'permanent' furnished tents for US$6.70 per person.

To find Sirikwa Safaris, look for the green concrete posts and the sign on a rise on the right-hand side of the road several km past the entrance to Saiwa Swamp National Park.

Places to Stay – middle

The *New Kitale Hotel* is the town's old colonial place but, these days, it wears a garb of total neglect bordering on dereliction. Despite this, and the feeling that everytime you open a wardrobe in one of the rooms that a skeleton dressed ready for a June ball will fall out, the rooms are spacious, self-contained and have a balcony. Rates are US$3.40/6.70 for singles/doubles without towels, soap or toilet paper. It's a shame that it has not been looked after – it could be beautiful.

The most popular place to stay in this range is the *Bongo Hotel* (☎ 20593) on Moi Ave which has singles/doubles with shared bath (no breakfast) for US$6/6.70, or US$7.80/10 with private bath and an excellent breakfast. There's hot water in the showers, clean sheets, and towel, soap and toilet paper are provided.

Also excellent value is the *Alakara Hotel* (☎ 20395) on Kenyatta St which offers spacious singles/doubles with shared bath for US$5.60/7.80. Twin-bed rooms with private bath cost US$8.90, and double-bed rooms with bath US$11.10. Single-occupancy rates are less. Prices include breakfast. Facilities include a good bar/restaurant, a car park and a residents' video room. The staff are friendly and helpful.

Outside of town, Jane and Julia Barnley's farmhouse is the place to head for (see Sirikwa Safaris earlier for directions). Apart from tents there are two very comfortable rooms with double beds for US$16/24 a single/double including breakfast. Half-board/full-board rates are US$20/32 and US$24/40 respectively. Children are half-price and babies stay free of charge. It's a very quiet and homely place and Jane and Julia are the perfect hosts.

Places to Eat & Entertainment

The *Wandi Café* on Kenyatta St is a popular place at lunch time. Meals are basic but tasty, and include dishes such as beef stew with rice, and chicken and chips. Another good place is the *Delicious Restaurant* on the same street.

The *Bongo Hotel* on the corner of Moi Ave and Bank St has a slightly more up-market restaurant which is a good place for an evening meal. It also serves alcohol. Right next door is the lively Bongo Bar and there's also a takeaway food section. Even better, though slightly more expensive, are the meals at the *Alakara Hotel* on Kenyatta St. You can either eat in the restaurant section or have meals brought to you in the popular bar.

Another lively bar here with loud music is

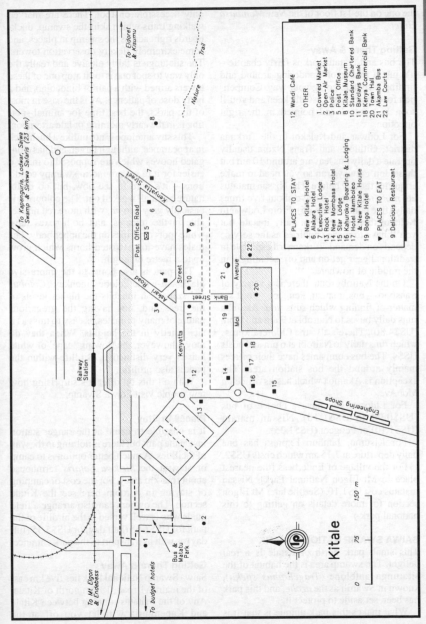

Kitale

PLACES TO STAY
4 New Kitale Hotel
6 Alakara Hotel
7 Executive Lodge
13 Rock Hotel
14 New Mombasa Hotel
15 Star Lodge
16 Kahuroko Boarding & Lodging
17 Hotel Mamboleo
& New Kitale House
19 Bongo Hotel

PLACES TO EAT
9 Delicious Restaurant
12 Wandi Café

OTHER
1 Covered Market
2 Open-Air Market
3 Police
5 Post Office
8 Kitale Museum
10 Standard Chartered Bank
11 Barclays Bank
18 Kenya Commercial Bank
20 Town Hall
21 Akamba Bus
22 Law Courts

the one on the 1st floor of the *New Mombasa Hotel.*

Getting There & Away

The bus and matatu park is fairly chaotic – it's just a matter of wandering around and finding a vehicle going your way. Competition for passengers is usually keen and you'll soon be spotted and pointed in the right direction.

For Lodwar and Kalekol in the Turkana district, Githiora and Trans Nzoia usually operate a daily bus leaving around 10 am but these don't always run so you need to make enquiries the day before. The Nissan matatus are more reliable and leave about five times daily (five hours, US$4.45). From Lodwar to Kalekol there's usually a daily matatu but you'll have to make enquiries as the service depends on demand. Turkana tribespeople in traditional gear get on and off, seemingly in the middle of nowhere.

On the Nairobi route there is a variety of transport – bus, matatu, Peugeot – so it's a matter of finding which suits you. Akamba runs daily buses to Nairobi at 9 am and 9 pm (US$4.80). There's also the Eldoret Express which runs daily to Nairobi at 6 pm and costs US$4. The bus companies have their offices mainly around the bus station area. The exception is Akamba which has its office on Moi Ave.

For Eldoret, you have a choice of bus (US$0.90 to US$1.10), Nissan matatu (US$1.10) or Peugeot (US$1.35).

For Kisumu, Jamhuri Express has one daily departure at 7.15 am which costs US$2.

For the village of Enderbess (the nearest place to Mt Elgon National Park), Nissan matatus cost US$1.10. (See the later Mt Elgon section for more details on getting to this national park.)

SAIWA SWAMP NATIONAL PARK

This small park north of Kitale is a real delight. The swamp area is the habitat of the sitatunga antelope *(Tragelaphus spekii),* known in Swahili as the *nzohe,* and this park has been set aside to protect it.

What makes this park unique is that it is only accessible on foot. There are marked walking trails which skirt the swamp, duckboards right across the swamp in places, and some extremely rickety observation towers. The sitatunga is fairly elusive and really the only way to spot one is to sit atop one of these towers armed with a pair of binoculars and a hefty dose of patience. As is the case in most of the parks, the best time for animal-spotting is in the early morning or late afternoon.

This shy antelope is not unlike a bushbuck in appearance, although larger, and has elongated hooves which are supposed to make it easier for it to get around in swampy conditions – it's hard to see how, but no doubt nature has it all worked out. The colouring is basically grey-brown, with more red noticeable in the females, and both sexes have white spots or stripes on the upper body. The males have long twisted horns which grow up to a metre in length.

The park is also home to the impressive black-and-white colobus monkey *(Colobus polykomos).* It inhabits the higher levels of the trees and, not having the gregarious nature of many primates, is easy to miss as it sits quietly in the heights. When they do move, however, the flowing 'cape' of white hair is very distinctive. Birdlife within the park is also prolific.

With all this on offer it's surprising how few people visit Saiwa Swamp.

Places to Stay

It is possible to camp at the ranger station inside the park but there is nothing in the way of facilities. A much better option is to camp or stay at the *Sirikwa Safaris* farmhouse about four km away. For the cost of camping or staying in a room here see the Kitale section. The owners can also arrange a field guide who is well versed in the birdlife of the park for US$2.65 (half day) or US$5.35 (full day) as well as transport to the park entrance.

Getting There & Away

Saiwa Swamp National Park lies five km east of the main A1 road, 18 km north of Kitale. Any of the matatus running between Kitale and Kapenguria will let you off at the

The Kalenjin

Kalenjin is a name formulated in the 1950s to describe the group of peoples previously called the Nandi by the British. The Nandi tag was erroneous as the people were all Nandi speakers (one of many dialects) but were not all Nandis; the other groups included Kipsigis, Marakwet, Pokot and Tugen (arap Moi's people). The word *kalenjin* means 'I say to you' in Nandi.

The Kalenjin people occupy the western edge of the central Rift Valley area which includes Kericho, Eldoret, Kitale, Baringo and the Mt Elgon area. They first migrated to the area west of Lake Turkana from southern Sudan around 2000 years ago and gradually filtered south as the climate changed and the forests dwindled.

Although originally pastoralists, most Kalenjin groups took up agriculture. Some, however, such as the Okiek, stuck to the forests and to a hunter-gatherer existence. Beekeeping was a common practice and the honey was used not only in trade but also for brewing beer.

As with most tribes, Kalenjin have age-sets into which a man is initiated after circumcision and remains for the rest of his life. Polygamy was widely practiced. Administration of the law is carried out at the *kok* – an informal gathering of the clan's elders and other interested parties in the dispute. Unusually, the doctors were usually women and they used herbal remedies in their work. Other specialist doctors practiced trepanning – taking out pieces of the skull to cure certain ailments – which is also practiced by the Bantu-speaking Gusii of the Kisii district.

Kalenjin in traditional dress

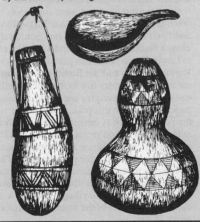

signposted turn-off, from where you'll probably have to walk to the park as there is little traffic along the dirt road.

MT ELGON NATIONAL PARK

Mt Elgon sits astride the Kenya-Uganda border and, while it offers similar trekking possibilities to Mt Kenya, its location makes it a far less popular goal. The lower altitude also means that the weather on the upper slopes is not quite as severe.

The mountain is an extinct volcano and the national park extends from the lower slopes right up to the border. The highest peak is Wagagai (at 4321 metres the fourth-highest in East Africa) and is actually on the far side of the crater in Uganda. The highest peak on the Kenyan side is Koitoboss. There are warm springs in the crater itself, the floor of which is around 3500 metres above sea level.

Access to the 170 sq-km national park is only officially allowed with a vehicle, but this may change when the hiking trails and huts being set up by the Mt Elgon Conservation & Development Project in Uganda are fully opened to the public. The project has its headquarters in Mbale. The plan is to link up the Ugandan trails with those on the Kenyan side.

The mountain's biggest attraction is the elephants, renowned the world over for their predilection for salt, the major source of which is in the caves on the mountain slopes. The elephants are such keen excavators that some have gone so far as to claim that the elephants are totally responsible for the caves! Sadly, the numbers of these saline-loving creatures has declined over the years, mainly due to incursions by poachers from the Ugandan side. There are three caves open to visitors – Kitum, Chepnyali and Mackingeny. Kitum is the one which you are most likely to see elephants in, while Mackingeny is the most spectacular. Obviously a good torch (flashlight) is essential if you want to explore the caves.

A less obvious attraction is the range of vegetation found on the mountain. Starting with rainforest at the base, the vegetation changes as you ascend to bamboo jungle and finally alpine moorland with the bizarre giant groundsel and giant lobelia plants. The lower forests are the habitat of the impressive black and white colobus monkey along with many other species of birds and animals. Those most commonly sighted include buffalo, bushbuck, giant forest hog and Sykes monkey.

Elgon can be a wet place at any time of the year, but the driest months seem to be December, January and February. As well as waterproof gear you are going to need warm clothes as it gets cold up here at night.

Walks

If you want to walk in the park, the most popular route is from **Kimilili**, a small village 36 km south of Kitale on the main A1 road to Webuye and Kisumu. There's basic accommodation here, and matatus run the seven km to **Kapsakwany**, from where you start walking. The Kimilili Forest Station is about five km past Kapsakwany and from there it's a further 20 km to the Chepkitale Forest Station, and another seven km past this station to the mountain hut. Obviously it's a long day's walk from Kapsakwany to the hut (32 km for those of you who can't add up) but the rangers at either of the forest stations shouldn't mind if you camp there.

From the hut it takes around four hours to reach the lake known as Lower Elgon Tarn, and from here it's a further one hour walk along a marked trail (cairns and white blazes) to Lower Elgon peak. The pass at the foot of Koitoboss peak and the **Suam hot springs** are around the crater rim to the right (north-east) and once here you are in the national park. If you reach this point and descend via the park entrance (Chorlim Gate), which is in fact illegal as you're not supposed to walk in the park, expect some difficult questions and be prepared to pay the park entry fee. The options are to return the same way, or via the third route, known as the Masara route, which goes to the small village of **Masara** on the northern slopes of the mountain, a trek of about 25 km.

Places to Stay

There are no lodges in the park itself but there is a beautiful camp site with good facilities close to the Chorlim Gate which you'll be allowed to walk to. You need to bring all your own food, camping and cooking equipment with you as there's none for hire and there are no shops. About one km before the Chorlim Gate is the *Mt Elgon Lodge* (PO Box 7 Enderbess, Kitale), one of the Msafiri Inns chain of hotels. Comfortable rooms with full board cost US$25/45 a single/double (US$60 for triples) in the low season, and US$40/65/85 in the high season. The hotel has its own bar and restaurant.

Getting There & Away

To get to the village of Enderbess (the nearest place to Mt Elgon National Park), there are normal matatus for US$0.55 or Nissan matatus for US$1.10 from Kitale. Part of this road is good tarmac but there are also some horrific sections with huge potholes.

The turn-off for Mt Elgon National Park (Chorlim Gate) is several km before Enderbess on the left-hand side (clearly signposted).

If you're hitching, you'll need to get to the turn-off but it's still a long way into the park from there and there's very little transport. Rangers' vehicles and support trucks do come along the road at least once a day but you could be waiting half the day.

Although the road into the park is a good gravel road, in the wet season the only way in is to have your own 4WD.

Northern Kenya

This vast area, covering thousands of sq km to the borders with Sudan, Ethiopia and Somalia, is an explorer's paradise hardly touched by the 20th century. The tribes which live here – the Samburu, Turkana, Rendille, Boran, Gabra, Merille and El-Molo – are some of the most fascinating people in the world. The whole area is a living ethnology museum. Like the Maasai, most of them have little contact with the modern world, preferring their own centuries-old traditional lifestyles and customs which bind members of a tribe together and ensure that each individual has a part to play. Many have strong warrior traditions and, in the past, it was the balance of power between the tribes which defined their respective areas.

As late as 1980 there was a clash between the Samburu and the Turkana over grazing land near South Horr which required army intervention. Since most of the tribes are nomadic pastoralists these sort of conflicts have a long history. Nevertheless, the settlement of disputes between the tribes is based on compensation rather than retribution so wholesale violence is a rare occurrence.

Change is slowly coming to these people as a result of missionary activity (there is an incredible number of different Christian missions, schools and aid agencies, many of them in very remote areas), their employment as rangers and anti-poaching patrollers in national parks and game reserves, the construction of dams and roads, and the tourist trade. You may well be surprised, for example, to see a young man dressed smartly in Western-style clothes doing some business in a small town and then later on the same day meet him again out in the bush dressed in traditional regalia. It might even turn out that he's a college student in Nairobi for much of the year. Pride in their heritage is one thing these people are very unlikely to lose.

Yet, such examples of sophistication aside, not only are the people another world away from Nairobi and the more developed areas of the country but the landscapes are tremendous. Perhaps no other country in Africa offers such diversity.

Geography

Much of northern Kenya is scrub desert dissected by luggas (dry river beds which burst into a brief but violent life whenever there is a cloud burst) and peppered with acacia thorn trees which are often festooned with weaver birds' nests. But there are also extinct and dormant volcanoes; barren, shattered lava beds; canyons through which cool, clear streams flow; oases of lush vegetation hemmed in by craggy mountains and huge islands of forested mountains surrounded by sand deserts. And, of course, the legendary 'Jade Sea' (Lake Turkana) – Kenya's largest lake and, as a result of the Leakeys' archaeological digs, regarded by many as the birthplace of humanity.

A long narrow body of water, Lake Turkana stretches south from the Ethiopian border for some 250 km, yet is never more than 50 km wide. While it looks fairly placid most of the time, it is notorious for the vicious squalls which whip up seemingly out of nowhere and are largely responsible for the fatalities among the local Turkana and El-Molo people who live along the lake shores.

The lake was first reached by Europeans in the late 19th century in the form of two Austrian explorers, von Hehnel and Teleki, who named it Lake Rudolf and it wasn't until the early 1970s that the name was changed to Turkana. The fossil hominid skulls discovered here by the Leakeys in the 1960s are thought to be around 2½ million years old. At that time it is believed that the lake was far more extensive than it is today and supported a richer plant and animal life. Around 10,000 years ago the water level was high enough for the lake to be one of the sources

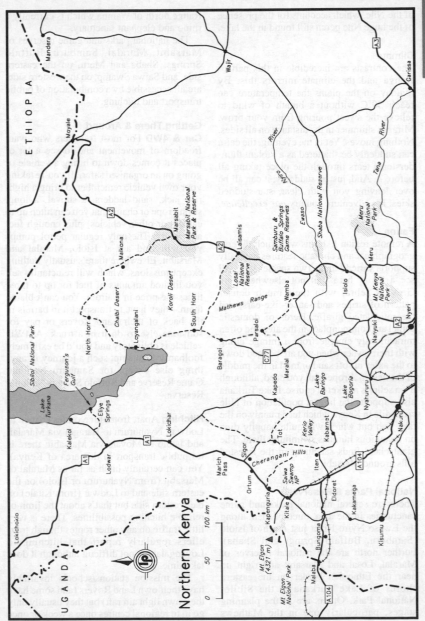

Northern Kenya

0   50   100 km

of the Nile, which accounts for the presence of the huge Nile perch still found in the lake.

Climate

The contrasts are incredible in this part of Kenya and the climate mirrors this. By midday on the plains the temperature can reach 50°C without a breath of wind to relieve the sweat pouring from your brow. Mirages shimmer in the distance on all sides. Nothing moves. Yet in the evening, the calm can suddenly be shattered as a violent thunderstorm tears through the place taking all before it. And, just as suddenly, it can all be over leaving you with clear, star-studded skies. It's adventure country *par excellence*.

Fauna

A remote region like this with such diverse geographical and climatic features naturally supports varied fauna. Two species you will see a lot of here (but not elsewhere) are Grevy's zebra, with their much denser pattern of stripes and saucer-like ears, and the reticulated giraffe. Herds of domestic camel are commonplace in the area and often miraculously emerge from a mirage along with their owner when you are bogged down to the axles in soft sand or mud in the middle of the desert. A rope is all you need, although it's a seller's market of course. Lake Turkana also supports the largest population of Nile crocodile in Kenya which feed mainly on the lake fish but which will quite happily dine on incautious humans swimming there. The giant eland finds sanctuary in the forested hills around Marsabit.

National Parks & Reserves

There are several national parks and game sanctuaries in the area, three of them along the Ewaso Nyiro River just north of Isiolo (Samburu, Buffalo Springs and Shaba). Further north are the national reserves of Maralal, Losai and Marsabit and right up near the Ethiopian border on the eastern shores of Lake Turkana is the Sibiloi National Park. Others are in the planning stages, particularly one in the Mathews Range north of Wamba which is currently a rhino and elephant sanctuary.

The national parks and game reserves of Marsabit, Maralal, Samburu, Buffalo Springs, Shaba and Meru, on the eastern side, and Saiwa Swamp, on the western side, are all accessible by a combination of public transport and hitching.

Getting There & Around

Car & 4WD For most travellers who want freedom of movement and to see a lot of places it comes down to hiring a vehicle or going on an organised safari. If you're taking your own vehicle remember to bring a high-rise jack, sand ladders, a shovel, a long, strong rope or chain (that you can hitch up to camels or other vehicles) plus enough fuel and water. The only regular petrol pumps you will find are at Isiolo, Maralal and Marsabit. Elsewhere there's usually nothing except missions, which will reluctantly sell you limited amounts of fuel for up to three times the price in Nairobi. You can't blame them – they have to transport it in barrels in the back of their Land Rovers or pay for someone else to do it in a truck. A 4WD vehicle is obligatory and you'd be extremely foolhardy to attempt such a journey in anything else except for Samburu National Game Reserve and Buffalo Springs National Reserve.

Hitching Apart from three routes (Kitale to Lodwar, Nyahururu to Baragoi via Maralal, and Isiolo to Moyale via Marsabit, there is no public transport in this area of Kenya). You can certainly hitch as far as Maralal or Marsabit (from Nyahururu or Isiolo) on the eastern side and to Lodwar (from Kitale) on the western side but that's about the limit of reliable hitching possibilities. There is *very* little traffic on any other routes though travellers regularly report that hitching to Loyangalani is not difficult although it does take time.

The mission stations/schools invariably have their own Land Rovers (and some have their own light aircraft) but they usually only go in to regional centres once a week or once a fortnight. Although most will try to help you out if you're stuck, you cannot be guaranteed a lift. The vehicle might be full of people who need urgent medical assistance or (on the return journey) full of supplies. Hitching is possible, of course, but you must have no deadlines to meet and you must be the sort of person who is quite happy to wait around for days for a ride. In some ways, this could be a very interesting way of getting around and you'd certainly meet a lot of local people but if it is lifts you want you can only hitch along the main routes.

You could, of course, buy a camel and do a John Hillaby but this isn't something to approach lightly. It is, however, a distinct possibility especially if you are part of a small group. You'd have the adventure of your life!

Safaris Most organised safaris last from seven to 10 days, though there are others which last 14 days, and they all seem to follow much the same route. Starting from Nairobi, they head up the Rift Valley to Lake Baringo, over to Maralal and then up the main route to Loyangalani on Lake Turkana via Baragoi and South Horr. On the return journey, again via Maralal, they take in Samburu National Game Reserve and Buffalo Springs National Reserve. Only one or two of them take in Marsabit National Park & Reserve since the only way of getting there from Loyangalani is directly across the Koroli Desert (hazardous after rain) or via the long loop north through North Horr and Maikona. Even this involves crossing the Chalbi Desert which, like the Koroli, is hazardous after rain.

The cost of safaris varies between US$265 and US$1650 depending on the number of days and the standard of accommodation. The price includes transport, all meals, park and camping fees, and camping equipment. Since the terrain is rough beyond Isiolo or Maralal, open-sided 4WD trucks are used for these safaris and it's a dusty journey. Don't expect any of life's little luxuries on these safaris (such as hot showers or cold beers), though these can be found with determination! The following

companies all offer Turkana tours, usually once a week but sometimes once a fortnight (see also the Safari section of the Kenya Getting Around chapter). Note also that these have been listed alphabetically, not in any order of preference:

Best Camping
Nanak House, 2nd Floor, on the corner of Kimathi and Banda Sts, PO Box 40223, Nairobi (☎ 28091, 27203).
Like the others, Best takes the usual route but its safari lasts eight days.

Bushbuck Adventures
Barclays Bank Bldg, Kenyatta Ave, PO Box 67449, Nairobi (☎ 212975/6/7; fax 218735).
Bushbuck offers a 12-day safari to Lake Turkana but it keeps well away from the usual route taking in the Mathews Range, the Ndoto Mountains and Shaba National Game Reserve. It leaves once a month in the dry season and costs US$1650. There's also an 18-day 'Northern Frontier Expedition' which takes in Samburu, the Ndoto Mountains, Lake Turkana and North Horr and, like the previous tour, keeps well away from the usual route. It costs US$1480 and includes a return flight from Loyangalani to Nairobi.

Exotic Safaris & Travel
1st Floor, Uniafric House, Koinange St, PO Box 54483, Nairobi (☎ 338811; fax 211701).
This company also offers a seven-day safari to Lake Turkana.

Gametrackers
1st Floor, Kenya Cinema Plaza, Moi Ave, PO Box 62042, Nairobi (☎ 338927; fax 330903).
This company is the only one which takes in Marsabit National Park and then crosses the Chalbi Desert to Lake Turkana. It takes eight days, costs US$330 and departs twice a month on Fridays. It also has an eight-day safari to Lake Turkana which takes the normal route, departs twice a month on Fridays and costs the same.

Safari Camp Services
PO Box 44801, on the corner of Koinange and Moktar Daddah Sts, Nairobi (☎ 28936, 330130; fax 212160).
This is the group which blazed the trail 17 years ago and recently celebrated its 600th departure. You won't find better. There's a seven-day safari (US$265) which leaves every second Saturday year-round (every Saturday in the high season).

Special Camping Safaris
Gilfillan House, Kenyatta Ave, PO Box 51512, Nairobi (☎ 338325; fax 211828).
This company takes the usual route but its safari lasts 10 days. The cost is US$370 and there are departures twice per month.

Yare Safaris
　1st Floor, Union Towers, Mama Ngina St, PO
　Box 63006, Nairobi (☎ 214099; fax 213445).
　Yare's 10-day safari covers the usual route and
　includes a night at its Maralal hostel and camp
　site. The cost is US$360 and there are departures
　twice (sometimes three times) a month on Satur-
　days.

West of Turkana

From Kitale the road north winds through the fertile highlands, passing the turn-off for the tiny Saiwa Swamp National Park (well worth a visit) before reaching **Kapenguria**, the town most famous for being the place where Jomo Kenyatta and five associates were held and tried in 1953 for their part in the Mau Mau Rebellion.

The road then snakes its way up along a forested ridge and through the narrow north-ern gorges of the Cherangani Hills, emerging on to the desert plains through the Marich Pass. The change in scenery is dramatic and there are some fantastic views of the plains. The only town in this part of the hills is **Ortum**, just off the road. If you want to stop and explore the area, there is basic accom-modation in the town but the best place to stay is the Marich Pass Field Studies Centre further north (see the following Marich Pass section).

Shortly after Marich Pass is a turn-off to the left (west) to the Turkwel Gorge. It's here that you'll find the huge hydroelectric project which is destined to supply electric-ity to a large area of the densely populated highlands – the northern areas will still have to rely on generators.

After km of endless plains and dry creek beds the town of **Lokichar** is little more than a collection of dismal dukas by the side of the road. The heat here is oppressive and the settlement seems to be gripped by a perma-nent torpor. The one redeeming feature of the place is that it is possible to buy basketware and other Turkana trinkets cheaper than you'll find them further north.

MARICH PASS AREA

The main reason for visiting this area is to stay at the Marich Pass Field Studies Centre (see Places to Stay & Eat) and use this as a base for a number of excursions in the area.

Those with their own vehicles should bring sufficient supplies of petrol as there are no service stations between Kapenguria and Lodwar. If you intend walking in the vicinity then you need to be adequately prepared for a variety of weather conditions.

A few km to the north-west, **Mt Sekerr** (3326 metres) can be climbed comfortably in a three-day round trip via the agricultural plots of the Pokot tribe, passing through forest and open moors. The views from the top are magnificent when the weather is clear.

To the south are the **Cherangani Hills**, which offer some of the best hill walks any-where in Kenya ranging from half-day excursions to week-long safaris by vehicle and on foot. Possibilities include a half-day walk along the old road perched high on the eastern side of the Marich Pass to a local Pokot trading centre; a hard day's slog up the dome of Koh which soars some 1524 metres above the adjacent plains; a safari of several days' duration along the verdant Weiwei Valley to Tamkal and then up to Lelan Forest and the main peaks of the Cherangani.

The **Elgeyo Escarpment** rises to more than 1830 metres in places above the Kerio Valley and offers spectacular views and waterfalls. It's only 1½ hours away from the field studies centre along a road that passes through several local market centres and intensively farmed garden plots.

The **South Turkana National Reserve** in dry and rugged hills north-east of the field studies centre is the domain of Turkana herders and rarely visited by outsiders. The 50-km drive to get there traverses grazing lands of the pastoral Pokot.

Lastly, the **Turkwel Gorge** hydroelectric station is only 30 km away along a fine tarmac road. Much of the gorge, with its towering rock walls, has not been affected by the construction, while the dam itself (the highest of its type in Africa) is spectacular.

The 35 km-long lake will eventually be available for fishing, sailing and other water sports.

Places to Stay & Eat

The best place to stay in this area is the *Marich Pass Field Studies Centre* (☎ (0321) 31541), PO Box 2454, Eldoret. This is essentially a residential facility for groups pursuing field courses in geography, botany, zoology, ecology, conservation, geology and rural development, but it's also open to independent travellers who want to spend a day, a week or a month in a little-known corner of Kenya.

The centre occupies a beautiful site alongside the Weiwei River and is surrounded by dense bush and woodland. The birdlife here is prolific, monkeys and baboons are 'in residence', while wart hogs, buffaloes, antelope and elephants are regular visitors. Facilities include a secure camp site (US$1.80 per person per night) with drinking water, toilets, showers and firewood, as well as dorm beds for US$2.20 and simple but comfortable bandas for US$6.20 (two people) and US$9.40 (three people).

English-speaking Pokot and Turkana guides are available on request. There's also a restaurant where you can get breakfast for

US$1.50, lunch for US$1.10 and dinner from US$1.70 (vegetarian) to US$2.10 (meat). Meals should ideally be ordered in advance since the very friendly manager often has to walk into the nearest village to buy the food. You can, of course, bring your own food with you and cook it at the centre. There's little available in the villages of this area.

Getting There & Away

To reach the field studies centre, take the main Kitale to Lodwar road and watch out for the centre's signpost two km north of the Sigor to Tot road junction (signposted) at Marich Pass. The centre is about one km down a clearly marked track.

There are three approaches to Marich Pass. The first and easiest is through Kitale and Kapenguria and then a further 67 km down a tarmac road (described as 'possibly Kenya's most spectacular tarmac road'). There are daily bus services from Nairobi to Kapenguria, and matatus (US$0.80 or US$0.90 in a Nissan) from Kitale to Kapenguria. There are also a few daily matatus which cover the stretch from Kitale to Lokichar via Marich Pass.

The second approach is through Iten either from Eldoret or via Kabarnet using the

---

The Samburu

Closely related to the Maasai, and in fact speaking the same language, the Samburu occupy an arid area directly north of Mt Kenya. It seems that when the Maasai migrated to the area from Sudan, some headed east (and became the Samburu) while the bulk of them continued south to the area they occupy today.

As is often the case, age-sets are an integral part of the society and the men pass through various stages before becoming a powerful elder at the top of the ladder. Circumcision is practiced in both sexes, although with the girls it is only done on the day of marriage, which is usually when she is around 16 years old. Men are often in their thirties by the time they pass out of warriorhood and become elders qualified to marry. ■

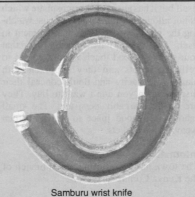

Samburu wrist knife

scenic road across the upper Kerio Valley from Kabarnet. The all-weather Cherangani Highway can be picked up from Iten to cross the main pass of the Cherangani Hills and join up with the Kitale to Lodwar road near Kapenguria.

The roughest of the three approaches is the road from Lake Baringo through the Kito Pass and across the Kerio Valley to Tot but its main advantage is that it gives you the chance to visit the hot waterfalls at **Kapedo**. From Tot, the track skirts the northern face of the Cherangani Hills and involves fording numerous streams which may be impassable after heavy rain, although an Italian-funded road project should soon make this an all-weather road.

LODWAR

The hot and dusty administrative town of Lodwar is the only town of any significance in the north-west. With a bitumen road connecting it with the highlands, and air connections with Nairobi, it is no longer the isolated outpost of the Northern Frontier District as the area was known during colonial days but is certainly lagging a few steps behind the rest of the country.

Lodwar is also the base for any excursions to the lake from the western side and you will probably find it convenient to stay here for a night at least. There's little to do in the town itself but it has an outback atmosphere which is not altogether unpleasant and just watching the garrulous locals is entertainment in itself. The Turkana have suddenly found that tourists are a good touch when it comes to selling trinkets and they approach with alarming audacity and don't conceal their disgust when you don't want to buy. They are also remarkably persistent. The small market is a good place to watch women weaving the baskets.

Information

The town has a post office and a branch of the Kenya Commercial Bank.

Places to Stay – bottom end

Lodwar is one place where it's worth spend-ing a bit more on accommodation – mainly to get a room with a fan. The rooms in the cheaper places are all hellishly hot and, as the mosquitoes are fierce, you need to cover up or burn coils if you don't have a net. It seems the recently surfaced road from the south has put Lodwar on the map, and there are new hotels springing up all the time.

Best of the cheapies is the *Mombasa Hotel*, almost next door to the JM Bus office which is where you'll be dropped if arriving that way from Kitale. The friendly Muslim owners charge US$1.40/2.10 for singles/doubles. The singles are cooler (it's all relative though) as they have high ceilings. If you have a mosquito net you can sleep in the courtyard.

The *Marira Boarding & Lodging* is a new place and could be worth a try. Another bottom-end cheapie is the *Ngonda Hotel*. Both charge the same as the Mombasa Hotel.

Places to Stay – middle

The *Turkwel Hotel* (☎ 21201) is the town's social focus and also has the best accommodation. Single rooms with fan and shared bath go for US$2.20, while singles/doubles with fan and bath cost US$4/5.40. There are also a few spacious cottages which are very pleasant and cost US$8 for two including breakfast.

It is rumoured that a luxury hotel of the African Tours & Hotels chain is to be built on the southern side of the Turkwel River on the approach into town.

Places to Eat

The restaurant at the *Mombasa Hotel* does reasonable local food and has excellent fresh mandazis (semisweet doughnuts) early in the morning. The *Marira Boarding & Lodging* has little variety but its chips are excellent and freshly cooked to order. For something a bit more sophisticated the *Turkwel Hotel* restaurant does standard Western fare such as steak, chips, etc. Breakfast here consists of a couple of eggs and a sausage, and non-guests are not served until all the hotel guests have finished. The bar here is also a popular place.

Getting There & Away

In theory, there are daily Githiora and Trans Nzoia buses from Kitale to Lodwar which generally leave around 10 am and (sometimes) at 2 pm but sometimes they don't run at all. The matatus are more reliable and there are usually five per day which leave when full. The trip takes around seven hours and costs US$4.50.

Matatus also run from Lodwar to Kalekol near the lake if demand warrants, but you can't count on them. The trip takes one hour. If you want to hitch to Kalekol the place where the locals wait is under the tree about 200 metres north of the Kobil station. To give an indication of how long you can expect to wait, there is a chai (tea) stall here which also sells mandazis.

KALEKOL

Most travellers head on from Lodwar to Kalekol, a fairly dismal little town a few km from the lake shore. The main building in this one-street town is the fish-processing factory built with Scandinavian money and expertise and, although fairly new is currently not operating. There is also an Italian-sponsored plant closer to the lake shore.

Places to Stay & Eat

A good place to stay is the rudimentary but friendly *George Oyavi's Hotel*. It is right next to the bus office and George meets all incoming buses. The rooms are only rough grass constructions and so thankfully get some breeze. There's a rough-and-ready shower rigged up and George and his staff somehow muddle through and cook meals although you need to order in advance. Warm beer and sodas are also available. If you want anything more sophisticated to eat than rice, chapatis or fish you'll need to bring it from Lodwar.

There's a second hotel called *Skyway Bar & Lodge* on the right-hand side as you enter Kalekol from the south. Rooms here cost US$0.80/2.70 a single/double with shared bathroom facilities. Next door is the *Safari Hotel* which has a reasonable restaurant.

Getting There & Away

Assuming one of the buses made it from Kitale the previous day, it generally leaves for the return journey at around 5 am. There is no danger of missing it as the driver revs the engine and honks the horn well before he leaves. Alternatively, there's usually a matatu which leaves later in the day. Make enquiries the night before if you want to be sure of leaving next day.

To get out to the lake it's a hot 1½-hour walk. Someone at George's will guide you, or just walk to the Italian fishing project and cut across the lake bed from there.

FERGUSON'S GULF

This is the most accessible part of the lake shore and while it's not particularly attractive, although the sense of achievement in just getting there usually compensates. The water has receded greatly, mainly due to drought in Ethiopia, so you have to walk a long way over the lake bed to actually get to the water. The birdlife along the shore is prolific. There are also hippos and crocodiles, so seek local advice before having a refreshing dip.

There's a small fishing village of grass huts on the far side of the Turkana Fishing Lodge and that's about the limit of development.

To get out on the lake you can hire the launches from the lodge to take you to **Central Island National Park**, a barren yet scenic volcanic island. By all accounts the trip is worthwhile but it's not cheap. A covered cruiser which takes eight people costs US$52, while the open four-seater long boat costs US$39. Talk to the fishers and they might take you out for a good deal less but make sure their craft is sound – the danger posed by the lake's squalls is not to be taken lightly.

Places to Stay

If you don't mind really roughing it, the local villagers will put you up for a few bob, otherwise you'll have to come here just for a day trip from Kalekol or stay at the lodge.

The *Lake Turkana Fishing Lodge* (☎ (2) 26623), PO Box 41078, Nairobi, is supposedly on an island but the level of the lake has fallen so far in recent years that it's now possible to drive to the lodge, in the dry season at least. It takes around 1½ very hot hours to walk out there from Kalekol – follow the track to the Italian fishing project then head across the lake bed from there. There are children with canoes who will paddle you across the 20 metres or so of channel. By car you just follow the main road through Kalekol and it takes a circuitous route to the far side of the lodge.

Although reportedly busy on weekends, the lodge was deserted when I visited on a weekday and the underworked staff were happy to pass the time playing darts in the bar. The cottages are all self-contained and cost US$48/96 for singles/doubles with full board. Day visitors are catered for in the restaurant if you're not staying the night. Although the water once used to lap at the edge of the bar terrace, it is now more than 100 metres away across a blinding expanse of sand.

ELIYE SPRINGS

This is a far more attractive place than Ferguson's Gulf but is inaccessible without a 4WD. The small village here has an army post, a couple of dozen grass huts, and a lodge which is of marginal status to say the least. The springs however do provide moisture enough for a curious variety of palm tree (the doum palm) to grow here which gives the place a very misplaced tropical island feel. This particular palm tree has an unusually shaped fruit which the locals eat.

If you do make it here you will be greeted by a number of Turkana girls and young women selling trinkets at absurdly cheap prices. With an average of one vehicle a week, it's a real buyer's market. Items for sale might include fossilised hippo teeth and fish backbones threaded into necklaces!

Places to Stay & Eat

The only way you can stay here is to camp and you must bring your own food with you.

The lodge fell apart years ago though there are still one or two workers milling around. Rumour has it that it may reopen one day.

Getting There & Away

The turn-off for Eliye Springs is signposted about halfway along the road from Lodwar to Kalekol. There are a few patches of heavy sand so a 4WD is advisable although you'd probably get through in a conventional vehicle. As there are so few vehicles, hitching is not an option and it's 35 long hot km if you plan to walk it.

LOKICHOKIO

This frontier town is the last on the Pan African Highway before the Sudan border. The road has been sealed all the way here and is in excellent condition but you can't get beyond Lokichokio without a police permit. Even if this was forthcoming, the area is not safe as long as the civil war in southern Sudan continues.

Places to Stay

There's a hotel of sorts here with a couple of mud huts out the back, and there's a bar in town. On the other hand, if you get this far, you'll probably find yourself staying with aid/famine relief workers who take care of the refugee camps around here.

East of Turkana

There are two main routes here. The first is the A2 highway from Nairobi to Marsabit, via Isiolo and Laisamis, and north from there to Moyale on the Ethiopian border. The other is from Nairobi to Maralal, via Gilgil and Nyahururu or via Nakuru and Lake Baringo, and north from there to Loyangalani on Lake Turkana, via Baragoi and South Horr. It's also possible to cross from Isiolo to Maralal. From Loyangalani you can make a loop all the way round the top of the Chalbi Desert to Marsabit via North Horr and Maikona.

Getting There & Around

Bus & Matatu Mwingi buses run from Isiolo to Marsabit but there is no real schedule so you could be stuck in either place for a few days waiting for the bus to arrive. The fare is US$6.80. There's no alternative except to simply hang around and wait or either negotiate a ride on a truck (relatively easy and usually somewhat less than the bus fare) or walk out to the police checkpoint north of Isiolo town where the tarmac ends and hitch a ride with tourists (not so easy). A convoy system is in operation in order to deter shiftas from stopping and robbing trucks, buses and cars.

Mwingi also operates buses from Isiolo to Maralal a few times a week (depending on demand) which cost US$6.50.

North of Maralal, the only public transport is a matatu which plies between Maralal and Baragoi once daily if demand warrants it.

Car & 4WD None of the roads in this region are surfaced and the main A2 route is corrugated *piste* which will shake the guts out of both you and your vehicle depending on your speed. The road connecting Isiolo with Maralal (which branches off the A2 north of Archer's Post) is similarly corrugated but otherwise in good shape. The road from Lake Baringo to Maralal and from Maralal to Loyangalani, however, is surprisingly smooth though there are bad patches here and there including a diabolical section of several km from the plateau down to Lake Turkana.

The main cross route between Isiolo and Maralal the two is via Wamba and Parsaloi (though you don't actually go through Wamba itself). This road leaves the main A2 about 20 km north of Archer's Post and joins the Maralal to Loyangalani road about 15 km south of Baragoi. Though a minor route, this road is very smooth most of the way with the occasional rough patch. Its main drawback is the steep-sided luggas, none of which are bridged. In the dry season you won't have any problems with a 4WD (impossible with a 2WD) but you can forget about it in the wet season. The worst of these luggas is just

outside Wamba and there's a way around it by taking the Maralal road from Wamba and turning first right along a dirt road once you've crossed an obvious bridge. You'll probably only use it if you want to visit the Mathews Range and the Ndoto Mountains.

Forget about the Maralal to Parsaloi road marked on the Survey of Kenya maps. It's all washed out and you won't even make it in 4WD.

NATIONAL PARKS & RESERVES

Just north of Isiolo are three national reserves, **Samburu**, **Buffalo Springs** and **Shaba**, all of them along the banks of the Ewaso Nyiro River and covering an area of some 300 sq km. They are mainly scrub desert and open savannah plain, broken here and there by small rugged hills. The river, however, which is permanent, supports a wide variety of game and you can see elephants, buffaloes, cheetahs, leopards and lions as well as dik-dik, wart hogs, Grevy's zebra and the reticulated giraffe. Crocodiles can also be seen on certain sandy stretches of the river bank. You are guaranteed close-up sightings of elephants, reticulated giraffe and various species of smaller gazelle in both Samburu and Buffalo Springs but other game is remarkably thin on the ground, particularly on the route into Samburu from Archer's Post. The rhino were wiped out years ago by poachers.

If you are driving around these parks in your own vehicle it's useful to have a copy of the Survey of Kenya map, *Samburu & Buffalo Springs Game Reserves* (SK 85).

The roads inside Buffalo Springs and Samburu are well maintained and it's easy to get around, even in 2WD, though you might need a 4WD on some of the minor tracks.

Entry to all three parks or game reserves costs US$12 per person plus US$1.50 per vehicle per day. Even though they're contiguous, if you drive from Buffalo Springs to Samburu (or vice versa) in one day then you'll have to pay two lots of park entry fees. However, if it's very late in the afternoon when you cross the boundary, the guards will

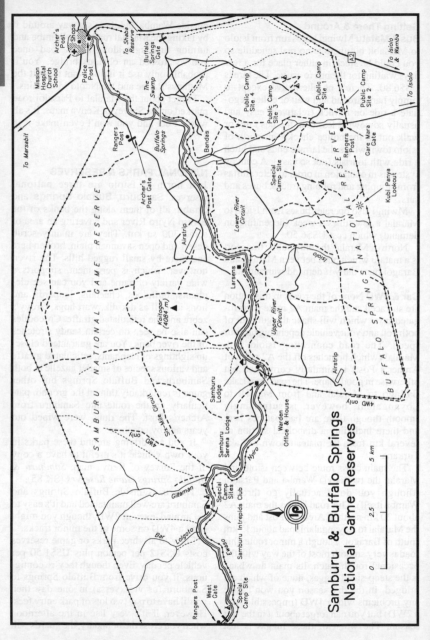

Samburu & Buffalo Springs
National Game Reserves

generally postdate your ticket for the following day.

These parks are much less touristed than Amboseli or Masai Mara so, once you're out of the immediate vicinity of the lodges and camp sites, you'll frequently have the place to yourself.

Places to Stay

Buffalo Springs In Buffalo Springs National Reserve there are four *public camp sites* close to the Gare Mara entrance gate (the nearest to Isiolo and accessible from the main Isiolo to Marsabit road). However, none of them are particularly safe as far as robberies go so stick with a group and make sure your tent is guarded when you're out on game drives or pack it up and take it with you. There's also a *special camp site* further west. Camping costs US$2.50 per person per night.

For those with adequate finances, there's the *Buffalo Springs Tented Lodge* (☎ (0165) 2234) up at the north-eastern end of the reserve just south of the Ewaso Nyiro River. The lodge consists of 30 tents shielded from the sun by makuti roofs and each with its own bathroom. There are also eight cottages which sleep two to four people. The lodge has a swimming pool and a bar/restaurant overlooking a natural spring where you can sit and observe the wildlife. In the high season, tents or cottages cost US$106/156 for singles/doubles with full board; the price includes a game drive. Advance bookings can be made through African Tours & Hotels Ltd (☎ (02) 221855), PO Box 30471, Nairobi. The best access to the lodge is either from the Gare Mara Gate or the Buffalo Springs Gate just south of Archer's Post.

Samburu In Samburu National Game Reserve, the most convenient places to stay are the *public camp sites* close to the Samburu Lodge and close to the wooden bridge which connects the western extremity of Buffalo Springs to Samburu across the Ewaso Nyiro River. The sites themselves are fairly pleasant and adjacent to the river but the facilities are minimal and the 'toilets' are

nothing short of pigsties. If you don't want to cook for yourself their only advantage is that they're very close to the lodge with its restaurant and bar. There are also two *special camp sites* further west. Camping costs US$2.50 per person per night.

For those with money, there's a choice of five top-range lodges/tented camps. The most popular is perhaps the *Samburu Lodge* which is part of the Block Hotels chain (☎ (02) 335807), PO Box 47557, Nairobi. It's built right alongside the river and consists of a main building (stone and makuti roof) which houses the restaurant, bar and reception area, and a series of self-contained cottages strung out along the river bank. The tariff depends on the season. In the high season it's US$123/182, whereas in the low season it's US$66/112 for singles/doubles, all with full board. Rates in the shoulder season are intermediate.

The lodge is the only place in the two parks where petrol can be bought. Game drives through the park can be organised at the lodge.

The supposed 'highlights' of any evening here are the appearance of a leopard across the other side of the river and the crocodiles which crawl up onto a sandy bank adjacent to the bar. The leopard, which is lured by a hunk of meat strung up from a tree by two very blasé employees just before dusk, is extremely contrived but Kodak make a fortune supplying film to fools who think they can get anything but a picture of midnight in the bush with an Instamatic from about 100 metres. The crocodile 'show' is equally contrived but at least it takes place right in front of you even if pieces of dead meat in the sand don't encourage dynamism.

Further east and also alongside the river is *Larsens* which is a luxury tented camp also owned by the Block Hotels chain. The rates depend on the season. In the high season (15 December to 31 March and 1 July to 31 August) full board costs US$166/242 in a tent and US$209/286 for a suite, whereas in the low season (1 April to 30 June) the corresponding rates are US$70/140 and US$83/166. For the rest of the year the costs are intermediate. All these rates include two game drives.

The *Samburu Intrepids Club* (☎ 338084 in Nairobi), further upstream on the northern side of the river, is another luxury tented lodge and more like a beach resort in many ways. A night here costs US$138/208.

The *Samburu Serena Lodge* charges US$124/156 for full board in the high season and US$46/91 in the low season. For bookings contact Serena Lodges & Hotels (☎ (02) 710511), PO Box 48690, Nairobi. The last place is the *Samburu Lodge*, which charges US$138/198 for full board.

You can take any of the park access gates to get to these lodges but remember that if you drive through Buffalo Springs and into Samburu on the same day then you'll be up for two lots of park entry fees. You can avoid this by entering through the Archer's Post gate.

Shaba The spectacular *Shaba Sarova Lodge* in Shaba National Game Reserve has single/double rooms with full board for US$165/208. For campers there's a beautiful camp site about 20 minutes' drive away. There's abundant firewood here but you need to bring water from the lodge.

WAMBA

Wamba is a small, essentially one-street town off the Isiolo to Maralal road north of Samburu National Game Reserve and a sort of provincial headquarters for the surrounding area. There's precious little here for the traveller and its only claim to fame is that it was from here that John Hillaby organised his camel trek to Lake Turkana which resulted in his book, *Journey to the Jade Sea*.

It has quite a few well-stocked dukas, a butchery, a hospital, schools and a large police station but no bank and no electricity despite its proximity to Isiolo.

Places to Stay & Eat

There's only one lodge in the village and that is the *Saudia Lodge* run by Jamal which is at the back of the main street off to the right-hand side coming into town (signposted). Jamal – and indeed his whole family – is very friendly and helpful. You get a pleasant,

clean room here (mosquito nets, soap, towel and toilet paper are provided) for just US$4/5.80 a single/double. Bathroom facilities are communal. A wholesome breakfast can be provided for you if you order it in advance.

There's a lively bar on the main street, on the right-hand side as you enter the main part of town, where you can drink your fill though there's no refrigeration. You can't miss it – just listen for the cassette player blaring away!

MARALAL

Maralal is high up in the hills above the Lerochi Plateau (essentially a continuation of the central highlands), north of Nyahururu and Nanyuki and north-west of Isiolo, and connected to all these towns by gravel roads. Surrounding it is the Maralal National Sanctuary which is home to zebras, impala, eland, buffaloes, hyenas and wart hogs, all of which you can see from the road leading into Maralal from the south or at the Maralal Safari Lodge which has the only permanent water hole in the area.

It's an attractive area of grassy undulating plains and coniferous forests which was once coveted by White settlers in the colonial era. However, their designs for taking it over were scotched by the colonial authorities due to anticipated violent opposition from the Samburu for whom it holds a special significance.

The town itself, while a regional headquarters, retains a decidedly frontier atmosphere. There's a sense of excitement blowing in the wind which frequently sweeps the plains and whips up the dust in this somewhat ramshackle, but very lively, township with its wide streets and wild west-type verandahs. It's also the preferred route and overnight centre for the safari companies which take people up to Lake Turkana. People here are very friendly and it's a great place to buy Samburu handicrafts.

There's a post office (with telephones), petrol stations, mechanics, the only bank north of Isiolo other than in Marsabit, shops with a good range of stock, hotels, bars, one

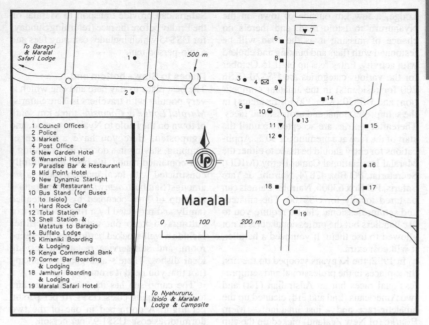

1 Council Offices
2 Police
3 Market
4 Post Office
5 New Garden Hotel
6 Wananchi Hotel
7 Paradise Bar & Restaurant
8 Mid Point Hotel
9 New Dynamic Starlight
   Bar & Restaurant
10 Bus Stand (for Buses
    to Isiolo)
11 Hard Rock Café
12 Total Station
13 Shell Station &
    Matutus to Baragio
14 Buffalo Lodge
15 Kimaniki Boarding
    & Lodging
16 Kenya Commercial Bank
17 Corner Bar Boarding
    & Lodging
18 Jamhuri Boarding
    & Lodging
19 Maralal Safari Hotel

Maralal

To Baragoi
& Maralal
Safari Lodge

500 m

To Nyahururu,
Isiolo & Maralal
Lodge & Campsite

of the best camp sites in Kenya, a surprising number of butchers' shops and regular bus transport to Isiolo. There are also matatus to Baragoi which leave from the Shell station. If you're not travelling with a safari company you may well consider spending a few days here. It's a bizarre but captivating place.

Information

The Kenya Commercial Bank is open during normal banking hours. This is the last bank going north apart from those in Marsabit so stock up on cash.

The post office is open normal hours and the staff are very helpful should you want to make national or international calls.

There are two petrol stations (Shell and Total) in the centre of town where you can be assured of getting what you need at regular prices. North of here you will only find petrol at Baragoi and Loyangalani, and if there is some it is always at a high price.

Safaris

Regular camel safaris depart from Yare Safaris' Maralal Lodge & Campsite and they can also arrange safaris to Lake Turkana by truck (see the Getting Around and Northern Kenya chapters for details).

Maralal International Camel Derby

Inaugurated by Yare Safaris in 1990, this annual event takes place on the Saturday of the third week of October. It's a great time to be here and the three races which are held (amateurs, semiprofessional, and professional) are open to everyone. It attracts riders and spectators from the four corners of the earth, there's substantial prize money to be won (US$10,000), the media is there in force, you can make excellent contacts which will stand you in good stead for the rest of your trip, it's good fun, and, last but not least, it's one hell of a binge! Even George Thesiger attends!

The races start and finish at Yare's Maralal

Lodge, a few km outside of town on the Nyahururu to Isiolo road, and there's no chance of missing it as the road will be festooned with flags and bunting and choked with activity. Entry fees up until 15 October for the various categories are US$20 (KSh 200 for residents) in the amateur competition; and US$30 (KSh 300 for residents) in the semiprofessional and professional races. Thereafter, entries are accepted up until the start of the race at a premium of 50%. Applications for entry should be made to either the Maralal International Camel Derby (MICD) Secretariat, PO Box 47874, Nairobi, or Yare Safaris, PO Box 63006, Nairobi. Camels can be hired locally for US$100. The amateur and semiprofessional classes require you to use handlers but the professional class is not allowed to use them. If you need a handler, it will cost extra.

In 1992, the Kenyans scooped up the first three places in the professional and semiprofessional races but an Australian (1st) and two Americans (2nd and 3rd) cleaned up the amateur race – just imagine! – Mem Bourke (of New Zealand) picked up the cup for 'Best Lady'.

To tie in with this event, Yare is also organising an annual Great Kenyan Camel Endurance Race (beginning 1993) which takes 18 days and covers around 660 km. The race begins at Isiolo and ends in Maralal on the day before the Camel Derby and the entry fee is US$700 per team (four people). The first prize is worth US$50,000. If you're thinking of entering, four camels, saddles and a handler can be hired for US$35 per day plus US$250 per team for camel insurance and US$250 per team for vet coverage.

A substantial amount of the money made on these events goes towards the provision of medical facilities for the Samburu people.

And just in case you're thinking this is a good laugh for the humans but a lousy deal for the animals, International Camel Races Association rules apply so the camels are checked daily by a vet and monitored by a KSPCA officer.

Get yourself up there! This is one of the major events on the Kenyan calendar. Yare Safaris can provide transport to Maralal on the Friday before the race (returning Sunday) for US$45 which includes camping fees and a two-person tent.

Places to Stay – bottom end

The best place to stay here and one which is very popular with travellers is Yare Safaris' *Maralal Lodge & Campsite*, three km south of town on the Isiolo to Nyahururu road, and signposted. Here you have a choice of camping, staying in a dormitory or renting a self-contained banda. It's been thoughtfully constructed with local materials and is set amongst Samburu *manyattas*. (A manyatta is a group of huts occupied by an extended family and protected by a ring of thorn tree cuttings to keep out wildlife.) Facilities include a well-stocked bar/lounge, reference room, and self-service restaurant serving local dishes. There's also guarded parking (not that you need it around here).

The camp site has its own showers and toilets. Camping costs US$1.70 per person per night. A dorm bed in one of the two dormitories costs US$1.95 per person.

The self-contained bandas are clean, comfortable and excellent value at US$8 a single and US$12 a double which includes breakfast.

Advance booking for the dormitories and camp site is not normally necessary but it's a good idea for the bandas. Advance booking is essential for any sort of accommodation here during the week of the camel derby (third week of October). For bookings, contact Yare Safaris (☎ 214099; fax 213445), 1st Floor, Union Towers, Mama Ngina St, PO Box 63006, Nairobi.

In Maralal itself the most popular place to stay is the *Buffalo Lodge* (☎ 2228) which is a fairly modern structure offering rooms with clean sheets, towels and hot water in the mornings for US$6.70 a single or double. It's a lively place and there's a bar/video room at the back. Sammy, the barman here, is a real live wire and very friendly.

Cheaper but excellent value is the *Kimaniki Boarding & Lodging* which is a two-storey wooden building offering good rooms for US$1.10/2.20 a single/double. Clean sheets are provided as well as hot showers (if requested) and vehicles can be parked safely in the hotel compound. There's also the *Mid Point Hotel* (☎ 2221) which offers good lodging for single people at US$1.10 plus hot water in the mornings. Also good value is the *Paradise Bar & Restaurant* which has singles/doubles for US$1.60/3.10 with hot water in the mornings.

Other possibilities include the *Corner Bar Boarding & Lodging, Jamhuri Boarding & Lodging, Maralal Safari Hotel, New Garden Hotel* and *Wananchi Hotel* – all rather basic.

Places to Stay – top end
The only top-range hotel in Maralal is the *Maralal Safari Lodge* (☎ 2060 in Maralal; 225641 in Nairobi), PO Box 70, Maralal and PO Box 42475, Nairobi. It consists of a main building housing a restaurant, bar and souvenir shop and a series of cottages. It costs US$68/90 for singles/doubles with half board and US$72/98 with full board. Children's rates are US$22/24 respectively. Meals are available to nonguests for US$4.60 (breakfast) and US$8.60 (lunch or dinner). The staff here are pleasant and Diners Club cards are accepted. There's a watering hole, which attracts a varied selection of game, right in front of the bar's verandah so you can watch the animals whilst sipping a cold beer. The lodge is quite a way from the centre of Maralal (about three km), off the road to Baragoi (signposted).

Places to Eat & Entertainment
The best place to eat here is the relatively new *Hard Rock Café* opposite the Shell station. The food is good and the staff are friendly and eager to please. As a result, it's the most popular place in town.

The liveliest bar – and one where you can get good, tasty, cheap food – is the improbably named *New Dynamic Starlight Bar & Restaurant* which, nevertheless, lives up to its name. The inside rooms are painted with the most bizarre and florid representations of African flora & fauna and there's even a traditionally dressed Samburu hooker here most evenings who does a roaring trade. Unfortunately, there's no refrigeration so the beers are warm but the company makes up for it and some of the characters who come in here have walked straight out of a Breugel canvas. It's a great spot to meet local live wires, get completely out of it and have numerous animated conversations.

The Buffalo Lodge also has two good bars but the one out at the back, although the best, is essentially a video lounge.

There's usually a disco on Friday and Saturday nights so, if you're interested, ask around.

Getting There & Away
If you're not coming in on a Yare Safaris' bus, Mwingi operates buses every second day to Isiolo which cost US$6.50. They leave from the dirt patch in front of the New Garden Hotel.

There are also matatus to Nyahururu daily which leave early in the morning, and usually one to Baragoi, though this only runs when there's sufficient demand. Matatus leave from in front of the Shell station.

MATHEWS RANGE
North of Wamba, off the link road between the Isiolo to Marsabit road and the Maralal to Loyangalani road via Parsaloi, is the Mathews Range. Much of this area is thickly forested and supports rhinos, elephants, lions, buffaloes and many other animal species. The highest peak here rises to 2285 metres. The whole area is very undeveloped and populated by Samburu tribespeople but the government is in the process of making it into a game sanctuary especially for the rhino. Some of the tribespeople are already employed to protect the rhino from poachers and there's a game warden's centre.

A few km from this centre (where you have to report on the way in, though there are no charges as yet) is a camp site with no facilities other than river water and firewood. At one time it was a well set-up research centre, as the derelict huts indicate. It's a superb site and a genuine African bush experience. You are miles from the nearest village and elephants are quite likely to trundle through your camp in the middle of the night – lions too. During the day, traditionally dressed Samburu warriors will probably visit you to see if you need a guide (which you will if you want to see game or climb to the top of the range as we did). Agree on a reasonable price beforehand, and remember you'll also have to pay for the one who stays behind to guard your vehicle.

Also, don't forget that the rules of hospitality will oblige you to provide them with a beer, soft drink or cup of tea, a few cigarettes and perhaps a snack when you get back to camp. They're extremely friendly people. One or two will be able to speak English (the nearest school is in Wamba) but most can converse in Swahili as well as Samburu.

Another accommodation possibility is the *Kitich Camp* (☎ (0176) 22053), on the banks of the Ngeng River, off the Wamba to Parsaloi road about 40 km from Wamba. It's mainly set up as a luxury tented camp with all the facilities, and it costs US$90 a double with full board. It's also possible to camp for US$4.50 per person, but the facilities for independent campers are minimal.

Getting There & Away

Getting to the camp site in the Mathews Range is not at all easy, even with 4WD. There are many different tracks going all over the place and you are going to have to stop many times to ask the way. Perhaps the best approach is from the Wamba to Parsaloi road. Just before Wamba you will get to a T-junction. Instead of going into Wamba, continue north and take the first obvious main track off to the right, several km after the junction. If there are tyre tracks in the sand – follow them. There are two missions down this track and both have vehicles. You will be able to ask the way at either.

One of the mission stations is right next to a large river course which generally has some water flowing through it and which you have to ford. If you get lost, ask a local tribesman to come along and guide you but remember that you will have to drive him

back to his manyatta after you have found the place. No-one in their right mind walks around in the bush after dark except in large groups – the buffaloes and elephants make it too dangerous. It might sound like a *tour de force* getting to this place but it's well worth it!

PARSALOI

Further north, Parsaloi (sometimes spelt Barsaloi) is a small scattered settlement with a few very basic shops but no petrol station. It has a large Catholic Mission which may or may not offer to accommodate you or allow you to camp. There are no lodges. The EC recently funded the building of quite a large school.

There are two very rugged and steep-sided luggas at this point on the road, one on either side of the village, and you'll definitely need 4WD to negotiate them.

BARAGOI

Next on is Baragoi, a more substantial settlement full of tribespeople, a couple of very basic lodges, a new and better appointed hotel, and a few shops. There's also a derelict petrol station but petrol can usually be bought here from a barrel – the local people will show you where to find it. If you're White, you'll probably be the only one in town and therefore an object of considerable curiosity. Quite a few people speak English around here. The town seems to get rain when everywhere else is dry so the surroundings are quite green.

Be careful not to take photographs in the town as it's supposedly forbidden and the local police are keen to enforce the rule and are not at all pleasant about it.

Places to Stay & Eat

If you ask at any of the restaurants in town they'll usually come up with accommodation but it will be very basic – just a bed in a bare room with no toilet facilities. Some will also allow you to camp in their back yards.

If you have camping equipment, the best place to stay is the camp site at the water-pumping station about four km to the north

The Turkana

Originally from the Karamajong district of north-eastern Uganda, the Turkana number around 250,000 and live in the virtual desert country of Kenya's north-west. Due to their isolation, the Turkana are probably the least affected by the 20th century of all Kenya's people.

Like the Samburu and the Maasai (with whom they are linguistically linked) the Turkana are cattle herders first, and more recently have taken up fishing the waters of Lake Turkana and even growing the occasional crops, weather permitting. But unlike these other two tribes the Turkana have discontinued the practice of circumcision.

The traditional dress of the Turkana people is amazing, as is the number of people who still wear it – catching a bus up in the north-west is a real eye-opener for a first-time visitor. The men cover part of their hair with mud which is then painted blue and decorated with ostrich and other feathers. The main garment they wear, despite the blast-furnace heat of the region, is a woollen blanket (usually a garish modern checked one) which is worn around one shoulder.

Traditional accessories include a small wooden stool carved out of a single piece of wood (used either as a pillow or a stool), a wooden stick with a distinctive shape, and a wrist knife. Both the men and the women wear with great flourish the lip plug through the lower lip which looks a bit gruesome. The women wear a variety of beaded and metal adornment, much of it indicating to the trained eye events in the woman's life. A half skirt of animal skins and a piece of black cloth are the only garments worn although these days pieces of colourful cloth are not uncommon for use as baby slings.

Tattooing is also surprisingly common and it

Turkana woman

too is usually indicative of something. Men are tattooed on the shoulders and upper arm each time they kill an enemy – the right shoulder for killing a man, the left for a woman – and it's surprising the number of men you still see with these markings. Witch doctors and prophets are held in high regard and tattooing on someone's lower stomach is usually a sign of witch doctors' attempts to cast out an undesirable spirit rather than any sort of decoration. ∎

---

of town. To get there, take the road north towards South Horr. After a while you'll go through a small gully and then, a little further on, across a usually dry river bed. Take the next track on the right-hand side and follow this for about one km. It will bring you to a concrete house and a fairly open patch of

ground. This is the camp site and there's always someone around. Facilities include toilets and showers and your tent will be guarded by Samburu warriors. It costs about US$2.50 per person per night. Trips can be arranged to nearby manyattas for a small fee and you'll be allowed to take photographs.

There's a large new *hotel* in town which costs US$5.80/12 for a clean single/double with shared bathroom. It's the first building you come to when arriving in Baragoi from the south.

For food in the town itself, the best is the *Wid-Wid Inn* run by Mrs Fatuma. It's on the top side of the main street and you'll know you've got the right place because all the staff wear garishly pink pinafores! She'll cook you up an absolutely delicious meat stew and chapatis for dinner as well as pancakes, omelettes and tea for breakfast.

There are also two bars in the town but only one of them – the *Sam Celia Joy Bar*, at the end of the main street going north – usually has beers. The other, on the back street, usually only has *conyagi* (local firewater) and other spirits.

SOUTH HORR

The next village is South Horr which is set in a beautiful lush canyon between the craggy peaks of Mt Nyiro (2752 metres) and Mt Porale (1990 metres) and Mt Supuko (2066 metres). It's a lively little place with a huge Catholic Mission but there's no petrol available.

There are two small and very basic hotels on the main street – the *Mt Nyiro Hotel* and the *Good Tourist Hotel* – where you can find accommodation of sorts as well as a reasonably tasty meal of meat stew, mandazi and tea for around US$2 per person. The hotels will generally need up to two hours' notice if you want to eat, but tea is usually immediately available.

There's a camp site (the signpost reads 'Camping' but it's easy to miss) about 12 km out of town on the right-hand side as you head north. It's a pleasant site owned by Safari Camp Services in Nairobi and facilities include showers and toilets. There's also plenty of firewood. The charge is US$2 per person per night. Guards can be arranged to watch your tent if you want to eat in town.

South Horr also sports a very lively bar – the *Serima Bar* – on the main road heading north out of town. It's only open in the evenings and seems to have a plentiful supply of beer though there is no refrigeration.

LAKE TURKANA (THE JADE SEA)

Further north, the lushness of the Horr Valley gradually peters out until, finally, you reach the totally barren, shattered lava beds at the southern end of Lake Turkana. Top the ridge here and there it is in front of you – the Jade Sea. It's a breathtaking sight – vast and yet apparently totally barren. You'll see nothing living here except a few brave, stunted thorn trees. When you reach the lake shore, you'll know why – it's a soda lake and, at this end, highly saline. The northern end of the lake isn't anywhere near as saline because it's fed by the Omo River from Ethiopia (is that where the name of the washing powder came from!?). At this point, most people abandon whatever vehicle they're in and plunge into the lake. If you do this, watch out for crocodiles. They're quite partial to a meal of red meat as a change from Nile perch.

LOYANGALANI

A little further up the lake shore and you are in Loyangalani – Turkana 'city'. There is an airstrip, post office, fishing station, luxury lodge, two camp sites, a Catholic Mission (which may reluctantly sell petrol at up to three times the price in Nairobi) and all of it surrounded by the yurt-like, stick and doum-palm dwellings of the Turkana tribespeople. Taking photographs of people or their houses here will attract 'fees'.

If you're an independent traveller, the Oasis Lodge can organise trips to the village where the El-Molo live. Otherwise, ask the safari-truck drivers at the camp sites if they have room for you – organised safaris to this part of Kenya usually include a trip to the El-Molo village. They're one of the smallest tribes in Africa and quite different from the Turkana though it seems their days are numbered as a distinct tribe. Tourism has also wrought inevitable changes in their lifestyle and you may feel that the whole thing has been thoroughly commercialised. You'll also pay handsomely for taking photographs. One traveller who felt the tribe had totally

Skull 1470

In the early 1970s, archaeologist Richard Leakey (now head of the Kenya Wildlife Service) made a significant fossil find on the shores of Lake Turkana. It was the discovery of a fossilised skull, which came to be known somewhat prosaically as 1470 (its Kenya Museum index number).

The almost complete, but fragmented, skull was thought to be from an early hominid. It was hoped that it would back up earlier fossil discoveries made by the Leakeys in the Olduvai Gorge in Tanzania in the '60s which suggested that the direct human ancestral line went back further than the 1½ million years that most people thought at the time.

The pieces of the skull were painstakingly fitted together – a demanding task in itself which kept two people fully occupied for over six weeks. The completed jigsaw confirmed what they had suspected: here was an evolutionary sophisticated hominid, named *Homo habilis*, which was a direct ancestor of *Homo sapiens*. It was 2½ million years old.

Since then *homo* fossil finds have been made which push the date back even further, but at the time the 1470 was a very important person'! ∎

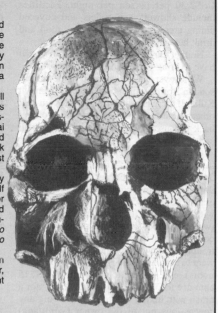

'prostituted' their traditional way of life to make money from tourists has put it this way, 'If they live on fish it must be smoked salmon and caviar'.

Trips to **Mt Kulal** and **Mt Porr** can also be arranged at the Oasis Club but they're expensive. The Mt Kulal trip is a part-drive, part-walking trip up to the forest there, and Mt Porr is a well-known fossicking spot. A better thing to do would be to get in touch with Francis Langachar who is a very friendly young Turkana man and ask him to organise something similar for you. He speaks fluent English, and his father accompanied John Hillaby on his trek to Lake Turkana, recounted in *Journey to the Jade Sea*.

Places to Stay & Eat

Of the two camp sites, it's hard to favour one over the other though only one has a restaurant and bar. Both are staffed by very friendly people and theft doesn't appear to be a problem at either of them. The first you come to is *El-Molo Camp* (☎ (02) 724384), PO Box 34710, Nairobi. It has excellent facilities including good showers and toilets, a swimming pool (US$4.50 for day use), a large dining hall and bar (with cold beers!) and electricity up to 9.30 pm at night (kerosene lanterns after that). Camping costs US$2.70 per person per night. There are also 20 self-contained bandas for rent which cost US$52/83 a single/double with full board. Meals can be ordered at short notice in the dining room here whether you are staying on the site or not, but they take a long time to arrive: 1½ hours is normal. The food, on the other hand, is very good. Cold beers naturally cost more than in Nairobi but are still very reasonably priced.

The other camp site adjacent to El-Molo is *Sunset Strip Camp,* which is also run by Safari Camp Services in Nairobi. It costs

US$2.30 per person per night. Facilities include showers and toilets and covered dining areas but you cannot buy food and drink here and there's no electricity.

Neither camp site has firewood so you'll have to bring your own from further south.

Whichever place you camp at, beware of sudden storms which can descend from Mt Kulal. If there is a storm, stay with your tent otherwise it may not be there when you get back because of the wind, and neither will anything else.

Other than the camp sites there is the luxury *Oasis Lodge* (☎ (02) 751190; PO Box 34464, Nairobi) which has 25 self-contained double bungalows with electricity (own generator) at US$105/150 for a single/double with full board. It's a beautiful place with two spring-fed swimming pools, and ice-cold beers and meals are available. The only trouble is, if you are not staying there but want to use the facilities (bar and swimming pools), it's going to cost you a US$15 entrance fee. It's a lot of money to pay for a brush with luxury but you won't wring any concessions out of the owner (Wolfgang) who can be quite belligerent about this. Basically, he doesn't want what he considers to be 'riffraff' marring the tone of the place.

Other than the El-Molo Camp, there are a couple of basic teahouses on the main street of Loyangalani and, if you ask around, you'll meet villagers who will cook up a meal of Nile perch for you in their houses.

Getting There & Away

There is no scheduled transport of any sort in or out of Loyangalani, so you need to be independent.

NORTH HORR

North of Loyangalani the road loops over the lava beds to North Horr. There is a short cut across the desert through the village of Gus.

There are no lodges here and no petrol available but the people at the Catholic Mission are very friendly and will probably offer you somewhere to stay for the night if you are stuck. It's staffed by German and Dutch people.

MAIKONA

Next down the line is Maikona where there is a large village with basic shops (but no lodges) and a very friendly Catholic Mission and school, staffed by Italian people, where you will undoubtedly be offered a place to stay for the night. Please leave a donation before you go if you stay here. The mission usually has electricity and the Father goes into Marsabit once a fortnight in his Land Rover.

MARSABIT

South of Maikona is Marsabit, where you are back in relative civilisation. Here there are three petrol stations, a bank, post office, dry cleaners, shops, bars and lodges, buses and an airport. The main attraction here though is the Marsabit National Park & Reserve centred around Mt Marsabit (1702 metres).

The hills here are thickly forested and in stark contrast to the desert on all sides. Mist often envelopes them in the early morning and mosses hang from tree branches. The views from the telecommunications tower on the summit above town are magnificent in all directions. In fact, they're probably as spectacular as any of the views from Mt Kenya or Kilimanjaro. The whole area is peppered with extinct volcanoes and volcanic craters (called *gofs*), some of which have a lake on the crater floor.

One of the most memorable sights in Marsabit is the tribespeople thronging the streets and roads into town. Most noticeable are the Rendille with their elaborate braided hairstyles and dressed in skins, fantastic multicoloured beaded necklaces and bracelets. These people graze camels and, like the Samburu and Maasai, show little interest in adopting a more sedentary lifestyle, preferring to roam the deserts and only visiting the towns when necessary for trade. They are the major non-Muslim people in what is otherwise a largely Muslim area.

The other major tribes are the Boran and the Gabra, both pastoralists who graze cattle rather than camels. They're allied to the Galla peoples of Ethiopia from where they originated several hundred years ago. Many

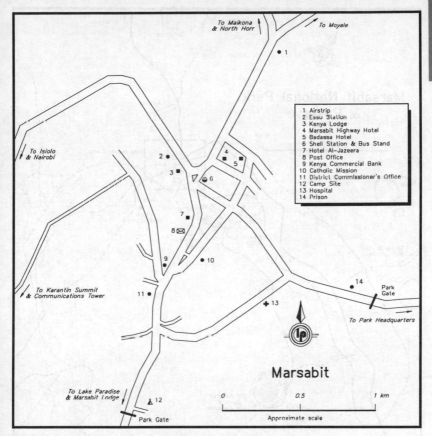

1 Airstrip
2 Esso Station
3 Kenya Lodge
4 Marsabit Highway Hotel
5 Badassa Hotel
6 Shell Station & Bus Stand
7 Hotel Al-Jazeera
8 Post Office
9 Kenya Commercial Bank
10 Catholic Mission
11 District Commissioner's Office
12 Camp Site
13 Hospital
14 Prison

To Maikona & North Horr

To Moyale

To Isiolo & Nairobi

To Karantin Summit & Communications Tower

Park Gate

To Park Headquarters

To Lake Paradise & Marsabit Lodge

Park Gate

Marsabit

0   0.5   1 km

Approximate scale

have abandoned their former transient life style and settled down to more sedentary activities. In the process, many have adopted Islam and the modes of dress of the Somalis with whom they trade and who have also migrated into the area. There are also quite a few Ethiopians in town as a result of that country's tragic and turbulent recent past.

Marsabit National Park & Reserve

The Marsabit National Park & Reserve is home to a wide variety of the larger mammals including lions, leopards, cheetahs, elephants, rhinos, buffaloes, wart hogs, Grevy's zebra, the reticulated giraffe, hyena, Grant's gazelle, oryx, dik-dik and greater kudu among others. Because the area is thickly forested, however, you won't see too much game unless you spend quite some time here and, preferably, camp at **Lake Paradise**. The lake, which occupies much of the crater floor of Gof Sokorte Guda, is appropriately named. It's an enchanting place and right out in the bush. Entry to the park, which is open from 6 am to 7.15 pm, costs US$12 per person plus US$1.50 for a vehicle.

The Survey of Kenya's map, *Marsabit*

KENYA

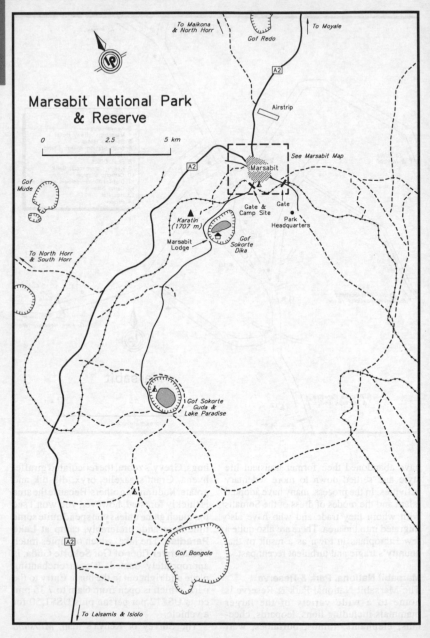

Marsabit National Park & Reserve

0   2.5   5 km

To Maikona & North Horr

Gof Redo

To Moyale

A2

Airstrip

See Marsabit Map

Marsabit

Gof Mude

A2

Karatin (1707 m)

Marsabit Lodge

Gof Sokorte Dika

Gate & Camp Site

Gate

Park Headquarters

To North Horr & South Horr

Gof Sokorte Guda & Lake Paradise

Gof Bongole

A2

To Laisamis & Isiolo

National Park & Reserve (SK 84) is worth buying if you are touring this park.

Places to Stay & Eat

In the Park Few camp sites in Kenya would rival the one at Lake Paradise. There are no facilities (except lake water and firewood) so bring everything with you. A ranger has to be present when you camp here so it costs more than an ordinary site (US$15 per group and only one group at a time) but you can arrange all this at the park entrance gate. There's also another good camp site next to the entrance gate (water and plenty of firewood) but the so-called showers are a joke. You could die of thirst waiting for enough water to wet the back of your ears here. Camping at this site costs US$1.90 per person.

There's also the *Marsabit Lodge* (☎ (0183) 2044), a luxury safari lodge overlooking a lake in another gof, Sokorte Dika. This costs US$51/79 for a single/double with full board, except from 1 April to 30 June when the price drops to US$29/57. Bookings can be made either directly with the lodge, or at Msafiri Inns (☎ (02) 229751), 11th Floor, Utalii House, Uhuru Highway, PO Box 42013, Nairobi.

In the Town If you have no camping equipment there's a good choice of lodges available in the town of Marsabit. One of the best is the *Kenya Lodge*. It's very clean and pleasant and rooms cost US$3.30/5.20 a single/double with soap and toilet roll provided. The showers are communal and the hotel has its own bar and restaurant at the front. The restaurant offers excellent Ethiopian food.

Almost as good is the *Marsabit Highway Hotel* which costs US$4.20 for a double with shower and toilet. It's a large place and very clean. The hotel has its own bar/restaurant which is open from 11 am to 2 pm and 5 pm to midnight. There is a disco on Friday and Saturday nights.

The cheapest place, though not such good value, is the *Hotel Al-Jazeera* which costs US$1.95 per person with communal

showers. There's a bar and restaurant at the front. For something vaguely mid-range, try the *Badassa Hotel*.

The best place for tea, mandazi and snacks is the *Bismillah Tea House* in front of the Catholic Technical School.

Getting There & Away

Mwingi buses run from Marsabit south to Isiolo and north to Moyale on the Ethiopian border. They supposedly run a couple of times a week depending on demand and breakdowns – be prepared for a wait. The cost to either place is US$6.80 and the trip to either takes six hours.

All vehicles, including buses travelling between Marsabit and Isiolo or Marsabit and Moyale, must travel in convoy. The reason for this is to minimise the danger of attack from shiftas.

MOYALE

Straddling the Kenyan-Ethiopian border, Moyale lies some 250 km north of Marsabit across the Dida Galgalu Desert. It's a small town of sandy streets with bars, a post office, police station, several shops selling basic commodities, and a small market area. Unlike Marsabit, however, where most of the roofs these days are of corrugated iron, there are still a large number of traditionally built houses here with sturdy pole frames supporting mud and stick roofs which can be up to half a metre thick thus ensuring that the interiors stay cool even when the outside temperature is 30°C and more.

There's not a great deal to do here, though the town attracts the occasional intrepid traveller either just for the hell of it or for the sake of an exotic passport stamp.

There is no bank in Moyale and only derelict petrol stations, so come prepared.

The Ethiopian side of the town is somewhat larger and the facilities are much better, with sealed roads, electricity, a number of bars and small restaurants, a hotel, and a lively market area.

Places to Stay & Eat

There are only three places to stay on the

Kenyan side of Moyale and they're all pretty basic. Probably the best of the bunch is the *Barissah Hotel* which also has the town's bar. Out at the back surrounding an earth compound there are several basic cubicles without locks where you can rent a bed for US$1.95 person. There are no showers (though you can order a bucket of water) and the place is far from clean but the staff are friendly. The Barissah is also the preferred place to eat, the usual fare being meat stew and chapatis.

If it's full, head for the *Bismillahi Boarding & Lodging* across from the Barissah and up behind the derelict Esso station. It's a family-run place and you'll find yourself sharing the same roof as the family. A bed here costs US$1.95 and facilities are absolutely minimal.

On the Ethiopian side of Moyale, the best place to stay is the *Bekele Molla Hotel* which is government owned and about two km from the border. It has a very lively bar – especially in the evenings – and the rooms are clean and self-contained.

For somewhere to eat closer to the border, try the *Negussie Hotel*, up on the hill to the left after you've crossed the border. It offers the standard Ethiopian fare of wat (a fierce hot sauce) and injera (bread made of millet flour), and there's also a bar here.

Kenyan shillings are acceptable when paying for meals and drinks.

Getting There & Away

Bus services between Marsabit and Moyale are detailed in the Marsabit section.

CROSSING TO ETHIOPA

Except for Kenyans and Ethiopians, this border was officially closed throughout Mengistu's regime but is now open, though you'll still need an Ethiopian visa to enter. This may well take some effort in Nairobi at the Ethiopian Embassy since you're required to have an airline ticket to Addis Ababa. References with clout obviously increase your chances of being able to enter overland. Otherwise, follow the rules to get your visa and trade in your Addis ticket later.

The North-East

Like the north of Kenya, the north-east up to the border with Somalia covers a vast area of desert and semidesert with very few centres of population and limited public transport possibilities. The main towns are Garissa and Wajir. Most of the area is relatively flat yet it's through here that one of Kenya's major rivers, the Tana, flows. The river enters the ocean about halfway between Malindi and Lamu and is the territory of the Orma, Pokomo and Bajun tribes. Straddling this river just north of Garsen is the Tana River Primate Sanctuary which is included on a few safari companies' itineraries but otherwise difficult to get to. The reserve was set up to protect the red colobus and crested mangabey monkeys both of which are endangered species. The other main river, the Ewaso Nyiro which flows through Samburu and Buffalo Springs national reserves, eventually peters out into the Lorian Swamp, never reaching the ocean.

Few travellers come this way except those taking the back route to Lamu via Garissa and Garsen. The area north and east of Garissa is now the domain of gun-toting 'refugees' from Somalia. When the UN/American troops went into Somalia in late 1992 to help in the distribution of food aid, many of those with guns sought shelter in Kenya where they could rustle cattle and create havoc with relative impunity. It's not a safe area to venture into unless you're with one of the aid agencies, and even then your safety is not guaranteed. Although the Somali border is still open, the country itself is pretty much a no-go area for the average traveller.

Other than a visit to Meru National Park, which would be worth it if security could be guaranteed, and the Tana River area, the north-east isn't a particularly interesting region even for desert fans, though Wajir, with its predominantly Somali population, Beau Geste fort and market, would definitely have the edge over Garissa, itself quite a nondescript town hardly worth stopping for.

Warning You should think twice before driving a vehicle around Meru National Park (or even taking an organised safari) until the poaching situation is resolved because tourists have been robbed at gunpoint and some of them actually shot dead. If you do go there and you're held up, don't mess about! Get your money and cameras out and hand them over. Any prevarication will invite a bullet in the head.

MERU NATIONAL PARK

On the lowland plains east of the town of Meru, the Meru National Park is a complete contrast to the more northerly reserves of Samburu, Buffalo Springs and Shaba where open bush is the norm. In Meru, abundant rainfall and numerous permanent streams flowing down from the Mt Kenya massif support a luxuriant jungle of forest, swamp and tall grasses which, in turn, provide fodder and shelter to a wide variety of herbivores and their predators. As in other parks, such as Marsabit, where the vegetation is dense, the wildlife is not so easily sighted so you need to spend a few days here if you're to fully appreciate what the park has to offer.

Unfortunately this area was one of the worst hit by poachers and shifta, and so there is not the abundance of wildlife that you find in other parks. With some difficulty, elephants, lions and cheetahs can all be seen. Buffaloes and giraffes are more common, and eland and oryx are the main antelope to be seen. Monkeys, crocodiles and a plethora of bird species are common in the dense vegetation alongside the watercourses.

Meru National Park was also the home of Kenya's only herd of white rhinos which were imported from the Umfolozi Game Reserve in South Africa. Jealously guarded 24 hours a day by rangers to protect them from poachers, these huge animals were quite unlike their more cantankerous cousins, the black rhino, in being remarkably docile and willing to allow their keepers to herd them around the camp sites and park headquarters area during the day and pen them up at night. Sadly, that's all gone now. Heavily armed poachers shot the lot of them and, for good measure, killed their keepers too.

The park is also famous for being Joy and George Adamson's former base where they raised orphaned lion and leopard cubs until they were old enough to be returned to the wild. Both paid for their efforts with their lives – Joy several years ago when she was murdered in Meru park by poachers, and George in 1989 when he too met the same fate along with two of his assistants in the nearby Kora National Reserve.

Security in the park has been beefed up since George Adamson was murdered but there is still a small risk of encountering poachers and bandits here so you need to bear this in mind, especially if you're driving your own vehicle. It's true to say, however, that the chances of running into bandits is just as great in Masai Mara or Tsavo as it is in Meru. The one major plus about Meru National Park is that you're unlikely to come across another safari vehicle anywhere in the park except outside the lodges.

The tracks through the park are well maintained and signposted though it's a good idea to have a copy of the Survey of Kenya's *Meru National Park* map with you.

Places to Stay

There are several public camp sites in the park, but the one at junction 12 is the only one operating. There's running water and an askari in attendance.

More expensive are the 10 self-contained bandas at *Leopard Rock Lodge* which have electricity, hot water, mosquito nets and fully equipped kitchens. These cost US$21 per person per night; children aged from two to 15 years pay US$4. There's a shop at the site which sells basic commodities including canned goods and beer. Bookings can be made through Let's Go Travel (☎ (02) 213033) in Nairobi.

At the top of the range is the *Meru Mulika*

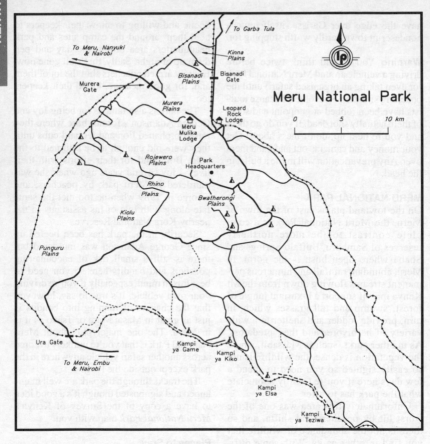

Meru National Park

To Garba Tula

To Meru, Nanyuki & Nairobi

Murera Gate

Bisanadi Plains

Kinna Plains

Bisanadi Gate

Murera Plains

Leopard Rock Lodge

Meru Mulika Lodge

Rojewero Plains

Park Headquarters

Rhino Plains

Bwatherongi Plains

Kiolu Plains

Punguru Plains

Ura Gate

To Meru, Embu & Nairobi

Kampi ya Game

Kampi ya Kiko

Kampi ya Elsa

Kampi ya Teziwa

0   5   10 km

Lodge (☎ (0164) 20000) which has all the usual facilities of a luxury lodge including a swimming pool and where full board costs US$70/96 for a single/double, except from 1 April to 30 June when it drops to US$39/70. Children aged from two to five years pay US$19, and from six to 11 years the charge is US$21. Bookings can be made with the lodge, or through Msafiri Inns (☎ (02) 229751), PO Box 42013, Nairobi.

Getting There & Away

Getting to Meru National Park by public transport is a problem. There are no buses or matatus which will take you either to the lodges or the camp sites and park headquarters. Likewise, attempting to hitchhike is basically a waste of time since so few vehicles come into the park and those that do are mainly tour groups so they won't pick you up. It's almost essential to have your own vehicle or be part of a tour group. Quite a few safari companies include Meru National Park on their itineraries but they are all liable to cancel visits at short notice if there has been any trouble with shiftas in the park. Dead or robbed tourists are no good for business.

TANA RIVER PRIMATE SANCTUARY

Well south of Garissa and not too far north of Garsen is the Tana River Primate Sanctuary which, as its name suggests, is a reserve for a number of endangered monkey species. It's possible to get close to the sanctuary by public transport but there's still a lot of walking involved and the facilities have long fallen into disrepair so you need to take everything with you. Very few safari companies include the reserve on their itineraries. Let's Go Travel (☎ (02) 340331) is the agency for a seven-day trip which takes in Tsavo, Tana River and Lamu for US$410.

GARISSA

The only reason to come to Garissa is if you are taking the back route to Lamu direct from Nairobi via Garsen. There's nothing much to see or do here and the heat and humidity are unrelenting but there's a bank (open normal hours), petrol stations, bars and a fair choice of places to stay.

Places to Stay & Eat

Perhaps the best place to stay for the night is the *Safari Hotel* which offers clean rooms with running water for US$4/6 a single/double. There's reasonable food in the attached restaurant.

The *Garissa Government Guest House*, a short distance out of town, is somewhat more expensive at US$6 per person for rooms with bathroom and breakfast, but is worth the extra money. If both are full then there's the more basic *Nile Lodging* or the *Kenya Hotel & Lodging*.

Getting There & Away

Garissa Express operates a bus from the KBS depot Eastleigh, Nairobi, to Garissa on Monday, Wednesday, Friday and Sunday at 8 am. The depot is a 10-minute matatu ride from Ronald Ngala St (route No 9). The fare is US$5.20 and the journey takes about eight hours.

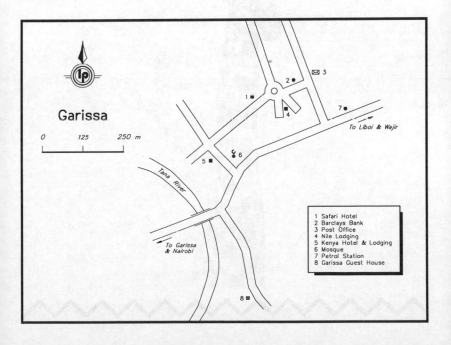

Garissa

0   125   250 m

Tana River

To Liboi & Wajir

To Garissa
& Nairobi

1 Safari Hotel
2 Barclays Bank
3 Post Office
4 Nile Lodging
5 Kenya Hotel & Lodging
6 Mosque
7 Petrol Station
8 Garissa Guest House

There's also a daily Garissa Express bus from Lamu (at Mokowe on the mainland) to Garissa which leaves at 7 am, costs US$9.40 and takes 10 hours when the weather is dry.

LIBOI

Liboi, right on the Kenya-Somalia border, is a staging post in the *qat* (drug) trade to Somalia. It has also become a major refugee centre following the civil war and famine in Somalia. It has only one place to stay, the *Cairo Hotel*.

GARSEN

If you're heading towards Lamu from Garissa then you may have to stay at Garsen en route – the bus from Garissa to Mokowe on the mainland opposite Lamu is not direct. There's nothing special about Garsen but there are several basic hotels to choose from. The best is the *3-in-1 Lodging & Restaurant* which is fairly clean and has its own restaurant.

For details of buses passing through Garsen, see either the Malindi or Lamu sections in the coast chapter.

Amboseli, Masai Mara, Tsavo & Taita Hills

AMBOSELI NATIONAL PARK

Amboseli is the next most popular park after Masai Mara, mainly because of the spectacular backdrop of Africa's highest peak, Mt Kilimanjaro, which broods on the southern boundary of the park.

At 392 sq km Amboseli is not a large park, and it certainly doesn't have the profusion of game which you find in Masai Mara but the game here is easy to spot. The western section of the park is the dry bed of Lake Amboseli, and although it is occasionally flooded in the wet season, for the majority of the time it is a dry, dusty, shimmering expanse.

Probably the best reason for visiting Amboseli is that you stand the best chance of spotting a black rhino. Amboseli also has huge herds of elephant, and to see a herd of them making their way sedately across the grassy plains, with Kilimanjaro in the background, may be a real African cliché but is an experience which leaves a lasting impression.

Other animals which you are likely to see here include buffaloes, lions, gazelle, cheetahs, wildebeest, hyenas, jackals, wart hogs, Masai giraffes, zebras and baboons.

Amboseli more than any other park has suffered greatly from the number of minibuses which drive through each day. It has a much drier climate than Masai Mara and so for much of the year is a real dust bowl. If you are driving through the park, stick to the defined tracks, and hopefully others will follow suit.

Outside the town's petrol station there are a couple of shops selling Maasai crafts. The first prices asked are totally ridiculous, so bargain fiercely.

Most visitors approach Amboseli through Namanga, the main border post between Kenya and Tanzania. If you're stuck, there's accommodation at the *Namanga Hotel* among others. The petrol station is a good place to ask around for lifts.

Places to Stay – bottom end

Once again the only budget option is a camp site. This one is right on the southern boundary of the park. The only facilities are a couple of long-drop toilets, and a kiosk where you can buy warm beer and sodas and pay the camping fees.

The water supply here is extremely unreliable so bring some water with you. Elephants are a real problem in this camp site at night and practically everyone who has stayed here has an elephant story to relate – there are some hilarious (and not so hilarious) ones doing the rounds. At night make sure all food is locked away inside your vehicle. *Don't* keep food in your tent as elephants have a habit of investigating, as do baboons during the day when you're out on a game drive.

Places to Stay – top end

The group of lodges in the centre of the park are strategically situated for views of Kilimanjaro. The *Kilimanjaro Safari Lodge* and the *Amboseli Lodge* are both run by the Kilimanjaro Safari Club in Nairobi (☎ (2) 227136), PO Box 30139. Prices at both lodges are approximately the same at US$92 per person with full board. The single-person supplement is US$55. Also in this group is the *Ol Tukai Lodge* (☎ 334863 in Nairobi) which consists of self-catering cottages. These are much cheaper than the Kilimanjaro lodges at US$13 per person, with a single-person supplement of US$9.20.

Close to the southern perimeter of the park is the *Amboseli Serena Lodge* (☎ 339800 in Nairobi), a sensitively designed and constructed lodge which blends in well with the landscape. The nearby Enkongo Narok Swamp ensures constant bird and animal

KENYA

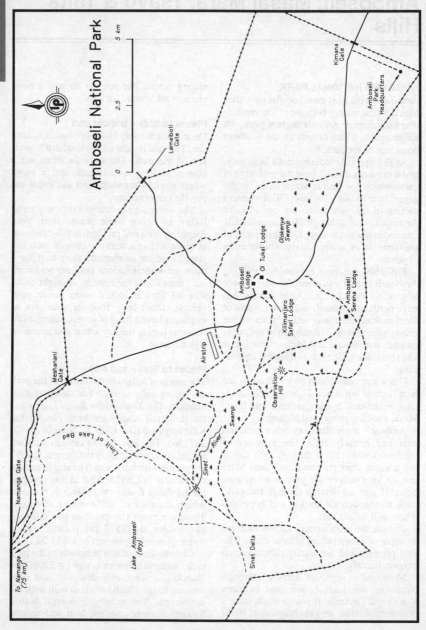

Amboseli National Park

5 km

2.5

0

Kimana Gate

Amboseli Park Headquarters

Lemeiboti Gate

Olokenya Swamp

Ol Tukai Lodge

Amboseli Lodge

Kilimanjaro Safari Lodge

Amboseli Serena Lodge

Meshanani Gate

Airstrip

Observation Hill

Sinet River

Swamp

Namanga Gate

Limit of Lake Bed

Sinet Delta

To Namanga (75 km)

Lake Amboseli (dry)

activity. Room charges are US$87 per person with full board and US$56 for the single-person supplement.

Getting There & Away
Air Air Kenya Aviation has daily flights between Wilson Airport (Nairobi) and Amboseli. These depart from Nairobi at 7.30 am and Amboseli at 8.30 am; the trip takes about an hour and costs US$65 one way.

Car & 4WD The usual approach to Amboseli is through Namanga, 165 km south of Nairobi on the A104, and the last fuel stop before the park. The road is in excellent condition from Nairobi to Namanga, however, the 75-km dirt road from Namanga to the Namanga Gate is fiercely corrugated and is guaranteed to shake your fillings loose. If you'd been wondering up until now why the suspension in your minibus was shot to pieces, here is the answer. The whole trip from Nairobi takes around four hours.

It's also possible to enter Amboseli from the east via Tsavo.

MASAI MARA GAME RESERVE
The Mara is the most popular game park in Kenya. Virtually every person who visits Kenya goes to Masai Mara, and with good reason as this is the Kenyan section of the wildly evocative Serengeti Plains and the wildlife abounds. This is also traditionally the land of the Maasai, but these people have been displaced in favour of the animals.

The Mara (as it's often abbreviated to) is a 320-sq-km slab of open grassland dotted with the distinctive flat-topped acacia trees tucked away in the south-west corner of the country. It is watered by the tree-lined Mara River and its tributary the Talek River. The western border of the park is the spectacular Oloololo Escarpment and it's at this edge of the park that the concentrations of game are the highest. It must also be said that it's the most difficult area of the park to get around in as the swampy ground becomes impassable after heavy rain. Conversely, the concentrations of tourist and minibuses are highest at the eastern end of the park around

the Oloolaimutia Gate and Talek Gate as it's these areas which are the most accessible by road from Nairobi.

Fauna
Wherever you go in the Mara, however, the one certain thing is that you'll see an astonishing amount of game, often in the one place at the one time. Of the big cats, lions are found in large prides everywhere and it's not at all uncommon to see them hunting. Cheetahs and leopards are harder to spot but are still fairly common. Elephants, buffaloes, zebras and hippos also exist in large numbers within the reserve. Of the antelopes, the black-striped Thomson's gazelle (Tommys) and the larger Grant's gazelle are found in huge numbers, while the impala, topi and Coke's hartebeest and of course the wildebeest are also profuse. Rhinos do exist in the park but are rarely seen. Other common animals include Masai giraffes, baboons (especially around the lodges), wart hogs, spotted hyenas and grey (or side-striped) jackals.

The highlight of the Mara is no doubt the annual wildebeest migration when literally millions of these ungainly beasts move north from the Serengeti in July and August in search of the lush grass, before turning south again around October. It is truly a staggering experience to be in the reserve at that time – and one which is likely to have a profound effect on your own feeling of insignificance.

Masai Mara doesn't have national park status. The fundamental difference between a national park and a game reserve is that in a game reserve people (in this case the Maasai) can graze their animals and can also shoot animals if they are attacked. In a national park however, the entire area is set aside exclusively for the wildlife and the natural environment.

Maasai Village
Just outside the Oloolaimutia Gate there's a Maasai village which has opened itself up as a tourist attraction. For around US$3.50 per person you can walk around and take as many pictures as you like. As you might

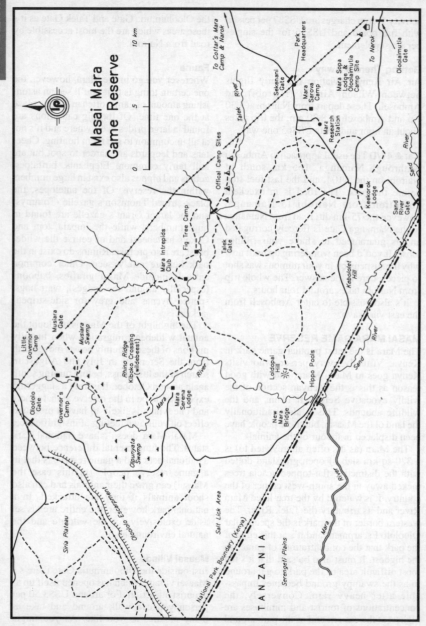

Masai Mara
Game Reserve

10 km

5

0

To Cortar's Mara
Camp & Narok

Talek River

To Narok

Park
Headquarters

Sekenani Gate

Mara Sarova
Camp

Oloolaimutia Gate

Mara Sopa
Lodge &
Oloolaimutia
Camp Site

Mara Research
Station

Official Camp Sites

Keekorok
Lodge

Kekololet Hill

Sand River
Gate

Sand River

Mara Intrepids
Club

Fig Tree Camp

Talek Gate

Loldopai
Hill

Hippo Pools

Musiara Gate

Musiara Swamp

Rhino Ridge
Kibokok Crossing
(wildebeest)

Little
Governor's
Camp

Governor's
Camp

Mara River

Mara Serena
Lodge

New Mara
Bridge

Olpunyata
Swamp

Mara River

Ololoolo Gate

Ololoolo Escarpment

Siria Plateau

Salt Lick Area

Serengeti Plains

National Park Boundary (Kenya)

TANZANIA

imagine, it's a real zoo when you have a couple of dozen tourists poking their video cameras and long lenses everywhere. *If* you can manage to visit when there are no other tourists it's not too bad and you can at least talk to the villagers. At other times you'll have the crap hassled out of you to buy trinkets and bead work.

Ballooning
If you can afford the US$300 price tag, balloon safaris are definitely the way to go. It's a superb experience. For more details see the Safaris section in the Kenya Getting Around chapter.

Narok
Narok is the main access point to the Mara and is a small provincial town a few hours' drive west of Nairobi. As most vehicles stop to refuel here (it's the last place to do so before the park itself) the town is chock-full with souvenir shops and hawkers. There are branches of Barclays and the Kenya Commercial banks, a post office, and a range of budget and mid-range hotels. For accommodation, try the *Spear Hotel* which has self-contained rooms.

A very popular place to grab a snack here is *Kim's Dishes* diagonally opposite the Agip station on the right hand side if you're standing with your back to the petrol station. It offers cheap fast-food items such as chips, sausages, etc. There are also several basic but busy bars on the main street as well as *Pussy's Bar* across the river from the main street about one km from the centre.

There are frequent buses and matatus buzzing between Nairobi and Narok which park outside Kim's Dishes.

Places to Stay – bottom end
There is no budget accommodation within the reserve so it's camp or pay high prices at the lodges and tented camps. It's possible to camp just outside the park at any of the gates for a small fee. There are no facilities but you can usually get water from the rangers. The Maasai run the *Oloolaimutia Campsite* between the gate of the same name and the

Mara Sopa Lodge at the western extremity of the park. This place is very popular with the budget safari outfits and is usually pretty lively. For US$2 per person the Maasai provide firewood and an askari at night. The water supply here is very limited and if you need any water you'll have to buy it from the Maasai. The staff canteen of the nearby Mara Sopa Lodge is usually a lively place and you can get meals and warm beer.

There are official camp sites at the usual price along the Talek River by the Talek Gate on the north-eastern border of the park, and just outside the reserve on the banks of the Mara River near the Oloololo Gate. If you want to use any of these sites it's advisable to book them in advance in Nairobi (at the Kenya Wildlife Service) but people who roll up unannounced generally seem to have no problems. The only problem with using these sites is that they are none too secure – baboons and thieves can both take their toll on your gear.

What isn't widely known is that it's possible to camp at *Cottar's Mara Camp* (see the following section) for US$3.40 per person. The owners certainly don't encourage it but won't turn you away.

Places to Stay – top end
The lodges and tented camps are all pitched at the top end of the market and should all be booked in advance. Prices for accommodation with full board vary between US$80 and US$150 per person per night. The lodges generally consist of separate self-contained bandas, while the tented camps are often almost identical, the difference being that the 'rooms' have canvas walls protected from the elements by an open-sided makuti-roofed structure. It's certainly stretching things to call them tents but it seems to satisfy the desire for a token of authenticity among those with money to burn.

The *Mara Sopa Lodge* (☎ (2) 336088; PO Box 72639, Nairobi) by Oloolaimutia Gate is one of the newer ones and has a commanding view plus it's been attractively designed and built. Singles/doubles with full board cost US$135/180. *Keekorok Lodge* is one of the Block Hotels (☎ (2) 335807; PO Box 47557, Nairobi) and is an older but well-maintained lodge on a grassy plain. Singles/doubles with full board cost US$129/187 in the high season, US$75/109 in the low season. Prices in the shoulder season are about halfway between the two. Keekorok is one of the two lodges which operates balloon flights.

The *Mara Sarova Camp* is part of the Sarova Hotels chain (☎ (2) 333233; PO Box 30680, Nairobi) and is not far from the Sekenani Gate and has the works, including a swimming pool. The room rates here with full board are US$78/157 a single/double in the high season, less in the shoulder and low seasons.

Along the northern banks of the Talek River are the *Fig Tree Camp* (☎ (2) 21439; PO Box 40683, Nairobi), and the *Mara Intrepids Club*. The Fig Tree Camp is attractively designed, has a swimming pool, and is approached across a wooden bridge from the car park on the opposite bank. It's a tented camp and has singles/doubles/triples for US$94/127/174 with full board. This is the other lodge from which you can take a balloon safari. It's wise to book them in advance at the Nairobi office though you can also do this at the camp. The Mara Intrepids Club is considerably more expensive at US$122/244 for singles/doubles with full board but the price does include game drives.

In the centre of the reserve is the *Mara Serena Lodge* (☎ (2) 339800) on a superb site overlooking the Mara River. It blends in beautifully with the surrounding countryside and was built to resemble a modern Maasai village. Singles/doubles with full board cost US$87/175.

Most expensive of all is the *Mara Safari Club* (☎ (2) 216940), part of the Lonrho chain of hotels (PO Box 58581, Nairobi). Singles/doubles with full board cost US$215/290 in the high season and US$155/205 in the low season. Shoulder-season prices are about halfway between the two, and all prices include game drives.

In the northern section of the park is another group of tented camps including the

Governor's Camp (☎ (2) 331871) and *Little Governor's Camp* (owned by the same people). Singles/doubles with full board plus game drives cost US$150/300.

Other accommodation outside the park north of Oloololo Gate includes the *Kichwa Tembo Camp* (☎ (2) 335887) at US$77/140; the *Mara River Camp* (☎ (2) 331191) at US$56/100, and the *Mara Buffalo Camp*.

About 15 km from Sekenani Gate is another tented lodge, *Cottar's Mara Camp* (☎ (2) 882408). The 'cottages' are dotted around a beautiful green clearing with shady trees, sweeping lawns and flowers. There's an open bar and dining room and a roaring log fire at night. Although it's not actually in the reserve there's a lot of game around the camp itself. There is a baited hide nearby and you have a good chance of seeing leopards. Dawn walks and night-time spotlight game drives are also organised from the camp.

Even if you can't afford to stay in one of these camps, they are usually great places to drop in for a cleansing ale and perhaps a snack although, not surprisingly, prices are relatively high.

The Mara Sarova Camp, Keekorok Lodge and Mara Serena Lodge all sell petrol and will usually part with it to nonguests, though prices are higher than in Narok or Nairobi.

Getting There & Away

Air Air Kenya Aviation has twice-daily flights between Nairobi's Wilson Airport and Masai Mara, departing from Nairobi at 10 am and 3 pm, and from the Mara at 11 am and 4 pm. The one-way fare is US$83, but to these you have to add the cost of chartering a vehicle in the park to collect you from the airstrip.

Car & 4WD The Mara is not a place you come to without transport. There is no public transport to or within the park, and even if there was there's certainly no way you could do a game drive in a matatu! If you are patient and persistent you should be able to hitch a ride with other tourists, but get yourself to Narok first.

From Narok onwards the bitumen runs out

and public transport dries up. It's almost 100 km from here to any of the park gates.

It's also possible to approach the reserve from Kisii and the west along reasonably well-maintained dirt roads. You can get closer to the park by public transport but there are far fewer tourist vehicles to hitch a ride with. Matatus run as far as Kilgoris directly south of Kisii, or Suna on the main A1 route close to Isebania on the Tanzanian border.

TSAVO NATIONAL PARK
At just over 20,000 sq km, Tsavo is the largest national park in Kenya, and for administrative purposes it has been split into Tsavo West National Park, with an area of 8500 sq km, and Tsavo East National Park, which covers 11,000 sq km.

The northern area of Tsavo West, west of the Nairobi to Mombasa A109 road, is the most developed and has some excellent scenery. Tsavo East is much less visited and consists of vast rolling plains with scrubby vegetation. The entire area north of the Galana River, and this constitutes the bulk of the park, is off limits to the general public. This is due to the ongoing campaign against poachers, who still find the relative remoteness of Tsavo a good prospect. Happily it seems the authorities are winning the battle, but in the meantime the rhino population has been absolutely decimated – from around 8000 in 1970 to less than 200 today.

When driving around the park, all track junctions have a numbered cairn which makes navigation fairly simple. Don't attempt this park without 4WD if you intend to get off the main routes. You can certainly get to Kilaguni Lodge and Ngulia Lodge on the main service road from Mtito Andei in a 2WD but you'll get into strife and possibly get hopelessly stuck on the minor tracks. You will not make it to the above lodges in a 2WD if you enter through the Tsavo Gate further south unless you're a rally driver and/or willing to risk damaging the car. There are some diabolical sections on this access road; the lava flows along here will rip with underside of any normal car apart.

Tsavo West National Park
The focus here is the watering holes by the Kilaguni and Ngulia lodges. The one at Kilaguni is the better of the two and attracts huge varieties of animals and birds, particularly during the dry season when water may be scarce elsewhere.

The **Mzima Springs** are not far from Kilaguni Lodge and the pools here are favourite haunts of both hippos and crocodiles. The much vaunted underwater viewing chamber was designed to give you a view of the hippos' submarine activities, but the hippos have retreated to the far end of the pool. There are, however, plenty of fish to be observed. The springs are the source of the bulk of Mombasa's fresh water and there is a direct pipeline from here to the coast.

Also in the area of the lodges is the spectacular **Shetani lava flow** and caves. Both are worth investigating, though for the caves you'll need to exercise caution and carry a torch (flashlight). The **Chaimu Crater** just south of Kilaguni Lodge can also be climbed. It's worth remembering while walking on any of these nature trails that the park animals are far from tame, and while there's little danger, you do need to keep your eyes on what's happening around you. These nature trails are also the only places where you are permitted to get out of the vehicle.

There is an information centre at the Kilaguni Lodge and if it's open it may be worth checking to see where the most recent animal sightings have been.

Places to Stay – bottom end Tsavo West has a number of camp sites, namely at each of the three main gates (Tsavo, Mtito Andei and Chyulu) and the *Ziwani Campsite* on the western boundary of the park. The usual camping fees apply.

The self-service accommodation at the *Ngulia Safari Camp* and the *Kitani Safari Camp* is, by park standards, quite cheap at US$19 per person (minimum charge of US$38 per banda) in the fully equipped bandas but you must bring all your own food and drink with you or eat at one of the lodges.

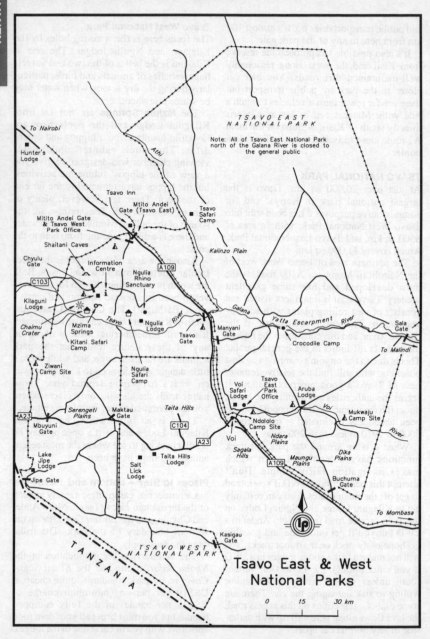

Tsavo East & West
National Parks

0   15   30 km

Both camps consist of self-contained one-bedroom bandas with bedding, towels, mosquito nets, a fully equipped kitchen, and kerosene lanterns. Take with you toilet paper, washing-up liquid, soap, matches, drinking water and an ice box. For reservations at either camp, contact Let's Go Travel (☎ (2) 340331), Caxton House, Standard St, Nairobi.

Places to Stay – top end The *Ngulia Lodge* (☎ (2) 336858) is part of the African Tours & Hotels group (PO Box 30471, Nairobi). It's not the most attractive of lodges but it is comfortable and the views are excellent. Singles/doubles with full board cost US$90/120 in the high season and US$42/85 in the low season. Prices in the shoulder season are about halfway between these. The water hole here is small but there's a leopard which visits each evening to pick up meat strung up on a dead tree outside the patio.

The *Kilaguni Lodge* is owned by the same hotel group and costs exactly the same, but the main attraction here is the water hole which attracts a wide variety of game. It's a more attractive lodge than the Ngulia and there are extensive views out to the west.

Here's an account of a day spent at Kilaguni Lodge:

The lodge is beautifully situated looking out over the rolling hills. The large water hole, floodlit at night, is right in front of the lodge and you can sit in the bar or restaurant, or on the verandah in front of your room, and watch the wildlife. You can even lie in bed with your binoculars to hand – every room faces a water hole. All this luxury, including a swimming pool and lush garden, doesn't come cheap, but where else do you need a pair of binoculars and a field guide at hand while you eat?

We arrive in time for lunch and watch the comings and goings at the water hole. To the left there are impala and a couple of waterbuck; back from the water there's a small group of ostrich, and off to the right there's a herd of oryx. Marabou storks lounge around in the foreground while right in front of the restaurant are groups of smaller birds and mongoose. There's so much activity it's hard to concentrate on lunch – and this is just after the wet season when the game are less concentrated at the water holes!

The scene is only spoilt by the idiots who persist, in spite of numerous posted warnings, in throwing bread out to the animals. This has already taught some of the storks (notoriously efficient scavengers) to line up in front of the restaurant wall. It would be all too easy to turn this wonderful scene into a cheap zoo with animals begging for hand-outs. This is the same Africa of Ethiopia and Mozambique and there's something obscene about dumb tourists hurling whole bread rolls just for amusement and a better shot with the Instamatic.

After lunch we watch from the verandah of our room – some zebras and two more ostriches appear but all the storks have left and gradually the animals wander off as the afternoon wears on. By 4.30 pm there's only the solitary waterbuck left; even the ostriches finally troop off in a stately line.

Down at the northern end of the lodge grounds is a tree full of weaver-bird nests with twittering hordes of these bright yellow birds furiously at work. Some of their nests, mainly older ones, have fallen out of the tree, and on close examination they are amazingly intricate and neatly woven; coconut-sized with a funnel-like entrance underneath. Right in front of our room a small squad of mongoose appears, cavorts around for a few minutes, then wanders away. By 5 pm it's baboon time again and the tribe wanders down to the water hole again for their evening visit. A few of them come up to our room to hassle us but soon give up. Rock hyrax scamper around, one even coming right into our room, and the mongoose come and go. Gradually the impala reappear.

Dinner time, unhappily, is the one blot on the perfect experience. Once again there are the idiotic food hurlers at work and a hyena trots up and waits expectantly for hand-outs, joined by a slender mongoose-like genet. With much shouting, loud conversation and cameras flashing madly there's a distinct theatre-restaurant feel to the whole meal and we're glad to get back to the quiet of our rooms.

The baboons leave soon after dark and by bedtime it's basically the impalas and zebras. I get up several times in the night to check what's up but, apart from bats swooping around, the scene seems static until dawn. The impala keep watch all night long.

At dawn the zebras wander off, the oryx reappear, the whole baboon tribe wanders back and immediately start carousing merrily. A couple of pairs of impala bucks square off for a morning duel and the whole cycle starts again.

Although we didn't see elephants or lions we still enjoyed every minute of it. Now if only they could put those 'don't feed the animals signs' on every table...

Tony Wheeler

In a fairly isolated spot on the western boundary of the park and almost on the Tanzanian border, the *Lake Jipe Lodge* (☎ (2)

27623) is one of the cheaper places but it's a long way from anywhere else.

If you don't have the money to stay at one of the lodges in the park but don't want to camp or go to the trouble of organising your own food, etc for one of the self-catering camps, then you have options though they involve staying just outside the park boundaries alongside the main Nairobi to Mombasa road. Even here, you're not looking at budget hotel options.

Right opposite the Mtito Andei Gate is the *Tsavo Inn* (PO Box 20, Mtito Andei) which is fairly pleasant but otherwise unremarkable. Doubles with breakfast cost US$52 (no singles) plus there are slightly more expensive half-board and full-board rates. For Kenyan residents it's considerably less expensive at US$16/19 for singles/doubles with breakfast.

Better is the *Hunter's Lodge* at Kiboko north of Mtito Andei at the extreme northern end of the park but also on the main Nairobi to Mombasa main road. Rooms here cost around US$13 per person per night including breakfast.

Getting There & Away The main access to Tsavo West is through the Mtito Andei Gate on the Mombasa to Nairobi road near the northern end of the park. The park headquarters is here and there's a camp site. From the gate it's 31 km to the Kilaguni Lodge.

A further 48 km along the main road away from Nairobi is the Tsavo Gate, where there's another camp site. This gate is 75 km from the Kilaguni area, so if you're hitching the Mtito Andei Gate is much closer and far busier. It's also worth taking into consideration the diabolical state of certain sections of the road between the Tsavo Gate and the lodges.

From Voi there is access past the Hilton-owned Taita Hills and Salt Lick lodges via the Maktau Gate. This road cuts clear across the park, exiting at the Mbuyuni Gate, to Taveta from where it's possible to cross into Tanzania and the town of Moshi at the foot of Kilimanjaro.

Tsavo East National Park

The southern third of this park is open to the public and the rolling scrub-covered hills are home to large herds of elephants, usually covered in red dust.

The **Kanderi Swamp**, not far into the park from the main Voi Gate and park headquarters, is home to a profusion of wildlife and there's a camp site here. Further into the park, 30 km from the gate, is the main attraction in this part of the park, the **Aruba Dam** built across the Voi River. Here too you'll encounter a wide variety of game without the usual hordes of tourists – very few people visit Tsavo East.

Places to Stay – bottom end There are camp sites at the Voi Gate, Kanderi Swamp (*Ndololo Campsite*), Aruba Lodge and the *Mukwaju Campsite* on the Voi River 50 km in from the main gate.

Places to Stay – top end The *Voi Safari Lodge* (clearly signposted in the town of Voi) is part of the African Tours & Hotels group (☎ (2) 336858; PO Box 30471, Nairobi) and is five km inside the park from the Voi Gate. As you might imagine, things are a good deal more peaceful here than at the lodges in Tsavo West. Singles/doubles with full board cost US98/120 in the high season. In the low season they are US$41/81 and somewhere between the two in the shoulder season. The *Crocodile Camp* is somewhat cheaper at US$46 per person per night with full board.

The *Aruba Lodge* (☎ 340331 in Nairobi) is in a good shady location by the dam but considerably more expensive, as is the *Tsavo Safari Camp*. Both cost US$80 per person with full board.

Getting There & Away The main access point and the park headquarters is Voi Gate near Voi off the Nairobi to Mombasa road. Further north near the Tsavo Gate entrance of Tsavo West is the Manyani Gate. The murram (dirt) road from here cuts straight across to the Galana River and follows the river clear across the park, exiting at Sala Gate on the eastern side, a distance of 100 km. From Sala Gate it's a further 110 km to Malindi.

TAITA HILLS & VOI

The Taita Hills to the west of the main Nairobi to Mombasa road cover a vast area and are scenically spectacular. They have the status of a game reserve despite the fact that the main Voi to Taveta road passes through it on the southern side. Game is prolific in this area and you can even see plenty of it along the road to Taveta. There are also two lodges on the south-western side – the Taita Hills Lodge and the Salt Lick Lodge.

Taita Hills

The cheapest of the lodges is the *Taita Hills Lodge* which has rooms with full board for US$102 per person per night. More expensive is the *Salt Lick Lodge* which has the same for US$136 per person per night.

There are matatus from Voi to Wundanyi (in the heart of the Taita Hills) for US$0.90,

and both trains (five hours) and matatus (2½ hours) from Voi to Taveta for US$2.60. The trains and matatus from Voi to Taveta will get you close to the lodges but, if you can afford to stay there, you'll probably be in your own vehicle anyway.

Voi

The town of Voi was described recently by a Peace Corps volunteer who works there as, 'an attractive spaghetti western-like setting surrounded by hills that are good for hiking and catching expansive views of the surrounding plains'. That's close to the truth but it's not Maralal and a lot of development is going on. Nevertheless, it's a pleasant, small town and worth considering as a base for exploring the Taita Hills and Tsavo National Park or even as an overnight stop between Mombasa and Nairobi.

The cheapest place to stay with decent facilities is *Johari's Guest House* (☎ 2079) where singles/doubles go for US$2.20/4

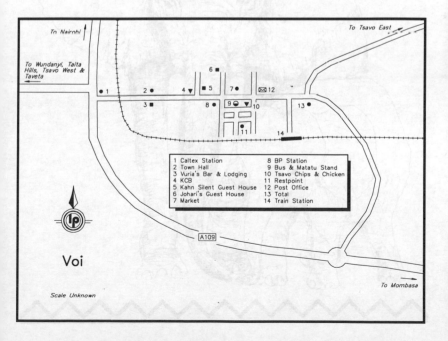

1 Caltex Station	8 BP Station
2 Town Hall	9 Bus & Matatu Stand
3 Vuria's Bar & Lodging	10 Tsavo Chips & Chicken
4 KCB	11 Restpoint
5 Kahn Silent Guest House	12 Post Office
6 Johari's Guest House	13 Total
7 Market	14 Train Station

To Nairobi

To Wundanyi, Taita Hills, Tsavo West & Taveta

To Tsavo East

A109

Voi

To Mombasa

Scale Unknown

with shared bath. The *Voi Restpoint Hotel*
(☎ 2079) is the only budget hotel with self-
contained rooms including fan and
telephone. Singles/doubles with breakfast
cost US$5.40/7.60. There are three restau-
rants in the hotel, including one on the
rooftop.

Slightly more expensive is the *Kahn Silent
Guest House* (☎ 2058), on Moi Hospital Rd.
It has singles/doubles for US$2.70/4 and is
working on budget tours of Tsavo National
Park.

Up in price is *Vuria's Bar & Lodging*,
opposite the town hall, which offers self-
contained rooms for US$3.40/5.60 including
breakfast.

All the guesthouses have reasonable restaurants plus there's *Tsavo Chips & Chicken*
at the matatu stand. Out on the main Nairobi
to Mombasa road at the roundabout is the
Caltex petrol station which has a whole
complex of shops, fast-food outlets and a bar.
The food here is OK and very reasonably
priced, plus beers in the bar are ice-cold.

Uganda

Introduction

Uganda's long string of tragedies since independence in 1962 have featured in the Western media to such an extent that most people probably regard the country as dangerously unstable and to be avoided.

Yoweri Museveni's National Resistance Army (NRA) has ruled effectively since coming to power in 1986. In the past, predictions of the stability of a regime have been premature. However, Museveni is taking Uganda into the 1990s with brighter prospects than it has had for many years. Stability has returned to most parts of the country, Kampala has virtually returned to normal and the process of getting the country back on a firm footing is well under way.

Before independence Uganda was a prosperous and cohesive country. Its great beauty led Winston Churchill to refer to the country as the 'Pearl of Africa', but by early 1986 Uganda lay shattered and bankrupt, broken by tribal animosity, nepotism, politicians who had gone mad on power, and military tyranny. While a lot of the blame can be laid squarely at the feet of the sordid and brutal military dictatorship of Idi Amin, who was overthrown in 1979, others have a great deal to answer for. Indeed, there was really little difference between any of Uganda's pre-1986 rulers. All appear to have been spawned from the same degenerate mould.

Yet despite the killings and disappearances, the brutality, fear and destruction of the past, Ugandans appear to have weathered the storm remarkably well. You will not meet a sullen, bitter or cowed people. Rather, though hard to believe, they still smile and find the enthusiasm to carry on and rebuild after the nightmare years. In fact these days,

there's an air of optimism as people realise that the years of terror and bloodshed are finally over.

Undoubtedly, the main reason for the improvement is the regime headed by Museveni which has made a clean sweep of the government, the civil service and the army. Despite the huge odds against him, and an empty treasury, during his early years in power Museveni made a big effort to get the country back on its feet. There was a clampdown on corruption, political meetings were banned to prevent a resurgence of intertribal rivalry and squabbling among power brokers, and a real effort was made to reassure tribal elders that Museveni's administration was balanced.

Perhaps of chief importance, Museveni's army is the most disciplined that Uganda has ever seen, despite the astonishing (to Westerners) sight of fatigued teenagers among its ranks – some as young as 14. Gone are the days when every road was littered with checkpoints staffed by drunken, surly soldiers intent on squeezing every last penny from civilians, or when soldiers took anything they wanted from stores at gunpoint. There are still some roadblocks, but politeness and courtesy are what you're most likely to encounter now.

For the traveller, all this means that Uganda is once again a safe and friendly country to visit. Certainly the level of comfort is not what you might be used to in Kenya, but the Ugandan people are among the friendliest on the continent and there are some unforgettable sights. Don't be afraid to go there. It's a beautiful country with a great deal to offer.

Facts about the Country

HISTORY
Early Settlement

Until the 19th century, there was very little penetration of Uganda from outside. Despite the fertility of the land and its capacity to grow surplus crops, there were virtually no trading links with the East African coast. Some indigenous kingdoms came into being from the 14th century onwards, among them Buganda, Bunyoro, Toro, Ankole and Busoga, with Bunyoro initially being the most powerful.

Over the following centuries, the Buganda people eventually created the dominant kingdom. They make up about 20% of Uganda's population and were once ruled by a *kabaka* (king).

During the reign of Kabaka Muteesa I in the mid-19th century, contacts were established with Arab traders who began to travel

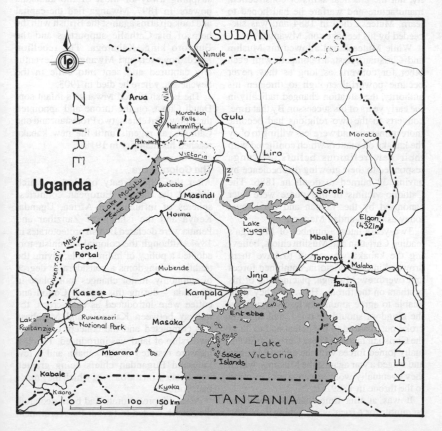

inland from Zanzibar in search of ivory and slaves. They brought with them Islam, and some of the practices of this religion were adopted by the Bugandan court. The first European visitor to Baganda was the explorer John Hanning Speke, who spent several months at the royal capital in 1862. He was followed by Henry Morton Stanley in 1875. Muteesa told Stanley he wanted to have teachers of European learning and religion sent out to live in his country, and this resulted in the arrival, in 1877, of the first Anglican missionaries. They were not quite what the kabaka had in mind, however, as they would only teach him about Christianity, not the practical skills of construction, manufacture and warfare he had hoped to learn. Muteesa died in 1884 and was succeeded by his teenage son, Mwanga.

While Muteesa had allowed his Muslim and Christian guests to compete with each other for converts as long as they never became powerful enough to threaten his authority, the situation changed radically in the early years of his successor. By that time, converts to the two religions had become more numerous and were less willing to obey the kabaka on matters which conflicted with their new religious beliefs. Mwanga responded to their growing disobedience by having 32 burned to death in 1886. The Catholic victims of this purge were later canonised by the Vatican and are known today as the Ugandan Martyrs.

Two years later, a number of Mwanga's leading Christian and Muslim chiefs, believing the kabaka was about to have them drowned in Lake Victoria, combined forces and overthrew Mwanga, placing one of his brothers on the throne. However, they were unable to agree among themselves on how the kingdom should be ruled, and fighting broke out, leading to the defeat and exile of the Christian faction. These Christians eventually joined forces with the exiled Mwanga and waged a war against the Muslims, which they eventually won. Mwanga was restored to the throne in 1889.

It was at this time that the European 'scramble for Africa' was reaching its height.

The British were the first to reach Buganda, in 1890, arriving with a small military force under the command of Captain Lugard, who established a base on Kampala hill near the royal capital. Fighting was still going on between the Muslim and Christian factions when Lugard arrived and there was also a rivalry developing between the Protestant and Catholic chiefs.

The Protestant chiefs regarded the British as their natural allies so, when it became clear that the kabaka was siding with the Catholics, they turned to Lugard for help. The ensuing power struggle led to a declaration of British control over Buganda and the stripping away of most of the kabaka's powers. In 1897, Mwanga fled the capital and took up arms against the British with the help of his Catholic supporters and the Bunyoro king, Kabarega. The rebellion failed, however, and Mwanga was eventually captured and sent into exile in the Seychelles, where he died in 1903.

The British placed Mwanga's infant son, Daudi Chwa, on the throne and appointed three powerful chiefs, two Protestant and one Catholic, as regents until the new kabaka reached his majority in 1918.

The Colonial Era

After the 1890 Treaty of Berlin, which defined the various European countries' spheres of influence in Africa, Uganda, Kenya and the islands of Zanzibar and Pemba were declared British protectorates in 1894. Although the colonial administrators adopted a policy of indirect rule, giving the traditional kingdoms a considerable degree of autonomy, major changes took place in Buganda – during this period. Cotton and coffee were introduced as cash crops, the railway between Kampala and Mombasa was completed and the concept of private ownership of land was introduced. This last measure resulted in the kabaka and a few thousand Bugandan chiefs being granted huge estates, on the basis of which they made their fortunes.

After the protectorate had been declared, the British tended to favour the recruitment of Buganda for the civil service. Other tribespeople, unable to acquire responsible jobs in the colonial administration or to make inroads into the Buganda-dominated commercial sector, were forced to seek other ways of joining the mainstream. The Acholi and Lango, for example, chose the army and became the tribal majority in the military. Thus were planted the seeds for the intertribal conflicts which were to tear Uganda apart following independence.

The Bugandan kabaka, Daudi Chwa, died in 1939 and was succeeded by his 15-year-old son, Muteesa II, who was educated at English-language boarding schools and later at Cambridge University. In 1953, however, a conflict developed between Muteesa II and the British governor over changes to the Ugandan constitution. Muteesa II was deposed and sent into exile in England. The action gave rise to a storm of protest in Buganda, and the British were eventually forced to back down and return the kabaka to his throne.

Independence

Unlike Kenya and, to a lesser extent, Tanzania, Uganda never experienced a large influx of European settlers and the associated expropriation of land. Instead, tribespeople were encouraged to grow cash crops for export through their own cooperative groups. As a result, nationalist organisations sprouted much later than those in neighbouring countries, and when they did, it was on a tribal basis. So exclusive were some of these that when independence began to be discussed, the Buganda even considered secession. By the mid-1950s, however, a Lango schoolteacher, Dr Milton Obote, managed to put together a loose coalition which led Uganda to independence in 1962 on the promise that the Buganda would have autonomy. The kabaka was the new nation's president and Milton Obote was its prime minister.

It wasn't a particularly propitious time for Uganda to come to grips with independence. Civil wars were raging in neighbouring southern Sudan, Zaïre and Rwanda and refugees streamed into Uganda, adding to its problems. Also, it soon became obvious that Obote had no intention of sharing power with the kabaka. A confrontation was inevitable.

Obote moved fast, arresting several cabinet ministers and ordering his army chief of staff, Idi Amin, to storm the kabaka's palace. The raid resulted in the flight of the kabaka and his exile in London, where he died in 1969. Following this coup, Obote had himself made president, the Bugandan monarchy was abolished, along with those of the kingdoms of Bunyoro, Ankole, Toro and Busoga, and Idi Amin's star was on the rise.

The Amin Years

Events started to go seriously wrong after that. Obote had his attorney general, Godfrey Binaisa (a Bugandan), rewrite the constitution to consolidate virtually all powers in the presidency. He then began to nationalise foreign assets.

In 1969, a scandal surfaced over US$5 million in funds and weapons allocated to the Ministry of Defence that could not be accounted for. An explanation was demanded from Amin. When it wasn't forthcoming, his deputy, Colonel Okoya, and some junior officers demanded his resignation. Shortly afterwards Okoya and his wife were shot dead in their Gulu home and rumours began to circulate about Amin's imminent arrest. It never came. Instead, when Obote left for Singapore in January 1971 to attend the Commonwealth Heads of Government Meeting (CHOGM), Amin staged a coup. The British, who had probably suffered most from Obote's nationalisation programme, were among the first to recognise the new regime. Obote left Singapore and went into exile in Tanzania.

So began Uganda's first reign of terror. All political activities were quickly suspended and the army was empowered to shoot on sight anyone suspected of opposition to the regime. Over the next eight years an estimated 300,000 Ugandans lost their lives, often in horrifying ways: bludgeoned to death with sledgehammers and iron bars or tortured to death in prisons and police stations all over the country. Nile Mansions, next to the Conference Centre in Kampala, became particularly notorious. The screams of those who were being tortured or beaten to death there could often be heard around the clock for days on end. Prime targets of Amin's death squads were the Acholi and Lango, who were decimated in waves of massacres. Whole villages were wiped out. Next he turned on the professional classes. University professors and lecturers, doctors, cabinet ministers, lawyers, businesspeople and even military officers who might have posed a threat to Amin were dragged from their offices and shot or simply never seen again.

Next in line was the 70,000-strong Asian community. In 1972 they were given 90 days to leave the country with virtually nothing but the clothes they wore. Amin and his cronies grabbed the US$1000 million booty they were forced to leave behind and quickly squandered it on new toys for the army and frivolous luxury items. Amin then turned on the British and nationalised, without compensation, US$500 million worth of investments in tea plantations and other industries. Again the booty was squandered.

Meanwhile, the economy collapsed, industrial activity ground to a halt, hospitals and rural health clinics closed, roads cracked and filled with potholes, cities became garbage dumps and utilities fell apart. The prolific wildlife was machine-gunned by soldiers for meat, ivory and skins and the tourist industry evaporated. The stream of refugees across the border became a flood.

Faced with chaos and an inflation rate which hit 1000%, Amin was forced to delegate more and more powers to the provincial governors, who became virtual warlords in their areas. Towards the end, the treasury was so bereft of funds that it was unable to pay the soldiers. At the same time, international condemnation of the sordid regime was strengthening daily as more and more news of massacres, torture and summary executions leaked out of the country.

About the only source of support for Amin at this time was Libya, under the increasingly idiosyncratic leadership of Gaddafi. Libya bailed out the Ugandan economy, supposedly in the name of Islamic brotherhood (Amin had conveniently become a Muslim by this stage), and began an intensive drive to equip the Ugandan forces with sophisticated weapons.

The rot had spread too far, however, and was way past the point where it could be arrested by a few million dollars in Libyan largesse. Faced with a restless army in which intertribal fighting had broken out, Amin was forced to seek a diversion. He chose a war with Tanzania, ostensibly to teach that country a lesson for supporting anti-Amin dissidents. It was his last major act of insanity and in it lay his downfall.

Post-Amin Chaos

On 30 October 1978 the Ugandan army rolled across north-western Tanzania virtually unopposed and annexed more than 1200 sq km of territory. Meanwhile, the airforce bombed the Lake Victoria ports of Bukoba and Musoma. President Julius Nyerere ordered a full-scale counterattack, but it took months to mobilise his ill-equipped and poorly trained forces. By the following spring, however, he had managed to scrape together a 50,000-strong people's militia composed mainly of illiterate youngsters from the bush. This militia joined with the many exiled Ugandan liberation groups (united only in their determination to rid Uganda of Amin). The two armies met. East Africa's supposedly best equipped and best trained army threw down its weapons and fled and the Tanzanians pushed on into the heart of Uganda. Kampala fell without a fight, and by the end of April, organised resistance had effectively ceased. Amin fled to Libya, where he remained until Gaddafi threw him out following a shoot-out with Libyan soldiers. He now lives in Jeddah on a Saudi Arabian pension.

The Tanzanian action was criticised, somewhat half-heartedly, by the Organization for African Unity (OAU), but it's probably true to say that most African countries breathed a sigh of relief to see the madman finally thrown out. All the same, Tanzania was forced to foot the entire war bill, estimated at US$500 million. This was a crushing blow for an already desperately poor country. No other country has ever made a contribution.

The rejoicing in Uganda was short-lived. The 12,000 or so Tanzanian soldiers who remained in the country, supposedly to assist with reconstruction and to maintain law and order, turned on the Ugandans as soon as their pay wasn't forthcoming. They took what they wanted from shops at gunpoint, hijacked trucks arriving from Kenya with international relief aid and slaughtered more wildlife.

Once again the country slid into chaos and gangs of armed bandits began to roam the cities, killing and looting. Food supplies ran out and hospitals could no longer function. Nevertheless, thousands of exiled Ugandans began to answer the new president's call to return home and help with reconstruction.

Usefu Lule, a modest and unambitious man, was installed as president with Nyerere's blessing, but when he began speaking out against Nyerere, he was replaced by Godfrey Binaisa, sparking riots supporting Lule in Kampala. Meanwhile, Obote bided his time in Dar es Salaam.

Binaisa quickly came under pressure to set a date for a general election and a return to civilian rule. Although this was done, he found himself at odds with other powerful members of the provisional government on ideological, constitutional and personal grounds – particularly over his insistence that the pre-Amin political parties not be allowed to contest the election.

The strongest criticism came from two senior members of the army, Tito Okello and David Ojok, both Obote supporters. Fearing a coup, Binaisa attempted to dismiss Ojok, who refused to step down and instead placed Binaisa under house arrest. The government was taken over by a military commission, which set the election for later that year. Obote returned from exile to an enthusiastic welcome in many parts of the country and

swept to victory in an election which was blatantly rigged. Binaisa returned to exile in the USA.

The honeymoon with Obote proved to be relatively short. Like Amin, Obote favoured certain tribes. Large numbers of civil servants and army and police commanders belonging to the tribes of the south were replaced with Obote supporters belonging to the tribes of the north. The State Research Bureau, a euphemism for the secret police, was re-established and the prisons began to fill once more. Obote was about to complete the destruction that Amin initiated. More and more reports of atrocities and killings leaked out of the country. Mass graves were unearthed that were unrelated to the Amin era. The press was muzzled and Western journalists were expelled. It was obvious that Obote was once again attempting to achieve absolute power. Intertribal tension was again on the rise, and in mid-1985 Obote was overthrown in a coup staged by the army under the leadership of Tito Okello.

The NRA Takeover

Okello was not the only opponent of Obote. Shortly after Obote became president for the second time, a guerrilla army opposed to his tribally biased government was formed in western Uganda. It was led by Yoweri Museveni, who had lived in exile in Tanzania during Amin's reign and who had served as defence minister during the chaotic administrations of 1979 and 1980.

From a group of 27 grew a guerrilla force of about 20,000, many of them orphaned teenagers. In the early days, few gave the guerrillas, known as the National Resistance Army (NRA), much of a chance. Government troops frequently made murderous sweeps across the notorious Luwero Triangle, and artillery supplied by North Korea pounded areas where the guerrillas were thought to be hiding. Few people outside Uganda even knew of the existence of the NRA, due to Obote's success in muzzling the press and expelling journalists. At times it seemed that Museveni might give up the battle – he spent several months in London at one point – but his dedicated young lieutenants kept fighting.

The NRA was not a bunch of drunken thugs like Amin's and Obote's armies. New recruits were indoctrinated in the bush by political commissars and taught that they had to be the servants of the people, not their oppressors. Discipline was tough. Anyone who got badly out of line was executed. Museveni was determined that the army would never again disgrace Uganda. Also, a central thrust of the NRA was to win the hearts and minds of the people, who learnt to identify totally with the persecuted Bugandans in the infamous Triangle.

By the time Obote was ousted and Okello had taken over, the NRA controlled a large slice of western Uganda and was a power to be reckoned with. Recognising this, Okello attempted to arrange a truce so that the leaders from both sides could negotiate on sharing power. However, peace talks in Nairobi failed. Wisely, Museveni didn't trust a man who had been one of Obote's closest military aides for more than 15 years. Neither did he trust Okello's prime minister, Paulo Mwanga, who was formerly Obote's vice president and minister of defence. Also, Okello's army was notorious for its lack of discipline and brutality. Units of Amin's former army had even returned from exile in Zaïre and Sudan and joined with Okello.

What Museveni wanted was a clean sweep of the administration, the army and the police. He wanted corruption stamped out and those who had been involved in atrocities during the Amin and Obote regimes brought to trial. These demands were, of course, anathema to Okello, who was up to his neck in corruption and responsible for many atrocities.

The fighting continued in earnest, and by late January 1986 it was obvious that Okello's days were numbered. The surrender of 1600 government soldiers holed up in their barracks in the southern town of Mbarara, which was controlled by the NRA, brought the NRA to the outskirts of Kampala itself. With the morale of the government troops at a low ebb, in February the NRA launched an all-out offensive to take the capital. Okello's troops fled, almost without a fight, though not before looting whatever remained and carting it away in commandeered buses. It was a typical parting gesture, as was the gratuitous shooting-up of many Kampala high-rise offices.

During the following weeks, Okello's rabble were pursued and finally pushed north over the border into Sudan. The civil war was over, apart from a few mopping-up operations in the extreme north-west and in Karamoja Province. The long nightmare had finally ended. Although there are occasional reports of units of Okello's army raiding frontier areas, it's a spent force. There is no mistaking which of the two armies Ugandan civilians prefer.

Despite Museveni's Marxist leanings (he studied political science at Dar es Salaam University in the early 1970s and trained with the anti-Portuguese guerrillas in Mozambique), he has proved to be pragmatic since taking control. Despite many of his officers' radical stands on certain issues, he appointed several arch-conservatives to his cabinet and made an effort to reassure the country's influential Catholic community.

In the late 1980s, peace agreements were negotiated with most of the guerrilla factions who had fought for Okello or Obote and were still active in the north and north-east. Under an amnesty offered to the rebels, by 1988 as many as 40,000 had surrendered, and many were given jobs in the NRA. In the north-west of the country, almost 300,000 Ugandans returned home from across the Sudanese border.

Since then Uganda has come a long way. Services have been restored, factories which lay idle for years are again productive, agriculture is back on line, the main roads have been resurfaced and the national parks' infrastructure has been restored and revitilised. As a result, the tourist industry is set to boom.

There was, however, still one thorn in Museveni's side: the refugee problem from neighbouring Rwanda. Western Uganda was saddled with some 250,000 Tutsi refugees who had fled Rwanda's intermittent tribal conflicts, and feeding and housing them was a severe drain on Ugandan resources. On several occasions Museveni tried hard to persuade Rwanda's President Habyarimana to set up a repatriation scheme, but to no avail. It seems Museveni's patience finally snapped, and in late 1991, Rwanda was invaded by a 5000-strong guerrilla force from western Uganda which included NRA units and weaponry.

The evidence supports the contention that Museveni knew of preparations for this, though he denies it. In any event, the rebels were thrown back across the border by the Rwandan army, assisted by troops from Belgium, France and Zaïre, and the ensuing witch-hunt of Tutsi inside Rwanda added to the number of refugees inside western Uganda. But it didn't last long. The rebels were back in force shortly afterwards and by early 1993 were in control of around one-third of the country.

Other than the occasional audible artillery barrage close to the Uganda-Rwanda-Zaïre border and the lines of Red Cross trucks in Kabale, life appears to be very peaceful and there are no visible army units anywhere. Nevertheless, the border between the two nations has been closed for some time. The spectre of thousands of refugees flooding into the area between Kisoro and the Uganda-Zaïre border is just journalistic fiction. I was there when the story appeared in the press and it was pure bullshit. There wasn't a refugee in sight!

Museveni, in common with many African rulers, is under pressure to reintroduce a multiparty system but has so far resisted the pressure on the contention that it's a premature move. He may be right. There were even reports in early 1993 that Idi Amin was in southern Sudan and planning a 'comeback'. Uganda certainly doesn't need anything of that nature ever again. Or the likes of Milton Obote. There are criticisms of Museveni's regime (some of them valid) but it has given the country a long period of stability and peace. If/when opposition parties are again legalised, let's hope they behave in a more mature fashion.

GEOGRAPHY

Uganda has an area of 236,580 sq km, of which about 25% is fertile arable land capable of providing a surplus of food. Lake Victoria and the Victoria Nile, which flows through much of the country, together create one of the best watered areas of Africa.

The land varies from semidesert in the north-east to the lush and fertile shores of the lake, the Ruwenzori Mountains in the west and the beautiful, mountainous south-west.

The tropical heat is tempered by the altitude, which averages over 1000 metres.

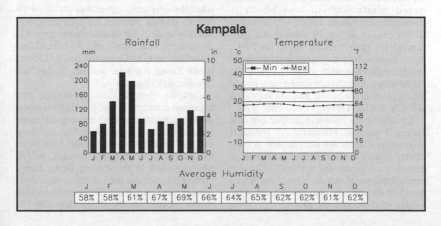

Kampala

Average Humidity											
J	F	M	A	M	J	J	A	S	O	N	D
58%	58%	61%	67%	69%	66%	64%	65%	62%	62%	61%	62%

CLIMATE

As most of Uganda is fairly flat, with mountains only in the extreme east (Mt Elgon), extreme west (Ruwenzori) and close to the Rwanda border, the bulk of the country enjoys the same tropical climate, with temperatures averaging about 26°C during the day and 16°C at night. The hottest months are from December to February, when the daytime range is 27°C to 29°C. The rainy seasons in the south are from April to May and October to November, the wettest month being April. In the north, the wet season is from April to October and the dry season is from November to March. During the wet seasons, the average rainfall is 175 mm per month. Humidity is generally low outside the wet seasons.

GOVERNMENT

Uganda is a republic and a member of the Commonwealth. The president is head of state, the government and the armed forces. The governing 80-member National Resistance Council (NRC) is made up of members of various political organisations, including the National Resistance Movement (the political wing of the NRA), the UPM, Democratic Party, Uganda People's Congress, the Conservative Party and two guerrilla organisations.

At the base of the NRM political policy is the Resistance Committee (RC) – a village-based administration tool which is responsible for village matters – members of which can, in theory, be elected and pass through the system all the way to the NRC. Apart from being a way to channel new faces into the political system, the RC provides the NRM with a direct line to disseminate policy information to the people and has improved security at a local level.

Constitutional reform is another big task facing President Museveni. A political system must be chosen and adopted. A multiparty system is not necessarily the best at present for Uganda, due to tribal and/or sectarian frictions. Hopefully a lot of the debate over reform will take place as planned at the village level through the RCs.

ECONOMY

Before Amin's coup, Uganda was approaching self-sufficiency in food and had a small but vital industrial sector and profitable copper mines. Boosting export income were the thriving coffee, sugar and tourist industries. Under Amin the country reverted almost completely to a subsistence economy. The managerial and technical elite was either expelled, killed or exiled and the country's infrastructure was virtually destroyed. Some cash crops made a tentative recovery under Obote, but Museveni's government inherited major problems.

In 1987 there was a massive devaluation, a new currency was issued, an International Monetary Fund (IMF) restructuring deal was accepted and the government made a real attempt to tackle its economic problems. Despite this, inflation was running at more than 100% within a year and another massive devaluation followed.

Uganda's problems stem from its almost total reliance on coffee, which accounts for 98% of exports, plus the fact that 60% of foreign earnings is used to pay off the country's large overseas debt.

The remainder of the exchange reserves are spent on items aimed at bringing about improvements in the long term. Short-term benefits are few and poverty is widespread.

One of the more interesting aspects of the Ugandan economy is the barter system, whereby the country makes deals with foreign trading partners, exchanging goods (usually coffee) for much-needed imports. So far it has struck deals with Algeria, Cuba, Czechoslovakia, Germany, Italy, Libya, North Korea, Rwanda, Somalia, Sudan and (the former) Yugoslavia.

Despite the obvious problems, the Ugandan economy is finally taking off again as the agricultural, manufacturing and construction sectors gather pace. The currency has also been put onto a rational basis with the introduction of Forex bureaus, which have resulted in the shilling being freely convertible against the US dollar and other hard currencies and has eliminated the black market. Gone are the days when the US dollar was being exchanged on the black market at up to 10 times the official rate.

Agriculture is the single most important component of the Ugandan economy. It accounts for 70% of gross domestic product (GDP) and employs 90% of the workforce. Coffee, sugar, cotton and tea are the main export crops. Crops grown for local consumption include maize, millet, cassava, sweet potato, beans and cereals.

The manufacturing sector's share of GDP has shrunk from 12% in 1970 to less than 4% now. Manufactured goods include textiles, soap, cement and steel products. Foreign aid is used mostly to supply vital imported fuel, purchase spare parts to get factories back to full production, and for other measures to repair the economic infrastructure.

POPULATION

Uganda's population of 16 million is increasing at the alarming rate of 2.8% per annum. It is made up of a complex and diverse range of tribes. Lake Kyoga forms the northern boundary for the Bantu-speaking peoples, who dominate much of east, central and southern Africa and, in Uganda, include the Bugandans and several other tribes. In the north live the Lango (near Lake Kyoga) and the Acholi (towards the Sudan border), who speak Nilotic languages. To the east are the Teso and Karamojong, who are related to the Maasai and who also speak Nilotic languages. Pygmies live in the forests of the west.

RELIGION

While about two-thirds of the population are Christian, the remaining one-third still practise animism, with a small percentage who follow Islam. There were sizeable numbers of Sikhs and Hindus in the country until Asians were expelled in 1972. The Asians are gradually returning, following a presidential invitation.

LANGUAGE

The official language is English, which most people can speak. The other major languages are Luganda and Swahili, though the latter isn't spoken much east of Kampala or in the capital.

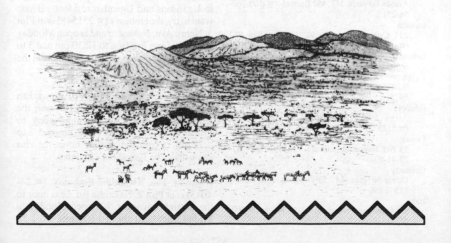

Facts for the Visitor

VISAS & EMBASSIES

Visas are required by all visitors to Uganda, except nationals of Denmark, Finland, Israel, Norway, Republic of Ireland, Sweden, and most Commonwealth countries (except Australia, Canada, India, New Zealand and Nigeria). Visa costs vary depending on your nationality: for most it's US$25. For others it's: Austria (US$24), Belgium (US$27), Canada (US$46), France (200 FF), Germany (DM 20), Italy (US$20), Netherlands (US$34), Switzerland (US$20) and USA (US$22). Two photos are required and the visas are issued in 24 hours. The above fees are for single entry; double entry costs twice as much.

Visas are available at the border on entry for the usual fee, though you probably won't need a photo. They may give you less than three months but the visa is renewable in the normal way.

Ugandan Embassies

There are Ugandan embassies in the following places:

Belgium
    Ave de Tervuren 317, 450 Brussels (☎ (02) 762-58-25)
Canada
    231 Cobourg St, Ottawa, Ontario Kin 8J2 (☎ (613) 233-7797)
Denmark
    Sofievej 15, DK 2900, Hellerup (☎ (01) 620966)
Egypt
    9 Midan El Messaha, Dokki, Cairo (☎ 348-5975)
Ethiopia
    Africa Ave H-18, K-36, N-31, Addis Ababa (☎ 513531)
France
    13 Ave Raymond Poincare, 75116 Paris (☎ 47-27-46-80)
Germany
    Duerenstrasse 44, 5300 Bonn 2 (☎ (0228) 355027/9)
Italy
    via Giuseppe Pisaneli 1, 00196 Rome (☎ 360-5211)

Japan
    5-1-1 Heimajima Ohta-ku, Tokyo 143 (☎ 768-3511)
Kenya
    Baring Arcade, 4th Floor, Kenyatta Ave, Nairobi (☎ 330801)
Rwanda
    Rue d'Epargne, Kigali (☎ 6495/6)
Sudan
    House No 9, Block 9L, St No 35, Khartoum (☎ 43049)
Tanzania
    Extelecoms Bldg, 7th Floor, Samora Ave, Dar es Salaam (☎ 31003/5)
UK
    Uganda House, 58/59 Trafalgar Sq, London WC2N 5DX (☎ (071) 839-5783)
USA
    5909 16th St NW, Washington DC 20011-2896 (☎ (202) 726-0416)
    Uganda House, 336 East 45th St, New York 10017 (☎ (212) 949-0110)
Zaïre
    17 Ave Tombalbaye/Ave de Travailure, Kinshasa (☎ 22740)
Zambia
    Kulima Tower, 11th Floor, Katunjila Rd, Lusaka (☎ 212462)

Foreign Embassies in Uganda

Burundi Don't plan on getting a visa for Burundi in Uganda, as these are only issued to Ugandans and Ugandan residents. If you want to try, the embassy (☎ 231548) is at Plot 5, Nehru Ave, Nakasero and is open Monday to Friday from 8.30 am to 12.30 pm and 3 to 5.30 pm. Otherwise, visas are available at the border on entry.

Kenya The Kenyan High Commission (☎ 231861) is at Plot 60, Kira Rd, near the Uganda Museum. It's open Monday to Friday from 8.30 am to 12.30 pm and 2 to 4.30 pm. If you apply before noon, the visa can usually be issued the same day.

Rwanda The Rwandan Embassy (☎ 24-4045) is at Plot 2, Nakaima Rd, next door to the Uganda Museum. It's open Monday to Friday from 8.30 am to 12.30 pm and 2.30

Top: Matatu station, Kampala, Uganda (GE)
Bottom: School children, Kampala, Uganda (GE)

to 5 pm. Visas cost USh 8400 (same for all nationalities) require two photos and are issued in 24 hours, or the same day if you apply early in the morning. It's advisable to get a multiple-entry visa if you plan to travel by road between Bukavu (Zaïre) and Bujumbura (Burundi). Remember that the border between Uganda and Rwanda is closed and has been for some time.

Sudan The Sudanese Embassy (☎ 243518) is at Plot 21, Nakasero Rd, and is open Monday to Friday from 9 am to noon. Visa applications are only accepted on Monday and Thursday. A one-month tourist visa costs US$10 (shillings are not accepted) and requires two photos, a letter of introduction from your embassy and an onward ticket. Visas can take anything up to a month to issue, as all applications have to be referred to Khartoum. The border between Uganda and Sudan is effectively closed due to the civil war in southern Sudan.

Tanzania The Tanzanian High Commission (☎ 56755) is at 6 Kagera Rd and is open Monday to Friday from 9 am to 3 pm. Visas are valid for three months, take two days to issue and require two photos. Costs vary according to your nationality.

Zaïre The Zaïrian Embassy (☎ 233777) is at 20 Philip Rd, Kololo, and is open Monday to Friday from 8 am to 3 pm. A one-month, single-entry visa costs US$75 (US$120 for multiple entry), a two-month, single-entry visa costs US$135 (US$180 for multiple entry), a three-month, single-entry visa costs US$200 (US$225 for multiple entry), and a six-month, single-entry visa costs US$270 (US$360 for multiple entry). Two photos are required, plus a letter of introduction from your embassy. The visa is issued in 24 hours.

There's also a Zaïrian Consulate in Kasese, open Monday to Friday from 8.30 am to 1 pm and 3 to 5 pm. Visa requirements are the same but you can get the visa the same day if you're polite but persistent.

MONEY
Currency
The Ugandan shilling (USh) is now a stable currency and floats against the US dollar. It is also fully convertible (ie you can buy Ugandan shillings with US dollars or US dollars with Ugandan shillings) since the introduction of Forex bureaus.

The only trouble with changing money is that the largest Ugandan note in circulation is USh 1000 (less than US$1), which means a lot of Ugandan notes if you change US$100. Other notes in circulation are USh 500, USh 200, USh 100, USh 50, USh 20 and USh 10. There are no coins.

Exchange Rates
US$1 = USh 1210 (cash)
US$1 = USh 1185 (travellers' cheques)
UK£1 = USh 1800 (cash/travellers' cheques)

Changing Money
Since the introduction of Forex bureaus, the Ugandan shilling trades at whatever it's worth against the US dollar/UK pound and there's very little fluctuation from day to day. Banks also trade at the same rate. There is no black market. As a result, it doesn't really matter too much where you change your money, though the Forex bureaus generally offer a slightly better rate than the banks. The trouble is that there are not Forex bureaus in every town and, where one doesn't exist, the banks take advantage of this by giving lousy rates. Likewise, hotels give lousy rates.

You will find Forex bureaus at both the Malaba and Busia border posts (Uganda-Kenya border), Jinja, Kampala (where there are scores of them), Masaka, Mbarara and Fort Portal. They don't exist in Tororo, Mbale, Kabale and Kisoro, so if you're going there, plan ahead.

If you're buying US dollars or UK pounds with hard currency cash or travellers' cheques or with Ugandan shillings, you'll have to pay a premium for them. This is negligible in the case of US dollars (USh 40 to USh 50 per dollar) but quite a bit more for UK pounds (USh 150 per pound).

Currency declaration forms have been abolished.

Costs

Since the elimination of the black market and the introduction of the Forex bureaus, Uganda is not the travel bargain it was a few years ago. Obviously, there are many ways of keeping costs to a minimum, but if you demand a reasonable level of comfort and facilities, you'll find your stack of Ugandan notes diminishing at what can be an alarming rate.

Uganda is just as expensive as Kenya – often more so because, unlike Kenya, where there is a large difference between the official rate of exchange and the rate at which the international banks trade, in Uganda there is no such difference. Here, a dollar is worth a dollar. End of story. And prices are pitched accordingly.

A mid-range hotel in Nairobi costing US\$15, for instance, will cost you US\$30 in Kampala and the facilities will be no better (and in some cases, worse). Transport is still cheap, as is food at a no-frills restaurant, but a splurge at a good restaurant will cost you more than it would in Kenya. National park entry and camping fees are much the same as those in Kenya.

BUSINESS HOURS & HOLIDAYS

Banking hours are Monday to Friday from 8.30 am to 2 pm (closed on Saturday and Sunday). Forex bureaus are generally open from 9 am to 6 pm Monday to Friday and 9 am to 1 pm on Saturday (closed on Sunday).

The following holidays are observed in Uganda:

January
  New Year's Day (1st)
  Start of NRM Government (26th)
March/April
  Good Friday
  Easter Monday
May
  Labour Day (1st)
October
  Independence Day (9th)

December
  Christmas Day (25th)
  Boxing Day (26th)

TOURIST OFFICES

There is a tourist office on Obote Ave (Parliament Ave) in Kampala but, although the staff are enthusiastic, they have very little printed information.

The Uganda National Parks office (☎ 256534, 258351), Plot 17-19, Nkrumah Rd, PO Box 3530, Kampala, is somewhat better funded and includes many expatriate workers amongst its staff. It's worth calling in here if you plan to visit any of the national parks, as it has all the latest information and an informative notice board in the reception area. On the other hand, it's not yet set up for an influx of information-seeking tourists and is generally pretty busy.

POST & TELECOMMUNICATIONS

Despite the ravages of the civil wars, international postal and telephone services are good, at least from Kampala. What is not well managed at present is the poste restante at Kampala's main post office. It's chaos, and letters are seemingly stuffed into any pigeonhole that is to hand. Checking the piles under my own initials, I came across others which spanned almost the entire alphabet. A polite request that someone sort it out was met with total indifference.

Postage rates for an airmail letter are USh 300. For parcels it's USh 1200 (one kg), USh 3300 (three kg) and USh 4500 (five kg), rising to USh 10,000 (20 kg).

Internal telephone connections have improved greatly in the past few years and are generally not a problem. International connections are good from Kampala but not from elsewhere in the country. They're also expensive. Never make an international call from a Kampala hotel unless it's a matter of life and death. They all load the bill by at least 50% (the Sheraton loads it by almost 100%!)

TIME

Ugandan time is GMT/UTC plus three hours.

MEDIA
Newspapers
Over the last few years, newspapers and magazines have mushroomed in Kampala and the pavements are awash with printed matter, though these publications are generally more expensive than their Kenyan equivalents. The daily *New Vision* is the government-owned newspaper. Unlike its equivalent in Tanzania, it's a good read, with plenty of African coverage, though less of other world events. Much better for gutsy, analytical journalism is the weekly *The Monitor*, which contains feature articles as well as better coverage of international news. It should keep you busy most of the day.

The Kenyan daily, *Nation*, is available in the late morning. International magazines like *Time, Newsweek, New African* and *South* are also readily available, but dailies are harder to find (try the shops at the Sheraton).

HEALTH
You must take precautions against malaria. Bilharzia is also a serious risk in all of Uganda's lakes and rivers. Avoid swimming and walking barefoot, especially where there are lots of reeds (the snails which are the intermediate host for the bilharzia parasite live in areas such as these).

AIDS continues to be a huge problem in Uganda. The epidemic is worst in the southwest of the country, where it is estimated that 20% of the population carry the AIDS virus. A government campaign focuses on preventing infection through fidelity and abstinence rather than through the use of condoms. Blood is screened in main medical centres and the incidence of cases arising from contaminated blood is declining. (For more information, see the Health section in the introductory Facts for the Visitor chapter.)

DANGERS & ANNOYANCES
More than any other East African country, Uganda has suffered incredibly from misgovernment, corruption, civil war, coups and badly disciplined armies. As a result, it has a lingering image as a dangerous and unstable country to visit. Only in the past few years

have tourists started to visit Uganda once more. With the stability that has been established under the Museveni government, travellers have found that Uganda is once again a safe, friendly and interesting country.

Having said that, there are still some places where your safety cannot be guaranteed, but these are limited to the area north of Murchison Falls National Park and Karamoja. If you want to visit these parts of the country, make enquiries before setting off. There's also a ratbag bunch of loony so-called Christian guerrillas who hang out in the north-west near Muchison Falls National Park and occasionally kidnap tourists (though they're generally released unharmed not too long afterwards). As for the rest of the country, it's safe to travel in.

FILM & PHOTOGRAPHY
Bring all your own equipment and film. In Kampala there are limited quantities of Kodak, Fuji, Agfa, Konica and Tudor print film but very little slide film. In other parts of the country, don't count on being able to get anything.

The *Camera Centre* (☎ 236991), Africa House, 42 Kampala Rd, Kampala, is a good place to find film. The cheapest is Tudor (USh 3700 for ·135/36) and Agfa 135/36 (USh 3950). More expensive is Kodak Gold 135/36 or Fuji 135/36 (USh 4850). This place will also do four passport photos for USh 3000 (24 hours) or USh 4500 (express).

Although there are no official restrictions on photography, there is a certain amount of paranoia about photos being taken of anything which could be interpreted as spying (military and civilian infrastructure) or of poverty or deprivation. Most of the time, there are no problems, but it's probably best to ask permission before taking photos of people. Usually they will be more than happy to be photographed, but respect their feelings if they aren't. Quite a few Ugandan homes are proudly displaying family portraits which I took, and having received the photos, they always write to wish you every happiness in the world. So if you promise a copy, please send it.

Getting There & Away

Possible access routes into Uganda are by air, land and lake. There are railways but no international trains, even though the line connects with the Kenyan system. One day it may be restored, making it again possible to travel all the way from Kasese to Mombasa by train. The only boat connection is between Uganda and Tanzania – Port Bell (Kampala) and Mwanza – across Lake Victoria. There are no passenger-boat connections between Uganda and Kenya.

AIR

International airlines serving Uganda include Aeroflot, Air Tanzania, British Airways, EgyptAir, Ethiopian Airlines, Kenya Airways, Sabena, Air Botswana and Uganda Airlines.

Few travellers enter Uganda by air because most of the discounted air fares available in Europe and North America use Nairobi as the gateway to East Africa. International airline tickets bought in Uganda have to be paid for in hard currency (though why this should be so when the Ugandan shilling is freely convertible is a mystery). However, unlike Nairobi, you will not find discounted fares available in Kampala, so if you fly out of Entebbe (Kampala's international airport), it will be more expensive.

If you intend flying from Entebbe to Nairobi, book at least a few days in advance, as flights are sometimes heavily subscribed. Flights cost US$106 one way and take between one and 1¾ hours, depending on the type of aircraft. Even if you book with Uganda Airlines, you may find yourself on an Air Botswana flight (no problem, it's a small jet and faster than an F27). In theory, Air Tanzania (☎ Kampala 234631) has flights from Kampala to Dar es Salaam on Wednesday via Nairobi and on Sunday direct (US$195 one way). It also has flights from Kampala to Kilimanjaro airport on Sunday (US$100 one way).

LAND
To/From Kenya
The two main border posts which most overland travellers use are Malaba and Busia, with Malaba being by far the more commonly used. You would probably use Busia only if you were coming from Kisumu and wishing to go directly to Jinja or Kampala, bypassing Tororo. On the other hand, the only advantage to crossing at Busia is that the border posts are right next to each other, so there's no long walk. At Malaba, you're up for a one-km walk between the two border posts.

Nairobi to Kampala via Malaba There are trains from Nairobi to Malaba via Nakuru and Eldoret on Tuesday, Friday and Saturday, leaving at 3 pm and arriving at 8.30 am the next day. In the opposite direction, they depart from Malaba on Wednesday, Saturday and Sunday at 4 pm and arrive at 9.30 am the next day. Fares are US$22/12.50/4.75 in 1st/2nd/3rd class. The trains don't connect with the Ugandan system, so you must go by road between Malaba and Tororo (and beyond, unless you want to take the extremely slow train from Tororo to Jinja or Kampala).

An alternative to the trains is the daily direct Akamba bus (either way) between Nairobi and Kampala. This leaves Kampala (Dewinton St) at 3 pm, costs USh 15,000 (about US$12.50) and arrives the following morning.

Doing the journey in stages, there are buses with different companies which travel daily between Nairobi and Malaba, departing from each place at about 7.30 pm and arriving at about 5.30 am the next day. The fare is US$5.40. If you prefer to travel by day, there are several daily buses between Nairobi and Bungoma, in each direction, which leave each place at about 8 am and arrive at about 5 pm the same day. There are also Peugeot share-taxis between Nairobi and Malaba for around US$12 per person.

There are plenty of matatus between Bungoma and Malaba (around US$1, 45 minutes). If you stay in Bungoma overnight, there are many cheap hotels to choose from.

The Kenyan and Ugandan border posts are about one km from each other at Malaba, and you will have to walk.

On the Ugandan side, there's a Forex bureau which is open seven days a week, where you can change money at the prevailing rate. You'll have to do this to pay for the matatu or taxi.

There are frequent matatus in either direction between the Ugandan side of Malaba and Tororo (US$0.30, less than one hour). Between Malaba and Jinja (US$2, two hours) or Kampala (US$3, three hours), matatus are frequent until the late afternoon. The road has been resurfaced and is excellent, though it does mean that drivers can reach terrifying speeds, especially between Jinja and Kampala. On the other hand, traffic density is far lower in Uganda than it is in Kenya.

There's also a train from Tororo to Kampala but it only runs three times a week, is diabolically slow (21 hours) and has only 3rd class. For the masochists, it costs USh 2950.

Taking a vehicle through this border crossing is fairly straightforward and doesn't take more than a couple of hours.

To/From Rwanda

Due to the civil war in Rwanda and the political tension between Uganda and Rwanda, the border between the two countries is closed. The only way you can get there is to fly or to enter via Tanzania or Zaïre.

To/From Sudan

As with the Rwandan border, overland entry into Sudan is impossible at present, and dangerous even if you managed to get that far. There's not much point in trying to do it via the Nimule border crossing anyway because you won't get any further north.

To/From Tanzania

Since the Rwandan and Sudanese civil wars cut off the south-western and northern Ugandan borders to overland traffic, the only ways to get west have been directly into Zaïre or via Tanzania into Rwanda or Burundi.

The route into Rwanda and Burundi via Tanzania goes through the Kagera salient from Masaka to Bukoba via Kyaka. This is the route which the overland companies take these days. Road conditions have improved considerably over the last few years (on the Ugandan section), so it's now possible to do the journey from Masaka to Bukoba in one day. There are matatus from Masaka to Kyotera (USh 1200, 45 minutes), and several daily pick-ups go from there to the border at Mutukula (USh 1500, one hour), departing when full. The border crossings are easy-going and there are moneychangers on the Tanzanian side, though they give a lousy rate. From the border, there's a daily Land Rover that goes to Bukoba (TSh 1500), which takes about four hours over appalling roads. If the Land Rover has departed before you arrive at the border, your only option is to hitch, and that's not easy because there's little traffic. At the checkpoint in Kyaka, you're obliged to stop and have your passport checked.

There's also a bus between Bukoba and Mutukula which departs from Bukoba daily (except Sunday) at 11.15 am, costs TSh 600 and takes about four hours. In the opposite direction, it leaves Mutukula for Bukoba at 5 pm.

We have had one report of a direct bus between Kampala and Bukoba, leaving Kampala at 7.30 am on Wednesday and Saturday, arriving in Bukoba at around 7 pm and costing USh 6000. It apparently returns from Bukoba to Kampala on Tuesday and Friday and costs TSh 3000. No other traveller has yet confirmed this, so it may no longer exist.

To/From Zaïre

The two main crossing points are south from Kisoro to Rutshuru via Bunagana, and north-west from Kasese to Beni via Katwe and

Kasindi. The Ishasha crossing between Kasese and Rutshuru is also open. There are less-used border posts further north, between Mahagi and Pakwach and between Aru and Arua. If you're thinking of crossing between Aru and Arua, you'd be wise to make enquiries about security before setting off – ratbag remnants of Amin's, Obote's and Okello's troops may still be a nuisance in this area.

Rutshuru to Kisoro The most popular and reliable crossing is that between Kisoro and Rutshuru, a distance of about 30 km, since this gives you direct access to Djomba, one of Zaïre's principal gorilla sanctuaries. The road from Kabale to Kisoro is not only spectacular but in excellent condition, even though it's a gravel road. There are daily pick-ups (very crowded) between Kabale and the border via Kisoro. Crossing into Zaïre is very straightforward and presents no hassles, but get there early in the day if you want to get to Rutshuru, as there are few pick-ups.

If you intend spending time in Zaïre, come here with a visa. Otherwise, you can buy a temporary three-day visa to visit the gorillas at Djomba (just over the border) for US$50 but you have to leave your passport at the Zaïre border post until you return. You also have to buy a new Ugandan visa to re-enter Uganda (unless you have a multiple-entry visa). This arrangement is very well established and there are no problems whatsoever. The border officials on either side are very friendly and helpful. You can even camp in front of Ugandan immigration and they'll probably join you for a beer after work. Meat (on the hoof) and beers are readily available on either side of the border.

There's reasonable accommodation in Kisoro and basic accommodation on the Zaïre side of the border.

Rutshuru to Kasese The Ishasha border is another possibility. As there's a Friday market at Ishasha, this is probably the best day to go because trucks from Rutshuru to Ishasha leave early in the morning (about 5.30 am) and return in the evening. There's also a Saturday market at Isharo (about halfway between Rutshuru and Ishasha), so there are trucks from Rutshuru early on Saturday mornings.

On the Ugandan side, the Ishasha River Camp is 17 km from Ishasha inside the Queen Elizabeth National Park. You'll have to wait for a lift, as walking in this part of the park is prohibited due to the lions. There are no supplies (apart from Primus beer from Zaïre), though the rangers will cook something up if you're desperate. Camping costs US$2 and *bandas* (circular, grass-thatched traditional-style houses) are US$4.

From Ishasha, the road to Katunguru (marked on most maps as a 2nd-class road) is impassable at present, so don't try it! The alternative route is the road through Kihihi and Rukungiri to Ishaka on the Kasese to Mbarara road. There is a steady trickle of traffic along this route, so hitching from Ishaka shouldn't be too much of a problem, and there's even the occasional matatu. The Ugandan customs official at the Ishasha border lives at Kihihi, so it may be possible to hitch with him.

Beni to Kasese The route from Beni to Kasese via Kasindi, Mpondwe and Katwe involves hitching unless you can find a matatu. Depending on the day you go, this could involve a considerable wait (hours rather than days), whichever of the two routes you use from the Ugandan border to Kasese.

Kasindi has a couple of hotels, a bar and a restaurant of sorts. It's three km from Kasindi to the border post at Bwero. You'll probably have to walk.

In Bwero, the *Modern Lodge Hotel* is a clean and very friendly concrete place. Rooms cost around US$1 per night, and coffee and omelettes are available across the road. Pick-ups leave at about 7 am for the trip to Kasese.

LAKE
To/From Tanzania
There's a regular lake service between Port Bell (Kampala) and Mwanza (Tanzania)

which departs from Port Bell on Monday at 6 pm and arrives in Mwanza on Tuesday at 10 am. In the opposite direction, it leaves Mwanza on Sunday at 3 pm and arrives in Port Bell on Monday at 7 am. It's a good trip and costs US$25/20 (USh 32,500/26,000) in 1st/2nd class, US$15 (USh 19,500) in 3rd

class. Tickets should be booked at 2 pm on the day of departure at the Port Bell port gate. This is going to involve you in a taxi trip, unless you want to hang around all day until the ferry leaves or you're staying at the nearby Silver Springs Hotel on Luzira Rd (somewhat expensive).

Getting Around

AIR

Uganda Airlines services all internal routes, but there are very few of these. Tickets must be paid for in hard currency unless you are a resident. There are usually several flights per week between Entebbe and most major centres of population but they're often cancelled at short notice. Not only that, but it's a mystery where to buy tickets outside Kampala. I didn't come across a single Uganda Airlines office anywhere else in the country.

BUS & MATATU

Uganda is the land of minibuses (matatus) and share-taxis, and there's never any shortage of them. Fares are fixed and vehicles leave when full. Unlike Kenya, where the concept of 'full' has no meaning, travel by matatu in Uganda is relatively civilised, even though many drivers are speed maniacs who go much too fast to leave any leeway for emergencies. Luckily, traffic density on Ugandan roads is much lower than on Kenyan roads, so accidents are much less frequent.

Normal buses also connect the major towns. They're cheaper than matatus, and much slower because they stop a great deal to pick up and set down passengers. They're also a lot safer.

Most towns and cities have a bus station/matatu park – simply turn up and tell people where you want to go. On the open road, just wave your hand.

TRAIN

There are two main railway lines in Uganda. The first starts at Tororo and runs west all the way to Kasese via Jinja and Kampala. The other line runs from Tororo north-west to Pakwach via Mbale, Soroti, Lira and Gulu.

Travelling by train is possibly a good way of getting from Kampala to Kasese, but frequent delays and breakdowns mean that travelling times often bear no relationship to stated times. On the rest of the system, you can forget about travelling by train – it takes forever. There are also only 3rd-class carriages available these days on Ugandan trains, so if you're looking for discomfort, this is the way to go.

Between Kampala and Kasese there is one train per week on Friday at 3 pm which supposedly arrives in Kasese at noon the following day and costs USh 2950 (3rd class).

Between Kampala and Tororo, there are trains on Monday, Wednesday and Friday at 9 am, arriving the following morning. The fare is USh 1950 (3rd class).

Between Tororo and Gulu, trains run once a week in either direction. They take about 21 hours and cost USh 3350 (3rd class).

CAR & 4WD

There's an excellent system of sealed roads between most major centres of population in the southern part of the country. Between Kampala and Mubende (on the road to Fort Portal), the road is superb, but after that it goes back to *murram* (dirt). Nevertheless, it's still easily negotiable in 2WD in the dry season. Between Fort Portal and Kasese there are several potholed sections where you need to be careful. The road between Kabale and Kisoro is gravel but is well graded and in excellent condition. In the north, minor roads are usually badly potholed and, after heavy rain, become impassable in anything other than a 4WD.

What is totally missing in Uganda, on the other hand, is road signs. There are hardly any, even outside major towns. Unless you know where you're going, it's possible to get hopelessly lost. I recently took off from Jinja and ended up at Kamuli (close to Lake Kyogya) along a beautiful tarmac road thinking it was the road to Tororo (no signs, of course). Luckily, an unemployed student who had never been to Tororo had the time to show me the right direction (which involved going back to Jinja first): a very convenient 160-km detour. I finally got there, but I'm glad he had the time of day. I think it's time the Ugandan authorities also had the time of day to put up a few signs. Are we all supposed to be clairvoyant?

Carrying a map is one suggestion, but you'll also need a compass, since there are no decent large-scale maps. Getting out of the vehicle and talking to local people is obviously the best idea, but sometimes, they don't know the way either!

What is good in Uganda is road safety. All the main roads you're likely to use are sealed and traffic volume is minimal.

Car Rental

Unlike Kenya, vehicle hire in Uganda is in its infancy and it's virtually impossible to find an agency which will hire for self-drive. A car *with* driver is the only option which most companies offer. This includes the internationals like Hertz, Avis, etc. As far as I could ascertain, the only company which will rent for self-drive is Nile Safaris (☎ 244331), Room 230, Farmers House, Parliament Ave, Kampala. James Bakeine, the owner of this company, is very helpful and has a number of Toyota Corollas (2WD) which he's willing to hire for self-drive at a negotiable rate (which is considerably less than what you would pay in Kenya, plus there are no mileage charges). Issues like deposits and insurance are, again, negotiable. The cars are not exactly new and you may need basic maintenance skills but they're essentially sound. If you have problems which cost you money to fix, James will generally discount this from the rental, so long as you have a receipt for repairs.

HITCHING

Without your own transport, hitching is virtually obligatory in some situations, such as getting into national parks to which there's no public transport. Most of the lifts you will get will be on trucks, usually on top of the load at the back, which can be a very pleasant way to travel, though sun protection is a must. Free lifts on trucks are the exception rather than the rule, so ask before you get on. Other sources for lifts are game wardens and rangers who work in the parks, international aid workers, missionaries, businesspeople and the occasional diplomat, but you may have to wait a long time in some places before anyone comes along.

BOAT

Lake Victoria Ferries

There's a regular ferry service between Port Bell (Kampala) and the Ssese Islands (Kalangala). See the Kampala chapter for details.

You can also get to the Ssese Islands from Bukakata, a small village on Lake Victoria 36 km due east of Masaka. This ferry docks at Luku, from where there's a daily bus to Kalangala. See the Ssese Islands and Masaka sections for details.

SAFARIS

Organised Safaris

When the first and second editions of this book were published, there was virtually nothing available in the way of organised safaris. This has all rapidly changed and there are now quite a few reliable companies which offer safaris to the national parks and other places of interest, including to the gorillas of Bwindi and Mgahinga in the extreme south-west of the country.

National parks which are covered by these companies include Murchison Falls, the Ruwenzori, Queen Elizabeth, Bwindi, Mgahinga and Lake Mburo. Other places of interest covered include Kibale Forest Primate Reserve, the Semliki Valley (hot springs, Pygmies), Lake Bunyonyi (Kabale) and the Source of the Nile (Jinja). None of them goes to Kidepo National Park or to Mt Elgon.

Costs Unlike Kenya, where budget travellers are well catered for with no-frills camping safaris, Ugandan companies rely heavily on lodge and hotel accommodation whilst on safari, so they're proportionally more expensive. Even where camping is involved, it's usually the luxury tented camp variety and thus no cheaper. Some companies even fly you back to Kampala from western Uganda at the end of their longer safaris. It's also true to say that the higher-priced companies tend to cater for package tourists who book in advance from overseas rather than for walk-ins. As a result, their safari prices include such things as transfers to and from Entebbe airport and first and last night accommodation at five-star hotels. On the other hand, they will discount the cost of these items from the price if you prefer to make your own arrangements.

Since none of the Ugandan companies offers genuine budget camping safaris such as those in Kenya, it's worth considering going with a Kenyan company which covers Uganda (and usually the gorillas of Zaïre). One or two even have departures from Kampala. Check out the Organised Safaris section of Kenya's Getting Around chapter.

Costs vary a great deal from one company to another and depend considerably on how many people are in the group – the more there are of you, the less you pay individually. As an example, the cost of a three-day safari to Murchison Falls National Park can vary from US$235 (two people) to US$165 (four people) or US$145 (seven people) with the cheaper companies and from US$688 (two people) to US$398 (four people) with the more expensive companies.

In general, if you assume US$55 to US$80 per person per day with the cheaper companies, US$115 to US$130 per person per day with the intermediate companies and US$220 to US$260 per person per day with the most expensive companies, you won't be too far off the mark. This should include all transport, three meals a day, accommodation (including all camping equipment where appropriate) and park entry fees (though some companies exclude park entry fees).

Note that with these prices, it is assumed that you're willing to share accommodation with one other person. If you're not, there will be an additional 'single person supplement' which will bump up the cost by quite a margin.

Departure Frequency Most companies have weekly departures (some more frequent) for all the safaris they offer. Even where departures are not so frequent, there are usually departures two or three times per month. As in Kenya, any safari company will lay on a trip almost immediately if you have a group of at least three (sometimes four) people.

Choosing a Company Among the companies which can be recommended are the following. However, note that these have been listed alphabetically and are not in any order of preference or reliability:

African Pearl Safaris
   Lower Ground Floor, Embassy House, Kampala (☎ /fax 235770) or 33 Scarborough St, Southport, Qld 4215, Australia (☎ (075) 880411; fax (075) 912583).
   This company offers three-day safaris to Murchison Falls National Park for US$398 and seven-day safaris to Queen Elizabeth National Park for US$814. It also has a five-day Mountain Gorilla Tracking safari to Bwindi National Park for US$845. As usual, these prices assume a minimum of four people. There are departures to all the above two to three times per month.
Blacklines Tours
   2 Colville St, PO Box 6968, Kampala (☎ 254240; fax 230008).
   Like African Pearl, this company is in the intermediate price range. It offers a three- day safari of Queen Elizabeth National Park (US$300), a three-day safari of Murchison Falls National Park (US$200) and a 12-day 'Circuit of the Kingdoms' which takes in Lake Mburo National Park, Lake Bunyonyi (Kabale), Queen Elizabeth National Park and Murchison Falls National Park (US$1400). These prices assume a minimum of three people. There are weekly departures to all these.
Hot Ice Ltd
   Spear House, Dewinton Rise, PO Box 151, Kampala (☎ 242733, 267441; fax 242733).
   This top-of-the-line company has been operating for years and is very well set up. It also maintains radio contact with its safaris so, if anything goes wrong, something can be done quickly. The company also owns the Rabongo Cottages in Murchison Falls National Park and recently completed a tented camp in Lake Mburo National Park. Hot Ices' short trips include a three-day Queen Elizabeth National Park safari for US$975 and a four-day Murchison Park National

Park safari for US$1140. Longer safaris include an eight-day Queen Elizabeth National Park trip for US$1987, an eight-day trip taking in the Source of the Nile, Queen Elizabeth National Park and Murchison Falls National Park for US$1590, or the same but leaving out the Source of the Nile for US$915.

Hot Ice is also one of the few companies which offer genuine camping safaris using light camping equipment. These 'Explorer Safaris' are individually tailored to your requirements and can be as short or as long as you like. They weigh in at US$187 per person per day (two people) down to US$112 per person per day (10 people), excluding park entry fees, hotel/lodge accommodation (where required) and alcoholic beverages. The parallel private tented safaris (luxury tented camps), are also tailored to your requirements, cost US$270 per person per day (two people) down to US$157 per person per day (10 people).

Hot Ice also offer 'Lake Safaris' on Lake Victoria using their own cabin cruiser based at Entebbe. Accommodation is on board the cruiser or in light tents. The cost is US$157 per person per day (two people) down to US$90 (six people), including everything except alcoholic beverages.

Jumbo Tours & Travel Ltd
PO Box 11420, Kampala (☎ 255317; fax 232716) or through Unique Travels Ltd, Plot 10 Kampala Rd, Uganda House Arcade Shop No 2, Kampala.
This company has prices similar to Nile Safaris but only offers three-day safaris to Queen Elizabeth National Park (US$285 per person) and to Murchison Falls National Park (US$185 per person). There are departures to both every Friday morning.

Nile Safaris Ltd
Room 230, Farmers House, Parliament Ave, PO Box 12135, Kampala (☎ 244331; fax 245967).
This company, which is run by James Bakeine, offers consistently cheaper safaris than anyone else. His three-day safaris to Murchison Falls National Park, and to Lake Mburo and Queen Elizabeth national parks cost US$165 and US$240 respectively. A six-day safari to Lake Mburo, Queen Elizabeth and Bwindi national parks comes to US$475 and a nine-day safari to the Source of the Nile and Lake Mburo, Queen Elizabeth and Ruwenzori national parks comes to US$695.
Nile Safaris also offers longer excursions,

such as a 14-day trip to Source of the Nile, Murchison Falls, Ruwenzori and Queen Elizabeth national parks for US$1115 and a 20-day safari which includes all the above plus Lake Mburo and Kibale Forest for US$1270. Lastly, there's a five-day Mountain Gorilla Tracking safari to Bwindi/Mgahinga for US$865. The prices assume a minimum of four people. There are departures for all these safaris every Monday, Wednesday and Friday.

This is not an exhaustive list of safari companies but most of the others are top-range. They include Belex Tours & Travel Ltd (☎ 244590) and Speedbird Tours & Travel Ltd (☎ 234669), both of which are based in the Kampala Sheraton Hotel shopping arcade.

Do-It-Yourself Safaris
The possibilities of doing this without your own transport are limited in Uganda, as there's so little traffic into the national parks. That doesn't mean you can't do it – plenty of travellers do – but it will involve a fair amount of hitching and waiting around for a ride. Climbing the Ruwenzori is much easier in this respect, as it's all very well organised and caters to walkers. All you have to do is get yourself to Kasese and contact the Rwenzori Mountaineering Services office there. They'll get you fixed up and arrange transport to the trail head at Nyabitaba. See the Ruwenzori Mountains section in the Uganda National Parks chapter for details.

Climbing Mt Elgon isn't so easy to arrange at present, as the Mt Elgon Conservation & Development Project is still in its infancy and there's a lot of work to be done. On the other hand, those who work on this project are very enthusiastic and will help out with information and even with transport where possible. See the Mt Elgon section in the Uganda National Parks chapter for details.

Kampala

The Ugandan capital, Kampala, suffered a great deal during the years of civil strife following Idi Amin's defeat at the hands of the Tanzanian army in 1979. The turmoil only ended with the victory of Yoweri Museveni's NRA in early 1986. The city still carries the scars of street fighting and looting, the enforced departure of its Asian population and the years of corruption.

Unless you've had previous experience of upheavals like these, it's hard to believe the amount of gratuitous destruction and looting that went on: office blocks and government offices had the bulk of their windows shattered; the buildings were riddled with rifle fire; plumbing and electrical fittings and telephone receivers were ripped from walls; buses were shot at and abandoned; and stores were looted of everything, down to the last bottle of aspirin or the last odd shoes.

Kampala is getting back on its feet, and is now much more like a normal city – the electricity works, water comes out of the taps, buildings are being rehabilitated and the shops and markets are once again well stocked. The major roads are in fairly good condition and matatus and taxis ply the streets regularly. Even the Asians are returning. Uganda also seems to be the flavour of the '90s with international aid agencies. A large proportion of the traffic on Kampala's roads obviously belongs to one or another of them.

The good thing about Kampala, in stark contrast to Nairobi, is that it's quite safe to walk around at any time of the day or night. You won't get mugged here, the city is green and attractive, and the people are friendly. There's also plenty happening these days.

Orientation

Kampala is said to be built on seven hills, though you'll probably spend most of your time on just one of them – Nakasero, in the city centre. The top half of this hill is a type of garden city, with its wide, quiet avenues lined by flowering trees and its large, detached houses behind imposing fences and hedges. Here you'll find many of the embassies, international aid organisations, top-class hotels, rich people's houses, the high court and government buildings.

Between Nakasero and the lower part of the city is Kampala's main thoroughfare – Kampala Rd (which turns into Jinja Rd at one end and Bombo Rd at the other). On this road are the main banks, the post and telecommunications office, the railway station and a few hotels and restaurants.

Below Kampala Rd, towards the bottom of the valley, are heaps of different shops and small businesses, budget hotels and restaurants, the market, the immense *gurdwaras* (temples) of the very much depleted Sikh community (one temple has been converted into a school), and the bus and matatu stations.

It's a completely different world to that on the top side of Kampala Rd. Here there are potholed, congested streets thronged with people, battered old cars and minibuses, overflowing garbage skips, impromptu street markets, and pavement stalls offering everything from rubber stamps to radio repairs. There are hawkers, newspaper sellers, hustlers, and one of the most mind-boggling and chaotic matatu stands you're ever likely to see. This is Kampala's answer to Nairobi's River Rd.

To the east, across the golf course, is Kololo, which is a fairly exclusive residential area. Many embassies are situated here, as are a few hotels and the Uganda Museum. To the west is Namirembe, on top of which stands the Anglican Cathedral.

To the south of the city centre lies Tank Hill, across the railway tracks, where there are a number of mid-range hotels, good restaurants and that famous Kampala landmark the Half London, to which everyone in search of good live music goes.

Information

Tourist Office The Ministry of Tourism & Wildlife (☎ 32971) acts as a tourist office. It's on Obote Ave (Parliament Ave), PO Box 4241, opposite the British High Commission and the US Embassy. The staff are very friendly and helpful and do their best under trying circumstances.

The Uganda National Parks office (☎ 256534, 258351), Plot 17-19, Nkrumah Rd, PO Box 3530, Kampala, is somewhat better funded and includes many expatriate workers amongst its staff. It's worth calling in here if you plan to visit any of the national parks, as it has all the latest information and an informative notice board in the reception area. On the other hand, it's not yet set up for an influx of information-seeking tourists and can be rather busy.

Post & Telecommunications The GPO is on the corner of Kampala and Speke Rds. It's open Monday to Saturday from 8 am to 5 pm, and on Sunday from 9 to 11 am.

The poste restante here is chaos, run by someone who doesn't know the difference between A and Z. The chances of finding anything under your initial are negligible. You'll have to check the lot, and that's not easy, as the person who staffs it is stroppy. Good luck!

The post office also houses the international telephone exchange, and there are public phones where you can ring overseas. First pay for the call, then they'll connect you.

Money Kampala Rd and the streets parallel to it going up the hill is where you'll find all the banks and Forex bureaus. The Forex bureaus generally stay open longer than the banks. If you want to change money at the weekend, there's also a branch of the Standard Chartered Bank in the shopping complex of the Sheraton Hotel which is open on Saturday from 9 am to 1 am and which changes at normal Forex rates. Also here is Express Uganda (☎ 236767, PO Box 353), the American Express agent, offering the usual range of Amex facilities, including a clients' mail service.

Bookshops For English-language publications, the best place to try is the Uganda Bookshop on Colville St. Excellent large-scale maps of Uganda (Series 1301, Sheet NA-36) with a lot more detail than any of the usual maps of East Africa (Michelin, Bartholomew's, etc) can sometimes be bought here. There are other bookshops along Kampala Rd but their stock is limited.

Things to See

Uganda Museum The Uganda Museum on Kira Rd was closed for years but is now open again Monday to Saturday from 10 am to 6 pm and on Sunday from 3 to 6 pm. Entry costs USh 1500 (USh 200 for Ugandan residents). It has good ethnological exhibits covering hunting, agriculture, war, religion and *juju*, as well as archaeological and natural history displays. Perhaps its most interesting feature is a collection of traditional musical instruments, which you're allowed to play.

A booklet for sale here, *Kasubi Tombs*, describes the history of the Buganda and the royal palace enclosure on the hill above Makerere University.

There's also an office of the East African Wildlife Society at the museum, open from 10 am to noon on Monday, Wednesday and Friday.

Kasubi Tombs Another 'must see' are the Kasubi Tombs (also known as the Ssekabaka's Tombs), on Kasubi Hill just off Masiro Rd, which were first built in 1881. Here you will find the huge traditional reed and bark cloth buildings of the kabakas (kings) of the Buganda people. The group of buildings contains the tombs of Muteesa I, his son Mwanga, Sir Daudi Chwa II, and his son Edward Muteesa II, the last of the kabakas. He died in London in 1969, three years after being deposed by Obote. As a result of recent political pressure by the Buganda, there are now moves to bring back his young son and reinstate him as kabaka,

UGANDA

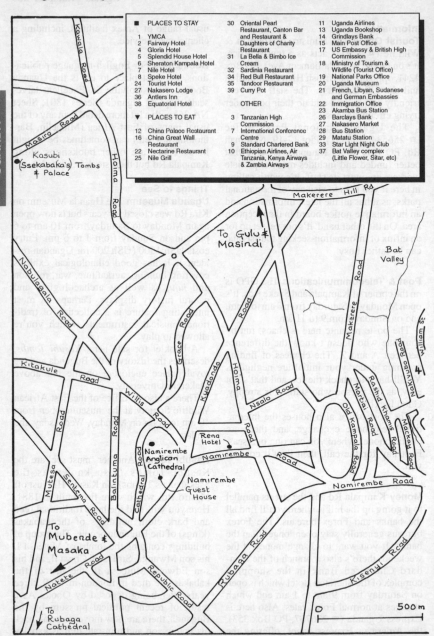

PLACES TO STAY

1 YMCA
2 Fairway Hotel
4 Gloria Hotel
5 Splendid House Hotel
6 Sheraton Kampala Hotel
7 Nile Hotel
8 Speke Hotel
24 Tourist Hotel
27 Nakasero Lodge
36 Antlers Inn
38 Equatorial Hotel

PLACES TO EAT

12 China Palace Restaurant
16 China Great Wall Restaurant
22 Nectarine Restaurant
25 Nile Grill

30 Oriental Pearl Restaurant, Canton Bar and Restaurant & Daughters of Charity Restaurant
31 La Bella & Bimbo Ice Cream
32 Sardinia Restaurant
34 Red Bull Restaurant
35 Tandoor Restaurant
39 Curry Pot

OTHER

3 Tanzanian High Commission
7 International Conference Centre
9 Standard Chartered Bank
10 Ethiopian Airlines, Air Tanzania, Kenya Airways & Zambia Airways

11 Uganda Airlines
13 Uganda Bookshop
14 Grindlays Bank
15 Main Post Office
17 US Embassy & British High Commission
18 Ministry of Tourism & Wildlife (Tourist Office)
19 National Parks Office
20 Uganda Museum
21 French, Libyan, Sudanese and German Embassies
22 Immigration Office
23 Akamba Bus Station
26 Barclays Bank
27 Nakasero Market
28 Bus Station
29 Matatu Station
33 Star Light Night Club
37 Bat Valley complex (Little Flower, Sitar, etc)

Kasubi (Ssekabaka's) Tombs & Palace

To Gulu & Masindi

Makerere Hill Rd

Bat Valley

Kitakule Road

Rena Hotel

Namirembe Anglican Cathedral

Namirembe Guest House

Namirembe Road

Namirembe Road

To Mubende & Masaka

To Rubaga Cathedral

0   500 m

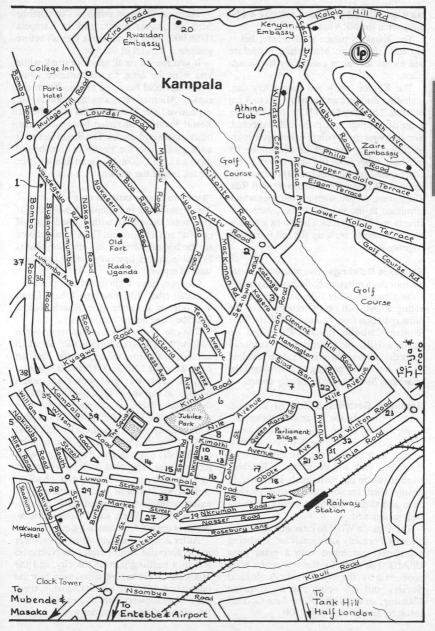

Kampala

Kira Road

20

Kenyan Embassy

Kololo Hill Rd

Acacia Drive

College Inn

Bombo Road

Paris Hotel

Mulago Hill Road

Lourdel Road

Rwandan Embassy

Athina Club

Windsor Crescent

Mabua Road

Elizabeth Ave

Zaire Embassy

Philip Road

Upper Kololo Terrace

1

Wandegeya Rd

Buganda Road

Nakasero Rd

Lumumba

Akii-Bua Road

Nakasero Hill Road

Mewate Road

Kyadondo Road

Kafu Road

Kitante Road

Golf Course

Acacia Avenue

Elgon Terrace

Lower Kololo Terrace

Golf Course Rd

37

Lumumba Ave

Lumumba Road

36

Old Fort

Radio Uganda

Nakasero Road

Sezibwa Road

Katonga Road

Kagera Road

2

3

Shimoni Road

Clement Hill Road

Golf Course

Hannington Road

Siad Barre

38

Kyagwe Road

Ternan Avenue

Victoria Road

Princess Ave

Speke Ave

Kintu Ave

Nile Avenue

7

22

Nile Avenue

Jinja / Tororo

23

5

Kampala Road

William Street

Wilson Road

34

35

39

The Square

Jubilee Park

Speke Rd

Pilkington

Kimathi St

Colville St

Queen Mary's Gdns

Parliament Bldgs

Obote Ave

De Winton Road

Jinja Road

Nakivubo Road

Allen Road

8

6

10 11

12 13

17

18

21 30

31 32

9

14

15

16

26

33

25

24

Nakivubo Place

Stadium

28

29

Luwum Street

Burton St

Market Street

Sikh St

Kampala Road

Nkrumah Road

Nasser Road

Rosebury Lane

19

27

Makwano Hotel

Clock Tower

To Mubende & Masaka

Nsambya Road

To Entebbe & Airport

Railway Station

Kibuli Road

To Tank Hill Half London

but it's a political hot potato and may not be quite what the NRA has in mind.

The kabaka's palace is also here, but is closed to the public. Meanwhile, the palace and tombs are taken care of by the Ganda clans.

The Kasubi tombs are open every day, including Sundays and holidays, from 8 am to 6 pm. The entry fee of USh 1000 includes a guide, though a tip is half expected. Remove your shoes before entering the main building. You can get to the tombs by minibus, either from the matatu park in the city centre (ask for Hoima Rd) or from the junction of Bombo and Makerere Hill Rds. The minibuses you want are the ones which terminate at the market at the junction of Hoima and Masiro Rds. The tombs are a few hundred metres' walk up the hill from here (signposted).

Religious Buildings Also worth a visit are the four main religious buildings in Kampala – the gleaming white Kibuli mosque dominating Kibuli Hill on the other side of the railway station from Nakasero Hill, the huge Roman Catholic Rubaga Cathedral on Rubaga Hill, the Namirembe Anglican Cathedral (where the congregation is called to worship by the beating of drums) and the enormous Sikh temple in the city centre.

Botanical Gardens & Zoo At Entebbe, outside Kampala, the Botanical Gardens are worth visiting if you have half a day available. Laid out in 1898 by A Whyte, the first curator, they're along the lake side between the sailing club and the centre of Entebbe. Even if you're not particularly interested in botany, there are some interesting, unusual trees and shrubs and the gardens are fairly well maintained.

The Uganda Wildlife Education Centre is close by. Formerly just a small zoo, it is being completely revamped with a grant from USAID. The plans for the new centre were produced by the New York Zoological Society and it's being run by Christen Manning, an associate of the Jane Goodall Institute. Entry costs USh 1000.

There are frequent minibuses to Entebbe from the central matatu park in Kampala (USh 900, 35 to 40 minutes). Get off before you reach the end of the line.

If you need a meal, snack or drink while you're in the area, try the Entebbe Club, which has cold beer and reasonably priced meals. Alternatively, try the popular but expensive Lake Victoria Hotel or the Beach Resort Entebbe for cheap barbecued meat, other snacks and drinks. The Beach Resort is quite a walk from the 'centre' of Entebbe and there's a USh 1750 entry fee on Sunday (free for the rest of the week).

Places to Stay – bottom end
Accommodation in Kampala is not cheap if you want anything with a modicum of comfort and a bathroom. There's little choice for the budget traveller and much of what is available in this bracket is in an appalling state of repair.

Campers have a choice of two places in Kampala (the YMCA and the Athena Club) and one in Entebbe (the Beach Resort Entebbe). See below for details.

The one saving grace in this range is the YMCA (☎ 230804) on Buganda Rd, about 15 minutes' walk from the city centre. You can camp here for USh 3500 (USh 3000 with a YMCA card) but you won't get much privacy, as the site is on a playing field. In the building itself, you can sleep on the floor with a mat for USh 4000 (USh 3500 with a YMCA card) or with a mattress for USh 5000 (USh 4500 with a YMCA card). It's a popular and friendly place to stay, though somewhat inconvenient (you must pack up and be out by 8 am each day, as it's used as a school on weekdays). The showers are erratic and the toilets could do with a good scrub, but otherwise it's OK. There's also a canteen here, which is open from 7 am to 8 pm.

As far as hotel accommodation goes, there is the Splendid House Hotel on Nakivubo Rd, in a bustling part of the city, and the Makwano Hotel on Nakivubo Place, near the bus station. Both are barely habitable, there are bucket showers only and the toilets are full of shit – only for the desperate.

Not much better, but habitable, is the *Hotel Gloria* (☎ 233638), just a few minutes' walk from the centre on William St. It has singles/doubles at USh 10,500/13,000 plus a restaurant (meals for USh 1200 to USh 2000), bar and laundry service. Checkout time is 9 am. In much the same league is the *Nakasero Lodge* opposite the Nakasero Market. It's convenient, the rooms are fairly clean and not too small and at USh 900/15,000/19,500 a single/double/triple with shared bath, it's reasonable value.

Far better but a long way from the centre is the *College Inn Bar & Restaurant*, just off the large roundabout at the top of Bomba Rd. Here you can get a single/double with shared bathroom facilities for USh 10,000/14,000 or the same with own bathroom for USh 12,000/16,000. The staff are friendly and the food in the restaurant is good. Just round the corner from here on Mulago Hill Rd is the *Paris Hotel*, which offers remarkably cheap singles/doubles with shared facilities for just USh 3800/5600. There's a clean and popular bar downstairs but the rooms are nothing special. They're basically for short-time use by the bar customers.

If you intend to take the ferry from Port Bell to Mwanza (Tanzania), a cheap place to stay the night before is *St John's Hostel*, next to the Silver Springs Hotel (expensive). It's very clean, has hot showers and mosquito nets and costs USh 5000 per person per night.

Places to Stay – middle

Cheapest in this range (though it only barely qualifies as mid-range) is the very central *Tourist Motel* (☎ 257426) on Kampala Rd. Self-contained singles/doubles here cost USh 10,900/13,800. There's no hot water and breakfast is extra. The trouble with this place is that because of its location and price, it's usually full. Try to book a room in advance, even if you stay elsewhere for a couple of days.

West of the city centre, the *Rena Hotel* (☎ 273504) on Namirembe Rd is good value, at USh 10,350 for a single with shared facilities or USh 14,950 with private bathroom.

A double with private bath is USh 23,000 and there are 'apartment suites' for USh 46,000. The hotel has its own bar and restaurant. Not far from here, up the hill and next to the Namirembe Cathedral, is the *Namirembe Guest House* (☎ 272071). It's set in spacious grounds in a quiet suburb and has a range of rooms available. Dormitory beds cost USh 5000 in the old wing and USh 6000 in the new wing. Singles/doubles/triples with shared bath cost USh 10,000/13,000/18,000 in the old wing; self-contained rooms in the new wing are USh 12,000/17,000/22,500. It's a pleasant place to stay. Meals are available for USh 2000 (breakfast), USh 3500 (lunch) and USh 4000 (dinner).

To get to either of the above, take a Namirembe matatu from the matatu park, or walk.

Up in price but in a noisy position along Bomba Rd is the *Antlers Inn* (no telephone), which offers self-contained doubles for USh 30,000. There are no singles. The hotel has its own bar and restaurant.

Out of the centre, off Makindye Rd, the *Calendar Rest House* (☎ 243727) has singles with shared facilities for USh 16,100 and self-contained singles/doubles for USh 17,250/20,000 (USh 34,000 for a twin-bed). It's a very pleasant spot with well-maintained gardens, a bar and restaurant and guarded parking. To get there, go down Entebbe Rd to the clock tower, then along Entebbe Rd to the first roundabout and turn left. It's signposted off to the right about 300 metres after the turn-off from the roundabout.

Places to Stay – top end

Most of the accommodation in this price bracket is quoted in hard currency (US dollars or UK pounds), and that's the manner in which you'll be expected to settle the bill, though there are exceptions.

Very popular is the *Speke Hotel* (☎ 254553/6), Nile Ave, PO Box 7036, Kampala. It has plenty of character and atmosphere. Renovations have been underway for some time, though work on the main block has yet to start. Most of the rooms are self-contained and spacious and the majority have a balcony. The cheapest single rooms with shared facilities cost US$50 and the same with own bathroom are US$60. 'Standard' singles/doubles are US$70/80, 'executive' singles/doubles are US$80/90 and twin-bed rooms cost US$100/110. All prices include breakfast. The terrace bar is a very popular meeting place, there's a snack bar/coffee shop and the new restaurant should be open by the time you read this. Credit cards are not accepted.

The *Fairway Hotel* (☎ 25957) on Kafu Rd, near the golf course, is essentially for those intending to stay a long time, though it will also rent rooms for the night. It's used mainly by expatriate workers. Self-contained singles with bed and breakfast cost US$58.50. Monthly rentals without breakfast cost US$805/920 for singles/doubles. There's a bar (open 12.45 to 2 pm and 5 to 10 pm) and restaurant. Credit cards are not accepted.

East of here, on Kololo Hill, is the *Athina Club* (☎ 241428) on Windsor Crescent. This is a great place to stay, with lots of atmosphere, and is run by Greek Cypriots (the Cypriot High Commission is also here). Overland safari companies use the Athina for camping (which costs USh 3000 per person per night) but it's not the best of sites – basically a gravel car park. Self-contained singles/doubles with hot water and full board cost US$60/70. Nonresidents can also eat here for USh 7500 (lunch or dinner). There's a guarded car park.

As this edition was being researched, a new hotel was nearing completion at the junction of Kampala and Kyagwe Rds. By the time you read this, the *Equatoria Hotel* should be open, but we have no details of cost as yet.

South-east of the city centre and very close to Port Bell is the *Silver Springs Hotel* (☎ 221231), on Luzira Rd in the Nakawa suburb. It's very convenient if you intend taking the Lake Victoria ferry from Port Bell to Mwanza (Tanzania) but is otherwise a long way out unless you have transport. It offers a number of self-contained cottages, which cost USh 23,300 (small), USh 28,750 (medium) or USh 34,500 (large), plus self-contained double rooms in the main block (USh 16,100). The hotel has a bar, restaurant, swimming pool and gym. To get there, take a Luzira matatu from the city centre.

On Tank Hill, also to the south-east, are two hotels popular with expatriate residents; but forget about staying here unless you have your own transport, as they are near the top of the hill and some considerable distance from a matatu route. The views from either, on the other hand, are excellent. First up the hill, and clinging to it like a Bhutanese temple on a rocky ledge, is the *Hotel Diplomate* (☎ 254240), which has an excellent range of suites on the upper floor ranging from US$50 to US$80 a double, all self-contained and with a TV/video. Prices are negotiable (if they're not busy, you can expect a discount of US$10 on any of the rooms). The staff are very friendly, there's a bar, restaurant and even a video bank. All major credit cards are accepted.

Up the hill a little further but off the same road is *The Pennine* (☎ 267145), predictably run by a northern Englishman. It's smaller than the Diplomate and offers spacious, self-contained double rooms with TV and full breakfast for US$60 (US$45 per night for long-stay visitors). There's a bar and restaurant and it's a popular place for a traditional English roast lunch on Sundays. Credit cards are not accepted.

At the very top end of this scale are two hotels in the centre of town, on Nakasero Hill. The *Sheraton Kampala Hotel* (☎ 244-590) on Ternan Ave just above the Speke Hotel, is situated in what used to be Jubilee Park (which is open to the public in daylight hours but closes at 7 pm). It has all the facilities you'd expect of a Sheraton Hotel, including swimming pool, several restaurants and bars, and a shopping precinct. There's live music in the enclosed bar every night and the same in the open-air bar on Sunday afternoon and evening (no charge for entry). Singles/doubles with breakfast cost US$150/168, though there are considerable discounts if you stay for a month or longer. All credit cards are accepted.

Even more expensive than the Sheraton is the *Nile Hotel* (☎ 235900), adjacent to the Uganda International Conference Centre on Nile Ave. It has all the usual facilities and offers singles/doubles for US$110/140 and executive suites for US$175/225, plus 15% government tax. Prices do not include breakfast. It's often fully booked when there is a conference in progress.

Places to Stay – Entebbe
Even though Entebbe is 35 km from Kampala, it's essentially a suburb of the capital and is also where the international airport is situated.

The cheapest place to stay here is the *Beach Resort Entebbe* (no telephone), right on the shores of Lake Victoria. You can camp on a fine grassy site here for USh 2300 per person but bring insect repellant with you as there are plenty of sandflies. Alternatively, they have pleasant, self-contained rondavels with double beds (USh 45,000 single or double). There's a large picnic area here with sheltered tables and benches. Beers and soft drinks are available, as well as meals and snacks. The camp site is used by a number of overland truck companies.

At the top end of the market is the well-appointed *Lake Victoria Hotel* (☎ 21096, 20027), which has standard singles/doubles for US$91/99 and executive suites for US$113/121, including breakfast and all taxes. There's a swimming pool, bars and restaurants. It's a very popular place among the well-heeled for a meal and drinks on the weekend.

Places to Eat – cheap
If you're staying at the YMCA (as many travellers do), there are a couple of cheap local restaurants by the roundabout, or eat at the YMCA's own canteen. There's also the *College Inn Bar & Restaurant*, which has good meals of roast chicken or steak and chips at very reasonable prices.

Down in the centre on Kampala Rd, diagonally opposite the Tourist Motel, is the *Sindbad*. This Italian-Ethiopian restaurant does very tasty and reasonably priced food which you can either eat there or take away.

In the Uganda House arcade (adjacent to the Nile Grill) is *Beatons Bakery*, which offers excellent cookies. Next door, the *Hot Loaf Bakery* does great pastries, samosas and bread.

Places to Eat – more expensive
A popular city centre meeting place on Kampala Rd is the *Nile Grill*. It's not the cheapest place to go but is popular with expatriate aid workers and well-to-do locals. Outside there are tables with umbrellas. The food is expensive and not that great, but if you're hanging out for a steak or roast chicken, it's one place to head for. Many people come here for just a coffee or a beer. It's open Monday to Saturday from 9 am to 10 pm and on Sunday from 9 am to 9 pm. There's a notice which says 'Cover charge of USh 3000 for guests sitting idle'.

For Chinese food, there's a good selection of places to go. Well regarded is the *China Palace Restaurant*, located on the 1st floor of the high-rise office building on Pilkington St (signposted, though inadequately, on the ground floor). Main dishes cost from USh 3000 to USh 5000. It's open Tuesday to Sunday for lunch and dinner. Also very good is the *China Great Wall* on Kampala Rd, up from and opposite the Nile Grill. It's open daily from noon to 11 pm. Right next door is the *Slow Boat Pub*. Similar to the China Great Wall is the *Oriental Pearl*, between Jinja Rd and Dewinton St, which has a similar range of dishes at much the same price. The Oriental is open from noon to 3 pm and 6.30 to 11.30 pm daily but they also offer fast foods and takeaways. Almost next door is the *Canton Bar & Restaurant*, and below it is the *Daughters of Charity Restaurant*, which is open from 7 am to 7 pm and offers economical Anglo-Ugandan breakfasts and lunches.

The place in town for ice cream is *Bimbo Ice Cream* opposite the Oriental and the Canton.

UGANDA

For Indian food, you probably can't beat a meal at the *Sitar Indian Restaurant* on Bomba Rd. Part of the Bat Valley nightclub complex, it's open for lunch and usually (but not always) in the evenings. There's also the *Tandoor*, 70 Kampala Rd, which puts on daily lunch-time buffets (eat-all-you-can) for USh 6500 plus tax. Another popular Indian restaurant is the *Curry Pot*, on Kampala Rd close to the Red Bull. It offers good curries and stews for USh 2500 to USh 3500.

On the other side of Kampala Rd, opposite Central Park, is *Burger Queen*, where you can sit outside on a balcony overlooking the road and have a good meal for USh 2000 to USh 5000.

For an absolutely superb, mouth-watering German-style meal cooked to perfection, head for the *Red Bull Restaurant* on Kampala Rd. This restaurant is famous in Kampala for its excellent food, and the German owner is quite a character. Even the Sheraton buys its meat from him (there's a butchery next door, which he also runs). It's a splurge – you're looking at around USh 10,000 including a beer – but you won't be sorry you ate here and you'll probably be back. The interior of the restaurant resembles something out of rural Bavaria.

The *Sardinia* on Dewinton St is also well-regarded for a splurge. It serves a range of grills for around USh 7000 to USh 8000 and puts on a Saturday lunch-time Chinese menu. If you're thinking of eating here in the evening, check that's it's going to be open beforehand – it may not be.

For Greek food, the best place to go is the *Athina Club*, on Windsor Crescent in Kololo. It's run by Greek Cypriots, so you know the food is authentic. You're looking at around USh 9000 for a meal. It's open for both lunch (buffet) and dinner (à la carte).

Despite its somewhat formidable reputation as an expensive place, the *Sheraton Kampala Hotel* also offers reasonable Western-style food for around USh 7000 to USh 8000, so long as you stick to the ground-floor terrace bars (the Rhino and Hippo bars) or the buffet at the Lion Bar (separate from

the main building but in the same grounds). The all-you-can-eat buffet meals are particularly good value. There's also live music at the Lion Bar on Sundays. The restaurants on the 1st floor of the Sheraton (Victoria and Crane Gourmet restaurants) are much more expensive. You might also want to check out the buffet breakfast at the Sheraton – for USh US$8, you can tuck into a mind-boggling array of food as often as you like. You won't need lunch when you've finished.

Further afield, a very popular place with excellent food is the *Half London* on Gaba Rd (sometimes spelt Ggaba). They offer a range of grills and Western-style food and the service is good but it's not just a restaurant. The bar is one of *the* places to go in the evenings amongst young people, both Black and White. It's packed every night and there's a live band which plays a mixture of African and Western music and never seems to take a break. You're looking at around USh 8000 for a meal.

Closer to town and just off Gaba Rd is the *Fasika* which, according to resident expatriates, has the best Ethiopian food in town. Main courses cost around USh 3500.

It's also possible to eat at *The Nectarine*, in the basement of the Crested Crane Towers at the roundabout on Nile Ave opposite the Uganda International Conference Centre. Like the Half London, it's basically a music joint, though it only has live music (jazz) on Thursdays. For the rest of the week, it's recorded music.

Entertainment

Nightlife in Kampala is much improved on what it was a few years ago. One of the cheapest and most informal nightclubs and one where there's always a good crowd is the *Star Light Night Club* (formerly known as the California Bar) on Luwum St. This is where the Centra Volcano Band has its residency, and they play here most nights (exclusively African music). They're very good and go on until late. Entry costs USh 2300 and beer prices are low. Up on Bombo Rd is the *Bat Valley* complex, next to UNICEF and near the YMCA. At the back is the *Little Flower Night Club*, which has been going for years but which only opens on Friday and Saturday nights. It's an open-air place under shady trees and costs USh 4200 entry.

Two popular all-night discos in the city centre are *Club Clouds*, Nkrumah Rd, and the *Club Tropicana One-Ten*, Jinja Rd. The Tropicana is open on Wednesday (USh 2000), Friday (USh 2500) and Saturday (USh 3000). Perhaps the most popular disco is the *Ange Noir* (pronounced locally as 'Angenoa'), which is off Jinja Rd east of the two main roundabouts leaving the city centre and behind buildings which line the road on the right-hand side. Everyone knows it but it's not signposted on the main road. It's open nightly and entry costs between USh 3500 and USh 4500, depending on the night.

As previously mentioned under Places to Eat, the *Half London* (on Gaba Rd below Tank Hill) is also a very popular place to pick up live music any night of the week but especially from Thursday to Sunday. It's partially open-air, partially enclosed, the crowd is multiracial, the bar is friendly and boisterous, the band never stops playing (and will let you sing or play an instrument if you're anywhere near half good) and the beers are normal price. There's no entry charge at the Half London. Get here early at weekends if you want a table or the luxury of parking anywhere within 500 metres of the joint. Without your own transport you'll need a taxi – there are very few matatus along this road at night.

A popular local bar in the city centre is the *Rooftop Bar*, across from the Florian Bar and close to the Mukwana Hotel. It has a live band every night, and the view of the bustling night market three levels below is magic. Chicken and salad is served for USh 1200.

Don't forget the open-air *Lion Bar* at the Sheraton on Sunday.

Much lower key is the *Nectarine*, in the basement of Crested Crane Towers on Nile Ave, opposite the Nile Hotel.

If you want to meet journalists and have a spirited discussion on politics and the like in the evening, try *La Bella* bar at the corner of Dewinton St and Siad Barre Ave. This is where the crew from *The Monitor* go after work.

The club bar at the British High Commission on Obote Ave (Parliament Ave) is open on Tuesday, Thursday and Friday evenings, though you need to be signed in by a member since, in order to buy drinks, you need coupons (cash is not accepted). If you're going to be staying in Kampala a long time, membership costs US£20 plus USh 5000. Contact Karen Bate (☎ 257054).

If you're interested in traditional dance and music, check out a troupe called the Ndere Troupe. It's composed of members of the many ethnic groups in Uganda and has gained international acclaim in Europe and North America. They perform every Saturday at the Sheraton Hotel in the barbecue area and every other Sunday at the Lake Victoria Hotel in Entebbe. They are also preparing a cultural village which will offer classes in dance and music on a personal basis as well as promoting traditional arts (such as woodcarving and instrument making). Additional information can be obtained from the troupe's director, Stephen Rwangyezi, who is also director of the National Theatre (☎ 254567/8), PO Box 11353, Kampala.

Theatre buffs should check out the National Theatre above Dewinton St. They have a regular programme of events and offer performances in English and vernacular languages. The Ndere Troupe (mentioned earlier) perform at the theatre and the Alliance Française is also located here.

Getting There & Away

Air Uganda Airlines (☎ 232990), Kenya Airways (☎ 233068), Zambia Airways (☎ 244007), Ethiopian Airlines (☎ 254796) and Air Tanzania all have offices on Kimathi Ave. Sabena (☎ 234200) is in the Sheraton Hotel and Aeroflot (☎ 231703) is on Parliament Ave. EgyptAir (☎ 236910) is in Metropole House, Entebbe Rd. British Airways (☎ 257414), which only recently resumed flights to Uganda, had no established office at the time this book was being researched.

Bus Buses leave for Kasese daily at 7 am and go via Mbarara. There is no advance booking, so be there an hour before and fight your way on or you could be standing the entire way. The trip takes eight hours to Kasese and costs USh 7000; to Fort Portal, it's one hour less and costs USh 6000. On this route, there's a fairly rough murram (dirt) stretch between Mubende and the Fort Portal-Hoima junction but a fine sealed road the rest of the way.

There are buses daily at 7 am to Kabale via Masaka and Mbarara. The entire trip takes 10 hours and costs USh 6500. Be there early to get your bum on a seat.

Matatu Tororo to Kampala by matatu costs USh 5000 and takes about 3½ hours. Jinja-Kampala costs USh 2500 and takes about one hour. By ordinary bus, the fare is less but the journey takes over two hours.

The matatu trip to Busia takes about four hours and costs USh 4500. There are also matatus between Kampala and Masaka and Mbarara.

Entebbe to Kampala by matatu costs USh 900 and takes about 35 minutes.

Train The train schedules from Kampala should be taken with a large pinch of salt. Delays and cancellations are the order of the day and passenger services have been severely curtailed.

Trains to Tororo depart on Monday,

Wednesday and Friday at 9 am and arrive the following morning. The fare is USh 1950 (3rd class only).

To Kasese, the trains depart Friday only at 3 pm and arrive the following day about noon. The fare is USh 2950 (3rd class). There's no 1st or 2nd class available.

Ferry From Kampala's Port Bell, there are ferries to the Ssese Islands (Kalangala) on Tuesday and Saturday at 8 am, arriving at around 6 pm. The fare is USh 3000 (1st class) and USh 2500 (2nd class). In the opposite direction, they leave on Wednesday and Sunday at 4 am. Tickets should be booked at the Port Bell ferry jetty.

Getting Around
The international airport is at Entebbe, 35 km from Kampala. There are public matatus between Kampala and Entebbe but only a taxi service for the last three km between Entebbe centre and the airport terminal. A private taxi from Kampala to Entebbe airport costs USh 20,000.

In Kampala itself, there are plenty of taxis but they're difficult to identify, since there's no standardised colour and they have no signs. Good places for finding them in the centre are outside the railway station, at the upper end of Colville St, and outside the Star Light Club on Luwum St. The drivers will be hanging around talking or asleep on the seat. A standard short-distance fare would be USh 2500. Negotiate a price for longer distances, including waiting time if that's what you want them to do.

South-Eastern Uganda

TORORO

At the eastern railhead of Uganda, not far from the border with Kenya, is Tororo. It must have looked particularly beautiful once, with its flowering trees, and it obviously had a substantial Asian community, as the two large Hindu temples suggest. These days, however, there's little of interest and the town wears a cloak of dereliction. Its only redeeming feature is the intriguing, forest-covered volcanic plug that rises up abruptly from an otherwise flat plain at the back of the town. The views from the top are well worth the climb.

For travellers, Tororo is a place to stop and rest en route to Mbale, Mt Elgon and points further north and west.

Information

There are no Forex bureaus in Tororo and it's difficult to change money after banking hours, even if you have cash. Bring sufficient local currency with you.

Places to Stay & Eat

The only cheap place worth considering is the *Tororo Christian Guest House*, diagonally opposite the Total petrol station on Mbale Rd. It's clean enough and the people who run it are very friendly. It costs USh 3500/4500 for singles/doubles with shared toilet. There are no showers.

The clean and friendly *Coop Hotel* is the next best and charges USh 4600/5600 for singles/doubles with shared bathroom facil-

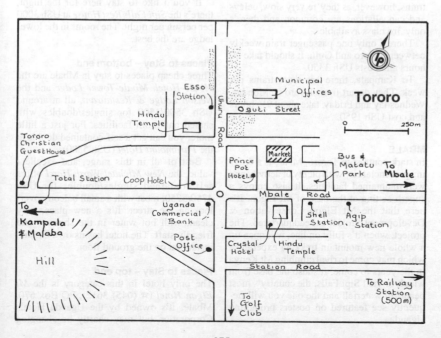

375

ities. Bucket showers are available and the toilets are kept clean. (Trivia lovers will be thrilled to know that the cisterns are genuine cast-iron Shanks 'Made in England'.) The hotel has its own bar and restaurant.

The best hotel in town and the only one with self-contained rooms is the *Crystal Hotel*, which has clean doubles (no singles) for USh 8600. There's a bar and restaurant. If you're not eating at your hotel, try the *New Safari Hotel*, on the corner of Mbale and Uhuru Rds.

Getting There & Away

Matatu A matatu to Kampala costs USh 4000 and takes about 3½ hours. The short ride to Malaba, on the Kenyan border, costs USh 1000.

Train Tororo is a railway junction for trains north to Mbale, Soroti and Gulu and west to Jinja and Kampala. Few travellers use the trains, however, as they're very slow, delays and cancellations are common and there's only 3rd class available.

There's only one passenger train weekly between Tororo and Gulu. It should take 20 hours and costs USh 3350.

To Kampala, there are three trains per week. They depart from Tororo on Monday, Wednesday and Friday, take about 9½ hours and cost USh 1950.

MBALE

In stark contrast to Tororo, Mbale is a thriving provincial city with plenty of activity and well-maintained facilities. It also enjoys a superb setting at the base of Mt Elgon. It's here that the Mt Elgon Conservation & Development Project is headquartered. The project, when it's fully on line, will open up a whole new mountain trekking experience which may come to rival climbing Mt Kenya in the years to come. It's also the base from which to visit Sipi Falls, the country's most beautiful waterfall and the one you will frequently see featured on posters promoting Uganda.

Information

There are no Forex bureaus in Mbale, so bring sufficient local currency with you. If you have to change money at the banks, you'll get a lousy rate of exchange.

The Mt Elgon Conservation & Development Project (☎ (045) 3179), PO Box 2690, Mbale, has its offices on the top floor of the building next to the main post office (see the Mbale map). For full details, see the Uganda National Parks chapter.

Sipi Falls

Sipi Falls is a truly beautiful sight, and it's well worth making the effort to get there. The falls are situated about 35 km north of Mbale, in the foothills of Mt Elgon and not far from the town of Kapchorwe. The cheapest way of getting there is to take a matatu to Kapchorwe and get off close to the falls, but these matatus are not very frequent, so it may be more convenient to put a small group together and hire a taxi for the day.

If you'd like to stay here for the night, there's the *Sipi Falls Rest House* at USh 3000 per person per night. The rooms in the lower lodge are the best.

Places to Stay – bottom end

Three cheap places to stay in Mbale are the *Mbale Hotel, Mbale Tower Lodge* and the *Nelson Lodge & Restaurant*, all at around USh 3500/4500 for singles/doubles with shared bathroom facilities. For just a little more, you can get a self-contained double at the *Paramount Hotel* (USh 5500).

Best of all in this range, and excellent value, the *New Michael Worth Hotel* offers self-contained singles/doubles for USh 4750/5750, most with a small balcony overlooking the street. It's a new place, very clean, with hot water in the showers and friendly staff. The hotel has its own bar and restaurant on the ground floor.

Places to Stay – top end

The only hotel in this category is the *Mt Elgon Hotel* (☎ (045) 3612), PO Box 670, Mbale. It's owned by the Uganda Hotels Corporation but may shortly be changing

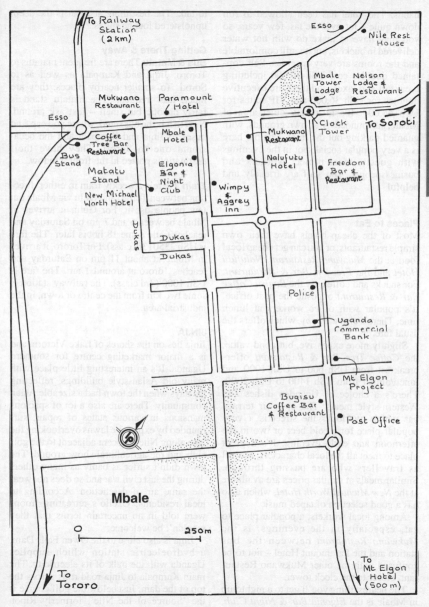

Mbale

0   250m

To Railway
Station
(2 km)

Esso

Mukwano
Restaurant

Paramount
Hotel

Esso

Coffee
Tree Bar
Restaurant

Bus
Stand

Matatu
Stand

New Michael
Worth Hotel

Mbale
Hotel

Elgonia
Bar &
Night
Club

Dukas

Dukas

Wimpy
& Aggrey
Inn

Dukas

Nile Rest
House

Mbale
Tower
Lodge

Nelson
Lodge &
Restaurant

Clock
Tower

To Soroti

Mukwano
Restaurant

Nalufutu
Hotel

Freedom
Bar &
Restaurant

Police

Uganda
Commercial
Bank

Mt Elgon
Project

Bugisu
Coffee Bar
& Restaurant

Post Office

To
Tororo

To
Mt Elgon
Hotel
(500 m)

UGANDA

hands. The hotel has been allowed to run down quite a lot over the last few years, so you may have to make do with hot water delivered in buckets, but it's still comfortable and the rooms are very spacious. Self-contained doubles cost USh 30,000 including breakfast and taxes, and there are executive doubles for USh 36,000 and VIP suites for USh 66,000. It's in a very quiet area of Mbale, surrounded by its own grounds, with guarded parking out the front. The bar here is a very popular social spot in the evenings with guests, local project workers and businesspeople. The staff are friendly and helpful.

Places to Eat

Most of the cheap hotels have their own simple restaurants, or you can get cheap local food at the *Mukwano Restaurant, Nalufutu Hotel* and the *Freedom Bar & Restaurant*. For snacks and coffee, try the *Bugisu Coffee Bar & Restaurant* opposite the post office. It's popular with office workers at lunch time. There's also a *Wimpy*, which offers the usual fare.

Slightly more expensive, but good value, the *Coffee Tree Bar & Restaurant* offers breakfast from USh 600 to USh 1000 and lunch/dinner from USh 1400 to USh 2000. There's a choice of Ugandan dishes and Western-style meals. The open-air terrace bar which overlooks the street is a very popular place for a cold beer or two in the afternoon and early evening. It's a great place to meet all the local characters, as well as travellers who are passing through. Similar meals at similar prices are available at the *New Michael Worth Hotel*, which also has a good selection of taped music.

Among local workers, a popular place to eat, especially in the evenings, is the *Mukwano Restaurant* between the bus station and the Paramount Hotel – not to be confused with the other Mukwano Restaurant, closer to the clock tower.

The nearest thing you'll get to a nightclub in Mbale is the *Elgonia Bar & Night Club*, which is basically a place where people come

to talk. The best thing about it is the deep, upholstered lounge suites.

Getting There & Away

Bus & Matatu There are frequent matatus to Tororo, Jinja and Kampala as well as to Soroti. To smaller nearby places, they are much less frequent. The matatu stand is fairly chaotic but small – just ask around. Next to it is the bus stand, where you can find buses to Jinja and Kampala and the occasional one to Soroti. They have their destinations posted in the front window.

Train There's a weekly train in either direction between Tororo and Gulu via Mbale but few people use it. For Gulu, it arrives in Mbale between 6 and 7 pm on Saturday and reaches Gulu some 18 hours later. The fare is USh 2350 (3rd class). For Tororo, it arrives in Mbale at about 11 pm on Saturday and reaches Tororo at around 1 am. The fare is USh 1000 (3rd class). The railway station is some two km from the centre of town, in the industrial area.

JINJA

Jinja lies on the shores of Lake Victoria and is a major marketing centre for southern Uganda. It's an interesting little place with many old Asian-style buildings, reflecting the days when the town had a sizeable Asian community. There are also a lot of spacious mansions in various states of repair, surrounded by expansive lawns overlooking the lake along Nile Crescent adjacent to the golf club and the agricultural show ground. The town didn't suffer as badly as many others during the last civil war and so does not wear the same air of dereliction. According to local residents, Okello's retreating troops were told in no uncertain terms that they wouldn't be welcome.

Jinja is also close to the Owen Falls Dam, a hydroelectric station which supplies Uganda with the bulk of its electricity. The main Kampala to Jinja road runs across the top of the dam. Just below the golf course is the 'Source of the Nile', formerly Ripon Falls.

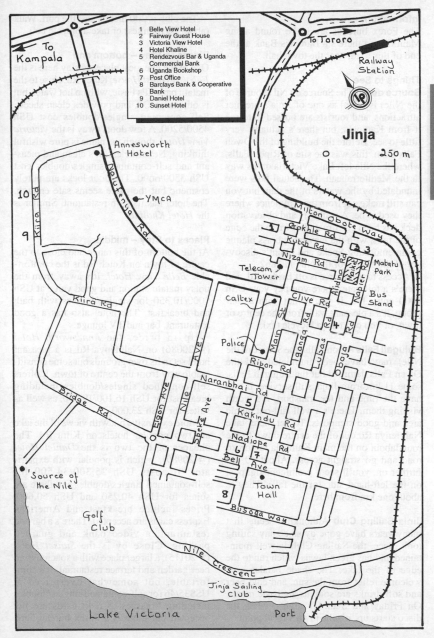

Jinja

0   250 m

1 Belle View Hotel
2 Fairway Guest House
3 Victoria View Hotel
4 Hotel Khaline
5 Rendezvous Bar & Uganda Commercial Bank
6 Uganda Bookshop
7 Post Office
8 Barclays Bank & Cooperative Bank
9 Daniel Hotel
10 Sunset Hotel

To Kampala

To Tororo

Railway Station

Annesworth Hotel

YMCA

Telecom Tower

Caltex

Police

Matatu Park

Bus Stand

Gokhle Rd

Kutch Rd

Nizam Rd

Clive Rd

Ripon Rd

Naranbhai Rd

Kakindu Rd

Nadiope Rd

Bell Ave

Busoga Way

Nile Crescent

Town Hall

Golf Club

'Source of the Nile'

Jinja Sailing Club

Port

Lake Victoria

Milton Obote Way

Nalufenga Rd

Kiira Rd

Kiira Rd

Nile AVE

Bridge Rd

Elgon Ave

Speke Ave

Main St

Ganga Rd

Lubas Rd

Oboja Rd

Napier Rd

Aldina Rd

Kampala Rd

Information
The Forex bureaus are to be found along Main St and there's a Barclays Bank at the end of this road, near the town hall.

Things to See
Source du Nil The Source du Nil (Source of the Nile) is billed as one of Jinja's premier attractions, and tourists are bussed in to see it from Kampala, but there's actually very little to see. Before the building of the Owen Falls Dam, this was the site of Ripon Falls, where the Nile left Lake Victoria on its way to the Mediterranean. The actual falls were inundated by the waters of the dam but you can still make out from the turbulence where they used to be. A walkway and observation deck has been constructed down to the edge of the falls, with the inevitable brass plaque commemorating Speke and Grant's discovery of the source of the Nile in 1862.

Access to the source is off Bridge Rd, and there's a toll gate where you pay your USh 1000 entry fee. If you're not with a tour group, it's a pleasant walk from the centre of town, or you can take a bicycle taxi.

Bujagali Falls Ripon Falls (the Source of the Nile) may have been inundated and the Owen Falls dammed but the Bujagali Falls, some 11 km from Jinja, still survive. If you have the time and the transport, it's worth visiting them. There's a well laid-out picnic area and good signposts. To get there, take Nalufenya Rd out of the centre down to the roundabout on the main Kampala to Tororo road and go straight across. About 10 km further on, you'll see a prominent signpost on the left-hand side for the falls. They're about one km from here.

Jinja Sailing Club Although it seems that many years have gone by since any sailing took place, the Sailing Club is well maintained and has green lawns which run to the edge of the lake. The shade bandas give welcome relief from the sun, and cold beer and soft drinks are sold, as are basic meals. On Friday and Saturday nights, when the disco starts up, it's the town's focal point.

The club is 200 metres past the port. Walk (about 20 minutes) or take a bicycle taxi.

Places to Stay – bottom end
One of the cheapest places to stay here is the *Fairway Guest House*, Kutch Rd, close to the matatu park. It's basic, with no hot water, but is otherwise OK and provides clean sheets. Self-contained singles/doubles cost USh 4500/5200. A few doors away is the *Victoria View Hotel*, though the name is pure wishful thinking. Nevertheless, it's clean and pleasant and self-contained singles/doubles cost USh 5500/6600. The door locks are purely cosmetic but the place seems safe enough. The hotel has its own restaurant. Similar is the *Hotel Khaline*.

Places to Stay – middle
At the bottom of this range and close to the centre of town on Kutch Rd is the comfortable *Belle View Hotel*. It's away from the noisy matatu station and good value at USh 9000/10,350 for singles/doubles with bath and breakfast. The hotel also has a good restaurant, bar and TV lounge.

Up in price, the *Annesworth Hotel* (☎ 20086) on Nalufenya Rd is a pleasant hotel set in its own grounds but some considerable way from the centre of town. It offers self-contained singles/doubles including breakfast for USh 16,100/19,550, as well as suites for USh 23,000.

More expensive but with views of the lake are two popular hotels on Kiira Rd. The cheaper of the two is the *Daniel Hotel* (☎ 20989), which is popular with expatriates. It costs USh 25,300/34,500 for self-contained singles/doubles and there are suites for USh 40,250 and USh 50,600. Prices include breakfast and American Express cards are accepted. There's a bar and restaurant, a video bank and guarded parking. Close by is the *Sunset Hotel* (☎ 20115), a larger place with a spacious bar, beer garden and terrace restaurant. It's comfortable, but somewhat overpriced at US$35/46 for self-contained singles/doubles including breakfast. Credit cards are not accepted but there is a Forex bureau here.

Even if you can't afford to stay, it's worth having a drink in the gardens.

Places to Eat

For a cheap local meal of beans, rice and vegetables, go to the market opposite the Victoria View Hotel. It closes at 9.30 pm.

The best eatery in town is the restaurant in the *Belle View Hotel*, where you can get a good lunch or dinner for around USh 2000. The beers are cold too. The *Victoria View Hotel* serves basic meals for lunch and omelettes and bread for breakfast.

Also popular is the *Rendezvous Bar & Restaurant*, along Main St.

The restaurants at the *Sunset Hotel* and the *Daniel Hotel* are also good but, if you're not staying there, are somewhat inconveniently located away from the centre of town. They're slightly more expensive than the Belle View.

Getting There & Away

Bus & Matatu The trip from Kampala to Jinja by matatu costs USh 2500 and takes about one hour on a very good road. By ordinary bus, the fare is marginally less but the journey takes more than two hours.

There is supposedly a direct bus (People's Bus Company) daily to Busia (Kenyan border), departing at 8 am, but it's unreliable. A better bet is a matatu to Busia or Malaba (USh 3300).

Train Jinja is on the Tororo-Kampala main railway line. A train runs in each direction three times a week (see the Tororo or Kampala Getting There & Away sections). The railway station is about one km out of town on the Tororo road.

Ferry Ugandan Railways ferries operate to Mwanza in Tanzania but they don't take passengers. To get to Mwanza, you'll have to take the ferry from Port Bell (see Getting There & Away in the Kampala chapter for details).

South-Western Uganda

FORT PORTAL

Fort Portal, a small, pleasant and quiet town at the north-eastern end of the Ruwenzori Mountains, is the centre of a tea-growing area. It's also the base from which to explore the Semliki Valley (hot springs and Pygmy villages) and the Kibale Forest Primate Reserve. Many travellers stay here overnight en route to Murchison Falls National Park.

Information

Kabarole Tours (☎ (0493) 2668), PO Box 384, Fort Portal, opposite the Glue Pot Bar and signposted 'Tour Agency', is an excellent tour agency and information bureau on all the area's places of interest. The people who staff it are very friendly and helpful, and tour prices are very reasonable, as long as you have a group to share the cost. See the following section for details of the tours offered.

For moneychanging, the Moons Forex bureau is across the road from the Wooden Hotel.

If you have your own transport but need repairs or maintenance done, ask for Ibrahim at the Total station diagonally opposite the Wooden Hotel. He's excellent and his charges are ridiculously reasonable.

Organised Tours

Unless you're intent on doing it the hard way, the best place to arrange transport and tours to the places of interest around Fort Portal is through Kabarole Tours (see the earlier Information section). Its office is open daily from 8 am to 6 pm and has scheduled departures to the Semliki Valley on Tuesday, Friday and Sunday (9 am to 4 pm, USh 30,000 shared between up to seven people), to Kibale Forest on Monday and Thursday (6 am to noon), to Queen Elizabeth National Park on Saturday (6 am to 6 pm), to the Nyakasura Caves on Monday (2 to 4 pm, USh 15,000 shared by up to seven people), to the crater lakes on Wednesday (2 to 4 pm,

USh 35,000 shared by up to seven people), and to a tea factory on Thursday (2 to 4 pm, USh 30,000 shared by up to six people). In addition, it offers a tour to Kibale Forest which leaves on Tuesday at 5 pm and involves an overnight stay with return transport to Fort Portal the following day at noon. These itineraries can be changed to suit demand, or you can simply charter a minibus for the day (12 hours) for USh 50,000 (plus fuel) shared between up to seven people.

Kabarole Tours also offer a trek across the lower levels of the Ruwenzoris which involves transport to Kichwamba (14 km), followed by a 28-km, 10-hour trek through tropical vegetation to Bundi (around 2650 metres), overnight accommodation at the Moonlight Hotel in Bundibugyo, and then public transport back to Fort Portal via the Pygmy villages and hot springs. The trek costs USh 20,000 per person plus guide fees (about USh 2000 per person), accommodation (USh 2500) and shared transport to the start of the trek. They can also arrange visits to the Toro Game Reserve and the fishing village of Ntoroko at the southern end of Lake Mobutu Sese Seko.

Kabarole is a reliable operation and can be recommended.

Places to Stay – bottom end

One of the cheapest and most popular places to stay is the *Kyaka Lodge* on Kuhadika Rd. Here you can get a simple but clean room with shared bathroom for USh 3000/4000. The showers have hot water. The hotel has its own bar and restaurant, but the bar isn't exactly vibrant, as everyone seems to mimic catatonia, gawping speechless at whatever video is on the TV.

If the above is full, try the *Hot Springs Lodge* on Rukidi III St, which is just as good, costs USh 3000/5000 for singles/doubles and has a restaurant. There's also the *Honest Rest House*, off the Kasese road, which offers singles/doubles with shared bathroom

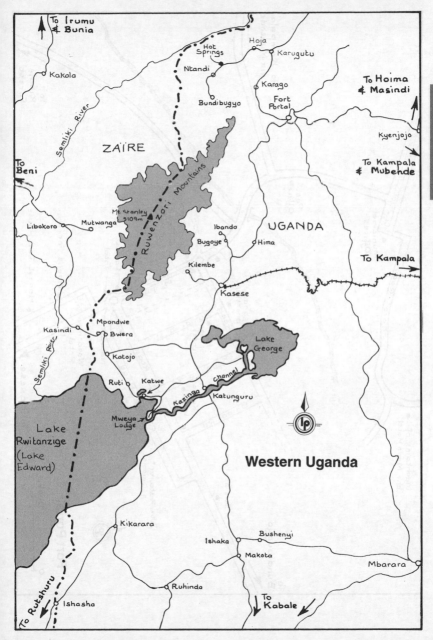

UGANDA

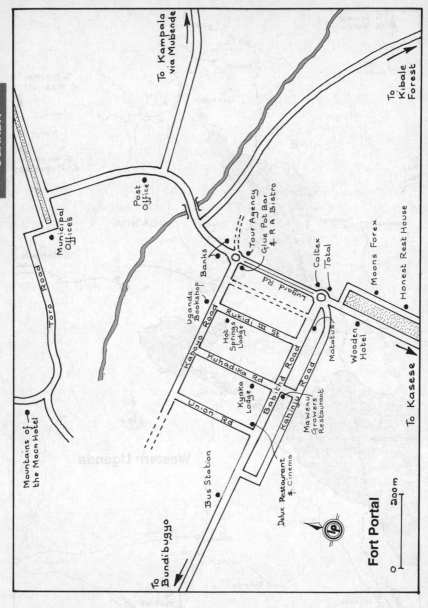

Fort Portal

Left: Rainforest, Ruwenzori Mountains, Uganda (CK)
Right: Katanguru, Uganda (GE)
Bottom: Fort Portal, Uganda (GE)

Top: Nyamulgira & Nyiragongo volcanoes, from Lake Kivu, Zaïre (GC)
Bottom: Gorillas, Ruhengeri National Park, Rwanda (GE)

facilities around a central courtyard for USh 3000/5500. It's bit overpriced considering the facilities. Close by and further up this same road are the *Economy Lodge* and the *Centenary Guesthouse*, which cost USh 3300/4400 for singles/doubles. The Centenary has its own bar and restaurant.

Places to Stay – middle

There's only one place to stay in this range in the centre of town and that's the popular *Wooden Hotel* (☎ 2560) on Lugard Rd, which is run by a coterie of apparently eccentric women. They're actually very friendly once they've seen your face a few times (and the colour of your money) and they certainly look after you. Very clean, comfortable, self-contained rooms here cost USh 8050/10,350 for singles/doubles. Bucket hot water is delivered to your room. The hotel has a bar/restaurant (good, tasty meals for around USh 2000) whose internal décor could have been inspired by a visit to a New Orleans brothel. Ask for a torch with your dinner. There's parking in the compound at the rear.

About eight km out of town on the road to Mubende, amid the Kiko Tea Estate, is the *Rwenzori Hotel* (☎ 2270) (known locally as the Tea Hotel). It's a typical plantation mansion and, although it has been allowed to deteriorate, it's still comfortable and spotlessly clean, and bucket hot water is available on request. Self-contained singles/doubles are reasonably priced at USh 6900/8050. Meals are extra and should be ordered in advance. It's signposted on the main road.

Places to Stay – top end

The only place in this category is the *Mountains of the Moon Hotel* (☎ 2513), on the hill above the centre of town. It's part of the Ugandan Hotels Corporation chain but may soon change hands. Like the rest of the hotels in this chain, it's been allowed to deteriorate, but it's still reasonably comfortable and the grounds are well maintained. Self-contained singles/doubles with breakfast but no hot water cost US$25/30 for nonresidents and USh 12,000/18,000 for residents. There are also suites for US$45 (USh 36,000 for residents). Credit cards are accepted and there's a bar and restaurant. The good news for budget travellers is that you can camp here for US$5 (or Ugandan equivalent) per tent. It's where the overland companies camp.

Places to Eat

There's good, reasonably priced food at the *Wooden Hotel* (if you can see what you're eating). It's also worth checking out the *Mawenu Growers Restaurant*, and the *Delux Restaurant* in front of the cinema.

The best food in town, however, is to be found at the *R A Bistro* on Lugard Rd, which serves Western-style food. It isn't that cheap, at USh 3500 to USh 4000 for a main course, but it's excellent, with good service and friendly staff. Have a good night out and eat here.

Entertainment

There are not many riveting places to go for a drink in Fort Portal. Most of the bars have turned into dreary video parlours where no-one talks to each other, and the bar at the Mountains of the Moon Hotel is terminally staid. Luckily, there's one bar which hasn't succumbed to video vacuity: the *Glue Pot Bar*, at the roundabout on Lugard Rd. It's definitely no-frills, but with a bit of luck, you can meet a good cross section of the town's vocal political intelligentsia and jesters here and go home still laughing. They'll stay open until you stop drinking.

Getting There & Away

The matatu 'stand' is on Babitha Rd, near the junction with Lugard Rd. As elsewhere, there's no schedule so you just hang around until they're full, but there are fairly frequent departures to Hoima and Masindi to the north, and to Kasese (USh 1000) to the south.

From the bus station at the other end of Babitha Rd, a daily bus runs to Kabale at 7 am (USh 7500) via Kasese and Mbarara. There's also a daily bus to Kampala at 7 am (USh 6000, seven hours), via Mubende. The road from the Fort Portal-Hoima junction to Mubende is a gravel track which isn't too bad for most of the course, though it would get sloppy in the wet season. From Mubende to Kampala, it's a new tarmac road.

AROUND FORT PORTAL
Kibale Forest Primate Reserve

This recently established reserve some 30 km south-east of Fort Portal is home to chimpanzees, baboons, red and white colobus monkeys, and larger mammals such as bushbuck, sitatunga, duiker, civet, buffaloes and elephants. It's said to have the highest density of primates in the world, including an estimated 500 chimpanzees, and Uganda's third-largest population of elephants.

The star attraction is the chimpanzees, five groups of which have been partially habituated to human contact. Nevertheless, you have only a 25% chance of seeing them on any particular day, though you'll almost certainly hear them as they scamper off into the bush on your approach. They'll obviously become more tame as time goes on, so the chances of seeing them will increase. If you want to be sure of sighting them, plan on spending a few days here.

The reserve headquarters is at Kanyanchu River Camp (fax (256) 493 2636), PO Box 700, Fort Portal, signposted on the left-hand side about six km before you reach the village of Bigodi coming from Fort Portal. It's from here that guided walks can be arranged along well-marked tracks (about a three-km round trip) in search of the chimps. There are daily walks from 7 to 11 am (the best time to go) and from 3 to 6 pm, costing USh 6000 and USh 3600, respectively, per person. The price includes a guide. The group size is limited to six people but any number of groups can set off, as long as they go off in different directions. Even if you don't see the chimps, you will see the colobus monkeys and the incredible number of butterflies and birds which live in this forest. The vegetation is equally lush.

You can camp at the headquarters for USh 2500 per person per night on the public site or USh 3000 on the 'private' site. There is one double tent for hire (USh 3000 for the first night and USh 1000 for each additional night). Facilities include water, firewood, a toilet and shower block and kerosene lanterns (the latter cost USh 800 per night). Car parking at the headquarters costs USh 2500 per night. There are only soft drinks for sale at the headquarters, so you must bring all your own food or (if you have transport) drive to Bigodi village and eat there. Reception at the headquarters closes at 6 pm sharp.

If you don't want to camp, there are two simple but very good places to stay at Bigodi village. Perhaps the best is *Mucusu*, at the back of the village, run by David Nyamuganya and his wife. It's a very cosy and friendly place which costs USh 2000/4000 for singles/doubles including breakfast. Excellent, tasty food is available if ordered in advance and includes stews, shepherd's pie (!), chops, rice, baked potatoes and peanut sauce. It's incredible what they turn out with minimal cooking equipment. The communal bathroom facilities are clean and bucket hot water is available.

The other place, right in the middle of the village, is the *Safari Hotel & Lodge*, which has singles/doubles for USh 2000/3000 including breakfast. You can also get excellent, tasty meals if you order in advance. Charles Lubega, the owner and chef, once cooked for the Belgian ambassador to Rwanda, so expect your meals to be served with a liberal amount of panache, wit and repartee. There's an amazing variety of food available on the menu and it's very reasonably priced. You can camp at this place free of charge if you eat there. You can even have your laundry done for you.

There are matatus from Fort Portal to Bigodi daily (except Sunday) between 10 and 11 am which pass the reserve headquarters. In the opposite direction, a matatu leaves Bigodi daily (except Sunday) between 6.30 and 7 am. Alternatively, you can charter a minibus from Kabarole Tours in Fort Portal to take you to Bigodi (USh 25,000 one-way shared between up to seven people). You can also arrange to have them collect you and take you back to Fort Portal, for the same price. The gravel road between

Fort Portal and Bigodi is in excellent condition, apart from one or two rough patches.

Semliki Valley

Just about everyone who comes to Fort Portal makes a day trip (at least) to the Semliki Valley and to **Bundibugyo** on the other side of the Ruwenzoris.

The two main attractions are the hot springs near Sempaya and the Pygmy villages near the village of Ntandi in the forest of the Semliki Valley, a few km before Bundibugyo, but the best part of this trip are the magnificent views over the rainforest and savannah of the Semliki Valley and into Zaïre. Unfortunately the Pygmy villagers have gone the way of those in eastern Zaïre and are now horribly commercialised, their culture moribund. And just to make sure I hadn't got it wrong, I went to visit them again in early 1993.

It was one of the most mutually degrading encounters I have ever had. If you want to contribute to the demise of these people, then keep on going there, flashing superficial smiles, buying tourist tat and giving them hand-outs. All you'll do is draw them further away from anything which was previously of value to them, and give the Christian missions and local authorities more reason to be totally and utterly condescending towards them.

If you don't believe this, buy the 'information' sheet available at the toll gate and read it. How would you like to be bleakly categorised thus: '...most of the males have a hairy body and most of the women are big breasted', without further qualification? And, 'Their standard of living is difficult and alarming. They do not perform any agricultural activities but have large families; eg their Chairman has a family of 12 within a small leaved grass thatched house 7 x 6 x 4 ft, all living in that bushel, bedless sleeping, no beddings, not even fine clothes to cover themselves'. There's now tremendous pressure on them to abandon their centuries-old hunter-gatherer ways and be dragged kicking and screaming into the tourist industry as a pathetic sideshow.

Still, the tourists roll in day by day, allowing themselves to be harassed and fleeced so they can tell their chic friends back home that they met a Pygmy and here's the photograph. Meanwhile, another unique culture hits the dust. It's sick.

If you insist on going, the 'official' charge for a visit to their village is USh 1500 per person, but you'll be lucky to get away with three times that amount and the pressure to buy rubbish is enervating.

The other 'attraction' is the hot springs. At least you won't get hassled here but the place is very much a let-down. This is not Bogoria National Park (Kenya) and it's worlds away from the geysers of Rotorua (New Zealand) and Iceland.

On the way into the Semliki Valley, there's a toll station where you have to pay a USh 4000 entry fee.

Places to Stay Near the toll station, there's a simple hotel where you can stay the night for USh 3000 a double. You can also stay at one of the two bandas run by Morence Mpora (☎ (0493) 2245) at Kichwamba/Nyankuku, on the way to Bundibugyo. Morence has been offering accommodation for several years now in an effort to help finance the ophanage he runs. Just ask the matatu driver to drop you in the right place – it's near the Kichwamba Technical College.

If you find yourself in Bundibugyo (the local administrative centre) and need to stay the night, there's the *Moonlight Hotel* which costs USh 2500 per person.

Getting There & Away The best way to get to the Semliki Valley is to put together a small group and go on one of Kabarole Tours' half-day excursions (USh 30,000 shared between up to seven people). Alternatively, hire a car and driver for the day. This will cost much the same. There are occasional matatus between Fort Portal and Bundibugyo, but as they're obviously not going to hang around while you visit the sights, you'll be left stranded. Hitching is a waste of time.

KASESE

Kasese is the western railhead of Uganda and the base from which to organise a trip up the Ruwenzori Mountains or to Queen Elizabeth National Park. It's a small, quiet town but was once important to the economy because of the nearby copper mines at Kilembe

UGANDA

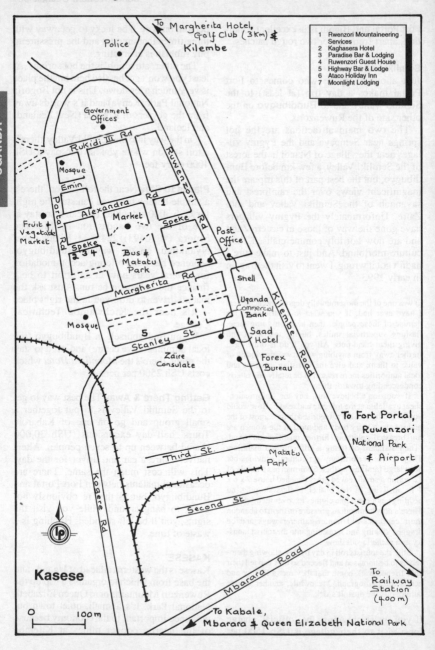

To Margherita Hotel, Golf Club (3km) & Kilembe

Police

1 Rwenzori Mountaineering Services
2 Kaghasera Hotel
3 Paradise Bar & Lodging
4 Ruwenzori Guest House
5 Highway Bar & Lodge
6 Ataco Holiday Inn
7 Moonlight Lodging

Government Offices

Rukidi III Rd

Mosque

Emin

Portal Rd

Ruwenzori Rd

Alexandra

Market

1

Speke

Fruit & Vegetable Market

Speke

2 3 4

Bus & Matatu Park

Post Office

7

Margherita Rd

Shell

Uganda Commercial Bank

Mosque

5

6

Stanley St

Saad Hotel

Zaire Consulate

Forex Bureau

Kilembe Road

To Fort Portal, Ruwenzori National Park & Airport

Kagere Rd

Third St

Matatu Park

Second St

To Railway Station (400m)

Mbarara Road

Kasese

0   100m

To Kabale, Mbarara & Queen Elizabeth National Park

UGANDA

(copper was Uganda's third most important export during the 1970s), though these are now closed.

Like Kabale, Kasese was controlled by the NRA for several years before Okello was thrown out and so was spared the looting and destruction which befell other Ugandan towns further east.

The town acquired a bad reputation several years ago on account of police harassment of travellers, who were required to register on arrival. This has now stopped.

Information

There's a Forex bureau on the ground floor of the Saad Hotel block but be prepared to accept a lot of small-denomination notes.

The Zaïrian Consulate is on Stanley St and is open Monday to Friday from 8.30 am to 1 pm and 3 to 5 pm. Visas cost the same as elsewhere but, if you bow and scrape, it's possible to get them the same day instead of having to wait 24 hours.

Rwenzori Mountaineering Services, or RMS (☎ (0493) 4115), PO Box 33, Kasese, has an information and booking office on Alexandra Rd. This is where you make arrangements for climbing the Ruwenzoris. For further details, see the relevant section in the Uganda National Parks chapter.

Things to See

Kasese has no attractions, but if you have half a day to kill, hire a bicycle and cycle the 13 km up to the copper mine at Kilembe for an interesting diversion. It is a long gradual uphill climb, which makes for hard work on the way there but is great fun on the way back! You can get a tour of the surface remnants (crushers, concentrators and separators, etc) free of charge but you're not allowed underground. The manager of the Saad Hotel can arrange bicycle hire. You can call off for a cold beer en route at the Margherita Hotel, three km from Kasese.

Places to Stay – bottom end

There's a choice of four places to stay in this range and they're all of much the same quality. Perhaps the most popular is the

Kaghasera Hotel on the corner of Speke and Portal Rds, which has singles with shared bathroom facilities for USh 4000 and self-contained doubles for USh 5000. There's no hot water in the showers but there is a restaurant on the ground floor. On the same block are the *Paradise Bar & Lodging* and the *Ruwenzori Guest House*, which are similar. Another fairly popular place is the *Moonlight Lodging*, at the junction of Margherita and Ruwenzori Rds. This is a large place fronted by a restaurant and bar with the rooms around a courtyard at the back. Doubles (no singles) with shared bathroom cost USh 6000.

Another good choice in this range is the *Highway Bar & Lodge* on Stanley St, which has doubles (no singles) with shared facilities for USh 5000.

Places to Stay – middle

The *Saad Hotel* (☎ 4157/9) on Ruwenzori Rd has been a very popular travellers' hangout for years, and just about everyone who climbs the Ruwenzoris stays here for rest and recreation both before and after the climb, though there is no bar (the owners are Muslim). The staff are very friendly and the rooms are pleasant and spotlessly clean. It has only self-contained double rooms (with two single beds) but they allow three people to share a room. For two people, it costs USh 15,000 and for three it's USh 22,500. The hotel has its own restaurant and upstairs TV/video lounge.

If the Saad is full, head for the *Ataco Holiday Inn*, also on Stanley St, which has self-contained doubles (no singles) for USh 12,000.

Places to Stay – top end

The *Margherita Hotel* (☎ (0493) 4015), three km out of town on the road up to Kilembe, is owned by the Ugandan Hotels Corporation and payment is expected in hard currency. Singles/doubles including breakfast cost US$25/30 (USh 12,000/16,000 for residents) and suites are US$35 and US$50, with a 10% discount on these rates for 'mountaineers' (presumably anyone with mud on their boots). There's also a free camp site with bathing facilities. The hotel is on a beautiful site looking out towards the Ruwenzoris on one side and the golf course on the other, surrounded by flowering trees. A film of the trek from the Margherita to Stanley peaks in the Ruwenzori is shown daily, if you want to know what you're up for. The restaurant here serves reasonable food at USh 2000 to USh 2500 for main courses.

Places to Eat
There are several inexpensive restaurants around the matatu park and market where you can get traditional staples like meat stews, matoke, beans and rice.

Otherwise, the meals at the *Saad Hotel* are hard to beat. There's a good selection of dishes, the food is tasty and the staff are friendly. You're looking at USh 1500 to USh 2000 for a main course. Breakfasts are also good value.

Entertainment
The liveliest bar for a cold beer is the *Ataco Holiday Inn*, which attracts a good crowd every lunch time and evening. The front terrace is a great place to hang out in the heat of the day. It basically stays open until the last person wants to go home.

Getting There & Away
Bus There are daily buses in either direction between Kasese and Kampala via Mbarara (USh 7000, about eight hours). From Kasese, the bus leaves at 6 am, so be there early to ensure that you get a seat.

There's also a daily bus in either direction between Fort Portal and Kabale via Kasese and Mbarara. It starts from Fort Portal at 7 am, arriving in Kasese at around 9 am. It then continues on to Kabale, taking about 7½ hours. The fare from Kasese to Kabale is USh 6500. The last part of the journey south crosses a mountain pass from which, weather permitting, you'll be rewarded with spectacular views to the west of the volcanoes along the Uganda-Rwanda border.

Matatu There are frequent matatus between Kasese and Fort Portal which take about one hour and leave when full.

Getting to Queen Elizabeth National Park by matatu is more problematical. There's usually one matatu daily to Katwe around 10 am (USh 2000, about an hour), which will drop you at the park gate, from where it's an eight-km walk. Alternatively, it's worth getting a group together and hiring a matatu for the day to take you around the park. You're looking at about USh 25,000 shared by up to six or seven people.

To get to the Nyabitaba/Ibanda trail head for the Ruwenzori climb, it is possible to take a matatu from Kasese but, since most people do this trek as part of a group, it's best to arrange transport through the Rwenzori Mountaineering Services office.

Train The weekly train in either direction between Kasese and Kampala leaves Kampala on Friday at 3 pm and arrives in Kasese (in theory) at noon the following day. From Kasese, it should depart late on Saturday, but this all depends on what sort of delays are encountered on the outward journey. In other words, play it by ear and be prepared to leave whenever you get the word. Only 3rd class is available and the fare to Kampala is USh 2950.

MASAKA
In 1979 Masaka was trashed by the Tanzanian army in the closing stages of the war which ousted Idi Amin. A lot of rebuilding has taken place since then, but the scars are still visible and the potholes in the streets are definitely something to behold – there's no way you'd drive a vehicle down some of these streets! There's very little to do in Masaka, and for most travellers it's just an overnight stop en route to the Ssese Islands in Lake Victoria or south into Tanzania. Masaka has a museum, but it's closed.

Information
Greenland Forex is the best place to change money here.

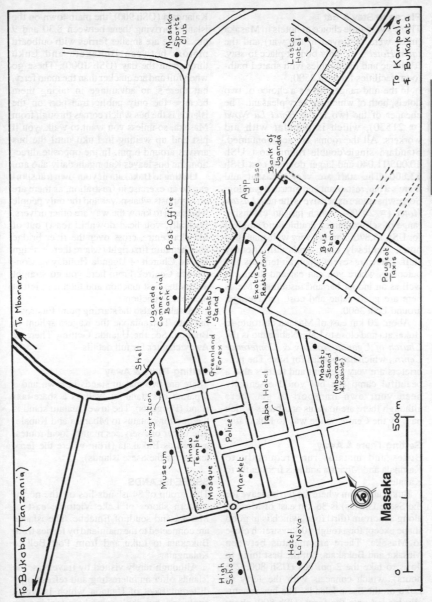

To Kampala & Bukakata

Laston Hotel

Masaka Sports Club

Bank of Uganda

Esso

Agip

Post Office

Uganda Commercial Bank

Bus Stand

Matatu Stand

Exotic Restaurant

Peugot Taxis

To Mbarara

Shell

Immigration

Museum

Hindu Temple

Police

Greenland Forex

Iqbal Hotel

Matatu Stand (Mbarara & Kabale)

To Bukoba (Tanzania)

Mosque

Market

High School

Hotel La Nova

Masaka

To Mbarara & Kabale

500 m

UGANDA

Places to Stay & Eat

There's very little choice of hotels in Masaka (most were destroyed in the war) and the *Iqbal Hotel* is the only budget place to stay. It's basic and has doubles with shared bathroom facilities for USh 3500.

In the mid-range, there's a choice of two hotels, both of which are very pleasant. The cheaper of the two is the *Hotel La Nova* (☎ 21520), which is popular with aid workers. All the rooms are self-contained. Standard single/double rooms cost USh 10,005/11,040 and larger doubles cost USh 13,800. The staff are very pleasant and there's a bar, restaurant and guarded parking. Somewhat more expensive is the new *Laston Hotel* (☎ 20309), which has an extensive range of self-contained doubles (no singles) for USh 15,870. This is a very well-managed hotel, spotlessly clean and with friendly staff. There are several open-air terraces and balconies where you can eat and drink, as well as an indoor bar and restaurant. Meals here are good value and cost, on average, around USh 3600.

About 20 km east of Masaka en route to Bukakata and close to Lake Nabugabo is the *Church of Uganda Holiday & Conference Centre*, which has bandas for hire. The proprietors are very pleasant and there's also a beautiful camp site but you'd essentially need your own transport to get there although there are matatus and buses which pass by the Centre on the way to Bukakata.

Getting There & Away

Buses and matatus run frequently to Kampala and Mbarara and less frequently to Kabale.

Bukakata (from where the ferries leave for the Ssese Islands) is 36 km east of Masaka along a murram (dirt) road, which is in good shape except for a rough 10-km stretch close to Masaka. There are matatus between Masaka and Bukakata, but the best thing to do is to take the 2 pm bus (USh 800, 2½ hours), which connects with the ferry to Luku on the Ssese Islands. The bus is actually loaded onto the ferry (USh 800, about one hour) and, on landing, continues on to Kalangala (USh 900), the main town on the islands, arriving there between 8.30 and 9 pm. There are smaller ferries with outboard motors between Bukakata and Luku throughout the day (USh 1000). These go when full and are quicker than the main ferry, but there's no advantage in taking them because the only public transport on the islands is the bus which comes through from Masaka, so unless you want to walk, you'll just end up waiting in Luku until the bus arrives around 6 pm. In the opposite direction, the bus leaves Kalangala daily at 6 am.

Getting to Bukakata in your own transport can be an exercise in frustration, as there are no signposts whatsoever and the only people who seem to know the way are other drivers. Basically, you head downhill (east) out of Masaka centre, cross over the river bridge and then turn first right (where there's a sign for the Church of Uganda Holiday & Conference Centre). From here you go straight across the first junction and then turn left at the next T-junction.

Masaka is also the starting point for crossing into Tanzania via the Kagera salient to Bukoba. See the Uganda Getting There & Away chapter for full details.

Getting There & Away

There are two matatu stands in town and a separate bus stand, as well as a share-taxi stand (Peugeots). The lower matatu stand is the one for matatus to Mbarara and Kabale. The upper one services mainly local routes, as well as Bukakata (from where the ferry leaves for the Ssese Islands).

SSESE ISLANDS

This group of 84 islands lies off the northwestern shores of Lake Victoria, east of Masaka and south of Entebbe. The islands are connected to the mainland by ferries from Bukakata to Luku and from Port Bell to Kalangala.

Although rarely visited by travellers, the islands offer an interesting and refreshingly different facet of Uganda which is worth exploring, but don't come here looking for 'action' – this is rest and recreation time.

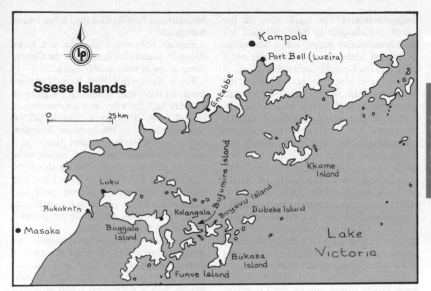

Ssese Islands

Kampala
Port Bell (Luzira)
Entebbe
Bufumira Island
Kampala
Kkome Island
Luku
Bukakata
Bugovu Island
Kalangala
Bubeke Island
Masaka
Buggala Island
Bukasa Island
Lake Victoria
Funve Island

0   25 km

Unlike the mainland, these islands escaped the ravages of the civil wars and so remain largely unspoiled. The people, known as the Basese, form a distinct tribal group, with their own language, culture and folklore. As so few foreigners visit the islands, you're assured of a warm welcome.

Most islanders are members of one or other of the various Christian sects. A minority are Muslims. Communities are tightly knit and there are no dangers associated with wandering around the islands on foot. In fact, this is the best way to see them.

The Basese are primarily fishers, and farmers of coffee, sweet potato, cassava, yams and bananas. As you might expect, fish forms a major part of their diet.

The main islands of Buggala, Bufumira, Bukasa, Bubeke and Kkome are hilly and, where not cultivated, are forested with a wide variety of trees. Animals you're likely to come across include various species of monkey, hippos, crocodiles and many different types of bird, but there are no large predators (other than crocodiles).

Many spots afford beautiful views over the lake and across to the other islands. You'll have no problems persuading the fishers to take you out on their boats. Swimming is also possible off most of the islands, as long as you observe the usual precaution about avoiding reedy areas (where the snails which carry the bilharzia parasite live).

All up, you're looking at a very mellow and peaceful time on these islands. There is a plentiful variety of food and, most of the time, there's not another tourist in sight.

Places to Stay & Eat

Most of the accommodation on the islands will be in private houses, and this is also where you'll eat. Simply ask around in any town or village and you'll quickly find somewhere to stay. There are no standard charges. Indeed, most people will probably offer you free accommodation and meals. If that's the case, remember the rules of hospitality and be generous in what you give. Be warned in advance: there's no electricity on any of the islands.

Buggala Island The main town on the islands is Kalangala on Buggala Island. It's the administrative centre, with a post office (telephone connections to Kampala) and a branch of the Uganda Commercial Bank.

The best place to stay here is the *Malaanga Ssese Safari Lodge* (☎ Kalangala 26), owned by Mr P T Andronico Ssemakula, a schoolteacher who speaks fluent English. Andronico has a well-deserved reputation for running the best lodge on the islands, and if cleanliness is next to godliness then he's got it right. It's spotless! A bed here costs USh 2500 and meals (cooked by his daughter, Josephine) cost USh 2000. You need to order meals in advance. Beers and soft drinks are also available and you can rent bicycles for USh 2000 per day. Andronico is working hard on getting his boat trips organised, so he should soon be able to take you to some of the other islands on day trips.

Other than Andronico's Lodge, there is the *Ssese Guest House*, run by the Church of Uganda, where you can camp for USh 500 per tent (no facilities) or rent a room for USh 1800. There are only two rooms with three mattresses in each. It's very basic accommodation and there are no meals available, though Stella, the pastor's wife, will cook for you if you ask.

The only other place to find food and drink in Kalangala is the *People's Bar & Restaurant*, right opposite Andronico's lodge. Food here is marginally cheaper than at Andronico's and you don't need to order in advance, but there's no choice – you eat whatever the dish of the day is.

Other Islands There are also several lodges and guesthouses in the other main towns on the islands. On Bukasa Island, ask for Mr J Lutaya Kaganda or for *Agne's House*. The latter is a very friendly place, but dark and run-down. It is cheap, though, at USh 1000 per person for bed, breakfast and dinner. Camping is allowed in the garden.

Getting There & Away
Two ferries go to the islands from the mainland departure points of Bukakata (east of Masaka) and Port Bell (in the Luzira area of Kampala).

Ferries between Bukakata and Luku (Buggala Island) are detailed in the Getting There & Away section of Masaka.

From Kampala's Port Bell, there are ferries to the Ssese Islands (Kalangala) on Tuesday and Saturday at 8 am, arriving at around 6 pm. The fare is USh 3000/2500 (1st/2nd class). In the opposite direction, they leave on Wednesday and Sunday at 4 am (but they sometimes leave earlier, so be there in plenty of time). Tickets should be booked at the Port Bell ferry jetty. There's no transport between the boat jetty and Kalangala town, so you're up for a half-hour walk. These ferries go via Kkome, Bubeke, Bukasa and Bufumira islands.

A third way of getting to the islands is by small motorised boats from Kasenyi, a fishing village on the Entebbe Peninsula. These go every day to the main islands, though there's no regular schedule – they leave when there are sufficient passengers or cargo.

Getting Around
There's no public transport on any of the islands, other than the daily bus which connects Masaka with Kalangala via Luku, but it's fairly easy to find local paddle or motorised boats between the islands. Simply ask around in the fishing villages or towns. Rates are negotiable.

MBARARA
The main town between Masaka and Kabale, Mbarara suffered a great deal during the war to oust Idi Amin but now bears few scars of those times. It's a very spread-out town, but pleasant, with a good range of facilities and is a good place to overnight between central and western Uganda.

The Nile Bank Forex is the best place to change money.

Places to Stay – bottom end.
A reasonable cheap place to stay is the *Super Tip Top Lodge, Bar & Restaurant*, which has singles/doubles with shared facilities for

UGANDA

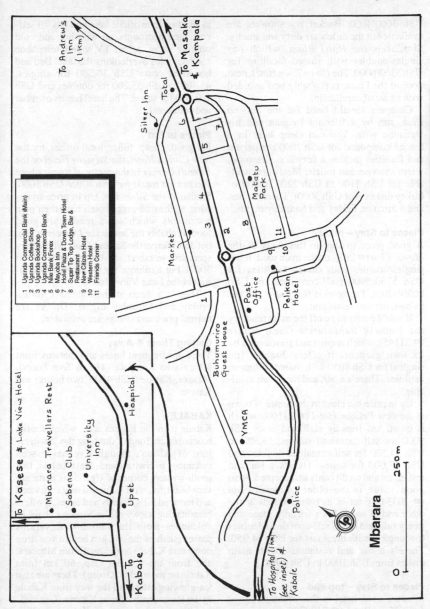

USh 3000/4000. Bucket hot showers are available but the toilets are dirty and smelly. Similar is the *Hotel Plaza*, which has singles/doubles with shared facilities for USh 3500/6000. The *Down Town Hotel*, next door to the Plaza, is probably best avoided with its air of dereliction.

Campers should head for the *Sabena Club*, run by a friendly Belgian and his Ugandan wife. You can camp here in a fenced compound for USh 1000 per person and facilities include a fireplace, firewood, warm showers and toilets. Meals are available for USh 1100 to USh 2200 (rabbit or turkey dishes cost USh 3000). There's a bar, and a disco on Friday and Saturday nights.

Places to Stay – middle

A good place to stay in this range is the *Mayoba Inn* (☎ 283), on the main road. It has singles/doubles with shared facilities for USh 5750/6900 (self-contained for USh 8050/9200). The hotel is fairly new and has its own bar and restaurant.

If you'd prefer to be off the main road, try the homely *Buhumuriro Guest House* (☎ 21145), which is quiet and surrounded by its own gardens. It offers doubles (no singles) for USh 8050 with shared bathroom facilities. There's a bar, and meals are available.

Up in price but close to the centre of town is the new *Pelikan Hotel* (☎ 21100), which is quiet, has friendly staff and costs USh 9000 for self-contained singles, 13,500 to USh 14,500 for self-contained doubles and USh 17,000 for suites. There's a bar and restaurant and credit cards are accepted. Also good value is the older *University Inn* (☎ 20334/5), set in its own grounds at the other end of town. It's a friendly place and rarely full, and offers self-contained doubles (no singles) with breakfast for USh 14,950. There's a bar and restaurant, with main dishes from USh 1000 to USh 2000.

Places to Stay – top end

Mbarara's top hotel is the recently opened *Lake View Hotel* (☎ 21397/8), on the outskirts of town off the road to Kasese. It's sited in front of an artificial lake and has 70 self-contained bedrooms, all with hot and cold running water, colour TV, video, telephone and balconies overlooking the lake. Bed and breakfast costs USh 30,300 for singles, 41,400 to USh 55,200 for doubles and USh 103,000 for suites. The hotel has its own bar and restaurant.

Places to Eat

For good, cheap, filling local dishes, try the *New Citizen Hotel*, the *Western Hotel* or the *Friends Corner* in the centre of town, where you can get meals for USh 800 to USh 1000. Similar is the *Silver Inn*. Up in price somewhat, all the mid-range hotels have their own restaurants which serve reasonably good food. Probably the best is the *University Inn*, but don't forget the *Sabena Club*, where they specialise in rabbit and turkey dishes (USh 3000). For a splurge, try the *Mariza Restaurant* at the Lake View Hotel.

There's a disco at the Sabena Club on Friday and Saturday nights. Drinks are normal price and snacks are available.

Getting There & Away

There are frequent buses and matatus from Mbarara to Kampala (4½ to five hours), Masaka, Kabale (USh 4000, two hours) and Kasese.

KABALE

Kabale is in the Kigeza area, which tourist brochures are fond of dubbing the 'Switzerland of Africa', though I've never seen volcanoes in Switzerland. Nevertheless, this south-western corner of Uganda is certainly very beautiful, with its intensively cultivated and terraced hills, forests and lakes. It offers breathtaking views of the Virunga chain of volcanoes from the summits of various passes (such as the one just before you drop down into Kabale on the road from Mbarara, and from the Kanaba Gap, 60 km from Kabale on the road to Kisoro). There are also tea-growing estates all the way from Kabale to the Rwandan border at Katuna (Gatuna).

Although the town of Kabale itself is nothing special, Kigeza is superb hiking

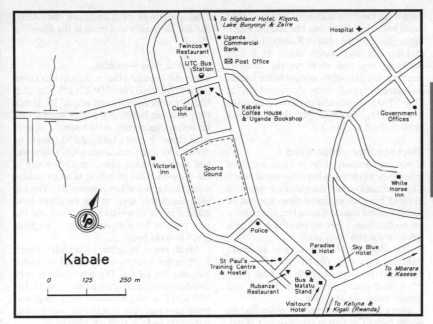

Kabale

0   125   250 m

UGANDA

country and the area is honeycombed with tracks and paths, hamlets and farms. A visit to Lake Bunyonyi is particularly recommended.

Kabale is Uganda's highest town (about 2000 metres) and turns cool at night, so have warm clothes handy.

Information

There are no Forex bureaus in Kabale, so bring sufficient local currency with you unless you want to change at a lousy rate at the Uganda Commercial Bank.

Things to See

Go walking down any of the tracks in this area and let them take you where they will. There are always good views over the surrounding countryside and local people are very friendly and keen to talk with you.

A *must* in this area is a trip to **Lake Bunyonyi**, a famous beauty spot over the ridge to the north-west of Kabale. It's a large and

irregularly shaped lake with a number of islands, and the surrounding hillsides, as elsewhere in this region, are intensively cultivated. Many of the villagers have boats and you shouldn't have any difficulty arranging a trip onto the lake, plus there are regular departures across the lake for USh 7000. If you'd like to stay up here overlooking the lake, go to the Hotel Bamboo, at the end of the tarmac road which skirts part of the eastern side of the lake. This is a beautiful place, newly constructed, and should have huts available by the time you read this. At the time of writing they had only a bar and restaurant operating.

It's also worth visiting **Bwama Island**, in Bunyoni Lake, where there's a community of disabled people producing crafts. There's also a guesthouse on the island, where you can find a bed for USh 500. It has a small restaurant.

To get to Lake Bunyonyi, you can either take a matatu (infrequent), hitch or walk (about six km from Kabale). The access road is off to the left about one km past the Highlands Hotel on the road to Kisoro (the Hotel Bamboo is signposted here). If you're walking, you can short-cut the road by heading straight uphill alongside the stream just past the small dams. A 'tourist tax' of USh 1000 is supposedly payable on the ridge overlooking the lake but there's rarely anyone there to collect it.

Places to Stay – bottom end
If you are camping, there is a free site close to the White Horse Inn but it has no facilities. The overland safari companies camp at a disused brickworks about three km out of Kabale on the road to Kisoro but, again, there are no facilities. Look for two red-brick gate posts on the left-hand side.

The cheapest place to stay is St Paul's Training Centre & Hostel (☎ 284), where dormitory beds are available for USh 1150. It's a clean place, the staff are friendly and simple meals are available.

There are also two very popular budget hotels here. The first is the Visitours Hotel, which is divided up into units of three rooms which share a common bathroom and toilet and a small lounge. It's very clean, towels are provided and singles/doubles cost USh 2000/3000 (dropping to USh 1000/2000 if business is slack). The hotel has a restaurant and there's an attractive upstairs verandah overlooking the street. The other option is the Sky Blue Hotel, which also has very clean rooms with towel and soap provided and bucket hot water on request. It costs USh 3450 a double (no singles) with shared bathroom facilities. The owner can arrange transport to the Zaïre border if you don't want to find it yourself.

Also cheap is the Capital Inn, which has rooms (single or double occupancy) for USh 2000 with shared bathroom facilities. It's fairly well maintained and clean but is basically a brothel – the female staff giggle if you're a single man asking about single occupancy. Bucket hot water is available on request. There's a restaurant and a lively upstairs bar with huge (and remarkably accurate) paintings of Kabale on the walls. Similar in quality and price is the Paradise Hotel.

Places to Stay – middle
The most popular place to stay in this range is the Highlands Hotel (☎ 22125). The staff here are very friendly and helpful but check the plumbing before you accept any particular room, since little maintenance has ever been done. It costs USh 12,650 (single or double) for a self-contained room with towel and soap provided and there's hot water in the showers if the plumbing is intact (otherwise, bucket hot water is provided). The big plus about this hotel is the excellent food offered in the downstairs restaurant and the very popular bar with its log fire. It's a great place to meet people.

Much better in terms of facilities which work is the recently restored and expanded Victoria Inn (☎ 22134), which offers very comfortable, self-contained rooms for US$10/13 a single/double with soap and towel provided. The hotel has its own bar and restaurant and the staff are friendly.

Places to Stay – top end
Kabale's best hotel is the White Horse Inn (☎ 22020), up on the hill overlooking the town. It's part of the Uganda Hotels Corporation chain but has not suffered from the same neglect as other hotels in this chain. It's a very attractive place and offers doubles (no singles) for USh 30,000 (nonresidents) or USh 18,000 (residents) including breakfast. The hotel has a bar and restaurant.

Places to Eat
You can find a good cheap breakfast (omelette, bread and tea or coffee) at the Visitours Hotel, Sky Blue Hotel or Twincos (opposite the post office). All three places also serve good local food for lunch and dinner. The Rubanza Restaurant is worth checking out for lunches and dinners.

The best value, however, is the restaurant at the Highlands Hotel. It's a minor splurge at around USh 2500 for a main course but it's well worth it, assuming they have what you want to eat (fish is frequently not available). You have the choice here of eating in the enclosed restaurant or in the partially open-air bar area with a log fire to warm your cockles. They also have the local banana wine, banapo, for sale by the bottle or the glass. One of these days I'll find the time to show them how to make a decent brew. In the meantime, rot your guts.

For a real splurge, but not necessarily better food, go for a meal at the *White Horse Inn*, which has a pleasant garden setting. Expect to pay around USh 3000 to USh 3500 for a main course.

Getting There & Away
Bus The UTC's daily bus to Kampala departs at 7 am, takes about 10 hours and costs USh 6500. To Fort Portal, there's a daily bus via Mbarara and Kasese at 7 am (USh 7500, about 10½ hours).

Matatu The daily matatus between Kabale and Kisoro in either direction cost USh 4000 (USh 4500 to the Zaïre border) and take about 2½ hours. They go when full, and 'full' means just that! Most of them are dan-

gerously overloaded but the ride, over an excellent gravel road, is absolutely magnificent and the views superb. On average, one of these matatus goes over the side every month, so on dangerous corners, get ready to jump off! The matatus depart from the Shell petrol station next to the Visitours Hotel.

KISORO
Kisoro is at the extreme south-western tip of the country on the Ugandan side of the Virunga Mountains, across from Ruhengeri in neighbouring Rwanda. Many travellers prefer to enter Rwanda this way rather than direct from Kabale, but its main draw for travellers is as a base from which to visit the gorillas in Mgahinga National Park to the south or the gorillas at Djomba just over the border to the west in neighbouring Zaïre.

Information
National Parks The Mgahinga National Park headquarters is on the main road in the centre of town, and it's here you should make enquiries about seeing the gorillas and arrange for transport to take you there. For full details about visiting the gorillas, see the

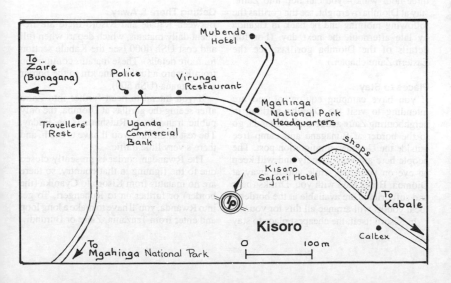

Kisoro

Mgahinga National Park section in the Uganda National Parks chapter.

Money There is no Forex bureau in Kisoro, so bring sufficient local currency with you, including enough to pay for food and guide tips for the trip to see the gorillas at Djomba (Zaïre) if you intend to go there. The Zaïrians in this area prefer payment in Ugandan shillings rather than zaïres, since zaïres are basically toilet paper. There's no bank at the border.

Immigration The Zaïre-Uganda border at Bunagana (nine km from Kisoro) is very easy-going. If you have no Zaïre visa and want to visit the Djomba gorillas and then return to Uganda, three-day visas can be issued on the spot (US$50) but you have to leave your passport with the immigration authorities at the border. You will also have to pay for a new visa to re-enter Uganda unless you have multiple entry on your original Ugandan visa. Everyone at the border is very familiar with travellers hopping over into Zaïre to see the gorillas for a day or two, so there are no hassles whatsoever.

From the border to Djomba it's just a three-hour walk – you can hop into Zaïre, stay at Djomba overnight, see the gorillas the following morning and be back in Uganda by late afternoon the next day. (For full details of the Djomba gorillas, see the Eastern Zaïre chapter.)

Places to Stay

If you have camping equipment and are intending to visit the Djomba gorillas in neighbouring Zaïre and return to Uganda, go to the border at Bunagana and camp free outside the Ugandan immigration post. The people here are very friendly and will keep an eye on your tent while you're away at Djomba. Bring food with you. Drinks (beer and soft drinks) are available at the border – local youths will arrange all this for you.

In Kisoro itself, the cheapest place to stay is the *Mubendo Hotel*, which has self-contained twin-bed doubles for USh 4400 and self-contained doubles with a double bed and sitting room for USh 5500. It's very clean, the staff are friendly and there's a bar and restaurant. The manager is a good conversationalist and reads a lot.

Somewhat more expensive is the *Travellers' Rest*, formerly part of the Uganda Hotels Corporation. This place must have been very pleasant in its heyday but has been allowed to deteriorate, though the atmosphere lingers on. It offers no-frills, self-contained double rooms (two beds) with bucket hot water. Reasonably priced meals here are tasty and good value but take some time to arrive, as the cooking facilities are limited. Cold beers are also available. Another possibility is the basic *Kisoro Safari Hotel*, which has no restaurant.

Places to Eat

For a cheap local meal, go to the *Virunga Restaurant* on the main street. Other than this, the only places to eat are the *Mubendo Hotel* and the *Travellers Rest*. Both offer much the same kind of food at similar prices.

Getting There & Away

Between Kabale and Kisoro there are frequent daily matatus, which depart when full and cost USh 4000 (see the Kabale section for more details). These matatus continue on from Kisoro a further nine km to the border at Bunagana (USh 500).

If you intend to head further into Zaïre after seeing the gorillas at Djomba, the only public transport to Rutshuru is on Friday. The rest of the time you'll have to hitch, and there's very little traffic.

The Rwandan border is presently closed due to the fighting in that country, so there are no matatus from Kisoro to Cyanika (the border) or further on to Ruhengeri. To get into Rwanda, you'll have to make a long loop and enter from Tanzania, Zaïre or Burundi.

Northern Uganda & National Parks

GULU

Gulu is the largest Ugandan town in the north of the country and is on the railway line between Tororo and Pakwach. It's a starting point for a visit to Paraa on the Victoria Nile, which runs through the spectacular Muchison Falls National Park. Thirty km north of Gulu at Patiko is Baker's Fort, built by the British in the 1870s as a base from which to suppress the slave trade.

This area hasn't seen tourists for years because of the threat of rebel activity. Even today, your safety cannot be guaranteed, so if you're thinking of coming to this area, check with an embassy in Kampala before setting off.

Places to Stay & Eat

A good, cheap place and excellent value is the *Church of Uganda Guest House*. Also excellent value is the *Uganda Red Cross Society*, which has a couple of rooms where travellers can stay – USh 2500/3000 for a single/double including all meals, it's an

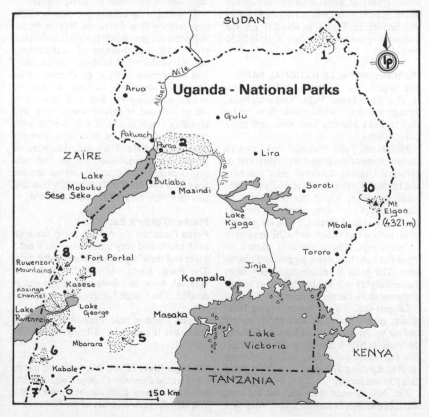

Uganda - National Parks

401

absolute bargain. Other places recommended are the *New Gulu Restaurant* in Pakwach Rd and the *Luxxor Lodge* opposite the truck park.

The top hotel is the *Acholi Inn* (☎ 108), part of the Ugandan Hotels Corporation. It has standard self-contained doubles for US$25 and 'executive' doubles for US$30. American Express cards are accepted.

Getting There & Away
Buses and trucks go between Kampala and Gulu. Those to Kampala leave around 5.30 am. Gulu is on the railway line between Tororo and Pakwach but trains only operate between Tororo and Gulu via Mbale and Soroti at present. There is a train once a week which departs from Gulu at 7 am on Saturday and arrives in Tororo at about 1 am the following morning. The fare is USh 2350 (3rd class).

MURCHISON FALLS NATIONAL PARK
The largest park in Uganda, at 3900 sq km, is the Murchison Falls National Park, through which the Victoria Nile flows on its way to Lake Mobutu Sese Seko (formerly Lake Albert).

Murchison Falls National Park used to contain some of the largest concentrations of game in Uganda. Unfortunately, poachers and retreating troops, both armed with automatic weapons, wiped out practically all game, except the more numerous (or less sought after) herd species. There are now no lions, only a few rhinos and a 20-head herd of elephants. There are still plenty of Ugandan kob, buffaloes, hippos and crocodiles. The game is recovering slowly from the onslaught but it will be a long time before it returns to its former numbers – if ever.

Despite this, it's still worth visiting Murchison, if only for the animals which are left and for the Murchison and Karuma Falls on the Victoria Nile within the park boundaries. The falls were once described as the most spectacular thing to happen to the Nile along its 6700-km length.

The Nile bisects the park, and the area south of the river is safe for travel. Also safe is the three-hour launch trip upriver to a point from which you can opt to walk for a couple of hours to the falls. En route you see crocodiles and hippos, thousands of birds and, usually, elephants. The only drawback with the launch is the price (US$40, payable in shillings and shared by up to 10 people), but as this is a popular place among aid workers and diplomatic staff, there's usually sufficient people to share the launch, especially on weekends.

Game drives north of the Nile are more problematic. There is a real (though slight) risk of ambush or kidnap. The last time this happened was in February 1993 but no-one was injured and all were set free several days later. Not all the rebels are so benevolent.

This area of the country gets quite hot. The best remedy is a dip in the Nile at Paraa. Bilharzia is a possibility but the fast-flowing river and the absence of settlements upstream reduce the likelihood considerably. You're far more likely to get chewed up by a hippo, so inspect the bathing site carefully before plunging in. You will inevitably attract a crowd of curious locals, who will probably laugh at you. If you're at all self-conscious, this may be more of a deterrent than the bilharzia. They will also warn of people-eating crocodiles, but the last incident occurred more than 20 years ago and the poor creatures have been so heavily poached that they steer clear of human habitation.

Places to Stay & Eat
Paraa Paraa has a very basic camp site with earth toilets and very little else – you'll need a tent and there's plenty of water in the Nile. The Paraa Lodge across the river was bombed, burnt and looted years ago and is derelict. The Chobe Lodge is likewise derelict.

Food supplies (and beer) are available in Paraa but it's cheaper to bring them from Masindi.

Waringo River If you don't want to camp, there are the *Rabongo Cottages*, about 30 km from Murchison Falls on the banks of the Waringo River, a tributary of the Nile. These are managed by Hot Ice (the Kampala safari company) on behalf of the Uganda National Parks office. Rabongo provides a choice of catering or self-catering arrangements and each cottage has a double and a single room with shower and toilet facilities and a verandah. There's a central lounge, a kitchen for self-caterers and radio communication with Kampala. The cottages cost US$42 per person per night (half that for children under 12 years of age). The only problem with this place is getting there. You must have your own transport or pay for someone to take you there (expensive). Game drives are available from the cottages (US$38). Hitching is a waste of time.

Getting There & Around

The usual access to Murchison Falls is via Masindi, along a good surfaced road from Kampala. There are plenty of buses and matatus between Kampala and Masindi. From Masindi to Paraa, transport is more problematical and you may have to hitch, but there is a regular bus three times a week which leaves Masindi at 2 pm from the 'new' bus station and goes to Bulisa via Butiaba (itself on Lake Mobutu Sese Seko). The fare is USh 2300 and the journey takes about four hours. There's also at least one matatu a day from Masindi to Bulisa (USh 2500, about three hours); however, you'll have to stay overnight at the rest house in Bulisa (singles only, USh 2000). From Bulisa to the falls you can rent a bicycle or bicycle taxi with peddler for USh 3000. It's 18 km to the national park entry gate and a further nine km to the camp site at Paraa.

Hitching from Masindi to Paraa is only really worth trying at weekends in the mornings, as a lot of expatriates visit the park at that time, but for the rest of the week, it's quiet.

From Paraa back to Masindi, you can either follow the procedure for getting there in the reverse order (decide how long you want to stay and ask the bicycle taxi to come and collect you – amazingly, they do come back) or ask around amongst those with vehicles at the rest camp for a lift back to Masindi or Kampala.

If you haven't the patience, time or inclination to hitch, go on an organised safari from Kampala. All the safari companies offer trips to Murchison Falls (see the Safaris section in the earlier Getting Around chapter for details).

QUEEN ELIZABETH NATIONAL PARK

Formerly the Ruwenzori National Park (until the mountains of the same name were made a national park recently), this park covers 2000 sq km and is bordered to the north by the Ruwenzori Mountains and to the west by Lake Rwitanzige (Lake Edward).

The Queen Elizabeth National Park was once a magnificent place to visit, with its great herds of elephant, buffalo, kob, waterbuck, hippo and topi. But like Murchison Falls, most of the game was wiped out by the retreating troops of Amin and Okello and by the Tanzanian army which occupied the country after Amin's demise. They all did their ivory and trophy-hunting best. There's now very little game in the park, apart from gazelle, buffaloes, hippos, a couple of small herds of elephant, and the occasionl lion. But it's worth a visit just to see the hippos and the birds. There are few places in Africa where you will be able to see so many hippos.

Every visitor takes a launch trip up the **Kazinga Channel** to see the thousands of hippos and the pelicans. If you're lucky you will also catch sight of one of the elephant herds and very occasionally see a lion or leopard. The two-hour trip costs US$50 shared by up to 10 people or US$5 per person if there are more than 10 of you. There are trips at 9 am (the best time) and 2.30 and 5 pm. Those in search of material for the game Trivial Pursuits will be interested to know that the launch was built in 1970 by Groves & Guttridge, East Cowes, UK.

Game drives covering around 80 km are also available from Mweya Lodge in the company of a ranger/guide (USh 800 per km plus USh 5000 for the ranger, shared by up to eight people).

A much less visited area of the park is that

around Ishasha, on the border with Zaïre. Once you get to Ishasha (see the Getting There & Away chapter), the only problem is getting a lift for the 17-km trip from the gate to the camp. Rangers usually visit the gate once a day and provide lifts. Hitching is prohibited because of the lions.

The lions in this area were once famous for their habit of climbing trees, but it seems they've given it up. The attraction now is the beautiful setting. You can bathe in the river (watch out for hippos) and walk in the forest, the only danger there being the buffaloes – make lots of noise as you walk.

Entry to the park costs US$10 (or the equivalent in Ugandan shillings); residents pay USh 7500. The price for a car is USh 2500 (trucks cost USh 6000) and there's a US$15 fee for movie cameras (USh 10,000 for residents).

The small **museum** next to Mweya Safari Lodge contains skulls and a few other things. It's open on weekdays from 3 to 6 pm and at weekends from 10 am till noon.

Places to Stay

Most of the places to stay are on the Mweya Peninsula close to the Mweya Safari Lodge. The cheapest way to stay is to camp, which costs USh 5000 per person per night (USh 2000 for residents). It's a reasonable site but has no shade. Hippos wander through the site at night. If you don't have a tent, there's the *Students' Camp*, where you can get a dormitory bed with shared bathroom facilities for USh 5000 (same price if you're a resident). More expensive is the *Ecology Institute*, where you can get a double room (no singles) with shared bathroom facilities for USh 9900 or US$10 per person. Bed linen and pillows are not provided.

Top of the line is the *Mweya Safari Lodge* (☎ Kasese 4266 or radio call 04 93), which has a stunning position on the raised peninsula, with excellent views over Lake Rwitanzige (Lake Edward) to Katwe and Zaïre and in the other direction along the Kazinga Channel. Sitting on the terrace with a cold drink at sunset is perfect. The lodge is part of the Uganda Hotels Corporation. It's

very comfortable, with self-contained rooms at US$35/55 for singles/doubles including breakfast (residents pay the same price). During the week the place is almost deserted but it gets busy on weekends. Good lunches and dinners are available here at reasonable prices and the restaurant is open to all. American Express cards are accepted. Watch out for the mongoose which come scampering across the lawns in the late afternoon on their way to the rubbish dump – rubbish is considered a throwaway item here and no attempt is made to conceal or bury it. Even the warthogs rummage through it. At night, hippos browse across the lawns, so watch what you're walking into!

The camp sites near Ishasha are very basic – toilets are all that's provided. The only supplies available are beer (Primus from Zaïre), so come prepared. If you're desperate, the rangers will cook some local stodge for you. If you don't have a tent there are several bandas, including one lovely old thatched colonial building which is falling down but is still infinitely more agreeable than the recently erected brick monstrosities. Camping costs the same as at Mweya and a double banda is US$10 per person per night.

Places to Eat

The *Ecology Hostel* provides basic meals. Otherwise, the *Mweya Safari Lodge* offers excellent meals for around USh 3500, but you must order in advance if you're not staying there. Snacks are also available.

Getting There & Away

The main gate is on the Kasese to Katwe road and there are several matatus from Kasese daily at about 10 am. The trip takes about one hour and costs USh 1500. A share-taxi from Kasese to the gate costs around US$10 one-way or US$16 return, including a drive in the park.

From the gate it's seven km to the lodge, and although the rangers don't seem too keen, they do actually let you walk this stretch. Vehicles are reasonably frequent, so you shouldn't have to wait too long if you decide to hitch.

There's another gate near the village of Katunguru where the Kasese to Mbarara road crosses the Kazinga Channel. There is much less traffic from this gate to the lodge, but you'd get there eventually. If you do get stuck, there is a basic lodge in Katunguru.

Hitching out of the park is easy – just stand by the barrier at the Mweya Safari Lodge and ask the driver for a lift. Better still, make arrangements the night before at the Lodge.

If you're not into hitching, arrange an organised safari from Kampala or from Fort Portal.

LAKE MBURO NATIONAL PARK

Between Mbarara and Masaka and covering an area of 290 sq km, this national park is mainly savannah with scattered acacia trees. There are five lakes, the largest of which is Lake Mburo. Created in 1983, the park features some of the rarer animals, such as impala, eland, roan antelope, reedbuck, klipspringer and topi, as well as zebras, buffaloes and hippos. Adjacent to the park are the ranches of the Bahima tribe, who herd the famed long-horned Ankole cattle which are a common sight. This is one of the parks you're allowed to walk through (accompanied by a ranger), or you can go on game drives. Canoes (either paddled or outboard-driven) are available on Lake Mburo.

Entry to the park costs US$10 (USh 2000 for residents).

Places to Stay

There are four camp sites in the park (USh 5000 per person per night, USh 2000 for residents), or you can stay at the *Rwonyo Rest Camp*, which has three double, two single and one four-bed bandas with bedding, mosquito nets and bathroom facilities. They cost USh 6000 a single and USh 4000 per person in a double. Meals are also available here or you can cater for yourself. Fresh fish is sold each morning by fishers from the lake. There's no electricity or refrigeration but storm lanterns, pit latrines and warm bucket showers are available. Bookings should be made through the Uganda

National Parks office (π 256534), Plot 17-19, Nkrumah Rd, PO Box 3530, Kampala.

Other facilities are constantly being improved by the Lake Mburo National Park Community Conservation Project, which is part of the African Wildlife Foundation project.

Getting There & Away

The park is on the main Masaka to Mbarara road. Coming from Masaka, turn left at the 50-km marker (13 km past Lyantonde) or turn left at Sanga Trading Centre (24 km past Lyantonde). Both entry points are signposted. It's possible to hitch lifts in the irregular but accommodating park vehicles from the main road. Alternatively, you can hire a taxi in Mbarara to take you there (US$25 to US$30 shared by up to four people). If you're taking your own vehicle, 4WD is recommended.

TORO GAME RESERVE

This is a small game reserve to the north of Fort Portal in the Semliki Valley. It stretches as far as Ntoroko on the shores of Lake Mobutu Sese Seko. You really need your own transport to see this reserve, as there has been nowhere to stay since the Semliki Safari Lodge burnt down quite a few years ago. The best way to see it is to go on an organised safari from Fort Portal, taking in the fishing village of Ntoroko. See the Fort Portal section for details of these safaris.

KIDEPO VALLEY NATIONAL PARK

Surrounded by mountains and notable for ostriches, cheetahs and giraffes, this park covers an area of 1450 sq km in the extreme north-east of Uganda, along the border with Sudan. It may still be a dangerous area to visit because of scattered bands of Okello supporters and Karamoja cattle-rustlers. Make enquiries in Kampala about safety before heading off in this direction. Entry to the park costs USh 2000 per day, plus a further USh 1000 per day if you require a cook. Vehicles for game-viewing (when available) cost USh 800 per km, plus USh 1500 per day for a ranger escort.

Places to Stay

There are four camp sites, all within two km of the park headquarters and the adjacent NRA camp. Camping costs USh 300 per person per night.

There's also the *Apoka Rest Camp* which, though somewhat run-down, has 16 twin-bedded chalets supplied with bedding and mosquito nets. All the chalets have their own showers and hot water is provided by wood-fired boilers. Other facilities include boiled and filtered water and an electric fridge, which works when the camp generator is running (7 to 11.30 pm). The charge is USh 2400 per person per night. There are only limited stocks of dried food available at Apoka, so bring all your own requirements with you.

Getting There & Away

Virtually the only way to get there at present is by chartering a light plane. This will cost you around US$1200 return for a six-seater. Driving to the park is not recommended.

RUWENZORI NATIONAL PARK

The fabled, mist-covered Ruwenzori Mountains on Uganda's western border with Zaïre are almost as popular with travellers as Kilimanjaro and Mt Kenya but definitely harder to climb. They have a well-deserved reputation for being very wet at times. This was best summed up by a comment on the wall of Bujuku hut: 'Jesus came here to learn how to walk on water. After five days, anyone could do it.' Be prepared and take warm, waterproof clothing.

The mountain range, which is not volcanic, stretches for about 100 km. At its centre are several mountains which are permanently snow and glacier-covered: Mt Speke (Vittorio Emmanuele) is its highest peak at 4890 metres); Mt Baker (Edward is its highest peak at 4843 metres); Mt Gessi (Iolanda, 4715 metres); Mt Emin (4791 metres) and Mt Luigi di Savoia (4627 metres). The three highest peaks in the range are Margherita (5109 metres), Alexandra (5091 metres) and Albert (5087), all on Mt Stanley.

Trekking on the Ruwenzori

The climbing varies from the easy ascent of Mt Speke, which requires only limited mountain experience, to the harder routes on Stanley and Baker, which should not be attempted unless you are of alpine standard. Climb to the top only if you want to – otherwise, the guides will be happy to take you around the lower reaches.

Five days is the absolute minimum for a visit to the range, but seven or eight days is better, with one or two days at the top huts. The best times to climb are from late December to the end of February and mid-June to mid-August, when there's little rain. Even at these times, the higher reaches are often enveloped in mist, though this generally clears for a short time each day.

Books & Maps Before attempting a trek in the Ruwenzori Range, it's strongly recommended that you obtain a copy of *Ruwenzori – Map & Guide*, by Andrew Wielochowski (1989). This is an excellent large-scale contour map of the mountains, with all the main trails, huts and camping sites marked (as well as other features).

On the reverse side are detailed descriptions of the various possible treks as well as sections on history, flora & fauna, weather and climate, necessary equipment, useful contacts, costs, and advice in the event of an accident. It's for sale in most Nairobi bookshops (KSh 100), or you can get it from Ian Munro/Mark Savage, PO Box 44827, Nairobi, Kenya, or from Andrew Wielochowski, 32 Seamill Park Crescent, Worthing BN11 2PN, UK.

Alternatively, buy a copy of the much less detailed *The Mountains of the Moon* (USh 2000), put out by the Rwenzori Mountaineering Services in Kasese. It will give you a good idea of what's involved in trekking around the summit.

It may still be possible to get hold of a copy of *Guide to the Ruwenzori* (Mountain Club of Uganda, 1972), by Osmaston & Pasteur. This was the first comprehensive account of the mountains to be published and, though somewhat out of date, is still

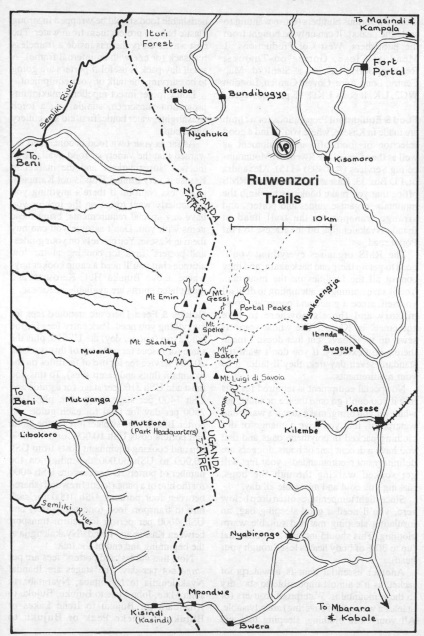

UGANDA

useful for serious climbers (those wanting to scale the peaks). It can only be bought from the publishers, West Col Productions, 1 Meadow Close, Goring-on-Thames, Reading, Berks, UK, and at Stanfords Map Centre, Long Acre, Covent Garden, London WC2, UK. It costs UK£8.95 plus postage.

Food & Equipment Preparations for a climb are made in Kasese, where you'll find a good selection of foodstuffs and equipment as well as the office of the Rwenzori Mountaineering Services (☎ (0493) 4115), Alexandra St, PO Box 33, Kasese. It's through the RMS office that you make bookings to climb the mountain, organise guides and porters, and arrange transport to the trail head at Ibanda/Nyakalengija, off the Kasese to Fort Portal road.

The RMS organises everything you'll need to get up there and back again, and they control all the facilities on the mountain. You'll save nothing by attempting to do it all yourself, since a guide and porter are compulsory and there's nowhere to hire equipment in Kasese. The whole scene is sewn up these days, but that doesn't mean there's no flexibility. If you don't want the standard seven-day trek, they'll tailor it to your requirements.

No special equipment is required for this trek if you don't go onto the ice or snow, but whatever you bring, make sure it's warm and waterproof, that you have a change of dry clothing packed in polythene bags and that you have a decent pair of boots. Joggers are definitely not recommended – your feet will get soaked walking through the bogs, making you cold and miserable all day.

Since night temperatures often drop below zero, you'll need a good sleeping bag, an insulating sleeping mat and suitable warm clothing. This should include a woollen hat (up to 30% of body heat is lost through your head).

Another essential item is a waterproof jacket, as it's almost impossible to stay dry in these mountains. Waterproof trousers (or at least a waterproof covering) are advisable. All your extra clothing, sleeping bag and

perishable food should be wrapped in strong plastic bags to protect them from water. The best way to carry them is inside a frameless rucksack (or one with an internal frame). A small day pack is useful if porters are going to be carrying the bulk of your equipment.

Don't forget insect repellent, maximum-protection sunscreen, sunglasses, a torch (flashlight), water bottle, first-aid kit, cutlery and a cup.

As far as your own food is concerned, be warned that the variety of food available in the two 'supermarkets' and the market in Kasese is very limited. This is not Kampala, much less Nairobi. If there's anything you particularly want to eat on the trek or you have any special requirements, bring these items with you. Don't assume you can buy them in Kasese. You can rely on your guides' and porters' fires for cooking at the low altitudes but you'll need a camp cooker anywhere above Bujuku Hut. Kerosene and methylated spirits are available in Kasese.

Guides & Fees There are standard fees for everything you need. Park entry fees for the whole trip (*not* per day) are US$10, plus the same for rescue fees. On top of this is a USh 20,000 service fee for use of facilities on the mountain (huts and camp sites). To this you must add USh 2100 per stage for a guide and USh 1400 per stage per porter, plus USh 2500 per day for food for each guide and porter. Blanket and sweater hire for the guide and porters costs USh 10,000 for the whole trip and cooking equipment costs from USh 10,000 to USh 30,000 depending on the number of porters. Other fees are USh 4000 for the hire of a panga to cut firewood (shared between four porters), USh 1000 for sack hire to transport food (one per porter) and USh 4000 per person for return transport between Kasese and Ibanda/Nyakalengija at the beginning and end of the trek.

Note that guides' and porters' fees are per *stage* not per day. The stages are Ibanda/Nyakalengija to Nyabitaba, Nyabitaba to John Mate, John Mate to Bujuku, Bujuku to Kitandara (or Bujuku to Irene Lakes or Bujuku to Speke Peak or Bujuku to

Margherita), Elena Hut to Margherita, Kitandara to Guy Yeoman (or Kitandara to Baker or Kitandara to Lugigi), Guy Yeoman to Nyabitaba, and Nyabitaba to Ibanda/Nyakalengija. If you walk more than one stage in the day, you have to pay for two stages.

These charges may soon increase, depending on negotiations between Uganda National Parks and the guides' and porters' union.

The cost of going onto ice or snow is proportionally higher, as you'll have to provide the guide and porters with appropriate equipment and clothing.

Assuming you don't go onto the ice or snow and take two porters per climber (more or less obligatory, due to food requirements and weight restrictions on porters), that works out at US$117 per person plus the cost of your food and drink and any equipment you need for the standard six-night, seven-day trek. That's pretty good value, however you see it.

Remember that if you want a good trip, befriend your guide and porters. These people are drawn from the Bakonjo, a hardy but friendly mountain people, most of whom have Biblical names. They'll be staying in rock shelters overnight while you stay in the huts or in your own tent, so be generous with small hand-outs and give a decent tip at the end of the journey.

Accommodation With heavy USAID investment, many improvements have been made to the tracks as well as the huts. There are new bridges over the larger rivers, the huts now have essentials such as walls and roofs (which they lacked not long ago) and some have a kitchen plus there's a wooden pathway over the bog. All this is being done to lessen the impact of walkers on the fragile environment.

It's important to be clear whether you'll be staying in the huts or in your own tent when booking with the RMS. Overbooking is not unknown, so if you don't have your own tent, it could be rough going.

There are a total of 10 huts on the mountain, but some accommodate only a few people, so if you have camping equipment, make sure you are booked to stay in them before setting off. The cost of hut accommodation and camping fees is covered in your USh 20,000 fee payable to the RMS.

Altitude Sickness Be aware of the dangers of high-altitude sickness. In extreme cases it can be fatal. High-altitude sickness usually becomes noticeable above 3000 metres and is a sign of your body adjusting to lower oxygen levels. Mild symptoms include headaches, mild nausea and a slight loss of coordination. Symptoms of severe altitude sickness include abnormal speech and behaviour, severe nausea and headaches, a marked loss of coordination, and persistent coughing spasms. When any combination of these severe symptoms occurs, the afflicted person should immediately descend 300 to 1000 metres. When trekking, such a descent may even have to take place at night.

There are no known indicators as to who might suffer from altitude sickness (fitness, age and previous high-altitude experience all seem to be irrelevant), and the only cure is an immediate descent to lower altitudes.

The Trails Ibanda/Nyakalengija is the starting point for a climb in the Ruwenzoris. There are two basic trails up the mountain starting from Ibanda/Nyakalengija which will take you between the peaks of Mt Baker and Mt Stanley. They both have the same approach as far as Nyabitaba Hut on the first day. After that you can either go clockwise or anticlockwise between the peaks.

The following is the clockwise route (the anticlockwise route is the reverse of the above and takes the same amount of time):

Day 1 Nyakalengija to the Nyabitaba Hut (2650 metres), the first stage, is a fairly easy walk taking four to five hours.

Day 2 From Nyabitaba Hut (2650 metres), you can either take the old route to the Guy Yeoman Hut (3450 metres, five to six hours) or the new but safer route (seven hours). Along the new route, you also have the choice of staying at Kuruguta Hut/camp site (2940 metres). The route takes you through tropical vegetation, over two minor streams, across the Mahoma River and finally up the side of a steep valley to the ridge on which the hut is situated.

Day 3 From the Guy Yeoman Hut, you pass through a bog to the Kabamba rock shelter (3450 metres) and waterfall, then via the Bujongolo rock shelter and the Freshfield Pass (4215 metres) to the Kitandara Hut (3990 metres). This takes about seven hours. The hut is picturesquely situated on the shore of the lake of the same name.

Day 4 This is possibly the most interesting part of the trek. After leaving the twin Kitandara lakes, you climb over boulders at the foot of Mt Baker on the one side and the glaciers of Savoia and Elena on the other. From here you cross Scott Elliot Pass (4372 metres) and proceed down to Bujuku Hut (3900 metres). The walk takes about four hours. If you intend to scale Mt Stanley or Margherita, on the other hand, you head for Elena Hut (4547 metres), in which case both you and your guide and porters will need appropriate equipment to deal with ice and snow.

Day 5 Assuming you don't scale Mt Stanley or Margherita, the trek from Bujuku Hut is all downhill to the John Mate Hut (3350 metres). The walk takes about five hours. En route you pass the Bigo Hut (3400 metres), where you have the option of taking a difficult track north leading to Mt Gessi, Mt Emin and the Lac de la Lune via a series of bogs. There are also three bogs between the Bujuku Hut and the John Mate Hut, but it's here you'll come across stands of giant heather, groundsel and bamboo. Should you decide to spend the night at Bigo Hut, it sleeps up to 12 people and there is room for tents. Firewood is available nearby for open-air cooking in fine weather.

Day 6 From the John Mate Hut, it's downhill again along a rough track to Nyabitaba (about five hours).

There are quite a few other minor trails, both up the mountain and across the top into Zaïre and down to Mutwanga (the Uganda-Zaïre border essentially crosses the peaks).

Organised Treks

If it's your time rather than your money that is limited, you can have all the necessary arrangements made for you by a safari company. For details of safari companies in Kampala which offer Ruwenzori treks, see the Getting Around chapter earlier in the Uganda section.

BWINDI & MGAHINGA NATIONAL PARKS

These are two of Uganda's most recently created national parks. They are in the south-western corner of the country, Bwindi (formerly known as the Impenetrable Forest) being north of Kisoro and Mgahinga south. Together the parks encompass two of the last remaining habitats of the mountain gorilla, where half of the surviving mountain gorillas in the world live – an estimated 320 individuals.

A major conservation effort has been going on here for the last three years to protect the gorillas' habitat, under the auspices of the German Animal Protection Society and Uganda National Parks. As a result, encroachment on the montane forest by cultivators has been stopped, poaching has ceased and the gorilla families have been gradually habituated to human contact. As of 1 April 1993, the gorillas can be visited (casual visitors were prohibited from visiting them for a number of years whilst the project got underway).

Gorillas are not the only animals to have benefitted from this project. Both parks contain elephants, at least 10 species of primates, including chimpanzees, colobus monkeys and baboons, duiker and bushbuck and the rare giant forest hog, as well as a host of bird and insect species. They encompass one of the richest areas in Africa for flora & fauna.

The gorillas in these parks are nowhere near as habituated to human contact as the ones in Zaïre, so you need to be patient and prepared to scramble through more bush than would be necessary at Djomba, but it's well worth it. There's an information office in Kisoro which can give you all the latest information. Otherwise, contact PO Box 723, Kabale (the project's headquarters) or the Uganda National Parks office in Kampala.

Fees for a gorilla visit are US$80 per person, plus US$10 (USh 7500 for resident foreigners) park entry fee, plus US$5 for a guide (compulsory) for half a day. The maximum group size is four people but it's planned to increase this to eight people.

Kisoro or Kabale are the best places to base yourself for these visits unless you have camping gear, in which case there's a camp site at Buhoma, though there are no facilities and you must bring everything with you.

The project, in terms of public access, is still in the early stages, so if you'd like more information or wish to help financially, contact the Mgahinga Gorilla National Park Project, PO Box 7487, Kampala, Uganda, or the Deutscher Tierschutzbund E V, Baumschulallee 15, 5300 Bonn 1, Germany. They need funds if this work is to continue and, if the fighting in neighbouring Rwanda continues, they need it *now*.

MT ELGON FOREST PARK

This is the most recently created of Uganda's national parks and encompasses the upper regions of Mt Elgon up to the Kenyan border.

The mountain (Wagagai is the highest peak at 4321 metres) is said to have one of the largest surface areas of any extinct volcano in the world and is peppered with cliffs, caves, gorges and waterfalls. The views from the higher reaches across the wide plains are some of the most spectacular in Uganda. The upper slopes are clothed in tropical montane forest, while above this lies a vast tract of alpine moorland which extends over the caldera, the collapsed crater which

covers some 40 sq km at the top of the mountain. **Sipi Falls**, north of Mbale in the foothills of the mountain, has to be the most beautiful and romantic waterfall in the whole of Uganda, regardless of what you might think about Murchison Falls. Don't miss it, even if you don't trek up the mountain.

The best time to climb the mountain is from December to March, but the seasons are unpredictable and it can rain at any time.

The national park is being supervised by a very enthusiastic and dedicated bunch of people under the umbrella of the Mt Elgon Conservation & Development Project (☎ (045) 3179), PO Box 2690, Mbale. External financial support comes from NORAD, the Norwegian international development agency.

The idea is to promote conservation and rehabilitation of the flora & fauna of Mt Elgon, encourage sustainable development in the communities surrounding the park, maintain the quality and quantity of the water flow to all areas affected by the forest, and develop the long-term tourism potential of the mountain.

In terms of overseas visitors, this comes down to trekking up the mountain, and to this end, they've already produced a leaflet which describes the possibilities.

Trekking on Mt Elgon The Mt Elgon Conservation & Development Project is still in its infancy as far as tourism is concerned, so you need to be resourceful, patient, self-sufficient and not expect well-worn paths such as those you find on Mt Kenya and Kilimanjaro. You obviously need your own camping and cooking equipment, your own food, appropriate clothing and a guide. Don't attempt the trek without a guide – you'll get lost. So far, there are three established camp sites along the Sasa River Trail, the usual route to the summit.

Give yourself a minimum of three days to do this trek and five if you want to reach Jackson's Point, Wagagai and Suam Gorge.

Guides and porters can be found at the *Wagagai Hotel* (☎ Budadiri 4) in Budadiri, 30 km north-east of Mbale, where you can also get a bed for USh 5000 per night. The usual rates for guides/porters are USh 5000/4500 per day, half payable in advance and the remainder at the end of the trek.

There are regular matatus to **Budadiri** (which, for the present, can be considered to be the trailhead). From here, a road leads to Bugitimwa, then it's about three hours' walk to the forest. Almost as soon as you enter the forest, you reach Mudangi cliffs, which are scaled by means of 'ladders' (piles of branches). From the top, the trail is less steep and the path well defined. Half an hour's walk down this path is the bamboo forest and a further half hour's walk across the other side of the Sasa River brings you to the first camp site. Getting across the river involves boulder-hopping or wading knee-deep in fast-flowing water, depending on the season.

The camp site is marked by a well-used fireplace and there are enclosed toilets and a rubbish pit. If it's still early in the day when you reach here, you have the option of continuing another two hours further up the trail to stay at the next camp site, some 300 metres to the left of the trail near the Environmental Task Force hut.

The next part of the trail goes up to the top of the forest and into the heathland, where there's another possible camp site close to a small cave (about three hours beyond the first camp site). The moorland is studded with giant senecio (groundsel) and you'll often see duikers bounding through the long grass and Lammergeier vultures overhead.

A further three hours' walk brings you to the caldera, after which the path splits, the left fork leading directly into the caldera and the hot springs at the head of the Suam Gorge, the right fork going to Jackson's Summit via Jackson's Pool. The latter path crosses a permanent stream, and is a possible camp site if you wish to stay up here.

Jackson's Summit and Wagagai can be reached in one day, allowing for a comfortable return to the second camp site in good light. The return journey from the second camp site to the road head can be done in five to six hours.

If you're heading over the border into Kenya via Suam Gorge, you can stay at *Kabyoyon Farm*, about eight km off the main road, but you need to bring your own food if you turn up unexpectedly.

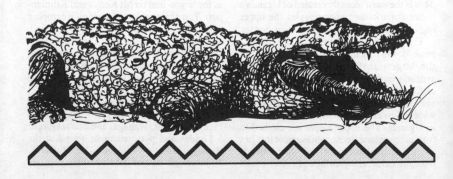

Rwanda

Rwanda

Many travellers come to Rwanda to visit the Parc National des Volcans in the north, where the borders of Rwanda, Uganda and Zaïre meet. The thickly forested slopes are one of the last remaining sanctuaries of the mountain gorilla.

Like Burundi, Rwanda is one of the world's most densely populated countries. To feed the people, almost every available piece of land is under cultivation, except for the Akagera (along the border with Tanzania) and the higher slopes of the volcanoes. Since most of the country is mountainous, this involves a good deal of terracing. The banded hillsides are similar to those in Nepal or the Philippines. Tea plantations take up considerable areas of land.

Warning As of October 1993 the Parc National des Volcans was a war zone due to ongoing hostilities between the Watutsi and Hutu (see the following History section). The border with Uganda is closed and much of Rwanda north of Kigali is off limits to travellers. Undoubtedly the park will reopen when a reconciliation between the two sides is brokered, but that may not be for some time.

Facts about the Country

HISTORY
Early Settlement
As in neighbouring Burundi, the original

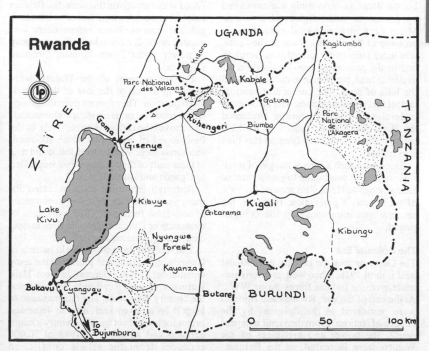

Rwanda

Parc National des Volcans

UGANDA

Kisoro

Kabale

Gatuna

Ruhengeri

Biumba

Kagitumba

Goma

Gisenye

Z A Ï R E

Lake
Kivu

Kibuye

Kigali

Gitarama

Parc National
de L'Akagera

T A N Z A N I A

Kibungu

Nyungwe
Forest

Kayanza

Bukavu

Cyangugu

Butare

B U R U N D I

To
Bujumbura

0   50   100 km

inhabitants of Rwanda, the Twa Pygmies, were gradually displaced from 1000 CE onwards by migrating Hutu tribespeople who, in turn, came to be dominated by the Watutsi from the 15th century. The Watutsi used the same methods here for securing domination over the Hutu as they did in Burundi – the introduction of a feudal land system and a lord-peasant relationship with regard to services and the ownership of cattle, which represented wealth. There the similarities with Burundi end. The authority of the Rwandan *mwami* (king) was far greater than that of his opposite number in Burundi, and the system of feudal overlordship which developed in Rwanda was unsurpassed outside Ethiopia.

Not only was the Rwandan mwami an absolute ruler in every sense of the word, with the power to exact forced Hutu labour and to allocate land to peasants or evict them, but the Watutsi overlordship was reinforced by ceremonial and religious observances. Military organisation, likewise, was the sole preserve of the Watutsi. Rwanda, however, was more intensively farmed than Burundi, and in the process of growing food on all available land, the Hutu eventually denuded the hills of trees. The consequent erosion, lack of fuel and competition with the Watutsi pastoralists for land frequently threatened the Hutu with famine. Indeed, in the 20th century alone, there have been no less than six famines.

Faced with such a narrow margin of security, something was bound to give sooner or later among the Hutu, who account for 89% of the country's population. However, the process was interrupted by the colonial period.

The Colonial Era

The Germans took the country in 1890 and held it until 1916, when their garrisons surrendered to the Belgian forces during WW I. At the end of the war, Rwanda and Burundi were mandated to the Belgians by the League of Nations. From then until independence, the power and privileges of the Watutsi were increased, as the Belgians found it convenient to rule indirectly through the mwami and his princes. They were not only trained to run the bureaucracy but had a monopoly on the educational system operated by the Catholic missionaries.

The condition of the Hutu peasantry deteriorated and led, in 1957, to a series of urgent demands for radical reform. Power and privilege are rarely given up voluntarily in Africa, however, and in 1959, following the death of Mwami Matara III, a ruthless Watutsi clan seized power and murdered Hutu leaders.

Independence

The Watutsi power grab was a serious miscalculation and provoked a massive Hutu uprising. About 100,000 Watutsi were butchered in the bloodletting which followed, and many thousands fled into neighbouring countries. The new mwami fled into exile. Faced with carnage on this scale, the Belgian colonial authorities were forced to introduce political reforms. When independence was granted in 1962, it brought the Hutu majority to power under Prime Minister Gregoire Kayibanda.

Certain sections of the Watutsi were unwilling to accept the loss of their privileged position. They formed guerrilla groups which mounted raids on Hutu communities, thus provoking further Hutu reprisals. In the fresh round of bloodshed which followed, thousands more Watutsi were killed and tens of thousands of their fellow tribespeople fled to Uganda and Burundi.

Although intertribal tensions eased for many years after that, there was a resurgence of anti-Tutsi feeling in 1972 when tens of thousands of Hutu tribespeople were massacred in neighbouring Burundi.

The slaughter reignited the old hatreds in Rwanda at that time and prompted the army commander, Major General Juvenal Habyarimana, to oust Kayibanda. He has ruled the country ever since, and has managed to keep it on an even keel, despite depressed prices for tea and coffee (the country's major exports) and an influx in 1988 of 50,000 refugees from the ethnic conflict in neighbouring Burundi. He also managed to stay clear of applying for IMF loans and the austerity measures which are a usual precondition.

Then, in October 1990, the whole intertribal issue was savagely reopened. On the first day of the month, Rwanda was invaded by some 5000 well-armed rebels of the Rwandan Patriotic Front, or RPF (essentially a Tutsi military front), from their bases in western Uganda. They were led by Paul Kagame, the former security chief of the Ugandan army, and assisted by officers and soldiers of the Ugandan NRA. All hell broke loose. Two days later, at Habyarimana's request, France, Belgium and Zaïre flew in troops to help the Rwandan army repulse the rebels.

With this support assured, the Rwandan army went on the rampage against the Tutsi and any Hutu 'suspected' of having collaborated with the rebels. Thousands were shot or hacked to death and countless others indiscriminately arrested, herded into football stadia or police stations and left there without food or water for days. Many died. Those that could, fled to Uganda. Zaïrian troops, likewise, joined in the carnage. President Museveni of Uganda was accused of having encouraged the rebels and supplied them with equipment. The accusations were denied but the evidence suggests otherwise. It's inconceivable that Museveni was totally unaware of the preparations which were going on, and it was also common knowledge that Uganda was keen to see the repatriation of the 250,000 Tutsi refugees in western Uganda.

The setback for the RPF was only temporary, however. They invaded again in 1991, this time better armed and prepared. The government forces were thrown back over a large area of northern Rwanda, and by early 1992, the RPF was within 25 km of Kigali, at which point a cease-fire was cobbled together and the warring parties brought to the negotiating table in Arusha (Tanzania).

The negotiations stalled several weeks later and hostilities were renewed. They have gone on ever since, though not at the same level of intensity. French troops, flown in ostensibly to protect foreign nationals in Kigali, have been accused by the RPF of assisting the Rwandese army, but these accusations have been denied. Meanwhile, with morale in the Rwandese army at a low ebb, Habyarimana is under increasing pressure to agree to a power-sharing deal with the RPF and an integration of the two armies. Whether this will ever eventuate, given the bitterness between the two sides, remains to be seen, but something must be done to pave the way for the return of the estimated one million refugees who have fled the fighting and who cannot return until their security is assured.

In the meantime, much of Rwanda north of Kigali remains off limits to travellers and the border with Uganda is closed. This also means you can no longer visit the gorillas in the Parc National des Volcans, north of Ruhengeri. (See the National Parks section later in this chapter.)

GEOGRAPHY
Rwanda's mountainous terrain occupies 26,338 sq km. Land use is about 35% arable, 20% pasture and 11% forest.

CLIMATE
The average day temperature is 30°C with a possible maximum of 34°C, except in the highlands, where the day range is 12°C to 15°C. There are four discernible seasons: the long rains from mid-March to mid-May, the long dry from mid-May to mid-October, the short rains from mid-October to mid-December and the short dry from mid-December to mid-March.

It rains more frequently and heavily in the north-east, where volcanoes are covered by rainforest. The summit of Kalisimbi (4507 metres), the highest of these volcanoes, is often covered with sleet or snow.

GOVERNMENT
The head of state is Major General Habyarimana, who is also leader of the only political party, the Mouvement Révolutionnaire National pour le Développement

RWANDA

(MRND). He has been re-elected three times since coming to power in a bloodless military coup in 1973. In each election he was the sole candidate. Multiparty elections have been mooted but are unlikely to take place until the present military standoff is resolved.

ECONOMY

The economy is agriculturally based, with coffee by far the largest export, accounting for about 75% of export income. Tungsten, tin, pyrethrum and tea are also important, but the tin industry is presently in limbo following the forced liquidation of the state mining company after the collapse of the International Tin Agreement in 1985.

The country is a major recipient of international aid, particularly from the People's Republic of China, Belgium and Germany.

Agriculture is the main employer and export earner, contributing about 40% of GDP. The principal food crops include plantain, sweet potato, beans, cassava, sorghum and maize.

The manufacturing sector accounts for nearly 20% of GDP. Local produce includes cigarettes, soap, plastics and textiles.

Inflation is running at a very respectable 4% per annum.

POPULATION

The population of about 6.7 million is increasing at the alarming rate of 3.7% annually (almost equal to Kenya). The country's population density is the highest in Africa. About 65% are Christians, 25% follow tribal religions and the rest are Muslims.

LANGUAGE

The national language is Kinyarwanda. The official languages are Kinyarwanda and French, which enables you to get by in most areas. Kinyarwanda is the medium of school instruction at primary level, French at secondary level (only 8% of the population reach secondary level). Little English is spoken but Swahili (more correctly known as Kiswahili) is useful in some areas.

Facts for the Visitor

VISAS & EMBASSIES

Visas are required by everyone except German nationals. Avoid applying for your visa outside East Africa, as this often involves a lot of red tape. They cost about US$10 in most countries, require two photos, allow a one-month stay and generally take 24 hours to issue.

There are a couple of points to consider when applying for a Rwandan visa. The first is that you have to give the exact date you intend to enter the country, as the visa becomes valid from that date and lasts only for the period you have specified. You cannot legally enter the country before the specified date, though some people have done so without any problems. It's best to get a one-month visa as it is not expensive, and it gives you some flexibility as to the date you turn up at the border.

The second consideration is whether to request a multiple-entry visa, especially if you intend to re-enter Rwanda from Zaïre. There's no extra cost and, again, it gives you flexibility. The main reason for this is that one of the routes between Bukavu (Zaïre) and Bujumbura (Burundi) is via Rwanda, and for this you may need a Rwandan visa, even though only one-third of the road is through Rwanda and you have no intention of getting off the bus, truck or car. As Rwandan transit visas (valid for 12 hours) cost about US$10, you might as well apply for a tourist visa initially. There are alternatives to this route, so a Rwandan visa is not absolutely essential.

Neither letters of introduction from your own embassy nor onward tickets are required and no-one will ask to see (or count) how much money you are carrying on arrival.

Rwandan Embassies

There are Rwandan embassies in Brussels (Belgium), Ottawa (Canada), Cairo (Egypt), Addis Ababa (Ethiopia), Paris (France),

Bonn (Germany), Abidjan (Ivory Coast), Tokyo (Japan) and Washington DC (USA).

In East Africa, visas can be obtained from Rwandan embassies in Bujumbura (Burundi), Nairobi (Kenya), Dar es Salaam (Tanzania), Kampala (Uganda) and Kinshasa (Zaïre). There's also a consulate in Mombasa (Kenya).

Burundi The embassy (☎ 26865) is at 24 Ave Zaïre, Bujumbura, next to the Zaïrian Embassy. One-month multiple-entry visas cost BFr 2500, require two photos and are issued in 24 hours. Office hours are Monday to Friday from 8 am to 4 pm and Saturday from 8 to 11.30 am.

Kenya The embassy (☎ 334341) is on the 12th floor, International House, Mama Ngina St, Nairobi. It's open Monday to Friday from 9 am to noon and 2 to 5 pm. One-month visas cost US$5.20, require two photos and take 48 hours to issue.

Tanzania The embassy (☎ 46502) is at 32 Upanga Rd. Visas cost TSh 8000 or US$20, require two photos and are issued in 24 hours. Office hours are Monday to Friday from 8 am to 12.30 pm and 2 to 5 pm.

Uganda The embassy (☎ 244045) is at Plot 2, Nakaima Rd, next to the Uganda Museum. It's open Monday to Friday from 8.30 am to 12.30 pm and 2.30 to 5 pm, but visa applications are accepted in the morning only. Visas cost USh 8400, require two photos and are issued the same day. It's advisable to get a multiple-entry visa if you plan to travel by road between Bukavu (Zaïre) and Bujumbura (Burundi). Remember that the border between Uganda and Rwanda is closed.

It's advisable to get a multiple-entry visa if you plan to travel by road between Bukavu (Zaïre) and Bujumbura (Burundi). Remember that the border between Uganda and Rwanda is closed and has been for some time.

Zaïre There are no Rwandan consulates at either Bukavu or Goma in eastern Zaïre, so it's advisable to get your visa in Kinshasa (or elsewhere) if you're coming from the west. On the other hand, Rwandan transit visas are available at the border for US$10.

Visa Extensions
Tourist visas can be extended in the capital, Kigali, at the immigration office, Rue du Commerce, next to the Air France office. The cost is about US$17. Transit visas obtained at a border can also be extended (for seven days) in Kigali, at a cost of US$40.

Foreign Embassies in Rwanda
Kigali, the capital of Rwanda, is a small city, and most foreign embassies are within easy walking distance of the centre.

Burundi The embassy (☎ 73465) is on Rue de Ntaruka off Ave de Rusumo. Visas are issued only to Rwandan residents, so don't waste your time. Visas are available at the border.

Kenya The embassy is on Rue Kadyiro near the Meridien Hôtel, on the way to the airport. It's open Monday to Friday from 8.30 am till noon and 2 to 4.30 pm. Visas cost US$10 or the equivalent in local currency, require two photographs and are issued the same day if you apply before 11.30 am. No onward tickets or minimum funds are asked for.

Tanzania The embassy (☎ 76074) is on Ave Paul VI close to the junction of Ave de Rusumo. Visas require two photos and generally take 48 hours to issue. The cost depends on your nationality (see the Tanzanian Facts for the Visitor chapter for details). The embassy is open Monday to Friday from 9 am to 2 pm.

Uganda The embassy (☎ 76495) is on the 3rd floor of the building on Ave de la Paix near the corner of Ave des Collines. It's open Monday to Friday from 8 am to 3 pm. Visas cost US$20 or US$25 (depending on your nationality), require two photos and issued in 24 hours.

Zaïre The embassy (☎ 75327) is on Rue Député Kamuzinzi off Ave de Rusumo. Visa costs are the same as elsewhere (see the Zaïre chapter for details), require three photographs and are issued in 24 hours. A letter of recommendation from your own embassy is generally not needed nor is an onward ticket, but these regulations change from time to time.

MONEY
Currency
The unit of currency is the Rwandan franc (RFr). It's divided into 100 centimes, but it's unlikely you'll come across these.

Exchange Rates
US$1 = RFr 135 (official)
US$1 = RFr 180 (black market, cash)

Changing Money
Travellers with only travellers' cheques are at a considerable disadvantage in Rwanda, since the bank commission rates are outrageous. Even at the Banque Commerciale de Rwanda in Kigali, it costs about US$2 per transaction. In other banks you can expect to lose up to US$4 per transaction. Bring cash to Rwanda and change it on the street market or in shops. The best rates are to be found in Kigali, Cyangugu and Gisenyi.

The Kigali street market is more or less controlled by a few individuals. Try walking around the Rue de Travail or the Blvd de la Révolution. You can often change money in minibuses on the way to Kigali. You'll find quite a few people around the petrol station on the main street in Gisenyi who will offer to change US dollars, Rwandan francs, zaïres, etc; their rates aren't too bad if you know what the current rate is. In Kigali, the moneychangers hang around the main post office.

The Banque Nationale de Kigali will change US dollar bank cheques into Bank America US dollar travellers' cheques for a 1% commission.

Rwandan banking hours are Monday to Friday from 8 to 11 am. Outside these hours, armed only with travellers' cheques, you are in dire straits. You can change travellers' cheques on the black market, but only in Kigali and only at a slight premium over the bank rate. Basically, only the banks want them. Don't come to Rwanda without at least some cash.

Credit cards are generally accepted only in relatively expensive hotels and restaurants in places such as Kigali and Gisenyi. The most useful cards are American Express, Diners Club and Visa. You cannot make cash withdrawals against a Visa card at any bank in Rwanda, but some banks will give you cash against a MasterCard, though only Rwandan francs (at the official rate).

Currency declaration forms are not issued at the border.

Costs
Rwanda is expensive, possibly because of the dense population and the many expatriates. In this landlocked country, a lot of export earnings are spent importing food, drink and transport requirements for the expatriates. As a budget traveller, you will be hard-pressed even if you stay in mission hostels. There is no way you can exist here on a Kenyan, Tanzanian or Ugandan budget, and student cards are only useful to get into the national parks at a discount.

Transport (by minibus) and food in roadside restaurants cost much the same as in the rest of East Africa, so long as you don't want meat with your meal. Meat will just about double the price. Anything on which culinary expertise has been lavished will cost you a week's budget. If you have a yen for French cuisine, however, there are some excellent restaurants in the capital.

TOURIST OFFICES
The tourist office (☎ 76514) in Kigali is open long hours (7 am to 9 pm) but its main function is to take bookings to see the gorillas. There is very little printed information or maps, though it does have a list of current prices for the middle and top-end hotels around the country.

BUSINESS HOURS & HOLIDAYS
Many shops and offices tend to be closed between 1 July and 5 July. The following days are public holidays in Rwanda:

January
    New Year's Day (1st)
    Democracy Day (28th)
March-April
    Good Friday
    Easter Monday
May
    Labour Day (1st)
    Ascension Thursday
    Whit Monday
July
    National Day (1st)
    Peace & National Unity Day (5th)
August
    Harvest Festival (1st)
    Assumption (15th)
September
    Culture Day (8th)
    Kamarampaka Day (25th)
October
    Armed Forces Day (26th)
November
    All Saints' Day (1st)
December
    Christmas Day (25th)

POST & TELECOMMUNICATIONS
Post
Overseas postal rates are relatively high. A postcard, for example, costs RFr 60 (well over US$0.50 at the official exchange rate).

Telephone
International calls are similarly expensive. In Kigali, you can dial your own calls at the main post office, so connection is immediate. Charges per minute are RFr 800 to Australia, RFr 500 to the USA and RFr 400 to the UK and Europe.

TIME
Rwanda time is GMT/UTC plus two hours.

MEDIA
Newspapers and periodicals are published mainly in Kinyarwanda and French.

There are two AM and five FM radio stations, which generally broadcast in either Kinyarwanda or French. There are also programmes in Swahili and English.

HEALTH
As with most African countries, you should take precautions against malaria whilst in Rwanda, but mosquitoes generally are not a problem.

Expatriate residents suggest that you should take special care in Rwanda to avoid illness and/or treatment which could require a blood transfusion. A recent study of prostitutes in this country indicated that about 80% carry the HIV virus. If you think you'll need any injections whilst you're there, buy your own disposable syringes.

There are certain parts of Lake Kivu where it is very dangerous to swim, as volcanic gases are released continuously from the lake bed and, in the absence of wind, tend to collect on the surface of the lake. Quite a few people have been asphyxiated as a result. Make enquiries or watch where the local people swim and you'll probably be safe.

Bilharzia is also a risk in Lake Kivu. Stay away from shore areas where there is a lot of reedy vegetation. Also keep away from slow-moving rivers. (See the Health section in the introductory Facts for the Visitor chapter for more information.)

It's advisable not to drink tap water. Purify all water used for drinking, except that obtained from mountain streams and springs above any human habitation. Soft drinks, fruit and beer are available in even the smallest places.

Other than the necessary precautions mentioned here, you'll find Rwanda a fairly healthy place to live, especially as much of the country is considerably higher than neighbouring Tanzania, Uganda and Zaïre. Cholera vaccination certificates are compulsory for entry or exit by air. If entering overland, the check is cursory but officials sometimes ask about it.

FILM & PHOTOGRAPHY
Bring plenty of film with you, as it is very expensive and the choice is extremely limited – usually only 64 ASA and 100 ASA

RWANDA

colour negative film and then only in places like Kigali and Gisenyi. Slide film is almost impossible to obtain. If you buy film, check the expiry dates carefully.

To take photos of the gorillas in the Parc National des Volcans, you will need high-speed film. It's often very dark in the jungle where they live, so normal film will produce very disappointing results when developed. Use 800 ASA or 1600 ASA fast film, which in East Africa can only be found in Kenya (and it's even difficult to find there).

Warning
Don't take photographs of anything connected with the government or the military (post offices, banks, bridges, border posts, barracks, prisons, dams, etc). Your film and maybe your equipment will be confiscated.

ACCOMMODATION
Camping
The national parks will burn a hole in your pocket unless you have your own tent, and unlike Kenya or Tanzania, organised safaris don't cater for budget travellers, concentrating only on intrepid mega-dollar travellers with two or three weeks to spare and plenty of money.

Hostels
If you don't mind dormitory accommodation at the mission hostels, you're looking at between US$2.50 and US$3.50 per night without food. A private double room at the hostels will cost from US$7 to US$12.50 per night.

Mission hostels seem to attract an exceptionally conscientious type of person who takes the old adage 'Cleanliness is next to godliness' fairly seriously. You might not get hot water but your bed and room will be spotless. The one catch with mission hostels is that they're often full, particularly on weekends or in places where there is only one mission hostel in town. Also, the door is usually closed at 10 pm (or earlier).

Hotels
Hotels, as opposed to mission hostels, are considerably more expensive and rarely worth the extra amount, especially at the bottom end, where hotels are little better than squalid flea pits. You're also likely to be woken up at dawn by the sound of chickens being strangled in preparation for lunch. There are exceptions, but not many.

Getting There & Away

You can enter Rwanda by air or road; there are no railways. Lake ferries on both the Rwandan and Zaïrian sides of Lake Kivu connect towns only on their respective sides of the lake.

AIR
International airlines flying into Rwanda are Aeroflot, Air Burundi, Air France, Air Tanzania, Air Zaïre, Ethiopian Airlines, Kenya Airways and Sabena.

Air Rwanda flies internationally from Kigali to Brussels (Belgium) and Goma (Zaïre) once a week, to Bujumbura (Burundi) twice a week and to Entebbe (Uganda) twice a week.

Its main office (☎ 73793) is on Blvd de la Révolution, BP 808, Kigali, opposite the US Embassy. There are offices at Kigali Airport (☎ 85472); Butare, c/o SORIMEX; Gisenyi (☎ 40282) c/o Hôtel Edelweiss; and Kamembe (☎ 407) c/o Garage Ruzimeca. Air tickets bought in Rwanda for international flights are very expensive and compare poorly with what is on offer in Nairobi.

Kenya Airways flies from Nairobi to Kigali and vice versa twice a week, on Tuesday and Friday.

LAND
To/From Burundi
Bujumbura to Butare The main crossing point between Rwanda and Burundi is via Kayanza, on the Bujumbura to Butare road. The road is sealed all the way. There are daily minibuses (BFr 300) from Bujumbura to Kayanza, from where there are minibuses to

the border on Tuesday, Friday and Sunday (BFr 150). Otherwise, hire a taxi or hitch.

The border crossing is easy, though there is usually a cursory baggage search on each side. The two posts are only about 200 metres apart. There are infrequent minibuses between the border and Butare (RFr 200, about an hour).

Bujumbura to Cyangugu It's also possible to go from Bujumbura to Cyangugu via the border at Bugarama, in the far south-western corner of Rwanda. This is another possibility for the Bujumbura to Bukavu (Zaïre) route. If that's where you're headed, this is the way to go if you don't have a visa to re-enter Zaïre (and you do have a Rwandan visa), as the road is in much better condition than the Uvira to Bukavu road.

There's no shortage of traffic along this route. Minibuses from Bujumbura to Rugombo cost BFr 200 and take about two hours. It's 12 km from Rugombo to the border village of Luhwa and a further eight km to the Rwandan border post of Bugarama. You'll probably have to hitch the entire 20 km. From Bugarama there are minibuses to Cyangugu. Using this route, it's easy enough to get from Bukavu to Bujumbura in one day. (See the Eastern Zaïre Getting There & Away section.)

To/From Tanzania

Getting into Rwanda from Tanzania is much easier than it used to be. First take a bus from Mwanza to Ngara (though you have to get off at Lusahanga). The buses leave Mwanza (usually daily) at 4 am and arrive after dark. They're operated by the New El-Jabry Bus Co in Mwanza. To make sure you catch the bus, stay at the Penda Guest House next to the bus terminal. It's a dump but it's convenient.

Lusahanga is an overnight truck stop for petrol trucks supplying Kigali and Bujumbura from the Tanzanian coast. It's easy to get a lift to Rusumo (the first Rwandan town) or even to Kigali. If you only get as far as Rusumo, there's a daily bus from there to Kigali (RFr 500). Alternatively, you can take a share-taxi from Rusumo to Kibungo (RFr 300) and a minibus from there to Kigali (RFr 400).

To/From Uganda

The border between Rwanda and Uganda has been closed for some time now. If and when the fighting in Rwanda stops and it becomes possible to cross the border again, there are two main crossing points: Kabale to Kigali via Gatuna/Katuna, and Kisoro to Ruhengeri via Cyanika.

To/From Zaïre

The two main crossing points from Rwanda to Zaïre are between Goma and Gisenyi (at the northern end of Lake Kivu) and between Bukavu and Cyangugu (at the southern end of Lake Kivu). These borders are open between 6 am and 6 pm (for non-Africans). For Africans, they are open from 6 am until midnight.

Goma to Gisenyi The two crossing points are the Poids Lourds crossing (a rough road) along the main road north of the ritzy part of Gisenyi, and a sealed road along the lake shore. It's only two to three km either way. From Goma, it's a couple of km to either post; a motorcycle will cost Z250.

The easier of the two routes is along the lake shore, but from the border, you'll have to take a taxi (RFr 350) or a taxi-motor (RFr 50) into Gisenyi. I arrived at this border at 7.30 am one morning and was through within five minutes! The officials at the Poids Lourds post are apparently not quite as amenable. There are minibuses into Gisenyi from this post.

Bukavu to Cyangugu From Bukavu, it's a three-km walk or a Z500 taxi ride to the Ruzizi border post. This is an easy border crossing and you can walk between the two posts.

On the Rwandan side, Cyangugu is the actual border post but Kamembe is the town and transport centre. From the border, minibuses make the half-hour ride to Kamembe for RFr 30. You'll be able to catch one to Bugarama if you're heading straight to Bujumbura.

Getting Around

AIR

Internally, Air Rwanda flies from Kigali to Gisenyi and Kamembe (close to Cyangugu). There are six flights a week to Kamembe and twice-weekly flights to Gisenyi. There are also connecting flights between Gisenyi and Kamembe.

BUS

Rwanda has an excellent road system, mainly due to massive injections of foreign aid. The only unsealed roads now are those to Kibuye, on the shore of Lake Kivu.

There are plenty of modern, well-maintained minibuses serving all the main routes. Between dawn and about 3 pm, at the bus station in any town, you can almost always find one going your way. Destinations are displayed in the front window and the fares are fixed (ask other passengers if you're not sure).

Minibuses leave when full, and this means when all the seats are occupied (unlike in Kenya and Tanzania, where most of the time they won't leave until you can't breathe for the people sitting on your lap and jamming the aisle). You should not be charged for baggage. Many minibuses have decent sound systems, so you might hear some good African music which isn't ear-splitting.

There are also modern government buses (many of them bearing the Japan-Rwanda assistance programme logo) on quite a few routes. These are cheaper than minibuses but take longer and are far less frequent.

CAR

Car hire isn't well established in Rwanda, so you'll have difficulty finding something. Try Rwanda Tourist, near the Tourist Office in Kigali. They may be able to rent you a small 4WD jeep for around RFr 7500 per day (RFr 7000 per day if taken for seven days or more).

Petrol costs RFr 134 per litre.

HITCHING

If you are hitching in Rwanda, you may find a list of vehicle licence plates useful, as they indicate the province of origin of the vehicle (though that doesn't mean they are going there):

AB	Kigali
BB	Gitarama
CB	Butare
DB	Gikongoro
EB	Cyangugu
FB	Kibuye
GB	Gisenyi
HB	Ruhengeri
IB	Byumba
JB	Kibungo

If you're looking for lifts on trucks from Kigali to Uganda, Kenya, Burundi or Zaïre, go to MAGERWA (short for Magasins Généraux de Rwanda) in the Gikondo suburb, about three km from the centre. Have your pick from the scores of trucks at the customs clearance depot. To get there, head down the Blvd de l'OUA and turn right when you see the sign. It's sometimes possible to find a free lift all the way to Mombasa, but usually it's a matter of negotiating a fare with the driver.

FERRY

The ferries on Lake Kivu used to connect Rwandan ports with Zaïrian ports, but these days Rwandan ferries only call at Rwandan ports and Zaïrian ferries only call at Zaïrian ports. The small modern motor ferry *Nyungwe* covers the route from Cyangugu to Kirambo, Kibuye and Gisenyi. It leaves Cyangugu on Mondays and Thursdays and Gisenyi on Wednesdays and Saturdays, all at 6 am. The full trip takes about six hours and costs RFr 765. This is just a tiny boat but it rarely gets crowded. In Gisenyi, make enquiries at the boat or, if it's not there, at the bus depot next to the post office.

LOCAL TRANSPORT
Taxi-Motor

Most towns are compact enough to get around on foot, but where you need transport, the taxi-motor is a good bet. It's just a motorcycle and you ride on the back. The driver can usually sling your pack across the petrol tank and they generally drive pretty safely, though of course there's no helmet for the passenger.

Kigali

The tourist organisation describes Rwanda as the 'Land of Eternal Spring'. Kigali, the capital, displays this appropriate motto to the full. Built on a ridge and extending down into the valley floors on either side, it's a small but beautiful city with an incredible variety of flowering trees and shrubs. From various points on the ridge, there are superb views over the surrounding intensively cultivated and terraced countryside. The mountains and hills seem to stretch forever and the abundant rainfall keeps them a lush green.

Many international organisations have bases here – the United Nations (UN), Food & Agriculture Organisation (FAO) and the European Community (EC), for instance – and there is a large number of resident expatriates, mainly from Europe and the Far East, so it's a fairly cosmopolitan city. Don't miss the Chinese Embassy, which must be one of the largest and most impressive buildings in the country and puts both the American and Russian embassies to shame. China funds many aid projects in Rwanda.

The only trouble with Kigali is that, unless you have friends or contacts who will introduce you to the social life of the city, there isn't much to do (apart from enjoying the tremendous views and pleasant walks). Restaurants, bars and cafés are few and far between. European-style restaurants, in particular, tend to be well outside most travellers' budgets.

Information
Tourist Office

The national tourist office, Office Rwandais du Tourisme et des Parcs Nationaux (☎ 76514), BP 905, is on the Place de l'Indépendance, opposite the post office (PTT). It's open daily, including Sundays and public holidays, from 7 am to 9 pm. It has a few leaflets (in French and English) about the mountain gorillas, but little else. Reservations must be made here to see the mountain gorillas in the Parc National des Volcans.

Post & Telephone

The poste restante is quite well organised and staff will let you look through the log book of letters, so it's unlikely that you'll miss anything sent to you for collection, including parcels. Each letter collected will cost RFr 20. The post office is open Monday to Friday from 7.30 am to 6 pm, and on Saturday from 8.30 am to 1 pm. The telephone office is also here and is open the same hours.

Foreign Embassies

Neighbouring countries with diplomatic offices in Kigali include Burundi, Kenya, Tanzania, Uganda and Zaïre – see the Visas & Embassies section under Facts for the Visitor earlier in this chapter. There are also embassies for Belgium (☎ 75551), the People's Republic of China, Egypt (☎ 75755), France (☎ 75225), Germany and the USA (☎ 75327). A British Consulate (☎ 75905) is at 55 Ave Paul VI.

Immigration

The immigration office is on Ave du Commerce, next to the Air France office, in a building set back from the road.

Bookshops

There are a few bookstores in Kigali, selling mainly French-language publications. The best is probably Librairie Caritas, next to the immigration office on Ave du Commerce.

Camping Goods

The so-called disposable Campingaz cartridges can be bought at the Rwanda Petrolgaz shop below the market, or at the Janmohammed's shop on Rue du

RWANDA

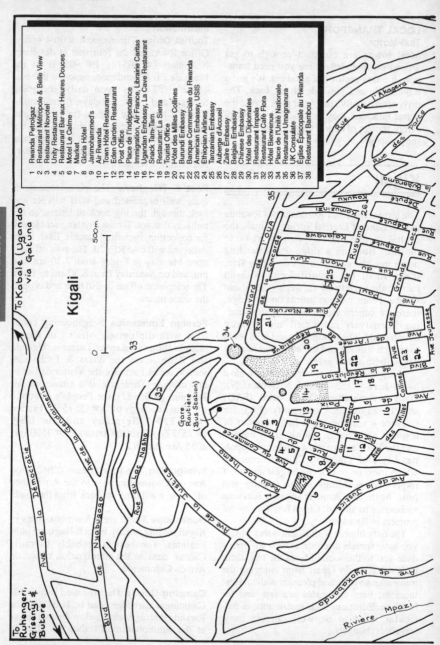

1 Rwanda Petrolgaz
2 Restaurant Métropole & Belle View
3 Restaurant Novotel
4 Unity Restaurant
5 Restaurant Bar aux Heures Douces
6 Motel Le Calme
7 Market
8 Gloria Hôtel
9 Janmohammed's
10 Air Rwanda
11 Town Hôtel Restaurant
12 Eden Garden Restaurant
13 Post Office
14 Place de l'Indépendance
15 Immigration, Air France, Librairie Caritas
16 Ugandan Embassy, La Cave Restaurant
17 Snack Tam-Tam
18 Restauran: La Sierra
19 Tourist Office
20 Hôtel des Milles Collines
21 Burundi Embassy
22 Banque Commerciale du Rwanda
23 American Embassy, USIS
24 Ethiopian Airlines
25 Tanzanian Embassy
26 Auberge d'Accueil
27 Zaïre Embassy
28 Belgian Embassy
29 Chinese Embassy
30 Hôtel des Diplomates
31 Restaurant Impala
32 Restaurant Café Flora
33 Hôtel Bienvenue
34 Place de l'Unité Nationale
35 Restaurant Umagnanura
36 UK Consulate
37 Église Épiscopale au Rwanda
38 Restaurant Bambou

Kigali

To Kabale (Uganda)
via Gatuna

To Ruhengeri,
Gisenyi
Butare

500m

Gare
Routière
(Bus Station)

Rivière Mpazi

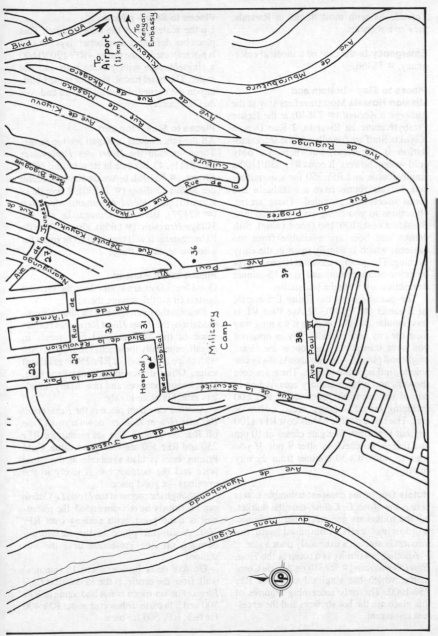

Travail. As with most things in Rwanda, they're not cheap.

Emergency In the case of a medical emergency, ☎ 76466.

Places to Stay – bottom end
Mission Hostels Most travellers stay at the *Auberge d'Accueil* (☎ 73640) at the Église Presbytérienne au Rwanda, 2 Rue Député Kayuku. Staff are friendly and the accommodation is excellent, but there are only cold-water showers. It costs RFr 650/1100 a single/double and RFr 350 for a dormitory bed. Private rooms have a washbasin and clean sheets are provided. There are no objections to you doing your own laundry. Breakfast costs RFr 150 (good value). Soft drinks and beer are available from the canteen, which is usually open in the early evening. The auberge closes at 10 pm, except by prior arrangement, and is a 15-minute downhill walk from the bus station.

The *guesthouse* at the Église Épiscopale au Rwanda (☎ 76340), 32 Ave Paul VI, is less popular, mainly because it's a long way from the city centre (really only an option if you have transport). The rooms are clean, bright and plentiful, so you should always be able to find accommodation. There are cold showers and a large laundry area. A bed in one of the six triple rooms costs RFr 600 including breakfast (eggs, bread, coffee or tea). The three double rooms cost RFr 1100 without breakfast. The gate closes at 10 pm and there's no check-in after 9 pm. If you want to walk, it's 30 minutes from the city centre.

Hotels One of the cheapest habitable hotels here is the *Motel Le Calme*, near the market, but the rooms are generally claustrophobic, windowless cells. Compared with the mission hostels, it's extremely poor value.

Another possibility is a room at the *Town Hôtel Restaurant* (☎ 76690) on Ave du Commerce, which has singles/doubles for RFr 750/1000. The only redeeming features of this place are the hot showers and the excellent restaurant.

Places to Stay – middle
Up the scale a bit is the *Gloria Hôtel*. This place has definitely seen better days but this is not reflected in the prices – RFr 1200/1600 a single/double with private bath and hot water. The hotel has no sign but is the building on the corner of Rue du Travail and Ave du Commerce.

Places to Stay – top end
All the other hotels in Kigali are top range. These include the *Hôtel des Diplomates* (☎ 75111), 43 Blvd de la Révolution, *Hôtel Kiyovu* (☎ 75106), 6 Ave de Kiyovu, *Hôtel des Milles Collines* (☎ 76530), 1 Ave de la République, *Hôtel Umubano-Méridien* (☎ 82177), Blvd de l'Umuganda, and the *Village Urugwiro* (☎ 6656), also on Blvd de l'Umuganda. It will cost US$50 or more for a double at any of these.

Places to Eat – cheap
Good breakfasts are available at the mission hostels (if you're staying there).

Despite the poor value of its hotel accommodation, the *Town Hôtel Restaurant* offers some of the cheapest and best meals in Kigali, especially for lunch. The tilapia (fish) with chips and salad for RFr 250 is excellent value. Other dishes include chicken, beef, goat, beans, potatoes and rice. Many travellers rate this place highly.

Another excellent place is the *Restaurant Bar aux Heures Douces*, down a small lane off Rue du Travail. The set menus for RFr 250 and RFr 300 are very good value. Cold Primus beer is also available at the usual price and the outdoor bar is lively in the evenings – a good place.

Although the rooms at the *Motel Le Calme* can't seriously be recommended, the restaurant is quite good, with nothing over RFr 200. A similar place is the *Restaurant Novotel*, on Rue Préfecture near the bus station.

On Ave de la Justice, about 15 minutes' walk from the centre, is the *Restaurant Café Flora*. The set menu is not bad value at RFr 500 and à la carte dishes cost about RFr 400 for fish, RFr 500 for meat.

For those staying at the Auberge d'Accueil, a good place to eat at night is the *Restaurant Umaganura*, on Blvd de l'OAU opposite the end of Rue Député Kayuku. This very basic African eatery is cheap and friendly and the food is quite OK.

The closest restaurant to the Église Épiscopale au Rwanda guesthouse is the *Restaurant Bambou*, around the corner on Ave Paul VI.

Places to Eat – more expensive
Going up-market, try the *Eden Garden*, Rue de Karisimbi, which offers Western-style food and bamboo dcor. Tilapia with French fries and salad costs RFr 600. Beef or chicken with French fries and salad costs RFr 700.

On Ave de la Paix close to the Ugandan Embassy is *La Cave*. Pizza, spaghetti or steak costs between RFr 400 and RFr 600 and breakfast is available for RFr 300. The entrance is down the steps under the photo-developing shop. Similar is *UMUCO*, Ave de la Justice, about 100 metres from the main roundabout. The food is good and prices are moderate.

Le Petit Kigali, next to the Hôtel Kiyovu at 6 Ave de Kiyovu, is a very popular Italian restaurant which serves excellent and substantial three-course meals for RFr 800. It's open for lunch and dinner.

For just a snack, try sitting outside at the *Snack Tam-Tam*, on Blvd de la Révolution. The service can be incredibly slow and the food is not that cheap, with sandwiches at RFr 300, salads for RFr 350 and pizza for RFr 600, but it's a good place for a beer or a coffee. Just a few doors along is the *Restaurant La Sierra*. This is an expensive place with full waiter service.

The *Restaurant Impala*, Blvd de la Révolution, next to the Hôtel des Diplomates, is worth a visit if you have the money. Brochettes (kebabs) are a lunch speciality and there's a good bar.

For a splurge, try the buffet at the *Hôtel des Milles Collines*. The cold buffet costs RFr 1000 and the hot one is RFr 1300.

Entertainment
Apart from bars, there is not much cheap entertainment available. There are night-clubs in the big hotels, but apart from being expensive, they require you to be well dressed to get in. Jeans and T-shirts don't make it. It's worth enquiring at both the US Information Service (USIS), next door to the US Embassy, and the Centre Culturel Français, Ave de la République close to the Place de l'Unité Nationale, to see if they have anything happening. The latter often puts on concerts and films in the afternoons and evenings. Local events are also advertised at the tourist office. There's a cinema on the Blvd de la Révolution, opposite the Banque Commerciale du Rwanda.

Getting There & Away
Air Airline offices in Kigali include Air Rwanda (☎ 73793), Air France (☎ 75566), Ethiopian Airlines (☎ 75045), Kenya Airways (☎ 73999), Sabena (☎ 75290) and Aeroflot (☎ 73646).

Matatu Matatus run from the main bus station to towns all over Rwanda, including Butare (RFr 400, about three hours), Gitarama (RFr 200), Katuna (RFr 250), Kibuye (RFr 400), Ruhengeri (RFr 300, about two hours), Rusumu (RFr 450), Cyangugu (RFr 800) and Gisenyi (RFr 450). See the respective town entries for more details.

Getting Around
The international airport is at Kanombe, 12 km from the city centre. A taxi costs RFr 2000, but you can get there more cheaply by taking a direct minibus from the bus station (RFr 60).

Western Rwanda

GISENYI
Gisenyi is a resort town for rich Rwandans and expatriate workers and residents. Their beautifully landscaped villas, plush hotels and clubs take up virtually all the Lake Kivu

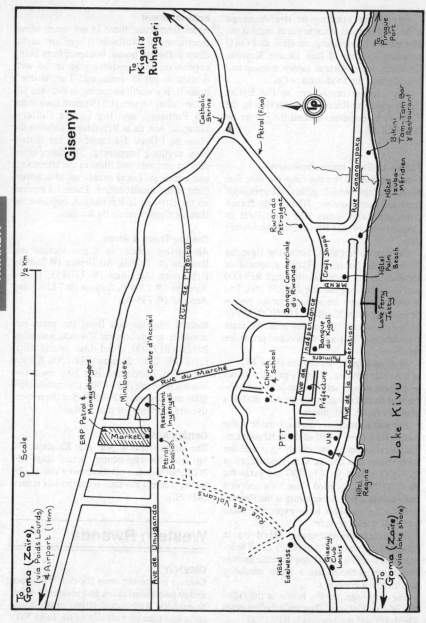

Gisenyi

frontage and are quite a contrast to the African township on the hillside above.

For those with the money, there's a wide variety of water sports available, plus nightclubs and restaurants. For those without, there are magnificent views over Lake Kivu and, looking north-west, the 3470-metre-high volcano of Nyiragongo. Swimming and sunbathing on the sandy beach are also free. It's a pleasant town to stay in but is, as you might expect, expensive, especially if you want some action.

Information

Money If you are carrying only travellers' cheques, try to avoid having to change money at the banks, as commission rates are outrageous (up to US$5 per transaction). Moneychangers (cash transactions only) hang out around the market and the ERP petrol station outside. There are others at the craft stalls on Ave de l'Indépendance, at the back of the Hôtel Palm Beach. Their rates are as good as you'll get in Kigali.

Visas & Embassies There is no Zaïrian consulate here, so you must obtain your visa elsewhere if you intend going to Zaïre. The nearest embassy is in Kigali.

Places to Stay – bottom end

There are a few small hotels up in the African part of town but they're hard to find (no signs) and the standard of accommodation is low. Most travellers stay at the Mission Presbytérienne's *Centre d'Accueil* (☎ 40-522), about 100 metres from the market and bus station. It costs RFr 300 per person in a dormitory or RFr 500/900 a single/double with shared facilities. The windows have mosquito netting, which is an important consideration when choosing somewhere to stay here. It's good value for money and rarely has more than a couple of guests. The views over the lake from the front lawn are excellent. This is better value than anything across the border in Goma.

Places to Stay – middle

Apart from the hostel, there is no decent cheap place to stay in Gisenyi. All the acceptable hotels are near the lake front. The most reasonably priced of these is the *Hôtel Edelweiss* (☎ 40282), run by a Belgian and his Zaïrian wife. As the name suggests, it's built in the style of an alpine cottage. Although a fairly old building, it's homely and clean and the verandah is a delightful place to sit and have a beer and watch the lake. It costs RFr 1700 for a double room with a private toilet and hot shower. There are no singles.

Next up in price are the *Hôtel Palm Beach* (☎ 40304) and the *Hôtel Regina* (☎ 40263), both on Ave de la Coopération, the palm-shaded lake-shore drive. Hôtel Palm Beach costs RFr 2600 a double with private toilet and hot shower, while the Regina is cheaper, at RFr 1500/2000 a single/double. The Palm Beach doesn't have single rooms and the staff are likely to treat backpackers with a considerable degree of disdain (as are the clientele).

Places to Stay – top end

The *Hôtel Izuba-Méridien* (☎ 40381) is the equivalent of the Hôtel des Diplomates in Kigali and costs from US$50.

Places to Eat

Several simple restaurants on the main road in the African part of town serve cheap meals (usually matoke, rice, beans and a little meat), but the standard isn't up to much. Much better is the *Restaurant Inyenyeli*, opposite the Centre d'Accueil. It has a reasonably priced and varied menu, with dishes for about RFr 150.

The restaurant at the *Hôtel Edelwiess* looks good, but unfortunately, the food is grossly overpriced and you can grow old waiting for your meal to arrive, so avoid eating here.

More reasonable is the curiously named *Bikini Tam-Tam Bar & Restaurant*, on the beach on Rue Kanarampaka. A main course costs about RFr 600. Alternatively, put your own meals together from the wide variety of fruit and vegetables available at the main market.

RWANDA

Entertainment

If you're looking for action at night, the *Gisenyi Club Loisirs*, close to the Hôtel Edelweiss, is open to nonmembers and puts on live music on Saturday nights. Entry to the hall where the band plays costs RFr 400, but you can go into the bar free of charge if you want to check the music out before paying.

If it's just a quiet drink you're after, the balcony of the *Hôtel Edelweiss* is hard to beat, or for something with a bit more local colour, try the bar next to the Restaurant Inyenyeli.

Getting There & Away

Air The Hôtel Edelweiss is the agency for Air Rwanda. There are twice-weekly flights to Kigali and one flight a week to Kamembe.

Matatu A matatu from Ruhengeri to Gisenyi takes about 1½ hours and costs RFr 150. It's a beautiful journey through upland forest and villages and there are panoramic views of Lake Kivu as you descend into Gisenyi. There are two border posts into Zaïre (see the Getting There & Away section earlier in this chapter for details).

Ferry The ferry across Lake Kivu operates twice a week to Kibuye and Cyangugu. See the Getting Around section earlier in this chapter for details.

KIBUYE

A small town about halfway along Lake Kivu, Kibuye has an excellent beach and water sports facilities. It's a pleasant place to relax for a few days. If coming here by road from Gisenyi, try not to miss **Les Chutes de Ndaba**, a waterfall at Ndaba. It's more than 100 metres high.

Places to Stay

A very popular place among travellers is the *Hôme St Jean*, about two km from town up the Kigali road. If you're not sure of the way, ask at the Catholic church in town. The Hôme St Jean is on a superb site overlooking the lake and is excellent value if you can persuade them to let you have a dormitory

bed at RFr 100 per night, though it seems they're reluctant to do this these days. What they will let you have are doubles/triples at RFr 800/1100. Towels and filtered water are provided.

The only other place to stay is the *Guest House Kibuye* on the lake side. It's expensive (RFr 2500/3370 for singles/doubles, RFr 4750 for triples), but does have a good outdoor bar, with cold beers at the usual price, and a diving board which anyone can use.

Places to Eat

Excellent meals are available at the *Hôme St Jean* for RFr 350 (fish, potatoes and vegetables) or RFr 450 (meat, potatoes and vegetables).

Two cheap places, the *Restaurant Nouveauté* and *Restaurant Moderne*, are at the eastern end of town. They have the same menu (goat stew, beans, rice, potatoes, omelettes) and you can eat well for about RFr 200. It also offers cold beers and soft drinks.

Getting There & Away

From Kigali, the road is partly sealed and minibuses cost RFr 400. The fare from Gitarama is RFr 250.

CYANGUGU

At the southern end of Lake Kivu and close to Bukavu (Zaïre), Cyangugu is an attractively positioned town on the lake shore and the Zaïre border. Kamembe, a few km from the border, is the main town and an important centre for the processing of tea and cotton. Nearby is the Rugege Forest, home for elephants, buffaloes, leopards, chimpanzees and many other mammals and birds.

The **waterfalls** of the Rusizi River and the **hot springs** of Nyakabuye are here, and it's also the ferry departure point for the other Rwandan towns on Lake Kivu: Kibuye and Gisenyi.

Places to Stay & Eat

A convenient place to stay if you're heading for Zaïre (or coming from there) is the *Mission St François* at the border. It's friendly, spotlessly clean and charges RFr 400/700/1050 a single/double/triple. The only problem is that couples may be separated. The meals there are excellent. Breakfast costs RFr 150, a three-course lunch or dinner costs RFr 250 and there's unlimited tea and coffee.

The only other accommodation option is the expensive *Hôtel du Lac* opposite.

Getting There & Away

Matatu Matatus cost RFr 30 between Cyangugu and Kamembe and RFr 450 from Kamembe to Butare (a total of four hours). This road is incredibly spectacular in parts and passes through the superb Nyungwe rainforest.

From Kamembe, matatus to Kigali (via Butare) cost RFr 800. If you're heading straight for Bujumbura, minibuses go from Cyangugu to Bugarama on the Burundi border.

Ferry The small ferry *Nyungwe* connects Cyangugu with Kibuye and Gisenyi twice a week. See the main Getting Around section at the beginning of this chapter.

RUHENGERI

Most travellers come to Ruhengeri on their way to or from the Parc National des Volcans. It's a small town with two army barracks, a very busy hospital and magnificent views of the volcanoes to the north and west – Karisimbi, Visoke, Mikeno, Muside, Sabinyo, Gahinga and Muhabura.

Forget any ideas you may have about climbing the hill near the post office, as it's a military area and access is prohibited.

Information

Money Banks are open Monday to Friday from 7.45 to 11 am and 2 to 3 pm. Commission rates for travellers' cheques are about the same as in Kigali.

Post The post office (PTT) is open Monday to Friday from 8 am till noon. It's also open Monday to Thursday from 2 to 6 pm and on Saturday from 8 am to 1 pm. Service can be slow.

Places to Stay – bottom end

The only place to consider seriously is the *Centre d'Accueil*, on Ave de la Nutrition close to the grass airstrip. It's clean and has dormitory beds for RFr 250 and singles/doubles for RFr 450/650. The communal showers have hot water and the toilets are clean. A taxi-motor from the bus stop costs RFr 50; otherwise it's a 10-minute walk.

In contrast, the *Hôme d'Accueil*, on Ave du 5 Juillet in the town centre, has eight small rooms and charges an outrageous RFr 1000 a double for what is basically a dump.

Places to Stay – top end

At the top end of the market is the *Hôtel Muhabura* (☎ 46296), Ave du 5 Juillet, which even local people rate as very overpriced at US$30 a double with private bathroom (hot water) and toilet. Breakfast costs from RFr 250 to RFr 400 and lunch or dinner costs RFr 1000.

Places to Eat

The *Centre d'Accueil* offers excellent dinners (stewed meat, beans, cabbage, sautéed potatoes) for RFr 250, but the breakfasts aren't such good value at RFr 100 (tea, bread, margarine, jam). Cold beers are available at the usual price and there's a common room for residents.

There are a couple of simple restaurants in the town centre which offer standard African food. One such place is the *Restaurant Amahoro* on the main street, where meals cost about RFr 200. The *Hôtel Urumuli*, down a small side street off Rue du Marché, has an outdoor area where you can get good meals in the evening (excellent brochettes for RFr 40) and very cold beers.

Very popular is the *Restaurant Sympathique*, which always seems to be full and which serves reasonable food.

For a splurge, it's well worth going to the *Restaurant Touristique*, Rue du Commerce, where the food is excellent. The four-course

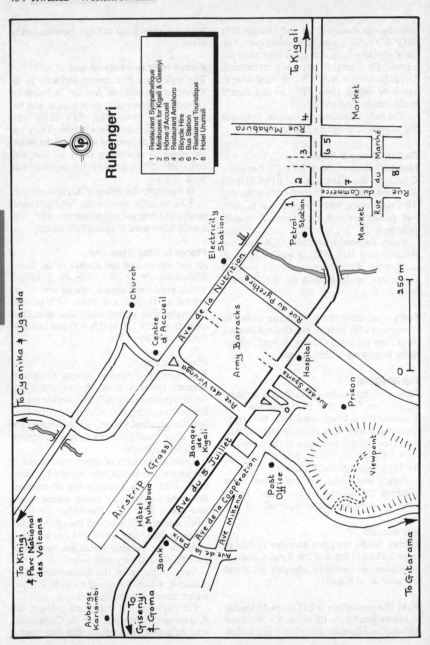

Ruhengeri

1 Restaurant Sympathetique
2 Minibuses for Kigali & Gisenyi
3 Hôme d'Accueil
4 Restaurant Amahoro
5 Bicycle Hire
6 Bus Station
7 Restaurant Touristique
8 Hôtel Urumuli

set menu is RFr 850, or you can order à la carte (about RFr 400 for a main course).

If you are putting your own meal together, there's a good variety of meat, fish, fruit and vegetables at the market in the town centre.

Getting There & Away

Matatu From Kigali, matatus take about two hours and cost RFr 300. The road ascends and descends magnificently over the intensively cultivated mountains. From Cyanika, on the Rwanda-Uganda border, matatus to Ruhengeri cost RFr 100. From Gisenyi, on the Rwanda-Zaïre border, they cost RFr 150 for the 1½-hour trip.

Taxi-Motor If you're heading for the Parc National des Volcans, the best way to get up to the entrance on the morning of the day of your visit is to get a ride on a taxi-motor. It costs RFr 500 and means that you don't have to stay overnight at the cottages if you don't have a tent. A safer way of getting there, perhaps, is to hitch, but you would need to do this the day before your gorilla visit, as there's no guarantee that you'd get there in time.

Getting Around

Bicycles are for hire near the market, but at RFr 500 per day, they're not that cheap.

Southern Rwanda

BUTARE

Butare is the intellectual centre of Rwanda, and it's here that you'll find the National University, the National Institute of Scientific Research (folklore dance displays) and the excellent National Museum.

In the surrounding area are several craft centres, such as **Gihindamuyaga** (10 km) and **Gishamvu** (12 km). If you're thinking of buying anything at these places, look first at the quality and prices of what's for sale at the two top-range hotels in town, the Hôtel Ibis and Hôtel Faucon.

Those interested in trees should visit the Arboretum de Ruhande.

National Museum

This huge museum was opened in 1989 and is probably the best museum in East Africa. It's certainly the most amazing building in the country. A gift from Belgium to commemorate 25 years of independence, it's well worth a visit for its ethnological and archaeological displays. The museum is open on Monday from 2.30 to 4.30 pm, Tuesday to Friday from 9 to 11.30 am and 2.30 to 4.30 pm, Saturday from 2 to 5 pm and Sunday from 9 am till noon and 2 to 5 pm. Entry is RFr 100, or RFr 50 if you have a student card. It's about 15 minutes' walk north of the centre, past the matatu park.

Places to Stay – bottom end

The best place to stay is undoubtedly the *Procure de Butare*, a very attractive building surrounded by flower gardens. It costs RFr 400 per person and, though there are double and triple rooms, it usually has only singles available. These are large, well furnished rooms and the sheets are crisp! There are no signs for this place, so you must ask directions, but it's at the opposite end of town to the matatu park (about a 20-minute walk), so take a taxi-motor. The door closes at 9 pm sharp.

If you want a hotel, there are a few along the street near the market. The clean and friendly *Weekend Hôtel* has singles/doubles for RFr 600/1000. Better value is the *International Hôtel* across the road. It has double rooms with good beds, a bath and hot water for RFr 1000.

Places to Stay – top end

There are two top hotels here: the *Hôtel Faucon* (☎ 30391) and the *Hôtel Ibis* (☎ 30335). The Ibis charges RFr 3000/3600 a single/double with all facilities. It also has a good terrace bar which serves drinks and snacks. The Faucon is more expensive.

Places to Eat

The *Procure du Butare* has good, cheap

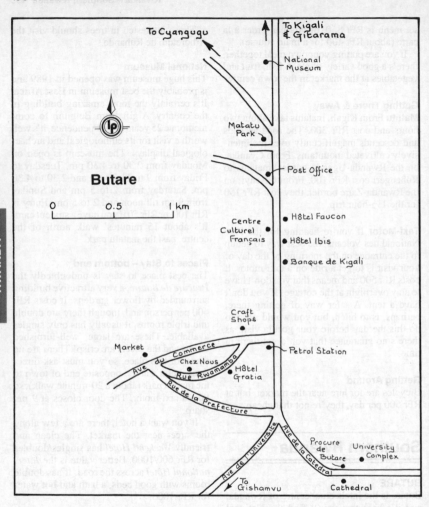

Butare

0   0.5   1 km

To Cyangugu

To Kigali & Gitarama

National Museum

Matatu Park

Post Office

Hôtel Faucon

Centre Culturel Français

Hôtel Ibis

Banque de Kigali

Craft Shops

Market

Ave du Commerce

Chez Nous

Rue Rwamamba

Hôtel Gratia

Petrol Station

Rue de la Prefecture

Ave de l'Université

Procure de Butare

University Complex

Ave de la Catedral

To Gishamvu

Cathedral

meals, with breakfast available for RFr 150 and excellent dinners for RFr 250 (three courses, all you can eat). Otherwise, the *Restaurant Chez Nous* near the market has good local food. Next door to the International Hôtel and in a pleasant setting, the *Jacaranda Restaurant* has a very good three-course set menu for RFr 400.

Other than the above, two travellers recommended the *Chic-Choc*, on Rue Santé, two blocks from the Procure de Butare, as 'the best restaurant in Africa'. That sounds like an extravagant claim, but they described it as '...very new and quaint with excellent service, sympathetic table settings, lots of plants and a menu to suit most budgets'. Dishes range from RFr 200 to RFr 600, with a three-course menu for RFr 550 (rabbit) or

RFr 750 (beef). It also does breakfasts for RFr 150 to RFr 250 (continental and American). Beers are normally priced.

Getting There & Away
The matatu park is just a patch of dirt about one km north of the town centre, by the stadium. Arriving matatus often drop you in the centre of town, but when leaving, you have to get yourself to the matatu park. Taximotors abound, so this is not a problem.

To Kigali, matatus cost RFr 400 and take about three hours. To Gitarama, it's about RFr 200, and to Kamembe (Cyangugu), it's RFr 450 along a road which is spectacular in parts. It passes through the Nyungwe Forest, which contains some amazing virgin rainforest between Uwinka and Kiutabe.

To the Burundi border, there are infrequent matatus, which cost RFr 200 and take about an hour once they set off. The one I travelled on waited for 1½ hours before it finally filled up and left.

National Parks

PARC NATIONAL DES VOLCANS
This area along the border with Zaïre and Uganda has to be one of the most beautiful sights in Africa. There is a chain of no less than seven volcanoes, one of them more than 4500 metres high.

But it's not just the mountains which attract travellers. On the bamboo and rainforest-covered slopes is one of the last remaining sanctuaries of the mountain gorilla *(Gorilla beringei)*. These animals were studied in depth by George Schaller and, more recently, by Dian Fossey.

Fossey spent the best part of 13 years living at a remote camp high up on the slopes of Visoke in order to study the gorillas and to habituate them to human contact. She'd probably still be there now had she not been murdered in December 1985, most likely by poachers with whom she made herself very unpopular. Without her tenacious efforts to have poaching stamped out, however, there possibly wouldn't be any gorillas left in Rwanda. It remains to be seen what will happen to the four known groups which survive.

It isn't just poaching which threatens the gorillas. Also clawing away at their existence is local pressure for grazing and agricultural land, and the European Community's pyrethrum project – daisy-like flowers processed into a natural insecticide. This project was responsible for the removal in 1969 of more than 8900 hectares from the park – almost half its area! The park now covers only 0.5% of the total land area of Rwanda.

Fossey's account of her years with the gorillas and her battle with the poachers and government officials, *Gorillas in the Mist* (Penguin Books, 1985), makes fascinating reading. Pick up a copy before coming here. Her story has also been made into a film of the same name, and following its success, the tourism industry in the country boomed for a while, until fighting between the government and the RPF put the area out of bounds to tourists.

Warning
At the time of writing, the Parc National des Volcans was a war zone, and even if you were allowed to visit it, you'd be extremely foolish to do so. You could well end up with a bullet through your head or step on a mine and blow yourself to bits.

Undoubtedly the park will reopen when a reconciliation between the two sides is brokered, but that may not be for some time.

Visiting the Gorillas
As with visiting the gorillas in Zaïre, many travellers rate a visit to these beautiful creatures as one of the highlights of their trip to Africa. It isn't, however, a joy ride. The guides can generally find the gorillas within one to four hours of starting out, but this often involves a lot of strenuous effort scrambling through dense vegetation up steep, muddy hillsides sometimes to more than 3000 metres. It also rains a lot in this area. If you don't have the right footwear and clothing, you're in for a hard time.

RWANDA

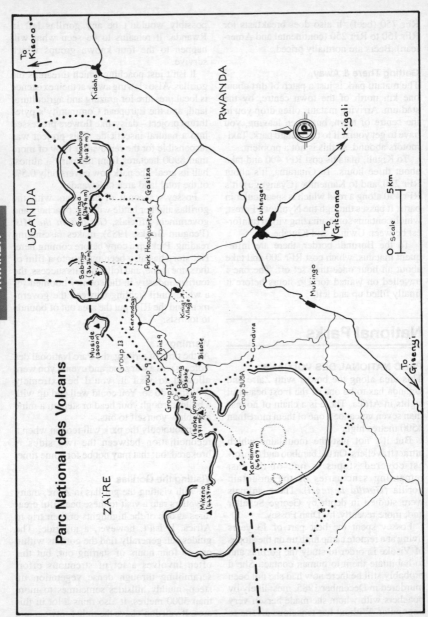

Parc National des Volcans

To Kisoro

Kidaho

RWANDA

UGANDA

Muhabura (+4127 m)

Gahinga (3474 m)

Gasiza

Park Headquarters

Sabinyo (3634 m)

Musida (3000m)

Karandagi

Kinigi Village

Group 13

Point 9

Bisate

Group 9

Group 11

Parking Block

ZAIRE

Group 15

Visoke (3711 m)

Karisimbi (+4507 m)

Group SUSA

Cundura

Mukingo

Mikeno (+4437 m)

To Gisenyi

Kigali

Ruhengeri

To Gitarama

0   5 km

Scale

RWANDA

An encounter with a silverback male gorilla at close quarters can also be a hair-raising experience if you've only ever seen large wild animals in the safety of a zoo. Despite their size, however, they're remarkably nonaggressive animals and are usually quite safe to be around. For most people, it's a magical encounter.

In the Parc National des Volcans, the four gorilla groups you can visit are known as Group 9 (six gorillas), Group 11 (12 gorillas), Group 13 (10 gorillas) and Group SUSA (29 gorillas, including two silverbacks). Any of the groups can be seen in one day, though a visit to Group SUSA involves a more rugged trip, starting at 5.30 am rather than 8 am.

Reservations To see any group, you must make advance reservations at the tourist office in Kigali, Office Rwandais du Tourisme et des Parcs Nationaux (☎ 76514), BP 905. Otherwise you can not be guaranteed a place on the day you want to go. Groups 11 and 13 are often booked up weeks ahead, especially during the European summer holiday season, but there are lots of cancellations, so it's often possible to join a group if you are at the park headquarters before 8 am. Also, a single person can often get a place in a group just two or three days in advance.

The maximum group size is eight people, but unfortunately (for the gorillas), the pressure of numbers means this limit is often exceeded. Children under 15 years of age cannot visit the gorillas.

Having made a booking, present yourself at the park headquarters between 7 and 8 am on the day of the visit to pay fees or have your permit checked. Be at the various departure points by 9.15 am. This can be problematical without your own transport. The park doesn't lay on any, tourists with cars are often reluctant to take you and there's very little local transport, so it may not be possible to hitch. A possible solution is to take a taxi-motor from Ruhengeri in the morning (RFr 500) or stay at the park gate the night before.

To see the SUSA gorillas, you must pay your fees at the park headquarters by 5 pm on the day before your visit. You then have to turn up at 5.30 am the next day at the park entry point at Gashinya. To get there, catch a Gisenyi minibus from Ruhengeri and get off at Busoyo, then walk the seven km to Gashinya. This entails an overnight stay at the park gate unless you have transport.

Kinigi village is about 18 km from Ruhengeri and the park headquarters is another two km from there (signposted 'Bureau du PNV'). It's not too difficult to hitch from Ruhengeri to the turn-off for the park headquarters (expect to pay about RFr 50 for a lift).

Park Fees Fees are US$126 per person (US$95 for students) for a gorilla visit (including compulsory guide), payable in hard currency. Resident foreigners can pay the equivalent in local currency. Porters are also available but you pay extra for this service. The guide and/or porters will expect a tip at the end.

Places to Stay & Eat Although camping is temporarily banned due to the hostilities, it used to be possible and may again be possible in the future. Assuming it is, there's a partially covered site 100 metres from the park headquarters for RFr 500 per person per night, with use of the same facilities as the chalets across the road. Be very careful about thieves at the camp site. Don't leave anything of value in an unguarded tent. Thieves even steal from tents in which the occupants are sleeping.

Without a tent (none for hire), you'll have to stay in one of the *chalets* opposite the camp site, of which there are four. Unfortunately, they were trashed during the hostilities and the beds were stolen, so it's going to take some time to restore them when peace comes. Assuming they are replaced, each chalet has five beds and a fireplace (a couple often get a whole chalet to themselves). They cost RFr 850 per person. Clean sheets are provided but firewood costs RFr 200 per bundle. Toilets and showers are communal and not very clean. Valuables left in the chalets appear to be safe.

A common room/bar, which is open all day until late at night, serves soft drinks, beer, wine and spirits. There's also a barbecue in another building in the same compound, which offers cheap brochettes, chicken and French fries.

Climbing the Volcanoes

There are several possibilities for trekking up to the summits of one or more of the volcanoes in the park. The treks range from several hours to two days or more. For all these, a guide is compulsory (at the usual fee) but porters are optional.

The ascents take you through some remarkable changes of vegetation, ranging from thick forests of bamboo, giant lobelia or hagenia on to alpine meadows. If the weather is favourable, you'll be rewarded with some spectacular views over the mountain chain. It is forbidden to cut down trees or otherwise damage vegetation in the park and you can only make fires in the designated camping areas. The following treks are among the more popular:

Visoke (3711 metres) The return trip takes six to seven hours from Parking Bisoke. The ascent takes you up the very steep southwestern flanks of the volcano to the summit, where you can see the crater lake. The descent follows a rough track on the northwestern side, from which there are magnificent views over the Parc National des Virunga (Zaïre) and Lake Ngezi.

Lake Ngezi (About 3000 metres) The return trip takes three to four hours from Parking Bisoke. This is one of the easiest of the treks, and if you get there at the right time of the day, you may see a variety of animals coming to drink.

Karisimbi (4507 metres) The return trip takes two days. The track follows the saddle between Visoke and Karisimbi and then ascends the north-western flank of the latter. Some five hours after beginning the trek, you

arrive at a metal hut, which is where you stay for the night (the hut keys are available at Parking Bisoke). The rocky and sometimes snow-covered summit is a further two to four hours' walk through alpine vegetation. You descend the mountain the following day. To do this trek, you need plenty of warm clothing and a very good sleeping bag. It gets very cold, especially at the metal hut, which is on a bleak shoulder of the mountain at about 3660 metres. The wind whips through, frequently with fog, so you don't get much warmth from the sun.

Sabinyo (3634 metres) The return trip takes five to six hours from the park headquarters at Kinigi. The track ascends the south-eastern face of the volcano, ending up with a rough scramble over steep lava beds along a very narrow path. There's a metal hut just before the start of the lava beds.

Gahinga & Muhabura (3474 metres & 4127 metres) The return trip takes two days from Gasiza. The summit of the first volcano is reached after a climb of about four hours along a track which passes through a swampy saddle between the two mountains. There is a metal hut here, which offers a modicum of shelter, but it's in a bad state of repair. The trip to the summit of Muhabura takes about four hours from the saddle.

PARC NATIONAL DE L'AKAGERA

This national park is something of a disaster zone at present due to the hostilities between the government and the RPF. The southern half is still open but the northern portion (north of Plage Hippos) is out of bounds because of land mines. Camping in the park is also currently prohibited.

Created in 1934 and covering an area of 2500 sq km, Akagera is one of the least visited but most interesting wildlife parks in Africa. One reason for this is its three distinct environments. Large areas of the park are covered with treeless savannah, but there is an immense swampy area about 95 km long and between two and 20 km wide along the border with Tanzania. This contains six lakes and numerous islands, some of which are covered with savannah, others with forest. Thirdly, there is a chain of low mountains (ranging from 1618 to 1825 metres high) which stretches through much of the length of the park. The vegetation here is variable, ranging from short grasses on the summits to wooded savannah and dense thickets of xerophilious (adapted to a dry habitat) forest on the flanks.

There's an extraordinary variety of animals to be seen here and they're often much easier to find than in other wildlife parks. In just a two to three-day trip, you can usually come across topi, impala, roan antelope, giant eland, bushbuck, oribi, various types of duiker, buffaloes, wart hogs, red river hogs, baboon, vervet monkeys, lions, leopards, hyenas, zebras, hippos, crocodiles and, at night, hares, palm civets, genet, galagos (bushbabies) and giant crested porcupine. There are also herds of elephant.

The best time to visit the park, in terms of access, is during the dry season (mid-May to mid-September). November and April are the wettest months.

Tsetse flies can be particularly troublesome in the north and east, but you could be bothered by the odd one anywhere in the park, so bring a fly swat and/or insect repellant.

Hiring a guide is a waste of money. You won't find any more animals with a guide than you will without. All you need is a map of the park, your eyes and a pair of binoculars. Park maps, for sale at the tourist office in Kigali, are remarkably accurate despite the way they appear – you can't buy these at the park. A wildlife handbook is also useful. Take all your own food, drinking and washing water, and fuel. It's best to assume you won't be able to get these in the park. Sometimes fuel is available at the hotels but they're very reluctant to sell it.

Park entry fees are RFr 1500 per person, plus RFr 800 for a car or RFr 1000 for a jeep. Camping costs RFr 1000 per person. A guide costs RFr 500 per day and a fishing licence costs RFr 1500 per day.

Places to Stay

There are two lodges in the park, but the *Gabiro Guest House* was trashed during the war and is closed. It's unlikely to open again in the near future. The only place which is currently open is the *Hôtel Akagera*, which is very expensive. It sits on the top of a hill and commands excellent views. A boat trip on the lake is recommended, as it's cheap and there are plenty of birds to be seen.

If you can't afford the lodge, you'll have to camp, and there are several designated sites but no facilities. One exception is at *Plage Hippos*, halfway up the park and close to the Tanzanian border. Here there are covered picnic tables, good waste bins and toilets but the site is no more protected than anywhere else. It's a beautiful place and there are plenty of hippos and crocodiles, monkeys and birdlife. Don't swim here, not only because of the hippos and crocodiles but also because there's a fair chance of catching bilharzia.

Getting There & Away

The only problem with getting to Akagera is that you need to have your own transport or to join an organised safari. Safaris do not, as in Kenya and Tanzania, cater to budget travellers. Check out car hire and safari prices in Kigali at Rwanda Travel Service (☎ 2210), Hôtel des Diplomates, 45 Blvd de la Révolution; Umubano Tours Agency (☎ 2176), BP 1160; and Agence Solliard (☎ 5660), 2 Ave de la République.

The best entry into the park is either at the Gabiro Guest House (in the mid-north) or the Akagera Hôtel (in the south), but the quickest is the Nyamiyaga entrance, about 16 km from the sealed road going through Kayonza.

NYUNGWE FOREST CONSERVATION PROJECT

Despite not being a national park, the Nyungwe Forest ranks among Rwanda's foremost attractions. One of the largest protected montane rainforests in Africa, it covers 970 sq km and offers superb scenery

RWANDA

overlooking the forest and Lake Kivu as well as views to the north of the distant volcanoes of the Virunga.

The conservation project began in 1988 and is sponsored by the American Peace Corps, the New York Zoological Society and the Rwandan government. It aims to promote tourism in an ecologically sound way while studying the ecology of the forest and educating local people about its value.

The main attraction is the guided tours to view large groups of black-and-white colobus monkeys (up to 300 per group). The lush, green valleys also offer outstanding hiking across 20 km of well-maintained trails passing through enormous stands of hardwoods, under waterfalls and through a large marsh. There are about 270 species of tree, 50 species of mammal, 275 species of bird and an astonishing variety of orchids and butterflies.

The guided tours depart from the project headquarters at Uwinka three times daily, at 8 and 11 am and 2 pm. An information centre is also at the headquarters. The tours cost RFr 500 per person and you should expect to walk for about an hour. Sturdy shoes, binoculars and rain gear are advisable.

Another guided tour (RFr 500 per person) goes to the Kamiranzovu Marsh, where the area's six remaining elephants reside in the forest.

In addition to the tours, there are six other trails, ranging from one km to nine km in length, along which you're free to hike without a guide.

Places to Stay

There are nine camp sites at the Uwinka headquarters but you must bring everything you need – tent, sleeping bag, cooking equipment, water, food and warm clothes (the nights are cool at 2400 metres). There is nothing here other than toilets, charcoal and wood. Camping fees are RFr 200 per person per night. The nearest towns for provisions are Cyangugu and Butare. Plans are being made to connect the existing trails with other camp sites to enable those who prefer backpacking to take two to three-day treks in the forest. Uwinka sits on a ridge overlooking the forest and offers impressive views in all directions. There's also a camp site at Karamba, about 14 km towards Cyangugu from Uwinka.

Getting There & Away

The Nyungwe Forest lies between Butare and Cyangugu. From Kigali, head south to Butare and then west towards Cyangugu. Minibuses leave from Kigali (RFr 800) and Butare throughout the day. Another option is to take the large, crowded green bus which leaves Kigali daily at 7 am and costs only RFr 600. The Uwinka headquarters is just past the 90-km post and is marked by a board on which a black-and-white colobus monkey is painted. The trip from Kigali takes between four and six hours.

From Cyangugu, take a minibus towards Butare and get off at Uwinka, which is just past the 54-km post. The journey takes about one hour and costs RFr 300.

Warning
Because of instability, political uncertainty and in some cases military action, travellers planning to visit this region are advised to check with the appropriate authority before leaving home, and/or with their diplomatic representatives abroad. ■

Burundi

Burundi

Burundi is a small and beautiful mountainous country. Sandwiched between Tanzania, Rwanda and Zaïre, there are magnificent views over Lake Tanganyika.

Burundi has had a stormy history of tribal wars and factional struggles between the ruling families. This has been further complicated in recent times by colonisation, first by the Germans and later by the Belgians. Even today, intertribal clashes are still occurring.

Burundi is one of the most densely populated countries in the world, with 145 people per sq km. Despite this, there are very few urban centres. The only towns of any size are the capital, Bujumbura, and Gitega. Most people live in family compounds known as *rugos*.

Facts about the Country

HISTORY
Early Settlement

The original inhabitants of the area were the Twa Pygmies, who now comprise only 1% of the population. They were gradually displaced from about 1000 CE onwards by Hutu, mostly farmers of Bantu stock, who now make up 85% of the population.

In the 16th and 17th centuries, the country experienced another wave of migration. This time it was the tall, pastoralist Watutsi from Ethiopia and Uganda, who now make up 14% of the population. The Watutsi gradually subjugated the Hutu into a type of feudal system, similar to that which operated

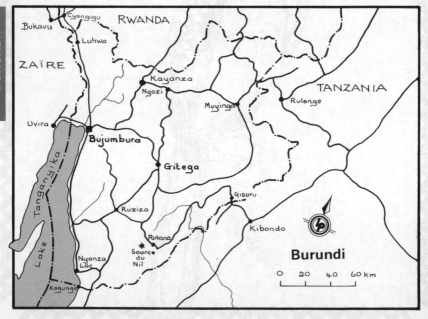

Burundi

0   20   40   60 km

in medieval Europe. The Watutsi became a loosely organised aristocracy with a *mwami*, or king, at the top of each social pyramid. Under this system the Hutu relinquished their land and mortgaged their services to the nobility in return for cattle – the symbol of wealth and status in Burundi.

The Colonial Era

At the end of the 19th century, Burundi and Rwanda were colonised by Germany. However, they were so thinly garrisoned that the Belgians were easily able to oust the German forces during WW I. After the war, the League of Nations mandated Burundi (then known as Urundi) and Rwanda to Belgium.

Taking advantage of the feudal structure, the Belgians ruled indirectly through the Watutsi chiefs and princes, granting them wide-ranging powers to recruit labour and raise taxes. The Watutsi were not averse to abusing these powers whenever it suited them. After all, they considered themselves to be a superior, intelligent people, born to rule, while the Hutu were merely hardworking but dumb peasants. The Christian missionaries encouraged this view by concentrating on educating the Watutsi and virtually ignoring the Hutu. As the missions had been granted a monopoly on education, this policy remained unchallenged.

The establishment of coffee plantations and the resulting concentration of wealth in the hands of the Watutsi urban elite further exacerbated tensions between the two tribal groups.

Independence

In the 1950s, a nationalist organisation based on unity between the tribes was founded under the leadership of the mwami's eldest son, Prince Rwagasore. However, in the run-up to independence, the prince was assassinated with the connivance of the colonial authorities, who feared their commercial interests would be threatened if he came to power.

Despite this setback, when independence was granted in 1962, challenges were raised to the concentration of power in Watutsi hands. It appeared that the country was headed for a majority government. This had already happened in neighbouring Rwanda, where a similar tribal imbalance existed.

Yet in the 1964 elections, even though Hutu candidates attracted a majority of votes, the mwami refused to appoint a Hutu prime minister. Hutu frustration boiled over a year later in an attempted coup staged by Hutu military officers and political figures. Though the attempt failed, it led to the flight of the mwami into exile in Switzerland. He was replaced by a Watutsi military junta. A wholesale purge of Hutu from the army and the bureaucracy followed, but in 1972 another large-scale revolt saw more than 1000 Watutsi killed.

The military junta responded to this challenge with what amounted to selective genocide. Any Hutu with wealth, a formal education or a government job was rooted out and murdered, often in the most horrifying way. Certainly few bullets were used, and convoys of army trucks full of the mutilated bodies of Hutu rumbled through the streets of Bujumbura for days on end, initially even in broad daylight. Many Hutu were taken from their homes at night, while others received summonses to police stations.

It is hard to believe how subservient the Hutu had become to their Watutsi overlords. Even the most uninformed peasant was aware of what was occurring. After three months, 200,000 Hutu had been killed and 100,000 had fled to Tanzania, Rwanda and Zaïre. More refugees have poured into Tanzania since.

Neither the Christian missions inside the country nor the international community outside raised any protest against this carnage. Indeed, whilst it was in full swing, an official of the Organization of African Unity (OAU) is on record as having visited Bujumbura to congratulate President Michel Micombero on the orderly way the country was being run!

In 1976 Jean-Baptiste Bagaza came to power in a bloodless coup, and in 1979 formed the Union pour le Progrès National (UPRONA), ruling with a central committee and small politburo. As part of a so-called democratisation programme, elections in 1982 saw candidates (mostly Watutsi and all approved by UPRONA) voted into the National Assembly. The elections gave the Hutu a modicum of power in the National Assembly, but it was limited by the fact that Hutu people have only ever held about 25% of government ministries.

During the Bagaza years, there were some half-hearted attempts by the government to remove some of the main causes of inter-tribal conflict, but these were mostly cosmetic. The army and the bureaucracy remained under Watutsi domination, with the Hutu confined to menial jobs, agriculture and cattle raising. The government even vetoed international aid when it suspected that this might be used to educate or enrich the Hutu, and thus sow the seeds of discontent.

In 1985 the government tried to lessen the influence of the Catholic Church, which it believed was sympathetic to the Hutu majority. Its fears of a church-organised Hutu revolt were heightened by the fact that in neighbouring Rwanda, Hutus were in power. Priests were put on trial and some missionaries were expelled from the country.

Bagaza was toppled in September 1987 in a bloodless coup led by his cousin Major Pierre Buyoya. The new regime did a reasonable job of mending fences between the government and the Catholic Church/international aid agencies. It also attempted to address the causes of intertribal tensions yet again by gradually bringing Hutu representatives back into postitions of power in the government but there was a renewed outbreak of intertribal violence in the north of the country in August 1988. As in previous clashes of this nature, the violence was unbelievable. Depending on whose figures you believe, somewhere between 4000 and 24,000 people were massacred and thousands more fled into neighbouring Rwanda.

Then, in 1992, Buyoya bowed to international pressure and announced that multiparty elections would be held the following year. For a time, it seemed that sense and reason might prevail over the endless cycle of bloodletting which has scarred the country's history. However, it was not to be.

Although elections were duly held in June 1993, which brought a Hutu-dominated government to power headed by Melchior Ndadaye (also a Hutu), a dissident army faction, led by Colonel Sylvestre Ningaba, staged a bloody coup in late October the same year, assasinated the president and went on the rampage. The coup failed when army generals disowned the plotters but, in the chaos which followed the assasination, thousands of people were massacred in intertribal fighting and an estimated 400,000 refugees fled across the border into neighbouring Rwanda. Surviving members of the government, who had holed up in the French Embassy in Bujumbura, were able to reassert some degree of control several days later with the help of loyal troops. Prime Minister Sylvie Kinigi has been negotiating with the dissident army officers, but the future is not bright.

We strongly suggest you keep your eye on developments in this country before contemplating a visit. This sort of violence doesn't usually affect foreign visitors, but you'd hardly want to be around when it happens.

GEOGRAPHY
Burundi occupies a mountainous 27,834 sq km. The capital, Bujumbura, is on the northern tip of Lake Tanganyika.

CLIMATE
Burundi has a variable climate. The lower land around Lake Tanganyika is hot and humid, with temperatures around 30°C. In the more mountainous north, the average temperature is around 20°C. The rainy season lasts from October to May, with a brief dry spell in December and January.

GOVERNMENT
Burundi held its first multiparty elections on 1 June 1993 after a lengthy process of democratisation. The incumbent president,

Major Paul Buyoya, who had been in power since his coup d'etat of 1987, was ousted and a new president, Melchior Ndadaye, was elected after winning two-thirds of the vote.

This was Burundi's first democratic election, and the first time that the majority Hutu tribe were able to return a Hutu to the presidency. It was also the end of military rule and the beginning of a democratic government.

The coup on 21 October was a reaction by an element in the army which was not happy to relinquish power to a Hutu president. Many of the top ministers were tipped off in advance and either fled the country or took refuge in foreign embassies.

ECONOMY

Burundi's economy is predominantly agricultural, with coffee, the main commercial crop, accounting for 65% of export income. The government has been trying to encourage development of the noncoffee sector in an effort to diversify the economy. Consequently, the production of tea has increased greatly in the past few years.

Agriculture is the mainstay of the economy and accounts for more than 50% of GDP. It employs about 85% of the workforce. Apart from coffee, cash crops include tea, cotton, palm oil and tobacco. Subsistence crops (which occupy most of the cultivated land) include cassava, bananas, sweet potatoes, maize and sorghum.

The manufacturing sector, based in Bujumbura, accounts for 15% of GDP, with output including cigarettes, glass, textiles, cement, oxygen and processed coffee.

Unfortunately, wood is used to meet most of the energy requirements at the village level. Major energy needs are met through oil imports from the Persian Gulf and electricity from Zaïre.

Inflation is running at about 7.5%.

POPULATION

The population of five million is about 14% Watutsi and 85% Hutu.

LANGUAGE

The official languages are Kirundi and French, and Swahili is also useful. Hardly anyone speaks English.

Facts for the Visitor

VISAS & EMBASSIES

Visas are required by all visitors to Burundi. Transit visas cost US$10 and a one-month tourist visa costs US$20. You will need two photos and can generally get your visa the same day, if you apply early enough.

There's no extra charge for requesting a multiple-entry visa, so if there's any chance you would need this, get it now rather than later.

For some reason, certain Burundi embassies (Nairobi in Kenya and Kigali in Rwanda are two) will not issue visas, telling you to get them at the border. They are still available at the embassy in Kampala (Uganda) and at the consulates in Kigoma (Tanzania) and Bukavu (Zaïre).

Tourist visas can be extended at the immigration office in Bujumbura. These cost BFr 1000 per month and take 24 hours to issue. Apply early in the morning, as it's very busy in the afternoon.

Burundi Embassies

Visas can be obtained from Burundi embassies in Addis Ababa (Ethiopia), Algiers (Algeria), Cairo (Egypt), Dar es Salaam (Tanzania), Kampala (Uganda), Kinshasa (Zaïre) and Tripoli (Libya). There are also consulates in Bukavu (Zaïre) and Kigoma (Tanzania). The embassies in Kigali (Rwanda) and Nairobi (Kenya) do not issue visas.

Outside Africa, there are Burundi embassies in Beijing (People's Republic of China), Bonn (Germany), Brussels (Belgium), Bucharest (Romania), Geneva (Switzerland), Moscow (Russia), Ottawa (Canada), Paris (France) and Washington DC (USA).

The visa application story in East Africa is as follows:

Kenya The Burundi Embassy is currently

not issuing visas and will tell you to get one on arrival at the border.

Rwanda The embassy (☎ 73465) is on Rue de Ntaruka off Ave de Rusumo. Visas are only issued to Rwandan residents, so don't waste your time. Visas are available at the border.

Tanzania At the consulate in Kigoma, visas cost TSh 4000, require two photographs and are issued while you wait. The consulate is open Monday to Friday from 8 am to 3 pm.

In Dar es Salaam the requirements are the same. The embassy (☎ 46307) is at Plot 1007 Lugalo Rd, next to the Italian Embassy, and is open Monday to Friday from 8 am to 2.30 pm.

Uganda Don't plan on getting a visa for Burundi in Uganda as these are only issued to Ugandans and Ugandan residents. If you want to try, the embassy (☎ 231548) is at Plot 5, Nehru Ave, Nakasero, Kampala, and is open Monday to Friday from 8.30 am to 12.30 pm and 3 to 5.30 pm. Otherwise, visas are available at the border on entry.

Zaïre At the consulate in Bukavu (SINELAC Bldg, 184 Ave du Président Mobutu), Burundi visas cost US$20, require two photos and take 24 hours to be issued. The consulate is open Monday to Friday from 7.30 am till noon and 2.30 to 5 pm.

Foreign Embassies in Burundi

Visas available in Bujumbura for neighbouring African countries include:

Rwanda The embassy (☎ 26865) is at 24 Ave du Zaïre, Bujumbura, next to the Zaïrian Embassy. A one-month multiple-entry visa costs BFr 2500, requires two photos and is issued in 24 hours. Office hours are Monday to Friday from 8 am to 4 pm and Saturday to 11.30 am.

Tanzania The embassy is on Ave de l'ONU, around the corner from the Rwandan and Zaïre embassies on Ave du Zaïre. Visas

require two photographs and are issued in 24 hours. Costs vary according to your nationality (see the Tanzania Facts for the Visitor chapter for details). The embassy is open Monday to Friday from 8 am till noon and 2 to 5 pm.

Zaïre The embassy is on Ave du Zaïre, next to the Rwandan Embassy. Visa costs are the same as in other countries (see the Zaïre chapter for details), three photos are required and the visa is issued in 24 hours. The embassy is open only in the morning, from 8.30 am till noon.

MONEY
Currency

The unit of currency, the Burundi franc (BFr), is divided into 100 centimes, which you're highly unlikely to come across. Notes in circulation are BFr 5000, BFr 1000, BFr 500, BFr 100, BFr 50 and BFr 10. The only coins are BFr five and BFr one.

Exchange Rates

US$1 = BFr 202 (official)
US$1 = BFr 230 (black market)

The exchange value of the Burundi franc fluctuates according to the international currency market, particularly the value of the US dollar and the French franc, and devaluations are not uncommon.

Changing Money

Commission rates for changing travellers' cheques are bad news at most banks – some charge up to 7%! The Banque de la République du Burundi is the best place to change, as it charges only a very small commission and may even change small amounts of dollar travellers' cheques to cash dollars. Banking hours are Monday to Friday from 8 to 11.30 am. Outside these hours, you can change travellers' cheques at one of the large hotels in Bujumbura (eg, Novotel, Chaussée du Peuple Burundi). Their rates are fractionally below those offered by the banks, though they charge no commission.

There's a relatively open street market in

Bujumbura. Dealers generally hang around the front of the main post office. Rates obviously vary according to the official exchange rate and the amount you want to change (large bills are preferred). For currencies other than the US dollar, you're better off at the bank.

Tanzanian shillings can also be bought here, which is handy if you're heading for Kigoma, but the rate is not that good. The nearest Tanzanian banks are in Kigoma.

If you take your own food on the Lake Tanganyika steamer (and don't intend to buy drinks), there's no need for shillings, but you'll need some for the Nyanza Lac and Gombe Stream route. If you're not providing your own food or are taking the steamer all the way to Mpulungu, you'll need shillings, as it's a Tanzanian boat and meals and drinks must be paid for in Tanzanian shillings.

At the border post between Uvira (Zaïre) and Bujumbura, you'll run into a lot of moneychangers. Their rates are quite reasonable, so long as you know the current street rates for the Burundi franc.

Currency declaration forms are not issued on arrival.

Costs

Burundi can be an expensive place to stay if you want to be near the town centre in Bujumbura, but there are reasonably cheap places in the suburbs. Elsewhere, meals can usually be found at a fair price and transport costs are about the same as in Rwanda.

BUSINESS HOURS & HOLIDAYS

Official business hours (other than banks) are Monday to Saturday from 8 am till noon and 2 to 5 pm. The following public holidays are observed:

January
New Year's Day (1st)
March/April
Good Friday
Easter Sunday
May
Labour Day (1st)
Ascension

July
National Day (1st)
August
Feast of the Assumption (15th)
September
(18th)
October
(13th)
November
All Saints' Day (1st)
December
Christmas Day (25th)

POST & TELECOMMUNICATIONS
Post

The postal service is reasonably efficient, but the poste restante service at the main post office (PTT) in Bujumbura is poorly organised. Make sure you check not only the pile for your surname but also those for any other possible combinations or spellings. It's open Monday to Friday from 8 am till noon and 2 to 4 pm, and on Saturday to 11 am.

Telephone

Rates for international telephone calls are extremely high; however connections from the main post office in Bujumbura take no more than a few minutes.

TIME

The time in Burundi is GMT/UTC plus two hours.

MEDIA

The main newspaper is the French-language daily, *Le Renouveau du Burundi*.

Local radio stations broadcast in Kirundi, French and Swahili. There are occasional broadcasts in English on the local FM station (98.10 MHz). This station also plays some pretty decent African music.

HEALTH

As with most African countries, you should take precautions against malaria in Burundi. There is a good beach (with expensive hotels and restaurants) at the northern end of Lake Tanganyika, between Bujumbura and the Burundi-Zaïre border. It's probably safe to swim there, but you should avoid bathing in

BURUNDI

this lake wherever there is reedy vegetation, due to the risk of contracting bilharzia. See the Health section in the introductory Facts for the Visitor chapter for more details.

Getting There & Away

You can enter Burundi by air, road or lake ferry. There are no railways.

AIR

International airlines servicing Burundi are Aeroflot, Air Burundi, Air France, Air Tanzania, Air Zaïre, Cameroon Airlines, Ethiopian Airlines, Kenya Airways and Sabena.

If you're heading for Tanzania and are thinking of flying internally from Kigoma to Dar es Salaam, it's worth making a reservation at the Air Tanzania office in Bujumbura. You don't have to pay for the ticket until you get to Kigoma but Air Tanzania staff will give you written confirmation of your reservation.

In theory, Air Tanzania flies Kilimanjaro to Bujumbura (and vice versa) on Sunday and Dar es Salaam to Bujumbura (and vice versa) on the same day, but cancellations are frequent.

LAND
To/From Rwanda

There is a choice of two routes. Which one you take will depend on whether you want to go from Kigali direct to Butare and on to Bujumbura, or via Cyangugu (Lake Kivu).

Butare to Bujumbura From Butare, take a minibus (infrequent) to the border for RFr 200. You'll be met by a gaggle of money-changers, who'll change dollars or Rwandan francs into Burundi francs.

The border is easy-going, though you should expect cursory baggage searches on both sides. From the Burundi border village, it's possible to catch a minibus to Kayanza (BFr 150) on Tuesdays, Fridays and Sundays (market days in Kayanza); at other times,

you'll have to hitch or hire a taxi. There are frequent minibuses to Bujumbura (BFr 300, two hours) from Kayanza.

Cyangugu to Bujumbura From Cyangugu, take a minibus to the border village of Bugarama. You'll probably have to hitch the next eight km to the Burundi border post at Luhwa and the following 12 km to the village of Rugombo. From Rugombo there are minibuses to Bujumbura (BFr 200, about two hours).

There's quite a lot of traffic along this route, so it's easy enough to travel between Cyangugu (or Bukavu in Zaïre) and Bujumbura in a day.

To/From Zaïre

There are two possible routes between Burundi and Zaïre.

Bukavu to Bujumbura via Cyangugu Having crossed from Bukavu to Cyangugu (in Rwanda), this route is identical to the route described above.

Bukavu to Bujumbura via Uvira This is the longer and less comfortable route. First read about travel between Bukavu and Uvira in the Eastern Zaïre chapter, as this route has two options, one through Rwanda and the other direct to Uvira.

Once in Uvira, the route into Burundi is across the top of Lake Tanganyika. From Uvira, share-taxis leave until late in the afternoon and take about 15 minutes. You'll probably have to walk the one km from the Zaïre border post to the Burundi border post, though bicycle taxis are available. You may be able to find a minibus going from the Burundi border post to Bujumbura, but usually you will have to get a share-taxi (BFr 100, about 15 minutes).

LAKE
To/From Tanzania & Zambia

The two routes available both use Lake Tanganyika at different points. A direct route is from Kigoma on the venerable MV *Liemba*. However, a more interesting route is via

Nyanza Lac and Gombe Stream National Park, the chimpanzee sanctuary across the border in Tanzania.

Ferry The MV *Liemba* connects Tanzania with Burundi (and Zambia). It used to operate in conjunction with a sister ship, the MV *Mwongozo*, but this boat now only services ports on the Tanzanian part of the lake (see the Tanzania Getting Around chapter).

The schedule for the MV *Liemba* is more or less regular but the ferry can be delayed for up to 24 hours at either end, depending on how much cargo there is to load or unload. Engine trouble can also delay it at any point, though usually not for more than a few hours.

Officially, the MV *Liemba* departs once a week from Bujumbura, on Monday at about 4 pm, and arrives in Kigoma (Tanzania) on Tuesday at 8 am. It leaves Kigoma at about 4 pm on Wednesday and arrives in Mpulungu (Zambia) on Friday at 8 am. It calls at many small Tanzanian ports en route between Kigoma and Mpulungu, but rarely for more than half an hour. The fares from Bujumbura are:

Port	1st class	2nd class	3rd class
Kigoma	US$31	US$21	US$11
Mpulungu	US$87		

In addition, port fees of BFr 300 are payable upon boarding in Bujumbura. Tickets for the ferry can be bought from SONACO, Rue des Usines (off Ave du Port), Bujumbura, on Monday morning from 8 am.

Tickets bought in Mpulungu for the trip north to Kigoma or Bujumbura and tickets bought in Bujumbura for the trip south to any of the ports en route must be paid for in US dollars. Local currency is not acceptable.

To save money when going all the way from Bujumbura to Mpulungu, buy a ticket to Kigoma, then once the boat docks, get off, immediately make a reservation for a 1st or 2nd-class cabin and change money into Tanzanian shillings. Pay for your ticket the following morning at 8 am using the shillings you changed. This will save you approximately US$40 in total.

When travelling from Bujumbura direct to Mpulungu, you have to stay on the boat for the 36 hours or so that it docks in Kigoma, though you are allowed into town during the day even if you don't have a Tanzanian visa (where required). Passports have to be left with immigration in the meantime.

Third class consists of bench seats either in a covered area towards the back of the boat or in another very poorly ventilated area with bench seats in the bowels of the vessel. The best plan is to grab some deck space. The 2nd-class cabins are incredibly hot, stuffy and claustrophobic. They have four bunks and are very poorly ventilated. If you want a cabin, go the whole hog and take a 1st-class one. These have two bunks, are on a higher deck, have a window and fan and are clean and reasonably cool. Bedding is available for a small fee.

Third class is not usually crowded between Bujumbura and Kigoma, so this is a reasonable budget option, especially as it's only overnight. It's no problem to sleep out on the deck – the best spot is above the 1st-class deck, though you need to be discreet, as it's supposedly off limits to passengers. On the lower decks, you need to keep your gear safe, as some petty pilfering does sometimes occur. If you're travelling 3rd class between Bujumbura and Kigoma and want to upgrade to a cabin for the Kigoma-Mpulungu leg, make sure you do this as soon as the boat docks in Kigoma. Third class is not recommended between Kigoma and Mpulungu, as it's usually very crowded.

Meals and drinks are available on board and must be paid for in Tanzanian shillings, so bring enough to cover this. Three-course meals of soup, chicken and rice followed by dessert are not bad value at TSh 400 for lunch, TSh 500 for dinner and TSh 300 for breakfast. You can buy cold Safari lager (Tanzanian) at TSh 400 or Primus (Zaïrian) at TSh 720.

Coming from Bujumbura, the MV *Liemba* arrives at Kigoma at about 5 am, but you can't get off until 8 am, when customs and immigration officials arrive. Instead of packing your bags and hanging around, it's a good idea to have breakfast.

Lake Taxi & Matatu The alternative to the MV *Liemba* is to travel partly by matatu and partly by lake taxi between Bujumbura and Kigoma, via the Tanzanian border village of Kagunga and the Gombe Stream National Park. The national park is primarily a chimpanzee sanctuary and is well worth a visit, but it does cost US$50 entry fee plus US$20 for accommodation. If you can't afford this, then simply stay on the lake taxi, which will take you all the way to Kigoma.

From Bujumbura, matatus go daily to Nyanza Lac (BFr 800). You must go through immigration here; the office is about one km from the town centre towards the lake. After that you take a matatu (BFr 100) to the Burundi border post. From this post to the Tanzanian border post at Kagunga, it's a two-km walk along a narrow track. From Kagunga, there are lake taxis to Kigoma (actually to Kalalangabo, about three km north of Kigoma), which cost TSh 500, leave some time before dawn and take most of the day. The taxis call at Gombe Stream (about halfway), where you can get off if you like. The fare to Gombe Stream is TSh 250, as is the fare from there to Kigoma.

The lake taxis are small, wooden boats, often overcrowded not only with people but with their produce, and they offer no creature comforts whatsoever. They're good fun when the weather is fine, though if there's a squall on the lake, you may be in for a rough time. If you have a choice, try to get a boat with a cover, as it gets stinking hot out on the lake in the middle of the day. These boats do not operate on Sunday.

Getting Around

AIR

Air Burundi, the national airline, does not have regular internal flights.

BUS

As in Rwanda, most of the major routes are sealed.

There are plenty of modern, Japanese minibuses, which are fairly frequent, not overcrowded and cheaper than share-taxis. Destinations are displayed in the front window and vehicles depart when full. You can usually find one heading in your direction any day between early morning and early afternoon at the *gare routière* (bus station) in any town or city.

Government OTRACO buses serve the area around Bujumbura.

Bujumbura

Sprawling up the mountainside on the northeastern tip of Lake Tanganyika, Bujumbura overlooks the vast wall of mountains in Zaïre on the other side of the lake. The Burundi capital is a mixture of grandiose colonial town planning (wide boulevards and imposing public buildings) and dusty crowded suburbs like those which surround many African cities. It's also one of the most important ports on Lake Tanganyika.

Like Kigali in neighbouring Rwanda, Bujumbura has a sizeable expatriate population of international aid organisation workers, medicos, missionaries and businesspeople. Even Colonel Gaddafi has made his mark here, in the form of a large and beautifully conceived Islamic Cultural Centre and mosque, which must have cost a small fortune. There is also a pleasant botanical surprise: like many places along Lake Tanganyika, Bujumbura sports coconut palms – most unusual at well over 1000 km from the sea!

More English is spoken here than in most parts of Rwanda or Eastern Zaïre. Also noteworthy is the height of many of the people – they are Watutsi and they're huge!

Bujumbura has a slightly sleazy atmosphere and is certainly not the friendliest place in the world. You are advised not to walk along Ave de la Plage between the

Cercle Nautique and the port, even during the day, as there have been reports of muggings. Rue des Swahilis, in the same area, should also be avoided.

Information
Tourist Office It's on Blvd de l'UPRONA, and the information available is limited. This office has a wide range of handicrafts for sale, but they're not cheap. They also sell maps of Burundi (BFr 1500). The office is open Monday to Saturday from 7.30 am till noon and Monday to Thursday from 2 to 5.30 pm.

Post & Telecommunications The main post office is in the city centre, on the corner of Blvd Lumumba and Ave du Commerce. The international telephone service is housed in the same building. Both are open Monday to Friday from 8 am till noon and 2 to 4 pm, and on Saturday to 11 am.

Foreign Embassies African countries with diplomatic representation in Bujumbura include Rwanda, Tanzania and Zaïre – see the Facts for the Visitor entry earlier in this chapter.

Other countries with embassies here include Belgium, Denmark, France, the Netherlands, Germany and the USA.

Cultural Centres The American Cultural Center on Chaussée Prince Rwagasore screens video news from the USA from Monday to Friday at 5.15 pm. Its library is open Monday to Friday from 2 to 8 pm and on Tuesday and Thursday from 9 am till noon. Alliance Française is across the road and has similar services and facilities.

The Islamic Cultural Centre and mosque is a beautiful building near the main square. Paid for by the Libyan government, it is well worth visiting. Sometimes there are public performances by dance troupes, drummers and singers.

Things to See & Do
Bujumbura's two museums and its reptile park are within a block of each other on the Ave du 13 Octobre, which leads down to the Cercle Nautique on the lake front.

Musée Vivant This is a reconstructed traditional Burundian village with basket, pottery, drum and photographic displays. Occasionally there are traditional drum shows. Entry costs BFr 100 (BFr 50 for students) and the museum is open daily from 9 am till noon and 2.30 to 5 pm, except Mondays.

Parc des Reptiles Adjacent to the Musée Vivant, this park (☎ 25374) exhibits just what you might expect. Entry costs BFr 200 but the park is only open on Saturday from 2 to 4 pm, or by appointment during the rest of the week.

Musée de Géologie du Burundi Opposite the reptile park, the geology museum is dusty and run-down but has a good collection of fossils. Entry is free. The museum is open on weekdays from 7 am till noon and 2 to 5 pm.

Swimming Pool To use the pool at the Novotel will cost BFr 500, whereas the public pool at the stadium costs BFr 300.

Places to Stay – bottom end
It can be difficult to find a reasonably priced place to stay in Bujumbura, especially at weekends or if you arrive late in the day. Also, many of the cheaper places are more or less permanently filled with expatriate aid workers. You may have to do some leg work!

For years now, budget travellers have found a warm welcome at the *Vugizu Mission* (☎ 32059), run by the Johnson family. In the garden of the mission, there's a two-bed caravan and a tent (which sleeps two) for travellers' use. These facilities plus an excellent breakfast are free and there are no chores to do. The mission is on a beautiful site overlooking the lake, near the University Hospital in Kamenge.

The mission is a considerable distance from the centre, so catch a taxi (about BFr 400) or a bus. The best bus is the OTRACO bus to Gisenyi, which takes you almost to the

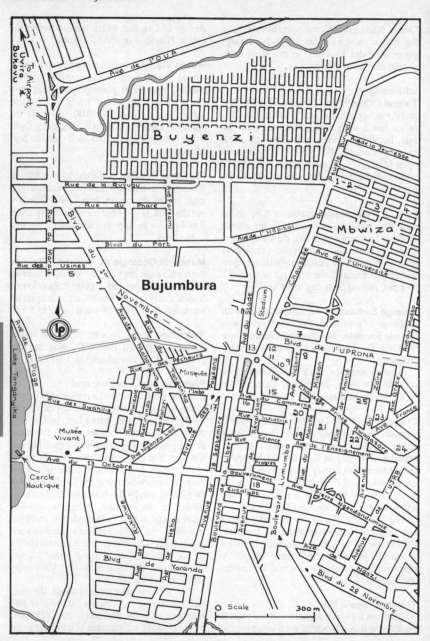

1	BP & FINA Petrol Stations
2	Hôtel Au Bon Accueil
3	Hôtel Panama
4	Au Château Fort Hôtel
5	SONACO (MV *Liemba* tickets)
6	Novotel
7	Tourist Office
8	Restaurant Pizza Oasis
9	Ethiopian Airlines
10	Alliance Française, Boulangerie-Pâtisserie Trianon
11	Aux Délices Restaurant
12	Hôtel Burundi Palace
13	Air Tanzania
14	American Cultural Center
15	Restaurant Aux Beaux Lilas, Airlines' Agent
16	Aeroflot
17	New Tourist Hôtel
18	Banque de la République du Burundi
19	Banque du Crédit de Bujumbura, Sabena
20	Post Office
21	Market & Minibuses
22	Banque Commerciale du Burundi, American Embassy
23	Zaïre & Rwanda Embassies
24	Hôtel Résidence
25	Tanzanian Embassy

mission, but there are only three buses each morning and afternoon. It's easier to get a minibus (from the main bus stand) to Kamenge. These leave frequently. Get off at the large road junction where there are the petrol stations and ask for directions to Johnson's – about a 500-metre walk.

If you're coming into Bujumbura on a bus from Kayanza or Bugarama, ask to be let off at the large road junction at Kamenge.

Another place to pitch a tent is at the yacht club (Cercle Nautique) on the lake shore, a 15-minute walk from the city centre, but if you don't eat and drink there, you'll have to pay for the site.

For regular hotels, the cheapest are in the suburb of Mbwiza, about 10 minutes' walk north-west of the city centre and 15 minutes east of the port. It's a fairly depressed district, with car bodies rusting in the dirt streets, inadequate drainage and an air of neglect. None of the streets is signposted, but 6th Ave

is the one which runs alongside the BP station, almost opposite the small post office on Chaussée du Peuple Burundi. Fifth Ave is the next one back towards the city centre, alongside the FINA station.

The cheapest of the habitable places is the *Hôtel Panama* on 5th Ave. Singles/doubles cost BFr 850/1250 and are basic but OK.

The *Au Château Fort Hôtel* is also on 5th Ave, a couple of blocks further from Chaussée du Peuple Burundi. It has a variety of rooms, ranging from BFr 630 for a cupboard to BFr 1250 for a double. There are so many security grilles and gates that the place seems like a prison. It also makes you wonder about the likelihood of getting out in a hurry if there was a fire.

A better place on the same street is the *New Bwiza Hôtel*, which charges BFr 800 for a single or BFr 1200 for a couple in the same room; there are no doubles. It's a friendly place and has mosquito netting on the windows.

If you can afford the extra, the friendly *Hôtel Au Bon Accueil*, on 6th Ave in Mbwiza, is well worth it. The rooms are all upstairs and have outward-facing windows which catch any breeze that's going. The communal bathroom facilities are kept reasonably clean and there's a good bar and restaurant downstairs. Singles/doubles cost BFr 1500/3000. If it's not busy and you are catching the MV *Liemba* at 4 pm, staff will often let you keep the room until 3 pm.

The *Hôtel Résidence* (☎ 23886) is close to the city centre and has a variety of rooms, ranging from BFr 2800 (no balcony) to BFr 3000 (with balcony) a double, plus 50% if you are two people of the same sex sharing a room.

Places to Stay – middle

The cheapest place to stay in the city centre is the *Hôtel Burundi Palace*, which has singles/doubles for BFr 2450/3150 plus BFr 1200 for an extra bed.

The *New Tourist Hôtel*, Place de l'Indépendence, has been renovated and charges BFr 3000 for a single or a double.

Up slightly in price is the *Hôtel de*

BURUNDI

l'Amitié, Rue de l'Amitié, which has self-contained rooms with fan, mosquito nets, soap and towel for BFr 3500 a double. The hotel has its own restaurant but the food is mediocre.

Better is the *Hôtel le Doyen*, Ave du Stade, a splendid colonial-style building set in beautiful grounds. All rooms have mosquito nets, and soap and towel are provided. Rooms with twin beds but shared showers and toilets cost BFr 3000 a double, or there are self-contained rooms for BFr 5000 a double. There are also self-contained, air-con doubles for BFr 8000. The hotel has a good restaurant but it's not cheap. Nonresidents can also eat and drink here.

Places to Stay – top end

The *Novotel*, Chaussée du Peuple Burundi, is the best hotel in Bujumbura and has all the facilities you would expect in a hotel belonging to this chain. As elsewhere in the world, you're looking at at least US$100 per night.

There's also the *Hôtel Club des Vacances* on the lake shore, which is popular at weekends with the local expatriate population. Entry to the beach costs BFr 500 and there's a nightclub as well. A taxi from the city centre costs about BFr 500.

Places to Eat – cheap

If you're staying in Mbwiza and want to eat basic African street food, try the *Restaurant des Jeunes*, behind the FINA petrol station on Chaussée du Peuple Burundi. It's as basic as you can get, but the food is fine and very cheap – rice and beans cost BFr 100, or try potato, plantains and spinach. No English is spoken, so you need to know the food names in Swahili.

On almost every corner in Mbwiza there seems to be a makeshift stall selling brochettes, though the hygiene at some places leaves a lot to be desired. Also in Mbwiza is the *New Nusura Restaurant* on 7th Ave.

We heard bad reports about the *Restaurant Aux Beaux Lilas*, Ave du Commerce, in the city centre. It has apparently become expensive and many items on the menu are missing, but people still eat here.

A good place for excellent coffee and home-made ice cream is the *Café Polar* on Chaussée Prince Rwagasore, one block back from Ave du Zaïre. Coffee costs BFr 50, ice cream BFr 100 and a tortilla BFr 250 (very filling). They also have hamburgers.

The *Cotton Club*, in the Asian part of town, has cheap food and good rock or folk music all the time. Don't be late, as food runs out early.

Super-Snack-Sympa, behind the market, has good pizzas, lasagna and a special 'hamburger', all with vegetables, cream and tortilla bread, for US$1.50.

Very popular not only with travellers but with local people is the *Acapulco* on the corner of Blvd de l'UPRONA and Caussée du Peuple Burundi, next door to the Hôtel Burundi Palace. It's very good, quite cheap and serves Western-style food.

For travellers staying at the Vugizu Mission in Kamenge, there's a place selling kebabs on the main road where you catch the buses to Bujumbura. The kebabs sell for US$0.50.

About one km further along the same road are several nice, cheap bars. There's also the *Mukate Papa* restaurant, which is good value.

Places to Eat – more expensive

The *Boulangerie-Pâtisserie Trianon* on Chaussée Prince Rwagasore is a popular place for breakfast. For good snacks and main meals, the nearby *Aux Délices* is also popular, though the main attraction seems to be the video rather than the food. Meals are from BFr 1000 to BFr 1500 and snacks range from BFr 500 to BFr 1000. The service is not exactly fast as the waiters also find the video interesting.

Back in Mbwiza, the *Hôtel Au Bon Accueil* has a good restaurant and bar. The back lawn becomes a very pleasant beer garden and al fresco restaurant in the evening. Cold Primus beer costs BFr 200.

For a splurge, you could do worse than try the *Restaurant Pizza Oasis* on the corner of Ave Victoire and Blvd de l'UPRONA. It's open Monday to Saturday from noon till

2 pm and 7 to 10 pm, and is expensive. Also expensive is the *Cercle Nautique* (☎ 2559) on the lake front at the end of Ave du 13 Octobre. You can eat very well here for between BFr 800 and BFr 1000 whilst enjoying the views, which include the occasional hippo. It's a great place to sip a cold beer even if you don't want to eat. The Cercle is open daily, except Tuesday, from 5 pm and on Sunday from 11 am.

Entertainment
Most nightclubs are by the lake shore in the vicinity of the Hôtel Club des Vacances. The best ones are the *Black & White* and the *Bamboo*. A taxi from the city centre costs about BFr 500; it's not safe to walk.

By far the best and safest beach is at **Resha**, where there are no crocodiles, hippos or risk of catching bilharzia. It's usually deserted and the sand is almost white and very clean. Resha is one hour from Bujumbura by car but there are also buses available. The one hotel here offers self-contained, circular thatched huts, with electricity until 10 pm. The huts cost BFr 5000 and mosquito nets are provided. The hotel also has a restaurant, but the service is slow and the food is not exactly cheap.

Getting There & Around
Air Air France (☎ 26310) has its main office on Blvd Lumumba and a branch office in the Novotel. The Air Tanzania office is also in the city centre on Place de l'Indépendence. The Sabena office is on Blvd Lumumba near the corner of Ave de la Croix Rouge. Other airlines, such as Kenya Airways, are represented by the travel agent on Ave du Commerce. The international airport is 11 km from the city.

Car If you're thinking of hiring a car, ask for Freddy, whose sister is one of the receptionists at the Hôtel le Doyen. He has a convertible Suzuki Samurai which he rents out for around BFr 9000 per day – less if you hire it for more than a few days.

Other Towns

GITEGA
Gitega is the second largest town in Burundi and is home to the National Museum. Although small, the museum is well worth a visit and is very educational. Entry is free. There might be a folklore performance – ask if the *tambourinaires* are playing. They usually play at Gishola, about 10 km away, on the last Sunday of every month.

A good day trip from Gitega is to the **Chutes de la Kagera**, near Rutana. They're spectacular in the wet season (October to January) but there's no public transport there, so you'll have to hitch. There's a Catholic mission here where you can stay.

Places to Stay & Eat
The *Mission Catholique* has a huge guesthouse and is probably the best place to enquire for budget accommodation.

A good place to eat here is the *Foyer Culturel*, which does good, cheap food but has slow service. For a small splurge, the Pakistani restaurant in the town centre is excellent value for money.

KAYANZA
Kayanza is on the road north to Kigali, near the Rwandan border. It has a good market on Monday, Wednesday and Saturday.

The missions won't take guests, so stay at the *Auberge de Kayanza*, which costs BFr 960 a double.

Matatus from Bujumbura cost BFr 300 and take about two hours. See the Getting There & Away section earlier in this chapter for details on getting from Kayanza to the Rwandan border.

KILEMBA
The principal attraction here is the **Kibabi Hot Springs**, 16 km from town. There are several pools of differing temperature, the main one hovering around 100°C. A little further uphill is a waterfall, and another deep pool where it's safe to swim.

BURUNDI

Most people stay at the *Swedish Pentecostal Mission*, which has a very good guesthouse. A bed in the dormitory costs BFr 200. Private rooms with a shower and toilet and the use of a fully equipped kitchen cost BFr 800 per person.

SOURCE DU NIL

This is supposedly the southernmost source of the Nile, though Ugandans dispute this. It is no more than a trickle – not exactly a riveting sight. You can stay at the *Mission Catholique* in Rutana, seven km away.

Warning
Because of instability, political uncertainty and in some cases military action, travellers planning to visit this region are advised to check with the appropriate authority before leaving home, and/or with their diplomatic representatives abroad. ■

BURUNDI

Eastern Zaïre

This section covers the southern jungles of the region north to northern as of Lake Tanga-nyika to Lake Albert. See Section above. Zaïre would not be appro-borders with Burundi, Rwanda, only a small part of Kivu is included in this book... and many of the natural integral part of the major... have taken place in the from the western wall of the... Valley... also considerably easier to get to from... Africa than from the west coast, which with everyone on the nearby borders.

Eastern Zaïre are an issue magnificent in our...

Eastern Zaïre

This section covers a narrow strip of eastern Zaïre from the northern tip of Lake Tanganyika to Lake Mobutu Sese Seko, along the borders with Burundi, Rwanda and Uganda. It is included in this book because it is an integral part of the mountainous area that forms the western wall of the Rift Valley. It is also considerably easier to get to from East Africa than from the west coast, which entails a journey through the jungles of the Congo Basin.

A full history of Zaïre would not be appropriate, since only a small part of Kivu Province is covered and many of the historical events which have taken place in the western parts of Zaïre have no connection with events on the eastern borders.

Eastern Zaïre has some magnificent coun-

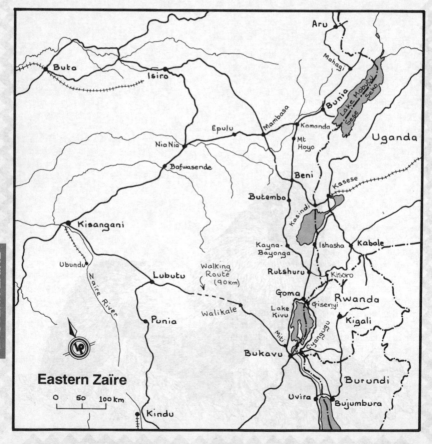

Eastern Zaïre

0   50   100 km

tryside and many things to see and do, such as mountain treks, and visits to gorilla and chimpanzee sanctuaries and Pygmy settlements.

Facts about the Country

HISTORY

Because of the altitude and the fertile soil in eastern Zaïre, the Belgian colonialists developed many coffee plantations early in the 20th century. They also built up the lake resort towns of Bukavu and Goma and several mountain retreats further north. These days it is Mobutu, president of Zaïre since 1965, and his cronies who maintain summer palaces here, partly to ensure that their presence is felt in this far-flung corner of the country.

Mobutu, however, is not alone in wanting to maintain a presence here. In few other areas of East Africa will you encounter so much Christian missionary activity. The number of different sects hard at work saving souls is little short of amazing. The whole range of Catholic and Protestant sects are involved, as are the ubiquitous Seventh Day Adventists, Mormons and Jehovah's Witnesses. It's probably a good thing that they have chosen to work this area so intensively, as their schools and hospitals provide many people with their only educational and medical facilities. Few funds are available for these sorts of facilities from the central government and, because Mobuto's regime is so corrupt, the funds shrink every year.

In the early years following independence in 1960, there was very little direct control of Kivu Province by the central government in Kinshasa and, consequently, local governors enjoyed virtual autonomy. The attempted secession by the southern province of Shaba (formerly Katanga) under Moise Tshombe, and the subsequent intervention by the United Nations is well known. These events prompted the overthrow and murder of Zaïre's first prime minister, Patrice Lumumba, and his replacement by

Joseph Kasavubu with assistance from Mobutu, the army commander at the time. What is less well known is that after the Katangan secession had been crushed, Kasavubu was faced with armed revolt by the governors of the eastern provinces, including Kivu Province. His failure to crush the rebellion and bring the governors to book led to his overthrow by Mobutu in 1965.

Mobutu has certainly restored a high level of centralised control to Zaïre, but the costs in terms of wasted resources, repression, jailings, executions, corruption and a decaying infrastructure have been enormous.

It is unlikely that Mobutu will be replaced until he dies though the pressure is definitely on both internally and internationally. He is a cunning and ruthless politician who has perfected a personality cult in a way few other African presidents have been able to match. These days he rules as a half god, half-chieftain, combining the sophisticated techniques of 20th-century communication with traditional tribal symbolism. His photograph is to be seen everywhere, often accompanied by one of the many slogans underlining his indispensability and benevolence, such as 'Mobutu: The Unifier', 'Mobutu: The Pacifier' and 'Mobutu: The Guide'. It would almost be a comic opera if it weren't so serious, as one day the people of Zaïre will have to pay for the extravagance, corruption and neglect.

In many ways, the pressure being applied internationally on Mobutu, especially by the USA, France and Belgium, is hypocritical: it was principally these countries which bankrolled his avarice for decades and then suddenly, when human rights became flavour of the month, demanded that he step down. In the intervening period, it's estimated that Mobutu amassed a personal fortune equal to Zaïre's foreign debt.

But it can't last forever as the country literally falls apart. There are serious power conflicts between Mobutu and the prime minister, Etienne Tshisekedi, and between both of these and the army commander, General Marc Bokungu. When Mobutu authorised the issue of a Z 5,000,000 banknote in early 1993, Tshisekedi promptly declared it illegal tender. Traders, therefore, refused to accept it. Unfortunately, it was in these Z 5,000,000 notes that the troops were paid. Faced with fistfuls of worthless paper, they rioted and, in the process, trashed and looted many cities, including Kinshasa, Goma and Bukavu. Large areas of these cities arc now in virtual ruin and economic activity has ground to a halt.

Embassies in East Africa will warn you not to go to Zaïre because of the serious security problems and the real danger of being robbed at gunpoint by rebellious troops. They're not wrong, but they're not entirely right either. Life doesn't come to a halt just because troops loot and riot. Food still has to be grown and money made, and people move from one place to another. And where there's money to be made, local people will look after their vested interests.

This is precisely the situation in eastern Zaïre, where the gorillas, chimpanzees and mountain climbing generate handsome incomes from visitors. At present, it's safe to visit the gorilla sanctuaries, though we can't promise you that you won't be fleeced for all you've got by troops who, effectively, haven't been paid for months. Just stay out of the towns and keep a low profile. The political situation must improve, but it could well get worse before it gets better.

GEOGRAPHY

Geographically this area is quite different from the rest of Zaïre. It is a land of huge volcanoes and vast, deep lakes. Some of the volcanoes, such as those at the northern end of Lake Kivu, have erupted in the last decade and Nyiragongo is still smoking, but the rest are currently dormant. Others, where the borders of Zaïre, Rwanda and Uganda meet, haven't erupted in living memory and their upper slopes are among the last remaining sanctuaries for the rare mountain gorilla.

The Ruwenzori Mountains along the border with Uganda are the highest in the region and the only ones with permanent snow cover on the peaks. These are not typical, as they are not volcanic. It's a wild and beautiful area of Africa.

CLIMATE

Eastern Zaïre enjoys a Mediterranean climate. This is one reason, apart from the magnificent views and water sports, why those with sufficient money (including the president) have made Goma and Bukavu, on Lake Kivu, into resort towns. The seasons are similar to those in Rwanda and Burundi. The main rainy season is from mid-March to mid-May and the dry season is from mid-May to mid-September. The short rains last from mid-September to mid-December and the short dry season from mid-December to mid-March.

GOVERNMENT

Executive power is held by the president, who has a seven-year mandate and the right to appoint a prime minister of his choice, though this is disputed and has led to serious riots and the virtual collapse of central government. The legislative council (parliament) consists of 210 deputies elected for a five-year term by universal suffrage. The only legal political party is the Mouvement Populaire de la Révolution (MPR). In practice, both the government and law and order have collapsed and the country is in chaos. The former government and the opposition are at each other's throats and an early resolution of the conflict is highly unlikely.

ECONOMY

Zaïre is potentially a rich country, with a huge array of natural resources. Unfortunately the years of colonial mismanagement and exploitation, followed by civil war, corruption and inefficiency, have prevented this potential being fulfilled. The country's vast size (Zaïre is the third-largest country in Africa) and its inadequate transport infrastructure have exacerbated the problems. Subsistence agriculture is the basis of most people's existence.

Copper, cobalt, oil, diamonds (Zaïre is the world's largest producer of industrial diamonds) and coffee account for the bulk of

Zaïre's export income. The country is at the mercy of world prices for these products. In particular, its dependency on copper led to an economic crisis when the copper price collapsed in 1975.

The agricultural sector contributes about 30% of GDP. Of that, 50% is subsistence farming, employing about 70% of the workforce. The main subsistence crops include cassava, maize and rice. With the terrible infrastructure, supplies are basically limited to urban areas. Zaïre was once self-sufficient in foodstuffs but now imports more than 125,000 tonnes each year. Cash crops include coffee, cocoa, rubber, tea, palm oil, cotton, sugar and tobacco.

POPULATION

Zaïre's population of about 35 million is divided between more than 200 tribes, several of which extend into neighbouring countries. Eastern Zaïre is one of the few areas in Africa where there are significant numbers of Twa people (the Pygmies). The forest-dwelling Twa have resisted attempts to integrate them into the wider economy, and many continue their nomadic, hunting and gathering existence. Tourist curiosity, on the other hand, has sadly commercialised many of these people.

LANGUAGE

The official language is French, but Swahili is widely spoken in Kivu Province. Most army personnel speak Lingala but this isn't widely known outside the army. Very little English is spoken. The following is a list of words and phrases in Lingala:

Greetings & Civilities

hello	mbote
What's new?	Sangonini?
nothing new	sangote
OK/thanks	malam

Useful Words & Phrases

go	nake
depart	kokende
Where?	Wapi?
Where are...?	Okeyi wapi...?
Why?	ponanini?
very far	musika
tomorrow	lobi
house	ndako
home	mboka
strong	makasi
a lot	mingi
new	sango
dog	mbwa

Food & Drink

to eat	kolia
to drink	komela
things to eat	biloko yakolia
water	mai
manioc	songo
bananas	makemba
rice	loso
beans	madeso
salted fish	makaibo
fresh fish	mbisi
meat	nyama
peanuts	injunga karanga
market	nazondo

Facts for the Visitor

VISAS & EMBASSIES

Visas are required by all visitors to Zaïre, and Zaïrian visas are some of the most expensive in the world. Transit visas (three days) cost US$45. A one-month single-entry tourist visa costs US$75 (US$120 for multiple entry), a two-month single-entry visa costs US$135 (US$180 multiple entry), a three-month single-entry visa costs US$200 (US$225 multiple entry) and a six-month single-entry visa costs US$270 (US$360 multiple entry). Visas take 24 hours to issue.

All visa applications must be accompanied by a letter of introduction from your own embassy (except in Bangui, Harare and Kasese). Some embassies issue these free but others charge for them. British embassies charge about US$10. You may also be asked for an onward ticket and vaccination certificates (cholera and yellow fever) but this isn't normal.

You don't need a visa if you simply wish to hop over the border from Kisoro (Uganda) to visit the gorillas at Djomba and return the following day. In that case, you pay US$50 to immigration at the border, leave your passport with them and collect it the following day. It's a scam to make money but it's cheaper than buying a normal one-month single-entry tourist visa.

Zaïrian Embassies
In Africa, visas can be obtained from Zaïrian embassies in Abidjan (Ivory Coast), Accra (Ghana), Addis Ababa (Ethiopia), Algiers (Algeria), Bangui (Central African Republic), Brazzaville (Congo), Bujumbura (Burundi), Cairo (Egypt), Conakry (Guinea), Cotonou (Benin), Dakar (Senegal), Dar es Salaam and Kigoma (Tanzania), Harare (Zimbabwe), Kampala and Kasese (Uganda), Khartoum (Sudan), Kigali (Rwanda), Lagos (Nigeria), Libreville (Gabon), Lomé (Togo), Luanda (Angola), Lusaka (Zambia), Maputo (Mozambique), Monrovia (Liberia), Nairobi (Kenya), Nouakchott (Mauritania), N'Djamena (Chad), Rabat (Morocco), Tripoli (Libya), Tunis (Tunisia) and Yaoundé (Cameroon).

Outside Africa, there are Zaïrian embassies in Berlin and Bonn (Germany), London (UK), Madrid (Spain), Paris (France), Rome (Italy) and Washington DC (USA).

Burundi The Zaïrian Embassy is on Ave du Zaïre in Bujumbura. Visas cost the same as in other countries, require three photos and are issued in 24 hours. The embassy is open from 8.30 am to noon only.

Kenya The Zaïrian Embassy (☎ 229771) is at Electricity House, Harambee Ave, Nairobi. Four photographs and a letter of introduction from your own embassy are required and the visa is issued in 24 hours. Staff are pleasant and the embassy is open Monday to Friday from 8.30 am till 12.45 pm and 2 to 5 pm.

Rwanda In Kigali, the embassy (☎ 75327) is on Rue Député Kamuzinzi off Ave de Rusumo. Three photographs are required for any visa, which is issued in 24 hours. A letter of recommendation from your own embassy is generally not needed, nor is an onward ticket.

There are no Zaïrian consulates in either Gisenyi or Cyangugu.

Tanzania In Dar es Salaam, the Zaïrian Embassy is on Malik Rd near the junction with United Nations Rd. You will need three photographs and a letter of introduction from your own embassy. Visas take 24 hours to be issued. The embassy is open Monday to Friday from 8 am to 3 pm.

There's also a Zaïrian consulate in Kigoma, on Lake Tanganyika. Office hours are Monday to Friday from 9 am till noon.

Uganda The embassy (☎ 233777) is at 20 Philip Rd, Kololo. It's open Monday to Friday from 8 am to 3 pm, though visa applications are only accepted before noon. You need a letter of introduction from your own embassy and three photos, and the visa is issued in 24 hours.

Foreign Embassies in Zaïre
Burundi The consulate in Bukavu is in the SINELAC building, top floor, 184 Ave du Président Mobutu. The consulate is open Monday to Friday from 7.30 am till noon and 2.30 to 5 pm.

Rwanda There are no Rwandan consulates at either Bukavu or Goma in eastern Zaïre, so it's advisable to get your visa in Kinshasa (or elsewhere) if you're coming from the west. Several travellers have reported that it's possible to get a *permis provisoire* (a type of transit visa), valid for one week, for about US$46 on demand at the Goma (Zaïre) and Gisenyi (Rwanda) border crossing. Alternatively, assuming you have the time, get a tourist visa from the Belgian Consulate in Goma for about US$17. The latter takes two weeks to be issued and you have to leave your passport with them. The same may be true for the Belgian Consulate in Bukavu.

The regulations change constantly, so don't rely on this possibility.

It's probably wise to have both Rwandan and Zaïrian multiple-entry visas if you intend to go by road between Bukavu and Bujumbura, as there are a couple of alternatives and a multiple-entry visa gives you flexibility. On the other hand, the latest reports indicate that Rwandan transit visas are available at the border for RFr 1600.

Kenya, Tanzania & Uganda There are no consulates for these countries in eastern Zaïre (the embassies are in the capital Kinshasa in the west). The nearest embassies are in Kigali (Rwanda) and Bujumbura (Burundi).

MONEY
Currency
The unit of currency is the zaïre, and incidentally, there are no surplus zeros on the exchange rate (mid-1993) given below.

Exchange Rates
US$1 = Z 2,500,000

The Zaïrian financial system is in total chaos and the inflation rate is astronomical. By the time you read this, it could be double the above exchange rate. What this means to travellers in eastern Zaïre is that you pay for everything in US dollars or Ugandan shillings. Zaïres are still acceptable but no-one wants them. They're toilet paper.

The largest denomination banknote which is acceptable is Z 1,000,000. Do not accept Z 5,000,000 banknotes (except as souvenirs). The president says they're legal tender; the prime minister says they're not. Traders will not accept them. Troops who were paid in Z 5,000,000 notes rioted and trashed Goma and Bukavu in early 1993.

It's obviously a ridiculous situation which cannot last much longer, but whilst it does, you'll have to wear it.

Changing Money
If you need zaïres, you'll have to change on the street because most banks simply don't have enough banknotes to change a travellers' cheque or a hard currency banknote. This is no problem and no-one will arrest you – it's completely acceptable.

The easiest way to get your head around this exchange rate nightmare (and keep pace with inflation) is to buy a bottle of Primus beer. This always costs around US$1 regardless of any other factors. After that, forget about zaïres and think in terms of bottles of Primus. It saves a lot of mental energy.

Currency declaration forms are not issued anywhere, except in Bukavu (when they have them, though no-one will ask for them when you leave).

BUSINESS HOURS & HOLIDAYS
January
   New Year's Day (1st)
   Day of the Martyrs for Independence (4th)
May
   Labour Day (1st)
   MPR Day (20th)
June
   Zaïre Day (24th)
   Independence (30th)
August
   Parents' Day (1st)
   (14th)
October
   President's Birthday (14th)
   (27th)
November
   Armed Forces Day (17th)
   Anniversary of the New Regime (24th)
December
   Christmas Day (25th)

POST
There's a small charge for each letter collected from poste restante.

TIME
Eastern Zaïre is GMT/UTC plus two hours.

HEALTH
Take precautions against malaria. If you stay in Zaïre a long time, you could pick it up. I've met very few American Peace Corps volunteers in Zaïre who haven't had at least one bout of malaria, despite the fact they were taking prophylactics.

Tap water is not safe to drink, so purify it first.

Another condition you might pick up, especially if you only wear thongs, is jiggers (tropical fleas which burrow under your skin). Get them pulled out at a clinic. They're easy to remove if you know what you're doing.

FILM & PHOTOGRAPHY

Bring all your film requirements to Zaïre. About the only places where you can buy film are Bukavu and Goma, and it's expensive. Check the expiry date carefully.

Since all civil servants are strapped for cash, immigration and customs officials may demand that you buy a 'photography permit' when you enter. This is nothing more than an unbridled act of creativity on their part but what can you do about it? Basically, you pay or you waste half the day messing around. You might even get your visa cancelled. Don't argue: pay the 'fee' and get moving. You won't encounter this at Bunagana on the Uganda-Zaïre border (between Kisoro and Rutshuru) – after all, you will already have paid them US$50 for a temporary 'visa' to visit the gorillas!

Warning Don't take photographs of anything vaguely connected with the military or of government buildings, banks, bridges, border posts, post offices or ports. If anyone sees you, the chances are you'll have your film confiscated and you'll have to pay a 'fine'.

Getting There & Away

AIR

The national airline, Air Zaïre, flies into Goma from Kinshasa and Kisangani on an irregular basis but it frequently gets diverted. Essentially, the airline caters to the requirements of the president and various other ministers. The president's wife recently commandeered one of the jets to transport

several *tonnes* of shopping back from France to Zaïre.

In other words, never rely on Air Zaïre. It's often quicker to go overland. Also, while the political uncertainties remain in Zaïre, no other airline is flying into Goma.

LAND

To/From Burundi

There are two routes to Zaïre from Burundi.

Bujumbura to Bukavu via Cyangugu (Rwanda) This route goes from Bujumbura via the Burundi-Rwanda border at Bugarama to Cyangugu in Rwanda, from where it's just a short hop across the Zaïre border into Bukavu. See the Rwanda Getting There & Away section for details on the Bujumbura to Cyangugu leg. For details of the Cyangugu-Bukavu border crossing, see To/From Rwanda in this section.

Bujumbura to Bukavu via Uvira (Zaïre) The second route goes from Bujumbura to Bukavu via Uvira (in Zaïre, just across the border from Bujumbura). This route has two variations: the first (and less comfortable) is the direct road between Uvira and Bukavu (see the Bukavu section); the second, also from Uvira to Bukavu, goes mostly through Rwanda to make use of the far superior Rwandan roads. To take this route you'll need a Rwandan visa, and a multiple-entry Zaïrian visa to re-enter Zaïre. In the past, border formalities have sometimes been dispensed with so that officially, you never left Zaïre. This was because the amount of time you spent in Rwanda was minimal and you had no intention of staying in that country. This doesn't seem to happen any more, so check that you have the necessary visa stamps. If you do have a Rwandan visa, the best bet is to use the route direct from Bujumbura to Bukavu via Bugarama and Cyangugu anyway. You certainly don't miss anything by bypassing Uvira.

To/From Rwanda

The two main crossing points between Rwanda and Zaïre are between Gisenyi and

Goma and between Cyangugu and Bukavu. These borders are open for non-Africans from 6 am to 6 pm.

Gisenyi to Goma There are two border crossing points between Gisenyi and Goma – the Poids Lourds crossing (a rough road) along the main road north of the ritzy part of Gisenyi, and a scaled road along the lake shore. It's between two and three km either way.

The easier of the two routes is along the lake shore, but you'll have to take a taxi (RFr 350) or a taxi-motor (RFr 50) or walk to it. I strolled through this border at 7.30 am one morning and was in Goma within five minutes! The officials at the Poids Lourds post are apparently not quite as amenable.

From either post, once on the Zaïre side it's a couple of km into Goma. Motorcycles are available if you don't want to walk.

Cyangugu to Bukavu Cyangugu is the actual border post here, but Kamembe is the town and transport centre and is where you'll be dropped off if arriving from elsewhere in Rwanda. From here, there are minibuses (RFr 30) for the 15-minute ride to the border at Cyangugu. It's an easy border crossing and you can walk between the two posts. From the Zaïre side, you can either take a taxi or walk the three km into Bukavu.

To/From Uganda
The two main crossing points are south from Kisoro to Rutshuru via Bunagana and north-west from Kasese to Beni via Katwe, Bwera and Kasindi. The Ishasha crossing between Kasese and Rutshuru is another possibility which quite a few travellers use. There are less-used border posts further north, between Mahagi and Pakwach and between Aru and Arua. If you're thinking of crossing between Aru and Arua, you'd be wise to make enquiries about the situation before leaving, as your security cannot be guaranteed.

Kisoro to Rutshuru The most reliable and frequently used crossing is between Kisoro and Rutshuru via Bunagana, a distance of

about 30 km. This is the crossing used by travellers who want to hop across the border into Zaïre for two days, see the gorillas at Djomba and return to Uganda the following day. Hundreds of people do this every year, the border officials are very familiar with it, and formalities are minimal.

There are crowded matatus/pick-ups from Kisoro to the border (nine km) for USh 1500. At the border, you go through Ugandan customs and immigration (no hassles), then the same through Zaïrian customs and immigration, which is right next door (again, no hassles). From here to Rutshuru, it's a rough road and transport is minimal. There are occasional minibuses and pick-ups but nothing regular, so you will probably have to hitch.

If you just want to see the gorillas at Djomba and return to Uganda the following day, you don't need a Zaïrian visa. You simply give the Zaïrian immigration officials US$50, leave your passport with them and walk to Djomba. After seeing the gorillas, you walk back to the border, collect your passport and re-enter Uganda (a visa costs US$20, unless you already have a multiple-entry visa).

Kasese to Rutshuru The Ishasha border between Katunguru and Rutshuru is less reliable. There's a steady trickle of traffic along this route, so hitching is feasible, and there's even the occasional matatu. There's a market on Fridays at Ishasha, so this is probably the best day to go. The Ugandan customs official stationed at this border post actually lives in Kihihi, so it may be possible to hitch to the border with him. For a place to stay in Kihihi, check out the *Hilltop Lodge*.

Kasese to Beni The route from Kasese to Beni via Katwe, Mpondwe and Kasindi involves hitching, unless you can find a matatu. Again, depending on the day you go, this could involve a considerable wait (hours rather than days), whichever of the two turn-offs you take going west. If you want to take this route, it would be a good idea to make enquiries in Kasese before you set off.

From Kasese, there are occasional matatus to the border post at Bwero, where accommodation is available on the Ugandan side for around US$1 per person at the *Modern Lodge Hotel*. Once across the border, there is accommodation in a basic hotel in Kasindi, and from here there are connections to Beni.

To/From Central Zaïre
Kisangani to Goma & Bukavu The traditional main route between eastern Zaïre and Kisangani, on the Zaïre River, is from Komanda on the Beni to Bunia road, via Mambasa, Epulu, Nia Nia and Bafwasende. There are some diabolical stretches of road en route but it's generally passable, even in the wet season. You're looking at hitching truck rides along this route but you should make it to Kisangani in under three days.

The alternative is the new highway between Kisangani and Bukavu via Lubutu and Walikale, which was due for completion in 1992 (though political unrest may have delayed completion). There's regular transport along this route and journey times are obviously much faster than on the traditional route.

LAKE
To/From Tanzania
SNCZ operates boats from Kalemie to both Uvira and Kigoma, usually once a week. The boat to Uvira generally leaves on Tuesday. For information on these boats in Kigoma, see the stationmaster at the railway station.

Tickets can only be bought the day before departure, early in the morning.

There's another privately owned boat, called the *Lwenge*, owned by a man called Fizi. He has a business in Kalemie called PGC, which is almost opposite the Hotel de la Gare. His boat runs once weekly (usually on Thursday) from Kalemie to Uvira and takes around 36 hours.

Drinks are usually available on board but you must take your own food. Tickets can be bought two to three days in advance of the trip.

Getting Around

AIR
Quite a few private airline companies operate small planes between various places in eastern Zaïre. If you're in a desperate hurry, these might be of interest. Virunga Air Charters (VAC) does the half-hour flight between Goma and Bukavu twice daily. Scibé-Airlift operates a similar service. VAC also flies between Bukavu and Kisangani.

BUS & TRUCK
There are very few regular buses of any description, and most of the time you will have to hitch lifts on trucks. Free lifts are the exception, unless you meet the occasional Somali or Kenyan driver. Usually you will have to pay for lifts, the price often reflecting the difficulty of the journey rather than the

---

Zaïrian Roads
With a few exceptions, getting around Zaïre is an exercise in initiative, imagination, patience, persistence and endurance. It's archetypal Africa and it promises some of the most memorable adventures you're ever likely to experience. To enjoy it and not end up with a frazzled brain, forget your fetish for getting from A to B in a certain time, or for eating food and staying in accommodation of a particular standard. Few things can be guaranteed, nothing runs on time and, in the wet season, you could be stranded for days or even weeks waiting for a lift or for the road to dry out sufficiently to give you a fighting chance of getting through. On the other hand, the beer rarely runs out. Aside from Australia and Germany, there are few countries which place such a high priority on their beer supplies.

Roads are often in a diabolical state of repair, with potholes large enough to swallow a truck, but they do tend to get smoothed out as the dry season progresses. ■

distance but being more or less 'fixed'. This doesn't mean you'll be quoted the price local people pay straight away. Negotiation is the name of the game. There's generally a truck park in every town where drivers congregate, and it's here that you'll find a lift. In small places, it's usually around the petrol station.

Transport on the main route (between Bunia on Lake Mobutu Sese Seko and Uvira on Lake Tanganyika) is more or less guaranteed, but once you leave the main route, you may well have to do a lot of walking. You must be in the right frame of mind to do this, and it helps if you have a light pack. Usually it's quite safe to walk around in this area but, if there are political problems or the troops haven't been paid, your safety cannot be guaranteed. In other words, don't set off uninformed. You may think you're a budget traveller but, to army personnel, you represent a wallet.

There's little point in quoting hitching costs on trucks, since these will change and, to some extent, will depend on your bargaining ability. To get the best price, don't be in a hurry and ask around before you have to leave. Free lifts are available in some places if you can make the contacts, but they're the exception.

BOAT

In theory, there are three boats which ply between Goma and Bukavu on Lake Kivu, but much of the time, at least two of them will be out of service. If they're running, it's a pleasant trip with incomparable views of the Virunga volcanoes across the lake. None of the boats call at Rwandan ports, nor do the Rwandan ferries call at Zaïrian ports.

The boats are the *Karisimbi*, the *Vedette* and the *Mulamba*. The first two are government owned and operated. The *Vedette* is purely a passenger boat, while the *Karisimbi* takes freight, including motorcycles. Both are crowded and not particularly comfortable.

The *Mulamba* is a privately owned vessel which carries beer from the Primus factory in Bukavu to Goma once a week. It is a far more comfortable boat to travel on (if you go

1st class) and is only slightly more expensive than the *Vedette*. The fares on the *Mulamba* are US$15 (1st class) and US$7.50 (2nd class). The 1st-class area is not crowded and there's a small lounge where reasonable meals are served. As you might expect, there's plenty of warm Primus beer for sale! Second class on the *Mulamba* is the cheapest way to cross the lake but it's is crowded and you're exposed to the elements – it's hot and often wet as well.

All three boats take from seven to eight hours to make the crossing. Tickets should be bought a day in advance, so you need to make enquiries in Bukavu or Goma regarding the schedules, which are variable. In Bukavu, tickets for the *Mulamba* can be bought at the ACT office on Ave du Président Mobutu.

Eastern Zaïre from North to South

BUNIA
This large town in the hills above Lake Mobutu Sese Seko is one of the starting points for the trip west to Kisangani via Komanda, Mambasa and Nia Nia.

If you get this far, it's worth making a side trip to the fishing village of **Tshoma**, on the lake, via the border post town of Kasenye. It's a lively village with bars open 24 hours a day to accommodate the fishers' unsocial hours. The hospitality is excellent and the fresh fish very cheap, but unfortunately, it's not safe to swim in the lake because of bilharzia.

Places to Stay & Eat
The *Hôtel Semliki* is a good place to stay. It also serves good food at reasonable prices. Nearby, and similar in price, is the *Hôtel Ituri*. Further down the hill in the *cité* are plenty of other cheapies.

Going up in price, the *Hôtel Rubi*, on the main street, is one of the best. Another that has been recommended is the *Butembo II*. It's friendly and has great food.

Getting There & Away

There are a few buses each week between Goma and Bunia but, as elsewhere in this region, transport is extremely variable.

KOMANDA

Komanda has a small market and a bakery. The *Hôtel LL*, about 50 metres from the monument on the Bunia road, offers spacious, clean rooms. Nearby, several small restaurants serve cheap meat and rice.

Trucks between Epulu and Komanda take eight hours along a very good road.

BENI

Beni is the starting point for climbing the Ruwenzori Mountains from the Zaïre side. Several of the hotels offer excess baggage storage facilities, though you can also leave gear at the park warden's office in Mutsora.

Places to Stay

One of the cheapest places is the *Hôtel Walaba*, about 100 metres down the Kasindi road from the roundabout. It's a good place to meet other travellers, and the Somalian owner, Mohammed, will change money if you're stuck. Both he and the predominantly Ugandan staff speak English. You can leave baggage safely here while you climb the Ruwenzori. They don't mind if you cook your own food, though they also have a cheap restaurant.

Another popular place is the *Hôtel Jumbo*, which offers good rooms with bucket showers but has no electricity. To get there, go down the main street to the roundabout, then walk west about 30 metres; the hotel is on the left. Also good value is the *Hôtel Basmie*, run by friendly Ugandan and Somalian owners. Cheap food is available there. They, too, will store baggage safely while you climb the Ruwenzori.

There are also the *Hôtel Sina Makosa* and the *Hôtel Majestic*, by the roundabout.

For a mid-range hotel, try the *Hôtel Beni* or the *Hôtel Isale*.

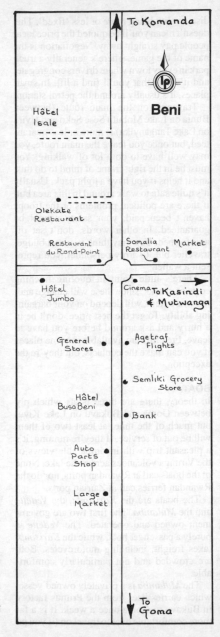

Places to Eat

The restaurant at the *Hôtel Lualaba* offers rice and beans, meat and rice and omelettes. Their bread is baked on the premises.

Good breakfasts are available from the *Restaurant du Rond Point*, on the roundabout. The snacks outside the *Paradisio Club* (a disco) are also recommended.

For a splurge, try the plat du jour (Z 5000) at the *Hôtel Busa Beni*.

Next to the Hôtel Lualaba is a small, well-stocked market. The Semliki Grocery Store has a good range of provisions. This is useful if you're organising a trek up the Ruwenzoris, as there's only a very limited range of foodstuffs at the market in Mutsora.

Getting There & Away

There are frequent pick-ups and minibuses available between Beni and Butembo. In Beni, both the minibuses and trucks leave from the petrol station, which is down the Komanda road from the roundabout. Pick-ups to Komanda take about six hours. Trucks to Mutwanga are also available.

For lifts out of Beni, ask at the CAPACO depot about trucks to Goma. The manager is very friendly and may organise a free lift. The journey often takes about 24 hours.

BUTEMBO

With a population of 100,000, Butembo is a large town about halfway between Goma and Bunia. It has a good market and excellent views of the surrounding countryside.

Places to Stay

Most of the cheapies are near the market. The *Logement Apollo II* has electricity in the evenings and bucket showers. The *Semliki Hôtel*, at the northern end of town on the main road, offers doubles without shower or toilet but does have a good restaurant.

Somewhat more expensive is the *Hôtel Ambiance*. It's very pleasant, with electricity, running water, showers and facilities for washing clothes.

The *Oasis Hôtel*, a deteriorating colonial place displaying a delightful air of neglected elegance, used to be popular but fell apart for

a while when the Belgian owner died in 1987. Things have improved since then and renovations have been undertaken. Excellent meals are available here and there's a bar and disco. Similar is the *Hôtel Kyavagnendi*, 55 Ave Bukavu.

Other travellers have recommended staying at one or other of the three missions close to town.

Places to Eat

Apart from the hotels, the *Restaurant Cafétéria*, near the market, is recommended.

Getting There & Away

There are four buses a week to Goma, depending on breakdowns. The journey takes at least 10 hours.

Hitching a truck ride along this stretch could take two days because of stops en route. If you do decide to hitch, trucks leave from outside a group of shops on the left towards the southern end of the main street.

Between Butembo and Beni, there are frequent pick-ups and minibuses available. The trip takes about five hours. To get to Komanda takes about 14 hours.

KAYNA-BAYONGA

This town is a truck stop on the road between Goma and Butembo, particularly if you're heading south, since drivers are not allowed to travel through the Parc National des Virunga at night. As far as views are concerned, this is to your advantage, as you would otherwise miss the Kabasha Escarpment.

Places to Stay

Although there are a few small places in the town centre, most truck drivers (and thus travellers looking for a lift) stay at the *Hôtel Italie*, about three km north of town. It has clean, concrete toilets and bucket showers (cold water). There's no electricity but kerosene lamps are provided.

Places to Eat

If you stay at the *Hôtel Italie*, you'll probably have to eat there too, though the food is

EASTERN ZAÏRE

relatively expensive. On the other hand, they don't mind cooking for those who arrive late (say, up to 10 pm).

If you stay in the town centre, there are three places where you can pick up food. Two are on the main street but one is really only a bar which has bread. The restaurant on the main street offers the best value, with meat, rice and tea, though the proprietor may try to charge you a tourist price. The other restaurant is down an alley off the main street and has similar food and prices. There's a good daily market if you want to put your own meal together.

Getting There & Away

The bus from Butembo to Goma is supposed to pass through here four times a week, but this depends on breakdowns.

Trucks leave for Goma early in the morning, between 5.30 and 6 am, either from the Hôtel Italie or from the market. Otherwise you'll have to rely on transport passing through from elsewhere.

RUTSHURU

Rutshuru is perhaps the most convenient departure point for a visit to the mountain gorillas in the Parc National des Virunga, where they are found on the slopes of Muside and Sabinyo volcanoes (which Zaïre shares with Rwanda and Uganda). First make your way to Djomba (sometimes spelt Jomba). The turn-off for this place is about two km south of Rutshuru and is clearly signposted.

If you're coming from or going to Uganda, you will probably also come through Rutshuru, unless you are going to cross the border further north between Beni and Kasese via Kasindi.

Places to Stay & Eat

Probably the best place to stay in Rutshuru is the *Catholic Mission Guest House*, about four km outside town. It's a friendly place and costs around US$3 per night per person. Showers and meals are available and you may be able to camp in the mission grounds free of charge.

A cheaper option is the unnamed *lodging*

house about 50 metres north of the police station on the opposite side of the road. It has basic rooms, bucket showers and an earth toilet. The owner is very friendly and may help you find transport.

The *Hôtel Gremafu*, close to the truck park, is very clean but has no electricity or running water. Bucket showers and candles are provided. There's a bar, and meals of meat, chips and salad are available at a reasonable price if you order an hour in advance. It's just beyond the truck park (on the main street) at the northern end of town and off to the right. It's possible to leave excess baggage here if you want to see the gorillas or Rwindi National Park.

Getting There & Away

There is a daily bus to and from Goma which takes about two hours. You can also hitch with a truck for about the same price, though, in this case, it's advisable to make an early start (say 5 am), as breakdowns and/or punctures often prolong the journey. To get to Butembo in a pick-up takes about 11 hours.

It's also possible to hitch to the Ugandan border and head for Kisoro. There's a basic hotel at the border. (See the Uganda Getting There & Away chapter.)

GOMA

Goma sits at the foot of the brooding Nyiragongo Volcano at the northern end of Lake Kivu. This is not far from the chain of volcanoes which make up the Parc National des Virunga, on the border between Zaïre and Rwanda. Like Bukavu, Goma is an important business, government and resort town and has a fairly cosmopolitan population. There's quite a contrast between the ritzy landscaped villas down by the lake shore and the cité behind it. President Mobutu maintains a palatial villa, but keep away from it.

Unfortunately, Goma was trashed and looted by rioting troops in early 1993 after they were paid with Z 5,000,000 banknotes, which traders refused to accept after the prime minister declared them illegal tender. Many foreigners abandoned their businesses

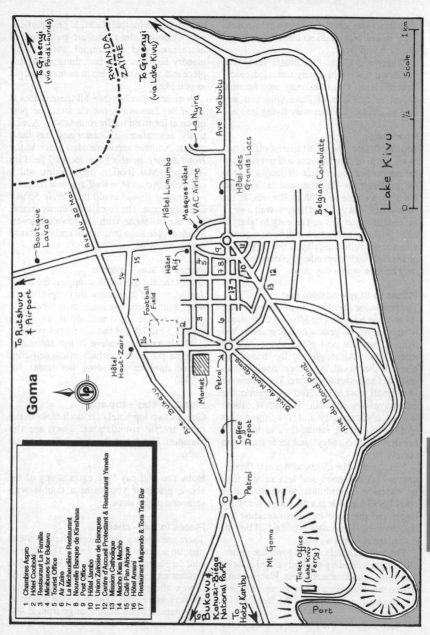

Goma

1   Chambres Aspro
2   Hôtel Cocholi
3   Restaurant La Famille
4   Minibuses for Bukavu
5   Tourist Office
6   Air Zaïre
7   La Michaudière Restaurant
8   Nouvelle Banque de Kinshasa
9   Post Office
10 Hôtel Jambo
11 Union Zaïroise de Banques
12 Centre d'Accueil Protestant & Restaurant Yeneka
13 Mission Catholique
14 Macho Kwa Macho
15 Café Pan Afrique
16 Hôtel Amani
17 Restaurant Mupendo & Tora Tina Bar

after this experience and have yet to return. They're unlikely to do so until the political situation improves.

Otherwise, Goma is a dusty, somewhat run-down town with many unsealed roads. Nevertheless, it has the only international airport in this part of Zaïre (not that any foreign airlines are presently flying into it).

Information

Tourist Office The small tourist office one block north of Ave Mobutu and not far from the post office is the place to book a visit to the gorillas in the Parc National des Virunga. It's also possible to book at Rwindi, at the radio shack, but you may have to wait a week for confirmation. It's just as easy to take pot luck, go direct to Djomba and book a gorilla visit for the following day at the park headquarters though, depending on demand, you may have to wait a day or so.

Places to Stay – bottom end

The best value for money in this category are the mission hostels. The *Mission Catholique* is an anonymous yellow building about 300 metres from the post office along Ave du Rond Point. Although not the friendliest place in the world, it's exceptionally clean and quiet and is totally secure. The rooms are very small, cost US$3.20/6 a single/double and have a washbasin. Breakfast (about US$1) is definitely not for big eaters (coffee/tea, bread, sausage). The hostel is usually full on Sundays and there's a 10 pm curfew.

Next door is the *Centre d'Accueil Protestant*, which is a good deal less austere than its Catholic neighbour. Accommodation costs US$9 a double but the rooms are much larger and the price includes breakfast and hot showers. The hostel is often full but the restaurant is worth a visit.

The budget hotels in this town are generally characterised by their advanced state of decrepitude and uncleanliness. Places which fit into this category are the *Chambres Aspro*, the *Macho kwa Macho* and the *Hôtel Haut-Zaïre*.

Much better is the *Hôtel Coaboki*, at the bottom of the football field. It's not particularly clean but the toilets are passable and there are good communal shower and laundry facilities. The best thing about this place is that you can cram in as many people as you like.

A much better bet than all these places is the *Hôtel Lumumba*, not far from the post office at the main traffic roundabout. A relatively new place, it's clean and has flush toilets. Another recommended place is the *Hôtel Amari*, north of the football field on Ave du 20 Mai. It offers single rooms which can sleep two and the staff are very friendly.

Campers should avoid the *Cercle Sportif* like the plague. The so-called security guards here are in league with the town's thieves. Many people have lost the lot and resistance will invite violence.

Places to Stay – middle

One of the cheapest in this range is the *Hôtel Jambo*, behind the Banque du Peuple (which itself fronts onto the main roundabout). It offers self-contained doubles from US$12.50 to US$18 but has no hot water.

Much more expensive is the *Hôtel Rif*, near the post office, which offers self-contained doubles including hot water for US$40.

Places to Stay – top end

Goma's two top hotels are both close to the main traffic roundabout. They are the *Masques Hôtel* and the *Hôtel des Grands Lacs*.

Note You will pay 50% extra at any of the above places if you share a double with someone of the same sex.

Places to Eat – cheap

There are a few good places where you can pick up a cheap African meal. The *Restaurant La Famille* (previously the Rendezvous Restaurant), run by a very friendly family, serves cheap and tasty food. The owner speaks some English and is a good source of information. Main dishes range from Z 400 to Z 900 and the breakfast of omelette, bread, butter, jam, cheese and tea or coffee for Z 700 is particularly good value.

In the same area is the restaurant in the *Hôtel Cooboki*, near the football field. It's a simple African eatery but is popular with locals.

The market in Goma has a good selection of food if you are doing your own cooking.

Places to Eat – more expensive

The *Café Tora*, on the southern side of the main roundabout opposite the post office, is highly recommended. The *Restaurant Yeneka* at the Centre d' Accueil Protestante is also worth a try – the food is unexciting but even the heartiest eaters should be satisfied with the portions.

Going up in price, *La Michaudière*, on Ave Mobutu, is quite a fancy place where you can pick up long-forgotten delicacies like hamburger, chips and salad, real coffee and good cakes. Similar but more expensive is the *Restaurant Mupendo*. The food here is excellent but the breakfasts are poor value.

Goma's best bar and restaurant is *La Nyira*, a few minutes' walk from the post office west along Ave Mobutu. It's a very new place, with over-the-top prices but excellent food and service. There's a good selection of French-language current affairs magazines in the bar.

One of the most pleasant surprises about Goma is the local cheese. You can buy cheeses either from street hawkers or from general stores. Salamis and pâtés are also produced locally.

Getting There & Away

Air VAC and Scibé-Airlift, both next to the Masques Hôtel near the main roundabout, have flights from Goma to Bukavu. See the Getting Around section at the beginning of this chapter. The Air Zaïre office on Ave Mobutu offers occasional flights to Kinshasa.

Bus There is a daily bus in both directions between Goma and Rutshuru. It's a bit hard to pin down, but it leaves in the early afternoon and takes a couple of hours. The customary place to wait for it is outside the Boutique Lavao, a small shop on the Rutshuru road, 500 metres north of Ave du 20 Mai. Sometimes there's a bus in the morning, too. The journey takes two to 2½ hours. You can also hitch this section on a truck for the same price, though it generally takes longer.

To get to Butembo, the connections are even more tenuous. The road is in a bad way and the bus is in equally poor shape. It's supposed to leave four times a week from outside the Centre d' Accueil Protestante. Buy tickets and make enquiries there as to where the bus is and its current state of disassembly – running repairs are carried out all the time. The trip takes at least 10 hours.

Minibus If you don't want to take a lake ferry, there are daily minibuses to Bukavu from near the Hôtel Rif. Buy your ticket the day before from the office with the corrugated iron front in the first building back from the main road which skirts the back of the post office.

Minibuses leave daily at about 7 am, but think seriously about doing this journey by road. The so-called road is diabolical – a single-lane dirt track full of large potholes – and the trip is exhausting. The minibuses are thoroughly overcrowded (up to 33 people plus produce), and though you may be told that the journey takes only 10 hours, it can take up to 24 hours. There are also articulated trucks to contend with which, if they break down, can block the road for days. Bring sufficient food and drink with you in case of difficulty.

Ferry The three ferries between Goma and Bukavu are the *Vedette*, the *Karisimbi* and the *Mulamba* – see the Zaïre Getting Around section for details. The port is about a 20-minute walk from the market area and slightly less from the mission hostels.

Hitching Often there are Kenyan trucks outside the coffee depot on Ave Mobutu, waiting to load coffee to haul to Mombasa. The drivers are mostly Somalis and are a

EASTERN ZAÏRE

friendly bunch. It shouldn't be too difficult to arrange a ride, though you won't be breaking any speed records if you go this way – they take about 10 days to get to Mombasa via Kigali (Rwanda) and Kampala (Uganda).

BUKAVU
Orientation
Built over several lush tongues of land which jut out into Lake Kivu, and sprawling back up the steep mountainside behind, Bukavu is a large and very attractive city with a fairly cosmopolitan population.

It's effectively divided into two parts, following the lines of Ave des Martyrs de la Révolution, which heads south straight up a valley from the lake shore, and Ave du Président Mobutu, which winds its way east above the lake shore. The two parts are separated by the grassy saddle of a hill. Most of the budget hotels and restaurants, the main market (Marché Maman Mobutu) and the truck parks are in the south of the city. The business centre, government offices, consulates, the huge cathedral and the ritzier parts of the city are along Ave du Président Mobutu.

Like Goma, Bukavu is still recovering from the trashing and looting which it received from rioting troops in early 1993 after they discovered that the Z 5,000,000 banknotes in which they'd been paid were worthless.

More English is spoken here than in the other francophone cities of the region, mainly because of the large American Peace Corps Training Center. The city also has a more than adequate number of mosquitoes, so have a net or coils on hand.

Information
National Parks Office The Institut Zaïrois pour la Conservation de la Nature (IZCN) is at 185 Ave du Président Mobutu and is open Monday to Friday from 8.30 am to 3 pm and on Saturday from 8.30 am till noon. The staff are friendly and helpful.

If you want to visit the plains gorillas in the Parc National de Kahuzi-Biéga, it's advisable to book at this office first. As this park is still not very popular, you can usually get on a group for the following day, though this cannot be guaranteed. If you can't get a booking, turn up at the park gate and hope there's a cancellation. This often happens, especially as it's not necessary to pay when booking. People often book and forget to cancel. Weekends are busier than weekdays. Your US$125 fee (payable in cash or travellers' cheques) is collected at the park gate on your arrival.

Foreign Consulates The Burundi Consulate is on the top floor of the SINELAC building, 184 Ave du Président Mobutu (look for the Burundi flag). Visas require two photographs, are issued in 24 hours and cost US$10 (transit visa) or US$20 (one-month tourist visa). The consulate is open Monday to Friday from 7.30 am till noon and 2.30 to 5 pm.

There is no Rwandan consulate in Bukavu, but transit visas can be bought at the Rwandan border.

Things to See & Do
The only real attractions in Bukavu are the views of the lake and the city's beautiful setting. If this was the Mediterranean, the place would be full of millionaires' mansions. Take a walk past the Hôtel Riviera and out along the peninsula to the Cercle Sportif. Along here are many old villas which must have been splendid in their day. Now they're generally tatty and poorly maintained.

For a good view of the city, take the minor road which heads uphill from the Place du 24 Novembre. Follow it past the girls' boarding school and keep going for another km or so. The entire city is laid out before you, with the hills of Rwanda in the background. The whole walk should take a couple of hours each way. There's no problem with taking pictures up here, as there's no-one about.

Places to Stay – bottom end
Most of the budget hotels are along Ave des Martyrs de la Révolution. One of the cheapest hotels is the Hôtel Taifa, which is pretty scruffy but costs only US$3.50/5 a single/

double with a washbasin and shower cubicle. Its bar is one of the liveliest in town and is a good place for a bop, though if you're staying here, it can be difficult to sleep before 1 am, when the music stops. Similar places in the same street include the very tatty *Hôtel de la Victoire* and, cheapest of the lot, the *Hôtel Moderne* (US$2.50/3.25 a single/double). Further up the hill towards the market are the *Hôtel Mu-ungu* and the *Hôtel Mundial*, both of a similar standard to the Taifa.

At the top of the hill where the minibuses for Uvira leave is the cosy *Hôtel Nambo*. It's really too far from the city centre for convenience but is a good place to stay if you're going to take an early morning bus to Uvira. Twin rooms are expensive (US$10), but for solo travellers or couples, US$5 a single is not bad value. Close by is the friendly but overpriced and noisy *Ngeza Guest House*.

For camping, the *Cercle Sportif* is on the lake shore. It's a very pleasant site but is overpriced at US$5 per person. Cars can be parked by tents but trucks and larger vehicles have to be left outside on the road. Entrance to the site's bar costs US$1 for nonmembers, but if you're heading west, this is a good place to ask around for lifts.

A cheaper place to camp, if you can persuade them to allow you to do so, is the lawn of the *Hotel Métropole* (US$1.20 per person).

Places to Stay – middle

These hotels are generally along Ave du Président Mobutu. One exception is the *Hôtel Joli Logis*, on Ave des Martyrs de la Révolution. Set in a garden and with plenty of parking space, it's popular and has large rooms with a bath and hot water for US$6.50/10 a single/double. Also recommended is the *Tsikoma Hotel*, close to Place du 24 Novembre, which costs US$6.50 a double. There's a bar, and a restaurant where you can get steak and chips for US$7.50.

On Ave du Président Mobutu, the best bet is the *Hôtel Canadien*. About one km east of the city centre, almost opposite the Burundi Consulate, it's a friendly place and some

English is spoken. Huge singles/doubles with a bath cost US$6/7, though the plumbing needs attention. Still, it's about the best value in this range.

Up the scale a bit is the *Hôtel Métropole*, very conveniently situated in the city centre. It's seen better days but is still not bad value at US$7.50/11.25 for a single/double in an ordinary room, up to US$12.50/17.50 for deluxe rooms. Almost next door is the *Hôtel Lolango I*, which charges US$8.25/12 for large singles/doubles without bath and up to US$20 for a double with bath and hot water. The shared bathrooms also have hot water. Breakfast is included in the prices. The *Hôtel Lolango II*, further up Ave du Président Mobutu, is owned by the same people and has similar prices. The beds here are large and there are good views.

Close to the Hôtel Résidence is the *Hôtel La Frégate*, an older-style place with good-sized doubles from US$7.50 to US$15. It's not bad.

Another mid-range hotel is the *Tourist Hotel*, at the eastern end of town on Ave du Président Mobutu.

Places to Stay – top end

The *Hôtel Résidence* is in the city centre, on Ave du Président Mobutu. Rooms start at US$30 and have all the facilities you'd expect for that price. Have a look at the downstairs bar if you want to see how the other half lives.

The *Hôtel Riviera* has a cramped location on the edge of the lake, at the bottom end of town. It's a comfortable hotel and the service is good. Prices are similar to those at the Résidence.

Places to Eat – cheap

There's a good choice of cheap, African eateries in Bukavu. One of the simplest, and perhaps the most atmospheric in the entire region, is the colourfully named *Restaurant Docteur Wa Tumbo*, near the Place du 24 Novembre. It's practically a hole in the wall, with no electricity and only bench seating for 10 people at a squeeze. The owner is very amenable and the food, though extremely

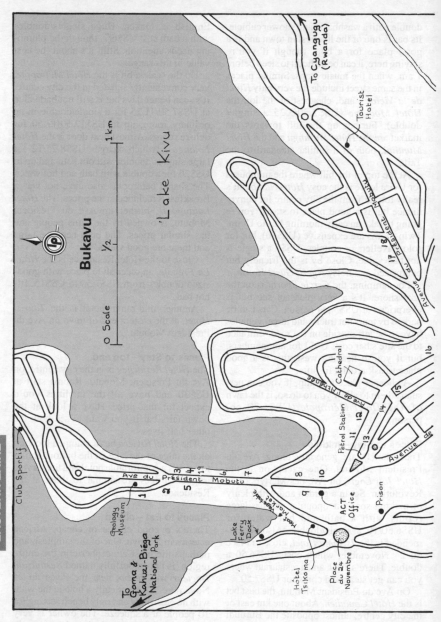

Bukavu

Lake Kivu

Scale

0   ½   1 km

To Cyangugu (Rwanda)

Tourist Hotel

Avenue du Président Mobutu

Avenue de

Cathedral

Petrol Station

Club Sportif

Ave du Président Mobutu

Geology Museum

To Goma & Kahuzi-Biéga National Park

Meat Market

Lake Ferry Dock

Hôtel Tsikoma

Place du 24 Novembre

ACZ Office

Prison

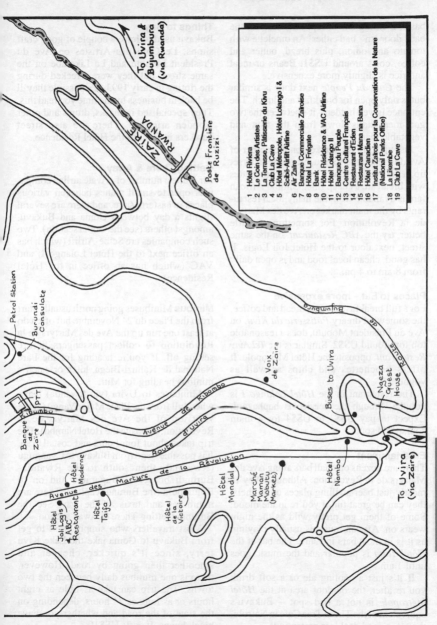

1   Hôtel Riviera
2   Le Coin des Artistes
3   La Terrasse, Pâtisserie du Kivu
4   Club La Cave
5   Hôtel Métropole, Hôtel Lolango I &
      Scibé-Airlift Airline
6   Air Zaïre
7   Banque Commerciale Zaïroise
8   Hôtel La Frégate
9   Bank
10 Hôtel Résidence & VAC Airline
11 Hôtel Lolango II
12 Banque du Peuple
13 Centre Culturel Français
14 Restaurant d'Eden
15 Restaurant Mana na Bana
16 Hôtel Canadien
17 Institut Zaïrois pour la Conservation de la Nature
      (National Parks Office)
18 La Likembe
19 Club La Cave

EASTERN ZAÏRE

basic, is filling and cheap. The view out the back door isn't bad either! An omelette with tomato and onion, plus bread, butter and coffee, costs around US$1. Beans or meat and rice is slightly more expensive.

The *Café du Peuple* next door is similar but is only open for breakfast and lunch. The entrance is well hidden – it's between the two goat-meat stalls down from the fruit and vegetable market.

Just up from the market, on the corner of Ave du Président Mobutu, brochette stalls set up in the evening, and a couple of brochettes with bread are a cheap filler. Similar African fare is available from the many local restaurants by the main market on Ave des Martyrs de la Révolution. For something a little better, try the *ABC Restaurant*, on the same street, next door to the Hôtel Joli Logis. It has good, cheap local food and is open daily from 8 am to 4 pm.

Places to Eat – more expensive
For a full breakfast of eggs, bread and coffee, the somewhat dreary *Pâtisserie du Kivu*, on Ave du Président Mobutu, does a reasonable job for around US$2. Similar is the *Tel Aviv Restaurant*, opposite the Hôtel Métropole. It offers brochettes and chips as well as yoghurt.

The restaurant in the *Hôtel Lolango I* is popular, though the service is haphazard. Expect to pay US$3 to US$4 for a main course and soup.

Entertainment
There are dozens of small bars along Ave des Martyrs de la Révolution. Although they're mostly just beer-swilling places or brothels, they can be great fun if you're in the mood. Some of them get pretty wild as the night wears on. African music is usually playing, as it is in most bars in Zaïre. The bar at the *Hôtel Taifa* is popular and the music goes until 1 am.

If it's just a cooling ale or a soft drink you're after, the outdoor area at the *Hôtel Métropole* is not a bad spot – Bukavu's equivalent of the Thorn Tree Café in Nairobi, though a good deal less pretentious.

Things to Buy
Bukavu used to have a couple of good craft shops, Le Coin des Artistes on Ave du Président Mobutu and La Likembe on the same street, but they were wrecked during the rioting in early 1993. It's possible they'll be back in business by the time you read this. They specialised in masks, drums and other wooden artefacts. There are also street hawkers in front of the Hôtel Résidence.

Getting There & Away
Air Quite a number of private airline companies operate small planes between various places in eastern Zaïre, and there are several flights a day between Goma and Bukavu, amongst others (see the Goma section). Two such companies are Scibé-Airlift (which has an office next to the Hôtel Lolango I) and VAC (which has an office in the Hôtel Résidence).

Minibus Minibuses going north usually start from the Place du 24 Novembre but often do at least one run up the Ave des Martyrs de la Révolution to collect passengers before setting off. If you're heading for the Parc National de Kahuzi-Biéga, hitch or catch a minibus heading for Miti.

Minibuses to Uvira (via Rwanda) leave when full from the Place Major Vangu (at the very top of the Ave des Martyrs de la Révolution, opposite the Hôtel Nambo). The trip takes about four hours and costs US$5. It is possible to go from Bukavu to Cyangugu (Rwanda), then south to the Rwanda-Burundi border at Bugarama and on to Bujumbura (the Burundi capital). There are minibuses and taxis all the way. See the Burundi Getting There & Away section.

Most travellers who simply want to get from Bukavu to Goma take the Lake Kivu ferry, since it's quicker, cheaper and smoother than going by road. However, there is one minibus daily between the two towns. The trip can take as little as eight hours or as long as 24 hours, depending on the state of the road and whether you have breakdowns. It costs US$10.

Top: Zanzibar, Tanzania (GC)
Middle: Wildebeest migration, Serengeti National Park, Tanzania (CK)
Bottom: Ngorongoro Crater village school, Tanzania (GH)

Top: Great Ruaha River, Tanzania (RvD)
Bottom: Looking south from Mt Kilimanjaro, Tanzania (HF)

Hitching The main truck parks are around the Marché Maman Mobutu and around Place Major Vangu.

From Place du 24 Novembre, you can hitch a ride to Walikale if you plan to do the 90-km walk to Lubutu. You can also pick up trucks going north from the BRALIMA brewery, about two km from the Place du 24 Novembre along the Goma road.

Ferry Three ferries ply between Bukavu and Goma on Lake Kivu: the *Vedette*, the *Karisimbi* and the *Mulamba* (see the Getting Around section at the beginning of this chapter).

The *Vedette* and *Karisimbi* dock at the port, just off Place du 24 November. The *Mulamba* does the beer run, so it docks at the BRALIMA brewery, two km along the Goma road, though when arriving from Goma, it often stops at a small jetty about halfway between the brewery and the port to let passengers disembark.

All ferries should be booked one day in advance. Tickets for the *Vedette* and *Karisimbi* can be bought at the port, while tickets for the *Mulamba* should be bought from the ACT office on Ave du Président Mobutu. You'll have to show your passport to buy a ticket, so if you're buying tickets for other people, make sure you have their passports as well.

Getting Around

There are plenty of dilapidated yellow taxis. Drivers generally hike up the prices when they see a foreigner, so bargain hard.

UVIRA

Uvira is on the north-western tip of Lake Tanganyika, facing Bujumbura across the lake. It's not a particularly attractive or interesting place. Avoid army personnel and keep that camera out of sight – there's a lot of mercenary paranoia in the area.

The actual port area, Kalundu, is four km south of Uvira. You'll be very lucky to find a boat going south – most travellers have drawn a blank – and the road south is not safe.

Places to Stay

One of the cheapest places is the *Hôtel Babyo 'La Patience'*, on Ave Bas-Zaïre near the mosque. If it's full, try the *Pole Pole*. There's no running water but it has a bar and good brochettes for sale. Another good place which is clean and quiet is the *Hôtel Rafiki*.

Places to Eat

A good place to eat is the *Tanganyika Restaurant*, down the road from La Patience hotel. Run by Ugandan refugees, the food is good, the staff are pleasant and English is spoken. For a splurge, try the *Hôtel La Côte*, which offers very good three-course meals.

Entertainment

For nightlife, try the *Lobe Disco*, which becomes very crowded after 9.30 pm. The *Nyanda au Grand Lac* sometimes has music.

Getting There & Away

There are two possible routes between Uvira and Bukavu. The first goes entirely through Zaïrian territory and involves finding a lift on a truck (there are usually several daily). The route takes a mountain road on the western side of the Rusizi River via Kamanyola and Nya-Ngezi through stunning countryside. Minibuses are available between Uvira and Kamanyola if you can't find a truck.

The second route goes some of the way through Rwanda, to take advantage of the excellent Rwandan road system, and there are plenty of minibuses. The trip takes three to four hours and costs US$5. If you use this route, you'll need a Rwandan transit or tourist visa, and a multiple-entry visa to get back into Zaïre, though in the past, this rule has not always been enforced; officially you never left Zaïre. Rwandan transit visas are available at the border for RFr 1600.

Taxi Taxis to the Zaïre border post run all day until late afternoon, take 10 minutes and cost about US$0.50. This is a very easy-going border. It's about one km from the Zaïre post to the Burundi post, and bicycle taxis are available if you don't want to walk. From the Burundi post, there are taxis into Bujumbura.

National Parks

PARC NATIONAL DE KAHUZI-BIÉGA

Lying between Bukavu and Goma, this park was created in 1970 with an initial area of 600 sq km but was expanded to 6000 sq km in 1975. It was primarily created to preserve the habitat of the eastern lowland (plains) gorilla *(Gorilla gorilla graueri)*, which was once found all the way from the right bank of the Zaïre River to the mountains on the borders with Uganda and Rwanda. Now this gorilla is an endangered species, as is the mountain gorilla which lives on the slopes of the volcanoes on the borders between Zaïre, Rwanda and Uganda.

Many other animals also live in this park. These include chimpanzee, many other species of monkey, elephant, buffalo, many species of antelope, leopard, genet, serval and mongoose. The birdlife is prolific.

The altitude varies between 900 metres and 3308 metres (Mt Kahuzi) and the average annual rainfall is fairly heavy (1900 mm), with the largest falls in April and November. The dry season runs through the months of June, July and August. Most areas of the park have a temperate climate with a fairly constant average temperature of 15°C.

Because of the heavy rainfall and the varying altitude, there's a wide variety of vegetation, ranging from dense rainforests at the lower levels, through bamboo forests between 2400 metres and 2600 metres, to heath and alpine meadows on the summits of the highest mountains. Many animals tend to live in the denser parts of the forest and so are often difficult to see.

Visiting the Gorillas

There are several groups of gorillas, though you will usually see only one of the groups which has become accustomed to humans. In 1990 there were 27 gorillas in the family group. Each year they become more and more accustomed to seeing humans. It's usually possible to get within a metre or two of the silverbacks and large females.

The gorillas can be visited any day of the year, including public holidays. Children under 15 years of age are not allowed. Ideally you should make a reservation at the IZCN national park office in Bukavu (Institut Zaïrois pour la Conservation de la Nature, 185 Ave du Président Mobutu), but often, if you just turn up at Station Tshivanga (the park entrance and departure point) by 8 am, there's no problem. As most people use Bukavu as a base, it's easy to make a booking, in which case there is no need to be at the gate until 9 am. The visit ends back at the gate at about 1 pm.

The cost is US$125, payable in hard currency (cash or travellers' cheques) at the park entrance on the day of your visit. Payment in zaïres is not accepted. The ticket you get is valid for seven days, but though you could stay in the park for seven days, it is only good for one trip to see the gorillas.

The fee includes a guide, trackers (who chop the vegetation to make a track) and a gun-toting guard (who scares off elephants). They all expect a tip at the end – so would I if I had to chop my way through thick jungle with a bunch of tourists every day! The average tip is US$2, given to each of them back at the gate.

You must have appropriate footwear and clothing, preferably a pair of stout boots and waterproof clothes – this is not a picnic. It's often very muddy and hard-going up steep slopes. You need to be careful about what you grab hold of to pull yourself up, as many vines and other plants carry thorns or will sting. A pair of gloves is a good idea. It can rain even in the dry season.

The guides can generally locate a group of gorillas within two hours, though it can take up to five hours or as little as five minutes (unusual). If you don't see any the first day, your fee covers you for another attempt the next. No refunds are possible if you can't return the next day.

To photograph the gorillas, you need the fastest film you can get – ASA 1600 is the

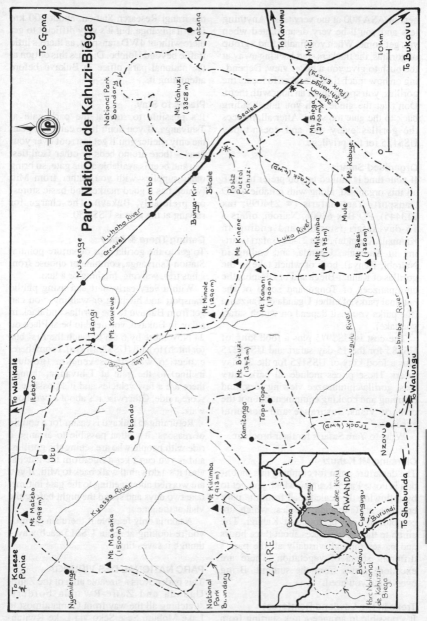

Parc National de Kahuzi-Biéga

To Goma

Katana

To Kavumu

To Bukavu

Miti

National Park Boundary

Mt Kahuzi (3308m)

Tshivanga Station (Park Entry)

Sealed

Mt Biéga (2790m)

Mt Kabuye

Hombo

Bunyia-Kiri

Bitale

Poste Putral Kaniza

Gravel

Luhoho River

Mt Kinene

Mt Mitumba (1275m)

Mt Mule

Musenge

Luka River

Track (4WD)

Mt Kaweue

Mt Mimole (1249m)

Mt Kanani (1700m)

Mt Besi (1850m)

Isangi

To Walikale

Itebero

Luka River

Mt Bituzi (1342m)

Lugulo River

Lubimbe River

Ntando

Kamibongo

Tope Tope

Nzovu

To Walungu

Utu

Mt Matebo (998m)

Mt Kitimba (913m)

To Shabunda

To Kasese & Punia

Kyassa River

Nyamilenge

Mt Masaka (1500m)

National Park Boundary

10km

To Kalese & Punia

ZAÏRE

Goma · Gisenyi

Lake Kivu

RWANDA

Bukavu · Cyangugu

Cyangugu

Burundi

Parc National de Kahuzi-Biéga

To Shabunda

best or ASA 800 at the very least. Anything less and you'll be very disappointed when you get home. When you finally find a group of gorillas, the trackers start hacking away at the bush to give you a better view. Depending on how much time it's taken to locate the gorillas, you spend about an hour with them. Don't let the guide rush you into heading back to the gate too soon. After all, he sees the gorillas every day and doesn't pay US$125 for the privilege.

Organised Safaris

If your time is limited or you prefer to have all this organised, along with reliable 4WD transport, Yare Safaris (☎ 214099; fax 213445), PO Box 63006, Nairobi, offers a 15-day safari (starting and ending in Kampala, Uganda) and a 21-day safari (starting in Kampala, Uganda, and ending in Nairobi, Kenya), both of which take in the gorillas of Kahuzi-Biéga and/or Djomba, the chimpanzees of Tongo and some of the national parks of either Uganda or Tanzania (the parks you visit depend on which safari you take).

The cost is US$975 plus a food kitty of US$85 for the 15-day safari and US$1275 plus a food kitty of US$125 for the 21-day safari. These prices include all park entry fees, gorilla/chimpanzee viewing fees, and camping and cooking equipment but not the cost of visas, insurance and personal expenses.

Write to Yare Safaris for their brochure.

Climbing Mt Kahuzi

The departure point for climbing this mountain is Poste Patrol Kahuzi, which you get to by following the sealed road from the park entrance at Tshivanga. Guides, which are compulsory, can be found at Kahuzi. The climb to the summit takes about three hours and passes through virtually all the park's different strata of vegetation. There are excellent views from the summit. Bring everything you need.

Treks in the Lowland Rainforest

It's possible to arrange a trek starting from the Irangi Research Station, about 100 km from Tshivanga, but it's very difficult to get there without 4WD transport, as there's little traffic beyond Hombo. Discuss this option at the national park office in Bukavu before attempting it.

Places to Stay

It's possible to stay at the park gate at Tshivanga. If you don't have camping gear, the only shelter you'll get is a roof over your head – there are no beds or other facilities. Tea and beer is available at the gate, so bring other supplies with you, either from Miti (which has a good market and basic stores) or, preferably, Bukavu. The charge for staying at the gate is US$2.50.

Getting There & Away

To get to the gorilla trips departure point at Station Tshivanga, combine or choose from a bus trip, walking, hitching or a taxi.

With a very early start and using public transport and hitching or walking, you can get from Bukavu to the gorillas and back in a day. In Bukavu, you need to be at Place du 24 Novembre by 6 am to catch the first bus (or hitch) to Miti (US$2, 18 km). From there, expect to walk the seven km (gradual incline) to the gate at Tshivanga, though there are a few vehicles and it's possible to score a ride. Otherwise it's about a two-hour walk.

Returning to Bukavu is easier for a couple of reasons: it's often possible to arrange a ride with people who are seeing the gorillas, and if you can't get a ride from the gate, at least it's a downhill walk back to Miti. If you are worried about getting to the gate in time, take two days and spend the night before the visit at the gate.

A taxi is only feasible if there's a group – you're looking at about US$15 each way – though it saves time.

PARC NATIONAL DES VIRUNGA

This park covers a sizeable area of the Zaïre-Uganda and Zaïre-Rwanda borders, stretching all the way from Goma almost to Lake Mobutu Sese Seko via Lake Rwitan-

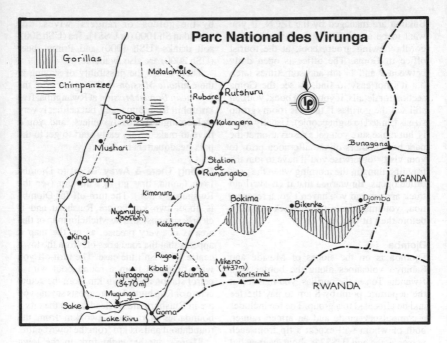

Parc National des Virunga

Gorillas

Chimpanzee

Motalamule

Rubare · Rutshuru

Tongo · · Kalengera

Mushari

Burunqu

Station de Rumangabo

UGANDA

Bunagana

Kimanura

Bokima · Bikenke · Djomba

Nyamulgira (3056m)

Kakamero

Kingi

Mikeno (4437m)

Rugo

Nyiragongo (3470m) Kibati Kibumba Karisimbi

RWANDA

Sake Mugunga

Goma

Lake Kivu

zige (Edward). Much of it is contiguous with national parks in Uganda and Rwanda.

Created in 1925, the Virunga was Zaïre's first national park. It covers an area of 8000 sq km. For administrative purposes the park has been divided into four sections. From the south these are: Nyiragongo, Nyamulgira and Karisimbi; Rwindi and Vitshumbi; Ishango; and the Ruwenzoris. Entry to any part of the Parc National des Virunga (except if you're passing straight through on transport between Rutshuru and Kayna-Bayonga) costs US$45 (UK£25) for a seven-day permit except for visits to the Djomba or Bukima gorillas which cost US$125 (UK£70) and the chimpanzees at Tongo which cost US$65 (UK£35). The higher fees cover you for a seven-day permit, but you're only allowed one gorilla or chimpanzee viewing in that seven-day period. If you want to see them more than once, you pay another US$125 or US$65, respectively, for each additional viewing. You can go from one part of the park to another without paying twice, so long as your permit is still valid.

If you have a video camera and intend to use it, there's an additional fee of US$25.

All these fees are payable in hard currency (cash or travellers' cheques). Local currency is not acceptable.

You might think these fees are extortionate, but they're not. Everyone who goes on a gorilla viewing enthusiastically agrees that they're worth every cent. I personally endorse that. It's a once-in-a-lifetime experience not to be missed. You should also remember that if the trackers and rangers (who are local people) couldn't make a reasonable living out of taking visitors to see the gorillas, and the national parks organisation didn't have money to maintain the sanctuaries and their facilities, the gorillas would probably have been wiped out by now. Your US$125 gives them a sporting chance at survival.

The gorilla sanctuaries at Djomba and

Bukima are managed by the IZCN. If you want to be absolutely sure of getting on a gorilla-viewing group, book at the tourist office in Goma. The office is open daily between 9 and 11 am and sometimes later, but it's not easy to find, so see the Goma section for details. If you don't book, you can still see the gorillas if there is room (group size is limited to eight people). Usually there is, but make sure you get a reservation at the park headquarters on the afternoon prior to your visit – otherwise you'll have to join the fray first thing in the morning when the park office opens. Be warned that if an overland truck arrives and you haven't got a reservation, you may have to wait several days before they fit you in.

Djomba

Djomba is on the slopes of Muside and Sabinyo volcanoes along the border with Rwanda. To see the gorillas, you must be at the departure point by 8 am to pay the fee and be allocated to a group. The fee includes a compulsory guide and an armed ranger, both of whom will expect a tip from each person at the end (US$2 is about average but many people tip more, since this is, after all, one of life's unique experiences).

There are two families of gorillas here, known as the Marcel family (23 animals) and the Oscar family (11 animals). The guides can usually find their allotted group of gorillas within an hour or two, sometimes less.

Note that other than gorilla viewing fees, which must be paid in hard currency, everything at Djomba has to be paid for in hard currency or in Ugandan shillings. No-one accepts zaïres.

Places to Stay & Eat There's an excellent hut at the park headquarters, containing two dormitories with four beds in each (good value at US$2 per bed). Clean sheets are provided and there's an earth toilet outside. There's also ample camping space with a tap and earth toilet. Camping costs US$1 per tent (if it's collected – often it's not). If you're not cooking your own food, you can buy very tasty meals at the park headquarters cooked

by the guides' or rangers' wives for Ugandan Sh 1000 (or US$1). Tea (USh 500), soft drinks (USh 1000) and Primus beer (USh 2000) are also available.

There's also the possibility of staying at the *Catholic Mission* in Bunagana or at the *American Baptist Mission* at Rwanguba, five km uphill from Bunagana, but neither is very welcoming towards travellers, and you'd have to make a very early start to get to the park headquarters by 8 am.

Getting There & Away To get to Djomba from Goma, first go to Rutshuru (see the Rutshuru section). The turn-off for Djomba is about two km before Rutshuru and is clearly signposted. The Michelin map of this area is not very precise, as on the map it appears that the road goes off from the town centre. This isn't the case. The turn-off you want branches from a roundabout with a petrol station about four km from the actual centre of Rutshuru. The signposts saying you are in Rutshuru are misleading, as the city's boundaries start about two km from the roundabout and six km from the town centre.

There's another right fork in the town centre which leads to Uganda via Ishasha. The bus from Goma goes into the centre, so make sure the driver knows that you want to be put down at the Djomba turn-off. From the turn-off on the Goma to Rutshuru road, it's about 26 km to the Zaïre border village of Bunagana over a very rough road. Transport is sporadic and there are no regular minibuses, so you'll have to hitch or walk.

At Bunagana, you'll be met by local children and youths who will offer to guide you up to the park headquarters at Djomba and/or carry your bags. Don't pass up their services or you'll get lost in the maze of farms and paths along the way. The usual tip is US$2 to US$3. The seven-km, gradual uphill walk to the park headquarters should take you two to 2½ hours.

Coming from Uganda, stay overnight at a hotel in Kisoro or camp (free of charge) on the Ugandan side of the border in the village of Bunagana. Next day, cross the border into Zaïre. You need a Zaïrian visa to do this *unless* you are only going to visit the Djomba gorillas and then return to Uganda afterwards. If you intend to return to Uganda after seeing the gorillas, you don't need a visa. Instead, immigration will charge you US$50, retain your passport and allow you to go to Djomba. When you return, you get your passport back. This is cheaper than buying a tourist visa (US$75 for one-month, single-entry). Re-entry into Uganda costs US$20 or US$25, depending on your nationality, unless you already have a multiple-entry visa.

Bukima

After booking in Goma, get to the Station de Rumangabo on the Rutshuru road, 45 km from Goma (about a two-hour drive). A guide will take you up the mountain (about a four-hour walk), where you stay overnight. The next morning there's a two-hour walk to find one or other of the three families of habituated mountain gorillas *(Gorilla gorilla beringei)*, after which you return the same day to Rumangabo – a long day. The guides will expect a tip at the end of the gorilla viewing (US$2 per guide is average). The maximum group size is six people but this may be stretched a little up to eight people.

Places to Stay & Eat There's a very pleasant hut with cooking facilities, firewood and clean sheets which costs US$2 per person, and there's also a cleared camp site here, though it has no facilities. Otherwise, get a room with one of the locals – they're open to negotiation. There's also a very basic mountain hut *(gîte)*, which you can use for US$1, but it has no beds, curtains or water.

Getting There & Away If you're coming from Kisoro in Uganda, a guide may meet you about one km past the border post, at the restaurant, and offer to take you to the hut. He knows a short cut which will get you to the hut in two hours (as opposed to eight hours via the road). The walk is through mountain villages and is very interesting. He expects US$5 per person for this, but large

groups can barter him down to between US$10 and US$20 for the group.

Tongo Chimpanzee Sanctuary

Tongo is Zaïre's first chimpanzee sanctuary, and it's a pity there are not more, since poachers are decimating these primates elsewhere in the country.

Viewing starts at 6 am, but as it can often take up to four or five hours before the group is located, expect a strenuous walk. There are also colobus monkeys and baboons to be seen, as well as a wide variety of birdlife. Butterflies are everywhere.

Places to Stay & Eat Besides a camp site with toilets, shower and kitchen (US$1 per person per night), there's also the *Sokomutu Lodge*, with very clean rooms, electricity and hot water for US$20 a double. Breakfast costs US$5 and lunch/dinner is US$7. The manager of the lodge was described by one traveller as 'a prize arsehole' but the lodge is on a beautiful site above the village of Tongo, looking out towards the Virunga Mountains.

Accommodation costs must be paid in hard currency.

Getting There & Away To get there, take transport from Goma to Rutshuru but get off at Kalangera village, about 10 km south of Rutshuru. From there, a 17-km dirt track leads you to Tongo. Market day in Tongo is Friday, so this is the best day to get a lift along this road. Otherwise, it's a pleasant four-hour walk.

Porters congregate at the turn-off for Tongo and will carry your pack to Tongo for US$1 to US$2 (though they start off asking a considerably higher price).

Nyiragongo

This volcano (3470 metres), which broods over Goma, used to be a spectacular sight when it was erupting but is now merely smoking. It's still worth climbing to the top for the views. Since it only takes five hours up and three hours down, it can be done in one day if you set off very early. However, a one-day trip isn't recommended because the summit is only clear of mist or cloud in the early morning and again, briefly, in the late afternoon; it's better to make it a two-day event.

The starting point is at Kibati, about 15 km north of Goma on the Rutshuru road. Here you find the Camp des Guides, a long, white, unmarked building set back above the road at the foot of the volcano. Either hitch or walk to this place.

The US$45 (UK£25) entry fee is paid at the camp and includes the services of a guide (who will expect a tip at the end – US$2 seems average). Porters can also be hired at Kibati. The trouble with porters and guides is that they'll set off with neither food nor bedding, so you'll have to provide this if you want to make the climb a two-day event. Bring all your food and drink from Goma, as there's nothing for sale at Kibati. Firewood is also in short supply.

On the first day, you need to start out before 1 pm, as it's a three-hour walk to the base of the crater cone proper and then another hour to the huts (which are in bad shape). On the way up, you pass some interesting geological formations and vegetation – tropical forest, hardened lava flows (recent, old and ancient) and giant lobelia.

On the second day, get up early and put on some warm clothes so you can set off by 6.30 am. It's a half-hour walk to the crater rim and the weather should be clear. Looking down into the base of the crater, you'll probably still see wisps of steam and vapour coming from the walls, while the base itself is an uneven cooled mass of lava. Sulphur fumes hang in the air. The views of Goma, Lake Kivu and over into Rwanda are terrific. By about 9.30 am the mist will start closing in for the day and you lose the views. The descent takes about three hours.

Places to Stay It's possible to stay at the *Camp des Guides* the day before you go up the mountain but there's no regular accommodation. Many travellers buy the head guide a bottle of beer and end up sleeping on his floor – he's a friendly and interesting man. Otherwise, you can camp at the free

camp site about two km south of the Camp des Guides.

Nyamulgira

You will need at least three days to climb Nyamulgira volcano (3056 metres), but you shouldn't have to pay the park entry fee again if you haven't used all your original seven days. As for Nyiragongo, you'll have to tip the guides extra. Bring all your food requirements and a tent, as there's nowhere to stay at the Nyamulgira base camp.

The trip starts at Kibati (as for Nyiragongo) and the first part involves a 45-km walk (two days) to the base camp through beautiful countryside. The next stage is a six-hour climb through an incredibly varied landscape ranging from old and recent lava flows (some of them pocked with lava pools) to dense upland jungles. You may be lucky to catch sight of elephants, chimpanzees, buffaloes and antelope, but you'll definitely see and hear hundreds of different birds.

The first night on the mountain is spent at a decaying but rambling hut (for which you pay extra), though it is possible to return to the base camp the same day if you set off early enough. Camping is an alternative. The guides generally cook their own food.

The next day you set off for the crater rim. It takes about one hour to reach the tree line and then another hour to get to the crater rim across recent lava flows (slippery when wet). The views from the summit are magnificent. You descend the mountain the same day.

Rwindi & Vitshumbi

The main attraction in this part of the park is the game – lions, elephants, hippos, giraffes, antelope, hyenas, buffaloes and many others. The Ruwenzori National Park in neighbouring Uganda (which is contiguous with the Parc National des Virunga) used to be much the same but was sadly depleted of wildlife during that country's civil wars. You cannot hire vehicles to tour this part of the Virunga, so you'll be reliant on tourists, who are not always keen to pick up strangers.

The lodge at Rwindi is somewhat expensive, though if you wait until the bar closes, it may be possible to bed down by the swimming pool. The more people do this, the sooner there will be a clampdown, as camping is officially forbidden in or around the lodge. If you can't afford to stay at the lodge, enquire about rooms in the drivers' quarters; you may be lucky and get a cheap room. There's also a small guesthouse in the nearby village but they're not keen on taking tourists.

While you're in this area, you should pay a visit to the fishing village of **Vitshumbi**, at the southern end of Lake Rwitanzige (Edward). A visit to the fishing village of Kiavinyonge at the northern end of the lake, near Kasindi, is also interesting.

Ishango

This is similar to the Rwindi/Vitshumbi part of the park except that there are no elephants. Ishango is just a park camping area with a small airstrip and a derelict lodge, which you can use free of charge – it's usually filthy with bat droppings. Camping is preferable but you'll be charged for this. There are no fences, so it's advisable to be careful at night. Campers have encountered hyenas and leopards that have come too close for comfort.

Those who know the area well say that it's possible to swim in either Lake Rwitanzige (Edward) or in the Semliki River, which flows into it. While there's apparently no danger of bilharzia, they do give a strong warning about hippos. If you decide to swim, watch closely for 10 to 15 minutes to make sure there are no hippos anywhere near you. One traveller who ignored the warnings had a buttock bitten. There are no hospitals close by in Zaïre, but he was lucky because the Ugandans allowed him through to their nearest hospital (after a long hassle). The wildlife and, particularly, the birdlife is prolific where the Semliki flows into the lake.

To get to Ishango, first travel to Kasindi either from Beni (Zaïre) or Kasese (Uganda). It's possible to hitch, as there are usually a fair number of trucks on the road between the two places. Wait at the turn-off in Kasindi for a lift into the park. If you get stuck at the turn-off, it's three km to the park entrance.

You can generally rent a bedroom in one of the park buildings, but you will have to pay the park entrance fee again if your seven-day permit expires. There is a way around this if you don't want to go to Ishango: tell them you are going to Kiavinyonge, which is 10 km beyond Ishango and is not strictly in the national park. No-one else pays to get there, as the only road in is through Kasindi and Ishango. The trip involves a ferry crossing over a river literally swarming with hippos.

Kiavinyonge

This large fishing village has a spectacular setting at the foot of a mountain range leading down to the northern end of Lake Rwitanzige (Edward). Herds of hippo wallow close to the beach and large marabou birds are everywhere. At about 6 am, the village becomes a hive of activity as fishing boats land their catches on the sandy beach in front of the restaurant and houses. The men look after the nets and the women sort the fish, which are then smoked during the day. Few tourists visit, so you're in for a treat.

Places to Stay & Eat The *Logement Spécial*, at the west end of the village, has cheap rooms. Don't be put off if they're not sure what to do with you when you turn up! There's a *restaurant* on the lake shore which sells coffee, tea, bread and hot corned beef (of all things!) but the best thing to buy is fish and rice – it won't be found fresher anywhere else. The restaurant is open from 6 am to 8 pm.

Getting There & Away To leave Kiavinyonge, enquire about trucks taking fish to Butembo. These leave at around 8 am and take about four hours. It's an incredible journey up over the mountains on a dirt road with many hairpin bends (not the normal Kasindi to Butembo road).

Ruwenzoris

This is the most northerly part of the Parc National des Virunga, and its major appeal for travellers is the climb up the Ruwenzori Mountains. It is also possible to climb from the Ugandan side, since the border between the two countries passes along the summits. Don't underestimate the difficulties of this trek from either side. It's much tougher than climbing up Kilimanjaro. True, some people do make it in joggers and normal clothes but they suffer for it. Anywhere above Hut Three (about 4200 metres), you can almost freeze to death without adequate clothing and a warm sleeping bag. Snow is not unusual at or above this point. Prepare for it properly and it will be one of the most memorable trips in your life.

Before even considering doing this trek, obtain the appropriate footwear, clothing and sleeping bag. Don't forget a woollen hat and gloves. Pots and pans are very useful and will repay their cost several times over, especially if you're trying to economise on weight by taking dried soups. You need to take *all* your own food, including enough to feed the guide and any porters hired. A stove is a good idea but is not absolutely essential.

The guide and porters are very partial to cigarettes at the end of a day. If you run out, they can become unpleasant. Leave your 'clean and healthy living' fetishes at home; these people are not trekking for fun. Sure, they're being paid, but it's not a king's ransom. Before setting off, make sure that all parties agree on what are your and their responsibilities, who pays for what, where exactly you are going and how many days the trip will take. Be firm, but remember that other trekkers will follow, so try to keep them happy. If they end up wanting to string you up from the nearest tree, I don't want to be on the trek which follows yours. Five days or more is a long time to be with people who want to battle with you at every turn.

The best selection of food is at Beni, but there are also some fairly well-stocked shops and a reasonable market (meat, fruit, vegetables, beer, soft drinks, etc) in Mutwanga. This is where the guides and porters get their supplies.

The actual trek starts when you get to the park headquarters in Mutsora, about four km from Mutwanga. Both of these places are about halfway between Beni and Kasindi on the road to Uganda.

Park Fees These are paid at the park headquarters in Mutsora, which is also where you arrange guides and porters. Fees are US$45 (park entry), US$5 (camera), US$2 (guide per day), US$2 (guide's porter per day), US$2 (other porters per day) and US$2 (hut fees per person per day). These fees must be paid in hard currency. The guide's and porters' fees supposedly include food but it's best to assume they don't, so bring enough food for them too. In addition, both the guide and porters will expect a good tip at the end of the trek.

Guides & Maps Before attempting to climb the Ruwenzori, it's a very good idea to get hold of a copy of *Ruwenzori – Map & Guide*, by Andrew Wielochowski. Published in 1989, it has an excellent large-scale contour map with the Ruwenzoris on one side and information on geology, flora & fauna, walking routes, hire of guides and porters, costs, equipment, useful contacts and weather on the other side. It's available from Nairobi bookshops or from 32 Seamill Park Crescent, Worthing BN11 2PN, UK (☎ (0903) 37565).

It may still be possible to get hold of a copy of Osmaston & Pasteur's *Guide to the Ruwenzori*, last published in 1972. The only places I know of where you can buy this book are West Col Productions, 1 Meadow Close, Goring-on-Thames, Reading, Berks, UK, and Stanfords Map Centre, Long Acre, Covent Garden, London WC2, UK.

Places to Stay & Eat A large, clean, well-furnished room at the park headquarters costs US$3/5 for singles/doubles. Camping costs US$1 per person per night, plus a vehicle charge if you have one. Most budget travellers, however, go to Mutwanga, about four km away. Here you will find what has become a legend among the travelling cognoscenti – an abandoned hotel, variously called the Hôtel Ruwenzori or the Hotel

Engles, with three swimming pools but no windows or furniture.

No-one, including the Belgian owner or the caretaker, minds if you stay the night, and it's completely free (but please leave a tip with the caretaker). You can also camp free of charge. It's a great place and anyone will tell you where it is. The caretaker will even chop wood for you (at a price) and sell you food. Don't forget that tip! The hotel has been left in this state due to a dispute between the local authorities and the owner.

All three huts on the normal route have been refurbished, so they're weatherproof and as clean as the last occupants left them. They have fireplaces and beds but no mattresses. Hut 1 accommodates 24 people, and Huts 2 and 3 accommodate 12 people each.

There's also a fourth hut (Moraine, at 4312 metres), on the edge of the moraine, but you'll be charged extra for this and you have to sign an indemnity releasing the national parks from any responsibility for whatever might happen to you – part of the route is across bare rock with only a rope to hold on to. Properly equipped climbers can also make the ascent of the peaks of Mt Stanley.

The Trek The standard trek takes five days. The trip is: Mutsora (1700 metres) to Kalongi (2042 metres), about five hours; Kalongi to Mahungu (3333 metres), about 5½ hours; Mahungu to Kyondo, (4303 metres), about 4½ hours; Kyondo to the summit and back to Kalongi, about seven hours; and Kalongi to Mutsora, about four hours.

Variations to this route and scheduling are possible , but you must arrange these before setting off.

Day 1 From Mutwanga/Mutsora (1700 metres), it's a two-hour walk along a gently rising path through the cultivated foothills to *Kiandolire Hut* (or Guides' Hut) at 1700 metres. Few trekkers stay here, though it will sleep 10 people and water is available. Leaving the hut, the path enters thick forest and fords two major streams. You'll reach *Kalonge Hut* (2042 metres) after a three-

hour trek; it appears about 10 minutes after fording the second stream. This hut can sleep 16 people and there's space for camping. It's in excellent condition and water and firewood are available.

Day 2 The path from Kalonge Hut veers off east and drops steeply to another stream before climbing to a ridge at 2440 metres and then to a knoll at 2910 metres. This section takes about three hours. From the knoll, it's two hours to *Mahungu Hut* (3333 metres), made tough by giant heather and deep mosses. This hut sleeps up to 16 people. There is space for tents and water is sometimes available from a small well close to the hut. If the well is dry, the porters know another water source a considerable distance from the hut.

This part of the trek and the first part of the following day is the toughest, as it's mostly uphill and is very hard going between roots and vines. For much of the way the ground is very wet, and rain can fall frequently even outside the wet season.

Day 3 The trek continues through giant heather and mosses for about two hours until the heather thins and a small stream is reached. A further hour takes you through more open countryside to Kampi ya Chupa, a ridge at 4030 metres, from which there are beautiful views over the rainforests of Semliki Valley on the one side and down to Lac Noir on the other. On the way up you'll pass some superb stands of giant groundsel, lobelia, senecio and helichrysum. A further hour from Kampi ya Chupa brings you to *Kyondo Hut* (4303 metres), from which there are fine views of the Stanley peaks, weather permitting. The hut can sleep 12 people and there's space for tents. Water is available from a nearby stream.

Day 4 This begins from a col just east of the hut, from which the path descends to a rocky step protected by a cable. It continues to descend more steeply, through a muddy gully to Lac Vert at 4160 metres, after which it climbs steeply from the northern end to Lac

Gris, where there is a good camp site. This section takes about two hours. About 45 minutes further on you arrive at *Moraine Hut* (or Glacier Hut) at 4495 metres, after which the snowfield starts. The hut can sleep four people and there's space for one tent nearby. The hut is damp and can be extremely cold at night, so be prepared. Going further requires suitable equipment and preferably experience of climbing on snow and ice. Porters will not go beyond this point.

Days 5 & 6 If you're reasonably fit, you can descend along the same route in two days, with an overnight stop at *Mahungu Hut*, which is about an eight-hour walk from Mutwanga.

Getting There & Away There are trucks from close to the H tel Lualaba in Beni to the turn-off to Mutsora and Mutwanga. From there you walk, though it is possible to get a lift all the way to Mutwanga. It's about 13 km from the turn-off on the Beni to Kasindi road to either Mutsora or Mutwanga.

Mt Hoyo

Mt Hoyo is about 13 km off the Beni to Bunia road, close to Komanda. Its drawcards are the waterfall known as the **Chutes de Vénus**, the **grottos** (small caves) and the **Pygmy villages** nearby. It also used to be possible to climb Mt Hoyo (a two-day trek) but the track is now overgrown and there's no longer a hut at the top. This shouldn't deter those who are determined; guides can be found at the hotel.

The waterfall and grottos are managed as an extension of the Parc National des Virunga, so you must pay for a seven-day permit, which includes the services of a compulsory guide. The guide may tell you that you have to pay him direct but this isn't true; you must pay at the Auberge. The tour of the waterfall and grottos lasts about two hours and takes you to three different cavern systems (illuminated with a kerosene lantern) and finally down to the base of the waterfall.

The Pygmy villages have seen too many tourists and are very commercialised. You'll be hassled to death and will have to pay for every photograph you take. If you have the time, spend a few days here and gradually build up a relationship with the Pygmies by trading with them or buying food from them before visiting their village.

A better place to visit the Pygmies is at **Loya**, at the first bridge over the Loya River south of the Mt Hoyo turn-off. There is a small car park south of the bridge (with a very small sign on the roadside). Park there and someone will soon appear. A trip to their village can then be arranged by pirogue. So far, these people are much less commercialised and don't give you the hard sell.

If you come here on the Eka Massambe bus from Butembo (Monday and Thursday from Butembo, about seven hours), it will drop you at the Mt Hoyo turn-off at about 5 pm, which means you'll have to make the 13-km walk to the hotel at night. It's possible to hire porters for this three-hour walk. Seven km down the road is a fruit plantation which has pineapples, papayas, avocados and bananas for sale. Buy some while you have the chance because food at the hotel is very expensive.

The hotel, *Auberge de Mont Hoyo*, is not cheap for a room with three beds, and you will literally have to beg for electricity. It's possible to camp cheaply, the cost for which includes use of a toilet and showers. If you have no tent and cannot afford the hotel, there's a small room adjoining the toilet and bathroom which you can rent fairly cheaply (it sleeps up to four people on the floor). Meals are very expensive. Some food can be bought from Pygmies who come up to the hotel.

Warning
Because of instability, political uncertainty and in some cases military action, travellers planning to visit this region are advised to check with the appropriate authority before leaving home, and/or with their diplomatic representatives abroad. ∎

Tanzania

Facts about the Country

Tanzania, with its magnificent wildlife reserves, is East Africa at its best. Famous parks such as Serengeti or the wonderful crater of Ngorongoro offer some of the best safari opportunities on the continent. While these two may be the best known of the country's numerous parks and reserves, many others deserve a visit. These range from the tiny Gombe Stream National Park chimpanzee sanctuary near the Burundi border to the huge and virtually untouched Selous Game Reserve in the south-east.

Parks and wildlife are not all Tanzania has to offer. In the north near the Kenyan border is snowcapped Mt Kilimanjaro, the highest mountain in Africa. Scaling this 5895-metre peak is the goal of many visitors. Offshore in the Indian Ocean are several islands, including exotic Zanzibar, with its labyrinthine old Stone Town, ruined palaces and Persian baths, fort and other reminders of the Omani period, not to mention its beaches and coral reefs.

HISTORY

No other African country has been moulded so closely in the image of a former president. Known as Mwalimu (teacher) in his own country and often referred to as the 'conscience of Black Africa' during his tenure, Tanzania's first president, Julius Nyerere, is one of Africa's elder statespeople.

He ruled his country as president for more than 20 years, until he stepped down in 1985 to become the chairman of his party, Chama Cha Mapinduzi (CCM, or the Party of the Revolution).

Like many other first presidents of postcolonial Africa, such as Nkrumah (Ghana), Sekou Touré (Guinea) and Kaunda (Zambia), Nyerere was firmly committed to radical socialism and nonalignment. He was always in the forefront of African liberation struggles, and Dar es Salaam has been home to many a political exile or guerrilla fighter.

Likewise, he never missed an opportunity to condemn the apartheid regime of South Africa during the years of confrontation.

Certainly his sincerity couldn't be faulted, but a more pragmatic attitude to solving his country's problems might well have been more realistic than rigid adherence to ideology. On the other hand, his popularity among the people cannot be doubted. In the 1975 and 1980 elections, he picked up more than 90% of the vote. None of his party colleagues has come even close to matching this performance.

Since November 1985, Ali Hassan Mwinyi has been the president though, out of respect to Nyerere, their photographs appear side by side in most offices, hotel foyers, restaurants, etc.

Early Settlement

Not a great deal is known about the early history of the Tanzanian interior except that by 1800 CE, the Maasai, who in previous centuries had grazed their cattle in the Lake Turkana region of Kenya, had migrated down the Rift Valley as far as Dodoma. Their advance was only stopped by the Gogo, who occupied an area west of the Rift Valley, and the Hehe to the south of Dodoma. Because of their reputation as a warrior tribe, the Maasai were feared by the neighbouring Bantu tribes and avoided by the Arab traders, so the northern part of Tanzania was almost free from the depredations of the slave trade and the civil wars which destroyed so many villages and settlements in other areas of the country.

Now the Maasai occupy only a fraction of their former grazing grounds and have been forced to share it with some of Tanzania's most famous national parks and game reserves. Although some of the southern clans have built permanent villages and planted crops, their northern cousins have retained their pastoral habits and are the least

Tanzania

0   100   200 km

TANZANIA

affected by, or interested in, the mainstream of modern Tanzania. Most of the other tribes of this country have more or less given up their traditional customs under the pressure of Nyerere's drive to create a unified nation which cuts across tribal divisions.

Arab Traders & Slavers

Though the coastal area had long been the scene of maritime rivalry, first between the Portuguese and Arab traders and later between the various European powers, it was Arab traders and slavers who first penetrated the interior as far as Lake Tanganyika in the middle of the 18th century. Their main depots were at Ujiji on the shores of Lake Tanganyika and at Tabora on the central plain. Their captives, generally acquired by commerce rather than force, were taken first to Bagamoyo and then to Zanzibar, where they were either put to work on plantations, or shipped to the Arabian Peninsula for sale as domestic servants.

It was, nevertheless, a sordid trade which devastated the tribes of the interior. The young and the strong were abducted, children and old people were left to die, and the few who resisted were eliminated. Mothers unable to carry both their babies and their ivory load were dispatched with a spear or machete. It's estimated that by the late 19th century, over 1½ million people had been transported to the coast and that 10 times that number had died along the caravan routes.

Zanzibar had been ruled for decades from Oman at the mouth of the Persian Gulf. By the first half of the 1800s, it had become so important as a slaving and spice entrepôt that the Omani Sultan, Seyyid Said, moved his capital there from Muscat in 1832. Though cloves had only been introduced to Zanzibar from the Moluccas in 1818, by the end of Seyyid Said's reign it was producing 75% of the world's supply.

British Influence

Britain's interest in this area stemmed from the beginning of the 19th century, when a treaty had been signed with Seyyid Said's predecessor to forestall possible Napoleonic French threats to British possessions in India. The British were only too pleased that a friendly Oriental power should extend its dominion down the East African coast rather than leave it open to the French. When Seyyid Said moved to Zanzibar, the British set up their first consulate there.

At that time, Britain was actively trying to suppress the slave trade, and various treaties limiting the trade were signed with the Omani sultans. But it wasn't until 1873, under the threat of a naval bombardment, that Sultan Barghash (Seyyid Said's successor) signed a decree outlawing the slave trade. Though the decree abolished the seaborne trade, slavery continued on the mainland for many years, as it was an integral part of the search for ivory. Indeed, slavery probably intensified the slaughter of elephants, since ivory was now one of the few exportable commodities which held its value, despite transport costs to the coast. Slaves were the means of transport.

European explorers began arriving around the middle of the 19th century, the most famous being Stanley and Livingstone. Stanley's famous phrase, 'Dr Livingstone, I presume', stems from their meeting at Ujiji on Lake Tanganyika. Other notable explorers in this region included Burton and Speke, who were sent to Lake Tanganyika in 1858 by the Royal Geographical Society.

The German Colonial Era

A little later, the German explorer Carl Peters set about persuading unsuspecting and generally illiterate chiefs to sign so-called treaties of friendship. On the strength of these, the German East Africa Company was set up to exploit and colonise what was to become Tanganyika. Though much of the coastal area was held by the Sultan of Zanzibar, German gunboats were used to ensure his compliance. The company's sphere of influence was soon declared a protectorate of the German state, after an agreement signed with Britain gave the Germans Tanganyika, Rwanda and Burundi while the British took Kenya and Uganda.

Like the British in Kenya, the Germans set about building railways and roads to open their colony to commerce, building hospitals and schools and encouraging the influx of Christian missionaries. However, unlike Kenya's fertile and climatically pleasant highlands, eminently suitable for European farmers to colonise, much of Tanganyika was unsuitable for agriculture. Also, in large areas of central and southern Tanganyika, the tsetse fly made cattle grazing or dairying impossible. Most farming occurred along the coast and around Mt Kilimanjaro and Mt Meru. A few descendents of the original German settlers still live in these areas.

The detachment of the sultan's coastal mainland possessions didn't go down too well with his subjects, and Bagamoyo, Pangani and Tanga rose in revolt. These revolts were crushed, as were other anti-German revolts in 1889. The most serious revolt against German rule, however, was the Maji Maji uprising between 1905 and 1906, triggered by resentment over a cotton scheme. Believing themselves invincible when annointed by 'holy water' ('maji' is Swahili for 'water') but inadequately equipped, some 75,000 to 120,000 Africans lost their lives before the revolt fizzled out in the face of superior German weaponry.

The German occupation continued until the end of WW I, after which the League of Nations mandated Tanganyika to the British and Rwanda and Burundi to the Belgians, but not before a long and hard campaign had been fought. The famous German cruiser *Königsberg* harrassed and sank British ships along the East African coast, including the *Pegasus* in Zanzibar harbour, before it was forced to take refuge in the Rufiji delta, where the British finally located it using aerial reconnaissance and sank it. Inland, the fighting was equally protracted. While steamers exchanged fire on Lake Victoria, the British were forced to transport gunboats all the way from South Africa to Lake Tanganyika to counter the German naval threat on that lake. On land, General Paul von Lettow Vorbeck led the British forces a withering cat-and-mouse game throughout the

war, including beating them soundly at Tanga and holding them at bay in the south. The armistice in East Africa was only declared two weeks after the same was declared in Europe and with von Lettow Vorbeck still unbeaten.

The British Period

Because of the tsetse flies that made much of central and southern Tanzania unsuitable for agriculture and stock raising, the British tended to neglect development of Tanganyika in favour of the more lucrative and fertile options available in Kenya and Uganda. Nevertheless, political consciousness gradually coalesced in the form of farmers unions and cooperatives through which popular demands were expressed. By the early 1950s, there were over 400 such cooperatives, which were shortly to amalgamate with the Tanganyika Africa Association (TAA), based in Dar es Salaam.

Independence

By 1953, Julius Nyerere had gained the leadership of the TAA, and quickly transformed it into an effective political organisation by amalgamating it with other political groups into the Tanganyika African National Union (TANU), which had as its slogan 'Uhuru na Umoja' (Freedom and Unity). The British would have preferred to see a 'multiracial' constitution adopted by the nationalists so as to protect the European and Asian minorities, but this was opposed by Nyerere. Sensibly, the last British governor, Sir Richard Turnbull, ditched the idea and Tanganyika attained independence in 1961 with Nyerere as the country's first president.

It was a smooth, bloodless transition and TANU was fortunate in having no tribal conflicts, dominant tribe or linguistic divisions which could have torn it apart.

The island of Zanzibar had quite a different experience in its push for independence. It had been a British protectorate since 1890, as had a 16-km-wide strip of the entire Kenyan coastline which was considered to belong to the sultan. The main push for independence came from the AfroShirazi Party

(ASP), which was formed in 1957. It was opposed by two minority parties, the Zanzibar & Pemba People's Party and the Arab Sultanate-oriented Nationalist Party, which were favoured by the British administration. The British actively intervened on behalf of the two minority parties, denying the ASP power in three preindependence elections so that, at independence in 1963, it was the two minority parties which formed the first government. But it didn't last long. Angered by continued victimisation, the ASP, led by Abeid Amaan Karume and supported by TANU on the mainland, initiated a bloody revolution which quickly resulted in the toppling of the sultan and the massacre or expulsion of the bulk of the island's Arab population. The sultan was replaced by a revolutionary council formed by the AfroShirazi Party. A short time later, Zanzibar and the other offshore island of Pemba merged with mainland Tanganyika to form the United Republic of Tanzania. Later, in 1977, in order to promote unity and collective leadership, TANU and ASP merged to form the Chama cha Mapinduzi (CCM), which still rules today.

Socialist Tanzania

Nyerere inherited a country which had been largely ignored by the British colonial authorities, since it had few exploitable resources and only one major export crop, sisal. Education had been neglected too, so that at independence, there were only 120 university graduates in the whole country.

It was an inauspicious beginning, and the problems it created eventually led to the Arusha Declaration of 1967. Based on the Chinese communist model, the cornerstone of this policy was the Ujamaa village – a collective agricultural venture run along traditional African lines. The villages were intended to be socialist organisations, created by the people and governed by those who lived and worked in them. Self-reliance was the key word in the hundreds of villages that were set up. Basic goods and tools were to be held in common and shared among

members, whilst each individual was obligated to work on the land.

Nyerere's proposals for education were seen as an essential part of this scheme and were designed to foster constructive attitudes to cooperative endeavour, stress the concept of social equality and responsibility and counter the tendency towards intellectual arrogance among the educated.

At the same time, the economy was nationalised, as was a great deal of rented property. Taxes were increased in an attempt to redistribute individual wealth. Nyerere also sought to ensure that those in political power did not develop into an exploitative class, by banning government ministers and party officials from holding shares or directorships in companies or from receiving more than one salary. They were also prohibited from owning rented properties. Nevertheless, corruption remained widespread.

In the early days of the Ujamaa movement, progressive farmers were encouraged to expand in the hope that other peasants would follow their example. This enriched those who were the recipients of state funds but resulted in little improvement in rural poverty. The approach was therefore abandoned in favour of direct state control and peasants were resettled into planned villages with the object of modernising and monetising the agricultural sector of the economy. The settlements were to be well provided with potable water, clinics, schools, fertilisers, high-yielding seeds and, where possible, irrigation. This new approach also failed, since the finance for this sort of venture was well beyond the country's resources, and there was a lot of hostility and resentment among the peasants towards what they regarded as compulsory resettlement without any consultation or influence over the decision-making process.

Following the second failure, a third scheme was adopted. This was based on persuading the peasants to amalgamate their small holdings into large, communally owned farms, using economic incentives and shifting the emphasis to self-reliance. In this way, the benefits reaped by the members of

Ujamaa settlements would be a direct reflection of the dedication of those who lived there. The scheme had its critics but was relatively successful and prompted the government to adopt a policy of compulsory 'villagisation' of the entire rural population.

Despite lip service to his policies, there was little development aid from the West, so Nyerere turned to the People's Republic of China as a foreign partner. Part of the aid package involved China building the TAZARA railway from Dar es Salaam to Kapiri Mposhi in the copper belt of Zambia, at a cost of some US$400 million. For a while it was the showpiece of eastern and southern Africa and considerably reduced Zambia's dependence on the Zimbabwean (at that time Rhodesian) and South African railway systems. OPEC's oil price hike at the beginning of the 1970s, however, led to a financial crisis and Tanzania was no longer able to afford any more than essential maintenance of the railway. There were also serious fuel shortages. As a result, the railway no longer functioned anywhere near as well as it did when first built, though things have recently been improving.

Tanzania's experiment in radical socialism and self-reliance might have been a courageous path to follow in the heady days following independence, and during the 1970s when not only Tanzania but many other African countries were feeling the oil price pinch. However, only romantics would argue with the assessment that it failed. The transport system fell into ruin, agricultural production became stagnant, the industrial sector limped along at well under 50% capacity, and virtually all economic incentives were eliminated. Obviously, numerous factors contributed to Tanzania's woes, and many of them were beyond its control, not least the fact that Tanzania is one of the world's poorest countries. At least, that was true of the mainland, for Zanzibar was one of the most prosperous countries in Africa at the time of independence.

Part of the trouble was that Nyerere had no intention of changing and he tolerated no dissent. In 1979, Tanzanian jails held more political prisoners than South Africa's, though over 6000 were freed late that year and a further 4400 the following year. Even though Nyerere is no longer president, his influence lingers on. Mwinyi (president of Zanzibar from 1984 to 1985) has successfully distanced himself from Nyerere and his policies, but the pace of change is slow and unlikely to accelerate until after Nyerere's death.

Tanzania has been one of the most consistently outspoken supporters of African liberation movements, particularly in the south. Nyerere joined with Zambia's Kaunda in supporting the guerrillas fighting for the independence of Angola and Mozambique from the Portuguese, and also those fighting to overthrow the White minority government of Rhodesia during Ian Smith's regime. This support cost both countries dearly and it will be a long time before they fully recover.

Tanzania also provided asylum to Ugandan exiles during Idi Amin's regime, including Milton Obote and the current president, Yoweri Museveni. This support almost bankrupted Tanzania. In October 1978, Idi Amin sent his army into northern Tanzania and occupied the Kagera salient, and also sent in his airforce to bomb the Lake Victoria ports of Bukoba and Musoma. It was done, so he said, to teach Tanzania a lesson for supporting exiled groups hostile to his regime, but it's more likely that it was a diversionary movement to head off a mutiny among his restless troops.

As Tanzania had hardly any army worth mentioning, it took several months to scrape together a people's militia of 50,000 men and get them to the front. They were ill-equipped and poorly trained but they utterly routed the Ugandans – supposedly Africa's best trained and best equipped army at the time. The Ugandans threw down their weapons and fled and the Tanzanians pushed on into Uganda. A 12,000-strong Tanzanian contingent stayed in the country for some time to maintain law and order and to ensure that Nyerere could exert a significant influence over the choice of Amin's successor. The war cost Tanzania around

US$500 million, and it received not a single contribution from any source.

Not only that, but Tanzania was half-heartedly condemned by other African countries within the Organisation of African Unity (OAU). One of the cardinal principles of the OAU is that African borders are inviolable and member states must not interfere in the internal affairs of others. It wasn't the first time Tanzania had interfered in the affairs of its neighbours. Nyerere had helped to topple two other regimes, once in the Comoros Islands in 1975 and again in the Seychelles in 1977.

GEOGRAPHY

A land of plains, lakes and mountains with a narrow coastal belt, Tanzania is East Africa's largest country. The bulk of its 945,087 sq km is a highland plateau, some of it desert or semidesert and the rest savannah and scattered bush. Much of the plateau is relatively uninhabited because the tsetse fly prevents stock raising. The highest mountains – Meru (4556 metres) and Kilimanjaro (Africa's highest at 5895 metres) – are in the northeast, along the border with Kenya.

Along the coast is a narrow low-lying strip and offshore are the islands of Pemba, Zanzibar and Mafia. More than 53,000 sq km of the country is covered by inland lakes, most of them in the Rift Valley.

CLIMATE

Tanzania's widely varying geography accounts for its variety of climatic conditions. Much of the country is a high plateau, where the altitude considerably tempers what would otherwise be a tropical climate. In many places, it can be quite cool at night.

The coastal strip along the Indian Ocean and the offshore islands of Pemba, Zanzibar and Mafia have a hot, humid, tropical climate, tempered by sea breezes. The high mountains are in the north-east, along the Kenyan border, and this area enjoys an almost temperate climate for most of the year.

The long rainy season is from April to May, when it rains virtually every day. The short rains fall during November and December, though it frequently rains in January, too.

GOVERNMENT

Executive power rests with the president and the ruling Chama Cha Mapinduzi (CCM or Party of the Revolution) of which there are 297 members in the national assembly. Both the president (Ali Hassan Mwinyi) and the national assembly are elected for five-year terms. Both the prime minister of Tanzania and the president of Zanzibar are vice-presidents of the Republic of Tanzania.

While the CCM was, until recently, the only legal political party, Tanzania was forced to bow to the winds of political liberalism sweeping Africa and accept multiparty politics in 1991. Since then, several parties opposed to the CCM have emerged, but progress towards free elections has been slow. Kenya's 1992 experiment in multiparty elections was watched with great interest by Tanzania's opposition parties which quickly saw the folly of dividing their strength and competing not just with the incumbent government but with each other.

While all this has been going on, there have been serious political moves in Zanzibar to dissolve the union and make Zanzibar, once again, independent. Zanzibar, it seems, wants to go its own way even though it has always enjoyed a considerable degree of autonomy. As any visitor to the island will know, there has always been a separate passport check on arrival and, until recently, a compulsory money change on arrival. Just why the island wants to secede isn't quite clear, but relevant factors probably include the island's exclusively Islamic culture (and its fear of Christian influence), the increase in tourism, and a desire to enhance overseas investment. The government of Zanzibar recently and unilaterally applied for membership of the Islamic Conference, a move which was vetoed by the union government on the grounds that this was the prerogative of the central government.

It may just be a hiccup, but there were riots related to the behaviour of tourists in 1992,

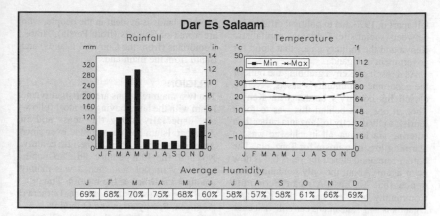

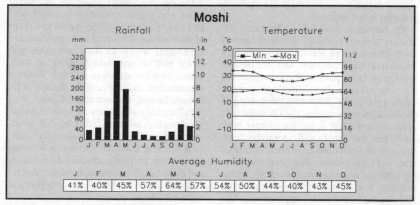

though these were probably politically motivated. On the other hand, the president, Ali Hassan Mwinyi is himself a Zanzibari.

ECONOMY

Tanzania, or Tanganyika as it once partly was, was always the poor cousin of the British colonial Kenya-Uganda-Tanganyika trio. Although it did not have the problem of a large influx of European settlers, Tanzania was still a seriously underdeveloped country at the time of independence. Things have not improved – the economy is still overwhelmingly agricultural and, overall, has been marked mostly by mismanagement and decline.

Sisal, a fibre plant used for cordage, is the leading export. Other cash crops are cloves (80% of world supply), coffee, cotton, coconuts, tea, cashew nuts and timber. Diamonds, gold, tin and mica are mined.

Perhaps Tanzania's economy wouldn't have got into such a parlous state if the East African Economic Community had been allowed to work. At the time of independence, Kenya, Tanzania and Uganda were linked in an economic union which shared a common airline, telecommunication and postal facilities, transportation and customs. Their currencies were freely convertible and there was freedom of movement. Any person from one country could work in another. It fell apart in 1977 due to political differences between socialistic Tanzania, capitalistic Kenya and the military chaos that stood for government in Uganda.

As a result of Kenya grabbing the bulk of the economic community's assets, Nyerere closed his country's border with Kenya. Though one idea behind this was to force tourists to fly directly to Tanzania rather than entering via Kenya, all it achieved was an alarming loss of tourism for Tanzania. The border remained closed for years but is now open again. About the only remaining evidence that an East African Economic Community once existed is that Kenyans, Ugandans and Tanzanians can still visit each other's country with a simple ID paper. A passport is not required.

On becoming president of Tanzania, Ali Hassan Mwinyi gradually distanced himself from Nyerere and introduced reforms to liberalise the economy and encourage foreign investment, but it was a slow process for many years. It is developing more momentum in the 1990s with the floating of the local currency against the US dollar and a determined effort to get the country back on its feet, but there's still a lot to be done. Some of the main roads have been resurfaced with aid from various European countries, the railways run somewhat more efficiently, tourism has increased dramatically and there's even talk of multiparty elections. But don't hold your breath. Roads outside the north-eastern region are appalling, the telephone system is frequently out of order, the national airline, Air Tanzania, is virtually defunct, the press is still essentially muzzled, and the capital, Dar es Salaam, is still very much down-at-heel. Try to find a bookshop in Dar es Salaam which sells anything other than dreary Marxist tomes or African liberation rhetoric dating from the 1960s.

POPULATION

The population of Tanzania is about 20 million. There are more than 100 tribal groups, the majority of which are of Bantu origin. The Arab influence on Zanzibar and Pemba islands is evident in the people, who are a mix of Shirazis (from Persia), Arabs, Comorians (from the Comoros Islands) and Bantu from the mainland.

RELIGION

The two main religions are Christianity and Islam with the latter having the most followers, especially along the coast and in Zanzibar. Islam has been around ever since Arab traders arrived here in the 12th century. Not until the 19th century did Christianity make any impact, and then it was mainly amongst the tribes of the interior. The principal Christian sects are Catholic, Lutheran, Anglican, Presbyterian and Orthodox.

On the other hand, there are still many tribes who follow neither of the above religions and prefer to worship the ancient spirit of their choice. Principal amongst them are the Maasai, who place their faith in the god *Engai* and his messiah, *Kindong'oi*, from whom their priests are descended. Worship is conducted under special fig trees or at Ol Doinyo Lengai, the mountain of god.

In Tanzania, as in many African countries, religion plays an important part in the availability of educational and medical facilities, as is obvious from the number of schools, clinics and hospitals attached to mosques and churches. It's claimed, however, that no religious bias exists in the country's political and civil administration.

LANGUAGE

Swahili (KiSwahili) is the official language but English remains widely spoken and is the principal language of commerce. There are also many local African languages, reflecting the tribal diversity of the country. Outside the cities and towns, far fewer local people speak English than you would find in comparable areas in Kenya. It's said that the Swahili spoken in Zanzibar is of a much purer form than that which you find in Kenya (at least, that's their story), and quite a few travellers come here to learn it, since the Institute of KiSwahili & Foreign Languages is on the island.

Facts for the Visitor

VISAS & EMBASSIES

Visas are required by all visitors to Tanzania, except nationals of most Commonwealth countries (Canada excepted), Scandinavian countries, the Republic of Ireland, Rwanda, Romania and Sudan. For these nationalities, a free visitor's pass, valid for one to three months, is obtainable at the border (you'll be asked how long you want to stay – three months is no problem).

For other nationalities, visa costs vary. Canadians are hardest hit (around US$40), while Israelis have it the easiest (around US$6.50). Others fall in between these two figures. Two photos are required and visas are generally issued in 48 hours (24 hours if you get there early in the morning). You generally get what you ask for, up to three months. Even South African passport holders can now get visas for Tanzania, despite all the years of official political hatred and rhetoric, but it does take some weeks for them to come through.

In the past, some Tanzanian borders acquired bad reputations for hassling travellers but this was connected either with currency or with suspected visits to South Africa. That's all finished with the introduction of Forex bureaus, the abolition of currency declaration forms and a reluctant *rapprochement* with South Africa. You shouldn't have any problems, except with the occasional overzealous official.

If you take a car across the border into Tanzania, you will have to buy a 90-day road permit for TSh 1000.

Tanzanian Embassies

You can obtain visas for Tanzania in the capital cities of the following neighbouring countries:

Burundi The Tanzanian Embassy in Bujumbura is on Ave de l'ONU, around the corner from the Rwandan and Zaïre embassies on Ave du Zaïre. As elsewhere, visa costs vary according to your nationality, two photographs are required and visas are issued in 24 hours. Opening hours are Monday to Friday from 8 am till noon and 2 to 5 pm.

Kenya In Nairobi, the Tanzanian High Commission (☎ 331056/7) is on the 4th floor, Continental House, on the corner of Harambee Ave and Uhuru Highway. It's open Monday to Friday from 8.30 am to 12.30 pm and 2 to 5 pm but visa applications are only accepted between 9 am and noon. Visas take 48 hours to issue and require two photographs.

Rwanda The Tanzanian Embassy (☎ 76074) is on Ave Paul VI close to the junction with Ave de Rusumo. Visas generally take 48 hours to be issued and require two photos. The embassy is open Monday to Friday from 9 am to 2 pm.

Uganda The Tanzanian High Commission (☎ 56755) is at 6 Kagera Rd, and is open Monday to Friday from 9 am to 3 pm. Visas take 48 hours to issue and require two photographs.

Other Countries There are Tanzanian embassies in Addis Ababa (Ethiopia), Bonn (Germany), Brussels (Belgium), Cairo (Egypt), Conakry (Guinea), Geneva (Switzerland), The Hague (Netherlands), Harare (Zimbabwe), Khartoum (Sudan), Kinshasa (Zaïre), Lagos (Nigeria), London (UK), Lusaka (Zambia), New Delhi (India), New York (USA), Ottawa (Canada), Paris (France), Rome (Italy), Stockholm (Sweden), Tokyo (Japan) and Washington DC (USA).

Foreign Embassies in Tanzania

Burundi The embassy (☎ 46307) is at Plot 1007, Lugalo Rd, Dar es Salaam, next door to the Italian Embassy and at the back of the Palm Beach Hotel. Office hours are Monday to Friday from 8 am to 2.30 pm and Saturday from 8 am to 12.30 pm. Visas cost US$20 (or the equivalent in local currency), require two photos and are issued in 24 hours. There's also a Burundi consulate in Kigoma on Lake Tanganyika.

Kenya The high commission (☎ 46362/6) is on the 14th floor, NIC Investment House, Samora Ave, at the junction with Mirambo St, Dar es Salaam. It is open Monday to Friday from 8 am to 3 pm but visa applications are only dealt with between 9 am and noon. Visas cost US$10 (or equivalent in local currency), require two photographs and take 24 hours to be issued.

Rwanda The embassy (☎ 46502) is at 32 Upanga Rd, Dar es Salaam. Visas cost US$20 (or equivalent in local currency), require two photographs and take 24 hours to be issued. They're valid for a stay of one month. Office hours for visa applications are Monday to Friday from 8 am to 12.30 pm and 2 to 5 pm.

Uganda The high commission (☎ 31003/5) is on the 7th floor, Extelecoms building, Samora Ave, Dar es Salaam. Visas cost US$20 or US$25, depending on your nationality, require two photographs and are issued in 24 hours. Office hours are Monday to Friday from 8 am to 3.45 pm.

Zaïre The embassy (☎ 24181/2) is at 438 Malik Rd, Dar es Salaam. A one-month, single-entry visa costs US$75 (US$120 for multiple entry), a two-month, single-entry visa costs US$135 (US$180 for multiple entry), a three-month, single-entry visa costs US$200 (US$225 for multiple entry), and a six-month, single-entry visa costs US$270 (US$360 for multiple entry). Three photographs are required, as well as a letter of recommendation from your own embassy. Visas are issued in 24 hours. Office hours are Monday to Friday from 8 am to 3 pm.

There's also a Zaïrian consulate in Kigoma. Office hours are Monday to Friday from 9 am till noon.

Zambia The high commission (☎ 46383/9) is at 5/9 Sokoine Drive, Dar es Salaam. Office hours are Monday to Friday from 8 am till noon and 2 to 4.30 pm.

Francophone Countries Dar es Salaam is a good place to stock up on francophone country visas (Central African Republic, Chad, etc). As there are very few of these embassies in the capital you must get them all from the French Embassy (☎ 66021) which is at the corner of Bagamoyo and Kulimani Rds. It's open Monday to Friday from 8 am to 4 pm.

MONEY
Currency
The unit of currency is the Tanzanian shilling (TSh). There are bills of TSh 1000, 500, 200, 100 and 50 shillings and coins of TSh 20, 10 and five shillings. There are two sizes of the TSh 1000 and TSh 500 bills in circulation, both of which are legal tender. The smaller notes are new issue.

Exchange Rates

US$1	=	TSh 440 (cash)
US$1	=	TSh 412 (travellers' cheques)
UK£1	=	TSh 620 (cash)
UK£1	=	TSh 600 (travellers' cheques)

Despite the liberalisation of the currency, there is still an official exchange rate, which is US$1 = TSh 345. This will only affect you if you use international credit cards, in which case you'll be billed at the official exchange rate – not the Forex rate. If you have the option, it obviously makes sense not to use credit cards.

Changing Money
Forex Bureaus In the past, Tanzania used to overvalue its currency to a ridiculous degree and the black market for foreign currency was rampant. That's all changed, and there are now Forex bureaus in most towns and cities where you can change cash or

travellers' cheques at the prevailing free market exchange rate. You can do the same at the Tanzania Commercial Bank. The day's rates are prominently displayed at both places and there's no messing about. A transaction takes a couple of minutes. A black market still exists but offers only marginally better rates than the Forex bureaus and banks. If you get offered substantially more, forget it – you're being set up for a robbery.

If you need to change money where there are no Forex bureaus, the banks will only change at the official rate. Why? Because you have no choice! The message is: stock up while you can at a Forex bureau.

There are Forex bureaus at Namanga, Arusha, Moshi, Dar es Salaam, Zanzibar and various other places, but none in Morogoro, for instance. The Forex bureau at Dar es Salaam airport offers rates comparable to those in the city centre, so you can change here with confidence.

In theory, the introduction of Forex bureaus meant you could not only trade hard currency for local currency but could also buy hard currency with local currency, albeit at a premium. In theory, that's true. If you want to buy US dollars with Tanzanian shillings, then they'll cost you US$1 = TSh 450 – if they have them and if they want to sell them. It's definitely possible but not easy. No-one really wants to part with hard cash. I've met people who have been waiting for hours trying to do this at a Tanzania Commercial Bank. I tried it, too, at a popular Forex bureau on Samora Ave in Dar es Salaam, but they said (or pretended) they had only US$25. I doubt it was the truth. It's a far cry from Uganda, where all this is very simple.

The only place where you can readily reconvert Tanzanian shillings into US dollars is at Dar es Salaam airport, but you must produce either a bank receipt or a Forex bureau exchange receipt and, in any case, their rates are lousy.

Kenyan currency used to be considered a more-or-less 'hard' currency in Tanzania. That no longer applies. As we go to press, KSh 1 = TSh 7.50 and it's on the way down.

Hard Currency Payments Despite the introduction of Forex bureaus in Tanzania, there are a lot of things which must be paid for in hard cash or travellers' cheques. This includes national park entry fees, most mid-range and top-end hotels, airline tickets and even the hydrofoil between Zanzibar and Dar es Salaam. The rest (cheap hotels, meals, transport, etc) are payable in local shillings. The problem here is that if you're paying in travellers' cheques and the amount of the cheque doesn't match the bill, you'll be given change in local currency at the official bank rate – US$1 = TSh 345)! In other words, bullshit still prevails to a degree. If you pay in cash US dollars but your banknote doesn't match the charge you have to pay, you have a sporting chance of getting the change in US dollars cash – but don't count on it. Have lots of small US dollar bills handy to counter this. It's not usually a hassle at the national park gates, since they generally have plenty of change in hard cash.

Credit Cards Diners Club, American Express and, to a lesser extent, Visa and MasterCard credit cards are generally acceptable in the more expensive restaurants and major hotels, as well as a few other places, but you'll be billed at the offical bank rate.

Currency Declaration The export of Tanzanian shillings is officially limited to TSh 200; import is offically prohibited. However, no-one cares about this any more.

TOURIST OFFICE

The Tanzania Tourist Corporation (TTC) has offices in Dar es Salaam (☎ 2761/4), Maktaba St, PO Box 2485; Zanzibar (☎ 32344), Livingstone House, PO Box 216; and Arusha (☎ 3842) on Boma Rd opposite Air Tanzania.

The TTC can make bookings for you at any of the large hotels and national park lodges under their control.

The TTC also has offices in the following countries:

Germany
    Kaiserstrasse 13, 6000 Frankfurt Main 1
    (☎ (0611) 280154)
Italy
    Palazzo Africa, Largo Africa 1, Milano
    (☎ 432870, 464421)
Sweden
    Oxtorgsgatan 2-4, PO Box 7627, 102 94 Stockholm (☎ (08) 216700)
UK
    43 Hertford St, London W1
USA
    201 East 42nd St, New York, NY 10017 (☎ (212) 986-7124)

USEFUL ORGANISATIONS

The national parks are managed by the Tanzania National Parks Authority (☎ 3471), PO Box 3134, Arusha. Its main administrative office is on the 6th floor, Kilimanjaro Wing, Arusha International Conference Centre. If you call in, there may be a range of descriptive leaflets about the national parks and a reasonably good road map of the Serengeti National Park (there's a nominal charge).

BUSINESS HOURS & HOLIDAYS

Banking hours are Monday to Friday from 8.30 am to 12.30 pm and Saturday from 8.30 to 11.30 am.

The following public holidays are observed in Tanzania:

January
    Zanzibar Revolution Day (12th)
February
    CCM Foundation Day (5th)
April
    Union Day (26th)
May
    Workers' Day (1st)
July
    Peasants' Day (7th)
December
    Independence Day (9th)
    Christmas Day (25th)

Variable public holidays are Good Friday, Easter Monday, Id ul Fitr (end of Ramadan) and Id ul Haji.

POST & TELECOMMUNICATIONS

The poste restante is well organised and you should have no problems with expected letters not turning up. The same is true for telegrams. There's a small charge for collecting letters.

Extelecoms House, on Samora Ave in Dar es Salaam, has an efficient international exchange. You can usually get a connection in just a couple of minutes, but it's expensive. Expect to pay US$10 *per minute*! A deposit is payable before you are connected. Reverse charge (collect) calls cannot be made from here.

You can also make overseas calls through a hotel switchboard, but they'll add on a commission of at least 25%.

While international calls are fairly easily arranged, domestic calls (including those to Kenya and Uganda) are another story. There are days when it's easy and days when it's all but impossible. If it happens to be one of the latter, forget it and try again the next day. One of the most notorious lines is that between Arusha and Nairobi.

TIME

The time in Tanzania is GMT/UTC plus three hours.

BOOKS

The *Tourist Guide to Tanzania* (Dar es Salaam, 1991), by Gratian Luhikula, is probably the best local guide available and is good value at TSh 3200 for 275 pages of information. The descriptive passages provide excellent background information on all places of interest, but accommodation and transport are inadequately covered. The maps, too, are of limited use. It's available in bookshops in Dar es Salaam.

Also worth buying, if you're going to Zanzibar and/or Pemba, is *A Tale of Two Islands – Zanzibar* (Zanzibar, 1992), by the Commission for Tourism. It covers all the places to see and the places to stay quite adequately and includes prices. The maps are not too bad.

There's also a recently published series of well-produced and illustrated booklets which cover most of Tanzania's principal national parks. Published by the Tanzania National Parks Authority in cooperation with the African Wildlife Foundation, they cost about US$5 each and are excellent safari companions. The series includes *Arusha National Park, Kilimanjaro National Park, Tarangire National Park, Ngorongoro Conservation Area, Mikumi National Park* and *Gombe Stream National Park*, among others. They're available from bookshops and hotel stores.

MEDIA
Newspapers & Magazines
Although 'liberalisation' is the name of the game these days, the government doesn't like criticism. As a result, it does its best to harrass independent newspaper publishers and journalists to the point where they either go bust or prepare themselves to carry on regardless. The government's official English-language newspaper is the *Daily News*, which you can get in most places. It's a dreadful rag and essentially a 'what the president did today' type of publication. Foreign news coverage is minimal.

International magazines and periodicals and the Kenyan *Nation* can be found at stalls along Samora Ave and Maktaba St in Dar es Salaam and around the post office in Arusha.

HEALTH
Make sure you have a valid vaccination certificate for yellow fever before arriving in Tanzania. You won't be asked for it at land borders and you probably won't be asked for it if you arrive by air through either Kilimanjaro or Dar es Salaam airports, but it's essential for Zanzibar and Pemba. Officially, you are prohibited from entering Zanzibar or Pemba without a valid certificate, and these will be checked on the dockside at Dar es Salaam before boarding any of the boats to Zanzibar or on arrival by air. In practice, it's just about negotiable but you're in for a major hassle. A Kenyan friend was refused permission to board the boat for Zanzibar in Dar es Salaam until the very last minute because she didn't have one. It must have

been her lucky day, as four Russians also turned up who didn't have certificates. They, too, were given a hard time but were eventually allowed on. After that, they couldn't refuse her without it appearing to be a case of racial discrimination.

As in most African countries, you must take precautions against malaria. Most of the lakes and rivers of Tanzania carry a risk of bilharzia if you bathe in them or walk along the shores without footwear, especially where the vegetation is very reedy. Tsetse flies are distributed over large areas of the central plateau, though they're only a real nuisance in a few places (insect repellant and a fly whisk are useful). Tarangire National Park is infested with them – keep the windows shut on game drives!

FILM & PHOTOGRAPHY
Bring all your photographic requirements with you, as very little is available outside Dar es Salaam, Arusha and Zanzibar. Even in these places, the choice is very limited and prices are high. Slide film is a rarity – colour negative and B&W film are what's mostly available. If you're desperate for film, the large hotels are probably your best bet. You'll be extremely lucky to find film at any of the national park lodges.

Don't take photographs of anything connected with the government or the military (government offices, post offices, banks, railway stations, bridges, airports, barracks, etc). If you do, you may well be arrested and your film confiscated. If you're on the TAZARA train from Dar es Salaam to Kapiri Mposhi (Zambia) and want to take photographs of game as you go through the Selous Game Reserve, get permission first from military personnel if possible or, failing that, from railway officials. You might think that what you are doing is completely innocuous but they may well think otherwise. Despite the reluctant *rapprochement* with South Africa, years of officially induced paranoia die hard.

Getting There & Away

It's possible to enter Tanzania by air, road, rail or boat. Rail access is only from Zambia. Even though the Tanzanian railway system is continuous with the Kenyan system, there are no through services. Boat connections on the lakes include a service on Lake Victoria between Port Bell (Uganda) and Mwanza (Tanzania) and another on Lake Tanganyika between Bujumbura (Burundi), Kigoma (Tanzania) and Mpulungu (Zambia). There are no connections on Lake Victoria between Kenya and Tanzania but there are dhows and a regular catamaran service between Mombasa, Zanzibar and Dar es Salaam.

AIR

International airlines serving Tanzania either through Kilimanjaro or Dar es Salaam international airports include Aeroflot, Air France, Air India, Alitalia, British Airways, EgyptAir, Ethiopian Airlines, Kenya Airways, KLM, Linhas Aereas Mocambique, Lufthansa, PIA, Sabena, SAS, Swissair and Uganda Airlines.

Quite a few travellers use Tanzania as a gateway to Africa, though it is not as popular as Nairobi. There's not a lot of difference between the fares to Nairobi and those to Dar es Salaam or Kilimanjaro. International flight tickets bought in Tanzania have to be paid for in hard currency, not local currency.

The departure tax for international flights is US$20 or UK£18, which must be paid for in hard currency. UK£1 coins are not acceptable.

To/From Kenya

The cheapest regular options to fly between Tanzania and Kenya are the Kenya Airways flights between Dar es Salaam and Nairobi (US$123 full fare one way but as little as US$110 bought from an agent) and Zanzibar and Mombasa (US$45), though you must add the US$20 departure tax to these prices. You can forget about Air Tanzania for the present because, although they schedule a Dar es Salaam to Nairobi flight, they have only one jet in their 'fleet' of just two planes and it's fully occupied servicing the Tanzanian domestic routes.

The Kenya Airways Mombasa-Zanzibar-Mombasa flight is very popular, so you need to book at least two weeks ahead if you want to be sure of getting a seat. It flies three times a week, on Sunday, Monday and Thursday.

Two private companies based in Zanzibar operate six and eight-seater propeller planes which occasionally fly between Zanzibar and Mombasa (US$45) or Nairobi (US$100). They are Air Zanzibar (☎ (054) 32512), 302 Kenyatta Rd, Shangani, Zanzibar, and Zan Air (☎ (054) 33670), Malindi, Zanzibar. To find out if they're going, contact their offices in Zanzibar or keep an eye on the notice boards at Africa House Hotel or the Fisherman Restaurant. They do not have offices in either Mombasa or Nairobi.

LAND

To/From Kenya

Dar es Salaam to Mombasa There are a number of bus companies (such as Coast, Cat and Tawfiq) which do the run from Dar es Salaam to Mombasa via Tanga and vice versa, though usually only once per week in either direction. The trip takes anything from 16 to 24 hours (eight to 12 hours from Tanga). The border at Lunga Lunga-Horohoro is quite straightforward, but it takes as much as four hours to clear all 50 or so people through both posts. The fare from Dar es Salaam to Mombasa is TSh 3000. The Cat bus office in Dar es Salaam is on Msimbazi St, close to the Kariakoo Market and the Caltex station. In Mombasa, it's on Kenyatta Ave.

Remember that buses are prohibited from travelling between 10 pm and 4 am within Tanzania (a government regulation introduced in early 1992 to cut down on the accident rate), so whatever they tell you in Mombasa about the arrival time in Dar es Salaam, don't believe it. The road between Dar es Salaam and Tanga is newly surfaced, but between Tanga and the border, it's diabolical.

You can also do the journey the hard way. From Tanga to the Tanzanian border post at Horohoro, there are a couple of buses per day along the rough single-lane dirt road (TSh 400). From Horohoro, it's a six-km walk to the Kenyan border post at Lunga Lunga, and there's very little traffic so hitching is difficult. Once through the Kenyan border post, however, there are frequent matatus for the one-hour journey to Mombasa.

Arusha & Moshi to Nairobi These days the trip between Nairobi and Arusha or Moshi is a breeze. There are at least three companies with direct buses/minibuses operating on a daily basis. The most expensive of them is the DHL Shuttle (run by the international courier company), which leaves Nairobi daily at 8.30 am from the Norfolk Hotel, and from Arusha at 2 pm from the Novotel Mt Meru. The fare from Nairobi is US$17. Advance booking is advisable, and this can be done at 8th floor, Town House, Kaunda St, Nairobi (☎ (02) 212804). In Arusha, the DHL office is in the foyer of the Novotel Mt Meru.

A similar shuttle service is operated by Tayler's Travel (☎ (02) 335365), Tubman Rd, Nairobi and on Swahili St, Arusha (☎ 3488).

Much cheaper is Arusha Express, which operates full-sized buses and has its office in amongst the cluster of bus companies down Accra Rd in Nairobi. In Arusha, the office is at the bus station. It operates a daily service, except Wednesday, leaving Nairobi at 8.30 am (US$5.70).

All buses take five hours, and getting through customs and immigration on them is straightforward.

It's also easy, but less convenient, to do this journey in stages, and since the Kenyan and Tanzanian border posts are next to each other at Namanga, there's no long walk involved. There are frequent matatus and shared taxis from Arusha to Namanga every day. These go when full and cost TSh 700 to TSh 1300 (negotiable). The taxis normally take about 1½ hours, though there are a number of kamikaze drivers who are totally crazy and will get you there in just one hour. From the Kenyan side of the border, there are frequent matatus (US$2.85, three hours) and share-taxis (US$4.30, two hours), which go when full. Both have their depot outside the petrol station on Ronald Ngala St, close to the junction with River Rd in Nairobi.

Moshi to Voi The crossing between Moshi and Voi via Taveta is also reliable as far as transport goes (buses, matatus and shared taxis). A matatu between Taveta and Voi (along a bumpy road) takes 2½ hours and costs US$2.60. There's also a train, which takes five hours and costs the same.

Musoma to Kisii It's much more difficult to cross the border between Musoma and Kisii via Isebania in the north; there are no matatus or buses which go all the way to the border, so you're looking at hiring a taxi or hitching. Hitching is difficult because there's very little traffic. On the other hand, this is one of the routes through to Zaïre which overland trucks use, so you may be lucky and get a lift all the way, though they don't come through that often.

Serengeti to Masai Mara If you look at any detailed map of the Serengeti National Park and Masai Mara Game Reserve, you'll see that there's a border crossing between Bologonja and Sand River, and so you would assume it's possible to cross here. It is if you're crossing *from* Kenya *to* Tanzania, assuming you have the appropriate vehicle documentation (insurance and temporary entry permit). But officially, it isn't possible to cross in the opposite direction because you must pay the park entry fee to Masai Mara and you must pay it in Kenyan shillings, which you ought not to have since, under Kenyan currency regulations, you're not allowed to export them. And the nearest place where you *might* be able to change money is at Keekorok Lodge, 10 km away. Just imagine! In practice, the border guards/park officials are very helpful, so if you just happen to have a sufficient stash of Kenyan shillings to pay the park entry fees, then like Nelson with his blind eye at Trafalgar, it's a question of 'I see no ships'.

To/From Malawi

The one crossing point here is between Karonga and Mbeya, at the top of Lake Malawi, via Tukuyu and Kyela. The Tanzanian side of this border was notorious for officialdom for years, though it should now have cooled off due to Tanzania's reluctant *rapprochement* with South Africa.

A daily bus from Karonga to the border at Iponga on the Songwe River departs between 2.30 and 3 pm and takes about four hours. The bus goes via Kaporo, where you get your Malawi exit stamp. The border closes at 6 pm, which means you'll get there too late to cross and will have to stay the night. You'll find this most inconvenient, as there are no facilities whatsoever – no food, accommodation or running water. Nor will you be allowed to sleep on the bus, so bring what you need to make an uncomfortable night tolerable. The bus returns to Karonga at 6 am the next morning.

In the morning you cross over to the Tanzanian side, after which it's about seven km to the main Kyela to Mbeya road. You'll have to hitch a ride or walk this stretch. Once on the main road, buses to Mbeya (about a five-hour trip) pass two or three times a day, but it's often more convenient to hitch a ride. There's no need to go into Kyela along this route, as the town is five km south-east of the junction and so in the wrong direction for Mbeya.

Going in the opposite direction from Tanzania, take a bus from Mbeya going to Kyela (TSh 600) but get off at the turn-off to the border. Alternatively, take a bus to Tukuyu, which is on the same road (TSh 400, about three hours), and then another to Kyela (TSh 200, 1½ hours), again alighting at the turn-

off to the border. At the turn-off you will find several youths with bicycles, who will perch you on the back and pedal away at a suicidal rate to the border for TSh 300. The border closes at 6 pm but it's still worth going there. Kyela is a dump and you'll probably be allowed to sleep on the veranda of the immigration office. There's food here and cold beers. Change money with the bicycle boys.

In the morning, you cross the border, but because there's a one-hour time difference between Tanzania and Malawi, by the time the Tanzanian border post opens, the bus to Karonga will have already left, so you'll have to hitch to the Malawi customs post (15 km). Should you manage to overtake the bus, it costs Kw 1.60 from the Malawi customs post to Karonga and takes 30 minutes.

Don't attempt to cross this border on a Sunday, as there's hardly any traffic and you'll have to do a lot of walking.

A fortnightly bus in either direction between Mzuzu and Dar es Salaam is operated by Momaga Motor Ltd. It leaves Mzuzu at 6 am on Wednesday and arrives at Karonga at noon, after which it continues on to Kyela, where you stay the night. It arrives at Mbeya at noon the next day and at Dar es Salaam at about 1 pm on Friday. The fare from Mzuzu to Dar es Salaam is Kw 60. In the opposite direction, the bus leaves Dar es Salaam on Sunday morning and arrives in Mbeya at about 7 pm on Monday. It continues on to Kyela, where you stay the night, and the next day goes on to Karonga, arriving at 9 am. Mzuzu is reached at 3 pm the same day. This bus can be picked up in Mbeya if there are spare seats.

To/From Rwanda

Entering Tanzania from Rwanda is much easier than it used to be. First take a matatu to Kibungo (RFr 350), from where you get a share-taxi (RFr 200) to the border at Rusumo (Chutes de Rusumo). Otherwise, take the 7 am direct bus from Kigali to Rusumo.

There's a small forest hut just down the road from the Tanzanian immigration post where you can stay the night (TSh 600/1200 for singles/doubles). It's clean and friendly but has no electricity.

From Rusumo, you will have to hitch to Ngara or Lusahanga. The Lusahanga to Kigali road via Rusumo is the main route used by petrol trucks supplying Kigali and Bujumbura, so there's plenty of traffic.

From Ngara, a bus (usually daily) goes to Mwanza via Lusahanga, setting off very early (about 4 am) and arriving after dark. The buses are operated by the New El-Jabry Bus Co in Mwanza. Lusahanga is an overnight truck stop for petrol tanker drivers and is where the tarmac road starts.

Alternatively, organise a lift all the way from Kigali. Take a Gikondo matatu from the Place de l'Unité Nationale in Kigali, go about three km down the Blvd de l'OUA to the STIR truck park and ask around there. Many trucks leave daily from here at about 9 am, heading for Tanzania. Most of the drivers are Somalis, and if you strike up a rapport with them, you may well get a free lift all the way to a major city in Tanzania. If not, you're looking at about US$20 from Kigali to Mwanza.

If you're entering Rwanda from Tanzania, get the bus from Mwanza to Ngara but make sure you get off at Lusahanga. Buses leave Mwanza (usually daily) at 4 am and arrive after dark. To make sure you catch the bus, stay in Mwanza at the Penda Guest House, next to the bus terminal. It's a dump but it's convenient.

To/From Uganda

The route into Uganda goes through the Kagera salient on the west side of Lake Victoria between Bukoba and Masaka, via Kyaka. This is the route which the overland companies take these days. Road conditions have improved considerably over the last few years, so it's now possible to do the journey from Masaka to Bukoba in one day. There are matatus from Masaka to Kyotera (USh 1200, 45 minutes) plus several daily pick-ups from there to the border at Mutukula (USh 1500, one hour), which go when full. The border crossings are easygoing and there are moneychangers on the

Tanzanian side, though they give a lousy rate. The border posts are right next to each other. From the border, a daily Land Rover goes to Bukoba (TSh 1500, about four hours) over appalling roads. If the Land Rover has departed before you arrive at the border, your only option is to hitch – not easy, as there's little traffic. There's a checkpoint in Kyaka, where you're obliged to stop and have your passport checked.

There's also a bus between Bukoba and Mutukula which departs from Bukoba daily (except Sunday) at 11.15 am, costs TSh 600 and takes about four hours. In the opposite direction, it leaves Mutukula for Bukoba at 5 pm.

We have had one report of a direct bus between Kampala and Bukoba, leaving Kampala at 7.30 am on Wednesday and Saturday, arriving in Bukoba at around 7 pm and costing USh 6000. It apparently returns from Bukoba to Kampala on Tuesday and Friday and costs TSh 3000. No other traveller has yet confirmed this, so it may no longer exist.

To/From Zambia

Bus The usual route is on the TAZARA railway, but there's also road transport from Mbeya to Tunduma on the Tanzania-Zambia border. From the border, you walk to Nakonde on the Zambian side and take a bus from there to Kasama and Lusaka. Not many people use the road route. This border used to be notorious for officialdom, and though it has cooled off a lot in recent years, it's wise to be on your guard.

Train The TAZARA railway runs between Dar es Salaam and Kapiri Mposhi, in the heartland of the Zambian copper belt, via Mbeya and Tunduma/Nakonde. The line was built by the Chinese in the 1960s and passes through some of the most remote countryside in Africa, including part of the Selous Game Reserve. It is Zambia's most important link with the sea, but unfortunately, maintenance hasn't matched the energy with which the Chinese first constructed the railway. As a result, schedules can be erratic. There are usually five trains per week in either direction, two express and three ordinary.

The express trains depart from Dar es Salaam on Tuesday and Friday at 4.55 pm and the ordinary trains on Monday, Thursday and Saturday at 11 am. The journey takes between 42 and 48 hours and the fares (in Tanzanian shillings) from Dar es Salaam are in the table below.

Tickets should be booked in advance in Dar es Salaam at the TAZARA Railway Station on Pugu Rd. This is not the same station as the one in central Dar es Salaam, where Central Line trains arrive and depart. The TAZARA station is about halfway to the airport. Get there on an airport bus from the junction of Sokoine Drive and Kivukoni Front, opposite the Cenotaph and Lutheran church. A taxi will cost TSh 1500.

Book tickets at least five days ahead. Don't expect any 1st or 2nd-class tickets to be available beyond this point, unless you have 'contacts' such as government officials and diplomats. It's remarkable how easy it is to get a 1st-class ticket the day before departure if you know someone like this! Third-class tickets are sold only on the day of departure.

Student discounts of 50% are available for International Student Identity Card (ISIC) holders, though getting authorisation for this can be time-consuming. The normal procedure is to pick up a form from the TAZARA station and take it to the Ministry of Education beside State House, where you fill in more forms and get the appropriate rubber stamp. Then you take the form back to the TAZARA station and buy your ticket. It's a lot of fuss for a few dollars!

As on Kenyan trains, men and women can only travel together in 1st and 2nd class if they occupy an entire compartment.

Meals are usually available on the train and can be served in your compartment, though food supplies generally run out towards the end of a journey. If this happens, there are always plenty of food and drink vendors at the stations en route. Don't take photographs on this train unless you have discussed the matter beforehand with the police.

LAKE

To/From Burundi & Zambia

Ferry The main ferry on Lake Tanganyika is the historic MV *Liemba*, which connects Tanzania with Burundi and Zambia. It operates a weekly service connecting Bujumbura (Burundi), Kigoma (Tanzania) and Mpulungu (Zambia). This is a great way to travel.

The MV *Liemba* is a legend among travellers and must be one of the oldest steamers in the world still operating on a regular basis. Built by the Germans in 1914 and assembled on the lake shore after being transported in pieces on the railway from Dar es Salaam, it first saw service as the *Graf von Goetzn*. Not long afterwards, following Germany's defeat in WW I, it was greased and scuttled to prevent the British getting their hands on it. In 1922 the British colonial authorities paid the princely sum of UK£4000 for it. Two years later they raised it from the bottom of the lake, had it reconditioned and put back into service as the MV *Liemba*. The fact that it's still going after all these years is a credit to its maintenance engineers.

The schedule for the MV *Liemba* is more or less regular, but the ferry can be delayed

Station	Express			Ordinary		
	1st	*2nd*	*3rd*	*1st*	*2nd*	*3rd*
Mbeya	8380	5800	2670	7930	5350	2230
Tunduma	9340	6440	2950	8850	5950	2460
Kasama	10,750	7420	3360	10,190	6860	2800
Mposhi	14,050	9690	4420	13,310	8950	3690

Top: Pride, Ngorongoro Crater, Tanzania (GE)
Bottom: Tusker, Ngorongoro Crater, Tanzania (GE)

Top: Children, Arusha, Tanzania (GE)
Left: Game drive, Ngorongoro Crater, Tanzania (GE)
Right: Makonde carvings, Tanzania (SB)

for up to 24 hours at either end, depending on how much cargo there is to load or unload. Engine trouble can also delay it at any point, though not usually for more than a few hours.

Officially, the MV *Liemba* departs from Bujumbura on Monday at about 4 pm and arrives in Kigoma (Tanzania) on Tuesday at 8 am. It leaves Kigoma at about 4 pm on Wednesday and arrives in Mpulungu (Zambia) on Friday at 8 am. It calls at many small Tanzanian ports en route between Kigoma and Mpulungu, but rarely for more than half an hour.

The fares from Bujumbura are:

Port	1st class	2nd class	3rd class
Kigoma	US$31	US$21	US$11
Mpulungu	US$87		

The fares from Kigoma (in Tanzanian shillings) are:

Port	1st class	2nd class	3rd class
Bujumbura	3015	2765	2295
Kibwesa	3445	3205	2690
Karema	4100	3870	3290
Kapili	4970	4750	4080
Kasanga	6705	6520	5675
Mpulungu	6925	6740	5875

In addition, port fees of BFr 200 are payable upon boarding in Bujumbura. Tickets for the ferry can be bought from SONACO, Rue des Usines off Ave du Port, Bujumbura, on Monday morning from 8 am.

Tickets bought in Mpulungu for the trip north to Kigoma or Bujumbura and tickets bought in Bujumbura for the trip south to any of the ports en route must be paid for in US dollars. Local currency is not acceptable. Tickets bought at any of the Tanzanian ports can be paid for in Tanzanian shillings.

To save money when going all the way from Bujumbura to Mpulungu, first buy a ticket to Kigoma, then once the boat docks, get off and immediately make a reservation for a 1st or 2nd-class cabin. Then change money into Tanzanian shillings and pay for your ticket the following morning at 8 am using the shillings you changed. This will save you approximately US$40 in total.

When travelling from Bujumbura direct to Mpulungu, you have to stay on the boat for the 36 hours or so that it docks in Kigoma, though you are allowed into town during the day even if you don't have a Tanzanian visa (where required). Passports have to be left with immigration in the meantime.

Third class consists of bench seats either in a covered area towards the back of the boat or in another very poorly ventilated area with bench seats in the bowels of the vessel. The best plan is to grab some deck space. The 2nd-class cabins are incredibly hot, stuffy and claustrophobic. They have four bunks and are very poorly ventilated. If you want a cabin, go the whole hog and take a 1st-class one. These have two bunks, are on a higher deck, have a window and fan, and are clean and reasonably cool. Bedding is available for a small fee.

Third class is not usually crowded between Bujumbura and Kigoma, so this is a reasonable budget possibility, especially as it's only overnight. It's no problem to sleep out on the deck – the best spot is above the 1st-class deck, though you need to be discreet as it's supposedly off limits to passengers. On the lower decks you need to keep your gear safe, as some petty pilfering does sometimes occur. If you're travelling 3rd class between Bujumbura and Kigoma and want to upgrade to a cabin for the Kigoma to Mpulungu leg, make sure you do this as soon as the boat docks in Kigoma. Third class is not recommended between Kigoma and Mpulungu, as it's usually very crowded.

Meals and drinks are available on board and must be paid for in Tanzanian shillings. Bring enough shillings to cover this. Three-course meals of soup, chicken and rice followed by dessert are not bad value at TSh 400 for lunch, TSh 500 for dinner and TSh 300 for breakfast. Cold Safari lager (Tanzanian) is for sale at TSh 400, and Primus (Zaïrian) costs TSh 720.

Coming from Bujumbura, the MV *Liemba* arrives at Kigoma at about 5 am, but you can't get off until 8 am when customs and immigration officials arrive. So, instead of packing your bags and hanging around, it's a good idea to have breakfast.

Lake Taxi & Matatu The alternative to the MV *Liemba* is to travel partly by matatu and partly by lake taxi between Bujumbura and Kigoma via the Tanzanian border village of Kagunga and the Gombe Stream National Park. The national park is primarily a chimpanzee sanctuary and is well worth a visit, but it does cost US$50 entry fee plus US$20 for accommodation. If you can't afford this, simply stay on the lake taxi, which will take you all the way to Kigoma.

From Bujumbura, matatus go daily to Nyanza Lac (BFr 800). You must go through immigration here – the office is about one km from the town centre towards the lake. After that, take a matatu (BFr 100) to the Burundi border post. From this post to the Tanzanian border post at Kagunga, it's a two-km walk along a narrow track. From Kagunga, there are lake taxis to Kigoma (actually to Kalalangabo, about three km north of Kigoma), which cost TSh 500, leave before dawn and take most of the day. The taxis call at Gombe Stream (about halfway), where you can get off if you like. The fare to Gombe Stream is TSh 250, as is the fare from there to Kigoma.

The lake taxis are small, wooden boats, often overcrowded not only with people but with their produce, and they offer no creature comforts whatsoever. They're good fun when the weather is fine, but if there's a squall on the lake, you may be in for a rough time. If you have a choice, try to get a boat with a cover, as it gets stinking hot out on the lake in the middle of the day. These boats do not operate on Sundays.

To/From Kenya
It's possible to go by dhow between Zanzibar, Pemba and Mombasa, plus there's a catamaran, the MV *Flying Horse*, which does the Dar es Salaam to Mombasa run via Zanzibar once a week in either direction (on Mondays from Mombasa). For full details, refer to the Mombasa section in the Kenya chapter.

There are no steamer services which connect Kenya with Tanzania on Lake Victoria.

To/From Uganda
There's a regular Lake Victoria service between Port Bell (Kampala) and Mwanza which leaves Port Bell on Monday at 6 pm and arrives in Mwanza on Tuesday at 10 am. In the opposite direction, it departs from Mwanza on Sunday at 3 pm and arrives in Port Bell on Monday at 7 am. It's a good trip and costs US$25/20 (USh 32,500/26,000) in 1st/2nd class, US$15 (or USh 19,500) in 3rd class. In Port Bell, tickets should be bought on the day of departure at 2 pm at the port gate. This is going to involve you in a taxi trip, unless you want to hang around all day until the ferry leaves or you're staying at the Silver Springs Hotel (close by on Luzira Rd).

To/From Zaïre
SNCZ operates boats from Kalemie to both Uvira and Kigoma on Lake Tanganyika, usually once a week. The boat to Uvira generally leaves on Tuesday. For information on these boats, see the stationmaster at the railway station. Tickets can only be bought the day before departure, early in the morning.

There's another privately owned boat, called the *Lwenge*. Its owner, a man called Fizi, has a business in town called PGC, which is almost opposite the Hotel de la Gare. His boat runs once weekly, usually on Thursday, from Kalemie to Uvira and takes around 36 hours.

Drinks are usually available on board but you must take your own food. Tickets can be bought two to three days in advance of the trip.

Getting Around

AIR

Air Tanzania, the national carrier, serves most of the internal routes but their 'fleet' consists of just one jet and one propellor plane. Their schedule (if you can get one) lists a fistful of destinations and includes international routes, but it's an unbridled work of fiction. Basically, the only domestic routes which function at present are the Kigoma/Mwanza to Kilimanjaro and Dar es Salaam and the Dar es Salaam to Zanzibar sectors.

Even so, *never ever* rely on Air Tanzania. Cancellations and long delays are the order of the day, and don't waste time and energy complaining about it because no-one is going to lift a finger to help you. There are a lot of employees with a lot of computers at their headquarters in Dar es Salaam but most of them would be better employed doing something constructive.

A number of private airlines operate light aircraft (six to eight-seaters). These mainly service the Dar es Salaam to Zanzibar, Zanzibar to Pemba and Dar es Salaam to Mafia sectors but occasionally fly from Zanzibar to Arusha, Mombasa and Nairobi. You can also charter them to fly anywhere in Tanzania at any time, if you're willing to pay the price. The private airlines are Air Zanzibar and Zan Air, both based in Zanzibar, and Tanzanair, based in Dar es Salaam. Details of their domestic flights can be found in the Zanzibar and Dar es Salaam sections, respectively.

Nonresident foreigners must pay for Air Tanzania tickets in hard currency (cash or travellers' cheques) or by credit card (American Express, Diners Club and Visa are acceptable). You cannot pay for flights in local currency. And beware: if you pay for a flight with cash or travellers' cheques and it's cancelled, any refund will be in shillings! There's no way you'll get your hard cash back. By contrast, you can talk sense with the private companies in the event of a cancellation.

Domestic airport departure taxes vary – TSh 500 at the large airports and TSh 300 at the smaller ones.

BUS & MATATU

Tanzania's economy is definitely on the mend but there's still very little spare cash for road or rail maintenance. So expect the worst, and when it's better than that, be grateful. Except for certain sections – Namanga, Arusha, Moshi, Himo and Dar es Salaam to Morogoro – the roads are poor. At one time many roads were sealed, but the tarmac has since broken up and large potholes have formed, making them worse than poorly maintained gravel roads. Traffic meanders from one side of the road to the other like a cavalcade of drunken ants, in an often vain attempt to avoid the larger holes. It's not particularly dangerous, especially during daylight hours, because no-one can travel at high speed.

On the main long-haul routes, there's generally a choice between luxury buses and ordinary buses. It's worth taking the luxury buses where there's a choice, as they're only marginally more expensive than the ordinary buses, are far more comfortable and get to their destination faster. Ordinary buses pick up and put down more frequently, so take longer.

Advance booking on long hauls is definitely advisable. Don't expect to turn up an hour or so before departure and be able to buy tickets.

On short hauls the choice is between ordinary buses and matatus and, for those who want to get somewhere fast and have the money, share-taxis. Ordinary buses and matatus leave when full and the fare is fixed. Only rarely will the conductor attempt to charge you more than what anyone else is paying. A few Tanzanian towns (Moshi and Arusha) have central bus and matatu stations, so it's easy to find the bus you want. Other places, Dar es Salaam being the prime example, don't have a central bus stand and buses depart from several locations, some of which are not at all obvious. In circumstances like this, you will have to ask around to find the bus you want.

Beware of pickpockets and thieves at bus stations. There are usually scores of them and they're all waiting for you! Don't let your attention wander, even for a moment. Arusha is notorious for them, with Moshi a close second.

If you have the option, it's always better to travel 1st or 2nd class on a train for long hauls than to go by bus. Take a look at the haggard faces of travellers who stumble off the ordinary buses between Dar es Salaam and Moshi and you won't need any further convincing!

Finding a place to put your pack on a bus can sometimes present problems. The racks above the seats are generally too small to accommodate rucksacks but there's usually room up front near the driver. On long hauls, don't allow your bag to be put on the roof if there's any possibility of passengers being up there with it. There won't be much left in it by the time you arrive at your destination. The safest thing to do is insist that it go under your seat or in the aisle where you can keep your eye on it. Another option on short hauls is to pay for an extra seat and pile your bags on that.

TRAIN

Apart from Arusha, Tanzania's major population centres are connected by railway. The Central Line linking Dar es Salaam with Kigoma via Morogoro, Kilosa, Dodoma and Tabora was built by the German colonial authorities between 1905 and 1914. Later it was extended from Tabora to Mwanza by the British. The other arm of this line links Dar es Salaam with Moshi and Tanga via Korogwe.

The other major line is the TAZARA railway linking Dar es Salaam with Kapiri Mposhi, in the heartland of the Zambian copper belt, via Mbeya and Tunduma/ Nakonde. It is Zambia's most important

link with the sea and passes through some of the most remote country in Africa, including part of the Selous Game Reserve. Built by the People's Republic of China in the 1960s, the line involved the construction of 147 stations, more than 300 bridges and 23 tunnels – the most ambitious project ever undertaken by the Chinese outside their own territory. Unfortunately, maintenance hasn't matched the energy with which the Chinese first constructed the railway, so schedules can be erratic, though there are usually three trains in either direction each week.

As with bus travel, keep an eye on your gear at all times, particularly in 3rd class. Even in 1st and 2nd class, make sure that the window is jammed shut at night. There is usually a piece of wood provided for this, as the window locks don't work. It's common practice for thieves to jump in through the window at night when the train stops at stations.

Classes

There are three classes on Tanzanian trains: 1st class (two-bunk compartments), 2nd class (usually six-bunk compartments) and 3rd class (wooden benches only).

Second class on the Dar es Salaam to Moshi and Dar es Salaam to Tanga trains is seats only. You'd have to be desperate to go any distance in 3rd class – it's very uncomfortable, very crowded and there are thieves to contend with. It's definitely not recommended. Second class is several quantum levels above 3rd class in terms of space and comfort (though the fans may not work) and is an acceptable way to travel long distances.

The difference between 1st and 2nd class is that there are two people to a compartment instead of six. Men and women can only travel together in 1st or 2nd class if they occupy the whole compartment.

Some trains (Dar es Salaam to Kigoma, Mwanza, Moshi and Tanga) have restaurant cars which serve good meals (TSh 400 for dinner, TSh 300 for breakfast), soft drinks and beer. Bed rolls are available in 1st and

2nd class at a cost of TSh 150, regardless of how long the journey is. These can be a good investment on the long runs from Dar es Salaam to Mwanza or Kigoma.

Reservations

Buying a ticket can be a daylight nightmare, especially in Dar es Salaam and Moshi. It's chaos at the stations and nowhere will you find any schedules. The only information that's usually posted is a list of fares (often out of date). Even when you try to book a ticket several days in advance, you may well be told that 1st and 2nd class is sold out. The Central Line station in Dar es Salaam is notorious for this. The claim is usually pure, unadulterated rubbish, but it helps to secure 'presents' for ticket clerks. If you are told this, see the station master and beg, scrape and plead for his assistance. It may take some time but you'll get those supposedly 'booked' tickets in the end. The claim is generally true, on the other hand, on the day of departure.

Schedules & Fares

The schedule for the TAZARA trains can be found in the To/From Zambia section of the earlier Tanzania Getting There & Away chapter.

Central Line trains from Dar es Salaam to Kigoma and Mwanza depart at 5 pm on Tuesday, Wednesday, Friday and Sunday. In the opposite direction, there are departures from both Kigoma and Mwanza for Dar es Salaam at the same time and on the same days. The journey normally takes about 36 hours but can take 40 hours.

Central Line trains from Dar es Salaam to Moshi and Tanga depart at 4 pm on Monday, Wednesday and Friday. In the opposite direction, there are departures from both Moshi and Tanga for Dar es Salaam at the same time and on the same days. The journey to Moshi takes 15 to 18 hours and to Tanga about 16 hours.

The fares in Tanzanian shillings from Dar es Salaam are as follows:

	1st class	2nd class	2nd (sitting)	3rd class
Dodoma	6790	2980	2185	1125
Kigoma	11,190	6805	5070	2540
Morogoro	2655	1710	1225	655
Moshi	5445	3375	2485	1270
Mwanza	11,025	6705	4995	2505
Shinyanga	9550	5825	4330	2180
Tabora	7905	4845	3590	1815
Tanga	3970	2490	1815	945

BOAT

Ferry

Lake Tanganyika See the earlier Tanzania Getting There & Away chapter for information about transport from Tanzania to Burundi aboard the MV *Liemba* on Lake Tanganyika. This connects Tanzania with Burundi and Zambia and also operates between Tanzanian ports on the lake.

The MV *Mwongozo* operates services only in Tanzania, connecting Kigoma with the small Tanzanian ports to the south and north. On Sundays it sails south from Kigoma to Kasanga, near the Zambian border. On Thursdays and Saturdays, it heads north for Kagunga, near the Burundi border.

Lake Victoria The MV *Victoria*, which connects Port Bell (Uganda) with Mwanza (Tanzania) once a week in either direction (see the Lake section in the Tanzania Getting There & Away chapter for details), spends the rest of the week sailing between Mwanza and Bukoba, along with two other internal ferries: the MV *Bukoba* and the MV *Serengeti*. There are departures from Mwanza at 9 pm on Monday (*Serengeti*), Friday (*Bukoba*) and Saturday (*Serengeti*), and at 10 pm on Tuesday and Thursday (*Victoria*) for Bukoba, which arrive next morning. The ferries sail back to Mwanza the following night at the same time and arrive the following morning.

The fares from Mwanza in Tanzanian shillings are:

Port	Victoria class	1st class	2nd class	3rd class
Bukoba	3300	2795	2540	1310
Musoma	3560	3015	2765	1430

Lake Malawi Two ferries operate on the Tanzanian part of Lake Malawi, sailing between Itungi and Mbamba Bay via a number of other small ports. The MV *Songea* departs from Itungi at 7 am on Monday and Friday, arriving at Mbamba Bay the same day at 11 pm. In the opposite direction, it leaves Mbamba Bay at midnight on Tuesday and Saturday and arrives in Itungi at 4 pm the same day.

The other ferry, the MV *Mbeya*, runs south from Itungi on Wednesday but only goes as far as Njambi.

The fares from Itungi in Tanzanian shillings are:

Port	1st class	2nd class	3rd class
Makonde	1710	1435	725
Lupingu	1710	1435	725
Manda	2145	1875	955
Ndumbi	2360	2100	1075
Lundu	2360	2100	1075
Nkili	2580	2320	1190
Njambi	2795	2540	1310
Liuli	3015	2765	1430
Mbamba Bay	3230	2980	1540

Offshore Islands & South Coast See the Dar es Salaam and Zanzibar chapters for details of services to the islands off the Tanzanian coast.

To the mainland ports south of Dar es Salaam as far as Mtwara, near the Mozambique border, there is the FB *Canadian Spirit*, operated by Adecon Marine Inc (☎ 20856), PO Box 63027, Dar es Salaam. The office is on Sokoine Drive in amongst all the other shipping companies which service the Dar es Salaam to Zanzibar route. There is no regular schedule for this boat – departures depend on passenger and cargo demand – but it usually goes once every two to three weeks from Dar es Salaam to Mtwara, calling at Mafia Island, Kilwa and other smaller ports. It can take up to 800 passengers and also vehicles but has no cabins, so take bedding with you or stay up all night drinking (it's an overnight journey between Dar es Salaam and Mtwara). The fares from Dar es Salaam are:

Port	Class 'A'	Class 'B'	Class 'C'
Mafia Island	TSh 4000	TSh 3500	TSh 3000
	US$25	US$20	US$15
Mtwara	TSh 7000	TSh 6000	TSh 5000
	US$30	US$25	US$20

Dhow

Dhows have sailed the coastal waters of East Africa and across to Arabia and India for centuries. Though now greatly reduced in number, they can still be found if you're looking for a slow and uncomfortable but romantic way of getting across to the islands or up to Mombasa.

Most of the dhows are motorised but it's still possible to find the smaller ones which rely entirely on their sail. Dependent on the wind and tides, they sail only when these variables are favourable; otherwise, too much tacking becomes necessary. This may mean that they sail at night which, on a full moon, is pure magic. There's nothing to disturb the silence but the lapping of the sea against the sides of the boat. Remember that they are open boats without bunks or luxuries. You simply bed down wherever there is space and where you won't get in the way of the crew. Fares are negotiable but are often more than you would pay on a modern vessel for the same journey.

The larger, motorised dhows used to be a standard form of public transport connecting Dar es Salaam to Zanzibar. They've been superseded with modern ferries, catamarans and hydrofoils, but still operate between Zanzibar and Pemba and between Tanga and Pemba. They usually run on a daily basis, but you need to negotiate with the captains personally regarding departure times and fares. It may also involve getting written permission from the district commissioner. See the Zanzibar, Pemba and Tanga sections for full details.

CAR & 4WD

Driving in Tanzania is a trade-off between speed and potholes. Traffic density is low outside the main towns, so collisions are rare. Wiping yourself out on a large pothole is another matter. Keep your speed down. The gravel roads in the national parks of the north-east (Serengeti, Ngorongoro, Lake Manyara, Tarangire and Arusha) are usually very good, as are the sealed roads leading to them, but there are some very rough stretches between Lake Manyara and the entrance to Ngorongoro. You could make it in a 2WD vehicle in the dry season but certainly not in the wet season.

Car & 4WD Rental

This is an expensive option for getting around Tanzania and, at present, you're unlikely to find anyone who is willing to rent for self-drive, except on Zanzibar Island. Few companies want to rent their vehicles for self-drive, since spares are both hard to get and expensive, and recovery, in the event of a breakdown, is equally expensive. In other words, if you rent a car, it inevitably comes with a driver.

Essentially, what this means is that without your own vehicle, you're down to organised safaris with a driver and public transport for the rest. This is not Kenya but things are slowly changing. The word was out, for instance, in early 1993 that Hertz was about to set up shop in Dar es Salaam and Arusha and would have self-drive vehicles available for hire, but it appears they are going to restrict this to city/town use only. Safari vehicles will still come with a driver.

Rental Costs

Typical rates for hiring a small car like a Toyota Corolla or a Nissan would be US$70 plus US$0.55 per km over 100 km. A 4WD Land Rover costs US$95 plus US$0.65 per km over 100 km for town use, and US$130 plus US$0.70 per km over 100 km plus US$15 driver's allowance for safari use. The rates for a six or 10-seater minibus are US$90 plus US$0.60 per km over 100 km for town use, and US$125 plus US$0.70 per km over 100 km plus US$15 driver's allowance for safari use. These rates are inclusive of fuel, insurance and, where no driver's allowance is specified, the driver as well.

Don't take these figures as gospel. I was able to rent an almost new 4WD Suzuki with unlimited mileage and no deposit on Zanzibar for just US$40 a day, but Zanzibar was the *only* place in Tanzania where this was possible. Elsewhere in Tanzania, you'll have to go through the safari companies for vehicle hire.

Safaris

ORGANISED VEHICLE SAFARIS

Going on an organised safari is the way most travellers visit Tanzania's national parks.

Safaris to Arusha National Park, Tarangire National Park, Lake Manyara National Park, Ngorongoro Conservation Area and Serengeti National Park are best arranged in Arusha, where there are plenty of companies to choose from. Kilimanjaro National Park is the exception here, with climbs best arranged in Moshi (but see the relevent section). Visits to Sadani Game Reserve, Mikumi National Park, Ruaha National Park and Selous Game Reserve are best arranged in Dar es Salaam, while those to Gombe Stream and Mahale Mountains national parks are best arranged from Kigoma. Getting to Rubondo Island National Park (in Lake Victoria) is only feasible by light aircraft.

As in Kenya, most of the safari companies offer a choice of camping safaris (the cheaper option) and lodge safaris (the more expensive option). If you haven't been to Kenya and haven't read the Safaris section in the Getting Around chapter for that country, do it now. There's no point in repeating all the same general points here.

Routes

From Arusha Arusha is the safari capital of Tanzania, and there's a plethora of companies which offer a range of possibilities to suit all tastes and pockets. Cost and reliability vary widely, and to a large extent, you get what you pay for.

The safaris available vary from just one day to 15 days. A one-day safari takes you to Arusha National Park and a two-day safari to Tarangire National Park. Most travellers, however, prefer longer safaris – four to seven days on average. You need a minimum of three days and two nights to tour Lake Manyara and Ngorongoro Crater, four days and three nights to tour Lake Manyara, Ngorongoro Crater and Serengeti, and six days and five nights to tour Lake Manyara, Ngorongoro Crater, Serengeti and Tarangire. These are absolute minimum tour lengths. If you can afford to stay longer, do so. You'll see a lot more and you won't come back feeling that half the driving time was taken up just getting to and from Arusha. A longer tour will also enable you to make more economical use of park entry fees. If you leave one park within 24 hours and enter another (between Ngorongoro Crater and Serengeti, for instance), you'll be up for two lots of park entry fees (US$30 per person) instead of one (US$15 per person).

If you want to have a good look at Lake Manyara, Ngorongoro Crater and Serengeti, plan on a five to six-day safari. On a seven-day safari, you could see Lake Manyara, Ngorongoro Crater, Serengeti and Tarangire at a relatively leisurely pace. On a 10-day safari, you could take in all the places mentioned plus Lake Natron and Arusha National Park, but not many companies offer safaris of that length.

From Dar es Salaam Safaris to Mikumi typically last two to three days, to Mikumi and Ruaha five days, and to Selous five days, though weekend visits are also an option on the latter. Safaris which take in all three parks last for around nine days.

The possibilities of camping in these parks are much more limited than in the northern parks and there are no public camp sites in the Selous. On most safaris, you'll stay in lodges or permanent tented camps.

From Kigoma Most travellers prefer to visit Gombe Stream and/or Mahale Mountains national parks independently rather than go through a safari company, though there is one company in Kigoma which can arrange this. Some companies in Dar es Salaam can

also arrange this, but it's generally part of a much longer trip and these are expensive.

Costs

The cost of a safari depends on two main factors: whether you camp for the night or stay in a lodge or permanent tented camp, and how many people are on the safari.

The two factors are closely linked, but a camping safari is obviously much cheaper than one which uses lodges for overnight accommodation. The exact cost depends partly on how long you want to go for and partly on where you want to go. In general, it's true to say that the longer you go for and the more people there are in your group, the less, proportionally, it will cost you per day. The rock-bottom outfits in Arusha were quoting US$50 per person per day in early 1993, assuming a minimum of four people on the trip. This was supposed to include park entry and camping fees, camping equipment, transport and meals. How they do this, considering that park entry and camping fees represent US$25 of that alone, I'm not sure. I'd say they were running on the edge of bankruptcy. A more realistic figure which others were quoting was US$70 per person per day, assuming a minimum of four people, or US$50 per person per day, assuming a minimum of six people. On that amount, you could certainly run a budget safari, though there would be no frills.

While it's alright to use the above figures as a benchmark, it's not that simple, as the prices quoted by various companies differ widely. A two-day camping trip to Lake Manyara and Ngorongoro varies from US$100 to US$210 (five to seven people) and US$315 to US$556 (one to two people). A three-day trip to the same parks varies from US$150 to US$200 (five to seven people) and US$260 to US$637 (one to two people). A five-day Lake Manyara, Ngorongoro and Serengeti safari costs US$250 to US$469 (five to seven people) and US$540 to US$690 (one to two people). These prices should be all-inclusive in the higher brackets but *may* not be in the lower brackets. Make sure you know whether park entry fees, camping fees and food are included. Never assume that they are.

The prices for safaris which involve staying in lodges or tented camps are considerably higher. A two-day Lake Manyara and Ngorongoro safari in this category costs US$192 to US$225 (five to seven people) and US$391 to US$692 (one to two people). A three-day trip to the same parks costs US$235 to US$480 (five to seven people) and US$425 to US$1100 (one to two people). A five-day Lake Manyara, Ngorongoro and Serengeti safari costs US$390 to US$780 (five to seven people) and US$565 to US$2015 (one to two people). These prices are all-inclusive.

Why such a wide variation in price for the same thing? This doesn't happen in Kenya, nor does it happen for the Kilimanjaro climb, where the various companies' prices are roughly comparable. Part of the difference undoubtedly reflects better facilities and services where the price is high, but it surely must also indicate that quite a few companies are simply out to squeeze as much money as possible from their clients. There's no logic, other than greed, in why one company finds it possible to take one or two people to Lake Manyara, Ngorongoro and Serengeti for five days including lodge accommodation for US$565 (Sunny Safaris) and another demands US$2015 (Simba Safaris) for the same thing. The lodges cost much the same, as does fuel for the vehicle; park entry fees are standard and meal prices are not exactly extortionate. By way of comparison, UTC, one of the more expensive companies, will do the above trip, including lodge accommodation, for US$791 per person regardless of numbers.

All this means that, whatever sort of safari you want to go on, there's no substitute for legwork. Collect as many leaflets as you can, decide where you want to go, compare prices, work out what's included and what isn't, and then make your choice.

One last thing to remember is that prices are based on the assumption that you will share accommodation (a tent or room) with one other person. If you don't want to do this,

you'll have to pay what's called a 'single room supplement'. This can be up to 50% above the daily per person rate.

Tipping Regardless of whether you go on a camping safari or a lodge safari, the driver/guide and the cook(s) (where provided) will expect a reasonable tip at the end of the journey. Be generous. You may think you've paid a lot of money for your safari but most of it will have gone to the national parks, the lodges and the safari company. The wages of the driver and cooks will have been minimal. Remember that others will come after you and there's nothing worse than a driver/guide and/or cooks who couldn't care less and who feel exploited.

Departure Frequency
This varies a lot from company to company but the larger outfits generally have guaranteed departures at regular intervals for the most popular parks, assuming there are at least two clients. Virtually any company will get you on the road either the same or the next day if you have a group together and if they have a vehicle and driver on hand.

Choosing a Company
The same general comments about safari companies outlined in the Kenya chapter apply to Tanzanian companies, though it tends to be easier to separate the wood from the trees in Tanzania because, on the one hand, Arusha is a much smaller place than Nairobi and, on the other, in Dar es Salaam, there are far fewer companies.

Arusha The majority of safari companies here have offices in the Arusha International Conference Centre (AICC). Others are along India St, Boma Rd, Sokoine Rd, Ngoliondoi Rd and Seth Benjamin Rd. We recommend you check out the following companies before deciding on a particular one. For camping safaris try:

Hoopoe Adventure Tours

India St, PO Box 2047, Arusha (☎ (057) 7011, 7541; fax (057) 8226).

This is a well-established company with an excellent reputation, top-notch vehicles and equipment, and keen, committed staff. It's run by Terry Rice, Stephen Laiser and Oliver Davidson, all of whom have been in the safari business for years and know it inside out. Apart from offering both the Kilimanjaro and Mt Meru climbs, they offer a three-day/two-night trip to Lake Manyara, Ngorongoro and Tarangire from US$150 (six people) to US$260 (two people); and a five-day/four-night trip to all of these plus Serengeti from US$350 (six people) to US$540 (two people). Hoopoe also owns and runs the Kirurumu Tented Camp above Lake Manyara. This company is highly recommended.

Tropical Tours Ltd

India St, PO Box 727, Arusha (☎ (057) 8353; fax (057) 8907).

This company specialises in walking and camping safaris off the beaten track. In its own words, 'Serengeti Safari Racing is not within our program and we do not participate in Ngorongoro Rush Hour'. Instead, it offers three to four-day walking safaris in the Monduli Mountains (where a treehouse has been built which can accommodate up to seven people); a climb up Mt Longido (halfway between Arusha and Namanga – US$210 per person for three days); a 'north Masailand' trek; a four-day Ngorongoro 'adventure walk' (US$710 per person); and treks up Mt Meru (US$570 per person for six days/five nights) and Kilimanjaro (Machame route – US$1360 for six days/five nights). These prices are all-inclusive (even sleeping bags are included). The people who run this outfit are very keen, so you can expect excellent facilities, food and service well away from the madding crowds.

Tropical Trails

Equator Hotel, Boma Rd, PO Box 6130, Arusha (☎ /fax (057) 8299).

Run by Mike Brydon, Tropical Trails is a reliable company which offers all the normal safaris. It also specialises in walking safaris in the Monduli Mountains just north-west of Arusha, which overlook the Rift Valley. A visitors' centre which resembles a Masaai village has been built here, and this is the place where you camp. The prices for any of Tropical Trails' safaris without food or a cook peak at US$155 (one person) and drop to US$55 (five people) per person per day. With food and a cook, costs are US$165 (one person) and US$65 (five people) per person per day. Tents, cooking utensils and sleeping bags are included in the price. Tropical Trails also own and run the Masaai Camp in Arusha.

Arumeru Tours & Safaris

Seth Benjamin Rd, PO Box 730, Arusha (☎ (057) 2885; fax (057) 8117).

This is a well-run and long-established company which gets many recommendations from budget travellers. Apart from day trips to Arusha and Tarangire National Parks, they do all the usual safaris to Lake Manyara, Ngorongoro and Serengeti. A three-day/two-night trip to Lake Manyara and Ngorongoro costs from US$328 (two people) to US$200 (five people), and a five-day/four-night safari to Lake Manyara, Ngorongoro and Serengeti costs from US$353 (five people) to US$541 (two people). A six-day/five-night trip to the same three parks costs from US$427 (five people) to US$652 (two people).

Shidolya Tours & Safaris

Room 616, Serengeti Wing, AICC, PO Box 1436, Arusha (☎ (057) 8506; fax (057) 8242).

This company, run by Lazarus Mirisho Mafie, is one of the smaller but reliable outfits. It offers all-inclusive camping safaris for US$70 per person per day regardless of numbers, but will negotiate down from this price if you're a large enough group (say, five people). It has good 4WD Nissan vans and can also fix you up with a Kilimanjaro or Mt Meru climb.

Equatorial Safaris Ltd

India St and Room 460/1, Serengeti Wing, AICC, PO Box 2156, Arusha (☎ (057) 7006, fax (057) 2617).

Equatorial is another reliable company which undertakes all the usual safaris to Tarangire, Lake Manyara, Ngorongoro and Serengeti. As its leaflet puts it, 'Ours is a comfortable, informative safari yet at budget prices.' Camping safaris cost US$70 per person per day all-inclusive.

Star Tours

Room 139/140, Ngorongoro Wing, AICC, PO Box 1099, Arusha (☎ 3181, ext 2281, 2379).

This long-established budget outfit has had a variable press over the years. I personally went on one of its safaris several years ago and had no complaints at all. Others haven't been so lucky. They quote US$495 (one person) to US$205 (six people) for three days/two nights to Lake Manyara/Ngorongoro, US$630 (one person) to US$240 (six people) for four days/three nights to Tarangire, Lake Manyara and Ngorongoro, and US$835 (one person) to US$310 (six people) for five days/four nights to Lake Manyara, Ngorongoro and Serengeti, all-inclusive.

Pelican Safaris

Joel Maeda Rd, PO Box 6148, Arusha (☎ (057) 8181).

This company offers all the usual safaris, ranging from day trips to Arusha and Tarangire National parks to seven-day Tarangire, Lake Manyara, Ngorongoro and Serengeti trips. It quotes an overall US$130 per person per day, including full board, park fees, transport and driver guide, for any of its safaris.

Ali Baba

Seth Benjamin Rd, PO Box 10558, Arusha (☎ /fax (057) 8929).

This is one of the cheapest outfits in town, quoting from US$50 per person per day (four or more people) to US$70 per person per day (two people), all-inclusive. Ali himself is an inscrutable Zanzibarian character with a reputation which some would define as 'roguish' but which he dismisses with a smile as pure professional jealousy. Certainly a lot of budget travellers take safaris with his company and many come away satisfied; others do not. The choice is yours.

Amango Tours & Services

Room 208, Serengeti Wing, AICC, PO Box 7280, Arusha (☎ 3181, ext 1234).

Some people recommend this company highly, but we've also received complaints about clients being overcharged for standard national park camping fees and about the attitude of the manager, Mr Prem, when confronted with this, so be wary.

This is by no means a comprehensive list of companies which offer camping safaris. There are plenty more on just about every floor of the AICC building. You could easily spend a whole day checking out the various offices.

Virtually all the companies which offer camping safaris can also arrange a lodge safari. If you want a lodge safari, Hoopoe Safaris Ltd, Tropical Trails, Arumeru Tours & Safaris and Equatorial Safaris Ltd (addresses above) can be recommended, as can the following companies:

Bushtrekker Safaris

New Arusha Hotel, PO Box 3173, Arusha (☎ (057) 3727; fax (057) 8085)

Bobby Tours & Safaris

Ngoliondoi Rd, PO Box 2169, Arusha (☎ /fax (057) 8176)

Wildersun Safaris & Tours

Joel Maeda Rd, PO Box 930, Arusha (☎ (057) 8848; fax (057) 8223)

Savannah Tours Ltd

PO Box 3063, Arusha (☎ (057) 8455)

United Touring Company

cnr Sokoine and Ngoliondoi Rds, PO Box 2211, Arusha (☎ (057) 7931; fax (057) 6475)

Takims Tours & Safaris

Room 421, Ngorongoro Wing, AICC, PO Box 6023, Arusha (☎ (057) 8026)

Pelican Safaris

Joel Maeda Rd, PO Box 6148, Arusha (☎ (057) 8181)

Ranger Safaris

Room 333, Ngorongoro Wing, AICC, PO Box 9, Arusha (☎ 3074)

Simha Safaris

Joel Maeda Rd, PO Box 1207, Arusha (☎ (057) 3509; fax (057) 8207)

Again, this is by no means a comprehensive list of companies offering lodge safaris. There are many more in the AICC building and elsewhere, but all the above have their own well-maintained vehicles and experienced staff and they have regular guaranteed departures. If you want to be absolutely sure of getting a place on a certain safari on a certain date, write to the above and ask for their brochures before you get to Tanzania. It could save you a lot of legwork.

Mwanza If you enter Tanzania via Isebania and Musoma and wish to tour Serengeti and/or Ngorongoro from the north, you can do this from Mwanza. Fortes Safaris Ltd (☎ (068) 40497; fax (068) 40536), PO Box 1904, Mwanza, has been on the go for some 19 years. The manager is Lucas Fortes.

Dar es Salaam There are far fewer safari companies in Dar es Salaam, and they are scattered throughout the city centre rather than being concentrated in one building as in Arusha. They cater mainly for safaris to Mikumi, Ruaha and Selous, and there are guaranteed departures, at least once a week, to all these parks. On the other hand, if you have a group together, most will lay on a safari any time you're ready.

Check out the following companies, which offer lodge-based safaris:

Takims Tours & Safaris

Jamhuri St, PO Box 20350, Dar es Salaam (☎ 25691, 30037).

This reliable, long-established company goes to all the parks within reach of Dar es Salaam and has regular departures.

Bushtrekker Safaris
PO Box 5350, Dar es Salaam (☎ 36811).
Also very reliable, this company goes to all three parks on a regular basis.

Savannah Tours Ltd
Kilimanjaro Hotel, PO Box 25017, Dar es Salaam (☎ (051) 25753; fax (051) 25237).
This company, run by the very efficient and friendly Tamsin Burfitt, offers safaris to all the above parks on a regular basis. It also specialises in much longer holidays which take you all over the country in 14 to 15 days. They're not cheap but the services is excellent.

A four-day safari to the Selous Game Reserve, staying at Rufiji River Camp and Mbuyu Safari Camp, costs from US$575 (five people) to US$805 (two people), all-inclusive (except for the charter flight, which is extra). The three-day trip to Mikumi National Park, staying at Mikumi Wildlife Lodge, costs from US$335 (seven people) to US$590 (two people), all-inclusive. It also has a 15-day safari to Selous, Ruaha and Mikumi, including two days at a beach hotel in Dar es Salaam, for US$3420 (two people) down to US$2220 (five people) all-inclusive.

Impala Tours & Safaris
Zanaki St, PO Box 4783, Dar es Salaam (☎ (051) 25779).
Anna Kasidi, who runs the office in Dar, is an excellent organiser and has all the details at her fingertips. This company specialises in safaris to Selous, and owns and runs the Impala Safari Camp in the game reserve. It can organise everything for you at a cost of US$65 per person per day with full board, plus park entry fees (US$10 per day), plus the cost of a chartered flight (TSh 147,000 return shared by up to five people). If you don't want to fly, they can also organise road transport (considerably cheaper).

Coastal Travels Ltd
Upanga Rd, PO Box 3052, Dar es Salaam (☎ (051) 37479/80, fax (051) 46045).
This is a well-established company which not only makes airline, hotel and lodge bookings but also specialises in safaris to Mikumi and Selous. It offers a two-day/one-night Mikumi trip which costs US$210 per person with full board at the lodge but excludes park entry fees. Extra days cost US$95 per person per day. The three-day/two-night Selous trips depart every Friday and Sunday and cost US$370, including air charter to/from Selous, full board at Rufiji River Camp and park fees. The same safari but for six days/five nights costs US$610 per person. Game drives, boat trips and walking safaris each cost US$22 extra per person.

OTHER SAFARIS

With the expansion of the safari business in Arusha in recent years, more and more companies are beginning to offer unusual safaris which don't just involve driving around the game parks in vehicles but demand more effort from you. These include walking safaris (usually outside the national parks) and camel safaris.

Walking Safaris

For details of walking safaris offered by companies in Arusha, check out Tropical Tours Ltd (☎ (057) 8353; fax (057) 8907), India St, PO Box 727, Arusha; and Tropical Trails (☎ /fax (057) 8299), Equator Hotel, Boma Rd, PO Box 6130, Arusha, under the earlier Choosing a Company section.

A new outfit was recently set up in Babati, south of Lake Manyara on the main Arusha to Dodoma road. It specialises in part-walking/part-driving safaris in the Babati area but outside the national parks. Its main aim is to introduce overseas visitors to rural life off the well-trodden tourist circuits, using selected local hotels for overnight stops. You will see some wildlife on some of the walks but the emphasis is on meeting local people, introducing you to their customs, visiting farms and climbing mountains in the area. The man who started this venture, Mr Joas Mahembe, is keen to see the concept catch on, so if you're interested, write to Kahembe's Hotel (☎ Babati 88), Box 366, Babati, for information.

Camel Safaris

This relatively new concept in Tanzania is now fully operational and is a beautiful way to see the country at a leisurely pace. It gives you the opportunity to become fully involved in the daily lives of the local Masaai people who walk with you, do the camel handling and the cooking and other camp chores. It was set up by Fran More and Sophy Grattan, two women who were born in Kenya and who have wide experience in the safari and hotel businesses both there and in Tanzania. Their tented headquarters is situated in the northern foothills of Mt Meru, about 85 km from Namanga and 50 km from Arusha, well off the main road to the Kenyan border. For further details and bookings contact Camels Only (☎ 502491, 506139; fax 502739), PO Box 56923, Nairobi. Its office is at Wilson Airport. You can also book one of its camel safaris through safari companies in Arusha.

Balloon Safaris

Balloon flights have been operating for years over the Masai Mara Game Reserve in Kenya, but you can now do it over the Serengeti. There are daily flights which last about two hours and cost US$275 per person, including a champagne breakfast after the flight. Demand for places is high, so advance booking is highly recommended. You can do this before you get to the Serengeti through UTC (☎ (057) 7931; fax

(057) 6475), Subzali Bldg, Ngoliondoi Rd, PO Box 2211, Arusha, or at either the Seronera Lodge or the Serengeti Sopa Lodge when you're in the park itself.

DO-IT-YOURSELF SAFARIS

Tanzania is not Kenya as far as this goes because of the difficulties of hiring self-drive vehicles. Essentially, it's not worth it without your own vehicle, and if you bring a foreign registered vehicle into Tanzania, the park entry fees for the vehicle alone will be US$30 per 24 hours, as opposed to just TSh 300 for a locally registered vehicle. Also, if you intend to stay at lodges, you won't be entitled to the discounts which agents can get for group bookings, so you'll be up for the full cost (the agents' commission for booking lodges is usually 10%).

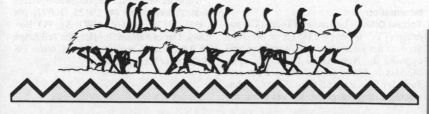

Dar es Salaam

Dar es Salaam, the 'Haven of Peace', started out as a humble fishing village in the mid-19th century when the Sultan of Zanzibar decided to turn the inland creek (now the harbour) into a safe port and trading centre. It became the capital in 1891, when the German colonial authorities transferred their seat of government from Bagamoyo, whose port was unsuitable for steamships.

Since then the city has continued to grow and now has a population of about 1½ million. Although quite a few high-rise buildings have appeared in the centre and at various places in the suburbs, Dar es Salaam remains substantially a low-rise city of red-tiled roofs, with its colonial character largely intact. The harbour is still fringed with palms and mangroves, and Arab dhows mingle with huge ocean-going vessels.

Like all large African capitals, there are substantial contrasts between the various parts of the city. However, you won't find here the glaring disparity in living standards between the slums and the more salubrious suburbs that you would in Nairobi. The busy, dusty streets and concrete buildings around the Kariakoo Market and clock tower are certainly a world away from the wide, tree-lined boulevards of the government and diplomatic quarters, but there's no way you would describe them as slums.

From being a relatively unrewarding place for nightlife in the mid to late 1980s, Dar es Salaam has considerably livened up, particularly if you're willing to head towards Oyster Bay.

Information

Tourist Office The Tanzania Tourist Corporation (TTC) office (☎ 2485) is on Maktaba St, near the junction with Samora Ave and opposite the New Africa Hotel. It's open Monday to Friday from 9 am to 5 pm and Saturday from 9 am till noon. The office has a limited range of glossy leaflets about the national parks and other places of interest, a (not too good) map of the city and, sometimes, a 1:2,000,000 scale map of Tanzania, though they're often out of stock of the latter. If the maps are unavailable, it can be difficult to find any street map of Dar es Salaam, but the road map is sometimes available from the Kilimanjaro Hotel shops.

The TTC can also make reservations at any of the larger hotels in Tanzania and at most of the beach hotels and national park lodges (payment in foreign currency only) but they can't help you with budget accommodation. It's better to book national park lodges through a travel agency, as they may offer special deals.

The TTC office has a folder with lots of information in it (which you have to ask for) but, although it's good on some things (railway fares, boat prices, etc), it's useless on others (departure times, journey times, bus company locations, etc).

You can forget about going to the TTC headquarters in the IPS building, diagonally opposite, since the people who work there are a bunch of arrogant ratbags who feel they should only have contact with presidents, cultural attaches, the World Bank and their computers.

Money Banking hours are Monday to Friday from 8.30 am to 12.30 pm and Saturdays from 8.30 to 11.30 am. If you need to change money at a bank outside these hours, the branch of the National Bank of Commerce in the Kilimanjaro Hotel is open Monday to Saturday from 8 am to 8 pm.

American Express is represented by Rickshaw Travels Ltd (☎ 29125, 35097; fax (051) 29125, 35456), UWT St, PO Box 1889, Dar es Salaam. It offers the full range of Amex travel services and can issue US dollar travellers' cheques.

Foreign Embassies Embassies in Dar es Salaam include:

Algeria
34 Upanga Rd (☎ 46250). Open Monday to Friday from 8 am to 2 pm.

Angola
10th Floor, IPS Bldg, Maktaba St (☎ 24292). Open Monday to Friday from 8 am to 3 pm and Saturday from 8 am till noon.

Belgium
7th Floor, NIC Investment House, Samora Ave (☎ 20244/5). Open Monday to Friday from 8 am to 12.30 pm.

Burundi
Plot 1007, Lugalo Rd (☎ 46307). Open Monday to Friday from 8 am to 3 pm.

Canada
38 Miramba St, Garden Ave (☎ 46000/9). Open Monday to Friday from 7.30 am to 3 pm.

Denmark
Ghana Ave (☎ 46319/20). Open Monday to Friday from 8 am to 1 pm.

Egypt
24 Garden Ave (☎ 32158). Open Monday to Friday from 8.30 am to 2.30 pm.

Finland
9th & 10th Floors, NIC Investment House, Samora Ave (☎ 46324). Open Monday to Friday from 7.30 am to noon and 12.45 to 3.30 pm.

France
Corner of Bagomoyo and Kulimani Rds (☎ 66021). Open Monday, Tuesday, Wednesday and Friday from 8.30 am to 2 pm and Thursday from 8 am to 4 pm.

Germany
10th Floor, NIC Investment House, Samora Ave (☎ 46334). Open Monday and Thursday from 7 am to 1.15 pm and 2 to 4 pm, and Tuesday, Wednesday and Friday from 7 am to noon.

India
11th floor, NIC Investment House, Samora Ave (☎ 46341). The consular section is at 28 Samora Ave (☎ 20295/6). Open Monday to Thursday from 8 am to 3.30 pm and on Friday from 8 am to 6 pm.

Ireland
Development Coop Office, 1st Floor, TDFL Bldg, corner of Ohio St and Upanga Rd (☎ 46492/3).

Italy
316 Lugalo Rd (☎ 46352/3). Open Monday and Tuesday from 7.30 am to 1 pm and 3.30 to 6 pm, Wednesday and Friday from 7.30 am to 1 pm, and Thursday from 7.30 am to 1 pm and 3.30 to 7 pm.

Japan
Plot 1018, Upanga Rd (☎ 46356/9). Open Monday to Friday from 8.30 am to 3.30 pm.

Kenya
14th Floor, NIC Investment House, Samora Ave (☎ 46362/6). Open Monday to Friday from 8 am to 3 pm (visa applications accepted from 9 am).

Madagascar
143 Malik Rd (☎ 29442). Open Monday to Friday from 8 am to 2 pm and Saturday from 8 am till noon.

Malawi
9th Floor, IPS Bldg, Maktaba St (☎ 46673/6). Open Monday to Friday from 8 am till noon and 2 to 5 pm.

Mozambique
25 Garden Ave (☎ 33062/5). Open Monday to Friday from 8.30 am to 4 pm.

Netherlands
New ATC Bldg, 2nd Floor, corner of Garden Ave and Ohio St (☎ 46391/2). Open Monday to Friday from 8 am to 3 pm.

Norway
Plot 160, Mirambo St (☎ 46815). Open Monday to Friday from 7.30 am to 2.30 pm.

Rwanda
32 Upanga Rd (☎ 46502). Open Monday to Friday from 8 am to 12.30 pm and 2 to 5 pm.

Spain
IPS Bldg, 7th Floor, Samora Ave (☎ 66018/9). Open Monday to Friday from 8.30 am to 2.30 pm.

Sudan
64 Upanga Rd (☎ 46509). Open Monday to Friday from 8.30 am to 3 pm.

Sweden
Extelecoms House, Samora Ave (☎ 46512/3). Open Monday to Friday from 7.30 am to 3.30 pm.

Switzerland
17 Kenyatta Drive, Oyster Bay (☎ 66008/9). Open Monday, Tuesday, Wednesday and Friday from 7.30 am to 2.45 pm and Thursday from 8 am to 3 pm.

Uganda
7th Floor, Extelecoms Bldg, Samora Ave (☎ 31003/5). Open Monday to Friday from 8 am to 3.45 pm.

UK
Hifiadhi House, Samora Ave (☎ 29601/5). Open Monday to Friday from 7.45 am to noon.

USA
36 Laibon Rd (☎ 66010/3). Open Monday to Friday from 7.30 am to 3.30 pm.

Zaïre
438 Malik Rd (☎ 24181/2). Open Monday to Friday from 8 am to 3 pm.

Zambia
5/9 Sokoine Drive at Ohio St (☎ 46383/9). Open Monday to Friday from 8 am till noon and 2 to 4.30 pm.

Dar es Salaam

1 National Museum
2 Main Post Office
3 Tourist Office
4 Buses to Moshi & Arusha
5 Extelecoms House & Ugandan Embassy
6 Roman Catholic Cathedral
7 Immigration Office
8 Buses to Iringa & Mbeya
9 Buses to Tanga
10 Malawi Embassy & Zambia Airways
    Zambian Airways
11 Zambian High Commission
12 Belgian, German, Finnish, Indian &
    Kenyan Embassies/High Commissions
13 British High Commission
14 Kariakco Market & Buses to Bagamoyo
15 Nyumba ya Sanaa
16 Air Tanzania
17 Bushtrekker Restaurant, KLM & Ethiopian
    Airlines
18 Kenya Airways, Air France & Lufthansa
19 Air India
20 Aeroflot
21 Rickshaw Travels & American Express
22 Mozambique Embassy
23 Canadian Embassy
24 Impala Tours
25 Coastal Travels

TANZANIA

Zimbabwe
408 Longido St, Upanga (☎ 46259). Open Monday to Friday from 8.30 am to 1 pm and 2 to 4 pm.

The nearest Australian and New Zealand high commissions are in Nairobi.

Bookshops Unless you're particularly fond of heavy Marxist tomes and anti-colonial rhetoric, there are no good bookstores in Dar es Salaam. The ones that exist stock only a very limited selection of the paperback Heinemann African Writers Series. For a much better selection, there's a second-hand stall on the street outside Tancot House, opposite Luther House, and others along Samora Ave between Maktaba St and Extelecoms House. At these stalls and similar ones along Maktaba St, as far as the main post office, you can buy international news magazines such as *Time, Newsweek, New African, South*, etc.

Things to See
National Museum The National Museum is next to the Botanical Gardens, between Samora Ave and Sokoine Drive. It houses important archaeological collections, especially the fossil discoveries of Zinjanthropus (Nutcracker Man), and has sections on the Shirazi civilisation of Kilwa, the Zanzibar slave trade and the German and British colonial periods. There are also displays of handicrafts, witchcraft paraphernalia and traditional dancing instruments. Entry costs TSh 200 for residents, TSh 800 for nonresidents (TSh 400 for nonresident students), and is free for resident students. The museum is open daily from 9.30 am to 6 pm.

Village Museum Another museum which is definitely worth visiting is the Village Museum, about 10 km from the city centre along the Bagamoyo road. This is an actual village consisting of a collection of authentically constructed dwellings from various parts of Tanzania, which display several distinct architectural styles. Open daily from 9 am to 7 pm, there's a small charge for entry

plus another charge to take photographs. Traditional dances are performed on Saturday and Sunday between 4 and 8 pm.

Mwenge Three km further down the Bagamoyo road at Mpakani Rd is Mwenge, a *makonde* (ebony-carving) community. It's an excellent place to pick up superb pieces of this traditional art form at rock-bottom prices. If you're heading this way by public transport, watch carefully, as it's not obvious from the Bagamoyo road. Stay up front with the driver and ask to be dropped off at the right spot.

Another good place to find makonde carvings, though at slightly higher prices, is the beer garden in front of the Palm Beach Hotel on Upanga Rd. Every evening, vendors do the rounds of the tables with examples of the craft.

Art Centre Local oil, water and chalk paintings can be seen at the Nyumba ya Sanaa building at the junction of Ohio St, Upanga Rd and UWT St, overlooking the Gymkhana Club. You can see the artists at work, and there are also makonde carvers and batik designers.

Kariakoo Market Between Mkunguni and Tandamuti Sts, this market has a colourful and exotic atmosphere – fruit, fish, spices, flowers, vegetables, etc – but very few handcrafts for sale.

Places to Stay
Finding a place to stay in Dar es Salaam can be difficult. The later you arrive, the harder it gets. It's not that there aren't a lot of hotels – there are – but they always seem to be full, and this applies as much to the expensive places as to the budget hotels. So, whatever else you do on arrival in Dar es Salaam, *don't* pass up a vacant room. Take the room and then look for something else if you're not happy with it. You can always make a booking for the following day if you find something better.

Most of the cheaper hotels are scattered between Maktaba and Lumumba Sts, with several others in the vicinity of the Kariakoo Market. The expensive places are either on Maktaba St or to the north and east of it.

All the TTC hotels – New Africa Hotel, Kilimanjaro Hotel, Kunduchi Beach Hotel – offer 50% discounts from the Monday following Easter Sunday until 30 June.

Dar es Salaam has water and electricity problems. Basically, supply doesn't match demand, so certain sections of the city are shut off from time to time. This affects practically all hotels, even the New Africa Hotel, but not the Kilimanjaro or Embassy hotels, which have their own generators.

Places to Stay – bottom end Don't expect too much for your money – a scruffy room with equally scruffy communal showers and toilets are the rule, but there are one or two exceptions.

Two places stand head and shoulders above the rest as being excellent value for money. The first is *Luther House* (☎ 46687), Sokoine Drive, PO Box 389, next to the characteristically German church at the junction of Sokoine Drive and Kivukoni Front. A single or double with communal bathroom facilities costs US$10 for nonresidents (TSh 3000 for residents). Breakfast is extra. It's clean and secure, mosquito nets are provided and there's hot water. As you might expect, it's a very popular place to stay. So popular in fact that it's likely to be booked out at least a week in advance, so to be sure of a room, write in advance requesting a booking and, preferably, enclosing a deposit.

Equally popular is the very clean and secure *YWCA* on Maktaba St, PO Box 2083, next to the main post office, which takes couples as well as women. There are a lot of rules (shorts are not allowed in the canteen, for instance), which are enforced, but everything works as a result. Mosquito nets and laundry facilities are provided. It's excellent value, at TSh 1500/2400 a single/double with communal bathroom facilities, including breakfast. Be polite and look clean and tidy when asking about accommodation here, otherwise they'll tell you it's full. Like Luther House, it's advisable to book in

advance, but there's more chance of getting a room here, as visitors can stay a maximum of seven nights.

The *YMCA*, Upanga Rd, isn't such good value, at US$10 for singles or doubles for nonresidents (TSh 3000 for residents). The bathroom facilities are communal but the price includes a (poor) breakfast.

There's another mission guesthouse, the *Sister Sandra Guest House* (☎ 22749), Kibasila Rd, at the back of the National Library, which is on UWT St. I've never heard of anyone staying there, but they offer double rooms with hot showers for much the same price as the YWCA. It's very clean and a large breakfast is included in the price.

Two of the cheapest hotels are the *Holiday Hotel*, Jamhuri St, which has singles/doubles with shared bath for TSh 1200/1300 and doubles with private bath for TSh 1500, and the *Traffic Light Motel* (☎ 23438), corner Jamhuri St and Morogoro Rd, which offers singles/doubles/triples with shared bath for TSh 800/1600/2400 and self-contained doubles for TSh 2400.

Going up in price a little, one of the best places to stay and one which has become very popular with travellers is the *Safari Inn* (☎ 38101), Band St, PO Box 21113, off Libya St behind the Jambo Inn. It's fairly new, very friendly and has a reasonably useful notice board. It's excellent value at TSh 2500/3500 for self-contained singles/doubles including breakfast. There are also a number of air-conditioned rooms, which go for TSh 4000 per person including breakfast. Checkout time is 11 am. There used to be a sign saying 'Women of moral terpitude not allowed', but it seems to have disappeared!

The *Jambo Inn* (☎ 30568) on Libya St is also reasonable value at TSh 2000/3000 for self-contained singles/doubles with fan, and TSh 3500 for superior doubles. The room rates include continental breakfast. The hotel has its own restaurant, which specialises in Indian non-vegetarian food.

Further afield, in the vicinity of the clock tower, are several other cheapies. The *Delux Inn* (☎ 20873), Uhuru St, is reasonable

Dar es Salaam
(Hotels & Restaurants)

1 Nyumba Ya Sanaa
2 Bushtrekker Restaurant
3 Mawenzi Hotel
4 Night of Istanbul
5 Amrapali's
6 Oriental Restaurant
7 Chick King
8 Jambo Inn
9 Open House
10 Pizza Villa
11 Mirror Palace
12 Azam Ice cream
13 Hotel Embassy
14 Pandya's
15 Margot's Disco
16 Club Bilicanas (disco)
17 Rendezvous
18 Foster's Ice cream
19 The Alcove
20 Salamander Coffee &
    Snack Bar
21 New Africa Hotel
22 Motel Agip
23 Hotel Skyways
24 Forodhani's
25 Kilimanjaro Hotel
26 Shalimar Restaurant
27 Sno-cream Parlour
28 Supreme Restaurant
29 Hotel Continental
30 Golden Dragon
31 DSM Chinese Restaurant
32 NBC Club
33 Jamaa Fast Foods
34 Cozy Cafe

value, at TSh 1500/2500 a single/double with shared bath, as is the *Kibodya Hotel* (☎ 31312) on Nkrumah St, which has doubles (no singles) with bathroom for TSh 2500. The Kibodya is a popular place to stay and is often booked out three days in advance. Both the Delux and the Kibodya are older-style places.

Nearby on Lindi St, the *Hotel Tamarine* (☎ 20233, 20573) has self-contained doubles (no singles) for TSh 2000 but is often full. On the opposite side of the road is the *Hotel Internationale* (☎ 22785), which is of a similar standard and charges the same rates as the Tamarine.

Places to Stay – middle Worth a try in this category is the *Hotel Continental* (☎ 22481), Nkrumah St. There are no singles, and self-contained doubles cost TSh 5490 including breakfast. The hotel has its own bar and restaurant. Similar in price is the *Motel Afrique* (☎ 46557), corner Kaluta and Bridge Sts, which has singles with shared bathroom for TSh 2500 and self-contained doubles with air-conditioning for TSh 5000. There are also self-contained suites with air-conditioning for TSh 7000. The room rates include breakfast. The hotel has a bar and restaurant on the 4th floor.

The *Hotel Skyways* (☎ 27061), corner Sokoine Drive and Ohio St, is very conveniently placed in the city centre and offers self-contained singles/doubles with air-conditioning at TSh 5500/6000 for residents (US$22/25 for nonresidents). Breakfast is included. The hotel has its own bar and restaurant.

A little further from the city centre is the *Mawenzi Hotel* (☎ 27761), at the roundabout on the corner of Upanga Rd and Maktaba St, opposite the YMCA. This hotel has undergone a major refurbishment and is now very good value and a popular place to stay. Tariffs for nonresidents are US$25/30/40 a single/double/triple (TSh 6500/7500/9500 for residents). All rooms are self-contained with air-conditioning and the hotel has a bar and restaurant.

If you're prepared to stay even further out

of the centre (a 15 to 20-minute walk), then you can't beat the Greek-owned *Palm Beach Hotel* (☎ 28892), Upanga Rd, near the junction with Ocean Rd. The outdoor beer garden/barbecue area is a favourite watering hole for expatriates from all over the world, as well as for Tanzanian entrepreneurs and for local women looking for a man to take them to the Oyster Bay Hotel disco or Club Bilicanas when the bar closes. It's an excellent place to make useful contacts. The hotel is efficiently run, secure and hassle-free, has friendly staff and is as clean as a whistle. There are a variety of rooms, all with air-conditioning and telephone, at TSh 4410/6405 a single/double with shared bath and TSh 7560/10,395 a single/double with private bath. Prices include breakfast (extra charge for eggs) and the hotel has a laundry service. The restaurant has an indoor area (basically seafood and meats), and a beer garden barbecue area where you can eat al fresco. It's very lively and well patronised.

Not far from the Palm Beach Hotel is *Etienne's Hotel* (☎ 20293) on Ocean Rd. This used to be a favourite Peace Corps volunteers hang-out, and some of them still stay here when they're in town. It has a kind of engaging leafy degeneracy about it with hints of a down-at-heel obscure rural English pub and comes complete with one of the world's most indolent bartenders. It's tropical languor *par excellence*. Fans groan lazily above your head, the springs on the lounge seats succumbed to posterior pressure long ago, the lights are dim and people talk in conspiratorial tones. There's a beer garden and meals are available. There are no singles, and doubles with shared bathroom cost TSh 3120. Self-contained doubles cost TSh 4620.

Last in this range is the *Twiga Hotel* (☎ 22561), Samora Ave, but it was being completely refurbished in early 1993, so you can assume that when it reopens, it will probably be considerably more expensive than it was previously.

Places to Stay – top end There are only four top-end hotels in the city centre, two of which are privately owned and the others operated by the TTC.

Of the privately owned, probably the best is the *Hotel Embassy* (☎ 30006), 24 Garden Ave (PO Box 3152), which has 150 rooms – all self-contained with air-conditioning, a telephone and 24-hour room service – at TSh 12,500/16,000 for singles/doubles including breakfast. There are also suites for TSh 20,500. Nonresidents have to pay in hard currency (cash or travellers' cheques), which makes the singles/doubles US$55/71. There's a swimming pool, bar, grill, restaurant and all the usual services. Credit cards are accepted.

Somewhat more expensive is the recently refurbished *Motel Agip* (☎ 23511/3), Pamba Rd, PO Box 529, at the back of the New Africa Hotel. Self-contained singles/doubles with air-con cost TSh 17,850/21,000 for residents and US$85/90 for nonresidents, including continental breakfast. The hotel has its own bar and restaurant and credit cards are accepted.

The first of the TTC hotels is the *New Africa Hotel* (☎ 29611) in Maktaba St. A well-known landmark, it's currently being extended to double its size. The rooms are well appointed and fully air-conditioned and the hotel has all the usual facilities, except a swimming pool. Singles/doubles, which include a continental breakfast, cost US$60/70 for nonresidents and TSh 7000/8500 for residents, plus 25% taxes and service charges. Credit cards are accepted.

Top of the range is the TTC *Kilimanjaro Hotel* (☎ 21281), Kivukoni Front, where singles/doubles/triples with a continental breakfast cost US$69/79/86 for nonresidents, plus 25% taxes and service charges. There's also a shopping and service hall on the ground floor. As at the New Africa Hotel, all the rooms are well appointed and fully air-conditioned and the hotel has all the usual facilities, including a swimming pool and a popular rooftop restaurant which overlooks the harbour. Credit cards are accepted.

Places to Eat – cheap

There are many small restaurants in the city centre where you can buy a cheap traditional African meal or Indian food (usually the latter). Some of these places are attached to hotels.

Currently popular with travellers is the *Sheesh Mahal*, India St, which offers good, cheap Indian food. Equally popular is the *Imran Restaurant*, Chagga St, offering Indian curries which are rated by some travellers as the best in town. Also very popular, especially for lunch, is the *Salamander Coffee & Snack Bar*, Samora Ave at Mkwepu St, where you can eat either inside or outside on the verandah. An average lunch costs about TSh 800. Other good cheapies include the *Pop-In*, the restaurant at the *Jambo Inn* (lunch-time specials such as mutton briyani and pilau or chicken for TSh 1200 and kebabs for TSh 600), and the *Nawaz Restaurant*, Msinhiri St, between Mosque St and Morogoro Rd, which has cheap rice and meat dishes.

Possibly the best vegetarian Indian restaurant in Dar es Salaam is the *Supreme Restaurant*, Nkrumah St. This place has been operating for years and has a well-deserved reputation. The *Royal Restaurant*, Jamhuri St, between Mosque and Kitumbini Sts, also does vegetable curries and the like.

For even cheaper stand-up-and-eat or takeaway snacks, try one of the cafés near the junction of Mkwepu and Makunganya (Indira Gandhi) Sts.

Ice-cream freaks should make at least one visit to the *Sno-Cream Parlour*, Mansfield St, near the junction with Bridge St. Mansfield St is between Samora Ave and Sokoine Drive. This place has the best ice cream in Tanzania and is well on the way to becoming a legend among travellers. You should see the number of Indian families who come here on Sundays! Lastly, for fruit juices, peanut brittle and gooey cakes, go to *Siefee's Juice Shop*, Samora Ave. It also has good samosas.

Places to Eat – more expensive

For a not-too-expensive splurge, the *DSM Chinese Restaurant* in the basement of the NIC building, Samora Ave at Mirambo St, is excellent value and has been a popular place for a small spree for years, especially if you want a break from Indian or African food. Likewise, you'll find a lot of travellers eating lunch at the restaurant on the ground floor of the *New Africa Hotel*. The cuisine varies from average to good and a full meal will cost around TSh 1200 including taxes. The food is basically continental, though they also attempt Chinese. For a good Indian meal, try the *Shalimar Restaurant* on Mansfield St, next door to the Sno-Cream.

Meals at the *Motel Agip* have been described by a few Italian travellers as 'as good as a first class restaurant in Rome with better service and at a fraction of the cost'. It's slightly more expensive than the New Africa Hotel.

For a very refreshing change, treat your taste buds to an evening meal at the *Night of Istanbul*, corner Zanaki and UWT Sts. This restaurant is owned and run by a Turk, so there's all the usual Turkish dishes (doner kebab, shish kebab, hummus, etc). It isn't particularly cheap, at TSh 1500 to TSh 2000 for a meal, but it's highly rated by everyone who goes there. Another place of similar standard is *Shari's Dar Bar*, UWT St, which offers huge servings of Tandoori chicken, beef and salad for about TSh 1000. Further out of town, it's worth heading for the very popular outdoor barbecue at the *Palm Beach Hotel*, Upanga Rd, especially if you're thinking of doing some serious drinking afterwards (they never run out of beer, even if you're not eating). Barbecued chicken or doner kebab with chips and salad costs less than TSh 1000. The indoor restaurant offers somewhat more expensive standard European dishes but the food is only average. The nearby *Etienne's Hotel*, Ocean Rd, also offers lunch and dinner and is recommended by Peace Corps volunteers. It's somewhat cheaper than the Palm Beach.

For a real splurge, there's a choice of three restaurants. One of the most popular is *The Alcove*, Samora Ave, which offers Indian and Chinese dishes in air-conditioned comfort amid soft lighting. The food would rate a mention in any international restaurant guide. Average prices for a main course are TSh 2000. Only imported beers are served, and these are (naturally) more expensive than Safari Lager. The Alcove is open for lunch and dinner. Get there early or reserve a table if you don't want to stand around. The restaurant was completely refurbished in early 1993.

More expensive still but a superb place to eat is the *Bushtrekker Restaurant*, overlooking the Gymkhana Club on the roundabout where Upanga Rd, Ohio St and UWT St meet. It's very up-market, with starched linen tablecloths and an extensive wine list, and you have the choice of eating al fresco on the covered balcony or inside with the air-conditioning on. Main dishes range from TSh 2000 up to TSh 5000 for such things as lobster and beef tenderloin. Starters range from TSh 800 to TSh 1500, soups are about TSh 800 and desserts range from TSh 500 to TSh 900.

Most people have at least one meal at the rooftop restaurant in the *Kilimanjaro Hotel*. The views over the harbour at night are superb and the food is usually good, though I have been served a very dry and tasteless fish meal here before now, so perhaps the quality is not consistent. It's popular with businesspeople, local expatriates and well-heeled tourists. Prices are roughly the same as those at The Alcove.

Entertainment

Definitely the most popular place for a cold cleansing ale in the city centre is the street-level patio bar of the *New Africa Hotel* on Maktaba St. Most travellers come here at one time or another and you can always get into a lively conversation. It gets very busy between 4.30 and 7 pm. Both imported beer and the Tanzanian brew, Safari lager are served, but before ordering, ask what is cold. The coldest are invariably the more expensive imported lagers.

Others have recommended the bar at the *Motel Agip*, but the mezzanine bar at the *Hotel Embassy* is much livelier and attracts a friendly and garrulous crowd of resident expatriates and Tanzanians every evening from around 5 pm onwards. You need to be fairly well dressed and wearing shoes or clean joggers at either the Agip or Embassy; otherwise you'll feel very much out of place.

Another lively bar is the one at the *Palm Beach Hotel*, Upanga Rd, though it is further out of town, so you'll have to take a taxi (TSh 300) at night. In the evenings it's always full of a gregarious mixture of Africans and working expatriates (both male and female), and although the beers get warmer as the night wears on, they never run out. The bar closes at about 11 pm. The nearby *Etienne's Hotel*, Ocean Rd, is also worth a visit, though it's generally much quieter.

Far and away the most popular disco in Dar es Salaam is *Club Bilicanas*, at the back of the former Mbowe Hotel on Mkwepu St. This is one of the best discos in East Africa. It's obviously had megadollars poured into it, has been imaginatively designed and has all the lighting and other effects you'd expect from a world-class disco. Drink prices are reasonable and the place is fully air-conditioned. It's open every night until around 4 am and entry costs TSh 2000 for a single person or TSh 3000 for a couple, except on Friday and Saturday nights, when the price is TSh 2500 and TSh 3000 per person, respectively.

There's another disco, which is open nightly, at the *Oyster Bay Hotel*, though you'll definitely need a taxi (TSh 500) to get there from the centre, unless you're offered a lift from the Palm Beach Hotel when its bar closes. This is an open-air disco with live bands (though the one I heard was very mediocre). Entry costs TSh 1000 per person. It used to be very popular but is often almost empty these days. The clientele has obviously deserted it in favour of Bilicanas. The problem with coming here without your own transport is that the taxi drivers have you over a barrel when you want to leave. Whatever fare they quote is what they'll take you for – they won't bargain. There's also a disco at the *Kilimanjaro Hotel* and at the beach resort hotels.

The *Yacht Club*, about four km beyond Oyster Bay, is recommended as a good place to meet expatriates. A taxi to the club from central Dar es Salaam costs TSh 1000.

The *British Council* (☎ 22716), Samora Ave, has free film shows on Wednesday afternoons or evenings and sometimes on Mondays. Similar social evenings are organised by the *Goethe Institute* (☎ 22227), in the IPS building on Samora Ave, and the *US Information Service* (☎ 26611) on Samora Ave.

Getting There & Away
Air Dar es Salaam is the major international arrival point for flights from overseas. See the earlier Getting There & Away and Getting Around chapters for Tanzania for details of international and domestic flights.

Airlines with offices in Dar es Salaam are:

Aeroflot
    Eminaz Mansion, Samora Ave (☎ 34602)
Air France
    Peugeot House, corner of Upanga Rd and UWT St (☎ 20356)
Air India
    Corner of Upanga Rd and UWT St (☎ 23525)
Air Tanzania
    ATC House, Ohio St (☎ 38300)
Alitalia
    Peugeot House, Upanga Rd
British Airways
    Coronation House, Samora Ave (☎ 560250)
EgyptAir
    Matasalamat Mansion, Samora Ave (☎ 23425)
Ethiopian Airlines
    TDFL Bldg, Ohio St (☎ 24174)
Kenya Airways
    Peugeot House, Upanga Rd (☎ 25352)
KLM
    TDFL Building, Ohio St (☎ 37519)
Lufthansa
    Peugeot House, corner Upanga Rd and UWT St (☎ 38843)
Pakistan International Airlines
    IPS Bldg, Maktaba St (☎ 26944)
Sabena
    AMI Bldg, Samora Ave (☎ 30109)
SAS
    Luther House, Sokoine Drive (☎ 34068)
Swissair
    Luther House, Sokoine Drive (☎ 34068)
Zambian Airways
    IPS Bldg, Maktaba St (☎ 21316)

Bus As there's no central bus station in Dar

es Salaam, buses to various parts of the country leave from a variety of places within the city.

Buses for Bagamoyo leave throughout the day until about 3 pm from outside the Kariakoo Market on Swahili St. They depart when full, cost TSh 200 one way and take between two and three hours.

Heading for Moshi and Arusha, buses depart from the bus station on the corner of Morogoro Rd and Libya St. Luxury buses depart daily and vary in price between TSh 6000 and TSh 7500. Freshya Shamba has the best buses (TSh 7500), followed by Bariadi Bus Service (TSh 6500) and Dar Express Bus Service (TSh 6000). They take about nine hours between Dar and Moshi. Ordinary buses cost around TSh 3000 and take longer. The road is rough as far as Korogwe but is newly surfaced between there and Moshi.

Buses to Tanga and Mbeya and other points west and south depart from the so-called Country Bus Station on Libya St, on the bottom side of the park between Uhuru and Nkrumah Sts. The buses to Tanga take between seven and eight hours and those to Mbeya take about 20 hours. See the individual towns for details of fares and schedules.

Train For information about the TAZARA line between Dar es Salaam and Kapiri Mposhi, see the earlier Tanzania Getting There & Away chapter. For details of the Central Line railway between Dar es Salaam and Kigoma, Mwanza, Tanga and Moshi, see the Tanzania Getting Around chapter.

Boat
To/From Zanzibar Transport between Dar es Salaam and Zanzibar and Pemba islands has undergone a remarkable transformation in the last two years. There's now a choice of five different boats, a hydrofoil, a catamaran and two ordinary ferry boats, as well as the traditional motorised dhows. It's all very well organised and there are daily departures on most.

The one thing you *must* have before you're allowed to board *any* boat to Zanzibar

is a yellow fever vaccination certificate. There will be a medical official checking that you have one before you board the boat and he's very strict. Avoid unpleasantness and disappointment by making sure you have one.

Whichever form of transport you take, there's a US$5 port charge in addition to the boat fare. Residents pay TSh 300.

The cheapest, but most tedious and uncomfortable, way to get to Zanzibar is by motorised dhow. These operate out of the Malindi Dock alongside Sokoine Drive. The fare is TSh 600 and the journey takes from six to eight hours. The dhows are large, wooden, motorised vessels which can take about 200 passengers – these are not the small dhows with lateen sails. There's usually one dhow per day in either direction.

To book, go down to the Malindi Dock and buy a ticket the morning before the dhow sails. The booking office is on the right-hand side just inside the metal gates at the bottom of the tarmac ramp which goes down from Sokoine Drive. It's labelled 'East & Southern Boat Transporters'. These dhows don't sail on Sundays or public holidays.

Departure times vary, but you have to check in at the customs shed two hours before departure – you'll be told what time when you buy the ticket. No food or drink is available on the boat, so bring your own. There's generally a toilet on board which hangs off the back of the dhow.

Getting off the dhow at Zanzibar is like extricating yourself from a rugby scrum. *Wazungu* (White people) are generally the last to leave, as it's a major effort to climb over the side of a dhow with a rucksack on your back and into a flimsy bucking aluminium motor launch whilst dozens of Zanzibaris claw and elbow you out of the way. Good luck!

Few travellers use the dhows these days, as the other boats are much more convenient, more comfortable and faster. They all have booking offices next to each other on Sokoine Drive, adjacent to the customs shed.

The cheapest ferry boat is the MV *Muungano*, operated by Azam Marine & Co

(☎ 26699 in Dar es Salaam, 31262 in Zanzibar). It departs from Dar es Salaam daily at 1 pm for Zanzibar. In the opposite direction, it leaves Zanzibar for Dar es Salaam at 4.30 pm. The journey takes 2½ hours and costs US$10 or UK£5 (TSh 2500 for residents). If you're in a group of six or more, one of you goes free.

The FB *Canadian Spirit*, operated by Adecon Marine Inc (☎ 20856 in Dar es Salaam), also does the Zanzibar run, as well as connecting Zanzibar with Pemba, but there are no regular departures. Most of the time, it's a car ferry cum passenger boat and sails between Dar es Salaam and Mtwara via Mafia island and Kilwa (as well as other smaller ports on the coast south of Dar), but it also has occasional services between Dar and Mombasa, Zanzibar and Mombasa, and Pemba and Mombasa. There are three classes: fares to Zanzibar are US$10 (Class 'A'), US$8 (Class 'B') and US$6 (Class 'C'). Residents pay TSh 2500, TSh 2000 and TSh 1500, respectively. Between Dar and Pemba, the fares are US$30, US$25 and US$20 in the appropriate classes. Residents pay TSh 6500, TSh 5500 and TSh 4500, respectively. Check with the office for departures.

More expensive, but faster, is the MV *Flying Horse*, operated by the Africa Shipping Corporation (☎ Dar es Salaam 33414, or Zanzibar 33031). This boat is a catamaran and leaves Dar es Salaam for Zanzibar Tuesday to Saturday at 10.15 am and 3.45 pm. In the opposite direction, it departs from Zanzibar for Dar es Salaam on the same days at 7 am and 1.15 pm. On Sunday, Monday and public holidays, there's only one departure (at 11.30 am from Dar). The journey takes two hours and costs US$50 (VIP cabin), US$30 (1st class), US$20 (2nd class) and US$10 (3rd class). Residents pay TSh 5000, TSh 3500, TSh 3000 and TSh 2400, respectively. Children pay half-fare.

The fastest of the lot is the *Sea Express*, which takes just 1½ hours and is operated by Sea Express Services Ltd. This is a hydrofoil which leaves Dar es Salaam for Zanzibar daily at 9 am and 2.30 pm; some days, there's an extra departure at 4.15 pm. In the opposite direction, it leaves Zanzibar for Dar es Salaam at 7 am and 2.20 pm. The fares are US$30 or UK£20 (1st class) and US$20 or UK£15 (2nd class). Residents pay TSh 6200 and TSh 4900, respectively. Children under 12 years old pay half-price. There's very little difference between 1st and 2nd classes. The only trouble with this hydrofoil is that you see very little en route, as you're fully enclosed, but it is fast.

To/From Mafia Island, Kilwa & Mtwara The only ferry connecting Dar es Salaam with places south towards Mozambique is the FB *Canadian Spirit* (mentioned earlier in this section). There are no regular departures, so you need to check with the office – they depend on cargo and passenger demand. The fares from Dar es Salaam to Mafia are US$25 (Class 'A'), US$20 (Class 'B') and US$15 (Class 'C'). Residents pay TSh 4000, TSh 3500 and TSh 3000, respectively. The fares from Dar es Salaam to Mtwara are US$30 (Class 'A'), US$25 (Class 'B') and US$20 (Class 'C'). Residents pay TSh 7000, TSh 6000 and TSh 5000, respectively.

Getting Around
To/From the Airport Dar es Salaam airport is 13 km from the city centre. Bus No 67 connects the two but, if you get on at the airport, make sure that it is going right into the city centre – some don't.

A shuttle bus between the centre of Dar es Salaam and the airport is operated by Takims Tours & Safaris. It leaves for the airport from the New Africa Hotel, Maktaba St, at 8 and 10 am and noon. In the opposite direction, shuttle buses from the airport to Dar es Salaam connect with incoming flights between 9 am and 6 pm and will take you direct to the hotel of your choice. The fare is TSh 500.

A taxi to or from the airport costs TSh 3000 (but first quotes are often TSh 4000 to TSh 5000). You can share this with up to four people.

Bus Local buses are operated by both government (UDA buses) and private firms

(Dala Dala). Neither type is numbered. Instead, buses have their first and last stop indicated in the front window. The bus to the TAZARA railway station is marked 'Posta Vigunguti'. Fares are fixed and are only a few shillings, but all buses are very crowded. It would be almost impossible to get onto them with a rucksack, let alone get off at your destination.

Taxi Taxis have no meters and charge a standard TSh 500 per journey inside the immediate city centre. Slightly outside this area, they'll charge TSh 600 to TSh 700. To Oyster Bay, taxis cost TSh 1000 to TSh 1500, depending on the time of day. To the TAZARA railway station, they should cost around TSh 1500 (negotiable).

Beaches

Oyster Bay is the nearest beach, six km north of the city centre and on the fringes of where the affluent and the foreign ambassadors have their residences. As you might expect, it's a particularly beautiful stretch of tropical coastline fringed with coconut palms, but keeping it that way has become a bone of contention between local environmental groups and the city council. It seems that various groups of young, well-to-do rev-heads have been chewing up the foreshore at weekends with their 4WD dune buggies and not giving a damn about the damage they do or the work which local residents have put into conserving the area. Some people have been arrested for attempting to plant coconut palms intended to replace those which will soon die. That's a sad indictment of the city council's policies, and very short-sighted. This beach is, after all, a major recreation area for the city.

There are other beaches a little further up the coast from here, but the major resort area is 25 km to 27 km north of the city, east of the Bagamoyo road. Strung out along the coast here, from south to north, are the Kunduchi Beach Hotel, Silversands, Rungwe Oceanic Hotel and the Bahari Beach Hotel. This is Dar es Salaam's answer to the Shelly, Tiwi and Diani beaches south of Mombasa. It's an idyllic mixture of sea, sand, sun and landscaped tropical extravagance. The only drawback, as with the Mombasa beaches, is the copious amount of seaweed, which makes swimming at high tide very unpleasant. When the tide goes out, however, the seaweed tends to stay on the beach, thus providing clear sea in which to enjoy yourself. There are also several wooded islands with good beaches offshore, to which the beach hotels run boats.

If you stay at any of these beach resorts, don't walk from one to the other either along the beach or along the connecting roads unless you're with a large group. Many people have been robbed, some violently. Always take a taxi or get a lift.

Boat trips to offshore islands such as Mbudya, where you can swim, snorkel or sunbathe, are available from the Kunduchi Beach Hotel, the Rungwe Oceanic Hotel and the Bahari Beach Hotel. There are usually several trips per day from Monday to Saturday and more on Sundays and public holidays. You need a minimum of four people, unless you're willing to pay a surcharge. You can also go sailing from these places or rent a catamaran but it won't be a cheap day out.

Some 28 km south of Dar es Salaam, there's another beach resort, the Ras Kutani Beach Resort, a relatively new place which is built of local materials but has the full range of creature comforts.

Places to Stay

The *Oyster Bay Hotel* (☎ 68062/4), Touré Drive, PO Box 2261, Dar es Salaam, about six km from the city centre, is the first of the beach hotels north of Dar es Salaam. All rooms face the sea and are self-contained and air-conditioned. Bed and breakfast costs US$90/110 for singles/doubles, and there are suites for US$150 and US$170. Credit cards are not accepted. The hotel has its own bar, restaurant and disco.

Of the other hotels further up the coast, the

TTC *Kunduchi Beach Hotel* (☎ 47621) is quite pleasant and all rooms face the ocean. Self-contained singles/doubles with continental breakfast cost US$36/45/52 for singles/doubles/triples, including taxes but excluding 5% service charges. Residents pay TSh 6300, TSh 6800 and TSh 8500, respectively. Temporary daily entry for nonresidents costs TSh 500, plus a further TSh 200 to use the swimming pool, but you don't pay this if you arrive on the State Transport Corporation shuttle bus, since they assume you're going to stay there or go further up the coast to one of the other hotels.

Next up the coast is the *Rungwe Oceanic Hotel* (☎ 47021), which is favoured by overland truck companies because it's the only beach hotel where camping is permitted. This makes it the only one within reach of the budget traveller. Camping costs TSh 500 per person per night, but the site is somewhat run-down and water is rarely available. It's possible to leave a vehicle here for a small nightly charge whilst you go to Zanzibar.

Top of the range is the *Bahari Beach Hotel* (☎ 47101), a stunningly beautiful construction in coral rag and makuti, and very thoughtfully landscaped with flowering trees and coconut palms. Apart from the reception and dining areas, the Bahari consists of a series of two-storey chalets, each with four bedrooms, private showers, individual balconies and air-conditioning. There's a swimming pool and a very popular weekend disco. Doubles (no singles) with continental breakfast cost US$90 and triples cost US$110 (TSh 12,000 and TSh 14,000, respectively, for Tanzanian residents) in the high season, including taxes. Temporary daily entry costs TSh 500 on weekdays and Saturdays and TSh 800 on Sundays, when there's live music. Bookings should be made through Bushtrekker Safaris (☎ 31957; telex 41178), PO Box 5350, Dar es Salaam.

South of Dar es Salaam is the new *Ras Kutani Beach Resort*, owned by the Selous

Safari Company (☎ 28485), PO Box 1192, Dar es Salaam. Built out of local materials (coral rag with makuti roofs, etc) to blend with the environment, it consists of 25 self-contained units built around a beautiful freshwater lagoon. The units cost US$96 per person for nonresidents and US$70 per person for residents, with full board and including taxes but excluding service charges (5%). There's a 50% supplement on the above rates during July and August, October and January and December.

Places to Eat

It's more than likely that you'll eat at the hotel where you're staying, but if you're just a day guest, you can also eat lunch and dinner at any of the hotels. The cost for either meal is about US$10 to $US12 (payable in shillings). Those relying on the State Transport Corporation shuttle bus from Dar es Salaam to the hotels only have the option of taking lunch, since the last bus back to Dar es Salaam leaves at about 6 pm. If you're staying for dinner, you'll need your own transport back.

Getting There & Away

It is possible to get to the Kunduchi beach resorts using local buses from the centre of Dar es Salaam, but these will drop you in the village, from where it's quite a walk to the hotels. Also, there's a good chance of being robbed. It's much safer and more convenient to take the State Transport Corporation shuttle bus from the New Africa Hotel in Dar es Salaam. The shuttle bus leaves the New Africa Hotel at 9 am, 2 and 5 pm Monday to Friday; 9 am, 1 and 5 pm on Saturday; and 9 and 11 am and 1 and 5 pm on Sunday and public holidays. In the opposite direction, ask at your hotel for the return times, and don't worry if the bus doesn't arrive on time – it's often half an hour late. The fare is TSh 600.

The Coast

BAGAMOYO

The name of this coastal town 75 km north of Dar es Salaam derives from the word 'bwagamoyo', meaning 'lay down your heart'. It's a reminder that this was once the terminus of the slave trade caravan route from Lake Tanganyika. This was the point of no return, where the captives were loaded onto dhows and shipped to Zanzibar for sale to Arab buyers.

Bagamoyo later became the headquarters of the German colonial administration, and many of the buildings which they constructed still remain. However, its history goes back to the 14th century, when the East African coast was being settled by Arabs and Shirazis from the Persian Gulf. The ruins they left at Kaole, just outside Bagamoyo, are similar to those at Gedi and around the Lamu archipelago further north in Kenya.

Warning The only trouble with staying anywhere in Bagamoyo is the very real possibility of being violently mugged. This can happen at any time of the night or day and your assailants will usually be armed with *pangas* (machetes), which they won't hesitate to use even if you don't resist. Quite a few travellers have been badly injured and their valuables stolen. Don't expect any help from the police – they're not going to lift a finger. The same danger exists anywhere along the beach.

Things to See

The tourist literature would have you believe that Bagamoyo is a miniversion of Zanzibar or Mombasa, with a historical centre of narrow, winding alleys, tiny mosques, cafés and whitewashed German colonial buildings. There's certainly a small section of town down by the waterfront which corresponds to such a description, but it has all seen better days and the most lasting impression is one of near-terminal decay.

Restoration is being carried out on the customs house at the beach but the other colonial buildings show only benign and mildewy neglect. All in all, it's debatable whether what remains is worth a four to six-hour return bus trip. Personally, I think not, and many other travellers agree with me.

Museum The Catholic Mission north of town maintains a museum, with relics of the slave trade and displays about the early European explorers Burton, Speke and Stanley. The chapel where Livingstone's body was laid before being taken to Zanzibar en route to Westminster Abbey is also here. Don't walk to this museum alone, as there's a good chance you'll get mugged.

Kaole Visiting the 14th-century ruins at Kaole involves a one-hour walk along the beach going south past Kaole village into the mangrove swamps. When the beach apparently ends, go inland and look for the stone pillars. The guardian, Mr Kajeri, has a hut nearby and is well informed about the ruins.

Entry costs TSh 400 (less if you don't want a receipt). Don't bring any valuables along this beach and make a determined effort to look poor; otherwise, robbery is a near certainty.

Art College At Chuo ya Sanaa, 300 metres south of the Badeco Hotel, you can watch students practise music and dance. There's a festival here each year in the last week of September.

Places to Stay & Eat

There's only one hotel (well signposted) in Bagamoyo itself, but it's very basic and essentially is used only by prostitutes and their clients. Most travellers head out to the *Badeco Beach Hotel*. Even this place is very run-down: hardly anything works, there are no mosquito nets and most of the beds are broken. It costs TSh 350 per person, though the manager is very creative about inventing other 'fees'. The cook at the hotel will prepare food for a small fee, but don't expect anything fancy. You can buy lobster and other seafood from the fishers near the old German customs building. They land their catches here in the late morning and late afternoon.

Much better but considerably more expensive is the new *Gogo Beach Resort*, which offers self-contained doubles, a restaurant, a picnic and camping area and a swimming pool.

Getting There & Away
Buses depart from Dar es Salaam throughout the day until about 3 pm from outside the Kariakoo Market. They leave when full, are very crowded, cost TSh 160 one-way and take two to three hours, depending on the number of stops en route.

PANGANI
Pangani is a small village north of Bagamoyo and some 50 km south of Tanga. It's on a beautiful stretch of coast, with many reefs and islands offshore. From Pangani you can organise fishing trips to the reefs and snorkelling at the two islands of **Mawe Mdogo** and **Mwamba Mawe**.

There's also a small marine park on the island of **Maziwi** and boat trips are possible to see the wildlife up the Pangani River.

Places to Stay & Eat
The *YMCA* is more than six km north of Pangani, so it's really only suitable for those with their own transport or a penchant for walking more than 1½ hours to the nearest restaurant. It costs TSh 250 per person; breakfast costs TSh 250 and dinner is TSh 400. It's basic but mellow, and though there are no locks on the doors, gear appears to be safe. The manager, Dickson, is a live wire and well worth tracking down for an animated conversation.

A more convenient place to stay in Pangani is the *Pangadeco*, at the beach end of the main street on the high-water mark,

about 50 metres through the coconut palms. The rooms are clean but mosquito nets are not provided and you may not be too impressed with the sky-blue décor. There's no running water, so bucket showers are the order of the day. It costs TSh 400 a double and food is available on request. There's also a good bar.

There are two other guesthouses: the *River Inn* is on the road running alongside the river, about halfway from the boat yard to the ferry stage, and the *Udo* is on the same road but nearer the ferry.

Entertainment
Pangani is a Muslim town and has only one bar, which is noisy despite an average clientele of only six people per night. However, here you can meet the district commissioner and district administrator, who are both charming when sober and are keen to help tourists have a good time.

Getting There & Away
Buses go to and from Tanga three times daily and depart between 8 am and noon. Trips by motorboat (from the frozen-fish factory) are expensive – TSh 2800 for two hours, for example.

TANGA
Strolling around Tanga, amid its sleepy, semicolonial atmosphere, you'd hardly be aware that this is Tanzania's second-largest seaport. Seen from the air, however, it's a remarkably large town which sprawls well into the hinterland. It was founded by the Germans in the late 19th century and is a centre for the export of sisal. Not many travellers come here, apart from those looking for a dhow to Pemba Island or heading north to Mombasa.

Tanga briefly hit the headlines in early 1990 when, after a tip-off, police uncovered hundreds of elephant tusks buried in the sand in gunny sacks on a tiny offshore island. Those involved were obviously intent on smuggling them out of the country one dark night but there were no reports of subsequent arrests. Sound like a familiar tale?

Tanga

To Korogwe, Moshi, Dar es Salaam & Airport

Marina Inn

St Anthony's Cathedral

Dhow & Fishing Boat Anchorage

To Bus Station

Station Rd

Railway Station

Government Offices

Tanga Library

Uhuru Park

Planters Hotel

Stadium

Market St

Bank

Bandarini Hotel

Independence Ave

Clock Tower

Pahwas Restaurant

Market

Four Ways Hotel

Post Office

National Bank of Commerce

Chinese Restaurant

To Beaches, Cement Factory & Tanga Bathing Club

Container Ship Dock

Scale

0   250m

Things to See

Amboni Caves This area is predominantly a limestone district, and the Amboni Caves, off the road to Lunga Lunga, are not too far from town.

Tongoni Ruins The Tongoni Ruins are 20 km south of Tanga on the Pangani road. There's a large ruined mosque and more than 40 tombs, the largest concentration of such tombs on the East African coast.

According to accounts which came into the hands of the Portuguese when they first arrived at Kilwa in 1505, both Kilwa and Tongoni were founded at the end of the 10th century by Ali bin Hasan, the son of Sultan Hasan of Shiraz in Persia. Certainly the method of construction of the mosque is unlike that used by the Arabs who came from the Arabian Peninsula in later centuries. Yet Persian script has only been found once, on one of the tombstones at Tongoni, though Persian coins are common at other sites along the coast, such as at Malindi.

Places to Stay – bottom end

Overlooking the harbour on Independence Ave, the *Bandorini Hotel* is a very twee place which many travellers rate highly, but Tush, the owner, is struggling to keep up standards since the recent death of his wife. Assuming he's coping, it offers English colonial-style living (reflecting the owners' nationality) and its seven rooms are often full. It costs TSh 750 per person without breakfast. The owner can arrange boat trips to Pangani and elsewhere.

The *Usabara Guest House* on Third St is similarly priced and its rooms have a fan, clean sheets and a towel. The staff are friendly and your belongings are secure when left in the rooms. You can't miss this place – it's painted in large, bright stripes.

If the Bandorini and the Usabara are full, try the *Planters Hotel* (☎ 2041) on Market St. It's a huge, rambling, old wooden hotel surrounded by an enormous verandah and with a bar and restaurant downstairs. Aussies from Queensland will love this place – it's home away from home. The rooms are clean

and have a hand basin but the communal showers have cold water only. It costs TSh 1100/1800 a single/double or TSh 3000 for a double with air-conditioning.

Other than these, there's the *Four Ways Hotel* (☎ 46097), also on Market St, which offers self-contained doubles with balcony, fan and clean sheets for TSh 1500. The hotel has its own bar and restaurant.

Places to Stay – middle

The most convenient mid-range hotel is the *Marina Inn*, which is a modern, well-maintained hotel offering air-conditioned doubles for around TSh 3000, including breakfast. There are no singles. The hotel has a bar and restaurant, but if you're going to spend this amount of money, it's probably better to stay at the *Baobab Hotel* (☎ 40638), about five km from the centre. It's slightly more expensive but a better place to stay.

Places to Eat

A good place to eat is the *Patwas Restaurant*, opposite the market in the town centre. This very clean and friendly Asian-run restaurant offers excellent curries for lunch and dinner, with snacks and tea in between, but is not particularly cheap. Some travellers criticise the place because they feel it caters too much to Western tastes. They suggest instead the *Baht*, a takeaway snack bar on Second Ave, between the two railway crossings. Here you can get an excellent selection of vegetarian bhajis, samosas and sweets.

The *Marine Restaurant* on Market St is very popular with local people for lunch. Meals are cheap but the food is only average.

The *Chinese Restaurant*, next to the post office, is also recommended. It offers good, cheap seafood and sweet and sour vegetarian meals.

For a minor splurge, you can eat at the *Planters Hotel*. The service is a bit on the slow side but the food is worth the wait. Fish, chips and salad or curried prawns with rice costs TSh 600.

The *Yacht Club* is the focus of the lives of resident foreigners (English, Dutch, Norwegian and German), though alcohol is the main motivation for coming here and the conversation is pretty uninspiring as a rule. Still, the club is a good place to track down people who are driving to Dar es Salaam, Mombasa and other places in relatively comfortable vehicles such as Land Cruisers, so it's worth checking this place out if you're heading in that direction.

Getting There & Away

Bus There are usually one or two buses daily from Dar es Salaam to Tanga. The trip takes seven to eight hours and costs TSh 800.

For the Tanzanian border post of Horohoro, try to catch one of the infrequent buses from the bus station. Otherwise, you'll have to hitch, though there's very little traffic. See the Tanzania Getting There & Away chapter.

Train There are departures at 4 pm on Monday, Wednesday and Friday in either direction between Tanga and Dar es Salaam. The fares are TSh 3970 (1st class), TSh 2490 (2nd class), TSh 1815 (2nd-class sitting) and TSh 945 (3rd class) and the trip takes about 13 hours.

From Tanga to Moshi, it's the same train, but it has to wait at Korogwe until the train from Dar es Salaam to Moshi arrives. There's a lively platform café at Korogwe which serves food and drink.

Boat Dhows operate between Tanga and Pemba but are irregular. Usually they go two to three times per week. You need to enquire down at the dhow sheds at the port. The fare is TSh 1500 plus a port tax of US$5.

Zanzibar

History

The annals of Zanzibar read like a chapter from *The Thousand & One Nights* and doubtless evoke many exotic and erotic images in the minds of travellers. Otherwise known as the Spice Island, it has lured travellers to its shores for centuries, some in search of trade, some in search of plunder

and still others in search of an idyllic home. The Sumerians, Assyrians, Egyptians, Phoenicians, Indians, Chinese, Persians, Portuguese, Omani Arabs, Dutch and English have all been here at one time or other. Some, notably the Shirazi Persians and the Omani Arabs, stayed to settle and rule.

It was early in the 19th century under the Omani Arabs that the island enjoyed its most recent heyday, following the introduction of the clove tree in 1818. Not long afterwards, the sultan's court was transferred from Muscat, near the entrance to the Persian Gulf, to Zanzibar. By the middle of the century, Zanzibar had become the world's largest producer of cloves and the largest slaving entrepôt on the east coast. Nearly 50,000 slaves, drawn from as far away as Lake Tanganyika, passed through its market every year.

As a result, Zanzibar became the most important town on the East African coast. All other centres were subject to it and virtually all trade passed through it. However, this changed with the establishment of the European protectorates towards the end of the 19th century and the construction of the Mombasa-Kampala railway. The Omani sultans continued to rule under a British protectorate until 1963, when independence was granted, but were overthrown the following year in a bloody revolution instigated by the Afro-Shirazi Party. This occurred prior to the union with mainland Tanganyika.

The many centuries of occupation and influence by all these various peoples has left its mark, and the old Stone Town of Zanzibar is one of the most fascinating places on the east coast. Much larger than Lamu or the old town of Mombasa, it's a fascinating labyrinth of narrow, winding streets lined with whitewashed, coral-rag houses, many with overhanging balconies and magnificently carved brass-studded doors. Regrettably, many of these doors have disappeared in recent years.

There are endless quaint little shops, bazaars, mosques, courtyards and squares, a fortress, two former sultans' palaces, two huge cathedrals, former colonial mansions,

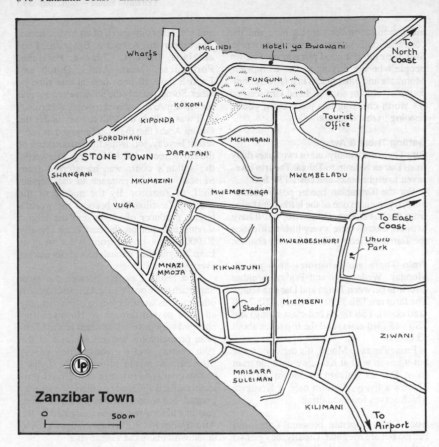

Zanzibar Town

0 500 m

a Persian-style public bathhouse and a bizarre collection of foreign consulates.

Outside town there are more ruined palaces, other Shirazi remains, the famous Persian baths and that other perennial attraction – magnificent, palm-fringed beaches with warm, clear water, ideal for swimming and snorkelling.

Information
Tourist Office The Tanzania Tourist Corporation (☎ 32344), PO Box 216, has an office in Livingstone House. It has an excellent map of Zanzibar town (1:10,000) and one of

the island (1:200,000). The town map is worth buying for exploring the alleys of the old town, though you'll probably still get lost from time to time. It costs TSh 800 and is also available at the tourist office in Dar es Salaam. They also sell the booklet *A Tale of Two Islands – Zanzibar*, in English and French. It's basically a guide book to the islands of Zanzibar and Pemba which lists hotels, restaurants, places to see, tour operators and beaches and gives a rundown on history, geography and transport connections. It's overpriced (TSh 6000) but might be useful if you're staying a long time.

Bookings for government-owned Zanzibar beach chalets must also be made at the Livingstone House tourist office.

There's a branch office on Creek Rd. The staff at both offices are very friendly and helpful.

Money As on the mainland, Zanzibar now has Forex bureaus, where you can change travellers' cheques and cash with the minimum of fuss – the day's exchange rates are chalked up on a board inside the office. There's also a Forex bureau in the foyer of the International Hotel.

Otherwise, there's the National Bank of Commerce, which is open Monday to Friday from 8.30 am to 4 pm and on Saturday from 8.30 am to 12.30 pm.

Foreign Consulates The island has consulates for Germany, the Sultanate of Oman, Egypt, India, Mozambique and the People's Republic of China. The first two are in the old Stone Town, while the others are on the road to the airport.

Immigration Although Zanzibar is part of the United Republic of Tanzania, it jealously guards its autonomy, and makes this point quite plain by requiring foreign visitors to go through its own immigration and customs on arrival and on leaving. You'll be required to fill in an immigration form and state how long you want to stay. It's best to ask for longer than you intend to stay (otherwise, you'll have to have the permit renewed, which is a hassle if you're not staying in Zanzibar town itself). Don't overstay your permit. Officials get shirty about this and may attempt to fine you.

The customs inspection on arrival is cursory – basically, all they do is chalk your bag without opening it.

Guide Books David Else, who writes a number of camping and mountain trekking guides to Kenya, has just brought out a new *Guide to Zanzibar & Pemba* (Bradt, UK, 1993). It promises to be a thoroughly comprehensive guide but was not available as we went to press.

Institute of KiSwahili & Foreign Languages This institute on Vuga Rd runs four-week courses in KiSwahili for beginners and intermediate-level students and a two-week advanced course. The price is US$60 per week. Class sizes are between two and five people and lessons are conducted from 8 am to noon five days a week. It's worth booking in advance.

Old Stone Town

The old Stone Town of Zanzibar is a fascinating place to wander around and get lost in, though you can't really get lost for too long because sooner or later, you'll end up either on the seafront or on Creek Rd. Nevertheless, every twist and turn of the narrow alleyways will present you with something of interest – be it a school full of children chanting verses from the Koran, a beautiful old mansion with overhanging verandahs, a shady square studded with huge old trees, a collection of quaint little hole-in-the-wall shops selling everything from Panadol to pawpaws, or a gaggle of women in *bui-bui* (veils) sharing a joke and some salacious local gossip.

You'll see a lot of crumbled and crumbling buildings as you walk around the Stone Town, and it's a great pity that so much of the fabric of this historic place has been allowed to fall into disrepair. A determined effort is now being made to restore a lot of the more important buildings, and you'll often come across expatriate aid workers wandering around with clipboards, making notes. Nevertheless, it would be a good idea if the entire Stone Town was declared a World Heritage site and appropriate funds provided to restore it to its former glory. The provision of a garbage service would be a good first step. Tourist receipts have gone done a lot to encourage the local authorities to halt the decay but priorities are elsewhere and money, as usual, is in short supply.

It's not really possible to suggest any sort of 'itinerary' or route, since it takes at least a week for a newcomer to come to grips with the town's layout, even with a map (though a map does help). Still, it's worth putting in the effort to see some of the town's major features.

Beit-el-Ajaib

One of the most prominent buildings in the old Stone Town is the Beit-el-Ajaib, or House of Wonders, formerly the sultan's palace and one of the largest structures in Zanzibar. Built in 1883 by Sultan Barghash (1870-88), it's an elegant four-storey structure surrounded by wide verandahs. In 1896 it was the target of a British naval bombardment, the object of which was to force Khalid bin Barghash (son of Sultan Barghash) to abdicate in favour of a British nominee. These days it's the local political headquarters of the CCM (Chama Cha Mapinduzi). Beside it is the more modest palace to which Barghash's successor moved after vacating the Beit-el-Ajaib in 1911.

Fort

On the other side of Beit-el-Ajaib is the 'Arab' fort, a typical massive, crenellated and bastioned structure. Originally built by the Portuguese in 1700, there's little inside other than a craft gallery in a poor state of repair, though restoration is soon to begin if the notice outside is to be believed. There might be an entry fee, but the last time I visited, the guard was fast asleep on the table.

The craft gallery has an excellent selection of first-rate batiks, worth a look even if you don't want to buy any.

Old Slave Market & UMCA Cathedral

Another prominent landmark is the UMCA Anglican cathedral. Completed in 1877 by the United Mission to Central Africa (UMCA), it was the first Anglican cathedral to be built in East Africa. It stands on the site of the Old Slave Market, alongside Creek Rd.

St Joseph's Cathedral

The towers of this Roman Catholic cathedral, set back from the fort, are easily spotted on arrival at the island by dhow. However, it's deceptively hard to find in the narrow confines of the adjacent streets. Designed by the French architect Beranger, it was completed in 1896.

Hamamni Persian Baths

Perhaps worth a visit are these baths, built by Sultan Barghash as public baths. They're a protected monument and are locked, but if you show a passing interest, the guardian (who runs a shop a few metres away) will rush up with the key and show you around, then ask you for a 'donation'. There's no water inside anymore, so it's not that interesting, especially if you've ever been inside a functional Persian/Turkish bath. They were built between 1870 and 1888 but ceased to be used from 1920.

Mosques

As Zanzibar is a strongly Muslim society, there are quite a few mosques – 50 in all – scattered around the Stone Town. Perhaps the most famous is the **Msikiti wa Balnara** (Malindi Minaret Mosque), originally built in 1831, enlarged in 1841 and extended again by Seyyid Ali bin Said in 1890. Others include the **Agha Khan Mosque** and the **Ijunaa Mosque**, which is currently being rehabilitated and extended. It's unlikely you'll be able to enter any of these, as they're all functional.

National Museum

The larger of the two buildings which make up the National Museum presents a catalogued history of the island from its early days up until independence. It contains Livingstone memorabilia, artefacts from the days of the Omani sultans and the British colonial period, as well as drums used by the sultans, and a priceless collection of old lithographs, maps and photographs dating mainly from the 19th and early 20th centuries. There are also stamp and coin displays. The smaller building houses a natural history collection specialising in butterflies, fish, small mammals, snakes and shells. There's also a collection of deformed animal foetuses. Outside is a pen housing two giant tortoises. Entry costs TSh 300.

Livingstone House

Outside the Stone Town, to the north-east along Malawi Rd, this was the base for the missionary/explorer's last expedition before he died. It's now the main tourist office.

Festivals

The festival of Id al Fitr (the end of Ramadan) lasts about four days, and if you visit the island at this time, don't miss the Zanzibarian equivalent of the tug-of-war at Makunduchi in the south of the island. Men from the south challenge those from the north by beating each other silly with banana branches. After that, the women of the town launch into a series of traditional folk songs, and the whole town then eats and dances the night away.

Places to Stay

Until 1991, accommodation in both Zanzibar town and on the beaches was limited, but since then, with tourist development now one of the island's priorities, many new hotels and guesthouses have opened their doors, ranging from budget to expensive.

A point to remember when choosing a budget hotel is that, a little while ago, the government ordered all guesthouses and hotels to charge a minimum of US$20 per person for accommodation. This caused temporary panic, as it threatened to wipe out the budget trade. The new minimum rates were duly posted in budget hotel reception areas but no hotelier ever attempts to charge these rates – they wouldn't get any trade if they did! The dust has now settled and everyone generally accepts that the measure was doomed from the start, so you can totally ignore it.

All accommodation on the island has to be paid for in foreign currency (preferably US dollars) unless you're a Tanzanian resident. There are no exceptions. Make sure you have sufficient small denomination travellers' cheques or bills to pay for this – otherwise, change is usually given in local currency, though not always (at one hotel, I was given change in dollar bills for travellers' cheques without paying any commission). If you haven't got small denominations, check out the Forex bureau.

Places to Stay – bottom end

One of the cheapest places to stay is the small *Flamingo Guest House* (☎ 32850), Mkunazini Bazaar. It's very friendly but lacks character. Rooms with a fan and mosquito net cost US$8 per person including breakfast. There are both single and double rooms and bathroom facilities are shared. Not far from here, just off Vuga Rd and close to the Omani Consulate, is the quite popular *Victoria Guest House* (☎ 32861). It's a modern place, the staff are friendly, and self-contained singles/doubles including breakfast cost US$8/16. A notice in reception says 'Unmarried couples will not be entertained', but I've never heard of them demanding to see marriage certificates. What they do ban is alcoholic beverages.

Across the other side of Vuga Rd is the *Florida Inn Guest House* (☎ 31828). The painted sign on the concrete gate post has faded over the years and is hard to spot, but it's there. It has cheap rooms with communal bathroom facilities for US$7 per person, plus more expensive self-contained rooms, but it's an old place and maintenance is minimal, so it can hardly be recommended. Somewhat further afield, adjacent to Africa House Hotel, is the *Wazazi Guest House*, which charges the same as the Florida, but it's a dump and you'd have to be desperate to stay here. The shared showers are Dickensian, the fans died years ago, there are no sheets or mosquito nets and, generally, the place is in an advanced state of decrepitude.

Up in the Malindi area of town, close to the docks and at the back of the Ciné Afrique, is another good cheapie, the *Warere Guest House* (☎ 31187). It's very clean and well kept and offers singles/doubles/triples for US$8/16/25 including breakfast. Bathroom facilities are communal.

My own nomination for best place to stay (with which many travellers would agree) is the *Malindi Guest House* (☎ 30165), Funguni Bazaar, also in the Malindi area. This is a beautiful place with bags of atmosphere, superbly maintained and constantly being repainted. The staff are very friendly. Bed and breakfast costs US$10/20/30 a

1 Boat Company Ticket Offices
2 New Gulf Restaurant
3 Malindi Guest House
4 Warere Guest House
5 Cine Afrique
6 Malindi Sports Club
7 Zan Air
8 Narrow Street Hotel
9 Tufaak Inn
10 Agha Khan Mosque
11 Hotel Kiponda & Restaurant
12 Spice Inn
13 Hotel International
14 Emerson House
15 House of Wonders (Beit-el-Ajaib)
16 Hotel Clove
17 Bottom's Up Guest House
18 Karibuni Inn & Restaurant
19 Mayur Indian Restaurant
20 Luis' Yogurt Parlour
21 Riverman Inn
22 UMCA Cathedral
23 Old Slave Market
24 Fisherman Restaurant, Stone Town
    Inn & Le Pêcheur
25 Post Office
26 Air Zanzibar
27 Dolphin Restaurant
28 Forex Bureaux
29 Green Garden Restaurant
30 Flamingo Guest House
31 Kenya Airways
32 Institute of KiSwahili & Foreign
    Languages
33 Air Tanzania
34 Florida Inn Guest House
35 Victoria Guest House
36 Garden Lodge
37 Zanzibar Hotel
38 Baghani House
39 Africa House Hotel
40 Camlurs Restaurant
41 Cave Resort
42 St Joseph's Cathedral

TANZANIA

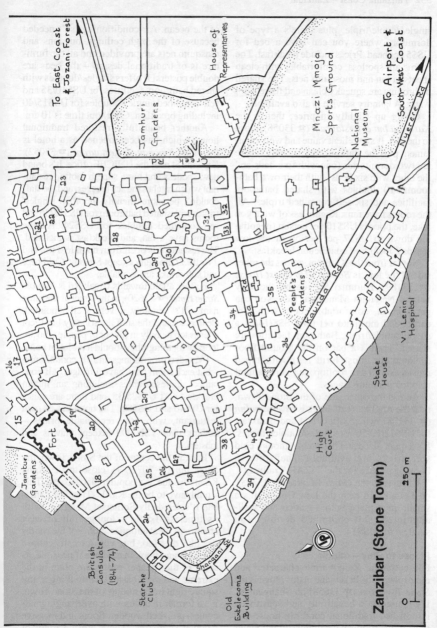

Zanzibar (Stone Town)

To East Coast
& Jozani Forest

House of
Representatives

To Airport
& South-West Coast

Nyerere Rd

Jamhuri
Gardens

Mnazi Mmoja
Sports Ground

National
Museum

Creek Rd

VI Lenin
Hospital

People's
Gardens

Kaunda Rd

Vuga Rd

State
House

Fort

High
Court

Jamituri
Gardens

British Consulate
(1841–74)

Starehe
Club

Old
Estelecoms
Building

Shangani St

250 m

0

single/double/triple, plus there's a type of dormitory where you can have a bed for US$5 per head. Prices include breakfast. The rooms are spotless, comfortable, with clean sheets, a fan and mosquito nets. The shared bathrooms are squeaky clean and there's hot water. A laundry service is also available.

Going up slightly in price, there's the *Karibuni Inn & Restaurant* (☎ 33058), close to the fort. It's excellent value and well maintained, plus the staff are very friendly. There are two dormitories (one with five beds and the other with six beds) with their own bathrooms, 10 doubles with shared bathroom facilities and six self-contained triples. All the rooms have fans. Regardless of what you take, the price is US$10 per person (negotiable down to US$7 per person in the low season), including continental breakfast.

Not far from the Karibuni, across the other side of the fort, is *Bottom's Up Guest House* (☎ 33189), Hurumzi St, run by the very helpful Narendra Mandania. Here you can get a clean, comfortable room with fan, carpet and mosquito net for US$8/14/21 a single/double/triple. Bathroom facilities are shared. There's a bar on the ground floor (painted the most lurid red) with taped music, as well as a rooftop area. A restaurant is in the planning stages.

Across the other side of the Stone Town, near the Anglican cathedral, is *Riverman Inn* (☎ 33188), which offers bed and breakfast for US$12/20/30 for singles/doubles/triples. It's a quiet place and has no bar, though cold soft drinks are available. They offer a booking service for the TAZARA railway.

Cheaper is the *Garden Lodge* (☎ 33298), on Kaunda Rd near the Law Courts. It's a small, quiet place with a garden and well-appointed, self-contained doubles (no singles) for US$14.

Places to Stay – middle

For authentic Zanzibarian character and atmosphere, the best value in this range is the *Stone Town Inn* (☎ 33658) on Shangani St. It's housed in a beautifully and sensitively refurbished traditional coral rag house and most of the rooms have uninterrupted views

of the ocean. Air-conditioning isn't needed because of the high ceilings, but fans and mosquito nets are provided and all the furniture is of traditional design – the beds are double posters! It offers singles/doubles with shared bathroom facilities for US$10/35 and self-contained singles/doubles for US$15/40 including breakfast. Checkout time is 10 am.

Another beautifully restored traditional house which has been opened as a hotel is the *Hotel Kiponda & Restaurant* (☎ 33052), Kiponda St near the UNICEF office. It's brand new, spotless and has a superb rooftop restaurant which catches the sea breezes, and the staff couldn't be more friendly. It offers singles/triples with shared bathroom for US$12/36 and self-contained doubles for US$24. All the rooms have a fan, and breakfast is included. The restaurant is open from noon to 3 pm and 7 to 10.30 pm daily except Sunday. Cold beer and soft drinks are available.

Further afield towards Creek Rd is *Narrow Street Hotel* (☎ 32620), in the street of the same name. It's certainly a very well-appointed, clean place and the staff are friendly but I feel it leans too heavily in favour of people who are looking for things they should have left at home – TV, video programmes and air-conditioning – but each room does have a fridge. Self-contained singles/doubles including an Indian breakfast cost US$25/35, and there are suites for US$40 and US$50. The hotel has its own restaurant, with very reasonable prices – nothing over TSh 900 (except prawns and lobster).

Back in the centre of the Stone Town, the *Spice Inn* (☎ 30728/9), close to the Agha Khan Mosque, is a popular place to stay. This would have to be the Raffles Hotel of Zanzibar. It's decidedly Somerset Maughan, with its timeless 1st-floor lounge full of easy chairs and local antiques. Some of the rooms are like this too, but you have to choose carefully and book in advance if possible, as some of the cheaper rooms are plain in the extreme and very basic. Overlooking a tiny square right in the middle of the Stone Town, it's a former mansion with overhanging balconies, polished wooden floors and massive wooden staircases. There are a variety of rooms, the best being those with a verandah overlooking the small square. Prices range from US$22 to US$45 a single and US$30 to US$50 a double, plus there are more expensive air-conditioned suites. Anything priced under US$33 involves shared bathroom facilities. All prices include breakfast, and lunch and dinner are also available. Visa and MasterCard are accepted.

About the same price is the rambling *Zanzibar Hotel* (☎ 30708/9), PO Box 392, tucked away in the narrow alleys of the Stone Town and only a three-minute walk from the Africa House Hotel. But while it's a gem of Zanzibari architecture, at least in the public areas, the rooms themselves are very plain and utilitarian and the plumbing antediluvian. What's needed here is someone with imagination to refurbish and refurnish the rooms and fix up the bathrooms. Basically, it needs money spent on it because what it charges doesn't match what it offers. Rooms cost US$25/40/50 for singles/doubles/triples without own bathroom, US$30/45/60 with own bathroom. There are also air-con rooms, which cost US$30/45/60 with shared bath, US$35/50/75 with private bath. Prices include breakfast and all taxes.

The same company which owns the Zanzibar Hotel also owns the *Africa House Hotel* (☎ 30708), which used to be the 'British Club' in the days when Zanzibar was a British protectorate. Esoteric reminders of those bygone years are still to be found around the place, but the billiard table has disappeared. All the same, it's one of the very few hotels actually on the waterfront and it's a popular place to stay, though like the Zanzibar, it's somewhat overpriced given the standard of accommodation it offers. Prices are exactly the same as at the Zanzibar. The staff are friendly but there are problems with the water supply on the upper floors (though none, apparently, downstairs). The hotel has a restaurant above the bar.

A better place to stay if you're looking for atmosphere is *Emerson House* (☎ 32153), close to the Empire Cinema and not too far from the Spice Inn. The rooms here have been beautifully decorated by a local artist and are furnished with antiques. There are nine rooms, two of them self-contained, and prices range from US$40 to US$70 per room (single or double) including breakfast. Dinner is served on the rooftop, from which there are good views of the town, but it's expensive (around TSh 4000 for a meal, plus the cost of drinks). On the ground floor is the *Africadabra Coffee Bar*, where light lunches and cakes are served in the morning and early afternoon.

In the same area is the new *Hotel International* (☎ 33182), a large hotel which has doubles (no singles) for US$35 and US$45, triples for US$50 and suites for US$70. All the rooms are self-contained, with air-conditioning and a fridge, and the price includes a full breakfast. Credit cards are not accepted. I felt this place was a little bit overdone but it is popular with package tourists. The hotel has its own bar, and a restaurant which serves Indian, Chinese and continental dishes, but the service is very slow.

Perhaps better, as far as modern hotels and atmosphere go, is the quiet and newly opened *Tufaak Inn*, which has eight self-contained rooms without air-conditioning for US$35, as well as air-conditioned singles/doubles (US$40/55). The price includes breakfast and Visa and MasterCard are accepted. This place, particularly the reception area, is very reminiscent of the Middle East.

There's also the *Hotel Clove* (☎ 31785), Hurumzi St, close to the Beit-el-Ajaib. This is very clean and good value but lacks character – it's essentially a concrete box. All the rooms are self-contained, with air-conditioning and a refrigerator, and cost US$24/30 a single/double. There are also deluxe doubles for US$35.

Far and away the best place to stay in this range, if you have the money, is *Baghani House*, adjacent to the Zanzibar Hotel. This magnificently restored former mansion furnished in local style is very comfortable indeed. All the rooms are self-contained and air-conditioned, costing US$40, US$50 and US$60 a double (no singles), depending on size. It's the up-market version of the Stone Town Inn – check it out before going anywhere else. There are only a few rooms, so it has a very intimate atmosphere.

There are other hotels outside the Stone Town, such as the *High Hill Hotel* (☎ 30000), Kilimani St, halfway between Zanzibar town and the airport, but they're generally expensive and why stay there anyway? If you've come to see Zanzibar, there's ample choice in the town itself. Another hotel out of town but at least on the shoreline is *Inn by the Sea* (☎ 31755), at Mbweni, 6½ km from town. The rooms are self-contained, but plain and have no mosquito nets. Air-con singles/doubles cost US$40/60. There's a free courtesy bus into town.

Places to Stay – top end

At the top of the range but totally characterless is the *Hoteli ya Bwawani* (☎ 30200), overlooking Funguni Creek. To think that someone had the opportunity and money to construct a top-range hotel in an historic place like Zanzibar and came up with something so utterly ordinary and boring is beyond belief! A German correspondent put it succinctly: 'The Bwawani Hotel still tries in vain to provide the charms of East Berlin's Karl Marx Strasse in the '70s. Obviously it has come out of fashion. In another 20 years it might probably be of historical interest to some students of architecture'. Still, for those without an ounce of imagination, this is it. All the rooms are self-contained with air-con and the price includes breakfast and all taxes. Ordinary singles/doubles are US$59/75, plus there are suites ranging from US$120 to US$200. Checkout time is noon. The hotel has all the usual facilities, including a swimming pool (often empty), tennis and squash courts, restaurant, bar (expensive beers!) and a disco (9 pm to 2 am and open to nonguests). American Express and Diners Club cards are accepted.

Places to Eat – cheap

Undoubtedly the cheapest place to eat in the evening, along with a good slice of the population of Zanzibar, is in the Jamituri Gardens in front of the fort. The townspeople gather here at that time to socialise, talk about what's happened and watch the sun go down. Food stalls sell spicy curries, roasted meat and maize, cassava, smoked octopus, sugar-cane juice and ice cream – all at extremely reasonable prices.

Just about as cheap and very popular, especially with local people, is the café at the *Ciné Afrique*, where basic African dishes are available.

Somewhat more expensive but very popular with travellers is the *Dolphin Restaurant* (☎ 31987), close to the GPO on Kenyatta Rd. The Dolphin has been going for years and offers all the usual seafood dishes plus a few other items.

Similar, when it's open, is the *Tropicana Café* at the junction of Kaunda and Vuga Rds.

Those staying at either the Warere Guest House or the Malindi Guest House should try the meals at the *New Gulf Restaurant/Golden Falcon*, opposite the entrance to the Malindi Guest House.

The best place on the island for a bowl of yoghurt is *Luis' Yogurt Parlour*, opposite the mosque at the back of the fort.

Places to Eat – more expensive

For a not-too-expensive splurge, there's a choice of three very popular restaurants. The first is the *Fisherman Restaurant* (☎ 33101), on Shangani St near the Starehe Club. Set up in a traditional Zanzibari house, which makes for an intimate atmosphere, the restaurant offers a full range of excellent seafood at very competitive prices. Salads and soups average TSh 300 and main courses are TSh 1450 to TSh 1650 (fish, calamari, etc), with prawns at TSh 3600 and lobster from TSh 3000 to TSh 5000. It's open daily from 9 am to 10 pm. Get there early for lunch or dinner if you want the best choice of tables. Ice-cold imported Löwenbräu is also available.

The second is *Camlurs Restaurant* (☎ 31919), close to Africa House. This beautiful little restaurant with a very intimate atmosphere offers Swahili food – meat, seafood and vegetable curries cooked with coconut. The food is excellent and prices are similar to those at the Fisherman. It's open Monday to Friday from 11.30 am to 2 pm and Monday to Saturday from 6.30 to 9 pm. The staff here are very friendly and eager to please.

The third choice is the *Sea View Indian Restaurant* (☎ 32132), on Mizingani Rd overlooking the harbour, on the 1st floor. This restaurant has one of the best locations of any on the island and offers a choice of eating outside on the balcony or inside. A full range of seafood is offered as well as Indian curries. It's a very pleasant place to dine but the service can be slow – so slow at times that the starters occasionally turn up after you've finished the main course! This is partly because the chefs insist on cooking everything in the traditional manner over charcoal and disdain the use of a gas oven, even though they have one. If you plan to eat here in the evening, it's advisable to pop in earlier in the day and choose your menu so that they have time to organise it. Book a table if you want to eat on the balcony.

Also very good, but not so well known, is the *Chit Chat Restaurant* (☎ 33003), 500 Cathedral St, which offers Goan Indian food. It's run by an Indian from Goa, so you know the dishes are authentic and spicy. A very tasty meals costs around TSh 1500, including a beer – excellent value. It's open Tuesday to Sunday from 6 to 11 pm. It's best to make a reservation in advance and find out what's on the menu by ringing Mr Lobow.

Another Indian restaurant well worth a try is the *Mayur Indian Restaurant*, just at the back of the fort.

Round the corner from the Flamingo Guest House is the *Green Garden Restaurant*, which looks like a very pleasant place to eat, though I didn't manage to check it out. Follow the signs from the Flamingo.

As far as hotel restaurants go, the *Spice Inn* and the *Hotel International* are definitely worth checking out. The food at both is reasonably priced and well prepared. Also very good is the rooftop restaurant at the *Hotel Kiponda*. Here you can eat in quiet style and catch the sea breezes, plus there are

cold beers. Prices are very reasonable. It's open for lunch from noon to 3 pm and for dinner from 7 to 10.30 pm. It's advisable to make an advance reservation if you want a certain dish.

The *Africa House Hotel* also has a restaurant above the bar but few people eat there, as it's not up to the standard of the other hotel restaurants.

Lastly, there's the *In By The Sea Resort* (☎ 31755), next to the Bwani ruins, off the road to the airport and just past the Chinese Consulate. The restaurant is right by the sea and is open for lunch and dinner. It serves chicken and chips for around TSh 1000 and has a fairly popular bar. It's a long way to go (6½ km from town) and you'd have to take a taxi, which would make it expensive unless a group of you shares the cost.

Entertainment

Virtually everyone goes to the *Africa House Hotel* for a cold beer in the late afternoon/early evening. The bar is on the 1st-floor terrace overlooking the ocean and is a favourite spot to watch the sun go down. The beers are reasonably priced and generally cold but, depending on demand, get warmer as the evening wears on. Safari Lager is available as well as imported beers (Stella Artois, Becks, Löwenbräu and even Aussie Castlemaine Forex). The bar is open throughout the day, from around 10 am to 11 pm. It's *the* place to meet old friends and acquaintances and to make contacts for visits to Changuu Island and the beaches on the east coast.

Also very popular, especially in the evening after dinner, is *Le Pêcheur*, right next door to the Fisherman Restaurant. It's a very lively place with a good notice board and has the best selection of local and imported beers and liquors on the island, plus an excellent selection of taped music. It's open all day, every day and basically doesn't close until the last customer leaves.

The bar at the *Bottom's Up Guest House* is another option. It, too, is open all day, every day and has a good selection of music. The beer is always cold, though the lurid décor might make you wonder whether you fell into purgatory en route to pleasure.

Another bar to which surprisingly few people go is the *Starehe Bar* on Shangani St. It's quite a large place right next to the beach overlooking the harbour. Since it rarely has too many customers, the beers are always ice cold. It has an occasional disco in the evenings, for which there might be a small cover charge.

The best disco on the island, however, is the newly opened *Carumbeta Club*, part of the Fisherman Restaurant, Stone Town Inn and Le Pêcheur complex. It's open nightly from around 8 pm until early in the morning. There's a small entry charge (free entry for women on Monday and Tuesday). Drinks are reasonably priced.

The *Hoteli ya Bwawani* also has a regular disco, which generally operates three times a week. There's a small cover charge but the beers are expensive. Make enquiries before going there.

Getting There & Away

Air In theory, Air Tanzania operates 12 weekly flights in either direction between Dar es Salaam and Zanzibar, but don't rely on them – cancellations are frequent.

The Air Tanzania office in Zanzibar is on Vuga Rd and is open Monday to Friday from 8 am to 12.30 pm and 2 to 4.30 pm and on Saturday from 8 am to 12.30 pm.

Much more reliable are the light six and nine-seater planes operated by two private companies based in Zanzibar. They are Air Zanzibar (☎/fax (054) 32512), 307 Kenyatta Rd, Shangani, Zanzibar (☎ Pemba 2398 and Dar es Salaam 30934), and Zan Air (☎ (054) 33670), Malindi, Zanzibar.

Air Zanzibar has two flights per day between Dar es Salaam and Zanzibar in either direction on Monday, Wednesday, Friday and Saturday. The one-way fare is US$40 or TSh 9000. It also flies from Zanzibar to Pemba and vice versa on Monday, Wednesday and Friday (two flights on Friday). The fare is US$40 or TSh 9000. Zan Air has similar departures and its fares are the same. Both these companies also occa-

sionally fly from Zanzibar to Arusha, Mombasa and Nairobi. For details about these, keep your eye on the notice boards at either the Africa House Hotel or the Fisherman Restaurant.

Another very popular flight is the thrice-weekly Kenya Airways run between Mombasa and Zanzibar return on Sunday, Monday and Thursday, which costs US$45 one way plus US$20 airport tax. Again, book well in advance to be sure of a seat. The Kenya Airways office (☎ 32041/2/3) in Zanzibar is off Vuga Rd, behind Air Tanzania.

Boat The majority of budget travellers come to Zanzibar by motorised dhow, ferry boat, catamaran or hydrofoil from Dar es Salaam and return the same way. The schedule for all these boats can be found in the Getting There & Away section of the Dar es Salaam chapter. Except for the motorised dhows, the ticket offices for all these boats in Zanzibar are just outside the dock gates.

The dhows have to be booked at the Malindi Sports Club directly opposite Zan Air on the morning before departure. Tickets are sold here. This is also where you book a passage on a dhow to Pemba Island – the dhows dock at Mkoani in the south of the island.

Dhows and other boats also run between Zanzibar and Mombasa, usually once or twice a week in either direction. To find out the schedule and to book, go to the Institute of Marine Science workshop on Mizingani Rd – there's a small sign at the gate (which is flanked by the Tanzanian and Zanzibari flags) which says, 'Tickets for Dar, Pemba, Mombasa'. The fare is about US$10 or TSh 4000 and the journey takes about 12 hours but can take quite a bit longer, depending on the currents.

Getting Around

To/From the Airport Municipal buses run between the airport and town for a few shillings. They're marked 'U'. A taxi will cost TSh 2000.

Car & Motorbike Renting mopeds, motorcycles and even self-drive cars has become a lot easier over the last two years, in stark contrast to the position on the mainland. Al Ridha Transport (see under Bicycle Rental) is the main renter of mopeds and motorcycles. Motorcycles cost around US$80 per week. Self-drive cars are a little harder to find. The best thing to do is to ask around for a young man named Secrete (pronounced as in French) at the bar of the Africa House Hotel (ask the head bartender). He offers Suzuki 4WD vehicles in excellent condition for around US$40 per day with no mileage or insurance charges or refundable deposit, and you don't even have to leave your passport with him as a guarantee. This is excellent value anywhere in East Africa. Secrete himself is a very pleasant and helpful man and totally trustworthy. Make sure you are, too. There are a few other places where you can rent self-drive but not on such favourable terms.

Bicycle There are at least two places where you can rent bicycles. The first is Al Ridha Transport, close to the Empire Cinema and Emersons off Creek Rd. Ask for Zameer or Wendy. The other is at Maharouky's Store, on Creek Rd next to the petrol station in Daranjani. It's signposted, so you can't miss it.

Bicycles can be put on the roofs of local buses if you get tired of pedalling.

Around Zanzibar

Historical sites around the island which are worth visiting include the **Maruhubi Palace**, built by Sultan Barghash in 1882 to house his harem but unfortunately largely destroyed by fire in 1899, the **Persian Baths** near Kidichi, built by Sultan Seyyid Said for his Persian wife at the highest point on the island (153 metres), and the **Mangapwani Slave Caves** (used for illegal slave trading after the legal trade was abolished by the British in the late 1800s), about 16 km north of Zanzibar town. To get to the Slave Caves under your

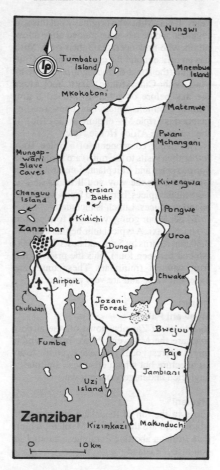

own steam, take bus No 2 from the bus station on Creek Rd, opposite the market in Zanzibar town.

SPICE TOURS

To visit all the above sites separately involves a lot of effort and backtracking. It's much better to take one of the popular Spice Tours. Perhaps the best person to tour with is an elderly Indian man named Mitu, who owns taxis and has been doing these trips for years. It was Mitu who originally put this trip together and he has since trained quite a few others who now operate on their own. Mitu has an office round the corner from the Ciné Afrique (the street on the right-hand side as you face the Ciné Afrique). Try to book a tour the day before or get there around 8 am. Another bunch which has been recommended is Triple M – enquire at the office in the bar of the Africa House Hotel.

The major components of a Spice Tour (other than visits to the ruins) are visits to the various spice and fruit plantations around the island. Along the way you'll be invited to taste all the spices, herbs and fruits which the island produces. Lunch is included.

To get a tour going, you need four people to share a taxi. A typical tour begins at about 9.30 am, returns by 5 pm and costs TSh 6000 (shared between four), plus the price of the fruit you eat (minimal). These tours are excellent value and are very popular.

RUINS

Mbeweni Palace

Just south of Zanzibar town off the airport road are the Mbeweni Palace ruins, which might interest you if you have a yen for Arab architecture but which otherwise are totally neglected and largely overgrown.

Mvuleni

Close to the top of the island and north of Mkokotoni are the ruins of Mvuleni, which date from an abortive Portuguese attempt to colonise the island.

Shirazi Mosque

Near Kizimkazi in the south are the ruins of the Shirazi Dimbani Mosque. An inscription around the mihrab is dated 1107 – the oldest inscription found in East Africa. Excavations have indicated the existence of an earlier mosque on the same site. Kizimkazi was the island's capital until the 17th century, and there are remnants of a wall which used to surround the settlement.

JOZANI FOREST

Some 10 km south-east of Zanzibar town,

between Chwaka and Uzi bays, is the Jozani Forest, a nature reserve for the rare red colobus monkey, the Zanzibar leopard, two antelope species and the Zanzibar duiker and sunni. To get there, you need to organise your own transport or get a group together and hire a taxi. The tourist office also offers tours of the forest (TSh 3900 shared between up to five people). Entry to the forest costs US$1 (payable in US dollars).

OFFSHORE ISLANDS

Just offshore from Zanzibar town are several islands ringed with coral reefs. Three are simply sandbanks which partially disappear at high tide, but the other four (including Chumbe Island to the south, where there is a lighthouse) are well-forested, idyllic tropical islands with small but superb beaches.

Changuu Island

The island which everyone seems to visit is Changuu Island, also known as Prison Island. It's the most famous of the offshore islands and in the 19th century was owned by an Arab who used it, as the sign says, for housing 'recalcitrant slaves'. It was later bought by a Briton who constructed a prison (which apparently was never used, though the ruins remain). Now it's used by day-trippers from Zanzibar as a pleasant day out.

The beach is superb, the sea is crystal clear and there's a whole family of (frequently copulating) giant land tortoises which roam around the main landing spot. It's thought they were brought to the island from Aldabra in the Seychelles at around the turn of the century.

The island has a two-storey house with a verandah, a bar and a restaurant, adjacent to which are several basic rooms to rent. Lunch (seafood, chips and salad) costs about the same as on the main island and cold beers are available (you can drink without eating).

The island is run by the Tanzania Tourist Corporation, which charges an entry fee of US$1, UK£1 or DM 2, payable in *cash* – neither shillings nor UK£1 coins are accepted. If you don't have that spare dollar you'll have to sit on the boat all day unless you can persuade them to give you change in dollars.

Activities here include windsurfing, sailing, scuba diving and and snorkelling, but you have to pay for equipment.

It's easy finding transport across from Zanzibar. Simply sit in the bar at the Africa House Hotel any evening and someone will ask if you want to go there the next day. Otherwise, enquire at Chemha Brothers Tours (☎ 31751), next to the Fisherman Restaurant, Fisherman Tours (☎ 30468), Creek Rd, or the tourist office, all in Zanzibar town. Motorised boats cost TSh 3000 shared by up to 10 people. They generally leave at 9 am and return by 4.30 pm (departure and return times are entirely up to you).

Bawe Island

The beach at the northern tip of this island is one of the best places in Zanzibar for snorkelling. There's a restaurant of sorts here but it only serves chips and omelettes, though fish is sometimes available. All the drinks are warm. On landing, you have to pay the English manager of the still nonexistent hotel a TSh 250 landing fee. A boat to Bawe should cost around TSh 7000.

Chumbe Island

A marine national park is being created here, as well as a diving educational centre, but it's not yet open to the public.

BEACHES

There are some superb beaches, particularly on the east coast of the island, which are as unspoilt as you're likely to find. This is rapidly changing, however, as new guesthouses open their doors each week. All the same, most of the accommodation available is for those who can do without electricity, hot and cold running water, swimming pools and night entertainment. Paradise here is still simple and uncomplicated and the local people have not yet jumped on the tourism gravy train. It's totally relaxing and, unlike many of the beaches on the western side of

the island close to Zanzibar town, there are no concerns about being robbed or mugged.

The roads to these places are also pretty rugged in parts, so a fair amount of effort is necessary to get to them, though the bulldozers and graders were hard at work in early 1993, so things could change in the near future. There's also been a surge in foreign investment on resort complexes, so if you want to experience the place before it begins to resemble the beaches north and south of Mombasa, get there soon.

The main beaches on the east coast, from the northern tip of the island, are: Nungwi, Matemwe, Pwani Mchangani, Uroa, Chwaka, Bwejuu, Paje, Jambiani and Makunduchi. Everyone has their favourite but there's actually not too much to choose between them. All are protected by coral reefs offshore and have white coral-sand beaches and, depending on the season, a soup of seaweed to swim in. Don't knock the seaweed – the local people harvest it for export, and you'll see it drying in the sun in all the villages.

Places to Stay & Eat

Until a few years ago, the only places you could stay at the beaches were government-owned bungalows, which you needed to book in advance at the tourist office in Zanzibar town. That's all now changed, except that you must still book and pay for government bungalows at the tourist office before turning up. On the other hand, there's now a choice of other bungalows and guesthouses which are privately owned.

If you wish to stay at any of the government bungalows, those at Bwejuu, Chwaka and Makunduchi (where there are two) cost US$30 shared between up to five people, and those at Chwaka, Jambiani and Uroa cost US$40 shared between five people. Kerosene lanterns are provided at all the above bungalows and water is usually drawn from a well. Most people opt to have food prepared for them by either the caretaker or local people, but you can, if you prefer, put your own meals together. At Jambiani, for instance, the caretaker, Hassan Haji, and his

English-speaking assistant, Abul, are very friendly and will cook you fresh seafood meals. They can also provide rice, potatoes, pineapples and other fruits and vegetables at very low cost. Soft drinks are available. Snorkelling on the offshore coral reef can be done from dugout fishing boats.

As far as private guesthouses on the east coast go, there are now plenty to choose from, many with a booking office in Zanzibar town. If you don't have your own transport and don't want to take pot luck on arrival, advance booking is probably not a bad idea, though by doing this, you'll essentially lose any opportunity to strike a cheaper deal. If you simply turn up and your choice of guesthouse isn't full, you can haggle over the price. The choices at the various beaches include the following:

Mnemba Island This is the only island off the east coast and is surrounded by its own coral reef. The island is owned by Archer's Ltd, which have an office (Archer's Aviation) facing the park in Shangani opposite the old Extelecoms building in Zanzibar town. It's an exclusive resort development and has all the facilities you might expect for US$300 per person. It's closed from April to June.

Matemwe The only choice here is *Matemwe Bungalows* (☎ (054) 31342), which you can book through its office, opposite the High Court in Zanzibar town (open during office hours, 8.30 am to noon and 1 to 3 pm). It consists of 12 bungalows, six of them self-contained, a bar and a restaurant, and water sports equipment is available. The staff is friendly and the food is good but there's no electricity. The price in the high season is US$45 per person with shared bathroom or US$55 per person with own bathroom, including full board. Boats can be hired but are very expensive (around TSh 35,000 for four hours).

Uroa The principal resort hotel here is the *Tamarind Beach Hotel* (☎ (054) 51859; fax 31859), where self-contained singles/doubles including breakfast cost US$35/50. Accommodation consists of beach cottages built in local style, plus there's a bar and restaurant. There's also a full range of water sports equipment available (which costs extra). Transport to the resort can be arranged from the docks or the airport on arrival with Fisherman Tours (☎ (054) 30468; fax 32387). Otherwise, bookings can be made at their office on Creek Rd, Daranjani, in Zanzibar town.

More expensive is the *Uroa Bay Hotel & Fishing Club* (☎ (054) 33552), which consists of 18 bungalows (36 rooms in total). Rooms are self-contained and cost US$60 to US$80 per person, including breakfast. There's a bar, restaurant, swimming pool, tennis court, diving centre and water sports equipment (most of it at no extra cost). The food here is excellent but somewhat expensive at TSh 4000 for a buffet lunch. Transport is available from Zanzibar town or from the airport.

Bwejuu The main place to stay here is the *Bwejuu Dere Beach Resort* (☎ (054) 31017), which consists of three main buildings and associated bungalows. Many of the rooms face the sea, giving you the benefit of sea breezes. Another main building is in progress. The staff is friendly and the bar/restaurant offers excellent seafood (fish & chips for TSh 700) plus egg and chicken dishes. The rooms themselves are simple but adequate, and bathroom facilities (clean) are shared. Singles/doubles cost US$20/30 in the high season and US$10 per person in the low season.

Close by is the *Palm Beach Inn*, which is good value at US$20 a double or US$10 per person in a room with four beds. All rooms are self-contained and spacious and the staff are friendly. There's a bar and restaurant, done in local style, and meals average TSh 1500, with lobster at around TSh 3500.

Between the above two places is *Durhani Villas*, which sems to be used mainly by Muslim Asians. There's no bar or restaurant here.

Not directly on the beach but cheaper than

the above, the *Kibuda Family Guest House* offers accommodation for just US$4 per person including breakfast. Bucket showers are available and meals can be arranged. Ask for Jamal in the village.

A little further south down the coast, at the entrance to Bwejuu village, the *Seven Seas Guest House* offers bed and breakfast for US$4 per person.

About four km north of Bwejuu is what's known as the 'lagoon', where there's a superb beach (which was deserted at the time of writing). There are magnificent snorkelling opportunities here, but you must wear shoes or fins, or you'll walk away on crutches. The sea urchins and stone fish are not keen on being squashed by unwary visitors' feet, as I discovered to my cost (I finally extracted the last of the spines two months later). Local youths will guide you there along the beach road. Otherwise, just walk up the beach until you get to the abandoned Italian beach resort project (about 1½ hours). And, in case you were wondering why the beach resort was abandoned, it was apparently because the Mafia were backing the project and using it to launder money. At least, that's the rumour.

Paje South of Bwejuu and just north of Paje, *Paradise Beach* bungalows are good value at US$20 per bungalow with private bathroom and including breakfast. There's a bar and restaurant, which specialises in Japanese and continental dishes. You can book in advance at the Warere Guest House in Zanzibar town.

In Paje itself are three simpler guesthouses, the *Ndame Village, Amani Guest House* and the *Ufukwe Guest House*. They cost US$10 to US$20 per person including breakfast.

Jambiani A few years ago, Jambiani was one of the favourite beaches to head for, so there's a good choice of guesthouses. It's a *long* village, so if you're coming in on the bus, make sure you get off near where you want to stay or you could find yourself walking up to two km. Some of the smaller guesthouses are basically just square boxes with the absolute minimum of facilities, so if you're looking for more than that, take a better place first and then check the others out later.

The best of them in terms of facilities is the *Jambiani Beach Hotel*, which has rooms arranged around a rectangular compound. Bathroom facilities are communal and no mosquito nets are provided but it has a bar and a good restaurant, there's a good selection of tape music and the staff are very friendly. Singles/doubles are US$20/30, including breakfast, and meals of fish, squid or octopus cost around TSh 1000.

Right at the end of Jambiani village is the *Gomani Guest House*, which you'll see advertised in Zanzibar town. It's a very pleasant place on a coral outcrop overlooking the sea, so there are plenty of sea breezes. Officially, it costs US$20 per person, but in the low season it can cost as little as US$10 a double. Bathroom facilities are communal. There's a restaurant, and beers are usually available.

Also popular is the *Shehe Guest House* (☎ (054) 33188), in the centre of the village, which offers rooms with shared bathroom facilities, two beds, fan and mosquito net for US$8 per person, including breakfast. Other meals can be arranged on request. Book in advance at the office in the Africa House Hotel bar.

Other travellers have recommended the *Horizontal Inn*, which is very clean, has toilets and showers with running water and costs US$5 per person including breakfast. Lunch and dinner cost TSh 500 (fish, rice, potatoes and coconut sauce).

Other simpler guesthouses in Jambiani include *East Coast New Mwambao Guest House* (☎ (054) 32789), *East Coast Rising Sun, East Coast Visitors Inn* and *Manufaa Guest House*. You're looking at US$10 to US$20 per person in all of these, depending on the season, including breakfast.

Getting There & Away

To get to the east coast beaches, you'll have to take a local bus, hire a taxi or rent your own motorcycle or vehicle. The bus station is on Creek Rd opposite the market.

Bus No 9 leaves for Jambiani at 10 am and 4 pm (TSh 500, three hours), and also goes to Bwejuu (different from the bus to Jambiani – ask). The return bus from Bwejuu to Zanzibar departs from the village at about 2 am and reaches the market in Zanzibar by 6.30 am. Otherwise, get a group together and rent a minibus (about TSh 4500 shared between nine people). Bus No 10 goes to Makunduchi, No 6 goes to Chwaka (1½ hours) and the No 6 'Special' goes to Uroa.

Share-taxis to the east coast are a little more expensive. Count on around TSh 1500 to TSh 2000 per person with a minimum of four people from Zanzibar to Bwejuu, Paje or Jambiani, more to Matemwe or Uroa.

DIVING

Compared to other famous diving places (Maldives, Red Sea, etc) Zanzibar is not the best of places for this, due to the low clarity of the water. The shallow waters of the west coast (seldom more than 20 metres deep) are moved twice a day by the coming and going tide, with few barriers to prevent turbulence. On the other hand, it's not that bad either, but it is expensive.

There are quite a few possibilities. The first is to stay at the *Mawimbini Hotel* (US$120 per night), in which case you can dive free of charge. Secondly, you could ask around for Mr Chung at the Hoteli ya Bwawani. He rents equipment (bottles and weight belts but not regulators) and can take divers out in his boat. A third possibility is to rent equipment (US$30) or go diving (US$50) with the *Mtoni Marine Centre*, just north of Zanzibar town on Bububu Rd (minibus 'B'). It also rents out a traditional dhow (US$40 per person) for excursions to the offshore islands and sandbanks. Lunch is included but diving is extra. Then there's the Uroa Bay Hotel & Fishing Club, which has a diving centre; a dive costs US$45 per person.

Possibly the best place to dive is the Mnemba Island reef, in front of the Matemwe Bungalows. The west side of

Kwale Island is also good. To get to the latter, rent a boat from Fumba, south of Zanzibar town (ask for Uhmudi at the harbour – he's a helpful and experienced fisherman and captain.

Other Islands

PEMBA

While most travellers make it to Zanzibar, very few ever make the journey to Pemba Island, north of Zanzibar. It's perhaps not surprising since, in terms of tourism, the island is in its infancy. It's not that there are no historic sites to visit or good beaches, because there are plenty of these, but it's very difficult to get to them because there is little public transport off the island's only main road. Most of the beaches are small, too, due to the extensive mangrove forests which ring the island. Nevertheless, it's quite a contrast to Zanzibar.

For a start, the island is much more hilly and far more densely wooded than Zanzibar, the result of higher rainfall and more fertile soil. There are no extensive historic sections in the island's three main towns, though Chake Chake works hard at this with its 18th-century fort.

The island is very laid back, and the people are friendly and interested in where you come from and why you're there. It's the sort of place where you make an effort to get to know people and find out what's going on rather than go to see things in the usual tourist mode.

My one enduring impression of the island is the number of schoolchildren who flock onto the roads twice a day on their way home. There are thousands and thousands of them, so one must assume that education has a very high priority on this island. It's heartening to see that all these children are taught practical agriculture as part of the curriculum. Indeed, when it's clove harvest time (about once every five months), the schools close and everyone turns out to help.

Cloves are the mainstay of the island's

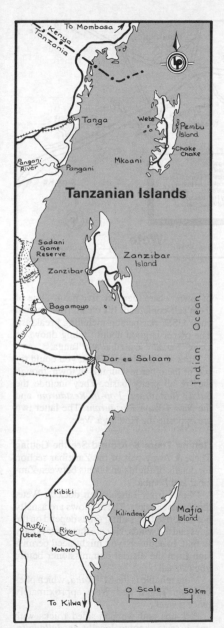

Tanzanian Islands

economy, and the crop is three times as large as the crop from Zanzibar. There are 3½ million clove trees on Pemba, many of which date from the early 19th century, when they were introduced from the Moluccas. Most are owned by farmers who would typically have between 10 and 50 trees on their plots. There are very few large plantations of the sort you might find on Zanzibar. Everywhere you go on this island, you'll see the ripe cloves laid out to dry in the sun and you'll smell their characteristic aroma.

Although Pemba was never as important as Zanzibar or other settlements on the Tanzanian coast, it has had some interesting and remarkable associations during its history. The island's earliest ruins are those of Ras Mkumbu, on the peninsula west of Chake Chake, where the Shirazis settled about 1200 CE. This site has several houses and pillar tombs and the remains of a large 14th-century mosque.

At Pujini on the island's east coast, there is a fortified settlement and the remains of a palace destroyed by the Portuguese in 1520. These were apparently built by conquerors from the Maldive Islands, though some scholars dispute this. It seems they were not particularly welcome, as one of the rulers of this town was known as Mkame Ndume (Milker of Men) because of the amount of work he extracted from his subjects. Later, after the expulsion of the Portuguese from this part of East Africa, Pemba was taken over first by the rulers of Paté in the Lamu archipelago, then by the rulers of Mombasa, and finally by the sultans of Zanzibar.

The trouble with the ruins on Pemba is that most are in poor condition, have never been excavated and are largely overgrown. Perhaps something will be done about them when the government has sufficient money or an international organisation provides the funds.

Come here if you want to see something different but don't expect historical romance or ready-made entertainment.

Wete

This is the most northern of the island's main

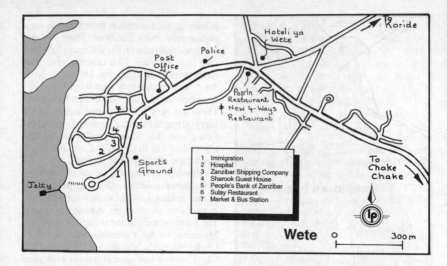

Wete

1	Immigration
2	Hospital
3	Zanzibar Shipping Company
4	Sharook Guest House
5	People's Bank of Zanzibar
6	Sulay Restaurant
7	Market & Bus Station

towns and has the second most important port, through which most of the clove crop is exported. It's essentially a one-street town which snakes up the hillside from the docks. A branch of the People's Bank of Zanzibar is on the main road, but it won't change travellers' cheques. You must go to Chake Chake for this.

Places to Stay & Eat There are only two places to stay in Wete. The main one is the *Hoteli ya Wete* (☎ 4301), a government-owned place on the main street at the top end of town. Rooms cost US$15 per person (payable in hard currency) whether you occupy them singly or as a double. Clean sheets, toilet paper, a towel and soap are provided and the price includes breakfast. All rooms are self-contained and have a fan. They're clean and well maintained, the staff are very friendly and English is spoken. Checkout time is 10 am. Lunch and dinner are priced at TSh 1700 each and ice-cold beers are available at normal prices (so long as the nearby police canteen still has a supply of them!).

The other place to stay is the simpler *Sharouk Guest House* (☎ 4386), in the centre

of town, where there are five rooms, one of them self-contained. It's clean, friendly and costs US$7 per person including breakfast. The owner is good about finding dhows to Dar es Salaam, Zanzibar and Tanga.

For a slight change of diet, you could try one of the other restaurants in town, though they're all pretty basic. They include the *Sulaly Restaurant, Pop-In Restaurant* and the *New 4-Ways Restaurant*. The latter two are opposite the Hoteli ya Wete.

Getting There & Around See the Getting There & Away part of the Zanzibar section for details of flights and boats between Zanzibar and Pemba.

Dhows from Tanga often dock at Wete, though not always. These dhows are usually not motorised, so sailing times depend on the tides and the winds. Nor are they always easy to find. In addition, you might need permission from the district commissioner before you can sail.

More reliable is the MV *Raha*, which plies between Tanga and Wete approximately twice a week.

Pick-ups and wooden-sided trucks with bench seats, known locally as *dalladalla,* (remarkably similar to the jeepneys of the Philippines) connect Wete with Chake Chake (No 6) and Koride (No 24) further north throughout the day. The journey to Chake Chake takes about 45 minutes. The people who use them are garrulous and good fun. The road is sealed and is in excellent condition.

Chake Chake

This is Pemba's principal town and a lively place to wander around in the early mornings and late afternoons. It has a well-defined but small old centre, complete with bazaar and the remains of a late 18th-century fort, and it sits on top of a ridge overlooking a largely silted-up creek into which dhows occasionally sail when the tides allow. The site of the fort is now occupied by a hospital, and only the eastern corner and tower survive. The overall impression of the town from the ridge is of a mixture of makuti and rusty old tin roofs, but times are changing rapidly here. Nearing completion is a brand-new hospital, funded by the European Community, and a huge sports stadium on the outskirts of town.

Chake Chake also has the island's only airport, about seven km from town off the road to Mkoani.

Information The tourist office (☎ 2121) is next door to the Hoteli ya Chake and is staffed by a very friendly woman. Unfortunately, they have no literature (only limited information) and can't supply you with a copy of the detailed map of Pemba which is on the office wall.

The People's Bank of Zanzibar changes travellers' cheques and can provide you with cash US dollars to pay your hotel bill against hard currency travellers' cheques (though they don't particularly like doing this). The staff are friendly and efficient.

As on arrival in Zanzibar, you will have to pass through immigration and customs and have your passport stamped.

Places to Stay & Eat The only place to stay in the centre of town is the *Hoteli ya Chake* (☎ 2069, 2189). This is exactly the same design as the hotel in Wete and has the same prices and facilities, including a bar (which

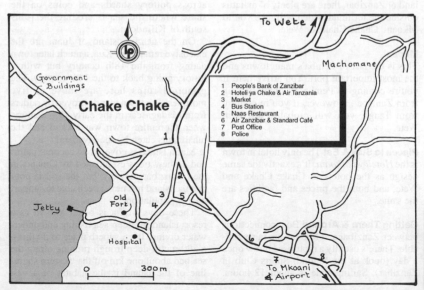

Chake Chake

To Wete

Machomane

Government Buildings

1 People's Bank of Zanzibar
2 Hoteli ya Chake & Air Tanzania
3 Market
4 Bus Station
5 Naas Restaurant
6 Air Zanzibar & Standard Café
7 Post Office
8 Police

Jetty

Old Fort

Hospital

0   300m

To Mkoani & Airport

TANZANIA

is frequently dry except for local spirits). There are also two private guesthouses, the *Guest House Nassir* at Machomane and the *Star Guest House* opposite the stadium, but they're both well outside the centre.

Getting There & Around The Air Tanzania office (☎ 2162) is on the main road which goes through town, below the hotel. The staff are friendly and helpful but there are currently no flights available.

Air Zanzibar flies from Zanzibar to Pemba on Monday, Wednesday and Friday at 7 am, and on Friday at 3.30 pm from Zanzibar to Pemba. Flights back to Zanzibar from Pemba depart one hour after the above times. The fare is US$40 or TSh 9000.

Pick-ups and dalladala go to Wete (No 6) and Mkoani (No 3) throughout the day.

Pick-ups and matatus only go to the airport when a flight is due (as that's the only time there's business at the airport). Ask around at the matatu station on the day your flight departs, or at the hotel – if you're staying there, they may give you a free lift. Air Zanzibar may also be able to help.

If you're arriving at Pemba from the mainland or Zanzibar, there are plenty of matatus outside the terminal which will take you to Mkoani, Chake Chake or Wete.

Mkoani

This is the last of Pemba's main towns and the most important port. You arrive here if you're coming to Pemba by dhow or ship from Zanzibar. However, if you're coming from Tanga, you will probably arrive in Wete.

Places to Stay & Eat The only hotel in town is the *Hoteli ya Mkoani*. It's exactly the same design as the hotels in Chake Chake and Wete, and both the prices and facilities are the same.

Getting There & Around Boat connections between Zanzibar and Mkoani are fairly reliable. There's usually a motorised dhow once a day (book at the Malindi Sports Club in Zanzibar). Sailing time is about 12 hours.

Otherwise, there are the MV *Mapinduzi* and the MV *Maendeleo*, which connect the two ports when cargo and passenger demand warrants, the MV *Butterfly* (presently out of service), and the FB *Canadian Spirit*, which connects Dar es Salaam with Zanzibar, Pemba (Mkoani) and Mombasa approximately twice monthly (see the Getting There & Away section in the Dar es Salaam chapter for details).

Pick-ups and wooden-sided trucks with bench seats (No 3) connect Mkoani with Chake Chake throughout the day.

MAFIA

Mafia Island lies south of Zanzibar off the mouth of the Rufiji River. It was an important settlement from the 12th to 14th centuries, in the days when the Shirazis ruled much of the East African coastal area. However, by the time the Portuguese arrived at the beginning of the 16th century, it had lost much of its former importance and had become part of the territory ruled by the King of Kilwa. Little remains above ground of the Shirazi settlement, though you may occasionally come across pottery shards and coins on the shore where the sea is eroding the ruins south of Kilindoni.

On the nearby island of Juani are the extensive remains of Kua, a much later town dating from the 18th century but with a history going back to the 14th century. The principal ruins here are those of five mosques. The town was destroyed by raiders from Madagascar in the early 19th century, when the entire town was sacked and the inhabitants eaten by the invaders!

Mafia Island is covered by coconut palms and cashew trees established by Omanis in their Zanzibari heyday, but the soil is poor and the island has never been able to support a large population.

These days Mafia is better known as a resort island for deep-sea fishing and underwater diving. It's a superb place to do this – a 200-metre-deep trough running along the sea bed about one km off the western shoreline of the island is the habitat of a vast

Map labels:

Zanzibar Shipping Company

Jetty

Shopping Area

Bus Station & Immigration

Post Office

Hoteli ya Mkoani

Petrol Station

To Chake Chake

Market

Bank

Market

Police

Mkoani

0   200m

number of different aquatic species. The coral formations are best off the small islands scattered around the main island, the best being the Okuto and Tutia reefs around Juani and Jibondo islands close to Chole Bay.

Mafia is also notable as a favourite breeding ground for giant turtles, which come up onto the white coral sands to lay their eggs. They do this principally on the uninhabited islands of Shungumbili, Burukini and Nyororo. Unfortunately, their numbers have been drastically depleted due to excessive hunting by local fishers, who also dig up and take away their eggs.

You're unlikely to meet any traveller who has been to Mafia Island. The reasons are simple – accommodation and transport. The accommodation available is expensive and transport can involve long waits in Dar es Salaam, as the boats operated by the Adecon Marine Inc are infrequent.

Places to Stay & Eat If you have a tent, you can find a suitable spot to pitch it and buy fruit, vegetables and fish from local people. If not, ask around among the locals for a room.

For those with money, the TTC-owned

Mafia Island Lodge (☎ 23491), Fisherman's Cove, has 30 air-con rooms with private showers and sea views for US$65 per person including breakfast. Other meals cost US$10. The hotel has its own generator but there's a 10 pm curfew and water is limited. Dhows can be rented for trips to the reef at TSh 1000 per hour – ask for Hasein.

Getting There & Around Air Zanzibar flies twice per day in either direction between Dar es Salaam and Mafia on Monday, Wednesday, Friday and Sunday. The fare is US$50 or TSh 10,000 one way.

See the Dar es Salaam chapter for details of shipping services between Dar es Salaam and Mafia Island.

MTWARA

This is Tanzania's southernmost port and almost on the border with Mozambique. It's a sleepy, relatively small place which rarely sees a traveller, though there are a number of expatriates living here who either have businesses or work with aid agencies. When in Dar es Salaam, you can find them drinking in the bar at the Embassy Hotel. They're a friendly and gregarious bunch and worth getting to know if you're heading that way.

Places to Stay & Eat Unless you are offered accommodation by one of the expatriates on the boat going down to Mtwara from Dar es Salaam, there's little choice of accommodation here. The best place is the *Beach Hotel*,

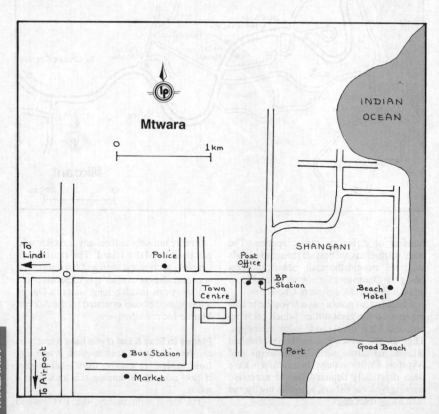

on the sea front, which has six double rooms, a bar and a restaurant (meals are available when ordered in advance). Prices are negotiable but reasonable. Fishing and diving trips can be arranged here.

Getting There & Away Virtually the only way to get to Mtwara without chartering a private light plane (expensive) is to take the FB *Canadian Spirit* from Dar es Salaam. It is operated by Adecon Marine and departures depend on cargo and passenger demand, which usually means about once a fortnight.

North-Eastern Tanzania

MOSHI

Moshi is the gateway to Kilimanjaro and the end of the Central Line railway from Dar es Salaam but is otherwise not a very interesting place. Rather than stay here, many travellers head straight out to Marangu and arrange a trek up the mountain from there, but this might not always be the best thing to do. The pros and cons are discussed in the Northern Tanzania & National Parks chapter.

Information

Money There are two Forex bureaus in Moshi, both in the same block as the Moshi Hotel, adjacent to the Dallas Supermarket and opposite the post office.

Telephone International telephone calls can be made from the post office, but there's only one booth and a long queue of very bored people.

Immigration The Moshi immigration office can renew your visa or stay permit. It's in Kibo House, close to the clock tower on the road leading to the YMCA. The office is open Monday to Friday from 7.30 am to 3.30 pm.

Places to Stay – bottom end

It used to be possible to sleep on the floor of the *Sikh Community Centre* and use the showers, though we haven't heard of anyone who's stayed there for a long time. To get there, turn left out of the railway station and continue until you see a football pitch on the left-hand side with a sign saying 'Members Only'. That's the place. If it looks closed, see the caretaker. Leave a donation if you stay.

The vast majority of travellers stay at the *YMCA*, on the roundabout some 300 metres from the clock tower. It's a large, modern building with a gymnasium, swimming pool, dining room and TV lounge/coffee bar. The rooms are spotlessly clean and well fur-

nished and some face Mt Kilimanjaro. It costs US$10/13 (TSh 500/600 for residents) for singles/doubles, including breakfast (fruit, eggs, bread and butter and tea/coffee). The showers (cold water only) and toilets are communal. Lunch and dinner are also available and are good value. Trans Kibo Travels are located here and can arrange treks up Kilimanjaro, plus there's a store which sells toiletries and the like. It's a friendly place and there's a guarded car park.

Cheaper but considerably more basic is the *Kilimanjaro Hotel*, just down from the clock tower towards the railway station. It offers self-contained singles/doubles (cold water only) for TSh 800/1500 and has a restaurant and bar. Opposite is the *Liberty Hotel*, which has very tatty doubles for TSh 600 – not recommended.

Good value, but further away from the centre and slightly more expensive, the *Green Cottage Hostel* is in a very pleasant area and has safe parking. Bathroom facilities are shared but there are hot showers. It's a small place run by friendly people. Just below the Green Cottage but approached from a different turn-off is the *Kizota Restaurant*, which has basic but adequate doubles with shared bathroom for TSh 1500. The verandah bar here is popular with local businesspeople.

Back in the town centre, close to the clock tower, is the *Coffee Tree Hotel*, on the 2nd and 3rd floors of the large office block. There's no prominent sign, so you might think it's not there, but the entrance is in the courtyard. Bed and breakfast costs TSh 1300 a single with shared shower, TSh 1850/3550 a single/double with private shower. There's also a self-contained suite for TSh 6800. There are great views of Kilimanjaro from the restaurant and some of the rooms.

Also good value is the *Haria Boarding & Lodging*, on Mawenzi Rd at the southern end of town, which is very clean and offers doubles (no singles) for TSh 2600 including

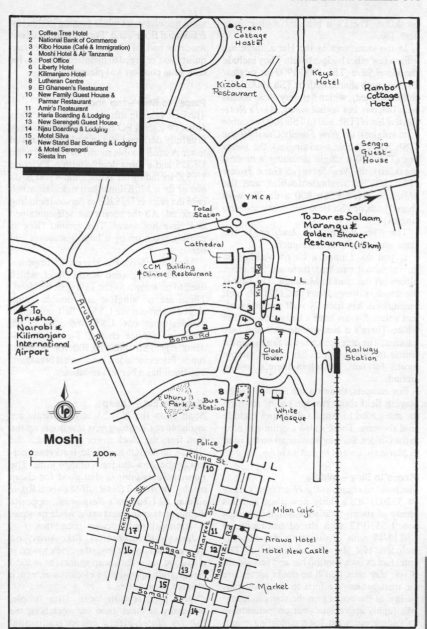

1 Coffee Tree Hotel
2 National Bank of Commerce
3 Kibo House (Café & Immigration)
4 Moshi Hotel & Air Tanzania
5 Post Office
6 Liberty Hotel
7 Kilimanjaro Hotel
8 Lutheran Centre
9 El Ghaneen's Restaurant
10 New Family Guest House &
   Parmar Restaurant
11 Amir's Restaurant
12 Haria Boarding & Lodging
13 New Serengeti Guest House
14 Njau Boarding & Lodging
15 Motel Silva
16 New Stand Bar Boarding & Lodging
   & Motel Serengeti
17 Siesta Inn

Green Cottage Hostel

Keys Hotel

Rambo Cottage Hotel

Kizota Restaurant

Sengia Guest House

YMCA

Total Station

To Dar es Salaam, Marangu & Golden Shower Restaurant (1·5 km)

Cathedral

CCM Building & Chinese Restaurant

Kibo Rd

To Arusha, Nairobi & Kilimanjaro International Airport

Arusha Rd

Boma Rd

Clock Tower

Railway Station

Uhuru Park

Bus Station

White Mosque

Police

Kilima St

Moshi

0   200 m

Milan Café

Arawa Hotel

Hotel New Castle

Kenyatta St

Market St

Mawenzi Rd

Chagga St

Somali St

Market

TANZANIA

breakfast. There's a pleasant rooftop area here, too.

In the same area as the Haria, there are quite a few other budget hotels. They include the *Motel Silva* (TSh 1400/1900 for singles/doubles with shared bath or TSh 1900/2400 self-contained), which has very clean rooms with balcony but no hot water, *Mlay's Residential Hotel* (TSh 800 to TSh 1000 a double – no singles), the *New Family Guest House* (TSh 700 a double – no singles), the *Siesta Inn* (TSh 950 a single including a modest breakfast), the *New Serengeti Guest House* (TSh 350/700 a single/double), and the *Motel Serengeti* (TSh 800 a double with shared bath, or TSh 1000 self-contained – no singles).

The *Njau Boarding & Lodging*, in the same area, won't take foreigners.

If you don't mind a bit of walking on arrival (about one km), there are two other places off the road to Marangu. The best is the *Rombo Cottage Hotel* (☎ 2112). It's well maintained, has friendly staff and is excellent value. Rooms have a bathroom and hot water. There's a bar, a restaurant and safe parking. The other place is the *Sengia Guest House* (☎ 4942), which has several simple rooms for rent, but often there's no-one around.

For campers, there's a site adjacent to the playing field about two km out of town on the main road to Arusha. Facilities include cold showers. There's also a camp site next to the Golden Shower Restaurant on the road to Marangu, owned by Let's Go.

Places to Stay – middle
The hotel of choice is the *Hotel New Castle* (☎ 53203). It's a fairly new place and has plenty of rooms available. Singles/doubles cost US$10/12 with shared bathroom, or US$13/15 with private bath; breakfast is included. Hot showers are available. The hotel has its own rooftop bar and restaurant. If you stay here, you'll no doubt appreciate the management's efforts to maintain tranquility, as the notices on the stairs indicate: 'We highly appreciate your cooperation in upholding our want for maintaining maxi-

mum noiselessness while passing in this last residential floor', and 'For the honour of our residents and all visitors who treasure tranquility you're urged to maintain calmness for their total comfort and pleasure'.

Places to Stay – top end
The best value in this range is the new *Keys Hotel* (☎ 2250), PO Box 933, which is very tastefully designed and in a pleasant area of town. A small double room (no singles) costs US$25 and a large double with a TV costs US$50 including breakfast, unless you go on one of their Mt Kilimanjaro treks, in which case the price is US$20 per person including breakfast. All the rooms are self-contained and have hot water. The ground floor is entirely taken up by a large restaurant and bar.

More expensive but somewhat impersonal is the TTC-owned *Moshi Hotel*, which used to be known as the Livingstone Hotel. There are no singles, and doubles with shared bathroom are US$21. Self-contained doubles/suites cost US$47/69 plus 22.5% taxes and service charge. Tanzanian residents pay TSh 4400/10,500 for doubles/suites. Prices include a continental breakfast. The hotel has a bar and restaurant.

Places to Eat – cheap
Apart from the YMCA, cheap meals are available at *Chrisburger*, a few doors up the road from the clock tower and towards the YMCA on the left-hand side. It serves excellent eggburgers and fresh orange juice. The *Parmar Restaurant* is also good for cheap meals. The *Arawa Hotel*, off Mawenzi Rd, is similar. *El Ghaneen's Restaurant*, opposite the bus station and next to the white mosque, is worth visiting for Asian specialities.

Helen's Restaurant & Take-Away, on Mawenzi Rd not far from the clock tower, is also good value for cheap snacks, as is *Kibo House*, right opposite the clock tower, which also has good coffee.

Very popular with local office people, especially at lunch time on weekdays, the *Liberty Hotel* offers cheap traditional

African fare, but it hardly functions at the weekend.

The *Rombo Cottage Hotel* is certainly worth visiting for lunch or dinner if you don't mind the walk. The food is very good and prices are competitive.

Places to Eat – more expensive

For a splurge, you have a choice of three places. Right in the centre of town, the *Moshi Hotel* offers a lunch or dinner menu of soup, main course and coffee for about TSh 1200 including taxes. It's also worth considering an evening at the *Keys Hotel* if you want to dine in style. Prices are similar to those at the Moshi Hotel.

For good Chinese food at moderate prices, try the *Chinese Restaurant* at the CCM building on the ring road.

My favourite, though it's a good 1½ km out of town on the Marangu road, is the *Golden Shower Restaurant*. This place has a much more intimate atmosphere and offers a choice of dining inside or outside in the garden. It also has a very cosy bar. The food is excellent and individually presented and the service is fast. Prices are slightly higher than those at the Moshi Hotel but the little extra is well worth it, plus there's nyama choma for TSh 500. Despite the distance from town, this restaurant is surprisingly popular with travellers, especially those who have climbed Kilimanjaro and feel like celebrating.

Getting There & Away

Air Kilimanjaro International Airport is halfway between Moshi and Arusha. Air Tanzania flies between Dar es Salaam and Kilimanjaro in either direction, usually once daily, but you must book well in advance to be sure of a seat. The Air Tanzania office is next to the Moshi Hotel. It's open Monday to Friday from 8 am to 12.30 pm and 2 to 4.30 pm and on Saturday and Sunday from 9 am to 12.30 pm.

Bus There are several buses daily in either direction between Moshi and Dar es Salaam. There's a choice between luxury buses (rec-

ommended) and ordinary buses (not recommended, especially with a backpack). The road is fine as far as Korogwe, but from there to Dar es Salaam it's rough, which is why it's worth spending those extra few dollars to take the luxury bus. The best of the luxury buses is Freshya Shamba, which departs daily at 10 am, costs TSh 7500 and arrives in Dar es Salaam at around 7 pm. If you prefer to get there earlier, take the Bariadi Bus Service luxury bus, which departs Moshi at 8.15 am daily, costs TSh 6500 and arrives at around 5 pm. There's also a luxury bus run by Dar Express Bus Service, which leaves Moshi daily at 8.15 am, costs TSh 6000 and arrives in Dar es Salaam at around 5 pm.

Ordinary buses cost around TSh 3000 but take considerably longer to get to their destination, are uncomfortable and are prone to breakdown.

Buses to Dodoma via Arusha depart daily at about 7 am, cost TSh 7000 and arrive at about 7 pm.

There are frequent daily buses and matatus between Arusha and Moshi which depart when full. The fare is TSh 200 and the trip takes about 1½ hours along a good, sealed road.

Matatus to Marangu also leave throughout the day when full and cost TSh 200.

Train Trains depart from Dar es Salaam for Moshi on Monday, Wednesday and Friday at 4 pm. In the opposite direction, they leave Moshi for Dar es Salaam on the same days at the same time. The journey takes from 15 to 18 hours and the fares are TSh 5445 (1st class), TSh 3375 (2nd class), TSh 2485 (2nd-class sitting) and TSh 1270 (3rd class). Bedding is extra and dinner is available in the buffet car. Advance booking is essential for 1st and 2nd class. Buying a ticket at Moshi station is an exercise in tenacity and determination. It's little short of chaos and you'll just have to join the rabble.

Getting Around

To/From the Airport State Transport Corporation shuttle buses to the airport leave from the Air Tanzania office about two hours before flight departure. The fare is TSh 1000. A taxi will cost you at least TSh 10,000, though they often quote up to TSh 15,000. The journey takes about one hour. The airport departure tax is TSh 500 for domestic flights.

Matatu & Taxi There are frequent matatus throughout the day between Moshi and Marangu (the village below the Kilimanjaro park entry gate). The fare is TSh 200. A taxi will cost around TSh 10,000 shared between four or possibly five people.

Taxis around Moshi cost TSh 300 per journey.

ARUSHA

Arusha is one of Tanzania's most attractive towns and was the headquarters of the East African Community in the days when Kenya, Tanzania and Uganda were members of an economic, communications and customs union. It sits in lush, green countryside at the foot of Mt Meru (4556 metres) and enjoys a temperate climate throughout the year. Surrounding it are many coffee, wheat and maize estates tended by the Waarusha and Wameru tribespeople, whom you may see occasionally in the market area of town. For travellers, Arusha is the gateway to Serengeti, Lake Manyara and Tarangire national parks and the Ngorongoro Conservation Area. As such, it's the safari capital of Tanzania. Mt Meru can also be climbed from here.

Arusha is a pleasant town to walk around and take in the sights, and the market area is particularly lively, but the main concern of most travellers will be arranging a safari and taking off for the national parks.

Orientation

The town is in two parts, separated by a small valley through which the Naura River runs. The upper part, just off the main Moshi to Namanga road, contains the government buildings, post office, top-class hotels, safari companies, airline offices, curio and craft shops, and the huge International Conference Centre. Further down the hill and across

the valley are the commercial and industrial areas, the market, many small shops, many of the budget hotels and the bus station.

Information

Tourist Office The tourist office (☎ 3842) is on Boma Rd just down from the New Safari Hotel. It generally has a few glossy leaflets about the national parks but its main function is to make bookings for TTC-owned hotels, including the national park lodges. Safari companies can also make these bookings if you're going on a trip with them, and may be able to arrange special deals which will save you money.

National Parks Office The Tanzania National Parks headquarters (☎ 3471, ext 1104), 6th floor, Kilimanjaro Wing, International Conference Centre, PO Box 3134, usually stocks a few leaflets about the national parks. Otherwise, you probably won't need to come here unless you're a journalist searching for information. The public relations manager, Cynthia Buretta, is very enthusiastic and helpful. The quarterly reports make interesting but often distressing reading, especially as far as poaching is concerned.

Money There are two Forex bureaus in Arusha, one at the junction of India St and Makongoro Rd (A Meir's) and the other on the bottom side of the stadium, at the junction of Makongoro Rd and Zaramo St (Hedal Bureau). You can also change money at the National Bank of Commerce at the junction of Sokoine and Sinoni Rds during normal banking hours. All these places chalk up the day's rates on blackboards outside their entrance doors.

Telephone The exchange is opposite the New Safari Hotel and is the best place from which to make calls, both domestic and international – when the lines are working! It's often crowded in the morning but is usually deserted in the evening. It's open Monday to Saturday from 8 am to 10 pm, and from 9 am to 8 pm on Sunday.

Immigration The immigration office is on Simeon Rd near the Makongoro Rd junction. The people here are reasonably efficient and helpful if you need a visa extension.

Media Local newspapers and Kenyan daily newspapers can be bought on the street, opposite the clock tower. International magazines and Kenyan daily newspapers can be bought from the bookstore at the New Arusha Hotel, which also has a reasonable selection of novels and national parks guide books.

National Museum
At the top of Boma Rd, this place simply has to be a joke. It consists of one corridor about 20 metres long by five metres wide with facsimiles of the evolutionary progress of Homo sapiens based on the digs at Olduvai Gorge. You've seen it all before. It's open Monday to Friday from 7.30 am to 5 pm, 7.30 am to 4.30 pm on Saturday. Entry costs TSh 50 (TSh 10 for Tanzanian residents).

Places to Stay – bottom end
The cheapest places to stay used to be the various religious mission guesthouses (St Theresa's Catholic Guest House, the Lutheran Centre and the Anglican Centre) but no-one seems to be able to get into them anymore without contacts and/or references. That leaves you with hotels or camping.

In common with the religious mission guesthouses, many of the budget hotels in the market area of town won't take foreigners. These include the *Town Guest House, Central Guest House, Amigo's Guest House* and the *New Central Hotel*. You can also forget about the *New Stanley Hotel*, which is a pigsty.

One of the cheapest and most basic places to stay is the *Alton Inn* (previously the Twiga Guest House), on Seth Benjamin Rd, which offers cardboard boxes with hot water (or so they claim) in the morning for TSh 800 per person. It's often full. On the same street, next door to Ali Baba's safari company, the *Pangani Guest House* is similar to the Alton Inn and costs the same.

Much better is the recently refurbished *Robannyson Hotel* on Somali Rd, which offers singles/doubles with shared bathroom facilities for TSh 800/1600. Hot showers are available, mosquito nets are provided and the hotel has its own restaurant (no bar). Similar in price is the *Friends Corner Hotel*, Sokoine Rd, which has singles/doubles for TSh 750/1500.

Excellent value in this range is the *Blue Bird Guest House* (☎ 8109). Owned by the same person who runs the Golden Rose Hotel, this very clean and newly renovated hotel with rooms arranged around a quiet courtyard costs TSh 1000/1500 for singles/doubles with shared bathroom facilities. The *Amazon Hotel*, Zaramo St, is older, but similar in standard and costs the same.

Also cheap is the *Greenland Hotel*, on Sokoine Rd between the two halves of town, but though relatively cheap, it's in an advanced state of decay and can't be recommended.

More expensive than the above and a very popular place to stay, though hardly worthy of a mid-range rating, is the *YMCA* on India St. It's fairly clean and well furnished but the toilets won't flush and the showers often don't work. Still, it's an excellent place to meet people, especially if you're trying to get a group together to go on safari. Bed and breakfast costs US$6/10 for singles/doubles with shared toilet facilities (cold water only). The breakfast isn't up to much – boiled egg, dry bread and butter, plus tea – but the staff are very friendly, your gear is safe and there's a laundry service. Downstairs is the Silver City Bar, but it closes early in the evening so there's no problem about noise. Get here early if you want a room.

Similar in price but with better facilities is the *Miami Beach Guest House*, north of the bus station. It's popular with travellers, well maintained, with friendly staff and hot showers. Singles/doubles/triples with shared bathroom facilities cost US$8/10/15. The hotel has its own bar and restaurant.

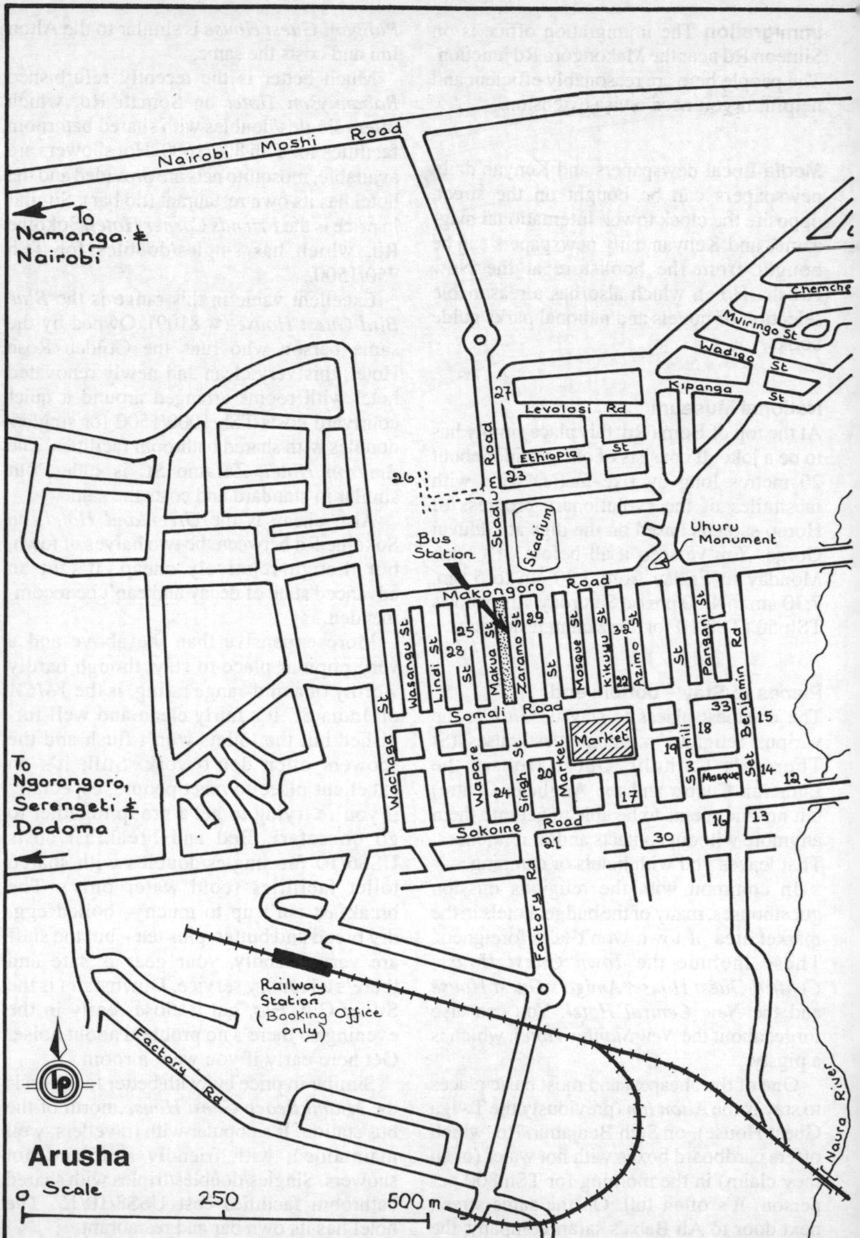

Nairobi Moshi Road

To
Namanga &
Nairobi

To Ngorongoro,
Serengeti &
Dodoma

Chemche

Mviringo St

Wadigo St

Kipanga St

Levolosi Rd

27

Ethiopia St

23

26

Bus
Station

Stadium
Road

Stadium

Uhuru
Monument

Makongoro Road

Wasangu St

Lindi St

25
28

Makua St

Zaramo St

29

Mosque St

Kikuyu St

32

Azimo St

Pangani St

Benjamin Rd

Somali Road

33

18

15

Wachaga St

Wapare St

Singh St

Market Road

Swahili St

Mosque

19

Market

24

20

17

14

12

Sokoine Road

21

30

16

13

Factory Rd

Factory Rd

Railway
Station
(Booking
Office
only)

Naura River

Arusha

Scale

0   250   500 m

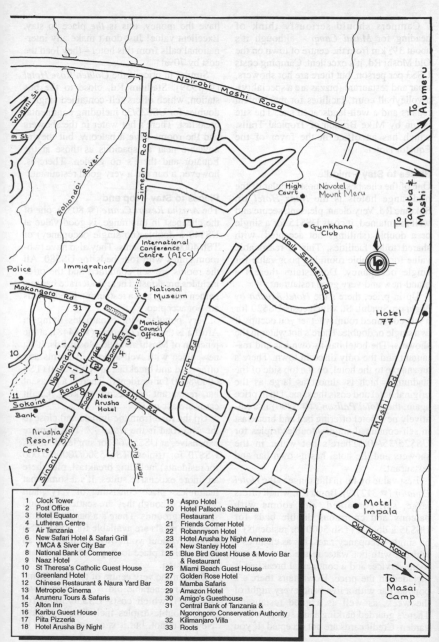

Campers should seriously think of heading for *Masai Camp* – although it's about 3½ km from the centre of town on the Old Moshi Rd, it's excellent. Camping costs US$3 per person, but there are hot showers, a bar and restaurant (pizzas are a speciality), a volleyball court, facilities for mechanical repairs and a well-landscaped site. The site is run by Mike Brydon of Tropical Trails, which has an office in the foyer of the Equator Hotel.

Places to Stay – middle

One of the cheapest and most popular of the mid-range hotels is the *Naaz Hotel* on Sokoine Rd. Very clean, pleasant, secure and well maintained, it costs US$15 for a single or a double (shillings not accepted) with shared toilet facilities. This is reasonable value for a double room but poor value for single occupancy. Downstairs there's a brand-new and very good restaurant.

Up in price, there's the *Hotel Arusha by Night* on Swahili St, which costs US$20 for a self-contained room whether you occupy it as a single or double. There's hot water in the showers. The hotel has its own bar and restaurant and the only disco in town. There's an annexe to the hotel, on the top side of the stadium, which is almost as large as the original hotel and costs the same. Up in price again, the *Hotel Pallson's* (☎ 3790) is a relatively new hotel offering bed and breakfast in self-contained singles/doubles/triples for US$25/35/40. There's hot water in the showers and the hotel has its own bar and restaurant.

Best value by far in this range is the *Hotel Equator* (☎ 3127/9), Boma Rd, which offers large, self-contained, airy rooms with balcony and enormous double beds for US$35 a double (TSh 5000 for residents) – no single-occupancy rates. It's as clean as a whistle, with hot water in the showers and room service, and a continental breakfast is included in the price. Downstairs there's a popular bar with a live band every night of the week, as well as a good restaurant. There's guarded parking and a spacious beer garden. Credit cards are not accepted. If you have the money, this is *the* place to stay. Excellent value! Just don't make any international calls from this hotel – they load the cost by 70%!

Similar in price is the *Golden Rose Hotel* (☎ 7959), Stadium Rd, close to the bus station, which offers self-contained singles/doubles for US$25/35 including continental breakfast. There's hot water in the showers and the rooms have a balcony, but they're nowhere near as spacious as those at the Equator and there's no garden. There is, however, a bar and a very good restaurant.

Places to Stay – top end

The *Arusha Resort Centre* (☎ 8033), one of the cheapest in this range, is good value at US$40 a double (no single occupancy) or TSh 4000 for residents. They also have two-room suites with four beds for US$80. All the rooms are self-contained and the price includes breakfast. There's a terrace bar in a garden setting, and a restaurant. Credit cards are not accepted.

Very popular with expatriates living in Arusha is the *Motel Impala* (☎ 8448), at the junction of Moshi and Old Moshi Rds. It's a new place with well-appointed rooms and offers bed and breakfast for US$30/40 (TSh 6000/8000 for residents). There's a pleasant bar, restaurant and secure parking. Credit cards are accepted.

Up the road from the Impala and close to the ring road is the *Hotel 77*. This is more expensive, at US$50/60 for singles/doubles, US$70 for triples (TSh 5500/7000/10,000 for residents) including breakfast, plus there are more expensive suites. It's a somewhat featureless place consisting of very plain 'cottages', though they are scattered around spacious grounds. There's a bar and restaurant, and meals are available for US$8 (TSh 2500). Without your own vehicle, it's an inconvenient place to stay. Credit cards are not accepted.

Back in the very centre of town on Boma Rd is the venerable old *New Safari Hotel* (☎ 2857), which costs US$30/50/80 for singles/doubles/triples including breakfast. 'New' it is not, but it is a popular place to stay. There's a bar, restaurant and a delightful beer garden/barbecue with makuti roof shelters. It's a good place to meet people. Credit cards are not accepted.

Better because of its extensive grounds is the *New Arusha Hotel* (☎ 8541), on the clock tower roundabout, which has good rooms for US$70/75/85 for singles/doubles/triples including a full breakfast. Residents' rates are TSh 6000/8000/10,000. There's a bar, restaurant, snack bar, shopping arcade, beer garden and secure parking.

At the top of the range is the *Novotel Mount Meru* (☎ 2712/28), set in landscaped grounds just off the main Arusha to Moshi road. It has all the usual facilities, including a swimming pool, shopping arcade and lounge/bar areas, and has singles/doubles for US$110/138, and triples for US$159, including breakfast and all taxes. The swimming pool can be used by nonresidents on payment of a temporary membership fee. The DHL shuttle bus office (to Nairobi) is in the foyer. You can also change money at the hotel – but only at official bank rates, not Forex rates.

If you prefer to stay outside Arusha in beautiful surroundings close to Mt Meru National Park, there's a choice of two places. The closest one to Arusha is the *Hotel Restaurant Dik Dik*, PO Box 1499, which is owned and managed by a Swiss team. It consists of nine bungalows with two double rooms in each, and a central amenties area which includes a swimming pool, spacious dining hall and a bar. No expense has been spared setting up this place and it's very comfortable. The rates are US$55/65 for singles/doubles including breakfast.

Further out and overlooking Lake Duluti is the *Mountain Village Lodge* (☎ 2699), PO Box 376. It's imaginatively designed to resemble a traditional African village and consists of 42 thatched bandas arranged in semicircular groups amongst tropical flowering trees. All the bandas are self-contained, furnished with a variety of local crafts and have a private verandah. There's a central amenities area (adapted from an old colonial villa), bar and restaurant. It's a superb place

to stay and costs US$62.80/73.80 for singles/doubles, plus there are suites for US$98.35. Breakfast is extra (US$7) and lunch/dinner costs US$10.

Places to Eat – cheap

Plenty of simple cafés and cheap restaurants in the lower part of town, along Sokoine Rd, offer standard Afro-Indian fare – curries, ugali or ndizi (plantains) with meat stew and beans, sambusa, biriyani and the like, for about TSh 400. Bars and discos usually have barbecued food – kebabs and chips or matoke for the same price. Try the *Silver City Bar*, attached to the YMCA, or the *Naura Yard Bar*, next to the Chinese Restaurant. Also very good and cheap is the *Moivo Bar & Restaurant*, next to the Blue Bird Guest House on Wapare St, which offers a kg of barbecued meat for just TSh 600, and has cold beers.

For cheap but tasty snacks such as yoghurt, fruit juices, samosas, sandwiches and salads, try the recently opened *Roots* on Seth Benjamin St, run by a very friendly Australian and Tanzanian couple. They have great music and nothing costs more than TSh 250.

Another good place for cheap vegetarian lunch-time food and one which has been recommended by quite a few travellers is *Johnnie's Ravalia Restaurant* on Sokoine Rd.

It's also worth wandering around the streets close to the bus station in the evening and looking out for verandah cafés. They're easily identified – just look for someone grilling kebabs over charcoal and frying chips in a large metal pan. I had some very tasty kebabs, chips and salad at such a place one evening and it was unbelievably cheap.

The fast-food cafeteria in the *New Arusha Hotel* has McDonald's-type food as well as samosas, but late in the day, only a fraction of what's on the menu is available.

Places to Eat – more expensive

The restaurant on the ground floor of the *Naaz Hotel* is worth trying for a better-than-average meal. It's brand new, very clean and offers Indian-style food.

For a splurge, most travellers go to one of two restaurants – the *Safari Grill*, next to the New Safari Hotel, or the *Chinese Restaurant*. Probably the most popular is the Safari Grill, which has a good range of fish and meat dishes as well as soups and desserts. The food is well cooked and presented and costs an average of TSh 300 for soups and TSh 600 to TSh 1000 for main courses, plus 15% taxes and service charge. It also serves very cold beers. There's cheaper barbecued meat (chicken or goat) in the New Safari's beer garden at the back of this restaurant if you prefer to eat al fresco. You can get a good plate of tasty food here for around TSh 500.

The Chinese Restaurant, on Sokoine Rd close to the bridge, is equally good and has a very extensive menu, which includes seafood, though this tends to be expensive. Prices are much the same as those at the Safari Grill but the food is very good and it's a popular place to eat. It's open for breakfast, lunch and dinner and menu prices include taxes.

A little further along Sokoine Rd is the new *Piita Pizzeria*, on the corner of Masai St. It's a pleasant place to eat and, as the name suggests, specialises in Italian food. It has soups for TSh 400 to TSh 500 and main dishes from TSh 1600 to TSh 2200. Cold beer is available. It's open Tuesday to Sunday from 11 am to 10 pm and is air-conditioned.

For excellent Indian Mughlai and Chinese cuisine, go for a meal at the *Shamiana Restaurant* at the Hotel Pallson's. Main courses cost around TSh 1500. It's closed on Tuesday.

The restaurant at the *Golden Rose Hotel* is also very good and the menu changes daily. The chef has obviously trained overseas, so watch out for some delicious Eastern European specialities. Average prices for lunch and dinner are TSh 800.

On Friday evenings, have a night out at the *Masai Camp*, some 3½ km out of town on the Old Moshi Rd, where they offer excellent pizzas from TSh 1000 to TSh 1300 and some of the cheapest cold beers in town.

Entertainment

Two of the liveliest and cheapest bars are the *Silver City Bar* next to the YMCA and the *Naura Yard Bar* next to the Chinese Restaurant. It's easy to strike up a conversation with local people or travellers at these places. Both have barbecue grills and the Naura has a deafeningly loud spit-and-sawdust disco each Sunday (free). Otherwise, in the afternoons, the beer gardens at the *New Safari Hotel* and the *New Arusha Hotel* are great places to relax and converse.

The indoor bar at the *Hotel Equator* is probably the best and most lively each evening. Everyone looking for action comes here. It kicks off with video films from around 6.30 to 8 pm, after which a live band plays until around midnight (later at weekends). There's no cover charge. At weekends live bands play during the day, but for these, there's a small cover charge.

The only nightly disco is at the *Hotel Arusha by Night*. This goes on until about 3 am and is popular with local people and wazungu. There are no hassles, drinks are the normal price and the sexes are about equally matched in number. There's plenty of dancing space and the lights are low. Entry costs TSh 500.

In the basement of the New Safari Hotel is the *Cave Disco*, which is very popular at weekends (nothing during the week), when it rocks all afternoon until very late at night. The tourist literature describes it as 'a sensation'. That's far from accurate, but deafening it certainly is. Entry costs TSh 500.

Things to Buy

There are several very good craft shops along the short street between the clock tower and Ngoliondoi Rd. These have superb examples of makonde carving at prices lower than in Dar es Salaam. If I wanted to buy an example of this beautiful and traditional art form, I would look for it here.

Don't allow yourself to be hustled into going into certain shops by touts. They're just after commission. Make your own choice.

Getting There & Away

Air Kilimanjaro International Airport is halfway between Arusha and Moshi and is serviced by Air Tanzania, Ethiopian Airlines and KLM. Air Tanzania generally has one flight per day between Dar es Salaam and Kilimanjaro in either direction. Advance booking is essential, as the service is heavily subscribed. The fare is US$124 (TSh 9000 for Tanzanian residents).

KLM flies Kilimanjaro to Amsterdam via Nairobi on Tuesday and Saturday. The fare is US$895 one way and US$1059 return. Ethiopian Airlines flies Dar es Salaam to Addis Ababa via Kilimanjaro on Wednesday, Friday and Sunday and Addis Ababa to Dar es Salaam via Kilimanjaro on Tuesday, Thursday and Saturday. Kilimanjaro to Addis Ababa costs US$231 one way and US$462 return.

The Air Tanzania office is open Monday to Friday from 8 am to 12.30 pm and 2 to 4.30 pm and on Saturday from 8 am to 12.30 pm. Bookings are computerised and American Express cards are accepted. KLM and Ethiopian Airlines are diagonally opposite Air Tanzania, next to the New Safari Hotel. You can book international flights here but they can't take you on internal flights.

Bus & Matatu For details of road transport to and from Arusha and Nairobi, see the earlier Tanzania Getting There & Away chapter.

There's a good selection of daily transport in either direction between Dar es Salaam and Arusha via Moshi, but if you have the choice, take a luxury. You won't regret the extra few dollars, as the road between Korogwe and Dar es Salaam is rough. The best is the Royal Class, a very comfortable bus with video, which departs every second day at 10 am, costs TSh 6000 and takes about nine hours. There are also fairly comfortable minibuses which do the same trip (eg TC Express) daily at 10 am, cost TSh 5500 and will take you to the hotel of your choice in Dar es Salaam. Ordinary buses along this route cost TSh 3300 and depart daily at 8 am.

To Mwanza, there's a choice of buses which go direct through Ngorongoro and the Serengeti National Park, and others which bypass the parks and go via Singida and Shinyanga. The difference is that those which go through the parks, despite being much quicker, cost much more because you have to pay two sets of park entry fees in addition to the fare. The two park entry fees total US$30 (payable in hard currency).

If you want to go through the parks, take Bangili's Bus Service, which departs from Arusha for Mwanza at 5 am on Monday, Wednesday and Friday, costs TSh 10,000 and takes 14 hours. If you don't want to go through the parks, take Haji's Bus, which departs daily except Monday and Thursday, costs TSh 7000 and takes about 36 hours. This involves an overnight stop because public transport is not allowed to move between 10 pm and 4 am.

For Tanga, Tawakal Bus departs daily at 10 am, costs TSh 2200 and arrives at around 7 pm.

It's advisable to book any of the above buses in advance at the bus station.

There are buses and matatus all day, every day until late between Arusha and Moshi, which leave when full. The fare is TSh 450 and the journey takes 1½ hours over a good, sealed road. Share-taxis between the two places cost TSh 7000.

Getting Around

To/From the Airport The State Transport Corporation operates shuttle buses to the airport about two hours before flight departures. The buses depart from outside the Air Tanzania office and cost TSh 1000. The journey takes about half an hour.

Taxi Arusha is a small place, so it's easy to get from one place to another on foot. Taxis charge TSh 200 per journey during the day and TSh 300 at night.

Organised Safaris Most of the safari companies have offices in the International Conference Centre and some are along Boma Rd, Sokoine Rd, India St and Ngoliondoi Rd, though there are others elsewhere. For a detailed breakdown of what is on offer regarding safaris, see the Organised Safaris section in Tanzania's Getting Around chapter.

USAMBARA MOUNTAINS

This area between Moshi and Korogwe and the Kenyan border is a spectacularly beautiful area which you shouldn't miss if you have the chance to visit. The Michelin map marks the road up to Soni and Lushoto as 'scenic', which is a major understatement. Getting up there involves negotiating a series of huge hairpin bends with sheer drops on the outer lane virtually the whole way. Yet despite the steepness, the mountains are cultivated from top to bottom (with the usual maize, bananas, pineapples, beans and tree plantations), so the landscape looks as if it's had a chequered green tablecloth thrown over it.

This is walking country, especially for those who like to get to the top of mountains without too much effort. There is an endless number of gently graded tracks which zigzag up the mountains, with breathtaking views at every turn. It's almost impossible to get lost as long as you stick to the track. One of the most popular tracks takes you to what's known as the Viewpoint – a slab of rock at the top of a cliff face looking out over the Mombo to Tanga road and the Masai Plain. The walk takes about one hour from Lushoto. To get there, head towards Irente and ask for the Children's Home (the regional orphanage). When you get there, ask someone to show you the right track. The views from here are simply incredible.

LUSHOTO

Lushoto, the main centre of population in the Usambara Mountains, sits in a valley, though the town is built on several levels, producing a feeling of space. Most of the houses are built from locally manufactured mud bricks and have pitched roofs. The main government buildings are European in style, and indeed Lushoto was once slated to become the capital of German East Africa back in colonial times. These days it's a religious centre of sorts, with a bewildering variety of churches, missions and mosques. Everyone is hard at it here making converts, and even if you're not hot on religion, it can be fun eavesdropping on religious politics.

Information

An interesting pair of wazungu here are Carter, a young American writer, and George, who live about an hour's walk from Lushoto. Both are keen hang-gliders and George is involved in training buzzards and falcons to assist glider pilots in staying airborne indefinitely, the idea being that these birds are far more capable than humans of reading the landscape and finding thermals. Once the pilot has been guided to the thermals, the birds sit on the steering bar until the glider wishes to land! You can often find these two at The Lawns Hotel or the Kilimani Guest House or at the Green Valley disco on Saturday nights.

A local youth named Bula has set himself up as a guide. He can take you to the Viewpoint, to Carter's house, or to anywhere else in the Lushuto area. Using local buses and lodgings in outlying villages, you can even go walking for a few days. Bula can be found by asking around at the Kilimani Guest House or the Green Valley.

Places to Stay

Owned by a resident expatriate, the most expensive place is *The Lawns Hotel*, which is positioned at the highest point with views over the valley. It's a fairly typical colonial-style hotel with a large front lawn mown by two cows, and has a verandah with easy chairs and a well-stocked bar. The rooms cost TSh 3500/4600/5700 for singles/doubles/triples. The service leaves a little to be desired.

The *Kilimani Guest House* has rooms set around a rectangular courtyard, at the centre

Post Office

Church

To Mlalo

Market & Bus Station

Bank

Green Valley Restaurant

Christian Bookshop

Shops

To 'Viewpoint'

Shops

Kilimani Guest House

The Lawns Hotel

To Soni & Mombo

Lushoto

0   500 m

of which is a bar. Singles/doubles cost TSh 300/600. The rooms are given privacy by an inner slatted fence that lines the courtyard. The beds are comfortable, with clean linen, and there's a table and chair. The women who run it can't speak two words of English between the four of them, but they're very friendly and helpful and are excellent cooks.

There's no running water, but a bucket of hot water and a mug will be provided on request.

To get there, leave the main street in Lushoto at the sign for the Lawns Hotel and continue past it. On your left, you come to a village green running along the top of the ridge. At the Lawns Hotel end is the guest-house.

Places to Eat

The *Green Valley Restaurant*, in the centre of town, is the best place to eat if you're not eating where you stay. The staff are pleasant and the food is very good.

Getting There & Away

To get to Lushoto, take a bus from Mombo on the main Moshi to Korogwe road. Anyone in Mombo will show you where the bus departs from. The journey takes about 1½ hours. Buses are usually crowded, but the road is well maintained and sealed all the way.

There are also direct buses between Tanga and Lushoto. If you have to stay in Mombo overnight, try the *Usambara Inn*, next to the petrol station on the corner of the road to Lushoto. It's something of a time warp but has a garden, bar and restaurant. Single rooms have a sink, a towel and a large fan and cost TSh 400.

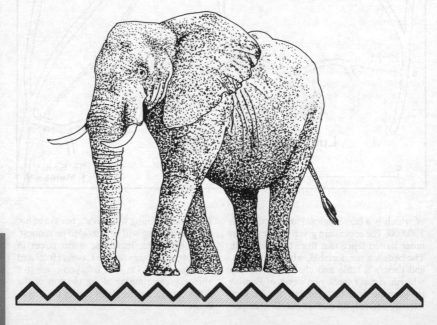

Lake Victoria

MWANZA

Mwanza is Tanzania's most important port on the shore of Lake Victoria and is the terminus of a branch of the central railway line from Dar es Salaam. It's a fairly attractive town flanked by rocky hills and its port handles the cotton, tea and coffee grown in the fertile western part of the country. The Wasukuma people, who live in the area, make up the largest tribe in the country. Lake ferries go from Mwanza to the Tanzanian ports of Bukoba and Musoma and to Port Bell in Uganda.

If you'd like to explore the area further north of Mwanza, there are regular ferries from Mwanza to Ukerewe Island.

Information

Money There are two Forex bureaus in Mwanza, one of which is indicated on the map. Otherwise, the National Bank of Commerce, Nyerere Rd, changes money at much the same rates.

Sukuma Museum

About 15 km east of Mwanza on the Musoma road, the Sukuma Museum (sometimes called the Bujora Museum) was originally put together by a Quebecois missionary. Its displays are about the culture and traditions of the Wasukuma tribe. There is an excellent drum collection, and about once a week the museum puts on traditional tribal dances, including the spectacular Bugobogobo, the Sukuma Snake Dance. It's well worth enquiring in town about when the next performance is to be. Entry costs TSh 100 (or TSh 200 if you want to take photographs). To get there, take a local bus from the bus station in Mwanza to Kisessa, from where it's about a one-km walk. It's also possible to camp at the museum or rent a banda.

Places to Stay – bottom end

You can generally camp for free at the *Sukuma Museum*, but if you have no tent, there are two-bed bandas for rent. It's a lovely spot and many travellers stay here. You can also camp free of charge at the *Saba Saba Showground*, about nine km from town on the airport road, though occasionally someone will masquerade as a guard and attempt to charge you a fee. Facilities consist of a tap and toilet only. There are no showers.

In Mwanza there's quite a choice of reasonably priced hotels. One of the cheapest is the *Furaha Guest House*, near the bus station, which costs TSh 600/700 for singles/doubles. The management is friendly but the place is poor value and very noisy, with useless mosquito nets and limited water, and you need your own lock. Better, and a fairly popular place to stay, is the *Zimbabwe Guest House*, which is basic but friendly and costs TSh 700/800 for singles/doubles. It's hidden behind market stalls, so if you can't find it, ask someone where it is. It tends to be a bit noisy, as the laundry staff often work through the night. Similar in price is the *Shinyanga Guest House*, which has rooms (single or double) for TSh 800 and family rooms for TSh 1200. The *Kishinapanda Guest House*, off Uhuru St, has also been recommended in the past. It has self-contained rooms with fan and mosquito nets.

Going up in price, the *Hotel Victoria*, though run-down, has doubles for TSh 1400. The restaurant here serves good, cheap food. Behind the Victoria is the *New Victoria Annexe*, which is good value at TSh 1800 for self-contained doubles, with hot water and soap, towel and toilet paper provided. The price includes breakfast. Also good value is the *Majukano Hotel*, which offers self-contained singles/doubles for TSh 1500/2000. It's clean and mosquito nets are provided. Similar is the *Deluxe Hotel*, which has self-contained singles/doubles for TSh 1700/2000 including breakfast.

Other travellers have recommended the

To Airport

1 Immigration
2 Kishinapanda Guest House
3 Deluxe Hotel
4 Salma Cone Ice-Cream Parlour
5 Grocery Store
6 National Bank of Commerce
7 Commercial & Rural Development Bank
8 Sitar Indian Restaurant
9 Forex Bureau
10 Hotel Victoria
11 Zimbabwe Guest House
12 Zam Zam Café
13 Lake Hotel
14 New Mwanza Hotel
15 Football Stadium
16 Post Office
17 New Tivoli Hotel

Hospital

Makongora Rd

LAKE VICTORIA

Ferry to Uganda & Bukoba

Clock Tower

Uhuru St

Local Ferries

Post St

Nyerere Rd

To Musoma & Sukuma Museum (15 km)

Bus Station & Markets

Lumumba St

Station Rd

Railway Station

Kenyatta Rd

Tilapia Hotel & Sky Blue Disco

Yacht Club

Mwanza

0   250m

To Shinyanga & Tabora

TANZANIA

New Tivoli Hotel (TSh 2000 a double) and the *New Avenue Guest House*. The proprietor at the latter was described by one traveller as an 'eccentric gentleman', but it's immaculately clean, with good beds, mosquito nets and fans in all rooms. The breakfasts are basic but dinners are good deep-fried fish meals.

Places to Stay – middle
The *Lake Hotel*, on Station Rd close to the railway station, is a reasonable choice in this category. It has self-contained singles/doubles with hot showers for TSh 3500/4100 and good meals are available for around TSh 1100. Also recommended is the *Ramada Hotel*, which offers self-contained rooms (single or double) for TSh 3500.

Places to Stay – top end
The only place to stay in this category is the *New Mwanza Hotel*, at the junction of Kenyatta Rd and Post St. Self-contained singles/doubles/triples cost US$50/70/80 including breakfast, plus 25% taxes and service charges. The hotel, which is owned by the Tanzanian Tourist Corporation, has a bar and a good but expensive restaurant.

Places to Eat
There are several good, cheap local restaurants along Lumumba St. Try the *Cairo*, next to the Shinyanga Guest House. In the evenings between 5.30 and 6.30 pm, you can eat well for a song at the food stalls opposite the Hotel Victoria.

A favourite with travellers is *Al Shah's African Restaurant*, where you can get a very cheap meal of fish or meat with vegetables and potatoes or rice. At the rear of this place, a lively weekend disco (African music) costs TSh 400 entry (free if you eat there). The *Seronera Hotel*, Uhuru St, has also been recommended for excellent cheap food.

For ice cream and fruit juices, two of the best places in town are the *Salma Cone*, near the Kishinapanda Guest House, and the *Blue Café*, on Post St. The *Nile Café*, across the road from the Blue Café, does excellent coffee.

Going up in price, the *Sitar Indian Restaurant*, on the corner of Lumumba St and Nyerere Rd, does the best Indian and Chinese food in town and the service is excellent. It's been recommended by many travellers. Also good for Indian Mughlai dishes is the restaurant at the *Deluxe Hotel*.

Getting There & Away
Bus From Mwanza to Arusha there's a choice of regular buses, some of which go through the Serengeti and Ngorongoro and others which go via Shinyanga and Singida. Those which go through the national parks are quicker, but you'll be up for two national park entry fees (US$30, payable in hard currency) in addition to the bus fare. Those which go through Shinyanga take much longer and the road is bad, but there are no national park fees to pay.

Buses which go through the national parks run three times a week, cost TSh 10,000 and take 14 hours. They're operated by Bangili Bus Service. The buses via Shinyanga run five times a week, cost TSh 7000 and take up to 36 hours, though usually less. They're operated by Haji's Bus. Both types of bus run during the daytime and advance booking is advised.

To Rusumo (on the Rwandan border), there's a direct bus every Friday at 4 am (TSh 1700, up to two days). It's a diabolical road, except for one stretch of just 90 km which is sealed. For details of doing this journey in stages, see the To/From Rwanda section in the Tanzania Getting There & Away chapter.

Train There are departures for Dar es Salaam and Kigoma at 5 pm on Tuesday, Wednesday, Friday and Sunday. In the opposite direction, there are departures from both Kigoma and Dar es Salaam for Mwanza at the same time and on the same days. The journey to either normally takes 36 hours but can take 40 hours. Going from Mwanza to Kigoma involves a change at Tabora. The fares from Mwanza to Tabora are TSh 3120 (1st class), TSh 1860 (2nd class), TSh 1405 (2nd class sitting) and TSh 690 (3rd class). From Mwanza to Dar es Salaam they are TSh

11,025 (1st class), TSh 6705 (2nd class), TSh 4995 (2nd-class sitting) and TSh 2505 (3rd class).

Travelling from Mwanza to Kigoma, there are only 1st and 2nd-class reservations available as far as Tabora. Beyond that point you cannot be guaranteed a reservation in the same class on the connecting train.

Boat See the Getting Around section for details of the ferries to Bukoba and the Getting There & Away section for details of the ferries to Port Bell (Uganda).

MUSOMA

Musoma is a small port on the eastern shore of Lake Victoria, close to the Kenyan border. It's connected to Bukoba and Mwanza by lake ferry.

Places to Stay & Eat

Most travellers stay at the very clean, cheap and friendly *Mennonite Centre*. The only drawback is that it's a long way from the ferry terminal. If it's too far, try the reasonably priced *Embassy Lodge* in the town centre, or the slightly more expensive *Musambura Guest House* around the corner.

More expensive but excellent value is the *Hotel Orange Tree*, Kawawa St off Iringa St, right by the lake. It offers singles with shared bathroom for TSh 1560 and self-contained singles/doubles for TSh 2400/3100 including breakfast. There's an attached restaurant with good meals for around TSh 650.

Another mid-range hotel is the *Railway Hotel*, about half an hour's walk from the town centre. It's worth coming here for a meal whilst you're in town, even if you don't stay.

Getting There & Away

There are buses twice daily to Mwanza, at 7 am and noon. They cost TSh 800 and take about four hours.

BUKOBA

Bukoba is Tanzania's second-largest port on Lake Victoria. It's become quite a popular

overnight stop for travellers on their way from Uganda to Tanzania and then on to Rwanda since the Uganda-Rwanda border was closed two years ago. The road route between Bukoba and Masaka in Uganda via Kyaka is now well traversed as a result, but is very rough as far as the Ugandan border. There are also ferry connections between Bukoba and Mwanza on Lake Victoria.

Information

Money There are no Forex bureaus in Bukoba, so you can only change money at the bank.

Places to Stay

The cheapest place to stay is the *Nyumba wa Vijana* (youth centre), at the Evangelical Lutheran Church on the road to the hospital. A dormitory bed costs TSh 300 and you can leave your gear here safely. The *Catholic Mission* has similar facilities.

For a cheap private room, there are many budget hotels around the bus station.

You can camp in the grounds of the *Lake Hotel* but it's not particularly cheap at US$2.20 per tent.

Other than the cheapies, a good place to stay here is the *Coffee Tree Inn* (☎ 412) which has self-contained doubles for TSh 1500. Others have recommended the *New Banana Hotel*, in the centre of town just a short taxi drive from the boat dock or the airstrip.

For a mid-range hotel, try the *Lake Hotel* (☎ 237), a beautiful old colonial building with a verandah overlooking the lake. It's about two km from the town centre, past the police station and the council offices.

Getting There & Away

Bus For details of the route between Bukoba and Masaka (Uganda) via Kyaka, see the Getting There & Away chapter.

Boat See the Getting Around section for details of ferries to Mwanza. The lake ferry jetty is about 2½ km from the town centre.

Central & North-Western Tanzania

MOROGORO

Sprawling over a relatively flat valley bottom between two huge verdant walls of mountains, Morogoro is a fairly attractive town, though there's not a great deal to do here unless you're into golf (it has one of Tanzania's most highly rated courses) or trekking to the top of the mountains. It is, however, the nearest town to Mikumi National Park, so you could use it as a base for safaris to the park and thus avoid having to stay at the expensive lodge in the park itself.

There is no Forex bureau in Morogoro, so you'll have to change money at the banks if necessary.

Places to Stay – bottom end

Those on a strict budget should try the *New Plaza Hotel* (very noisy), the *Sanga Guest House* or the *Nighesha Lodging* (both quiet). All three are basic.

More expensive but a quantum leap in comfort is the *Hotel New Tegetero* (☎ 2571), on the main street and very close to the bus station. Good rooms with clean sheets cost TSh 1500 a double (no singles) with shared bathroom facilities or TSh 1800 self-contained. Breakfast is not included in the price but the hotel has its own restaurant.

Similar in standard and just a few doors up is the *Hotel Luna*, which has doubles (no singles) with shared bathroom facilities for TSh 1200 or TSh 1800 self-contained. Breakfast is extra.

At the opposite end of town but close to the railway station is the *Acropol Hotel*, which offers doubles (no singles) with shared bathroom facilities for TSh 1600 or TSh 1850 self-contained. It's an old place, but the staff are very friendly and there's a good bar and restaurant.

Places to Stay – middle

Just outside the railway station is the *New Savoy Hotel* (☎ 2345) on Station Rd, which offers self-contained doubles (no singles) for TSh 2640, but there are no fans in the rooms. It's another old place and, considering the facilities, is overpriced but it does have a popular bar and restaurant. Much better, but more expensive, is *Mama Pierina Restaurant* (☎ 7172), also on Station Rd. This is essentially a family residence for the expatriates who run the restaurant but it does have a few rooms. It offers doubles with continental breakfast for TSh 3600 but there are no fans in the rooms. The restaurant here is possibly the best in town and very popular.

Cheaper and centrally located is the *Hotel Sofia* (☎ 4848), which is popular with businesspeople. It has singles/doubles with shared bath for TSh 1500/2500 and self-contained doubles for TSh 3600. The hotel has its own bar and restaurant.

At the eastern end of town is the fairly new *Roof Garden Hotel* (☎ 4404), which offers doubles (no singles) for TSh 2800 with shared bathroom facilities or self-contained doubles for TSh 4000. It's good value, the staff are friendly and, as the name suggests, there is a rooftop bar and restaurant.

Best in this category is the *Hilux Hotel* (☎ 3066), which is set back from the road in leafy surroundings. It's quiet and has self-contained doubles for TSh 4500 including continental breakfast. The hotel has its own bar and restaurant.

Places to Stay – top end

The best place to stay in this category is the *Morogoro Hotel* (☎ 3270/2), part of the Bushtrekker group. It's an imaginatively designed building set in its own grounds opposite the golf course but is a long way from either the bus station or the railway station. It offers comfortable, self-contained singles/doubles for US$45/50 (TSh 5400/6600 for residents) and air-conditioned doubles at US$55 (TSh 7800 for residents)

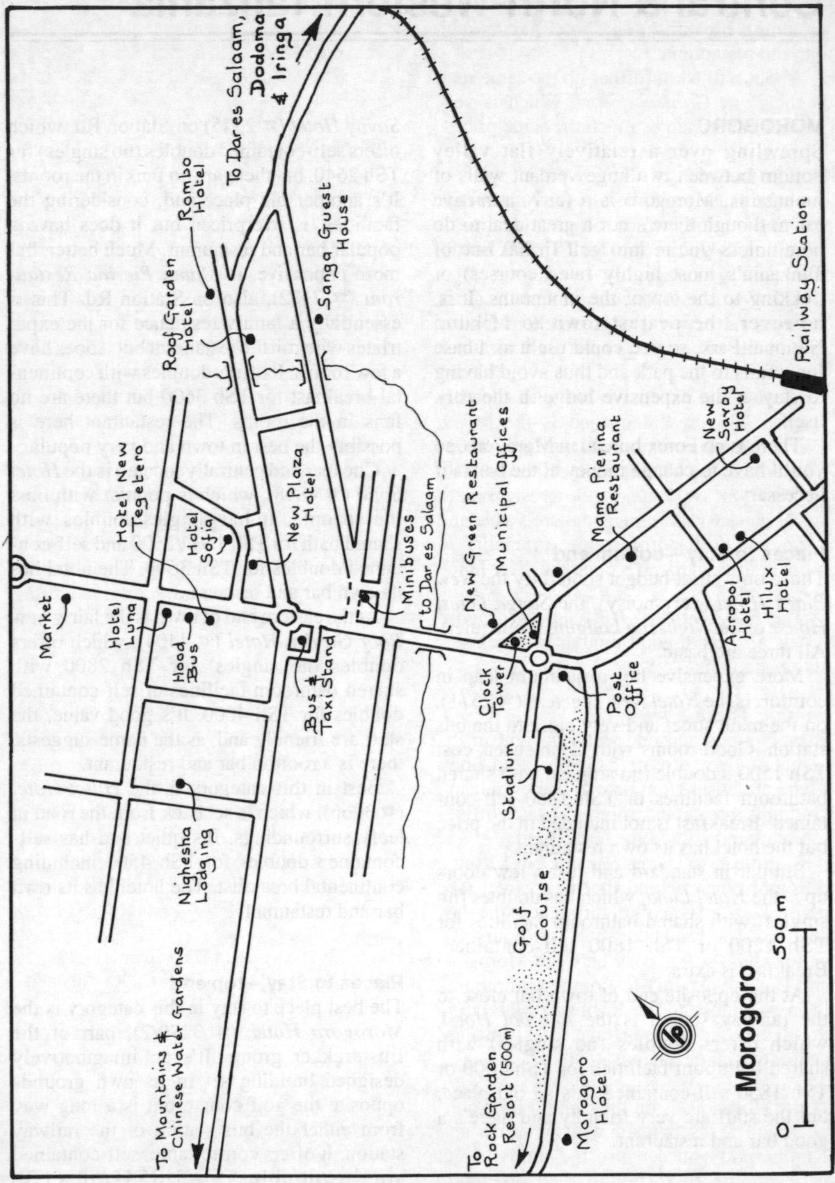

To Dar es Salaam, Dodoma & Iringa

Railway Station

Rombo Hotel

Sanga Guest House

Roof Garden Hotel

Hotel New Tegetero

New Plaza Hotel

Hotel Sofia

New Green Restaurant

Municipal Offices

Mama Pierina Restaurant

New Savoy Hotel

Acropol Hotel

Hilux Hotel

Minibuses to Dar es Salaam

Market

Hotel Luna

Hood Bus

Bus & Taxi Stand

Clock Tower

Post Office

Stadium

Nighesha Lodging

Golf Course

To Mountains & Chinese Water Gardens

To Rock Garden Resort (500m)

Morogoro Hotel

Morogoro

500 m

including breakfast. The hotel has its own bar and restaurant.

About half a km further up the same road is the *Rock Garden Resort*, which is very pleasant and charges much the same prices.

Places to Eat

A cheap place to eat here is the *Pop In* near the bus station, which offers main meals (traditional African fare) for TSh 300, but the food is only average.

The *New Green Restaurant* near the clock tower is far better. It does excellent food at reasonable prices and is open daily for lunch and dinner.

Much more expensive but with superbly cooked and presented food is the *Mama Pierina Restaurant* on Station Rd. Soups here cost TSh 440 and main dishes are TSh 1200 to TSh 1800. It's the best restaurant in town, service is prompt, and there's a bar and verandah with comfortable armchairs to relax in afterwards. It's open daily for lunch and dinner.

The *Roof Garden, Hilux* and *Morogoro* hotels also have good though fairly expensive restaurants.

Getting There & Away

Bus The bus and taxi stand is right in the centre of town, just off the main roundabout. There are buses from here to Dar es Salaam, Dodoma, Iringa and Mbeya. Ticket offices are scattered around the compound.

Minibuses to Dar es Salaam leave from a different place behind the main street (see map). They go when full throughout the day, cost TSh 1000 and take about two hours. It's an excellent sealed road between Morogoro and Dar es Salaam. Most of these minibuses drop you close to the Kariakoo Market, so you'll have to walk or take a taxi into the centre of Dar es Salaam.

Train Morogoro is on the Central Line connecting Dar es Salaam with Mwanza and Kigoma, so you can use the trains to get between the two, though they are much slower than the buses and minibuses and, if you're coming from Dar es Salaam, you

won't arrive until well after dark. Fares from Dar es Salaam are TSh 2655 (1st class), TSh 1710 (2nd class), TSh 1225 (2nd-class sitting) and TSh 655 (3rd class). See the Tanzania Getting Around section for the schedule.

DODOMA

Dodoma is the CCM party political headquarters and the official capital of Tanzania, though so far, none of the embassies and high commissions in Dar es Salaam has moved there. Nor are they likely to do so in the near future. Who would want to live there? It's a wasteland with nothing to do and minimal facilities – a far cry from the other new African capitals of Yamoussoukro (Côte d'Ivoire) and Abuja (Nigeria).

It is, however, the only wine-producing area of Africa south of Morocco/Algeria and north of South Africa. Bacchanalians shouldn't get too excited though, as Tanzanian viniculture has a long way to go before it will interest those with a taste for anything other than wine vinegar.

Places to Stay & Eat

One of the cheapest places to stay is the *Ujiji Guest House*, near the bus station. It has clean showers and toilets, provides mosquito nets and costs TSh 500 a single. Also within walking distance of town is the *Horombo Malazi*, Nyumba wa Wagena, a simple local guesthouse where you can get a cheap double room. The owner is friendly and you'll probably be the only wazungu there.

The best value, however, is the *Christian Council of Tanzania Guest House* (ask people for the 'CCT'), which has double rooms with a cold shower, towels and mosquito nets for TSh 1120 including *one* continental breakfast. The canteen serves reasonable meals for about TSh 400 (omelette and chips).

Somewhat more expensive is the *Jamboree Hotel & Restaurant*, which is friendly, good value and costs TSh 1350/2600 for singles/doubles including breakfast.

The *Central Province Hotel* (☎ 21177) is also a reasonable place to stay. To get there, leave the front entrance of the railway station and turn right along the road running parallel with the tracks. Continue to the first roundabout and turn right. Walk to the next roundabout and turn right again. The hotel is 50 metres down the first street on the left.

For a top-end hotel, the *Dodoma Hotel* offers self-contained doubles for US$35. Its restaurant serves excellent breakfasts and dinners. The bar is a popular hang-out for local people and expatriates.

Getting There & Away
Bus The daily bus to Arusha departs at 9.30 am, costs TSh 1600 and takes about 15 hours. It's operated by Sahib bus service and tickets can be bought from the office opposite the Caltex station. Book a day in advance. The road is diabolical.

Train The railway line from Dar es Salaam to Kigoma/Mwanza runs through Dodoma. See the Tanzania Getting Around section for details of the schedule. Fares from Dar es Salaam are TSh 6790 (1st class), TSh 2980 (2nd class), TSh 2185 (2nd-class sitting) and TSh 1125 (3rd class).

TABORA
Tabora is a railway junction town where the Central Line branches for Mwanza and Kigoma. You may have to stay the night if you're changing trains and can't get immediate onward reservations.

If you have time to spare, there is a small museum in one of Livingstone's former homes, just outside town.

Places to Stay & Eat
The *Moravian Guest House* is probably the best place to stay and is exceptionally cheap. It's pleasant and the staff are friendly.

As far as hotels go, the *Vatican Guest House, Deluxe Guest House* and the *Golden Eagle Guest House* are all reasonable places to stay at around TSh 1000 a double.

An English woman who worked here for a year highly recommends the *Hotel Wilca* (☎ 3488), which is in the centre of town about half a km from the railway station. It

offers self-contained doubles with hot water for TSh 2000, including breakfast, and it has its own bar, restaurant and garden. The restaurant does excellent beef masala for TSh 400, including rice or chips. The owner, William Camara, is a very friendly and helpful man who loves a conversation.

If you'd like more creature comforts, try the more expensive *Railway Hotel*. It is an attractive building with some lovely old rooms but otherwise has little to offer.

Getting There & Away
Train The railway line north-west of Dar es Salaam splits at Tabora, one line continuing west to Kigoma on Lake Tanganyika, the other heading north to Mwanza on Lake Victoria. See the Getting Around section for details of departures. The fares from Dar es Salaam are TSh 7905 (1st class), TSh 4845 (2nd class), TSh 3590 (2nd-class sitting) and TSh 1815 (3rd class).

KIGOMA
Kigoma is the most important Tanzanian port on Lake Tanganyika and is the terminus of the railway from Dar es Salaam. Many travellers come through here en route to or coming from Bujumbura (Burundi) or Mpulungu (Zambia) on the Lake Tanganyika steamer MV *Liemba*. It's a small but pleasant town, its one main street lined with huge, shady mango trees. Life ticks over at a slow pace. If you get stuck waiting for the train (a few days is not uncommon) or the boat (a day or two), you'll have to amuse yourself with walks around town and visits to Ujiji. There's very little of interest in the Kigoma township, but it's a good base for visits to Gombe Stream National Park (see the Northern Tanzania & National Parks chapter).

Don't bother trying to climb any of the hills that flank the town in search of a view – these are military zones and are off limits to mere mortals. The best (accessible) view of the town is from outside the new church, which is just to the left of the main road as you head up the hill towards Muwanga.

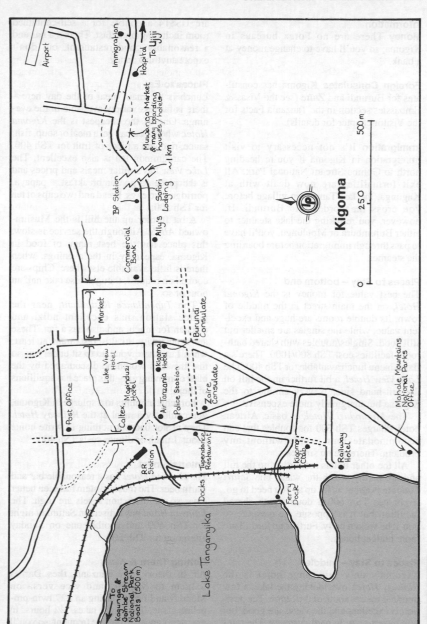

Kigoma

500 m

250

To Ujiji

Airport

Immigration

Hospital

Mwananza Market & many boarding houses/hotels

1 km

BP Station

Ally's Safari Lodging

Commercial Bank

Market

Lake View Hotel

Caltex

Majinduzi Hotel

Post Office

Air Tanzania Hotel

Kigoma Hotel

Police Station

Burundi Consulate

Zaire Consulate

Mahale Mountains National Parks Office

Tupendance Restaurant

RR Station

Docks

Kigoma Club

Railway Hotel

Ferry Dock

Lake Tanganyika

To Kagunga & Gombe Stream National Park Boats (500 m)

TANZANIA

Information
Money There are no Forex bureaus in Kigoma, so you'll have to change money at a bank.

Foreign Consulates Kigoma has consulates for Burundi and Zaïre (see the Visas & Embassies section in the Tanzania Facts for the Visitor chapter for details).

Immigration It's not necessary to visit immigration in Kigoma if you're heading north to Gombe Stream National Park. All exit formalities are now dealt with at Kagunga, the last Tanzanian village before you cross the border into Burundi. If, however, you're taking the lake steamer to either Bujumbura or Mpulungu, you'll have to pass through immigration before boarding the steamer.

Places to Stay – bottom end
The best value for money is the *Kigoma Hotel*, on the main street in the middle of town. Its double rooms are huge and excellent value, while the singles are smaller but still good. Singles/doubles with shared bathroom facilities cost TSh 800/1000. There's a fixed-menu lunch available for TSh 400. The *Lake View Hotel*, a bit further up the hill on the left-hand side, is very similar to the Kigoma but marginally more expensive.

The *Mapinduzi Hotel*, a basic African hotel, charges TSh 500 for doubles that can accommodate four people without any problem. There are no singles.

All the other hotels are further up the hill and are hardly worth the walk. The *Safari Lodging* is about as far up as you need to go. It charges TSh 600 a double with shared facilities, but it is opposite the mosque, so you'll be woken early. Further up the hill are more budget hotels.

Places to Stay – middle
Kigoma's only mid-range hotel is the *Railway Hotel*, overlooking the lake, a few hundred metres south of the centre. The position is excellent and the views are good, but you have to pay in hard currency. The rates

are US$14 a double for a self-contained room including breakfast. There's a bar and a reasonably good restaurant, but don't expect anything fancy.

Places to Eat
Lunch is the main meal of the day here – there is far less variety available in the evenings. One of the cheapest is the *Kigoma Hotel*, where you can get a meal of soup, fish, sauce, rice and a piece of fruit for TSh 400. The cardammon tea is also excellent. The *Lake View* has similar meals and prices and is the place to go for breakfast – papaya, porridge, two eggs, bread and two cups of tea for TSh 300.

A bit further up the hill is the Muslim-owned *Ally's*. Although the service is slow, this place has the best range of food in Kigoma, especially in the evenings, when there is little available elsewhere. Chips are cooked on request, though these take half an hour or so.

The *Tupendance Restaurant*, near the police station, has excellent ndizi and chicken for lunch, and also has a fan. These are a necessity, in this restaurant at least; when I ate there you had to sit under one so that the flies would be discouraged by the blast of moving air – this place has squillions of them!

For what amounts to a splurge in Kigoma, you could try a meal at the *Railway Hotel*. They're not bad but nothing to write home about. Lunch or dinner costs TSh 400.

Entertainment
The *Kigoma Hotel* has a reasonable bar and warm beer. The music system has seen better days, so the distortion levels are high. The *Railway Hotel* has a disco on Saturday night for TSh 400 and another one on Sunday afternoon for TSh 200.

Getting There & Away
Air In theory, Air Tanzania flies Dar es Salaam to Kigoma and vice versa on Monday and Friday, using an F27 twin-propellor plane. The flight takes 3¾ hours. In practice, cancellations are frequent, so you'll

have to play it by ear and make sure you have a reservation.

If you're coming from Burundi and want to fly to Dar es Salaam from Kigoma, you can make a reservation in advance in Bujumbura. You pay for the flight in Kigoma.

Train There are departures at 5 pm on Tuesday, Wednesday, Friday and Sunday for Dar es Salaam and Mwanza. The journey normally takes about 36 hours but can take 40 hours.

The fares from Kigoma to Dar es Salaam are TSh 11,190 (1st class), TSh 6805 (2nd class), TSh 5070 (2nd class sitting) and TSh 2540 (3rd class). See the Chief Booking Clerk at the station in Kigoma for 1st-class bookings. The train is often booked out in 1st and 2nd class, but with persistence you can usually get a booking, at least as far as Tabora. From there you're at the mercy of the travelling ticket examiner on the train. He will try to find you a berth on to Dar es Salaam or Dodoma, but this is not always possible, in which case you'll end up in 3rd class for the night.

Bus & Truck The buses in this area only serve local towns, but it is possible to find trucks to Mwanza if you are prepared to wait a few days. Ask around in the shops on the main street.

Ferry For details of the MV *Liemba's* services to Mpulungu and Bujumbura, see the Tanzania Getting There & Away chapter.

The 'dock' for lake taxis to the Gombe Stream National Park is about an hour's walk up the railway tracks from the station.

Getting Around
Air Tanzania runs a minibus from their office in town to the airport about 1½ hours before flight departures. There's a small charge.

UJIJI
Down the lake shore from Kigoma, Ujiji is one of Africa's oldest market villages and is a good deal more interesting than Kigoma. This is where the famous words 'Dr Livingstone, I presume' were spoken by the explorer and journalist Henry Stanley. There's the inevitable plaque at the site where this event is alleged to have occurred; there is a similar plaque in Burundi! The site is to the right of the main road (when coming from Kigoma), down the side street next to the Bin Tunia Restaurant – just ask for Livingstone and the bus driver will make sure you get off at the right place.

The two mango trees growing in the walled compound at the site are said to have been grafted from the original tree growing there when the two men met. There's also a museum, which houses a few pictorial representations by local artists of Livingstone's time here. The pictures bear captions such as: 'Dr Livingstone sitting under the mango tree in Ujiji thinking about slavery'. Entry costs TSh 200, which seems to go straight into the caretaker's pocket.

About 500 metres past the compound along the same street is the beach and the local boat builders. This seems to be a thriving local industry, and there may be as many as a dozen boats in various stages of construction. No power tools are used and construction methods have hardly changed in generations.

Places to Stay
The *Matunda Guest House*, on the main street, is a cosy place to stay and costs TSh 400 a double.

Getting There & Away
There are frequent buses to Ujiji from outside the railway station in Kigoma. The fare is TSh 30.

Southern Tanzania

MBEYA

Mbeya lies in a gap between the verdant Mbeya mountain ranges to the north and the Uporoto Mountains to the south-east. It was founded in 1927 as a supply centre for the gold rush at Lupa (to the north) but is now an important staging centre on the main road and TAZARA railway between Tanzania and Zambia. Many travellers also stay here overnight en route to Malawi via the Songwe river bridge to Karonga.

The surrounding area is very fertile, with banana, tea, coffee and cocoa plantations, and though few travellers seem to stay more than a night, there are many places of interest in the vicinity.

Things to See & Do

Kaluwe For those with just a day to spare, it's worth climbing this 2834-metre peak in the Mbeya Range, which overlooks the town to the north. The views from the top are amazing, though it's probably wise to stay away from the radio mast or people might think you're a spy. To get there, head from the roundabout towards the waterworks but turn left before you reach the gates, along a gravel track (about 150 metres from the roundabout). You will pass a quarry on the right-hand side after 50 metres or so and then a few houses below a eucalypt forest. The track then goes to the left of a clearing where maize is grown. From there, follow one of the paths which go to the mountain top. It will take about two hours to get to the top.

Ngozi This 2621-metre volcanic peak in the Uporoto Mountains is to the east of the Mbeya to Tukuyu road and is well worth the attention of enthusiastic hikers. Other than the hike up to the summit, which takes you through thick rainforest and out onto alpine heathland, you'll be rewarded on the summit with a view of the Ngozi Crater Lake, some 2½ km long by 1½ km wide, surrounded by sheer cliffs dropping 200 metres down to the lake. Ngozi is approached from a track off the main road, and you'd be advised to engage a local guide. The walk to the summit should take about two hours.

Natural Bridge & Kijungu A little further south and, again, off the Mbeya to Tukuyu road is the Natural Bridge, which spans a small waterfall. Estimated to have been formed some 1800 million years ago by water flowing through cooling lava spewed out from the nearby erupting Rungwe Volcano, it is situated eight km from Kiwira Prison College. A further three km up the steep gorge from the Natural Bridge is Kijungu ('cooking pot'), where the entire Kiwira River tumbles into a seething sump in the riverbed. It's an impressive sight, even during the rainy season when the river overflows its banks.

Places to Stay – bottom end

If at all possible, you should arrive early in the day, as places fill up rapidly by late afternoon. One of the most popular places to stay is the *Moravian Youth Hostel* on Jacaranda Rd. It's excellent value, clean and friendly and costs TSh 600 a double, but there are no meals available. A similar place, but a considerable distance from the centre of town, is the *Karibu Centre*, 500 metres off the Tanzam Highway in Forest Area. It's run by Swiss missionaries and is very clean and friendly, though alcoholic drinks are prohibited on the premises. According to local people, it has the best food in town.

There are many other cheap lodges scattered around town but they're mostly basic. One which is good value is the *Nkwenzulu Hotel*, opposite the bus station on Mbalizi Rd, which has doubles with shared bath for TSh 1100 and self-contained doubles for TSh 1700. The rooms are spacious but there are only cold showers available. There's a bar, and a restaurant which serves good, cheap food. Also pretty good value is the *Central Visitors' Lodge* on Waseni St.

Further out to the east, near the junction of Sokoine Stadium Rd and Lumumba Ave, the Asian-run *Holiday Inn* is clean and good value, at TSh 1000 a double. Mosquito nets are provided. It's been recently renovated and has a good restaurant.

Places to Stay – middle

Not far from the Holiday Inn, just 100 metres off Lumumba Ave on Chunya Rd, is the *New Joseph Hotel*, which is highly recommended by local people. It's in the lower mid-range category.

Going up in price, there's the *Mbeya Hotel*, at the junction of Lumumba and Karume (Kaunda) Aves. This is owned by Tanzania Railways Corporation and is a pleasant, colonial-style hotel with comfortable rooms, clean sheets, mosquito nets and hot showers. Self-contained singles/doubles cost US$10/14 (payable in hard currency) including breakfast. There are also cheaper rooms with shared bathroom facilities. The hotel has a bar, and a restaurant which serves good food for TSh 600.

Places to Stay – top end

Top of the line are three hotels which offer amentities and cuisine comparable to other top-end hotels throughout Tanzania. They are the *Mt Livingstone Hotel, Mbeya Peak Hotel* and *Rift Valley Hotel*. You're looking at around US$35 to US$45 a double at any of them. They're all fairly close to the town centre and all have bars and restaurants.

Places to Eat

Most of the good bars and restaurants are in the above-mentioned hotels, though there others in the town centre, close to the market and bus station.

The Tanzanian Coffee Board has a coffee shop on the corner of the market square, where you can get a good cup of coffee for a few shillings.

Getting There & Away

Bus There are five daily express buses between Mbeya and Dar es Salaam via Iringa and Morogoro (TSh 2500, 20 hours). The road is rough as far as Morogoro, after which it's an excellent sealed road. Zainabs bus company has been recommended as being fast and comfortable. Advance booking is essential. The Dar es Salaam to Mbeya road goes through the Mikumi National Park, and there's a lot of game visible during the day, including elephant, giraffe, zebra and gazelle.

For details on the trip from Mbeya to Karonga (Malawi), see the To/From Malawi section in the Tanzania Getting There & Away chapter.

Train Trains on the TAZARA railway to Dar es Salaam or Kapiri Mposhi (Zambia) are heavily booked, so make a reservation well in advance (see the Train section in the Tanzania Getting Around chapter for details of the schedule). Fares between Mbeya and Dar es Salaam are TSh 7930 (1st class), TSh 5350 (2nd class) and TSh 2230 (3rd class), or TSh 8380 (1st class), TSh 5800 (2nd class) and TSh 2670 (3rd class) on the express train. Reservations can be made at the railway station, or at the Tanzania Railways Corporation office in town, at the junction of Station Rd and Post St.

KYELA

If it's early in the day and you're on your way to the Malawi border, there's no need to come to Kyela, as the turn-off to the border is about five km back up the road towards Mbeya. From the turn-off, it's seven km to the border, which is open until 6 pm. If it's late, you may have to stay the night at Kyela.

Places to Stay

The *Ram Hotel*, not far from the bus stand, is excellent value at TSh 600 a double with clean sheets and mosquito nets. The hotel has its own generator (so there are lights after dark) and good food is available. The *Salaam Hotel*, on the main road, has beds for TSh

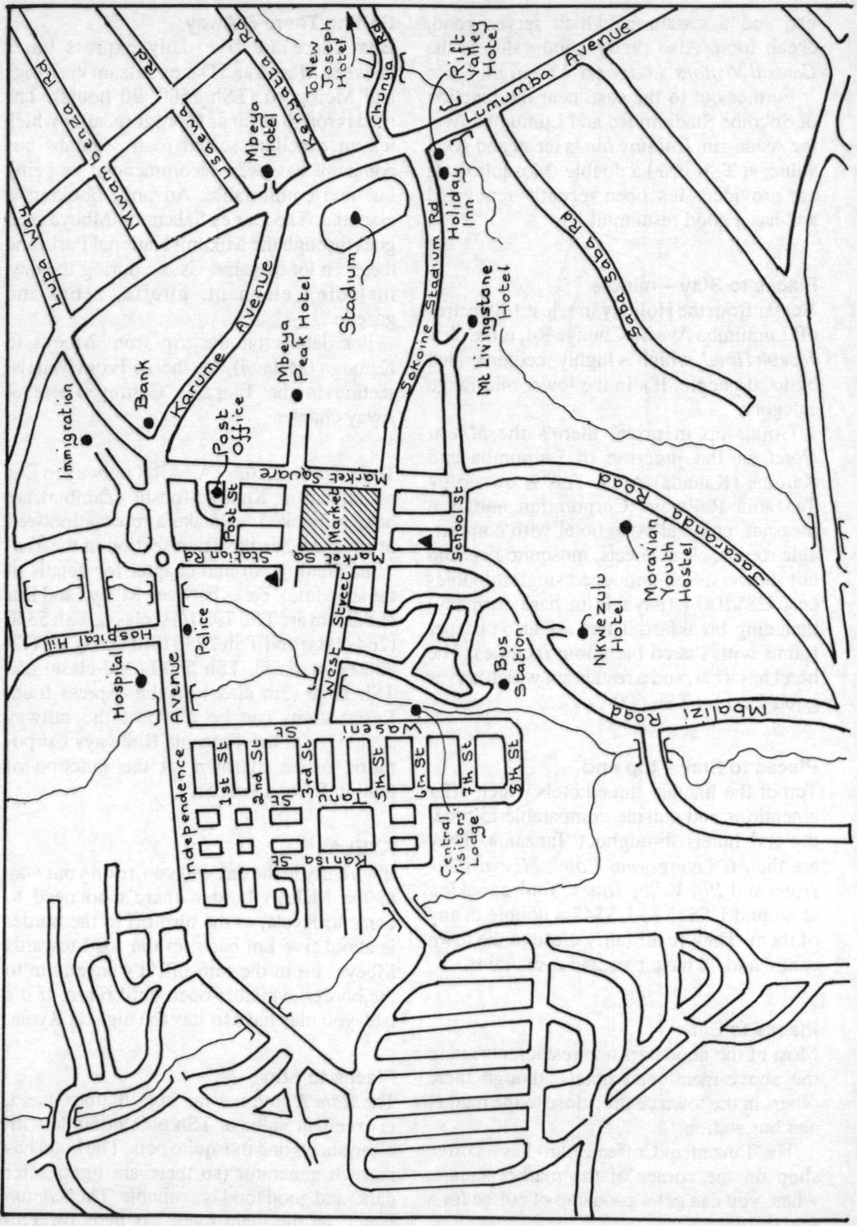
Lupa Way
Mwambenza Rd
Kenyatta Rd
To New Joseph Hotel
Chunya Rd
Rift Valley Hotel
Lumumba Avenue
Mbeya Hotel
Holiday Inn
Stadium
Sokoine Stadium Rd
Saba Saba Rd
Karume Avenue
Mbeya Peak Hotel
Mt Livingstone Hotel
Immigration
Bank
Post Office
Market Square
Post St
Market
Station Rd
Market Sq
West Street
School St
Jacaranda Road
Moravian Youth Hostel
Hospital Hill
Police
Hospital
Independence Avenue
Nkwezulu Hotel
Bus Station
Mbalizi Road
Maseni St
1st St
2nd St
3rd St
Tanu St
5th St
6th St
7th St
8th St
Kanisa St
Central Visitors Lodge

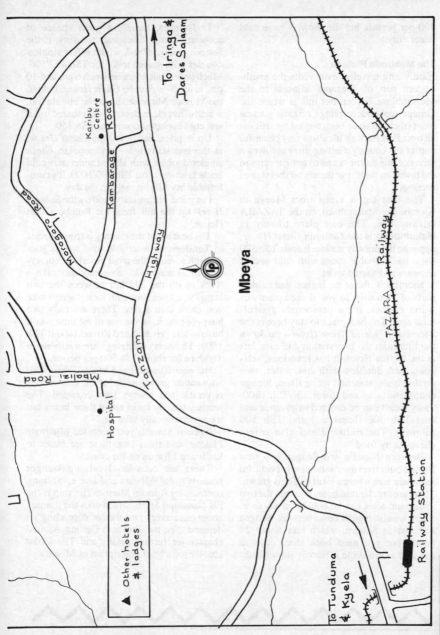

To Iringa & Dar es Salaam

Karibu Centre

Kambarage Road

Morogoro Road

Mbeya

Highway

Tanzam

Mbalizi Road

Hospital

TAZARA Railway

Railway Station

To Tunduma & Kyela

▲ Other hotels & lodges

400 per person, but the showers have cold water only.

The Makonde Plateau

Hardly any traveller ever visits the south-eastern part of Tanzania adjacent to the Mozambique border, but this is where the famous makonde carvings originally came from (they've since been copied by artisans all over East Africa). It's also a very beautiful part of the country. Getting there involves a series of bus journeys and overnight stays in the towns en route, but there's no shortage of transport.

The first leg is a bus from Mbeya to Njombe via Makumbako, on the TAZARA railway line. The best place to stay in **Makumbako** is the *Lutheran Guest House*, opposite the railway station. It costs TSh 500 for a basic double room with cold bucket showers and shared toilet.

Njombe is one of the highest and coldest parts of Tanzania, so you'll need plenty of warm clothes. It's a prosperous agricultural area. The best place to stay here is the *Njomba Highland Green Hotel* – go down the hill from the bus station and turn left at the Eidina Hotel. It has luxurious, self-contained doubles with hot water, two double beds, starched white linen, lounge chairs and soap and towel, for TSh 1800. Tasty meals can be ordered in advance and cost TSh 300 (breakfast) and TSh 500 (dinner). The *Eidina Hotel* also offers cheap, tasty food.

Between Njombe and Songea is a new British-built road over a stunningly beautiful mountain area where a lot of coffee is grown. There are regular minibuses between the two towns and seats can be booked in advance. There are also regular buses between Songea and Dar es Salaam, which take about 24 hours, but you must book three days in advance as this route is heavily subscribed.

In **Songea**, there's a good choice of accommodation. Cheapest, but dirty, is the *Songea Deluxe Hotel*, which offers singles/doubles with shared toilet for TSh 450/500. Much better, but noisy between 6 am and 10 pm, is the *New Rombo Guest House*, behind the Mossile Music studio at the bus station, which offers clean doubles with shared toilet and cold bucket showers for TSh 750.

Up in price, the *New Nipu Guest House*, at the bus station, is very popular. Clean singles/doubles with shared toilet and cold bucket showers cost TSh 800/1000. It's comfortable but fills up early in the day.

For good, cheap, tasty food try the *Salama Hotel*, up the hill from the Rombo Guest House.

The next leg of the journey is from Songea to **Tunduru** on a terrible road which goes through some of the most deserted countryside in Tanzania. It can sometimes take a week to do the 272 km between the two towns in a truck, but with luck it won't take you more than a day. There are only two buses per week, so the rest of the time you'll have to hire private Land Rovers (about TSh 1500, 12 hours). Lodgings are available in Tunduru for about TSh 500 per person.

Between Tunduru and Masasi, there's an all-weather gravel road, but the bus service is erratic and always very crowded. The journey usually takes about three hours but it can occasionally take 10.

Once at Masasi, you're on the Makonde Plateau, and from here there are buses to Lindi and Mtwara on the coast.

There are occasional cargo/passenger boats between Mtwara and Dar es Salaam, operated by Adecon Marine. The ship is the FB *Canadian Spirit*, which does the journey about once every two weeks, depending on demand. See the Tanzania Getting Around chapter for further details and The Coast chapter for a brief description of Mtwara.

National Parks

Kenya may well have the better-stocked game parks, and easier access to them, but Tanzania has the world famous Serengeti National Park and Ngorongoro Crater, with the Olduvai Gorge sandwiched between them. It also has Mt Kilimanjaro. Less famous but no less of a drawcard are Arusha, Tarangire and Lake Manyara national parks. All of these are within striking distance of Arusha, though Kilimanjaro is generally more easily approached from Moshi.

Serengeti has a huge animal population, and they're easy to see in the flat grassland of the park, especially in the dry season. At Ngorongoro, the park is in the crater of a huge extinct volcano, which is said to be the world's largest caldera.

Tanzania has many other national parks, but getting to those in the more remote western or southern parts of the country can be problematical, expensive or both. Accommodation at these more remote parks also tends to be limited if you're not camping. This doesn't mean that they're not worth the effort – they certainly are, especially the Selous Game Reserve, which is Tanzania's largest park. The Selous was also the very first game park to be set up in Tanzania, yet it remains a vast wilderness with facilities available only on the north-eastern fringes.

The partial border closure with Kenya which began in 1977 and lasted until the mid-1980s did a great deal of damage to Tanzania's tourist industry. During that period, tourist facilities were nowhere near as numerous or as easily accessible as Kenya's, except in the northern parks and game reserves. This all quickly changed once the border was reopened. Since then, safari companies mushroomed and there's a wide variety of both budget and luxury safaris to choose from. The industry was given an extra fillip during 1991 and 1992 due to political tensions and violence in Kenya, during which time many visitors preferred Tanzania over Kenya.

The national parks are open from 6 am to 7 pm. You are not permitted to drive in the parks at any other time.

Conservation & Wildlife Groups

If you want to get involved in anti-poaching measures and conservation activities in Tanzania (and help is needed in a big way), contact either the Tanzania Wildlife Protection Fund, PO Box 1994, Dar es Salaam, or the African Wildlife Foundation, PO Box 48177, Nairobi, Kenya (also 1717 Massachusetts Ave NW, Washington DC 20036, USA). The Wildlife Conservation Society of Tanzania, PO Box 70919, Dar es Salaam, does similar work.

All these societies do their best to protect wildlife and their habitats, help the recovery of endangered animal and plant species, and fund research into the management of wildlife and the impact of human beings on their habitats. Enquiries are welcome.

Park Entry Fees

All national park fees must be paid in hard currency (cash or travellers' cheques) unless you are a Tanzanian resident, in which case you pay in local currency. The following fees are for each 24-hour period or part thereof:

Fees	Nonresident	Resident
Adult entry	US$20	TSh 5000
Vehicle entry (up to 2000 kg)	US$30	TSh 1000
Vehicle entry (over 2000 kg)	US$150	TSh 10,000
Camping (established sites)	US$20	TSh 5000
Camping ('special' sites)	US$40	TSh 10,000
Guide (where appropriate)	US$10	TSh 500

Entry for children between the ages of five and 16 years is US$5 (TSh 1000 for residents), and for those under three years of age is free. Camping costs US$5 (TSh 500) for

Tanzania – National Parks & Game Reserves

children in established sites, US$10 (TSh 2000) in 'special sites'.

The only exception to this fee structure is at the Gombe Stream National Park on Lake Tanganyika, where the park entry fee is US$100, or TSh 10,000 for residents (the fees for children are US$20 and TSh 3000, respectively).

Charges for vehicle recovery in the event of an accident are TSh 50,000 (up to 2000 kg) and TSh 100,000 (over 2000 kg).

On Mt Kilimanjaro and Mt Meru, there are additional fees for use of mountain huts, rescue fees and fees for guides and porters, but these are specific to those national parks (see under relevant sections for details).

Foreigners must pay the above fees in hard currency (cash or travellers' cheques), and it's important to bear in mind that if you don't have the exact amount in hard currency to pay these fees, the park officials are entitled to give you the change in local currency at the official rate of exchange (ie not at Forex rates). Usually, they're more accommodating than this *if* you pay in cash dollars. If that's the case, you can usually arrange for the change to be paid in cash dollars, *if* they have it. Rather than assume this, it's better to sort this out between yourselves before you arrive at a park entry gate.

You may well hear (as we do) of travellers who have managed to negotiate part or all payment in local currency at some entry gates. You can safely assume that they've been very lucky. At most entry gates, attempting to do this would simply be a waste of time.

You should also take heed of the warning in the Organised Safaris section of the Getting Around chapter regarding companies which cater for budget travellers and their commitment to pay park entry fees as part of the price of a safari. Some are banned from entering the parks because their cheques have bounced.

Books & Maps

In contrast to the mid-1980s, there's now a considerable amount of literature available on the various national parks. The best is a series of booklets written in association with the Tanzania National Parks, the African Wildlife Foundation or the Wildlife Conservation Society of Tanzania. These are priced between TSh 1000 and TSh 1500 and include detailed descriptions of the national parks, their geography, flora & fauna and tourist facilities, and include sketches and maps. The series includes *Kilimanjaro National Park, Ngorongoro Conservation Area, Serengeti National Park, Tarangire National Park, Arusha National Park, Mikumi National Park* and *Gombe Stream National Park*. These booklets are available at the bookshops of the large hotels in Arusha and Dar es Salaam and sometimes at park entry gates.

Another excellent booklet which covers all of the national parks and includes maps and sketches is *A Guide to Tanzania National Parks* (Travel Promotion Services Ltd, 1988), by Lilla N Lyogello. It costs only TSh 70, which is an absolute bargain – if you can find it. It seemed to be out of print in 1993.

There's also an excellent large-scale (1:250,000) map of Serengeti National Park and Ngorongoro Crater put out by the Frankfurt Zoological Society (TSh 3500). It's very useful if you're driving your own vehicle and don't know the park.

Getting There & Around

You can safely assume that attempting to hitch into the national parks is a complete waste of time. You may well be able to get to the entry gates of the most popular parks but it's very unlikely you'll get any further, and the only parks you are allowed to walk in are Selous, Mahale and Gombe Stream. Most people arriving at a park entry gate will be either part of an organised safari group (in which case you've got next to no chance) or in their own vehicle (in which case they probably have lodge bookings and/or are loaded to the roof with supplies and camping equipment, etc, so they'll be extremely reluctant to overload the vehicle with you and your gear or get involved in complications about where you're going to stay).

This being so, there are basically only two

ways to visit a national park: go on an organised safari, bring your own vehicle or rent your own vehicle.

KILIMANJARO NATIONAL PARK

An almost perfectly shaped volcano which rises sheer from the plains, Mt Kilimanjaro is one of the African continent's most magnificent sights. Snowcapped and not yet extinct, at 5895 metres it is the highest peak in Africa.

From cultivated farmlands on the lower levels, it rises through lush rainforest onto alpine meadow and finally across a barren lunar landscape to the summit. The rainforest is home to many animals, including elephants, buffaloes, rhinos, leopards and monkeys. You may encounter herds of eland on the saddle between the summits of Mawenzi and Kibo.

History

Geologically, Kilimanjaro is a relative newcomer to the Rift Valley and didn't even exist between one and two million years ago. At that time, where Kilimanjaro now stands there was just an undulating plain with a few old eroded mountains. But that all changed with movements of the earth's crust associated with the rift. Lava poured out from the fractures that were created and eventually gave rise to an enormous ridge, which is now represented by the nearby peaks of Ol Molog, Kibongoto and Kilema.

Kilimanjaro began to grow about 750,000 years ago as a result of lava spewing out of three main centres – Shira, Kibo and Mawenzi. It kept growing until their cones reached a height of about 5000 metres about half a million years ago. About this time, Shira collapsed into a caldera and became inactive, but Kibo and Mawenzi continued to erupt until their peaks reached about 5500 metres. Mawenzi was the next to die, but Kibo continued to be active until about 360,000 years ago, during which time there were some particularly violent eruptions, including one which filled the old eroded caldera of Shira with black lava.

From an estimated final height of 5900 metres, Kibo gradually fell silent, and though intermittent eruptions continued for thousands of years, the whole mountain began to shrink and Kibo's cone collapsed into a series of concentric terraces. Erosion, in the form of glaciers which came and went, wore the peaks down even more, as did a huge landslide about 100,000 years ago which created the Kibo Barranco.

Kibo finally died after a last fling of violent activity which created the present caldera and the lava flows known as the Inner Crater and Ash Pit. Then the glaciers returned to continue their work. Meanwhile, the forests and alpine vegetation claimed what they could of the mountain, and streams sculpted the sides of the massif into the shape it is now. Interestingly, it appears that Kilimanjaro, like Mt Kenya, is gradually losing its glaciers.

Climbing Kilimanjaro

Kilimanjaro can be climbed at any time of year, but there's usually a lot of rain during April, May and November. It's also best to avoid climbing during the Christmas/New Year period, as all the huts will be fully booked.

It is a traveller's dream to scale the summit, watch the dawn break and gaze out over vast expanses of East African bushland. Who would come to East Africa and not climb Kilimanjaro? Certainly not many, but you should know that it's going to cost you between US$320 and US$380 for a standard five-day climb along the Marangu route (plus US$70 to US$80 for each additional day). These costs include park entry fees, hut fees, rescue fees, food, guide, porters and, usually, transport to Marangu but exclude the hire of camping gear and clothing/footwear. The bulk of this is payable in hard currency – cash or travellers' cheques – as it represents national park fees. See later in this section for a list of tour companies.

Safety Too many people try to scale Mt Kilimanjaro without sufficient acclimatisation and end up with altitude sickness or, at the very least, nausea and headaches. This is

Kilimanjaro National Park

obviously going to detract from your enjoyment of going up there and prevents quite a few people from reaching the summit. Scaling a 5895-metre mountain is no joy ride!

To give yourself the best chance of reaching the top, it's a very good idea to stay at the Horombo Hut for two nights instead of one, though this will not guarantee you plain sailing. You won't get the same benefits from staying two nights at the Kibo Hut, as it's too high and you won't be able sleep very much. Remember the old mountaineering adage: 'Go high, sleep low'. Also, whatever else you do, walk *pole pole*, drink a lot of liquid, suck glucose tablets and don't eat too much (you won't feel like eating much anyway). Other travellers recommend taking Diamox (usually prescribed for elderly patients to treat glaucoma). It's useful in treating altitude sickness. Staying two nights at the Horombo Hut is going to make the trek into a six-day affair and increase your costs, so bear this in mind and make sure that the guides and porters understand what you have in mind before setting off.

There's a very funny but accurate description of what it's like climbing Kilimanjaro in Mark Savage's *Kilimanjaro – Map & Guide*. Make sure you read it!

Books & Maps The best map of Kilimanjaro is *Kilimanjaro – Map & Guide* (1:75,000), by Andrew Wielochowski. It has an excellent topographical map of Kilimanjaro on one side and details of the geology, flora & fauna, weather and climate, history, walking and climbing routes on the other side. Similar is *Kilimanjaro – Map & Guide* (1:50,000), by Mark Savage, except that this cuts off the trail heads. Both are available from most bookshops in Nairobi, or you may be able to get one or the other from the bookshop in the New Arusha Hotel in Arusha.

An excellent booklet to take on your trek is *Kilimanjaro National Park* (1987), written by Jeanette Hanby in association with the Tanzania National Parks and the African Wildlife Foundation. It contains descriptions of all the possible routes up Kilimanjaro, the climate, flora & fauna, mountain medicine and tourist facilities, complete with maps and illustrations. It's for sale in Arusha (at bookshops in the large hotels) and in Dar es Salaam.

For those intending to rock climb, as opposed to walk, the *Guide to Mt Kenya & Kilimanjaro* (Mountain Club of Kenya, 1981), edited by Iain Allan, is also worth chasing up, though it's presently out of print. You may be able to get a copy from the Mountain Club of Kenya (PO Box 45741, Nairobi) or from bookshops in Nairobi. You will not be able to buy it in Tanzania.

For any other information, get in touch with the Kilimanjaro Mountain Club, PO Box 66, Moshi, Tanzania.

Clothing & Equipment No specialist equipment is required to climb Kilimanjaro but you do need a strong pair of good boots, and plenty of warm clothing, including gloves, a woollen hat and waterproof overclothes. You also need a sleeping bag and small mattress or air bed. If you lack any of these, they can be hired from the two hotels in Marangu village or at the park entrance. Approximate costs are:

sleeping bag	TSh 500
boots	TSh 500
sweater	TSh 400
raincoat	TSh 400
rain trousers	TSh 400
dacron jacket	TSh 400
water bottle	TSh 200
gloves	TSh 200
balaclava	TSh 400

These fees are for a five-day trek and your passport will have to be left as a deposit. The gear, from all accounts, is of reasonable quality.

If the huts are fully booked you'll have to camp, and if that's the case, make absolutely sure there are sufficient tents and sleeping bags for all of you *before* setting off.

Organising Your Own Climb
This is doing it the hard way! You won't save much money over what's on offer in Moshi

from the cheapest outfits and you'll have to do a lot of running around, including buying and transporting food from Moshi and arranging transport to the park entry gate plus, where necessary, hiring equipment or extra clothing.

A saving of US$50 overall is about all you can expect, and for that you'll have to carry all your own gear and do your own cooking on the climb. Nevertheless, if you're determined you can do it. It's not compulsory to do the trek through a safari company. A guide (compulsory) and porters (optional) can be arranged at the park entry gate. Clothing and the like can be hired from the park entry gate or from the hotels in Marangu. See the later Organised Climbs section for a list of tour companies.

Park Fees Whichever way you climb Kilimanjaro, there are fees to be paid, since this is a national park. These are:

Fees	Rate
Park entry fee	US$20 per day
Hut fee	US$15 per day
Rescue fee	US$20 per trek
Camping fee	US$40 per trek

Assuming you use the huts, the minimum fee is US$170 for the standard five-day trek, and this must be paid in hard currency.

If you organise your own trek, there's a further fee of US$5 'park commission', plus you'll have to pay for a guide (compulsory) and any porters (optional) which you require, and both their entry and hut fees. See the next section.

Guides & Porters Daily wages are TSh 1200 for guides and TSh 1000 for porters. Their daily park entry and hut fees are TSh 100 per person. Guides' and porters' wages are higher on trails other than Marangu.

Whether you take an organised climb or organise your own, the guide and porters will expect a tip at the end of the trek. Be generous about this but don't be profligate. Unfortunately, a lot of affluent tourists have been tipping excessively over the last few

years (eg US$50 to the guide and US$20 for each porter), so these are the sort of tips they have come to expect – and even demand – from everyone. This is crazy when you consider that a Tanzanian schoolteacher earns around TSh 12,000 (US$30) per *month*. About US$30 from each member of your group to be shared between the guide and porters is more than generous. Nevertheless, you can expect a hassle and even threats to abandon you on the summit unless you tip them *before* the descent and by an amount which the guide considers he can squeeze out of you. A lot of people have had nasty altercations about this.

You must head this sort of nonsense off before you start the climb. Have it clearly understood that the tips will be given *only on completion of the climb*, and don't compromise on this.

Another ruse which is becoming common is for the guide to claim that there were more porters than there actually were so your tip must be increased. Be sure how many porters there actually are, and if any of them 'disappear' during the climb, adjust your tip accordingly. And don't put up with any threats – tell the guide firmly to get his act together and pull his head in. And report it to the park authorities.

Accommodation The first hotel you encounter on the road into Marangu from Moshi/Himo is the *Marangu Hotel* (☎ (055) 50639), PO Box 40, Moshi. It consists of a collection of self-contained cottages set in pleasant, leafy gardens and costs US$100 a double (including hot water showers, breakfast and dinner). Single occupancy of the rooms costs US$70. The hotel is owned by the Brice-Bennett family, who have lived here for decades. Their son, Seamus, took over responsibility for daily operations and marketing in 1992 after spending 14 years in the UK. It used to be possible to camp here (for a small fee) but this is no longer possible. The hotel is seven km from the park entry gate.

By turning left over the river bridge in Marangu village and continuing on for several hundred metres, you will come to the *Kibo Hotel* (☎ Marangu 4), PO Box 102, Marangu. This hotel has a superb position overlooking the surrounding countryside and, like the Marangu Hotel, is set in landscaped gardens. Bed and breakfast costs US$70/80/100 for singles/doubles/triples, US$120 for a four-bed room and US$140 for a five-bed room, plus 5% service charges. Half-board rates are US$80/100/130 for a single/double/triple, US$150 for four people and US$190 for five people, plus service charges. All the rooms are self-contained and the parking lot is guarded. Campers are welcome and are charged US$6 per person per night. The restaurant is open to non-guests. Breakfast costs TSh 1000, lunch is TSh 1800 and dinner is TSh 2200, plus 10% sales tax and 5% service charge. The Kibo is about 5½ km from the park entry gate.

On the other side of the village from the Kibo Hotel (turn right just before the river bridge) are two other places to stay. They're both considerably cheaper than the Kibo and both accept payment in local currency. The nearest is the *Babylon Bar & Restaurant*, above the road on the left-hand side (signposted). A self-contained double room (no singles) costs US$30 including breakfast. There's hot water in the showers and towels, soap and toilet paper are provided. Camping in the grounds costs US$5 per person. The restaurant is reasonable and the beautiful beer garden, filled with exotic flowers, is popular with local people.

Much further down the track (about 3½ km from Marangu village) is the *Ashanti Lodge* (☎ Arusha 2745), PO Box 6004, Arusha. Run by the very friendly Ali and his family, this is a relaxing place to stay and has a restaurant which serves breakfast, lunch and dinner. There's a bar, a pleasant garden and a climbing gear hire service. Campers are welcome, too. There are also hot showers. To get there from Marangu, either walk or hitch a ride with whatever is going down this gravel road – tractors, pick-ups and trucks – there's not much else.

Up at the park entry gate (five km beyond Marangu), you can either camp for the usual fee or stay in one of the two hostels. These cost US$10 per bed per night (TSh 500 for residents) and there are four to six beds per room. A canteen offers breakfast, lunch and dinner.

Organised Climbs

Competition for business is fierce in both Moshi and Arusha, so it's fairly easy to find either a tout or a company who will offer you the climb for US$240 to US$260. Some people come out of these cheap deals smiling; others do not. A great deal depends on your own attitude. If you're very fit and prepared to carry your own gear the whole way, not fussy about food quality, don't care whether there's a bed for you at the huts and are used to roughing it, then you might come out smiling. Otherwise, you will not.

Most people who climb Kilimanjaro, unlike Mt Kenya, opt to go on an organised tour. There are good reasons for this. Most of the charges are standard and a guide is compulsory in any case. Also, as the climb takes a minimum of five days, organising your own climb involves a lot of running around, which is difficult without your own transport – food supplies are very limited at Marangu, so you'll have to do most of your shopping in Moshi. By the time you have the whole thing together, you will have saved very little. Not only that, but most people find that they have very little energy left for cooking at the end of a day's climb. Having someone to do it for you can very well make the difference between loving and hating the trek. Likewise, hiring porters to carry the bulk of your gear is going to add considerably to your enjoyment of the mountain. Are you seriously going to climb the highest mountain in Africa without hiring a porter to carry your heavy gear at what amounts to US$2.50 a day plus tip!? If you are, then you're either crazy or an athlete.

It's probably true to say that the cheapest deals are available in Moshi rather than Arusha, but this is not always the case, particularly if you want good accommodation the night before and the night after a trek, as some safari companies in Arusha can offer deals on the hotel accommodation which you would not be able to match through your own efforts.

Moshi Tour Companies Those in search of rock-bottom treks and negotiated prices should check out the following companies in Moshi:

Mauly Tours & Travels
> PO Box 1315, Moshi (☎ (055) 52787).
> This outfit can offer you climbs on any of the routes to the summit and quote US$350 for the standard five-day Marangu route, including transport to Marangu, but will negotiate. For the Machame route, they quote US$750 (seven days).

Kilimanjaro Guides & Tours
> This is a new outfit which operates out of a wooden hut (signposted) directly opposite Moshi Hotel/Air Tanzania in Moshi. They people are friendly, know the scene and will negotiate on prices.

Shah Tours & Travels Ltd
> PO Box 1821, Moshi (☎ (055) 2370).
> This company can also fix you up with either the Marangu or Machame routes at much the same prices as above and will negotiate, but be wary of invented 'conditions' and extra charges – we have had complaints.

Marangu Hotel
> PO Box 40, Moshi (☎ (055) 50639).
> Although there is no negotiation on prices, this hotel at Marangu is quite willing to organise what it calls 'hard way' climbs on the standard five-day Marangu route (US$290 including transport to the park entry gate).

If you go with any of the above, check exactly what is included in the price and what is not. It's not that they're unreliable; it's just that, at those prices, they're cutting a fine line between profitability and bankruptcy. Don't expect any frills!

If you'd like a little more grease on the wheels and basic creature comforts without the organisational headaches, check out the following. You can safely assume that the prices quoted by all of these outfits include park fees, hut fees, guide fees, porters, cooked food, guaranteed hut bookings and transport to Marangu:

Key's Hotel
> PO Box 933, Moshi (☎ (055) 52250).
> These guys just shave it into the cheapest bracket at US$345 for the standard five-day Marangu trek. They also offer concesssional rates for accommodation at the hotel if you go on one of their treks. Extra days cost US$75. They will organise a Machame route climb for US$660 all-inclusive, but you must bring your own tents and equipment for this.

Trans Kibo Travels Ltd
> PO Box 558, Moshi (☎ (055) 52017).
> This outfit, based at the YMCA in Moshi, has been in business for years and is very reliable. It has daily departures for Kilimanjaro at 9 am and quotes US$440 to US$400 all-inclusive for the five-day Marangu trek (depending on the number of people) plus US$80 per person for each extra day. However, this can drop to US$360 if you feign disinterest and avoid signing travellers' cheques as soon as you sit down. The Machame, Umbwe and Mweka routes cost US$680 per person (six days).

Marangu Hotel
> PO Box 40, Moshi (☎ (055) 50639).
> In addition to offering the 'hard way' climbs, this outfit offers fully serviced climbs for US$490 to US$470 (depending on numbers) plus US$130 for each extra day, including transport to and from the park entrance gate. Like the Key's, it offers concessional rates for hotel accommodation if you go on one of its treks.

Kibo Hotel
> PO Box 102, Marangu (☎ Marangu 4).
> The Kibo, though an expensive hotel, offers daily departures at 9 am on the Marangu route from US$300 to US$350 (depending on numbers), plus US$100 for each extra day over five, all-inclusive. It can also cater for the Machame route at US$700 to US$860 (depending on numbers), plus US$150 for each extra day.

Tropicana Safari Tours
> PO Box 884, Moshi (☎ (055) 51977).
> This company, right opposite the Coffee Tree Hotel on Kibo Rd, is highly rated by Arusha safari operators and offers treks for much the same price as the above.

Arusha Tour Companies If you do book through an Arusha tour company, make sure they're not going to subcontract it out to a Moshi company – otherwise, you'll have given up your ability to negotiate and will end up paying two lots of commission.

Hoopoe Adventure Tours

PO Box 2047, India St, Arusha (☎ (057) 7011, 7541).

This very reliable company offers five-day climbs of Kilimanjaro to walk-in clients for US$380 (minimum two people) or US$390, which includes one night at the Key's Hotel. This is a very good deal, since a night at the Key's normally costs US$50 a double. Booked in advance, including two nights at the Key's (seven days total), the price is US$780 to US$900, depending on numbers.

Kili Trekking Agency

PO Box 2171, Arusha (☎ (057) 8247).

This outfit offers five-day climbs on the Marangu route for US$350 all-inclusive, regardless of numbers, but transport to and from the park entrance gate is extra. If you want to extend the climb to six days, this costs US$70 extra.

Shidolya Tours & Safaris

Room 616, Serengeti Wing, AICC, PO Box 1436, Arusha (☎ (057) 8506).

This small but reliable company offers Kilimanjaro climbs for US$330 all-inclusive.

Bobby Tours & Safaris

PO Box 2169, Goliondoi Rd, Arusha (☎ (057) 8176).

Up considerably in price, this company offers five-day Marangu treks plus two nights at the Kibo Hotel for US$680 to US$1095 (depending on numbers) all-inclusive.

Tropical Tours Ltd

PO Box 727, Arusha (☎ (057) 8353).

This company offers six-day treks at US$780 per person (minimum two people), including transport to and from the park entrance gate but no lodge accommodation before or after the trek. It also caters for the Machame route (six days), at US$1360 per person.

Savannah Tours Ltd

PO Box 3063, Arusha (☎ (057) 8455).

Savannah offers five-day Marangu treks plus two nights at the Kibo Hotel for US$755 to US$950 (depending on numbers) all-inclusive.

Simba Safaris

PO Box 1207, Arusha (☎ (057) 3509).

This company offers possibly what is the most expensive trek available, at US$805 to US$1225 (depending on numbers) for seven days, but it does include two nights at the Kibo Hotel and transport to and from the Kenyan border at Namanga. It obviously caters for those with extremely tight schedules and money to burn.

The above is not an exhaustive list of companies offering Kilimanjaro treks. There are plenty more but we can't vouch for them.

Getting to the Trekking Routes

The Marangu trail is the route most taken by tourists, being the easiest way up the mountain. At the head of the trail is Marangu village, set below the park entry gate.

There are minibuses all day, every day until late in the afternoon between Moshi and Marangu via Himo, terminating in Marangu village at a spot below the post office. The fare is TSh 200 and the journey takes about one hour. A taxi over the same distance will cost about TSh 8000 shared between up to four people, though drivers' initial quotes are often higher.

Marangu has a post office, a petrol station, a small market and several shops selling a limited range of goods. There are several places to stay in the village or close by. It's an attractive place with an alpine atmosphere and a boulder-strewn stream which flows through the centre.

At the park entry gate is a general store, which stocks items such as candles, flour, beer, soft drink, whisky, *konyagi*, tinned meat and vegetables, dried soup, biscuits, fresh bread, cooking fat, margarine, chocolate, cigarettes and matches. There's no fresh fruit or vegetables available (limited quantities of these can be bought in Marangu and at various houses between there and the park entry gate).

Marangu Trail

This is the trail most visitors take.

Day 1 Starting from the Marangu park entry gate at 1800 metres, it's a fairly easy three to four-hour walk through thick rainforest to the *Mandara Hut* (2700 metres). (This hut and the Horombo Hut (3720 metres) might be better described as lodges, since they consist of a large central chalet surrounded by many smaller huts. They almost constitute villages.) There's often quite a lot of mud along this route, so wear good boots. The Mandara Hut consists of a group of comfortable wooden A-frame huts with bunk beds and mattresses and has a total capacity of 60. Water is piped in from springs above the hut and there are flush toilets. There's a dining area in the main cabin.

Day 2 The route climbs steeply through giant heath forest and out across moorlands onto the slopes of Mawenzi and finally to the *Horombo Hut* (3720 metres). It's a difficult 14-km walk and you need to take it slowly. Reckon on five to seven hours. If your clothes are soaked through by the time you arrive at the Horombo Hut, don't assume you will be able to dry them there. Firewood is relatively scarce and is reserved for cooking. The Horombo Hut is similar to Mandara Hut but can accommodate 120. There are both earth and flush toilets.

Days 3 & 4 If possible, spend two nights at this hut and on the fourth day go to *Kibo Hut* (4703 metres), about six to seven hours away. Porters don't go beyond the Kibo Hut, so you'll have to carry your own essential gear from here to the summit and back. Don't skimp on warm clothing. It's extremely cold on the summit and you'll freeze to death if you're not adequately clothed. Kibo Hut is a stone block house which is more like a mountain hut of the type you are likely to find on Mt Kenya. It has a small dining area and several dormitory rooms with bunk beds and mattresses (total capacity of 60). There are earth toilets but no water, so bring sufficient water from the stream above Horombo Hut.

Day 5 Most people find it difficult to sleep much at Kibo, so as you have to start out for the summit very early (1 or 2 am) to get to it just before sunrise, it's a good idea to stay awake the evening before. You'll feel better if you do this rather than try to grab a couple of hours of fitful sleep. The mist and cloud closes in and obscures the views by 9 am and sometimes earlier. The route over the snow to the summit is sometimes like a technicolour dream if it hasn't snowed recently, due to the deposits of those who have vomited as a result of trying to get to the top too quickly! Expect to take five to six hours from Kibo

Hut to Gillman's Point and a further one to two hours from there to Uhuru Peak.

On the same day, you will descend from the summit to the Horombo Hut and spend the night there.

Day 6 On the last day, you return to the starting point at Marangu.

Mweka Trail
Starting from Mweka village directly north of Moshi, this is the most direct, fastest and steepest route to the summit.

To get to the trail head, you will have to drive or get a lift from Moshi to Mweka village. Vehicles can usually be left safely at the College of Wildlife Management if you ask permission.

From here you follow an old logging track, which is often very slippery. Two hours later the track turns into a path, which follows a gully. This path will take you up above the tree line to a ridge where the *Mweka Huts* (3000 metres) are. Expect this leg of the trek to take six to eight hours. The huts are two round metal constructions which each sleep eight people. They are not furnished and there are no toilets. Water can be found below the huts.

From the Mweka Huts, continue up the ridge to the west until you reach the *Barafu Huts* (4600 metres). These are exactly the same as the Mweka Huts and sleep eight people each but there are no toilets and no water. The walk will take six to eight hours.

From the Barafu Huts you can ascend straight up to the rim of Kibo, but the trail is very steep and will take you about six hours. Uhuru Peak is another hour away.

Umbwe Trail
This is another relatively short but steep route (west of Moshi), and it's probably better to descend it from either the Mweka or Machame trails rather than attempt the ascent.

To get to the trail head, take the main Moshi to Arusha road and turn off right to Weru Weru and Mango. Drive past Weru Weru for some 15 km along the Lyamungu road and turn right at the T-junction towards Mango. About 150 metres after crossing the Sere River, turn left and you'll find the Umbwe Mission, where vehicles can be left (with permission).

From the mission, follow an old forestry track up to 2100 metres and then follow the path along a narrow ridge between the Lonzo and Umbwe rivers. If it's getting late by the time you get up here, stay at *Bivouac I* (2800 metres), an all-weather rock shelter with water close by. The walk up here from Umbwe village takes four to six hours.

From Bivouac I, continue up to *Bivouac II* (3780 metres), which is a rock overhang. Water is available from a spring about 15 minutes down the ravine to the west. Next go up the ridge to the end of the tree line. From here a path marked by cairns goes up to *Barranco Hut* (3900 metres). This hut, an unfurnished metal cabin with a wooden floor, sleeps up to five people. There's an earth toilet and water is available from nearby streams. The walk from Bivouac I to here takes about five hours.

From Barranco Hut, head up to *Lava Tower Hut* and the summit via what's known as the Great Western Breach. The walk from Barranco to Lava Tower takes about three hours.

Machame Trail

Some people regard this as the most scenic of the trails up Kilimanjaro. The ascent through forest is gradual until you emerge onto the moorland of Shira Plateau, from which there are superb views of the Kibo peak and the Great Western Breach.

The turn-off on the main Moshi-Arusha road is even further west than that for Umbwe. Once you get there, head north for Machame village. If you have your own transport you can leave the vehicle at either the school or the hotel. From the village, a track leads through coffee plantations and forest to the park entry gate (about four km). From the park entry gate there's a clear track which continues up through more plantations and forest to a ridge between the Weru Weru and Makoa

streams and on to the *Machame Huts* (3000 metres). These consist of two unfurnished metal huts which sleep up to six people. There are earth toilets and water is available about five minutes' walk down the valley. From Machame village to the Machame Huts takes about nine hours, so an early start is recommended.

From Machame Huts, cross the valley and continue up the steep ridge, then west into a gorge and up again to the *Shira Hut* (3800 metres), an unfurnished metal cabin which sleeps up to eight people. There is no toilet, but water is available in the stream about 50 metres north of the hut. The walk takes about five hours.

From the Shira Hut you have the options of continuing on to the *Barranco Hut* (five to six hours), the *Moir Hut* (two hours), or the *Lava Tower Hut* (4600 metres, four hours). The Lava Tower Hut is an unfinished metal cabin which sleeps up to eight people. There are no toilets but water is available close by.

Loitokitok Trail

Coming in from the north, this trail is officially closed to the public and, in any case, you're strongly advised to avoid it. Doing the rounds in Nairobi are stories of murders along this route.

ARUSHA NATIONAL PARK

Although it's one of Tanzania's smallest parks, Arusha is one of the most beautiful and spectacular. It's also one of the few that you're allowed to walk in (accompanied by a ranger). Yet few travellers appear to visit it, possibly because of their haste to press on to the more famous parks of Ngorongoro Crater, Serengeti and Mt Kilimanjaro. This is a profound mistake, since it has all the features of those three parks, including a superb range of flora & fauna.

The park's main features are Ngurdoto Crater (often dubbed Little Ngorongoro), the Momela Lakes and rugged Mt Meru (4556 metres), which overlooks the town of Arusha to the north. Because of the differing altitudes within the park (from

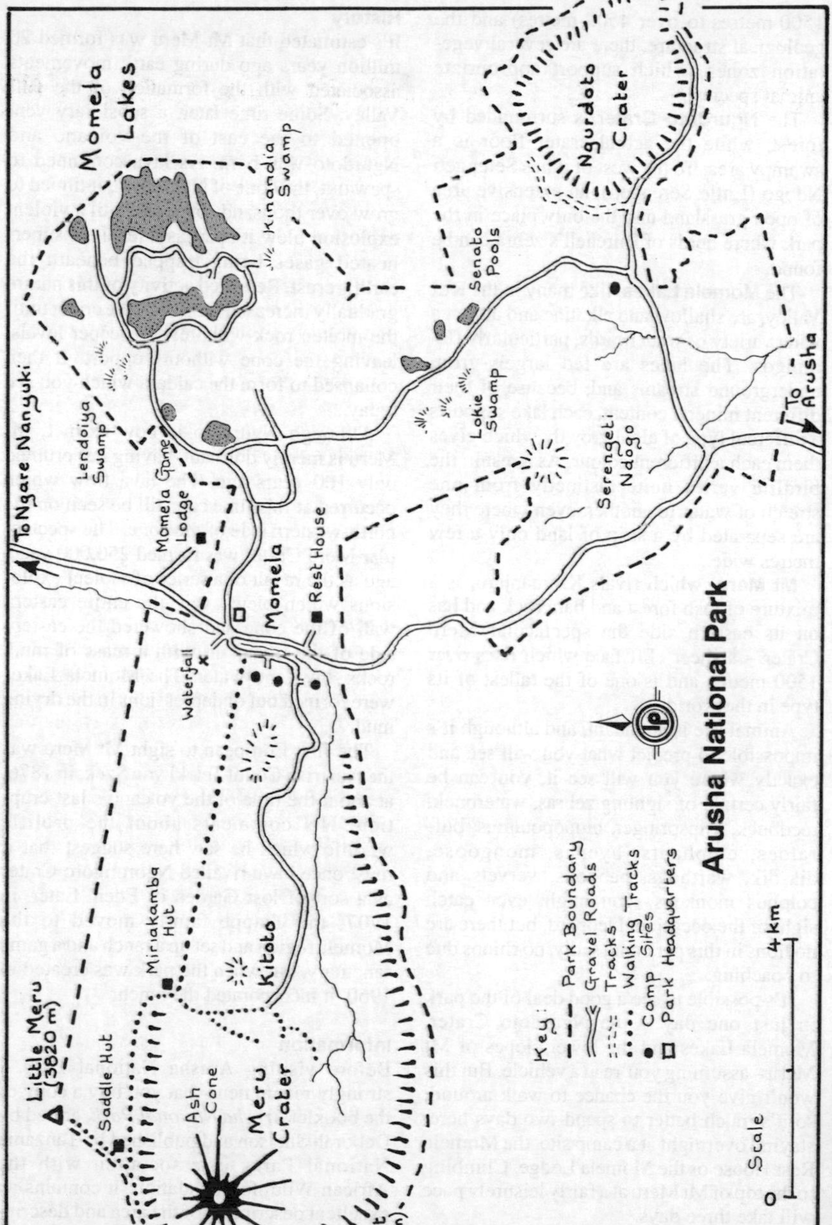

Arusha National Park

Momela Lakes

Kinandia Swamp

Ngurdoto Crater

Senato Pools

Lokie Swamp

To Arusha

Serengeti Ndogo

Lendoiya Swamp

To Ngare Nanyuki

Momela Gate Lodge

Momela

Rest House

Waterfall

Little Meru (3820 m)

Saddle Hut

Miriakamba Hut

Kitoto

Ash Cone

Meru Crater

Meru Summit (4556 m)

Key:
- — — — Park Boundary
- Gravel Roads
- Tracks
- .... Walking Tracks
- ● Camp Sites
- □ Park Headquarters

Scale

0   4 km

TANZANIA

1500 metres to over 4500 metres) and the geological structure, there are several vegetation zones, which support appropriate animal species.

The **Ngurdoto Crater** is surrounded by forest, while the actual crater floor is a swampy area. To the west of it lies Serengeti Ndogo (Little Serengeti), an extensive area of open grassland and the only place in the park where herds of Burchell's zebra can be found.

The **Momela Lakes**, like many in the Rift Valley, are shallow and alkaline and attract a wide variety of wader birds, particularly flamingos. The lakes are fed largely from underground streams and, because of their different mineral content, each lake supports a different type of algal growth, which gives them each a different colour. As a result, the birdlife varies quite distinctly from one stretch of water to another, even where they are separated by a strip of land only a few metres wide.

Mt Meru, which rivals Kilimanjaro, is a mixture of lush forest and bare rock and has on its eastern side the spectacular Meru Crater – a sheer cliff face which rises over 1500 metres and is one of the tallest of its type in the world.

Animal life is abundant, and although it's impossible to predict what you will see and exactly where you will see it, you can be fairly certain of sighting zebras, waterbuck, reedbuck, klipspringer, hippopotamus, buffaloes, elephants, hyenas, mongoose, dik-dik, warthogs, baboons, vervets and colobus monkeys. You might even catch sight of the occasional leopard, but there are no lions in this park and, sadly, no rhinos due to poaching.

It's possible to see a good deal of the park in just one day – the Ngurdoto Crater, Momela Lakes and the lower slopes of Mt Meru – assuming you're in a vehicle. But this won't give you the chance to walk around, so it's much better to spend two days here, staying overnight at a camp site, the Momela Rest House or the Momela Lodge. Climbing to the top of Mt Meru at a fairly leisurely pace will take three days.

History

It's estimated that Mt Meru was formed 20 million years ago during earth movements associated with the formation of the Rift Valley. Some time later, a subsidiary vent opened to the east of the volcano and Ngurdoto was born. As lava continued to spew out, the cone of Ngurdoto continued to grow over thousands of years until a violent explosion blew it apart as a result of superheated gases being trapped beneath the earth's crust. Repeated activity of this nature gradually increased the size of the crater until the molten rock withdrew to deeper levels, leaving the cone without support. It then collapsed to form the caldera which you see today.

Although Ngurdoto is now extinct, Mt Meru is merely dormant, having last erupted only 100 years ago. The lava flow which occurred at this time can still be seen on the north-western side of the cone. The spectacular Meru Crater was formed 250,000 years ago as the result of a series of violent explosions which blew away the entire eastern wall of the cone and showered the eastern side of the mountain with a mass of mud, rocks, lava and water. The Momela Lakes were formed out of depressions in the drying mud.

The first European to sight Mt Meru was the Austrian Count Teleki von Szek, in 1876, at about the time of the volcano's last eruption. His comments about the prolific wildlife which he saw here suggest that it must once have rivalled Ngorongoro Crater as a sort of lost Garden of Eden. Later, in 1907, the Trappe family moved to the Momela region and set up a ranch and a game sanctuary, but when the park was created in 1960, it incorporated the ranch.

Information

Before visiting Arusha National Park, I strongly recommend that you buy a copy of the booklet *Arusha National Park*, edited by Deborah Snelson and published by Tanzania National Parks in association with the African Wildlife Foundation. It contains an excellent description of the area and descriptions of all the animals, birds and plants to be found there, as well as notes on accommodation, transport, climbing Mt Meru and park management. You can find it at the bookshop in the New Arusha Hotel, and elsewhere.

Climbing Mt Meru

To climb Mt Meru, you have the choice of going on an organised climb or arranging your own. If you're organising your own, hitch to the Momela park headquarters or charter a taxi (if you're part of a group). The trek to the summit starts from the park headquarters.

The climb up Mt Meru possibly rivals that up Kilimanjaro. There are numerous animals and changes of vegetation to be seen along the way. Parts of the climb are very steep, particularly along the saddle, but the views are absolutely stunning.

In the dry seasons, jogging shoes are sufficient, but if there's a possibility of rain, you're advised to have a stout pair of boots. As for Kilimanjaro, bring along plenty of warm clothing. Temperatures drop to below zero at night up on the saddle and around the peak, and there's often snow there, too. You'll need to bring all your own food from Arusha. A guide is compulsory and can be hired from the park headquarters at Momela. Porters are available and their fees are the same as for porters on Kilimanjaro.

Bookings for the two mountain huts should be made in advance through the park warden. It's also a good idea to book a guide in advance here so that you don't waste time waiting around park headquarters. If you go on an organised climb, the company will arrange all these bookings for you. Companies in Arusha which offer climbs of Mt Meru include Hoopoe Adventure Tours (US$250 per person for three days, minimum two people), Star Tours (US$210 to US$240, depending on numbers, for three days) and Tropical Tours Ltd (US$480 per person for five days or US$570 per person for six days). These charges include transport to and from the park, food, park entry and hut fees, rescue fees and ranger fees.

It's obvious from the walking times mentioned below that Mt Meru can be scaled in just two days, which makes this an option if your time and/or money is limited, but it does limit what you will see on the way and you need to be fairly fit. It may not be Kilimanjaro, but it's not that small either.

Assuming you take three days to climb the mountain, the usual route is:

Day 1 The first part of the walk is from the Momela park headquarters to *Miriakamba Hut*. This takes about three hours and leaves you the rest of the day to explore Meru Crater. The hut accommodates up to 48 people and firewood is provided.

Day 2 From Miriakamba Hut, it's a three-hour walk to *Saddle Hut* and an afternoon climb up to the summit of Little Meru (3820 metres). Saddle Hut accommodates up to 24 people and firewood is provided.

Day 3 From Saddle Hut, you can walk around the rim of Meru Crater to the summit of Mt Meru and then return to the Momela park headquarters.

Places to Stay

There are three camp sites at Momela (close to the park headquarters) and another at Ngurdoto. All cost the usual US$20 per person per night and all have water, toilet facilities and firewood.

There's also a very pleasant self-help *Rest House* near the Momela Gate which accommodates up to five people. There are superb views from here up through Meru Crater to the peak of Mt Meru. Bookings can be made through The Warden, Arusha National Park, PO Box 3134, Arusha.

Just outside the park, north of the Momela Gate, is the *Momela Wildlife Lodge* (☎ (057) 6423), PO Box 999, Arusha, which can accommodate up to 40 people. Bed and breakfast costs US$50/63/75 for self-contained singles/doubles/triples. The rates for residents are TSh 4250/6150/8033, respectively. Lunch and dinner are both TSh 2050 and lunch boxes can be arranged for TSh

1500. The lodge has excellent views of Mt Meru and Mt Kilimanjaro.

Getting There & Around

The park is 21 km from Arusha and is reached by turning off the main Arusha to Moshi road at the signpost for the national park and Ngare Nanyuki.

There's an excellent series of gravel roads and tracks within the park which will take you to all the main features and viewing points. Most are suitable for saloon cars, though some of the tracks get slippery in the wet seasons (October and November and between March and May). There are also a few tracks which are only suitable for 4WD vehicles.

When driving around the park, you don't need a guide, but if you intend to walk, an armed guide/ranger is compulsory because of the danger of buffaloes. A guide/ranger is also compulsory if you intend to climb Mt Meru. Guides/rangers can be hired for US$10 a day from the park headquarters at Momela. While you can drive or walk around the Ngurdoto Crater rim, you are not allowed to walk down to the crater floor.

Several safari companies in Arusha arrange day trips to the park, but they're expensive unless you're part of a group of between five and seven people. If that's the case, you're looking at US$30 to US$50 per person. If you're just a couple, it's going to cost US$80 to US$145 per person. Companies in Arusha which offer day trips include Bushtrekker Safaris (US$30 to US$80 for two to seven people), Arumeru Tours & Safaris (US45 to US$100 for two to six people), Hoopoe Adventure Tours (US$95 to US$242 for one to six people), UTC (US$79 regardless of numbers), Golden Arrow Safaris (US$50 to US$145 for one to five people) and Sunny Safaris (US$50 to US$130 for one to five people).

TARANGIRE NATIONAL PARK

This national park covers quite a large area south-east of Lake Manyara, mainly along the course of the Tarangire River and the swamp lands and flood plains which feed it

from the east. During the dry season, the only water here flows along the Tarangire River. The park fills with herds of zebra, wildebeest and kongoni, which stay until October when the short rains allow them to move to new pastures. Throughout the year, however, you can see eland, lesser kudu, various species of gazelle, buffalo, giraffe, waterbuck, impala, elephant and the occasional leopard and rhino. For ornithologists, the best season is from October to May.

Tsetse flies can be a pest in this park at certain times of year (eg February and March), so keep the windows of your vehicle closed when not taking photographs.

Places to Stay & Eat

There are two public camp sites where you can pitch a tent for the usual price (US$20 per person per night, $US5 for children between the ages of five and 16). Also, there are six so-called special camp sites at US$40 per person per night (US$10 for children).

The beautifully sited *Tarangire Safari Lodge* (☎ (057) 7182), PO Box 2703, Arusha, set on a bluff overlooking the Tarangire River, is run by Serengeti Select Safaris. It consists of 35 luxury double tents shielded from the sun by makuti roofs. Each tent has comfortable beds, a solar-heated shower, a flush toilet, electricity until midnight and a verandah, and there's a swimming pool. In the low season (1 April to 31 May) it costs US$30/35 plus 5% service charge for singles/doubles including breakfast. In the high season it costs US$52/65 plus 5%, respectively. Tanzanian residents pay about 35% less and can pay in local currency. The restaurant offers both Western and African dishes – lunch and dinner cost US$10 each (or the equivalent in local currency).

Just outside Tarangire to the east is *Oliver's Camp* (☎ (057) 3108), PO Box 425, Arusha. This is a luxury tented camp set amongst an almost two-km-long set of kopjes known as Kikoti by the Maasai. (Kopjes are slight rises strewn with huge, smooth granite boulders. They generally support a few trees and are often the lookouts of cheetahs.)

The camp takes a maximum of 12 guests at a time, thus ensuring intimacy and closeness to nature. The emphasis is on walking and observing, which you do with an armed ranger. Only occasionally do you drive, and then usually at night to hides overlooking waterholes. The twin-bed tents are individually sited with all the necessary facilities (chairs, table, shower and toilet and covered verandah), plus there's a large dining tent and a library tent where wildlife videos are shown in the evenings after dinner. Full board costs US$100 per person per night (or US$160 for single occupancy) plus a US$12 'conservation fee'. You pay a further US$5 per day if you bring your own vehicle. Bush walks (two to three hours) using Oliver's Camp guides cost US$30 per person. Visiting guides are charged US$112 in main accommodation or US$27 per night in the staff camp.

LAKE MANYARA NATIONAL PARK
Lake Manyara National Park is generally visited as the first stop on a safari which takes in this park and Ngorongoro and Serengeti. It's generally a bit of a letdown, apart from the hippos, since the large herds of elephant which used to inhabit the park have been decimated in recent years. Because the park is too small, the elephants invade adjoining farmland for fodder during the dry season. Naturally, local farmers have been none too pleased, and once outside the park boundaries, the elephants are fair game (and their ivory is worth a lot of money).

Even the waterbirds which come to nest here (greater and lesser flamingos in particular) can usually only be seen from a distance because there are no roads to the lake shore, though this may have changed recently as the level of the lake has shrunk and there are large expanses of open sand. You will certainly see wildebeest, giraffes and baboons and you may well see the famous tree-climbing lions. The trouble is, most safaris to Manyara only spend a day here, so what you see is limited.

There is a reasonably interesting market in the nearby village of Mto-wa-Mbu – mainly fabrics and crafts – but they see a lot of tourists here, so it's overcommercialised and bargains are hard to find. Indeed, it's possibly cheaper to buy what is for sale here in Arusha.

Places to Stay & Eat
There are two camp sites just outside the park entrance, which is just down the road from the village of Mto-wa-Mbu (River of Gnats or Mosquito Village, according to various translations, and whichever one you choose, it's true).

Camp Site No 2 is probably the best. You can either pitch a tent here or rent one of the bandas, which contain two beds, blankets and sheets and have running water, a toilet and firewood. Insect repellant and/or a mosquito net would be very useful and you need to beware of thieving baboons.

Avoid camping at any sites within the park, as they're all so-called 'special camps', which will cost you US$40 per person per night (US$10 for children between the ages of five and 16).

Budget and mid-range accommodation is available in Mto-wa-Mbu village. There are several budget hotels around the market/craft square, including the *Rift Valley Bar & Hotel*, which has doubles with two single beds, clean sheets and shared bathroom facilities for TSh 1000 per person including free condoms, and the *Camp Vision Traders Ltd*, which costs TSh 1000/2000 for singles/doubles with shared bathroom facilities. The beds are comfortable and clean sheets are provided, but very little English is spoken. Despite the name, you cannot camp here and there's no restaurant. There's also the *Kibo Guest House*, which has doubles for TSh 2000 without breakfast and a restaurant which offers nyama choma, and the *Rombo Star Guest House* (very basic).

The best place to stay in Mto-wa-Mbu, however, is the popular *Holiday Fig Resort* (☎ 2), which is set in its own leafy grounds off the main street and has a swimming pool, bar and restaurant. It's a very friendly place run by Zulekha and her daughter Shaina. The beds are large and clean and the rooms self-contained. It costs US$15/30/45 for singles/doubles/triples including breakfast. You can also camp here for US$5 per person, and there's guarded parking as well as vehicles which can take you into the national park. Look for the hotel's signpost on the main street.

Further down the street which takes you to the Holiday Fig Resort are the *Manyara Guest House* and the *Lutheran Evangelical Guest House*. The latter offers full-board facilities.

Up on top of the escarpment overlooking Lake Manyara is the *Starehe Bar & Hotel*. It's about 100 metres off to the left along the turn-off for the Lake Manyara Hotel (signposted) on the main road from Mto-wa-Mbu to Ngorongoro. It's rustic but very clean and comfortable and there are no bugs, mosquitoes or electricity (though candles are provided). There are hot showers, and the staff are eager to please, very friendly and will cook you superb, generous meals of tasty stewed chicken, sautéed potatoes, haricot beans, mung beans, gravy and rice and great breakfasts of two eggs, bread, butter, jam and tea/coffee. Accommodation costs TSh 3000 per person.

Lake Manyara Hotel (☎ 3300, 3113) is the place to stay for luxury hotel accommodation. It sits right on the edge of the escarpment overlooking Lake Manyara, about three km along the same turn-off on which the Starehe Bar stands. It's part of the Tanzania Tourist Corporation chain. Singles/doubles/triples cost US$85/95/108 including breakfast, plus a 22.5% tax and service charge. From Easter Monday to 30 June, there's a 15% discount on these prices. The hotel has flower gardens, a swimming pool, petrol pumps and a curio shop.

Also up on top of the escarpment overlooking the lake, but on the opposite side of the main Lake Manyara to Ngorongoro road, is Hoopoe Adventure Tours' *Kirurumu Tented Camp* (☎ (057) 7011). It's about 13 km from the main road (signposted) and has

become very popular with safari companies. The twin-bed tents are clean and comfortable and the showers (bucket hot water provided) and toilets are shared. It costs US$20/25 for singles/doubles (children under 10 years are half-price), or you can camp for US$5 per person (tent provided) or US$3 per person (own tent). Delicious meals are available in the mess tent for US$2.50 (breakfast) and US$7 (lunch/dinner) and there's a plentiful supply of cold beer.

NGORONGORO CONSERVATION AREA

There can be few people who have not heard, read or seen film or TV footage of this incredible 20-km-wide volcanic crater with its 600-metre walls packed with just about every species of wildlife to be found in East Africa. The views from the crater rim are incredible, and though the wildlife might not look too impressive from up there, when you get to the bottom you'll very quickly change your mind. It's been compared to Noah's Ark and the Garden of Eden, and though this is a little fanciful, it might have been just that around the turn of the century, before wildlife in East Africa was decimated by the 'great White hunters' armed with the latest guns and a total lack of concern and foresight regarding conservation.

It doesn't quite come up to Noah's Ark expectations these days, but you definitely see lions, elephants, rhinos, buffaloes and many of the plains herbivores such as wildebeest, Thomson's gazelle, zebras and reedbuck, as well as thousands of flamingos wading in the shallows of Lake Magadi – the soda lake on the floor of the crater.

Despite the steep walls of the crater, there's considerable movement of animals in and out – mostly to the Serengeti, since the land between the crater and Lake Manyara is intensively farmed. Yet it remains a favoured spot for wildlife because there's permanent water and pasture on the crater floor. The animals don't have the crater entirely to themselves. Local Maasai tribespeople have grazing rights, and you may well come across some of them tending their cattle. In the days when Tanzania was a German colony, there was also a settler's farm there, but that has long since gone.

You can visit Ngorongoro at any time of year, but during the months of April and May it can be extremely wet and the roads difficult to negotiate. Access to the crater floor may be restricted at this time, too, though a major grading effort was in progress in early 1993.

History

Ngorongoro and the nearby craters and volcanoes are fairly recent additions to the landscape, geologically speaking. Though there has been a considerable amount of volcanic activity in the area for about 15 million years, Ngorongoro is thought to date back only 2½ million years and may at one time have rivalled Mt Kilimanjaro in size. Its vents filled with solid rock, however, and the molten material was forced elsewhere. As the lava subsided, circular fractures developed and the cone collapsed inwards to form the caldera. Nevertheless, minor volcanic activity continued as lava found cracks on the caldera floor and in the flanks of the mountain, creating the small cones and hillocks which you can see on the floor of the crater.

Only in the 1930s was a road constructed through Ngorongoro and a lodge built on the rim, but even before WW II the crater had acquired international fame as a wildlife area. In 1951 it was included in the newly created Serengeti National Park. It was hived off five years later due to conflict between the park authorities and the local Maasai, who felt that being excluded from the Serengeti was bad enough but that to have their grazing rights to Ngorongoro also withdrawn was going too far. As a result it became a conservation area for the benefit of pastoralists and wildlife alike. In recognition of its importance and beauty, it was declared a World Heritage site in 1978.

Places to Stay & Eat

On the crater rim, there is a choice of four places to stay and two camp sites.

Of the four lodges, the *Rhino Lodge* is the first one you come to, off to the left. It costs US$45/70/95 for singles/doubles/triples including breakfast in the high season (1 July to 31 March) and half that price in the low season. Tanzanian residents are entitled to a 25% discount on the above prices and can pay in local currency. Children under the age of 12 pay half-price. Breakfast (for casual visitors) is US$7 and lunch/dinner is US$10. It's on a beautiful site but is somewhat out of the way and doesn't overlook the crater. You might be able to camp here if you have a tent. Bookings can be made in Arusha at the Ngorongoro Conservation Area Authority (☎ (057) 3339), PO Box 776, Arusha. Its office is by the roundabout at the junction of Makongoro and Ngoliondoi Rds.

Next is the *Ngorongoro Wildlife Lodge* (☎ (057) 2711/2), PO Box 877, Arusha, a very modern building set right on the edge of the crater rim and with superb views. All rooms are centrally heated, have a bath and toilet and face the crater. It used to be owned by the Tanzania Tourist Corporation but has been taken over by Accor Tanzania/Serengeti Safari Lodges. Half-board rates are US$98/121 a single/double, plus 25% taxes and service charge in the high season. Full-board rates are US$110/144 plus 25% taxes. There is a 50% discount in the low season (1 April to 30 June). Meals are excellent and can be paid for in local currency. The bar is a good place to meet people and, like the one at the Crater Lodge, has a log fire. Bookings can be made at the TTC office (☎ (057) 3842), PO Box 3100, Sokoine Rd, Arusha.

The *Ngorongoro Crater Lodge* (☎ Arusha 3300, 3114), an old rustic lodge built in 1937 and overlooking the crater, is managed by Windsor Hotels Ltd. Book through Abercrombie & Kent (☎ 7803, 3181), Sokoine Rd, PO Box 427, Arusha. It's a very pleasant place to stay and costs US$70/88/120 a single/double/triple including breakfast and all taxes and service charges. Full-board rates are US$105/162/230, respectively. Tanzanian residents pay US$52/67/90, respectively for bed and breakfast. There's a 50% discount between 1 April and 30 June. Meal prices are US$6 (breakfast), US$12

Ngorongoro Conservation Area

To Mwanza, Musoma & Seronera Lodge

Naabi Gate

Serengeti National Park

Olduvai Gorge

Olduvai Museum

Lake Ndutu

Ndutu Safari Lodge

Lemaguru Hills

Oninaingarngar Hills

Kiruma Plain

Enduleni

Escarpment

Endamagnay

Kakesio

Escarpment

Lake Eyasi

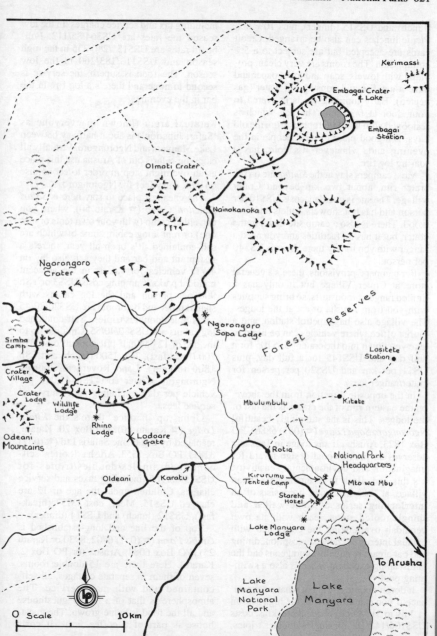

(lunch) and US$15 (dinner), plus 10% tax. Picnic lunches can also be arranged. Credit cards are accepted but are subject to a 5% commission. The rooms are very clean, provided with towels, soap and toilet paper and have a gas fire and nonstop hot water (gas heated). Early morning tea is delivered to your door at 6.30 am. The bar, which is festooned with hunting trophies from the old days, is a good place to meet people in the evening and, whenever it's cold, has a roaring log fire.

Most campers stay at the *Simba* site on the crater rim, about two km beyond Crater Village. The site is guarded, costs US$10 per person and has hot showers, toilets and firewood. There is also a camp site down in the crater, but it has no facilities and you need a ranger with you to stay there. It costs US$40 per person.

For campers' provisions, there's a general store at Crater Village but it only has a limited range of foodstuffs, so bring supplies with you from Arusha or eat at the lodges. The village also has a petrol station, and a tourist office where vehicles can be hired to take you down into the crater (US$105 for a half day and US$145 for a full day, plus US$1 per km and US$20 per person for crater/ranger fees).

In the opposite direction from the above, on the eastern rim of the crater, is the last of the lodges. This is the stunningly beautiful *Ngorongoro Sopa Lodge* (☎ (057) 6886), PO Box 1823, Arusha. If any lodge in Tanzania deserves an international design award for imagination and environmental sensitivity, it's this one. Built to resemble an African village, at least in layout, it consists of an interlocking series of stone-walled and shingle-roofed suites, each with its own verandah overlooking the crater and with palatial interiors. The vast reception, dining and bar areas are equally courageous and the landscaping excellent. There's also a swimming pool.

It doesn't come cheap but what an experience if you can afford it! In the high season (1 July to 31 March) bed and breakfast costs US$106/142/187 for singles/doubles/triples,

including tax and service charges. In the low season the rates are US$64/85/112. Full-board rates are US$155/240/335 in the high season and US$113/183/260 in the low season. The food is superb, the service is second to none and there's a log fire in the bar in the evenings.

Karatu Karatu (known to everyone as 'Safari Junction') is about halfway between Lake Manyara and Ngorongoro. Virtually all camping safaris out of Arusha use this place as an overnight stop in order to economise on park entry fees for Ngorongoro.

The cheapest place to stay here is *Safari Junction Camp* (☎ Karatu 50), where you can either camp (with your own tents or hire one) or rent a log cabin, some of which are self-contained. It's open all year, there's a restaurant and bar and they can also lay on 4WD vehicles for safaris in the adjacent national parks. Camping costs US$3 or TSh 900 per person and the log cabins with shared toilet and bathroom are US$20/30/45 for singles/doubles/triples. Self-contained log cabins are US$30/40/55. Children up to the age of 12 pay half-price. Meals cost TSh 700 (breakfast), TSh 1500 (lunch) and TSh 1800 (dinner). Land Rovers for touring Ngorongoro Crater cost TSh 45,000 per vehicle per day, excluding park entry and service fees.

Going up in price, there's the *Kifaru Lodge* (☎ Karatu 20), PO Box 20, Karatu, managed by Big Game Safaris Ltd (☎ (057) 3181), PO Box 7553, Arusha. It offers self-contained singles/doubles/triples for US$75/88/105, including taxes and service charges. Children under the age of 12 are charged US$15. Meals cost US$7 (breakfast), US$12 (lunch) and US$14 (dinner).

Top of the line and long-established is *Gibb's Farm* (☎ (057) 6702, 8930 or Karatu 25), PO Box 6084, Arusha (or PO Box 2, Karatu). Here there are 15 double rooms, seven of them in separate cottages, all self-contained and with maid service. The atmosphere is that of a family guesthouse and all the food is home-grown. The guesthouse is part of a coffee farm. It costs

US$85/105/125 for singles/doubles/triples plus 5% service charge. Children under the age of 12 pay US$16. The discount for Tanzanian residents is about 40% (even more in the low season). Meals cost US$7 (breakfast), US$14 (lunch) and US$16 (dinner) plus 15% tax and service charges. The hotel is closed during the months of April and May. The farm is signposted on the main road into Karatu coming from Lake Manyara.

Getting There & Away

If you are trying to get to the crater under your own steam, there are private buses from Arusha at least as far as Karatu but it may be difficult to find anything going beyond there. There are also plenty of trucks as far as Karatu.

Only 4WD vehicles are allowed down in the crater, except at times during the dry season when the authorities *may* allow conventional vehicles in. The roads into the crater, except from the Sopa Lodge, are very steep, so if you are driving your own vehicle, make sure it will handle the roads. It takes between 30 and 45 minutes to get to the crater floor. Whether you are driving your own vehicle or are on an organised tour, you must take a park ranger with you (US$20 per day). It's also possible to hire a 4WD Land Rover from the tourist office at Crater Village from the same place where you collect a ranger (prices above). The lodges also offer this service but they charge more for it than does the tourist office.

OLDUVAI GORGE

The Olduvai Gorge made world headlines in 1959 following the discovery by the Leakeys of fossil fragments of the skull of one of the ancestors of Homo sapiens. The fragments were dated back 1.8 million years. The Leakeys were convinced by this and other finds that the fragments represented a third species of early humans, which they dubbed *Homo habilis*. They proposed that the other two, known as *Australopithecus africanus* and *Australopithecus robustus*, had died out and that *Homo habilis* had given rise to

modern humankind. The debate raged for two decades and is still unsettled.

Meanwhile, in 1979, Mary Leakey made another important discovery in the shape of footprints at Laetoli which she claimed were of a man, woman and child. They were dated back 3.5 million years, and since they were made by creatures which walked upright, this pushed the dawn of the human race much further back than had previously been supposed.

The gorge itself isn't of great interest unless you are archaeologically inclined. However, it has acquired a kind of cult attraction among those who just want to visit the site where the evolution of early humans presumably took place. There is a small museum on the site, which is only a 10 to 15-minute drive from the main road between Ngorongoro Crater and Serengeti. The museum closes at 3 pm and in the rainy season is often not open at all. It's possible to go down into the gorge at certain times of the year if you would like to see the dig sites.

Places to Stay

There is nowhere to stay at Olduvai, but at the western end of the gorge, where the creek which flows through it empties into Lake Ndutu, the *Ndutu Safari Lodge* (☎ (057) 6702), PO Box 6084 in Arusha or PO Box 1501 in Karatu, sits on the borders of the Serengeti National Park. The lodge offers 32 self-contained double rooms, six tents with separate toilet and washroom facilities, and an open-air bar and dining area with an excellent view of the lake. Bed and breakfast in the high season is US$85/105/125 for singles/doubles/triples plus 5% government taxes. The low-season rates (April to June, September to November and 1-15 December) are US$52/70/86. Children under 12 years of age pay US$16 and US$10, respectively. Other meals cost US$14 (lunch) and US$16 (dinner). The lodge is open all year and can provide 4WD vehicles for game drives in the area.

SERENGETI NATIONAL PARK

Serengeti, which covers 14,763 sq km, is Tanzania's most famous game park and is

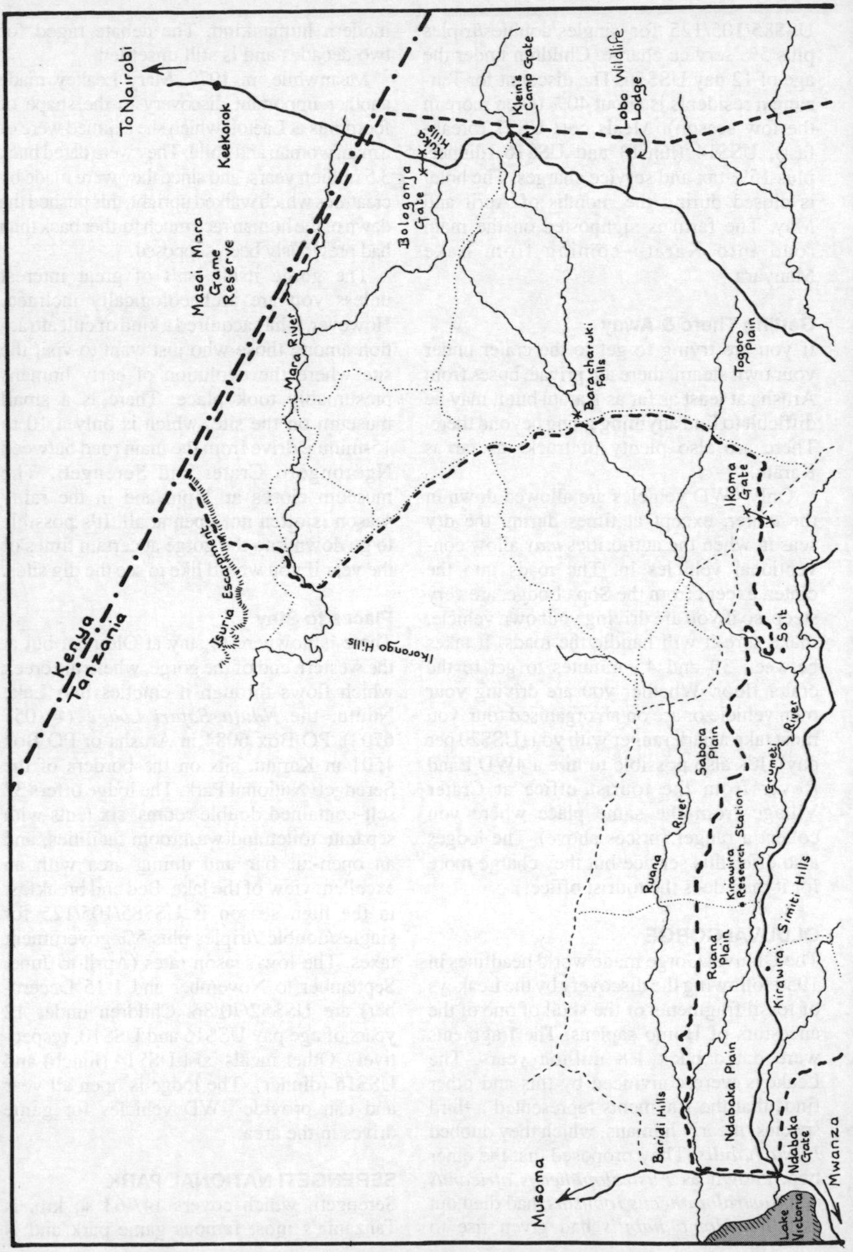

To Nairobi

Keekorok

Masai Mara
Game
Reserve

Klein's
Camp Gate

Kiba
Hills

Lobo
Wildlife
Lodge

Bologonja
Gate

Mara River

Baracharuki
Falls

Togoro
Plain

Ikoma
Gate

Kenya
Tanzania

Isuria Escarpment

Korongo Hills

Soit

Sabora
Plain

Kirawira
Research
Station

Ruana River

Grumeti River

Simiti Hills

Ruana
Plain

Kirawira Hills

Baridi Hills

Ndaboka
Plain

Ndaboka
Gate

Lake
Victoria

Musoma

Mwanza

TANZANIA

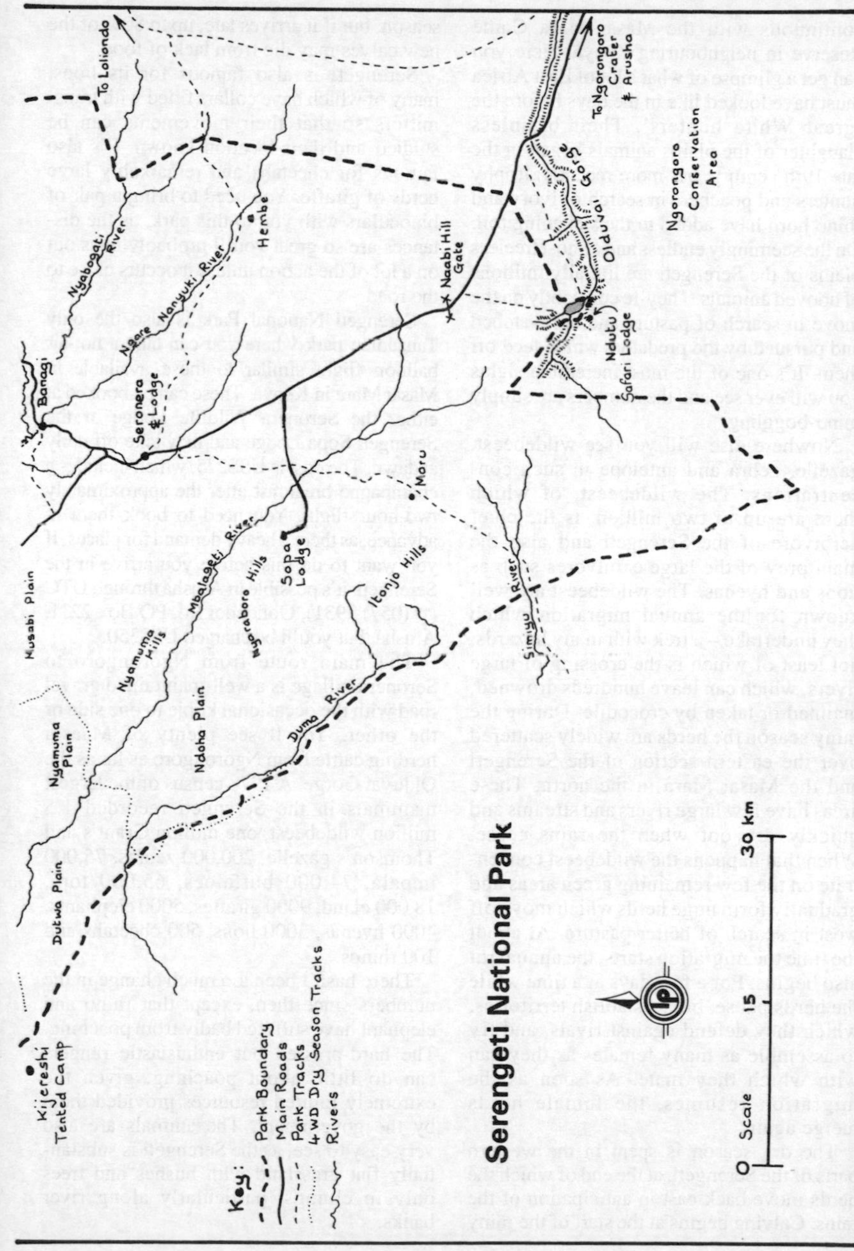

Serengeti National Park

Key:

- — — Park Boundary
- ———— Main Roads
- – – – Park Tracks
- · · · · 4 WD Dry Season Tracks
- ∿∿∿ Rivers

Scale: 0 — 15 — 30 km

To Loliondo

To Ngorongoro Crater & Arusha

Ngorongoro Conservation Area

Olduvai Gorge

Ndutu Safari Lodge

Naabi Hill Gate

Seronera Lodge

Banagi

Ngare Nanyuki River

Hembe

Ngabogat River

Seronera

Mbalageti River

Ngarabora Hills

Sopa Lodge

Itonjo Hills

Moru

Simyu River

Duma River

Ndoha Plain

Nyamuma Hills

Nyamuma Plain

Ndoha Plain

Dutwa Plain

Nyanuma Plain

Musabi Plain

Kijereshi Tented Camp

TANZANIA

continuous with the Masai Mara Game Reserve in neighbouring Kenya. Here you can get a glimpse of what a lot of East Africa must have looked like in the days before the 'great White hunters'. Their brainless slaughter of the plains animals began in the late 19th century, but more recently, trophy hunters and poachers in search of ivory and rhino horn have added to the sickening toll. On the seemingly endless and almost treeless plains of the Serengeti are literally millions of hooved animals. They're constantly on the move in search of pasture and are watched and pursued by the predators which feed off them. It's one of the most incredible sights you will ever see and the numbers are simply mind-boggling.

Nowhere else will you see wildebeest, gazelle, zebra and antelope in such concentrations. The wildebeest, of which there are up to two million, is the chief herbivore of the Serengeti and also the main prey of the large carnivores such as lions and hyenas. The wildebeest are well known for the annual migration which they undertake – a trek with many hazards, not least of which is the crossing of large rivers, which can leave hundreds drowned, maimed or taken by crocodile. During the rainy season the herds are widely scattered over the eastern section of the Serengeti and the Masai Mara in the north. These areas have few large rivers and streams and quickly dry out when the rains cease. When that happens the wildebeest concentrate on the few remaining green areas and gradually form huge herds which move off west in search of better pasture. At about the time the migration starts, the annual rut also begins. For a few days at a time while the herds pause, bulls establish territories, which they defend against rivals, and try to assemble as many females as they can with which they mate. As soon as the migration resumes, the female herds merge again.

The dry season is spent in the western parts of the Serengeti, at the end of which the herds move back east in anticipation of the rains. Calving begins at the start of the rainy season, but if it arrives late, up to 80% of the new calves may die from lack of food.

Serengeti is also famous for its lions, many of which have collars fitted with transmitters so that their movements can be studied and their location known. It's also famous for cheetahs and remarkably large herds of giraffe. You need to bring a pair of binoculars with you to this park, as the distances are so great you'll probably miss out on a lot of the action unless it occurs close to the road.

Serengeti National Park is also the only Tanzanian park where you can take a hot-air balloon flight similar to those available in Masai Mara in Kenya. These can be booked at either the Seronera Wildlife Lodge or the Serengeti Sopa Lodge and they take off daily at dawn. The cost is US$275, which includes a champagne breakfast after the approximately two-hour flight. You need to book them in advance, as there's heavy demand for places. If you want to do this before you arrive in the Serengeti, it's possible in Arusha through UTC (☎ (057) 7931), Goliondoi Rd, PO Box 2211, Arusha, but you'll be charged US$350.

The main route from Ngorongoro to Seronera village is a well-maintained gravel road with the occasional kopje to one side or the other. You'll see plenty of Maasai herding cattle from Ngorongoro as far as the Olduvai Gorge. A 1978 census of the largest mammals in the Serengeti recorded 1.5 million wildebeest, one million Grant's and Thomson's gazelle, 200,000 zebras, 75,000 impala, 74,000 buffaloes, 65,000 topi, 18,000 eland, 9000 giraffes, 5000 elephants, 4000 hyenas, 3000 lions, 500 cheetahs and 100 rhinos.

There hasn't been too much change in the numbers since then, except that rhino and elephant have suffered badly from poaching. The hard-pressed but enthusiastic rangers can do little about poaching, given the extremely limited resources provided them by the government. The animals are also very easy to see, as the Serengeti is substantially flat grassland with bushes and trees only in clumps, particularly along river banks.

Places to Stay & Eat

Most budget travellers stay at one or other of the *public camp sites* (US$20 per person). There are 12 of these – six at Seronera, two at Kirawira, one at Ndabaka, two at Lobo and one at Bologonja – but facilities are minimal. Some don't even have water, so it's best to bring with you everything you'll need. In addition, there are six *special camp sites* (US$40 per person) – one at Seronera, two at Kirawira, two at Lobo and one at Bologonja – and 12 *wilderness camp sites* (US$40 per person) – three at Moru, one at Hembe, one at Soit le Motonyi, two at Naabi Hill and five at Lake Lagarja (Ndutu).

Outside the park itself and south of the Ndabaka Gate, near the north-western extremity of the park, is *Kijereshi Tented Camp* (☎ Mwanza 40139), PO Box 190, Mwanza. This luxury tented camp costs US$70 a double including taxes and breakfast, and there are more expensive suites. Tanzanian residents pay TSh 6500/9500 for singles/doubles plus 5% service charge. To get there, you drive from Mwanza to Ramadi (140 km), then one km after Ramadi turn right at the sign for the camp. It's 16 km from there.

In addition to *Ndutu Safari Lodge* (see Olduvai Gorge), there are three other lodges within Serengeti. The *Seronera Wildlife Lodge* is a stunningly beautiful and very imaginative building constructed on top of and around a kopje, with hyrax (a small rodent-like creature) running around everywhere. They're so tame you can almost touch them. The enormous bar and observation deck at this lodge is right on top of the kopje, with the boulders incorporated into the design. Getting up to it on narrow stone steps between massive rocks is like entering Aladdin's Cave!

The rooms are very pleasantly furnished and decorated (though there seems to be a lack of electric light bulbs) and they all have a bathroom with hot water – when water is available (they've had water problems here for years). Singles/doubles/triples (with breakfast) cost US$67/74/84, plus 25% taxes and service charge, in the high season. Full-

board rates are US$110/144/183. There's a 50% discount in the low season (1 April to 30 June). Meals cost US$10 (lunch) and US$11 (dinner) plus 10% tax. The lodge has a generator but it's only switched on between sunset and midnight. The shop at the lodge specialises in local craft work. Don't expect to find guidebooks, maps, postcards or film for sale. If you can possibly afford to stay here, do so – it's absolutely superb!

Equally superb is the *Lobo Wildlife Lodge*, which is built into the faults and contours of a massive rock promontory overlooking the plains. It's very similar to the Seronera Lodge in terms of what it offers but is slightly less expensive. Bed and breakfast costs US$45/55/65 plus 25% taxes for singles/doubles/triples in the high season. Full-board rates are US$85/121/158. Costs in the low season are half the above rates. Meals cost the same as at the Seronera Wildlife Lodge.

Both the Seronera and Lobo wildlife lodges are owned by the Tanzania Tourist Corporation and can be booked through Serengeti Safari Lodges (☎ (057) 3842), PO Box 3100, Arusha.

The other lodge in Serengeti is the new *Serengeti Sopa Lodge* (☎ (057) 6886), PO Box 1823, Arusha, which was still being completed in mid-1993. Most of the lodge is up and running, but the design is nowhere near as imaginative as that used for the Sopa Lodge on Ngorongoro Crater. While it is luxurious and everything works, it's a fairly bland structure. On the other hand, the staff are friendly and helpful. It costs exactly the same as the Ngorongoro Sopa Lodge (see that section for details).

MIKUMI NATIONAL PARK

Mikumi National Park covers 3237 sq km and sits astride the main Dar es Salaam to Mbeya highway, about 300 km from Dar es Salaam. Not many budget travellers seem to visit this park, probably because of the lack of cheap accommodation, but there is a lot of wildlife to be seen. Elephants, lions, leopards, buffaloes, zebras, impala, wildebeest and warthogs can be viewed at any time of year.

One of the principal features of Mikumi is the Mkata River flood plain, an area of lush vegetation which particularly attracts elephants and buffaloes. Hippos can also be seen at Hippo Pools, about five km from the park entrance gate.

Mikumi is often visited as a weekend outing from Dar es Salaam (with an overnight stay on Saturday night) – most of the safari companies with branches in Dar es Salaam offer trips there.

Places to Stay

For those on a budget, there are three camp sites in the park (US$20 per person per night), or a *youth hostel* at the park headquarters, which has a capacity for 50 people. None of the camp sites has water, but they do have toilets and firewood. If you're staying at the youth hostel, bring your own bedding. There are toilet and cooking facilities. If you're camping, bring everything you need except firewood. Bookings for the youth hostel can be made through the Chief Park Warden, Mikumi National Park, PO Box 62, Mikumi, Morogoro.

Considerably higher in price is the *Mikumi Wildlife Tented Camp* (☎ 68631 in Dar es Salaam), a luxury tented camp which costs slightly less than the lodge and has 10 tents at present. It's managed by the Oyster Bay Hotel in Dar es Salaam, through which bookings should be made (see the Dar es Salaam chapter for the address and telephone number).

The *Mikumi Wildlife Lodge* is built around a watering hole and is the place to stay if you're looking for creature comforts. It's owned by the TTC (☎ 27671), PO Box 2485, Dar es Salaam, and costs US$45/55/65 a single/double/triple including breakfast, plus 25% tax and service charges. Between Easter Monday and 30 June, there's a 50% discount. Meals are available for US$10 (lunch) and US$11 (dinner), plus 10% tax. The lodge has a swimming pool, gift shop and petrol station.

SELOUS GAME RESERVE

The little-visited, 54,600-sq-km Selous is probably the world's largest game reserve. It's the quintessential East African wilderness. Wild and largely untouched by people, it is said to contain the world's largest concentration of elephants, buffaloes, crocodiles, hippos and hunting dogs, as well as plenty of lionz, rhinoz and antelope and thousands of dazzling bird species. Poaching probably makes the estimates of wildlife populations overly optimistic, but there are supposedly about 100,000 elephants in this reserve and there is a good chance of seeing a herd several hundred strong.

Established in 1922, for many years it remained largely the preserve of the trophy collectors and big-game hunters, even though only the northern tip of the reserve has ever been adequately explored. Most of it is trackless wilderness and is almost impossible to traverse during the rainy season, when floods and swollen rivers block access. The best time to visit is from July to March. In any case, the lodges and camp sites are closed from April to June.

One of the main features of the reserve is the huge **Rufiji River**, which has the largest water catchment area in East Africa. Massive amounts of silt are dumped annually during the wet season into the Indian Ocean opposite Mafia Island. For the rest of the year, when the floods subside and the water level in the river drops, extensive banks of shimmering white and golden sand are exposed.

In the northern end of the reserve, where the Great Ruaha River flows into the Rufiji, is **Stiegler's Gorge**, probably the best known feature of the park. On average it's 100 metres deep and 100 metres wide. A cable car spans the gorge, for those who are game enough to go across. It's in the area where most of the safari camps and the lodges are. The gorge is named after the German explorer of the same name who was killed here by an elephant in 1907.

The Selous is one of the few national parks which you are allowed to explore on foot. Walking safaris are conducted by all four camps in the reserve. Boat trips up the Rufiji

River are also offered by two of the camps (Rufiji River and Mbuyu Safari Camps) and are a very popular way of exploring the area.

Places to Stay

All park facilities are concentrated in the extreme northern end, and consist of four lodges and luxury tented camps. There are no budget facilities or camp sites available.

At the north-eastern tip of the park is the *Rufiji River Camp*, built on a high bank overlooking the Rufiji River and the plain beyond. It has 10 double tents, each with twin beds, and there are toilets and showers close by. There's also a dining room and bar, as well as three boats and three Land Rovers which can be hired for safaris. Accommodation with full board and including the entry fee is US$60 per person per day (Tanzanian residents TSh 15,000). Land Rover hire costs US$20 per person (Tanzanian residents TSh 7000) for each half-day. Sport fishing facilities are also available. The camp is operated by Tanzania Safari Tours Ltd (☎ 64177, 63546), PO Box 2005, Dar es Salaam, through which bookings should be made. Its office is on Pugu Rd, diagonally opposite the TAZARA railway station, and is open Monday to Friday from 8 am to 5 pm. The camp is closed during April and May (the main rainy season).

About 30 km from the Rufiji River Camp is *Mbuyu Safari Camp*, which is also built on a high bank overlooking the Rufiji River. This camp provides luxury tented accommodation with electric lights and sisal mats, and the tents are sheltered from the sun by makuti roofs. Each tent has a shower, flush toilet, twin beds, mosquito netting and a verandah. Set amongst baobab trees, there's a dining room, lounge, bar and reception area. Land Rovers are available for safaris, boats are available for river trips and you can arrange a walking safari. Fishing gear can also be hired. The camp is owned by Bushtrekker Safaris (☎ 31957/32671), PO Box 5350, Dar es Salaam, through which bookings should be made. There's an airstrip near the camp.

Also overlooking the Rufiji River, between Mbuyu Camp and Rufiji River Camp, is *Impala Safari Camp*, another luxury tented camp. It costs US$65 per person per day with full board (TSh 16,500 for Tanzanian residents). The camp has facilities for boat trips on the river, game drives and foot safaris. It's owned by Impala Tours & Safaris (☎ 25779), Zanaki St, PO Box 4783, Dar es Salaam, through which bookings should be made.

Lastly, there is the *Stiegler's Gorge Safari Camp*, which was built in 1977 for Norwegian scientists and engineers who were working in the area, but it's currently closed.

Getting There & Away

Hitching to Selous Game Reserve is virtually out of the question. To get there, you'll need to join an organised safari, have your own vehicle, or go by train and arrange to have a lodge pick you up.

There are three ways to get to the Selous. The easiest but most expensive is to fly in by chartered light aircraft. All the camps have an airstrip. Most safari companies in Dar es Salaam offer package deals on accommodation and flights to the Selous. A typical price would be US$370 for three days/two nights and US$610 for six days/five nights.

Those going in by train should take the TAZARA line as far as Fuga railway station. From Fuga, the lodges will collect you in one of their vehicles, but you must make arrangements for this before you leave Dar es Salaam. Being collected won't be cheap unless you're sharing the cost with others.

Those coming by road in their own vehicle have two options. The first is to take the Dar es Salaam to Mkongo road (via Kibiti) to either the Rufiji River Camp or Mbuyu Safari Camp. The road is sealed as far as Kibiti, after which it's a rough track. The last petrol station is in Kibiti and the distance from Dar es Salaam is about 250 km. The other way is to take the northern Dar es Salaam to Kisaki road via Morogoro and Matombo and then on to Stiegler's Gorge Camp.

The companies which own the camps can arrange road transport for you if you don't have a vehicle, but it's an expensive option.

RUAHA NATIONAL PARK

Ruaha National Park was created in 1964 from half of the Rungwa Game Reserve. It covers 13,000 sq km. Like the Selous, it's a wild, undeveloped area and access is difficult, but there's a lot of wildlife here as a result. Elephants, hippos and crocodiles, and kudu, roan and sable antelope are particularly numerous. The **Great Ruaha River**, which forms the eastern boundary of the park, has spectacular gorges, though a lot of the rest of the park is undulating plateau averaging 1000 metres in height with occasional rocky outcrops.

Visiting the park is only feasible in the dry season, from June to December. During the rest of the year the tracks are virtually impassable. The grass is long between February and June, restricting game-viewing.

If you're interested in helping this park to expand facilities, control poaching, reduce fire risks, and provide suitable equipment to undertake park maintenance, contact the Friends of Ruaha Society (☎ 20522, 26537, 37561), PO Box 60 in Mufindi or PO Box 786 in Dar es Salaam. These people are doing an excellent job to help the chief park warden and the 50 rangers to conserve the flora & fauna of this park (there's one ranger for every 260 sq km).

Places to Stay

Camping is permitted around the park headquarters at Msembe and at various other sites for the usual fee (US$20 per person per night). Also at the park headquarters is a permanent camp, consisting of bandas equipped with beds. Most of the essential equipment is provided but you must bring your own food and drink. This is also essential if you intend to camp. There are no shops in the vicinity, so bring supplies from Iringa, the nearest town. Bookings for the bandas can be made through the Park Warden, Ruaha National Park, PO Box 369, Iringa.

The nicest place to stay if you leave the money is *Ruaha River Camp*, which is constructed on and around a rocky kopje overlooking the Great Ruaha River. It consists of a number of beautiful bandas, which

blend into their surroundings, and a central dining and bar area (in the same style) on an elevated position, from which there are spectacular views. The food is excellent and the owner, Chris Fox, is very gracious and helpful, as are the staff. A double banda with full board costs US$50. It's excellent value and highly recommended. Make prior arrangements to hire 4WD vehicles or to make camp excursions to other parts of the park. Reservations should be made through Foxtreks Ltd, PO Box 84, Mufindi.

Getting There & Away

There is a good all-weather road from Iringa to the park headquarters via Mloa (112 km). This involves crossing the Ruaha River by ferry at Ibuguziwa, which is within the park. The drive should take about four hours. Hitching isn't really feasible, so you'll need to have your own vehicle or go on an organised safari.

GOMBE STREAM NATIONAL PARK

Primarily a chimpanzee sanctuary, this tiny park covers 52 sq km on the shores of Lake Tanganyika between Kigoma and the Burundi border, stretching between the lake shore and the escarpment a little further inland. In recent years, it has become very popular with travellers going north to or coming south from Burundi. It's well worth the effort to get here, and the journey by lake taxi makes an interesting alternative to the MV *Liemba*.

The park is the site of Jane Goodall's research station, which was set up in 1960. It's a beautiful place and the chimps are great fun. A group of them usually come down to the research station every day, but if they don't, the rangers generally know where to find them. You must have a guide whenever you are away from the park headquarters at Kasekela on the lake shore. The guides are mellow, interesting people and you can share the guide fee of US$10 between however many people are with you.

Entry to the park costs US$100 per person for each 24-hour period (US$20 for children between the ages of five and 16).

Places to Stay & Eat

Camping is only possible with special permission, which for most travellers means staying at the 'hostel'. It consists essentially of caged huts, each with six beds and a table and chairs (they're caged to keep the baboons out). A bed costs US$10 per night.

Bring all your own food, though eggs and fish are sometimes available at the station. If you run out of food, you can get more at Mwamgongo village, about 10 km north of here at the northern extremity of the park. The village has a market twice a week (enquire at the station as to the days). Be careful when walking between the cookhouse and the huts at the station, especially if you are carrying food. Baboons have jumped on quite a few people and robbed them of food. The hostel also has a well-stocked library.

Getting There & Away

There are no roads to Gombe Stream, so the only way in is to take one of the lake taxis – small, motorised wooden boats which service the lake-shore villages all the way from Kigoma to the Burundi border.

From Kigoma, the lake taxis leave from the small village of Kalalangabo, about three km north of town, usually between 9 and 10 am. The trips to Gombe Stream and from there to Kagunga (the last village in Tanzania) take about three hours each and cost TSh 250 per person for each leg of the journey. These boats do not operate on Sundays. When catching a lake taxi, try to get one with a cover, as it gets stinking hot out on the lake in the middle of the day. The boats are often overcrowded, not only with people but also with their produce, and they offer no creature comforts whatsoever. They're good fun when the weather is fine, but if there's a squall on the lake, you may be in for a rough time.

Since the boats don't operate on Sunday, it's important not to arrive on a Saturday, otherwise you'll be up for two days' park entry fees (US$100) and hostel fees (US$20).

MAHALE MOUNTAINS NATIONAL PARK

This national park, like Gombe Stream, is mainly a chimpanzee sanctuary but you won't find it marked on most maps since it was only created in mid-1985. It's on the knuckle-shaped area of land which protrudes into Lake Tanganyika about halfway down the lake, opposite the Zaïrian port of Kalemie. The highest peak in the park, Nkungwe (2460 metres), ensures that moist air blowing in from the lake condenses there and falls as rain. This rain supports extensive montane forests, grasslands and alpine bamboo. Numerous valleys intersect the mountains, and some of these have permanent streams which flow into the lake. The eastern side of the mountains are considerably drier and support what is known as miombo woodlands. It's a very isolated area.

The animals which live in this park show closer affinities with western than with eastern Africa. They include chimpanzee, brush-tailed porcupine, various species of colobus monkey (including the Angolan black-and-white colobus), guinea fowl and mongoose. Scientists, mainly from Japan, have been studying the chimpanzees for 20 years, during which time more than 100 of the animals have been habituated to human contact. The population has dramatically increased since 1975, when local people were moved to villages outside the park, thus putting a stop to poaching and field-burning activities. This relocation has also led to the reappearance of leopards, lions and buffaloes, which were never (or very rarely) seen in the past.

Unlike other national parks in Tanzania, this is one which you can walk around – there are no roads in any case. Very few tourists come here because of the remoteness of the area, but it's well worth it if you have the time and initiative.

The best time to visit is between May and October.

Places to Stay

Camping is allowed in specific areas if you have equipment (otherwise there may be a limited amount for hire). Camping fees are

US$20 per person per day. There's also a guesthouse at Kasiha village, though the facilities are still very limited. Bring all your food requirements from Kigoma, since meals are not available. It's a good idea to check with the park headquarters in Kigoma about current conditions, transport and accommodation before setting off.

Getting There & Away

The only way to get to the park is by lake steamer from Kigoma using either the MV *Liemba* or the MV *Mwongozo*. You have to get off at Lagosa (otherwise known as Mugambo), usually in the middle of the night, and take a small boat to the shore.

From Lagosa, charter a small boat from the local fishers or merchants for the trip to Kasoge (about three hours). For the MV *Liemba* schedule, see the To/From Burundi section in the Tanzania Getting There & Away chapter. For the MV *Mwongozo* schedule, enquire in Kigoma.

Because you will be reliant on the lake steamers for getting into and out of Mahale, you may have to stay there for a whole week. This is obviously going to be expensive in terms of park entry fees and camping fees, so you need to think seriously about this before you go. It also means you'll have to bring enough food with you from Kigoma to last a week.

Index

TEXT

Thanks

From Geoff Without listing them in any order of preference, Geoff would like to sincerely thank the following people for their friendship, help, encouragement, hospitality and constructive criticism:

George Pavlu of Brisbane, Australia, who I took with me on my previous trip to East Africa and who hasn't been able to stay away from the place ever since. George contributed to the research, maintained his usual highly explosive degree of humour (most of the time), and amazed all and sundry by his prodigious consumption of Tusker lager. A professional photographer and film scriptwriter, he has maintained his ability to introduce me to facets of Kenya about which I might otherwise have remained ignorant. More power to your elbow, my friend.

Malcolm Gascoigne of Yare Safaris, Nairobi, who enthusiastically met me at Nairobi airport on arrival with a Tusker lager and never let up until the day I left. A good head and shoulders above anyone else I met in Kenya, Malcolm's humour was contagious. He helped me with facts and figures which I wouldn't have had access to otherwise, and his consumption of Tusker lager was at least the equal of George's. I also have to thank him for introducing me to my first ever Maralal International Camel Derby, keeping me informed of important changes whilst I wrote the book, and for his bottomless fund of hospitality both in Nairobi and Maralal.

Alice Njoki Chege, a Kikuyu from Kiambu who accompanied me on several trips and contributed to the research with an impressive speed and thoroughness. Alice also introduced me to life on the 'wrong side of the tracks' where all you meet is smiling children's faces, tenacity and hardship. Alice showed me a Kenya which I would otherwise not have seen.

Ian North, formerly of Kumuka (an overland safari company) who first greeted me with the words, 'I used to hate you', but subsequently became one of my best friends, gave me his Karen house for a month, and helped me in so many other ways. Good luck with your negotiations, mate!

Don Cornes and Margaret, a Kiwi and Kikuyu, respectively, from Nairobi, both of whom injected sense into nonsense when nothing else prevailed and did it with humour. What's also not generally known is that he makes the best spaghetti bolognaise in Nairobi (invitation only) and that he has a very discerning eye for African art.

Philip Jackson (and Purity – or was it Catherine? – only time will tell), a bearded, bespectacled, Yorkshire tyke and ex-overland safari driver who never let up on the jokes and who now runs a safari/travel agency (in between Tusker lagers) in Nairobi.

Alex McCafferty, Australian balloon pilot at Fig Tree Lodge, who gave me a free flight over Masai Mara – my first ever. What an experience!

Mem Bourke, an ebullient Kiwi based in Nairobi with Kumuka, who took me to Masai Mara after the Maralal Camel Derby (where she won the cup for 'Best Lady'). Keep riding those camels, Mem!

Aidan Flannery, former Africa representative for the *Observer* and *Guardian* and now an advertising director based in Nairobi, for his astute analysis of political trends, his good humour and for looking after excess research material whilst I was in Tanzania. Even after a crate of White Cap, his BBC delivery would have David Attenborough green with envy.

Jane and Julia Barnley of Sirikwa Safaris, Kitale, for their warm hospitality and interesting conversation whilst I was in that area.

Paul 'Sliderule' Marsh and Jackie of Nairobi, a fruitcase of an Englishman and a Kikuyu, respectively, for whose wedding I was best man. Shame on you, Paul, you couldn't even pronounce Jackie's Kikuyu names at the ceremony, but then you were never circumcised! I trust your marriage will be as tumultuous as your courtship.

Brian Mitchell, technical officer at the British High Commission in Nairobi, who gave me a lift to Kampala. We couldn't believe it when we discovered that we were born only half a km from each other in the same town (Todmorden) yet had never met.

James Bakeine, former manager of the Saad Hotel, Kasese in the '80s who now runs Nile Safaris in Kampala and gave me an excellent deal on a self-drive car when no-one else in Kampala would even consider self-drive. Thanks for your trust in me, James.

Katie Aston of the UK, an unflappable traveller of like mind and inclination, who was matchless company on the trip around western Uganda and who helped considerably in the research.

Terry Rice, Stephen Laiser, Oliver Davidson and Augustino Mtemi of Hoopoe Adventure Tours, Arusha, for a memorable safari to Tarangire, Manyara, Ngorongoro and Serengeti and for bags of information and subsequent help.

Thanks also to Cynthia Buretta, the public relations manager of Tanzania National Parks, Arusha for details on the national parks; Lucy Ndesamburo, director of the Key's Hotel in Moshi, Tanzania, for keeping me informed of the ins and outs of the Kilimanjaro climb; and Harold Attu, a journalist in Dar es Salaam for giving me a map of Mbeya (his home town) which I would never otherwise have found.

Finally, thanks to all the regulars at Buffalo Bill's and The Pub: 'Welsh' Gareth, 'Kenyan' Kevin, 'Maori' Kevin, big Don Fergie, 'Goan' Sonny, Colin 'The Water Man', big fat Dougie 'The Primus Man', plus many of those mentioned above, and that inimitable and boisterous trio, Margaret Zemei, 'Cutie' and Gladys, who were the originators of the now-famous Nairobi phrase and saying: 'Just imagine! No problem! Even you!'

640

From the Publisher Thanks to all those travellers who took the time and effort to write in with comments and suggestions; apologies if we have misspelt any names:

Peter Ackland (Uga), Jerry Adler (USA), David Alexander (Aus), Hamish Allan, David Allan (Aus), V Arnim (DK), Guy Atherton (UK), F Bakker (NL), Simon Barne (Tan), Catherine Barrett (Aus), Joan Bartz (C), Piers Beagley (Aus), H G Becker (Tan), Karl Beringhs (B), Michael Birnmeyer (USA), Mwijage Bishota, Joe Bivona (USA), Magnus Bjornsen (NL), Neil M Blencowe (UK), Jill Blevins (USA), Jane Boot (Aus), Jonathan Booth, Pia Borjesson (S), Rauline Bossema (NL), Pam Bowers (UK), Louise H Bowers, Josiane Brauer (F), Anke Brettnich (DK), Brian & Barbara (UK), Jutta Brielich (DK), Adam Broadway (UK), Louisa Bungey (UK), Nick Cameron (Tan), Marcel Canoy (NL), Julius Carricho, Anne Casley (Aus), Hayley Cavill (UK), Theresa P Caynes, Stephen Chopyk (C), Horatio Clare (UK), Mary Jane Clarke (USA), Matthew Clarke (UK), Joyce Clarke (UK), Faye Clarke (Aus), Alison Cockerill, Richard Colbey (UK), Christopher Coleridge (UK), Carl Corneliussen (DK), Robert Cox (UK), John Cross (USA), Chris Curtis (USA), Igno Dalmijn (NL), Sarah Davies (UK), Andrew Deakin (UK), Kevin Dean (UK), Michael Deane (UK), Lisa Doan (USA), Heinz Eisenhome (DK), Miriam Elkan (UK), Soren Ericsson (S), Jake Evans (UK), Ursula Fait (I), Sascha Faxe (DK), Debbie Finch (UK), Magnus Fiskesjo (USA), Miss L Fletcher (UK), Jennifer Forsdyke (UK), Ian Fraser (UK), P W Frew (UK), Mark Fulcher (Aus), Clare Gilliam (UK), Chris Glover (C), Mark Goldstein (USA), Edith Gommers (NL), Mark Goodger (Aus), Anne & Roy Goodman (Aus), Mia Granvik (S), Rachel M Gravett (UK), Simon Gustafson (S), David Guthrie (UK), Noralee Halpert (Uga), Peter Harnetty (C), David Harris (UK), Patty Haybach (USA), Mark Hayman (USA), Elizabeth Hayward (UK), John Healey (Aus), Lydia Heard (NZ), Kevin Hester (NZ), Jim Hinds (UK), James Hoskins (NZ), Chris & Cath Howell (NZ), Cissie Hultberg (Tan), John Hunwick, D Ihrmach (DK), Mark Infield (Uga), Bill & Judith Ingram (UK), Timothy Insoll (UK), Pavel Ivanyi (NL), Jim Jackson (UK), Paul-Erik Jensen (DK), Shirley Johnson (USA), Evan Jones (Aus), Amanda Joyce (Aus), Joas Kahembe (Tan), Elisa Karamage (Uga), Richard Kiddle (Aus), Michael Kilsby (NZ), M Kingham (UK), Justa Kiondo, Mikael Kirkensgaard (DK), Ruth & Drew Klee (USA), Frans La Cour (DK), S Lane (UK), Dr Andrew Langley (UK), R Larson (USA), Rebecca Lawson (UK), James Lawton (USA), Cristina Lazzaroni (I), Bob Le Seur (UK), Dr Jim Leppard, Juliet Lesser (UK), Dr Sandro Lionello (I), Michele Lischi, Joanne Liu (C), Dave & Judy Lugers (USA), Edwin & Sarah Mackaness (UK), Adam MacKenzie (NZ), Chris Marshall (Ken), Philippa Marshall (UK), Stuart Martin (UK), Andrea Martin (C), Per Mattsson (S), Sean McCollum (USA), Ruth McCoy (UK), G J McGrath (UK), B McLaren (NZ), Darren McLean (Aus), Helen Meads (UK), Jane Mejer Larsen (DK), John Moffatt (UK), Collie Moran (Irl), Ken & Naomi Morrice (UK), Jenny Mothoneos (Aus), Jane Mumford (UK), Mervi Mustakallio (Ken), K F Neeves (UK), Dave Nelson (UK), Elaine Newkirk (USA), Steve Nicolle (UK), Gail Nolan-Neylan (Aus), Charlotte Oakes (UK), Ulrich Offersen (DK), Mike Osborn (UK), Wayne Patterson (USA), D Peaty, Jo Pegler (Aus), Francisco J S Perez (Sp), Sarah Pitman (NZ), Jo Plant (UK), Kees Punt (NL), Gunter Quaisser (DK), Luk Raeymaekers (B), AA Abdul Rahman (Ken), Steve Rainbow (UK), John Rashak (USA), Kari Rempel (C), Sijtze Reurich (NL), Terry Rice (Tan), Penny Richards (Aus), Ruth Riley (UK), Lucy Robertson (UK), Susan Robinson (UK), Steve Rogowski (UK), Ian Ross (C), Lionello Sandro (I), Manjit Schat (UK), Rolf Schenker (CH), Wiebke Schlomer (DK), Helena Schluter (DK), W J Schouten (NL), Falko Schube (DK), Hans-Joachim Schultze (DK), Marneo Serenelli (I), Charles Sewell (USA), Mr & Mrs Shahaf (Isr), Peter Shanks (USA), Raimond Siebesma (NL), Pat Silton (UK), Kwang Poh Sim (UK), Alberto Paulo Simoes (P), Chris Smith (USA), Kate Smith (UK), Jonathon H Spear (UK), Stacey Spencer (Aus), Mark Stanley Price (Ken), Maud Steeman (NL), Annie Stockley (UK), Raimund Strodza (I), Herman Stuijver (NL), Paul Sullivan (USA), Bert Taken (NL), Phil Tancock (UK), Fenella Taylor (UK), Mrs M N Tejpar (Ken), Judy Thompson (Aus), Whitney Tilson (USA), Justine & Todd, Jane Tompsett (UK), Marymae Trench (Aus), Tim K A Turner (UK), Herman Van der Kuil (NL), Arie van Engelenburg (NL), Liesbeth van Seumeren (NL), Erik Verbeek (B), Carinne Vernaillen (B), Thomas Wagensonner (DK), Harriet Wansink (NL), Marie Ward (Aus), Theodora H Washer (USA), J Christine Wattelet (F), Gillian Wells (UK), E Brooke Whitaker (Ken), Eric T Wiberg, Miss E A Williams (UK), Martin Williamson (UK), Jeanette Worrell (UK), Patsy Wright-Warren (UK), Mike Wylie (Ken), Arnon Yaffe (Isr) and Nicole Zwager (NL)

Aus – Australia, B – Belgium, C – Canada, DK – Denmark, F – France, I – Italy, Irl – Ireland, Isr – Israel, Ken – Kenya, NZ – New Zealand, NL – Netherlands, Sp – Spain, S – Sweden, Tan – Tanzania, Uga – Uganda, UK – United Kingdom, USA – United States of America

Update – March 1996

Travel in most parts of the region remains fairly safe. However, Rwanda is still suffering from its inter-tribal war and Burundi is sliding towards civil war. Avoid both countries. Areas that were dangerous for muggings in the past are still at least as dangerous.

Kenya

Kenya is experiencing a rough time on the political scene. Its relations with Rwanda are at an all-time low, due to Kenya's alleged support for Hutu extremists. On the domestic scene, Richard Leakey, the famous anthropologist, has helped to create Safina, a new party with a platform of stamping out corruption, mismanagement and incompetence. That a white Kenyan should set up a political party and possibly be a presidential candidate has apparently upset President Moi.

Visas A traveller reports that transit visas issued at the airport are valid for only three days and are definitely not extendible.

Money & Costs Entry fees for some national parks have increased by about 40%, while some have been reduced by about 25%.

In March 1996 the exchange rate was approximately US$1 = KSh58.

Dangers & Annoyances Vehicles on roads in the vicinity of the Kenya/Somali border have been attacked by Somali armed gangs. Virtually the only safe way to pass through the region is in convoy. Apparently all buses take this option.

Nairobi ('Nairobbery') is still a muggers' paradise and in some coastal areas crime is increasing. There have been reports of travellers being drugged by robbers, so be careful about accepting food or drink from strangers. There have also been reports of visitors to Masai Mara Game Reserve being attacked and robbed.

Health In 1995, the *Sunday Standard*

Dear traveller

Prices go up, good places go bad, bad places go bankrupt...and every guidebook is inevitably outdated in places. Fortunately, many travellers write to us about their experiences, telling us when things have changed. If we reprint a book between editions, we try to include the best of this information in an Update section. We also make travellers' tips immediately available on our award-winning World Wide Web Internet site (http://www.lonelyplanet.com) and in a free quarterly newsletter, *Planet Talk*.

Although much of this information has not been verified by our own first-hand research, we believe it can be very useful. We cannot vouch for its accuracy, however, so bear in mind it could be wrong.

We really enjoy hearing from people out on the road, and apart from guaranteeing that others will benefit from your good and bad experiences, we're prepared to bribe you with the offer of a free book for sending us substantial useful information.

I hope you do find this book useful – and that you let us know when it isn't. Thank you to everyone who has written.

Tony Wheeler

reported that 75 out of 78 brands of bottled water sold in Kenya were Nairobi tap water.

Tanzania

Tanzania's first multi-party elections, held in late 1995, resulted in a victory for the ruling Chama Cha Mapinduzi Party. However, the elections were something of a shambles, with complaints about irregularities from independent observers and the withdrawal of the opposition from the re-runs which were granted in a few high-profile seats.

Visas Readers report that Tanzanian visas are much more expensive in Kenya than in overseas countries.

Money In March 1996 the exchange rate was approximately US$1 = TSh 552.

Dangers & Annoyances Muggings seem to be on the increase. Bagamoyo is particularly dangerous, and we've had a report from a traveller who was mugged in Dar es Salaam's Kiriakoo market at noon. The western border area, affected by fighting in Rwanda and Burundi, is tense.

Many people have problems with safari organisers. A new association that brings together Tanzanian tour operators and travel agents, the Association of Tanzanian Travel Operators (ATTO), was formed to ensure that members adhere to ethics governing the industry. The ATTO has published a set of guidelines for visitors to follow when seeking a safari operator in Tanzania. These guidelines can also be used in Kenya. The ATTO's guidelines are:

- never entertain street boys trying to offer safari deals
- never seal a deal, buy a safari or pay money to anyone purporting to be a tour operator anywhere outside official company premises
- don't pay money to anyone for safaris in hotels, guesthouses, restaurants or any other places other than company premises
- always demand a safari contract, itinerary and a receipt (all on company stationery or with an official company stamp)

In case of doubt about any safari company or person, seek the assistance of the Tanzania Tourist Board or the ATTO. The latter has offices in Arusha, in the International Conference Centre (AICC), Ngorongoro Wing, 2nd Floor, Room No 234/5.

Getting Around A group of travellers report that it might be cheaper for a group to charter a plane between destinations like Dar es Salaam and Zanzibar or Serengeti and Zanzibar, than it is for each person to buy a train, bus or boat ticket. It also saves a great deal of time. Naturally, you need to bargain for a good price.

The passenger train between Dar es Salaam and Tanga seems to have stopped running. There are plenty of buses.

The boats that ply the Dar es Salaam/Zanzibar route have changed their departure times: the MV *Muungano* departs Dar es Salaam at 11.15 am and returns at 10 pm; FB *Canadian Spirit* departs Dar es Salaam at 9

am on Mondays and Thursdays; MV *Flying Horse* departs Dar es Salaam at 12.30 pm and returns at 10 pm; and the *Sea Express* has many daily departures from Dar es Salaam at 8 am, 10 am, noon, 2.30 pm and 4.30 pm, returning from Zanzibar at 7 am, 10 am, noon, 2.30 pm and 4.30 pm.

Uganda

Guerilla activity along the Sudanese border has made northern Uganda very dangerous. It's currently safe to visit Murchison Falls National Park south of the Pakwatch/Karuma Falls road. Get the latest information before going, however.

US and Canadian citizens reportedly do not require visas to enter Uganda.

A traveller reports that the Kabale border between Rwanda and Uganda has reopened.

The Greenland Bank opposite the GPO in Kampala is open until at least 8.30 pm on weekdays, so if you're arriving on the Nairobi/Kampala bus (which is now direct) don't change too much money at the border – you'll get a better rate in Kampala. There are now Forex bureaus in Kabale and Kisoro.

The National Parks office in Kampala (☎ 53 0158, fax 53 0159) has moved to Plot 31, Kanjokya St (off Kira Rd about one km past the museum).

In March 1996 the exchange rate was approximately US$1 = USh 1013.

Zaïre

The outbreak of the deadly Ebola virus in the Kikwit district in 1995 caused worldwide concern, but by late 1995 the World Health Organization had declared that the outbreak was over. However, Ebola could reappear.

In March 1996 one new zaïre (NZ) was worth about US$0.000087.

Acknowledgements

The information in this Update was compiled from various sources, including reports by the following travellers: E Davies & P Brown, Muganyizi Theophil Kashasha (Tanzania), Steven Smith (UK), Steve Susswein (USA) and Susan Wood (UK).

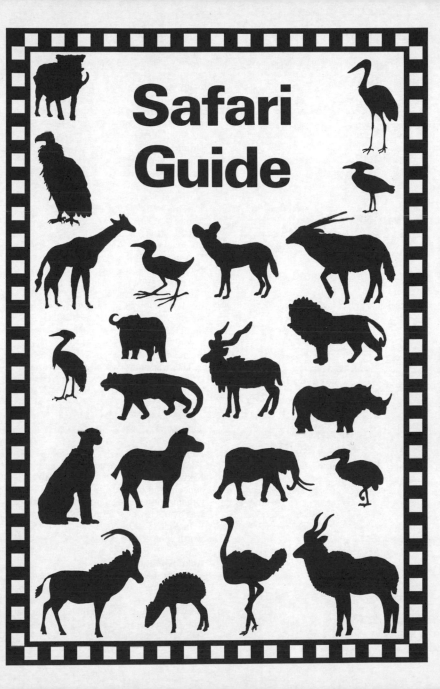

Safari
Guide

Safari Guide

ANTELOPES

The large, striped bongo antelope is rarely seen. About your only chance of sighting one is in Aberdare National Park. They live close to water in dense forest, only leaving the forest cover to graze at night in open clearings.

The bongo stands around 120 cm high at the shoulder and measures around 250 cm from head to tail. Mature males are a beautiful dark mahogany-brown colour, while the females are a much lighter reddish-brown. Both sexes have distinctive vertical white stripes on the body, never less than nine, never more than 14. Horns are sported by both males and females, and these are slightly spiralling (lyre shaped) with yellow tips, with those on the male being slightly shorter and sturdier than on the female.

The bongo grazes mainly on leaves and will often stand on its hind legs to increase its reach. It also digs for roots with its horns. Bongos are usually found in small family herds although bulls often lead a solitary existence, meeting up with other animals only to mate.

Bongo
(Tragelaphus eurycerus)
Swahili: *bongo*

Although the small bushbuck antelope exists in fairly large numbers in most of Kenya's game parks, it is a shy, solitary animal and is rarely sighted.

Standing at about 80 cm at the shoulder, the bushbuck is chestnut to dark brown in colour with a variable number of white vertical stripes on the body between the neck and rump, as well as (usually) two horizontal white stripes lower down which give the animal a 'harnessed' appearance. There are also a number of white spots on the upper thigh and a white splash on the neck. Females are reddish brown. Horns are usually only grown by males but females have been known to grow them on rare occasions. They are lyre shaped with gentle spirals and average about 30 cm in length.

Bushbuck are rarely found in groups of more than two and prefer to stick to areas with heavy brush cover. When startled they take off and crash loudly through the undergrowth. They are nocturnal animals and browsers yet rarely move far from their chosen spot. Though shy and elusive they can be aggressive and dangerous when cornered. Their main predators are leopards and pythons.

Bushbuck
(Tragelaphus scriptus)
Swahili: *pongo*

Dik-dik
Kirk's dik-dik
(Madoqua kirki)
Swahili: *dik-dik*

Kirk's dik-dik is the more common of the two dik-diks found in Kenya (the other is Gunther's dik-dik, found only in Marsabit National Park & Reserve) and is commonly seen in Nairobi, Tsavo, Amboseli and Masai Mara reserves. Its name comes from the 'zic-zic' call it makes when alarmed.

The dik-dik is a tiny antelope, standing only around 35 cm at the shoulder. It is a reddish-brown colour on the back, with lighter flanks and white belly. Size is usually the easiest way to identify a dik-dik, but other telltale marks are the almost total lack of a tail and the tuft of dark hair on the forehead. Horns (found on the males only) are so short (around six cm) that they are often lost in the hair tuft.

Dik-diks are usually seen singly or in pairs and are often found in exceedingly dry places – it seems they don't have a great dependence on water. They are territorial creatures, each pair occupying an area of around five hectares. They are mainly nocturnal but can be seen grazing in acacia scrub in the early morning and late afternoon; like so many animals they rest in the heat of the day.

The females bear a single offspring twice a year. After six months the young dik-dik reaches sexual maturity and is then driven out of the home territory.

Duiker
Common or bush duiker
(Sylvicapra grimmia)
Swahili: *nsya*

This is the most common of the duikers, of which there are at least 10 species. Even so, they are not often sighted as they are largely nocturnal, usually only live in pairs and prefer areas with good scrub cover. They are known to exist in Marsabit, Tsavo, Nairobi, Amboseli, Meru and Masai Mara reserves.

The duiker stands only 60 cm at the shoulder, is a greyish light-brown colour with white belly and a dark brown vertical stripe on the face. The horns (males only) are short (around 20 cm), pointed, and grow straight.

Duikers are widely distributed and can be found in a variety of habitats ranging from open bush to semidesert and up to the snow line of the highest mountains except for bamboo forest and rainforest. This ability to survive in many different habitats explains their survival in cultivated areas where other herbivorous species have been exterminated.

They are almost exclusively browsers and only rarely eat grasses though they appear to supplement their diet with insects and guinea fowl chicks. They are capable of doing without water for long periods but will drink it when available.

The eland looks similar to some varieties of cattle seen on the Indian subcontinent, and is found in Nairobi, Marsabit, Tsavo and Masai Mara parks/reserves.

The biggest of the antelopes, the eland stands about 170 cm at the shoulder and a mature bull can weigh up to 1000 kg. Horns are found on both sexes and these are spiralled at the base, swept straight back and grow to about 65 cm. Males have a much hairier head than the females, and their horns are stouter and slightly shorter. They are a light greyish-brown in colour, and bear as many as 15 vertical white stripes on the body, although these are often almost indistinguishable on some animals.

The eland prefers savannah scrub to wide open spaces, but also avoids thick forest. It grazes on grass and tree foliage in the early morning and late afternoon, and is also active on moonlit nights. It needs to drink once a day, but can go for a month or more without water if its diet includes fodder with high water content.

Eland are usually found in groups of around six to 12, but there may be as many as 50 in a herd. A small herd normally consists of several females and one male, but in larger herds there may be several males, and there is a strict hierarchy. Females reach sexual maturity at around two years and can bear up to 12 calves in a lifetime. The young are born in October-November.

Eland
(Tragelaphus oryx)
Swahili: *pofu*

The gerenuk is probably the easiest of all antelopes to identify because of its inordinately long neck, which accounts for its Swahili name, *swala tiga*, meaning giraffe-gazelle. Its distribution is limited to Meru, Samburu, Tsavo and Amboseli national parks.

Growing to around 100 cm at the shoulder, the gerenuk is a dark fawn colour on the back which becomes much lighter on the sides and belly. The horns (found on the male only) curve gently backward and grow up to 40 cm long.

The gerenuk's habitat ranges from dry thorn bush country to semidesert and its food consists mainly of the tender leaves and shoots of acacia bushes. It is quite capable – in the same way as a goat – of standing on its hind legs and using one of its forelegs to pull down the higher branches of bushes to get at the leaves and shoots. Also like goats, they are quite capable of doing without water.

Gerenuk
(Litocranius walleri)
Swahili: *swala tiga*

Grant's Gazelle
(Gazella granti)
Swahili: *swala granti*

This is one of the most common antelopes and exists in large numbers in Nairobi, Amboseli, Masai Mara, Tsavo and Marsabit reserves.

Grant's gazelle are most easily identified by their colouring and long horns: sandy brown on the back, clearly demarcated from a lighter colour on the flanks and white belly, and white around the tail and hind legs. They are not a large gazelle, standing around 90 cm at the shoulder. Horns are found on both sexes and are heavily ridged with around 25 rings; in the male they grow to around 60 cm (although they often appear longer because of the relatively small body) and curve gracefully and evenly up and back, usually with some outward curving as well; in the female the horns are much shorter but follow the same pattern.

You usually come across herds of Grant's gazelle in open grassy country where there is some forest cover, although they are also occasionally found in heavily wooded savannah country. Herd size is usually between 20 and 30, with one dominant male, does and young. Food consists mainly of leaves and grass. As water is obtained through dietary intake these gazelles do not need to drink.

Greater Kudu
(Tragelaphus strepsiceros)
Swahili: *tandala mkubwa*

The greater kudu is one of the largest of the antelopes but it's a rare sight and only found in any numbers in Marsabit National Park & Reserve. Elsewhere, kudu prefer hilly country with fairly dense bush cover. The kudu stands around 1.5 metres at the shoulder and weighs up to 250 kg, yet it's a very elegant creature, light grey in colour, with broad ears and a long neck. The sides of the body are marked by six to 10 vertical white stripes and there is a white chevron between the eyes. Horns are carried only by the males and are both divergent and spiralling.

Kudu live in small herds of up to four or five females with their young but these often split up during the rainy season. The males are usually solitary though occasionally they band together into small herds.

They are mainly browsers and only seldom eat grasses but are capable of eating many types of leaves which would be poisonous to other animals.

Although somewhat clumsy animals when on the move, they are capable of clearing well over two metres when jumping.

The hartebeest is a medium-sized antelope and is found in Nairobi, Tsavo, Amboseli and Masai Mara parks. It is easy to recognise as it has a long, narrow face and distinctively angular short horns (on both sexes) which are heavily ridged. Colouring is generally light brown on the back, becoming paler towards the rear and under the belly. The back slopes away from the humped shoulders. They prefer grassy plains for grazing but are also found in lightly treed savannah or hills.

The hartebeest feeds exclusively on grass, and usually drinks twice daily, although it can go for months without water if necessary.

They are social beasts and often intermingle with animals such as zebras and wildebeest. Their behaviour is not unlike the wildebeest's, particularly the head tossing and shaking.

Sexual maturity is reached at around 2½ years and calving goes on throughout the year, although there are peak periods in February and August. Predators are mainly the large cats, hyenas and hunting dogs.

Hartebeest
(Alcelaphus buselaphus)
Swahili: *kongoni*

The graceful impala is one of the most common antelopes and is found in virtually all national parks and reserves in large numbers.

A medium-sized antelope, it stands about 80 cm at the shoulder. The coat is a glossy rufous colour though paler on the flanks with the underparts, rump, throat and chin being white. A narrow black line runs along the middle of the rump to about halfway down the tail and there's also a vertical black stripe on the back of the thighs but, unlike in Grant's gazelle, this does not border the white buttocks. It's also distinguishable from Grant's gazelle by having a tuft of long black hair above the heels of the hind legs. Only the males have horns which are long (averaging 75 cm), lyre-shaped and curve upwards as they spread.

Impala are gregarious animals with each male having a 'harem' of up to 100 females, though more usually around 15 to 20. Males without such a 'harem' form bachelor groups. There is fierce fighting between males during the rutting season but otherwise they are fairly placid animals.

One of the most noticeable characteristics of impala is their speed and prodigious ability at jumping. They are quite capable of clearing 10 metres in a single jump lengthwise or three metres in height and this they frequently do even when there are no obstacles in their path.

Impala are both browsers and grazers and are active during the day and by night. They are quite highly dependent on water but are capable of existing on just dew for fairly long periods. Their main predators are leopards, cheetahs and hunting dogs.

Impala
(Aepyceros melampus)
Swahili: *swala pala*

Klipspringer
(Oreotragus oreotragus)
Swahili: *mbuzi mawe*

The distinctive klipspringers inhabit rocky outcrops in Tsavo, Amboseli, Masai Mara, Marsabit and Meru reserves.

Standing about 50 cm at the shoulder, they are easily recognised by their curious 'tip-toe' stance (the hooves are designed for balance and grip on rocky surfaces) and the greenish tinge of their speckled coarse hair. Horns (found on the male only) are short (10 cm) and widely spaced.

Klipspringers are most often seen on rocky outcrops, or in the grassland in the immediate vicinity, and when alarmed they retreat into the rocks for safety. They are amazingly agile and sure-footed creatures and can often be observed bounding up impossibly rough rock faces. These antelope can also go entirely without water if there is none around, getting all they need from the greenery they eat. They are most active just before and after midday, and single males often keep watch from a good vantage point. The klipspringer is usually found in pairs, or a male with two females, and inhabits a clearly defined territory.

Klipspringers reach sexual maturity at around one year, and females bear one calf twice a year. Calves may stay with the adult couple for up to a year, although young males usually seek their own territory earlier than that.

Predators are mainly the leopard and the crowned eagle, but also include jackals and baboons.

Lesser kudu
(Tragelaphus imberbis)
Swahili: *tandala ndogo*

The lesser kudu is a smaller model of the greater kudu, the major differences being the lack of a beard, more numerous and more pronounced vertical white stripes on the body, and two white patches on the underside of the neck. As with the greater kudu, only the males have horns. The coat colour varies from brownish grey to blue-grey. It stands around a metre high at the shoulder.

Kudu usually live in pairs accompanied by their fawns though females occasionally form small herds. They are very shy animals and spend much of the day hiding in dense bush, only moving out of cover to feed in the early morning and at dusk. This makes them difficult to spot.

Kudu are browsers and feed on a mixture of leaves, young shoots and twigs and, though they drink regularly if water is available, they are capable of doing without it for relatively long periods – more so than the greater kudu.

The most likely places you will find them are Tsavo and Marsabit national parks where they prefer the drier, more bushy areas.

Not unlike a duiker in appearance, the small oribi is relatively uncommon, and your best chance of spotting one is in the Masai Mara reserve.

The oribi's most distinguishing mark, although you'll need binoculars to spot it, is a circular batch of naked black skin below the ear – it is actually a scent gland. Another useful indicator is the tuft of black hair on the tip of the short tail. Otherwise the oribi is a uniform golden brown with white on the belly and insides of the legs. Short straight horns about 10 cm in length are found on the males only.

Oribi usually graze in grassy plains with good shelter. If water is available they will drink willingly but can also go without it entirely. When alarmed they bolt and then make bouncing jumps with a curious action – all four legs are kept completely stiff. It is thought this helps them to orient themselves in places with poor visibility. After 100 metres or so they stop and assess the danger.

Oribi are usually found in pairs and are territorial. Sexual maturity is reached at around one year, and the females bear one calf twice a year.

Being quite small, the oribi has many predators, including the larger cats.

Oribi
(Ourebia ourebi)
Swahili: *taya*

The fringe-eared or Kilimanjaro oryx *(Oryx gazella callotis)* is found in Kenya's Amboseli and Tsavo national parks and is a large antelope standing around 120 cm at the shoulder. The coat is a sandy fawn with a black spinal stripe which extends to the tip of the tail. The underparts are white and separated from the lower flanks by another black stripe. There are also two black rings just above the knee of the forelegs.

The related galla oryx *(Oryx gazella gallarum)* is reddish-grey and is most commonly seen in the Marsabit reserve and along the Tana River. (Note that the oryx species name may also be referred to as *beisa*.) Both types of oryx have ovate, pointed ears with the main distinguishing feature being, as the name suggests, a tuft of black hair on the ears of the fringe-eared one. Oryx are easy to distinguish from other antelopes due to their straight, very long and heavily ridged horns which are carried almost parallel. Both the males and females have horns. These horns come into their own when the animal is forced to defend itself. Held down between the forelegs, they are formidable weapons and used to impale an enemy.

Oryx are principally grazers but will also browse on thorny shrubs. They are capable of doing without water for long periods but will drink daily if it is available.

Herds vary from five to 40 individuals and sometimes more though the bulls are usually solitary. Oryx are often found in association with zebra and Grant's gazelle.

Oryx
Fringe-eared oryx
(Oryx gazella callotis)
Swahili: *choroa*

Reedbuck
Bohor reedbuck
(Redunca redunca)
Swahili: *tohe*

The best places to spot the dusty brown reed-buck is in Nairobi and Amboseli national parks, and they are occasionally seen in Tsavo National Park.

The reedbuck is a medium-sized antelope, standing around 80 cm high at the shoulder. The most distinctive features are the forward curving horns (found on the males only) and the bushy tail. The underbelly, inside of the thighs, throat and underside of the tail are white.

The reedbuck frequents open grassy plains or hills and is never found more than around eight km from a water supply. It is very territorial and is found in small groups of up to 10 animals. The groups usually consist of an older male and ac-companying females and young. Its diet consists almost exclusively of grass but does include some foliage.

At mating time males fight spiritedly. After reaching sexual maturity at around 1½ years, females bear one calf at a time.

The bohor reedbuck's main predators include the big cats, hyenas and hunting dogs.

Roan Antelope
(Hippotragus equinus)
Swahili: *korongo*

The roan antelope is one of Kenya's less common antelope species. The best place to see one these days is in the Shimba Hills National Reserve, where they have been translocated from other parts of the country, although there are still a few small herds in Masai Mara.

The third largest of the antelopes after eland and kudu at up to 150 cm at the shoulder, a roan bears a striking resemblance to a horse. The coat varies from reddish fawn to dark rufous with white underparts and there's a conspicuous mane of stiff, black-tipped hairs which stretches from the nape to the shoulders. Under the neck, there's another mane of sorts consisting of long dark hairs. The ears are long, narrow and pointed with a brown tassel at the tip. The face is a very distinctive black and white pattern. Both sexes have curving backswept horns which can measure up to 70 cm.

Roan are aggressive by nature and fight from a very early age – a characteristic which fre-quently deters predators. For most of the year they live in small herds of up to 20 and sometimes more, led by a master bull, but in the mating season, the bulls become solitary and take a female out of the herd. The pair stay together until the calf is born after which the females form a herd by themselves. They eventually return to their former herd. Herds congregate during the dry season.

Being principally grazers, roan rarely move far when food is plentiful but they are susceptible to drought and during such periods they may be constantly on the move.

Also found only in the Shimba Hills National Reserve, the sable antelope is slightly smaller than its cousin the roan, but is more solidly built. The colouring is dark brown to black, with white face markings and belly. Both sexes carry long back-swept horns which average around 80 cm, those of the male being longer and more curved.

The sable antelope is active mainly in the early morning and late afternoon, and is found in herds of up to 25 and sometimes more in the dry season. They are territorial and each group occupies a large area, although within this area individual males have demarcated territories of up to 30 hectares. Sables feed mainly off grass but leaves and foliage from trees account for around 10% of their diet.

Females start bearing calves at around three years of age, and the main calving times are January and September.

Like the roan, the sable is a fierce fightor and has been known to kill lions when attacked. Other predators include the leopard, hyena and hunting dog.

Sable Antelope
(Hippotragus niger)
Swahili: *pala hala*

The sitatunga is a swamp antelope with unusual elongated hooves which give it the ability to walk on marshy ground without sinking. It is restricted solely to the Saiwa Swamp National Park near Kitale, and it's well worth a visit to this small, walkers-only park.

Very similar to the bushbuck in appearance, except that the coat of the male is much darker and the hair of both sexes much longer and shaggier, the sitatunga stands something over one metre at the shoulder. The females have a lighter, reddish coat and the males have twisted horns up to 90 cm long. It is a fairly shy antelope and sightings are not all that common. A good swimmer, the sitatunga will often submerge itself almost completely when alarmed.

It feeds largely on papyrus and other reeds and is usually nocturnal though in places where it remains undisturbed it can be diurnal. Animals normally live singly or in pairs but sometimes come together in small herds numbering up to 15.

Sitatunga
(Tragelaphus spekei)
Swahili: *nzohe*

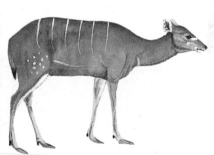

Thomson's Gazelle
(Gazella thomsonii)
Swahili: *swala tomi*

The small and frisky Thomson's gazelle is instantly recognisable by the black slash across the side which separates the brown back from the white underbelly. They are very common in the plains country – Amboseli, Masai Mara and Nairobi reserves, but very rare in different habitats such as Tsavo National Park.

Standing around 60 cm at the shoulders, the 'Tommy' is one of the smaller antelopes. Horns on the male grow to about 30 cm and almost straight with just a gentle curve towards the tips; in the female the horns are straighter and much shorter. Another easy to identify characteristic is the short black tail which seems to be constantly twitching. Along with the oribi, Tommys also do the stiff-legged bouncing jump when alarmed.

Group size varies: one old (largely territorial) male may be accompanied by anything from five to 50 females, or there may be herds of up to 500 young males without territory. When food is plentiful the herds tend to be smaller and more territorial. In times of drought herds of several thousand may gather and roam for food. They are often found in close proximity to other animals, including Grant's gazelles and wildebeest.

Sexual maturity is reached at around one year but males only mate after establishing their own territory, which occurs sometime after two years of age. Calving occurs throughout the year though tends to peak at the end of the rainy season.

Being a small animal, Tommys have many predators, including the big cats, hunting dogs, hyenas and servals.

The topi is not unlike the hartebeest in appearance, but is a dark almost purplish colour and has black patches on the rear thighs, front legs and face. Its horns, which are found on both sexes, also differ in shape from the hartebeest in curving gently up, out and back. Although fairly widely distributed in East Africa, in Kenya it is only found in Masai Mara where it exists in large numbers.

A highly gregarious antelope which lives in herds numbering from 15 up to several hundred individuals, topi congregate at certain times of year in gatherings of up to 10,000 in preparation for a migration to fresh pastures. They are often found mingling with wildebeest, hartebeest and zebra.

In the mating season, bulls select a well-defined patch of ground which is defended against rivals and this is where mating takes place. At this time females are free to wander from one patch to another. After mating, the herds split into single-sex parties.

Topi are exclusively grazers and prefer flood plains which support lush pasture though they are capable of thriving on dry grasses which other antelopes will not eat. When water is available they drink frequently but they are also capable of surviving long periods without water so long as there is sufficient grass available.

Their main predator is the lion.

Topi
(Damaliscus lunatus)
Swahili: *nyamera*

Waterbuck
Defassa or common waterbuck
(Kobus ellipsiprymnus)
Swahili: *kuru*

The defassa waterbuck is a fairly solid animal and is easily recognisable by its thick, shaggy, dark brown coat, and white inner thighs. It is fairly common and easily seen in Nairobi and Nakuru national parks, and in Masai Mara. A second variety, the ringed waterbuck (also *Kobus ellipsiprymnus*), so-called because of the white ring around its rump, is also seen in Marsabit, Tsavo and Amboseli parks. Both varieties have white facial and throat markings.

Only the males have horns, and these curve gradually outwards then grow straight up to a length of about 75 cm. As you might expect from the name, waterbuck are good swimmers and readily enter the water to escape from predators. Their habitat is always close to water, and males have marked territories by the water's edge. Females and younger males tend to wander at random through male territories. Herds are small and usually consist of cows, calves and one mature bull – the other bulls live in small groups apart from the herd.

The bulk of the waterbuck's diet is grass but it does eat some of the foliage of trees and bushes.

Sexual maturity is reached at just over one year, although a male will not become the dominant bull in the herd until around five years of age.

Waterbuck are usually only preyed on when other food is scarce. The reason being that when mature the flesh is tough and has a distinct odour. Predators such as lions, leopards and hunting dogs go for the young calves and females.

Wildebeest are to the African savannah what the bison once were to the North American prairies. Numbering in their millions in certain areas, particularly Masai Mara and over the border in Serengeti, they are unmistakable for their prehistoric appearance. Wildebeest (also known as blue wildebeest or brindled gnu) are well known for their eccentric behaviour which includes loud snorting, tossing and shaking of the head, bucking, running around in circles and rolling in the dust (thought to be a reaction to the activity of the botfly larva which manage to find their way right up into their nostrils). They are heavily built with a massive head and wild mane, are somewhat clumsy, and have been described as having the forequarters of an ox, the hind parts of an antelope and the tail of a horse.

Their sheer numbers, nevertheless, are testimony to their superb adaptation to the environment.

Almost entirely grazers, they are constantly on the move in search of good pasture and water, and their annual migration between the Serengeti and Masai Mara (and vice versa) has to be one of the world's most spectacular sights. Thousands lose their lives in this annual event – drowning in rivers, being taken by crocodiles and other predators or just through sheer exhaustion. The migration north from Serengeti takes place in July and the return trip from Masai Mara in October.

They're very gregarious animals and are usually seen in large herds numbering up to tens of thousands in association with zebra, Thomson's gazelle and other herbivores.

During the mating season, groups of up to 150 females and their young are gathered together by one to three bulls which defend a defined territory against rivals even when on the move. There's apparently no hierarchy amongst the bulls and, at the end of the mating season, the breeding herds are reabsorbed into the main herds.

Although they graze in a scattered fashion without any apparent social organisation during the rainy season, they coalesce around water holes and remaining pasture in the dry season. Wildebeest prefer to drink daily and will walk up to 50 km to secure water but are capable of surviving for up to five days without it. They're also a noisy animal when grazing, constantly producing a series of snorts and low-pitched grunts.

Their main predators are lions, cheetahs and hunting dogs though hyenas are also very partial to young calves.

Wildebeest (Gnu)

Blue wildebeest or brindled gnu
(*Connochaetes taurinus*)
Swahili: *nyumbu*

BIRDS

Flamingo
(Phoenicopterus minor,
Phoenicopterus ruber)
Swahili: *heroe*

Flamingos are found by the million in Kenya. They are attracted by the proliferation of algae and crustaceans which thrive in the soda lakes of Baringo, Bogoria, Nakuru and Magadi in the Rift Valley, and Lake Natron across the border in Tanzania.

There are always some birds at each lake but large concentrations seem to move capriciously from one to another over a period of years. Lake Nakuru is the current hot spot but this may well change. It is thought that the changing water levels may be one reason why they change locations. Whatever lake they are presently at, the best time of the year for flamingo viewing is in January-February when they form huge pink masses around the shores of the lakes.

Flamingos have a complicated and sophisticated system for filtering the foodstuffs out of the water. This is because the highly alkane water would be toxic if consumed in large quantities. The deep-pink lesser flamingo, *Phoenicopterus minor*, filters algae and diatoms out of the water by vigorous suction and expulsion of the water in and out of its beak several times per second. The minute particles are caught on fine hairlike protrusions which line the inside of the mandibles. This is all done with the bill upside down in the water. The suction is created by the movement of the thick and fleshy tongue which lies in a groove in the lower mandible and works to and fro like a piston. Where the *Phoenicopterus minor* obtains its food largely by sweeping its head to and fro and filtering the water, the greater flamingo, or *Phoenicopterus ruber*, is more a bottom feeder and supplements its algae diet with small molluscs, crustaceans and other organic particles from the mud. It has been estimated that one million lesser flamingos consume over 180 tons of algae and diatoms daily!

The very distinct and instantly identifiable ostrich is the largest living bird. It is widely distributed throughout the savannah plains of Kenya, and so is most widely seen in the southern parks and reserves – Masai Mara, Amboseli and Tsavo.

The adult ostrich stands around 2½ metres high and weighs as much as 150 kg. The neck and the legs are bare, and all these areas of bare skin turn bright red in breeding males. The bushy plumage on the males is black, with white feathers in the redundant wings and the tail. The females are a uniform greyish brown and are slightly smaller and lighter than the males. The ostrich's long and strong legs can push it along at up to 50 km/h.

Ostriches tend to be territorial and are rarely seen in groups of more than six individuals. They feed on leaves, flowers and seeds of a variety of plants. When feeding, the food is gradually accumulated in the top of the neck and then passes down to the stomach in small boluses, and it's possible to see these masses of food actually moving down the neck.

The ostrich breeds in the dry season, and the males put on quite an impressive courtship display. Having driven off any possible rival males, the male trots up to the female with tail erect, then squats down and rocks from side to side, simultaneously waving each wing in the air alternately. Just for good measure the neck also waves from side to side. The males may couple with more than one female, in which case the eggs of all the females (up to five) are laid on the same nest, and so it may contain as many as 30 eggs. The eggs are incubated by the major female (the one first mated with) by day, and by the male at night. The other female birds have nothing further to do with the eggs or offspring.

Ostrich
(Struthio camelus)
Swahili: *mbuni*

Vulture
Nubian vulture
(Torgos tracheliotus)
Swahili: *gushu*

Vultures are a large, eagle-like bird belonging to the Accipitridae family, of which hawks and eagles are also members. There are a whole range of different species, the most common ones in Kenya being the Egyptian *(Neophron percnopterus)*, hooded *(Necrosyrtes monachus)* and white-headed vulture *(Trigonoceps occipitalis)*. Others include Ruppell's vulture *(Gyps ruppellii)*, a common nester in Kenya's Hell's Gate National Park, and the white-backed vulture *(Gyps bengalensis)*, found in all East African national parks. Vultures prefer savannah country with high concentrations of game.

These large birds, with a wing span of up to three metres and weighing up to five kg, feed almost exclusively by scavenging. They are fairly inefficient fliers and so rely to a large degree on finding rising hot-air thermals on which to glide and ascend. For this reason you won't see them in the air until well into the morning when the upcurrents have started.

African vultures have no sense of smell and so depend totally on their excellent eyesight, and that of their colleagues, for locating food. Once a kill or a fallen animal has been sighted a vulture will descend rapidly and await its turn at the carcass. Of course other vultures will follow the first downwards and in this chain reaction they may come from as far afield as 50 km. They are very efficient feeders and can rapidly strip flesh from bone, although they are not good at getting a start on a completely intact carcass. A large group of vultures (and they congregate in groups, often of up to 100) can strip an antelope to the bone in half an hour. Because they are poor fliers, however, vultures often cannot fly with a belly full of food and so after gorging will retreat a short distance and digest their meal.

BUFFALO

The buffalo is another animal which appears in great numbers in all the major parks, with the exception of Nairobi National Park.

The massive animal is said to be the most dangerous (to humans) of all African animals and should be treated with caution, although for the most part they will stay out of your way. Females protecting young calves, and solitary rogue bulls, are the most aggressive, and having 800 kg of angry animal thundering towards you is no joke.

Both sexes have the distinctive curving horns which broaden and almost meet over the forehead, although those in the female are usually smaller. The buffalo's colour varies from dark reddish brown to black.

Buffalo are often found in herds of 100 or more and never stray too far from water, especially in the dry season. When food and water are plentiful the herds often disperse. They are territorial in that they have a home range of about 50 km outside of which they don't stray.

Syncerus caffer
Swahili: *mbogo*

Cheetah
(Acinonyx jubatus)
Swahili: *duma*

CARNIVORES

The cheetah is one of the most impressive animals you can hope to see – sleek, streamlined and menacing. It's found in small numbers in all of Kenya's major game reserves – Nairobi, Amboseli, Masai Mara, Tsavo, Samburu, Buffalo Springs, Marsabit and Meru.

Similar in appearance to the leopard, the cheetah is longer and lighter in the body, has a slightly bowed back and a much smaller and rounder face. It stands around 80 cm at the shoulder, measures around 210 cm in length (including the tail) and weighs anything from 40 to 60 kg.

When undisturbed, the cheetah hunts in early morning or late evening, although these days with the number of tourist vehicles around, it is often found hunting at midday when the rubbernecks are back in the lodges stuffing their faces and the poor animal has a chance to stalk some dinner undisturbed. This forced change in habit is particularly stressful for the cheetah as it relies on bursts of tremendous speed for catching its prey, and this speed (up to 110 km/h) is only sustainable for a very short time. Obviously, as the midday heat is much greater than morning or afternoon, hunting for the cheetah becomes much more difficult. During a hunt the cheetah stalks its prey as close as possible and then sprints for 100 metres or so; if by that time it hasn't caught its victim, it will give up and try elsewhere. The prey (usually small antelope) is brought to the ground often with a flick of the paw to trip it up. Other food includes hares, jackals and young wart hogs.

Cheetah cubs reach maturity at around one year but stay with the mother much longer than that as they have to learn hunting and survival skills. Cubs are usually born in litters numbering from two to four, and the main breeding period is from March to December.

The cheetah rarely fights but predators (mainly of cubs) include lions, leopards and hyenas.

Civet
(Viverra civetta or *Civetticus civetta)*
Swahili: *fungo*

The civet is a medium sized omnivore around 40 cm high at the shoulder and 90 cm long (excluding the tail), with some canine features and short, partially retractile claws. Its coat of long coarse hair is basically grey but with a definite and variable pattern of black spots over most of the body, along with two black bands stretching from the ears to the lower neck and two black bands around the upper part of the hind legs. The tail is bushy at the base becoming thinner towards the tip, held out straight when the animal is on the move, and black except for three to four greyish bands near the base. The head is mostly greyish white and the ears are quite small, rounded and tipped with white hairs.

Civets are solitary, nocturnal animals which hide in thickets, tall grass or abandoned burrows during the day and so are rarely sighted. The most likely places to spot one are in Marsabit or Tsavo West reserves, although they are also known to inhabit Nairobi, Amboseli and Masai Mara.

It has a very varied diet consisting of rodents, birds and their eggs, reptiles, amphibians, snails, insects (especially ants and termites) as well as berries, the young shoots of bushes and fruits.

Litters consist of up to four cubs and these have a similar, though slightly darker colouring.

The other conspicuous feature of the civet is the presence of musk glands in the anal region which produce a foul-smelling oily substance used to mark territory. This musk is used in the manufacture of perfumes though in Western countries it is collected from animals held in captivity.

Genet
Small-spotted or common genet
(Genetta genetta)
Swahili: *kanu*

Unlike the civet, the genet distinctly resembles the domestic cat though the body is more elongated and the tail longer and bushier. The coat is long and coarse with a prominent crest along the spine. The basic colour varies from grey to fawn and is patterned from the neck to the tail with roundish dark brown to blackish spots. The tail is banded with nine to 10 similarly coloured rings and has a whitish tip. Another species of genet, the large-spotted or rusty-spotted genet *(Genetta tigrina)*, is similar in appearance to the common genet, but has a brownish-black spinal stripe and larger spots.

The genet lives in savannah and open country and is a very agile tree climber but not frequently sighted since it is entirely nocturnal. During the day it sleeps in abandoned burrows, rock crevices, hollow trees or up on high branches and seems to return to the same spot each day. The animals live singly or in pairs.

Its prey is generally hunted on the ground though it will climb trees to seek out nesting birds and their eggs. Like the domestic cat, it stalks prey by crouching flat on the ground. Its diet consists of a variety of small animals (mostly rodents), birds, reptiles (including snakes), insects and fruits. It is well known for being a wasteful killer, often eating only a small part of the animals it catches.

Litters typically consist of two to three kittens. Like the domestic cat, the genet spits and growls when angered or in danger.

Hunting Dog
(Lycaon pictus)
Swahili: *mbwa mwitu*

The hunting dog is the size of a large domestic dog and is found in all the reserves, or where there is a high concentration of game animals.

The dog's unusual coloration makes it quite an ugly creature – the black and yellowish splotches are different in each animal, ranging from almost all black to almost all yellow. The only constant is the white tail tip. Prominent physical features are the large rounded ears.

Hunting dogs tend to move in packs ranging from four or five up to as many as 40. They are efficient hunters and work well together. Once the prey has been singled out and the chase is on, a couple of dogs will chase hard while the rest pace themselves; once the first two tire another two step in and so on until the quarry is exhausted. Favoured animals for lunch include gazelle, impala and other similar sized antelope. They rarely scavenge, preferring to kill their own.

Hunting dog cubs are usually born in grass-lined burrows in litters averaging seven, although litters of up to 15 are not unheard of. By six months they are competent hunters and have abandoned the burrow. The hunting dog has no predators, although unguarded cubs sometimes fall prey to hyenas and eagles.

The spotted hyena is a fairly common animal throughout most of Kenya and especially where game is plentiful. Bearing a distinct resemblance to dogs, it is a large, powerfully built animal with a very sloping back, broad head and large eyes but with rather weak hindquarters. The sloping back is what gives the animal its characteristic loping gait when running. Its coat is short, dull grey to buff and entirely patterned with rounded blackish spots except on the throat. Its powerful jaws and teeth enable it to crush and swallow the bones of most animals except the elephant.

Hyenas are mainly nocturnal animals but are frequently seen during the day, especially in the vicinity of lion or cheetah kills impatiently waiting for their turn at the carcass along with vultures. Otherwise, the days are spent in long grass, abandoned aardvark holes or in large burrows which they dig out up to a metre below the surface of the soil. It's a very noisy animal and when camping out in the bush at night you'll frequently hear its characteristic and spine-chilling howl which rises quickly to a high-pitched scream. This is only one of the sounds which the spotted hyena emits. Another is the well known 'laugh', though this is generally only produced when the animal finds food or is mating.

The hyena has highly developed senses of smell, sight and sound, all important in locating food (carrion or prey) and for mutual recognition among pack members and mating pairs.

Hyenas are well known as scavengers and can often be seen following hunting lions and hunting dogs, usually at a respectable distance, though they will occasionally force these animals to abandon their kill. On the other hand, although carrion does form an important part of their diet, hyenas are also true predators and are more than capable of bringing down many of the larger herbivores. To do this they often form packs to run down wildebeest, zebra and gazelle, and are able to reach speeds of up to 60 km/h. They also stalk pregnant antelope and, when the female gives birth, snatch and kill the newly born foal and occasionally the mother too. Domestic stock are also preyed on.

In the mating season, hyenas assemble in large numbers especially on moonlit nights. All hell breaks loose on these occasions and the noise is incredible. The gestation period is about 110 days and litters number up to four though usually less. The young are born in the mother's burrow. The pups are weaned at around six weeks old and become independent shortly afterwards.

Humans are the hyena's main enemy, though lions and hunting dogs will occasionally kill or mutilate hyenas if they get too close to a kill. Although they are reputed to be cowardly, you're advised to keep your distance from them as they do occasionally attack humans sleeping in the open.

Hyena
(Crocuta crocuta)
Swahili: *fisi*

Jackal
Common or golden jackal
(Canis aureus)
Swahili: *bweha*

There are two species of jackal found in Kenya: the common or golden jackal, and the black-backed jackal *(Canis mesomelas)*, which is a common sight in the major reserves. The black back which gives it its name is usually more silvery than black, is wide at the neck and tapers to the tail. The golden jackal is similar, though without the back markings. Although the jackal is in fact a dog, its bushy tail and long ears are more like those of a fox than a dog.

The jackal is mostly a scavenger and so is commonly seen in the vicinity of a kill. The jackal will hunt for itself – insects, small mammals and birds, even the occasional small antelope. They are also found on the outskirts of human settlements and will attack sheep, poultry and calves.

Jackals are territorial and a pair will guard an area of around 250 hectares. Cubs are born in litters of five to seven and, although they don't reach maturity until almost a year old, they usually leave the parents when just two months old.

Enemies of the black-backed jackal include the leopard, cheetah and eagle.

Leopard
(Panthera pardus)
Swahili: *chui*

The leopard is perhaps the most graceful and agile of the large cats. A powerfully built animal which uses cunning to catch its prey, it is present in all the major game reserves but is difficult to find as it is nocturnal and spends the day resting on branches of trees, often up to five metres above the ground. It is as agile as a domestic cat in climbing such trees and this is also where it carries its prey so that it's out of the way of other scavengers which might contest the kill.

The leopard's coat is usually short and dense with numerous black spots on a yellowish background. The underparts are white and less densely spotted. In addition, the coats of leopards found in open country are generally lighter than those in wooded country.

Leopards are solitary animals except during the mating season when the male and female live together. The gestation period is three months and a litter usually consists of up to three cubs. They prey on a variety of birds, reptiles and mammals including large rodents, rock hyrax, wart hogs, smaller antelopes and monkeys (especially baboon), though they occasionally take domestic animals such as goats, sheep, poultry and dogs. This wide range of prey explains why they are still able to survive even in areas of dense human settlement long after other large predators have disappeared. But their presence is generally unwelcome since they do occasionally turn human-eater. It also explains why they are found in very varied habitats ranging from semidesert to dense forest and as high as the snow line on Mt Kenya and Kilimanjaro.

Lions are one of the main attractions of the game reserves and are found in all the main ones. They spend most of the day lying under bushes or in other attractive places and when you see a pride stretched out in the sun like this, they seem incredibly docile. It is possible to drive up very close to them in a vehicle – they either don't sense humans or realise that humans in vehicles are not a threat. Whatever the case, don't be tempted to get out of a vehicle at any time in the vicinity of a lion. Loud noises and sudden movement also disturb them. They're at their most active for around four hours in the late afternoon, then spend the rest of the time laying around.

Lions generally hunt in groups, with the males driving the prey towards the concealed females who do most of the actual killing. Although they cooperate well together, lions are not the most efficient hunters – as many as four out of five attacks will be unsuccessful. Their reputation as human-eaters is largely undeserved as in most circumstances they will flee on seeing a human. However, once they have the taste for human flesh, and realise how easy it is to make a meal of one, lions can become habitual killers of people. This mostly occurs among the old lions which no longer have the agility to bring down more fleet-footed animals.

Lions are territorial beasts and a pride of one to three males and accompanying females (up to 15) and young will defend an area of anything from 20 to 400 sq km, depending on the type of country and the amount of game food available.

Lion cubs are born in litters averaging two or three. They become sexually mature by 1½ years and males are driven from the family group shortly after this. Lions reach full maturity at around six years of age. Unguarded cubs are preyed on by hyenas, leopards, pythons and hunting dogs.

Lion
(Panthera leo)
Swahili: *simba*

Mongoose
Banded mongoose
(Mungos mungo)
Swahili: *kicheche*

The banded mongoose (the one most commonly found in Kenya) is usually seen in groups in Tsavo, Amboseli and Masai Mara reserves. It is brown or grey in colour and is easily identifiable by the dark bands across the back which stretch from the shoulder to the tail. The animal is about 40 cm in length and weighs between 1.3 and 2.3 kg.

Mongoose are very sociable animals and live in packs of between 30 and 50 individuals which stay close to one another when foraging for prey. They are often very noisy, having a wide variety of sounds which they use to communicate with each other. When threatened they growl and spit in much the same manner as a domestic cat. Being diurnal animals, they prefer sunny spots during the day but retire to warrens – rock crevices, hollow trees and abandoned anthills – at night. A pack frequently has several warrens within its territory.

The mongoose's most important source of food are insects, grubs and larvae but they also eat small amphibians, reptiles, birds' eggs, fruits, berries and birds. Their main predators are birds of prey though they are also taken by lions, leopards and hunting dogs. Snakes rarely pose a danger since these would-be predators are attacked by the entire pack and the snake is frequently killed.

Mongoose are one of the creatures which have become very habituated to humans in some places and come right up to the game lodges scavenging for scraps.

Serval
(Felis serval)
Swahili: *mondo*

The serval is a wild cat, about the size of a domestic cat but with much longer legs. It is found in all the major game reserves in Kenya.

The serval's colouring is a dirty yellow with large black spots which follow lines along the length of the body. Other prominent features are the large upright ears, the long neck and the relatively short tail. It stands about 50 cm high and measures 130 cm including the tail. Being a largely nocturnal animal, the serval is usually only seen in the early morning or late evening. It lives on birds, hares and rodents and is an adept hunter – it catches birds in mid-flight by leaping into the air.

Serval cat young are born in litters of up to four and although independent at one year, don't reach sexual maturity until two years of age.

ELEPHANT

Everyone knows what an elephant looks like so a description of them is unnecessary except perhaps to mention that African elephants are much larger than their Asian counterparts and that their ears are wider and flatter. A fully grown bull can weigh up to 6½ tonnes and sometimes more. In Kenya they are found in all the major game parks with the exception of Nairobi National Park where they would be too destructive to the environment to make their long term presence viable. They have been encountered as high as 3600 metres on the slopes of Mt Kenya.

The tusks on an old bull can weigh as much as 50 kg each, although 15 kg to 25 kg is more usual. The longest tusks ever found on an elephant in Kenya measured 3½ metres! Both the males and females grow tusks, although in the female they are usually smaller. An elephant's sight is poorly developed but its senses of smell and hearing are excellent.

Elephants are gregarious animals and are usually found in herds of between 10 and 20 individuals consisting of one mature bull, a couple of younger bulls, cows and calves, though herds of up to 50 individuals are sometimes encountered. Old bulls appear to lose the herding instinct and often lead a solitary existence, only rejoining the herd for mating. Herds are often very noisy since elephants communicate with each other by a variety of sounds, the most usual ones being various rumbles produced through the trunk or mouth. The most well known elephant sound, however, is the high-pitched trumpeting which they produce when frightened or in despair and when charging.

Herds are on the move night and day in order to secure sufficient water and fodder, both of which they consume in vast quantities – the average daily food intake of an adult is in the region of 250 kg. They are both grazers and browsers and feed on a wide variety of vegetable matter including grasses, leaves, twigs, bark, roots and fruits and they frequently break quite large trees in order to get at the leaves. Because of this destructive capacity, they can be a serious threat to a fragile environment especially in drought years and are quite capable of turning dense woodland into open grassland over a relatively short period of time. Because of Africa's rapidly increasing human population and the expansion of cultivated land, they also come into conflict with farmers when they destroy crops such as bananas, maize and sugar cane.

The other essential part of an elephant's diet are various mineral salts which they obtain from 'salt licks'. These are dug out of the earth with the aid of their tusks and swallowed in considerable quantities.

Loxodonta africana
Swahili: *ndovu* or *tembo*

Elephants breed year-round and the period of gestation is 22 to 24 months. Expectant mothers leave the herd along with one or two other females and select a secluded spot where birth occurs. They rejoin the herd a few days later. Calves weigh around 130 kg at birth and stand just under a metre high. They're very playful and guarded carefully and fondly by their mothers until weaned at two years old. After that, they continue to grow for a further 23 years or so, reaching puberty at around 10 to 12 years. An elephant's life span is normally 60 to 70 years though some individuals reach the ripe old age of 100 and even longer.

GIRAFFE

Rothschild's Giraffe
(Giraffa camelopardalis rothschildi)
Swahili: *twiga*

Rothschild's giraffe, one of three types of giraffe common to East Africa, is found in western Kenya around Lake Baringo, and Uganda. The Masai giraffe *(Giraffa camelopardalis tippelskirchi)* is more widespread in Kenya and is found in all the parks south and west of Nairobi. Rothschild's is paler and more thickset than the Masai, with less-jagged patches, and is usually unmarked below the knee. The Masai giraffe has irregular, star-shaped patches and is usually buff-coloured below the knee. However, it is often difficult to identify a particular giraffe type because individual and regional variations in colour and pattern are wide.

The average male stands around 5½ metres; females are mere midgets at 4½ metres. Horns are found on both sexes, but are merely short projections of bone covered by skin and hair. These are all that's left of what would once have been antlers. Despite the fact that the giraffe has such a huge neck, it still has only seven vertebrae – the same number as humans.

Reticulated Giraffe
(Giraffa camelopardalis reticulata)
Swahili: *twiga*

The reticulated giraffe differs from the Masai and Rothschild's giraffes in both colouring and pattern. It is a deeper brown and its body has a much more regular 'tortoiseshell' pattern, with white rather than buff-coloured outlines. It is found in the north and north-east of the country – Meru, Marsabit and Samburu reserves. You can easily come across them at the side of the road between Isiolo and Marsabit but probably the biggest herds are to be seen in Samburu and Buffalo Springs reserves.

Giraffes graze mainly on acacia tree foliage in the early morning and afternoon; the rest of the time they rest in the shade. At night they also rest for a couple of hours, either standing or lying down.

HIPPOPOTAMUS

In Kenya the hippo is found in greatest numbers in Masai Mara but can also be observed at Amboseli, Nairobi and Tsavo national parks and at Lake Baringo. At Tsavo there is a submarine viewing tank but the hippos are not very cooperative and seem to have deserted the immediate area.

Hippos are too well known to need description except to note that these huge, fat animals with enormous heads and short legs vary between 1350 kg and 2600 kg when fully grown. Their ears, eyes and nostrils are so placed that they remain above water when the animal is submerged.

Hippos generally spend most of the day wallowing in shallow water, coming out to graze only at night. They are entirely herbivorous and feed on a variety of grasses in pastures up to several km away from their aquatic haunts. They are voracious feeders and can consume up to 60 kg of vegetable matter each night. They urinate and defecate in well-defined areas – often in the water in which case they disperse the excreta with their tails.

Hippos are very gregarious animals and live in schools of 15 to 30 individuals though, in certain places, the schools can be much larger. Each school consists about equally of bulls and cows (with their calves) and, like other herd animals, there's an established hierarchy. Hippos may appear to be placid but they fight frequently among themselves for dominance and this is especially so among the males. The wounds inflicted in such fights are often quite horrific and virtually every hippo you see will bear the scars of such conflicts. They're not normally dangerous to humans unless cornered or frightened but you should definitely keep your distance. They may look sluggish but they are capable of running at considerable speed.

Hippos breed all year and the period of gestation is around 230 days. The cows give birth to a single calf either in the water or on land and suckle it for a period of four to six months after which it begins to graze on a regular basis. Sexual maturity is reached at about four years old and the life span is about 30 years (longer in captivity).

The only natural predators of hippos are lion and crocodile which prey on the young. Though hippos occasionally foul up fishing nets, they're considered to be beneficial since their wallowing stirs up the bottom mud and their excreta is a valuable fertiliser which encourages the growth of aquatic organisms.

Hippopotamus amphibius
Swahili: *kiboko*

HYRAX or DASSIE

Procavia capensis
Swahili: *pimbi*

The species of hyrax you're most likely to encounter (especially on Baboon Cliffs in Nakuru National Park but also in Nairobi, Tsavo, Masai Mara and Marsabit reserves) is the cape rock hyrax *(Procavia capensis)* or cape dassie. It's a small but robust animal about the size of a large rabbit with a short and pointed snout, large ears and thick fur. The tail is either absent or reduced to a stump.

Hyrax are extremely sociable animals and live in colonies of up to 60 individuals, usually in rocky, scrub-covered locations. They're diurnal, feeding mostly in the morning and evening on grass, bulbs and roots, and on insects such as grasshoppers and locusts. During the rest of the day they can be seen sunning themselves on rocks and chasing each other in play. Where habituated to humans, they are often quite tame but in other places, when alarmed, they dash into rock crevices uttering shrill screams. Their senses of hearing and sight are excellent.

Hyrax breed all year and the period of gestation is about seven months – a remarkably long period for an animal of this size. Up to six young are born at a time and the young are cared for by the whole colony. Predators include leopards, hunting dogs, eagles, mongoose and pythons.

Despite being such a small creature, hyrax are more closely related to the elephant than any other living creature by virtue of certain common physical traits.

PRIMATES

Baboon
(Papio cynocephalus)
Swahili: *nyani*

The yellow baboon is just one of at least seven subspecies of baboon and is the one most commonly sighted in Kenya. The other relatively common one is the olive baboon *(Papio anubis),* most often seen in Nairobi National Park. The main difference between the two is that the olive baboon has long facial hair and a mane on the shoulders, especially the males.

Baboons have a dog-like snout which gives them a much more aggressive and less human-like facial appearance than most other primates. They are usually found in large troops (of up to 150 animals, with a dominant male) which will have a territorial area ranging from two to 30 sq km. They spend most of the time on the ground searching for insects, spiders and birds' eggs. The baboons have also found that the lodges in the game parks are easy pickings, especially when idiotic tourists throw food to them so they can get a good snap with the Instamatic.

Baboons are fierce fighters and their only real natural enemy is the leopard, although young cubs are also taken by lions and hunting dogs.

Looking more like an Australian possum, the bushbaby is in fact a small monkey and is about the size of a rabbit. It is found in all major reserves, although being a nocturnal creature it is rarely sighted by day. The head is small with large rounded ears and, as might be expected on a nocturnal animal, relatively large eyes. The thick fur is dark brown and the bushbaby sports a thick bushy tail. Your average bushbaby measures around 80 cm in length, of which the tail is around 45 cm, and weighs less than two kg.

The lesser bushbaby *(Galago senegalensis)* is about half the size of the greater bushbaby. It is a very light grey in colour and has yellowish colouring on the legs.

Greater Bushbaby
(Galago crassicaudatus)
Swahili: *komba*

This forest-dwelling colobus monkey is a handsome creature found only in the forest parks – Mt Kenya, Mt Elgon, Aberdare and Saiwa Swamp.

The monkey is basically black but has a white face, bushy white tail and a white 'cape' around the back which flows out behind when the monkey moves through the trees – an impressive sight. An average colobus measures about 140 cm, of which about 80 cm is tail, and weighs from 10 kg to 23 kg.

The black and white colobus spends most of its time in the forest canopy and is easily missed unless you keep a sharp eye out. It is unusual for them to leave the trees; they get most of their water from small puddles formed in the hollows of branches and trunks.

Colobus monkeys are usually found in troops of up to 12 animals, consisting of a dominant male, females and young. Newborn monkeys are initially white, gaining their adult coat at around six months.

Eastern Black & White Colobus
(Colobus quereza caudatus)
Swahili: *mbega*

The playful vervet is the most common monkey in Kenya and is seen in parks and reserves throughout the country. It is easily recognisable with its black face fringed by white hair, and yellowish-grey hair elsewhere except for the underparts which are whitish. The males have an extraordinary bright blue scrotum.

Vervets are usually found in groups of up to 30 and are extremely cheeky and inquisitive – as you may well find if camping in the game reserves; they are often very habituated to humans and will come right inside tents or minibuses in search of a hand-out. Normally they live in woodland and savannah but never in rainforest or semi-desert areas.

Vervet
Green monkey or grivet
(Cercopithecus aethiops)
Swahili: *tumbili*

RHINOCEROS

Diceros bicornis
Swahili: *kifaru*

One of Africa's most sought-after species by poachers, the numbers of black rhino in Kenya have fallen dramatically in the past, though they are now once again on the increase, thanks to some determined conservation efforts. They are now thought to number around 500, compared with around 20,000 in 1970!

Rhinos are one of the more difficult animals to sight, simply because they're so few in numbers compared to other wildlife. They are seen in Amboseli quite often, and also in Masai Mara, Tsavo East (rarely), Nairobi National Park and Nakuru. Rhinos usually feed in the very early morning or late afternoon; at other times they tend to keep out of sight.

The eyesight of the rhino is extremely poor and it relies more on its keen senses of smell and hearing. Usually when alarmed it will flee from perceived danger, but if it decides to charge it needs to be given a wide berth, though with its poor eyesight chances are it'll miss its target anyway. Rhinos have been known to charge trains and even the carcasses of dead elephants!

A rhino's territory depends on the type of country and the availability of food, and so can be as little as a couple of hectares or as much as 50 sq km. The diet consists mainly of leaves, shoots and buds of a large variety of bushes and trees.

Rhinos reach sexual maturity by five years but females do not usually become pregnant for the first time until around seven years of age. Calves weigh around 40 kg at birth and by three months of age weigh around 140 kg. Adult animals weigh in at anything from 1000 kg to 1600 kg! They are solitary animals, only coming together for some days during mating. Calves stay with the mother for anything up to three years, although suckling generally stops after the first year.

WART HOG

Although there are a number of wild-pig species in Kenya, the one you're most likely to see is the wart hog. It is found in all the major parks – Amboseli, Masai Mara, Nairobi, Tsavo, Meru, Marsabit and Samburu.

Phacochoerus aethiopicus
Swahili: *ngiri*

The wart hog gets its name from the somewhat grotesque wart-like growths which grow on its face. They are usually found in family groups of a boar, a sow and three or four young. Their most (or perhaps only) endearing habit is the way they turn tail and trot away with their thin tufted tails stuck straight up in the air like some antenna.

The males are usually bigger than the females, measuring up to one metre and weighing as much as 100 kg. They grow upper and lower tusks; the upper ones curve outwards and upwards and grow as long as 60 cm; the lower ones are usually less than 15 cm.

Wart hogs live mainly on grass, but also eat fruit and bark, and, in hard times, will burrow with the snout for roots and bulbs. They rest and give birth in abandoned burrows or sometimes excavate a cavity in abandoned termite mounds. The young are born in litters of up to eight, although two to four is far more usual.

ZEBRA

Equus burchelli,
Equus grevyi
Swahili: *punda milia*

Zebras are one of the most common animals in the Kenyan parks and are widely distributed. You'll find them in great numbers in Nairobi, Tsavo, Amboseli, Samburu, Buffalo Springs, Maralal and Marsabit reserves as well as Masai Mara where they are present in the thousands.

Zebras often intermingle with other animals, most commonly the wildebeest but also with topi and hartebeest.

There are two species to be seen in Kenya, the most common being Burchell's zebra which is found in all the western and southern parks all the way up to Samburu and Maralal. In the more arid north-west and north-east, however, the most common species is the Grevy's zebra which differs from Burchell's in having much narrower and more numerous stripes, prominent, broad, rounded ears, and a pure white underbelly.

Some taxonomists classify Burchell's zebra into various 'races' or subspecies but this is a contentious issue since it is impossible to find two zebras exactly alike even in the same herd. What is more certain is that although Burchell's and Grevy's zebra often form mixed herds over much of their range, they do not interbreed in the wild.

Zebras are grazers but will occasionally browse on leaves and scrub. They need water daily and rarely wander far from a water hole, though they appear to have considerably more resistance to drought than antelope.

Reproductive rituals take the form of fierce fights between rival stallions for control of a group of mares. The gestation period is about 12 months and one foal is born at a time.

The most usual predator is the lion, though hyenas and hunting dogs will occasionally take zebras too.